CONSTITUTIONAL LAW, ADMINISTRATIVE LAW, AND HUMAN RIGHTS

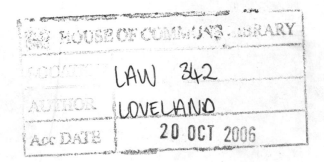

A Critical Introduction

To
Carol,
Madison and Daniel

CONSTITUTIONAL LAW, ADMINISTRATIVE LAW, AND HUMAN RIGHTS

A CRITICAL INTRODUCTION

Fourth Edition

PROFESSOR IAN LOVELAND
City University, London
Barrister, Arden Chambers

OXFORD
UNIVERSITY PRESS

OXFORD
UNIVERSITY PRESS

Great Clarendon Street, Oxford OX2 6DP

Oxford University Press is a department of the University of Oxford.
It furthers the University's objective of excellence in research, scholarship,
and education by publishing worldwide in

Oxford New York

Auckland Cape Town Dar es Salaam Hong Kong Karachi
Kuala Lumpur Madrid Melbourne Mexico City Nairobi
New Delhi Shanghai Taipei Toronto

With offices in

Argentina Austria Brazil Chile Czech Republic France Greece
Guatemala Hungary Italy Japan Poland Portugal Singapore
South Korea Switzerland Thailand Turkey Ukraine Vietnam

Oxford is a registered trade mark of Oxford University Press
in the UK and in certain other countries

Published in the United States
by Oxford University Press Inc., New York

British Library Cataloguing in Publication Data
Data available

Library of Congress Cataloging in Publication Data
Data available

Typeset by RefineCatch Limited, Bungay, Suffolk
Printed in Great Britain
on acid-free paper by
Ashford Colour Press, Gosport, Hants

ISBN 0–19–929041–5 978–0–19–929041–3

3 5 7 9 10 8 6 4 2

PREFACE TO THE FOURTH EDITION

The fourth edition of this book is a slightly expanded and modified version of its predecessor. The major alteration has been a substantial rewriting of chapter twelve, which addresses the early development of the effet utile jurisprudence of the European Court of Justice. As with previous editions, I have tried to resist the temptation of embarking on an 'every new case on the point' update to other chapters. I have however added substantial new sections addressing the appellate decisions in *Jackson v Attorney-General* and some of the post-2003 leading judgments on the impact of the Human Rights Act. Beyond those changes, amendments to the text have been limited to elaborating some key issues, correcting errors in the text and smoothing away some infelicities of style. The book therefore retains its initial concern to provide a cross-disciplinary introduction to the subject of public law, with a continuing emphasis placed on material drawn from political theory, political science and legal and social history. The companion casebook website to the textbook has been substantially expanded for this edition, in order to enable readers who are using the book as a main teaching text to have easy access to edited version of the relevant legislation and case law.

Ian Loveland
London, Summer 2006

ABOUT THE ONLINE RESOURCE CENTRE

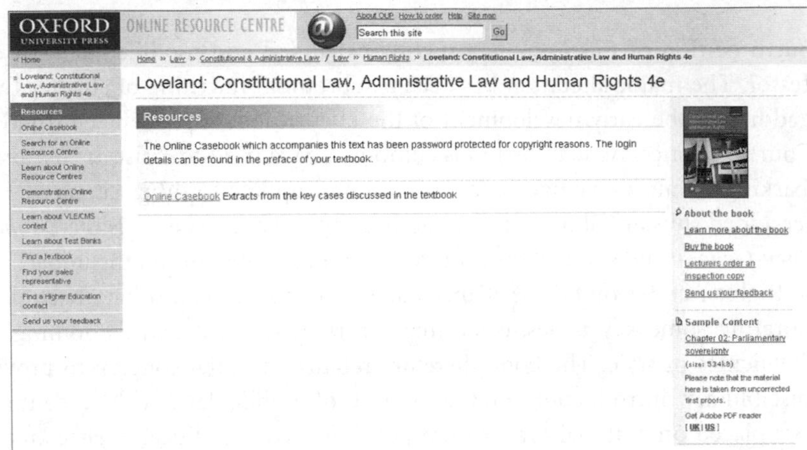

This book is complemented by an Online Resource Centre that provides a fully linked online casebook. Edited versions of leading cases discussed in the main text are listed under the same chapter headings that are in this book. This resource is available free of charge and is updated twice annually to ensure you are kept up-to-date with the latest judicial developments.

Please follow these instructions:

1) Go to: **www.oxfordtextbooks.co.uk/orc/loveland4e**

2) Click on the '**Online Casebook**' link

3) Enter the login details below (both are case sensitive)
username: **loveland4e**
password: **casebook**

4) Scroll through the list of cases and click on the link you are interested in

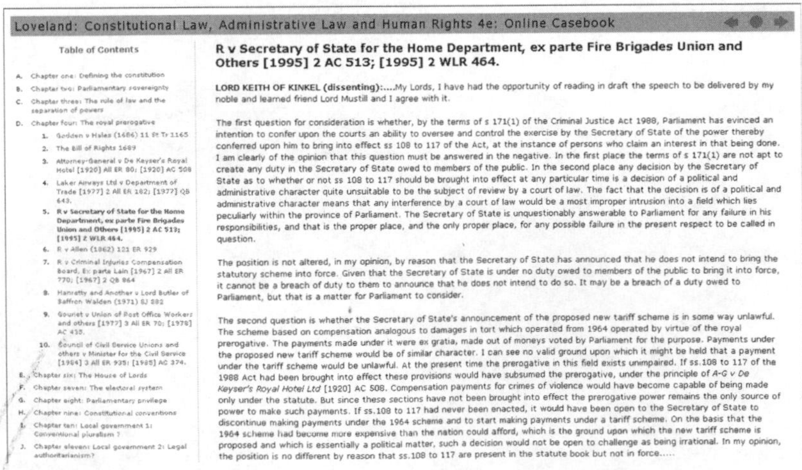

Should you experience any difficulty in accessing this resource, please contact *booksites.europe@oup.com* for assistance.

CONTENTS

TABLE OF LEGISLATION

STATUTES

STATUTORY INSTRUMENTS

Foreign Legislation

Australia

Ceylon

France

Italy

New Zealand

South Africa

United States

TABLE OF TREATIES AND CONVENTIONS

REGULATIONS

DIRECTIVES

LIST OF CASES

Decisions of the European Court of Justice are listed below numerically. These decisions are also included in the preceding alphabetical list.

1

DEFINING THE CONSTITUTION?

'We hold these truths to be self-evident. That all men are created equal. That they are endowed by their creator with certain inalienable rights. That among these are life, liberty and the pursuit of happiness. That to secure these rights, governments are instituted among men, deriving their just powers from the consent of the governed. That whenever any form of government becomes destructive of those ends, it shall be the right of the people to alter or abolish it, and to institute new government, laying its foundations upon such principles, and organising its powers in such form, as shall seem to them most likely to effect their safety and happiness.'

Thomas Jefferson, Philadelphia, 4 July 1776.

It may initially seem odd to begin a textbook analysing the law and politics of the British constitution by quoting several sentences from the United States' Declaration of Independence, a document drafted by Thomas Jefferson in 1776. The Declaration of Independence was written because the American colonists, most of whom were then the descendants of British émigrés, had rejected the British constitutional system under which they had previously been governed. Jefferson's words were intended firstly to provide an explanation for and justification of the American colonists' decision to rebel against British rule, and secondly to outline the broad moral and political principles that the revolutionaries would try to preserve in their new country.

This book begins with Jefferson's words in part because there is much common ground between American and British perceptions as to the moral principles which should be served by a country's constitutional arrangements.[1] However, they have been chosen primarily because, some 230 years after they were written, they continue to provide a succinct and eloquent statement of the issues and ideas with which constitutional lawyers in any modern democratic country should be concerned.

We might contrast the sentiments of the Declaration with the various definitions of the British constitution offered by the authors of several recent textbooks. Colin Turpin suggests that the constitution is: 'a body of rules, conventions and practices

[1] See Harlow C (1995) 'A special relationship? American influences on judicial review in England'; and Allan T (1995) 'Equality and moral independence: public law and private morality', both in Loveland I (ed) *A special relationship?* (Oxford: Clarendon Press).

which regulate or qualify the organisation and operation of government in the United Kingdom'; deSmith's classic introductory text regards the constitution as 'a central, but not the sole feature, of the rules regulating the system of government'.[2] A slightly longer version is offered by Vernon Bogdanor, for whom the constitution is:

> 'a code of rules which aspire to regulate the allocation of functions, powers and duties among the various agencies and officers of government, and defines the relationship between these and the public'.[3]

These authors seem to be trying to tell us what the constitution *is* – to *describe* the *form* that it takes. The Declaration, in contrast, is trying to tell us what a constitution *is for* – to *analyse* the *functions* it performs. This book follows Jefferson's approach in attempting to present a functionalist view of the British constitution. It is concerned more with the 'Why?' than with the 'What?' of contemporary arrangements. It assumes that the purpose of a constitution is to articulate and preserve a society's fundamental moral principles. This is not to suggest that a knowledge of the form that the constitution takes is unimportant, nor that issues of form and function are unrelated phenomena; it is simply to stress that one cannot understand the law of the constitution without looking beyond and behind its surface image.

The book does not, however, offer a one sentence 'definition' of the constitution, on the grounds that such a task cannot sensibly be performed. Rather, the entire book may be seen as a 'definition'. But this book amounts to only one definition, no more or less conclusive than any other formula that a student may encounter. British constitutional law is a subject as much concerned with social history and political practice as with legal rules. In consequence, definitive answers to particular problems are almost invariably elusive, and it is almost always possible to advance plausible alternatives to the solutions that have apparently been adopted.

This introductory chapter is intended merely to identify certain evaluative criteria which readers might wish to keep in mind when considering the description and analysis of Britain's current constitutional arrangements presented in the rest of the book. The following pages explore several abstract questions concerning the functions that a constitution might perform in order to illustrate the complex nature of the subject we are studying. We also devote some attention to the solutions which the American revolutionaries adopted to resolve the constitutional difficulties which they faced when the United States became an independent country. This is not a comparative book, nor is it suggested that the American solution is necessarily 'better' in any particular sense than the British model. The British and American systems are however very different in the form that they take. This is highly significant for our purposes, because the Americans claimed that their revolution was fought not against

[2] Respectively in (2nd edn, 1990) *British government and the constitution* p 3 (London: Weidenfield and Nicolson); Street H and Brazier R (5th edn, 1985) *deSmith's Constitutional and administrative law* p 15 (Harmondsworth: Penguin).

[3] Bogdanor V (1988) 'Introduction' p 4 in Bogdanor V (ed) *Constitutions in democratic politics* (Dartmouth Publishing: Aldershot).

the moral principles of the British constitution, but against the corruption of those principles by the British Parliament, the British government, the British judiciary, and the British people.

We will return to these historical matters shortly. Before doing so however, we may usefully spend some time considering the meaning of what we might (from a late twentieth century vantage point) intuitively regard as the most important function a constitution should perform – to ensure that a country is governed in accordance with 'democratic principles'.

I. THE MEANING(S) OF 'DEMOCRACY'?

The notion that modern Britain is a democratic country is perhaps a contemporary example of a 'self-evident truth': the point is so obvious that few observers would ever feel a need to question it. But if we dig beneath the surface of such widely held assumptions, we may find that we hold different views about the essential features of a democratic state.[4] We might also find that we would reach different conclusions about how democratic a country Britain actually is.

That, however, is a judgement best reserved to later chapters. At this point, we might more sensibly ask what yardsticks we might use in answering the question. The following hypothetical example assumes that the constitution of the countries concerned provide simply that laws shall be made by referendums, in which all adult citizens are granted one vote each. A law is passed if 50%+1 of those citizens who vote support the proposal. Let us assume that a majority of citizens in both countries A and B decide that they are not prepared to tolerate the poverty caused by an economic depression which has left 20% of the adult population unemployed.

In country A, the law is amended to provide for a very generous scheme of unemployment benefits, which are financed by heavy income taxes on the wealthiest 30% of the population. In doing this, the law frees the poorest members of society from the threat or reality of starvation and homelessness. But it also deprives the richest citizens of a substantial slice of their income, which they had planned to spend in pursuit of their own favoured forms of happiness.

In country B, the law is amended to require the government to deport unemployed citizens to an inhospitable, uninhabited island where they are left to survive according to their own devices. The cost of the scheme is met by fining the deportees themselves for being unemployed. In doing this, the law rids the country of the problem of unemployment at no financial cost to the majority of the population, but exposes the formerly unemployed citizens to the dangers and isolation of a new homeland.

How would we decide if these laws were 'democratic'? Should we ask only if the law

[4] For an introduction see Bealey F (1988) *Democracy in the contemporary state* esp chs 1 and 2 (Oxford: Clarendon Press); Holden B (1988) *Understanding liberal democracy* esp ch 1 (Oxford: Phillip Allan).

has majority support, and if the answer is yes, go no further? If so, both laws (and presumably the constitutional arrangements under which they were passed) would be democratic. Or should we demand that there be an inter-relationship between the level of support a law attracts and the severity of its consequences for particular minorities – the more severe the law, the greater the degree of support it must attract to be democratic? If we accepted that principle, could we then agree that deporting the unemployed is more 'severe' than imposing heavy taxes on the rich? If so, could we further agree that deportation would be 'democratic' if it enjoyed 55% (or 66% or 75% or 100%) support, while 50%+1 would be sufficient to 'democratise' large tax increases? Or thirdly, should we conclude that there are some laws whose consequences would be so severe that they may never be enacted by a democratic society, even if they attract the consent of 100% of the population? If so, would either deportation or large tax increases fall into that category?

Alternatively, let us suppose that country C declares war on countries D, E, and F. Country D immediately passes a law forbidding any criticism of its government's war effort and providing for the execution of citizens who do so, for fear that such freedom of speech could undermine morale and so increase the risk of defeat. Country E enacts a law which allows the government to imprison (without trial, and for an indefinite period, but in humane conditions) anybody suspected by a designated group of government employees of having connections with the enemy country, for fear that such people might be spies or saboteurs. Both laws achieve the desired effect, and country C's attacks are repelled. In country F, the majority decides that it must accord priority to freedom of speech and liberty of the person, and enacts neither of those measures. Subsequently, enemy agents (whose sympathies are suspected but unproven) succeed in sabotaging military facilities and undermining the citizenry's morale to such an extent that country F is defeated, and subjugated by country C.

Which country has acted in a democratic fashion here? Does a desire to preserve the country's independence justify interference with freedom of speech and physical liberty? Does the answer to this question depend on the severity of the interference – or on the severity of the threat from the aggressor? Or on the outcome of the war? Would one again wish to know the size of the majority supporting each measure before deciding if it was democratic?

We can rapidly make the questions raised by such 'laws' more elaborate by bringing the hypothetical law-making process under closer scrutiny. Would our conclusions about 'democracy' alter if it transpired that the law enacted in country A was supported by the 70% of the population who would not have to pay extra taxes to finance it, but opposed by the 30% who would suffer reduced income if the new system was introduced? Or alternatively, that it was supported by all of the richest 30% but opposed by many of the unemployed, who regarded it as a patronising erosion of their dignity and self-respect? Similarly, would our views as to the democratic nature of the new law made in country B change if we learned that it had been enthusiastically supported by the overwhelming majority of the people to be sent overseas? Would either law become more or less democratic in our eyes if we discover that neither country permits unemployed people to cast votes in the law-making process?

Constitutions as a social and political contract?

We might readily agree that the issue of 'consent' permeates the many plausible answers that might be offered to those hypothetical questions. As a statement of general principle, it is difficult to find fault with Jefferson's suggestion that 'government derives its just powers from the consent of the governed'. Problems begin to arise when we go rather further and ask what exactly the concept means.

The notion of a constitution as some form of 'contract', negotiated either among the citizenry themselves, or between the citizenry and their rulers, was not a novel idea, if only in philosophical terms, in 1776. The French philosopher Jean-Jacques Rousseau had explored the concept of 'direct democracy' through an idealised small city state, in which all citizens participated personally in fashioning the laws under which they lived.[5] In such a society, the legitimacy of all laws would rest on the citizenry's constant, express consent to the process of government. Rousseau rejected the idea of a divine, or natural, or God-given system of government; his men and women were not sculpted by their creator and endowed with those 'inalienable rights' that the American revolutionaries were so keen to defend. Rousseau's social order resulted from agreements between every individual citizen and the citizenry as a whole, from which government was formed. All government action therefore had a 'contractual' base; the citizens' rights and obligations under their constitution derived from covenants that they willingly made.

John Locke's celebrated *Second Treatise on Government*, first published in 1690, pursued the concept of constitutions as contracts in a slightly different form. Unlike Rousseau, Locke maintained that society was subject to a form of natural or divine law which imposed limits on individual behaviour. Government existed in order to provide mechanisms for enforcing the substance of such natural laws, the terms of which would serve as the constitution within which the government operated:

'it is unreasonable for Men to be Judges in their own Cases . . . Self-love will make Men partial to themselves and their friends . . . Ill Nature, Passion and Revenge will carry them too far in punishing others. And hence nothing but Confusion or Disorder will follow, and therefore God hath certainly appointed government to restrain the partiality and violence of Men'.[6]

Locke and Rousseau were of course engaging in an exercise in abstract, academic philosophising: they were sketching ideal solutions to hypothetical problems, rather than offering a detailed programme capable of immediate implementation in their respective countries.[7] Indeed, in the early 1700s it was difficult to identify any historical

[5] Rousseau J (1987) *The social contract* (edited and translated by Betts C) (Oxford: OUP).

[6] Laslett P (ed) Locke – *Two treatises of government*, II para 13 (Cambridge: CUP).

[7] There is debate among Lockean scholars as to whether the *second treatise* was written as an ex post facto justification for the 1688 English revolution, of which more will be said in chapter two; see Laslett P (1988) 'Two Treatises of Government and the revolution of 1688', in Laslett (ed) op cit.

examples of such idealised sentiments being put into practice. David Hume's famous 1748 essay on the formation of constitutions and governments, 'Of the Original Contract', recorded that:

'Almost all governments which exist at present, or of which there remains any record in story, have been founded originally either on usurpation or conquest, or both, without any pretence of a fair consent or voluntary subjection of the people'.[8]

Nonetheless, the writings of Locke and Rousseau provided an important frame of reference for the American and French revolutionaries whose armed struggle was waged so that their countries might try to construct a new, 'ideal' form of constitutional order. But even at a hypothetical, abstract level, the idea of constitutions as political contracts or covenants raises major difficulties, the foremost among which is, as Rousseau recognised 'to determine what those covenants are'.

Locke presented the emergence of government as a prerequisite for protecting individual citizens' 'property', a concept which he construed broadly as encompassing their lives, their physical and spiritual liberty, and their land and possessions.[9] These matters could thus be construed as entitlements which citizens derived from 'natural law', and are an obvious source of inspiration for Jefferson's notion of 'inalienable rights'. The terms are too vague to permit any exhaustive definition. Yet by focusing on the specific grievances and objectives of the American revolutionaries we can gain some indication of the issues they might encompass.

The Declaration's complaints against the British government concerned both the way that laws were made and their content. The overall thrust of the argument was that Britain was seeking to establish 'an absolute Tyranny over these States', but the general accusation was made up of many more specific complaints. Jefferson accused the British of, for example, 'imposing taxes on us without our consent' and '[keeping] among us, in times of peace, standing armies without the consent of our legislatures'. Jefferson is not arguing here that the levying of taxation or the maintenance of an army in peace-time are per se unacceptable features of government power, but that they are acceptable only if 'the people' affected by the measures have agreed to them.

At other points, in contrast, Jefferson identified British actions which apparently were unacceptable per se. The British had, for instance:

'dissolved Representative Houses repeatedly. . . . [and] refused for a long time, after dissolutions, to cause others to be elected. . . . [and] refused to pass laws for the accommodation of large districts of people, unless those people would relinquish the right of Representation in the Legislature, a right inestimable in them and formidable to tyrants only'.[10]

[8] Reproduced in Hume D (1994) *Political writings* p 168 (edited by Warner D and Livingston D) (Cambridge: Hackett).

[9] A useful introduction to Locke's use of 'property' is offered in Laslett P (1988) 'The social and political theory of *Two Treatises of Government*', in Laslett (ed) op cit.

[10] For the Lockean roots of this complaint see the *Second treatise on government* paras 215–216.

This grievance, so keenly felt, suggests that Jefferson considered that no part of the government process can be acceptable if 'the people' cannot choose their preferred law-makers at regular intervals. Without this power of choice, the people could not 'consent' to the laws under which they were governed, and therefore those laws could not be 'just'.

A third category of complaints suggests that there were some laws to which 'the people' could not give their consent even if they wished to. The Americans were outraged, for example, that Britain had subjected them to laws which 'depriv[ed] us in many cases of the benefits of Trial by Jury' and 'transport[ed] us beyond seas to be tried for pretended offences'. The presumption that one's guilt in criminal matters be established by a jury of one's peers, and that the scope of the criminal law be clear and stable, were seemingly regarded as fundamental principles of social organisation by the colonists. One might attach similar importance to Jefferson's claim that the British King had:

> 'obstructed the Administration of Justice, by refusing his Assent to Laws for establishing Judiciary powers. He has made Judges dependent on his Will alone, for the tenure of their offices, and the amount and payment of their salaries'.

But it is perhaps easier to identify precisely those aspects of government behaviour which the revolution was fought against, than those it was fought for. The rhetoric of 'All men being created equal' and sharing 'inalienable rights to life, liberty and the pursuit of happiness' is beguiling, almost perhaps bewitching. We might (again intuitively) regard such sentiments as integral ingredients of a democratic constitutional order. But what do such concepts mean? Their concern, broadly stated, appears to be with the nature both of the legal powers that a government possesses and of the processes through which that power is exercised. The bulk of this book explores those concerns in the British context, but we might first dwell on the answers which Jefferson and his contemporaries offered to these questions.

II. THE FIRST 'MODERN' CONSTITUTION?

The following pages offer a simplistically drawn picture of the constitutional settlement at which the American revolutionaries finally arrived in 1791.[11] It is intended to operate not as a yardstick against which to measure the adequacy of the details of the British constitution, which we examine in subsequent chapters, but as a comparator which indicates alternative ways in which modern societies might organise their constitutional structures.

[11] Readers seeking a more detailed introduction might usefully refer to McKay D (1989) *American politics and society* chs 3 and 4 (Oxford: Basil Blackwell).

THE PROBLEM – MAJORITARIANISM

The central principle informing the deliberations of the framers of the American constitution could be described as a pervasive distrust of human nature. This sentiment was best expressed by one Jefferson's contemporaries, James Madison, in *The Federalist Papers No 10*:

'As long as the reason of man continues fallible, and he is at liberty to exercise it, different opinions will be formed. . . . A zeal for different opinions concerning religion, concerning government and [above all] the unequal distribution of property. . . . have, in turn, divided mankind into parties, inflamed them with mutual animosity, and rendered them much more disposed to vex and oppress each other than to co-operate for their common good'.[12]

Madison saw no merit in trying to suppress diversity of opinion per se. That men would take different views on all manner of questions was an inevitable and indispensable component of both individual and collective liberty. He was however greatly concerned to draw lessons from history concerning the dangers that a country faced from within its own borders by the combination of citizens sharing the same 'vexatious' or 'oppressive' sentiments into distinct political 'factions', a faction being:

'a number of citizens, whether amounting to a majority or minority of the whole, who are united and actuated by some common impulse of passion, or of interest, adverse to the rights of other citizens, or to the permanent and aggregate interests of the community'.[13]

A form of government in which laws were passed to express the wishes of the electoral majority would ensure that any irrational or oppressive schemes favoured by minority factions would not be given legal effect. But, Madison, suggested, this 'majoritarian' system of law-making offered no protection to society when oppressive or irrational ideas were favoured by a majority of the population. That an idea enjoyed majority support did not necessarily make it conducive to the 'public good': majorities might proceed on the basis of false information, be temporarily persuaded to abandon their better judgement by the seductive rhetoric of charismatic leaders, or simply be prepared to sacrifice their country's long term welfare to gain a short term, sectional advantage. Consequently, Madison argued that perhaps the most important characteristic of the Constitution he was urging his fellow Americans to adopt was its attempt to ensure that 'the majority . . . be rendered unable to concert and carry into effect schemes of oppression'.

12 *The Federalist Papers* were a collection of essays written by James Madison, Alexander Hamilton and John Jay in the mid- to late 1780s. The US Constitution which exists today was adopted in 1789, and was the second Constitution which the revolutionaries adopted after having won the War of Independence. *The Federalist Papers* were part of an intense argument between advocates of the new Constitution and defenders of the then extant first Constitution, which was known as the Articles of Confederation.

13 *The Federalist Papers No 10.*

THE SOLUTIONS – REPRESENTATIVE GOVERNMENT, FEDERALISM, A SEPARATION OF POWERS, AND SUPRA-LEGISLATIVE 'FUNDAMENTAL' RIGHTS

Madison suggested that the dangers of faction could be reduced by adopting a form of 'representative government', in which laws would be made not directly by the people themselves, but by representatives who the people had chosen to exercise law-making power on their behalf in a legislative assembly. Madison hoped:

'to refine and enlarge the public views by passing them through the medium of a chosen body of citizens, whose wisdom may best discern the true interest of their country and whose patriotism and love of justice will be least likely to sacrifice it to temporary or partial considerations'.[14]

We might take something of a diversion at this point, and wonder how Madison's notions of 'wise' legislators fits with contemporary understandings of 'democratic' government. Let us return to countries A and B, and assume that laws are made not by the people directly, but by 100 legislators who are selected by the people to act on their behalf; a law is enacted if a simple majority of legislators support it. We may further assume that for the purposes of selecting its legislators, both countries are divided into electoral districts with equal populations, each of which returns one member to the legislature; all adult citizens have one vote in choosing their representatives, and the legislative seat is won by whichever candidate receives the most votes.

Would we consider the law enacted in country A as democratic if we learned firstly, that 10 of the 55 legislators who voted for it represented areas where the majority of electors opposed any tax increase, and secondly that the ten legislators concerned had promised their electors they would vote against any such measure? Would it make any difference to our answer if the reason for the ten legislators' change of heart was the force of the arguments presented in favour of the law during a debate in the legislature prior to the vote? The answer to this question presumably depends on how we would answer the logically precedent question of whether we accept that the role of a legislator is simply to transmit the wishes of her electors into law, or is rather to exercise her judgement as to the 'best' response to particular issues and act accordingly, even if her electors would wish her to reach a different conclusion?

A constitution in which law-making power is delegated or entrusted to a small number of citizens makes the task of judging the democratic nature of laws more complex, for we immediately become concerned not just with the merits of the particular law per se, but also with the merits of those laws which determine the way that legislators are selected and the ways that they behave during the legislature's law-making process. Might we question the 'democratic' basis of every law country A enacted, for example, if some electoral districts contained twice as many electors as others, but still returned only one member? Or, to revisit a familiar question, if

[14] Ibid.

unemployed people were not permitted to vote in the electoral process? Similarly, would a law to the effect that candidates for election were not permitted to advocate large tax increases compromise the constitution's democratic base? Might we also feel uneasy about the law-making process if we learned that many seats in the legislature had been contested by four or five candidates, all of whom attracted approximately equal electoral support, so that the winner was voted for by barely 30% of the people qualified to vote in each area?

A less contentious matter, at least from the American revolutionaries' perspective, was the presumption that the people's representatives, once elected, should enjoy unimpeded freedom to discuss any subject they chose, and to cast their law-making votes in any manner they wished. The colonists' aforementioned complaints over British interference with the operation of their colonial legislatures have clear philosophical roots in Locke's suggestion that 'consent' to government demanded that the people's legislature should not be hindered by any legal rules:

> 'from assembling in its due time, or from acting freely, pursuant to those ends for which it was constituted, the Legislative is altered. For tis not a certain number of men, no nor their meeting, unless they have also Freedom of Debating, and Leisure of perfecting, what is for the good of the Society wherein the Legislature exists. . . . For it is not Names that Constitute governments, but the use and exercise of those powers that were intended to accompany them'.[15]

The issue of representative government invites us to consider further dimensions of the concept of liberty adverted to in the Declaration. Jefferson's condemnation of imprisonment for 'pretended offences' addresses liberty in a physical and individual sense. Yet the Declaration also suggests that liberty bears more abstract and collective meanings, particularly in respect of matters concerning freedom of speech and conscience.

This leads us once again to consider the notion of 'consent' to government. Jefferson and his contemporaries assumed that 'man' was a rational, autonomous being; the preservation of his liberty demanded that 'he' make decisions on the basis of full and accurate knowledge. Consent had to be *informed consent.* The American revolutionaries thus placed a considerable premium on safeguarding individual citizens' freedom of conscience and expression in relation to moral and political matters. Consequently, the restrictions which Britain had placed on the activities of representative colonial legislatures were perceived by the colonists as an intolerable infringement of their collective liberty.

This particular strand of 'liberty' can be compromised in many ways, and it is intimately tied to our contemporary understandings of 'democratic government'. Would we conclude, for example, that no law made by the legislative assembly of our hypothetical country A could be democratic if it was a criminal offence for any person to reveal details of legislators' speeches or votes on the proposals before them. In such

[15] Locke J (1690) *Second treatise on government* para 215 (reproduced in Laslett op cit).

circumstances, electors would not know which legislators had supported or opposed tax increases, and so could not make informed choices as to their preferred candidate at the next election. Would we draw the same conclusion about country B if we learned it was a crime in that society for anyone to voice criticisms of the laws enacted by the legislature, with a view to convincing electors to choose different representatives at the next election? These issues are obviously of major significance to any attempt to gauge the adequacy of the mechanism through which legislatures are elected.

Madison's particular vision of 'representative government' clearly demands that one accept the desirability of fostering a certain degree of elitism in one's governors, and as such demands that law-makers ignore the irrational or oppressive sentiments of the citizens they represent. But this elitism may substantially dilute the 'representativeness' of the laws enacted. The preamble to the US Constitution begins with the words: 'We the people of the United States, in order to form a more perfect union . . .'. Yet it is evident that 'The People' who chose the legislators who framed the Constitution comprised barely 10% of the populace of the colonies.[16] Voters were all male, almost all were white, and the great majority were atypically well educated and affluent. The consent of the poor, the uneducated, and women was not presumed to be necessary to the establishment of the United States' newly created form of government, seemingly because the framers of the Constitution doubted that such groups, which comprised the mass of the populace, could be relied upon to support rational constitutional provisions.

Such discriminatory principles might lead us to conclude that the 'consent' which the revolutionaries sought was somewhat illusory, on the basis that consent should be a universal rather than selective phenomenon. This question is one to which we will frequently return in the context of British constitutional history and practice. Yet we may also consider it prudent to be concerned with the powers that legislators might wield once they have assumed (in accordance with whatever notion of popular consent determines their selection) their law-making powers. Madison recognised that it was by no means a complete answer to the spectre of tyranny simply to hope that a system of representative government, in which legislators were selected by an elitist electorate, would invariably produce rulers who would have the wisdom and capacity always to forswear sectional or irrational objectives favoured by factions of the population. One could not always rely on 'patriotism and love of justice' rather than 'temporary and partial considerations' being the dominant forces in the minds of one's chosen law-making representatives, no matter how carefully they were chosen. Madison considered that it was:

'In vain to say that enlightened statesmen will be able to adjust . . . clashing interests and

[16] See, for contrasting views, Beard C (1990) 'An economic interpretation of the Constitution', in Ollman B and Birmbaum J (eds) *The United States Constitution* (New York: New York University Press): and Brown R (1987) 'The Beard thesis attacked: a political approach', in Levy L (ed) *The making of the Constitution* (New York: OUP).

render them all subservient to the public good. Enlightened statesmen will not always be at the helm'.[17]

In those circumstances, the problem of majoritarianism was simply displaced from the arena of the 'people' themselves to the much smaller number of citizens who served as legislators. For the designers of the US Constitution, this indicated that preserving 'the public good' might demand that the helmsmen steering the ship of state either be precluded from embarking on voyages to certain undesirable destinations, or at the very least, be subject to constraints that made such journeys very difficult to undertake.

Federalism and the separation of powers

At the time of the revolution, the American colonists' sense of themselves as citizens of a single nation was not well developed. Each colony had been created, in the legal sense, by 'Charters' granted by the British monarchy.[18] These had been granted at different times, and on rather different terms. In consequence, by 1776, the (then) 13 colonies (from a British perspective) or States (in the revolutionaries' eyes) had developed distinctive political and social cultures, which were expressed in their respective laws.[19] Yet the colonists also shared many common practical and philosophical concerns. The most pressing was obviously justifying and then succeeding in their revolutionary war against British rule: this was a task that could be achieved only if the colonies acted in a co-ordinated manner, in pursuit of shared objectives; aspects of their individual identities would have to be surrendered to a 'national' military and political project. But having won their independence through such unified action, the revolutionaries then faced the dilemma of how best to structure the inter-relationships between the nation, the States and the people. Their eventual solution was to fashion a 'federal' constitution.

In the modern era, 'federalism' is a concept that may bear many meanings. As perceived by the American revolutionaries, their federal constitution would have the positive virtue of creating a multiplicity of powerful political societies within a single nation state, each wielding significant political powers within precisely defined geographical boundaries. However, the Constitution placed limits on the political autonomy of each State by granting sole responsibility for certain types of governmental power to the newly created national government. Those matters left within the sole competence of the States, while important in themselves, were not regarded as crucial to the well-being of the nation as a whole. It would not therefore be dangerous to allow the people of each State to devise their own 'internal' constitutional arrangements to determine their respective preferences on these issues: if

[17] *Federalist Papers No 10.*

[18] The grant of Charters was a part of what were known as the Monarch's 'prerogative' powers. We examine these powers more closely in ch 4.

[19] See Bailyn B (1967) *The ideological origins of the American revolution* pp 191–193 (Cambridge, Mass: Harvard UP). A contemporaneous perspective is offered by Madison in *The Federalist Papers No 39.*

they chose to indulge factional sentiment within their own borders, so be it; but their choices would have no legal force in the other States within the country. Each State could quite lawfully enact different laws to deal with matters within their geographical and functional jurisdiction.

The principle underlying the creation of a federal nation again derives from a particular view of the meaning of 'consent'. It assumes that a 'people' within which divergent factions held differing views on major (if not fundamental) political matters would be more likely to agree to live under a constitutional order which offered many opportunities for those views to be given legal effect at the same time, albeit within limited geographical areas, than a system which allowed a majority of the entire population, acting through a national legislature, to impose its preferences on all issues on the entire country.

Even if one accepts this principle as desirable, however, there remains the problem of deciding which powers should be allocated to which level of government. This is a question to which the many federal constitutions which now exist have given quite different answers. The American revolutionaries initially adopted a constitution known as the Articles of Confederation, which gave virtually no powers to the national government. The Articles were rejected within ten years, in favour of a new constitutional settlement which granted the national government considerably more authority.[20] The national government would be empowered to conduct foreign policy, to grant national citizenship, to maintain military forces and wage war, to issue the national currency, to impose customs duties on imported and exported goods, to levy sales taxes (but not income taxes) on a uniform basis throughout the country, to run the nation's postal service and to regulate commerce among the States and with foreign nations. The States were not permitted to enact laws concerning these matters.

Thus, if our hypothetical countries A, D and E were organised on the same federal lines as the United States' constitution, country A's central legislature would apparently have been unable to introduce its proposed anti-unemployment law, irrespective of how many legislators supported it, since the constitution seemingly did not give it the power to levy income taxes. Alternatively, if we accepted that the laws introduced by countries D and E were an element of the central legislatures' war powers, they could be enacted even if the majority of people in several of the States heartily disapproved of their contents.

Madison's concern with the dangers of faction and majoritarianism was initially directed at placing limits on the power of national government, acting at the behest either of a majority of the people or a majority of the States,[21] to produce irrational or oppressive laws. This safeguard was to be achieved in part by a further development on the theme of representative government. The Constitution eventually devised a representative form of national government which produced a balance between the

20 See Jensen M (1990) 'The Articles of Confederation', in Birnbaum and Ollman op cit; Levy L (1987) 'Introduction – the making of the Constitution 1776–1789', in Levy op cit.

21 Since the States were not of equal (population) size, the two concepts are not coterminous.

people as a whole and the people as citizens of their respective States. The framers of the Constitution created an elaborate separation (or fragmentation) of powers within the institutions of the national government. The national legislature, the Congress, would have two component parts. Seats in the House of Representatives were to be apportioned among the States in proportion to their respective populations. In contrast, each State, irrespective of its population size, would have two members in the Senate. The approval of a majority in both chambers would be required to enact laws.[22] Thus, in simple terms, neither a majority of the States nor a majority of the population could impose its wishes on the other. The dual nature of the national legislature did not however exhaust the fragmentation of power to which the Constitution subjected the national government.

The task of implementing Congressional legislation was granted not to the Congress itself, but to a separate, 'executive' branch of government headed by an elected President. In addition to possessing a limited array of personal powers, the President was also afforded a significant role in the legislative process. Measures which attracted majority support in both chambers of Congress would become laws only when signed by the President. Should he refuse his assent to the measure, it would be enacted only if it returned to Congress and was then approved by a two-thirds majority in both the Senate and the House. The President was thus empowered to block the law-making preferences of a small Congressional majority, but he could not frustrate the wishes of an overwhelming majority in both houses.

The framers' initial distrust of populist sentiment was further emphasised by the electoral arrangements made for choosing the President and the legislators who staffed the two chambers of Congress. While members of the House were to be elected directly by the 'people' of each State, Senators would be selected by each State's own legislative assembly, and the President would be chosen by an 'electoral college' of representatives from each State.

Thus two branches of the national government were to be placed in office by what was in effect an 'electorate within an electorate', whose members might be thought likely to (in Madison's words) 'refine and enlarge the public views'. Madison assumed that this elitist process would much reduce the possibility that the occupants of the most important national government offices would be motivated by 'temporary or partial considerations' when they performed the task of enacting and implementing laws made within the boundaries of their respective constitutional competence. But the Constitution took one further step in its efforts to guarantee that the federal and institutional separation of powers which the revolutionaries considered fundamental to the nation's long-term security and prosperity would be preserved against the threat of internal factions, even if that faction should prove to be of sufficient size to control the national law-making process.

22 Jefferson's aforementioned reiteration of Locke's analysis of the prerequisites of effective legislatures was met by the Constitution's requirements that Congress meet at least once every year, and that its proceedings, including the voting behaviour of its members, be published.

Fundamental rights and a supra-legislative constitution

It perhaps sounds fatuous to record that the Americans assumed that their Constitution would function as a 'constituent' document but, as we shall see in chapter two, the point is of considerable significance. The framers regarded the rules they had created as 'the highest form of law' within American society. The Constitution was to be the source of all governmental powers; its terms identified the fundamental or basic moral and political principles according to which society should be managed.

Federalism was clearly a fundamental political value to the framers of the Constitution. This was evident not only in the proposed allocation of powers between the national and State governments, but also in the procedures through which the Constitution itself was to gain legal force. As Madison explained in *The Federalist Papers No 39*:

'assent and ratification is to be given by the people, not as individuals composing one entire nation, but as composing the distinct and independent States to which they respectively belong. . . . The act, therefore, establishing the Constitution will not be a *national* but a *federal* act'.[23]

The Constitution would come into being, and the Articles of Confederation disappear, only if at least 9 of the 13 States agreed to this new allocation of powers.[24] The States would thus willingly surrender some of their previously existing powers to the national government which they themselves created. An individual State might, if its citizens so wished, refuse to consent to the new Constitution. But once that consent had been given, an individual State would not have the legal authority to take any of those powers back.

Madison and the other architects of the Constitution rejected the Lockean notion of 'divine' law in the sense of considering human beings subservient to a rigid set of rules emanating from a Deity. Similarly, they were not persuaded that the moral values which they wished to control the government of their new nation should be subject to an eternally fixed code of 'natural' law, which could never be altered. They nevertheless concluded that once they had succeeded in identifying the mutually acceptable principles according to which the foundations of government should be laid, those 'fundamental laws' should enjoy a considerable degree of fixity. The moral and political principles expressed in the Constitution had not lightly been arrived at: they were not lightly to be discarded; they were not to be left at the mercy of the ordinary institutions of government.

But the framers were not so arrogant as to assume that the views they held in 1789–1791 amounted to eternal truths, which would control the government of American society for all time. The federal Congress, the federal president, and the

23 Original emphasis.

24 The Articles themselves required that all 13 States assent to any amendment. This had led to suggestions that the Constitution was itself a 'revolution', albeit a peaceful one, fought against the United States' initial constitutional order: see Levy op cit; Jensen op cit.

various State governments would all be bodies of limited legal competence: they possessed only those powers which 'the people' had granted to them in the Constitution, and had no capacity to create new powers for themselves. The ultimate, or sovereign legal authority, was 'the people'. If the Congress, or the President, or one or more of the States wished to acquire new powers, they would have to persuade 'the people' to amend the Constitution. The framers of the Constitution decided that 'the people' would express themselves for this purpose through a special law-making process, involving both the Congress and the States, which demanded extremely large majorities in favour of change. Article 5 of the Constitution permits amendments only if the change attracts the support of a two thirds majority of both houses of Congress and three quarters of the states.[25]

'The people' was therefore not a law-making body that would be in constant, or even regular session. It would act only on those rare occasions when the overwhelming majority of members of Congress, and an even larger majority of the States, considered that the time had come for aspects of the country's fundamental laws to be altered.

The Constitution was in fact substantially altered almost as soon as it was introduced, although this initiative might more sensibly be regarded as the final stage of the original settlement rather than a rejection of its initial premises. The Constitution was adopted by the requisite number of States on the assumption that Congress' first task would be to formulate amendment proposals to send to the States for their approval.

Ten amendments, colloquially referred to as the 'Bill of Rights', were introduced in 1791. The first eight amendments listed a series of individual liberties (clearly much influenced by the litany of complaints in the Declaration) with which the institutions of national government could not interfere. These need not be listed in their entirety here, but we might note some of their most important provisions. The First Amendment precluded Congress from enacting laws which abridged freedom of speech, the freedom of the press, and freedom of religious belief. The Fourth Amendment forbade national government officials from conducting arbitrary searches of citizens' houses and seizure of their possessions. The Fifth Amendment prevented the national government from appropriating citizens' property, or interfering with their lives or liberty, without 'due process of law', and required that just compensation be paid if such property was taken for public use. The Fifth and Sixth Amendments in combination guaranteed the right to trial by jury in criminal cases, granted the accused the right to legal representation, and excused her from having to provide self-incriminatory evidence; while the Eighth Amendment prohibited the infliction of 'cruel and unusual punishments'.

Madison and his supporters had initially argued that the 'Bill of Rights' was superfluous. Congress and the Presidency possessed only those powers which the Constitution had granted them. Since no powers had been given to infringe the 'liberties' later listed in the Bill of Rights, the Constitution implicitly forbade the national

25 This somewhat oversimplifies the position, but the description is adequate for our limited purposes.

government acting in such a manner. The Madisonian 'faction' was later convinced that giving such liberties explicit protection was a beneficial course to follow. In part this shift of position was for the tactical reason of assuaging opposition to the new Constitution and thereby facilitating its adoption. However Madison also accepted that the Bill of Rights would have an intrinsic, declaratory value, by laying further emphasis on the basic moral principles the revolution had been fought to defend. These provisions themselves could only be altered or abolished in future in accordance with the Article 5 amendment process.

The importance which the framers accorded to maximising the political autonomy of the States within the Constitution's federal structure is illustrated by their decision to apply the provisions of the Bill of Rights only against the national government, not against the States. If the people of the States wished to impose similar restraints on their respective State governments, they were free to do so. But they were equally free not to do so. Madison himself, once he accepted the desirability in principle of the Bill of Rights, had favoured its extension to State as well as Federal governments. He found little support for this argument either in Congress or among the States; nothing in the text of the first eight amendments indicated that they were to control the States as well as Congress and the Presidency.

The constitutional role of the Supreme Court

The Constitution could be no more than a framework document. It sought to outline the broad principles within which the government process should be conducted, not to promulgate detailed rules which would provide answers to every foreseeable (or unforeseeable) problem that might arise. The framers anticipated that there would frequently be ambiguity in respect of the national/State separation of powers. Alternatively, within the context of the Bill of Rights, doubt might arise as to whether a Congressional law or Presidential action 'abridged the freedom of the press', or imposed a 'cruel and unusual punishment'. The framers entrusted the task of answering such questions to the United States Supreme Court.

The intended role of the Supreme Court was outlined by Alexander Hamilton in *The Federalist Papers No 78.* Hamilton envisaged that the Court would serve as the ultimate arbiter of the meaning of the Constitution. 'The people' had intended that the Constitution would impose agreed limitations on the powers of government bodies, and in Hamilton's view:

> 'Limitations of this kind can be preserved in practice no other way than through the medium of courts of justice, whose duty it must be to declare all acts contrary to the manifest tenor of the Constitution void'.

The Court would therefore stand:

> 'between the people and the legislature, to keep the latter within the limits assigned to their authority . . . A constitution is, in fact, and must be regarded by the judges as fundamental law. . . . the Constitution ought to be preferred to the [legislature's] statute, the intention of the people to the intention of their agents'.

This did not mean that the Supreme Court was to be in any sense 'superior' to the Congress:

> 'It only supposes that the power of the people is superior to both, and that where the will of the legislature [or the Presidency] . . . stands in opposition to that of the people, the judges ought to be governed by the latter and not the former'.

Unlike the Presidency, the Legislature, or the States, the Court had 'neither sword nor purse'; the effectiveness of its judgments would depend not on any coercive power, but on their legitimacy, which we may construe as their capacity to convince the citizenry that they were in conformity with the meaning of the Constitution.

Great care would thus have to be exercised in selecting the judges who sat on the Supreme Court, for they bore a heavy constitutional burden. Hamilton suggested that:

> 'there can be but few men in the society who will have sufficient skill in the laws to qualify them for the stations of judges. And making the proper deductions for the ordinary depravity of human nature, the number must be still smaller of those who unite the requisite integrity with the requisite knowledge'.

The Constitution did not specify either the intellectual or moral qualifications that Supreme Court nominees should possess, but involved both the President and the Senate in their selection. The President would nominate candidates for judicial office, but his nominees could assume their seats only after receiving the approval of the Senate. The President could thus not 'pack' the Court with appointees who did not enjoy the confidence of the legislature, although a President and Senate majority who adhered to the same faction could do so. Hamilton had placed much emphasis on a pre-revolutionary custom or tradition, developed (as we shall see in chapter three) within the British constitution, but corrupted in the colonies, that both politicians and the judiciary themselves should regard the courts' 'interpretation' of the law as a matter above factional politics. Politicians should thus forswear considerations of personal or party advantage in selecting members of the judiciary, while the judges themselves should exclude such considerations from their judgments.

But the framers did not rely solely on Presidential and Congressional self-restraint to safeguard the independence of the Supreme Court. Once the Judges were in office, neither the President nor the Congress would be able to remove them simply because they disapproved of the decisions the Court subsequently reached. Unless convicted of criminal offences, or guilty of grossly immoral behaviour, Supreme Court Justices were to enjoy lifetime tenure, with payment of their salaries expressly guaranteed in the Constitution itself.[26]

The enormous power and responsibility entrusted to the Supreme Court under the American constitution can be illustrated by returning to our hypothetical nations. If countries A, D and E had federal constitutions modelled on the initial American

[26] Provisions which obviously met the Declaration's aforementioned complaints as to the pre-revolutionary judiciary's lack of independence.

settlement, country A's tax-raising law would seem to have been illegal as the national legislature had no power to levy income tax. In contrast, the imprisonment and censorship measures enacted in nations D and E would seem to be constitutional exercises of the legislature's war powers.

Let us suppose, however, that the Supreme Court of country A concluded that the law in question was in reality a measure to regulate commerce among the nation's various States (a matter clearly within the national legislature's competence) by stimulating economic growth, and the tax thereby raised was merely an incidental side effect. As such, the measure would be constitutional. Similarly let us suppose that the Supreme Court of country D decided that the censorship measure contravened the free speech clause of the First Amendment, while in country E the Supreme Court held that the law introducing indefinite imprisonment without trial amounted to cruel and unusual punishment and thereby breached the Eighth Amendment. Would we conclude that such judgments represented a judicial attempt to subvert the fundamental principles of the Constitution, or that they were merely a rather surprising but nevertheless defensible interpretation of an ambiguous constitutional text?

It would be misleading to suggest that Supreme Court decisions which frustrated the wishes of the elected Congress or President were necessarily 'undemocratic' simply because the Judges themselves were not elected officials. Such accusations would have conclusive force only if one equates 'democracy' with a constitutional order which gives unfettered supremacy to the wishes of a legislative majority. They would be less convincing if one took a view of 'democracy' which entailed the protection of 'higher laws' against the possibly transient and ill-informed views of the greater number of one's legislators. Within that constitutional context, accusations of 'anti-democratic' conduct might as readily be levelled at the elected politicians who were apparently seeking to subvert the wishes of 'the people' from whom their powers derived.

CONCLUSION

Two hundred and thirty years ago, it took a revolutionary war for the American colonists to rid themselves of what they considered to be an unacceptable constitutional order. The new constitution which the United States subsequently fashioned marked a radical departure from traditional British understandings of the appropriate way for a country to regulate the relationship between its people and its government: its principles have been widely copied by many nations who have created or redesigned their own constitutional arrangements in the modern era. Lest it be assumed that the Americans created an 'ideal' constitutional order, we might note that the framers preserved the institution of negro slavery by leaving its abolition to the individual States. Thus while slave-owners had 'property' (guaranteed by the Fifth Amendment) in their slaves, slaves themselves enjoyed no inalienable rights, either of a physical or spiritual nature. Jefferson, for whom all men were supposedly created equal, was himself a slave-owner. And those framers who found slavery morally abhorrent were prepared to tolerate its continued existence in the Southern States rather than take the risk that some States would reject the new constitutional settlement.[27]

But, as we shall begin to see in chapter two, the contemporary British constitution retains many important elements of the system which the Americans rejected as tyrannical and oppressive in 1776. In modern Britain, there is no likelihood of a violent revolution to overhaul our constitutional arrangements. The country has, by and large,[28] avoided the difficulties posed by armed conflict between factions of its population for over 300 years. For some observers, that basic political reality might be sufficient grounds for concluding that there is no need even to question the adequacy of the constitution, still less to expend energy on proposals advocating fundamental or even partial reforms to its substance. Yet as we enter the twenty-first century, the workings of the constitution are the subject of wide-ranging and critical debate. We will examine the sources and nature of that debate throughout the remainder of this book. The modest objective of this opening chapter has been to identify some of the general ideas we might use to evaluate Britain's existing constitutional arrangements. In chapter two, we turn to what many commentators regard as perhaps the most important part of Britain's constitutional heritage – the doctrine of parliamentary sovereignty.

27 See particularly Madison's *Federalist Papers No 54*; Du Bois W (1990) 'Slavery and the Founding Fathers', in Ollman and Birmbaum op cit: Kelly A, Harbison W and Belz H (1983) *The American Constitution* ch 14 (New York: WW Norton).

28 As noted in the preface, this book does not address the history of Britain's relationship with Ireland in any systematic way. That history does of course demand that we qualify the notion of internal peace to an appreciable extent.

2

PARLIAMENTARY SOVEREIGNTY

For the purposes of analysing the way that constitutions work, it might be helpful to think of 'laws' as a formal way in which a 'democratic' society expresses its consent to the way in which it is governed. If we recall the references made to the American revolution in chapter one, we might say that the US Constitution is a clear example of a society making fundamental changes to its legal and political structures because its people no longer consented to their existing form of government.

The foundations of the USA's constitution reflect its architects' commitment to what is now regarded in many modern western societies as a basic, if contentious, point of democratic theory. Simply put, that principle asserts that in a democratic nation, the more important that a particular law is to the way that society is governed, the more difficult it should be for that law to be changed. One might suggest the reason for this is that it would be undesirable for fundamental features of the way in which a country is run to be vulnerable to reform which does not attract the 'consent' of the governed. The difficult questions that face designers of modern constitutions are: firstly, how much importance should one ascribe to particular values; secondly, how much consent should one need to change those values; and thirdly, in what ways should that consent be expressed?

As noted in chapter one, most of the terms of the United States' Constitution can only be amended with the consent of two thirds of the members of the federal Congress and the legislatures of three quarters of the 50 states. Because this level of consent is quite difficult to obtain, the Federal Constitution has been amended fewer than 30 times in over 200 years. This degree of permanence might justifiably lead us to say that the Constitution marks out stable and predictable legal boundaries which define the nature of the American people's consent to the powers of their government. This does not mean that the USA's Constitution invariably prevents a tyranny of the majority – but it does preclude a tyranny of *small* majorities.

It is also the case that most law-making in the USA takes place *within* the boundaries of consent outlined by the Constitution. These laws affect issues which are not fundamental to society's basic values, and so can be changed in less difficult ways. Some can be altered by the Congress, some fall within the remit of individual states. A straightforward majority vote in the particular legislature is often enough to change those parts of the law which are not regarded as essential to society's continued welfare.

PRE-1688 – NATURAL OR DIVINE LAW

The American system seeks to protect fundamental values by making their reform subject to a cumbersome law-making process requiring extremely high levels of popular consent. An analysis of early seventeenth century English case law reveals several judgments in which the courts suggested that were certain values that were *so fundamental* to the English constitution that they could not be changed by any process at all. These principles are perhaps analogous to the 'inalienable rights' of which Thomas Jefferson spoke in the US *Declaration of Independence.* Some judges seemed ready to suggest that there was a system of 'natural law' or 'divine law' which placed limits on what the various branches of government might do.

For example in *Dr Bonham's Case*[1] in 1610, Chief Justice Coke had said:

'And it appears in our books, that in many cases, the common law will controul Acts of Parliament, and sometime adjudge them to be utterly void: for when an Act of Parliament is against common right or reason, or repugnant, or impossible to be performed, the common law will control it, and adjudge such Act to be void'.

Five years later, in *Day v Savadge*, Chief Justice Hobart felt able to conclude that; 'even an Act of Parliament, made against natural equity, as to make a man judge in his own case, is void in itself, for jura naturae sunt immutabilia, and they are leges legum'.[2] Similarly in the 1653 case of *R v Love*, Keble J had pronounced that; 'Whatsoever is not consonant to the law of God, or to right reason which is maintained by scripture, . . . be it Acts of Parliament, customs, or any judicial acts of the Court, it is not the law of England'.[3]

The intricacies of the legal arguments expounded in these cases need not detain us here. The only point one would want to stress is that there have been periods in English constitutional history when it seems that it was widely believed that there were basic moral or political principles that it was not within the power of any number of the people, through any type of law-making process, to change in any way at all; and that the substance of those principles would be protected against legislative intrusion by the courts.[4]

[1] (1610) 8 Co Rep 114a at 118a. The case concerned legislation passed in 1561, which appeared to give the College of Physicians in London monopolistic control over the practice of medicine in London, and powers to punish (by fine and imprisonment) anyone who practiced without the College's approval. The key issue in the case for our purposes is whether statute could authorise a government body to operate as – in effect – a judge in a case where it was one of the parties.

[2] (1614) Hob 85; 80 ER 235 at 237. Loosely translated, the Latin maxim means that: 'natural law is immutable and the highest form of law'. The case concerned, prosaically, trespass to a bag of nutmegs. As in *Dr Bonham's Case*, the legal point in issue was whether a governmental body, had the competence to act as a judge in a cause to which it was also a party even if it appeared to have been given that competence by statute.

[3] (1653) 5 State Tr 825 at 828.

[4] The cautious language indicates that commentators hold divergent views as to the principles that Coke and his fellow judges were espousing. Several analysts have suggested that *Bonham* is merely advancing an unusual rule of statutory interpretation; see Thorne S (1938) '*Dr Bonham's case*' *LQR* 543–552: Plucknett T (1928) '*Doctor Bonham's Case* and judicial review' *Harvard LR* 30–70. In contrast see Dike C (1976) 'The case

THE DICEYAN (OR ORTHODOX) THEORY

Modern Britain does not have such a complex constitutional structure. We no longer seem to recognise the natural law doctrines of the seventeenth century. And unlike the Americans, we have not accepted that our fundamental constitutional values should be safeguarded by a complex and difficult amendment process. Things are more straightforward here. The 'basic principle' of the British constitution can be summed up in a fairly bald statement. A statute, that is a piece of legislation produced by Parliament, is generally regarded as the highest form of law within the British constitutional structure. The British Parliament, it is said, is a sovereign law-maker.

In describing this concept of parliamentary sovereignty, we are drawing mainly on two sources. The first is the political events of the late seventeenth century, when England experienced its last civil war. The second is a legal theory articulated in the late nineteenth century by an Oxford law professor, A V Dicey, in the first edition of a celebrated textbook, *An introduction to the study of the law of the constitution.* We will return to the late seventeenth century shortly; but it is helpful to begin by looking at Dicey's legal theory.

Dicey wields an enormous influence on British constitutional law. This is in many senses rather unfortunate. Some of the political views which Dicey held at the time that the first edition of . . . *the law of the constitution* was published would be considered entirely unacceptable from a contemporary moral standpoint. Dicey certainly did not approve of democracy as that concept is now understood. For example, he was very much opposed to allowing women or the working class to vote in parliamentary elections.[5] Nevertheless, it is important to understand the basic features of his theory. Dicey suggested that the concept of parliamentary sovereignty has two parts – a positive limb and a negative limb.

The positive and negative limbs of Dicey's theory

The principle articulated in the *positive limb* of the Diceyan theory of parliamentary sovereignty is that Parliament can make or unmake any law whatsoever. If a majority of members of the House of Commons vote in favour of a particular bill, and this is then approved by both a majority of members in the House of Lords and by the Monarch, that bill becomes an Act, irrespective of its contents. In technical legal terms there are no limits to the substance of statute law; Parliament can make any law that it wishes. Nor does it matter how big the majority in Parliament is for a particular measure; an Act passed by a majority of one in both the House of Commons and the

against Parliamentary Sovereignty' *Public Law* 283–297: Maitland F (1908) *The constitutional history of England* (Cambridge: CUP) at p 300: 'It is always difficult to pin Coke to a theory, but he does seem to claim distinctly that the common law is above the statute'.

5 See McEldowney J (1985) 'Dicey in historical perspective', in McAuslan P and McEldowney J (eds) *Law, legitimacy and the constitution* (London: Sweet and Maxwell): Loughlin M (1992) *Public law and political theory* ch 7 (Oxford: Clarendon Press).

House of Lords is as authoritative as legislation which receives unanimous support. Relatedly, no distinction is drawn between 'ordinary' and 'constitutional (or 'fundamental') law. Parliament may legislate in just the same way in respect of trivial matters as it does in respect of vitally important issues.

The proposition advanced in the *negative limb* is that the legality of an Act of Parliament cannot be challenged in any British court. According to the traditional view of the sovereignty of Parliament, there is no mechanism within the British constitution for declaring an Act of Parliament legally invalid. Adherents to Dicey's theory clearly reject the idea that the courts could invoke natural law or divine law to conclude that a statute was 'unconstitutional'. In the Diceyan theory of the Constitution, there is no higher form of law than the will of Parliament as expressed in the text of an Act.[6]

These two propositions, the negative and positive limbs of Dicey's theory, seem to offer us a simple and straightforward principle upon which to base an analysis of the constitution. As we examine the subject of parliamentary sovereignty further, it will become evident that the picture is not quite as clear cut as Dicey's modern day disciples would suggest. But before examining criticisms of this orthodox theory, it is useful to consider the sources on which contemporary adherents to Dicey's thesis rely to support his arguments. Why has it for so long been accepted by legal scholars that statute is the highest form of law in modern Britain?

THE POLITICAL SOURCE OF PARLIAMENTARY SOVEREIGNTY – THE 'GLORIOUS REVOLUTION'

When trying to make sense of contemporary constitutional practice, it is often helpful to turn our attention to the events of 1688. One might immediately sound a note of warning here. Readers might quite reasonably ask why events that happened over 300 years ago, in a pre-industrial society, where hardly anybody had the right to vote, should be regarded as relevant to shaping the constitutional structure of a modern, industrialised and apparently democratic country. That is a question to which we shall constantly be returning in later chapters. For the present, we will simply focus on the question of what is, rather than what should be, and so adopt (briefly) a formalist rather than functionalist approach to our subject.

The central theme of seventeenth century British political history is a struggle for power between the House of Commons and House of Lords and the Monarchy. In its most acute form, the conflict produced the civil war, the execution of Charles I, the brief rule of Oliver Cromwell, the restoration of Charles II to the throne, followed by the overthrow of his brother, James II, in 1688, and the installation of William of

6 Cf Dicey op cit at p 39: 'These then are the three traits of Parliamentary sovereignty as it exists in England: first, the power of the legislature to alter any law, fundamental or otherwise, as freely and in the same manner as other laws; secondly, the absence of any legal distinction between constitutional and other laws; thirdly, the non-existence of any judicial or other authority having the right to nullify an Act of Parliament, or to treat it as void or unconstitutional'.

Orange and his wife Mary as joint monarchs.[7] But in less dramatic terms, seventeenth century England had been continually beset by squabbles between the King, the Commons and the Lords as to the extent of their respective powers. This argument was waged as frequently in the courts as on the battlefield: both the King and the respective houses of Parliament hoped that the courts would supply rulings which favoured their own preferences. As we shall see in chapter four, the courts tended to switch their allegiance in these disputes as expediency and principle demanded. But on some occasions they struck an independent line; in the natural or divine law cases mentioned earlier, the judges were effectively saying that neither Acts of Parliament nor the actions of the Monarch were supreme. Both were subject to the laws of God and nature, and of course only the judges could identify the content of these immutable principles. In functionalist terms, adoption of this principle would have made the judiciary the 'highest source of law' within the English constitution.

Such reasoning did not commend itself to the Stuart monarchs, who were firm believers in the doctrine of the divine right of kings.[8] The doctrine placed complete legal authority in the person of the King himself. James I explained the rationale behind this theory thus in 1610:

> 'Kings are not only God's lieutenants on earth . . . but even by God himself they are called Gods. . . . [They] exercise a manner or resemblance of divine power on earth. . . . they make and unmake their subjects; they have power of raising and casting down; of life and of death; judges over all their subjects, and in all causes, and yet accountable to none but God only'.

James I would have rejected any assertion that this claimed power amounted to tyranny, for he considered himself bound by an oath he took upon his coronation to exercise his powers in accordance with the laws of the land. Yet since he also claimed the power to alter such laws at will, the substantive value of the oath was somewhat limited. The previous Tudor dynasty, in which the foundations of a recognisably modern government structure were laid,[9] had made no such sweeping claims. Nor, as a consequence, was James' doctrine uncontested by the House of Commons and the House of Lords. Both bodies invoked constitutional principles of considerable antiquity to place limits on the Stuart kings' effective legal powers.

Since the signing of the *Magna Carta* in the thirteenth century it had been accepted

[7] It is not possible to examine the details of this period in any depth in this book. Readers might usefully refer to the following sources for further information: Russell C (1971) *The crisis of Parliaments* (Oxford: Clarendon Press): Hutton R (1985) *The Restoration* (Oxford: Clarendon Press): Underdown D (1985) *Revel, riot, and rebellion* (Oxford: Clarendon Press): Speck W (1986) *Reluctant revolutionaries* (Oxford: Clarendon Press). A useful, succinct guide to the events of 1688 itself is provided in Miller J (1983) *The glorious revolution* (London: Longmans).

[8] See Plucknett T (11th edn, 1960) Taswell-Langmead's *English constitutional history* pp 329–333 (London: Sweet and Maxwell).

[9] See Elton G (1953) *The Tudor revolution in government* (Cambridge: CUP): Loach J (1990) *Parliament under the Tudors* (Oxford: Clarendon Press).

that the King could not levy taxation without 'Parliament's' approval.[10] Magna Carta could be compared to the American revolution in some respects. Both events represented a severe rupture in the fabric of society's previously dominant political values. They signalled that the present government no longer commanded the consent of 'the people', and they led to the digging of new political foundations upon which the constitution's legal structure was based. This is not to suggest that Magna Carta was a democratic constitutional settlement as we now understand the term.[11] It simply transferred some powers from one person, the King, to the few aristocrats who effectively controlled 'Parliament'.[12] Nevertheless, Magna Carta broadened, albeit very slightly, the basis of consent required to make law in English society. The Monarch's grip on the reins of constitutional power remained particularly firm because she retained the personal legal power (or 'prerogative') to summon and dissolve Parliament as and when she thought fit.

By the seventeenth century the Commons and Lords had become increasingly reluctant to give approval for the levying of taxes without a guarantee that the Monarch accepted certain limits on his personal powers. Although (as we shall see in chapter four) the Stuart Monarchs on occasion found ways to subvert this principle, Charles II and James II had generally sought to govern the country by proclamation or prerogative powers, bypassing Parliament and entrusting the administration of government to their own appointees. To a degree it was feasible for a Monarch to do this; the difficulty arose whenever the Crown needed money above and beyond its own resources – whenever it wanted to go to war for example.

The Triennial Act of 1641 was a measure passed by Parliament which purportedly required the Monarch to summon Parliament at least once every three years. Yet following the restoration of the Stuart Monarchy in 1660, Charles II did not regard himself as obliged to obey its terms. The long term causes of the 1688 revolution are many and varied, and cannot sensibly be addressed in any detail in this work. It is nevertheless clear that James II's evident contempt for the (admittedly limited) notion of citizen 'consent' to the government process, which was made apparent by his disinclination to allow Parliament to sit on a regular basis,[13] was a major contributor to his eventual downfall. The complaints of the English revolutionaries were outlined in the 1688 '*Declaration of Right*'. The broad thrust of the *Declaration of Right* was that:

10 Article 14 of Magna Carta. 'Parliament' did not then exist in a recognisably modern form; Article 14 refers to 'the archbishops, bishops, abbots, earls, and greater barons, by writ addressed to each severally, and all other tenants *in capite* by a general writ addressed to the sheriff of each shire'. One can discern here the outline of the subsequent distinction between the House of Lords and the House of Commons.

11 Professor John Millar argued for example that Magna Carta was intended 'to establish the privileges of a few individuals. A great tyrant on one side [King John], and a set of petty tyrants on the other, seem to have divided the kingdom, and the great body of people, disregarded and oppressed on all hands, were beholden for any privileges bestowed on them, to the jealousy of their masters' (1803) *Historical view* vol II pp 80–81, quoted in Loughlin (1992) op cit p 7.

12 An accessible introduction both to the events leading to the signing of Magna Carta, and the terms of the document itself, is provided in Plucknett (1960) op cit ch 4.

13 See Plucknett (1960) op cit pp 524–526.

'the late King James, by the assistance of diverse evill councellors, judges, and ministers imployed by him, did endeavour to subvert and extirpate the Protestant religion, and the laws and liberties of this kingdom'.

In the same way as the American revolutionaries' *Declaration of Independence*, the English revolutionaries' *Declaration of Right* supported its general accusation with a myriad of specific charges, and it seems that the similarities between the two documents extended to matters of substance as well as mere methodology. James II, it was alleged, had infringed upon the 'liberties' of the English people in, inter alia, the following ways:[14]

> By levying money for and to the use of the Crown by [pretence] of prerogative for other time and in other manner than . . . granted by Parliament;
>
> By assuming and exercising a power of dispensing with and suspending of lawes and the execution of laws without consent of Parliament;
>
> By violating the freedom of elections of members to serve in Parliament;
>
> By raising and keeping a standing army within this kingdom in time of peace without consent of Parliament and quartering soldiers contrary to law;
>
> Corrupt and unqualified persons have been returned and served on juries in trials;
>
> And excessive fines have been imposed and illegal and cruell punishments inflicted.

The 1688 revolution, like Magna Carta and the Civil War before it, marked the crossing of a political watershed. A new political 'contract'[15] was struck between Parliament and the Monarchy, and consequently a new constitutional foundation was laid. Having deposed James II, the victorious revolutionaries offered the throne to James II's (protestant) daughter Mary and her (protestant) husband, William Prince of Orange.[16] In return for the throne, William and Mary accepted that the Crown's ability to govern the English nation through its prerogative powers would be severely limited in future. The Monarch might still be responsible for governing the country, and she/he could appoint the Ministers who would do that job, but those Ministers would govern the country according to laws defined by Parliament. And if Parliament changed the law, the King's government would have to respond accordingly.

The initial 'terms' of the contract were specified in the text of the Bill of Rights produced by the Parliament of 1689. As one might expect, they address directly the complaints made in the *Declaration of Right*:[17]

> 1. That the pretended power of suspending of laws or the execution of laws by regall authority without consent of Parliament is illegal;

[14] The following quotations are actually drawn from the Bill of Rights of 1688, the first major statute passed by the post-revolutionary Parliament. The phraseology of the *Declaration* and the first parts of the Bill of Rights are virtually identical; Plucknett (1960) op cit pp 447–450.

[15] On the notion of the settlement as a 'contract' see Slaughter T (1981) ' "Abdicate" and "contract" in the Glorious Revolution' 24 *The Historical Journal* 323–337: Miller J (1982) 'The Glorious Revolution: "contract" and "abdication" reconsidered' 25 *The Historical Journal* 541–555.

[16] Who we might note was also James II's nephew.

[17] The numbers are those used in the Bill itself; they have been re-ordered thematically here.

13. And that for redresse of all grievances and for the amending, strengthening and preserving of the laws Parliaments ought to be held frequently;

8. That elections of members of Parliament ought to be free;

9. That the freedome of speech, and debates or proceedings in Parliament ought not to be impeached or questioned in any court or place out of Parliament;

4. That levying of money for or to the use of the Crown by pretence of prerogative without grant of Parliament . . . is illegal;

6. That the raising or keeping of a standing army within the kingdom in time of peace unlesse it be with consent of Parliament is against law;

11. That jurors ought to be duly impannelled and returned . . .

10. That excessive bail ought not to be required nor excessive fines imposed nor cruel and unusual punishment inflicted.

By virtue of their enactment in the Bill of Rights, these moral principles were henceforth to possess a superior legal status to any personal legal powers retained by the Monarchy. Furthermore, in addition to placing the Monarch's prerogative powers beneath statute in the hierarchy of constitutional importance, the 1688 revolution is generally regarded as having settled the question of the relationship between Parliament and the courts. The notion aired in *Dr Bonham's Case* and *R v Love* that 'natural' or 'divine' law provided the courts with a constitutional principle of more importance than statute was disregarded. And it was also assumed that the common law was subordinate in terms of its legal authority to legislation. We will examine the constitutional importance of the royal prerogative and the common law in more detail in chapter four; the basic principle one needs to remember at this point is that both are assumed to be less important than statute.

Despite the evident similarities between the functional underpinnings of the *Declaration of Independence* and the *Declaration of Right*, the English revolutionary settlement expressed in the 1688 Bill of Rights is substantially different from the American settlement articulated in the 1789–1791 Constitution. It is clear, for example, that while the American revolutionaries presumed that sovereignty should lie with the American 'people', their English predecessors assumed that sovereignty would rest with 'Parliament'. Consequently, the terms of the Bill of Rights could not be regarded as a constituent framework for the country's subsequent governance in the legal sense provided for by the Constitution in the United States.

This is not to say that the English revolutionaries were less sincere in the moral principles they expressed than were the Americans. Rather it means that there was nothing 'special' in the legal sense about the terms of the English settlement. Parliament, as the country's sovereign law-making power, was competent to alter, repeal or add to the supposedly 'fundamental' provisions of the Bill of Rights whenever it chose, through exactly the same process as it might enact laws on the most trivial of subjects. The British Bill of Rights was not secured against attack by the national legislature in the same way as its American namesake was protected against infringement by Congress. Parliament was to be the ordinary as well as the extraordinary legislative assembly of the newly created English nation. It would sit in regular, perhaps almost constant session. And it alone would wield all the law-making powers that were subsequently so carefully and elaborately divided by Madison and his colleagues among the Presidency, the Congress, and the people of the United States.

Moreover, England was a unitary rather than federal state. If geographically discrete parts of the country wished to be governed in different ways, in order to reflect local traditions or political sentiments, they could do so only with Parliament's permission. It was within Parliament's power to designate the boundaries of any sub-central units of government in England, to determine the powers such bodies might possess, and to specify the manner in which the officials running them were to be appointed or elected. And, of course, Parliament might change its mind on such matters whenever it chose. There were thus to be no constitutional rights which a citizen or group of citizens could expect the English courts to enforce against Parliament, for the wishes of Parliament were 'the highest form of law' known to the English constitution.

That the American revolutionaries framed their rebellion against Britain's post-revolutionary constitution in much the same terms as the architects of that constitution had framed their own complaints against the Stuart Kings some ninety years earlier might suggest that the 1688 settlement had not provided effective protection for 'the liberties of the people'. We might therefore wonder if the sovereignty of Parliament, a constitutional device created to safeguard the nation and its empire against the tyranny of its King, had succeeding merely in transferring tyrannical authority into different hands? In what sense, if any, did the English revolution ensure that the laws of England enjoyed the consent of the governed?

What is (was) 'Parliament'?

The 1688 Parliament was not 'representative' of the English population as we would now understand that term. But it would be rash to dismiss the principles underlying the 1688 settlement too quickly. For in some ways it was based on ideas that we might consider valid today. It is important to clarify what the revolutionaries of 1688 meant by the institution of 'Parliament' for instance. Parliament was not a single body, but had three parts, the House of Commons, the House of Lords, and the Monarch. At that time, all three parts of Parliament had equal powers within the law-making process. If one part refused to approve a bill, that bill could not become law.

From a modern day perspective, we might think that the 1688 Parliament simply represented the views of elite groups and effectively excluded the mass of the population from any means of consenting to the law-making process. However many political theorists of the late seventeenth century sincerely believed that a Parliament composed of these three bodies was the most effective way to secure that laws accurately expressed the national interest.[18] We should recall that Jefferson used a very selective

[18] See particularly Judson M (1936) 'Henry Parker and the theory of parliamentary sovereignty', in Wittke C (ed) *Essays in history and political theory in honour of Charles Howard McIlwain* (Cambridge, Mass: HUP). For an overview of the debate, on both sides of the Atlantic, see Bailyn op cit pp 198–229.

definition of 'The People' in the *Declaration of Independence*; for law-making purposes, many poor men, all women and all slaves were not 'people' in late eighteenth century America. Similarly, in seventeenth century England, it was assumed that only the King, the aristocracy, the Church, and the affluent merchant and landowning class which elected members of the House of Commons, had any legitimate role to play in fashioning the laws within which society was governed. Orthodox political theory argued that the Commons, the Lords, and the Monarch formed the three 'Estates of the Realm'. These estates, acting in concert, were presumed to be the only legitimate arbiters of the national interest.

So the 1688 settlement could be perceived as democratic in a twisted or primitive sense of the term; not because it gave all citizens a role in the law-making process, but because it gave such a role to everyone who was presumed to be entitled to participate. This might be seen as a more extreme version of Madison's subsequent advocacy of elitist representative assemblies, staffed only by legislators who could be trusted to act in the national interest. But the 1688 settlement had a further purpose in mind. The objective of the 1688 revolution was to create a 'balanced' law-making process within a 'balanced' constitution.[19] Because Acts of Parliament could only be made if the Commons, Lords, and King were in agreement with each other, the legislature could not produce statutes which represented the interests of only one or two of the three Estates of the Realm.[20] This supposed solution to the problem of potentially tyrannical law-makers did not spring, Athena like, from the heads of the 1688 revolutionaries. Rather it represented the culmination of a long process of theorisation and practice which had exercised the minds of philosophers and politicians throughout the seventeenth century.[21]

We should also remember that the Parliament of 1688 was not organised along party political lines as it is today. There were some fairly firm party based alliances among groups of members;[22] but the seventeenth century Parliament was intended to function as an arena both for local interests to be aired and for discussion of national priorities – the House of Commons was initially conceived as the *House of Communities*. Many individual members came to the Commons as representatives not of a political party, but of their town or county.

[19] See Vile M (1967) *Constitutionalism and the separation of powers* ch 3 (Oxford: Clarendon Press).

[20] Contemporary commentators expressed the principle in more hyperbolic language; 'Lest . . . the Crown should lead towards arbitrary government, or the tumultuary licentiousness of the people should incline towards a democracy, the wisdom of our ancestors hath instituted a middle state of nobility. . . . The excellence of this government consists in the due balance of the several constituent parts of it, for if either one of them should be too hard for the other two, there is an actual dissolution of the constitution'; Trenchard J and Moyle W (1697) *An argument showing that a standing army is inconsistent with a free government*, quoted in Miller (1983) op cit p 114.

[21] Perhaps the most helpful survey of the ebbs and flows of opinions and events is offered in Sharp A (1983) *Political ideas of the English civil war* (London: Longman).

[22] Plucknett (1960) op cit pp 436–438. For some estimate of the strength of recognisably modern party loyalties in the revolution Parliament see Horwitz H (1974) 'Parliament and the glorious revolution' *Bulletin of the Institute of Historical Research* 36–52: Plumb J (1937) 'Elections to the Convention Parliament of 1689' *Cambridge Historical Journal* 235–254.

From a contemporary perspective, one might readily ask how the formal structure of our constitution has responded to changing definitions of 'the people', and to what we might call the growing 'nationalisation' of politics? As chapter seven will explain, it is now a fundamental tenet of modern British society that virtually every adult is entitled to vote in parliamentary elections. It is also clear that parliamentary elections are contested by nationally organised politically parties, and are won and lost primarily on national rather than local issues. It might seem obvious that a constitutional structure designed to adduce the consent of a tiny minority of the small population of an agrarian country would be ill-suited to securing the consent of some forty million people in a modern industrialised society. It is perhaps instructive to observe for instance that no other modern democracy has fully copied the British constitutional model: the American system has proved much the more influential blueprint. But in many respects, the formal constitutional principles which emerged as a result of political revolution in England at the end of the seventeenth century remain largely unchanged in the Britain of today. And it is probably accurate to say that parliamentary sovereignty is the most important of those unchanged principles. It is therefore important that we begin to consider the ways in which the doctrine has been both criticised and vindicated in rather more recent times.

I. LEGAL AUTHORITY FOR THE PRINCIPLE OF PARLIAMENTARY SOVEREIGNTY

As mentioned earlier, our constitution no longer seems to offer any role for the courts to invoke natural law or common law as a source of legal authority having a higher constitutional status than Acts of Parliament. One must look very hard indeed to find any suggestion that after 1688 the courts entertained the idea that statutes might be invalidated if they conflicted with natural or divine law. The 1701 case of *City of London v Wood*[23] offers some albeit, confused support for the *Bonham* principle. At one point in his judgment, Holt CJ argued that:

'What my Lord Coke says in *Dr Bonham's Case* is far from any extravagancy, for it is a very reasonable and true saying, that if an Act of Parliament should ordain the same person should be party and judge, it would be a void Act of Parliament'.[24]

But having offered this apparent support for Coke's ideas, Holt CJ continued by concluding that; 'an Act of Parliament can do no wrong, though it may do several things that look pretty odd'.[25] So contradictory a judgment cannot be considered a powerful authority for natural law ideas. Nor can one find more helpful precedents in

[23] (1701) 12 Mod Rep 669. A helpful discussion of the case is offered in Plucknett (1928) op cit.

[24] (1701) 12 Mod Rep 669 at 687.

[25] Ibid, at 688.

the post-revolutionary case law.[26] The principle was last seen in *Forbes v Cochrane* in 1824, when the court suggested it would not enforce a law permitting slavery, as this would be 'against the law of nature and God'.[27]

On the other hand, one will not find much case law prior to 1800 which lends explicit support to the idea of parliamentary sovereignty. In his celebrated *Commentaries*, first published in 1765, Blackstone drew the following conclusion about the constitutional status of legislation:

'I know it is generally laid down . . . that acts of parliament contrary to reason are void. But if the parliament will positively enact a thing to be done which is unreasonable, I know of no power that can control it . . . for that were to set the judicial power above that of the legislature, which would be subversive of all government'.

As we saw in chapter one, the American colonists were contemporaneously trying to fashion a constitutional order which avoided the problem of subversion by setting the power of the people above both legislature and judiciary. Blackstone was manifestly unimpressed by such theorisation, but one might also note that he could find little direct judicial authority for his proposition as to Parliament's supremacy.[28] The dearth of authority may be because everybody took it for granted that this was the way things were; sometimes the most important values are those which go unspoken and therefore unexamined. But that may be a rash assumption to make. Several strands of case law supporting the orthodox understanding of parliamentary sovereignty appear in the nineteenth century. The first strand deals with what has been termed call 'the enrolled bill rule'.

SUBSTANCE OR PROCEDURE? THE ENROLLED BILL RULE

The plaintiff in *Edinburgh and Dalkeith Rly Co v Wauchope*[29] was a landowner affected by a private Act of Parliament authorising construction of a railway. He

26 Readers interested in exploring the esoterica of post-revolutionary natural law jurisprudence might consult *R v Inhabitants of Cumberland* (1795) 6 Term Rep 194 and *Leigh v Kent* (1789) 3 Term Rep 362.

27 (1824) 2 B & C 448 at 470; 107 ER 450. Forbes was suing Cochrane for the price (£3,800) of thirty-eight slaves (legally owned by Forbes under Spanish colonial law) who had escaped from Spanish territory in the Americas during an Anglo-Spanish war on to a British ship under Cochrane's command. The issue before the court was whether English common law should afford a remedy to a slave-owner in such circumstances. The court concluded that neither common law nor statute gave such a remedy. In a comment which was not strictly necessary to the outcome of the case, Best J observed that:

'If indeed, there had been any express law, commanding us to recognise those [ie a slave-owner's] rights, we might then have been called upon to consider the propriety of that which has been said by the great commentator on the laws of this country, "That if any human law should allow or injoin us to commit an offence against the divine law, we are bound to transgress that human law" '.

The 'great commentator' is Sir William Blackstone; the quotation is drawn from *Blackstone's Commentaries* Vol 1, p 42.

28 One might point to an ambiguous endorsement of this position in *Thornby d Duchess of Hamilton v Fleetwood* (1712) 10 Mod 114. A stronger authority appears in *Greate Charte Parish and Kennington Parish* (1742) 2 Stra 1173.

29 (1842) 8 Cl & Fin 710, 8 ER 279, HL.

claimed that the court should invalidate the legislation because its promoters had not given notice to affected parties in accordance with the House of Commons' standing orders which regulated its internal procedures in respect of such measures. Lord Campbell thought that judging the constitutional adequacy of proceedings in either the Commons or the Lords was entirely beyond the court's powers:

'All that a court . . . can do is to look to the Parliamentary Roll: if from that it should appear that a Bill has passed both Houses and received the Royal Assent, no court . . . can inquire into the mode in which it was introduced . . . or what passed . . . during its progress in its various stages through Parliament'.[30]

A similar conclusion was reached by the court in the factually similar case of *Lee v Bude and Torrington Junction Rly Co* where Wile J commented that; 'if an Act of Parliament has been obtained improperly it is for the legislature to correct it by repealing it; but so long as it exists as law, the Courts are bound to obey it'.[31]

This principle was also forcefully restated by the House of Lords in the 1974 case of *British Railways Board v Pickin.*[32] The facts of *Pickin* are very similar to the *Wauchope* and *Lee* litigation. Mr Pickin alleged that British Rail had steered a private bill through Parliament without giving the necessary notices to affected landowners, and had also misled Parliament about the bill's intentions. Somewhat surprisingly, the Court of Appeal thought this raised a triable issue: Lord Denning indicated that he thought one could draw a valid distinction between public bills and private bills.[33] But that view was rapidly overruled by the House of Lords. Lord Reid was quite explicit in denying that the courts had any power to question the legality of a bill's passage through Parliament. He thought any such investigation by the court would bring it into conflict with Parliament. Lord Reid said that he could entertain such a course only if compelled to do so by clear authority, but he was quite certain that 'the whole trend of authority for over a century is clearly against permitting such an investigation'.[34] In Lord Simon's opinion:

'a concomitant of the sovereignty of Parliament is that the houses of Parliament enjoy certain privileges. . . . Among the privileges of the Houses of Parliament is the exclusive right to determine their own proceedings'.[35]

The enrolled bill rule has been widely construed as offering an unambiguous judicial affirmation of the principle of parliamentary sovereignty. Whether this view is analytically defensible (in either formal or functionalist terms) is a question to which we shall return in subsequent chapters. For the moment, attention turns to a second series of cases, setting out what has come to be known as the 'doctrine of implied repeal', which is also presumed to provide similarly unequivocal support for the theory that Parliament enjoys unlimited legal powers.

30 Ibid, at 285. 31 (1871) LR 6 CP 576 at 582. 32 [1974] AC 765, HL.
33 This distinction is addressed in ch 5. 34 [1974] AC 765 at 788.
35 Ibid, at 788–789. We address the issue of the 'privileges of Parliament' in depth in ch 8.

THE DOCTRINE OF IMPLIED REPEAL

The two cases we are concerned with here, *Vauxhall Estates Ltd v Liverpool Corpn*[36] and *Ellen Street Estates Ltd v Minister of Health*[37] both focused on the Acquisition of Land Act 1919. That Act was a slum clearance measure which laid down levels of compensation for property owners whose houses were demolished. The Housing Acts of 1925 and 1930 made these compensation provisions less generous. Not surprisingly, the landowners affected looked for some way to have compensation assessed on the basis used in the 1919 Act.

The landowners seized on s 7 of the 1919 Act. This said that any Act affecting compensation provisions would 'cease to have or *shall not have effect*' (emphasis added) if it was inconsistent with the 1919 legislation. That phraseology is arguably looking towards future Acts as well as those already existing. But the plaintiffs did not argue that the 1919 Act was completely protected from amendment by a subsequent Parliament. Instead they drew a *distinction between express and implied repeal*.

The landowners conceded that if a subsequent Act said expressly that the 1919 Act was overturned, the courts could not challenge the new Act's effect. However, it was argued that the courts could safeguard the 1919 Act against *accidental or implied repeal*; if Parliament did not expressly say it was changing a statute that seemed to have been intended to prevent future amendment, the court should assume that the original Act should be upheld.

This argument seems to reach out towards constitutional principles founded on notions of consent theory. It suggests that it would be unconstitutional to allow legislation to have unintended effects because 'the people' could not have knowingly consented to the law that had been passed. This seems to offer a variation on the theme of 'functionalist' approaches to parliamentary sovereignty; if that function is to ensure that laws enjoy the consent of the governed, it would be logical to assume that the courts should not permit Parliament to enact legislation premised on false information.

The argument reached the Court of Appeal in *Ellen Street* – where it was uncategorically dismissed. The courts rejected any notion of a functionalist interpretation of the parliamentary sovereignty doctrine. The judges adopted instead a 'formalist approach'. That formal rule simply demanded that the courts unquestioningly obey the most recent Act of Parliament. And if that Act appeared inconsistent with previous legislation, the previous legislation must give way.[38] Questions about the existence of the people's consent, or Parliament's unspoken intentions, were not something the courts were prepared to entertain.

Despite the vigour with which the Court of Appeal delivered its opinion, it could not draw on much past case law to support its proposition. The main precedent it relied on was the decision in *Vauxhall Estates* two years earlier. That seems a flimsy

36 [1932] 1 KB 733. 37 [1934] 1 KB 590, CA.

38 The rule is sometimes expressed in the Latin maxim 'lex posterior derogat priori' (a later Act overrules an earlier one).

legal base on which to build so important a constitutional principle.[39] We can however find a further line of supportive decisions in cases dealing with the relationship between British statutes and international law.

INCONSISTENCY WITH INTERNATIONAL LAW

The first case we might consider is *Mortensen v Peters*.[40] One of the most important areas of international law relates to defining the extent of a country's jurisdiction over the oceans by which it is surrounded. By 1906, most nations had accepted that their respective jurisdictions should extend for some three miles from their coastline and had signed Treaties with each other to that effect. In 1889, the British Parliament passed the Herring Fishery (Scotland) Act. This Act gave Scotland's Fishery Board the power to make bye-laws to control fishing in the Moray Firth. Much of the Moray Firth is more than three miles from land, so the 1889 Act would seem to be inconsistent with international law obligations to which Britain was supposedly a party.

Mortensen was the captain of a Norwegian trawler. He was arrested for breaching the bye-laws that the Fishery Board had made. His defence was that the Act was 'unconstitutional' because it breached accepted international standards, and therefore could not have any legal effect. The court peremptorily dismissed this argument:

> 'In this Court we have nothing to do with . . . whether an act of the legislature is *ultra vires* as in contravention of generally acknowledged principles of international law. For us, an Act of Parliament duly passed by Lords and Commons and assented to by the King, is supreme, and we are bound to give effect to its terms'.[41]

This conclusion is entirely consistent with both traditional Diceyan theory and the political outcome of the 1688 revolution. Under Britain's constitutional arrangements, treaties are negotiated and formally entered into by the Crown (or 'the government') through its prerogative powers, not by Parliament. Orthodox constitutional theory maintains that a treaty signed by the British government can only have legal effect in Britain if it is *incorporated* into British law by an Act of Parliament. This is a logical consequence of the parliamentary sovereignty doctrine. The 1688 revolution

[39] See Marshall G (1954) 'What is Parliament? The changing concept of Parliamentary Sovereignty' *Political Studies* 193–209. There is also some ambiguity in Maugham LJ's judgment, in that he suggests implied repeal will only be effective 'if Parliament chooses to make it plain that the earlier statute is being to some extent repealed': [1934] 1 KB 590 at 597, CA. This suggests implied repeal will apply in situations where the later Act 'envelopes' the former, but not when there is simply an 'overlap' of inconsistent provisions.

[40] (1906) 14 SLT 227.

[41] Ibid, at 230. The term ultra vires literally means 'beyond the legal powers'. If a body is legally sovereign, nothing can be beyond its powers. The ultra vires doctrine thus could not be applied to Parliament, but as we shall see in subsequent chapters, it has an important role in respect of other governmental organisations.

produced an agreement between William of Orange and Parliament which provided that the constitutional role of the King's government was to govern within the laws made by Parliament. The government itself could not create new laws simply by coming to an agreement with foreign countries. If one allowed that to happen, one would essentially be saying that it is the government rather than Parliament that is the sovereign law-maker, as the government could bypass the refusal of the House of Commons and/or the House of Lords to consent to its proposed laws.

The principle is further illustrated by the case of *Cheney v Conn.*[42] Mr Cheney was a taxpayer who appealed against the Inland Revenue's assessment of his income tax liability. The Inland Revenue made its assessment in accordance with the Finance Act 1964. Mr Cheney claimed that some of his tax money was being used to build nuclear weapons, contrary to the principles of the Geneva Convention, a 1957 treaty which the British government had signed.

Parts of the Treaty had been incorporated into British law, but these were not helpful to Mr Cheney's argument. His case rested on sections of the Treaty that remained unincorporated. Mr Cheney argued that since these parts of the Treaty forbade the use of nuclear weapons, it must be illegal for Parliament to enact a statute that raised money so that such weapons could be built. The judge, Ungoed-Thomas J, had no doubt that this was a pointless argument:

> 'what the statute itself enacts cannot be unlawful, because what the statute says is itself the law, and the highest form of law that is known to this country. It is the law which prevails over every other form of law, and it is not for the court to say that a parliamentary enactment, the highest law in this country, is illegal'.[43]

Parliament was at liberty to forbid the manufacture of nuclear weapons in Britain, and should it ever do so the British courts would be obliged to apply that legislation. But an unincorporated Treaty could not have that effect.

Having sketched the basic political and legal foundations of the parliamentary sovereignty doctrine, we turn in the second half of this chapter to the various challenges to the Diceyan theory that have been aired before the courts and in academic fora in recent years. It might be noted at the outset that none of these challenges has thus far proved effective – but that does not necessarily mean that one will not become so in the future. We will consider three of these arguments in some detail. Firstly, we will look at the 'manner and form' technique of safeguarding certain basic constitutional values against reform by a simple majority vote in Parliament. Secondly, we will assess the status of the Treaty of Union of 1707 between England and Scotland. And thirdly, we will explore the notion that there might still be some moral or political values which the courts suggest Parliament can only change through *express* legislative statements.

42 [1968] 1 All ER 779, [1968] 1 WLR 242. 43 Ibid at 782.

II. ENTRENCHING LEGISLATION – CHALLENGES TO THE ORTHODOX POSITION

The positive limb of Dicey's theory seems to maintain that Parliament possesses the competence to give legal effect to any political or moral values it considers desirable. But there appears to be one basic flaw of logic in the Diceyan formulation of the parliamentary sovereignty doctrine. Simply put, the problem is how can Parliament have supreme legislative power if there is still one thing it cannot do? That one thing seems to be that Parliament cannot pass an Act which is binding on its successors. If Parliament is truly a sovereign law-maker, then one would have assumed that it must have the power to place limits on its own law-making capacity?[44] This apparent conundrum presents us with the distinction between the *continuing* and *self-embracing* theories of parliamentary sovereignty.[45]

The *continuing* theory maintains that the sovereign Parliament is a *perpetual institution.* Its unconfined legislative power is created anew every time it meets, irrespective of what previous Parliaments have enacted. This is the position which Professor Dicey supported. As far as Dicey was concerned, Parliament need pay no heed at all to what its predecessors have done. And this remains the orthodox interpretation of Parliament's legal powers.

The *self-embracing* theory advocates a radical position. It has aroused much academic interest. With one important exception,[46] it has not had any practical political effect in this country, but it has had considerable influence in countries which used to be British colonies. The self-embracing theory holds that Parliament's sovereignty does include the power to bind itself and its successors. Supporters of the self-embracing theory argue that it is possible to enact legislation which is safe from subsequent amendment – that certain measures can be *entrenched* within the legal system and rendered immune from repeal by a future Parliament.

When we talk of entrenchment in the British context, we are not dealing with a single device. The concept simply means any constitutional mechanism which makes some laws immune to repeal by the usual legislative formula of a simple majority vote in the Commons and the Lords plus the royal assent. In principle, a particular political

[44] This does not amount to the same thing, however, as asserting that a sovereign Parliament must be an ever-present feature of Britain's constitutional landscape; cf Dicey op cit at p 24:

> 'A sovereign power can divest itself of authority in two ways. . . . It may simply put an end to its own existence. Parliament could extinguish itself by legally dissolving itself and leaving no means whereby a subsequent Parliament could be legally summoned . . . A sovereign body may again transfer sovereign authority to another person or body of persons. . .'.

Whether the previously sovereign Parliament could then in some fashion be 'resurrected' at a future date is a nice question.

[45] Winterton G (1976) 'The British grundnorm: parliamentary sovereignty re-examined' 92 *LQR* 591–617.

[46] This relates to the United Kingdom's membership of the European Community. The development is of recent origin, and is discussed in detail in ch 13 below.

value might be entrenched in either a *substantive* or *procedural* sense. *Substantive entrenchment* would entail acceptance of the principle that *Parliament cannot legislate at all* about specific subjects. It implies that there are basic human values which can never be changed. This argument is reminiscent of the old and discredited natural law or divine law ideas, and has not been vigorously pursued in recent times. The obvious drawback to substantive entrenchment would be that a society would be stuck with particular values forever; it is a completely rigid form of safeguard for basic principles.

In the modern era, commentators who oppose Dicey's theory have sought to limit Parliament's power through the device of procedural entrenchment. It is important to stress that *procedural entrenchment would not necessarily produce a rigid constitution* – it produces a relative rather than absolute degree of permanence in respect of certain laws. In theory, one would have entrenched a particular piece of legislation if a majority of two rather than one in the House of Commons was needed to change it. That legislation would not be entrenched very firmly of course; but as one makes reform procedures more rigorous, so legislation becomes more securely entrenched. Constitutional values which could only be changed with the support of, for example 70% of MPs, would be quite deeply entrenched; if amendment required near unanimous support within each house of Parliament, then change might be virtually impossible.[47]

JENNINGS' CRITIQUE AND THE 'RULE OF RECOGNITION'

The starting point for analysis of this theory is to ask ourselves why it is that the courts recognise statutes as the highest form of law? There is obviously no supra-legislative constitution which articulates this rule. Similarly, we cannot find the doctrine of parliamentary sovereignty laid down in a statute. But the haziness surrounding the legal status of this so-called '*rule of recognition*' has given some assistance to constitutional lawyers opposed to the Diceyan view.[48]

The most forceful exponent in the modern era of what has come to be known as the '*manner and form*' strategy of procedural entrenchment was Sir Ivor Jennings.[49] Jennings based his critique of the orthodox theory on a version of the self-embracing understanding of sovereignty. His argument goes through three apparently logical steps. Firstly, the rule of recognition is a common law concept. Secondly, statute is legally superior to the common law. Thirdly, Parliament can therefore enact legislation changing the rule of recognition and requiring the courts to accept that some Acts of Parliament are protected from repeal by a simple majority vote in both houses plus the royal assent. Jennings formulated the argument in the following terms:

' "Legal sovereignty" is merely a name indicating that the legislature has for the time being

47 One could thus say that most parts of the United States' constitution are deeply, but not permanently entrenched.

48 The term is that of Professor H Hart; see (1961) *The concept of law* p 161 (Oxford: OUP). For an overview of related theories see Winterton (1976) op cit.

49 See especially (5th edn, 1958) *The law and the constitution* pp 140–145 (London: Stevens and Sons).

power to make laws of any kind in the manner required by law. That is, a rule expressed to be made by the Queen, [the House of Commons and the House of Lords] will be recognised by the courts, *including a rule which alters this law itself* ... The power of a legislature derives from the law by which it is established. ... In the United Kingdom ... it derives from the accepted law, which is the common law.'[50]

There seems to be an obvious legal logic to this argument. Jennings' analysis also appears to make sound political sense. If the judges are subordinate to Parliament, then surely Parliament can tell them what rules they should follow when assessing whether or not a statute is unconstitutional.

The manner and form argument draws its theoretical basis largely from Jennings' work. One would be quite justified in assuming however that academic theories are rather less important than case law in assessing the legal status of constitutional ideas. The legal basis of the manner and form argument relies heavily on three cases,[51] all of them rooted in the process of former British colonies gaining independence. The first, *A-G for New South Wales v Trethowan*,[52] was an Australian case decided by the Australian High Court and the Privy Council in 1932.

A-G for New South Wales v Trethowan

The New South Wales Parliament was created by a British statute, called in New South Wales 'The Constitution Statute 1855'. In many respects, the New South Wales constitution followed the British model. Legislation required the support of a simple majority in an upper house (the Legislative Council) and lower house (the Legislative Assembly), and the royal assent was provided by the Governor-General qua the Monarch's representative. However, s 5 of a subsequent British statute, the Colonial Laws Validity Act 1865, provided that statutes enacted by certain colonial legislatures (including the New South Wales Parliament) which sought to alter their own 'constitution, powers or procedures' would have legal effect only if passed 'in such manner or form' as the law then in force in the colony demanded. The terms of s 5 were left unchanged when the New South Wales' Constitution Act was passed by the New South Wales Legislature in 1902. The 1902 Act, inter alia, made provisions concerning the composition and respective powers of the two houses.

In 1929, the Liberal Party government, which had majorities in both houses of the NSW Parliament, promoted the Constitution (Legislative Council Amendment) Bill 1929. The Bill was passed by both houses, received the royal assent, and thus became an Act. The Act introduced a new s 7A into the Constitution Act 1902, to the effect that a bill seeking to abolish the Legislative Council could not be sent for the royal assent unless it had been approved by a majority of both houses and by a majority of the electorate in a special referendum. Section 7A therefore seemed to change the

50 Op cit at pp 152–153 and 156; original emphasis.

51 Jennings himself relied on the first two cases discussed here. The third case was decided after the 1958 edition of Jennings' book *The law and the constitution* was written.

52 (1931) 44 CLR 394; affd [1932] AC 526, PC.

'manner and form' of the legislation needed to abolish the upper chamber, by adding an additional step to the usual legislative process. Furthermore, s 7A(6) provided that s 7A itself could not be repealed unless the repealing legislation had also been approved by a majority of electors in a special referendum. It appeared that the government expected to be defeated in the imminent general election, and wished to ensure that the opposition party could not carry out its stated intention to abolish the upper house without first putting that specific question to the 'people' of New South Wales.

After the New South Wales elections of 1930, the previous opposition party secured a majority in both houses. Both houses thereafter approved bills respectively repealing s 7A and abolishing the Legislative Council. Neither measure was subjected to a referendum before it was submitted for the royal assent. Several members of the Legislative Council immediately began an action before the New South Wales courts requesting an injunction to prevent the bills being sent for the royal assent; if granted, the injunction would therefore prevent the bills becoming legislation. Their argument, quite simply was that s 7A could be repealed only in the 'manner and form' which it had itself specified.

The new government argued that successive New South Wales Parliaments, just like the British Parliament, could not be bound by any legislation passed by their predecessors. A Parliament might pass any 'manner and form' provisions it thought fit, but those provisions would cease to have effect when a future Parliament, acting by the 'simple majority plus royal assent formula', passed legislation to repeal them. That had indeed happened here, and thus s 7A had been lawfully repealed.

In the High Court of Australia,[53] two of the five judges accepted that argument. However the majority held that the Court was bound to prevent any Bill dealing with the subject matter of s 7A being sent for the royal assent unless it had been approved in a referendum. The special 'manner and form' of s 7A did provide an effective form of procedural entrenchment, safeguarding the existence of the Legislative Council. The majority reasoned that, unlike the British Parliament, the New South Wales legislature owed its existence and powers to two British statutes, the Constitution Statute 1855 and the Colonial Laws Validity Act 1865. Those Acts continued to provide the basis of the New South Wales Constitution, and until s 5 of the 1865 Act was itself repealed, the New South Wales legislature was subject to its terms. The majority saw this as a straightforward *legal rule*, which, Rich J explained (in terms very reminiscent of Madison's warnings as to the dangers of factionalism) served an obvious *political purpose*:

> 'There is no reason why a Parliament representing the people should be powerless to determine whether the constitutional salvation of the State is to be reached by cautious and well considered steps rather than by rash and ill considered measures'.[54]

On a further appeal to the Privy Council, the majority opinion, and the reasoning underlying it, was upheld unanimously.[55]

[53] (1931) 44 CLR 394. [54] Ibid, at 420. [55] [1932] AC 526, PC.

Harris v Dönges (Minister of the Interior)

The second case, *Harris v Dönges (Minister of the Interior),*[56] was decided by the Appellate Division of the South African Supreme Court in 1952. Once again, the story begins with the slow process of Britain disengaging itself from its former Empire. In 1909 the British Parliament passed the South Africa Act, which united the four South African colonies under a single legislature. The South African Parliament mirrored that of Britain in most respects. It had a lower house (the house of assembly) and an upper house (the senate) and retained the King's power of royal assent. In respect of almost all laws, South Africa's legislature had the same legal competence as the British Parliament – a Bill receiving a simple majority in both the house and the senate and thereafter receiving the royal assent was generally the 'highest form of law' within South Africa's constitution. However the 1909 Act contained some exceptions to the 'simple majority in both houses plus royal assent' formula.

Firstly, the South African Parliament could not, under any circumstances, pass laws 'repugnant' to British statutes intended to have effect within South Africa. The supremacy of British law vis à vis South African law was a substantively entrenched feature of South Africa's 1909 constitutional settlement. Secondly, ss 33–34 of the 1909 Act prevented the South African Parliament altering the composition of the house or the senate for ten years. Those provisions were thus substantively, but temporarily, entrenched. After the ten years had expired, the composition of the house and senate could be altered by simple majority legislation. Thirdly, s 35 provided that the right of Cape coloured citizens to be registered on the same electoral roll as whites could not be removed by South African legislation unless that legislation had been supported by a two thirds majority of the house and senate sitting in joint session. Fourthly, s 137 provided that the status of both Afrikaans and English as the country's official languages could only be changed by the two thirds majority procedure. Section 152 thereafter provided that s 35 and s 137 themselves could be amended only by a South African statute also attracting a two thirds majority in a joint legislative session. Section 35 and s 152 imply that the British Parliament in 1909 considered that coloured citizens' 'right' to vote on the same basis as whites was too important a political value to be left at the mercy of a bare legislative majority. It was not an 'inalienable right', but was to be more difficult to change than most other aspects of the South African constitution.[57]

In 1931, the British Parliament passed the Statute of Westminster which recognised South Africa (and several other former colonies) as independent sovereign states,

[56] (1952) 1 TLR 1245. The following pages present a simplified version of a series of complex judgments, all of which merit close study. For comment see particularly Griswold E (1952) 'The "coloured vote case" in South Africa' 65 *Harvard LR* 1361–1374: Note (1952) 68 *Law Quarterly Review* 285–287: Cowen D (1952) and (1953) 'Legislature and judiciary: parts I and II' 15 and 16 *Modern Law Review* 282–296 and 273–298. For a detailed treatment of the case and its background and aftermath see Loveland I (1999) *By due process of law? Racial discrimination and the right to vote in South Africa 1850–1960* (Oxford: Hart Publishing).

[57] For insight into why the British Parliament thought this additional protection appropriate see Loveland (1999) op cit ch 4: Lewin J (1956) 'The struggle for law in South Africa' 27 *Political Quarterly* 176–181.

possessing what was termed 'Dominion' status within the British Empire. The Statute of Westminster made, inter alia, the following provisions. Section 2 released the newly created Dominions from the controls imposed by the Colonial Laws Validity Act 1865.[58] Section 4 then provided that:

'No Act of Parliament of the United Kingdom passed after the commencement of this Act shall extend, or be deemed to extend, to a Dominion as part of the law of that Dominion unless it is expressly declared in that Act that that Dominion has requested and consented to the enactment thereof.'[59]

As a matter of British constitutional law, s 4 had little significance. If Parliament chose to pass legislation contravening s 4, the statute concerned would undoubtedly be applied by domestic courts. But the Statute of Westminster may more sensibly be seen as an exercise in *constitutional politics rather than constitutional law.* It affirmed an existing practical reality – namely that the Dominions were now capable of acting as independent States in respect both of their internal affairs and their international relations.[60] Some Dominions took the opportunity to modify their constitutions at the time that they gained independence. However, no changes were made to the South Africa Act 1909 at this time. The entrenchment provided for in ss 33–34 of the South Africa Act 1909 had by then elapsed. But the 1931 Act did not expressly repeal ss 35, 137 and 152; indeed, both houses of the South African legislature had resolved that the terms of the 1931 Act should 'in no way derogate from the entrenched provisions of the South Africa Act'.[61]

From the late 1940s onwards, the white Afrikaaner National Party possessed a majority in both houses of the legislature. The National Party had committed itself to introducing apartheid, a policy demanding rigid and (to non-whites) oppressive separation of different racial groups.[62] One element of this policy was to create separate electoral registers and voting systems for white and Cape coloured citizens. The Separate Representation of Voters Act was passed in 1951 by a simple majority, with both houses sitting separately. The Act's 'constitutionality' was then challenged

58 Section 2 was drafted in the following terms:

2(1) – The Colonial Laws Validity Act 1865 shall not apply to any law made after the commencement of this Act by the Parliament of a Dominion.

(2) No law . . . made after the commencement of this Act by the Parliament of a Dominion shall be void or inoperative on the ground that it is repugnant to . . . the provisions of any existing or future Act of Parliament of the United Kingdom . . . and the powers of a Dominion Parliament shall include the power to repeal or amend any such Act, order, rule or regulation in so far as the same is part of the law of the Dominion.

59 In effect, s 4 transformed the United Kingdom's Parliament into an additional part of the Dominion's own legislature.

60 The point is perhaps best conveyed by the comment of Lord Sankey in *British Coal Corpn v R* [1935] AC 500 at 520, PC; 'It is doubtless true that the power of the Imperial Parliament to pass on its own initiative any legislation that it thought fit extending to [a Dominion] remains in theory unimpaired: indeed, the Imperial Parliament could as a matter of abstract law, repeal or disregard s 4 of the Statute. But that is [legal] theory and has no relation to [political] realities'.

61 See Loveland (1999) op cit pp 179–187.

62 See Loveland (1999) op cit pp 231–247.

by several coloured voters, on the basis that the procedures used to enact it did not comply with the 'manner and form' specified in s 35.

Before the Appellate Division of South Africa's Supreme Court, the South African government argued that this special procedure was no longer necessary. The government maintained after the Statute of Westminster was passed in 1931 South Africa had become a sovereign state, and therefore its Parliament was not bound by the country's initial constitution, which was enacted while South Africa was still a colony.[63] As a matter of South African constitutional law, the government argued, the South African legislature had thus acquired all the legal attributes of Britain's Parliament: it could enact any law whatsoever by a simple majority; and no domestic court was competent to question the legality of any such Act.

All five of the judges then sitting in the Appellate Division rejected this argument, and concluded that the Act was unconstitutional. The court did accept that South Africa was a sovereign country. The Appellate Division also held that the South African courts would no longer consider British legislation superior to South African statutes. The court also accepted that South Africa had a sovereign Parliament. The Appellate Division nevertheless held that the Separate Representation of Voters Act was an illegal measure.

The judgment hinges on two presumptions. The first is the conclusion that it is possible to have a sovereign country without having a sovereign legislature. Pointing to the United States as an example, Centlivres CJ observed it was entirely feasible for a country's constitutional arrangements to withhold some legal powers from its central legislature. As we saw in chapter one, the USA's constitution reserves control of most of its basic principles to the cumbersome 'two thirds of Congress plus three quarters of the States' amendment process.

The second presumption, in respect of which the US model is not a helpful analogy, is that a country can have a sovereign Parliament without according complete legal competence to a simple majority procedure. The Court held that South Africa had adopted the terms of ss 35 and 152 of the 1909 Act as part of its constitutional settlement when it gained independence in 1931. Its Parliament therefore existed in two forms. For every purpose but three, Parliament could pass an Act by a simple majority with the houses sitting separately. But for those three purposes of repealing s 35, or s 137 or s 152, Parliament had to act by a two thirds majority in joint session. Until such time as that high percentage of the legislature's members wished to repeal those provisions, they remained entrenched within South Africa's constitution.

Bribery Commissioner v Ranasinghe

Ceylon, yet another former British colony, became an independent sovereign state in 1947. The terms of its Constitution were initially set by British law. In respect of many issues, Ceylon's Parliament (comprised of the House of Representatives and Senate

[63] There already seemed to have been a decision by a lower court to this effect: *Ndlwana v Hofmeyr* 1937 AD 229 (SA). See Loveland (1999) op cit pp 202–209.

plus the royal assent given by the Governor-General) would be competent to legislate by a simple majority.[64] However the Constitution also contained several principles (dealing primarily with religious discrimination) which were permanently and substantively entrenched. In addition, the Constitution contained various procedurally entrenched provisions. Section 29 of the Constitution provided that the procedurally entrenched provisions could be amended or repealed only by legislation which had been certificated by the Speaker of the House of Representatives as having been passed by at least two thirds of the members of the House. Among the entrenched provisions was s 55, which provided that junior members of the judiciary could be appointed only by a body called the Judicial Services Commission, comprised entirely of senior judges.

In 1958, Ceylon's Parliament passed the Bribery Amendment Act. The Act was not certificated in accordance with s 29. The Act established a body known as the Bribery Tribunal, which was in effect a court exercising jurisdiction over alleged bribery offences. Its members were appointed by the Ceylonese government, not by the Judicial Services Commission.

Ranasinghe had been tried before and convicted by the Bribery Tribunal. He then appealed against his conviction on the basis that the Bribery Amendment Act – since it had not been passed in the manner and form specified by s 29 of the Constitution – was inconsistent with s 55 of the Constitution and should therefore be regarded as void.

At that time, Ceylon's Constitution retained the House of Lords (sitting in its capacity as the Privy Council) as the country's highest court of appeal. Lord Pearce, delivering the Privy Council's sole judgment, had little difficulty in concluding that Mr Ranasinghe's argument was well-founded:

> '[A] legislature has no power to ignore the conditions of law-making that are imposed by the instrument which itself regulates its [ie the legislature's] power to make law. . . . [T]he proposition which is not acceptable is that a legislature, once established, has some inherent power derived from the mere fact of its establishment to make a valid law by the resolution of a bare majority which its own constituent instrument has said shall not be a valid law unless made by a different type of majority. . .'.[65]

Lord Pearce was also careful to echo the point made by Centlivres CJ in *Harris* that this conclusion did not mean that Ceylon lacked a sovereign Parliament, still less that it was not a sovereign state:

> 'No question of sovereignty arises. A Parliament does not cease to be sovereign whenever its component members fail to produce among themselves a requisite majority. . . . The minority are entitled under the constitution of Ceylon to have no amendment of it which is not imposed by a two-thirds majority. The limitation thus imposed on some lesser majority does not limit the sovereign powers of Parliament itself which can always, whenever it chooses, pass the amendment with the requisite majority'.[66]

64 See Jennings I and Tambiah H (1952) *The dominion of Ceylon* pp 73–75 (London: Stevens and Sons Ltd).

65 *Bribery Comr v Ranasinghe* [1965] AC 172 at 198, PC. 66 Ibid, at 200.

Are Trethowan, Harris and Ranasinghe relevant to the British situation?

Initially it might seem that *Ranasinghe, Harris* and *Trethowan* provide a model to bind Parliament in Britain. Suppose Parliament enacts a statute – the Bill of Rights Act 2007 – which replicates the terms of the United States' Bill of Rights, for example, and includes within the statute a section which specifies that Parliament may legislate in a way that is inconsistent with the Bill of Rights only if at least two thirds of the members of the House of Commons and House of Lords vote in favour of the Act concerned.[67] If a subsequent Parliament wished to enact a statute which did contravene the terms of the new Bill of Rights Act, surely *Harris, Ranasinghe* and *Trethowan* are precedents for saying that it could not do so by a simple majority: the 'manner and form' of two thirds support would be required before a British court would enforce any subsequently enacted statute breaching the provisions of the Bill of Rights. This proposition has attracted the support of several eminent commentators, in addition to Jennings himself.[68]

However there would seem to be little force to such arguments. Much the more persuasive analysis of these cases is that they are completely irrelevant to questions concerning the sovereignty of the British Parliament. This position, most forcefully argued by Wade in 1955,[69] contends that if one transposes these cases to the British context, they are revealed simply as instances of statutory bodies created by Parliament acting beyond the confines of the authority which Parliament has bestowed upon them. In both cases there was a 'higher law' to which the Acts in question were subordinate, namely an Act of the British Parliament: the New South Wales' and South African legislatures were acting 'ultra vires' (beyond their legal powers).[70] If these two *subordinate legislatures* had acted beyond the legal limits of the powers granted to them by the legislature which created them, it was quite consistent with the theory of parliamentary sovereignty for the courts to intervene. Indeed, the courts in those countries would as a matter of law be obliged to intervene – even if the countries had by then become independent sovereign states – for so long as the sovereign law-making power within each jurisdiction had not removed or amended the terms of the initial British statutes.[71]

67 We might also assume that the two-thirds majority provision is also protected by another two-thirds majority clause.

68 See Friedmann W (1950) 'Trethowan's case, parliamentary sovereignty and the limits of legal change' 24 *Australian Law Journal* 103–108; Keir D (6th edn, 1978) *Cases in constitutional law* p 7 (Oxford: Clarendon Press): Griswold op cit. Heuston R (1964) *Essays in constitutional law* ch 1 (London: Stevens). For a recent overview see Craig P (1991) 'Sovereignty of the United Kingdom Parliament after *Factortame*' *Yearbook of European Law* 221–255. The argument has recently been enthusiastically supported by Eric Barendt; see Barendt (1998) *An introduction to constitutional law* pp 86–93 (Oxford: Clarendon Press).

69 Wade HRW (1955) 'The basis of legal sovereignty' *Cambridge LJ* 172–197.

70 Professor Wade put a rather different gloss on *Harris*, suggesting that the South African Supreme Court was effectively in a revolutionary situation, in which its judgment was determined by political rather than legal principles; (1955) 'The basis of legal sovereignty' *Cambridge LJ* 172–197.

71 Jennings acknowledged that neither *Trethowan* or *Harris* were determinative authorities in the British context, but did mainatin that they were illustrative of the principle that; 'the power of a legislature derives from the law by which it was established'; op cit at p 156. And, as noted above, Jennings asserted that 'the law' here in issue was the common law.

Britain, in contrast, has no higher source of law than Parliament. Nor is there any obvious colonial master to which the British Parliament owes its existence.[72] To borrow Lord Pearce's formula in *Ranasinghe*, there is no 'constituent instrument' specifying the way in which Parliament should make laws on particular subjects. Consequently it would not seem to be possible for Parliament ever to exceed its legal authority. Indeed, it is perhaps puzzling that the earlier decision in *Trethowan* was ever invoked to suggest that the British Parliament could enact manner and form limitations on its own sovereignty, given the comments of the Australian judges hearing the case. Rich J stated quite clearly that: 'The Legislature of New South Wales is not sovereign, and no analogy can be drawn from the position of the British Parliament'.[73] Similarly, in Starke J's opinion: 'the Parliaments of the Dominions or Colonies are not sovereign and omnipotent bodies. They are subordinate bodies; their powers are limited by the Imperial [British] or other Acts which created them'.[74] In the same vein, Dixon J observed that:

> 'The incapacity of the British legislature to limit its own power . . . has been explained as a necessary consequence of a true conception of sovereignty. But in any case it depends on considerations which have no application to the legislature of New South Wales, which is not a sovereign body and has a purely statutory origin'.[75]

Advocates of the Jennings thesis might however draw on the following passage from Dixon J's judgment:

> 'It must not be supposed, however, that all difficulties would vanish if the full doctrine of parliamentary supremacy could be invoked. [If] an Act of the British Parliament . . . contained a provision that no Bill repealing any part of the Act . . . should be presented for the Royal Assent unless the Bill were first approved by the electors. . . . [i]n strictness it would be an unlawful proceeding to present such a Bill before it had been approved by the electors. . . . [T]he Courts would be bound to pronounce it unlawful to do so'.[76]

Dixon J's statement was merely obiter, and while one should acknowledge his subsequent reputation as one of the foremost of constitutional scholars, his opinion has yet to be embraced in the English courts.

The logic of the manner and form argument rests on the assumption made by Professor Jennings that the 'rule of recognition' is a common law principle. But as Professor Wade suggests, that logic disintegrates if one regards the *rule of recognition as a political fact rather than a legal principle.* In Wade's view, the rule of recognition is not part of the common law, but something prior to and superior to the common law. It is in essence a basic political reality, not a technical legal rule. It represents the courts' acceptance of the new political consensus brought about by the 1688 revolution. As a result of that revolution, the political underpinnings of British society were

72 The suggestion that one might identify *two* 'masters' (albethey not colonial in nature) is pursued in the following section.

73 (1931) 44 CLR 394 at 418. 74 Ibid, at 422. 75 Ibid, at 425–426.

76 Ibid, at 426.

radically changed. Parliament was in a position to establish its superiority over both the King and the Courts – and both the King and the Courts had no choice but to acquiesce to these new circumstances.

Thus from Wade's 1955 perspective, the theory and practice of parliamentary sovereignty could not be altered by 'legal' means, no matter how ingenious an argument we came up with. The only thing that could have removed the legislative sovereignty of Parliament was another revolution. This need not be a war or a violent insurrection, but it would have to be some momentous break in legal and political continuity, some fundamental redefinition of the way that the country's citizens bestow law-making power on their legislature.

Subsequently, in a series of lectures he delivered in 1980,[77] Wade appeared to adopt a rather different position. He suggested that the only feasible way forward was the very simple device of Parliament introducing legislation to change the judiciary's oath of loyalty. The new oath would require the judges to swear eternal obedience to a statute entrenching certain fundamental rights or liberties that we would never want to have removed, or which could only be removed by a special form of parliamentary procedure above and beyond the bare majority plus royal assent formula. If the courts subsequently found themselves presented with a situation analogous to the one that the South African Supreme Court faced in *Harris v Dönges (Minister of the Interior)*, their loyalty to the new oath would require them to declare the so-called legislation unconstitutional. The obvious drawback of that proposal is that one could envisage a future Parliament introducing legislation to change the oath back again. The idea does indeed look very simple – but perhaps that is because it seems most unlikely that it would work unless it was a part of a more wide-ranging revolutionary overhaul of the constitution that Wade talked of in 1955.

It will be suggested in the final chapter of this book that no such 'revolution' is necessary, and that the *Trethowan, Harris* and *Ranasinghe* episodes do now provide the legal tools with which to entrench legislation in Britain, even though one cannot remove Parliament's omnicompetent 'simple majority plus royal assent' legislative powers. That argument must however be withheld until we have explored other relevant aspects of Britain's constitutional arrangements.

IS PARLIAMENTARY SOVEREIGNTY A BRITISH OR ENGLISH CONCEPT?

The mid-1950s were an interesting time for opponents of the parliamentary sovereignty doctrine. As well as producing the *Harris* case, that era also lent a new impetus to a Scots challenge to the legal supremacy of the British Parliament. This chapter has stressed that parliamentary sovereignty initially emerged in *England, not in Britain.* The Glorious Revolution happened in 1688. At that time, England and Scotland shared a King, and had done so since 1603. But each country had its own Parliament.

77 *Constitutional fundamentals* (London: Stevens).

There was no doubt that Scotland and England were at that time both sovereign states, each with its own particular constitutional structure. *Britain* was not created until 1707, when the Scots and English Parliaments each passed an Act of Union approving the terms of a Treaty of Union negotiated between the governments of each country. In those nineteen years between 1688 and 1707, parliamentary sovereignty may have been accepted as the foundation of the constitution in England, but it is far from certain that the idea enjoyed that status in Scotland.[78] Quite what happened in legal and political (and hence constitutional) terms when Britain was created as a country is a matter open to several interpretations.[79]

Orthodox British theory suggests that what happened in 1707 was essentially a *takeover* or absorption of the Scots Parliament by the English Parliament. That is to say that the constitution of the newly created country of Britain was based on the same principles that underpinned the English constitution between 1688 and 1707. This analysis is presumably underpinned at least in part by the brute fact that the British Parliament sat in the same place as the English Parliament, and while Scots MPs were admitted to both the House of Commons and the House of Lords, no English seats in either house were removed.[80]

An alternative perspective would be to argue that what happened in 1707 was *not a takeover, but a merger*.[81] This argument would further maintain that the terms of that merger were set out in the Treaty of Union itself, and that the Treaty does provide a form of higher law, a higher law which places some limits on the legal powers of the British Parliament.

A third, and perhaps more appropriate characterisation of the events of 1707 is that; 'The union . . . cannot be described as the merging of two states. It was more accurately two renunciations of title and a new state acquiring title over the same territory immediately thereafter'.[82]

As with the second perspective, this view of the union maintains that the Treaty should be seen as a 'constituent instrument', restricting the legislative powers of the British Parliament.

'Entrenched' provisions within the Treaty of Union?

The Treaty does not at any point specify how Parliament should make laws: ie there are no enhanced majority or manner and form provisions to suggest that certain political values were to be entrenched in **procedural** terms. However, if interpreted in

78 Smith T (1957) 'The Union of 1707 as fundamental law' *Public Law* 99–121: Munro C (1987) *Studies in constitutional law* ch 4 (London: Butterworths): MacCormick N (1978) 'Does the United Kingdom have a constitution?' 29 *Northern Ireland Law Quarterly* 1–20.

79 For a fascinating survey and analysis see Upton M (1989) 'Marriage vows of the elephant: the constitution of 1707' *LQR* 79.

80 The Treaty of Union Art XXII made provision for 45 Scots MPs to sit in the Commons, and 16 to sit in the Lords. For a fascinating account of what one might term the 'cultural' basis of the union, see Colley L (1996) *Britons* (London: Vintage).

81 See especially MacCormick, op cit.

82 Wicks E (2001) 'A new constitution for a new state? The 1707 union of England and Scotland' *LQR* 109.

a literal fashion, parts of the text of the Treaty of Union create the impression that various types of **substantive** entrenchment were intended by the framers of the Treaty.

Art XXV certainly confirms that the provisions of the Treaty should supercede all existing laws incompatible with its terms – be they statutory or common law in origin – in both England and Scotland:

'Article XXV. That all Laws and Statutes in either Kingdom so far as they are contrary to or inconsistent with the Terms of these Articles . . . shall from and after the Union cease and become void. . .'.

This is of course a repealing rather than entrenching provision, but nonetheless a term that speaks to the supremacy of future legislation over existing law.

Various substantive entrenchment provisions are however easily identifiable. Article I provided that:

'That the Two Kingdoms of England and Scotland shall upon the First Day of May which shall be in the Year One thousand seven hundred and seven and for ever after be united into One Kingdom by the name of Great Britain. . .'.

Article II contained the following rule:

'. . . [A]ll Papists and Persons marrying Papists shall be excluded from and forever incapable to inherit possess or enjoy the Imperial Crown of Great Britain. . .'.

The permanent entrenchment of assorted religious principles was continued in an annex to the Treaty, which reproduced the text of an Act passed by the Scots Parliament in 1706. This included, inter alia, terms to the effect that the form of Protestantism then used in the Church of Scotland; 'shall remain and continue unalterable'. Relatedly, the Act provided that only adherents to this particular faith could hold positions in the then existing Scots universities.

Article VI was concerned with matters of fiscal rather than religious policy:

'That all Parts of the United Kingdom for ever from and after the Union shall . . . be under the same Prohibitions Restrictions and Regulations of Trade and liable to the Same Customs and Duties on Import and Export. . .'.

In addition, the Treaty contained what might best be termed 'substantively but contingently' entrenched provisions. For example, Article XVIII indicated that the British Parliament would be able to alter all laws concerning matters of public law and private law in Scotland. But this provision was limited in two ways. Firstly, alterations to matters of private law were permissible only if they were for the 'evident Utility of the Subjects within Scotland'. (Quite what was meant by 'evident utility', and who was to be responsible for deciding if a new law satisfied that test were matters on which the Treaty was silent). Relatedly, Article XIX stated that Scotland's Court of Session should; 'remain in all time coming within Scotland as it is now constituted by the Laws of theat Kingdom'. However, this unequivocal pronouncement was then qualified by the proviso that the British Parliament could modify the Court of Session in any fashion that was for; 'the better Administration of Justice'. As with the 'evident utility' clause of Art XVIII, the Treaty did not explain by who or against what criteria the notion of 'better administration of justice' would be gauged.

Notwithstanding these provisions, obvious criticisms can be levelled against both the second and third perspectives on the legal consequences of the Anglo-Scots union. Two such criticisms are schematic in nature. Firstly, the Treaty does not contain any suggestion as to how the entrenched provisions might be safeguarded against subsequent statutory infringement. Certainly no jurisdiction is given to any Court to invalidate any such legislation. Secondly, if the higher law perspective is correct, Britain was created without the benefit of a sovereign law-maker. Article III of the Treaty expressly abolishes the Scots and English Parliaments in creating the British Parliament. But the Treaty contains no mechanism for resummoning those Parliaments, nor any other device for amending or removing the entrenched provisions. A third criticism is rooted in practical historical fact. Most of the supposedly entrenched provisions of the Treaty of Union are apparently no longer in force.[83] Successive generations of parliamentarians and of judges seem to have accepted unquestioningly until the 1950s that the legal status of the Treaty of Union was the same as any other statute – its provisions were open to amendment by either express or implied repeal by subsequent legislation.[84]

However, the constituent instrument's understanding of the Treaty has been tested on several occasions since then in the Scots courts, and the Scots judges have not dismissed it out of hand. The 1953 case of *McCormick v Lord Advocate*[85] concerned a challenge to the constitutionality of the Royal Titles Act 1953. Under the terms of this Act, the former Princess Elizabeth succeeded to the British throne with the title of Elizabeth II. McCormick argued that Britain had never had a Queen Elizabeth I – the woman who stepped on Walter Raleigh's cloak in the sixteenth century was Elizabeth I of England – and so could not have an Elizabeth II.

The Scots Court of Session dismissed McCormick's claim on the facts, but it offered some unexpected opinions on the wider issue of the constitutional status of the Act of Union. The leading judgment was delivered by Lord Cooper, who observed that:

'The principle of the unlimited sovereignty of Parliament is a distinctively English principle which has no counterpart in Scottish constitutional law. . . . Considering that the Union legislation extinguished the Parliaments of Scotland and England and replaced them by a new Parliament, I have difficulty in seeing why it should have been supposed that the new

83 Wicks notes some disagreement between Scots constitutional scholars on the extent of the repeal; op cit p 18.

84 Cf Dicey's comment in *The Law of the Constitution* concerning the 'entrenched' provisions of the Treaty; 'The history of legislation in respect of these very Acts affords the strongest proof of the futility inherent in every attempt of one sovereign body to restrain the action of another equally sovereign body'. One need not be a rigorous critic of Dicey's position to see that in this passage he assumes rather than proves that the British Parliament possesses sovereign powers.

85 1953 SC 396.

Parliament of Great Britain must inherit all the peculiar characteristics of the English Parliament but none of the Scottish Parliament, as if all that happened in 1707 was that Scottish representatives were admitted to the Parliament of England. That is not what was done.'[86]

Lord Cooper then alluded to the various 'entrenched' provisions of the Treaty, and made the following observation:

'I have never been able to understand how it is possible to reconcile with elementary canons of construction[87] the adoption by the English constitutional theorists of the same attitude towards those markedly different types of provisions.'

It might also be noted that while many of the terms of the Act of Union have been repealed, some of its most important provisions remain in place. Scotland retains its own legal system for example,[88] and its own established church. It is interesting to speculate how the courts in England and Scotland would respond if Parliament passed legislation changing either of these two features of Scottish society.[89] Some indication of the likely answer to this question was offered in 1975 by the judgment in *Gibson v Lord Advocate*[90] Mr Gibson was a Scots fisherman who objected to recently enacted legislation which – in his contention – adversely affected his livelihood by opening access to Scots coastal waters to fishing boats and companies from other European Community countries. Mr Gibson based his legal challenge to the validity of the Act on Article VXIII of the Treaty of Union,[91] which if literally construed appeared to prevent the British Parliament from altering matters of 'private law' in Scotland unless such alterations were for 'the evidently utility of the subjects within Scotland'. Mr Gibson argued firstly that the question of fishing rights was a matter of 'private' rather than 'public' law. As such, he further argued, the legality of a statute altering such rights rested on an evaluation of whether or not the Act was indeed for the 'evident utility' of Scots subjects; this being a question which, in Mr Gibson's submission, it was for the court to resolve.

Mr Gibson's suit fell at the first hurdle on the court's conclusion that fishing rights were a matter of 'public' rather than 'private' law. As such, the question of whether or not any changes to laws on this subject were for the 'evident utility' of Scots subjects did not arise. For present purposes however, the significance of the judgment delivered by Lord Keith[92] perhaps lies in the fact that he did not simply

86 Ibid, at 411.

87 By which is meant the principles that 'British' courts have traditionally invoked to ascertain the meaning of statutory provisions. This point is adressed in an introductory form in chapter three below.

88 For illustrations of the significant differences between the two systems see Richardson T (1995) 'The War Crimes Act 1991', in Loveland I (ed) *Frontiers of criminality* (London: Sweet and Maxwell).

89 Cf. the comment by Lord Cooper in *MacCormick*; 'it is of little avail to ask whether the Parliament of Great Britain "can" do this or that, without going on to inquire who can stop them if they do'; 1953 SC 396 at 412.

90 (1975) SC 136.

91 See [p46] above.

92 Notwithstanding the judge's title, the judgment was a first instance opinion of the Outer House of Scotland's Court of Session.

dismiss the action on the basis of a Diceyan proposition that any attempt to challenge the legality of a statute was futile. Lord Keith did not rule out the possibility that such an action could plausibly be argued. He doubted that any court would be competent to assess whether a law affecting 'private' rights in Scotland met the evident utility requirement. But, echoing Lord Cooper in *MacCormick*, Lord Keith also observed:

'I prefer to reserve my opinion on what the position would be if the United Kingdom Parliament passed an Act purporting to abolish the Court of Session or the Church of Scotland or to substitute English law for the whole body of Scots private law'.[93]

It would seem rather unlikely that legislation with that intended effect would ever be enacted by Parliament. But both *MacCormick* and *Gibson* offer at least the theoretical possibility that an argument before a court questioning the validity of a statute might succeed.[94]

WOMEN'S ENFRANCHISEMENT

The common law also provides one often overlooked example of the courts disapplying orthodox notions of parliamentary sovereignty in defence of the traditional moral or political values. As we shall see in chapter seven, the 1832 Great Reform Act extended the parliamentary franchise to affluent middle class men. Further nineteenth century reforms gave the right to vote to an increasing percentage of the male population. Parliament declined explicitly to enfranchise women: but in the 1860s, women's suffrage campaigners formulated an argument that Parliament had done so impliedly.

Section 4 of Lord Brougham's Act, passed in 1850, provided that 'in all Acts words importing the masculine gender shall be deemed and taken to include females . . . unless the contrary as to gender is expressly provided'. The 1867 Reform Act did not expressly exclude women. John Stuart Mill, then an MP and supporter of women's suffrage, had suggested during the Bill's passage that such phraseology impliedly extended the vote to women. The government declined to introduce a clause expressly disapplying Lord Brougham's Act to the franchise issue, suggesting that interpretation of the statute would have to be left to the courts.[95]

In *Chorlton v Lings*,[96] a woman who satisfied all the criteria specified to entitle a man to vote argued that women had indeed been impliedly enfranchised by the 1867 Act. However, the Court of Common Pleas held that Parliament could not possibly have intended to extend the right to vote to women. To do so would overturn centuries of constitutional tradition and practice. Willes J explained the essentially

93 (1975) SC 136 at 145.

94 As suggested in chapter 22 below, recent changes in the structure of government within Scotland have lent an added practical significance to these previously rather esoteric theoretical debates.

95 Kent S (1989) *Sex and suffrage in Britain 1860–1914* ch 8 (New Jersey: Princeton University Press).

96 (1868) LR 4 CP 374.

political and moral reasoning behind this practice, in language no doubt considered diplomatic at the time:

'the absence of such a right is referable to the fact that . . . chiefly out of respect to women, and a sense of decorum, and not from their want of intellect, or their being for any other reason unfit to take part in the government of the country, they have been excused from taking any share in this department of public affairs'.[97]

The court's unanimous rejection of the argument that Parliament could impliedly amend basic constitutional values was most clearly expressed by Keating J; the legislature, 'if desirous of making an alteration so important and extensive, would have said so plainly and distinctly'.[98]

The *Chorlton v Lings* scenario was replayed some 40 years later in *Nairn v University of St. Andrews.*[99] The Representation of the People (Scotland) Act 1868 extended the franchise in university constituencies to all of the university's graduates. The Universities (Scotland) Act 1889 empowered Scots universities to award degrees to women. Nairn was one of several woman graduates who contended that the 1889 legislation necessarily implied that she was now entitled to vote. The House of Lords saw little merit in such an argument. Lord Loreburn LC was particularly adamant that female suffrage could be introduced only by the *most explicit* of statutory provisions: 'It would require a convincing demonstration to satisfy me that Parliament intended to effect a constitutional change so momentous and far-reaching by so furtive a process.'[100]

Keating J's holding in *Chorlton* that Parliament may introduce 'important and extensive' changes to the nature of a citizen's relationship to the state only through 'plain and distinct' statutory language is a principle of potentially wide application. One could draw the same conclusion about Lord Loreburn's observation that the common law does not permit Parliament to achieve policy objectives through 'furtive' legislative devices.

What the courts seem to be saying in these two cases does not seem easy to reconcile with the legal principles advanced in orthodox interpretations of the decisions in *Vauxhall Estates* and *Ellen Street Estates*, which are assumed to have established the doctrine of implied repeal. However, one can see convincing 'democratic' reasons for preferring the *Chorlton/Nairn* rationale. If we assume that Parliament derives its political authority from the consent of the people, it would seem sensible that Parliament is candid about the objectives it is seeking. Without such honesty in the legislative process, it would not be possible for citizens to decide whether or not they wished to continue to consent to what Parliament was doing. That is however essentially a political argument rather than a legal one, and as yet it is one that the British courts have not generally been prepared to accept.

97 Ibid, at 392. 98 Ibid, at 395.

99 [1909] AC 147, HL. On the background to the case see Leneman L (1991) 'When women were not "persons": the Scottish women graduates case, 1906–1908' *Juridical Review* 109–118.

100 [1909] AC 147 at 161, HL.

CONCLUSION

We might at this juncture draw some initial conclusions about the status of parliamentary sovereignty within our constitution. Perhaps the most important point to remember is that the principle was not designed for a modern, democratic society which has large political parties which contest general elections on a nationwide basis. It is a 300-year-old idea.

In order to do justice to Dicey's theorisation of the principle in the 1880s, we ought to note that his concern was to illustrate the relationship between Acts of Parliament and the courts – to stress that as *a matter of legal principle* the courts were invariably subordinate to the will of Parliament. Dicey took pains to stress that political sovereignty was a very different thing. When it came to the practicalities of government, it was simply nonsense to say that Parliament could enact legislation on any subject it chose. Because one part of Parliament, the House of Commons, was an elected body, and its members could periodically be changed by its citizens, MPs would always have to be conscious of what measures the electorate would accept, and temper the legislation they produce accordingly. Thus, to evaluate the *political acceptability* of Dicey's legal doctrine we must examine long term changes in other areas of Britain's law-making and government processes. In particular, we must assess the *voting system* through which members of the House of Commons are elected, the *relationship between the House of Commons and the government*, and the *changing balance of power within Parliament* between the Commons, Lords, and Monarch.

These inquiries will repeatedly lead us to a point of considerable importance which frequently resurfaces in any study of the British constitution; namely a *distinction between legal formality and political reality*. These two concepts do not always coincide, and one of the great difficulties facing constitutional lawyers is deciding in what circumstances law gives way to politics, and vice-versa. We will often return to this problem in subsequent chapters. But for the present, we might leave our discussion of parliamentary sovereignty with a quotation from the 1969 case of *Madzimbamuto v Lardner-Burke*.[101] Lord Reid observed that:

> 'it is often said that it would be unconstitutional for . . . Parliament to do certain things, meaning that the moral, political and other reasons against doing them are so strong that most people would regard it as highly improper if Parliament did these things. But that does not mean it is beyond the power of Parliament to do such things. If Parliament chose to do any of them, the courts could not hold the Act of Parliament invalid'.[102]

As later chapters suggest, the United Kingdom's accession to the European Economic Community in 1973 has cast considerable doubt on certain aspects of the orthodox theory of parliamentary sovereignty. But it would be an adventurous lawyer who

[101] [1969] 1 AC 645, PC. [102] [1969] 1 AC 645 at 723, PC.

suggested that we can currently find purely *domestic* limitations to the principle that Parliament's legal powers are unconfined. Yet as we shall begin to see in the following chapter, it would be rash to assume that the continued dominance of the orthodox theory of parliamentary sovereignty necessarily and invariably places obvious limits on the constitutional authority of the courts.

3

THE RULE OF LAW AND THE SEPARATION OF POWERS

The 'rule of law' is another taken-for-granted element of the British constitution, often invoked – as is democracy' – to convey the essential adequacy of Britain's constitutional arrangements. But 'the rule of law', like 'democracy', is not a concept with just one accepted meaning. 'The rule of law' is not a legal rule, whether in the context of the British constitution or any other, but a political or moral principle. As such, it will necessarily mean different things to different people according to their particular moral or political positions. In later chapters, we will assess whether one can identify characteristics of 'the rule of law' which traverse party political, national, and chronological boundaries, and we will question whether Britain's model is found wanting when measured against such a yardstick. At present, we concentrate on exploring the various meanings that the principle has been accorded in the post-revolutionary British constitution.

For analytical purposes, it is helpful to view the rule of law as a vehicle for expressing 'the people's' preferences about two essentially political issues. Firstly, it relates to the *substance* of the relationship between citizens and government. Secondly, it deals with the *processes* through which that relationship is conducted. Phrased more simply, the rule of law is concerned with what government can do – and how government can do it.

Many legal and political theorists have presented variations on these two themes.[1] In addition to analysing several seminal cases, in which one can discern the varying ways in which principles are put into practice, this chapter deals briefly with three theoretical analyses, those of A V Dicey, Friedrich Hayek, and Harry Jones, which in chronological and political terms, span the spectrum of mainstream debate about the nature of the rule of law in Britain's modern constitution.

[1] Perhaps the most helpful introduction is offered in Harlow ,C and Rawlings R (1984) *Law and administration* chs 1–2 (London: Weidenfeld and Nicolson). See also Munro op cit ch 9: Thompson E (1975) *Whigs and hunters* pp 258–266 (London: Penguin): Raz J (1977) 'The rule of law and its virtue' 93 *LQR* 195–211.

I. THE DICEYAN PERSPECTIVE: THE RULE OF LAW IN THE PRE-WELFARE STATE

Before examining Dicey's views on the rule of law, we should again recall why we might prudently view his theories with a sceptical eye. Firstly we must remember that Dicey was the product of an undemocratic society in the sense we would understand it: as we shall see in chapter seven, fewer than half the adult population were entitled to vote in parliamentary elections when Dicey completed his famous *Study of the law of the constitution* in the 1880s. Dicey himself also vehemently opposed the nineteenth century trend towards increased government intervention in social and economic affairs.[2] His ideas about the relationship between government and citizens were not shaped by political values which most modern observers accept as entirely orthodox. Nevertheless, as we saw in respect of parliamentary sovereignty, the British constitution is built upon a foundation which pre-dated modern concepts of democracy. Consequently, Dicey's theories provide us with a good place to start our examination of the meaning of the rule of law.

The essence of the Diceyan approach to this issue can be extracted from several short passages in the *Law of the constitution*:

> 'We mean, in the first place, that no man is punishable or can be lawfully made to suffer in body or goods except for a distinct breach of the law established in the ordinary legal manner before the ordinary courts of the land. . . . [And] we mean in the second place . . . that every official, from the Prime Minister down to a constable or collector of taxes, is under the same responsibility for every act done without legal justification as any other citizen'.[3]

This definition can be divided into three parts. Firstly, 'no man can lawfully be made to suffer in body or goods'. That indicates that Dicey's primary concern is with protecting individual rights and liberties, (and as such is a more modern restatement of Lockean principles). Dicey stressed that this protection had to be effective against both other citizens and against the government. Acting in an official capacity did not per se amount to a defence for a civil servant or Minister accused, for example, of theft, or being sued for breach of contract, or for trespass on private property. A government official, just like every other citizen, had to find some legal justification for behaving in an apparently unlawful way. Secondly, 'except for a distinct breach of the law' . . . This reinforces the conclusion that government has to operate within a framework of laws in some way superior to the mere actions of government officials: behaviour does not become lawful simply because a government official claims it is so. The third factor is that any breach of the law 'must be established in the ordinary legal

[2] McEldowney (1985) op cit.

[3] Dicey A (1915, 8th edn) *Introduction to the study of the law of the constitution* (London: Macmillan) pp 110 and 114.

manner before the ordinary courts of the land'. The implication of this is that the courts, rather than the government, have the power to determine whether or not the law has been broken. In combination, these three elements of Dicey's rule of law lead us towards another taken-for-granted component of the constitution; the principle of the separation of powers.

Readers interested in pursuing the philosophical foundations of the principle in the modern era might usefully consult John Locke's *Second Treatise of Civil Government* (1690) and Montesquieu's *Spirit of the Laws* (1748). Such works had a profound influence on theoretical analyses of the British constitution, and, in an obviously different way, on the constitutional principles adopted by the American revolutionaries.[4] For our introductory purposes, the basic point to distill from the separation of powers doctrine as it applies to the British constitution is that the government function can be divided into three discrete activities.

The first is legislation. One part of government has to make the laws under which people live. To put the matter simply, if we return to the idea of the British constitution as a social contract discussed in chapter one, we could say that the legislative function is to produce the terms of the contract under which government is conducted. In the British context, the legislative function rests with Parliament. But if a society drafts a contract, the people must also design some way of carrying that contract out.

This second part of the governmental function, the carrying out or 'execution' of the laws, is presumed to be undertaken by the executive branch of government. Dicey's version of the rule of law regards the second function of government with great suspicion. The assumption that underpins Dicey's view is that the executive will always be inclined to try to do things that the legislature has not authorised. It must be stressed that, according to orthodox British understandings of the principles of the rule of law and the separation of powers, the executive branch of government has no autonomous power to make law through legislation.[5] The power to make legislation rests exclusively with Parliament. Consequently, a third arm of government must exist to offer citizens some way of securing a remedy if the executive acts in ways that contravene the laws the legislature has enacted.

This third arm of the governmental system is the courts. The citizen can seek a remedy 'in the ordinary courts of the land' if she believes herself the victim of a government action conducted without statutory authority. In addition to determining if executive action falls within the limits approved by parliament, courts possess a limited law-making power of their own through the development of the common law. An executive action which has no legislative foundation may nonetheless be lawful if it can be justified at common law. It must be stressed that the executive branch of

[4] On the differential impact of these theories on Britain, France and the United States see Vile op cit.

[5] As we saw in ch 2, the Monarch (whom for present purposes we may treat as the head of the executive branch of government) has the power to make international law through the signing of Treaties. But as the decision in *Mortensen v Peters* makes clear, international law has no force in domestic law until the relevant Treaty has been 'incorporated' by an Act of Parliament; see pp 35–36 above.

government has no autonomous power to make law through altering the common law. The power to develop the common law rests exclusively with the courts.

This threefold division within the Diceyan version of the rule of law can best be understood by analysing a celebrated eighteenth century case – *Entick v Carrington.*[6]

ENTICK V CARRINGTON

The mid-eighteenth century was a turbulent time in British constitutional history. In addition to facing rebellion in the American colonies, the government was under continuous pressure from an indigenous radical movement which accused it of corruption and incompetence, and advocated far more extensive participation in the electoral process. Technological advances in the printing industry enabled radicals to spread their ideas far and wide. London in the 1760s was awash with numerous pamphlets which criticised or satirised the government.

The focus of much opposition was a man called John Wilkes, a radical politician who was elected to the House of Commons several times. But on each occasion the Commons had refused to permit him to take his seat.[7] This made him a hero to many American colonists, who felt he shared their struggle against an increasingly tyrannical government and insensitive Parliament.[8] The British government adopted various draconian tactics to stem the flow of critical literature being produced by Wilkes and his colleagues. One technique that the Home Secretary deployed was to issue a 'general warrant' empowering his civil servants to raid the premises of radicals suspected of producing seditious literature. The warrant purportedly authorised government officials to enter private premises without the owner's permission, and without offering the owner any opportunity to rebut their suspicions, and to seize every document that they found there. In 1764, the Home Secretary authorised a raid on the home of a Mr Entick, a printer and Wilkes sympathiser. The Home Secretary's messengers broke into Entick's house and removed his papers.

We might assume that the government's action contravened some basic principles of consensual constitutional government discussed in chapters one and two. There was little point in electors choosing Wilkes as their MP if the 'government'[9] prevented him from taking his seat. And it would be difficult for electors to make an informed choice about their law-makers if the government was suppressing radical publications. Since eighteenth century Britain was not a democratic country in the modern sense, one could not expect governments to respect modern democratic principles. But was it a society subject to the rule of law as Dicey later defined it?

Entick had obviously been made to suffer in goods – his papers had been taken away. But had he committed 'a distinct breach of the law established in the ordinary

6 (1765) 19 State Tr 1029.

7 The basis of this power, and its application to Wilkes and others, is explored further in ch 8.

8 See Maier P (1963) 'John Wilkes and American disillusionment with Britain' *William and Mary Quarterly* 373–395.

9 The word is used guardedly for reasons addressed in ch 8.

manner before the ordinary courts of the land'? The answer would seem to be no. He had not been accused nor convicted of a crime, nor brought before any court. In contrast, the government's officials appeared to have contravened the common law by trespassing on Mr Entick's property and seizing his papers.

Consequently, Mr Entick sued the messengers for trespass to his land and goods. At trial, the messengers' defence was that the Home Secretary's warrant provided them with a lawful excuse for their actions. However, the defence proved difficult to sustain. The defendants could not point to any legislation in which Parliament had authorised the Home Secretary to remove Mr Entick's papers in this manner. Such legislation had existed in the past, but was no longer in force.[10] Nor did there seem to be any common law precedent which made this government activity lawful.

In the absence of a clear statutory or common law authority to justify their actions, the government officials based their defence on two grounds. The first was an argument of 'state necessity'. The Home Secretary essentially claimed that he thought Entick's papers presented a serious threat to public order and social stability; it was necessary to seize the papers in order to prevent political unrest. The second argument might best be described as one of 'custom and tradition'. The Home Secretary pointed out that this power had been used many times, and had never been challenged by anyone. So, surely the practice could not be unlawful? Chief Justice Camden was not interested in what the government thought was necessary, or in what it had done in the past. All he was interested in was finding the law. And one element of 'the law' was entirely clear:

> 'By the laws of England, every invasion of private property, be it ever so minute is a trespass. No man can set his foot upon my ground without my licence. . . . If he admits the fact, he is bound to show by way of justification, that some positive law has empowered or excused him. . . . If that cannot be done, that is a trespass'.[11]

Furthermore, so 'exorbitant' a power as that deployed against Mr Entick could be justified only by extremely clear statutory or common law authority. Camden CJ put the point simply: 'If it is law, it will be found in our books. If it is not to be found there, it is not law'.[12] The lawyers arguing the messenger's case could not find any such authority. In consequence, the entry to Mr Entick's property and seizure of his papers were straightforward instances of trespass. Mr Entick was thus entitled to recover damages from them to compensate him for his loss. The jury awarded the then substantial sum of £300.

Decisions such as *Entick v Carrington* led one legal philosopher to characterise the courts as the 'lions under the throne' of the British constitution.[13] The aphorism lends itself to several interpretations, but for our purposes might be seen as conveying the idea that the judges were ready to spring out and fiercely defend the rights and liberties of individual citizens from unlawful government interference. *Entick* provides a classic

10 Anson op cit pp 309–311; Plucknett (1960) op cit pp 661–666.

11 (1765) 19 State Tr 1029 at 1066.

12 (1765) 19 State Tr 1029.

13 See Heuston R (1970) '*Liversidge v Anderson* in retrospect' 86 *LQR* 33–68.

example of the courts upholding the rule of law in the sense of the theory that Dicey later produced. The theory does not entail that government always acts lawfully, but that the citizen always has a legal remedy when the government acts unlawfully, and that the government respects the courts' judgment when it is held to have breached the law.

But *Entick* offers only a partial picture of either the principle or practice of the rule of law's constitutional role in modern Britain. Lord Camden's reasoning reveals the depths with which Lockean notions of 'property' and 'liberty' were embedded within the eighteenth century common law tradition. He noted at one point that: 'The great end, for which men entered into society, was to secure their property. That right is preserved sacred and incommunicable in all instances, where it has not been taken away or abridged by some public law for the good of the whole'.[14] But even if we accept that defence of 'property' and 'liberty' against arbitrary government is the courts' primary constitutional responsibility – and that is itself a controversial proposition – we again encounter the problem, adverted to in chapters one and two, of just what 'liberty' and 'property' might mean?

DICEY'S RULE OF LAW – PROCESS OR SUBSTANCE?

The concept of the separation of powers, coupled with the application of that principle in *Entick*, might lead us to think that the Diceyan theory of the rule of law is concerned only with the process of the way laws are administered, and not with the substance or content of those laws.[15] However Dicey's overt focus on process went hand in hand with a less visible political view about the 'correct' substance of the laws which the legislature should make. Dicey was much concerned that the laws which government administered had a high degree of *predictability or forseeability*. People needed to know where they stood if they were to run a business, get involved in politics, or start certain types of social relationships. So Dicey thought the rule of law demanded that Parliament did not give government any arbitrary or wide discretionary powers. A statute which said, for instance, that the Home Secretary can imprison anyone she likes, whenever she likes, for as long as she likes, for whatever reason she likes, would not meet the tests of predictability and forseeability, and would therefore seem to contradict Dicey's version of rule of law.

But we automatically encounter a major problem with this element of the rule of law. Dicey seems to be saying that there are limits to the type of governmental powers which Parliament can create through legislation if society is to remain subject to the rule of law. Yet the theory of parliamentary sovereignty tells us that there are no legal limitations on the statutes which Parliament can enact. One cannot go to court and ask for a statute which (for example) bestows very wide discretionary powers on

14 (1765) 19 State Tr 1029 at 1066.

15 On this point generally see Craig P (1997) 'Formal and substantive conceptions of the rule of law' *Public Law* 467–487.

the Home Secretary to search people's homes and seize their papers to be declared unconstitutional because it contravenes the Diceyan rule of law.[16] It appears from the judgment in *Entick*, that had Parliament previously passed a statute authorising the Home Secretary to seize people's papers whenever he thought such action desirable, the civil servants' intrusion would have been lawful, and Entick's suit would have failed. It was suggested earlier that notions of the inviolability of 'property' and 'liberty' were by then 'embedded' in the common law. They were not 'entrenched' in the constitution, for, as a matter of legal theory, Parliament might impinge upon property rights and personal liberties whenever and however it thought fit. After *Entick*, Parliament could if it had wished have passed legislation affording 'general warrants' an entirely lawful status.[17]

The logical conclusion would therefore seem to be that the rule of law is a less important constitutional principle than the sovereignty of Parliament. But we must remember that both the Diceyan rule of law and Dicey's theory of parliamentary sovereignty are at root political or moral concepts. Perhaps they are both, to borrow Professor Wade's terminology, 'ultimate political facts'. The difficult question which then arises is how can one have two 'ultimate' facts: one value must presumably give way to the other?[18] Later in this chapter, and in subsequent chapters, we will consider the ways in which this apparent tension between parliamentary sovereignty and Dicey's rule of law has been addressed. For the moment, we might just note that the two concepts seem theoretically irreconcilable.

THE 'INDEPENDENCE OF THE JUDICIARY'

A second contradiction between the rule of law and parliamentary sovereignty appears when we consider the concept of the 'independence of the judiciary'. Before the 1688 revolution, and in the years immediately thereafter, English judges held office 'at the King's pleasure'. This meant quite simply that not only did the King appoint the judges, but also that judges who subsequently displeased the King or his government could be dismissed. This fate befell Chief Justice Coke in the early seventeenth century; the cumulative effect of judgments such as *Dr Bonham's Case* (and others we consider in chapter four) led Coke into such disfavour with the Crown that he was removed from office.[19]

16 One can do so in the United States; the Fourth and Fourteenth Amendments of the Constitution limit the amount of discretion that Congress and the States can bestow on the executive arms of the federal and State governments; search warrants may only be issued 'upon probable cause . . . and particularly describing the place to be searched and the persons or things to be seized'.

17 As indeed it had already done in the American colonies; see Brogan H (1986) *History of the USA* ch 8 (Harmondsworth: Pelican). See particularly the judgment of the US Supreme Court in *Boyd v United States* 116 US 616 (1886).

18 An incisive analysis is provided by Allan T (1985) 'Legislative supremacy and the rule of law: democracy and constitutionalism' *Cambridge LJ* 111–143.

19 See Plucknett (1928) op cit; Corwin E (1928) 'The higher law background of American constitutional law (parts I and II)' *Harvard LR* 149–182 and 365–409.

The continuance of this situation after the 1688 revolution would have undermined parliamentary sovereignty, since the King could have used his dismissal powers to 'persuade' judges to interpret laws in a manner inconsistent with Parliament's intentions. The solution to this problem, adopted in 1701, provides a further example of a 'balanced' constitution. The Act of Settlement 1700 provided that while the Crown had the power to appoint judges, judges would hold office 'during good behaviour'. This means a judge can only be removed by a joint address of the House of Lords and House of Commons, after the judge has committed a crime or engaged in some gross form of moral misbehaviour. She cannot simply be sacked by the Crown for interpreting the law in a way that the government does not like.

As we saw in chapter one, a chief complaint of the American revolutionaries was that the Act of Settlement did not extend to the colonies. Their judges were appointed for limited terms by the Colonial Governors, acting on behalf of the Crown. And so they could be dismissed if they made decisions of which the Governor disapproved. This meant of course that the judiciary was not very independent of the Governor; judges wishing to stay in office had to keep one eye over their shoulders when deciding a case to see what the government wanted. In contrast, Lord Camden was able to produce a judgment of which the government disapproved in *Entick v Carrington* because, unlike colonial judges, he was not dismissible at the whim of the government. Alexander Hamilton presumably had such principles in mind in *The Federalist Papers No 78*, when he advocated that the United States Supreme Court Judges should hold office during good behaviour, noting that: 'The experience of Great Britain affords an illustrious comment on the excellence of the institution'.

One must observe however that the Act of Settlement only secured the independence of the judiciary against the Crown, not against Parliament. Parliamentary sovereignty meant both that an individual judge could be dismissed by a majority in the Commons and the Lords, and that the rules in the Act of Settlement could be changed at any time by new legislation. This theoretical possibility has yet to emerge in reality: only one High Court judge has ever been dismissed (in 1830); and while the Act of Settlement has been subjected to minor modifications, its basic provisions remain intact. We might therefore plausibly conclude that in practice the British constitution affords the judiciary independence (from both government and Parliament) in the tenure of their office. The force of this tradition in the 'British' context is perhaps best illustrated by returning once to the aftermath of the *Harris* decision in South Africa in the 1950s.

Harris v Minister of the Interior – the aftermath

The only entrenched clauses remaining in South Africa's constitution in 1952 were s 35, s 137 and s 152. Everything else could seemingly be changed by a simple majority house plus senate vote (and the royal assent). The government decided to use its majorities in the legislature to bypass or overcome the Supreme Court's defence of the constitution. Its first initiative was to enact a measure, the High Court of Parliament Act 1952, which purported to turn Parliament itself into a new Court, empowered to hear appeals from the Appellate Division on constitutional matters. The 'Act' was passed by simple majority. The plaintiffs in *Harris* immediately challenged this legislation, arguing that any such measure could only be enacted through the s 152 procedures. In *Minister of the Interior v Harris*,[20] the South African Supreme Court invalidated the 1952 Act, albeit through a somewhat more inventive strategy than the one deployed in *Harris (No 1)*.

A unanimous court found that s 152 impliedly contained a provision demanding that any legislation dealing with matters protected by s 35 or s 137 be subject to scrutiny by a 'court', which would ensure the Act had been passed in conformity with s 152. This implied term was a necessary inheritance of the British constitutional tradition on which South Africa's own constitution was based. Furthermore, a 'court' in this sense had to be institutionally independent from the legislature and the government, and had to be staffed by legally qualified 'judges'. The supposed 'High Court of Parliament' met neither criteria. It could not be a 'court' simply because a majority of the two houses so labelled it. To entrust such a body with the legal protection of s 35 and s 137 would render that protection illusory. A 'High Court of Parliament' with jurisdiction to hear cases involving the entrenched clauses could therefore only be created via the s 152 procedures.[21]

The government's second strategy was more straightforward. The government had re-introduced the Separate Representation of Voters Act as a bill to Parliament in both 1953 and 1954. On each occasion, the bill failed to attract a two thirds majority. But the Constitution did not prevent the legislature increasing the size of the Appellate Division. Consequently, the government invited the legislature to enact the Appellate Division Quorum Act 1955. This legislation – passed by simple majority – added six further judges, appointed by the government, to the existing five. All six of the new appointees ostensibly met the requirement identified in *Harris (No 2)* that they be legally qualified: they were all either judges in lower courts or law professors. All six were also however known to be firm supporters of government policy. Parliament then enacted, again by a simple majority process, the Senate Act 1955. This measure enlarged the senate from 48 to 89 members, chosen by a method which ensured that they were almost all National Party supporters. The government thereby gained a two thirds majority when the two houses sat in joint session. Then, in 1956, Parliament passed a new Separate Representation of Voters Act legislation in accordance with the manner and form required by s 35 which placed Cape coloured citizens on a separate electoral register. A majority of the new eleven judge Supreme Court promptly held that the new Separate Representation of Voters Act was constitutional in *Collins and Brikkels v Minister of the Interior*.[22]

All these steps were 'legal' in the formal sense, although we would from a contemporary British perspective question their moral acceptability.[23] Yet even the

20 1952 (4) SA 769 (A). 21 See Loveland (1999) op cit ch 9.

22 1957 (1) SA 552 (A). The majority included four of the original five judges.

23 For perspectives from within South Africa see Lewin op cit: Le May G (1957) 'Parliament, the Constitution and the doctrine of the mandate' 74 *South African Law Journal* 33–42. See also Loveland (1999) op cit ch 10.

apartheid government paid some regard to the rule of law and independence of the judiciary principles in its efforts to disenfranchise Cape coloured voters. The National Party government did not consider that attempting to sack the five obstructive Supreme Court judges who sat in *Harris (No 1)* and *Harris (No 2)* was a politically acceptable way to proceed. Nonetheless, the message that is clearly conveyed by the Appellate Division Quorum Act 1955 and the judgment in *Collins* is that there is more to the concept of an 'independent' judiciary than job security. Legislatures (as in South Africa) may create compliant courts by packing them with new judges rather than sacking the existing ones. 'Independence' may be as much a question of a judge's state of mind than the fixity of her legal hold on office.[24]

II. THE RULE OF LAW IN THE WELFARE STATE

As already stressed, Dicey formulated his constitutional theories in the Victorian era. His views were shaped by the experience of living in a society which permitted few citizens to vote in parliamentary elections, and in which government performed only a limited number of functions. By the 1950s, Britain was a society in which virtually all adults were enfranchised,[25] and government had assumed a significant role in managing economic and social affairs. At virtually the same time that Dicey was writing his *Law of the constitution*, Parliament had begun to make greater use of legislation which gave government bodies loosely defined discretionary powers and duties. This trend accelerated markedly between 1900 and 1940, and continued to accelerate immediately after World War II. It is beyond the scope of this book to consider questions of political theory and history in any great depth, but it is important that we grasp the rudiments of the arguments which have informed British political life in the modern era. There have been two main currents of opinion as to how best to govern a capitalist society in the post-war period.[26]

The first theory, representing right wing political views, we might call 'market liberalism', to which Dicey was an early adherent. Its most celebrated defence in the modern era was put forward by an Austrian economist, Friedrich von Hayek, in a 1944 book entitled *The Road to Serfdom*.[27] The second theory, social democracy, emerged from the centre-left of the political spectrum, and from a lawyer's viewpoint,

[24] We might also note that this episode serves as a warning against the principle that there are simple solutions to the entrenchment conundrum in the British context. Even if we were able to fashion a legal device which safeguarded basic moral values by demanding that they could be infringed only by super-majorities within Parliament, the protection would be of limited worth if we did not also ensure that the power to appoint judges and select members of Parliament was regulated in a similarly super-majoritarian fashion.

[25] The historical development of this element of the constitution is traced in chapter seven below.

[26] The most helpful introduction is perhaps George V and Wilding P (1976) *Ideology and state welfare* (London: RKP).

[27] London: RKP.

is best explained by the American jurist Harry Jones in a 1958 article in the *Columbia Law Review*.[28]

HAYEK – THE ROAD TO SERFDOM

Hayek is essentially a latter day exponent of the orthodox Diceyan viewpoint. For Hayek, the function of the rule of law is to ensure that: 'government in all its actions is bound by rules fixed and announced beforehand'.[29] Citizens must be able to predict precisely the exact limits of the government's legal powers. This concern encompasses both process and substance.

In respect of process, Hayek follows Dicey in demanding that all citizens must have access to an independent judiciary before which they can challenge the legality of government action; is it the case that what government has done is in accordance with a pre-existing common law or statutory rule? The courts' first and only duty when deciding a case of this sort is to protect the citizen against the government; judges must not succumb to the temptation to bend legal rules in order to facilitate the government process. Hayek's reference to 'rules' is of fundamental importance to his analysis. There is minimal scope within his ideal society for laws which give government discretionary powers, as such powers make it impossible for citizens to predict the exact extent of government authority. This preference for a rule bound government process co-exists with a desire for a government which is minimalist in substance. Hayek's political and economic theories exercised a great deal of influence on the Thatcher administrations which governed Britain between 1979 and 1990.[30] Hayekians believe that society's interests are best served by reducing the power and size of government to a minimum, thereby giving individual citizens as much freedom as possible to organise their social and economic affairs. Government must provide an army to defend the country from external aggression; it must provide a police force to uphold the criminal law; and it must provide a court system to settle disputes over crimes, contracts, and property. But it should go no further. In its most extreme form, market liberalism would maintain that government should have no role at all in the provision of health services, education, housing, or social security. If such things were beneficial to society, they would be provided by private entrepreneurs and purchased by individual citizens.

Hayek accepts that there will be great inequalities of wealth in such a society. This is considered regrettable, but is regarded as a natural consequence of people's varying

[28] Jones H (1958) 'The rule of law and the welfare state' 58 *Columbia LR* 143–156. For a specifically contextualised explanation of the political objects such a theory should serve see Crosland C (1952) 'The transition from capitalism'; and Jenkins R (1952) 'Equality', both in Crossman R (ed) *New Fabian Essays* (London: Turnstile).

[29] (1944) op cit p 54.

[30] A useful introduction is provided by Hall S (1983) 'The great moving right show' and Gough I (1983) 'Thatcherism and the welfare state'; both in Hall S and Jacques M (eds) *The politics of Thatcherism* (London: Lawrence and Wishart).

attitudes and abilities. Hayek considers such inequality to be a lesser evil than the intrusion upon individual freedom which would result if the government took positive steps to address this 'natural' state of affairs. The bottom line of the Hayekian analysis is that society cannot have both the rule of law and a welfare state. Since Parliament is sovereign, it may choose one value or the other, but it would be quite wrong for legislators to claim that they could simultaneously pursue both ideals. The *rule of law is an absolute value*, which can exist only in constitutions which prevent legislators intervening in social and economic affairs. From this viewpoint, the rule of law; 'has little to do with the question whether all actions of government are legal in the juridical sense'; rather 'it implies limits to the scope of legislation'.[31] Hayek denies that the legislature can perform a balancing act between economic equality and the rule of law; 'any policy aiming directly at a substantive ideal of redistributive justice must lead to the destruction of the rule of law'.[32]

JONES – THE RULE OF LAW IN THE WELFARE STATE

While Hayek's theory was very influential in Britain in the 1980s, it enjoyed little support among either the Conservative or Labour parties between 1945 and 1975. The political consensus in that era fell within the broad confines of a *social democratic* approach to government. The period is often referred to as 'Butskellism'. This is a combination of the names of R A Butler and Hugh Gaitskell, leading figures in the Conservative and Labour parties respectively, and stresses the similarity of the political objectives which the two parties pursued.[33] This perspective assumes firstly that government ought to play an extensive role in economic affairs, and secondly that individuals must accept quite restrictive limits on their autonomy if the legislature deems such restraints to be in the public interest. Social democracy must be distinguished from those forms of socialism and communism which have as their objective absolute economic equality between citizens. Social democracy is concerned with ameliorating, not eliminating inequality.

Some of the earliest examples of this theory of government were introduced by the Gladstone and Disraeli administrations in the late nineteenth century, in legislation which placed limits on the use of child labour for example, or which prevented factories from emptying their effluent into rivers or the streets. The justification for such government intervention comes from two sources. Firstly, it is considered 'just' and 'fair' insofar as it protects individuals from exploitation. Secondly, it is thought to be rational for society as a whole; for example the cost of ill health and death which might result from not having controls on pollution outweighs the expense involved in disposing of waste in a satisfactory manner.

By the 1950s, this twin rationale underpinned an immense network of government

31 (1944) op cit at pp 61–62. 32 (1944) op cit, p 59.

33 A helpful introductory guide to these various theories of government is George and Wilding op cit chs 2–4.

activities; a national health service, millions of publicly owned houses; government control of the coal, steel, water, gas, and electricity industries; old age pensions; unemployment benefits; and free schooling for all children until the age of 15. This clearly represented, in Hayek's words, a 'substantive ideal of redistributive justice'. The welfare state also required Parliament to give government officials large numbers of discretionary powers; it was simply not feasible to run a complex welfare state in accordance with legislative 'rules'. Government was now doing so much, and dealing with so many different situations, that it would simply be impossible for legislators to produce a rule for every foreseeable situation. This necessarily meant that there was some reduction in the degree to which citizens could precisely predict the limits of government's legal authority. However, some constitutional lawyers denied that this meant that society could not be governed in accordance with the rule of law.

In contrast to Hayek, Harry Jones suggests that the *rule of law is a relative rather than absolute political value*; that one can dilute the Diceyan model without removing its basic features. Like Hayek, Jones accepts that 'the rule of law's great purpose is protection of the individual against state power holders'.[34] But he also suggested that the rule of law would continue to exist as long as legislators, government officials, and the judiciary accepted what he termed an 'adjudicative ideal'.

While legislation in Hayekian society would take the form of rigid rules, the statutory basis of a welfare state would also contain flexible standards, permitting government to make various responses to given situations. However the adjudicative ideal demands that although the legislature can bestow wide discretion on government bodies, it may not grant them arbitrary powers. Jones' version of the rule of law does not dismiss the importance of predictability and certainty; rather it accepts that in some areas of government activity it is only necessary that citizens can foresee the general boundaries rather than the precise location of government authority.

Nor does Jones' theory reject the need for a separation of powers. Citizens must be able to challenge the legality of government through a 'meaningful day in court'. Jones differs from Hayek in assuming that this need not entail resort to the 'ordinary courts'; specialist tribunals could serve this purpose in respect of some government functions, since they might be more informal, more expert and less time consuming and expensive than the normal judicial process.

The task which faces the courts and tribunals in social democratic society is not simply to protect the individual at all costs. Since Parliament has given the government discretionary powers, the courts must accept that the legislature has intended that individuals might suffer some minor detriment or restraint on their autonomy in order to further the public interest. This may present courts with a difficult problem – how much discretion did Parliament intend the government to have? Jones recognised that this set 'a harder and wider task for the rule of law', but he suggested that Hayek

[34] Op cit at p 145.

was being unduly pessimistic in suggesting that the concept had to be abandoned altogether.

Although a welfare state may be difficult to reconcile with a Diceyan or Hayekian view of the rule of law, it would seem consistent with some of the notions of democracy in the sense of government by consent discussed in chapter one. If 'the people' have decided that they are willing to dilute the Diceyan ideal to achieve certain economic or social objectives, there would seem to be no obvious barrier to them doing so. Whether that conclusion is, from a political perspective, a sound one, is a question to which we shall return in later chapters. We might note for instance that it would be quite possible for a society to adhere to Hayek/Dicey's version of the rule of law without being a democracy. A dictator who preserved market autonomy and stuck rigidly to pre-announced limits on her/his powers would pass Hayek's test. Whether one can have a democratic constitution without respect for at least a diluted version of the rule of law is a more difficult question, which we shall pursue at a later stage.

However, from a lawyer's perspective, Jones' and Hayek/Dicey's competing viewpoints about the 'what and the how' of modern government are neatly encapsulated in what Carol Harlow and Richard Rawlings term the 'red light' and 'green light' theories of legal control of executive behaviour.[35] Red light theorists such as Hayek, echoing Dicey's suspicion of the executive, maintain that the rule of law's primary concern should be to stop government interfering with individual autonomy. Green light theorists such as Jones, in contrast, believe that the Diceyan pre-occupation with individual rights is misplaced in modern society. It is assumed that Parliament and the courts should loosen the legal constraints on government discretion, enabling government to curb individual autonomy in order to promote society's collective well-being.

As we shall see below and in subsequent chapters, the reality of court regulation of government action in the modern British constitutional context does not fit neatly into one or other of these theoretical perspectives. Harlow and Rawlings suggest that we can identify a third theoretical position – 'amber light' theory – lying between the two extremes. This does not mean that, in practice, legal controls lie at the precise mid-point of the theoretical continuum, but that individual cases tend to be located at various positions on the spectrum. Sometimes they approach the green light extreme, sometimes the red.

Within this theoretical framework, legal controls are designed to provide government with some flexibility, but not too much flexibility. That naturally raises the question of 'How much is too much?'. There is no easy answer to this question; the point is perhaps best illustrated by the gradual accumulation of many examples; a task to which, after a brief schematic diversion, we shall shortly return.

35 Op cit chs 1 and 2.

III. JUDICIAL REGULATION OF GOVERNMENT BEHAVIOUR: THE CONSTITUTIONAL RATIONALE

The origins, structure, and powers of the present judicial system is a subject best explored in detail in textbooks dealing with the English legal system. However some very broad points must be made here about the nature both of the court system and the 'judicial law-making process'. All courts in Britain are now in technical terms statutory creations. Prior to the revolution, the legal landscape was littered with many different courts, each exercising nominally independent but frequently overlapping jurisdictions. An inevitable consequence of the emergence of the parliamentary sovereignty doctrine was that the powers (and indeed even the existence) of particular courts could be amended or abolished by legislation. Numerous piecemeal reforms affecting the court system (such as the Act of Settlement 1700) were introduced during the next 200 years, but for our purposes the most significant legislative initiative was the passage of the Judicature Acts of 1873 and 1875. These Acts merged the many so-called 'superior' courts into the newly created High Court and Court of Appeal, and defined both the new courts' respective jurisdictions and the qualifications required of the judges who would sit in them. Subsequent statutes confirmed the House of Lords' position (in its judicial capacity) at the apex of the British judicial system, where it functions as the final court of appeal.

However, while Parliament has periodically altered the structure and jurisdiction of the courts, and while the 'common law'[36] is undoubtedly inferior to statute in circumstances where a statutory and common law rule seemingly demand different solutions to a particular problem, Parliament has never enacted legislation which has sought systematically to control either the method or outcome of the judiciary's law-making process. The 1688 revolution did establish that statute could alter or abolish any common law principles whenever Parliament wished, but virtually all of those principles initially remained in place. Thus, in the absence of statutory controls, the content of the common law remains a matter for the courts to control. And within the present court system, it is the House of Lords in its judicial capacity which is the ultimate arbiter of the substance of common law principles.

Such judicial power is not inconsistent with the notion of parliamentary sovereignty, because it is assumed that Parliament always intends that government will exercise its statutory powers in accordance with the precepts that the common law currently requires. One might say that common law principles are the implied terms of the government process, and that Parliament is generally considered to have 'contracted in' to these limits on executive autonomy. If Parliament does not want a particular government action to be subject to judicial control, it must say so in the

[36] The term is used here in a loose sense, to denote laws made by courts rather than by Parliament. The technical distinctions between common law, equity and other forms of judicial law-making are an unnecessary complication for this study.

statute which grants the power. Because Parliament is sovereign, it would seem that in theory Parliament can if it wishes 'contract out' of the common law principles which allow the court to regulate government activities. Such legislation might seem (to borrow Lord Reid's terminology in *Madzimbamuto v Lardner-Burke*) 'politically or morally improper', in so far as it arguably derogates from orthodox understandings of the rule of law, but there is no **legal** impediment to Parliament enacting it.

This book uses the term 'administrative law' to encompass the various common law controls that the courts place on the government process. In many instances, administrative law may take the simple form of an action in contract or (as in *Entick v Carrington*) tort against a government body where the government has breached a contract or committed a tortious act. However, the concept of *judicial review* is the main component of administrative law. We will explore that concept in detail in later chapters; but, if one wishes to gain a proper understanding of the basic features of constitutional law, it is necessary at this point to consider the fundamental ingredients of, and justification for the doctrine of judicial review of executive action.

Broadly stated, the modern form of judicial review is designed to uphold a certain interpretation of the rule of law and the separation of powers – its function is to ensure that executive bodies remain within the limits of the powers that the legislature has granted, or which are recognised by the courts as existing at common law.[37] One of the earliest judicial statements of the principle is provided by Coke CJ in *Baggs Case*,[38] which concerned the attempts of the Mayor and Burgesses of Plymouth to expel one of their number from the city's council. In addition to holding that the expulsion was unlawful, Coke CJ made a more general statement of the scope of the court's powers;

'[T]his court hath not only jurisdiction to correct errors in judicial proceedings, but other misdemeanours extrajudicial tending to the breach of the peace or the oppression of the subject . . . or any other manner of misgovernment; so that no wrong or injury, either publick or private, can be done but this shall be reformed or punished'.[39]

The intricacies and complexities of the emergence and consolidation of the judicial review jurisdiction no doubt merit closer examination than they can be given here.[40] For our more limited purposes, a preliminary understanding of the basic features of judicial review is perhaps best gleaned from the 1948 Court of Appeal decision in *Associated Provincial Picture Houses Ltd v Wednesbury Corpn*[41] which has often been invoked in modern times as the clearest restatement both of the constitutional basis

37 In the United States, as we saw in chapter one, judicial review has a further dimension, for the Supreme Court is also responsible for ensuring that the legislature remains within the limits of the powers that the Constitution has granted.

38 (1615) 11 Co Rep 93b.

39 (1615) 11 Co Rep 93b at 98a.

40 For comment on *Baggs' Case*, and on the emergence and consolidation of the judicial review principle more generally, see de Smith S (1951) 'The prerogative writs' *Cambridge LJ* 40: Jaffe L and Henderson G (1956) 'Judicial review and the rule of law: historical origins' *LQR* 345.

41 [1948] 1 KB 223, CA. The case did not create new principles, but merely restated well-established concepts.

for judicial review of government action and of the principles which a court will deploy to establish if a government body's action is lawful.

The case itself concerned a substantive issue of evidently minor importance. Local authorities in England and Wales (of which there were over one thousand at this time) were empowered by s 1 of the Sunday Entertainments Act 1932 to place 'such conditions as the authority think fit to impose' on cinemas in the authority's area which wished to open on Sundays. The Wednesbury Corporation imposed a condition which forbade children under the age of fifteen from attending cinemas on Sundays. The cinema company, facing an obvious threat to its profits, sought to establish that the condition was unlawful. The Court of Appeal's judgment in *Wednesbury* suggests that there are three grounds on which a court may find that executive action is 'ultra vires', that is to say 'beyond the limits' of parliamentary (or sometimes common law) authority.

The first ground could be described as 'illegality'. If Parliament passes a statute for instance which allows the government to provide schools, the government could not invoke that statute as a justification to build houses. Similarly, a government body empowered by a statute to employ teachers could not invoke the legislation to justify its employment of nurses or train drivers. Clearly, the Corporation's condition in the *Wednesbury* case did not fall into this category.

Wednesbury also makes it clear that a government body exceeds its statutory powers if it exercises them in a way that is 'unreasonable' or 'irrational'. This ground of review is particularly important in respect of discretionary powers. The concept of 'unreasonableness' bears a special meaning in administrative law. An action is only unreasonable if it is so bizarre that no reasonable person could have assumed Parliament would have intended it to happen. As an example, assume that a statute gives government the power to employ teachers in primary schools 'on such terms as it thinks fit'. The exercise of that power would only be unreasonable if it was used in a way that appeared to bear no relation at all to rational objectives; if the government body decided not to employ anyone with red hair for instance. In contrast, reasonable people might reach rather different conclusions about precisely how much teachers should be paid, for example, or what level of qualifications teachers should have. Such diversity is perfectly lawful: administrative law accepts that when a statute uses a discretionary term, Parliament has expected that there will be some variation in the substance of decisions reached. The notion of irrationality functions to ensure that those variations remain within the boundaries of political consensus that Parliament envisaged. The condition attached by the council in the *Wednesbury* case could not plausibly be classified as 'irrational' in this sense, even if it was noticeably more restrictive than the conditions imposed by other nearby local authorities.

The third ground of review identified in *Wednesbury* is sometimes referred to as 'natural justice'. This ground of review is not concerned with the substance or content of a given decision, but rather with the way in which the decision has been reached. Administrative law requires that government bodies exercise their statutory or common law powers through fair procedures. Broadly stated, this means firstly that decision-makers should not have a personal interest in the decision being made; and secondly that people affected by the decision should have an opportunity to state their case before a conclusion is reached.

Judicial review is a *supervisory* rather than *appellate* jurisdiction. A court which holds a government action unlawful will not substitute its own decision for the one made by the government body concerned, but will return the question to the original decision-maker so that the decision can be made again, this time in accordance with legal requirements. In contrast, in an action for (for example) trespass or breach of contract, the court will impose its solution on the dispute before it.

It should again be stressed that the theoretical rationale for judicial control of government behaviour derives from the constitution's 'ultimate political fact' of parliamentary sovereignty. This requires that the government may only perform those tasks that Parliament (or the common law) permits. The courts' constitutional role is therefore to police the boundaries of legislative intent,[42] and ensure that government cannot overstep those boundaries without incurring legal liability.

Yet one should beware of concluding from this that the courts' role is one of mere mechanical obeisance to legislative texts. We will return to this point in more detail below. But here, we might note that since the *Wednesbury* grounds of review are common law concepts, it is entirely legal for the courts to amend, abolish or add to those grounds as they think fit. We will shortly, when examining the concept of *stare decisis*, encounter the moral or political principles which have led the courts to be cautious in developing new grounds of review or redefining existing ones. But until such time as Parliament enacts legislation which seems to 'freeze' aspects of the common law at a particular point in their development, there is no legal barrier to radical judicial reform of any existing common law principle.

This necessarily leads us to ask to whom, or to what, does a judge's constitutional loyalty ultimately lie? This is not so much a question of a judge's personal predisposition, but of the principles which the judges sitting in the High Court, Court of Appeal and House of Lords deploy when interpreting the meaning of statutes and deciding the content of the common law. Both issues are more appropriately discussed in detail in textbooks on jurisprudence or the English legal system, but they are integral elements of the contemporary constitutional order, and so must be adverted to at least briefly in this work.[43]

[42] This point applies as much to legal justifications for government behaviour rooted in common law rather than statute, for one assumes that particular common law rules exist only because Parliament has not seen any need to abolish or amend them. Judicial regulation of the government's common law powers is addressed in ch 4.

[43] I am much indebted in the following pages to Michael Zander's (4th edn, 1994) *The law-making process* chs 3–4 (London: Butterworths).

IV. PRINCIPLES OF STATUTORY INTERPRETATION

While the words of a statute have traditionally been regarded as the 'highest form of law' known to the British constitution, the task of attaching a specific legal meaning to the words that Parliament has used has generally fallen to the courts. The inherent ambiguity and imprecision of language necessarily entails that even legislation which is expressed in the form of rigid rules may sometimes raise questions concerning its applicability to particular situations. Such uncertainty is much increased when Parliament chooses to employ statutory formulae which bestow discretionary powers on government bodies. Since the resolution of such uncertainty is a judicial function, the process of statutory interpretation is thus a crucial element both of the rule of law and the sovereignty of Parliament.

Parliament has on occasion enacted legislation instructing the courts as to the meaning to be accorded to particular words or phrases which constantly reappear in various statutes. We saw one example of a so-called 'interpretation act' in chapter two when we looked at the role played by Lord Brougham's Act of 1850 in the *Chorlton v Lings* litigation. However such legislation pertains to technicalities, rather than to sweeping instructions as to broad interpretative techniques. That latter component of the constitution is one that has traditionally been controlled by the courts themselves.

Three such techniques, respectively referred to as the 'literal rule', the 'golden rule', and the 'mischief rule' have traditionally been recognised as legitimate. The literal rule, which has been by far the dominant approach, suggests that the court's duty is to attach the orthodox, grammatical meaning to the statute's phraseology, even if that leads to ostensibly unjust or even bizarre results. The literal rule was perhaps most clearly expressed by Lord Esher in 1892 in *R v Judge of the City of London Court*: 'If the words of the Act are clear, you must follow them, even though they lead to a manifest absurdity. The court has nothing to do with the question of whether the legislature has committed an absurdity'.[44] The literal rule betokens a very dogmatic judicial acceptance of the common law's constitutional inferiority to statute. Since Parliament may if it wishes enact 'absurdities', the court would be questioning Parliament's sovereignty if it tried to attach a 'sensible' interpretation to statutory formulae whose literal meaning pointed in a different direction. If the absurdity or unjust result was a mistake rather than an intended consequence, the solution would be for Parliament to enact a new statute amending the meaning of the former Act.

The so-called 'golden rule' credits the legislature with a somewhat greater degree of rationality. It suggests that when a literal reading of a particular statutory provision would lead to an absurdity, the court should examine the statute in its entirety to see if another, more sensible meaning might be attached to the relevant words in the light of the legislative context in which they appear.

The third strategy, the 'mischief rule' neatly illustrates the hierarchical relationship

[44] [1892] 1 QB 273 at 290, CA.

between statute and common law. The rule requires that the court ask itself which 'mischief' or defect in the common law (or a previous statute) that the statute was intended to amend, and thereafter to construe the Act in a manner that minimises the possibility of the mischief recurring. In its initial form, the judges' interpretation of the mischief rule did not empower them to look beyond the statute and the relevant common law rules to ascertain the 'mischief' Parliament was supposedly trying to remove. Thus, if a logical parliamentary intent could not be deduced from the words of the Act itself, the rule could not be applied. By the mid-1970s, the courts had begun to refer to government policy documents explaining the policies underlying particular legislative reforms as an aid to interpretation.[45] That initiative certainly enhanced the potency of the mischief rule. But its utility continued to be greatly limited by the courts' presumption that their search for Parliament's intentions did not permit them to clarify the meaning of statutory texts by referring to speeches made about the legislation during its passage through the Commons and the Lords. We will consider the basis and implications of that principle, and the House of Lords' more recent departure from it, at a later stage, for neither can be fully understood until we have examined the nature of the legislative process in rather greater detail.[46]

All three traditional strategies seem to draw a clear distinction between the legislative and judicial role, and emphasise the subordinacy of the latter to the former. They did not, however, find favour with all members of the judiciary, some of whom thought a rather more radical approach was desirable. Lord Denning, in the 1950 case of *Magor and St Mellons RDC v Newport Corpn*, advanced a rather different understanding of the court's 'interpretative' duty:

> 'We do not sit here to pull the language of Parliament and of Ministers to pieces and make nonsense of it. . . . We sit here to find out the intention of Parliament and of Ministers and carry it out, and we do this better by filling in the gaps and making sense of the enactment than by opening it up to destructive analysis'.[47]

Lord Denning's initiative may be seen as an example of a fourth interpretative technique, now known as the 'purposive' or 'teleological' approach. This strategy rejects the presumption that a judge should restrict her search for the meaning of law to the statute itself, but rather tries to imagine what the framers of the legislation would have done if faced with the problem now before the court. The teleological strategy was by then already a common feature of many continental European legal systems, and was widely used in the United States. But Lord Denning's efforts to 'import' it into the English constitutional tradition found little favour with the House of Lords. On further appeal, the House of Lords firmly rebutted Lord Denning's presumptions as to the judiciary's appropriate constitutional role. According to Lord Simonds:

> '[T]he general proposition that it is the duty of the court to find out the intention of

45 *Black-Clawson International Ltd v Papierwerke Waldhof-Aschaffenburg AG* [1975] AC 591, HL.

46 In ch 8 below.

47 [1950] 2 All ER 1226 at 1236, CA.

Parliament – and not only of Parliament but of Ministers also – cannot by any means be supported. The duty of the court is to interpret the words that the legislature has used'.[48]

As to Lord Denning's suggestion that the court might 'fill in the gaps' left by the statute's text, Lord Simonds identified fundamental constitutional objections. For a court to adopt such techniques would be; 'a naked usurpation of the legislative function under the thin guise of interpretation . . . If a gap is disclosed, the remedy lies in an amending Act'.[49]

Lord Simonds somewhat overstated the 'naked usurpation' criticism. In the absence of legislation specifically forbidding 'purposive' interpretative techniques, the House of Lords (as the ultimate arbiter of common law principles) was in theory quite competent to jettison the three traditional rules and adopt Lord Denning's preferred option. That the majority in *Magor* chose not to do so was an indication that they considered such an innovation 'unconstitutional' in the sense of its political illegitimacy, not of its legal impossibility. Denning's judgment was overturned by the House of Lords not because it was unconstitutional in some objective sense, but because the Law Lords felt that it was unconstitutional.

The case does however emphasise the point that the dividing line between 'interpretation' and 'legislation' may on occasion be difficult to draw. We can confidently state that, as a matter of constitutional theory, Parliament legislates and the courts interpret. It is more difficult to ascertain whether, as a matter of constitutional practice, that theory is always respected. This problem is perhaps best illustrated by examining the judgments delivered in two leading cases; *Liversidge v Anderson* from the 1940s and *R v IRC, ex p Rossminster* from 1980.

LIVERSIDGE V ANDERSON (1942)

Liversidge v Anderson[50] arose in 1942 out of the Defence Regulations 1939, a measure enacted at the start of World War II to strengthen the government's powers to protect the country from sabotage or treason by enemy agents. Regulation 18b provided that:

> 'If the Home Secretary has reasonable cause to believe any person to be of hostile origins or association . . ., he may make an order against that person directing that he be detained'.

Between May and August 1940, the Home Secretary, Sir John Anderson, used reg 18b to detain 1500 people. Over 1,100 detainees were quickly released when it became clear that the government's suspicions about them were not well founded.[51]

One person detained was Robert Liversidge. Liversidge sued Anderson for false imprisonment. Liversidge had obviously been made (to borrow from Dicey's formulation of the rule of law) to 'suffer in body' – he had been confined in prison. The question before the court was whether the executive action which had led to Liversidge's detention was lawful. Was there a statutory or common law power which

48 [1951] 2 All ER 839 at 841, HL. 49 [1951] 2 All ER 839, HL. 50 [1942] AC 206, HL.

51 See the fascinating study by Simpson A (1991) *In the highest degree odious* (Oxford: Clarendon Press).

entitled the government to lock Mr Liversidge up? Liversidge's contention was that although the Defence Regulations empowered the Home Secretary to detain people in some circumstances, those circumstances did not exist in this particular case. The detention was therefore either 'illegal' or 'irrational' in the *Wednesbury* sense.

To understand the basis of Mr Liversidge's argument, we must examine the precise wording of reg 18b. It says that the Home Secretary can detain an individual if: 'he has reasonable cause to believe' that person is of hostile origin or association. The insertion of the 'reasonable cause to believe' clause seems to fit with the Diceyan idea of the rule of law which disapproves of any statute in which Parliament grants the government wide discretionary powers. The clause seems to limit the possibility of the Home Secretary using the power arbitrarily. Detention would not be lawful unless a court was satisfied that the Home Secretary's beliefs were underpinned by 'reasonable cause'. Regulation 18b apparently requires the Home Secretary to show the court the evidence on which his suspicions were based, and to convince the judges that the evidence did indeed amount to a 'reasonable cause'. The obvious meaning of reg 18b would therefore seem to be that if there was insufficient evidence to support the conclusion that a detainee had hostile origins, the power could not lawfully be used.

The government itself had acknowledged that this was the correct interpretation of the regulations in the first case challenging their use, *Lees v Anderson*.[52] In a subsequent case, *R v Home Secretary, ex p Budd*,[53] the government changed its argument, and contended that no such evidence need be presented. In short, the government's contention was that as long as the Home Secretary believed that a person was of 'hostile origins or association', that belief was necessarily 'reasonable'. That argument did not initially succeed; the court had ordered Mr Budd to be released because the Home Secretary was unable to produce any convincing evidence of his 'hostility'. Mr Budd then suffered the misfortune to be detained a second time. On this occasion, the court accepted the government's arguments as to the effect of reg 18b and saw no need to make any examination at all of the sufficiency of the evidence which led the Home Secretary to exercise his powers of detention.

When *Liversidge v Anderson* reached the House of Lords, the meaning of reg 18b was therefore in need of clarification. Four[54] of the five members of the House of Lords in *Liversidge* accepted the government's interpretation of reg 18b. They concluded that the Home Secretary could use reg 18b to imprison anyone he thought was of hostile origins. He did not need to offer the court any evidence to show that his belief was reasonable. He could imprison anyone at all. He did not have to say why. And anyone who was detained was wasting her time coming to the courts to challenge the adequacy of the Home Secretary's belief. Lord Wright encapsulated the majority sentiment by concluding that:

52 (1940) Times, 13 and 21 August; discussed in Simpson op cit pp 62–63 and ch 14.

53 [1942] 1 All ER 373. Mr Budd subsequently, and unsuccessfully, attempted to sue the Home Secretary for false imprisonment in relation to the first detention; *Budd v Anderson* [1943] 2 All ER 452; see Simpson op cit pp 318–321.

54 Viscount Maugham, Lord Macmillan, Lord Wright, and Lord Romer.

'All the word "reasonable", then, means is that the minister must not lightly or arbitrarily invade the liberty of the subject, He must be reasonably satisfied before he acts, but it is still his decision, and not the decision of anyone else. . . . No outsider's decision is invoked, nor is the issue within the competence of any court'.[55]

One Law Lord took a different view. Lord Atkin thought that reg 18b could bear only one possible meaning. If Parliament said 'reasonable cause to believe', it must have intended that there be **some** plausible evidence on which that view was based. If legislators had intended to give the Home Secretary an arbitrary power, they would simply have said 'if the Home Secretary believes'. Regulation 18(b)'s parliamentary history seems to support Lord Atkin's view.[56] The original version of the regulation had not included the 'reasonable cause' requirement. It had been inserted as an amendment because MPs had feared that leaving it out would give the Home Secretary too arbitrary a power. This suggests that the majority judgment effectively permitted the government both to disregard the principle of parliamentary sovereignty and to contravene Dicey's version of the rule of law. It seems that only Lord Atkin had upheld the orthodox tradition that the courts should interpret the words used in legislation in accordance with their literal meaning.

But despite the apparently 'unconstitutional' nature of the majority judgment, it was Lord Atkin who received considerable criticism from the government, from fellow judges, and from the public at large. In part, this criticism was directed at the substance of his opinion. The country was after all at war. People were greatly concerned about saboteurs, traitors and spies. Atkin was accused of wanting to tie the government's hands in its efforts to root out these potential enemies. Hayekian theory, for example, would accept that the rule of law could legitimately be 'suspended' during war, on the grounds that the most important political value (another 'ultimate political fact'?) was the preservation of the country's very existence as an independent state.[57] From that perspective, Lord Atkin's attachment to rigorous legal principle could almost be construed as treasonable.

However, Lord Atkin also antagonised many people (including fellow judges) by the language that he used to express his opinions.[58] He accused his four colleagues in the Lords of being 'more executive minded than the executive'.[59] Lord Atkin had found only one possible 'authority' to justify the majority's interpretation of reg 18b. There is a scene in *Alice through the looking glass* where Alice and Humpty Dumpty discuss the use of language:

' "When I use a word", Humpty Dumpty said in rather a scornful tone, "it means just what I choose it to mean, neither more nor less". "The question is" said Alice, "whether you can

55 [1942] AC 206 at 268–270, HL.

56 For reasons discussed in ch 8, courts did not then examine records of parliamentary debates when interpreting statutes. Cf Lord Macmillan [1942] AC 206 at 256: 'I do not know, and it would not be proper for me to inquire, why a change was made . . .'.

57 The principle is sometimes expressed in the latin maxim *salus populi est suprema lex*.

58 See Heuston op cit.

59 [1942] AC 206 at 244, HL.

make words mean different things". "The question is", said Humpty Dumpty, "which is to be master – that's all" '.[60]

The important inference that we ought to draw from Lord Atkin's dissent is that there is little point in regarding the relationship between citizens and the government as a 'political contract' in which Parliament creates a legal framework to which the people consent, nor to assume that the constitution rests on the twin bedrocks of parliamentary sovereignty and the Diceyan rule of law, if the words that the legislature uses in statutes to express its wishes can be interpreted by the courts to mean things Parliament did not intend. Such an outcome might be seen as a judicial subversion of the power of Parliament. One might meet this point by suggesting that the majority decision in *Liversidge* must have been 'correct', because Parliament took no steps to reverse it. As we shall see on later occasions, that argument rather oversimplifies the nature of the relationship between Parliament and the courts. It also fails to meet the objection that the House of Commons, the House of Lords or the Monarch might seek to mislead each other (or combine to mislead the people) by deliberately passing bills in the expectation that the courts will lend the resultant statute an interpretation that seems to defy accepted understandings as to the meaning of language.

In the aftermath of *Liversidge*, one of Lord Atkin's fellow judges (Stable J) wrote to him to say the majority decision brought the judiciary into disrepute. The judges were no longer 'lions under the throne, but mice squeaking under a chair in the Home Office'.[61] The case once again suggests that effective functioning of the rule of law, at least as Dicey understood it, requires judges who possess an independence of mind, as well as an independence of office.

R V IRC, EX P ROSSMINSTER LTD

The Taxes Management Act 1970, s 20C seemed to bestow sweeping search and seizure powers on Inland Revenue employees. Section 20C – which was added to the original Act in 1976 – empowered the Inland Revenue to seek a search warrant from a circuit judge. If the judge was satisfied that there were reasonable grounds to assume that evidence of a tax fraud might be found on particular premises, she could issue a warrant authorising a named officer to: 'Seize and remove any things whatsoever found there which he has reasonable cause to believe may be required as evidence . . .'. The Act did not explicitly require that the warrant specify the precise offence being investigated, nor identify the suspected perpetrator(s).

Acting under such a warrant, Inland Revenue officials raided Rossminster's premises and, without offering details of the matter under investigation, seized many documents. The legal background to the *Rossminster* seizure is distinguishable from the background to the *Entick* case, since the seizure was purportedly rooted in a

60 [1942] AC 206 at 245, HL.

61 Quoted in Heuston op cit at p 51. Stable J had issued a dissenting judgment in *R v Home Secretary, ex p Budd* [1942] 1 All ER 373, in terms similar to those used by Lord Atkin in *Liversidge*.

statutory power. Rossminster nevertheless claimed that Lord Camden's reasoning was relevant to interpretation of s 20C. Rossminster argued that the court should presume that Parliament intended s 20C to be construed consistently with the common law principles informing *Entick* – namely that the power would only be used in a precisely targeted way, and would not be invoked by Revenue officials to enable them to embark upon a speculative trawl through all of a company's or an individual's private papers.

The Court of Appeal accepted this argument.[62] Lord Denning's leading judgment was particularly forceful. He couched his argument in resonant, almost melodramatic terms, portraying the Inland Revenue's behaviour as incompatible both with contemporary moral standards and long established legal principle:

> '[T]here has been no search like it – and no seizure like it – in England, since that Saturday, April 30 1763, when the Secretary of State issued a general warrant by which he authorised the King's messengers to arrest John Wilkes and seize all his books and papers . . .'.[63]

Denning's judgment seemingly rested on the presumption that the bare words of the Act had to be read against a background (or contextual) legal principle; namely that Parliament would always be sensitive to the need to protect individual liberty when enacting legislation. As Lord Denning put it: 'it is, as I see it, the duty of the courts so to construe the statute as to see that it encroaches as little as possible upon the liberties of the people of England'.[64]

This was in effect a teleological or purposive approach to the interpretation of s 20C. The 'purpose' being served was ensuring that government behaviour did not interfere unduly with citizens' common law entitlements. This interpretative strategy then led Lord Denning to the following conclusion:

> '. . . as a matter of construction of the statute and therefore of the warrant – in pursuance of our traditional role to protect the liberty of the individual – it is our duty to say that the warrant must particularise the specific offence which is charged as being fraud on the revenue'.[65]

Since the warrant did not do so, it was invalid.

The Court of Appeal's judgment was subsequently reversed in the House of Lords, which adopted a straightforwardly literalist approach to s 20C. Lord Wilberforce, delivering the leading judgment, saw no point in referring to old cases such as *Entick* to support Rossminster's contention. He concluded that the 'plain words' of s 20C authorised the Inland Revenue to engage in behaviour which could not be justified at common law. Nor could he see any basis for finding an implied term in the statute which required much greater specificity in the terms of the warrant: Parliament's intention had been to override common law principles.[66] Lord Wilberforce's

[62] [1980] AC 952. [63] [1980] AC 952 at 970. [64] [1980] AC 952 at 972.
[65] [1980] AC 952 at 974.
[66] Lord Wilberforce was led to this conclusion in part by what he perceived as the 'substantial safeguards' the Act introduced to minimise the prospect of the power being used arbitrarily, namely that the warrant could only be sought by two senior officials, and it could only be granted by a circuit judge rather than, as was often the case, by a magistrate.

invocation of the literal rule was entirely orthodox, and quite consistent with traditional understandings of the separation of powers:

'while the courts may look critically at legislation which impairs the rights of citizens and should resolve any doubt of interpretation in their favour, it is no part of their duty, or power, to restrict or impede the working of legislation, even of unpopular legislation; to do so would be to weaken rather than advance the democratic process'.[67]

Lord Wilberforce nevertheless cast some doubt on the political acceptability of the legal rule which the statute had enacted, by observing that: 'I cannot believe that this does not call for a fresh look by Parliament'.[68] Lord Dilhorne expressed similar sentiments: 'It may be that there are many persons who think that in 1976 too wide a power was given to the revenue. If it was, and I express no opinion on that, it must be left to Parliament to narrow the power it gave'.[69]

The House of Lords evidently considered that the judges in the Court of Appeal had allowed their moral distaste for s 20C to push them into adopting illegitimate interpretative strategies, and thus to overstep the boundaries of their proper constitutional role. This is most clearly illustrated by Lord Wilberforce's comment that courts should not 'restrict or impede the working of legislation'. That is however a simplistic view. Lord Denning would no doubt have agreed with the sentiment that courts should not impede the working of legislation. Where he differed from Lord Wilberforce was in his understanding of how the legislation was supposed to work. In Denning's opinion it would work as Parliament intended if it did not trample over established common law principles. In Wilberforce's view it was designed to have just that intensely intrusive effect. Neither perspective can be regarded as legally 'correct' in any definitive sense. Rather the case shows us that there is much unpredictability in the way that courts may approach their constitutional responsibility of giving meaning to the text of statutes.

CONCLUSION

It is also helpful to compare *Liversidge* and *Rossminster* to illustrate the point that a court's adoption of a particular interpretative strategy does not determine the substantive character of the result that the court produces in a given case. If one looked solely at *Rossminster*, one might be tempted to assume that teleological interpretation would restrain governmental power to a greater degree than literal interpretation. Yet in *Liversidge*, Lord Atkin's robust defence of individual liberty against government interference is founded on a zealously literalist interpretative technique. In that case, it was the majority who engaged in teleological strategies. The 'purpose' the majority sought to promote was the successful prosecution of the war, which led them to construe the literal words of reg 18b against a background or context which demanded that government powers be very generously interpreted. In Viscount Maugham's view:

67 [1980] AC 952 at 988, HL.

68 [1980] AC 952 at 999.

69 [1980] AC 952 at 1006.

'The suggested rule (viz that legislation dealing with the liberty of the subject must be construed, if possible, in favour of the subject against the Crown) has no relevance in dealing with an executive measure by way of preventing a public danger when the safety of the State is involved'.[70]

Lord Macmillan put the argument in similar terms: 'The purpose of the regulation is to ensure public safety, and it is right so to interpret emergency legislation as to promote, rather than to defeat, its efficacy for the defence of the realm'.[71]

Lord Atkin – in contrast – (and much like Lord Wilberforce in *Rossminster*) seemed to consider resort to those background principles illegitimate, and invoked an alternative context against which to construe reg 18B:

'In this country, amid the clash of arms, the laws are not silent. They may be changed, but they speak the same language in war as in peace. It has always been one of the pillars of freedom, one of the principles of liberty for which on recent authority we are now fighting, that the judges are no respecters of persons and stand between the subject and any attempted encroachment on his liberty by the executive'.[72]

To put the matter in rather more abstract terms, cases such as *Rossminster* and *Liversidge* tell us that while Parliament *may do* anything which it wishes, the constitutional responsibility to tell us what Parliament actually *has done* rests with the courts.

V. STARE DECISIS

The principle of legal certainty – that citizens be able to predict the limits the law places on individual and governmental behaviour – is an essential ingredient (albeit one respected with varying degrees of stringency) in all theoretical analyses of the rule of law. The principle has only a precarious legal basis in the British constitution, since Parliament may at any time change any law in any way whatsoever. For much of the modern era, the common law has, in contrast, possessed an almost absolute degree of legal certainty.

The common law's attachment to an inflexible doctrine of *stare decisis* (a maxim best translated as meaning 'let the previous decision stand') was confirmed in the 1898 case of *London Tramway Co v LCC*.[73] For a unanimous House of Lords, Lord Halsbury claimed that the judgments of that court bound not only all inferior courts, but also the House of Lords itself. He acknowledged that such rigidity might on occasion produce substantively unjust solutions to given problems because the common law could not be adapted to meet changing social conditions:

'but what is that . . . as compared with the inconvenience – the disastrous inconvenience – of

70 [1980] AC 952 at 218–219. 71 [1980] AC 952 at 251. 72 [1980] AC 952 at 244.
73 [1898] AC 375, HL.

having each question subject to being reargued and the dealings of mankind rendered doubtful by reason of different decisions, so that in truth and in fact there would be no final court of appeal'.[74]

Lord Halsbury's reasoning obviously has strong roots in Diceyan perceptions of the need to avoid unpredictability and arbitrariness in the content of the legal framework within which citizens live. It may thus be seen as a legal expression of the political principles underpinning red light variants of the rule of law. It should however be emphasised that the courts' adherence to a rigid *stare decisis* principle (like its preference for a literal rule of statutory interpretation) was a common law rule, fashioned by the House of Lords itself, not a requirement imposed upon the courts by Parliament. Clearly, in cases involving intolerable injustice in which the House of Lords felt itself bound by a previous decision, Parliament could if it wished pass legislation altering the substantive law. Similarly, Parliament could at any time enact a statute ordering the courts to depart from the *London Tramways* rule in any way on any occasions they thought fit, or to abandon the principle altogether. But furthermore, in the absence of any legislation on the point, the House of Lords itself retained the power to amend or reject the rule: common law rules are as much at the mercy of the final court of appeal as of the legislature.

Lord Halsbury's suggestion that the House of Lords could bind itself is therefore a nonsense, as a matter both of abstract logic and constitutional principle. Binding legal rules depend for their force on the existence of a higher source of law than the rules themselves. The members of the House of Lords qua final court of appeal in 1898 could no more 'bind' their successors than the Parliament of that year could 'bind' future Parliaments. Lord Halsbury might expect his successors to respect his rule because of its intrinsic merits; he could in no legal sense compel them to do so.

The House of Lords did not avail itself of its undoubted constitutional power to overrule *London Tramways* until 1966. In a Practice Statement issued on 26 July,[75] the Lord Chancellor announced that the House of Lords would in future modify its approach to *stare decisis*, and depart from its previous decisions to avoid injustice in particular cases and to facilitate the development of common law principles in a way that reflected changing social and economic conditions. The House of Lords has however rarely availed itself of this new power, and has developed quite rigorous criteria which must be met before a previous decision is overruled.[76] The initiative may thus be seen as a classic example of the green light approach to the rule or law, in which red light principles are not abandoned entirely, but are nevertheless appreciably diluted. While important in itself, the significance of the 1966 Practice Statement should not be exaggerated. The House of Lords will only infrequently find itself faced by legal problems which cannot in some way be distinguished from previous decisions on similar points. And for constitutional lawyers, the more pressing

74 [1898] AC 375 at 380, HL.
75 *Practice Statement (Judicial Precedent)* [1966] 1 WLR 1234.
76 See Zander (1994) op cit pp 190–199.

question is not what the House of Lords will do when faced with a common law rule it considers unpalatable, but what it will do when its distaste is triggered by a statutory provision.

VI. PARLIAMENTARY SOVEREIGNTY V THE RULE OF LAW

Dicey's notions of parliamentary sovereignty and the rule of law only function in the sense that he intended if the courts accept that their allegiance lies to the legislature rather than to the executive or the citizenry. We must stress again that in orthodox constitutional theory, the courts' allegiance is not to the people, nor to a supra-legislative constitution, but simply to the will of Parliament as expressed in the words of a statute. But as our knowledge of the law of the constitution increases, so we come to see that orthodox theory may present a misleading picture. *Liversidge* seemingly provides an example of the courts in effect giving allegiance to the executive rather than to Parliament. Insofar as the constitution places the task of interpreting legislation in the hands of the courts, *Liversidge* respects parliamentary sovereignty because it is only the court which can tell us what Parliament intended. But that is a very formalistic view of 'law'; if we look behind this legal facade to the political principles underpinning traditional views of the rule of law and the separation of powers, *Liversidge* can plausibly be portrayed as a manifestly 'unconstitutional' decision.

But one can also find episodes in constitutional history when the judiciary apparently considered that its ultimate allegiance lay not to the executive, nor even to Parliament, but rather to a version of the rule of law which possessed a higher constitutional status than the clear words of legislation. Such appears to be the lesson offered by the judgment of the House of Lords in the 1969 case of *Anisminic Ltd v Foreign Compensation Commission*[77] and the Court of Appeal's decision a decade earlier in *R v Medical Appeal Tribunal, ex p Gilmore.*[78]

OUSTER CLAUSES – *GILMORE* AND *ANISMINIC*

In the 1950s and 1960s, Parliament made increasing use of statutes seeming to oust the courts' common law power of review. These so-called 'ouster clauses' were a logical ingredient of the drift towards 'green light' theories of administrative law. Often Parliament sought to exclude the courts because the legislation concerned established alternative fora for review, appeal, or inquiry. Relatedly, it was widely felt that much government activity did not lend itself to resolution by judicial methods.[79] Such statutes would contradict the Diceyan version of the rule of law, but since

77 [1969] 2 AC 147, HL. 78 [1957] 1 QB 574, CA.

79 See particularly Titmuss R (1971) 'Welfare rights, law and discretion' *Political Quarterly* 113–131.

Parliament can make any law whatsoever, there is theoretically no impediment to it passing legislation which excludes the common law power of review.

One might take as an example the system of welfare payments established under the National Insurance (Industrial Injuries) Act 1948. Decisions as to a claimant's entitlement were initially to be made by a government employee. The Act allowed applicants who were dissatisfied with the original decisions to appeal to a specialised medical tribunal. Section 36(3) provided that the tribunal's decision 'shall be final', a formula which seemed to remove the individual's right to seek review of the tribunal's decision in the courts. However in *R v Medical Appeal Tribunal, ex p Gilmore* Lord Denning, faced with an apparent error of law on the tribunal's part, concluded that, notwithstanding s 36(3)'s apparently unambiguous instruction, judicial review:

> 'is never to be taken away by any statute except by the most clear and explicit words. The word "final" is not enough. That only means "without appeal". It does not mean without recourse to [review]'.[80]

This apparently presents us with a modification to the doctrine of implied repeal, which we discussed in chapter two. Section 36(3) implies that Parliament had decided to 'contract out' of judicial review with respect to industrial injury compensation. Lord Denning's judgment appears to echo the decisions in *Chorlton v Lings* and *Nairn v University of St Andrews*, where the courts held that the enfranchisement of women would represent such a fundamental reform to society's political order that Parliament could not effect it through implied or 'furtive' legislative terms. In *Gilmore*, Denning seems to attribute the same high political status to a Diceyan principle of the rule of law – namely that individual citizens should always be able to challenge the decisions of government bodies before 'the ordinary courts'. Denning suggests that Parliament may 'suspend' this principle if it wishes, but only by adopting absolutely unambiguous statutory formulae.

One might have assumed that Parliament had adopted 'the most clear and explicit words' in the ouster clause in s 4(4) of the Foreign Compensation Act 1950. The Act established a Commission to distribute limited funds among British nationals whose overseas property had been seized by foreign governments. Section 4(4) stated that the Commission's 'determinations . . . shall not be called in question in any court of law'. 'Calling into question' would appear to reach both appeal and review. Nevertheless, in *Anisminic Ltd v Foreign Compensation Commission*,[81] the House of Lords assumed jurisdiction to review the Commission's activities. It did so on the grounds that the Commission had made an error of law in its decision-making process. Consequently, the decision that the Commission had produced was not a determination, but 'a purported determination'. Since the ouster clause made no reference to 'purported determinations', the court was not challenging parliamentary sovereignty by declaring the Commission's action unlawful.

Like the majority judgment in *Liversidge*, such reasoning commends itself only to

[80] [1957] 1 QB 574, CA. [81] [1969] 2 AC 147, HL.

the most formalistic of constitutional analyses. *Gilmore* and *Anisminic* can more plausibly be presented as examples of the judges steeling themselves to resist orthodox understandings of the hierarchy of legal authority within the constitution in order to safeguard a political principle – that government action always be subject to judicial review, irrespective of Parliament's intentions. In each case, the judges adopted a rather narrow view of legislative sovereignty. Parliament could indeed exclude judicial review; but it could do so only by initiating the protracted and highly visible process of passing legislation explicitly overturning the courts' decisions. One might say that the House of Lords was rejecting a formal, legalistic interpretation of parliamentary sovereignty in favour of a functionalist, political interpretation – namely to ensure that the exclusion of judicial review really did attract the consent of the people.

The House of Lords' judgment might lead some observers to recall the oft-quoted words of Bishop Hoadly, delivered in a sermon to the King in 1717:

> 'Whoever hath an absolute authority to interpret any written or spoken laws, it is he who is truly the lawgiver, to all intents and purposes, and not the person who first spoke or wrote them'.

Anisminic clearly presented a judicial challenge to Parliament's sovereignty, but that challenge lay in the sphere of the legitimacy rather than legality of parliamentary intentions. Parliament could if it wish reverse *Anisminic*, but only at the risk of being seen to abrogate orthodox understandings of the rule of law. The government initially seemed prepared to take that risk, and prepared a bill containing a more extensive ouster clause. This provided that not only the 'determinations' of the Commission, but also any 'purported determinations' should not be called in question in any court of law'. Whether the courts would have been prepared to 'defy' that legislation by a further exercise in creative statutory 'interpretation' is a matter for speculation. The proposal was abandoned in the face of opposition within Parliament, and replaced by a measure granting the Court of Appeal appellate jurisdiction over the Commission's determinations.[82]

Leading constitutional theorists took different views of *Anisminic's* implications. Professor John Griffiths felt that the courts were intruding in an unconstitutional way on the sovereignty of Parliament.[83] In contrast, Professor Wade suggested that the threat to the constitution came not from the judges' apparent challenge to parliamentary sovereignty, but from Parliament's increasing predisposition to deploy ouster clauses to limit or remove the courts' powers of judicial review. In Wade's view, such legislation showed an unhealthy disrespect for orthodox principles of the rule of law.[84] Both viewpoints are obviously defensible, a fact which further strengthens the presumption that constitutional analysis must operate as much in the realm of practical

82 Foreign Compensation Act 1969, s 3. See Wade HRW and Forsyth C (1994) *Administrative law* pp 734–739 (Oxford: Clarendon Press).

83 (1977) *The politics of the judiciary* pp 123–124 (Harmondsworth: Penguin).

84 (1969) 'Constitutional and administrative aspects of the *Anisminic* case' 85 *Law Quarterly Review* 198–212; (1980) *Constitutional fundamentals* pp 65–66 (London: Stevens).

politics as of legal theory. However if the *Anisminic* saga was seen by some constitutional physicians as a symptom that their patient was a little under the weather, the legislative response to the *Burmah Oil* judgment might have suggested that she required a prolonged course of intensive care.

VII. RETROSPECTIVE LAW-MAKING

The objection that Diceyans would make to Parliament's growing preference for granting the executive discretionary powers in statutes is that citizens may find it difficult to predict what government bodies are legally entitled to do. That objection is met only in part by the *Wednesbury* principles of administrative law; those principles may enable the citizen to predict the outer limits of lawful government action, but not the precise point at which a given decision may be located. But unpredictability would be taken to an extreme degree if Parliament enacted legislation which had retrospective effect; for example by enacting a statute in 2003 which provided that everybody who had bought a foreign car since 1983 had to pay a 'patriotism levy' of £50; or by introducing legislation in 2003 which made it a criminal offence to have written anything critical of government policy before 2001. Since Parliament is sovereign, there is no legal impediment to it introducing such legislation. In doing so however, Parliament would surely be undermining all three versions of the rule of law which have been discussed in this chapter. For students who might suppose Parliament could never do such a thing, the events which followed the 1964 case of *Burmah Oil Co (Burmah Trading) v Lord Advocate*[85] may come as a surprise.

RETROSPECTIVITY IN LEGISLATION – THE WAR DAMAGE ACT 1965

The saga began in 1942, when the British government, acting under what it presumed to be a common law power,[86] ordered its army in Burma to destroy one of Burmah Oil's refineries to prevent it falling into the hands of the advancing Japanese forces. After the war, the government offered Burmah Oil an *ex gratia* payment of £4.6 million as compensation. The oil company launched an action in the courts, claiming some £31 million compensation, and arguing that the common law power used required that owners be fully reimbursed by the government for any loss suffered. There did not appear to be any clear authority for the House of Lords to follow in this case. The judges thus faced the task of deciding the extent of the government's common law prerogative power to destroy property in war-time. The details of the

85 [1965] AC 75, HL.

86 These 'royal prerogative powers' are considered in detail in chapter four. The only point one need note here is that the claimed power had a common law rather than statutory origin.

judgment need not concern us;[87] suffice to say that the majority upheld Burmah Oil's claim.

The government was alarmed by this decision, since it might mean that not only Burmah Oil, but also many other individuals or companies whose property had been destroyed in similar circumstances, would be entitled to large sums of compensation. Such claims could have major implications for public expenditure. The government therefore introduced the War Damage Bill into Parliament to reverse the judgment. There could be no objection in terms of constitutional principle to Parliament changing the common law by statute in the sense of providing that *in future* the payment of compensation in such circumstances will be determined by statutory rule *x* rather than common law rule *y*. Such action is permitted by the doctrine of parliamentary sovereignty, and is consistent with all versions of the rule of law. However, the War Damage Bill was intended to overrule the common law not just for future instances of property loss, but also for those which had already happened – the statute was to have retrospective as well as prospective effect.

As stressed above, Diceyan theory tells us that such legislation is entirely consistent with the legal doctrine of parliamentary sovereignty, but utterly inconsistent with the political principle of the rule of law. The Bill generated appreciable controversy as it progressed through Parliament.[88] That it emerged as the War Damage Act 1965 provides further compelling evidence that the rule of law, insofar as it can be construed as a moral code embedding certain political values in Britain's democratic structure, may on occasions be regarded by our sovereign legislature as an expendable rather than indispensable ingredient of Britain's constitutional recipe. But one might also identify controversies of relatively recent origin where the same accusation might plausibly be levelled at the courts.

RETROSPECTIVITY AT COMMON LAW? RAPE WITHIN MARRIAGE

To modern day observers, one of the more obviously objectionable moral principles informing social and legal affairs in the mid-eighteenth century was the proposition advanced by the distinguished jurist Sir Matthew Hale in his *History of the Pleas of the Crown*:

'[a] husband cannot be guilty of a rape committed by himself upon his lawful wife, for by their mutual matrimonial consent and contract the wife hath given herself up in this kind unto her husband which she cannot retract'.[89]

The notion that a woman was in effect legally obliged to accommodate her husband's desire to have sex with her whenever he wished rested on the cultural or moral assumption that a wife was the 'subservient chattel'[90] of her husband. The questions

87 A useful summary is provided by Jackson P (1964) 'The royal prerogative' *Modern Law Review* 709–717.
88 See Jackson P (1965) 'War Damage Act 1965' *Modern Law Review* 574–576.
89 Quoted in *R v R (rape: marital exemption)* [1991] 4 All ER 481 at 483, HL; per Lord Keith.
90 [1991] 4 All ER 481 at 484, HL.

before the House of Lords in *R v R (rape: marital exemption)*[91] in 1991 were whether that assumption remained valid, and – if it was not – whether the common law should be altered to reflect new cultural or moral assumptions.[92]

If the court had considered itself still bound by the *London Tramways* view of *stare decisis* then the answer to the second question – irrespective of the answer to the first – would have had to have been 'No'. In *R v R*, however, the House of Lords accepted the view that the common law could legitimately be regarded as a dynamic and flexible source of legal rules. As Lord Keith put it:

> 'The common law is, however, capable of evolving in the light of changing, social, economic and cultural developments. Hale's proposition reflected the state of affairs in these respects at the time it was enunciated . . . Since then, the status of women, and particularly of married women, has changed out of all recognition . . . In modern times any reasonable person must regard [Hale's proposition] as quite unacceptable'.[93]

The House of Lords then concluded that the overturning of the previous common law rule was a task that could appropriately be undertaken by the courts. There was no need to wait for Parliament to enact legislation changing the law.[94]

R v R is a significant judgment in many respects. For our present purposes, the key question it raises is that of *when* it became a crime for a husband to rape his wife? The House of Lords settled the legal question in October 1991. The (attempted) 'rape' in issue was committed some two years earlier. The change in the law could thus be seen as retrospective, in the sense that any person who consulted law reports or legal textbooks in 1989 would understandably have concluded that – notwithstanding the morally abhorrent nature of such an action – a husband could not, save in very limited circumstances, be convicted of raping his wife. To put it in Diceyan terms, such an action would seemingly not have involved any breach – and certainly not a distinct one – of the law.

We would presumably have expected – if the House of Lords had felt it appropriate for the law to be changed by Parliament rather than the courts – that any legislation attaching criminal liability to a husband's rape of his wife would have only prospective effect. Had such a statute been given retrospective effect, sufficient to bring R (and presumably any other husband who had raped his wife since October 1989) within its terms, it would no doubt have attracted criticism on the grounds that it infringed the rule of law. But innovative judicial law-making – which either alters rules of common

91 [1991] 4 All ER 481 at 483, HL.

92 The rule had been narrowed somewhat by subsequent case law of fairly modern vintage. A husband could be convicted of raping his wife if they were legally separated prior to the finalisation of divorce proceedings. See the discussion in *R v R* at 486–489.

93 [1991] 4 All ER 481 at 483, HL.

94 On this point, the House of Lords followed the lead given by Lord Lane CJ when the case was before the Court of Appeal: 'The remaining and no less difficult question is whether . . . this is an area where the court should step aside to leave the matter to the parliamentary process. This is not the creation of a new offence, it is the removal of a common law fiction which has become anachronistic and offensive and we consider that it is our duty having reached that conclusion to act upon it' [1991] 2 All ER 257 at 256, CA.

law or attaches new meanings to existing statutory provisions – is generally retrospective in nature. One might in formalistic terms rebut that contention by pointing out that when R attempted to rape his wife the law had already changed. We (and he) just did not find out about that change until two years later when the House of Lords finally delivered judgment on the issue. And quite when the law changed is a mystery.[95]

It is perhaps curious that the British constitutional tradition has so normalised the retrospective impact of common law innovation that it is evidently not seen as 'really' retrospective at all. It might of course be suggested that most sensible observers in the 1980s would have anticipated that the marital rape exemption might well soon be substantially amended or even abolished by the courts, given that the rule rested on such obsolete and objectionable moral foundations and had already been narrowed by modern judicial decisions. But if one's understanding of the rule of law incorporates a concern with establishing with certainty the substantive content of laws – or at least those laws whose breach imposes heavy costs on a defendant – *R v R* can readily be regarded as a problematic decision in both specific and general terms.

That difficulty becomes more pronounced when one considers the Court of Appeal's subsequent judgment in *R v C*.[96] The defendant in *C* had been convicted in 2002 of – inter alia – raping his wife. The rape in issue had occurred in 1970; that is over 20 years prior to the House of Lords' decision in *R v R*. On appeal, C's counsel argued that the prosecution of the offence of rape should be regarded as an abuse of process and therefore be quashed by the Court of Appeal. C's argument conceded the propriety of the House of Lords' conclusion in *R v R* that by *1989* it was entirely foreseeable that courts would be prepared to reject Hale's assumption as to the legal impossibility of a man raping his wife. The argument asserted however that no such conclusion could sensibly have been drawn in *1970*. This contention might be thought to be reinforced by the observation that three significant judgments which weakened the general applicability of Hale's doctrine by disavowing its relevance in respect of spouses who were undergoing divorce or separation proceedings had been issued in 1974, 1976, and 1986 respectively.[97] In more prosaic terms, C's submission was that while the law had indeed changed prior to *R v R*, it had not changed by the time he 'raped' his wife in 1970.

The Court of Appeal saw no need to engage with the question left open by the House of Lords in *R v R*; namely when precisely did it become a crime for a man to rape his wife. The Court nonetheless had little difficulty concluding that the law had certainly changed by 1970. The judgment posed the question of what a solicitor might then have been expected to say to a client who inquired if he might be guilty of rape if he forced his wife to have non-consensual sexual intercourse. In the Court's view:

95 Cf the comment in the *Practice Statement (Judicial Precedent)* 1966 that in considering whether to depart from previous decisions, the House of Lords would bear in mind; 'the especial need for certainty in the criminal law'; [1966] 1 WLR 1234.

96 [2004] 3 All ER 1.

97 *R v O'Brien* [1974] 3 All ER 663; *R v Steele* (1976) 65 Cr App R 22; *R v Roberts* [1985] Crim LR 188.

'The solicitor would have started by pointing out to his client that to rape his wife would be barbaric, and that he would not condone it. He would then have told his client that the courts had developed and could be expected to continue to develop exceptions to the supposed rule of irrevocable consent, and that if ever the issue were considered in this court, the supposed immunity of a husband from a successful prosecution for rape of his wife might be recognised for what it was, a legal fiction.'[98]

The judgment did not offer any evidence to support this perhaps rather extravagant conclusion. It is certainly difficult to reconcile it with the observation of the Court of Appeal in 1986 in *R v Roberts* to the effect that the general presumption that a husband could not rape his wife remained valid, albeit subject to a growing number of exceptions:

'In our judgment the law is now quite plain on this topic. The status of marriage involves that the woman has given her consent to her husband having intercourse with her during the subsistence of the marriage. She cannot unilaterally withdraw it. The cases show that in a number of circumstances that consent can be terminated. If it has been terminated and the husband has intercourse with his wife without her consent he is guilty of rape.'[99]

The Court's conclusion in *R v C* might have acquired some cogent support by invoking the view of the leading criminal law text in the 1970s and 1980, Professor Glanville Williams' *Textbook of Criminal Law*; in which the author observed: 'It would be an understatement to say that this example of male chauvinism fails to accord with current opinion as to the rights of husbands'.[100] The Court of Appeal did not invoke this or indeed any other authority in support of its assertion as to common understandings of the law on this point in 1970, an omission which rather undermines the persuasiveness of its conclusion. We still do not know of course when the law on this point changed. We know simply that it had changed by 1970. Perhaps it had changed by 1960? Or 1950? This presumably means that there are an appreciable number of men who are now in principle liable to prosecution and conviction for having committed an act which was not identified as a crime by either statute or common law at the relevant time, but which carries a sentence of life imprisonment.

It may readily be conceded that C's behaviour was utterly barbaric. But that point should not be allowed to obscure the broader question of constitutional principle which the case raises; namely the aforementioned 'retrospective' impact of change in the substantive content of the common law. The principle might be thought difficult to reconcile with Diceyan notions of the rule of law, which demand inter alia that governmental interferences with the 'body or goods' of citizens are justifiable only if authorised by 'distinct' laws.[101]

98 [2004] 3 All ER 1 at para 19, per Hale LJ. 99 [1985] Crim LR 188.

100 (1978) p 195. It might nonetheless be noted that Professor Williams went on to observe that a husband who did so behave at that time (1978) would be 'morally guilty' rather than 'guilty' of rape.

101 See p 57 above.

The common law's attachment to what is often termed 'retrospective overruling' was premised in large part on the theoretical proposition that the courts simply 'declare' what the law is.[102] According to this declaratory theory of the common law, courts never actually make law when promulgating new rules or principles; rather they draw our attention to a state of legal affairs which has existed unnoticed for some (perhaps considerable) time. The modern status of this declaratory theory may be best illustrated by the following passage from Lord Browne-Wilkinson's judgment in *Kleinwort Benson Ltd v Lincoln City Council*:

> 'According to this theory, when an earlier decision is overruled the law is not changed; its true nature is disclosed, having existed in that form all along. This theoretical position is, as Lord Reid said, a fairy tale in which no-one any longer believes. In truth, judges make and change the law'.[103]

The difficulties which attend the practice of retrospective overruling in cases such as *R v R* or *R v C* might be avoided if the House of Lords were to accept (or Parliament were to require through statute) that overruling of previous decisions or the fashioning of entirely new common law principles would have only 'prospective effect'. That is the law would become effective only in respect of factual situations which occurred after the judgment was issued. This approach to the temporal effect of judicially created change to the law is by no means uncommon in modern western legal systems.[104] Given its sovereign law-making power, Parliament could at any time impose such a requirement on the courts, either in general or selective terms. Similarly, since our constitution's attachment to retrospective judicial innovation is a common law phenomenon, the House of Lords qua final court of appeal could alter the rule. From the late 1990s onwards, the question received continued judicial scrutiny. In *Re Spectrum Plus Ltd*[105] the House of Lords acknowledged that there was no insurmountable obstacle preventing a change of traditional practice. Affording a change in the previously accepted meaning of the law only prospective effect could be appropriate in 'exceptional' or 'extreme' circumstances. But neither the courts nor Parliament have as yet shown any obvious enthusiasm for making prospective overruling a principle of even extensive let alone general application.

102 My thanks to Terence Ingman's (9th edn, 2002) *The English legal process*, ch 9 for prompting me to allude to this issue.

103 [1998] 4 All ER 513 at 518. The reference to Lord Reid relates to the latter's comments in 'The judge as lawmaker' (1972–73) *Journal of the Society of Public Teachers of Law* 22.

104 See the discussion in Ingman *op cit* pp 387–388. For a broader consideration of the issue see Rodger A (2005) 'A time for everything under the law: some reflections on retrospectivity' *LQR* 57; Atrill S (2005) 'Nulla poena sine lege in comparative perspective . . .' *Public Law* 107.

105 [2005] UKHL 41; [2005] 4 All ER 209.

CONCLUSION

We will revisit both the legality and legitimacy of the *R v R* judgment later in the book.[106] At this early stage, our conclusions might sensibly be limited to observing that we should exercise caution when presented with the general proposition that Britain's constitutional tradition rests securely on the three supporting pillars of parliamentary sovereignty, the rule of law and the separation of powers, which are themselves securely rooted in the foundation stone of democracy. Chapters one and two indicated that our constitution's foundation is itself shifting and unstable; in addition, the theoretical analyses and historical events discussed in this chapter have suggested that those pillars may at times lean in contradictory rather than complementary directions. Whether this is a desirable situation is a question to which we shall return; it may be that one can argue it is preferable for a constitution to bend to the wind of changing times, rather than to stand rigid and so risk destruction in the face of a political or social hurricane. To sustain or refute that argument however, we need to gather more knowledge of the constitution's historical and contemporary make-up. In chapter four, we begin that task by examining the royal prerogative.

106 In ch 19 below.

4

THE ROYAL PREROGATIVE

The courts' traditional readiness to accept the Diceyan notion of parliamentary sovereignty meant that there was no scope for the judiciary overtly to challenge the substance of legislation. The House of Lords' decision in *Anisminic* would suggest that there may be some instances in our constitutional history when the courts seem *in effect* to dispute Parliament's supremacy. But, the court took care in *Anisminic* to root its arguments in a constitutional framework which was theoretically legitimate.

The existence of a gap between theoretical and practical legitimacy in judicial behaviour is less evident in respect of review of government action taken under statute. That government bodies be subject to judicial review is clearly necessary to maintain the sovereignty of Parliament. If the courts permitted government to cross the legal boundaries which Parliament has laid out, they would be saying that it was government action, rather than legislation, which was the most important value in the constitutional hierarchy. As suggested by *Anisminic* and *Liversidge v Anderson*, one sometimes finds cases where, in practice, the court's interpretation of a statute seems impossible to reconcile with parliamentary intent as expressed in the words of the Act. In such circumstances, we might plausibly argue that the theory of parliamentary sovereignty – in so far as it rests upon judicial obeisance to the obvious, literal meaning of the text of an Act – is being subverted. However, as noted in chapter two, statute is not the only source of the British government's legal authority. The government also possesses various common law powers. Constitutional lawyers gather these powers together under the label of the royal prerogative.

THE SOURCE OF PREROGATIVE POWERS

In its initial, pre-1688 form, the 'royal prerogative comprised the personal powers of the Monarch. Despite the apparent wishes of some of[1] the Stuart kings, the English monarchy was never absolutist – medieval kings had neither the financial or military resources to rule without the active support of the nobility. That support was essentially dependent on the Monarch accepting some constraints on her/his power to govern.

[1] See A Tomkins (2005) *Our republican constitution* (Hart: Oxford) pp 91–93 for a suggestion that Charles I might credibly be seen as favouring a more broadly based consensual approach to governance.

Those constraints were articulated in both statute and the common law – neither of which the Monarch could change without the support of Parliament or the courts.

The origins of current constitutional doctrines are often to be found in seventeenth century political history, and the law relating to the prerogative is no exception to that rule. As suggested in chapter two, this period of constitutional history was marked by a series of disputes between King and Parliament over the distribution of governmental power. There was an ongoing struggle between the King's effort to rule by prerogative powers or 'proclamations', and Parliament's power to restrain the King's autonomy through statute. And until such time as that struggle degenerated into civil war, the courts were usually the site of the battle.

Prerogative cases before the 1688 revolution

Seventeenth century, pre-revolutionary case law on the questions of how and for what purpose prerogative powers could be used was riddled with ambiguity and inconsistency. The fundamental legal issue at stake was whether, both in principle and in practice, the Monarch's prerogative powers had a superior constitutional status to Acts of Parliament. Judges tended to produce opinions which adopted inconsistent positions on this question, a fact which, given the political instability of that era, is perhaps readily understandable. In a climate of constant 'revolution', the ultimate source of legal authority within the constitution was likely to be an unstable phenomenon.

Prior to the 1688 revolution, the courts had on occasion robustly resisted the King's preferences. In the 1607 *Case of Prohibitions*,[2] James I had claimed a divine right to sit as a Judge and to develop the common law as he thought appropriate; 'The King said that he thought the law was founded upon reason, and that he and others had reason, as well as the judges'. The common law judges, led by Chief Justice Coke, rejected this claim. While the judges confirmed that the King was not subject to any man, he was subject to the law, and until such time as he had gained sufficient expertise in the law's many rules he had no entitlement to sit as a judge. This expertise was not a matter of 'natural reason' or 'common sense', but demanded mastery of 'an artificial reason . . . which requires long study and experience, before that a man can attain to the cognizance of it'.[3]

As well as placing restraints on the Monarch, this ruling enhanced the powers of the courts. We might recall that 'common reason' was the formula invoked in *Dr Bonham's Case* to overrule statute; if that common reason was something that only the judges were competent to discern, one would be saying in effect that the courts were the ultimately authoritative source of law in the pre-revolutionary constitution. Similarly, in the 1611 *Case of Proclamations*,[4] Chief Justice Coke seemingly placed quite

[2] (1607) 12 Co Rep 63.

[3] One sees here an early statement of a pervasive trend in British constitutional theory, subsequently embraced by other countries, which tied the 'independence' of the judiciary to its competence; see for example the sentiments of Alexander Hamilton in *The Federalist Papers No 78* (at pp 17–18 above) and Centlivres CJ in *Harris (No 2)* (at pp 63–64 above).

[4] (1611) 12 Co Rep 74.

stringent limits on the King's ability to rule by prerogative powers. He held that the King only had those prerogative powers which the common law *already recognised;* he could not grant himself new ones.[5] However not all judges were as committed to keeping the King's personal powers within legal boundaries as Coke. There are several examples in the seventeenth century of the judges interpreting prerogative powers in a way that completely undermined the principles laid down in the *Case of Proclamations.*

The Case of Impositions,[6] or *Bate's Case,* in 1606, centred on the King's prerogative power to regulate foreign trade, and Parliament's statutory power to prevent the King levying taxation without parliamentary consent. Bate had refused to pay an import duty that the King had placed on currants, his argument being the tax was illegal because it did not have Parliamentary approval. The King's response was that this was not a tax at all, but a measure to regulate trade. As such it was quite lawful – the money raised was just an incidental side effect of the regulatory power. The integrity of that argument is obviously questionable. However, the court was prepared to accept it, and so provided a back door route for prerogative powers to override statutory provisions. That was not necessarily unconstitutional at the time; we must remember that the supremacy of statute had not been established by then. Condemnation of this type of monarchical behaviour was subsequently to prove a major component of the 1688 *Declaration of Right*; as noted in chapter two, it was expressly prohibited by Article 4 of the Bill of Rights.[7]

A similar scenario arose in the *Case of Ship Money (R v Hampden)*[8] in 1637.[9] It was generally accepted at that time that the Monarch possessed a power to compel coastal areas of the country to furnish him with ships and crews in times of military emergency in order that he could better defend his realm. In the 1630s, Charles I sought to establish that his power in this regard extended to all parts of the country and permitted him to charge a sum of money (in effect a tax) rather than simply insist on the provision of a ship. When Charles I sought to levy such a charge in 1637, John Hampden – who was a member of the House of Commons and an opponent of much of the King's policy – refused to pay. Hampden accepted that the prerogative power existed, and also appeared to accept that it could be levied throughout the country in the form of a tax. However he argued that it could only be invoked when a military emergency was imminent.

The case was heard by a court of 12 judges.[10] Ten of the twelve resolved the argument in the king's favour. The majority opinion rested essentially on the presumption that only the king had the legal competence to assess if an emergency

5 Such activities were not the exclusive preserve of the Stuart kings. The decision in the *Case of Monopolies* (1602) 11 Co Rep 84b placed a judicial limit on Elizabeth I's use of prerogative powers, on the grounds that her attempt to create a monopoly in the manufacture and import of playing cards was against the 'public interest'.

6 (1610) 2 State Tr 371.

7 See p 28 above.

8 (1637) 3 State Tr 826.

9 My thanks are owed here to Adam Tomkins, whose stimulating book *Our republican constitution* (at pp 83–87) has led me to revisit the case and amend my treatment of it.

10 See Keir D (1936) 'The case of ship-money' *LQR* 546–574 for a lengthy account of the various judgments.

existed, and if so whether it was of an imminent nature. The court would not address concerns relating either to the good faith or the accuracy of the king's conclusion on this point. In effect, the judgment provided the king with a legal mechanism to bypass the generally accepted principle that the levying of taxation by the king could only be done with the approval of Parliament.

That narrow conclusion was itself thoroughly unacceptable to many members of Parliament. But the *Ship-money* judgment raised broader concerns. Several of the judges had used the case to make what appeared to be very sweeping statements as to the locus of sovereign legal power within the constitution. Judge Vernon went so far as to say: '[T]he king may charge pro bono publico notwithstanding any Act of Parliament . . . [A] statute derogating from the prerogative doth not bind the King, and the King may dispense with any laws in the case of necessity.'[11] Chief Justice Finch put the point in this way: 'They are void Acts of Parliament [which seek] to bind the King not to command the subjects, their persons and goods, and I say their money too; for no Acts of Parliament make any difference.'[12]

The *Ship-money* saga is a graphic example of the ongoing struggle in seventeenth century English constitutional history to establish where sovereign power actually lay. Within a few years of the judgment, Charles I responded to parliamentary discontent on the narrow implication of the judgment by assenting to a bill (which thereby became an Act) which not only purported to abolish his right to levy taxation through the ship-money power, but which also asserted that no such power had ever existed. Several of the judges who had found in his favour in the case were also removed from office and imprisoned. If, however, the king did indeed possess a power to dispense with Acts of parliament whenever he thought it necessary – and if necessity was a matter which only the king could assess – the efficacy of any such statute might prove to be rather limited.

Protection against unlawful taxation was clearly an important element of the citizens' property rights in pre-revolutionary England. It was however perhaps less important than 'property' in one's physical liberty, in the sense of being able to call upon the courts for protection against unlawful arrest or imprisonment. The writ of *habeas corpus* has common law origins which predate even the Magna Carta. Its purpose, crudely put, was to empower the common law courts to order any person detaining a citizen to bring that person before the court and show lawful authority for the detention. If no such authority could be shown in the gaoler's 'return', the prisoner would be released.

Habeas corpus was, in practice, hedged about with many limitations. Its utility was particularly compromised during the reign of Elizabeth I. Elizabeth and her Privy Councillors[13] claimed an entirely arbitrary power to imprison anyone who displeased them, without charge or trial, for as long as they wished. The constitutionality of such

[11] (1637) St Tr iii 1125; cited in Keir *op cit* at pp 568–569.
[12] (1637) St Tr iii 1215–16; cited in Keir *op cit* at p 569.
[13] On the status of the Privy Council see p 115 below.

commitment was widely questioned, and caused sufficient disquiet for the judges to deliver an opinion to the Crown assessing its legality. The so-called *Resolutions in Anderson* began with what seems a spirited defence of individual liberty: 'her highnesses subjects may not be detained in prison, by commandment of any nobleman or councillor, against the laws of the realm'. This suggests that the judges were claiming authority to examine the justification for any such detention and thereafter pronounce upon its legality. However, the *Resolutions* concluded by accepting that the courts had no power to question the factual basis of a claim by the Crown that the person detained had, in the Crown's view, committed treason.[14] Thus, as long as Privy Councillors complied with this formality, their actions would be within 'the laws of the realm', and their effective powers of arbitrary imprisonment would remain untouched.[15]

Anderson offers an obvious precedent for the *Bate's Case* and *Ship Money* principle that the Monarch was the sole judge of whether the factual prerequisites of a prerogative power actually existed. Unsurprisingly, Charles I relied upon the opinion as a justification for imprisoning those of his subjects who declined to pay the 'unlawful' taxes that he levied. Sir Thomas Darnel was one of five knights (including John Hampden's cousin, Edmund) who had refused to pay a compulsory loan to the King. Charles I immediately ordered their arrest and imprisonment. In *Darnel's Case*,[16] the knights' application for writs of *habeas corpus* were met by a return stating simply that they were held 'by special command of the King'. Darnel's counsel argued that this was in itself insufficient justification for committal, since it disclosed no breach of any known law. The court however concluded that the King's power fell within that considered acceptable in the *Resolutions in Anderson*: the judges would not investigate either the factual or legal basis of the King's opinion. In effect, it seemed, the King retained an arbitrary power.

Following the Civil War, the Commons and Lords persuaded Charles II and James II to assent to a series of Habeas Corpus Acts which appeared to extend the reach of the remedy, and relatedly, to curb the Crown's capacity to evade it. But, as the principle articulated in the following case suggests, the then uncertain status of statute vis a vis the prerogative cast considerable doubt on the efficacy of any such legislation.

James II was eager to take advantage of the courts' flexibility to rule by prerogative powers rather than with parliamentary consent in the 1680s. The case of *Godden v Hales*[17] in 1686 is the most obvious example of this trend. James was a King with strong Catholic sympathies trying to rule a country whose Houses of Parliament were dominated by Protestants. Parliament had passed several Acts disqualifying Catholics from government office. James attempted to override these acts on behalf of a Catholic citizen, Sir Edward Hales, by announcing that Hales need not swear loyalty to Protestantism before assuming office. Although this obviously breached an Act of

14 Plucknett (1960) op cit pp 308–311.

15 Which, on a cynical view, one might suggest was precisely the conclusion reached by the House of Lords in *Liversidge* in respect of the powers granted to the Home Secretary by reg 18b.

16 (1627) 3 State Tr 1.

17 (1686) 11 State Tr 1166.

Parliament, the court – by a majority off 11–1 – held that it was part of the Monarch's prerogative to dispense with laws in particular cases if it was necessary to do so. And as in *Ship Money*, the King was to be the sole judge of necessity. The court concluded its judgment with a succinct summary of the constitutional position:

'We were satisfied in our judgments before and, having the concurrence of eleven out of twelve, we think we may very well declare the opinion of the court to be that the king may dispense in this case; and the judges go upon these grounds:

1. that the kings of England are sovereign princes;
2. that the laws of England are the king's laws;
3. that therefore it is an inseparable prerogative in the kings of England to dispense with penal laws in particular cases and upon particular necessary reasons;
4. that of those reasons and those necessities, the king himself is sole judge; and then, which is consequent upon all;
5. that this is not a trust invested in, or granted to, the king by the people, but the ancient remains of the sovereign power and prerogative of the kings of England; which never yet was taken from them, nor can be.'

The obvious implication of *Godden v Hales* – an implication that was intolerable to many members of the House of Commons and the House of Lords – was that sovereign legal power within the English constitution rested with the king. Under this analysis of the constitution, the enactment of legislation in which the Commons, Lords and Monarch had reached and expressed a consensual position on particular political issues would be a legally futile endeavour, since the king would at any point have the power to 'dispense' with the measure that Parliament had produced.

POST 1688 – THE REVOLUTIONARY SETTLEMENT

It was arguably James II's persistent disregard of parliamentary authority that eventually triggered the 1688 revolution. The Bill of Rights 1688, which we could plausibly regard as the 'contract of government' between William and Mary and the revolutionary Commons and Lords, placed clear statutory limits on the extent of prerogative powers.

Reversing the effect of *Godden v Hales* – and denying the correctness of the judgment at the time it was made – were important elements of the revolutionary settlement. *Godden v Hales* is clearly the target of Art 1 of the Bill of Rights of 1689: 'That the pretended power of suspending the laws or the execution of laws by regal authority without consent of Parliament is illegal.' The correctness of the judgments in cases such as *Ship Money* and the *Case of Impositions* was also forcefully repudiated by the Bill of Rights; Art 4 provided that: 'levying money for or to the use of the Crown by pretence of prerogative, without grant of Parliament, for longer time, or in other manner than the same is or shall be granted, is illegal.' Two further points of great significance appeared to emerge from the political deal that was struck.

Firstly, the *scope of prerogative powers was fixed* – it was not open to the King to claim new ones. What William and Mary received in 1688 was the *residue* of the previous King's powers. That residue has been shrinking ever since. As Diplock LJ observed in the 1965 case of *BBC v Johns*:

> '[it was] 350 years and a civil war too late for the Queen's courts to broaden the prerogative. The limits within which the executive government may impose obligations or restraints on citizens of the UK without any statutory authority are now well settled and incapable of extension'.[18]

One must however note that while it is generally accepted that the 1688 settlement had imbued the prerogative with a residual character, the exact extent of that residue was far from clear. As we saw in *Burmah Oil*,[19] the courts have on occasion been called upon to decide the precise limits of prerogative powers, which, even 300 years after the revolution, remain poorly defined. *Burmah Oil* provides another example of the loose fit between the form and the reality of constitutional principles; while the Crown cannot *de jure* create new prerogative powers or duties, the courts could achieve that result by holding that the Crown had rediscovered a 'forgotten' part of the 1688 residue.

The second point, and the reason why the residue has been getting smaller, is that the 1688 settlement acknowledged that it was within the power of Parliament to amend or abolish prerogative powers through legislation. The prerogative was recognised as being a common law power, subordinate to statute. Thus, as in the *Burmah Oil* saga, Parliament may always respond to inconvenient judicial decisions concerning the scope of an existing prerogative power by introducing legislation to alter or reverse the courts' decisions.

Similarly, Parliament may at any time create a statutory framework which limits the ways prerogative powers may be used. This principle is perhaps best illustrated in the immediate post revolutionary era by legislative regulation of the Monarch's power to summon and dissolve Parliament. We may recall that Article 13 of the Bill of Rights had provided that 'Parlyaments ought to be held frequently'. Parliament defined that timescale more precisely in the Triennal Act 1694. This statute required the King to summon a new Parliament within three years of the dissolution of the previous Parliament, and also obliged him not to permit Parliament to sit for more than three years before the next dissolution. Within these statutory time limits, the Monarch enjoyed unfettered legal power to summon or dismiss the Commons and the Lords; but he/she had no legal power to exceed those periods. Parliament could extend or shorten the time scale if it wished, and indeed in the Septennial Act of 1715 it chose to increase its maximum duration to seven years.

While the Bill of Rights clearly and powerfully addressed the issue of the prerogative's status vis a vis Acts of Parliament, it was much less explicit about the question of how the Monarch's common law powers should be approached by the courts. Both *Bate's Case*, and *Darnel's Case* can be read as judgments in which the courts held

[18] [1965] Ch 32, [1964] 1 All ER 923, CA. [19] Pp 87–88 above.

that the judiciary was not competent to question the way in which a power that the king was accepted to possess could be used. A common law principle which effectively excused some of the Monarch's personal powers from judicial regulation presented an obvious threat to the sovereignty of Parliament. Moreover, the principle would not seem compatible with the various theories of the rule of law which subsequently emerged within the British constitutional tradition; and nor, one assumes, could they have survived unscathed the aftermath of the English revolution.

Since 1688, the personal political powers of the Monarch have declined significantly in practical terms. As we shall see in later chapters, the Queen is now largely just a figurehead, performing ceremonial and symbolic functions within the contemporary constitution. But this does not mean that the prerogative powers have disappeared. For most practical purposes, prerogative powers are exercised on the Monarch's behalf by the government. But before considering a brief list of the residue of prerogative powers which the government can use in the modern era, we ought to make some reference to a *definitional problem.* What was originally meant by the notion of the *personal powers* of the sovereign?

What is the prerogative? A definitional controversy

There are two schools of thought on this point.[20] The first, 'narrow' or 'restrictive' interpretation was advanced by Blackstone. For Blackstone, prerogative powers were only those 'singular and eccentrical' to the King himself – that is things which only the King could do. So for example the power to enter into contracts, to lend money, to employ people, should not be considered as part of the prerogative because any other citizen was legally competent to do those things. Only powers such as declaring war, or granting peerages were exclusive to the King, and so correctly labelled as prerogative powers.

The second, wide definition comes from Dicey. In Dicey's view everything that government can lawfully do that does not have its roots in a statute, but which could be enforced in the courts was a prerogative power. Dicey's usage is generally accepted today – although there are still some influential commentators who favour the Blackstone version.[21] But assuming we take the wider view as the more authoritative version, which prerogative powers does the government still possess?

The most important one is probably the conduct of foreign affairs and the signing of treaties. In the domestic sphere such actions as the summoning and dissolution of Parliament, the appointment of Ministers, the granting of peerages, appointing judges, giving pardons to convicted criminals or stopping criminal proceedings, and the terms and conditions on which civil servants were employed were all components of this residual source of legal authority. This is not an exhaustive list, but it is sufficient to convey the point that the prerogative remains a substantively important source of governmental authority.

20 See generally Markesenis B (1973) 'The royal prerogative revisited' *Cambridge LJ* 287–309.
21 See particularly Wade HRW (1985) 'The civil service and the prerogative' 101 *LQR* 190–199.

Most of these powers can be exercised in two ways, either directly or indirectly. Direct exercise of the prerogative need not take any documentary form. Foreign policy for example is usually carried on in this way. The prerogative is exercised indirectly through a device known as the Order in Council, which is in some respects analogous to a statute, in that it often grants Ministers the legal authority to exercise a range of discretionary powers. Changes to the terms of employment of civil servants are usually made through this indirect procedure.

Irrespective of the way they are used, the continued existence of prerogative powers raises two substantial constitutional issues – one of which is legal, the other political. The legal issue is essentially the question of the relationship between the government and the judiciary; which prerogative powers will the courts subject to judicial review, and in what circumstances and according to which criteria will the courts intervene to regulate government activity? The political issue centres on the relationship between the government and the houses of Parliament. Is it desirable that important political decisions such as going to war, signing treaties, or granting pardons should be taken without the explicit prior approval of a majority of MPs? We will return to the political issue at a later stage of the book. This chapter considers the fate of the prerogative in the courts during the twentieth century.

I. THE RELATIONSHIP BETWEEN STATUTE, THE PREROGATIVE AND THE RULE OF LAW

In the early twentieth century, after some initial hesitancy in the lower courts, the House of Lords produced two forceful opinions curbing the way that prerogative powers could be exercised. One of the most sweeping prerogative powers exercised by Monarchs was to seize property for military reasons in times of war, if the seizure was necessary to safeguard national security.[22] The power was invoked frequently during World War I. The government evidently believed its actions to be legal, but not all of the 'victims' of this power shared that view, and some seizures were challenged in the courts. The most controversial point was whether any such requisition of private property obliged the government to pay compensation to the owners.[23]

The first significant judgment addressing the issue was *Re Petition of Right*.[24] The case concerned the army's seizure of a commercial airfield for military purposes. The owners contended that the prerogative power to requisition the property without compensation arose only in emergency situations such as an actual invasion in which foreign troops landed on British soil, and not for the more long term purpose of

22 *R v Hampden* (1637) 3 State Tr 826. This was of course the power at issue in *Burmah Oil*; see pp 87–88 above.

23 The government's practice was to offer compensation *ex gratia*, ie not as a matter of right.

24 [1915] 3 KB 649, CA.

establishing an airbase. The High Court and Court of Appeal accepted that the power existed only in 'invasion' situations. The owners' claim nonetheless failed, as all of the judges considered that the notion of 'invasion' was to be interpreted in the light of modern military technology. A German plane or airship flying into British airspace was as much an invasion in 1915 as the disembarkation of belligerent troops at Dover would have been in 1637. This interpretive principle is of some importance, for it means that the practical reach of the supposedly residual prerogative could legitimately be extended – as a result of changing social, political or technological development – into areas it had not hitherto affected.

The Petition of Right judgment was also significant in another respect. If we recall *Ship Money*, we will remember that the question of deciding what was 'necessary' to protect national security was held be the sole preserve of the Monarch; it was an issue which the court considered itself unable to address. In *Petition of Right*, the courts seemed to require that the government demonstrate that an 'invasion' situation actually existed and that the requisition of the property concerned was necessary to counter the threat. However this did not appear to be a taxing obligation; the judges expressed no willingness to allow any challenge to a senior military officer's assertion that the seizure of the airport was necessary.

This approach was subtly modified by the Privy Council in *The Zamora*.[25] *The Zamora* was a ship from a neutral country carrying a cargo of copper. The government seized the ship and its cargo when it docked at a British port. The court accepted that judges were neither sufficiently expert, nor constitutionally entitled to argue the case with the government as to the adequacy of the national security justification for using this prerogative power. National security was still regarded as matters in respect of which the court could not evaluate the legal adequacy of the government's decision. However, in this case the government had not produced any evidence at all that the copper was needed for national security reasons. The court accepted that the prerogative power to seize the ship was available in certain circumstances. But the House of Lords also held that the government had not shown that the factual prerequisite for using the power had arisen. And unless those facts were shown to exist, the power could not be invoked. Thus the seizure was unlawful.[26]

The Zamora displays a shift from the position which the courts adopted in *Ship Money*. The decision seems to make essentially the same point as Lord Atkin's subsequent dissent in *Liversidge*; namely in the absence of a clear legislative provision to the contrary, the executive must convince the court that the facts which trigger the use of a legal power do indeed exist. What is less clear is how much evidence would be required to confirm that national security issues were involved. That is a point to which we will devote further attention later in the chapter.

25 [1916] 2 AC 77, PC.

26 See Holdsworth W (1919) 'The power of the Crown to requisition British ships in a national emergency' *LQR* 12–42.

A-G V DE KEYSER'S ROYAL HOTEL LTD (1920)

The judgments offered by the House of Lords in *A-G v De Keyser's Royal Hotel Ltd*[27] make this among the most instructive of all constitutional law cases. In addition to dealing authoritatively with the nature of the relationship between statute and prerogative powers, the court's use of principles of statutory interpretation tells us a great deal about the interaction between the doctrines of parliamentary sovereignty and the rule of law.

The 'property' at stake in *De Keyser* was the occupancy of a hotel, which the government wished to use to accommodate the administrative headquarters of the Royal Flying Corps. The owners of the hotel did not dispute that the government had the legal power to requisition it. Two substantial questions were however in issue. Firstly, did that power derive from statute or the prerogative? And secondly – whatever its source – was the power one which required the government to pay compensation to the owners of affected property?[28] The House of Lords[29] dealt with these questions in an holistic way, but for our purposes the decision may best be divided somewhat artificially into three parts; dealing respectively with the existence (or non-existence) of specific prerogative powers, the precise meaning of relevant statutory provisions, and the general issue of the relationship between statute and the prerogative.

On the first issue, two subsidiary questions arose: did the prerogative power identified in *Re Petition of Right* extend to these particular circumstances; and if it did not, did the Crown possess an alternative prerogative power to take property without compensation in war-time which did arise on these facts?

The court did not accept that this case fell within the *Re Petition of Right* principle. The property was not being commandeered to form an immediate defence against invasion (even in the modern sense of that term). Lord Sumner also made it quite clear – in an obvious departure from the *Ship Money* principle – that the court was competent to inquire if the factual circumstances amounting to an emergency actually existed; it would not simply defer to the government's view on that question.[30]

27 [1920] AC 508, [1920] All ER Rep 80, HL. The Attorney-General is the senior of the government's two 'law officers'; (the Solicitor-General is the junior officer). He/she is generally an MP sitting in the Commons, and will on occasion argue cases on the government's behalf in the courts. He/she is not usually a member of the cabinet.

28 These grand constitutional questions arose from the more prosaic matter of an argument about money. The government had initially claimed to take the hotel under statutory powers, and had begun to negotiate a compensation fee with De Keyser. After protracted discussions, the government made a final offer of £17,000 while De Keyser insisted on £19,500. In a mood of evident irritation, the government broke off negotiations and subsequently claimed it could take the hotel under prerogative powers and not pay any compensation.

29 All five judges who heard the case – Lords Dunedin, Parmoor, Sumner, Moulton and Atkinson – delivered opinions.

30 '[This] seems to me to be an . . . obvious proposition – namely that when the court can see from the character and circumstances of the requisition itself that the case cannot be one of imminent danger, it is free to inquire whether the conditions, resting on necessity, which were held to exist in [*Re Petition of Right*] are applicable to the case in hand' [1920] All ER Rep 80 at 105, HL. As in *The Zamora* however, no indication was given as to how rigorous the court would be in conducting such inquiries. A principle permitting judicial inquiry would be of no practical significance if the inquiry was satisfied by the mere statement of a Minister or government official that a situation of 'imminent danger' existed.

Nor was any member of the court convinced that the Crown had ever possessed a prerogative power to take property without paying compensation in non-emergency war-time situations. The power to take property in such circumstances was undoubtedly part of the residue of prerogative powers left to the Crown after the revolution; what was not so readily evident was whether the power could be exercised without granting the owner compensation. The court explored this issue through historical rather than legal analysis, as it could find no case law which offered clear guidance. The court's inquiries into the practical conduct of such requisitions indicated that they had all been accompanied by the payment of compensation. As Lord Atkinson put it:

'The conclusion, as I understand it, is that it does not appear that the Crown has ever taken for these purposes the land of the subject, without paying for it, and that there is no trace of the Crown having, even in the time of the Stuarts, exercised or asserted the power or right to do so'.[31]

In effect, the Attorney-General was arguing that the court should grant the government a new prerogative power. This was a request to which the court was not constitutionally competent to accede. This conclusion necessarily meant that if the government was empowered to requisition the hotel without paying compensation, that power had to derive from statute.

The court also engaged in something of a history lesson in deciding just what statutory powers the government possessed. Its conclusion on this point is not directly pertinent to the question of prerogative powers. Nonetheless, it merits some attention here because it enables us to add a further (at this stage thin) veneer of sophistication to our understanding of the way in which the courts' use of techniques of statutory interpretation can reconcile ostensible tensions between the principles of parliamentary sovereignty and the rule of law.

Their Lordships' judgments suggested that Parliament had begun to legislate on this matter in the eighteenth century primarily because the limited prerogative powers of emergency requisition were becoming increasingly inadequate to deal with the growing complexities of modern warfare. At the outbreak of World War One, the main legislation in this field had been the Defence Act 1842. The Act gave the government very substantial powers of requisition. At the same time, it attached quite rigorous procedural conditions to the exercise of those powers, and also provided that the owners of requisitioned property should be compensated, the amount to be decided by a jury in the relevant area.

The court's presumption was that the legislation was enacted to achieve three objectives which – to borrow Harlow and Rawlings' terminology – reveal a mix of green and red light concerns. The extended powers of requisition were intended to enhance the country's capacity to conduct war successfully; the procedural conditions were intended to reduce the likelihood that the power could be used arbitrarily or

31 [1920] All ER Rep 80 at 92, HL.

unjustly; and the compensation provisions were intended to place the cost of conducting a war on (via the government) the whole population rather than on the few people whose property was taken.

The 1842 Act was not repealed in 1914. Its effect was however likely to be extended by the powers contained in the Defence of the Realm (Consolidation) Act 1914. Section 1 of that Act provided that: 'His Majesty in Council has power to issue regulations for securing the public safety and the defence of the realm . . .'. Section 1(2) detailed a more specific example of that general power: 'Any such regulations may provide for the suspension of any restrictions on the acquisition or user of land . . . or any other power under the Defence Acts 1842–1875 . . .'. A regulation was subsequently passed in November 1914 which empowered an authorised military officer to take possession of any land or building when it was necessary to do so 'for the purpose of securing the public safety or the defence of the realm'.

The government's contention in *De Keyser* was that the duty to pay compensation laid down in the 1842 Act was a 'restriction' on the government's ability to acquire land for defence purposes, and as such could be suspended by regulation. The regulation passed in November was claimed to have this effect. De Keyser's response to this argument was that the notion of 'restrictions' reached only to the procedural conditions contained in the 1842 Act, and not to the separate issue of compensation.

The way in which the judges addressed this issue illustrates forcefully how blurred the edges might be between the literal and teleological approaches to statutory interpretation.[32] It is not fanciful to argue that having to pay for something is likely to operate as a 'restriction' on one's readiness to take it, in the sense that the cost may act as a disincentive to its acquisition. However the House of Lords rejected that interpretation of the term. Lord Moulton's reasoning on the point was cursory, implying that the literal meaning of 'restriction' simply could not bear that construction:

'The duty of paying compensation cannot be regarded as a restriction. It is a consequence of the taking, but in no way restricts it, and therefore . . . [De Keyser] are entitled to the compensation provided by that [1842] Act'.[33]

This is an assertion rather than an explanation.[34] The explanation for the conclusion is best provided in Lord Atkinson's judgment. One way of characterising his reasoning would be that the literal meaning of 'restriction' was conditioned by a contextual (or background) principle derived from a rigorous understanding of the rule of law intended to protect the property of private citizens:

'The recognised rule for the construction of statute is that, unless the words of the statute

[32] As we saw in chapter three, the literal rule was the dominant technique at that time. Teleological interpretation was not (formally) recognised as a legitimate judicial strategy. See the discussion of *Magor and St Mellons RDC* at pp 75–76 above.

[33] [1920] All ER Rep 80 at 98, HL.

[34] See also Lord Sumner: 'The obligation to pay compensation to a dispossessed owner . . . is not a restriction on the acquisition of his land. It might discourage the power of acquisition, but it does not limit that power' ibid, at 102.

clearly so demand, the statute is not to be construed so as to take away the property of a subject without compensation'.[35]

One might alternatively characterise his reasoning (and here one slips into the then heresy of teleological interpretation) as 'making sense'[36] of the 1914 Act and subsequent regulation by regarding them as devices to sweep away procedural impediments to the effective conduct of the war without compromising the substantive principle that its cost should be borne by the country as a whole.

The judgment also addressed several issues whose significance extends beyond the details of the case itself. Lord Atkinson firmly rejected the Attorney-General's contention that a prerogative power and a statutory power dealing with the same issue could exist side-by-side – that they were as the Attorney-General put it 'merged' – and that the government could choose to deploy whichever of the two powers best suited its purpose. Lord Atkinson considered the notion of 'merger' to be inapposite. Rather the enactment of a statute:

'abridges the royal prerogative while it is in force to this extent – that the Crown can only do the particular thing under and in accordance with the statutory provisions, and that its prerogative power to do that thing is in abeyance'.[37]

The notion that the passage of a statute sends the affected prerogative power into some form of constitutional suspended animation was not shared by all members of the court. Lord Dunedin in particular implied that he thought the prerogative power remained in place, but the place it now occupied was distinctly inferior to that inhabited by the new statutory provisions. This distinction is of little functional significance. The essential point common to both views concerns the hierarchical relationship between statute and the prerogative. On this question, Lord Dunedein and Lord Atkinson were at one. While Lord Dunedin indicated that the prerogative retained some degree of constitutional sentience: 'it is equally certain that if the whole ground of something which could be done by the prerogative is covered by the statute, it is the statute that rules'.[38]

35 Ibid, at 94. The court's methodology is much like that subsequently deployed by the Court of Appeal in *Gilmore* and the House of Lords in *Anisminic* (see pp 84–87 above), where the contextual principle concerned the jurisdictional question of access to the courts rather than the substantive issue of receiving compensation for property.

36 The term is borrowed from Denning LJ's opinion in *Magor and St Mellons RDC*; see p 75 above.

37 [1920] All ER Rep 80 at 92, per Lord Atkinson.

38 Ibid, at 86. Both standpoints would accept that Parliament is competent expressly to provide in legislation that prerogative powers covering a matter now affected by statutory rules continue to exist side-by-side with the Act concerned. For a more modern example of this principle in practice see the Immigration Act 1971. There is nothing in the judgments to suggest that Parliament can only override the prerogative by express suspension of the relevant prerogative powers. Any such rule would contradict the implied repeal facet of the parliamentary sovereignty doctrine. If statute is a superior form of law to the prerogative, and if existing statutes must give way if they are inconsistent with later legislation, it would be a nonsense if an existing prerogative power was considered more authoritative than an inconsistent statute. Yet there is some illogicality about the 'abeyance argument'. It would not be maintained for example that an Act of 1920 which amended a statute passed in 1910 'suspended' the earlier legislation, in the sense that the 1910 provisions

FITZGERALD V MULDOON[39]

The evidently clear conclusion in *De Keyser* that prerogative powers were constitutionally inferior to statute had not however fully impressed itself upon the legal sensibilities of all politicians in the modern era. In the mid-1970s, the constitution of New Zealand (a former British colony) was in most respects identical to that of Britain itself.[40] In particular, British law on prerogative powers was assumed as applicable in New Zealand as in Britain.

In the 1975 general election campaign, the then opposition party had announced that if it won the election it would promote a bill to repeal a statute called the New Zealand Superannuation Act 1974, which imposed a compulsory scheme of national insurance on employers and employees. The opposition won the election, and its leader, Muldoon, became Prime Minister. He immediately announced at a press conference that the government would soon introduce 'legislation'[41] repealing the 1974 Act, that in the interim the 1974 Act would not be enforced, and that the new statute would include retrospective provisions absolving anybody who failed to comply with the 1974 Act from various criminal sanctions that the 1974 Act imposed.

Fitzgerald claimed that this amounted to an unlawful 'suspension' of the law within the meaning of Article 1 of the Bill of Rights 1688. In effect, Muldoon was attempting to do what James II had done in *Godden v Hales* – to release the government from a statutory obligation which it found politically distasteful.[42] The New Zealand Supreme Court[43] agreed with this contention. The Prime Minister's action was clearly unconstitutional:

'[He] was purporting to suspend the law without the consent of Parliament. Parliament had made the law. Therefore the law could be suspended or amended only by Parliament or with the authority of Parliament'.[44]

would regain their legal effect if the 1920 Act were itself repealed. Nor would it be argued that the 1910 Act retained a legal status, albeit one inferior to the 1920 Act. The presumption would be that the 1910 statute no longer existed at all. It would thus seem peculiar that the prerogative, which is a common law power and thus inferior to statute, should enjoy a greater legal longevity than a statutory provision covering the same point. The illogicality can perhaps be reasoned away by suggesting that the courts could legitimately conclude that it would always be Parliament's intention to reinstate the prerogative whenever it repealed an Act which had itself put a prerogative power into abeyance. Such reasoning is however difficult to reconcile with orthodox understandings of the court's interpretive role.

39 [1976] 2 NZLR 615. 40 Its legislature had only one (elected) chamber.

41 It should be stressed that a government does not and cannot introduce 'legislation'. Nor does either the House of Commons or the House of Lords consider or pass 'legislation'. The government introduces a bill, which is then considered by each house. 'Legislation' comes into being only when a bill has been passed by both houses and received the royal assent.

42 The analogy cannot be pushed too far. Unlike Muldoon, James II could have had no realistic expectation that the legislature would soon pass an Act to achieve a similar effect.

43 Rather confusingly, the New Zealand Supreme Court is the equivalent of the English High Court. The highest domestic court in New Zealand is the Court of Appeal, from which a further appeal lies the to House of Lords (acting under the soubriquet of the Privy Council).

44 [1976] 2 NZLR 615 at 622.

LAKER AIRWAYS LTD V DEPARTMENT OF TRADE (1977)[45]

The judgment of the English Court of Appeal in *Laker Airways* further emphasised the prerogative's inferior constitutional status relative to statutes by a logical extension of the *De Keyser* principle. Following the passage of the Civil Aviation Act 1971, airlines which wished to operate a service between Britain and the USA required two forms of authorisation. Firstly, the airline had to be granted a licence by the Civil Aviation Authority (CAA). The CAA exercised powers granted under the 1971 Act, and awarded licences according to criteria laid down in s 3(1), which required the CAA to promote low fares, high safety standards, and competition on major routes. Under s 3(2) the Department of Trade (DoT) could give the CAA 'guidance' concerning the way it exercised its licensing function. Under s 4(3), the DoT could give the CAA 'directions' concerning matters which affected national security or diplomatic relations with other countries. Secondly, the airline had to be granted landing rights in the USA. These were not statutory rights, but derived from a Treaty called the Bermuda Agreement which the government, using its prerogative powers, had negotiated with the USA.

In 1972 Laker Airways applied for a licence to operate a very cheap London to New York service. At the time, the only British companies flying on these routes were British Airways and British Caledonian. The CAA granted Laker a licence under s 3(1), and the DoT used its prerogative power to make arrangements under the Bermuda Treaty for Laker to be given landing rights in New York. After the 1974 general election, the new Labour government decided that it wanted to protect British Airways and British Caledonian from Laker's competition, and so sought to withdraw Laker's permission to fly. The government could not use s 4(3) to give 'directions' to the CAA to revoke Laker's licence, since no questions of national security or diplomatic relations arose. Consequently, the DoT attempted to use its prerogative powers to cancel Laker's landing rights under the Bermuda Treaty, and issued the CAA with 'guidance' under s 3(2) instructing it to withdraw Laker's licence. Laker claimed that both actions were ultra vires.

The Court of Appeal supported Laker's contention; neither statute nor prerogative provided a lawful basis for the government's action. Lord Denning first considered the meaning of 'guidance' in s 3(2). He felt that Parliament's intention in using this term had been to 'explain', 'amplify' or 'supplement' the policy of the Act, but not to 'reverse' or 'contradict' that policy. However, Lord Denning concluded that the effect of the government's new policy would be to reduce competition and so raise prices on the London-New York route. This was entirely inconsistent with the objectives Parliament had enacted in s 3(1), namely to encourage competition and reduce prices. The policy could not therefore be 'guidance', and so lacked a statutory foundation.

Lord Denning also rejected the argument that the government's prerogative power to negotiate treaties with other states provided a lawful justification for withdrawing

45 [1977] 2 All ER 182, CA.

Laker's landing rights. He did so on the grounds that the government was trying to use its prerogative powers to contradict a statutory objective. In contrast to *De Keyser, Laker* presented a situation in which statutory and prerogative powers were not overlapping, but interlocking. The statute therefore was not intended to replace the prerogative, but to be used in conjunction with it. Nevertheless, in such circumstances, statute's superior constitutional status demanded that the prerogative be exercised only in ways that furthered, rather than obstructed Parliament's intentions. If the government wished to pursue a policy which contradicted the objectives of the 1970 Act, it would have to persuade Parliament to enact new legislation which repealed or amended the limits placed on the DoT's powers by Parliament in 1970.[46]

R V SECRETARY OF STATE FOR THE HOME DEPARTMENT, EX P FIRE BRIGADES UNION (1995)[47]

This principle was followed – and extended – in 1995, in a judgment concerning the administration of the Criminal Injuries Compensation scheme. The Criminal Injuries Compensation Board (CICB) was established in 1964 to provide compensation to the victims of violent crime or to their dependents. It was not set up under statute, but under the prerogative. The then Labour government also publicised criteria which the Board would use to assess compensation; criteria which were broadly based on the amount of compensation that a person could expect to receive if she had suffered a similar injury as a result of tortious action. Some twenty-four years later, Parliament enacted the Criminal Justice Act 1988. Sections 108–117 of the Act in essence gave a statutory basis to the existing common law scheme. However, the sections were not brought into force immediately. Rather, under s 171(1) of the Act, the Home Secretary was empowered to place the original entitlement criteria on a statutory basis 'on such day as he may appoint'. The government chose not to exercise this power immediately. In 1993, the government concluded that the existing scheme was proving too expensive. Consequently, rather than exercise his s 171 power, the then (Conservative) Home Secretary Michael Howard concluded that he would use his prerogative powers to amend the original scheme and introduce a cheaper system. In a manner rather reminiscent of Prime Minister Muldoon's behaviour in New Zealand twenty years earlier, the government announced in a policy paper that: '[T]he provisions in the Act of 1988 will not now be implemented. They will accordingly be repealed when a suitable legislative opportunity occurs'.[48] The government took the view that it was able to amend the existing scheme without infringing the 1988 Act, as ss 108–117 had no legal force until such time as the Home Secretary decided to exercise his power under s 171 to implement them.

46 See Wade HRW (1977) 'Judicial control of the prerogative' 93 *LQR* 325–327.

47 [1995] 2 AC 513, CA; affd [1995] 2 AC 513 at 544, HL.

48 Home Office (1993) *Compensation for Victims of Violent Crime: Changes to the Criminal Injuries Compensation Scheme* (London: HMSO; Cm 2434). Like Mr Muldoon, Mr Howard had evidently forgotten that it was for the legislature rather than the executive to enact statutes.

The Fire Brigades Union challenged the decision on various grounds, one of which maintained that the Home Secretary was attempting to disregard a statutory limit on his prerogative powers. Their argument was rejected in the High Court,[49] but accepted in the Court of Appeal. The Court of Appeal reasoned that s 171 did not place the Home Secretary under a duty to place the scheme on a statutory basis by any particular date. However, it did have the effect of channelling or curbing the Home Secretary's prerogative powers in respect of the scheme, in the sense that they could no longer be used in a way that contradicted Parliament's intentions. By enacting s 171, Parliament had in effect given a statutory seal of approval to the way in which the prerogative had been exercised when the CICB was established in 1964. For the Home Secretary to alter the scheme would therefore be inconsistent with Parliament's wishes. If the government wished to introduce a different set of entitlement criteria, it would first have to ask Parliament to repeal ss 108–117.

The Court of Appeal's decision was subsequently upheld in the House of Lords, albeit only by a three to two majority.[50] Lords Mustill and Keith suggested that ss 108–117 had as yet no legal force, and thus could not be seen as a statutory curb on the Home Secretary's prerogative powers. The majority[51] disagreed. The rationale underpinning the majority's conclusion is perhaps best put by Lord Lloyd. Lord Lloyd considered that it was mistaken to assume that ss 108–117 had no legal existence at all until such time as the s 171 power was deployed:

'True, they do not have statutory force. But that does not mean that they are writ in water. They contain a statement of Parliamentary intention, even though they create no enforceable rights. . . . The Home Secretary has power to delay the coming into force of the statutory provisions, but he has no power to reject them or set them aside, as if they had never been passed'.[52]

Shortly thereafter, the government announced that it would introduce a bill to modify the existing scheme. The bill was promptly enacted.[53]

II. THE TRADITIONAL PERSPECTIVE ON JUDICIAL REVIEW OF PREROGATIVE POWERS: AND ITS EROSION

As we saw in chapter three, orthodox constitutional theory assumes that Parliament 'contracts in' to administrative law when creating government powers through statute. If Parliament does not wish the implied terms of administrative law to apply to

[49] [1994] PIQR P320. [50] [1995] 2 AC 513 at 544.

[51] Lords Browne-Wilkinson, Lloyd and Nicholls.

[52] Ibid, at 570–571. For further comment on the judgment see Barendt E (1995) 'Constitutional law and the criminal injuries compensation scheme' *Public Law* 357–366.

[53] The bill was castigated as mean-spirited by both *The Times* and *The Guardian* newspapers; see *The Times* 20 June 1995 *The Guardian* 11 November 1995.

particular statutory activities, it must make that intention clear in the legislation. In the absence of such express 'contracting out', a government body's exercise of statutory power will (according to the *Wednesbury* principles) be ultra vires if no such power has been granted, if the power has been exercised 'unreasonably', or if decisions have been made through 'unfair procedures'. Such decisions were subject to what we might term 'full review'.

However, in relation to judicial review of government action taken under the prerogative, the courts traditionally applied only the first of the three *Wednesbury* principles. The judges were, as in *De Keyser* or *BBC v John*, willing to say whether or not a claimed prerogative power actually existed. This is clearly consistent with the notion that the prerogative was a collection of residual powers – the courts would not permit the government to claim new ones. Relatedly, as Lord Atkinson had stressed in *DeKeyser*, a court would accept jurisdiction to examine if the requisite factual triggers for an exercise of the power were present in the case before it.

The deployment of prerogative powers was in contrast widely regarded to be subject only to what we might term 'limited review'. Prior to the 1980s, the orthodox view among constitutional lawyers was that the courts were unwilling to say in what way, or for what objectives, the powers which did exist should be used. The concepts of 'unreasonableness' or 'procedural fairness' to which the use of statutory powers was subjected were seemingly not applied to government's use of the prerogative. Thus while the courts were concerned with the existence and extent of a claimed prerogative power, they were not concerned with the way in which that power was exercised.[54]

This differential treatment of prerogative and statutory powers would seem difficult to reconcile with orthodox understandings of the function performed by the principle of the rule of law within democratic constitutions – namely to minimise the possibility of government being able lawfully to exercise power in arbitrary, irrational, or procedurally unfair ways. From a functionalist perspective, such a dichotomy would be defensible only if prerogative powers were in some qualitative sense quite distinct from powers exercised under statute. In the absence of such a distinction, the common law's varying treatment of these two types of government powers could be justified only on purely formalist grounds – that prerogative powers were not fully reviewable simply because they were prerogative powers.

One can thus discern a 'rule of law' as well as a 'parliamentary sovereignty' basis for the *De Keyser* principle which forbade the co-existence of prerogative and statutory powers. To permit co-existence would allow the government to evade the judicial review principles to which it was assumed Parliament had subjected it by passing

54 There is a hint in Lord Parmoor's judgment in *De Keyser* that the exercise of prerogative and statutory powers should both be subject to full review ('this authority . . . is in itself part of the common law, not to be exercised arbitrarily, but *per legem* and *sub modo legis*' [1920] All ER Rep 80 at 105–106, HL) but his hint is not echoed in any of the other judgments. Relatedly, a close reading of *Petition of Right* reveals that Warrington LJ took the view that the power of property requisition during invasions had to be exercised 'reasonably and in good faith' [1915] 3 KB 649 at 667, CA.

legislation in an area where executive powers previously derived solely from the prerogative.

The principle that prerogative powers be subject to only limited review is given ringing endorsement in Blackstone's *Commentaries*:

'In the exertion therefore of those prerogatives, which the law has given him, the King is irresistible and absolute, according to the forms of the constitution. And yet if the consequence of that exertion be manifestly to the grievance or dishonour of the kingdom, the Parliament will call his advisers to a just and severe account'.[55]

This would however seem to have been an orthodoxy which rested on somewhat shaky foundations: judicial authority for the rule is rather less forthright. This is perhaps unsurprising, given that the rule seems to provide the government with a sweeping exemption from having to comply with an expansive understanding of the rule of law. In an influential article,[56] Markesenis pointed to two oft-cited authorities for the proposition; *R v Allen*[57] and *China Navigation Co Ltd v A-G.*[58] Both cases sustain the conclusion that the particular prerogative powers with which they were concerned should be subject only to limited review. Yet neither provides obvious support for the rule that all prerogative powers should be subjected to this very diluted conception of the rule of law.

R v Allen concerned the *nolle prosequi* power retained by the Attorney-General, a device which enables her to bring an end to any ongoing criminal trial. Allan had been charged with perjury. His trial was however halted when the Attorney-General issued a *nolle prosequi*. This intervention was challenged by the prosecuting authorities, on the ground that the *nolle prosequi* had been issued in a procedurally incorrect way, in so far as the Attorney-General had in this instance failed to conform to his usual practice of allowing the prosecution to give its views on the desirability of continuing the case before reaching his decision. The prosecuting authorities thus contended that the *nolle prosequi* should be quashed. The court clearly viewed the Attorney-General's failure to consult the prosecution lawyers with disfavour,[59] but nonetheless saw no grounds for reviewing his decision:

'Suppose it is possible that there could be an abuse of his power by the Attorney-General or injustice in the exercise of it, the remedy is by holding him responsible for his acts before the great tribunal of this country, the High Court of Parliament'.[60]

It is not possible to extract from the (extremely short) judgments any clear reason as to why the *nolle prosequi* should be treated in this way. Cockburn CJ alluded to the 'great inconvenience' that would result if the power were to be subject to full review,

[55] Volume 1 p 251. A less sweeping statement is offered in Chitty's 1820 volume on *Prerogatives of the Crown* p 6: 'in the exercise of his lawful prerogatives, an unbounded discretion is, generally speaking, left to the King'. Chitty seems to imply that there are some prerogatives powers that may be subject to full review.

[56] (1973) op cit. [57] (1862) 12 ER 929, 26 JP 341, 5 LT 636. [58] [1932] 2 KB 197, CA.

[59] '[The Attorney-General] would act wisely in calling the prosecutor before him. . . . I think that is a wholesome practice' (1862) 12 ER 929 at 931; per Cockburn CJ.

[60] Ibid.

but did not explain how this 'inconvenience' would arise. It is however clear that the various opinions in the case were all limited to the specific power of *nolle prosequi*: none of the judges made any reference to the prerogative in general.

The Court of Appeal's 1932 judgment in *China Navigation* was similarly specific in its scope. The prerogative power in issue was the government's control of the armed forces. The Court of Appeal noted that in some specific respects, this prerogative power had been restricted by statute. Those powers that remained, however, were: 'left to the uncontrolled discretion which [the King] exercises through his Ministers. The Courts cannot question it . . .'.[61] As in *R v Allen*, there is no indication that the Court regarded this conclusion as applicable to all prerogative powers.

DEVELOPMENTS IN THE 1960S AND 1970S

From the late 1960s onwards, the courts' attachment to the orthodox proposition that prerogative powers were subjected only to limited review began to change. Four cases from this period merit close attention. The first is the 1967 High Court decision in *R v Criminal Injuries Compensation Board, ex p Lain*.[62]

Mrs Lain was the widow of a policeman. She was seeking to argue that the amount of compensation she had been offered in respect of her husband's injuries and subsequent death had not been properly assessed in accordance with the published criteria. In other words, she was questioning the way in which the Board had exercised its powers. The Board contended that the court had no power to review the exercise of the prerogative.

However, the court held that this particular prerogative power should be reviewed as if it derived from a statute. The main reason for this appeared to be that the Board was performing an essentially 'judicial' task. It had the straightforward duty of awarding compensation on the basis of the published rules. Unlike the complex national security question raised in cases like *Ship Money*, this was an issue which the courts were well equipped to decide.

Lain apparently made a distinct break with traditional theory, although it received little attention in the academic press. At this time, the judgment lent itself to one of three interpretations. Firstly, that it was an aberrant decision, which if not overruled would be confined solely to the CICB and not extended to other prerogative actions. Secondly, that it laid the ground for future judgments to conclude that all prerogative powers should be fully reviewable. Or thirdly, that it intimated that full review should apply only to prerogative powers which raised issues that the court regarded as intrinsically well-suited to be subject to judicial scrutiny.

The *Hanratty* case in 1971 suggested that the third interpretation might be finding favour with the Court of Appeal. *Hanratty v Lord Butler of Saffron-Walden*[63] was a

[61] [1932] 2 KB 197 at 217, CA, per Scrutton LJ. See also Lawrence LJ at 229: 'The manner in which the Crown exercises its powers is not a matter which can be inquired into by a Court of law'.

[62] [1967] 2 QB 864.

[63] (1971) 115 Sol Jo 386, CA.

negligence action brought against a former Home Secretary by the relatives of a man executed in 1962 after having been convicted of murder. The plaintiffs claimed that Butler had negligently failed to take proper account of new evidence when advising the Queen whether or not to grant mercy to Hanratty and commute his sentence to life imprisonment.

The plaintiff's claim had been rejected in the High Court, a judgment which was upheld on appeal. Lord Denning MR (supported by Salmon and Stamp LJJ) rejected the assertion that the courts were competent to assess the way in which this particular prerogative power had been exercised:

> 'The high prerogative of mercy was exercised by the Monarch on the advice of one of her principal secretaries of state who took full responsibility and advised her with the greatest conscience and care. The law would not inquire into the manner in which that prerogative was exercised'.[64]

One might wonder how Lord Denning MR was able to conclude that Butler had acted 'with the greatest conscience and care' if the court 'would not inquire into the manner in which that prerogative was exercised'. However, for present purposes, the significance of the judgment lies in the way Denning confined the principle of limited review to this particular power. He gave no indication that this was a principle of general applicability.

Several years later, in *Laker Airways*, Denning lent further weight to the argument that prerogative powers per se should not be subject only to limited review. In that case, Denning again restricted his judgment to a particular prerogative power – designation of an airline under the Bermuda agreement – but this time concluded that the power should be subject to full review:

> 'Seeing that the prerogative is a discretionary power to be exercised for the public good, it follows that its exercise can be examined by the courts just as any other discretionary power which is vested in the executive [ie by statute]'.[65]

The 1978 case of *Gouriet v Union of Post Office Workers*[66] suggests that the higher courts had adopted different interpretations of the *Lain* decision. One prerogative power exercised on behalf of the government by the Attorney-General is the *relator* proceeding. This enables the Attorney-General to initiate civil proceedings in defence of the public interest in situations where an individual is either unable or unwilling to take action.

The Post Office Union had decided to boycott mail to and from South Africa for twenty-four hours, as a gesture of disapproval of the South African government's apartheid regime. This constituted a criminal offence under the Post Office Acts. However, for political reasons, the government decided that the union would not be prosecuted. Mr Gouriet was a member of a group called the Freedom Association, which greatly disapproved both of the union's activities, and of the government's

64 Ibid. 65 [1977] 2 All ER 182 at 193, CA. 66 [1978] AC 435, HL.

failure to start a prosecution. Consequently, Mr Gouriet approached the Attorney-General, asking him to initiate a *relator* action for an injunction to stop the mail embargo going ahead. When the Attorney-General refused to proceed, Mr Gouriet asked the courts to review his decision.

Before *Gouriet* there was no case law supporting the argument that the *relator* power could be reviewed in the courts. There was however precedent for the converse proposition; namely whether or not to launch *relator* proceedings was a prerogative power solely within the control of the Attorney-General. The *Gouriet* case produced a divergence of opinion between Lord Denning in the Court of Appeal and the House of Lords. Denning thought that the time had come to question traditional perceptions of the *relator* action as being completely beyond the supervision of the courts. He was cautious in doing this however. Denning drew a distinction between a situation where the Attorney-General launched *relator* proceedings, and circumstances where he refused to do so. In the former case, use of the prerogative power was not open to question in the courts. However a refusal to begin proceedings could be challenged; Denning suggested that if the courts did not intervene in situations like this it would allow the criminal law to be infringed with impunity. In such circumstances, Denning asked himself; 'Are the courts to stand idly by?'. In his opinion, the answer was no.

There was nothing unconstitutional, in the legal sense, about Denning's analysis. Since the prerogative is a common law concept, and since the common law is dynamic and open to constant amendment by the courts, Denning's innovative judgment could be thought legally defensible. He was not overriding a statute – but simply saying that an old common law rule should be replaced by a new one. From an orthodox theoretical perspective, Denning's decision was certainly less contentious than *Anisminic* for example.

However, as far as the House of Lords was concerned, the courts should indeed stand idly by when this particular prerogative power was being employed – and when it was not being employed. The Law Lords were unanimously critical of Denning's radical judgment. In the House of Lords' opinion, whether or not to launch a *relator* action was a public interest question which only the government was competent to decide. It was another example (like the test of 'necessity' in *Ship Money* perhaps) of a legal power which could not be subjected to review on the basis of either irrationality or procedural unfairness. The judgment suggested that it would be unconstitutional, in the political if not legal sense, to overturn government policy over this issue.[67]

Denning's perception of constitutionality accorded the highest priority to seeing that the criminal law was not ignored. In contrast, the House of Lords' version was most concerned with not overruling the policy preferences of an elected government. Despite the House of Lords' strong stance, there was a suggestion that the judges' reluctance to intervene owed more to the highly contentious nature of the power concerned rather than simply its source in the prerogative. In contrast to *Lain, Gouriet* raised an issue which had immense party political implications. For the court to have

67 This was perhaps the 'great inconvenience' to which Cockburn CJ had cryptically alluded in *Allen*.

told the government that it could not act in the way it wished would have exposed the judges to accusations of subverting the democratic process.

But would the courts infringe parliamentary sovereignty by changing the common law in order to place review of the prerogative on the same basis as review of action taken under statute? Clearly, any such alteration in the common law would be unconstitutional if it contradicted the clear terms of a statute. But even in the absence of an expressly contradictory statute, the constitutionality of such a reform to the law could perhaps be questioned. One might argue that if Parliament was dissatisfied with the courts' traditional reluctance to subject prerogative powers to full review, it could do one of two things. Either it could pass a statute saying that all prerogative powers would henceforth be reviewable in the same way as statutory powers. Or, less radically, it could place specific prerogative powers on a statutory basis, and so make them amenable to full *Wednesbury* review. If the legislature took neither of these steps, it would seem plausible to assume that Parliament approved of the present situation of limited review. Consequently, if the courts changed the common law, they might in effect, if not in theory, be 'usurping the legislative function'.

Nevertheless, the suggestion was being floated in the early 1980s that the time was ripe for the courts to reject the traditional idea that all exercises of the prerogative were beyond judicial supervision. If the courts could say that executive action taken under statute was unlawful in some circumstances, surely the same argument could be applied to the less party politicised aspects of prerogative power. As suggested above, this is another illustration of a constitutional argument rooted in a functionalist rather than formalist conceptual framework. If the function of the rule of law is to protect citizens from arbitrary or unpredictable government activity, why should the source of that government power be of any relevance? Use of the prerogative could impact just as seriously on individuals as action taken under statute. There was no logical, functional reason why the two sources of governmental authority should be distinguished. The scene was set therefore for the courts to question, or perhaps even to overturn, the orthodox constitutional theory. The opportunity for them to do so was provided by *Council of Civil Service Unions v Minister for the Civil Service*, a case which reached the House of Lords in 1985.

III. FULL REVIEWABILITY – THE *GCHQ* CASE

Council of Civil Service Unions v Minister for the Civil Service[68] is now the pivotal case in the development of judicial review of the prerogative. The litigation is generally known as the *GCHQ* case, since it concerned employees at the Government

[68] [1985] AC 374, [1984] 3 All ER 935, HL. For comment see Lee S (1985) 'Prerogative and public law principles' *Public Law* 186–193.

Communication Headquarters in Cheltenham. GCHQ was responsible for monitoring radio and satellite transmissions in overseas countries; it was linked in some ill-defined way with the security services. Many of its employees belonged to one or other of the civil service trade unions. At that time, civil servants did not have contracts of employment. Their terms and conditions of work were generally regulated by Orders in Council, the indirect exercise of the prerogative.[69] One term under which civil servants at GCHQ worked was that their conditions of service should not be altered until the Minister for the Civil Service had consulted with the trade unions about the proposed change.

In the early 1980s, the trade unions engaged in industrial action which to some extent disrupted GCHQ's intelligence gathering activities. The then Prime Minister, Margaret Thatcher, was also Minister for the Civil Service. She decided to respond to the disruption by forbidding GCHQ employees from belonging to a trade union. Employees who refused to resign from their union would be redeployed to less sensitive posts. The Prime Minister did not consult the trade unions before introducing this change.

The trade unions challenged the action on the grounds that the Prime Minister had acted in a procedurally unfair way by failing to consult them; (their argument was essentially the same as that employed by the prosecuting authorities in *Allen*). In effect, the unions were asking the courts to apply standards of statutory review to prerogative powers. The government advanced two defences. The first was simply that this was a prerogative power, and thus not subject to review on grounds of procedural unfairness. The second defence was that even if principles of procedural fairness did apply to this prerogative power, the court should not intervene here because the issue concerned 'national security'.

In a marked break with traditional doctrine, the House of Lords rejected the government's first defence. Lord Fraser perhaps put the point most clearly:

> 'There is no doubt that if the Order in Council of 1982 had been made under the authority of a statute, the power delegated to the Minister would have been . . . subject to a duty to act fairly. I am unable to see why the words conferring the same powers should be construed differently merely because their source was an Order in Council made under the prerogative'.[70]

This point was made with similar force by Lord Roskill, who could not see:

> 'any logical reason why the fact that the source of the power is the prerogative and not statute should today deprive the citizen of that right of challenge to the manner of its exercise which he would possess were the source of power statutory. In either case the act in question is the act of the executive. To talk of that act as the act of the sovereign savours of the archaism of past centuries'.[71]

[69] For subsequent developments on that point see Morris G and Fredman S (1991) 'Judicial review and civil servants: contracts of employment declared to exist' *Public Law* 485–490.

[70] [1985] AC 374 at 399, HL. [71] Ibid, at 417.

Such comments confirmed that the availability of judicial review in the modern era would depend upon *the nature of government powers, not their source.* But victory on this point of general constitutional principle did not mean that the trade unions were ultimately successful. The House of Lords' concern with the nature of government powers takes us to the second important part of the *GCHQ* decision. Lord Diplock suggested that government powers would not be what he termed 'justiciable', and so would not be subject to review on the basis of irrationality or of procedural impropriety, if the dispute was of a sort which does not lend itself to resolution by judicial type methods. The non-justiciable issue is not simply a case of A versus B. Rather it presents a great many competing points of view, all of which have to be weighed and balanced in the search for an overall political solution. Elected politicians, rather than non-elected judges, are the appropriate people to make these kinds of decisions. Lord Diplock described this type of decision as 'a balancing exercise which judges by their upbringing and experience are ill-qualified to perform'.[72] He considered that national security was 'par excellence a non-justiciable question. The judicial process is totally inept to deal with the sort of problems which it involves'.[73]

In effect, the House of Lords refused to investigate either the honesty or the reasonableness of the Prime Minister's claim that she had revoked trade union membership without consultation because of national security reasons. If we are looking for old parallels to elements of the *GCHQ* decision, it might be more appropriate to focus on the court's approach to this question of national security. In the pre-revolutionary *Ship Money* case, the court held that the King need not offer any evidence to support his assertion that the security of the realm was in jeopardy. In the 1916 *Zamora* case, in contrast, the court had required at least some evidence that the government had bona fide grounds for believing national security to be threatened. The *GCHQ* decision seems to follow the *Zamora* principle. The court required the government to produce an affidavit confirming that the Minister had genuinely considered the issue. But this does not seem to be a very difficult hurdle for the government to clear, and it implies that we have to trust the government never to invoke national security reasons for dishonest or bizarre reasons.

The final important point advanced in *GCHQ* was the court's conclusion that it was not just national security issues which were non-justiciable. Lord Roskill produced a list of what we might call 'excluded' categories – aspects of the prerogative where review would relate only to the existence of the claimed power, not to its exercise. The powers that Lord Roskill had in mind were: 'the making of treaties, the defence of the realm, the prerogative of mercy, the grant of honours, the dissolution of Parliament and the appointment of Ministers'.[74]

This list perhaps suggests that the court's definition of non-reviewable prerogative powers closely resembles Blackstone's old notion of the prerogative as consisting solely of those powers which are 'singular and eccentrical to the Crown', which

[72] Ibid, at 411. [73] Ibid, at 412. [74] Ibid, at 418.

indicates that one may always find a historical precedent for supposedly radical developments in constitutional law.

IV. POST-*GCHQ* DEVELOPMENTS

Cases decided since 1985 seem to build on rather than contradict the rather more functionalist analysis which the House of Lords' adopted in *GCHQ*. The central question the case raised, but perhaps could not answer, was whether 'justiciability' was a concept with a fixed meaning, or whether if, like other common law principles, it would prove to be an unstable concept, prone to sudden and substantial change. Before the courts offered answers to that question however, the Court of Appeal took a rather unexpected approach to the issues both of the existence of claimed prerogative powers and the capacity of such powers to co-exist with statutory provisions addressing the same matters.

R V SECRETARY OF STATE FOR THE HOME DEPARTMENT, EX P NORTHUMBRIA POLICE AUTHORITY (1988)[75]

The legal structure of the police forces in this country is quite complex; but to put the matter simply, some powers rest with central government, some with local police authorities, and some with the Chief Constable of each force.[76] The *Northumbria* case arose when the central government decided to set up a central supply store for plastic bullets and CS gas, on which Chief Constables could draw when they thought it necessary. Northumbria Police Authority did not want its Chief Constable to use these weapons without its approval, and so it initiated judicial review proceedings in an effort to establish that central government had no legal power to pursue this policy. The government claimed such power emanated from one or both of two sources. Either it came from the Police Act 1964, or it came from the old prerogative power 'to keep the peace'.

The Court of Appeal eventually decided that the 1964 Act did include the power to set up a central weapons depot. That was a controversial conclusion, but we need not dwell on it here. What we do need to consider is the court's answer to the questions of whether there was a prerogative power to keep the peace, and if so, what types of action came within the confines of that power in the mid-1980s?

Northumbria's case rested on two main contentions. The Police Authority's first argument was that there was no mention in nineteenth century text books or case law

75 [1988] 1 All ER 556, CA. See also Bradley A (1988) 'Police powers and the prerogative' *Public Law* 298–303.

76 An excellent analysis is offered in Lustgarten L (1989) *The governance of police* (London: Sweet and Maxwell). For a more concise introduction see Marshall G and Loveday B (1994) 'The police: independence and accountability', in Jowell and Oliver op cit.

of a prerogative power to keep the peace. This would seem a strong argument in the Police Authority's favour. If we recall Lord Camden's judgment in *Entick v Carrington*, we will remember that he was quite clear about how to determine if the Crown had a legal power to seize Mr Entick's papers; 'If it is law, it will be found in our books. If it is not to be found there, it is not law'. In effect, the Police Authority was contending that the residue of prerogative powers left to the Crown after the 1688 revolution never extended to equipping a police force.

The Court of Appeal dismissed this contention. Its somewhat innovative attitude is perhaps best expressed by Nourse LJ:

> '[The] scarcity of reference in the books to the prerogative of keeping the peace within the realm does not disprove that it exists. Rather it may point to an unspoken assumption that it does'.[77]

It is not difficult to agree with the first of those sentences; we should be cautious about assuming that eighteenth century textbooks and law reports offered a comprehensive map of that era's legal landscape.[78] But the meaning of the second sentence seems a little odd. Nourse LJ appears to argue that we should assume a legal power exists becomes no judge or textbook writer has ever recognised it. It seems hard to reconcile that reasoning with definitions of the rule of law which demand predictability and certainty in the scope of government's legal powers. Nevertheless, as we have already stressed, the *Burmah Oil* case serves as a salutary reminder that while there is no doubt that the prerogative is residual, there yet remains considerable uncertainty that all parts of that residue have thus far been identified. Nourse LJ's analysis might therefore be defended on the basis that he was perspicacious enough to find a 'lost' power which no other judge had previously managed to spot.

Northumbria's second argument drew on the *De Keyser Hotel* and *Laker Airways* principle. The first police force was created by statute in the early nineteenth century. So Northumbria contended that whatever prerogative powers to keep the peace may have existed between 1688 and 1800 would have been superceded by any overlapping statutory provisions. Section 4 of the Police Act 1964 granted the power to provide clothing and equipment to the police to Police Authorities. Northumbria argued that if one applied the *De Keyser* principle to s 4, one could only conclude that whatever prerogative power to supply equipment the Home Secretary might have had before 1964 had now been removed.

But the Court of Appeal also rejected this argument. It held that s 4 did not 'expressly grant a monopoly' in respect of equipment provision to the Police Authority, but rather created a situation in which the Police Authority's statutory power

[77] [1988] 1 All ER 556 at 575, CA.

[78] Cf Nourse LJ at 574: 'It has not at any stage in our history been practicable to identify all the prerogative powers of the Crown. It is only by a process of piecemeal decision over a period of centuries that particular powers are seen to exist or not exist'. The House of Lords' decision in *Burmah Oil* (above) is a pertinent example of what might best be described as a 300-year time lag in the judiciary's discovery of a hitherto hidden legal rule.

co-existed with the Home Secretary's prerogative power. But unlike the situation in *Laker*, the co-existence appeared to be contradictory rather than interlocking. This is a rather surprising argument, for it seems to be saying that the doctrine of implied repeal, discussed in chapter two, does not apply to prerogative powers. The court is apparently suggesting that Parliament can only abolish or curtail the prerogative through express statutory provisions.[79]

This initially appears to takes us into a seemingly illogical train of thought. Firstly, we accept that statute has a superior legal status to the prerogative. Secondly, we accept that statutes can be impliedly repealed by subsequent, impliedly inconsistent legislation. Thirdly, we accept that prerogative powers cannot be impliedly repealed by subsequent, impliedly inconsistent legislation. The third contention obviously contradicts points one and two. It is difficult to reconcile the Court of Appeal's decision about the status of the prerogative with orthodox constitutional theory, which might perhaps lead us to conclude that if we look hard enough we will usually find that our constitution harbours exceptions to even the most evidently straightforward of rules.

On further reflection however, Northumbria's acceptance of the co-existence of statutory and prerogative powers is, post-*GCHQ*, arguably unproblematic. Since the nature of the Crown's prerogative power to keep the peace and the powers afforded to the Home Secretary by the Police Act 1964 is the same, whichever method the government chose to apply its preferred policies would be subject to precisely the same degree of judicial scrutiny. There is thus no longer any functionalist justification for assuming the grant of statutory powers impliedly suspends or abolishes analogous prerogative authority.

FOREIGN AFFAIRS?

The courts have also given further guidance as to the reach of the justiciability principle. Three cases merit some attention; the first two nominally fall under the excluded category of 'foreign policy' to which Lord Roskill referred in *GCHQ*, while the third concerns the grant of pardons for the commissions of crimes which – per *GCHQ* – would also seem to be a non-justiciable power.[80]

Ex p Molyneaux[81] arose from the Anglo-Irish agreement signed by the British and Irish governments in 1985. The Agreement established an Inter-Governmental Conference which would meet to try to develop initiatives which might resolve the problems afflicting Northern Ireland. Molyneaux was one of several Protestant Northern Irish politicians who opposed the Agreement. He sought judicial review of the Agreement on the grounds that it implemented policies which could only be

79 This sets a somewhat improbable test; it would presumably have been rather unlikely that the 1964 Parliament would have expended energy on expressly abolishing a prerogative power which was not then known to exist.

80 For a perspective from a commonwealth jurisdiction on the extent of non-justiciable prerogative powers see *Patriotic Front-ZAPU v Minister of Justice, Legal and Parliamentary Affairs* 1986 (1) SA 532.

81 [1986] 1 WLR 331.

achieved through legislation. This was a very speculative argument, and the court dismissed it out of hand. The Agreement was a Treaty with a foreign state; it was quite clear that the government had a prerogative power to negotiate Treaties; and it was equally clear that the exercise of that power was not justiciable.

The court reached a different conclusion in the 1989 case of *R v Secretary of State for Foreign and Commonwealth Affairs, ex p Everett.*[82] Mr Everett was an alleged criminal who had taken up residence in Spain, a country with which Britain did not then have an extradition agreement which covered Mr Everett's alleged offence. When Mr Everett's passport expired, the Foreign Office declined to renew it. The government maintained a policy of not renewing passports when the applicant was the subject of an arrest warrant. The issuance of passports has not been put on a statutory basis, and so was clearly a prerogative power. The Foreign Office's refusal meant that Mr Everett would not be able to leave Spain. The Foreign Office did offer him a one way trip back to Britain, but since he would have been arrested as soon as he arrived, this was an offer which Mr Everett decided to refuse.

Mr Everett subsequently sought a review of the Foreign Office's decision. The government's primary defence was that the issue and renewal of passports was a question of foreign policy, and so within Lord Roskill's 'excluded categories'. The Court of Appeal rejected this argument. O'Connor LJ. held that:

> 'the issue of a passport fell into an entirely different category. [I]t would seem obvious to me that the exercise of the prerogative. . .is an area where common sense tells one that, if for some reason a passport is wrongly refused for a bad reason, the court should be able to inquire into it'.[83]

'Common sense' is perhaps not a very precise legal tool. Taylor LJ's reasoning is more helpful. He suggested that non-justiciability in foreign relations issues only extended to questions of 'high policy'. He did not define this precisely, but he seems to mean matters which had national security implications or which directly affected Britain's relationship with a foreign state. He felt that the grant of a passport was not a matter of high policy, but merely an administrative decision. As such, it should be subject to full review.

EXCLUDED CATEGORIES: A SHRINKING LIST?

The prerogative of mercy figured prominently in Lord Roskill's list of non-justiciable prerogative powers in *GCHQ*. But barely 10 years later, in *R v Secretary of State for the Home Department, ex p Bentley*,[84] the court effectively extended its power of review to

[82] [1989] QB 811, [1989] 1 All ER 655, CA.

[83] [1989] 2 WLR 224 at 228. That common sense was the appropriate tool to decide the extent of legal powers was of course the argument advanced by James I in the 1611 *Case of Proclamations.* As noted above, Coke CJ thought common sense (even kingly common sense) a most inapposite device to control legal interpretation.

[84] [1993] 4 All ER 442.

this aspect of the prerogative. Derek Bentley, a 19-year-old youth of very limited intellectual capacity, had been convicted of murder in 1952 and was hanged in 1953. Bentley had been an accomplice to the actual murderer, a 16-year-old, who was too young to be executed. Despite a recommendation from the jury that Bentley not be executed, the trial judge imposed the death sentence. The then Home Secretary declined to grant mercy to Bentley, despite advice to that effect from his senior officials.

The *Bentley* case was a final step in a 40-year campaign fought by Iris Bentley, the accused's sister, to establish either that her brother was innocent of the crime, or, at the very least, that he should not have received a capital sentence. By the early 1990s, Iris Bentley had managed to convince many people that her brother had been unjustly treated, and in 1992 she asked the Home Secretary to grant her brother a posthumous free pardon. The Home Secretary (then Kenneth Clarke) refused to do so. Mr Clarke suggested that he personally believed that Bentley should not have been hanged, but that he was unable to grant a pardon because he had not been presented with any evidence to indicate that Bentley was morally and technically innocent of the murder.

Before the High Court, Iris Bentley argued that the Home Secretary had misdirected himself in law, by failing to appreciate that 'a pardon' could take several forms, not all of which required a presumption of innocence. The Court rejected the Home Secretary's assertion that this particular prerogative power was per se unreviewable, concluding that Lord Roskill's apparent assertion to that effect in *GCHQ* was simply obiter. The Court based its analysis on a seemingly logical extension of the *GCHQ* principle that: 'the powers of the court cannot be ousted merely by invoking the word "prerogative" '.[85] The High Court then turned for guidance to a recent New Zealand decision, in which the New Zealand Court of Appeal held that while the prerogative of mercy was 'peculiar' to the Crown:

> 'it would be inconsistent with the contemporary approach to say that, merely because it is a pure and strict prerogative power, its exercise or non-exercise must be immune from curial challenge. . . . [T]he rule of law requires that challenge shall be permitted in so far as issues arise of a kind with which the courts are competent to deal'.[86]

The issue before the Court in *Bentley* was not the essentially non-justiciable question of how the Home Secretary should have balanced the various moral and political factors involved in determining whether a pardon should be granted in this case, but the eminently 'legal' question of whether the Home Secretary should be required to re-make his decision when his original response was based on a fundamental misunderstanding of the scope of his power. In such circumstances, the Court saw no constitutional barrier to the availability of review.

But having assumed the power to declare that Mr Clarke's decision was unlawful, the Court then declined to use it. Rather, Watkins LJ 'invited' the Home Secretary to look at the question again and 'devise some formula which would amount to a

[85] Ibid, at 452.

[86] *Burt v Governor-General* [1992] 3 NZLR 672 at 678.

clear acknowledgment that an injustice was done'.[87] In such circumstances, the distinction between an 'invitation' and an 'order' is perhaps merely semantic: the practical effect of the Court's decision was to pull a hitherto legally unregulated aspect of the government process within a recognisably Diceyan notion of the rule of law.

V. 'JUSTICIABILITY' REVISITED – ARE ALL STATUTORY POWERS SUBJECT TO FULL REVIEW?

Before ending this initial assessment of the royal prerogative, it is important to remember that the notion of justiciability is something of a two-edged sword. If, post-*GCHQ*, the courts' concern is now with the nature of a government power rather than its source, it would seem plausible to assume that there are (and always have been) some statutory powers whose nature makes them unsuitable for review. Once more therefore, we are drawn towards a functionalist rather than formalist interpretation of constitutional principle. *Chandler v DPP*[88] offers an example of this principle being put into practice.

Section 1 of the Official Secrets Act 1911 made it an offence for anybody to enter any prohibited place 'for any purpose prejudicial to the safety . . . of the state'. This is obviously a national security related issue, but one dealt with by statute rather than the prerogative. As part of a political campaign against nuclear weapons, Chandler had entered such a prohibited place, a military airfield, and tried to immobilise planes by sitting on the runway. He was subsequently prosecuted under s 1.

His defence was to argue that his efforts to publicise the cause of disarmament were in fact beneficial to the safety of the state. However the House of Lords declined to be drawn into this argument. The Lords held that the question of evaluating threats to national security was not a justiciable issue. National security was an issue that could only be gauged by the government of the day.

This was not quite a judicial retreat back to the *Ship Money* situation. At least technically, the court seemed to follow the precedent set in the *Zamora* case by requiring some evidence that the protestors' activities had jeopardised national security. That requirement did not seem to be very demanding however – the court was satisfied by an affidavit from an Air Commodore simply saying that the air strip was an important defence installation, and that any intrusion into it was 'prejudicial to the safety of the state'.

This result is obviously very similar to the one reached twenty years later in *GCHQ*. In theory, the government is subjected to a burden of proof to demonstrate that it was indeed motivated by national security considerations. But in practice, that

87 [1993] 4 All ER 442 at 455.

88 [1964] AC 763, HL.

requirement is merely a formality; it is discharged by the most flimsy evidence. So one must beware of falling into the trap of assuming that simply putting prerogative powers on a statutory basis will make them subject to the full rigour of judicial review. National security, whether invoked under a statute or under the prerogative, seems likely always to be a non-justiciable issue.

There may perhaps come a point where there seems to be no justification for claiming that national security issues arise. One might speculate for example how the Court of Appeal would have responded in *Laker* to a DoT claim that it was indeed entitled to issue 'directions' under s 4(3) – a power which arose only in respect of national security or diplomatic concerns – because in the Minister's considered opinion Laker's service did indeed have adverse national security implications. However this theory has not as yet been put to the test.

CONCLUSION

It is obvious that the courts supervise the government's use of prerogative powers more closely now than they did in the pre-revolutionary era. It is also quite clear that there has been some increase in the *theoretical* reach of the courts' power of review since the 1967 decision in *Lain*. We can also conclude that administrative law now seems to treat prerogative and statutory powers in the same way.

The more difficult issue is to decide if the concept of non-justiciabiity is too widely defined? Are the courts allowing too much government action to take place free from the control of judicial review? We might recall that after *Liversidge v Anderson*, Stable J had written to Lord Atkin suggesting that the House of Lords' decision meant that the judges were not so much 'lions under the throne' as 'mice squeaking under a chair in the Home Office'. We cannot apply such emotive language to the *GCHQ* or *Northumbria* judgments. But what we should remember is that the courts' control of the common law concept of judicial review gives the judges considerable power. By extending the scope of justiciability, the courts can place tighter controls on government's ability to behave in ways that seem inconsistent with traditional understandings of the rule of law. That looks very much like a 'red light' interpretation of the judicial function, and is a desirable result if one is suspicious of government, and fears that government powers might be used for unmeritorious ends. Alternatively, if one favours a 'green light' judicial role, believing that it is important for government to have great freedom to pursue policies which it thinks advance the national interest, one might prefer that the courts decide that more and more types of government action are non-justiciable. At present, the common law's power to extend review to currently non-justiciable issues obviously exists, but it is not clear under what circumstances, if any, it will be used.

The limits of the courts' willingness to expand the notion of justiciability were indicated by the Court of Appeal's 2002 judgment in *R (Abbasi) v Secretary of State for*

Foreign and Commonwealth Affairs.[89] Abbasi was a British national, alleged by the US government to have been a Taliban fighter, and imprisoned without trial in the Guantanamo Bay prison camp. His mother began judicial review proceedings on his behalf, seeking to establish that the Foreign Secretary was obliged to use his foreign policy prerogative to urge the US government to treat Mr Abassi more favourably. The Court of Appeal saw little scope for intervention:

'Whether to make any representations in a particular case and if so, in what form, was left entirely to the Secretary of State's discretion. The Secretary of State had to be free to give full weight to foreign policy considerations, which were not justiciable.'[90]

We should however remember that resort to the courts is not the only means to regulate the government's use of the prerogative, nor of a government body's deployment of powers it is granted by statute. In addition to having analysed the legal mechanism of judicial review, we must also assess political methods of control. This is a consideration which is as pertinent to the question of parliamentary sovereignty and government bodies' exercise of statutory powers as it is to control of the prerogative. As we shall see in subsequent chapters, political controls take various forms. In chapters five and six, we turn our attention to two of those forms – the House of Commons and the House of Lords.

89 [2002] EWCA Civ 1598, [2002] 47 LS Gaz R 29.
90 Ibid, per Lord Phillips MR.

5

THE HOUSE OF COMMONS

This chapter does not offer a comprehensive picture of the historical development and modern role of the House of Commons.[1] Rather, it sketches certain aspects of the relationship between the government and the legislature, in order to develop more fully arguments concerning the doctrines of parliamentary sovereignty and the separation of powers within the contemporary constitution.

CROWN AND COMMONS – THE ORIGINAL INTENT AND THE SUBSEQUENT RISE OF 'PARTY' POLITICS

The necessarily fragmentary and unreliable historical records of mediaeval England make it impossible to state with certainty when a body which might be regarded as the predecessor of the Commons first emerged. By 1270, several national assemblies, whose members included 'commoners' as well as aristocrats had met under the King's authority to assist in devising solutions to political or fiscal difficulties.[2] The consolidation of the Commons, Lords and Monarch as the three 'Estates of the Realm' occurred by 1300. Members of the Lords were individually summoned by the Monarch; the members of the Commons comprised representatives of each county and borough.[3] Nevertheless another 100 years passed before the Commons became a routine component of England's government structure. The Commons' early history need not be dwelt on here, although certain episodes are considered in subsequent chapters. For analytical purposes however, if we accept 1688 as the birth date of the modern constitution, it is helpful to focus briefly on then prevailing perceptions of the Commons' correct constitutional functions, and, relatedly, the political and moral source of its authority within the law-making and governmental processes.

The Commons initially performed two distinct formal legislative roles. The first,

1 For that see Silk P (1992) *How Parliament works* (London: Longman): Adonis A (1991) *Parliament today* (Manchester: Manchester University Press): Walkland S and Ryle M (eds) (1977) *The Commons in the seventies* (London: Martin Robertson): Ryle M and Richards (1988) *The Commons under scrutiny* (London: Routledge): Norton P (1985) *The Commons in perspective* chs 1–2 (London: Martin Robertson); (2nd edn, 1991) *The British polity* chs 8 and 11 (London: Longman).

2 Plucknett (1960) op cit pp 130–140.

3 The electoral system through which members of the Commons are chosen is discussed in chapter seven. The Commons is often referred to as the 'lower house' or 'lower chamber' of Parliament; the Lords as the 'upper house' or 'upper chamber'. The book uses these three labels for each house inter-changeably.

inherent in its status as the embodiment of one Estate of the Realm, was to safeguard the interests of non-aristocratic elite groups in society against the possible incursions of the Lords and/or the Crown.[4] As such, it provided a weak representative base to the governmental process. As is explained in chapter seven, 'the people' from which the Commons was drawn prior to 1832 was a very narrowly defined concept. But the notion that legitimate government demanded the consent of 'the people' rather than merely their submission – that they be persuaded rather than coerced to respect the law – was then an accepted (if flexible) principle of constitutional morality. The second was to provide a voice for local interests within the national legislature. Members of the Commons were 'elected' on a geographical basis, as the representatives of particular areas known as 'constituencies' and were expected to act as advocates for the areas they represented: the Commons was thus as much an aggregation of localities as a 'national' forum.

The MP – representative or delegate?

By 1688, the 'national' dimension of the Commons' role was becoming dominant.[5] This is illustrated by subsequently accepted perceptions of the nature of the relationship between an MP and his local electors, a perception famously articulated by Edmund Burke in his 1774 *Address to the electors of Bristol:*

> 'it ought to be the happiness and glory of a representative to live in the strictest union, the closest correspondence, and the most unreserved communication with his constituents. It is his duty to sacrifice his repose, his pleasures, his satisfaction to theirs; . . . and in all cases to prefer their interest to his own. But his unbiased opinion, his mature judgement, his enlightened conscience, he ought not to sacrifice . . . to any set of men living. . . . Your representative owes you, not his industry only, but his judgement: and he betrays, instead of serving you, if he sacrifices it to your opinion'.

One clearly sees echoes of Burke's thesis in Madison's notion of representative government.[6] Legislators were not the mere delegates of their electors. Madison's words would fit unproblematically into Burke's rationale; as representatives, MPs' legislative task would be to 'refine and enlarge the public view', to 'discern the true interest of their country' and to resist pressure from their electors to sacrifice that interest to 'temporary or partial considerations'. Electors who concluded that their MP had succumbed to such pressures, or, alternatively, who favoured 'temporary and partial considerations' which their representative did not support, might choose a different MP at a subsequent election. But what Parliament had thus far never done was pass legislation which empowered disgruntled electors to dismiss an MP who failed to follow their instructions.

Burke offers an idealised picture of the Commons; a vision of a legislative chamber in which several hundred independently minded MPs address every question before them in a mature, enlightened and impartial manner, free from the fetters both of

[4] As chapter seven suggests, this rather oversimplifies the political reality.

[5] Plucknett (1960) op cit pp 618–619.

[6] See pp 9–10 above.

blinkered parochialism and inviolable factional allegiances. In such circumstances, one might plausibly assume that the decisions the house reached would indeed best represent the 'national interest'. Whether such a governmental idyll ever did (or could) exist within the British constitution (or any other) is a moot point; more certain is that the practicalities of political life in the Parliaments which sat from 1750 onwards contained the seeds of a countervailing trend, which by 1900 had hardened into a rigid orthodoxy. In formal, legal terms the Burkean position still exists today. MPs are not legally obliged to structure their voting behaviour or work in the Commons in accordance with anybody else's wishes. Yet, in practice, the contemporary MP can defensibly be portrayed as a delegate; not of her constituents, but of her party.

THE FUSION OF POWERS, THE RISE OF THE PARTY SYSTEM AND CABINET DOMINANCE OF THE COMMONS

The concept of the 'independent' MP fits comfortably with idealised versions of the separation of powers, in which the legislature and the executive were entirely discrete bodies. Yet a pure separation of powers has always been a myth within the English (and later British) constitution. The 1688 constitutional settlement did not effect an extreme separation of powers. The Monarch, then the formal and functional core of the executive branch of government, was also part of the legislature. Similarly, many of his/her advisers and Ministers were members of the House of Lords: the holding of Ministerial office did not preclude (nor require) fully active membership of either house. The Monarch's advisers were collectively known as the Privy Council,[7] a body with as many as 50 members, many of whom were members of the Lords or Commons. Two of the three branches of government were from the very outset of the post-revolutionary era 'fused' rather than separated.

Yet it would be too simplistic to assume that an overlap of personnel necessarily precluded an effective divergence, if not quite separation, of powers between the Commons and the executive in the immediate post-revolutionary period. Given the turbulence of seventeenth century political history, so shaped by conflict between the King and the lower house, it is readily apparent that many members of the Commons would regard the Monarch with suspicion, even though his/her legal powers were now inferior to those of Parliament.

The emergence of the parliamentary sovereignty doctrine produced a substantial redefinition of contemporary constitutional understandings. Yet as noted in discussing the royal prerogative, certain pre-revolutionary principles continued to structure judicial perceptions of the relationships between the other two branches of government. Such continuities had a political as well as a legal dimension.[8]

Charles II introduced the first recognisably modern 'cabinet' within the executive,

[7] The term was in common usage by 1540; Plucknett (1960) op cit p 255. The Privy Council still exists, but it has little practical relevance other than on those occasions when (staffed by Law Lords) it sits as a final Court of Appeal for some Commonwealth countries.

[8] See Plucknett (1960) op cit pp 610–647.

when in 1671 he effectively marginalised the Privy Council and chose to formulate government policy with a so-called 'Cabal' of just five Ministers. Charles' initiative attracted considerable criticism; the Cabal was seen as a factional vehicle, rather than, as was the much larger Privy Council, a source of diverse and (ideally) disinterested counsel. Yet despite the revolution's apparent distrust of factional government, the more centralised Cabinet rather than the Privy Council formed the core of the executive in the immediate post-revolutionary era. Furthermore, the nature of the relationship between the Monarch and his/her Ministers within the core also began to shift. Neither George I nor George II took much interest in government affairs. By 1740, practical control of the Cabinet rested with the occupant of the newly emergent office of 'Prime Minister'. Sir Robert Walpole is generally regarded as the first holder of the post, but his position had no legal basis, and it was not until 1800 that the label came into common usage. George III took close control of the government process, but since he suffered periodic bouts of insanity,[9] his ability to reverse the drift towards Prime Ministerial pre-eminence within the government was limited.

The eighteenth century Monarchs' disinclination and/or inability to lead 'their' Cabinets coincided with the emergence of a sophisticated system of party political organisation. Outside the Commons, the rise of the national political party was facilitated by advances in technology. Improved transport facilities and cheaper printing meant that, for the first time, like-minded citizens throughout the country could constantly plan and act in concert on political issues.

The perception of the two houses containing 'a government' and 'an opposition' is again associated with Walpole, who from 1717 led a group of MPs which for first time saw its raison d'etre as being to 'oppose' the government, although it is not until 1826 that the label 'The Opposition' (meaning the second largest grouping of MPs in the house) became commonplace.[10] By then, the Cabinet, comprised almost exclusively of members of the Commons and/or Lords, was generally formed from the leading members of the party commanding majority support in the lower house.

As chapters six and seven suggest, the Commons had in practice become the dominant chamber within Parliament by the 1830s. Equally clearly, the Commons was beginning to be dominated by a majority party pursuing a coherent set of policy objectives, over which the Cabinet and the Prime Minister exercised an appreciable, increasing degree of control.

For modern observers, the perception that the Commons is little more than an arena within which the Labour and Conservative parties alternately form the government and the opposition is a strong one. It is given considerable force simply by the physical layout of the Commons' main chamber. The 'floor of the house' places government and opposition members directly opposite each other on several rows of

[9] The Monarch's standing qua the head of the government was not aided by George III's disastrous policies towards the American colonies: see Bailyn op cit pp 145–146, 152–153.

[10] Norton P (1988) 'Opposition to government' p 100, in Ryle and Richards op cit. The position of Leader of the Opposition is now a salaried public office.

benches. Government ministers and their opposition 'shadows' occupy the front benches on each side, with the rest of their party members sitting behind them.[11] That the lower house is now in practice a body in which party factions are clearly demarcated and constantly jostle for advantage cannot seriously be disputed. Equally clearly, that contemporary reality bears little relation to the Commons' initial role in the post-revolutionary constitution. The desirability or otherwise of this situation is a point to which we shall frequently return. For the moment however, our concern is with the ways in which party discipline in the lower house is maintained.

Party discipline in the Commons: the whips and the appointment of Ministers

MPs have never been legally obliged to support their party within the house. Parties are in effect voluntary organisations, within which maintaining co-operation between members is an entirely internal matter. Within the Commons, the larger parties have developed a relatively sophisticated control mechanism known as the 'whipping system'.[12] Several MPs in each party serve as whips. They function as the party's personnel managers, ensuring that their party's MPs are deployed in whichever way maximises achievement of party objectives.

'The whip' is also used to refer to the weekly timetable of Commons business produced by each party. This alerts MPs to the significance which their party's leadership attaches to particular issues. Specific items of business will be marked with 'one line', 'two line' and 'three line' whips; the higher the number, the more important it is presumed to be that MPs be present to participate in the business in hand and/or to cast their votes in support of their party.[13] Not all house business is whipped in this way. On issues in respect of which a party's leadership has no particular view, it may permit a 'free vote' in which its MPs follow whichever course they consider appropriate.

Party whips are often portrayed as a purely coercive force, whose role is to persuade or threaten MPs to support party policy. That is a role they frequently perform; but they also serve as a channel for exchanging information between the front and backbenches, and will sometimes be concerned more with convincing the Cabinet that its plans will not attract sufficient backbench support than with compelling backbenchers to support every item on the party agenda. Party whips also oversee their MPs' 'pairing' arrangements, whereby two MPs of opposing parties who expect to vote in different ways agree with each other not to vote on particular occasions, thereby freeing themselves to undertake activities elsewhere. Like most aspects of Commons procedures, 'pairing' is not a legally enforceable concept, and pairs have on occasion been broken in close votes.

[11] Hence ministers and shadow ministers are often referred to as 'front-benchers'. Members who do not hold governmental office or shadow positions are referred to as 'backbenchers'.

[12] See particularly Norton P (1979) 'The organisation of parliamentary parties', in Walkland S (ed) *The House of Commons in the twentieth century* (Oxford: Clarendon Press).

[13] Votes in the house are often referred to as 'divisions', as members register their vote by dividing into two lines and physically walking into different parts of an area of the house known as 'the division lobby'.

MPs who consistently flout party policy may have the whip withdrawn.[14] This can have severe long term consequences for the MP. Since an MP is legally the representative of her constituency rather than her party, losing the party whip has no impact on her presence in the Commons. However, as we shall see in chapter seven, election to the Commons is now determined primarily by a candidate's party allegiance. A member who is not adopted as her party's candidate at the next general election is unlikely to retain her seat.

If the whipping system is in some senses the stick with which parties discipline their MPs, granting governmental or shadow office may be seen as the carrot. The power to appoint people to ministerial office nominally rests with the Monarch through her prerogative powers. The government is technically 'Her Majesty's Government', just as the largest opposition party is 'Her Majesty's Opposition'. In effect, the appointment, promotion, transfer, demotion and dismissal of Ministers are matters for the Prime Minister. An MP's progress up (or down) what is disparagingly referred to as 'the greasy pole' is contingent on many factors, relating both to the qualities of the individual concerned and the wider political situation prevailing at any given time. But one may safely conclude that MPs who diverge from party policy on a regular basis are unlikely to enter ministerial or shadow ministerial ranks, still less to rise within them. Not all MPs seek to hold ministerial office; some will have returned to the backbenches after having previously served in government. For such members, the influence of the lure of office on their loyalty to their party is limited. For the careerist MP, however, the prospect of promotion is a powerful incentive for tailoring her own political cloth to the pattern drawn up by the party leadership.

There are no formal degrees of seniority within the Cabinet, but there is an informal hierarchy. Cabinet members are generally 'Secretaries of State' of particular government departments.[15] The three most important (often referred to as the 'great offices of state') are Home Secretary, Foreign Secretary, and the Chancellor of the Exchequer. There is no fixed limit to the number of Ministers who may serve in the Cabinet; (although at present no more than 21 Cabinet members may hold paid posts as Secretaries of State).[16] The number has risen over the past hundred years, from barely a dozen in the 1870s to as many as two dozen now. Nor is there any legal requirement that Cabinet Ministers be members of either house, although it is now unheard of for a minister not to be a member of Parliament.

'Ministers of State', several of whom are appointed for each department, occupy a lower rung of the Ministerial ladder, and are rarely Cabinet members. They may nevertheless wield very substantial executive responsibilities, and if their particular Secretary of State is a member of the Lords, they will bear primary responsibility for representing their department in the lower house. At a lower level, are junior ministers known as 'Parliamentary Under Secretaries'. At the bottom of the ministerial

14 See Cross J (1967) 'Withdrawal of the Conservative Party whip' *Parliamentary Affairs* 169–175.

15 Cabinet Ministers without any departmental responsibilities are known as 'Ministers without Portfolio'.

16 Ministerial and other Salaries Act 1975, s 1.

hierarchy are 'Parliamentary Private Secretaries' (PPSs), who are often rather pejoratively referred to as Ministerial 'bag carriers'. The PPS is not a salaried position. Occupants are nevertheless assumed to be part of the government, rather than simply, as are backbenchers, members of the governing party.

The House of Commons Disqualification Act 1975 currently precludes the government from having more than 95 ministers drawn from the Commons. The maximum number is not a sacrosanct moral principle; it has been periodically increased throughout the twentieth century. This may be attributed in part to the post-war era's growing acceptance of green light theories of the state; since twentieth century governments have assumed greater responsibilities than their predecessors, it is unsurprising that they feel a need for more Ministers. However, the increase may also be explained by successive governments' wishes to exercise more control over party members in the Commons.[17] This argument has the force of numbers behind it; since a party needs only 340 MPs to enjoy a comfortable Commons majority, the presence of nearly 100 members in the government points to a significant merging of the executive and legislative branches.

Sections two and three below consider whether this merging might defensibly be presented as an executive takeover of the lower house by assessing the Commons' roles as a contributor to the legislative process, and as a mechanism to scrutinise government behaviour. But before reaching those specific issues, it is necessary to add more detail to our picture of the context within which those roles are performed.

I. SETTING THE CONTEXT

This section focuses on three elements of the Commons' constitutional identity. The first concerns the roots of its procedural rules; the second addresses the role of 'the Speaker'; while the third considers the resources to which MPs have access in carrying out their duties.

THE SOURCES OF THE COMMONS' PROCEDURAL RULES

Parliament has passed little legislation controlling the Commons' proceedings. Nor has there been any significant judicial intervention through the common law in this area. As noted in chapter two, the courts have generally considered that each house enjoys unfettered control over its own affairs as a concomitant aspect of Parliament's sovereignty.[18]

Such questions have been left primarily to the house itself. Its rules currently derive from three main sources; traditional customs or 'ancient usage'; various 'Standing

17 deSmith op cit pp 264–265.

18 See pp 32–34 above. The issue is examined further in ch 8.

Orders' passed by the house; and Speakers' rulings. In the absence of legislation controlling the matter in issue, the house may amend any of its procedures by a simple majority vote.[19]

Significant changes are rarely introduced in so peremptory a fashion. The notion that the house's procedures should rest on the basis of consensual reciprocity has generally been a strongly held moral principle among MPs. Major reforms are generally instigated at the recommendation of the Commons Procedure Committee.[20] This committee has no permanent status, but is established whenever the house considers aspects of its procedures may require reform.

The leading source of guidance (for both commentators and MPs themselves) on Commons' procedure is *Erskine May's Treatise on the Law, Privileges, Proceedings and Usage of Parliament.*[21] But it would be misleading to consider such guidance, or indeed the procedures themselves, as 'laws'. Perhaps the most important element of the house's working practices is the phenomenon known as 'the usual channels' – the various informal agreements made between the government and opposition parties as to how the Commons' time should be allocated. Managing the usual channels is a task allocated primarily to the Leader of the House (a senior member of the Cabinet) and the government chief whip, together with their opposition counterparts.

The house's procedural rules can be regarded as a series of presumptions to which members voluntarily acquiesce: in part because they consider the rules intrinsically correct; in part because they feel the wishes of a majority of members should be respected; and in part because they would hope that should they form part of the Commons majority in future, the then minority would be similarly co-operative. The presumptions are not, however, irrebuttable.

The dominant presumption is that government business takes priority in each parliamentary session. This presumption is currently given force in a standing order – but that merely reflects rather than creates the government's ability to control the house's proceedings. The crucial informants of the way the Commons conducts its business are the willingness of its members to respect traditional practices, and, should that respect break down, the government's capacity to marshall majority support for its preferences.

The Commons generally sits for between 150 and 200 days per session; sessions usually begin in the autumn and run for eleven months. Each begins with 'The Queen's Speech', in which the Monarch outlines the government's planned legislative programme. There is no rigid rule as to how precisely time will be divided between the Commons' various functions. In recent years, 30%–35% of time spent on the floor of the house has been devoted to government Bills; 15%–17% has been used for motions (general debates) and ministerial statements on subjects of the government's

[19] Although as chapter eight suggests, there are instances when the house has apparently successfully defied legislative regulation of its behaviour.

[20] Griffith and Ryle op cit pp 174–175.

[21] References here to *Erskine May* are to the 21st edition, edited by Boulton C (1989) (London: Butterworths).

choosing; 7%–8% has been granted to Opposition motions; 8%–10% has been for backbenchers' Bills and motions, and similar amounts have been devoted to questions to Ministers, and passing delegated legislation.

There is great scope for inter-party disagreement as to the propriety of government efforts to manage the house's workflow. Since the Commons' procedural rules are not legal phenomena, and so not subject to judicial oversight, some other arbiter is required to resolve disputes. That function is one of several performed by the Speaker.

THE SPEAKER

The role of the Speaker, an office which dates from 1376, is of considerable significance. It is her task to interpret and apply the various customs and standing orders structuring the house's proceedings. To some extent, her role is that of judge whenever disputes arise as to how parliamentary business should be managed; when, for example, the usual channels cannot produce agreement, or backbenchers feel that the government and opposition front benches are paying insufficient attention to backbench concerns. Her jurisdiction is both extensive and multi-faceted. It embraces such diverse issues as deciding which amendments are to be debated (and for how long) at the report and third reading stages of a Bill's passage; choosing which members may speak; and disciplining members whose behaviour in the house breaches accepted standards.[22]

Before 1688, the Speaker often functioned largely as an emissary of the Crown. Given the then fairly effective separation of powers between the Commons and the government, the office could be uncomfortable in times of acute antagonism between the Commons and the Monarch.[23] For Speakers who felt their loyalty lay to the house rather than the Monarch that discomfort might grow into personal danger.[24] It was not until 1750 (when the fusion rather than separation of the executive and legislature was becoming apparent), that the Speaker had clearly become a defender of the Commons' interests against the wishes of the government.[25]

The Speaker is elected by members of the house. It is now accepted that the office is a non-party political post. The Speaker resigns from her political party on election. She nevertheless remains an MP, and acts on behalf of her constituents. She must also seek re-election to the Commons at subsequent elections, in which she stands as 'the Speaker'. She does not vote in the house except when there is a tie; in such circumstances, tradition requires her to vote for the status quo. In the modern era, Speakers

22 For an overview see Borthwick R (1988) 'The floor of the house', in Ryle and Richards op cit: Adonis (1990) op cit ch 4: Silk op cit pp 71–76: Laundy P (1979) 'The Speaker and his office in the twentieth century', in Walkland op cit.

23 Plucknett observes: 'Sir Peter de la Mare was imprisoned, but worse befell some of his successors . . . Bussy, William Tresham, Thorpe, Wenlock, Catesby, Empson, Dudley, Sir Thomas More – all came to violent ends on the scaffold, in civil war, or by assassination' (1960) op cit pp 210–211.

24 This explains the bizarre ritual during which a newly elected Speaker is dragged apparently unwillingly by other Members to assume office.

25 We examine this issue further in chapter eight.

have generally been members of the majority party. However, one recent incumbent, Betty Boothroyd, was a Labour MP prior to assuming office in 1992, even though the Commons then contained a Conservative majority. Ms Boothroyd could not have won the election without the approval of many Conservative members; a forceful indicator of the extent to which the Speaker is now perceived, in functional as well as formal terms, to be above party politics.[26] However, the Labour Party majority which controlled the Commons after the 1997 general election rejected the leading Conservative candidate, a former Cabinet Minister named Sir George Young, in favour of a rather obscure Labour backbencher, Michael Martin. Various parliamentarians and commentators cast doubt on Mr Martin's suitability for the post, and criticism was also levied at the rather arcane procedures through which his election was achieved.[27]

It would be inaccurate to characterise the Speaker as exercising coercive powers. In so far as a Speaker effectively controls the house, she does so because members voluntarily submit to her authority, even when it might appear that their immediate party political interests would be better served by defiance. As such, the Speaker performs the important (if largely symbolic) task of stressing that the Commons should function as more than a vehicle for dogmatic pursuit of short-term factional advantage.

RESOURCES

It is perhaps an exaggeration to classify MPs as poor relations of their legislative contemporaries in other modern democracies. Yet when compared to members of the US Congress, MPs receive little assistance in carrying out their tasks.[28] In the USA, members of Congress enjoy substantial research and administrative staffs. The rationale underpinning such expansive provision is rooted in the notion of informed consent to government. Legislators are unlikely effectively to contribute to the legislative process, nor searchingly evaluate the merits of government behaviour, if they lack access to expert analysis of relevant information.[29]

Yet in the mid-1980s, the Commons offered only 350 offices to its 650 members. Many MPs were consequently forced to share office space. Many offices were extremely small – few could accommodate secretarial and research staff as well as the MP herself. We might however observe that MPs are not richly endowed with supporting staff. Members presently receive an allowance of some £70,000–80,000 per year

26 The Speaker is not always in the chair when the Commons is in session. His/her presence is generally reserved only for the most important parts of the Commons' timetable. On other occasions, his/her role in the Chamber is taken by one of three deputy speakers, first among whom is the 'Chairman of Ways and Means'.

27 See Cowley P and Stuart M (2001) 'Parliament: a few headaches and a dose of modernisation' *Parliamentary Affairs* 238–257 at 253–255.

28 See generally Bennet P and Pullinger S (1991) *Making the Commons work* (London: Institute for Public Policy Research).

29 For a more expansive account see Lock G (1988) 'Information for Parliament' in Ryle and Richards op cit: Griffith J (1974) *Parliamentary scrutiny of government bills* ch 8 (London: George Allen & Unwin).

for these purposes. This is sufficient to employ a competent secretary and a junior researcher, but not to maintain an extensive information base.

The Commons has what might initially seem a substantial library. The library employs some 150 staff, many of whom devote all their time to researching MPs' queries. The Commons library is however a modest affair compared to the US Library of Congress. The Commons employs fewer than 700 staff to service its 650 MPs; the slightly smaller number of legislators in the US Congress have some 20,000 employees.[30]

It is difficult to accept that successive governments' unwillingness to afford MPs more substantial logistical support is motivated by financial considerations: facilities comparable to those in the USA would add only a tiny amount to public expenditure. Adequate resourcing would impose a 'cost' upon a government (of whatever party), but the cost would be political rather than financial in nature. A comment from a recent edition of *The Economist* offers a cynical explanation of the current situation:

> 'the government of the day has little to gain by giving Parliaments their own source of knowledge and advice. Why spend money providing information for backbenchers, when ignorance keeps them so much more malleable?'[31]

Any substantial increase in expenditure would require the support of a majority of MPs, which is unlikely to be forthcoming without government approval. By the mid-1990s, repeated expressions of backbench dissatisfaction with Commons' working conditions had apparently borne some fruit; the government accepted that sufficient resources should be provided to ensure that every MP at least had her own office within or adjacent to the Palace of Westminster.

Nor are MPs' salaries particularly high. They are currently about £60,000 per year, which obviously would not permit the member to finance the research and secretarial assistance she might consider appropriate.[32] This sum compares poorly with the remuneration paid to senior members of the professions. MPs were not paid at all until the early twentieth century. The present rather low level of salaries perhaps provides members with a financial incentive for seeking ministerial office, for which a substantial additional salary is payable. However, being a backbench MP need not be a 'full-time job': many backbench MPs derive income from other forms of employment, such as journalism, legal practice, directorships of companies, or 'consultancies' for commercial organisations.

The involvement of many MPs in paid extra-parliamentary activities also has some bearing on the Commons' traditionally bizarre working hours. Until very recently, activity on the floor of the house generally did not begin until 2.30 pm and frequently did not end until the early hours of the morning. Mornings are thus free for other activities. This is very convenient if an MP is in practice at the Bar or is serving as a

30 Adonis (1990) op cit p 62. 31 Cited in Lock op cit at p 52.

32 This is supplemented by travel expenses and, for MPs who live outside London, an allowance to finance a London home. MPs who have substantial personal wealth, and who choose to spend some of it on assistance in carrying out their political duties, have a distinct advantage over their less affluent counterparts.

director or consultant for commercial interests. Modest timetable reforms were introduced in 1994. The reforms introduced a limited number of morning sittings in the chamber, abolished some Friday sittings and proposed an earlier end to business on Thursdays. The change marked at least a modest first step towards a more far-reaching normalisation of MPs working hours. Further steps in this direction were taken in 2002.

There are some MPs who regard membership of the Commons as a full-time occupation. When not in the chamber, they will be found attending to matters arising in their respective constituencies, or participating in the work of the Commons' various committees.[33] Such backbenchers appear to be a minority however. This may be because some members now see election to the Commons as a means to other professional or financial ends, rather than as an end in itself. But it may also be, as sections three and four suggest, because realistic backbench MPs doubt that their individual and collective presence in the house will often have a significant impact, either on the content of legislation or the behaviour of the government.

Financial support for the opposition

In addition to the salaries paid to the Leader of the Opposition, the opposition chief whip, and the shadow Leader of the House, some financial support is now provided to the opposition parties to assist them in carrying out their activities.[34] This is referred to as 'Short money', after Edward Short, the Leader of the House in the Labour government in power when the scheme was introduced in 1975. For the main opposition party the sum is a useful addition to its resources (the Labour Party and Conservative Party when in opposition in the 1990s received around one million pounds per year of 'short' money), but is insufficient to finance extensive political activities. 'Short money' is paid to party leaders rather than shared equally among the party's MPs. One need not be overly cynical to wonder if the leadership might find good reasons for spending the money on activities which were not likely to undermine its preferred policies. A Committee of Inquiry chaired by Lord Houghton was established by the Labour government in the mid-1970s to consider whether far more substantial financial assistance, on a statutory footing, should be granted to all major political parties. The Committee made recommendations – ignored by all subsequent governments – to that effect.[35]

What has been said so far might suggest that the balance of power between the government and the Commons is weighted heavily in the government's favour. This is hardly surprising given the fused nature of the government/Commons relationship: in that context, the notion of a meaningful separation between the house and the executive is a misleading dichotomy. The following sections consider whether the dichotomy currently has any merit at all.

33 Of which more is said below.

34 Griffith and Ryle op cit pp 117–118. The scheme does not have an explicit statutory basis.

35 (1976) *Report of the Committee on financial aid to political parties* (Cmnd 6601 – London: HMSO).

II. THE PASSAGE OF LEGISLATION

Commentators now seem to agree that the modern House of Commons is rarely a law-*making* body in any meaningful sense. Norton suggests, for example:

'Although some writers continue to list "legislation" as one of the functions of the House of Commons, it is a function which for all intents and purposes has not been exercised by the house in the twentieth century'.[36]

Gavin Drewry expresses a similar scepticism:

'[S]ome would question whether in reality the Westminster Parliament, dominated as it is by a powerful executive, able in most circumstances to mobilise majority support in the division lobbies, can properly be called a "legislature" at all'.[37]

John Griffith's comprehensive study of the Commons in the 1967–1971 sessions, concluded that:

'[T]he direct impact of the House on Government proposals for legislation was unimpressive. . . . On no occasion was the government either defeated or forced to make a tactical retreat . . . [T]he visible result of a great deal of Opposition and Government backbench activity was very small indeed'.[38]

Such critiques contend that the content of legislation is effectively determined in Cabinet. Governments formulate policies which they expect to command the support of their party's members in the Commons, and it is rare that their preferences will be rejected or significantly amended during a Bill's passage in the house. Thus one might suggest that in examining the significance of the Commons' legislative role, one should direct attention to considering its efficacy in influencing or pressurising the government to modify or withdraw its proposals.

The various stages a Bill undergoes in its passage through the Commons seem now to possess a sacrosanct constitutional status. The process begins with the 'first reading'; a purely formal step, in which the measure is introduced to the house. Consideration of the Bill's main principles occurs during 'second reading', a major set piece debate on the floor of the house. If the Bill is approved,[39] its details are addressed in a 'standing committee', which is empowered to amend the original text. On leaving the standing committee, the Bill returns to the floor for its 'report stage', when any committee amendments (or new ones proposed by the government) are considered. On completing its report stage, the Bill (as amended) enters its third reading. If approved by the house, it is then sent to the Lords.[40] This process has no legal basis. It

36 Norton (1985) op cit p 81. 37 Drewry (1988) op cit p 122. 38 (1974) op cit p 206.

39 At all stages of the legislative process, a bare majority of members voting in favour amounts to approval.

40 A bill may originate in the Lords, in which case it would be sent for the Royal Assent after the Commons' third reading. For an informative study of the passage of a relatively recent, controversial measure see Rose H (1973) 'The Immigration Act 1971: a case study in the work of Parliament' *Parliamentary Affairs* 69–91.

is a matter purely of custom and tradition within the house. The various stages are designed to fulfil different functions, and, as suggested below, the process' broad outlines have become encrusted with detailed provisions.

There are no rigid rules concerning the time taken for a Bill to pass through the legislative process, although until 2003 a government or private member's Bill had to complete all its stages in a single parliamentary session. In emergency situations, a Bill may be passed in days or even hours. In such circumstances, the measure is unlikely to have received mature consideration. Conversely, controversial Bills on major issues may spend six months or more in the Commons.[41]

But even Bills in the latter category are not debated or scrutinised until all members are satisfied that the house has been apprised of all relevant viewpoints. In the 1870s and 1880s, Irish MPs dissatisfied with government policy towards 'Home Rule' for Ireland engaged in a protracted campaign of 'filibustering' – continuing debate until the Commons ran out of time – with the result that Bills were simply talked out. To prevent a minority of MPs sabotaging the government's legislative programme in this way, the house introduced (and subsequently refined and added to) several time management initiatives. The standing committee system, which dates from the 1870s and was firmly established as an integral part of the legislative process by 1910,[42] is one such device which has become entirely uncontroversial. Two other techniques, 'the guillotine' and 'the closure' have proved more problematic.

The guillotine and closure

A government with majority support in the house may at any stage of a Bill's passage subject it to an 'allocation of time order', colloquially referred to as the 'guillotine'.[43] The guillotine specifies in advance precisely how long shall be allocated to discussion of a Bill's provisions. Once that time expires, debate ends, irrespective of how much of a Bill remains undiscussed. The guillotine is generally used to regulate proceedings in committee. Standing orders currently require that guillotine motions be debated on the floor.

Allocation of time orders raise sensitive issues. They may from one perspective be viewed as elevating governmental expediency above the principle that proposed legislation should receive rigorous and exhaustive Commons discussion. Alternatively, they can be seen as an entirely legitimate means for the government to overcome bloody-minded obstructionism by minority parties. Before 1980 governments were most reluctant to deploy the guillotine, evidently for fear of the adverse publicity such a move might generate.[44] However, recent Conservative governments had fewer qualms about the constitutional propriety of doing so.[45] Feelings in the house over this issue were sufficiently inflamed in 1994 for the Labour Party to withdraw from

41 See Adonis (1990) op cit ch 5 : Silk op cit pp 138–139.
42 Norton (1985) op cit pp 89–90: Adonis op cit p 102.
43 See Erskine May op cit pp 409–416: Griffith and Ryle op cit pp 225–228.
44 For the 1974–1988 period see the helpful table in Griffith and Ryle op cit p 303.
45 Adonis op cit p 70.

the usual channels and commit itself to being as obstructive as possible to the conduct of government business.

A less draconian, but more frequently invoked (especially at the report stage), time-management device is the closure. Standing orders provide that any member may propose, at any time, that 'the question now be put'. If a majority of MPs present (of whom there must be at least 100 in total) support the motion, debate on the question is ended, and the house moves to its next business. The Speaker may reject the proposal if she considers it to be 'an abuse of the rules of the House'. There are no legal rules controlling the exercise of this discretion. Griffith and Ryle suggest that the Speaker would take into account such matters as how many (and which) members have already spoken on the issue and its substantive importance; it seems unlikely that closure would be permitted on a significant question before two or three hours of debate had been conducted.[46]

THE SECOND READING

Second reading debates on government Bills are opened and closed by speeches from the Bill's sponsoring Ministers, each of whom is followed by her opposition counterpart. During the central period of the debate, the Speaker controls the order in which MPs are called to speak, although tradition demands that she alternately chooses members of the government and opposition parties. In major debates, demand to speak is intense. This demand has been met to some extent since 1988, when a standing order was introduced which permitted the Speaker to limit individual speeches to a maximum of ten minutes.[47] This goes some way towards ensuring that the house is exposed to a wide range of views on the merits of the government's proposed policy.

It is unlikely that a contribution by an individual MP, or even a series of like-minded speeches, will persuade members to vote other than on party lines. To some degree, labelling the second reading stage as a 'debate' is misleading. Proceedings are rarely characterised by the cut and thrust of attack and immediate defence. Many members merely recite prepared speeches which outline a particular element of party policy. This is not to say second reading debates are worthless – but that they have little immediate impact on the content of Bill.[48]

The rapidity of a member's entry to (and subsequent rise up) the ranks of ministerial or shadow ministerial office is significantly affected by her oral performance on the floor of the house. Impressive performances will mark out a backbencher as a ministerial prospect. Conversely, Ministers who cannot command respect during debate will find their governmental careers grinding to a halt or slipping into decline.

46 Op cit pp 222–227. See also Griffith (1974) op cit pp 20–24: Erskine May op cit pp 405–408.

47 Silk op cit p 92.

48 Ministerial speeches have latterly assumed a significant legal status; see the discussion of *Pepper v Hart* in chapter eight below.

Second readings are also valuable simply because of their visibility to the wider public. Debates on major Bills are widely reported in the press, and excerpts broadcast on radio and television. Such coverage does not alert voters to the details of government and opposition arguments, but the aggregated effect of the constant glare of publicity may be an important incentive for both government and opposition to ensure that their policies do not markedly diverge from the wishes of the general public.

STANDING COMMITTEES

The Commons' capacity to pass Bills would be much reduced if their details, as well as their principles, had to be debated on the floor of the house. Thus, while measures of major constitutional significance[49] may undergo their committee stage on the floor, most Bills are sent 'upstairs' to be examined by a standing committee of between sixteen and fifty MPs. As many as eight standing committees may sit at one time.

The membership of standing committees reflects the party balance in the whole house. Thus a government with a comfortable majority is assured of a proportionate advantage at the committee stage. Standing committees on government Bills always include the sponsoring Minister and her shadow. Other members are formally chosen by the house's own Committee of Selection, which is required to take into account a member's fields of expertise when making its choice. But selection is in practice controlled by the party whips, and it is unlikely that the whips would support inclusion of an MP whose expertise might lead her to reject party policy.

That said, Ministers face more rigorous questioning in committee than on the floor. This is due in part to the nature of the committee's task: effective scrutiny of detail demands expertise and intellectual precision, rather than the rhetorical skills that may suffice on the floor. In addition, committee proceedings generally attract much less media attention than second reading debates. In so far as MPs are playing to an audience when in committee, it is to an audience of colleagues, who are most likely to be impressed by an incisive and knowledgeable dissection of the Bill's provisions.

At the committee stage (unless a guillotine has been imposed), the allocation of time to particular clauses is determined by the Chairman. The Chairman also decides which amendments may be moved. Amendments may not contradict the Bill's main principles as approved at second reading, but should be directed at questions of detail.[50] In practice, it appears that most committee amendments are introduced by the government itself, either to correct unnoticed errors, or to respond to what the government regards as acceptable concerns expressed by MPs or other interest groups.[51]

There must however be doubt as to the efficacy even of the standing committee's

49 This is not a legally defined categorisation.

50 Although so-called 'wrecking amendments' are occasionally introduced at other stages of the legislative process.

51 See especially Griffith (1974) op cit ch 3: Norton (1985) op cit ch 5.

more searching and informed deliberations when dealing with a government dogmatically attached to the details as well as principles of its legislative programme. This point is forcefully made by Adonis' discussion of the passage of the Thatcher government's Bills to privatise the water and electricity services.[52] The electricity Bill consumed over 100 hours of committee time. It was amended 114 times. 113 amendments were moved by the government. The other was 1 (of 22) moved by a Conservative backbencher. None of the 227 opposition amendments were carried.

REPORT AND THIRD READING

Since the mid-1960s, the report stage of government Bills has consumed some 10% of time spent on the floor of the house.[53] This gives some indication of its potential importance within the legislative process. The report stage enables the house to consider a Bill in its entirety as amended in committee. It also offers the opportunity for further amendments to be moved. Controversial Bills may require several full days of the house's time. Procedure is regulated by complex rules concerning the type of amendments admissible and which amendments are debated.

For most Bills which complete the report stage, the third reading is a mere formality. A debate may be held if six members request one. It is possible for a government Bill to be rejected at the third reading debate, but it is difficult to conceive of circumstances (other than those where a government has only a minority of MPs in the house) when this might occur.

CONCLUSION

It has become a cliché to suggest that the Common's role in respect of government Bills is now 'legitimation rather than legislation'. The inference seems to be that because the Commons is an elected body, the wishes of the majority of its members necessarily ensure that its decisions have a 'democratic' basis. As chapter seven will suggest, that assumption is itself problematic: as was noted in chapter one, legitimacy and democracy may demand rather more than simple majoritarianism.

Yet, seemingly paradoxically, there now also appears to be an academic consensus that backbench MPs have become more assertive since 1970 in resisting government policies of which they disapprove.[54] An MP's capacity to do this effectively depends in part on the size of the government's majority, and in part on the number of like-minded colleagues who support her cause. The first Wilson government (1964–1966), which had a majority of only three, found its plans to bring the steel industry into public ownership were blocked by the refusal of two Labour MPs to vote with the

52 (1990) op cit pp 103–104.

53 Griffith and Ryle op cit p 237: Silk op cit p 135.

54 For statistical information see Griffith and Ryle op cit pp 118–130. More generally see Johnson N (1988) 'Departmental select committees', in Ryle and Richards op cit: Norton P (1980) *Dissension in the House of Commons* 1974–1979 (London: Macmillan).

government.[55] One may also point to several instances in the mid-1980s when the Thatcher government, which had substantial Commons majorities, misread the mood of its backbenchers and found itself obliged to abandon Bills. The most spectacular example was provided by the Shops Bill 1986, a measure designed to liberalise Sunday trading laws. The government had correctly anticipated that Labour MPs would oppose the measure because of its impact on shopworkers. The government had not expected that many backbench Conservatives would support a campaign orchestrated by religious groups to 'Keep Sunday Special'. Squeezed by this unlikely alliance, the Bill was defeated on second reading.[56]

We will examine several more examples of such behaviour over significant policy issues (by both Labour and Conservative MPs) in subsequent chapters. Such episodes may defensibly be regarded as exceptions to a more general rule; namely that the passage of government Bills through the Commons is dependent not so much on the intrinsic merit of their contents, nor on the skill which Ministers display in defending them on the floor or in committee, but on the size and cohesiveness of the governing party's majority. But government measures are not the only Bills which the Commons considers. In respect of 'private members' Bills', different considerations may apply.

PRIVATE MEMBERS' BILLS

A few Bills are introduced every session by backbench members. Twelve Friday sittings per session are currently allocated for dealing with such measures. There is in theory no limit to the number of Bills that an MP can introduce. Many Bills are presented to the house simply because the sponsoring MP may wish to draw attention to herself or to a particular issue. But if the Bill is to have any realistic prospect of being enacted, it must be initiated through one of two mechanisms.

The most significant is the annual ballot under SO 13. Any backbencher may enter the ballot. Twenty 'winners' are drawn. The first six are allocated top place in the order of business on a given Friday for a second reading. These six then assume priority on subsequent Fridays for their report and third reading over the second readings of the other 14 Bills. If a Bill is to pass, it must complete its second reading on the first day. If a Bill is opposed, its sponsor must be able to force a closure to ensure it is not talked out. This may not be easy – it is often difficult to ensure that the 100 sympathetic members needed are in the house late on Friday afternoon, when many will wish to return to their constituencies.

The popularity of the procedure is due in part to the high profile that a full second reading debate can give to its sponsor. But the attractiveness is not solely a matter of publicity. Almost 200 Bills introduced through this method were enacted

55 See Pimlott B (1992) *Harold Wilson* pp 357–359 (London: Harper Collins).

56 Three other bills were withdrawn during that Parliament, for less dramatic reasons and in less dramatic circumstances. None could be regarded as of great importance. See Drewry (1988) op cit pp 134–136.

between 1974 and 1989.[57] It thus offers some MPs a good opportunity to make a legislative mark.

Such Bills have sometimes introduced important legislative reforms in areas which generate considerable moral controversy, but in respect of which opinion does not divide along traditional party lines. The most obvious (and oft-quoted) example of such legislation is the Abortion Act 1967 (sponsored by David Steel MP).[58] The process is also frequently deployed to rationalise archaic legislation, or to introduce a regulatory framework around newly emergent social or legal problems.[59]

There is little immediate point in backbenchers launching initiatives to which the government is opposed. The carrot and stick modes of intra-party discipline wielded by the Prime Minister and the whips do not suddenly disappear just because a Bill emanates from a backbencher. The government has no obligation to allow free votes on such Bills, although there is perhaps some moral pressure to do so. However, allowing a free vote may sometimes suit a government's purposes very well. An obvious benefit of so doing is to foster the impression that the government respects the independence of MPs as individuals, and of the Commons as a collectivity. On issues about which the government has no strong policy preferences, such action is a substantively painless way of rebutting suggestions that the executive wields an unhealthy degree of control over the legislative process. Equally, a government may conclude that facilitating the passage of a private member's Bill in respect of a policy which it supports, but which might be unpopular among its MPs or the electorate, is a useful way of achieving preferred outcomes without having to take responsibility for having done so.

The backbencher's need for government support also has a more mundane dimension. Pressures on the Commons' legislative timetable make it unlikely that Bills other than the first three or four in the ballot could be passed if the government does not allocate some of its own time for their passage. For a government with time to spare, making a little available to backbench initiatives is a painless way to curry favour with the house. The Labour governments of 1964–1970 offered time to over 20 backbench Bills.[60] In contrast, during the 1980s, successive Conservative governments did not appear concerned to facilitate such expression of backbench opinion: the Thatcher administrations were notably reluctant to devote government time to private members' Bills.[61]

Conversely, the private member's Bill can also offer governments with over-full legislative programmes a means to grab an even-greater share of the Commons' time. A backbencher promoting a Bill with which the government sympathises may find

57 Silk op cit p 117.

58 For an illuminating discussion of both the background to and passage of the Bill see Richards P (1970) *Parliament and conscience* ch 5 (London: Allen and Unwin).

59 For examples see Silk op cit pp 117–118: Griffith and Ryle op cit pp 386–390.

60 Norton (1985) op cit p 102.

61 Griffith and Ryle op cit p 398.

herself invited to modify her measure in accordance with ministerial preferences in return for assistance in finding the necessary Commons time to push it through.[62]

In contrast, there have been instances of governments covertly deploying backbench MPs to block a private member's Bill. An egregious example occurred in 1994. The government had not initially indicated that it opposed the Civil Rights (Disabled Persons) Bill, intended to prohibit discrimination in terms of employment and access to public facilities against disabled people. It was however widely thought that the government considered the Bill too expansive. Suspicions as to the government's true preferences were roused when Conservative backbenchers suddenly tabled 70 amendments. The amendments generated sufficient debate to ensure the Bill was talked out at second reading. It later transpired that the amendments had been provided by the government, which wanted the Bill to fail but feared the public criticism that would result if it achieved its objectives by ordering Conservative MPs to vote against the second reading. Such furtive tactics on the government's part betoken disrespect both for the Commons and for the general public. The behaviour of the compliant backbenchers is perhaps even more reprehensible.

In addition to the ballot, backbenchers may try to initiate legislation though the 'ten-minute rule Bill' process provided by SO 19. One such Bill may be introduced each Tuesday and Wednesday. Its sponsoring member is permitted time to make a brief (hence 'ten minute' rule) statement to the house outlining its objectives; an equal time is given to a member wishing to oppose the measure.

The procedure offers MPs a public platform when the house is often packed. But ten minute rule Bills are not a serious component of the legislative process. While most are formally allowed to proceed by the house, there is minimal chance that they will be enacted as there is so little time available for them. It is not unusual for periods of several years to pass without a single ten minute rule reaching the statute book. Their function might more sensibly be seen as affording an MP a high profile public forum from which to raise an issue of current concern, in the hope that either a government department or another MP who tops the private member's ballot will introduce a like measure. There are, as always, exceptions to the general rule. The Sexual Offences Act 1967, which repealed legislation criminalising homosexual acts between consenting adults, emerged from the ten minute rule. It is however clear that its passage was largely dependent on the government's willingness to find time for it to be enacted.[63]

It would be incorrect to assume that private members Bills are an unimportant part of the Commons' workload. Quantitatively, they are insignificant compared to government Bills. Equally, many of them address minor issues. Nevertheless they do occasionally effect major changes on matters of considerable substance. What they

[62] For example the Chronically Sick and Disabled Persons Act 1970 and Sexual Offences Act 1967; see Griffith and Ryle op cit pp 392–393 and Silk op cit pp 116–117. See also my discussion of the passage of the 1977 Housing (Homeless Persons) Act; *Housing homeless persons: administrative law and practice* ch 3 (Oxford: OUP).

[63] Richards (1970) op cit ch 4.

manifestly do not do is provide a vehicle through which the 'independence' of the Commons is promoted over and above party loyalties on a substantial and systematic scale.

PRIVATE BILLS

'Private' Bills are an entirely different form of legislative creature than private members Bills, which are technically, like government Bills, 'public' measures. Private Bills are intended to confer certain benefits or obligations on a narrowly defined class of persons or companies, or to authorise specific works or activities in a particular area.[64]

The Bills are introduced to the Commons not by a government department or an MP, but by the interested parties themselves. The parties are represented in the house by lawyers styled as 'parliamentary agents'. As chapter two suggested when discussing the *Wauchope* litigation, the house's standing orders impose rigorous requirements which oblige the promoters to notify any affected third parties of the Bill's intentions. After second reading, a private Bill is sent to a special committee of four members which examines it in great detail. It is at this stage that the significance of the need to notify affected parties becomes apparent. Clearly, if affected persons have not been notified of the Bill's passage, they will be unable to present their point of view to the Committee, which will thus proceed on the basis of incomplete information.

The very different process used to enact private statutes, and the generally sectional interests which they serve, perhaps lend force to Lord Denning's suggestion in *Pickin* that the courts should reconsider their traditional refusal to assess the procedural propriety of the legislative process. The mechanism was subject to an intensive investigation by a joint Lords/Commons select committee in the late 1980s, but as yet no significant reforms have been introduced.[65]

HYBRID BILLS[66]

A hybrid Bill is a government measure which affects a particular individual or organisation in a different manner to other individuals or companies in the same class; it thus bears some resemblance to a private Bill. There are no definitive rules for determining if a Bill is hybrid in substance; the decision is entrusted, via the Speaker, to a House of Commons official designated as the 'Examiners of petitions for Private Bills'.[67] It is thus quite possible that a government may unexpectedly find itself promoting a private measure, with potentially severe consequences for its legislative timetable.

64 As noted in ch 2, the device was often used in respect of the construction and management of railways.

65 Private Bills comprised a much more significant proportion of the Commons workload 150 years ago than they do now. They were frequently promoted by local authorities to enable them to carry out specific tasks, or by private companies constructing transport infrastructure. Such activities are now often subsumed within the government's own legislative programme.

66 See generally *Erskine May* pp 519–524.

67 On the origins of the post see *Erskine May* pp 811–812.

Hybrid Bills broadly follow the public Bill procedure. However they must go through a further stage before a select committee in both the Commons and the Lords before undergoing their standing committee stage. These select committees[68] are empowered to hear petitions from opponents of the Bill, and thus can obstruct the passage of legislation. Nevertheless, a government may dispense with this additional procedure if it can muster a Commons majority to do so.

DELEGATED LEGISLATION

It would be inaccurate to suggest that the bulk of the laws under which the British people now live have received searching Commons scrutiny. This is due only in part to the logistical and party political constraints operating on the house's analysis of Bills. Its major cause is the government's increasing tendency to promote Bills which delegate secondary law-making power to Ministers through the mechanism of 'regulations' or 'statutory instruments' (SIs).[69] Under this form of law-making, the 'parent' Act sketches the broad confines of the power conferred upon the government, leaving the Minister to fill in the details in SIs. The mechanism represents something of a half-way house in procedural terms between purely legislative and purely executive law-making.

SIs spare Ministers the time-consuming and potentially problematic task of putting their policy preferences into a Bill and trying to pilot it through the Commons. SIs have been favoured by governments of both parties in the modern era, largely because the growing scope of government intervention in social and economic life means that the house would not have time to deal with all matters through primary legislation. Since 1980, the government's resort to SIs has continued apace: over 1000 per year have been passed on average. It is not possible to form any general conclusion on the significance of such measures. Some are exceedingly trivial – a favourite example being the Baking and Sausage Making (Christmas and New Year) Regulations 1985.[70] Others have profound constitutional implications; the law under which Mr Liversidge was imprisoned was an SI, and delegated legislation can afford Ministers sweeping powers in important areas of governmental activity.

A political party's protests (when in opposition) against SIs should consequently be regarded sceptically – it seems likely that any 'principles' which underlie them would be quietly forgotten when that party next formed a government. For constitutional lawyers, however, the issues of principle have more force, since they bear directly on the questions of the sovereignty of 'Parliament' and the separation of powers, and thereby also bear indirectly on the question of what type of 'democracy' the constitution currently upholds. To explore these issues one must ask how closely do MPs

[68] Again the terminology is unfortunately confusing, since, as we shall see below most of the Commons' 'select committees' do not have any legislative role.

[69] This somewhat oversimplifies the terminology; see Griffith and Ryle op cit p 245: *Erskine May* pp 539–541.

[70] See Silk op cit pp 148–149.

oversee the creation of statutory instruments? Are they a sub-stratum of the legislative process, or would it be more realistic to regard them as 'law-making by the executive'?

Contemporary principles and practice

The use of delegated legislation assumed considerable prominence in the late 1920s, following the publication of a book called *The new despotism* by Lord Chief Justice Hewart.[71] Hewart, in a Diceyan vein, deplored Parliament's practice of affording Ministers what he regarded as arbitrary bureaucratic powers. The critique was hyperbolic, but is helpful in focusing attention on the distinction between substantive and procedural conceptions of the rule of law. A parent Act does not (and indeed cannot) bestow an unfettered power upon a Minister: she does not thereby become in any sense a 'sovereign legislature'; her powers are confined by the terms of the 'parent' legislation. Consequently, the terms of statutory instruments are subject to judicial review to ensure that they do not exceed the competence Parliament has granted.[72] But neither does the process require that the Commons consider every detail of each SI 'enacted'.

Hewart might plausibly be seen as concerned entirely with matters of process; it is not what government does that is the problem, but how government does it. Its intervention would be acceptable if only it had exposed its plans to the rigorous scrutiny attaching to the passage of primary legislation. An obvious response to such an argument would be to highlight the Commons' limited role even in respect of most statutes.

That dichotomy is somewhat misleading. Issues of process and substance are necessarily linked. It is simply not possible to govern a highly interventionist unitary state solely through primary legislation.[73] To reject altogether the process of delegated legislation therefore is to reject the substance of social democratic government. Hewart's attack led the government to establish the Donoughmore Committee,[74] which responded to Hewart much as Harry Jones later critiqued Hayek's minimalist notion of the rule of law.[75] Delegated legislation was a necessity in modern society. The issue therefore become one of how best to ensure that this unavoidable fact of political life departed as little as possible from orthodox constitutional understandings of the legislative/executive relationship.

Donoughmore recommended that a Standing Committee on delegated legislation be created in both the Lords and Commons. Such Committees would examine the technicalities and vires of proposed SIs. Their purpose would not be to question the merits of government policy per se, but to 'supply the private member with

71 See Harlow and Rawlings op cit pp 119–130.

72 See *Chester v Bateson* [1920] 1 KB 829.

73 The problem of 'legislative overload' is less acute in a federal state; its scale varying in inverse proportion to the scope of the powers afforded to the central legislature.

74 Donoughmore, Lord (1932) *Report of the Committee on Ministers' Powers* (Cmnd 4060) (London: HMSO).

75 See pp 67–69 above.

knowledge which he lacks at present and thus enable him to exercise an informed discretion whether to object or criticise himself'.[76]

Neither Parliament as a whole, nor the Commons itself made an immediate, far-reaching response to the Donoughmore report. A Commons Committee on Statutory Instruments was established in 1944, and the procedures through which SIs were to pass were rationalised by the Statutory Instruments Act 1946. The Act sketches out principles as to the processes to be followed; subsequent parent Acts may opt out of the 1946 Act if the enacting Parliament so wishes, and (ironically) ss 8–9 allow the legislation's scope to be altered by subsequent delegated legislation. A further step supposedly intended to enhance MPs' awareness of and control over the contents of SIs was made in 1972, when a Joint Commons/Lords Committee on Statutory instruments (the 'scrutiny committee') was established.

A small percentage of SIs receive no consideration in the house at all. Most are however dealt with by either the 'affirmative' or 'negative' resolution procedure specified in the 1946 Act. The affirmative procedure prevents the passage of an SI into law unless it is approved by majority vote in the house. The initiative thus rests with the government (within 40 days) both to defend the measure in debate, and to ensure its supporters are present in sufficient numbers to vote it through. Debates on affirmative resolutions on the floor are infrequent and short (generally up to 90 minutes) in duration. Most examination is undertaken 'upstairs' in the Standing Committee on Statutory Instruments, although the support of 20 members is sufficient to compel the Minister to schedule debate for the floor of the house. Committee debates rarely exceed 90 minutes per SI. The Committee's role is merely that of consideration. It cannot amend the SI: nor does it exercise delegated power to pass the measure; the subsequent vote is still taken by the whole house.

It is accepted that the more important SIs should be subject to the affirmative procedure, although this is not a legally enforceable provision, and there is obvious scope for disagreement between government and opposition on how to gauge an SI's importance. During the 1980s, some 20% of SIs were subject to affirmative resolutions.[77]

The 'negative resolution' procedure passes the initiative to the opposition parties, who may invite the house to vote against the instrument's passage into law, again within a 40 day period. Debate may be taken either on the floor of the house (generally late at night) or in standing committee. Once again, access to both fora is controlled by the government. Little time is allocated for debate before the whole house: Silk notes for example that the 9,500 SIs subject to the negative resolution procedure between 1974 and 1985 attracted barely 200 hours of debate.[78] One might therefore be forgiven for thinking that the process serves little useful purpose beyond enabling

[76] Donoughmore op cit at pp 63–64; quoted in Himsworth C (1995) 'The delegated powers scrutiny committee' *Public Law* 34–44 at p 37.

[77] Silk op cit p 151.

[78] Op cit p 152. See also Griffith and Ryle op cit pp 345–350.

a determined opposition to inconvenience a government with a small majority by disrupting its parliamentary timetable.[79]

The Joint Committee on Statutory Instruments (the 'scrutiny committee') plays, in quantitative terms, a more significant role. It is generally chaired by an opposition MP, which lends it an aura of independence. Its members are supposed to eschew party political issues, and to refrain from questioning the merits of a given SI's policy, and to focus instead on the narrower, legal question of the SI's compatibility with its parent Act. In the event of apparent inconsistency, the Committee will draw the SI to the house's attention, which may then proceed as it wishes. Neither the government nor the house is obliged to accept the Committee's opinions. Nor would a court be precluded from holding an SI ultra vires because the Committee had concluded its contents lay within the Minister's powers.

The vast quantity of SIs approved by the house each year, and the obvious limitations which attach to MPs' scrutiny of such measures, are forceful illustrations of the extent to which the government effectively controls the legislative process. They are not however the most draconian example of the constitution's seeming capacity to reconcile the de jure sovereignty of 'Parliament' with the de facto supremacy of the executive.

'HENRY VIII CLAUSES'

The Donoughmore Committee expressed grave reservations about the growing (but still quantitatively insignificant) parliamentary practice of enacting 'Henry VIII' clauses in primary legislation. Such provisions empower a government Minister to use SIs to amend or even repeal existing Acts of Parliament. The label stems from the Statute of Proclamations 1539. Henry VIII, presumably having doubts about the constitutional status of his prerogative powers vis à vis legislation and other common law rules, prevailed upon an unwilling Commons and Lords to pass a Bill confirming that the Monarch's proclamations were equal in force to Acts. Once enacted, this legislation would, by virtue of the *lex posterior* rule, enable the King to repeal or alter existing statutes without further recourse to Parliament; to – as Plucknett put it – 'play the despot by the co-operation of Parliament'.[80]

Applying the Henry VIII nomenclature to contemporary manifestations of this practice has the unfortunate tendency of belittling their constitutional significance. As noted in chapter four, the relative superiority of statute to the prerogative was not established in the sixteenth century; the King might plausibly have achieved the same result through direct exercise of his proclamatory power. Furthermore, the Statute of Proclamations itself was hedged about with restrictions which substantially

79 See Punnet R (1968) *British government and politics* p 333 (London: Heinemann). See also Drewry (1988) op cit.

80 Plucknett (1960) op cit p 233.

compromised its utility.[81] And, most importantly, neither Henry VIII, nor Tudor Parliaments, had any need to justify their behaviour in terms of 'democratic' principle.

There is no legal impediment to Parliament granting what is formally a 'circumscribed portion of legislative competence to a subordinate Minister'.[82] The power may at any time be withdrawn, and subsequent Parliaments may undo whatever 'legislative' work the designated Minister has done. Different issues arise if one asks if the practice is politically legitimate in modern society?

Until recently, the dubious moral basis of Henry VIII clauses seems to have led Parliament to enact them sparingly. The authors of the 1985 edition of deSmith's *Constitutional and Administrative Law* concluded that:

'this formulation is not widely used, and it is normally innocuous if the grant of power is confined to a limited period for the purpose of enabling draftsmen to make consequential adaptations to miscellaneous enactments that may have been overlooked when the principal Act was passed'.[83]

This view of Henry VIII clauses sees them essentially as time-saving devices for remedying unintended omissions or errors in primary legislation. As such they would be only mildly objectionable, in so far as they spare the government the consequences of its own incompetence. More recently however, governments have seemingly regarded Henry VIII clauses as an acceptable means to implement sweeping policy programmes. This trend scaled new heights of executive law-making in the Deregulation and Contracting Out Act 1994 introduced by the Major government.[84] The Act empowered the Secretary of State for Trade and Industry to make regulations to suspend any existing legislation which he/she considered imposes a burden on any economic activity, and to transfer many government functions allocated by statute to a Minister to any private sector organisation.

The Act suggested that the Major government regarded the legislative process as an unwelcome obstacle which it was entitled to circumvent whenever convenient. Whether that is construed as a welcome development depends presumably on the observer's party affiliation; and that is in itself perhaps a telling indictment of the extent to which the Commons is prone, even on significant issues, to operate simply as a vehicle for promoting the wishes of whichever faction currently forms a majority of its members.

81 Plucknett (1960) op cit pp 233–234: Elton G (1960) 'Henry VIII's Act of Proclamations' *English Historical Review* 208–222: Bush M (1983) 'The Act of Proclamations: a reinterpretation' *American Journal of Legal History* 33–53.

82 Turpin C (2nd edn, 1990) *British government and the constitution* p 369 (London: Weidenfield and Nicolson).

83 Op cit p 352.

84 See Freedland M (1995) 'Privatising *Carltona*: Part II of the Deregulation and Contracting Out Act 1994' *Public Law* 21–27.

CONCLUSION

From a legislative perspective, therefore, a House of Commons 'independent' of the executive is likely to occur only when the government cannot command a reliable majority. Yet it would seem likely that such circumstances will promote paralysis rather than consensus in the house. The implications that the Commons' essentially factional, antagonistic approach to the legislative process has for the democratic basis of the constitution cannot fully be appreciated until we explore the relationship between the Commons and the Lords, and between the Commons and the people. We return to these questions in later chapters. In the remainder of this chapter, we address another dimension of the relationship between the Commons and the government, which we might term 'scrutiny of the executive'.

III. CONTROLLING THE EXECUTIVE

Although a government's legislative programme is often viewed as its raison d'être, much government activity does not require legislative initiative. Ministers retain substantial legal powers under the prerogative, through which (within the boundaries set by judicial review) important policy decisions may be taken. Similarly, Ministers may also deploy existing statutory powers, which, if cast in sufficiently loose terms, may permit the government lawfully to pursue quite different objectives from those favoured by its predecessors. In neither case is the government legally dependent on maintaining majority Commons support to exercise its authority.[85] Nevertheless, the house may play an important constitutional role by monitoring the government's implementation of its preferred policies.

MOTIONS ON THE FLOOR OF THE HOUSE[86]

Approximately twenty days per session are devoted to general debates on topics chosen by the opposition parties. These occasions are directed towards a critical attack on particular aspects of government policy. Governments with a reliable majority have no difficulty in defeating such motions, but the outcome of the vote is of little significance. The main purpose of 'Opposition days' is to provide a very visible forum in which to display the adversarial character of the British political system. Leading speeches are made by Ministers within whose remit the chosen topic falls and by senior opposition frontbenchers. Backbenchers depend on 'catching the Speaker's eye' if they wish to contribute.

One might doubt if 'debate' is the correct label to apply to such proceedings.

85 As chapter nine suggests, there are occasions when it is so dependent in practical terms.

86 See generally Norton (1985) op cit ch 6: Irwin H (1988) 'Opportunities for backbenchers', in Richards and Ryle op cit.

Observers are more frequently presented with the recitation of a collection of opposing views rather than an intimately interactive argument. Nevertheless, the process serves certain tangential purposes. Impressive (or poor) speeches can further (or undermine) an MP's prospects of government or shadow front bench office. Additionally, the high profile such debates attract offers the wider public some opportunity to form opinions about the merits of government and opposition policies.

The house has also latterly devoted some 6% of its time to motions on topics chosen by the government. The format of these proceedings is as for opposition motions, although the government will select only those topics in respect of which if feels that public discussion will enhance rather than undermine its reputation.

Motions on subjects chosen by backbenchers have recently occupied around ten days per session, all on Fridays. The slots are allocated by ballot. Three motions may be scheduled for each day, although it is rare for more than one debate to be initiated.[87] Government whips prefer backbenchers to move uncontroversial motions which will not provoke a division, since this frees other government MPs to return to their constituencies or attend to other interests. This concern has less force for opposition MPs, for whom debate on a contentious issue offers the opportunity either to threaten the government with an embarrassing defeat, or at least to compel recalcitrant government backbenchers to wait around the house until a division is called.

EMERGENCY DEBATES AND ADJOURNMENT DEBATES

Any member may at the start of business on Monday to Thursday request that an 'emergency adjournment debate' be granted on a topic of current importance. The Speaker has wide discretion in deciding whether to permit such a debate. If the request is opposed by any other MP, its proposer requires the support of 40 colleagues. Few emergency debates are permitted, primarily because they would have an extremely disruptive effect on the Commons' timetable.[88]

If granted, the debate is held at 3pm on the next working day, or (exceptionally) at 7pm on the day the request is made. Emergency debates are obviously concerned with matters of intense public controversy. That substantive characteristic, combined with their timing at a high profile period in the Commons' working day, ensures that the speakers enjoy considerable publicity. As such, they offer a useful tool for the Opposition to embarrass the government.

'Adjournment debates' in contrast, occur regularly, for thirty minutes at the close of business on each working day. The Monday to Thursday slots are allocated by ballot; the Speaker chooses a member to speak on Fridays. Adjournment debates generally entail a fifteen minute speech by a backbencher member, and a similar reply by a (junior) Minister. They usually concern aspects of government policy which impact with particular intensity on a member's constituency. Adjournment debates

87 For a fuller account see Griffith and Ryle op cit pp 400–403.
88 There have on average been two per year since 1974; Griffith and Ryle op cit p 350.

rarely attract a sizeable audience in the house, nor much press coverage. They nevertheless offer an opportunity for the government to dwell on the details of its policies, and for a member to demonstrate her assiduity in defence of local interests to her constituency party.

QUESTIONS TO MINISTERS

The adversarial character of party politics in modern Britain is well illustrated by oral questions to Ministers put by backbenchers and shadow ministers. The procedure was an established feature of the Commons' working practices by the mid-nineteenth century, and by 1900 the government fielded some 5000 questions each year on the floor of the house.[89] Questions were taken as the first item of business, and 'question time' continued until all had been answered. This meant that other business was frequently not reached until the early evening. While this practice emphasised (literally as well as metaphorically) the principle that the government should be answerable to the Commons, it offered great opportunities for opposition MPs to upset the government's timetable; the time-tabling of innumerable questions was another tactic favoured by Irish nationalist MPs to disrupt government business.

Proposals for reform were introduced by Arthur Balfour, Leader of the House in the 1901 Conservative government.[90] Balfour's plans generated considerable controversy in the house, which eventually accepted that question time would in future be held before the commencement of public business, but for a limited time of between 45 and 55 minutes. Questions not reached on the floor would receive a prompt written answer. Individual MPs were limited to a maximum of eight questions per day.[91]

Questions are now taken at the beginning of business on Mondays to Thursdays, for around 45 minutes. Ministers answer in rotation, so that the conduct of each government department is examined at three-to four-week intervals. At present, up to 150 questions may be tabled for answer every day. It is unlikely that many more than two dozen will be dealt with in the short time available. Those questions not reached on the floor are answered in writing. Oral proceedings attract considerable attention, both from MPs and the media. Members are thus extremely keen to ensure that their particular question is delivered and answered on the floor. To have any chance of securing this objective, members must submit questions ten days in advance to the 'Table Office', which numbers them at random. Ministers thus have the opportunity to arrange for their officials to provide them with detailed answers to the specific questions raised, and to anticipate follow-up questions ('supplementaries') which might be put immediately after the Minister gives her reply.

Both the content and the style of questions to Ministers are subject to convoluted

89 Chester N (1977) 'Questions in the house', in Walkland and Ryle op cit.

90 Balfour, when Secretary of State for Ireland in the late 1880s, had experienced this tactic at first hand; Chester N and Bowring M (1962) *Questions in parliament* p 58 (London: OUP).

91 The daily maximum is now two per member per day, and no more than eight may be tabled in any 10 sitting days.

rules, interpretation of which is entrusted to the Speaker.[92] The Speaker exercises virtually unconfined discretion over the number of supplementary questions which may be put, both by the mover of the question and other MPs. The Speaker also chooses which members will speak. Successive Speakers have adhered to rather different policies on this issue, with some favouring more expansive exploration of a small number of questions, and others preferring to maximise the number of members called upon to speak.[93]

Erskine May tells us that: 'the purpose of a question is to obtain information or press for action'.[94] However one might doubt whether such sentiments underlie many of the questions currently tabled. Griffith and Ryle suggest that in the past 30 years questions have become considerably less specific. Rather than request that a Minister comment upon a particular detailed issue, often affecting the member's constituency, contemporary questions and the associated supplementaries are increasingly likely to be couched at a general level.[95] One might now be forgiven for thinking that the primary purpose of questions moved by opposition MPs is to use a supplementary to expose a Minister's inability to think on her feet, while government backbenchers offer Ministers the opportunity to engage in self-congratulation.

Despite the evidently increasing frequency of sycophantic questions from government backbenchers,[96] it would be an oversimplification to suggest that party loyalties create an absolute rule, rather than merely a strong presumption, of deference between a government's backbench MPs and its Ministers during questions. Small handfuls of MPs, generally acting in collective defence of their individual constituency interests can deploy the high public profile that question time provides severely to undermine a Minister's standing in the house and in Cabinet. A forceful recent example is provided by the furore which met the announcement in April 1995 by the then Health Secretary (Virginia Bottomley) that several London hospitals were to be closed to curb rising public expenditure. The policy was substantively unpalatable to Conservative MPs whose constituencies contained such hospitals. MPs were however further aggrieved by the procedures used for the announcement – a written answer in Hansard rather than orally in the house. Peter Brooke MP (a former Cabinet colleague of Bottomley) accused her in the house of 'lacking moral courage' by not making a personal statement. The insult ensured that the episode gained considerable publicity, to the extent that rumours circulated suggesting Bottomley would be sacked by the Prime Minister. No such consequences immediately ensued, but it was widely assumed that Bottomley's chances of assuming higher office had been fundamentally damaged by her humiliation in the house.

Vigorous defence of isolated constituency interests has always been a hallmark of

[92] Griffith and Ryle op cit pp 254–258. In practice, the Speaker delegates this role to clerks in the Table Office. The most important rule is that the question's subject matter must fall within the particular Minister's sphere of departmental responsibility.

[93] Griffith and Ryle op cit pp 369–70: Laundy op cit.

[94] Op cit at p 337.

[95] Op cit pp 254–258.

[96] See for example Hattersley R (1992) 'The beggaring of PM's question time' *The Guardian* 28 January.

backbench behaviour, and serves as a constant reminder that the localist origins of the Commons' representative system has not been entirely subsumed beneath the demands of party politics. Government whips may take a benevolent view of individual members who defy party policy in order to be seen to support their constituents' concerns, especially when such a 'rebellion' raises no prospect of defeat for the government. It would take an unusual combination of circumstances for this aspect of the MP's role to present a serious threat even to an individual Minister, still less to the government as a whole. The Bottomley incident was noteworthy because the government then had a Commons majority of barely a dozen, and had announced hospital closures in the constituencies of several of its backbench MPs.

Private notice questions

This mechanism allows members to raise a question for oral answer by the relevant Minister on matters of urgency and importance. The Speaker decides whether the question merits oral answer. In the 1980s, an average 30 to 40 PNQs were permitted. Exchanges lasted for an average of 20 minutes; appreciably longer than the Commons devotes to individual questions raised at question time.[97] Since 1980, 30–40% of PNQs accepted by the Speaker have been tabled by the opposition front bench, with most of the remainder coming from opposition rather than government backbenchers.[98]

PRIME MINISTERIAL ACCOUNTABILITY ON THE FLOOR OF THE HOUSE

Between 1960 and 1999, the Prime Minister took questions on the floor for 15 minute periods on Tuesday and Thursday afternoons. This practice began following a recommendation of the Select Committee on Procedure. Prior to that date, questions to the Prime Minister enjoyed no special priority over and above questions to other Ministers, which meant that on many days the Prime Minister was never called upon to give oral answers.[99]

Proceedings are now generally dominated by a ritualised clash between the Prime Minister and the Leader of the Opposition. The Leader of the Opposition is generally permitted to put as many as three questions consecutively to the Prime Minister. The opportunity this offers for immediate argument is perhaps as close as the house ever gets to witnessing a debate in the cut and thrust sense of the word. The exchanges are perhaps most significant for the impact they have on MP's perceptions of their respective leader's abilities. In the factionalised arena the house offers, a Prime Minister who continually bests the Leader of the Opposition is unlikely to find her ascendancy in her party under threat, while opposition MPs may be tempted to conclude that their prospects of future electoral success are much hampered by their Leader's

97 See Griffith and Ryle op cit pp 374–376.

98 Griffith and Ryle op cit pp 357 and 375 respectively.

99 See Jones G (1973) 'The Prime Minister and parliamentary questions' *Parliamentary Affairs* 260–272.

evident inadequacies on the floor. All recent Prime Ministers have devoted much time and effort to preparing themselves for this brief exposure to the house.[100]

For opposition MPs, the opportunity to speak is little more than a chance to attract a good deal of publicity by indulging in splenetic rhetoric designed to demonstrate their ideological purity either to their party leaders or their local constituency activists. Government backbenchers, in contrast, are likely to produce questions which enable the Prime Minister to lavish praise on particular aspects of government policy.

Immediately after the 1997 general election, Prime Minister Blair appeared to favour a more thoughtful approach to Prime Minister's question time by proposing that the previous two 15 minute slots be replaced with a single half hour session, evidently to enable issues to be examined in more depth. In practice, that worthy ambition seems to have been disregarded. The first years of the Blair government saw question time used increasingly by Labour MPs to indulge the government's apparent fondness for being showered with meaningless compliments couched in inane language, many of which were evidently extracted by the backbenchers concerned from lists of prepared questions produced by the government.[101] Some of the more egregiously sycophantic questions put by Labour backbenchers included the following gems of intellectual rigour and probing inquiry. In December 1997, Barry Sheerman MP came up with this inquiry to the Prime Minister:

> 'Does my right honourable friend agree that 18 years of the Conservatives' misguided policies have done great damage to our town and city centres?'.

That the Prime Minister was able to answer 'Yes' is hardly a surprise, a state of affairs replicated by his similar replies to the following question from Don Touhig MP on 21 October 1998:

> 'May I tell my right hon Friend that the people who sent me to this House warmly welcome the extra £40 Billion promised for health and education. They see it as an investment in their future. Will he make clear that cutting spending on schools and hospitals is the Tory way? It is not our way.'

and to the question placed by Alan Johnson MP a week later:

> 'Will [the PM] assure me that the Government will continue to promote fairness in the workplace, thus ensuring that the Conservative Party, which opposes the minimum wage and minimum standards, will remain a very minimum party?'

That MPs and ministers feel it appropriate to waste the Commons' evidently limited and supposedly valuable time on such nonsense is in itself regrettable. That such questions are also manifestly an insult to the intelligence of voters provides further justification for the contention that the House of Commons is a quite inadequate vehicle for the sensible representation of political opinion in a modern democratic society.

100 See Jones (1973) op cit for a detailed explanation of the mechanics of Prime Ministerial preparation.

101 See the Diary column in *The Guardian* 24 February 1999.

The copious media attention which Prime Minister's Question Time attracts both in the house and in the media may create a rather misleading impression. A revealing study published in 1990 noted that since 1945 Prime Ministers have contributed far less frequently to life on the floor of the house than their predecessors.[102] James Callaghan, Labour Prime Minister from 1976–1979, and Margaret Thatcher were particularly reluctant to participate in general debates, whether on government or opposition motions or during the passage of legislation. The study suggests that both Prime Ministers (but especially Thatcher) saw their role predominantly as that of running the executive rather than making themselves answerable to the Commons. Tony Blair's Premiership has seemingly continued this trend. If this view is correct, it identifies a thus far overlooked but nevertheless highly significant aspect of the executive's contemporary dominance of the Commons.

EARLY DAY MOTIONS

'Early day motions' provide what is in effect a noticeboard on which MPs can register their concern about particular issues. The mechanism enables a member to table a motion to which supportive MPs may append their signature. There are no limits either on the number of such motions that an individual MP may propose, nor on their contents. The number of motions tabled has risen precipitately since 1945, from fewer than 100 per year to over 1500 by the late 1980s.[103]

EDMs are very rarely debated in the house. Their primary purpose tends to be as an initial step in a campaign to generate publicity within the house, often in the hope that the issue concerned will subsequently be picked up by the government, the opposition, or a private member who has won a slot for an adjournment debate or private member's Bill, and thereby receive relatively extensive discussion. The device is a particularly helpful way for government backbenchers to demonstrate their strength of feeling on particular matters, and thereby occasionally 'persuade' Ministers to reverse significant policy decisions.[104]

QUESTIONS FOR WRITTEN ANSWER

For MPs whose main concern is with eliciting information from the government rather than simply confronting a Minister, the 'question for written answer' may prove a more effective tool than seeking an oral answer.[105] There is no limit on the number of such questions that MPs may table. In recent years, as many as 40,000 have

102 Dunleavy P, Jones G, and O'Leary B (1990) 'Prime Ministers and the Commons: patterns of behaviour 1868–1987' *Public Administration* 123–140.

103 Griffith and Ryle op cit pp 380–381.

104 For a pertinent recent example see Drewry G (1983) 'The National Audit Act – half a loaf' *Public Law* 531–537. See also Norton (1985) op cit ch 6.

105 For a useful guide to the emergence, growth and current utility of written questions see Borthwick R (1979) 'Questions and debates', in Walkland op cit.

been raised in a single session. Questions for written answer are often less partisan than proceedings on the floor. They are often more precisely targeted and more fully answered than their oral counterparts. As such, they represent a valuable resource for backbenchers, since in effect they force the government to undertake research which neither the member herself nor the Commons' library may have the capacity to carry out.[106]

INFORMAL PROCESSES

It may be that the most important vehicle for backbench influence on government behaviour is one that defies any straightforward calibration – namely the informal (and often invisible) processes of consultation and lobbying of Ministers by individual members on matters of constituency or general concern. Quite often, such influence will be entirely pre-emptive in nature – potential conflicts between front bench policy and back bench opinion are filtered out by modification to government policies before they make even an initial appearance. Party whips play an important part in this process, by acting as a conduit of backbench sentiment to the Cabinet and individual Ministers.

One can only speculate on the extent to which such pressure is effectively applied through channels hidden from public view.[107] Equally, there is no reliable way of knowing whether governments engage in self-censorship of some of their preferred policy objectives simply because they doubt their proposals would find favour in the house.

Thus far, this section has been concerned with the role MPs play in an individual capacity, or as members of ad hoc alliances over specific policy issues. But the Commons' efforts to oversee and influence executive behaviour are also expressed in a more formal, collective manner through the mechanisms of 'select committees'.

THE DEPARTMENTAL SELECT COMMITTEE SYSTEM

The 'domestic committees' of the Commons, which are concerned primarily with regulating the House's internal proceedings, will be considered in chapter eight. This section considers the role played by those Commons select committees which supposedly facilitate MPs' scrutiny of government behaviour.

'Select committees' have a potted parliamentary history. Their modern origins derive from an ad hoc Committee established in 1855 to examine the government's conduct of the Crimean War, when the Army frequently found itself lacking basic supplies. The initiative came from John Roebuck, a radical MP, and was staunchly

106 Although the government does sometimes decline to answer questions on the grounds that the cost of doing so would be prohibitive; see Griffith and Ryle op cit pp 373–374.

107 See Norton P (1982) '"Dear Minister" . . . The importance of MP to minister correspondence' *Parliamentary Affairs* 59–72.

resisted by the government which considered it incompatible with orthodox understandings of the separation of powers. Gladstone, in seeking to persuade the house not to establish the Committee, condemned it as an unprecedented and unconstitutional intrusion into the sphere of executive responsibility. On being overwhelmingly defeated in the subsequent vote, the government resigned, expecting that the Committee's inquiry would reveal grave errors in its policies.[108]

The Crimea committee was a single issue body of limited duration. The Public Accounts Committee (PAC), created in 1861, has in contrast been a permanent feature of the Commons' organisational landscape. The PAC scrutinises the implementation of the government's expenditure plans. It is chaired by an opposition MP, frequently one who was formerly a Treasury Minister. It has extensive investigatory powers and substantial resources to carry out its tasks. Its reports invariably attract a prompt and considered Treasury reply, and many of its recommendations have influenced subsequent government practice. In consequence, the PAC has gradually acquired a formidable reputation, and is widely regarded as an effective tool for the Commons to raise concerns about government expenditure.[109] But as we shall see below, it might justly be regarded as something of an exception to the general trend.

The Crossman reforms

It would be inaccurate to suggest that there was a select committee *system* until the 1960s. Prior to that date, most such committees were ad hoc bodies, established to deal with specific problems. In 1965, the Labour Prime Minister Harold Wilson supported proposals formulated by one of his Ministers, Richard Crossman, that the house should create two permanent select committees, which would scrutinise government policy in the areas of Science and Agriculture. Crossman presented his initiative as in part a means of enhancing government performance. He envisaged Committees of a dozen or so backbench members, who would gain some expertise in a particular policy field. The committees would have a functional rather than departmental remit, and could conceivably find themselves examining the behaviour of several Ministries. Their membership would reflect party balance in the house, but it was intended that their members would put aside party loyalties and advance the collective interest of the Commons overall. Thus constituted, the Committees 'could provide an astringent stimulus to . . . our Departments by ventilating issues and exploring corners which had been covered up in the past'.[110]

Crossman was concerned to redress what he saw as an undesirable imbalance of power between the Commons and the Cabinet:

'Ministers aren't bothered by Parliament, indeed they're hardly ever there . . . The amount of

108 See Magnus P (1963) *Gladstone* pp 118–119 (London: John Murray).

109 See Bates St J (1988) 'Scrutiny of administration': and Robinson R (1988) 'The House of Commons and public money', both in Ryle and Richards op cit: McEldowney J (1988) 'The contingencies fund and the Parliamentary scrutiny of public finance' *Public Law* 232–245.

110 Crossman R (1979) *Diaries* pp 200–201 (London: Mandarin).

time a Minister spends on the front bench is very small. The Executive reigns supreme in Britain and has minimum trouble from the legislature'.[111]

The policy had been strongly opposed by some Ministers. The Treasury feared that Committees would act as lobbyists for additional departmental expenditure, while others resented in principle the notion that their Departments' workings should be exposed to constant Commons scrutiny.[112]

It is not clear if Crossman and Wilson were sincere about enhancing the Commons' role vis à vis the Cabinet. Wilson's biographer records that they saw the Committees as: 'a means for keeping bored backbenchers out of mischief, rather than as a rod for their own backs'.[113] Four further Committees were established.[114] But the government quickly displayed little tolerance for Committee activities which effectively questioned government policy. The chief casualty of Wilson's disenchantment was the Agriculture Committee, which was disbanded after displaying considerable investigative independence on the issue of the impact that British accession to the EEC would have on the domestic farming industry.

It is worth noting that this episode also demonstrates how our constitutional culture has normalised the presumption that the government should control the Commons. Technically, of course, the government could neither create nor disband a Commons committee. That is a matter for the house itself. It seems however quite clear that when the house did indeed vote to abolish the Agriculture Committee, the Labour majority in favour of doing so was responding more to pressure from government whips rather than to a considered review of the merits of the case.

One might therefore crudely (but defensibly) conclude that the Crossman Committees did sometimes prove effective as a vehicle for enhancing MPs' knowledge on issues which cut across the party divide. What they seemingly did not do was convince MPs that their primary loyalty lay to their country, their constituents, or the Commons, rather than to their party.

The 1979 reforms

It is perhaps no coincidence that the Crossman reforms were promoted by a government with (initially) a very small Commons majority. The 1974–1979 Labour government which accepted far more systematic proposals from the Commons' Procedure Committee had similarly precarious support. This might suggest that governments

111 Crossman R (1979) *Diaries* p 275.

112 Crossman records the First Secretary to the Treasury, Michael Stewart, as arguing in Cabinet that: 'a backbench MP has a perfectly satisfactory job to do and there is no reason to create work for him to keep him happy. Indeed, our backbenchers should be thankful that . . . we want to keep the Executive strong, not to strengthen Parliamentary control. Michael's remarks had been applauded by many people around the table'; Crossman R (1979) *Diaries* p 275.

113 Pimlott op cit p 518. Note also the extract from Crossman's *Diaries* with which Griffith and Ryle preface their book on Parliament: 'The government has had its summer recess – a delicious time for any government. Now we have got to settle down to the dreary nagging strain of Parliament'.

114 Dealing respectively with Education and Science, Race Relations and Immigration, Scottish Affairs and Overseas Aid.

are more likely to accommodate the supposed independence of the Commons when they cannot invariably rely on a working majority.[115] However, the proposals were adopted by the subsequent Conservative government (which did enjoy a sizeable majority),[116] and were implemented (if only in part) under the tutelage of the then Leader of the House, Norman St John Stevas.

The reform's supposed objective (according to both St John Stevas and his Labour predecessor Michael Foot) was to reverse a perception that the Commons was becoming increasingly impotent in the face of government majorities in the house: the Procedure Committee had argued in 1978 that: 'the day-to-day working of the Constitution is now weighted in favour of the government to a degree which arouses widespread anxiety'.[117]

The method adopted to address this supposed problem was to create a dozen Select Committees, each having eleven to thirteen members, which would closely scrutinise the work of particular departments.[118] Membership was to be fixed for the life of a Parliament, so that MPs could develop specialised knowledge of particular issues. Members were to be chosen by a special Committee of Selection rather than by party whips. A principle nevertheless emerged to the effect that a government with a majority in the house would retain a majority on each committee. It also appears that both government and opposition whips have in practice succeeded in gaining de facto control of the appointment process.[119] Ministers could not serve on committees, and there was a hope, if not an expectation, that members would approach their task in an independent and fair-minded spirit. Their activities were to be overseen and co-ordinated by a Liaison Committee comprising the chairpersons of the individual committees.

The new select committees have been in operation long enough for us to form tentative impressions about their impact on the government/Commons relationship by noting several issues of general applicability and by focusing on some of the more significant episodes in their thus far brief history.[120]

The Committees have undoubtedly been prolific in terms of the number and diversity of reports which they have produced. On a few occasions, these reports seem to have led directly to shifts in government policy. Others are intended either to filter in

115 Although the then Labour chief whip, Michael Cocks, had little empathy with the proposals: 'I didn't want any bloody select committee examining what we were up to!' quoted by White M and Norton-Taylor R (1995) 'Commons watchdogs lack full set of teeth' *The Guardian* 22 March.

116 For the figures see table 7.5.

117 Quoted in Drewry (1985a) op cit p 136. See Baines P (1985) 'The history and rationale of the 1979 reforms', in Drewry G (ed) *The new select committees* (Oxford: Clarendon Press): Johnson op cit.

118 The Committees being Agriculture, Defence, Education, Employment, Energy, Environment, Foreign Affairs, Home Affairs, Scottish Affairs, Social Services, Trade and Industry, Transport, Treasury and Civil Service, and Welsh Affairs.

119 See Griffith and Ryle op cit pp 417–420.

120 For examples see Nixon J and Nixon N (1983) 'The social services committee' *Journal of Social Policy* 331–355: Hawes D (1992) 'Parliamentary select committees: some case studies in contingent influence' *Policy and Politics* 227–235. More generally see Drewry (1985) (ed) op cit.

the longer term into the general process of governmental policymaking, or merely to draw attention to issues whose complexities have thus far remained unappreciated.[121] This gradual accumulation of expert knowledge on a wide variety of issues is perhaps the most successful area of Committee activity thus far. In other respects, their impact has been far more limited.

Unlike the PAC, the departmental select committees are not well-resourced in terms of accommodation in the house and research and administrative support. The Committees do not control any resources of their own; their expenditure is determined by the House of Commons Commission. In this respect, they fare very poorly in comparison with the legislative committee system of the US Congress, which enjoys considerable power and prestige within the US government process. The two systems are not of course directly comparable, since the US constitution adheres to a more rigid separation of powers than Britain's, and often finds itself accommodating a national executive and legislature controlled by different political parties. Nevertheless, the select committees' paucity of resources undermines their capacity to be fully informed on relevant aspects of government policy.

A further significant constraint on the committees' efficacy derives from their (practically) limited powers to extract information from unwilling government departments. St John Stevas announced to the house in 1979 that:

> 'I give the House the pledge on the part of the government that every Minister from the most senior Cabinet Minister to the most junior Under-Secretary will do all in his or her power to co-operate with the new system of Committees and make it a success'.[122]

One cannot know if such a promise was made in good faith. Nor can one know if Committee members exercise their power 'to send for persons, papers and records' in fearless disregard of Ministerial sensibilities. But it is evident that a Minister may simply refuse to attend a Committee inquiry. Or she may decline to answer questions on particular subjects. It may be politically embarrassing for a Minister to behave in this way, and may expose her to both parliamentary and public criticism. But one must surely assume that she is non-cooperative because a candid discussion would reveal information of an even more embarrassing or damaging nature.

Ministers are frequently reluctant to permit senior civil servants to contribute to Committee inquiries. The Employment Committee's inquiry into the GCHQ affair was severely hindered by the government's refusal to allow the Director of GCHQ to give evidence. Similarly, the controversy engendered by the so called Westland Affair,[123] prompted inquiries by both the Defence Committee and the Treasury and Civil Service Committee; both were hampered by the government's decision not to allow particular civil servants to appear.[124]

121 See generally Griffith and Ryle op cit pp 423–428.

122 *HCD*, 25 June 1979 c 45; quoted in Turpin op cit p 384.

123 We will revisit Westland below in ch 9.

124 Hennessy P (1986) 'Helicopter crashes into Cabinet: Prime Minister and constitution hurt' *Journal of Law and Society* 423–432.

A further indication of the government's somewhat restrictive interpretation of 'full co-operation' was provided by a 1980 *Memorandum of Guidance* which indicated that certain types of documentary evidence would not be available. The text of the *Memorandum* lent itself to extremely broad interpretation. The forbidden territory included, for example, 'Questions in the field of political controversy'; 'advice given to Ministers by their departments'; the discussions of Cabinet committees; and 'inter-departmental exchanges on policy issues'.

The list suggests that the Thatcher government was no more willing than previous administrations to open its activities up to searching Commons' scrutiny. It is technically within the power of the house to insist that persons attend committee hearings, or that documents be produced. Defying an order would amount to contempt, which, as we shall see in chapter eight, may still lead to imprisonment. It is however difficult to envisage any circumstances in which a government would find itself unable to persuade its MPs to vote against any such action. Thus while the power may be significant in respect of private individuals, it is largely illusory in the context of government/Commons relations.

Most commentators seem to suggest that while the Committees have become accepted as a legitimate part of the parliamentary landscape, it is only the PAC which exercises a continuously significant influence over government behaviour: the reform clearly does not merit the label of a 'revolution' in the workings of government with which St John Stevas initially cloaked it.[125] The suggestion that governments would tolerate select committees only for so long as they did not prove a constant thorn in the executive's side was reinforced after the 1992 general election. Prior to the election, the Health Committee was chaired by Nicholas Winterton MP, an independently minded Conservative who had been a voluble critic of government health policy. The government seemingly wished to remove him from this post, but did not wish to do so candidly. Conservative whips thus formulated a rule that Conservative MPs could not serve for more than 12 years on the same Committee. Not, one assumes, by coincidence, it transpired that Winterton fell into this category. His initial reaction was one of blustering indignation, couched in the rhetoric of constitutional impropriety:

> 'What we have now is government by whips' dictat. They are now saying free speech and an independent mind can have no role in Parliament. . . . They [the Cabinet] are being seen as dictators who will not brook any dissent'.[126]

Yet Mr Winterton did not feel compelled to demonstrate his commitment to 'free speech and independence' by resigning from the Conservative Party. Nor was his outrage shared by a sufficient number of his colleagues for the Conservative whips to

125 See Johnson op cit: Drewry (1985a) op cit: Griffith and Ryle op cit pp 430–434. Some of the most enthusiastic endorsers of the efficacy of the new system are backbenchers who were formerly members of a Thatcher cabinet; cf Michael Jopling MP in 1995: 'The most important development in Parliamentary procedure in my 30 years in the House. Select Committees are giving backbenchers teeth with which to challenge the executive'; quoted in White and Norton-Taylor op cit.

126 *The Guardian* 14 July 1992.

doubt that a Commons majority would support their new policy. The episode may indeed have been, as one anonymous Conservative MP complained, 'a gross interference with the work of Parliament'.[127] Yet in formal terms, the government has no power to determine the rules controlling Committee membership; that is a matter for the house itself. That the whips' gambit was successful reveals the true significance of the Winterton 'sacking' – namely that so very few Conservative members regarded maintaining the independence of their house as a higher loyalty than pandering to the convenience of their party.

Perhaps curiously, given the size of the New Labour government's Commons majority, the significance of select committees within the house seemed to grow after the 1997 election. This resulted in part from a decision to experiment with the idea of using select committees to explore the merits of proposed legislation prior to its introduction to the house: an experiment which, in respect of the government's proposed freedom of information legislation, proved something of an embarrassment to Ministers.[128] But some committees also seemed to pursue their traditional role with increased vigour. The Treasury Committee became notably more assertive in its attempts to monitor the mechanics of the government's economic policy. More significantly, the Foreign Affairs committee subjected the Foreign Secretary and his officials to aggressive questioning over the government's involvement in the supply of arms – in breach of a United Nations embargo – to the government of Sierra Leone.[129] The next year, the Deputy Prime Minister, John Prescott, was sufficiently rattled by the Transport Select Committee's strong criticism of government transport policy to launch an intemperate attack on the committee's members.[130] Simultaneously, the Trade and Industry committee accused the government of a systematic failure to respect human rights concerns by promoting the sale of arms to repressive foreign regimes.[131]

In other respects, however, the effectiveness of the committee system was open to doubt. The first Blair government appeared to connive in several episodes in which backbench Labour MPs sought wilfully to undermine the independence of the Committees on which they sat. Ernie Ross MP, a Labour member of the Foreign Affairs Committee, deliberately sought to sabotage the Committee's investigation of the 'Arms to Sierra Leone' controversy by leaking information to the Foreign Office. Ross was required to resign from the committee when his duplicity was uncovered.[132] His example was subsequently followed by another Labour MP, Kali Mountford, who leaked a report on welfare benefits from the Social Security select committee to the Chancellor of the Exchequer's parliamentary private secretary, Don Touhig. Mountford then dishonestly denied any involvement with the leak during a subsequent

[127] *The Guardian* 14 July 1992. [128] *The Guardian* 23 June 1999.

[129] *The Guardian* 26 June 1998; *The Guardian* 1 July 1998.

[130] *The Guardian* 28 September 1999: *The Guardian* 11 August 1999.

[131] *The Guardian* 5 August 1999.

[132] *The Guardian* 24 February 1999: *The Guardian* 5 March 1999.

committee investigation.[133] Episodes such as this might suggest that ministers' unwillingness to accept that the great power they wield is in itself sufficient reason to subject their behaviour to rigorous, inconvenient examination by an informed and relatively autonomous Commons is not the exclusive preserve of the modern Conservative Party.

CONCLUSION

The Labour Party's sweeping victory at the 1997 general election (in which it gained a Commons majority of some 180 seats) did not herald any radical changes in the Commons' de facto subordination to the government. The Blair government did establish a cross party committee to investigate ways in which the Commons might modernise its internal procedures. Its proposals were mild. Foremost among them were the scheduling of more Commons business for the mornings and – in a nod to MPs' family commitments – short closures of the Commons during school half term holidays.[134] MPs whose constituencies were far from London would be assisted by a decision to make minimal use of Friday sittings, thereby offering MPs the chance to depart for their constituencies on Thursday evenings. The committee also suggested that more MPs should be enabled to speak in debates by empowering the Speaker to place stricter time limits on the duration of each speech. Whether that proposal would actually enhance the quality of debate, rather than just permit a greater number of anodyne contributions by inexpert speakers, remains to be seen. Some indication of how absurdly archaic the Commons' procedures are is given by press coverage of the cross-party committee's recommendations; the proposal that attracted most attention was the abolition of the requirement that an MP could only make a point of order during a division if she was wearing a top hat.[135]

A government with a Commons majority of 180 is unlikely to find its legislative timetable substantially inconvenienced by the lower house. The first Blair government suffered few episodes of major backbench rebellion. All came from the left of the party, in response to what rebels regarded as unacceptably harsh social policy initiatives. The most serious arose late in 1997, in respect of Bill designed to cut welfare payments to single parent families. Some 120 Labour MPs publicly opposed the changes. Only 47 eventually voted against the second reading, another 14 abstained. One junior Minister, Malcolm Chisholm, preferred to resign his office rather than support the government.[136] The government did not make any significant concession

133 She subsequently admitted her role, and attributed her dishonesty (which she characterised as 'rather silly') to ill health and naivety. See *The Guardian* 28 July 1999.

134 The Commons still has no on-site childcare facilities. A proposal by some women members that a nursery be built in the large space now occupied by the house's rifle range (!) has not been pursued.

135 *Independent on Sunday* 8 March 1998; *Independent on Sunday* 28 June 1998.

136 *The Times* 11 December 1997: *The Guardian* 11 December 1997.

to the rebels; but the episode was sufficiently embarrassing for the Prime Minister to feel obliged to sack the then Secretary of State for Social Security, Harriet Harman, shortly afterwards.

No such draconian consequences ensued in June 1998, when some 40 Labour MPs voted against the government's plans to abolish student grants.[137] Once again, backbench pressure was insufficient to persuade the government to alter its policy. In contrast, the Home Secretary was persuaded by the prospect of 50 or so Labour MPs voting against the government to modify the contents of his decidedly illiberal Bill to discourage refugees from seeking asylum in Britain.[138] Planned cuts in welfare benefits – this time to the disabled – caused further difficulties to the Blair administration late in 1999. The government offered minor concessions to the rebels, but refused to countenance major modifications. Some 54 Labour MPs eventually opposed the Bill at third reading, reducing the government's majority to 60. A further substantial revolt was triggered in May 2000 by the government's plan to privatise the air traffic control system, a policy which it had condemned as wholly undesirable when in opposition.

Notwithstanding such episodes, which attracted much press coverage, the first Blair government ended its term without having been defeated even once on a whipped vote. No other post-war government had achieved such a feat.[139]

The first Blair government also appeared unwilling to enhance the power of Commons Select Committees. In 2000, the Liaison Committee (comprised of the Chairs of other Select Committees) produced a report which urged, inter alia, that party whips should no longer play any part in choosing Committee members and that Committee membership should be structured in a fashion that offered an alternative career structure to the ministerial greasy pole. The government dismissed the proposals. Labour backbenchers were sufficiently quiescent to allow the government to resist demands that the report should be subject to a vote in the house.

The Commons appeared to have become more assertive in defence of its Committees in the immediate aftermath of the 2001 general election. In a manner reminiscent of the Major government's treatment of Nicholas Winterton, the government attempted to remove two of its most effective backbench critics, Donald Anderson and Gwyneth Dunwoody, from their respective Chairs of the Foreign Affairs and Transport Select Committees. The risible justification for the proposal was that Anderson and Dunwoody had sat on the Committees for too long. Ms Dunwoody had recently expressed the view that the government was so irritated by her Committee's behaviour that Ministers were co-ordinating a smear campaign among MPs and in the press to undermine her credibility.[140] The government then suffered the ignominy of a substantial defeat on the floor of the house when both MPs were voted back into their chairs. It should perhaps be stressed however that the election of Committee chairs is, at least in principle, a matter for a free vote. Whether Labour MPs would

[137] *The Times* 6 June 1998. [138] *The Guardian* 6 June 1999.
[139] Cowley and Stuart (2001) op cit. [140] *The Guardian*, 10 June 2002.

have proved such staunch proponents of the Commons' autonomy in the face of a whip is a matter for speculation.[141]

Hopes were raised that more extensive reforms might attract government support when the former Foreign Secretary, Robin Cook, was appointed as Leader of the House in the second Blair government. In an interview given shortly after his appointment, Cook professed himself much concerned to increase the authority and effectiveness of the house vis à vis the government.[142] Shortly thereafter, he announced that the government favoured change along the lines proposed by the Liaison Committee two years earlier. The plans were enthusiastically received in the press. Mr Cook had evidently failed however to convince his Cabinet colleagues and the Prime Minister of the benefits of his plans. In May 2002, government whips succeeded in persuading Labour backbenchers to vote against the reforms.[143] The only reform of any note introduced in the first year of the second Blair government's term was that the Prime Minister agreed to undertake a regular, televised question-and-answer session on all facets of government policy with the Liaison Committee.[144]

A forceful argument has however been made by Philip Cowley that backbench Labour MPs have demonstrated a remarkably high degree of independence from (or opposition to) the Blair government since 2001.[145] The point is overtly evidenced by the decision of 139 Labour MPs in March 2003 to vote against the government's motion in the House of Commons seeking approval of its planned invasion of Iraq. The motion was ultimately carried only because the government was supported by the Conservative opposition. A perhaps more graphic illustration is provided by the government's first defeat on a whipped vote in the Commons in November 2005, over its wish to have legislation enacted which would authorise the detention of terrorists suspects for up to 90 days without either charge or trial. Forty-nine Labour backbenchers joined the opposition parties in voting against the government's proposal.[146]

Cowley's study suggests that backbench Labour MPs have exerted considerable influence over government policy in rather more subtle ways. He identifies several major bills promoted by the government during the 2001–2005 Parliament which were substantially amended during their passage as a result of government concerns that backbench Labour support might not be forthcoming. After the 2005 general election, the government' majority in the Commons fell to 61; a scenario which suggested that Prime Minister Blair's third administration might have to be substantially more accommodating to the wishes of its backbenchers than its predecessors had been.

141 See Cowley P and Stuart M (2002) 'Parliament: mostly continuity, but more change than you'd think' *Parliamentary Affairs* 270.

142 *The Guardian* 7 January 2002.

143 One Labour MP who favoured change, Gordon Prentice, subsequently asked on the floor of the house; 'Is it in order for government whips to be standing outside the voting lobbies on a free vote and pointing to the No lobby and saying "parliamentary Labour Party this way"?'; *The Guardian* 15 May 2002.

144 For an account of the first session, see *The Guardian* 17 July 2002.

145 Cowley P (2005) *The rebels* (London: Politico's). The book offers a very detailed and engaging portrait of the realities of the law-making process within our modern Parliament.

146 Ibid, ch 5

Notwithstanding this recent trend, it is clear that for most of the modern era the House of Commons has been a body in which party politics is the dominant determinant both in the legislative process and in respect of executive accountability.[147] The house is manifestly now a factional rather than national assembly for most purposes. But it would as yet be premature to conclude that the constitution therefore permits factional concerns to determine both the content of legislation and the parliamentary accountability of government behaviour. To answer that question, our analysis must consider several further issues. Firstly, the constitutional role played by the House of Lords – the second limb of our tripartite Parliament. Secondly, the nature of the relationship between factional Commons majorities and 'the people'. And thirdly, the uses to which factional governments put whatever power is at their disposal. This last question is perhaps the most important of all. For even if one accepts that a factional constitution is undesirable in a modern democracy, it does not necessarily follow that such a constitution will lead to the production of factional laws, nor, in the event that it does, that the laws concerned do not attract the consent of the governed.

[147] A recent critique to this effect, coupled with a seven prong plan for reform, is offered by a report of the Hansard Society (2000) *The challenge for Parliament: making government accountable* (London: Vacher Dod).

6

THE HOUSE OF LORDS

Chapter five began to explore how accurately Parliament's current role reflects the intentions of the 1688 settlement; those being firstly to secure that elite groups monopolised law-making power, and secondly to ensure that no one or two factions within that elite could seize legislative power to pursue majoritarian or minoritarian ends. Chapter five suggested there has been a significant change in the Commons' role since 1688, from a body providing the voice of one distinct segment of society, counterposed to those of the Lords and the Monarch, to a forum in which the divergent political philosophies of the entire population are given expression. The rise of nationwide party politics, and the fusion rather than separation of powers between the legislature and the government, create the danger of a majoritarian lower chamber, in which pursuing factional party advantage rather than safeguarding national interests could be legislators' main occupation. Chapter seven considers how development of the parliamentary electoral system has affected this trend. This chapter asks whether the upper chamber plays an effective anti-majoritarian legislative role.

BICAMERAL LEGISLATURES: A FUNCTIONALIST JUSTIFICATION

Most modern democracies have two houses in their central legislature. They are referred to as having a bicameral Parliament: countries with only one legislative assembly have unicameral Parliaments. For example, the United States' Congress comprises the House of Representatives and the Senate. Before returning to the institutional mechanics of the United Kingdom's Parliament however, it is helpful to pause to consider once again why the USA adopted this bicameral system.[1]

The Americans' division of their central legislature was in part a continuation of the theme of the separation of powers. By requiring that federal legislation attracted the consent of more than one body, Madison and Jefferson hoped to reduce still further the likelihood that Congress could enact tyrannical laws. In addition, the two houses of the United States Congress fulfil different representative functions. The Senate has two Senators from each State, irrespective of the size of the State's population. Senators represent State interests within the national legislature, thereby

[1] On the reasoning behind several other countries' choice of this institutional framework see Shell D (1992) *The House of Lords* ch 1.

stressing the Constitution's federal nature. In contrast, members of the House of Representatives are chosen on a population basis; the number from each State reflects that State's share of the national population. This emphasises that the United States' Federal legislature was responsible to individual citizens as well as to the States. Bicameralism is intended to maximise the chances that Congress, acting within the legislative competence granted by the Constitution, produces laws that strike an acceptable balance between the interests of the States and of individual citizens.

Most countries with bicameral legislatures consider the composition and powers of both houses as part of their fundamental laws. In the USA, the structure of Congress is delineated in the text of the Constitution. Similarly, if we recall *Trethowan*, we see that the New South Wales constitution used procedural entrenchment to safeguard the Legislative Council's existence. Bicameralism was a 'higher' law within that constitutional settlement.

For practical purposes, the two parts of the United Kingdom's legislature are the Commons and the House of Lords. In theory, Parliament has a third part – the Monarch. And, again as a matter of legal theory, the Monarch retains the power to veto proposed legislation by withholding the Royal Assent. However, as a matter of practical politics, this particular Monarchical power is no longer used. In respect of the Royal Assent, the theory and practice of the constitution no longer coincide.[2]

Appreciating the distinction between *theory and practice*, or between what is sometimes referred to as *law and convention*, is essential to understanding the constitutional status and function of the House of Lords. Indeed, by pursuing this 'gap' between theory and practice at this point, we address ideas which later chapters will show to be central to understanding how and why the constitution functions as it does. The law/convention distinction is, again, an issue where Dicey's legacy provides an important starting point; we examine his ideas and Jennings' criticism of his analysis more fully in chapter nine. For present purposes, we might distinguish law and convention in the following simple way. Both are vehicles through which political power is exercised in an effective and legitimate manner. However, while laws may be enforced by an action before the courts, conventions have no actionable legal basis. Rather, they control the exercise of political power because the wielders of that power either believe that conventional restraints are morally correct, or they fear the political consequences of departing from conventional understandings.

The first two sections of chapter six sketch the historical background by examining several major episodes from the mid-nineteenth century onwards in which the Lords' legal and conventional roles underwent radical redefinition. The third section discusses briefly the various functions that the Lords performs today, offers some evaluation of how well it does those particular jobs, and assesses the reform initiatives promoted by the Blair government.

[2] We assess the nature of the Monarch's power in ch 9.

I. THE HISTORICAL BACKGROUND

The House of Lords' origins may be traced to the 'Great Council' of the mediaeval period, a body which gradually assumed a recognisably modern shape in the fifteenth century.[3] In the pre-revolutionary era, the Lords was regarded as a 'fundamental' element of the English constitution.[4] In 1688, the Lords and Commons were, in terms of their legal powers, co-equal partners in the legislative process. The 1688 revolution established the legal supremacy of Parliament, not of the House of Commons. So if the House of Lords disapproved of a Commons Bill, that Bill could not go any further. We have already noted the theory of the 'balanced' constitution. For present purposes, we might re-label that balance as one demanding compromise between monarchical (the Queen/King), aristocratic (the Lords), and democratic (the Commons) forms of government.[5]

Co-equality extended to the formation of governments as well as enacting legislation. Until the late nineteenth century, the Cabinet was as likely to contain a majority of members from the Lords as from the Commons: only one member of Lord Grey's 1830 Cabinet was not either a peer or the son of a peer: Gladstone assembled a cabinet of 12 in 1880; one was a duke, one a marquess, and five were earls.[6] Not until well into the twentieth century had the conventional practice arisen that the Prime Minister should be a member of the Commons. Furthermore, as chapter seven suggests, senior members of the Lords exercised appreciable control over the identity and voting behaviour of MPs until the mid nineteenth century.

In 1688, the peers who sat in the Lords were either hereditary peers or bishops. The Lords was a combination of the church and the land-owning aristocracy: it was not a democratic chamber in the modern sense. But neither was the Commons, whose members were then 'elected' (the word is used guardedly) by a tiny minority of the (male) population.[7] Co-equality was a co-equality of elites, not of the mass of the population. Such elitism was readily understandable from a functionalist perspective. The constitutional morality of that era discerned a vital purpose for an aristocratic veto within the legislative process: to preserve existing patterns of political and economic power.

As we shall discuss in chapter seven, the impact of the industrial revolution on both

[3] See Adonis (1993) op cit p 193. For a detailed description see Weston C (1965) *English constitutional theory and the House of Lords* ch 1 (London: RKP).

[4] England had a unicameral legislature between 1649 and 1657, when Cromwell's revolutionary House of Commons purported to abolish the Lords. Charles II, when restored to his throne in 1660, recalled the Lords, accepting that the Upper House should again enjoy 'that authority and jurisdiction which hath always belonged to you by your birth, and the fundamental law of the land': see Smith E (1992) *The House of Lords in British Politics and Society 1815–1911* p 1 (London: Longman).

[5] See Weston op cit ch 1.

[6] Turbeville A (1958) *The House of Lords in the Age of Reform* p 256 (London: Faber and Faber); Jenkins R (1968) *Mr Balfour's Poodle* p 27 (London: Heineman); Smith op cit p 64.

[7] The electoral process is examined in detail in ch 7.

the nature and distribution of wealth was immense, and led to equally significant realignments in the basis of political influence. However even as late as 1800, land ownership was the predominant form of economic power: and members of the House of Lords were the predominant class of landowners. In 1876, almost half of the country's thirty million acres was owned by barely 500 peers,[8] many of whom were also deriving substantial incomes from industrial, commercial, and residential development in addition to the more traditional vehicle of agriculture.[9]

CO-EQUALITY TO COMPLEMENTARITY: A CONVENTIONAL CHANGE

The situation of equal status between the two Houses within both the legislative process and the formation of the government continued in force in legal terms until the twentieth century. But it very quickly began to undergo a political change. From the outset of the post-revolutionary period, both Houses appeared to accept that the House of Lords should not veto legislation dealing with the raising of government revenue. The original sources of this conventional understanding are obscure,[10] but its scope was clearly delineated in a 1678 Commons resolution:

> [A]ll Bills for granting such Aids and Supplies ought to begin with the Commons: And that it is the undoubted and sole right of the Commons to direct limit and appoint in such Bills the Ends, Purposes, Considerations, Conditions. Limitations, and Qualifications of such Grants: which ought not to be changed or altered by the House of Lords.[11]

Quite how effective this principle, or indeed any other conventional under-standings, have proven in regulating the legislative process is a question perhaps best answered by example.

The Treaty of Utrecht

A major conflict between the post-revolution Lords and Commons arose in the early eighteenth century. The immediate cause was a disagreement between the government, which commanded a majority in the Commons, and the majority of peers in the Lords over the terms of the Treaty of Utrecht. The stalemate was resolved when the government asked Queen Anne to use her prerogative powers to create enough new peers who supported the government to ensure that it had a reliable majority in the Lords. The Queen accepted that she should follow her ministers' advice, and created twelve new peers.[12]

The Utrecht episode demonstrated that the Lords' theoretical co-equality could be undermined in practice if the Monarch supported a government which enjoyed

[8] Turbeville (1958) op cit p 408. [9] Turbeville (1958) op cit. See also Smith op cit pp 52–54.

[10] Smith op cit p 34.

[11] We address the legal status of resolutions in ch 8. At this point we need only note that since they are the product of only one limb of Parliament, they should not be equated with statutes.

[12] Plucknett (1960) op cit pp 540–542: Turbeville A (1927) *The House of Lords in the eighteenth century* pp 111–118 (Oxford: Clarendon Press).

majority Commons support. The affair is constitutionally significant, for it reveals a pro-majoritarian legal loophole sewn into the fabric of the 1688 settlement. For a government and Monarch to collude in this way would undermine the anti-majoritarian sentiment informing the original understanding of parliamentary sovereignty, but it would not be illegal.

A more important focus for constitutional change was provided by the Great Reform Act 1832. The passage of this legislation is examined in detail in chapter seven. Here we might simply note that the Act was vigorously opposed by many Tory peers, who feared it undermined the traditional 'balance' of the constitution and thereby threatened the distribution of economic power on which they assumed the security of the nation to rest.

The reasons behind the Lords' eventual acquiescence to the Bill are also discussed in chapter seven. That acquiescence meant however that from 1832 onwards one can begin to see a democratic justification for regarding the Lords as constitutionally subordinate to the Commons. The Commons was increasingly a body which could plausibly claim to derive its authority from the consent of the governed, as chapter seven will indicate. Consequently, it would be misleading to suggest that the Commons in 1833 was a truly representative body. But after 1832, the legislative trend was heading steadily and consistently in that direction.

The doctrine of the mandate

The more 'democratic' basis of the post-Reform Act Commons had significant implications for the power that a non-elected Lords could realistically expect to wield. By the 1880s the two Houses were in legal theory still equal legislative partners, but in practice their relationship had changed profoundly. By 1900 a convention had emerged that the Lords would not block bills that had gone through the Commons unless it seemed that the Commons itself was trying to introduce legislation that could not command popular support. The legitimate limits to the Lords' intransigence were described by Lord Lyndhurst in 1858:

> 'I never understood, nor could such a principle be acted upon, that we were to make a firm, determined and persevering stand against the opinion of the other House of Parliament when that opinion is backed by the opinion of the people'.[13]

Lord Lyndhurst viewed the Lords' capacity to block legislation as a power, which it might deploy when it thought the Commons was pursuing policies which lacked electoral support.

In contrast, Lord Salisbury, then leader of the Tory peers, suggested in 1872 that the veto was a constitutional duty. The upper house was obliged to defy the Commons on major issues unless 'the judgement of the nation has been challenged at the polls and decidedly expressed'.[14] This so-called 'doctrine of the mandate' or 'referendal theory' emerged in the late 1860s, when the Lords vetoed a government bill to reform the

[13] Cited in Jenkins (1968) op cit p 28.

[14] Jenkins (1968) op cit p 31.

Irish Church. Lord Salisbury justified the Lords' position on the grounds that the policy was not part of the manifesto on which the Liberal government had fought the last general election, and that another general election was shortly to be held.[15]

The defensibility of this position rested largely on the hardening of party allegiances in both the Commons and the country at large which had occurred by then. Party membership was all-pervasive in the Lords in 1880: E A Smith notes that '280 peers described themselves as 'Conservative and 203 as Liberal, against only thirteen of no party'.[16]

Party discipline was less rigidly enforced in the Lords than in the Commons, but was nevertheless generally sufficiently effective to assure the Conservatives of a majority whenever required.[17] Unsurprisingly, Tory governments experienced fewer problems in piloting Bills through the Lords than their Liberal counterparts. The administrations led by Sir Robert Peel in the 1840s and Lord Darby and Disraeli in the 1860s and 1870s generally secured Lords majorities for modest programmes of social, economic and political reform, although even Peel found his policies rejected on occasion.[18]

The doctrine of the mandate presents a paradox – a body composed primarily of the landed gentry[19] saw one of its crucial constitutional roles as upholding 'democratic' principles against the elected chamber. The Lords portrayed itself as the 'watchdog of the constitution', able to 'overreach' the House of Commons and seek the views of the people by insisting that a government with radical proposals test its popularity in a general election. Cynical observers might wonder if the upper house's defence of public opinion would be staunch only when public sentiment coincided with that of the majority of Tory peers. Salisbury was certainly prepared to amend his formula when the original version did not meet his needs. The Lords rejected the Liberal government's Irish Home Rule Bill on the basis that it had been approved by the Commons only with the support of Irish MPs. Most MPs from England, which was the 'predominant partner' in Parliament, had opposed the measure, which Salisbury considered sufficient justification to force the Liberals to put the issue to the electorate again.[20] This 'predominant partner' principle is of more than historical significance, for it emphasises the general point that the substance of a convention may be unilaterally altered by the individuals or groups who have considered themselves bound to it.

Such 'overreaching' was sporadically deployed in the late 1800s. The Lords and Commons clashed on several issues during the late Victorian era – especially policy

15 Smith op cit pp 166–168; Jenkins (1968) op cit pp 28–31. 16 Smith op cit p 157.

17 Smith op cit ch 5; Large D (1963) 'The decline of the "Party of the Crown" and the rise of parties in the House of Lords, 1783–1837' *English Historical Review* 669–695; Brock M (1973) *The Great Reform Act* pp 216–217 (London: Hutchinson).

18 See Turbeville op cit pp 347–351, 397–399, 411–416.

19 From the mid-nineteenth century onwards newly created peers had a slightly more meritocratic profile – outstanding service in the law, armed forces or government service were seen as legitimate ladders up which commoners could climb to the lower ranks of the aristocracy: Turbeville (1958) op cit pp 369–370.

20 Smith op cit pp 168–169.

towards Ireland[21] – but disputes were always defused before reaching a constitutional crisis. But the Lords' deference was a matter of political self-regulation. The Lords chose not to frustrate the Commons. This choice may have been influenced by the fear that the government might ask the Monarch to swamp the upper chamber with new peers if the Lords rejected a Commons Bill. But there was no legal impediment to the Lords simply blocking government policy.

There was perhaps an inverse correlation between the Lords' conventional power and the breadth of the Parliamentary franchise; as more people obtained the right to vote for members of the Commons, so it became more difficult for the Lords to find a 'democratic' justification for obstructing the majority party in the Commons. By 1900 almost all adult men were entitled to vote in elections for members of the Commons and, at the same time, the Lords' political role was shifting from *co-equality to complementarity*.

The Lords complemented the Commons by acting as a scrutiniser of Bills, a forum for debate on issues of general importance, and a vehicle to bring important questions to the nation's attention. As *The Times* had predicted in 1831, the Lords' political role was drifting towards one in which it might persuade, but not compel the Commons to forgo factional legislative programmes:

> 'among the uses of an Upper Chamber ought to be accounted that of . . . subjecting that which may be but a light or transient caprice, to the test of calm, laborious, and reiterated deliberation'.[22]

Between 1909 and 1911 however, the Lords appeared to reject its new conventional role of complementarity in favour of its traditional legal status of co-equality.

LLOYD GEORGE AND THE 'PEOPLE'S BUDGET'

A convention cannot be legally enforced. It is effective only for as long as the people supposedly bound by it agree to be bound. By 1909, the Lords no longer accepted conventional constraints on its formal legal power to veto Bills passed in the Commons. The long-term cause of this problem was the consolidation of the party system within national politics, in which substantial blocs of opinion had developed irreconcilable views around several major issues. An acute political fault line appeared over matters of social and economic policy, which, put simplistically, offers an early example of the dichotomy between green light and red light theories of the state in modern British political history.

In 1906, the House of Commons had 671 members. In the 1906 general election, the Liberals and the smaller parties supporting them won 514 seats. The opposition Conservative and Unionist parties had 157 seats. This gave the government an effective

21 See Smith op cit ch 9.

22 3 October 1831; quoted in Smith op cit p 118. One could find few better British examples of a recipe to counter Madisonian fear of faction.

majority of 357. Between 1906 and 1909 the Liberal government promoted various radical social policy programmes.[23] The Finance Bill of 1909, popularly known as Lloyd George's 'People's Budget', planned to raise taxes substantially to pay for a greatly expanded welfare state and enlargement of the navy. From a modern viewpoint, Lloyd George's tax plans seem very modest; for even the wealthiest people, income tax would be levied at only nine pence in the pound. Nevertheless, as Roy Jenkins records, the plans provoked furious Tory opposition:

'It "means the beginning of the end of all rights of property" said Sir Edward Carson. "It is a monument of reckless and improvident finance," said Lord Lansdowne [leader of the Conservative peers]. "It is inquisitorial, tyrannical and socialistic," said Lord Roseberry'.[24]

The opposing views of the 1906 budget neatly encapsulate one difficulty inherent in applying Jeffersonian constitutional principles to modern government. Carson might be seen as espousing the wealthy's 'inalienable right' not to have their property taken away by taxation. Lloyd George, in contrast, might plausibly have argued that the Liberals' substantial Commons majority made it clear that 'the people' had now consented to a more egalitarian route in their 'pursuit of happiness'.

Given the size of the Liberal majority, one might have thought that convention demanded that the Lords should not obstruct the Finance Bill. However, the Lords' Conservative majority persistently refused to pass the Bill, claiming that since the Bill's provisions had not been clearly put to the electorate in 1906 the doctrine of the mandate required the government to call a general election to decide if the citizenry supported the policy.

The Liberal government requested the King to create enough Liberal peers for the government to push the Bill through the Lords. Edward VII was reluctant to do this, and he was supported by Arthur Balfour, the Conservative leader in the Commons. Balfour had urged the Lords' Conservative majority to block the government's Bill. This led Lloyd George to suggest that the Lords was not the 'watchdog of the constitution', but 'Mr Balfour's poodle. It fetches and carries for him. It barks for him. It bites anybody that he sets it on to'.[25] The Conservative's upper house majority was almost as substantial as that of the Liberals in the Commons. Three-hundred and fifty-four peers took the Conservative whip, while fewer than 100 were Liberals, and only 43 claimed to have no party allegiance (the so-called 'cross-benchers').[26]

One might here pause to consider which party was acting 'unconstitutionally'. From a contemporary perspective, we might readily accuse the Conservatives, since the Liberals had won the 1906 general election. But to suggest that the Liberal government and its small party allies represented the mass of the people is misleading. We have already referred to the limited franchise which then existed; over half of the adult population were not entitled to vote in 1906. Moreover, as noted in table 6.2, only

[23] See Hay J (1975) *The origins of the Liberal welfare reforms 1906–1914* (London: MacMillan).

[24] (1968) op cit at p 76.

[25] Quoted in Butler D and Sloman A (1975) *British political facts* p 223 (London: Macmillan).

[26] Smith op cit p 157; Jenkins (1968) op cit pp 24–25.

Table 6.1 House of Lords: Historical Shifts in Party Allegiance

	1880	1906	1930	1955	1975	1992	2001
Conservative	280	354	489	507	507	475	222
Labour	–	–	17	55	149	119	197
Liberal	203	98	79	42	30	58	62
Crossbench	13	43	140	251	281	263	216

Sources: Compiled from information in Shell (1992) op cit p 67 : Adonis (1993) op cit p 205: Butler D and Sloman A (1975) op cit p 175: *The Guardian*, November 8 2001.

Table 6.2 The 1906 and 1910 General Elections

	Seats	(% vote)	Seats	(% vote)	Seats	(% vote)
	1906		1910 (1)		1910(2)	
Liberal	400	(49.0%)	275	(43.2%)	272	(43.9%)
Labour*	30	(5.9%)	78	(7.6%)	56	(7.1%)
Irish Nat*	83	(0.6%)	82	(1.9%)	84	(2.5%)
Conservative	157	(43.6%)	273	(46.9%)	272	(46.3%)
Turnout	82.6%		86.6%		81.1%	
Electorate	7,264,608		7,694,741		7,709,981	

* Aligned with the Liberals
Source: Compiled from information in Butler D and Sloman A (1975) op cit, pp 182–183.

55% of voters supported the Liberal bloc; 45% of voters preferred an opposition party. The Liberal position was therefore democratic only in the narrow sense of commanding majority support among a 'people' which was in itself only a minority of the population.

One might argue, (as did Professor Dicey)[27] that it was the Conservative peers who remained true to the traditional constitution. The tripartite, sovereign Parliament was created to preclude enactment of factional legislation. The factionalist label could clearly be attached to the People's Budget. In vetoing a bill of which a substantial minority of the people apparently disapproved, the Lords was presumably upholding the spirit of the 1688 settlement. The Liberal government assumed that electoral majoritarianism was the constitution's 'ultimate political fact'. Accusing the Lords of 'a breach of the Constitution' in blocking the Finance Bill, Prime Minister Asquith requested a dissolution of Parliament in December 1909.

The general election of January 1910 was fought primarily on the issue of the People's Budget. The Liberals achieved a substantial (albeit reduced) effective majority,

27 Jenkins (1968) op cit p 96.

and proposed a Parliament Bill greatly reducing the Lords' veto powers. While the Lords subsequently accepted the Finance Bill, it refused to approve a Bill reducing its own legal powers. King Edward VII also appeared hostile to the latter Bill, and equivocated about whether or not he would create the hundreds of new peers needed to outvote the Conservative majority. His successor (as of 6 May 1910) George V seemed equally reluctant to follow the Treaty of Utrecht precedent.

Facing such uncertainty, Asquith continued to seek a negotiated settlement with the Lords. A cross-party conference was established to find a solution, but failed to do so. Asquith called another general election for December 1910, squarely on the issue of constitutional reform to curb the Lords' power. The Liberals 'won' this election as well. In the aftermath of this it seemed that the King had agreed to create enough new peers to force the Bill through both houses.

A moderate grouping of Tory peers had proposed that the composition, rather than the powers of the upper house should be reformed.[28] Lord Lansdowne, Tory leader in the Lords, introduced a Bill in May 1911. The Bill proposed an upper house of some 350 members; one third elected by MPs, one third appointed by the government in proportion to parties' strength in the Commons, and one third comprised of so-called 'Lords of Parliament' – hereditary peers who had previously held important public office. The Bill did not envisage reduction in the Lords' powers. Lansdowne's initiative was designed to reinforce the Lords' legitimacy as a chamber co-equal to the Commons by reducing the obviously unrepresentative character of its members, and simultaneously increasing their apparent expertise and political impartiality. The Lords would become a meritocratic rather than an aristocratic assembly, designed to restrain the potentially impetuous wishes of a factional Commons majority by embodying a national interest owing more to sagacity and public service than wealth and genealogy.

The reform proposal was cursorily rebuffed by the government, which maintained that its plans to reduce the Lords' power would remain unchanged irrespective of the upper house's composition. Asquith recognised that Lansdowne's new House would still contain an in-built Conservative majority. Had the Cabinet supported the bill, it would have created a chamber no less powerful and potentially obstructive to Liberal policy than the existing house, but better positioned to defend any such obstruction by pointing to its reformed composition. At this point, a substantial number of moderate peers decided that further resistance to government policy was futile, and the Parliament Bill 1911 was passed in the upper house, albeit by only 17 votes.[29]

THE PARLIAMENT ACT 1911

The preamble to the Act announced that it was intended as an interim measure only, pending more thoroughgoing reform of the composition of the House of Lords,

[28] Jenkins (1968) op cit pp 139–144, 200–205.

[29] This oversimplifies the complexity of the inter- and intra-party manoeuvrings on this issue. Perhaps the most informative guide is provided by Jenkins (1968) op cit.

which would be 'constituted on a popular instead of hereditary basis'. However no such reforms were introduced. The World War I coalition government established the Bryce Commission to explore the question of reform of the Lords. The Commission's recommendations were not acted upon, but its analysis of the functions a second chamber should perform has attracted widespread support.[30] Bryce identified four main tasks for the Lords: examining and revising Commons bills; initiating bills on non-party political subjects; offering a forum for untrammelled debate on major issues; and, more controversially, delaying bills for sufficient time to allow public sentiment to be made clear.[31] We will shortly assess the success with which the Lords has performed these functions. But before doing so we should focus attention on an argument thrown up by the 1911 Act concerning the nature of 'Parliament' and its supposedly 'sovereign' law-making powers.

Three Parliaments? Or one?

The Act introduced several innovations in the way that laws might be made. The most significant provision was the grant of law-making powers to the Commons and king in circumstances where the House of Lords refused to pass a bill which had been approved in the lower house. Two distinct scenarios were identified in which the Commons and King would acquire this new authority.

Section 1 dealt with what were termed 'money bills'. It provided that:

> 'If a Money Bill, having been passed by the House of Commons, and sent up to the House of Lords at least one month before the end of the session, is not passed by the House of Lords without amendment within one month after it is so sent up to that House, the Bill shall, unless the House of Commons direct to the contrary, be presented to His Majesty and become an Act of Parliament on the Royal Assent being signified, notwithstanding that the House of Lords have not consented to the Bill.'

Section 1(2) contained a substantial number of examples of the type of bill that would be regarded as a money bill. However s 1(3) further provided that the Speaker would certify whether a bill did indeed fall within the 'money bill' definition.

Section 2 then addressed certain measures other than 'money bills' in the following terms:

> '(1) If any Public Bill (other than a Money Bill or a Bill containing any provision to extend the maximum duration of Parliament beyond five years) is passed by the House of Commons in three successive sessions (whether of the same Parliament or not), and, having been sent up to the House of Lords at least one month before the end of the session, is rejected by the House of Lords in each of those sessions, that Bill shall, on its rejection for the third time by the House of Lords, unless the House of Commons direct to the contrary, be presented to His Majesty and become an Act of Parliament on the Royal Assent being signified thereto, notwithstanding that the House of Lords have not consented to the Bill: Provided that this provision shall not take effect unless two years have elapsed between the date of the second

30 (1918) (Cd 9038); see Shell op cit pp 11–13.

31 *Idem*; Jenkins (1968) op cit pp 280–282.

reading in the first of those sessions of the Bill in the House of Commons and the date on which it passes the House of Commons in the third of those sessions'.[32]

Section 2(2) required that the Speaker attach a certificate to any bill sent to the king under this provision, confirming that the necessary events had indeed occurred.

Section 3 further provided that the Speaker's certificate on this matter (as in respect of a s 1(3) certificate) 'shall be conclusive for all purposes, and shall not be questioned in any court of law'. Section 4 then added the requirement that any law produced under the s 1 or s 2 procedures should contain the following statement:

'Be it enacted by the King's most Excellent Majesty, by and with the advice and consent of the Commons in this present Parliament assembled, in accordance with the provisions of the Parliament Act 1911, and by authority of the same, as follows . . .'

Section 7 of the Act reduced the maximum period between general elections to five years from the previous maximum of seven years.

If subjected to interpretation in accordance with either the literal or golden rule of statutory construction, the 1911 Act produces quite peculiar results. Perhaps the most notable textual provision of the Act was the characterisation in both s 1 and s 2 of the laws produced by the Commons and king as 'Acts of Parliament'. Read in conjunction with the statement in the preamble to the Act that the Act's objective was, inter alia, 'to restrict the powers of the House of Lords', the 'Act of Parliament' label in ss 1–2 indicates that legislators may have presumed that the 1911 Act created two 'new' or 'alternative' 'Parliaments'; these being the 'money bill Parliament' per s 1 (ie Commons and king after a one-month delay) and the 'other public bill Parliament' per s 2 (ie Commons and king after a three-session/two-year delay). This is, for three reasons, a difficult presumption to accept.

The first reason is that the presumption is flatly irreconcilable with the orthodox notion that Parliament *qua enacter* of statutes is a tripartite institution, and that the assent of each of its three parts is required for a measure to be recognisable as an Act of Parliament. We might readily concede that there can be no objection in legal terms to the proposition that Parliament can create law-making bodies which may exercise almost unlimited law-making powers. Nor need one take issue with the suggestion that the laws produced by such a body may be equivalent in terms of hierarchical legal status to Acts of Parliament in the orthodox sense.[33] Such laws might also be called 'Acts of Parliament'; albeit that styling them in that way would be confusing, misleading and constitutionally ill-informed. But whatever form that body might take, and whatever its powers might be, that body would be the creation of Parliament and its laws would be the progeny of the 1911 Act. To put the matter more simply, the body

[32] The original version of the bill had not included the 'duration of Parliament' provision. During the bill's passage, Conservative peers in the Lords proposed a large number of additional specific restrictions on the powers of the Commons and King qua law-maker. None save the duration of Parliament clause were accepted by the Commons.

[33] And so would override any contradictory rule of common law and would – either expressly or impliedly – override any existing and contradictory statutory provision. See the discussion at pp 34–35 above.

would be a subordinate 'legislature' and the laws it produced would be delegated legislation. From this perspective, a 'better' way for Parliament to have expressed its wishes would have been for the 1911 Act to have characterised the laws made by the Commons and King as measures 'equivalent in effect to Acts of Parliament' and to have styled them not as 'Acts of Parliament' but as 'Parliament Act legislation'.

The second reason relates to the intrinsic illogicality of s 1 and s 2. The 'money bill Parliament' is manifestly stated – in unambiguously literal terms – to be a law-making body of very limited competence: its powers are restricted to measures dealing with the subject matter identified in s 1 itself. Similarly, s 2(1) places express limitations on the results that can be produced by the 'other public bill Parliament'; namely that it cannot 'enact' a money bill or a bill which would extend the duration of a Parliament (ie the period between general elections) beyond five years. The notion expressed in both s 1 and s 2 that a law-maker can be both sovereign and subject to clear restraints on the scope of its powers is inherently oxymoronic.

The third reason – again stemming from the text of the Act itself – is the presence of the s 3 ouster clause. The purpose of an ouster clause is to protect governmental bodies from judicial review.[34] And the purpose of judicial review is to provide a mechanism for establishing that governmental bodies are acting within the limits of their powers. But there is of course no need to protect 'Parliament' from judicial review, since Parliament's powers are unlimited. In seeking to protect the 'money bill Parliament' and the 'other public Act Parliament' from judicial review, the 1911 Act necessarily acknowledges that it was creating a law-maker of limited competence.[35]

The difficulties outlined above might indicate that any attempt to discern the meaning of the Act would have to attempt to reconcile its text with the purpose that it was intended to serve; or to frame the issue in another way, to identify the 'mischief' the Act was intended to cure. Perhaps the clearest indication of the way in which Asquith's government saw the issue is found in Asquith's addresses to his constituency voters in the January and December 1910 general elections.

In January, Asquith identified the problem in the following terms:

'The claim of the House of Lords to control finance is novel, and a mere usurpation. But the experience of the Parliament which has today been dissolved shows that the possession of an unlimited veto by a partisan people, however clearly expressed, is always liable to be rendered inoperative . . . [A] Liberal majority in the House of Commons, as has been demonstrated during the last four years, is, under existing conditions, impotent to place on the Statute-book the very measures which it was sent to Westminster to carry in to law.

It is absurd to speak of this system as though it secured to us any of the advantages of a

[34] See the discussion at pp 84–87 above.

[35] One might further wonder why such a provision was thought necessary if one recalls that Art 9 of the Bill of Rights provides a general ouster clause in respect of 'proceedings in Parliament'. The Speaker's certificate would presumably be a 'proceeding' for these purposes. See further p [25] above and pp [242–249] below. It might also be noted that Art 9 is a device intended to protect not Parliament, but the House of Commons and the House of Lords, from judicial scrutiny. The point is discussed fully in ch 9 below.

Second Chamber, in the sense in which that term is understood and practically interpreted in every other democratic country.

The limitation of the veto is the first and most urgent step to be taken; for it is the condition precedent to the attainment of the great legislative reforms which our party has at heart . . .'.

In December, he presented the issue in this way:

'The appeal which is now being made to you and to the country at large may almost be said to be narrowed to a single issue. But upon its determination, in one sense or the other, hangs the whole future of Democratic government.

Are the people, through their freely chosen representatives, to have control, not only over finance and administrative Policy, but over the making of their law? Or are we do continue in the one-sided system under which a Tory majority, however small in size and casual in creation, has a free run of the Statute Book, while from Liberal legislation, however clear may be the message of the polls, the forms of the Constitution persistently withhold a fair and even chance?'

The 'mischief' which Asquith identifies here is quite a narrow one; namely that the House of Lords has the capacity to prevent legal effect being given to government-promoted bills ('Liberal legislation') addressing policy matters for which there is discernible popular approval ('the message of the polls').

The legal question raised by the 1911 Act is essentially this: would the courts accept the argument that the Commons and Monarch (using either the s 1 or s 2 procedure) were in legal terms a 'subordinate legislature', and thus entertain the possibility that a measure produced by the Commons and Monarch could be ultra vires their law-making power? The consequential question then arising if the first proposition was accepted would be: 'Just what was the extent of the vires granted to the Commons and King by the 1911 Act?'

The s 2 procedure was used twice shortly after the 1911 Act came into force. The government of Ireland Act 1914, which provided for the creation of an Irish Parliament with substantial law-making powers within Ireland was 'enacted' in 1914 under s 2, the bill on which it was based having been rejected by the House of Lords on three separate occasions. The same procedure was used in respect of the Welsh Church Disestablishment Act 1915. Both related to matters which had been the subject of substantial party political controversy prior to the 1910 elections, and in respect of which the intentions of the Asquith government were entirely clear. Neither measure was subjected to any legal challenge as being used to achieve an objective beyond the powers of the King and Commons.[36]

[36] That no challenge was made is not of course any indication that a challenge – if made – would have been unsuccessful. See the discussion of the 'custom and practice' argument unsuccessfully offered by the defendant in *Entick v Carrington* at pp 59–60 above.

THE SALISBURY DOCTRINE AND THE PARLIAMENT ACT 1949

The scope for conflict between the Commons and Lords was reduced virtually to vanishing point for much of the period between 1916 and 1945. For many of these years, the government was a multi-party coalition involving the Conservative, Liberal and Labour parties. In that political context, the government had no need to resort to law-making powers granted to the Commons and King by the 1911 Act. The evident convergence of policy objectives for Conservative, Liberal and (most) Labour MPs necessarily meant that there was no obvious opposition faction for Conservative peers to represent, and little scope for the Lords to claim it represented the national interest against a partisan Commons. In one commentator's view, the Lords in 1945 was 'a wasted and powerless assembly. It had long ceased to play any remotely significant role in government.'[37]

The failure of successive governments since 1911 to promote any legislation to give effect to the declaration in the 1911 Act's preamble that the composition of the Lords would be given a representative basis also lent the upper house an increasingly anachronistic character. From 1930 onwards, the electorate had embraced virtually all adult men and women; the Commons could plausibly be portrayed as the representative of 'the people' in a comprehensive sense. The upper house, in contrast remained an almost entirely hereditary body.

The 1945 general election produced a large majority in the House of Commons for the Labour Party. The Labour Party had fought that election on the basis of a radical policy program which included commitments to introduce a comprehensive welfare state and to nationalise many private sector industries. It was not however clear that the Lords, whose members remained overwhelmingly Conservative,[38] would pass the necessary bills. The prospect arose that the Lords would exercise its powers under the 1911 Act to delay such bills for two parliamentary sessions.

This stance would have been quite legal. Moreover, the Labour Party's massive Commons majority had been achieved with only 48% of the popular vote. One could see, as in 1906, some basis for arguing that the Labour government's radical plans did not enjoy universal support. Nonetheless, in recognition of these changed political circumstances, Conservative peers adopted a new convention concerning their powers under the 1911 Act. The convention, known as the Salisbury doctrine (after the fifth Marquess of Salisbury, then leader of the Conservative peers and a descendant of the Lord Salisbury mentioned above), was that the Lords would not even delay any bill which had been canvassed in the government's 1945 election manifesto.

The inverse correlation between the degree of 'democracy' shaping the composition of the Commons and the conventional extent of the Lords' powers again seems to explain this change. But the Salisbury doctrine structured the Lords' legislative role only while the majority of peers accepted its principles. For the 1945–50 Labour government, the doctrine had two flaws. The first was that a Lords' majority

[37] Adonis (1993) op cit p 230. [38] See table 6.1 above.

for self-restraint could not always be relied upon. The second was a question of time. Because the Lords retained a three-session/two-year suspensory power in respect of public bills other than money bills, the government could only be sure of getting its proposed legislation through both houses if it began more than two sessions before the end of Parliament's five-year term.

The Labour government found this possible obstacle to 'enactment' of its planned legislative program unacceptably restrictive, so used the 1911 Act procedure to introduce the Parliament Act 1949. This second Parliament Act reduced the Lords' delaying power to two sessions/one year. The bill was introduced in 1947,and was rejected three times in the House of Lords. The Lords' refusal to pass the bill was arguably quite consistent with the new Salisbury doctrine convention, as the Labour Party had not expressly intimated prior to the 1945 election that it wished to see the 1911 Act amended in this way. The Labour Party's 1945 election manifesto had included the statement that: '[W]e give clear notice that we will not tolerate obstruction of the people's will by the House of Lords.' This might readily be thought to fall some way short of being 'clear notice' that the electorate was being asked to approve a governmental programme which might involve further curtailment of the upper house's powers by use of the 1911 Act. Some suggestions were made during the bill's passage that use of the 1911 Act procedure would be 'unconstitutional', in that the 1911 Act had not been intended to be used to curb the Lords' powers any further. As in 1914 and 1915, however, that assertion was not put to a legal test before the courts.

The 1949 Act coincided with a cross-party initiative to produce agreement on reforms to the Lords' composition and powers. The Bryce recommendations as to functions of a second chamber were broadly approved; agreement was reached on the principles that this body should be a reformed House of Lords rather than a new institution, and that its composition 'should be such as to secure as far as practicable that a permanent majority is not secured for any one political party.'[39]

No significant changes were made, and it appeared that the Lords might simply fade into obsolescence. In the mid–1950s, attendance averaged 60 members. It seemed the upper house would become a quaint and curious historical relic; a tourist attraction without any significant constitutional power. However things did not turn out like that.

II. THE HOUSE OF LORDS IN THE MODERN ERA

This section examines four episodes in the Lords' recent history: the introduction of life peerages; the proposed 1968 reforms; the Lords' role in the 1974–1979 Parliament; and some aspects of the relationship between the upper house and the Thatcher governments.

[39] Jenkins op cit pp 281–282.

LIFE PEERAGES

In the late 1800s, the constitutional theorist Walter Bagehot had observed that:

'with a perfect Lower House it is certain that an Upper House would scarcely be of any value. But . . . beside the actual House [of Commons] a revising and leisured legislature is extremely useful.'[40]

By the mid-1950s, the House of Commons was getting evermore overloaded, both as a legislator and as a scrutiniser of the executive. We saw in chapter five that successive governments have promoted various changes to the Commons' internal workings to try to address this problem; a task which, we might defensibly conclude, they have undertaken with varying degrees of sincerity. In the 1950s, rather than radically reform the lower house, the Conservative government looked to the Lords to lighten the Commons' burden.

The 1958 Life Peerages Act introduced a new category of member to the Lords. 'Life peers' were appointed by the monarch on the advice of the Prime Minister. They were entitled to sit, speak and vote in the upper house, but could not pass on their titles when they died. Life Peers have generally been people who made distinguished contributions to public life, such as MPs, trade unionists, military personnel, businessmen and women, and a smaller number from the arts or universities.[41] The new class of peer meant that the upper chamber was better equipped to perform its complementary function. The infusion of life peers with broad expertise and experience enabled the Lords to counter criticism that it was just peopled by elderly landowners who could not make an informed contribution to the legislative and governmental process. The characteristics of life peers do not mirror those of the general population – but neither of course do those of MPs.[42]

The shift by 1911 in the Lords' role from co-equality with the Commons to complementarity had lent some impetus to arguments in favour of diluting the hereditary element in the upper house. As expertise and ability became increasingly important requirements for the second chamber, so the intellectual shortcomings of hereditary peers caused greater dissatisfaction, and the pressure for adding appointed members intensified. Such pressures were not sufficiently acute to merit an immediate response, but had become so by the late 1950s. The 1958 Act enjoyed some cross-party support, and was designed to strengthen the Lords' complementary relationship to the Commons. Complementarity was not viewed solely as a matter of doing some of the Commons' work. Viscount Samuel, 87 years old and a Minister in Asquith's 1911 government, attributed the need for reform to the entrenchment of party politics in the Commons. While regarding parties as a necessity, he feared that the rigidity of

40 Quoted in Griffith and Ryle op cit p 455.

41 Shell notes that of 601 life peers created between 1958 and 1991 204 were formerly MPs, 86 businessmen/women, 26 trade unionists, 65 academics, 35 local councillors, 19 civil servants, 9 military personnel, 30 lawyers, 11 doctors, 15 journalists, and 50 other types of public servant: (1992) op cit p 40.

42 See Adonis (1993) op cit ch 3; Silk op cit ch 2.

party discipline had produced: 'a considerable crushing of the independent mind' thereby excluding 'men and women who might be of the greatest value to the community, but who have not the time or the temperament . . . to face the turmoil and the preoccupations of strenuous Parliamentary life'.[43]

Quite how effective life peers have been in equipping the Lords to perform its complementary functions is considered below. We might conclude this section by making a simple party political point. Even by 1990 life peers remained very much in the minority within the Lords.[44] Consequently, they made only a limited impact on the Conservative majority, given the Conservative predispositions of most hereditary members. Labour Prime Ministers made substantial efforts to increase non-Conservative representation (see table 6.3), but among Conservative governments, only the Macmillan and Home administrations followed suit. Barely a quarter of the peers created by the Thatcher governments took the Labour or Liberal whip,[45] and since cross-benchers voted predominantly for Conservative policies,[46] it is difficult to avoid the conclusion that the introduction of life peers led the Lords some way towards the situation advocated by Lord Lansdowne, and feared by Asquith, in 1911 – namely a Conservative house which could invoke its more expert members as at least a partial justification for obstructing Labour government policy. Appointing peers remained a non-justiciable issue, although a 'political honours committee', comprising

Table 6.3 Party Allegiance of Life Peers Created Between 1958 and 1991

Prime Minister	Period	C	L	Lib	CB	Total	Hereditary Peers
Macmillan/ Home	1958–64	17	29	1	18	65	870
Wilson	1964–70	11	78	6	46	141	850
Heath	1970–74	23	5	3	15	46	820
Wilson/ Callaghan	1974–79	17	82	6	34	139	805
Thatcher	1979–90	99	45	10	45	199	780
Major	1990	6	5	1	1	13	777

Key: C = Conservative: L = Labour: Lib = Liberal/SDP: CB = Cross-bench. Figures for hereditary peers are approximate only

Source: Compiled from information in Shell D (1992) op cit, table 2.2; Griffiths and Ryle op cit, p 457: Adonis (1993) op cit, p 194.

43 Quoted in Weare V (1964) 'The House of Lords – prophecy and fulfilment' *Parliamentary Affairs* 422–433.

44 In July 1992, the house had 1205 members. 26 were clerics, 20 were Law Lords, 382 were life peers. 777 were hereditary peers; Adonis (1993) op cit p 194.

45 Adonis op cit pp 232–233.

46 Shell op cit pp 91–92.

three privy councillors, played a limited role in ensuring that the Prime Minister's nominees were not entirely unsuitable.[47]

THE 1968 REFORMS

The policies pursued by Harold Wilson's 1966–1970 Labour government were intended to 'modernise' the economic, social and political fabric of British society. Such modernisation was often expressed in institutional reform, such as the introduction of comprehensive schooling and the expansion in university provision, the reorganisation of local government in London, and the emergence of the National Economic Development Council to encourage co-operation between government, trade unions and employers.[48] Wilson's initiatives were less successful in respect of Parliament itself: the attempt to establish Commons Select Committees made little impact. Reform of the Lords promised to be a more fruitful endeavour.

In 1964, Wilson warned the upper house that if it delayed government bills: 'we shall seek a mandate to amend the Parliament Act so as to end the Lords' power to block Commons legislation'.[49] The Salisbury convention made such obstruction unlikely. However the Lords initially blocked the War Damage Bill 1965, which, as noted in chapter four, retrospectively reversed *Burmah Oil*. A Lords amendment removed the bill's retrospective element, but this was promptly reversed by the Commons, whereupon the Marquess of Salisbury, defending the convention bearing his name, persuaded peers to allow the bill to proceed. The Act provides an interesting example of a dispute between the Lords and Commons which did not have a simple party political basis, since the bill enjoyed cross-party Commons support. Given the Act's incompatibility with most perceptions of the rule of law, the Lords' stance might be thought consistent with the role of 'watchdog of the constitution'. Equally important however, is the indication the controversy gives of the Lords' impotence when opposing policies supported by Conservatives in the Commons.

The episode may have strengthened the government's resolve to maintain a bipartisan approach to reform, for it established an All Party Committee to consider the future of the upper house. The Committee's main innovation was to recommend dividing the Lords into two categories – voting and non-voting peers. Only life peers would be entitled to vote. The monarch could bestow life peerages on hereditary Lords, but they would have to give up their titles to vote in the new house.

The bipartisan approach collapsed in June 1967, when the Lords used for the first time the power left to them by the 1949 Parliament Act to veto delegated legislation.[50] In November 1968 the Labour government produced a White Paper, *House of Lords Reform*.[51] The continuity in this area of constitutional development is well illustrated

47 Shell op cit p 39.
48 For an overview see Gamble A (1981) *Britain in decline* ch 4 (London: Papermac).
49 Quoted in Weare op cit p 432.
50 The issue being an Order in Council imposing economic sanctions against Rhodesia.
51 Cmnd 3799.

by the close correspondence between the White Paper's view of the Lords' appropriate legislative role, and that of the Bryce Commission. The second chamber should serve as a forum for public debate; as a reviser of bills introduced in the Commons; as an initiator of bills on less party politicised issues; and as a scrutiniser of the executive and of delegated legislation.

The White Paper's proposals closely resembled the ideas of the All Party Committee, and was enthusiastically endorsed by the Lords. However the Bill introducing the proposals encountered substantial Commons opposition. Right wing Conservatives attacked it for going too far, while Labour's left wing thought that it did not go far enough.[52] The government subsequently withdrew the Bill in 1969. Between 1969 and 1999 there were no governmental attempts to promote legislation to alter the upper house's powers or composition. This does not mean, however, that the Lords did not generate appreciable constitutional controversy in that period.

THE 1974–1979 PARLIAMENT

Between 1974 and 1979, Britain had a Labour government which never had a majority of more than four in the Commons. Consequently, the government found it very difficult even to get Bills through the lower house. It faced even more difficulties in the Lords. As table 6.4 shows, these Labour governments enjoyed only minoritarian support in terms of the share of the vote they won at the two general elections of that year. Furthermore, the government suffered several by-election defeats and defections in the course of the Parliament, which temporarily left it in a Commons minority.

For a brief period after 1977, the Labour and Liberal parties formed a 'pact', in which the Liberals guaranteed their support in return for some policy concessions. This might be argued to have enhanced the government's legitimacy (in a crude majoritarian sense), in so far as the parties combined share of the vote at the last general election exceeded 50%. However the pact had not been part of either party's manifesto, and there is no way of knowing how any such coalition proposal might have affected voter behaviour. Despite its weak Parliamentary and electoral position,

Table 6.4 The 1974 General Elections – Seats Won and Share of Vote

	February	October
Labour	301 (37.1%)	319 (39.2%)
Liberal	14 (19.3%)	13 (18.3%)
Conservative	297 (37.9%)	277 (35.8%)
Others	23 (5.7%)	26 (6.7%)

Source: Butler and Sloman op cit p 186.

52 Shell op cit pp 21–23.

the 1974–1979 government was committed to pursuing radical economic policies. This combination of a clearly factional legislative programme by a government with a precarious Commons majority and limited popular support presented the upper house with several difficult questions as to its 'correct' constitutional role.

During the 1959–1964 Parliament, when the Conservatives were in government, there were 299 votes or divisions in the Lords. The government was defeated on 11 occasions – 3.7% of the time. Between 1974 and 1979, the Lords had 445 divisions. The Labour government was defeated on some 355 occasions – 80% of the time.

Such bald statistics obviously support arguments that the Lords continued to be a Conservative chamber. However we ought to qualify those figures a little. In almost all cases between 1974 and 1979 the Lords gave way if the Commons sent the Bill back. The government's policies were not being vetoed (a power which the Lords no longer possessed), nor even being delayed for the full period permitted by the 1949 Act. Nevertheless, they were being obstructed. Passing a Bill can be a protracted process, and as noted in chapter five, the Commons only has limited time for this task. By constantly refusing to approve the government's measures, and requiring the Commons to discuss and vote on issues again, the Lords significantly impeded government policy. Whether it was constitutionally acceptable for the Lords to do so raises a difficult question, which we might try to answer by briefly considering two of the measures on which the houses disagreed.

The Trade Union and Labour Relations (amendment) Bill and the Aircraft and Shipbuilding Industries Bill[53]

The first Bill was intended to amend the 1974 Trade Union and Labour Relations Act, which, because of the government's weak Commons position, had been subjected to several opposition amendments. The Act had been primarily concerned with regulating compulsory trade union membership (the 'closed shop') in the workplace; the amending Bill was intended to restrict the circumstances in which employees could refuse to join a union without risking dismissal from their jobs.

Table 6.5 Government Defeats in the Lords 1964–1986

Period	Governing Party	Number of defeats
1964–70	Labour	116
1970–74	Conservative	26
1974–79	Labour	355
1979–86	Conservative	100

Source: Brazier R (1990) *Constitutional texts* p 527 (Oxford: OUP).

53 See Burton I and Drewry G (1978) 'Public legislation: a survey of the sessions of 1975/76 and 1976/77' *Parliamentary Affairs* 140–162.

The substantive issue seized upon by Conservative and cross-bench peers was their wish to provide additional safeguards for newspaper editors whose freedom of expression was thought to be jeopardised if they had to join a trade union. The government proposed a 'Charter' safeguarding editorial independence, but declined to give it legal force. A Lords amendment to make the Charter enforceable in the Courts was passed, reversed in the Commons, but then insisted upon by the Lords. Amid government threats both of a mass creation of peers and of resort to the Parliament Acts, the government's position was eventually accepted by a Lords majority of 37.

The controversy over the Aircraft and Shipbuilding Industries Bill, intended to bring these industries into public ownership, was equally intense. This policy was an acute source of disagreement between the Conservative and Labour Parties. On this measure, that substantive controversy was exacerbated by procedural factors. The Bill's Commons passage, during which the government's proposals were substantially amended, provoked furious controversy. The government made frequent resort to the guillotine to curtail debate, and on one occasion a government whip was accused of deliberately breaking a pairing agreement in a division which the government won on the Speaker's casting vote.[54] Conservative peers, joined by cross-benchers and some Labour members, insisted upon several wrecking amendments. The government then initiated the Parliament Act procedures, but following consultation with the opposition, a much amended Bill was passed some months later.

The constitutionality of the Lords' behaviour on these occasions is debatable. Both measures had been included in the Labour Party's 1974 election manifesto, and so were nominally within the Salisbury convention. Yet both were highly contentious matters, for which there were only the barest of Commons majorities, which had passed the lower house amidst widespread accusations of procedural impropriety and a collapse of the usual channels. Lord Carrington, then leader of the Conservative peers, saw no legal shortcomings in the Lords' position. The Lords was invoking its powers: 'for the purpose for which they were given to us – that is as an opportunity for further consultation, for second thoughts'.[55]

Again, however, we are drawn to the impact of convention in undermining the legitimacy of an undoubtedly legal course of action. Donald Shell has suggested that the Lords committed a serious tactical blunder in the 30 years following World War II by adopting the conventional practice of appearing unwilling to use its delaying powers. Shell argues that this lent an unwarranted degree of constitutional significance to a power which had been envisaged by the framers of the 1911 and 1949 Parliaments as a routine, rather than exceptional part of the legislative process. It was precisely because this power had become delegitimised through disuse that the events of 1976 and 1977 provoked such a constitutional furore.[56]

The experience of the 1974–79 Parliament led the Labour Party to pledge to abolish

[54] This being the celebrated occasion when Michael Heseltine is reputed, inaccurately, to have seized the Speaker's Mace and advanced, in a threatening manner, towards the government benches.

[55] Quoted in Adonis (1993) op cit p 227.

[56] Shell (1992) op cit pp 246–253.

the House of Lords altogether if it managed to win a general election. It did not succeed at the polls however, and subsequent Conservative governments displayed no inclination formally to amend the status quo. Yet one would be mistaken in assuming that the relationship between the upper house and the Thatcher governments was unproblematic.

THE HOUSE OF LORDS AND THE THATCHER GOVERNMENTS[57]

The Thatcher governments of 1979–1990 assumed office, as did Asquith's Liberals in 1906, and Attlee's Labour Party in 1945, committed to implementing a radical policy agenda which would overturn many existing understandings of the appropriate role of government in contemporary society. Furthermore, just like Asquith's and Atlee's administrations, the Thatcher governments enjoyed substantial Commons majorities gained with less than 50% electoral support.

Shell records that the Thatcher administrations were defeated 155 times in the Lords between 1979 and 1990. Sixty-three defeats were accepted by the government, and on 30 occasions a compromise was reached; the remainder were rejected.[58] As the decade progressed, the government became increasingly unwilling to accommodate their Lordships' opinions, with the result that Conservative MPs experienced the inconveniences engendered by the need to be present in the Commons to vote to reverse Lords amendments.

The reasons for the frequency of conflict between the Lords and Commons in this era are difficult to quantify precisely. One contributory explanation may be that Conservatives in the Commons had become significantly more right wing in their political beliefs than the Conservative peers; such differences of opinion were clearly evident in respect of criminal justice legislation in the early 1980s. Another factor may have been the profound disarray among the Labour, Liberal and Social Democrat parties in the Commons, which perhaps convinced some peers that they were the only people capable of providing effective parliamentary opposition to Thatcherite policies. In addition, the Thatcher government apparently took some time to realise that many Conservative peers were not as susceptible to unquestioning party obedience as their Commons counterparts; their loyalty and approval had to be won in more subtle ways.

The most acute cause of tension between the Thatcher government and the Lords arose over differences in opinion as to the appropriate constitutional role of local government. We will consider the philosophical roots of this disagreement in detail in chapter eleven; here we might just briefly note its practical impact within the legislative process. The government suffered temporary defeats on several minor issues, such as an attempt to abolish free bus passes for schoolchildren in rural areas, and a clause

57 See particularly Shell D (1985) 'The House of Lords and the Thatcher government' *Parliamentary Affairs* 16–32: Adonis A (1988) 'The House of Lords in the 1980s' *Parliamentary Affairs* 380–401.

58 Shell (1992) op cit ch 7.

Table 6.6 The 1979, 1983 and 1987 Elections – Seats Won and Share of Vote

	1979	1983	1987
Conservative	339 (43.1)	397 (42.4)	376 (42.3)
Labour	269 (36.9)	209 (27.6)	292 (30.8)
Liberal*	11 (13.8)	23 (25.4)	22 (22.6)

* 1983 and 1987 includes the SDP.

Source: Compiled from information in Norton P (1991) *The British Polity* pp 97–99 (London: Longman).

in the 1985 Housing Bill which sought to force local authorities and housing associations to sell special sheltered accommodation for the elderly. The Lords inflicted more significant reversals on government plans to reform the structure of local government in 1985, and the system of local taxation in 1987 and 1988.[59]

Backwoodsmen – the voting house and the working house

The government's eventual success on the latter issues required it to draw on the so-called 'backwoodsmen'. Backwoodsmen were hereditary Tory peers who took no real part in the life of the house – they rarely attended or contributed to debates. They were however occasionally prepared to turn up at the house to vote when it seemed likely a Conservative government would be defeated on a major issue. No such resource was ever available to a Labour government, but backwoodsmen were a weapon of last resort even for a Conservative government in serious parliamentary difficulties. Because these peers were so disinterested in the day-to-day responsibilities of legislative activity, they were not very responsive to the government whip. Two or three calls in any parliamentary session was the most that a Conservative government could rely on.

For many observers, even one call was one too many. Since the Lords' continued legitimacy depended upon its members gaining a reputation for independent thought and expert abilities, the rapid influx of peers who never demonstrated any legislative skills, and who were clearly acting under party orders, enhanced neither the dignity nor the authority of the house.

The problem of Backwoodsmen led to the suggestion that one could draw a distinction between the 'Working House' and the 'Voting House'.[60] In the 1980s, the working house – those peers who attended regularly and contributed to debate – was fairly evenly divided between government and the opposition. This can create the impression that the Lords could be as powerful an obstacle to a Conservative government as to a Labour administration. However the voting house, which included the backwoodsmen, was so heavily Conservative that government policies were not seriously

59 See Welfare D (1992) 'The Lords in defence of local government' *Parliamentary Affairs* 205–219; and ch 11 below.

60 Adonis (1985) op cit (1993) op cit pp 198–199; Griffith and Ryle op cit pp 465–466.

threatened.[61] This led to the apparently unsatisfactory circumstance in which Lords debates suggested that majority sentiment opposed the government, only for the non-working Lords to appear and safeguard government policy when the vote was held.

The backwoodsmen problem would have disappeared had the 1968 reforms been enacted. It would no doubt have been a simple matter for a determined government with a reliable Commons majority to enact a third Parliament Act to achieve that objective. A rather more difficult question, to which the next section of this chapter is directed, is how effectively the 'working house' performed its role.

III. THE WORK OF THE HOUSE OF LORDS TODAY

Most commentators agree that the Lords became a more important element of the government process from 1960 onwards. Adonis speaks of a 'remarkable revival'; Shell of a 'much better attended and a partly professional House'.[62] As table 6.7 indicates, the amount of time which the Lords devotes to its tasks has increased markedly since 1950. The House has climbed out of the legislative gutter into which it had sunk by the mid–1950s. In assessing how high it has since climbed, this section centres on four areas in which the Lords might have played an obviously complementary role to the Commons, areas canvassed in the Bryce Report and/or the 1967 White Paper; deliberation on matters of public concern; revision and initiation of legislation; consideration of delegated legislation; and scrutiny of the executive.

We might note several characteristics of the Lords which distinguished it from the

Table 6.7 House of Lords : Sitting Hours and Attendance 1950–1985

Session	Sitting Days	Sitting Hours	Attendance
1950–1951	96	292	86
1960–1961	125	599	142
1970–1971	153	966	265
1980–1981	143	920	296
1985–1986	165	1213	317
1995–1996	136	885	372

Source: Griffith and Ryle op cit, p 472: Baldwin N (1999) 'The membership and work of the House of Lords', p 47, in Dickson and Carmichael (eds) *The House of Lords: its parliamentary and judicial roles* (Oxford: Hart Publishing).

61 See particularly Adonis' demolition of the claim made by Lord Denham, government chief whip, that: 'However you calculate it, the Conservative Party has no overall majority in your Lordship's House' (1988) op cit pp 381–382.

62 (1993) op cit p 226; (1992) op cit p 28.

Commons. Perhaps most significant was its less structured party discipline. In part this resulted from peers' non-elected status, which freed them from any need to cater to the prejudices of their local constituency association. The weaker grip exercised by party loyalties over peers' behaviour also accrued from their age and backgrounds; for peers at the end of their careers or with substantial extra-parliamentary interests 'the bait of Ministerial office dangled so effectively in the Commons is missing'.[63] The major parties maintain formal organisations within the house, for which they receive limited public funds, and also have a whipping system, albeit of an exhortatory rather than directory nature. A peer's behaviour must be egregious before he/she suffers withdrawal of the whip.[64]

The Lords preserved a more negotiatory approach to timetabling its business than the Commons. Government business has no formal priority; that it enjoys that status de facto is the result of the maintenance of conciliatory relations between the parties and cross-benchers through the upper house's variant of the 'usual channels'.

The more loosely disciplined nature of the Lords was further evidenced by the absence of a Speaker with coercive powers over procedure. The Lord Chancellor presides over the House in a formal sense, but regulation of peers' behaviour is a matter for the peers themselves. The chamber is 'guided' on such matters by the Leader of the House. The Lords has sporadically considered the desirability of creating a Speaker, but until 2006 preferred to rely on members' good manners to maintain decorous standards. The consensual conduct of Lords' business is exemplified by the fact that although the Leader of the House is also the Leader of the government in the Lords, it has never seriously been suggested that he/she has compromised the house's interests to further party political objectives.

DELIBERATION

It is often said that debates on matters of general public concern in the Lords are of a higher quality than in the Commons. This is partly because many members have considerable expertise in particular areas, and partly because party loyalty is not as unswerving as in the Commons. As Griffith and Ryle suggest: 'such subjective judgements are impossible either to prove or to refute'.[65] One can undoubtedly point to debates on major issues where speakers have brought a formidable body of knowledge and experience to bear on the issue concerned; reform of the legal profession, the administration of justice, and foreign and commonwealth relations are areas where the upper house possesses considerable expertise.[66] The quality of debate, in the sense of its capacity fully to explore the substance of the issue in question, rather than simply advance a partisan response, is aided by the more muted nature of party politics and the more relaxed procedural regime. However, if one construes the 'quality' of debate in terms of its influence on subsequent policy, the Lords' success is far

63 Griffith and Ryle op cit p 510.

64 For examples see Shell (1992) op cit pp 93–94.

65 Op cit p 497.

66 Shell (1992) op cit pp 188–194: Adonis (1993) op cit p 194.

more difficult to quantify. Adonis concludes that Lords' debates 'rarely have an impact on policy which is more than minor and indirect'; while Shell maintains that: 'Almost everyone involved with the House acknowledges that a great deal of what is said there is worthless'.[67]

Less cynically, one might suggest that as a deliberative chamber the Lords is intended to function more as a sounding board than as crucial contributor to policy formation over the full range of government activities. Debate in the upper house seems to have significant influence only in areas where the Lords combines expertise with personal interests in matters which are fairly non-contentious in the party political sense, such as legal reform, issues concerning the elderly, and policies affecting agriculture and the countryside. The percentage of the Lords' workload devoted to deliberative activities has declined markedly since 1980; from over 25% in 1979 to barely 14% in 1988.[68] This could be construed as an indication that the upper house has become less enamoured of its reflective role in recent years, but it may also be due to rather more practical pressures.

REVISION OF LEGISLATION

The reduction in the percentage of Lords' time spent on general debate has been more than matched by an increase in attention devoted to its purely legislative role. By 1989, 60% of the house's sitting hours were consumed by the revision of legislation, the overwhelming majority of which originated in the Commons.[69] We have already considered the (now limited) circumstances in which the Lords might either reject a Bill or pass a wrecking amendment. In quantitative terms, however, the Lords' revisionary role is primarily concerned with constructive rather than destructive amendment.

The lower profile of party loyalty and greater procedural flexibility in the Lords supposedly enables the upper house to do a better job of revising proposed legislation than the Commons. Peers are assumed to be less firmly wedded to party ideology, and so more willing to accept that bills may contain technical flaws. The presence of a substantial number of cross-bench peers reinforces this assumption. Relatedly, the growing breadth of experience and expertise among life peers make it unlikely that the upper house will be unable to muster an informed audience for even the most esoteric of government legislative proposals.

Superficially, a Bill's passage through the Lords mirrors that in the Commons. There are however certain important differences. In the absence of a Speaker, the house itself decides whether proposed amendments will be discussed. Neither does the house have a guillotine procedure: rather it relies on peers themselves to ensure that their spoken contributions are pertinent and concise.

Perhaps more importantly, the Lords traditionally did not have a standing committee structure: the committee stage is generally taken on the floor of the house. The

67 Adonis (1993) op cit p 216: Shell (1992) op cit p 198.

68 Griffith and Ryle op cit p 473. 69 Griffith and Ryle op cit p 473.

committee stage is presided over by the Chairman of Committees, a salaried post, to which a peer is appointed by the house each parliamentary session. During this period, the Chairman must detach her/himself from any party political activities.

The committee stage has latterly accounted for almost half of the time the upper chamber has given to its legislative functions.[70] The Lords has conducted sporadic experiments with standing committees in the past 30 years, but none have been regarded as a success.[71] In 1993/94, the Lords made a further effort in this regard, by considering five relatively uncontroversial bills under the so-called 'Jellicoe procedure'. As yet, one cannot predict how successful this strategy has been. Pressure on time is further increased, almost comically, by the physical process of walking through division lobbies whenever a vote on an amendment is taken: 40 hours were spent simply on voting in the 1985–1986 session.[72]

Table 6.7 charts the apparently substantial growth in the Lords' activities. One should beware of reading too much into workload statistics, for crude figures often conceal vast variations in the complexity or importance of nominally equivalent subject matter. Many amendments for example, may be introduced at the government's request, to remedy defects which escaped the Commons' attention. While this may frequently be a valuable function for the upper house to fulfill, it does raise the danger of the Lords becoming a convenient dumping ground for dealing with the minutiae of the legislative process which the Commons is unwilling to address.[73] A related problem is the government's recurring failure to spread the Lords legislative load evenly through the parliamentary session, with the result that the upper house faces impossibly onerous tasks which cannot be discharged in any meaningful way.[74]

Given the then Conservative majority in the Lords, it is safe to conclude that many of the amendments carried against government wishes during the 1980s were not motivated by simple party political bias. Yet as Adonis observes: 'On not a single occasion since 1979 has the Lords insisted on one of its amendments once overturned by the Commons'.[75] A Lords amendment against the government may be significant when the government has only a small Commons majority, for the reasoning behind the Lords' decision might persuade wavering backbench MPs not to follow the party line. But when faced with a cohesive Conservative majority in the lower house, the Lords currently resembles a constitutional watchdog which has long been deprived of any significant bite, and is only rarely willing to bark.

One notable recent exception to this trend was the Lords' refusal to pass the War Crimes Bill. This bill was intended to impose retrospective criminal liability for war crimes committed in World War II by foreign nationals who had subsequently

70 Griffith and Ryle op cit p 483.

71 Shell (1992) op cit pp 140–142: Borthwick R (1973) 'Public Bill Committees in the House of Lords' *Parliamentary Affairs* 440–453.

72 Adonis (1993) op cit p 241.

73 Adonis (1993) op cit pp 240–242.

74 The problem has been posed by governments of both parties; see Shell (1992) op cit pp 139–141: Drewry and Burton op cit.

75 (1993) op cit p 237.

Table 6.8 Lords Amendments to Government Bills 1970–1990

Period	Bills	Bills amended	Total amendments
1970–1973	79	31	2366
1974–1977	68	49	1859
1979–1982	82	39	2231
1983–1986	69	43	4137
1987–1990	61	38	5181

Source: Shell (1992) op cit, p 144.

become British citizens. The bill received clear cross-party support in the Commons. However a similar cross-party consensus in the Lords rejected it for what would appear to be, *pace* the War Damage Act, 'rule of law' type reasons – namely opposition in principle to retrospective legislation, and a belief that in practice it would be impossible to provide a fair trial to the accused.[76] The Lords' behaviour prompted even some Conservative MPs to question the undesirability of a non-elected chamber frustrating the elected house, but predictions of a constitutional crisis when the government used the Parliament Acts procedure to send the Bill for the Royal Assent proved unfounded.

The upper house also inflicted a series of defeats on the Major government's Criminal Justice Bill in 1994, relating to matters of sentencing policy and the conduct of criminal trials. Most of the defeats were subsequently reversed in the Commons, but the government made several concessions to the upper house.[77] The bill had been announced as a major plank of government policy by Home Secretary Michael Howard at the 1993 Conservative Party Conference. The Lords' intransigence might thus be seen either as an unacceptable barrier to the wishes of an elected government, or, alternatively, as an entirely prudent means to ensure that important legislation was not unduly influenced by unacceptably partisan objectives.

The Lords' greater procedural flexibility also extends to the introduction of private members' bills, although any such bill successfully introduced in the upper house is at the mercy of the government, since passage through the Commons will depend on the allocation of government time. In contrast, Bills which successfully proceed through the Commons are invariably (and rapidly) approved in the Lords.[78] Bills introduced in the Lords frequently perform a 'pathfinding' role, in which proposals for reform in controversial (but largely non-party political) matters are aired, with a view both to testing and perhaps moulding public opinion, in the hope that an initial failure will nevertheless weaken resistance to future reform. Issues such as the decriminalisation of homosexuality, the liberalisation of laws controlling abortion, and a tightening of

76 See Richardson (1995) op cit.

77 *The Guardian* 19 July 1994.

78 See Shell (1992) op cit pp 151–156.

the statutory framework regulating animal experimentation provide good examples of this episodic, incremental approach to social policy.[79]

CONTROL OF DELEGATED LEGISLATION

The Lords retains co-equal status with the Commons in respect of private Bills, although this is perhaps insufficiently important a topic to merit attention here. A more significant issue is the Lords' continued co-equality in respect of statutory instruments. Given the much greater resort made to such measures by modern governments, and the Commons' obvious shortcomings in monitoring their use, one might have expected this to be an area in which the upper house might function as a meaningful curb on government excesses. The formal parity between the two houses is emphasised by the their equality of representation on the joint select committee which examines the technical propriety of such measures.

In respect of the substantive policy merits of delegated legislation, however, we can once again discern a large gap between the Lords' legal and conventional authority. The Lords has only once vetoed an order, that being the aforementioned sanctions order against Rhodesia in 1967. By the mid–1980s, it appeared widely accepted that a repeat of such behaviour would breach convention.[80] The Lords' reticence may spring from a fear that exercising its veto would simply lead to a third Parliament Act removing their legal co-equality, but quite what purpose is served by possessing a legal power one will never use is unclear. Shell points to the 1967 Labour government's decision not to present an instrument designating Stansted as London's third major airport as a response to obvious opposition in the Lords as an example of an upper house 'pre-emptive strike', but it is hard to place any precedential value on such an event. This is perhaps another situation in which the Lords' legal powers have been delegitimised through disuse.

The house has fashioned several devices for expressing disapproval of government proposals without rejecting them. Motions signalling disagreement with or regret at an instrument may be moved and voted upon. Such devices may prove an embarrassment to the government, especially if they attract press publicity, but their value would appear to be more a symbolic affirmation of the Lords' independence than a practical constraint on executive action.

SCRUTINY OF THE EXECUTIVE

As Bagehot observed, there would be little need for upper house scrutiny of executive behaviour if the Commons adequately performed that task. But as we saw in chapter five, the intensity of party discipline, and paucity of investigatory resources in the lower house places stringent restrictions on the effectiveness of MPs' supervisory

79 Shell (1992) op cit.

80 Shell (1992) op cit p 219.

capacities. Consequently, there is appreciable scope for the Lords to complement the Commons in this respect.

Like the Commons, however, the Lords' scrutinising role is subject to resource constraints. These arise not simply, as in the Commons, from the limited office space and research assistance financed by the government, but also from more structural institutional sources. While it was commonplace for as many Ministers to sit in the Lords as in the Commons in the nineteenth century, almost all Ministers are now members of the lower house. Although modern Conservative governments have included several senior Ministers from the Lords, it is likely for a Labour government that the Lord Chancellor and Leader of the House will be the Lords' only two Cabinet Ministers. This poses obvious problems of accountability, simply because the politician responsible for the activities of most government departments is never present in the chamber. Occasional suggestions have been floated that all senior Ministers should be entitled to speak in either house, but none has been adopted.

The government's limited representation in the house also poses problems of competence. The practice which has consequently evolved is for politicians of sometimes limited experience to assume quite substantial and wide-ranging departmental responsibilities at an early stage of their careers. The Labour Party suffered particular problems in finding sufficient front bench spokespersons, particularly in opposition. Almost all Labour members were life peers, and as well as being older than many of their hereditary Conservative counterparts, they were ending rather than beginning their political careers – a junior ministerial or shadow post was therefore not an attractive proposition.

With the exception of a limited number of Ministerial posts, Leader of the Opposition, and Opposition Chief Whip, and the non-party political offices of Chairman and Principal Deputy Chairman of Committees, membership of the Lords is not salaried. While peers may claim reasonably generous expense allowances (over £200 per day) for days on which they attend the house, those lacking independent means cannot afford to be full-time politicians, a factor which necessarily reduces the time and energy peers can devote to examining government activities.

Within these constraints, the Lords has developed various mechanisms to monitor executive behaviour. Members may ask up to four 'starred questions' on two afternoons per week, when they are taken first in the order of business. They are intended to elicit information from the government, and while peers may place a supplementary, the exchange is not supposed to turn into a debate. Sessions may last for half an hour, and are a popular, well attended part of the house's activities. 'Unstarred questions', in contrast, trigger a debate in which the appropriate Minister delivers the final speech. Griffith and Ryle suggest they are the Lords' equivalent of Commons' adjournment debates.[81] They are the final item on the business agenda, and despite the late hour at which they are taken, are regarded as a useful forum by the working peers.

'Private notice questions' offer an emergency procedure to discuss issues too urgent

81 Op cit pp 474–475.

to have been scheduled on the order paper. The house itself, advised by the Leader, decides whether to admit such questions. They are infrequently accepted; fewer than three per year were taken during the 1980s. 'Questions for written answer' have expanded substantially in recent years. 283 were placed in 1970; over 1400 were posed in 1988. 'Motions for debate' and 'take note' motions are scheduled for one day per week to examine the merits of general or specific aspects of government policy. They are often limited to two and a half hours duration, generally conducted in a non-contentious fashion, and usually withdrawn by their mover without a division being held.

House of Lords' select committees

Lords' select committees are quite different creatures from their Commons' counterparts. Most are concerned purely with the house's own domestic and procedural matters.[82] The two permanent Committees which have an explicitly extra-parliamentary outlook are the European Communities Committee and the Science and Technology Committee. Both are more appropriately seen as part of the Lords' deliberative rather than supervisory functions.

The EC Committee dates from 1974. Its main function is to evaluate proposed EC legislation before it is enacted, thereby equipping the British government with a wider knowledge base upon which to draw when participating in the EC's legislative process. The House has a salaried post, the Principal Deputy Chairman of Committees, primarily concerned with overseeing the EC Committee's activities. The Committee is also (relatively) quite well resourced, having a dozen research and secretarial staff, and being able to appoint paid advisers to offer specific expertise. Twenty-four peers sit on the Committee, which may appoint sub-committees to undertake detailed investigations of particular topics. The Committee produces many reports each year. Most attract a considered government response, but like much of the Lords' work, their practical impact is hard to discern.

The Science and Technology Committee has succeeded in becoming a highly regarded investigative forum. The Committee was established in 1980, and fills a gap left by the coverage of the Commons departmental select committees. Its 15 members include life peers who are distinguished scientists, and it has sufficient resources to produce a substantial body of detailed reports. Griffith and Ryle neatly capture its character by describing it as 'the non-party political voice of the scientific community'.[83]

As noted in chapter five, a major weakness of the Commons' select committee system is that Committee reports are frequently not debated in the house. In the Lords, all reports come before the house for consideration. As we have already seen however, the impact of any Lords' debate on government policy is generally slight.

[82] The upper house has also made occasional use since 1972 of ad hoc select committees to inquire into matters of current public concern. For a list and evaluation see Griffith and Ryle op cit pp 494–495.

[83] Op cit p 494.

IV. THE 1999 REFORMS

Both the Labour and Liberal parties fought the 1992 general election on manifestos which included proposals to abolish the upper house and replace it with some form of elected assembly. The Conservatives' victory at that election forestalled any possibility of reform to the upper house, but did nothing to reduce the obvious weaknesses of the upper house. The most evident of these derived from the house's composition. The Labour and Liberal parties saw no defensible basis for an hereditary form of membership in our modern society – expert and independent judgement is not a genetically transmitted trait. The essentially corrupt (because it is neither meritocratic nor representative) nature of the hereditary system was powerfully illustrated when the Earl of Hardwicke took his seat in 1995. This young man of 24 had been brought up in the West Indies and, according to a profile in *The Times*,[84] supplemented his inherited wealth by 'organising raves' and 'working in public relations'. Hardwicke, who seemingly possessed neither any formidable intellectual powers, nor any substantial record of public service, did not however find taking his seat a daunting experience: 'I had hundreds of cousins in the Lords . . . My cousin Lord Hesketh, the chief whip, was there when I took the oath and he led me to the Tory benches'.[85] He also observed that the Lords was: 'a wonderful place to take friends for lunch – although it should have a snooker table – and you always end up sitting next to someone interesting'.[86]

The indefensibility of this situation arises not just from the significant (and quite unearned) political status which Hardwicke himself acquired, but also from the equally unearned addition which his seat in the Lords made to the voting power of the Conservative Party. The Labour Party's 1997 election manifesto included a pledge that a Labour government would introduce a Bill that would remove hereditary peers from the Lords, although the manifesto did not make it clear if the party's preference was to simply retain the Lords on a life peer only basis, or whether it envisaged that the Lords might be transformed into an elected second chamber. The Bill's prominent place in the manifesto should, in principle, have ensured that its passage was not blocked in the upper house. For peers to have rejected the Bill would have been a clear breach of the Salisbury convention. If the convention were to be respected, there would be no need for the government to invoke the Parliament Acts to bypass the Lords' refusal to approve the Bill. Lords reform was not an immediate priority for the new government,[87] but it seemed likely that legislation would be enacted before the next general election.

The Conservative majority in the Lords did not however take this as a cue to defer to the overwhelming Labour majority in the Commons. In 1998, the government

84 See *The Times* 5 April 1995.

85 *The Times* 5 April 1995.

86 *The Times* 5 April 1995.

87 The new Prime Minister did begin to reduce the Conservative bias in the Lords by appointing a large number of Labour life peers: *The Guardian* 2 August 1997; *The Times* 9 June 1998.

introduced its sweeping Crime and Disorder Bill in the House of Lords. The Bill's initial passage through the upper house was uncontroversial. However, when the Bill came to the Commons, a Labour MP moved an amendment which was intended to equalise the age of consent to sexual relations for people of both heterosexual and homosexual/lesbian orientation. The amendment received a majority of over 200 in the Commons in July 1998. On 23 July, the Bill was rejected by 290 votes to 122 in the Lords. Rather than risk losing the entire Bill, the government withdrew the amendment. The amendment had not been part of Labour's election manifesto, so its rejection by the Lords could not be regarded as a breach of the Salisbury convention. However the sentiments expressed by many peers who had opposed equalising the age of consent were distinctly bigoted and intolerant, and were widely represented in the press as an indication of how far many of the Lords were from newly emergent social values. More significantly, the Lords' behaviour undermined the suggestion that the upper house served as a moderating force against a narrowly partisan Commons.

The Blair government subsequently affirmed its support for the equal age amendment by including an identical provision in its Sexual Offences (Amendment) Bill in 1998. This measure was supported by all three major parties in the Commons, but was again rejected by the Lords. And once again, the rejection was cast in such intolerant and antediluvian terms that one might wonder if the government had deliberately offered the upper house the opportunity to discredit itself in public opinion; an opportunity which – if taken – would pre-emptively reduce any public disquiet about subsequent Lords reform.

It was evident that by the end of 1998 the Conservative majority in the Lords had angered the government substantially by failing to respect the terms of the Salisbury convention. The Labour Party's 1997 election manifesto had promised that a Bill to reform the electoral system used to select British members of the European Parliament would be introduced in time for the elections scheduled in May 1999. In the autumn of 1998, the Lords consistently refused to pass the Bill, on the disingenuous grounds that since the Labour manifesto had not specified precisely the new system that would be introduced, rejecting the measure did not breach the Salisbury convention. As in 1910 and 1911, the Conservative majority in the Lords was fully supported by the Conservative opposition in the Commons – a characterisation of the Lords majority as 'Mr Hague's poodle'[88] would seem entirely apposite.

Had the Blair government harboured any doubts about proceeding with reform of the Lords, the European elections controversy would have dispelled it. The details of the reform emerged late in 1998, amid an extraordinary breakdown of discipline within the Conservative shadow cabinet. In an attempt to forestall opposition to reform in the upper house, the Blair government had negotiated an agreement with the leader of the Conservative peers, Lord Cranborne, that 92 hereditary peers would be permitted to continue to sit in the house. Cranborne had not informed his shadow

[88] William Hague had replaced John Major as leader of the Conservative Party following the 1997 general election.

cabinet colleagues of these negotiations, and was promptly dismissed from the shadow cabinet when they were revealed. Bizarrely, the Conservative Party then decided to support the arrangement.[89]

The last weeks of the unreformed Lords' life were to be a farrago of pantomime and farce. The government had decided that the 92 hereditary members who would sit in the new house should be 'elected' by the hereditary peers.[90] Candidates were permitted to issue a 75-word 'manifesto' in support of their cause. The documents which emerged prompted the thought that the Blair government had again taken the chance to allow the hereditary peers to make themselves appear ridiculous. So, for example, Viscount Monckton's manifesto announced:

> 'I support the Queen and all the royal family . . . All cats to be muzzled outside to stop the agonising torture of small birds. . . . LEVEL UP, not level down. God willing'.

Earl Alexander of Tunis invoked more nationalistic sentiments:

> 'By the living God who made me, but I love this country. . . . I will struggle with all I have to offer: For her democracy, her integrity, her sovereignty, her independence, her self-government, her crown and the rights and ancient freedoms of her people'.

Having entered the realms of the absurd in the run-up to the hereditaries' 'election', the house then moved to the surreal in October 1999 at the Bill's third reading stage. As the debate began, the Earl of Burford leapt onto the Lord Chancellor's seat to shout out a tirade of hysterical nonsense. As peers from all sides of the house watched in stunned silence, soon followed by mutters of disapproval, Burford informed his audience the Bill was 'Treason', promoted by Prime Minister Blair as a first step in the abolition of Britain: 'Before us lies the wasteland. No Queen, no culture, no sovereignty, no freedom. Stand up for your Queen and country and vote this down'.[91] Had supporters of the reform of the Lords been invited to conjure a scenario in which the anachronisms of the upper house were revealed most starkly to the public at large, it is unlikely that they could have imagined anything quite so effective as Burford's intervention. His pleas fell – unsurprisingly – on deaf ears. The Cranborne deal was respected by most peers, and the Bill passed its third reading by a majority of 140.

The house saved a final irritation to the government for the next day, when they voted again against some provisions of the government's contentious welfare reform Bill – a measure that was already promoting rebellion among Labour MPs in the Commons. Perhaps ironically, the house's behaviour on this matter offered a perfect example of the role a subordinate second chamber might legitimately play within

89 See *The Guardian* 3 December 1998; 4 December 1998.

90 The government had indicated that the reform legislation would contain retrospective authorisation for this 'election'.

91 See *The Guardian* 27 October 1999; *The Times* 27 October 1999. The ludicrous nature of Burford's behaviour is magnified when one learns he himself was not a member of the Lords, but, as the eldest son of the Duke of St Albans, had the right to sit in the house during debates. The Dukedom was, incidentally, created by Charles I and bestowed upon one of the children borne for him by one of his mistresses, Nell Gwynne.

parliament. The arguments against the Bill were calm and measured, the votes against it drawn from all sides of the house. In rejecting the government's proposals, the Lords provided a voice for one of the most disadvantaged sections of society, a voice submerged in the Commons by the feebleness of those Labour MPs for whom the demands of party loyalty overrode any qualms of conscience.

THE 'REFORMED' HOUSE OF LORDS

Given the significance of its impact on the composition of Parliament, the House of Lords Act 1999 is a remarkably short and slender document. Section 1 provides simply that: 'No-one shall be a member of the House of Lords by virtue of a hereditary peerage'. Section 2 permits up to 92 persons to be exempted from s 1, in accordance with Standing Orders made by the house. As consolation for losing their seat in the Lords, hereditary peers not exempted under s 2 were to be allowed to stand for election to the Commons and to vote in Commons elections.

The Act creates a second chamber with obvious similarities to the Landsdowne proposals of 1911, proposals which Asquith rejected, for fear that a more legitimately composed house would be more obstructive to the Commons that a predominantly hereditary chamber. The Blair government had evidently overlooked this possibility, as it appeared to be wholly surprised in January 2000 when a multi-party grouping (including prominent Labour peers) in the Lords blocked the government's proposals to restrict the right to trial by jury by a majority of 100.[92] The legislation seemed an ideal candidate to be legitimately delayed in the new upper house. It was controversial in substance, impacted heavily on civil liberties, and raised the type of question which many life peers – by virtue of their legal experience – were well-equipped to evaluate and criticise. The government did not accept this proposition however. Home Secretary Jack Straw complained that the Lords' threat was 'undemocratic'. This comment was rather ill-conceived. Since the Blair government had presumably promoted the Lords reform Bill in the belief that the house's new composition was (if only temporarily) the most appropriate for a body possessing delaying and scrutinising powers, it could hardly be 'undemocratic' for those powers to be used; unless, of course, the government accepted that the reformed house was per se an 'undemocratic' institution. The episode rather indicated that the Blair government's view of the Lords' democratic credentials rested primarily on a majority in the upper house agreeing with the majority in the Commons, a perspective which suggests there is little point in having a second chamber at all.

An immediate consequence of the 1999 Act however was greatly to reduce the Conservative Party's strength in the upper chamber. As of November 2001, the Conservatives held 222 seats in the Lords, the Labour Party 197, the Liberals 62, and the crossbenchers (including the bishops and law lords) some 216. Given the (C)conservative predispositions of many crossbenchers, the government could certainly not

92 See *The Times* and *The Guardian*, 20 January 2000.

expect to command reliable majority support in the upper house. Frequently aired objections that the Blair government had 'packed' the Lords with its own supporters therefore had little basis in fact; rather the Prime Minister had used 'his' powers of appointment to begin to redress the huge historical imbalance within the house in favour of the Conservative Party.

THE RECOMMENDATIONS OF THE WAKEHAM COMMISSION

The Royal Commission established in 1999 to made recommendations for long term reform to the House of Lords published its report, *A house for the future*,[93] in January 2000. The Wakeham Commission had proceeded on the assumption that the powers of the upper chamber would remain largely unchanged. Its task was therefore to consider how to reform the composition of the Lords in ways which would enhance its existing complementary role to the Commons.

Effective complementarity would seem to require independence and expertise within the upper house. If we accept that the Lords should be both subordinate to the Commons and independent of the prevailing patterns of party affiliation in the lower house, there is no need for its members to be elected. Indeed, for those purposes an elected second chamber could be quite dysfunctional. If elected on the same basis as the Commons, the Lords might simply reproduce its party alignment, and so lose any plausible claim to independence. If chosen through a different electoral system, the Lords might be construed as a more legitimate expression of the people's wishes, and so pose a threat to the lower house's 'democratically' justified superiority. And whatever form of election was used, there remains the risk that members would be elected because of their appeal to transient popular prejudice, and so produce a chamber intellectually unsuited for its role of bringing to bear a supra-party political influence on legislative and governmental processes.

The life peerage system therefore appears well suited as a selection process for a complementary house. Reform to the Life Peerage Act to place some justiciable limits on the Prime Minister's powers to nominate peers might seem desirable, but the greatest weakness in the membership of the Lords that selection through life peerages would produce would seem to be not one of political bias or limited ability, but of age: a more vigorous house may demand that we have a younger house.

Given the predominance of the party in modern political life, it would be facile to think one could remove party politics from the Lords. Even if one abolished formal party organisation, it is certain that members' behaviour would continue to be structured by their party loyalties. And, indeed, since one of the functions we wish the Lords to perform is scrutiny of the executive, there must be a sufficient number of competent Ministers in the house for other peers to question. Consequently, rather than wondering how to abolish party influence, a more pertinent inquiry would be to

93 (London: HMSO; Cm 4534.)

ask how much influence should be accorded to party discipline in respect of each of the house's various functions.

Objections to the Lords' powers to delay or amend government Bills derive not so much from the delay per se, as from its differential party impact. That the Lords indulged in such behaviour prior to 2000 far more frequently when a Labour government controlled the Commons suggests that their Lordship's stance owed less to a principled belief in the integrity of their position than to a knee jerk mobilisation of their Conservative majority. There is no justification for according party ideology such scope in a complementary chamber. This suggests the Lords' composition as a corporate entity would have to be based on a quota system which ensured that a government Bill could be delayed or amended only if opposition peers won over a substantial body of cross bench opinion, and perhaps some governing party peers as well. One would thereby increase the likelihood that any legislative difficulties the government encountered derived from flaws in its policies, rather than the simple factional opposition intransigence. Nor should a house of life peers experience any conventional reluctance to use such legal powers – their very purpose would be to cause the government difficulties if it appeared that legislative policy ignored public sentiment. In this context, as with its scrutinising functions, the Lords' role is to expose government policy to the oxygen of publicity by alerting the electorate to criticism of the government's position.

The Wakeham Commission did not propose any increase in the upper chamber's legislative powers. Indeed, to the contrary, the Commission recommended that the Lords' veto power over delegated legislation be replaced with a much lesser power to delay such measures for up to three months. It did, however, recommend a modest extension of the Lords' role in scrutinising executive behaviour, primarily through an expansion of the house's select committee system. The Commission also suggested that – while members should not be salaried – they should receive appreciably enhanced attendance allowances, which raised the possibility that some members would be able to sit in the chamber on much more than an occasional basis.

The modesty of these proposals was matched by the Commission's recommendations for altering the composition of the house. Wakeham saw no place for the remaining 92 'hereditary' peers in a reformed house. The Commission suggested that the great majority of members of the new house, of whom there would be some 550, should be appointed to office. The Commission saw no valid role for the Prime Minister in the appointment process. Rather appointments should be made by an independent 'Appointments Commission', with ten members selected on a non-partisan basis. Appointees would serve for a 15-year fixed term. The Appointments Commission would ensure that the party balance among appointed members bore a close resemblance to each party's share of the vote at the most recent general election. In a further break with tradition, the Commission proposed that the overall composition of the house should better represent women and ethnic minorities than had been the case in the previous house and in the Commons. The Commission also recommended that a small proportion of the new house's members should be elected.

The various commissioners could not agree on how many members should be chosen in this way. Three options were suggested, ranging from barely 10% of the house to a maximum of around 35%. These modest figures led Shell to observe; 'One senses throughout the report a fundamental antipathy towards including elected members'.[94] The proposals attracted little enthusiasm from the opposition parties or constitutional reform pressure groups, most of whom had favoured the creation of a wholly elected second house. As suggested above, that perspective has little to commend it. That it was appointed peers who rejected the government's jury trial proposals so decisively (coincidentally on the same day that the Wakeham report was published) provides compelling evidence that an elected house is not necessary to ensure that the second chamber makes an effective contribution to the legislative process. The Commission was perhaps ill-advised in suggesting that any members be elected. In so doing, it implicitly acknowledged that it saw force in this argument yet, by recommending that so few members be chosen in this way, it opened itself to the criticism of being hypocritical or fainthearted. That view was strengthened by repeated rumours that the cabinet had made it known to Lord Wakeham that a wholly or predominantly appointed house would be its preferred option.

Despite its preferences being granted, the government made no immediate attempt to promote legislation further reforming the upper house. It seemed likely that any such proposal would be delayed until after the next general election. It also seemed likely, unless the present house proves to be habitually obstructive to government Bills, that the rather modest nature of the Wakeham Commission recommendations would offer the government a good reason for not pursuing any further reform at all.[95]

THE 2001 WHITE PAPER

That the second Blair government harboured no great enthusiasm for radical Lords reform was clearly evident from the contents of the white paper published in 2001, *Completing the reform*.[96] The government had formed the view that creating an entirely or substantially elected upper house was not a viable option, as this might lead to a situation of legislative 'gridlock' between the houses.[97] While there is undoubtedly some force in this position, the government rather undermined the

94 Shell D (2000) 'Reforming the House of Lords' *Public Law* 193.

95 See especially Bogdanor V (1999) 'Reform of the House of Lords: a sceptical view' *Political Quarterly* 375–381.

96 Lord Chancellor's Department (2001) *Completing the reform* (London: HMSO; Cmnd 5291).

97 Whether such 'gridlock' would be of a symbolic or practical kind would of course depend on the powers that the reformed Lords would exercise. The government did embrace Wakeham proposals that the Lords' powers over delegated legislation be reduced. No enhancement of powers in respect of primary legislation was supposed. Any gridlock that might ensue if this weakened house were to be composed of elected members would be of a sort that would embarrass a government with a Commons majority rather than block its legislative programme.

potency of its own favoured reform by proposing a house whose members would be selected in an incoherent mish-mash of ways.

The white paper accepted that hereditary peers should be removed from the house. It then recommended a chamber composed of some 600 peers:[98] 120 would be elected on a regional basis, 120 would be appointed by a statutory, non-partisan Appointments Commission, and 360 would be selected by party leaders in shares approximately equal to the parties' popularity at the previous general election. This represented a significant dilution of the Wakeham proposals, which had envisage that all non-elected peers be selected by the Appointments Commission.[99]

The white paper attracted little positive comment in the press or within Parliament. More radical proposals were advanced, including – with what one might regard as breathtaking hypocrisy – a suggestion from the Conservative Party that a reformed house be entirely elected. More significantly, in a rare display of independence, substantial numbers of backbench Labour MPs voiced strong opposition to the white paper, with many seemingly favouring a largely or wholly elected upper house.

The sentiments of Labour backbenchers were reflected in a report by the Commons Public Administration Select Committee, published early in 2002.[100] The report offered a cogent illustration of the capacity of the Commons to pursue a line quite independent of that favoured by the government. The Committee saw little merit in the white paper's proposals, and was not substantially more impressed by the recommendations of the Wakeham Commission. Perhaps rather naively, the Select Committee considered that the legitimacy of the second chamber – and thus its capacity effectively to act as a revising or delaying chamber within the legislative process – would be fatally compromised if it did not contain a substantial elected element. The report suggested that at least 60% of the members of the reformed house should be elected, with the remainder chosen by a non-partisan Appointments Commission of the sort suggested by Wakeham. It was also recommended that the Law Lords and Bishops should be removed from the reformed house. In the Select Committee's view, a chamber composed in this way would not function as a rival to the Commons, and its limited powers as identified in the Parliament Acts should not be extended.

The government apparently did not see the question of further reform to the House of Lords as a matter of sufficient importance to warrant an open fight with its backbenchers,[101] and in May 2002 the government announced that more far-reaching proposals for reform would be considered by a joint Commons and Lords Committee. Quite how receptive the Blair government would be to the Committee's plans

[98] The government envisaged that it might have to offer existing peers substantial 'redundancy packages' to persuade them to support the abolition of their own seats in the house.

[99] Prompting the unflattering comment that the white paper would; 'allow the party leaders to use the Lords as a patronage bin'; Constitution Unit (2001 – December) *Monitor* p 2.

[100] *Continuing the reform* (HC 4941 2001–2002) (London: HMSO).

[101] We might note the difference in backbench and government attitudes on this issue and the respective approaches taken to the strengthening of the Commons Select Committee system discussed in ch 5 at pp 161–168.

remained to be seen. The Leader of the House, Robin Cook, announced in May 2002 that; 'The matter is now in the hands of parliament and the speed and the radicalism with which we can now move is very much down to how MPs proceed in this matter and how they subsequently vote'.[102] Notwithstanding this statement of intent, press stories in June 2002 suggested that the government had been at some pains to place its own supporters on the joint committee, which was to be chaired by Jack Cunningham, a cabinet Minister in the first Blair government.[103]

The Joint Committee's report, which was published in the autumn of 2002,[104] could variously be described as a document which kept all options open or as a masterpiece of indecision. The report sensibly concluded that there was little point in addressing the issue of whether any changes should be made to the powers of the Lords until the matter of its composition was settled. The Joint Committee also identified various criteria which the reformed house should meet; 'legitimacy'; 'representativeness'; 'no domination by any one party'; 'independence'; and 'expertise'. Those criteria, while undeniably vague, would seem wholly unobjectionable. On the question of altering the composition of the House, however, the Joint Committee was rather more opaque. Its core recommendation was that MPs should be given a free vote on a variety of reform options, ranging from creating a fully elected chamber to retaining a fully appointed body through a number of hybrid elected/appointed options.

The government nominally accepted that the matter should be left to a free vote. However, shortly before the Commons addressed the issue, the Prime Minister made it clear that he was firmly supportive of a fully appointed second chamber. Mr Blair appeared to be concerned that a fully or partly elected upper house would act in effect as a rival rather than revising chamber to the Commons. His intervention was subject to some criticism both in the media and within Parliament, on the grounds that some of the more quiescent Labour MPs would not wish visibly to vote against his wishes irrespective of their own views on the merits of the issue.

In the event, the Commons' vote on further reform descended into farce. MPs were eventually presented with seven proposals for reform. Amid allegations that Labour whips were exerting pressure on Labour MPs to follow the Prime Minister's line, none of the proposals mustered majority support.[105] It was expected that the joint committee would make further attempts to fashion a proposal that would carry a majority in the Commons. But as of the spring of 2003, it seemed likely that little further progress would be made on this matter in the near future.

Notwithstanding the press criticism levied at the Blair government for its failure to take a radical lead on this issue, the status quo might be thought to have certain benefits. The partially reformed house has continued to prove a more potent obstacle to government policy than the Commons. As the reform debate raged at the end of

[102] *The Guardian*, 14 May 2002. [103] *The Guardian*, 20 June 2002.

[104] Joint Committee on House of Lords Reform (2002) *First report* (HL 171/HC 17) (London: HMSO).

[105] See Cowley (2005) op cit pp 34–36; 97–100.

2002, the Lords succeeded in persuading the government to make a number of important changes to Bills dealing with asylum and animal health issues.[106] In 2003, the upper house proved similarly obstructive towards the government's flagship bill to reform the National Health Service[107]; and in both 2004 and 2005 the House of Lords inflicted a series of defeats on the government in respect of proposed anti-terrorism legislation. It might also be suggested that the current House of Lords is reasonably representative of the public at large, at least in respect of the issue of party political affiliation. In the 2001 general election, the proportion of eligible voters who supported the Labour, Conservative and Liberal parties were 24%; 19% and 11% respectively. At that time, Labour peers held 28% of seats in the Lords; the Conservatives 32%; and the Liberals 9%; with the balance held by cross-benchers. As we shall see in chapter seven, the Lords might plausibly claim to be better representative of contemporary voting patterns than is the Commons. Whether that is in fact a beneficial characteristic for a second chamber is of course a matter for debate.

ONE PARLIAMENT OR THREE? JACKSON V ATTORNEY-GENERAL

While neither Parliament nor the Blair government displayed any obvious enthusiasm for further reform to the Lords, the courts did offer, in 2004 and 2005, a series of answers to the legal questions raised by the Parliament Act 1911; namely were the Commons and King a 'subordinate legislature'; and, if so, what were the limits on their legislative power?

In the postwar era, two distinct views had emerged among academic commentators as to the legal effect of the 1911 Act. The first view, championed by Professor de Smith was that the Parliament Act had 'redefined Parliament' in way which; 'provided a simpler, optional procedure for legislation on most topics'.[108] Any measure produced by the Commons and King was indeed therefore as much an 'Act of Parliament' as a statute enacted in the orthodox manner. That Professor de Smith also accepted that this (these) redefined Parliament(s) could not legislate to achieve objectives prohibited by s 1 and s 2 respectively did not deflect him from his initial assertion. De Smith's view on this point appeared to be much influenced by the Commonwealth legislature cases discussed in chapter two.[109] Quite why these cases should be regarded as relevant to the nature of the British Parliament is, for reasons outlined in chapter two,[110] something of a mystery.

The second view, proposed by William Wade, seems much the more persuasive. That view, initially advanced in 1955 and reiterated in 1980[111] was that measures passed by the Commons and King under the Parliament Act procedures were delegated legislation. While the Commons and Monarch might indeed be a 'legislature',

[106] *The Guardian*, 1 November 2003; 8 November 2002. [107] Ibid, pp 152–154.

[108] De Smith S (5th edn, 1985) *Constitutional and administrative law* p 100.

[109] See pp 39–44 above. [110] Pp 45–47 above.

[111] (1955) 'The basis of legal sovereignty' *Cambridge LJ* 172–197; (1980) *Constitutional fundamentals* (London: Stevens and Sons).

they could only be a subordinate legislature; their subordinacy being of course to the Parliament that created their law-making power:

'The acid test of primary legislation, surely, is that it is accepted by the courts at its own face value, without needing support from any superior authority. But an Act passed by Queen and Commons only has no face value of its own. As Coke put it in The Prince's Case, "If an Act be penned, that the King with the assent of the Lords, or with the assent of the Commons, it is no Act of Parliament for three ought to assent to it scil. The King, the Lords and the Commons." An Act of Queen and Commons alone is accepted by the courts only because it is authorised by the Parliament Act – and indeed it is required to recite that it is passed "in accordance with the Parliament Acts 1911 and 1949 and by authority of the same". This is the hall-mark of subordinate legislation'.[112]

The matter was eventually subjected to thorough judicial analysis in 2004 and 2005. The episode was triggered by the passage of a measure styled as the Hunting Act 2004. The law stemmed from an attempt by the Blair government to persuade Parliament in 2002 to regulate the hunting of wild animals – primarily foxes and deer – by groups of people who chased their prey on horseback accompanied by packs of dogs which tracked and killed the pursued animals. The proposal attracted considerable controversy in both Houses of Parliament and in the press. An amendment moved by a backbench Labour MP to ban such hunting entirely was approved in the Commons but then rejected in the Lords. It soon became clear that the government was far from enthusiastic about pursuing the issue at all. There was nonetheless substantial support for the hunting ban among many Labour, and opposition, party MPs in the Commons, and the Bill was re-introduced into the Commons in September 2004. Majority opinion in the House of Lords opposed the measure however and, when efforts to find a broadly acceptable compromise measure failed, the House of Lords again refused to pass the Bill even though the proposal had attracted a very large majority in the Commons. The measure was therefore sent to the Queen for her approval under the provisions of the Parliament Act 1949.[113]

Having lost the political argument in the House of Commons, opponents of the Hunting Act 2004 then sought to make a legal argument before the courts. The core of their case was that the Parliament Act 1949 was a legally invalid measure. If this contention was correct, then any subsequent measure purportedly enacted under the Parliament Act 1949 procedure – including the Hunting Act 2004 – would also be invalid. The argument endorsed Wade's analysis, to the effect that the law-making body – the Commons by simple majority plus the royal assent – created by the 1911 Act was a 'subordinate' rather than 'sovereign' legislature. As such, there had to be limits on its powers. One such limit was laid out expressly in the text of the 1911 Act; namely that the Commons and Queen could not extend the period between general elections beyond five years. It was further contended that the powers of the Queen and Commons were also subject to implied limits, in particular the limit that they

112 Ibid, pp 27–28.

113 See Banner C and Boutle T (2004) 'Challenging the Commons' *New Law Journal* 1466.

could not increase the scope of their own law-making authority. It was then suggested that because the Parliament Act 1949 sought to increase the powers of the Commons and Queen by reducing the Lords' power of delay, it was a measure beyond the powers of the Queen and Commons to produce.

The judgments of the High Court and Court of Appeal

The High Court saw little force in these arguments. In its view, the Commons and Queen was as much 'Parliament' as was the Commons, Lords and Queen. The Court's judgment suggested that the correct way to portray the effect of the 1911 Act was that it had 'remodelled' or 'redefined' Parliament in a fashion which enabled the Parliament qua Commons and Monarch to enact Acts of Parliament, albeit that these new Parliaments had to comply with the terms of the 1911 Act if their 'Acts' were to be valid. On this view, the Parliament Act 1949 – and any 'Act' subsequently passed under the 1949 Act procedure – were validly enacted primary legislation.

The three members of the Court of Appeal issued a single judgment.[114] Although the Court of Appeal reached the same conclusion as the High Court, it did so on the basis of quite different reasoning. The Court of Appeal was clearly much influenced by Wade's analysis of the Commons and Queen as a subordinate legislature. The judgment did not go so far as, in explicit terms, to class measures produced by the Commons and Queen as 'delegated legislation'. However, drawing on both the express limitation placed on the power of the Commons and Queen by the 1911 Act and the context of the Act's passage, the Court accepted that the Commons and Queen could not be regarded as the equivalent of Parliament in the orthodox sense:[115]

'[42]. The purpose of the 1911 Act was to establish a new constitutional settlement that limited the period during which the Lords could delay the enactment of legislation first introduced to the Commons but which preserved the role of the Lords in the legislative processes. In our view it would be in conflict with the 1911 Act for it to be used as an instrument for abolishing the House of Lords. . . . The preamble indicates that the 1911 Act was to be a transitional provision pending further reform. It provides no support for an intention that the 1911 Act should be used, directly or indirectly, to enable more fundamental constitutional changes to be achieved than had been achieved already.

[43]. Thus, it does not necessarily follow that because there is compliance with the requirements in the 1911 Act, the result is a valid Act of Parliament. . . .

[44]. This concession recognises that there are differences between the traditional powers of Parliament when legislating, and its powers when legislating under the 1911 Act . . .

[45]. Once it is accepted that the use to which the 1911 Act could be put is limited, the question arises as to the extent of the limitation. It is when we reach this stage that it becomes important to recognise that what could be suggested here is the power to make fundamental constitutional changes. If Parliament was intending to create such a power, surely it is right to expect that the power would be unambiguously stated in the legislation. This is not the case with s. 2 of the 1911 Act.'

114 Lord Woolf CJ, Lord Phillips MR, May LJ [2005] EWCA Civ 126.
115 The most important section of the judgment is at paras 30–48.

The logic of this argument in abstract legal terms seems compelling. To regard the Commons and Queen as 'Parliament' would entail accepting the proposition that the United Kingdom has since 1911 had two sovereign law-makers. The obvious practical objection to the Court of Appeal's reasoning is that the concept of 'fundamental constitutional change' is a very imprecise one. The Court of Appeal considered that the reduction of the Lords' delaying power in the 1949 'Act' was not fundamental in this sense, while a measure such as the abolition of the House of Lords or a measure excluding much government activity from judicial review would have a 'fundamental' character.

The Court's reasoning is avowedly teleological or purposive in nature. This makes it rather curious that neither the judgment – nor indeed the claimant's submissions – seemed to attach any significance to the 'purpose' that had evidently led Asquith to promote the original 1911 Bill; namely to ensure that the Lords could not prevent legal effect being given to policy proposals that a government with a Commons majority had put clearly to the electorate.[116] By 1945, the political parties fought election campaigns on the basis of broad policy manifestoes. The Labour Party manifesto of that year had said a good deal about the party's radical legislative plans; but those expressly stated plans did not include any explicit proposal to seek amendment of the 1911 Act in order further to limits the powers of the upper house.[117]

The judgment of the House of Lords

The House of Lords regarded the issue raised in *Jackson* as of sufficient importance to merit consideration by a panel of nine judges rather than the usual five. The House of Lords unanimously upheld the decision reached by the Court of Appeal, but did so on the basis of markedly different – and thoroughly unsatisfactory – reasoning.[118] Eight of the nine judges delivered reasoned judgments. Some elements of those opinions will be considered in the final chapter of this book in relation to the current status of the orthodox understanding of the principle of the sovereignty of Parliament. For the present, our analysis is limited to the conclusions offered by the Court as to the legal status both of the Commons and Queen as a law-maker and of the measures which they produce.

Lord Bingham delivered the longest judgment, which began with a careful study of the historical context within which the 1911 Act was produced. In Lord Bingham's view;:

'[24] . . . The 1911 Act did, of course, effect an important constitutional change, the change lay not in authorising a new form of sub-primary parliamentary legislation, but in creating a new way of enacting primary legislation. . . .

[25] [T]he overall object of the Act was not to enlarge the powers of the Commons but to restrict those of the Lords.'

Lord Bingham was apparently led to this conclusion in part by his reading of the

116 See pp 184–185 above. 117 See pp 187 above. 118 [2005] UKHL 56.

historical background to the Act. But his reasoning seemed to rest primarily on a literal construction of the text of the 1911 Act – and especially by ss 1(1) and 2(1) which provide that any measure passed by the Commons and Monarch would be an 'Act of Parliament'. In Lord Bingham's opinion, there are thus no substantive limits on the legislative competence of the Commons and Monarch. Acting in concert; they could enact a statute on any subject matter whatsoever. This would include a measure which overrode the express provision in s 2(1) of the 1911 Act that the new procedure did not apply to bills which extended the duration of a parliament beyond five years. There are obvious and substantial deficiencies in this analysis.

The first difficulty is that Lord Bingham's reasoning necessarily accepts the presumption that the United Kingdom now has two sovereign law-makers. This is a logical absurdity in an abstract jurisprudential sense. Lord Bingham is evidently not offering a scenario in which sovereignty is divided between differently identified Parliaments, each of which has limited competence, as was the case in South Africa in the 1950s.[119] Each of Lord Bingham's Parliaments is evidently legally omnipotent.

The second flaw in the argument is evident when one considers the practical consequences of Lord Bingham's unquestioning reliance on the literal wording of s 1(1) and s 2(1). On this reasoning, had the 1911 Act dispensed altogether with any need for the Lords or Monarch to assent to legislation, and had provided simply that any measure approved by a bare majority in the Commons at third reading was 'an Act of Parliament', then the House of Commons alone would have become a(nother) sovereign legislature. And had the 1911 Act attributed 'Act of Parliament' status to a written government policy proposal supported by a majority of the Cabinet and certified as such by the Prime Minister, then it seems a Cabinet majority would also be 'Parliament' and thus a sovereign law-maker. Moreover, according to Lord Bingham's analysis, either of those additional 'sovereigns' could now be brought into being by the Commons and Queen acting under the 1911 or 1949 Act procedures; and the additional sovereigns would then in turn, since their wishes would be 'Acts of Parliament', have the legal capacity to create yet more sovereign law-makers.

The judgment offered by Lord Nicholls is even more problematic. Like Lord Bingham, Lord Nicholls relies on the use of the 'Act of Parliament' label in s 1(1) and s 2(1) to support his assertion that the Commons and Monarch are not a subordinate legislature: 'To describe an Act of Parliament made by this procedure as "delegated" or "subordinate" legislation, with all the connotations attendant on those expressions, would be an absurd and confusing mischaracterisation.'[120] Rather the 1911 Act created 'a parallel route' for the creation of legislation. However, Lord Nicholls – unlike Lord Bingham – also held that his 'parallel route' could not be used by the Commons and Lords to repeal the substantive restrictions on its use laid out in s 2(1).[121] This must mean that the Commons and Monarch are a law-maker of limited competence.

119 See pp 41–43 above. 120 At para 64.

121 Ie that it did not apply to money bills or bills seeking to extend the duration of Parliaments beyond five years.

Yet they are also apparently not 'subordinate' to the Parliament composed of the Commons, Monarch and Lords. This is an intrinsically incoherent position to adopt. Lord Nicholls then offers as; 'the second source of confirmation'[122] of his conclusion the peculiar suggestion that any measures produced by the Parliament Act 1911 or 1949 procedures must be 'Acts of Parliament' because laws produced in such fashion have been recognised as such or amended by subsequent statutes enacted by (the three-part) Parliament.

Lord Hope approves much of Lord Nicholls reasoning, accepting both that the Commons and Queen are not a subordinate legislature but that they cannot pass an Act to extend the duration of a Parliament. But Lord Hope adds a further surreal twist to this bizarre assertion by also holding that the Commons and Monarch could not achieve that result through the indirect route of passing two 'Acts', the first of which simply repealed the relevant provision of s 2(1), and the second of which subsequently increased the period. For Lord Hope; 'such an obvious device to get around the express prohibition would be as vulnerable to a declaration of invalidity as a direct breach of it'.[123] This bald and unequivocal assertion might lead one to wonder if a government with a Commons majority might 'get around the express prohibition' by the expedient of having the Commons and Queen produce an 'Act' which altered the composition of the Lords in a fashion that gave the governing party a majority in the upper house, thereby making reliance on the Parliament Act procedures unnecessary to extend the duration of Parliament. Or would Lord Hope feel obliged to declare such an Act invalid? What degree of causal (or indeed chronological) proximity is required before 'obviousness' occurs.[124]

Lord Carswell was the only member of the House of Lords who offered any support for the Court of Appeal's conclusion that the Commons and Monarch might also be precluded from enacting a 'statute' which brought about other, undefined constitutional reform of a 'fundamental' nature. Notwithstanding these observations, Lord Carswell still managed to accept the premise that the Commons and Monarch could not be regarded as a subordinate law-maker.

Lord Steyn's judgment began in terms which seemed rather more sophisticated than those deployed by his colleagues. He appeared to take some care to avoid characterising the legal measures produced by the Commons and Queen as 'Acts' which were 'enacted' by Parliament. Instead he referred to: 'the manner and form in which laws may be made.... [T]he new method of making law.... [T]his new

[122] At para 67.

[123] At para 122. Baroness Hale evidently shared this view: see para 164. Lord Roger, while in broad agreement with Lord Nicholls, was not prepared to endorse the conclusion that a multi-part scheme by the Commons and Queen to overcome s 2(1) would necessarily be invalid: para 139.

[124] Lord Hope also offers the extraordinary observation – which might be attributed to careless drafting – that the House of Commons alone is sovereign. Lord Brown also couched his analysis in terms indicating that it was the Commons alone, rather than the Commons and Monarch – which could use the 1911 Act procedures to 'enact its legislative programme': at para 185.

method of expressing the will of Parliament'.[125] However, he eventually adopted the view that the 1911 Act had 'redefined Parliament', and rejected the suggestion that the Commons and Queen were a subordinate legislature: 'in manner and form the 1911 Act simply provides for an alternative mode by which Parliament, as reconstituted for specific purposes, may make laws'.[126]

An unsatisfactory judgment?

The reasoning – and thence the conclusions – of the members of the House of Lords are profoundly unsatisfactory. At root, the problem lies in the Court's evident unwillingness to accept the point so clearly made by William Wade that the sovereignty of Parliament is *not a phenomenon that derives from a legal source*, and as such *neither is it a phenomenon that can be altered by a legal source.* The 'ultimate political fact' of the constitution is that Parliament's sovereign power cannot by non-revolutionary means be restricted nor given away. However powerful qua law-maker the Commons and Monarch might be, they are not and cannot be Parliament and so cannot possess sovereign power. From this perspective, the judgment of the Court of Appeal offers a far more – if not thoroughly – convincing analysis of the constitutional consequences of the 1911 Act than do the various opinions offered by the House of Lords.

CONCLUSION

The number of variations on the theme of reforming the Lords are legion, as are the pros and cons of each scheme proposed.[127] But most reform plans present us with a great paradox. The more we ask a second chamber to perform functions complementary to those of the Commons, the more we demand of its members that they be (as individuals and as a body) 'expert', 'experienced' and 'non-partisan', and so the more we reveal the crushing dominance of party politics in the lower house, and the incapacity and/or unwillingness of backbench MPs to exert a restraining influence on government activities. This perhaps suggests that the key division within the legislative process is now not Lords versus Commons, nor Labour versus Conservative, but party versus national interest. If that is indeed the case, it is very difficult to identify effective reforming strategies for the Lords without simultaneously considering the merits and drawbacks of 'Parliament' more broadly, in terms both of its legislative powers and its relationship with the 'people'. Discussion of Lords reform frequently

125 Ibid, at para 75.

126 Ibid, at para 94. He also held however that the lifetime of a parliament could not be extended either directly or indirectly by the Commons and Queen.

127 See for example Oliver D (1990) *United Kingdom government and constitution* ch 3 (Buckingham: Open University Press): Brazier R (1992) *Constitutional reform* ch 4 (Oxford: OUP): Bogdanor (1999) op cit: Shell D (1999) 'The future of the second chamber' *Political Quarterly* 390–395: Dickson B and Carmichael P (eds) *The House of Lords: its parliamentary and judicial roles* (Oxford: Hart Publishing): Russell M (2000) *Reforming the House of Lords. Lessons from overseas* (London: OUP).

proceeds on the assumption that the upper house's legal and conventional subordination to the Commons is desirable because of what one might intuitively regard as 'democratic' reasons. The Lords may be portrayed as an elitist, unelected body, which has no legitimate power to obstruct the wishes of 'the people', such wishes invariably being accurately expressed by the elected representatives in the lower house. The recommendations of the Wakeham Commission, and the proposals outlined in the 2001 White Paper, do not go very far towards meeting that criticism. But before concluding that it is only the House of Lords (in both its unreformed and reformed states) that lacks a democratic underpinning within Parliament, we ought to revisit the House of Commons, and consider not its powers, but the methods through which its members are chosen.

7

THE ELECTORAL SYSTEM

This book began by suggesting various ways to assess if a society's constitution was 'democratic', in the substantive sense of the content of the country's laws, and the procedural sense of the way laws are made. The first six chapters sketched some characteristics of the British version of democracy. Parliament has traditionally been regarded as sovereign, capable of amending all laws by the simple majority in both houses plus royal assent formula. The Life Peerages Act 1958 and the House of Lords Act 1999 show that Parliament can alter the membership of its component parts. There is no obvious reason[1] why the parliamentary sovereignty doctrine should not also apply to the Commons' electoral system. The questions we might therefore ask are why Parliament has exercised its powers in this area in the way that it has; and how far does this choice satisfy democratic requirements?

To begin, we might return to the US *Declaration of Independence* claim that governments 'derive their just powers from the consent of the governed'. The claim is one most people would consider fundamental to any democratic society. But how do citizens choose their lawmakers? How effective is that choice in controlling the legislature's composition? And how do we decide if our choice ensures that the law's substance attracts our consent?

A recent survey of electoral laws in modern societies identified six fundamental characteristics of democratic systems.[2] Firstly, that virtually all adults may vote; secondly, that elections are held regularly; thirdly that no large group of citizens is prohibited from fielding candidates; fourthly, that almost all places in the legislature are contested; fifthly, that election campaigns are conducted fairly and honestly; and sixthly, that votes are secretly cast and accurately counted.

This chapter asks how well Britain's electoral system measures up to these yardsticks. Section two reviews the contemporary picture. Section one traces the route Britain has followed in reaching its present system of electoral law and practice, picking up the threads of issues previously encountered but left untied, and weaving a more tightly knit picture of the constitution.

[1] Ch 8 suggests there may be obscure ones.

[2] Butler D, Penniman H and Ranney A (1981) *Democracy at the polls* ch 1 (Washington DC: American Enterprise Institute for Public Policy Research).

I. THE EVOLUTION OF A 'DEMOCRATIC' ELECTORAL SYSTEM?

This section focuses on four issues: the Great Reform Act 1832; the Chartism movement; the reforms of 1867–1884; and voting rights for women.

THE GREAT REFORM ACT 1832

The Commons' progress towards becoming a fully representative institution dates from the 1832 Great Reform Act. The Act retained many features of earlier electoral law.[3] Nevertheless, its passage provoked a constitutional crisis. This arose in part from the House of Lords' decision to wreck a Bill that had majority Commons support, from the Monarch's (William IV) unwillingness to exercise his prerogative powers to create new pro-government peers, and in the apparent readiness of middle and working class[4] communities to use violence to secure the Bill's enactment. This complex web of forces makes the Act a useful vehicle for exploring the meaning of 'democracy' in British constitutional history.

By 1830, the nature of elite groups in British society was undergoing rapid change. Wealth had moved away from the landed and merchant classes towards manufacturing industry.[5] The technological advance which triggered this trend also facilitated the 'nationalisation of politics'; improved communications and transport systems permitted people in different regions to identify common interests transcending 'local concerns'. One can identify 'public opinion' as a distinct political force from 1800.[6] The Commons may still have been a House of Communities; but the nation was increasingly divided by economic class into several large segments, rather than by physical geography into innumerable cities, towns, and villages.

Dissatisfaction with the electoral system had four principal foci. The first related to the geographical distribution of seats; the second concerned the qualifications needed to vote; the third centred on candidate selection; the fourth on the conduct of election campaigns.

The constituency system

The Commons now has 650 members, each representing a given geographical area, or 'constituency'. This geographical division was a firmly embedded principle by 1688. Constitutional theory then accepted that the Commons existed as much to protect

3 Gash N (1953) *Politics in the age of Peel* p x (London: Longmans); Mandler P (1990) *Aristocratic government in the age of reform* ch 4 (Oxford: Clarendon Press).

4 'Class' was then a nascent concept, and is used here in a loose sense. See Hobsbawm E (1969) *Industry and empire* ch 4 (Harmondsworth: Penguin); Ward J (1973) *Chartism* pp 46–48 (New York: Harper Row).

5 Hobsbawm op cit chs 2–3.

6 Brock op cit p 17. Of the many studies of the 1832 Act, Brock's is the most engaging, and is heavily drawn upon here.

local interests as to define national issues. In 1830, 658 MPs sat in the Commons. The population was approximately sixteen million. Representation was divided broadly between counties and boroughs, with most English counties (39) and boroughs (around 200) each returning two members, and each Scots and Welsh county and borough returning one member. Ireland had two-member counties (32) and (mostly) one-member boroughs (31). Oxford and Cambridge Universities returned two members each; one MP represented Trinity College Dublin. This framework was established in 1675, and had remained broadly unchanged ever since.[7] Seat allocation bore no relation to population patterns; Parliament had not established any mechanism for altering representation to reflect demographic trends. In 1830, large industrial towns such as Birmingham and Manchester had no representatives at all.

In contrast, over 100 so-called 'rotten boroughs' had fewer than 100 voters. The system also threw up startling anomalies between ostensibly similar constituencies; Bristol had 5000 voters, Bath had 30.[8] Boroughs were created by the Royal Prerogative; the ways in which the Monarch exercised the power was not subject to judicial control.

Qualification for the franchise

Entitlement to vote arose in many ways, most of them deriving from land ownership. The value of the land required was generally set high enough to exclude most local residents, but in the 14 'potwalloper boroughs' enfranchisement extended to any resident man with a family who had facilities to boil water, and in the 38 'scot and lot' boroughs to any man paying poor rates. Residence was generally not required, which meant that many so-called 'out-voters' lived beyond borough boundaries and possessed votes in several places. The English county qualification was more

Table 7.1 The Size of the Electorate

	Adult Population	Electorate	% Enfranchised
1830	13,900,000	435,000	3.2%
1840	15,900,000	700,000	4.4%
1870	22,700,000	1,900,000	8.7%
1900	24,930,000	6,730,935	27.0%
1919	27,900,000	21,755,583	78.0%
1949	34,970,000	34,269,770	98.2%

Sources: Compiled from data in Seymour C (1970) *Electoral reform in England and Wales* Appendix 1 (Newton Abbot: David and Charles): Coleman D and Salt J (1992) *The British population* p 41 (Oxford: OUP): Butler and Sloman op cit p 200. Figures prior to 1900 are approximate only and are for England and Wales only. Later dates are for the UK.

[7] Cannon J (1973) *Parliamentary reform 1640–1832* p 29 (Cambridge: CUP).

[8] Cannon op cit p 31.

Table 7.2 Voting Population of Two Member English Boroughs 1830

Number of electors	Number of boroughs
0–50	56
51–100	21
101–300	36
301–600	24
601–1000	22
1001–5000	36
5000 +	7

Source: adapted from Brock op cit p 20.

straightforward – freehold ownership of land worth £2 per year; (the sum was fixed in 1430). Residence was not needed.[9]

Defenders of the status quo invoked the theory of 'virtual representation' to justify the non-enfranchisement of the bulk of the population. This saw no need for most citizens to have a vote, since there would be some MPs whose dominant constituency interest would coincide with those of the disfranchised group (generally defined in occupational terms), thus ensuring that representations would be made on that group's behalf within the Commons.[10] The British government had made this argument to the American colonists in the 1770s when dismissing their demand for seats in Parliament; the colonists considered the theory specious.[11] By 1830, its efficacy in countering domestic discontent had also substantially weakened.

The conduct of election campaigns

Three 'traditional' activities attracted considerable criticism by 1830: bribery, 'treating', and intimidation.[12] Bribery is a self-explanatory term. The explicit purchase of votes for cash had technically been illegal since 1696, but the law was so rarely enforced that the practice had almost acquired conventional status. Offers of employment, public office, or advantageous transfers of land in return for votes were also widespread.

'Treating' was indirect bribery, in which voters were 'persuaded' to support a candidate by lavish provision of food, drink and entertainments. Treating was much facilitated by the use of pubs as voting centres. While technically illegal since 1696, treating was so routine a part of elections that candidates who could not afford to 'entertain' voters were effectively debarred from entering contested elections, particularly as the 'price' of votes increased in closely fought constituencies. Treating was

9 This oversimplifies the issue; see Brock op cit ch 1.

10 See Rawlings H (1988) *Law and the electoral process* ch 1 (London: Sweet and Maxwell).

11 Bailyn op cit pp 161–170.

12 See generally O'Leary C (1962) *The elimination of corrupt practices in British general elections 1868–1911* ch 1 (Oxford: Clarendon Press).

further encouraged by the fact that many constituencies had only one polling booth. However, voters had many days to register their choice. This was a necessity for outvoters, who needed time to journey to their various electoral homes. Outvoters could also expect to have their travel, accommodation and refreshment bills met by their preferred candidate.[13]

The cost of candidacy was further increased by the rule that candidates themselves had to pay all the administrative costs of the election, such as hiring the polling station. This particular provision survived until well into the twentieth century.

Intimidation took various forms. Mob violence was common, as was assault of voters by supporters of particular candidates. Somewhat more subtle was economic intimidation, entailing dismissal from employment or eviction from property if the employer/landlord's voting instructions were not followed. 'Spiritual intimidation' was less tangible, but one cannot doubt the occasional efficacy of a tactic which involved local clergy informing impressionable voters that it would be a sin to vote for anyone other than the priest's favoured candidate.

The impact of all three practices was exacerbated by the lack of a secret ballot. Public voting was justified on the basis that the right to vote was akin to a trust, and so necessarily open to scrutiny.[14] Reformers regarded this as a guarantor of corruption and intimidation: candidates who bought votes could check they gained value for money and penalise voters of independent inclinations.

The incentive for candidates to engage in corruption was magnified by the political, rather than legal, nature of the way corruption was policed. Until 1604, defeated candidates alleging malpractice pursued their case before the courts. From 1604–1770, disputed election petitions were heard by the Commons sitting as a whole house. Since so many MPs owed their seats to corrupt practices, only the most egregious misbehaviour led to disqualification. In 1770, a private members' Bill was enacted which granted jurisdiction to a 13 member Commons committee, in the hope that the task could be approached in a less partisan manner.[15]

A corrupt contest was a lesser ground for concern than having no contest at all. Elections with just one candidate per seat were the norm rather than the exception of pre-1832 practice, and frequently resulted from an agreement by groups of candidates of opposing parties to allow each other a clear run in neighbouring constituencies.

Selecting candidates

Since 1710, MPs representing county constituencies had to own landed property worth at least £600; for borough members the sum was £300. These criteria clearly excluded most of the population, including many of the emergent middle classes, from the electoral contest, and indicates the formal influence of landed wealth on the Commons' composition. More noteworthy was the informal influence exercised by members of the Lords. The lack of contestation in many seats, the exorbitant cost of

[13] Cannon op cit p 209. [14] O'Leary op cit p 26. [15] O'Leary op cit pp 9–12.

contested campaigns, the small size of many electorates and the open voting process, combined to enhance local aristocrats' control of voters' behaviour.

There would have been little point in peers controlling voter behaviour if they could not subsequently control the MP's behaviour. For many local magnates, 'their' MP was as much a part of their property as their land or their livestock. In 'nomination' or 'pocket' boroughs, voters were economically dependent on the local aristocrat, and the candidates were often his sons. Such familial feeling frequently ensured a co-incidence of political opinion between the members of the lower and upper house. Similarly, candidates were frequently protegees of peers. They were selected to do their patron's bidding, and although they were, in legal terms, answerable to no-one for their opinions or voting record until the next election, they could not win that election without their patron's continued support. In 1830, 270 MPs represented such constituencies. Some senior peers reputedly controlled as many as 12 MPs.[16] And for patrons whose interest in politics might wain, a pocket borough was a saleable commodity, fetching as much as £180,000 (at 1830 prices).[17] One would err in assuming that nomination boroughs ensured that the Commons automatically followed the Lords' wishes. But their existence on such a scale undermined the Commons' supposed role as a balancing force arraigned against the aristocracy and the Monarch.

Perhaps the most extraordinary illustration of the pre-1832 system is an election at Bute where, according to Brock: 'the candidate had proposed and seconded his own nomination, and then voted for himself, he being the only person present . . .'.[18] Such tales may be apocryphal. That they could be given any currency at all indicates the electoral system's profound inadequacy for a rapidly industrialising and urbanising society.

The original Bill

The Bill presented by Lord Grey's Whig (Liberal) government[19] sought to shift the formal balance of power in the Commons away from the landowning aristocracy towards the newly emergent manufacturing and professional classes. Grey was not, however, advocating a 'democratic' society. As Brock suggests, the government wished 'to make aristocratic government acceptable by purging away its most corrupt and expensive features'.[20] Grey himself was candid as to his intentions:

> 'A great change has taken place . . . in the distribution of property, and unless a corresponding change can be made in the legal mode by which that property can act upon government, revolutions must necessarily follow. This change requires a greater influence to be yielded to the middle classes, who have made wonderful advances both in property and intelligence'.[21]

Grey established a four-member Committee to produce a reform plan sufficiently radical to defuse popular discontent, yet sufficiently conservative to ensure the continued dominance of aristocratic ideas within the lower house. The Committee recommended

16 Turbeville (1958) op cit pp 244–247. 17 Brock op cit ch 1. 18 Brock op cit p 32.
19 For a concise account see Cannon op cit pp 206–210.
20 Brock op cit p 44. 21 Brock op cit p 152.

that large counties should gain two extra MPs; boroughs with fewer than 2000 inhabitants would lose both members; boroughs with fewer than 4000 would lose one; unrepresented towns with over 10,000 residents would gain one MP. The Committee retained the property qualification, but recommended a uniform £10 freehold threshold. Outvoting was to be abolished by introducing a residence requirement, and, most radically, voting would be by secret ballot. These plans would produce a substantially increased electorate, voting in constituencies which acknowledged contemporary population patterns, under conditions encouraging independent voting behaviour.

While agreeing to most of these proposals, the Cabinet rejected the secret ballot. Grey personally opposed secrecy, as did William IV, considering it: 'inconsistent with the manly spirit and free avowal of opinion which distinguish the people of England'.[22]

The Bill's parliamentary passage

In the Commons, the Bill passed second reading by 302 votes to 301. In Committee, however, the Tories carried a wrecking amendment. Grey subsequently resigned, and was granted a dissolution by William IV. At the ensuing election, fought entirely on the basis of reform, the government gained a majority of 130 seats. The legislative battle ground subsequently shifted to the Lords.

As chapter six suggested, Conservative peers who regarded Liberal policies as revolutionary were not persuaded even in 1911 to defer to a newly elected Commons majority. In 1831, the convention that the Lords should do so had yet to be established. The Commons was asking the Lords to approve a measure which would have greatly reduced the aristocracy's direct control over the lower house's composition. Tory peers lacked Grey's faith that a middle class electorate would vote for aristocratic principles of government, and remained intransigent.

As noted in chapter six, one way to view the constitutional function of the Lords' (then) legislative co-equality was as a guarantor of traditional distributions of 'property'. The common law had accepted that an entitled voter could maintain a tortious action against a government official who unlawfully prevented him from exercising the right.[23] Casting one's vote could therefore be seen as 'property' in the same sense as security in one's home (*Entick*) or one's physical liberty (*Liversidge*).

But for many Tories, the vote was regarded as 'property' in a rather different sense, belonging not to the individual voter, but to the aristocrat on whom the voter was economically dependent, as tenant or employee. In 1829, the Duke of Newcastle responded to criticism of his decision to evict tenants who voted against his preferred candidate by saying: 'Is it presumed then that I am not to do what I will with my own'.[24] The point was clearly put by Lord Eldon when criticising the Bill's plan to abolish pocket boroughs: 'Parliament had no more right, Eldon told the Lords in 1832, "to take away the elective franchise from the present holders of it, than . . . to

[22] Quoted in Cannon op cit p 211.
[23] *Ashby v White* (1703) 2 Ld Raym 938. See ch 8 below.
[24] Brock op cit p 63.

take away from them the property in houses or land which conferred it".'[25] The idea that voting for one's legislators was a 'right' that all possessed simply by being a citizen, to be freely exercised according to one's conscience, was adhered to only by the radical fringes of early nineteenth century society.

The first weeks after the election were taken up with delicate negotiations between Grey and William IV concerning a mass creation of peers to ensure the Bill would be passed. William was unwilling to create the 50 peers needed to ensure a government majority, and the Lords rejected the Bill by 41 votes at second reading. The veto triggered widespread public protest. Riots in Bristol led to over 400 deaths, and several Tory peers found themselves and their property under attack.[26] The government was sufficiently alarmed to use its prerogative power to issue a proclamation, stressing that the formation of private militia was illegal.[27] Many observers feared violent revolution was at hand.

Modification of the Bill

Rather than resign again, the government produced a modified Bill, designed to mollify its Tory opponents. As in 1909 and 1911, the Tory Party split into two factions – the 'waverers' and the 'die-hards'. The former, fearing either that a further government defeat would lead either to its resignation and possibly civil war, or to a mass creation of peers, advocated amendment rather than veto. The latter favoured resistance, irrespective of the consequences. Initially, the die-hards kept the upper hand.

The amended Bill received a Commons majority of 162, but was subject to a wrecking amendment in the Lords. William continued to refuse a mass creation, whereupon Grey once more resigned. Given the party balance in the Commons, there was no likelihood of a Tory government being formed, although this was William's preferred solution. The King asked the Tory leader, the Duke of Wellington, to form a government, but he could not muster sufficient Commons support. 'Public opinion' voiced many protests against a possible Wellington administration. The 'Days of May' embroiled radical reformers in a co-ordinated effort to destabilise the currency by withdrawing gold from the banks (the movement's slogan being 'To Stop the Duke, Go for Gold'), and reformers in several towns prepared for armed struggle.[28] Grey subsequently agreed to continue in office if the King agreed to create as many peers as necessary to push the Bill through. At that point, sufficient Tory peers capitulated for the Bill to pass.

For Wellington, the Act was 'a revolution by due process of law'.[29] What Professor Wade later termed the 'ultimate political fact' of parliamentary sovereignty remained unchanged – but Parliament now reflected a changed concept of 'the people' upon whose consent the stability of constitutional government would depend.

25 Brock op cit p 36. 26 Cannon op cit pp 226–228: Brock op cit pp 247–259.
27 Cannon op cit p 227. 28 Cannon op cit pp 236–240. 29 Cannon op cit p 204.

CHARTISM AND THE PURSUIT OF A 'DEMOCRATIC' ELECTORAL SYSTEM

Wellington's 'revolution' created only an elitist electorate of the aristocracy and middle class. Like the Framers of the American Constitution 50 years earlier, the 1832 reformers distinguished carefully between 'the people' and 'the populace'. The emergent professional and commercial classes, could safely be enfranchised; their property and education led them to accept existing socio-economic norms. The 'populace', in contrast, were the urban working class, who – it was feared – would elect a Commons committed to far-reaching redistribution of wealth and political power.[30]

That the 1832 Act fell far short of real 'revolution' is indicated by the disintegration of the radical movement in the 1837 election. The new electorate appeared as conservative as its predecessor. Further reform disappeared from the parliamentary agenda: 'The reformed electorate was not radical enough to vote for its own enlargement'.[31] It was therefore among the 'populace', and through extra-parliamentary methods, that the next phase of Britain's journey towards a democratic constitutional settlement occurred.

Chartism: objectives, methods – and failure?

Modern democrats might regard the 'Six Points' of 'The People's Charter' as eminently reasonable. The demand for annual elections may embody too short a time span, but universal adult suffrage, constituencies of equal size, the secret ballot, the payment of MPs, and removing the requirement that MPs be substantial property owners now appear quite modest objectives. But to most Parliamentarians in the 1840s, the objectives, and the methods through which Chartists pursued them, struck at the roots of constitutional propriety.[32]

Chartism has been variously described as the 'first working class political party' or 'the first organised effort to stir up class consciousness on a national scale'.[33] It was an umbrella movement, with many local variations on a central theme which linked economic redistribution with democratisation of the political process; it owed as much to its members' poverty as to abstract notions of democracy.

Chartism was also beset by a tension between 'respectable' and 'revolutionary' factions – the former seeking reform through the persuasive and lawful route of 'moral force', the latter prepared to take up arms and usher in the democratic age through 'physical force'. Both factions were united however, in regarding the 1832 Reform Act as a Whig betrayal of 'the people'.

Chartism's many strands coalesced sufficiently for a National Convention to meet to formulate detailed demands and present The People's Charter to the Commons.

30 One might reflect here on the contents of the People's Budget, the product of a government returned by an electorate in which virtually all adult men were enfranchised.

31 Brock op cit p 317.

32 I am indebted to J Ward's (1973) *Chartism* (Harper and Row: New York) for the following pages.

33 Ward op cit p 7 and p 245.

Should it be rejected, a general strike would be called to persuade Parliament to enact the Six Points. The Convention met in February 1839, but its deliberations rapidly exposed divisions in Chartist ranks. Many delegates resigned as the majority mood swung increasingly towards violent action and evidence emerged that many Chartists were preparing for civil war.

The Commons debated the Charter only briefly, voting overwhelmingly to give it no further attention. The general strike attracted few supporters. Many leaders were gaoled for public order offences, and an abortive 'revolution' in Newport resulted in capital sentences for treason for some conspirators. In 1842, Chartism re-emerged in a distinctly less abrasive form. The National Charter Association dedicated itself to educative and lobbying initiatives, and by April had some 350 branches. Nevertheless, a second petition and National Convention were accompanied by widespread strike action in the north.

On this occasion, the Commons refused even to accept the Chartist's petition. Strikes were met by prompt prosecutions for any breaches of public order, criminal damage or conspiracy laws. Many of the movement's activists diverted their attention to social reform issues such as temperance and child labour laws. In combination with a distinct upturn in the economy, these factors again pushed Chartism to the margins of the political process.

Chartism's third and final phase began in 1845. The movement enjoyed considerable successes in local government elections in Leeds, and in 1846 a Chartist MP was returned for Nottingham. A third petition and National Convention were planned in early 1848. The Convention coincided with several revolutions in continental Europe. There was widespread fear among aristocrats and parliamentarians that a similar fate would shortly befall the British constitution when the Chartists planned to march *en masse* to Parliament to demand radical electoral reform. Such fears proved misplaced. Following a substantial mobilisation of military forces, the Chartists called off the march. The subsequent presentation of the petition further undermined the movement. Chartist claims of six million signatures were grossly inflated, and many names were obvious forgeries.

It is tempting to view Chartism simply as an isolated historical anachronism, but as Julius West has suggested, that underestimates its constitutional significance:

> 'The movement's failures lay in the direction of securing legislation . . . Judged by its crop of statutes, Chartism was a failure. Judged by its essential . . . purpose, Chartism was a success. It achieved not the Six Points, but a state of mind'.[34]

States of mind, like principles of constitutional morality, are invariably elusive concepts. Quite how great an influence the Chartist legacy exercised on subsequent electoral reform is impossible to gauge. Yet as a vehicle for demonstrating the importance of class divisions in the evolution of constitutional orthodoxies and heresies, and for emphasising the links between economic and political reform, it has few rivals.

[34] Quoted in Ward op cit p 245.

THE 1867–1884 REFORMS: TOWARDS A UNIVERSAL 'RIGHT' TO VOTE AND A 'FAIR' ELECTORAL CONTEST

Minor reforms were enacted in the 35 years following 1832. The requirement that MPs be substantial landowners was modified in 1838 – personal as well as real property would now suffice. The requirement was abolished altogether, without opposition from the Lords, in 1858. Nevertheless, the system remained manifestly 'undemocratic' as we now understand that term. In the 1847 election, over 60% of seats had only one candidate; in 1866 one could identify over 1200 different qualifications for the franchise.[35] Parliament undertook some ad hoc initiatives to remove the most blatant instances of electoral corruption. Legislation passed in 1844 and 1847 disenfranchised the boroughs of Sudbury and St Albans respectively; their seats were reallocated to the larger counties.[36] More systematic revision occurred in 1867.

Disraeli's 1867 Reform Bill attracted no substantial opposition in the Lords.[37] Its Commons passage, in contrast, was extraordinarily tortuous. Disraeli led a minority Tory Party in the Commons in an administration headed by Lord Darby. It assumed office following the resignation of Lord John Russell's Liberal government when a backbench Liberal rebellion defeated Russell's own reform plans; the rebels (known as 'the Cave') thought Russell's proposals too extensive. The 1867 Act introduced a modest redistribution to take some (limited) account of demographic trends. Its main focus, however, was on qualification for the franchise. Over a million voters joined the electoral roll, doubling its size. This was more than twice as many as envisaged by Russell's measure. Yet those very MPs who had voted against Russell subsequently supported Disraeli. Perhaps the most striking feature of the 1867 controversy is that a matter of such great constitutional significance was resolved not according to its substantive merits per se, but according to what Disraeli calculated would best serve his party's short term survival in government.[38]

Disraeli's great achievement was to produce a Bill supported not only by moderate Conservatives, but also by radical Liberals and reactionary Tories. At this time, the centre ranks of the Tories and Liberals (the Liberals led in effect by Gladstone) had become so mutually antagonistic that it was inconceivable either would support the other on any reform measure. It was also generally believed (as a legacy of 1832) that the Liberals favoured more far-reaching reform than the Tories.

The Bill detached the radicals from the Liberal Party by proposing to reduce the county franchise qualification from £50 to £15, and to extend the borough franchise to any adult male who paid poor rates. However it simultaneously placated reactionary Tories by creating 'fancy franchises' to give additional votes to individuals who had certain property or educational qualifications. Furthermore, borough ratepayers could vote only if they paid their rates personally: those who paid their rates to their

[35] Brock op cit pp 326–333. [36] O'Leary op cit p 22. [37] Turbeville (1958) op cit pp 422–425.

[38] A fascinating study is provided in Cowling M (1967) *1867: Disraeli, Gladstone, and revolution* (Cambridge: Cambridge University Press). A rather different version of events is offered in Turbeville (1958) op cit pp 396–428.

landlord as part of their rent (predominantly poorer tenants) would not be enfranchised. Initially one might think Disraeli's concessions would have alienated radical support. But Disraeli had tacitly agreed with radical MPs to acquiesce if they removed those restrictions in Committee, where the government was in a minority. The Committee stage modified the Bill in both progressive and reactionary directions. The personal payment and fancy franchise provisions were removed, and the county franchise reduced to £12, but the radicals could not muster majority support for the secret ballot, for voting by written form rather than in person, for government subsidy of election expenses, and for the explicit enfranchisement of women.[39]

Commons manoeuvrings were accompanied by extensive public agitation. A Reform League of London-based journalists and artisans lent the campaign a strident, working class edge. In April 1867, the League announced it would hold a mass rally in Hyde Park. The Cabinet initially wished to prohibit the event, but Walpole, the Home Secretary, could find no statutory power for doing so. Shortage of time precluded new legislation, so Walpole invoked the prerogative to issue proclamations warning protestors the meeting was illegal, despite his own lawyers' advice that the proclamatory power did not extend to such matters.[40] The protestors ignored the warnings. The meeting passed peacefully, embarrassing the government and setting a potentially important precedent concerning the status of freedom of speech and assembly within Britain's constitutional traditions.

In 1867, neither Disraeli nor Gladstone could be regarded as 'democrats'. Gladstone's Liberalism did not extend to enfranchising 'the poorest, the least instructed and the most dependent members of the community'.[41] Nevertheless, Gladstone was regarded in some quarters, both reactionary and radical, as coming closer to an embrace of 'democracy' than any other leading politician. And barely 20 years later, Gladstone led Parliament a considerable way along such a path.

The dawning of the democratic age?

Shortly after the passage of the 1867 Act, Disraeli steered the Election Petitions and Corrupt Practices at Elections Act through Parliament. The Act returned jurisdiction over disputed elections to the courts. The measure had both practical and symbolic effects; the former in ensuring that a coherent body of precedent defining unacceptable behaviour would emerge; the latter in suggesting that the electoral process was henceforth subject to orthodox rule of law principles.

The secret ballot was introduced in 1872. The 1868 general election had been attended by substantial corruption and intimidation.[42] A Select Committee established in 1869 identified the ballot as the most effective anti-corruption device. Gladstone's Liberal administration introduced a Bill in 1871, which was opposed by the Tories in

39 Cowling op cit pp 223–226.

40 See the *Case of Proclamations* at pp 95–96 above.

41 Cowling op cit p 40.

42 For contemporaneous accounts of the era see Rover C (1967) *Women's suffrage and party politics in Britain 1866–1914* pp 40–41 (London: RKP).

the Commons, and vetoed by the Lords. Gladstone submitted a similar Bill in 1872, and threatened to request a dissolution if it was rejected. The Bill was grudgingly approved. Equally significant was the Corrupt and Illegal Practices Prevention Act 1883. This limited the amount of money that individual candidates could spend on their local campaign, the amount being based on a (small) *per capita* sum for each voter in the constituency.

Both measures indicated a further cultural shift towards a meritocratic rather than aristocratic constitutional morality. The political process itself was increasingly structured by middle class values of fair competition, in which political power was fought and won on the basis of rational argument, rather than the unthinking deference previously accorded to landowning interests. By the mid-1880s, that rationality had extended to include a substantial proportion of working class men.

The key element of Gladstone's 1884 reform was a uniform borough/county voting qualification, set at the lower borough level, which would enfranchise two million additional voters.[43] The Tories initially opposed the Bill. Although the Liberals had a reliable Commons majority, they were a minority in the Lords. Lord Salisbury, leader of the Tory peers, was ready to apply his 'referendal theory' of the veto power,[44] and force a dissolution.

Many Liberal MPs relished the prospect of a veto, seeing an opportunity to curb the upper chamber's powers. Gladstone himself described any such veto as 'A precedent against Liberty'.[45] As in 1832, the Lords' intransigence provoked widespread public agitation in support of reform. In the Commons Tory MPs failed to follow Salisbury's advice to give the Bill 'a good parting kick at third reading'.[46] The Lords was thus unable to point to a clear split in electoral opinion on the issue. Crisis was avoided by negotiation between a handful of each party's leaders, without any substantial debate in either house, which prompted the leading Liberal newspaper (*The Manchester Guardian*) to describe the outcome as 'a usurpation of the office and powers of Parliament'.[47]

This contrasted markedly with the passage of the 1867 Bill, where the Commons committee stage was of paramount importance to the Act's final shape. The statutory label one may attach to both measures conceals substantial differences in the realities of the legislative process. The origins and passage of the Representation of the People Act (RPA) 1918, through which some women were enfranchised, took still another form.

GENDER DISCRIMINATION: WOMEN'S RIGHT TO VOTE

As chapter two observed, English and Scots courts in the Victorian era considered it an axiomatic constitutional principle that women did not vote. While Parliament could amend that principle, the political change entailed would be so profound that it could only be achieved through the most explicitly phrased statutory formulae. But

[43] See generally Jones A (1972) *The Politics of reform 1884* (Cambridge: Cambridge University Press).
[44] See pp 176–177 above. [45] Jones op cit p 149. [46] Jones op cit at p 148.
[47] Jones op cit at p 221.

Chorlton v Lings and *Nairn v University of St Andrews* were merely minor parts of a bitter, protracted dispute which ranged over Britain's constitutional landscape from the 1830s, embracing spirited debate in Parliament, determined public protest, and deliberate crimes of violence. There are few better illustrations of the complex nature of 'constitutionality' in British political history than the campaigns for women's suffrage.[48]

'Democracy' – a class or gender issue?

The 1832, 1867 and 1884 Reform Acts were contests conducted principally around the dividing lines of class and urbanisation. Women's enfranchisement was decisively rejected in the Commons in 1867 and 1884, and the Chartists had (briefly) entertained, but (promptly) dropped the women's cause.[49]

One strand of opposition to female suffrage had a 'natural law' basis, typified by E Wright's 1913 book, *The unexpurgated case against women's suffrage.* This contended that women should never be permitted to vote because their relative physical frailty meant they could not fight for their country, and their emotion-laden psyches led them 'to look upon their minds not as an instrument for the pursuit of truth, but as an instrument for providing them with creature comforts. . . .'.[50] Such sentiments were shared in 1892 by Asquith, who barely 15 years later embroiled his party in radical constitutional battle against the Tory peers. Democracy, for Asquith, demanded legislation to remove only man-made inequalities: 'not those indelible differences of faculty and function by which Nature herself has given diversity and richness to human society'.[51] Women and men were simply created unequal, at least when choosing their lawmakers.

A related belief was that political activities would drain women of the energies needed to bear children. Opponents of female suffrage also invoked virtual representation theory – women did not need a vote because they were adequately represented by their fathers, brothers or husbands. For Professor Dicey, women's enfranchisement should be resisted because it raised the spectre of Parliament being dominated by majoritarian sentiments. Women, Dicey noted, formed the majority of the population, and he assumed that they would vote in an homogenous bloc in pursuit of gender discriminatory policies. Such a Parliament would have no automatic claim to sovereignty:

> 'Is it certain that in such circumstances Englishmen would obey and enforce a law that punished as a crime conduct which they in general held ought to be treated as an offence, not against law, but against morality'.[52]

Supportive arguments were initially championed by John Stuart Mill. One proposition

48 The most informative guide continues to be Rover op cit.

49 Brock op cit p 322.

50 At pp 35–36.

51 Quoted in Pugh M (1980) *Women's suffrage in Britain 1867–1928* p 8 (London: The Historical Association).

52 Quoted in Rover op cit at p 45.

drew directly on an intensifying philosophical belief in the centrality of the individual as the repository of rights and obligations. Mill, invoking Diceyan notions of the rule of law for ends of which Dicey strongly disapproved, suggested it was capricious to deny women's individuality solely on the basis of their sex. Women increasingly possessed those attributes traditionally regarded as necessary for men to acquire the vote; namely education, ownership of land or commercial property, and liability for taxation.

The opposition case was also undermined by institutional factors – women had been enfranchised for local government elections since 1869. Gender equality in this sphere attracted little controversy as it was assumed that local government's parochial, social welfare responsibilities coincided with women's 'natural' role as wives and mothers.[53] Opponents of enfranchisement blundered rather by enlisting women as campaigners – thereby creating the absurd situation in which the campaigners could win their argument only by successfully doing what they argued they could not do. Consolidation of the national party system also weakened the opposition case. Installing and maintaining party loyalty among a growing electorate required many volunteers, ideally possessed of spare time, economic independence and some education. Middle class women were obvious recruits.

To speak of the 'Women's Suffrage Movement' is misleading, since the pressure for reform came from many quarters. Rover's leading study describes it as 'a political movement run by middle class women',[54] concentrated in London. Many reformers sought enfranchisement only on the same terms as men, which, even after 1884, would have prevented many women from voting. Nevertheless, working class women also devoted considerable time and effort to the reform movement. That they achieved less prominence in subsequent studies may be in part because they left less extensive records of their activities than their middle class contemporaries, and in part because, like the Chartists, their demand to vote was inextricably linked with economic policy issues arising from their unfavourable employment situation.[55]

Much like Chartism, the suffrage movement harboured a divide between activists favouring 'physical force' (the suffrag*ettes*) and those prepared only to employ moral force (the suffrag*ists*). The suffragists emerged in 1867, led by the National Society for Women's Suffrage (NSWS). The NSWS pursued only lawful (indeed genteel) routes to reform: 'In the 1870s, great store was set on presenting petitions to Parliament',[56] and much energy was expended on educative strategies aimed both at public opinion, and at potentially supportive MPs. In 1906, the NSWS claimed over 300 Commons supporters. Since 1870, sympathetic backbenchers of both parties had introduced appropriate private members' Bills. None attracted government support.

The militant Women's Social and Political Union was founded in 1903, in response to the perceived failure of 'constitutional' methods. Its own constitution implored

53 See Pugh op cit p 13. 54 Op cit p 12.

55 To redress the balance, see Liddington J and Norris J (1979) *One hand tied behind us* (London: Virago).

56 Driver op cit p 60.

members to engage in: 'Vigorous agitation upon lines justified by the position of outlawry to which women are at present condemned'.[57] Such agitation entailed increasingly serious illegality. It began in 1905 with the disruption of public meetings addressed by anti-suffrage MPs, escalated to confrontations with the police during public marches from 1907, and culminated in arson attacks on public buildings.

Activists frequently welcomed arrest and imprisonment as opportunities for publicity. Many convicted women engaged in hunger strikes, which presented the Liberal government with the dilemma of either allowing them to starve to death, and so emerge as martyrs to a political cause, or to release them and thereby allow them to evade the criminal law. An attempt to solve the dilemma by forced feeding attracted widespread public condemnation.

Successive Tory and Liberal leaders made determined efforts to present enfranchisement as a non-party issue. Women activists generally subscribed to this bi-partisan approach until 1912, when the suffragists formally aligned themselves with the Labour Party, which was the only party committed to the women's right to vote.[58] The various supporters of female suffrage coalesced between 1910 and 1912 around a 'Conciliation Bill', which would enfranchise women already entitled to vote in municipal elections. The Bill was defeated. Several reasons contributed to the defeat. One is that the Bill was 'torpedoed' by Asquith's announcement that the government would introduce a wide-ranging Reform Bill in 1913, which might be amended to include women's enfranchisement. A second is that Asquith secretly threatened to resign if the Bill was carried, a threat which prompted many Liberals and Irish members to renege on previous pledges of support. A third is that wavering MPs were tipped against the cause by the WSPU's extremism.

The subsequent government Bill was in turn 'torpedoed' by the Speaker's ruling that the women's suffrage amendment was inadmissable. Asquith was pleased by the outcome: 'The Speaker's coup d'etat has bowled over the Women for this session – a great relief'.[59] Moreover, Asquith hoped that if the amendment had passed in the lower house, the Lords would exercise its new delaying powers and enable the Commons to change its mind.[60]

At the outbreak of World War One, both suffragists and suffragettes suspended their campaigns. The issue thereafter assumed a consensual air. Asquith appointed a 'Speaker's Conference' composed of 32 MPs, which proposed a franchise for men aged over 21, and women aged over 30, based solely on residence. The proposals were enacted in the RPA 1918. The war undoubtedly contributed to the timing of enfranchisement, but the movement's eventual success was as much a symptom of the

[57] Reproduced in Rover op cit p 76.

[58] See Pugh M (1985) 'Labour and women's suffrage' in Brown K (ed) *The first Labour party* (London: Croom Helm).

[59] Quoted in Rover op cit p 196.

[60] Rover op cit p 96. This perfectly illustrates the point that constitutional law covers a sufficiently wide range of issues to permit a politician or judge to combine radicalism on some issues with rigid conservatism on others.

erosion of pervasive gender inequality in the social and economic spheres as of a sudden recognition of a need to restructure the political basis of the constitution.

CONCLUSION

The Speaker's Conference offered a formal and transparent device through which major constitutional reform could be planned in a way that transcended the generally partisan nature of parliamentary politics. But in 1918, matters of substance were at least as important as those of process. In addition to proposing female suffrage, the Conference made several other recommendations which, when enacted in RPA 1918, ironed out most of the obvious remaining anti-democratic creases in the fabric of Britain's electoral system.[61]

Adult male suffrage was now granted solely on the basis of six month's residence in a constituency (women under 30 had to wait until further reform was enacted in 1928). Some citizens still had two votes, since the university franchise and a business premises franchise were retained, but multiple outvoting was eliminated. The Act also acknowledged the desirability of maintaining constituencies with electorates of equal size, although it did not demand exact mathematical equality. Additionally, the RPA 1918 made several significant financial innovations. Parliament finally accepted that the government, rather than the candidates, should bear the administrative costs of the election. To discourage frivolous candidates, a deposit of £150 (then a substantial sum) was required. This was returned if a candidate attracted more then 12.5% of the vote. To impose further economic equality on candidates, the spending limits introduced by the 1883 Act were almost halved in real terms. The principle that MPs should receive a salary had been accepted in 1912. It was nevertheless not until 1955 that all seats were contested.

This chapter has dwelt at length on the historical dimension of electoral law and practice, both because the episodes considered illustrate themes which continue to inform constitutional practice, and to stress that the contemporary constitution is the product of much messy, hard fought political development. But longtitudinal analysis also reveals the temporal ephemerality of even 'fundamental' constitutional

Table 7.3 Uncontested seats in General Elections

1906	*1910**	*1918*	*1924*	*1929*	*1931*	*1935*	*1945*	*1951*
114	163	107	32	7	67	40	3	4

* Second election.

Source: Adapted from Butler and Sloman op cit pp 180–182.

61 For a summary see Butler D (1953) *The electoral system in Britain 1918–1951* ch 1 (Oxford: Clarendon Press).

orthodoxies. In a few decades, analysts might consider the present law, to which we now turn, as anachronistic as the situations of 1831, 1885 or 1917 appear to our eyes.

II. THE CONTEMPORARY ELECTORAL PROCESS

Despite the evidently 'democratic' credentials of Britain's electoral system, the contemporary political environment has contained many voices in recent years advocating electoral reform. Critics have three foci of discontent. The first relates to constituency apportionment. The second concerns the conduct of election campaigns, especially the cost and content of party political advertising. The third, and most significant, is the nature of the counting system through which citizens' choices are transmitted.

APPORTIONMENT – DRAWING CONSTITUENCY BOUNDARIES

The Parliamentary Constituencies Act 1986 is a consolidating statute which defines the powers and responsibilities of a body called the Boundary Commission. The Commission determines the size and shape of constituencies in Scotland, Northern Ireland, Wales and England. This is obviously a task which has to be sensitive to accusations of political bias. It is conceivable that boundaries could intentionally be drawn in ways that bestow a political advantage on one party. To minimise this problem, each country's Commission (although nominally chaired by the Speaker) is headed by a high court judge. She is assisted by two other members. Members are appointed by the government, but, as a matter of convention, are also approved by the opposition parties. A Commission taking this form was first established in 1944. Earlier legislation had created bodies with less clearly structured apportionment responsibilities, staffed by party politicians, which consequently had great difficulty rebutting accusations that they could not be objective.[62] At 15 year intervals, the Commission holds local inquiries concerning reapportionment proposals. The Commission then presents a report to the Home Secretary making recommendations. The Home Secretary must then lay the report, with an implementing Order In Council (which may amend the proposals), before the Commons and Lords for approval.

Apportionment criteria – a non-justiciable issue?

The Commission's discretion is structured by 'rules' contained in the House of Commons (Redistribution of Seats) Act 1949, Sch 2 (as amended). The 'rule' label is an unfortunate misnomer, since the legal status of Sch 2 provisions is frequently merely guidance to which the Commission must have regard. Rule 1 specifies (with some precision) the total number of constituencies. Rule 7 requires the Commission to calculate an electoral quota – a figure arrived at by dividing the total number of

62 See for example Cowling op cit pp 231–232.

registered voters by the number of constituencies. At present, the quota is approximately 66,000.

Thereafter, the Commission must apply rather more discretionary criteria, seemingly ranked in the following order of importance. Rule 4 provides that, 'as far as practicable', constituencies should not cross county or London borough boundaries. Rule 5 then directs the Commission, subject to r 4, to make all constituencies as near to the electoral quota as possible: it may only depart from r 4 if respecting county or London borough boundaries would produce 'excessive disparity' between a constituency's size and the electoral quota. Rule 6 then permits the Commission to override rr 4 and 5 if 'special considerations, including in particular the size, shape and accessibility of a constituency, appear to render a departure desirable'.

The legislation therefore does not require mathematical equivalence in constituency sizes. The original 1944 Act did make numerical equality the most important apportionment consideration, but this was amended in 1947 in favour of affording top priority to producing constituencies based on traditional local 'communities'.[63] Parliament clearly still viewed the Commons as the 'House of Communities'.

In practice, the Act produces substantial discrepancies in constituency size. Prior to the 1983 reapportionment, Buckingham constituency had 116,000 voters, while Newcastle Central had only 24,000.[64] Despite the 1983 reforms, by 1987 over 100 hundred seats deviated from the quota by over 20%. At the various extremes were the Orkney and Shetland constituency with 31,000 voters, and the Isle of Wight with over 98,000.[65]

Such variations provoke criticisms of anti-democratic practice, on the grounds that the system ignores the principle of 'one vote one value'.[66] This complaint has a collective and individuated dimension. Collectively, the votes of Orkney residents were 'worth' more than three times as much as those of Isle of Wight residents, since both constituencies returned only one MP. More generally, the 'value' of a given constituency's voting power increases/decreases according to the extent by which its electorate is smaller/larger than the electoral quota. All communities are not created equal for electoral purposes.

The effective 'value' of an individual vote is more difficult to gauge. If, for example, residents in Newcastle Central and Buckingham voted in 1983 in identical proportions for the Conservative, Labour and Liberal Parties, the relative sizes of the constituencies would not affect the parties' overall performance. However, if a party had only 12,001 supporters in the two areas combined (ie 9% of the total electorate), it could nonetheless win one (50%) of the two seats if they all lived and voted in Newcastle Central. This is an extreme illustration of the more general point that a party benefits greatly if its supporters are disproportionately concentrated in small

63 See Craig J (1959) 'Parliament and Boundary Commissions' *Public Law* 23–45.

64 Alder J (1994) *Constitutional and administrative law* p 161 (London: Macmillan).

65 Norton (1991) op cit p 94.

66 See especially Wade (1980) op cit ch 2.

constituencies. Conversely, parties whose supporters reside predominantly in large constituencies are disadvantaged.

The apportionment criteria undoubtedly contain appreciable scope for unintended political bias,[67] and, thus, one might have thought, wide scope for legal challenges to the Commission's recommendations. However Parliament sought to curtail litigation by providing in s 4(7) that any Order in Council *purportedly* made under the Act 'shall not be questioned in any legal proceedings'. The use of 'purports' presumably safeguards the Act against the judicial 'threat' posed by *Anisminic.* This suggests that legislators see apportionment as a non-justiciable issue, to which Diceyan notions of the rule of law cannot apply. Thus far the courts appear to agree with that analysis.[68]

The 1969 controversy

The court's limited supervisory role has contributed to an explicitly partisan mode of dispute settlement within Parliament, as evidenced by events in 1969. The Commission's 1969 recommendations, reflecting substantial population movement away from the cities, seemed likely to cost the Labour Party a dozen seats in the next general election. James Callaghan, the Home Secretary, decided not to introduce an implementing Order. Instead, the government introduced a Bill effecting only some of the Commission's proposals, and also removing the Home Secretary's statutory obligation to lay the Order. The government (feebly) defended its strategy on the grounds that constituency reapportionment should be carried out in tandem with the redrawing of local government boundaries expected within the next few years.

The Conservative opposition considered the government was acting for partisan purposes. Consequently, the Lords' Conservative majority passed several wrecking amendments to the Bill, which was then withdrawn. Rather than reintroduce the Bill and invoke the Parliament Act procedures, the government instructed Labour MPs to vote against the Orders when Callaghan laid them before the Commons. The boundary changes could therefore not be introduced before the next election. This was perfectly legal; the Act did not require either House to approve the Orders, it merely commanded the Home Secretary to present them. The cynicism underlying the cabinet's strategy is neatly revealed in Crossman's *Diaries:*

> 'We agreed to have all the Orders put to the Commons and the trick would be to put them but not approve them, so that . . . we would negate the lot. [Wilson has won]. We have not been discredited because the ordinary public are convinced that both the Government and the Tories are concerned for our own self-interest . . . '.[69]

67 Some commentators convincingly argue substantial bias is invariably unavoidable; see Taylor P and Gudgin G (1976) 'The myth of non-partisan cartography' *Urban Studies* 13–25.

68 See *Harper v Home Secretary* [1955] Ch 238, [1955] 1 All ER 331, CA. For comment see Craig J op cit; De Smith S (1955) 'Boundaries between Parliament and the courts' *Modern Law Review* 281–286.

69 Op cit p 660.

The 1983 controversy

While Orders cannot be challenged in court, there is no ouster clause preventing litigation trying to stop the Commission presenting its report to the Home Secretary. Whether such litigation enjoyed any prospects of success was, until 1983, an open question – to which the courts then offered a curt answer.

The Labour Party feared that the Commission's recommendations for the 1983 election would significantly benefit the Conservative Party. In *R v Boundary Commission for England, ex p Foot*,[70] the party's leader, Michael Foot, sought a judicial review of the Commission's findings. Mr Foot contended that the Commission had misconstrued its responsibilities by regarding the statutory 'rule' requiring approximate parity in constituency sizes as subordinate to the 'rule' that constituencies should not straddle county or London borough boundaries. Mr Foot argued that the substantial divergences in constituency size envisaged by the proposals: 'offend[ed] against the principle of equal representation for all electors which is required by our modern system of Parliamentary representation'.[71] The applicants sought a court order to prevent the Commission from submitting its recommendations to the Home Secretary. The application was dismissed at first instance and on appeal.

Given the wording of the 1949 Act, the applicants were advancing an optimistic argument. Whether the constitution recognises a principle of 'equal representation' in electoral districting which demands mathematical equality is a moot (and political) point, but not one expressed unambiguously in the Act. In effect, Mr Foot was asking the court to attach the same constitutional significance to the moral principle of 'one vote one value' as it had attached to the moral principle of the 'rule of law' in *Anisminic*. The court declined to do so. Sir John Donaldson MR categorised the Commission's task as presumptively non-justiciable in the absence of all but the most egregious malfeasance.

In 1999, the Labour government introduced the Political Parties, Elections and Referendums Bill which would transfer the Boundary Commissions' function to a new statutory body, the Electoral Commission.[72] The Commission would consist of between five and nine members, nominally appointed by the Queen (in effect by the Prime Minister) following approval by the House of Commons. The Bill also proposed the creation of a body called the Speaker's Committee to oversee the activities of the Commission. Rather bizarrely, the Speaker would not sit on the Committee, which would comprise the Home Secretary, the Minister responsible for local government, the Chair of the Home Affairs Select Committee and six backbench MPs. The Bill requires the Committee to approve candidates selected to sit on the Commission. On its face, the proposal seems to be an attempt not so much to depoliticise the apportionment question as to ensure that it functions on the basis of multi-party agreement. The Bill was enacted in 2000 as the Political Parties, Elections and Referendums Act (hereafter the PPERA 2000). The timetable for the Electoral Commission

[70] [1983] QB 600, CA. [71] [1983] QB 600 at 617, CA.

[72] See Oliver D (1999) 'An Electoral Commission: an ingenious idea' *Public Law* 585–588.

to take on the functions of the Boundary Commission was rather relaxed. The Commission took over responsibility for delineating local government boundaries in April 2002; its powers in respect of parliamentary constituencies have yet to be assumed.

The new Commission and Committee will per se do little to redress the arithmetical inequities which pervade the constituency system, and might be seen as a piece of procedural window dressing designed to divert attention from a more significant substantive problem. 'One vote one value' is an idea whose time has not yet come within the British constitution. The potential shortcomings of the apportionment process should not however be seen in isolation from other aspects of electoral law, especially the vote counting method discussed below. But before broaching that question, we briefly explore the conduct of election campaigns.

THE CONTENTS AND CONDUCT OF ELECTION CAMPAIGNS

This section discusses four subjects: the voters, the candidates, and the financing and content of electoral advertising. The following pages do not offer a comprehensive guide to the minutiae of the law, but merely identify some of the more important elements of the electoral process. Jurisdiction over disputed elections is still vested in the High Court, which is empowered to invalidate results and disqualify malfeasors from subsequent elections. Few petitions are now presented, a state of affairs primarily attributable to an apparently pervasive acceptance of the moral propriety of electoral law.

The voters

Voter registration was introduced in 1832 as a device to minimise fraudulent voting. The RPA 1918 introduced a more rigorous process, in which local authorities assumed responsibility for ensuring the register's accuracy. In the modern era, there have been few suggestions that the registration process is abused.

Constitutional morality now accepts that voting is not a privilege earned through property or educational qualifications, but a right extending to virtually all adult citizens, forfeited only in very limited circumstances. The principle now underlying the grant of the franchise is that of *residence*. Since the passage of the RPA 1948, all other citizens over 18 years old may vote if their names are entered on the electoral register of the constituency(ies) where they have a place of residence.[73] Until 2000, the register was compiled annually in October by local government officials. This had the unfortunate consequence that prospective voters who just missed the October deadline could not register in their new constituencies until the next October, and so would be unable to vote there if an election was held in the interim. The RPA 2000 removed this difficulty by permitting the register to be updated on a continual basis.

[73] 'Residence' is a justiciable concept. See *Ferris v Wallace* 1936 SC 561; *Fox v Stirk* [1970] 2 QB 463, [1970] 3 All ER 7, CA; *Hipperson v Newbury District Electoral Registration Officer* [1985] QB 1060, [1985] 2 All ER 456, CA.

While there is no legal obligation compelling registered citizens to vote, failure to respond to registration forms is an offence.

The university and business franchises were abolished in 1948, since when no-one has been entitled to more than one vote in any general election. Rather curiously however, it remains possible to be **registered to vote** in multiple constituencies. Voters with many residences can thus choose where to cast their vote; and indeed it appears that they may cast votes in several constituencies if by-elections happen to be held on the same day in constituencies where they are registered.[74]

In recent years, several minor initiatives have been undertaken to increase the size of the electorate still further. The RPA 1985 made it possible for previously registered voters who now lived overseas to maintain a vote in their old constituencies. The RPA 2000 promoted by the first Blair government further eroded the linkage between voting rights and residence by making it possible for homeless people to register a notional residence for electoral purposes. A homeless person may give as his/her address; 'a place in the UK where he commonly spends a substantial part of his time (whether during the day or night)'.[75] The 2000 Act also entitles prisoners held in gaol on remand to use the prison as their residential address.

The only citizens[76] presumptively excluded from the franchise because of their status are the monarch, life peers and the remaining hereditary members of the Lords. Other disqualifications are premised on failings of behaviour or competence. Individuals may not vote if they are serving prison sentences, or have recently been convicted of electoral malpractice. Some parliamentary consideration was given during the passage of the RPA 2000 to enfranchising convicted prisoners, but the government held the view that disenfrachisement was a logical additional penalty to be suffered by persons gaoled for having committed crimes.[77] The RPA 2000 also removed the previous disqualification of people detained in hospital under the Mental Health Act 1983. It appears that there is an archaic common law test of 'competence' which may serve to disenfranchise mentally ill or mentally disabled people, but this has not been applied in recent years and its scope and currency are uncertain.[78]

The candidates

There are few collective prohibitions on candidacy. Parties advocating extremist political philosophies such as the British National Party and Socialist Workers Party regularly field candidates, albeit never victorious ones. Nor is there any prohibition on parties such as Plaid Cymru, the Scottish Nationalists, or Sinn Fein, whose primary policy objective is to secure their respective country's independence. The entitlement to contest elections does not however extend to certain 'proscribed organisations',

74 RPA 1981, s 1; s 61.

75 RPA 2000, s 6, amending RPA 1983, s 7.

76 'Citizens' in this context is broadly defined to include not just UK citizens, but also citizens of Ireland and Commonwealth countries.

77 For a helpful critique of the Act and the principles underlying it, see Lardy H (2001) 'Representation of the People Act 2000' *Modern LR* 63–81.

78 See the discussion in Lardy op cit.

designated under the Prevention of Terrorism Acts. The justification for this is presumably that the groups concerned have chosen to pursue their political objectives outside the democratic process.

The requirement that MPs be wealthy was abolished in 1872. Current electoral law retains a modest financial barrier to candidacy itself. All candidates must produce a deposit of £500, which is forfeit if they fail to gain 5% of the vote. The rationale for the election deposit is not that impecunious candidates are per se unsuitable legislators, but that it prevents frivolous candidates from belittling the election process and/or making it harder to administer.

Candidates need not reside in their chosen constituency, but must be nominated by ten registered voters. Various statutes also disqualify a miscellaneous collection of citizens from candidacy, including those under 21 years old, Church of England and Roman Catholic clergymen, bankrupt debtors, and some categories of criminals and the mentally ill. This is overall a residual and quantitatively insignificant restriction, although as chapter eight suggests, individual exclusions can provoke great controversy.

The legal framework regulating candidacy is directed towards the candidate as an individual. Unlike most other 'democratic countries', Britain has no legislation dealing explicitly with such issues as the selection of parliamentary candidates, the formation of party policy, and the election of party leaders. These are all matters where Parliament has chosen not to interfere directly with party autonomy. Nor is there as yet anything to indicate that the courts consider such matters justiciable. An opportunity to test that assumption arose in 1990, when the Conservative Party ignored its rules for electing its leader when John Major succeeded Margaret Thatcher.[79] No challenge was issued however. Nor do constitutional lawyers appear to consider the question of much importance: intra-party democracy is an issue few legal commentators have examined.[80]

In 1994 it was suggested that legislation prohibiting gender and race discrimination might apply to political parties' internal membership and candidate selection practices, but this has yet to be confirmed by the courts. This raises a further dimension of the 'electoral equality' principle: women and citizens of minority ethnicity are severely under-represented both as MPs and candidates, and, as candidates, are disproportionately concentrated in unwinnable seats.[81]

A further lacuna in electoral law was revealed by a curious episode in 1994. The plaintiff in *Sanders v Chichester*[82] was a Liberal Democrat candidate in the 1994 election for members of the European Parliament,[83] although the issue it raised was of

79 See Alderman R and Smith M (1990) 'Can British Prime Ministers be given the push by their parties' *Parliamentary Affairs* 260–276; Alderman R and Carter N (1991) 'A very Tory coup: the ousting of Mrs Thatcher' *Parliamentary Affairs* 125–139.

80 The notable exception being Dawn Oliver; see her chapter in three successive editions (1985, 1989, and 1994) of Jowell and Oliver op cit.

81 Norton op cit pp 101–103.

82 [1995] 03 LS Gaz R 37.

83 An institution of the European Community, a topic broached below in chapters twelve and thirteen.

equal relevance in elections to the Commons. Mr Sanders was seeking to have the result of his constituency's election set aside.

The defendant was the successful candidate for the seat, although it was not his behaviour that was in question. A Mr Huggett had stood in the election as a 'Literal Democrat'. In Mr Sanders' view, Mr Hugget was seeking to mislead careless Liberal Democrat supporters into voting for him rather than Mr Sanders, in order to enhance the Conservative candidate's chances of winning. If that was Huggett's intention, he succeeded admirably. He attracted some 10,000 votes. The seat was won by Mr Chichester, the Conservative candidate, by fewer than 800 votes.[84]

The judgment turned on the meaning of rr 6(2) and (3) of Sch 1 of the RPA 1983. These rules require candidates to list their full name and address on the ballot paper. Candidates need not list any further information. They may add a description of up to six words. The description is generally used to confirm a candidate's party political affiliation.[85]

The court concluded that it could invalidate an election result only if a candidate had mis-stated her full name and address, since Parliament had made this aspect of candidate identification mandatory. However, the court held that Parliament had not intended that the permissive, description element of the information that candidates might enter on the ballot form could provide grounds for overturning an election result. The Act did not provide a legal mechanism to protect voters and candidates against potentially misleading entries on the ballot form: 'the rules did not prohibit candidates, whether out of spite or a wicked sense of fun, from describing themselves in a confusing way or indulging in spoiling tactics'.[86]

This was an unfortunately sterile interpretation of the statute. Parliament's failure to grant explicit protection against spoiling candidates to parties (and, more importantly, their supporters) was reprehensible in the context of a modern party-based electoral contest, but this was not necessarily a barrier to the court producing that result. Teleologically construed, the candidate's power to add a description to his/her name and address could readily be seen as a device intended to aid voters to make an informed decision when casting their vote. Descriptions which manifestly hampered that outcome would thus be unlawful.

The scope for abuse left open by *Sanders* was reduced by the Registration of Political Parties Act 1998. The Act permits parties to register particular emblems with the Registrar of Companies, and empowers them to prevent other parties using the emblem. More importantly, the Act prohibits candidates from describing themselves on the ballot paper in terms likely to mislead voters into assuming the candidate represents a registered party. The PPERA 2000 introduced a more extensive system of party registration, overseen by the Electoral Commission, which effectively precludes

84 Mr Huggett denied this was his intention. There was no suggestion that he had been encouraged to stand by the Conservative Party.

85 Permission to add the description was only introduced in 1968. Until then, candidates had not been allowed to identify their party on the ballot paper.

86 [1995] 03 LS Gaz R 37 at 39.

candidates standing for non-existent or 'spoiling' parties. This would seem a welcome – if belated – reform to electoral law, which clearly recognises the primacy of party affiliation in guiding voter behaviour.

Financing elections

A similar conclusion might now be drawn in respect of laws regulating electoral finance.[87] British campaigns are no longer marked by the violence and intimidation which so concerned the 1832 reformers. Nor do bribery or treating affect the contemporary process.[88] Similarly, the practice of spiritual intimidation seems to have faded away. Such threats would technically be caught by the crime of 'undue influence' (now RPA 1983, s 115), but s 115 prosecutions are more likely in respect of activities such as defacing a candidate's posters or pulling leaflets from voters' letterboxes.[89]

But there is more to fairness than an absence of physical force and financial corruption. This becomes apparent when one observes that until enactment of the PPERA 2000 the discrepancy between the historically local form of the electoral system and the nationalisation of political choice evident in the apportionment process was also apparent in the laws governing the amounts of money that parties and candidates can spend on election campaigns.

The reasoning behind the limits on expenditure first introduced by the Corrupt and Illegal Practices Prevention Act 1883 makes obvious democratic sense. The restrictions ensure that the merits of a candidate's arguments, rather than the size of her advertising budget, determine her electoral popularity. The letter of the 1883 law has been retained, with regularly updated financial thresholds. At present, each candidate is allowed by RPA 1983, s 76 to spend around £5,000, plus a few pence for every registered voter in the constituency. Rich candidates cannot derive an advantage from their wealth by, for example, employing dozens of full time helpers, or sending out glossy leaflets for weeks on end. Doubts exist as to when the expenditure clock starts ticking. The announcement of the dissolution of Parliament would appear the most likely point. This means of course that a wealthy candidate could spend unlimited amounts of money on publicity prior to the dissolution, but there is no indication that this is done on a significant basis.

Early efforts to enforce expenditure limits were handicapped by the law's limited focus. Only the candidate himself or his agent were covered by the rule: expenditure by 'independent' individuals or companies was not subject to any ceiling. This provoked ingenious efforts by candidates and their supporters to establish 'independent' financial relationships, and much litigation ensued as defeated opponents sought to disprove the supporter's allegedly autonomous status.[90] This loophole was plugged by RPA 1918, s 34(1) (now RPA 1983, s 75), which prohibited any expenditure intended

[87] On the pre-2000 position see particularly Rawlings op cit ch 5; Ewing K (1987) *The funding of political parties in Britain* (Oxford: Clarendon Press).

[88] See Rawlings op cit pp 146–149.

[89] *Roberts v Hogg* [1971] SLT 78.

[90] O'Leary op cit pp 54–55.

to promote a candidate unless written authorisation was received from the candidate's agent. Any such expenditure counts towards the candidate's overall limit.[91] The candidate's agent must compile an election return detailing all expenses. This is a public document, open to inspection by other candidates. Failure to produce the return is also an offence. However there is no mechanism for independent official scrutiny of returns. Any challenge to the legality of a candidate's expenditure is dependent upon the initiative of other candidates or voters.

The Fiona Jones case

Prior to 2000, the law on this question was in a state of considerable confusion. This was illustrated by an episode involving Fiona Jones, the successful Labour candidate for Newark at the May 1997 election. The defeated Liberal candidate accused Ms Jones of falsifying her expenses. She was subsequently prosecuted and convicted at Nottingham crown court under s 82 of the RPA 1983 for dishonestly making a false declaration of her election expense. Jones protested her innocence, and announced she would appeal. The Act seemed to require that any person convicted of such a crime vacate her seat in the Commons. The Speaker subsequently declared the seat to be vacant. Shortly thereafter, before any by-election was held, the Court of Appeal quashed the conviction.[92]

The Court's judgment dwelt primarily on the extraordinarily imprecise nature of the law in this area. Section 76(1) of the 1983 Act provides that:

> '(1) No sum shall be paid and no expense shall be incurred by a candidate at an election or his election agent, whether before, during or after an election, on account of or in respect of the conduct or management of the election, in excess of the maximum amount specified in this section'.

Section 118 then defined 'election expenses' as: 'expenses incurred, whether before, during or after the election, on account of or in respect of the conduct or management of the election'.

Lord Bingham CJ suggested that the meaning of ss 76 and 118 was obscure:

> 'There is no simple and decisive test to determine whether an expense is or is not an election expense. . . . Some expenses obviously are, some obviously not. But there may be some expenses about which reasonable people, applying themselves to the question in all good faith, could reach different conclusions. . . . In this intermediate area, questions of judgment may arise'.[93]

The Court accepted that it was possible that certain expenditures that Mrs Jones had incurred were indeed 'election expenses'. Particularly at issue were the cost of renting an office, shared with candidates in local elections, prior to the general election being called, and the use on polling day of a pre-existing database recording the names and

[91] For the background to the 1918 reform, its precise terms, and an example of its early implementation, see *R v Hailwood and Ackroyd Ltd* [1928] 2 KB 277, CCA.

[92] [1999] 2 Cr App Rep 253, CA.

[93] [1999] 2 Cr App Rep 253 at 260, CA.

addresses of likely Labour voters. But there was room for doubt on that point. And in the light of that doubt, there was no evidence to suggest that Jones had acted *dishonestly*; ie that she had *knowingly* made a false declaration. The jury had thus had no basis on which to convict her.[94]

The issue which then arose before the High Court in *A–G v Jones*[95] was whether Ms Jones' vacation of the seat should be regarded as invalidating the Newark election – thus requiring a by-election to be held – or whether it was merely a temporary incapacity, which if removed by a successful appeal against conviction under s 82, did not prevent Ms Jones resuming her seat.

It seems unfortunate, on a matter of such significance to both the MP concerned, her opponents and their electors, that the RPA 1983 did not offer a clear answer to this question. In a short, but very technical judgment, the court held that the Act imposed different consequences on candidates who filed false returns dependent on the forum before which the impugned behaviour was challenged. The court held that the RPA provided for invalidation of the election only if proceedings were undertaken before an election court. A criminal conviction did not invalidate the election result, and an MP in Mrs Jones' position could resume her seat as long as a by-election had not been held in the interim. The result makes obvious sense, but required some ingenuity on the court's part, which suggested that a more streamlined statutory scheme might be desirable.

The PPERA 2000 proposed some amendments to this area of the law. But these did not obviously cure the uncertainties highlighted by the Jones case, particularly in the way that account is taken of what might be termed 'spending in kind'; that is to say a candidate's use of office space or campaign personnel donated by supporters.[96]

A local not national limit on party spending

Prior to 2000, the limits on spending only applied to local campaigns. As Alder observes: 'The kind of campaign envisaged by the law is centred upon knocking on doors and holding meetings in public halls'.[97] As with apportionment, the law did not recognise the concept of a 'general election' for financial purposes; rather it saw 660 individual elections.

This is illustrated by the *Tronoh Mines* case.[98] Shortly before the 1951 General Election, the Tronoh Mines company placed an advertisement in *The Times*, part of which read:

[94] 'It is not a crime to declare an honest belief in a declaration of election expenses in which some expenses which should have been included have been omitted . . . unless the person making the declaration knows that it is false in one or other respect or both. Honest belief in the truth of the declaration, and thus in the completeness and accuracy of the figures disclosed, is a complete defence': [1999] 2 Cr App Rep 253, CA, per Lord Bingham CJ.

[95] [2000] QB 66, [1999] 3 All ER 436.

[96] See Ewing K (2000) 'Transparency, accountability and equality: the Political Parties, Elections and Referendums Act 2000' *Public Law* 542.

[97] Alder op cit p 163.

[98] *R v Tronoh Mines Ltd* [1952] 1 All ER 697, CCA.

'The coming general election will give us all the opportunity of saving the country from being reduced, through the policies of the Socialist government, to a bankrupt "Welfare State" '...

The advert clearly disparaged the Labour Party, and thus indirectly boosted the Conservatives' prospects. The company and *The Times* were prosecuted (under what is now RPA 1983, s 75) for making unauthorised expenditure designed to promote the candidacy of the Conservative in the constituency where the paper was printed. McNair J, held that there was no case to answer. He considered that the advert's purpose was 'to advance the prospects of the anti-Socialist cause generally' by influencing public opinion as a whole.[99] The Act however, addressed only efforts to promote 'a candidate at a particular election, and not candidates at elections generally'.[100] Since the advert played to a national, not constituency audience, it was not prohibited.

The inference of the judgment was that there was no legal limit to the funds a party could spend on its national campaigns. Parties could put as many adverts as they could afford in national newspapers; or buy as many poster sites they as could afford all over the country. Rawlings observed that *Tronoh Mines:* 'is an excellent illustration of the blindness of our electoral law to the realities of national election campaigning'.[101] That is an unduly harsh criticism of McNair J, whose interpretation of the Act was entirely logical. If the law was unsatisfactory, blame was more appropriately laid at Parliament's feet.

The courts have however concluded that the rules apply to locally targeted expenditure intended to secure the defeat of a particular candidate. This point was first made in *R v Hailwood and Ackroyd Ltd.*[102] The defendant, a disaffected Conservative, distributed leaflets in his constituency which urged voters not to support the Conservative candidate, but which did not expressly advise them to support any other candidate. The Court of Appeal upheld the conviction, on the grounds that such activities indirectly improved the chances of all other candidates in the constituency and should be construed as a financial contribution to their campaigns. The principle was confirmed 50 years later by the House of Lords in *DPP v Luft.*[103] Luft had circulated leaflets in several constituencies urging voters not to support the National Front candidate, but did not specify a favoured candidate. A unanimous court approved Lord Diplock's conclusion that: 'to persuade candidates not to vote for one candidate in order to prevent his being elected must have the effect of improving the collective prospects of success of the other candidates'.[104] Had Hailwood and Luft expressed their distaste via an advert in *The Times*, their expenditure would have been permissible.

In the Britain of 1883, a concept of financial equality limited to local campaigns was perhaps defensible. The party system was clearly well-established by then, but one still had 'independent' candidates, and the relative technological backwardness of the

[99] [1952] 1 All ER 697 at 698. [100] [1952] 1 All ER 697 at 699. [101] Op cit p 135.
[102] [1928] 2 KB 277, CCA.
[103] [1977] AC 962. See Munro C (1976) 'Elections and expenditure' *Public Law* 300–304.
[104] [1977] AC 962 at 983.

news media and transport infrastructure made local campaigns an important contributor to voter choice. Party loyalties influenced voter behaviour, but they were not obviously the dominant factor.

In modern Britain, political realities are very different. General elections are fought and won and lost in the national arena. Voter choice is motivated primarily by party affiliation. Similarly, the information on which that choice is based is more likely to have been gleaned from the national news media than from localised techniques such as listening to a candidate's local speeches or reading her election literature. One might plausibly conclude therefore that the more money a party spends on its national campaign, the more likely it is to persuade people all over the country that they should vote for that party's local candidate. There is no guarantee that spending lots of money will win a party lots more support. But as table 7.4 indicates, campaign expenditure has been rising in recent years.

Whether one can establish a correlation between the Conservative Party's higher spending and its electoral success is a question offering no easy answer. Deciding whether the constitution should tolerate the possibility of electoral choice being swayed by party wealth would seem more straightforward. The spirit of the 1883 Act was to sever the direct link between financial and political power; the retention merely of its letter in a quite different political context ensured that that objective was no longer being effectively achieved.

An equally significant omission was the absence of any legal requirement that parties reveal the sources of their income. This raised the possibility that powerful economic interests may 'buy' legislative influence. Neither were there any limits on the size of contributions that individuals or corporations might make to a political party. In the 1980s and 1990s, stories occasionally appeared in the national press alleging that life peerages have in effect been 'bought' by leading industrialists whose companies have made large donations to Conservative Party funds. Such allegations were unproven, but if substantiated would clearly further undermine the Lords' legitimacy. A greater concern was that substantial numbers of MPs may be predisposed to favour policies benefiting a substantial donor, irrespective of the policies' intrinsic merits. In

Table 7.4 Party Campaign Spending in Recent General Elections

	1983	1987	1992	1997	2001	2005
Conservative	£3.6m	£9.0m	£11.2m	£20.0m	£12.8m	£17.85m
Labour	£2.2m	£4.2m	£10.2m	£13.0m	£11.1m	£17.93m
Liberal/SDP	£1.9m	£2.0m	£1.8m	£0.7m	£ 1.4m	£4.3m

Source: Compiled from data in Butler D and Kavanagh D (1988) *The British general election of 1987* pp 235–236 (London: Macmillan); (1993) *The British general election of 1992* p 260 (London: Macmillan); (1998) *The British general election of 1997* p 242 (London: Macmillan): *The Guardian* 17 December 2001; Electoral Commission (30 November 2005) 'Spending by political parties and campaign groups at the 5 May UK parliamentary election' www.electoralcommission.org.uk.

the mid-1990s, particular concern was engendered by reports that the Conservative Party consistently accepted huge sums of money from overseas business interests, which created the suspicion that the donors were attempting to buy legislative influence. Such suspicions were intensified during the first term of the Blair government. Particular controversy arose over the gift of £1m given to the Labour Party by Bernie Ecclestone, the motor racing tycoon. The gift 'coincided' with an apparent abandonment by the government of a plan to ban tobacco advertising. Since Ecclestone derived vast amounts of his fortune from tobacco advertising, the inference that he had bought the change in government policy appeared well-founded. That the Labour Party subsequently returned the donation did little to allay suspicion that its financial integrity was as compromised as that of the Conservatives. Shortly afterwards, a further scandal arose when it appeared that the government had granted an exclusive and lucrative contract to provide smallpox vaccine to a company that had just made a large donation to Labour Party funds. The owner, Paul Drayson, was subsequently granted a peerage and was appointed as a minister in the third Blair government.

Such gaps in the law emphasised that the formal structure of this part of the constitution had not kept pace with changing political circumstances. The PPERA made a wide-ranging attempt to bring the rules of electoral finance law into line with contemporary political realities. Several important initiatives were introduced. Most significantly, Part V and Sch 8 of the Act place limits on a party's national campaign expenditure.[105] The sum was fixed at £30,000 per constituency contested. Parties contesting only a few seats may spend a maximum of £810,000 in England, £120,000 in Scotland and £60,000 in Wales. The Act requires that each party would have to appoint a Treasurer and Deputy Treasurers who are the only persons permitted to authorise campaign expenditure. Following the campaign, the party Treasurer is to be responsible for submitting detailed accounts to the Electoral Commission. A copy of the accounts will be available for public inspection. Exceeding the limits is now a criminal offence. In the light of party spending at the 1997 and 2001 elections, the ceiling proposed would not actually restrict parties' spending plans.

The Act also provides that only individuals registered to vote in the UK and corporate bodies established in the UK can make donations to political parties. Any donations from non-permitted donors must be returned, and a knowing breach of the rules by a party Treasurer or a donor would be a criminal offence. All donations of over £200 must be recorded in the party's accounts, which must be submitted to the Electoral Commission and made available for public inspection at the end of each financial year.

These are valuable initiatives.[106] The rationale underlying the Bill was that political parties should be entirely candid about the sources of their income, thereby enabling voters to make a more informed choice about who to support in future elections. Importantly, the Bill enjoyed a measure of multi-party support in the Commons and the Lords and was enacted in largely unchanged form by the end of the year. In so far

105 These sums would be additional to sums spent by individual candidates in constituency campaigns.

106 For a helpful analysis see Ewing (2001) op cit.

as the original Bill had an obvious weakness, it was in limiting penalties for breach of its provisions to individuals (in particular the party Treasurer). A penalty which involved invalidation of general election results in their entirety would not be practical. But the deterrent effect of the provisions might have been enhanced if their breach led to large fines being imposed on a party.[107]

Both the Labour and Conservative Parties fell some way short of spending the maximum permissible amount in the 2005 general election.[108] This rather suggests that the concern evinced by the Act that the larger parties might be augmenting their vote through unrestrained spending on campaigning was exaggerated. However the Act has evidently brought more intense public and press focus to bear on the ways in which political parties raise their money. The Electoral Commission maintains an online database which contains detailed listings of all registrable donations to the political parties. This innovation substantially enhances the transparency of party funding by making the relevant information widely available and thereby enabling other political parties, the press or interested individuals to raise questions about the legality of donations made.[109]

In 2002, continuing scandals over the main parties' (but especially the Labour Party's) evident predilections to take large sums of money in dubious circumstances from commercial sources led to renewed calls in the press, and within Parliament, for state financing of political parties, accompanied by calls for low limits on the amounts that individuals or companies could donate. The suggestion would seem to be a sound one. On the surface it appears profligate to allocate several million pounds of public money each year to political parties. But such expenditure would be substantially less damaging to the public purse than the status quo, in which it seems that parties in government are willing to channel large amounts of public expenditure in the form of subsidies, or sell-offs of public property, or contracts for services which represent poor value for money but whose beneficiaries have made a proportionately miniscule donation to party funds.

The Electoral Commission took the matter under review in the summer of 2002, and published a report in 2004.[110] The report did not advocate any radical changes to the existing system, offering instead the modest suggestion that individuals should be encouraged to make small donations to political parties either by the provision of matching public funds to supplement such gifts or by making donations eligible for tax relief.

However pressure for further legislative reform arose early in 2006. A series of

[107] The Bill did envisage that unlawful donations would be forfeited. [108] See table 7.4 above.

[109] Accusations were made in late 2005 that the Liberal Democrats had accepted several large donations – one of them totalling some £2.4m – from individuals and companies which were not 'British' in the sense required by the Act. The matter was still under investigation by the Electoral Commission in early 2006.

[110] The Electoral Commission (2004) *The funding of political parties* (London: Electoral Commission). For comment see Rowbottom J (2005) 'The electoral Commission's proposals on the funding of political parties' *Public Law* 468–476. For a sophisticated analysis of the issue see Marriot J (2005) 'Alarmist or relaxed? Election expenditure limits and free speech' *Public Law* 764–784.

stories ran in the press claiming that Prime Minister Blair had either solicited or accepted on the Labour Party's behalf very substantial loans from wealthy businessmen. These loans were not declared to the public, nor even it seems to the Labour Party's Treasurer and some senior members of the Cabinet. Strictly speaking, there was no legal requirement that the loans be declared, as the PPERA is concerned only with donations. It is of course conceivable that the terms of the 'loans' were so beneficial to the Labour Party that they might credibly be regarded as being at least partial donations. But the main criticism levelled at the Prime Minister was that it appeared that the makers of some of the loans were subsequently nominated by the Prime Minister for life peerages. The obvious and simple – and to many observers essentially corrupt – inference to be drawn from this was that Prime Minister Blair was selling seats in Parliament to wealthy supporters of the Labour Party. Accusations were also raised that the other main political parties had engaged in a similarly distasteful attempt to evade the spirit of the PPERA regime. In an attempt to contain the criticism made of the Prime Minister, the government announced in March 2006 that it would promote an amendment to the PPERA rules that would make loans declarable in future.

Television and radio broadcasting

The British approach to the regulation of television and radio broadcasting by political parties has been a markedly non-legal affair. On this point, there has long been widespread acceptance that candidates' and parties' wealth should have no bearing on their access to the public. Broadcasting time is not for sale to politicians. Air time was initially allocated by a body called the Committee on Party Political Broadcasting, composed of representatives from television and radio organisations, and members of the main political parties. The Committee allocated a small amount of air time to each party, the share being roughly in accordance with the party's portion of the vote at the last general election.

While both the BBC and the IBA are legally obliged to maintain political impartiality in their programming decisions, the Committee itself has no explicit legal basis. Nor could the Committee be described as a 'conventional' institution in the formal sense. The process in fact broke down in 1987, when decisions were made solely by the broadcasting organisations themselves. In the run up to the 1987 general election, the three main parties had five television broadcasts and the Greens one. It may seem anomalous that so important a part of the electoral process is not regulated by an explicit statutory framework. Yet paradoxically this is one of the few aspects of the system attuned to the realities of contemporary campaigns. There are no technical obstacles preventing Parliament intervening in this area; as yet no government has invited it to do so.[111] It may be the case that there is little practical need for such

[111] See generally Boyle A (1986) 'Political broadcasting, fairness and administrative law' *Public Law* 562–596. The PPERB proposed that broadcasters should have to take into account the Electoral Commission's views on broadcasts when allocating air time.

regulation, as the broadcasts themselves seem to have little (and declining) influence on voter behaviour: the broadcasts in the 2005 election were described by one commentator as: '[A] shrunken shadow of their former selves.'[112]

'Decent, honest and truthful'? The content of political advertising

Parliament has yet to take steps to regulate the content of party advertising. Hyperbolic claims and vitriolic abuse now seem a staple ingredient of election campaigns, as are lurid tales of opposing parties' hidden political agendas. Clearly one would not wish voters' choices to be influenced by lies. But 'truth' is an elusive concept, and has little bearing on matters of political opinion such as 'A Labour government would ruin the economy' or 'A Conservative government will produce increased unemployment'.

In 1895, a private members Bill was enacted which forbade the making of a 'false statement of fact' intended to hamper a candidate's prospects of success. Matters such as a circular letter falsely announcing a candidate's withdrawal from the contest, and press accusations of salmon poaching, were offered by MPs as evidence of such unworthy practices. The courts subsequently held that the Act extended only to statements concerning a candidate's personal characteristics, not his political views. A private members' Bill to reverse this decision failed through lack of government support in 1911.[113] The present law, RPA 1983 s 106, maintains the personal/political distinction: falsely calling a candidate a 'communist' or 'fascist' does not contravene the Act.

This measure is directed solely at individual candidates. False statements (assuming their falsity could be established) directed at parties are not covered. Publicity deployed in the notorious 'khaki election' of 1900, in which the Conservatives accused the Liberals of supporting the Boers against whom Britain was then conducting a war, was consequently not illegal. The problem is perhaps intensified by the fact that party manifestos have no legal status in respect of subsequent central government policy.

One therefore depends on the electorate being sufficiently sophisticated to recognise when parties are making unfounded claims. Whether such an assumption is justified is an open question. But press coverage in recent elections, and the extravagance of claims made by the political parties, might suggest that politicians and journalists have a low opinion of voters' analytical capacities.[114]

COUNTING THE VOTE

There is no evidence to suggest that the integrity of modern elections is compromised by irregularities in the physical process of adding up individual votes. Ballot slips are not altered after the voter fills them in; forged papers are not added to the ballot box; and ballot boxes do not go astray. The count is an open process, which all candidates

[112] Butler and Kavanagh (2005) op cit p 111.

[113] O'Leary op cit pp 179–181, 216–226.

[114] See the sections on press coverage in Butler D and Kavanagh D (1984; 1988; 1993; 1998; 2002) *The British general election of 1982; 1987; 1992; 1997; 2001* respectively (London: Macmillan).

may scrutinise. But the concept of 'counting' votes can also bear a rather wider meaning. The most frequently voiced complaint concerning the present system is the limited correlation between the votes that a party receives and the number of seats it wins. Chapter one adverted to the problems posed in a democratic state by the tyranny of the majority. Table 7.5 reveals that modern Britain has never suffered the problem of majoritarian government, since (except for the dubious exception of the 1977 Lib/Lab pact) it has never had a peacetime government enjoying majority electoral support. No government elected since 1945 has secured over 50% of the vote. The best Conservative performance was 49.7% in 1955. Labour's highest ever share was 48.8% in 1951. However, Labour lost the 1951 election. The Conservatives, with fewer votes, gained seven more Commons seats. Moreover, by no means everybody chooses to vote. The Thatcher governments elected in 1979, 1983 and 1987 had the positive support of one third of the population. The Blair governments elected in 1997 and 2001 enjoyed even lower levels of active support. In 2001, the Labour Party amassed a majority of over 160 in the Commons. It did so having won just 40% of the

Table 7.5 Votes Gained and Seats Won at General Elections since 1945

Year	Conservative		Labour		Liberal *		Turnout
	Vote %	Seats	Vote %	Seats	Vote %	Seats	
1945	39.8	213	47.8	393	9.0	12	72.7%
1950	43.5	298	46.1	315	9.1	9	84.0%
1951	48.0	321	48.8	295	2.5	6	82.5%
1955	49.7	344	46.4	277	2.7	6	76.7%
1959	49.4	365	43.8	258	5.9	6	78.8%
1964	43.4	304	44.1	317	11.2	9	77.1%
1966	41.9	253	47.9	363	8.5	12	75.8%
1970	46.4	330	43.0	287	7.5	6	72.0%
1974 [1]	37.9	297	37.1	301	19.3	14	78.7%
1974 [2]	35.8	277	39.2	319	18.3	13	72.8%
1979	43.9	339	36.9	269	13.8	11	76.0%
1983	42.4	397	27.6	209	25.4	23	72.7%
1987	42.3	376	30.8	292	22.6	22	75.3%
1992	41.9	336	34.4	271	17.8	20	77.7%
1997	30.7	165	43.2	418	16.8	46	71.2%
2001	31.7	166	40.7	412	18.3	52	59.8%
2005	32.4	198	35.2	356	22.0	62	61.2%

* 1983 and 1987 votes include the Social Democratic Party.

Source: Compiled from data in Norton (1991) *op cit* pp 97–99: Butler and Kavanagh (1993) op cit p 246; (1998) op cit p 255; (2002) op cit p261; 2006 op cit.

vote. Since turnout at the election slumped to less than 60% of eligible voters, the Labour Party was actually voted for by less than 25% of the registered electorate.

The figures for the 2005 general election appear similarly startling. The turnout was again very low. Only 61.2% of eligible electors exercised their right to vote. The Labour Party won 356 seats – and a majority in the Commons of over 60 – with a 35.2% share of the votes cast. The Conservatives' 32.4% of the vote yielded some 198 seats. The Liberal Democrats attracted 22% of the popular vote, yet secured only 62 seats. The third Blair administration thus enjoyed the dubious distinction of having won the lowest share of the vote of any twentieth century government.[115]

These ostensibly extraordinary results arise because the British electoral system permits minority rule, not simply majoritarianism. If one's concern as a constitutional lawyer is to ensure that government derives its powers from the consent of the governed, this may seem unsatisfactory, especially since – as chapters five and six have suggested – that government frequently has de facto control of Parliament's supposedly unlimited legal competence. Majorities or minorities are not necessarily tyrannical or undemocratic – both tyranny and democracy can be construed as concepts concerned with what government does with power, as well as how government acquires it. Equally, one might wonder if merely avoiding tyranny is an adequate ambition for a democratic constitution? These are points to which we shall return. For the present, we might consider how the seat/vote discrepancy arises.

This situation is an almost inevitable consequence of a country where most electoral support is closely divided between two political parties choosing the 'plurality' counting system in single member constituencies. The 'plurality' or 'first past the post' rule means that one wins a constituency simply by polling more votes than any other candidate. In a two-party contest, the winner must gain 50%+1 of the votes cast, an outcome which raises the prospect of barely majoritarian government. However, should four candidates compete, the seat could be won with as few as 25%+1 votes. The more candidates, and the more evenly balanced their support, the fewer votes needed to win.

Supporters of defeated parties in our hypothetical four candidate constituency have exercised only indirect, negative power over the selection of their MP, insofar as if they did not vote for losing candidates A, B, or C, winning candidate D would need fewer votes to succeed. But these 75%–1 voters have not exercised any direct, positive control over the choice of their legislative representative. This is often referred to as the 'wasted vote' problem. In legal terms, one votes not for one's party on a national basis, but for an individual representative of one's party in an individual constituency. It was not until 1969 that candidates were permitted to record their party affiliation on the ballot paper. The 'general election' label is a misnomer; rather one has 650 simultaneous local elections. Supporters of defeated parties cannot pick up their wasted votes and use them to support another of their party's candidates somewhere else.

115 Butler D and Kavanagh D (2005) *The British general election of 2005* (Basingstoke: Palgrave Macmillan), App 1.)

Within an individual constituency, there will always be a mismatch between votes cast and seats won in contested elections unless every voter supports one candidate, since there is only one seat to win. But the potential shortcomings of the single member plurality system are magnified when one aggregates the results of all constituencies to determine whose representatives gain de facto control of Parliament's unlimited legal sovereignty.

If modern Britain had only two political parties, enjoying approximately equal popular support, a party could theoretically take every seat by winning each constituency with 50%+1 votes: the party which won 50%–1 votes in every constituency would have no MPs at all. In a country with an electorate of over 40 million, a party would need only 650 or so votes more than its only rival to control every Commons seat.

Such theoretical extremes do not occur in practice. But candidates regularly win constituencies with only 40% of the votes, because the majority of electors have split their vote among several other parties: (see table 7.6). A constituency is rarely won by a candidate who gains more than 65% support. Consequently at least a substantial minority of votes are always 'wasted'. In the 2005 general election, 419 of the 646 constituencies were won by candidates who attracted fewer than 50% of the votes cast.[116] The problem was particularly acute in Scottish constituencies in the 2005 general election. Of the 59 seats contested in Scotland, 42 were won by candidates (26 of whom were Labour candidates) with under 50% of the vote. And of those 42 newly returned MPs, 13 (8 of them Labour candidates) failed to reach 40% level.[117]

Table 7.6 Minoritarianism in Parliamentary Constituency Elections

Constituency	Year	Con	Lab	Lib*	Nat
Carlisle	1983	37.3%	**37.5%**	25.1%	–
Stockton North	1983	33.3%	**37.1%**	29.6%	–
Brecon and Radnor	1987	34.7%	29.2%	**34.8%**	1.3%
South Stockton	1987	**35.0%**	31.3%	33.7%	–
Nairn and Lochaber	1992	22.6%	25.1%	**26.0%**	24.7%
Renfrew West	1992	32.9%	**36.6%**	10.0%	20.2%
Falmouth and Cambourne	1997	28.8%	**33.8%**	25.2%	–
Colchester	1997	31.4%	30.6%	**34.4%**	–
Hastings and Rye	1997	29.2%	**34.4%**	28.0%	–
Ochil and South Perthshire	2005	21.5	**31.4**	13.3	29.9
Perthshire North	2005	30.4	18.7	16.1	**33.7**

* Includes SDP.

Source: Compiled from data in Butler and Kavanagh (1983); (1988); (1993); (1998); (2005) op cit.

116 My thanks to my research assistant Roderic Jones for doing the counting on this point.

117 Butler and Kavanagh (2005) op cit App 1.

In a two-party system, where each party enjoys approximately equal support, the parties' wasted votes may cancel each other out. If one examines just the Conservative and Labour performances in table 7.5, one sees that the party with more votes generally (but not always) wins more seats, and that the Commons majority increases as the voting share expands. But table 7.5 also shows that the percentage of the total vote shared between the Labour and Conservative parties has declined sharply since 1945.[118] Other parties have attracted growing electoral support. They have not as a consequence gained growing parliamentary representation. The Liberal Party has suffered acutely from the vote/seat discrepancy. In 1983 the SDP/Liberal Alliance won 25.4% of the vote but only 23 seats. In 1987, their 22.6% of the vote produced only 22 MPs. Liberal support is spread relatively evenly throughout Britain. Consequently, Liberals often come second in both Labour and Conservative constituencies. But in a single MP constituency system, there are no direct rewards for coming second.

Alternative voting systems

The plurality model is generally contrasted with a voting mechanism described as 'proportional representation' (PR). PR is an umbrella term, embracing many electoral systems. Insofar as these systems share a common theme, it is an intention to produce a closer relationship between the votes cast for and seats won by parties attracting substantial national or regional voter support.

PR is not a novel idea in British constitutional theory.[119] John Stuart Mill coupled his advocacy of women's enfranchisement with support for the 'Hare' scheme of PR (named after its inventor).[120] This system was adopted in Tasmania shortly thereafter,[121] and a variant of it is described below. The 1867 Reform Act contained a Lords' amendment which might now be regarded as a form of PR. The 'minority voting' provision created three member constituencies in Liberal dominated areas in which voters were allowed only two choices – the three candidates with the most votes being returned. This virtually guaranteed the return of a Tory member in constituencies where the Tory Party could muster 34+% support.

PR generated a particular flurry of parliamentary and extra-parliamentary activity during the passage of the 1884 Reform Act. Many proponents were motivated by a purely sectarian desire to safeguard the representation of the minority protestant community in Ireland. Others, including E C Clark, then Regius Professor of Civil Law at Cambridge, saw PR as a Madisonian guard against factional legislation, which would remove any incentive for parties to offer sensationalist policies in the hope of appealing to the bigotry or ignorance of an 'impulsive' electorate.[122] The Speaker's Conference established during World War I had indeed recommended that the

118 On the reasons for this decline, which appear broadly to reflect a breakdown of traditional working class/middle class divisions, see Norton op cit pp 105–115.

119 See Hart J (1992) *Proportional representation: critics of the British electoral system 1820–1945* (Oxford: Clarendon Press).

120 Hart (1992) op cit ch 2.

121 Brown W (1899) 'The Hare system in Tasmania' *LQR* 51–70.

122 Jones op cit pp 99–100.

plurality method be replaced by a PR scheme. This was put to a free vote in both houses, where it attracted substantial, if not sufficient support.[123]

It is not entirely sensible to consider electoral reform in isolation from other constitutional issues; the method one adopts to choose one's legislature may well be affected by one's choice as to its powers. It is nonetheless helpful to outline the basic features of alternatives to the plurality/single member model.

The party list system

A national list system maximises the correlation between seats cast and votes won; a party gaining x% of the votes wins x% of the seats. There is in effect only one constituency – namely the entire country – under a national list system. Voters choose a party, not an individual candidate. The parties themselves draw up lists of candidates. Parties which gained sufficient votes for 10, 20 or 50 seats respectively would send the first 10, 20 and 50 members on their list to the legislature. Israel operates the purest list system. In its 120 member Knesset, a party will gain a legislative seat with only 1% of the popular vote.

A national list system completely eliminates both the wasted vote problem and the difficulties of apportionment. Whether it is however more 'democratic' is a complex question. The Israeli system affords legislative representation to extremist political parties, thereby lending an unwarranted legitimacy to their policies. In the British system, in contrast, given the existence of three mainstream parties, an extremist candidate will need at least 25%+1 support in a given constituency to win its seat. This danger may be countered by having a representation threshold – a party receives no seats at all unless it passes a 5% or 10% or 15% of the vote barrier. The higher the threshold, the more difficult it becomes for extremist parties to gain representation.

The list method also offers opportunities for small parties to enter government by forming coalitions with larger parties. If such coalitions result from post-election negotiation, one may end up with a government for which no-one has actually voted. That objection could be overcome if parties were to announce their prospective coalition partners prior to the poll.

Critics also point out that the list places complete control of candidate selection in the hands of party officials, although this criticism may be met by a legal framework which opens up parties' selection processes to all of their members. Similarly, accusations that the list precludes any identification between a given legislator and particular parts of the country can be reduced (if not eliminated) by compiling lists on a regional rather than national basis.

The single transferable vote

The single transferable vote (STV) method, (a development of the Hare system), offers the advantage of being tried, tested and evidently approved in Ireland, Malta and Australia. STV employs multi-member constituencies. Parties field as many

123 See Butler (1953) op cit ch 1.

candidates as they wish, while voters mark candidates in order of preference. A candidate is successful if she attains first preference votes equivalent to one more than the number of electors divided by the number of candidates + 1. In a four member constituency this figure would be 20%+1; in a three member constituency 25%+1, and so on. That candidate's second preference votes are then allocated as new first preference votes to the remaining candidates. Any candidates thereby reaching the quota are also elected, and their second preferences are in turn divided among remaining candidates until all seats are filled. If all seats cannot be filled by working from the top down, one begins to redistribute from the bottom up. The candidate with the fewest first preference votes is eliminated, and his second preference allocated to the others. If need be, the process is repeated until all seats are filled.

STV is time-consuming and complex, and also requires large and potentially unwieldy constituencies. Nevertheless, particularly in constituencies returning four or more members, it minimises the wasted vote problem. It also enables voters not wishing to support a straight party line to express a preference between individual candidates as well as between parties.

Absolute majority systems

Absolute majority systems are not strictly concerned with proportionality, but with ensuring that the winning candidate in a single member constituency attracts majority electoral support, thereby reducing but not eliminating the wasted vote problem. This may be achieved through the 'alternative vote' method. Voters list candidates in order of preference. If a candidate secures 50%+1 first preference votes she is elected. If no candidate does so, the least popular is eliminated and his second preference votes are re-allocated to the remaining candidates. This process is repeated until one candidate passes the 50% barrier.

Another route to a similar end is offered by the 'second ballot' method. Should more than two candidates run, the first ballot operates solely to eliminate all but the two most popular. These two candidates then contest a run-off election shortly after the initial contest. This both ensures majority support, and also offers voters the chance to reflect on their final choice.

The German system

Elections to Germany's *Bundestag* employ a mixed method of plurality voting in one member constituencies coupled with a regional list.[124] Half of the *Bundestag* seats are allocated to candidates gaining a plurality in their constituencies, half to candidates on the lists. However, voters also have a second vote in which they express a party preference. After the constituency candidates take their seats, each party's representation in the *Bundestag* is increased to that number which equates in percentage terms to its share of the party votes.

124 See Bogdanor V (1983) *What is proportional representation* ch 4 (Oxford: Martin Robertson): Pulzer P (1983) 'Germany' in Butler D and Bogdanor V (eds) *Democracy and elections* (Cambridge: CUP).

The process can usefully be illustrated by returning to the absurd example canvassed above in which Party A gains 50%+1 votes in every constituency, while Party B gains 50%–1. In Britain, Party A wins every seat. In Germany, (assuming voters follow a straight party line), Party A wins every constituency seat, but only one party seat, the rest of which go to Party B. Party A thus gains the slimmest of *Bundestag* majorities to reflect its tiny lead in the popular vote.

The German method offers the benefits of almost perfect proportionality along with constituency representation. It also addresses the criticisms made of national list systems that MP selection is utterly dominated by parties, and that legislators have no ties to particular areas.

The prospects of reform

One can identify shortcomings as well as benefits in all voting systems. This section has thus far dwelt solely on the drawbacks of our single member plurality system; one ought also to focus on its claimed merits. One would assume these are considerable, given that since 1945 both Labour and Conservative controlled Houses of Commons have chosen to retain an electoral system in which unlimited legal power is bestowed upon the representatives of a minority of the citizenry.[125]

The first is the so-called 'strong government' thesis. This stresses the importance of ensuring that the country always has a stable government, able to implement a clearly defined set of legislative priorities, unencumbered by the need to compromise its beliefs to maintain the support of minority parties. Relatedly, the electorate knows where to attribute responsibility for failure or success, and can react accordingly at the next election. A second argument points to the simplicity and transparency of the present system. It is easy both for voters to understand and for government to administer. A third dwells on the importance of small constituency representation, which ensures both that MPs are not too distanced from the concerns of ordinary voters, and that all candidates are directly exposed to popular, rather than simply party scrutiny.

Those points may be promptly rebutted. The strong government thesis is unconvincing if one views the project of government as a long- rather than short-term process. It may not be beneficial for a country to march strongly in one direction during the lifetime of one or two Parliaments, and then equally strongly in an altogether different direction for the next five or ten years. Similarly, if alternative systems are deemed too complex for the electorate to understand, the appropriate solution may be more extensive voter education. Thirdly, the necessity or desirability of having members of the national legislature play a substantial role as constituency representatives is contingent on the powers and structure of sub-central elected government, an issue addressed in chapters ten and eleven.

125 For the defence see Maude A and Szemerey J (1981) *Why electoral reform? The case for electoral reform examined* (London: Conservative Political Centre). For a demolition of the defence see Oliver D (1982) 'Why electoral reform? The case for electoral reform examined' *Public Law* 236–239.

The Labour Party's 1997 election manifesto had included a commitment to hold a referendum in which voters would be presented with a choice between the existing system and some form of proportional alternative. The government promptly established a commission headed by Lord Jenkins of Hillhead, a former Labour Cabinet Minister and subsequently a Liberal life peer, to recommend the most appropriate alternative system. The Jenkins report[126] canvassed a wide variety of alternative mechanisms, before eventually settling on a device of its own creation. The proposal retained the constituency based, system to elect the majority (around 80%) of MPs. Constituency MPs would be elected by the absolute majority method; ie the winner would have to gain at least 50%+1 of the vote. However constituencies were to be clustered in groups of five or six. Each cluster would be given an additional so-called 'county' MP, (in total some 20% of the Commons' members) whose seat would be allocated in a way that ameliorated (if only slightly) any disproportionality between aggregate votes cast and seats won in the cluster constituencies. The proposed system seemed extremely difficult to understand, and the Blair government showed no obvious enthusiasm for making preparations for a referendum. No referendum was held before the 2001 election, and since then the government has given no indication that the issue will be put to voters during its second term. In the medium term at least, the first past the post, constituency system will continue in evidently robust political health.[127]

Enhancing turnout

One of the various powers created by the RPA 2000 enables local councils to explore ways of enhancing voter turnout in local elections. That allocation of responsibility seems particularly timely given the lamentably low figure of voter participation in the 2001 general election. Various experiments were tried out in local government elections in 2000 and 2001, such as allowing universal postal voting, opening polling booths in supermarkets, and spreading voting over several days. No startling increases in turnout were reported. The PPERA 2000 gave the Electoral Commission the responsibility of approving further innovations and keeping the issue under review. The Commission produced a wide-ranging report on the issue in 2002 which surveyed and analysed a series of innovations which were tried on an experimental basis in various local government elections.[128] Whether low turnout is a problem that can be dealt with by tinkering with the details of the electoral system remains to be seen. More extensive use was made of postal voting in the 2005 general election. This seemed to lead to modest increases in voter turnout in some constituencies. However this beneficial reform was counterbalanced by substantial concerns that the postal

126 Jenkins R (1998) *Report of the independent commission on the voting system* (London: HMSO). For an intriguing analysis see McLean I (1999) 'The Jenkins Commission and the implications of electoral reform for the UK' *Government and Opposition* 145–160.

127 As noted in chapter twenty-two below, rather different systems have latterly been introduced for elections to the newly created Scots Parliament and Welsh Assembly.

128 Electoral Commission (2002) *Modernising elections* (London: Electoral Commission.)

vote system was being abused by 'over-zealous' political party workers in some parts of the country.[129] A more radical and no doubt more effective solution would be to make voting in general elections compulsory, as is the case in – inter alia – Australia, Italy and Belgium. As yet there is little indication that such a proposal commands significant support within Parliament or the country at large.[130]

CONCLUSION

It would be facile to assume that there is an 'ideal' electoral system waiting to be discovered. In leaving this topic, we might again try to assess the extent to which electoral law ensures that the political party controlling the legislature enjoys the consent of the governed. In chapters five to seven, it has been suggested that the sovereignty of Parliament is in effect the sovereignty of the Commons, which is in turn the sovereignty of the majority party in the lower house, which is in turn the sovereignty of the minority of voters supporting that party. The constitution is, in legal terms, a vehicle facilitating factional government on all issues.

Yet factionalism in the law-making process need not lead to factionalism in the law's content. We must also consider what objectives factional parties pursue when they control Parliament's sovereign legal authority. If major parties share similar views on those elements of the constitution regarded as 'higher law' in other democracies, majoritarian or minoritarian control of the Commons is less problematic – factional differences will only be given legal expression in respect of non-fundamental issues. Supporters of the losing party may find such policies unpalatable, but not intolerable, and accept defeat because they anticipate that their opponents would do likewise if they lost the next election. Chapter nine will explore the extent of such similarities between the major parties in the modern era, and ask whether even if one can identify short term consensus, one should rely on its continued long-term existence. The thorny question of how one identifies a 'fundamental' law is then returned to repeatedly in subsequent chapters. But before broaching either of these extra-parliamentary issues, we turn briefly in chapter eight to a question of narrower scope – that of the 'privileges of Parliament'.

129 Butler and Kavanagh (2005) op cit pp 78–79, 174–175.

130 For a contemporaneous analysis of the issue with a particular focus on the 2001 and 2005 elections see Curtice J (2005) 'Turnout: electors stay home again' *Parliamentary Affairs* 776–785.

8

PARLIAMENTARY PRIVILEGE

'Parliamentary privilege' began to assume a coherent form on the constitutional landscape by 1450, from when the Speaker of the House of Commons began each session of Parliament with an address to the Monarch claiming 'the ancient rights and privileges of the Commons'. The scope of parliamentary privilege is both multi-faceted and uncertain. In broad terms, it embraces such issues as the two houses' power to control their own procedures, to admit and expel MPs and regulate their behaviour, and to punish non-members for obstructing the houses' business.

Early analysis of privilege assumed the Commons and Lords were superior 'courts', possessing exclusive, inherent power over all matters within their claimed jurisdiction. The point is best expressed by Coke CJ:

> 'Every court of justice hath rules and customs for its directions . . . It is lex et consuetudo parliamenti that all weighty matters in any Parliament moved concerning the peers of the realm, or commons in parliament assembled, ought to be determined, adjudged, and discussed by the course of the parliament, not by the civil law nor yet by the common laws of this realm used in more inferiour courts'.[1]

Coke's treatise was written in the pre-revolutionary era, and offers no clear guidance on the legal status of the *lex et consuetudo parliamenti* (law and custom of Parliament) vis à vis statute and the common law.[2] This is partly the consequence of a misleading use of terminology. Coke's attention was focused not on 'Parliament', but on two of its component parts – the Commons and Lords – qua independent constitutional actors. But the inexactitude is not merely linguistic. It also has an historical base in the blurred origins of 'Parliament' as a law-making body. Unlike the United States Congress, which was established to fulfil an exclusively legislative function within a limited sphere of legal competence, the two English houses had initially been judicial as well as legislative bodies.

The revolutionary settlement retained many features of the pre-revolutionary legal and political order. The common law's substantive provisions were left largely intact; the courts remained unwilling to examine the exercise of prerogative powers; and Charles II's move towards 'Cabinet' government was adopted by his successors.[3]

[1] 1 Inst 15; cited in Keir and Lawson op cit p 251.

[2] 'Common law' in the wide sense alluded to at p 70, n 36 above.

[3] See pp 70, 100–101 and 130–131 respectively.

Similarly, the Commons' and the Lords' eclectic 'judicial' powers were not systematically re-evaluated and redefined. Several theoretical questions (with significant practical consequences) were thus left unanswered. How far did the powers of each house extend? Were they residual powers, or could each house create new ones? Were such powers constitutionally superior to Acts of Parliament and/or the common law whenever a clash occurred? And in that event, would responsibility for answering the third question rest with the courts or with the house?[4]

In this area, legal theory and political practice rarely coincide. Matters are further complicated by the frequency with which theory and practice are themselves categories riven with internal inconsistencies. In conceptual terms, parliamentary privilege is a fascinating component of the modern constitution. And while it has in the twentieth century been relegated rather to the status of an historical anachronism, recent events (discussed in section V below) have lent it renewed significance.

There is no scope here to analyse in detail the pre-revolutionary history of the houses' respective privileges. However, three significant episodes merit discussion, with a view to identifying issues which assumed considerable significance after 1688.

Strode's case (1512)

Strode was an MP who had promoted bills to regulate the tinning industry. His activities antagonised members of the Stannary Courts of Cornwall and Devon. The Stannary Courts were created by Edward I, and had a geographically limited jurisdiction immune from oversight by the common law courts. The Courts convicted Strode of 'vexing and troubling' local tin miners, and imprisoned him.[5]

The imprisonment triggered a swift response, not simply from the Commons, but from Parliament. Legislation (generally referred to as Strode's Act) was rapidly passed, both condemning the action taken by the Stannary Court and warning other such bodies against pursuing such a course in future:

> 'sutes, accusments . . . punyshmentes etc, put or had, or hereafter put or had unto . . . the said Richard, and to every other . . . person of this present Parliament, or that of any Parliament hereafter, for any bill spekying, reasonying, or declaring of any mater or maters concerning the Parliament, to be communed and treated as utterly void and of no effecte'.

The contemporaneous legal status of 'Strode's Act' is necessarily unclear, given the then prevailing uncertainty as to the relative importance of statute vis à vis other sources of legal authority. It is also unclear whether Parliament assumed it was creating new law, or, as seems more likely, merely restating what the Commons believed to be one of its existing privileges. The Act's significance is perhaps better construed as a

[4] The Commons generally assigns questions concerning its privileges to its Committee of Privileges (recently renamed as the Committee on Standards and Privileges). The report of the Committee is then considered by the whole house. See Griffith and Ryle op cit ch 3: Marshall G (1979) 'The House of Commons and its privileges', in Walkland op cit.

[5] Plucknett (1960) op cit pp 248–249.

symbolic affirmation of the Commons' increasing confidence in its role as a central component of the law-making process.

Peter Wentworth's defence of freedom of discussion in the Commons

That the 1688 revolution was fought against a Stuart monarch tends to divert attention from significant tensions between the Crown and the Commons in earlier periods. Elizabeth I fell on several occasions into profound disagreement with both houses over her failure to marry or nominate an heir, and her unwillingness to countenance legislation promoting religious reform.[6] Elizabeth made frequent efforts, both directly and via her supporters in the lower house, to prevent the Commons even discussing such matters.

The tension became acute in 1587, when Anthony Cope MP introduced a Bill to the Commons advocating radical religious reform. Elizabeth had expressed a wish that the Bill should not even be presented, still less debated. She had an ally in the Speaker, who both attempted to stop the reading of the Bill, and thereafter furnished the Queen with a copy of its text.[7] This prompted considerable controversy within the house. A question was placed by Peter Wentworth MP, asking:

> 'Whether this house be not a place for any member freely and without controlment of any person, or danger of laws, by bill or speech, to alter any of the griefs of the Commonwealth whatsoever touching the service of God, the safety of the Prince and this noble realm?'.

Wentworth had by then been imprisoned several times under the *Anderson* principle, and was once more confined to the Tower of London, this time by a lower house fearing the Queen's likely response to his temerity in drawing attention to an entitlement which the Commons itself had so staunchly defended in respect of Strode.

Strode's Act was clearly not then regarded as an adequate legal defence against the Monarch's prerogative powers of imprisonment. Wentworth's misfortune also demonstrated that Commons' privileges did not fasten themselves inviolably on all its members, but could be diluted or waived by the house acting collectively. At least in its early years, the meaning of parliamentary privilege was less a question of legal niceties than of stark political realities. A second episode illustrates that point even more forcefully.

The Case of the Five Members (1641)

Notwithstanding Elizabeth's evident enthusiasm for invoking the *Resolutions in Anderson*, and her similarly pronounced distaste for liberty of discussion in the Commons, neither she nor her Tudor predecessors sought to rule as entirely absolutist Monarchs. Under that form of constitutional arrangement, there would be no legal protection for legislation, for the common law, or for the privileges of each house against the prerogative.

[6] The following paragraphs are drawn from Plucknett (1960) op cit pp 312–328 and Wittke op cit pp 26–28.

[7] This being an era when the perception of the Speaker's role as the Commons' champion against the Crown was not accepted; see pp 136–137 above.

Charles I had ruled between 1629 and 1640 without summoning Parliament. By 1640, his political and fiscal weakness made that course unsustainable. The newly summoned houses rapidly addressed what they perceived as the worst abuses wrought by the King. MPs agreed to levy taxation only after securing (reluctant) royal support for the Triennial Act, an Act abolishing ship money (which also gaoled the judges who had found for the King), and legislation subjecting the Monarch's detention power under *Anderson* to (limited) judicial scrutiny.

For many MPs however, such measures inadequately expressed what they perceived as the growing significance of Parliament within the constitution (and of the Commons within Parliament). A motion was subsequently moved in the house to present to the King (and for publication) the 'Grand Remonstrance' of 1641 which detailed an extensive list of political and religious grievances. The motion offers the first recorded instance of the house 'dividing' on a vote, rather than presenting a united front behind which its internal divisions were hidden. A narrow majority of members voted in favour of presenting and publishing the Remonstrance. An enraged Charles I demanded of the Commons that the five leaders (including one John Hampden)[8] of this 'opposition' to his government be tried for treason. The Commons did not comply with this request, regarding it as a gross interference with its deliberative autonomy.

As tension mounted, the house prepared to equip itself with an armed guard, fearing that the King would abduct the five members by force. Charles subsequently entered the house, backed by 400 armed men, and commanded that the MPs identify the impugned members. No MP would do so. In an act of some personal courage, the Speaker William Lenthell (in words frequently invoked to demonstrate the Speaker's role as the Commons' defender against executive interference) defied the King's direct command to reveal the five members' whereabouts: 'May it please your majesty, I have neither eyes to see, nor tongue to speak in this place but as this House is pleased to direct, whose servant I am here.'

Charles' 'invasion' of the Commons was perhaps the precipitate cause of the civil war. His Stuart successors nevertheless remained reluctant to accept that the constitution forbade such direct Monarchical interference with the house's internal proceedings. As noted in chapter two, the *Declaration of Right* stressed the constitutional importance of the Commons' 'independence' from interference either from the Crown directly or (since judges were then appointed by the King and dismissable at his pleasure) indirectly via the courts. The crucial provision was subsequently expressed in Article 9 of the Bill of Rights.

ARTICLE 9 OF THE BILL OF RIGHTS 1689

'That the freedom of speech, and debates or proceedings in Parliament ought not to be impeached or questioned in any court or place out of Parliament'.

[8] See p 90 above.

Quite what status Article 9 possessed in England's revised constitutional order was (and remains) uncertain. One interpretation would suggest that, by enacting Article 9, Parliament abolished all pre-existing privileges and replaced them with a new statutory formula. The meaning to be attached to 'freedom of speech', 'debates', 'proceedings', 'Parliament', 'impeached' and 'questioned' would then become purely a question of statutory interpretation entrusted to the courts, in respect of which the previous *lex et consuetudo parliamenti* might serve as a persuasive authority if the judges so wished.

Much academic, judicial and political opinion has until very recently rejected such an interpretation. The preferred view appears to have been that Article 9 was merely 'declaratory' of the legitimacy of the pre-revolutionary situation.[9] Yet such an opinion is conceptually very problematic. The Bill of Rights, like any other post-revolutionary legislation, enjoys an entirely different constitutional status to any pre-revolutionary statute. In respect of Acts passed before 1688 'declaring' the extent of privilege, there is no difficulty in assuming that Parliament was merely bestowing added legitimacy on a political concept which arguably enjoyed equal but separate status to legislation. In the absence of a clear consensus as to the 'sovereignty' of Parliament, such statutes would merely mirror the *lex parliamenti*. But one might readily assume that legislation passed by the newly sovereign Parliament could no longer be merely declaratory, but necessarily transformed the constitutional status of the issues it addressed.

Any claim by the Commons or Lords that the interpretation of Article 9 was a matter for them alone has no textual basis in the Bill of Rights itself. Such a claim would also contradict orthodox understandings of parliamentary sovereignty and the rule of law, which entrust the task of interpreting statutes to the ordinary courts. But one can discern a contextual basis for the Commons' wish to exclude judicial interpretation of Article 9. This would derive in part from a suspicion that the Crown could interfere indirectly with the Commons' operations through its power to appoint and dismiss the judges. However, that contextual justification would largely have disappeared following the Act of Settlement 1700, which empowered the Commons to veto the dismissal of members of the judiciary.

The Act of Settlement displaced rather than extinguished the Commons' understandable fears about losing control of its claimed interpretive power. Despite the then eclectic structure of the English court system, the House of Lords unarguably enjoyed a dual 'judicial' status, exercising jurisdiction over both its own *lex parliamenti* and most facets of the common law. For the scope of the Commons' privileges to be determinable by the common law would mean in effect that they were controlled by

9 Thus in *Pickin v British Railways Board* (p 31 above) Lord Simon denied that Article 9 'created' the enrolled bill rule. Rather, Article 9 'reflected' an existing functional imperative – namely preserving uninhibited discussion in a democratic Parliament. This analysis is inept. The pre-1689 Parliament was in functional terms nothing like its present day successor; the 1688 revolutionaries had no inclination to produce a 'democratic' legislature. Article 9 could not 'reflect' democratic sentiment, because no such sentiment existed. The judgment does however raise important methodological issues, in that it suggests the scope of privilege falls to be determined by judicial (rather than house) perceptions of what is 'necessary' for the conduct of parliamentary business. See further Denham CJ in *Stockdale v Hansard* (pp 282–284 below), and Lord Browne-Wilkinson in *Pepper v Hart* (pp 254–287 below).

the Lords. As we saw in chapter seven, the Lords exercised sufficient influence over the composition of the Commons to make it inaccurate to suggest that the two houses held invariably antagonistic views on all issues. The tensions were nevertheless sufficient for the lower house consistently to deny the ordinary courts' authority in matters of claimed privilege. It was not until the passage of the Judicature Acts of 1873 and 1875 that one could plausibly argue that the House of Lords qua 'ordinary court' was both formally and functionally independent of the Lords qua legislative assembly; although as suggested below, this initiative was not sufficient to induce the Commons to disclaim its purported interpretive authority.

We will revisit the conceptual problems flowing from the uncertain status and meaning of Article 9 below. But other issues also merit attention. The following pages sweep broadly over three hundred years of the history of parliamentary privilege in five general areas. Firstly, the houses' power to regulate their own composition through the admission, retention and expulsion of their members; secondly, the publication of details of house business; thirdly, the admissibility before the courts of such published material; fourthly, the concept of 'contempt of the house'; and fifthly, the regulation of MPs' ethical standards.

I. THE ADMISSION, RETENTION AND EXPULSION OF MEMBERS

The tortuous development of the Commons' electoral system was traced in chapter seven. However the Acts which gradually extended the franchise do not fully identify the constitutional principles which have determined the lower house's composition. The relationship between the 'people' and the Commons has also been affected by questions of privilege.

ASHBY V WHITE REVISITED

As noted in chapter seven, the courts had accepted shortly after the revolution that enfranchised citizens enjoyed common law 'rights of property' in their entitlement to vote. Thus the plaintiff in *Ashby v White* could maintain an action in tort against the returning officer in Aylesbury who had prevented him from voting.[10] The judges hearing the litigation had however held sharply divergent views on the issue. As we saw in chapter seven, the Commons enjoyed statutory authority to determine the outcome of disputed elections between 1604 and 1868.[11] The result in the Aylesbury election was not in doubt, and thus the Commons had no statutory jurisdiction over Ashby's suit. The point of contention which Ashby raised was whether a freeholder's

[10] (1703) 1 Bro Parl Cas 62. See p 227 above. [11] P 225 above.

right to vote was a matter of common law, or a facet of the Commons' power to control its own composition. The question had profound consequences; if the latter claim were accepted, it would effectively empower the Commons alone to determine the allocation of the franchise.

The majority of the judges hearing Ashby's case at first instance accepted that latter viewpoint. His claim bore directly on an established Commons privilege, with which the court was not competent to interfere. For White and Gould JJ, the matter was a question of hierarchy – in these matters, the *lex parliamenti* overrode common law. Powys J added a further point (which we would now recognise as one of justiciability): 'we are not acquainted with the learning of elections, and there is a particular cunning in it not known to us'.[12]

Holt CJ dissented. Ashby's claimed right to vote was firmly based in common law. The judges' duty was to uphold that law. The court should thus hear his claim, and if the case was well-founded, decide in his favour. To do otherwise would breach the court's constitutional duty: 'We must not be frighted when a matter of property comes before us, by saying it belongs to the parliament; we must exert the Queen's jurisdiction'.[13] For Holt, the extent of privilege was a question for the courts, not the house to decide.

PATY'S CASE

The House of Lords (qua final court of appeal) supported Holt's dissent, and reversed the judgment. It is tempting to see this as a victory for the 'rule of law' over the arbitrary inclinations of the Commons. For the lower house, it perhaps appeared as an illegitimate intrusion by the upper house (qua legislative body) into its sphere of responsibility. The Commons immediately passed a resolution rejecting the Lords' decision in *Ashby*:

> '[N]either the qualifications of any elector, or the right of any person elected, is cognisable or determinable elsewhere, than before the commons of England. . . . whoever shall presume to commence any action [before] any other jurisdiction . . . except in cases especially provided for by act of parliament . . . are guilty of a high breach of privilege of this house'.[14]

Shortly thereafter, five other voters in Aylesbury who had suffered similar obstructions to Ashby initiated legal actions. To do so, defying the Commons' resolution, was a bold undertaking, for the lower house immediately held them to have breached its privileges and gaoled them. The equivocal role adopted by the courts was then illustrated by a majority judgment which declined jurisdiction over writs of habeas corpus issued on the voters' behalf.[15]

Holt again dissented, stressing the subordinacy of privilege to both common law and statute:

[12] (1703) 92 ER 126 at 130.
[13] (1703) 92 ER 126 at 138.
[14] Quoted in Plucknett (1960) op cit pp 582–583.
[15] *R v Paty* (1705) 2 Salk 503, 91 ER 431.

'bringing such actions was declared by the house of Commons to be a breach of their privilege; but that declaration will not make that a privilege that was not so before. . . . The privileges of the house of Commons . . . are nothing but the law. . . . This privilege of theirs concerns the liberty of the people in a high degree, by subjecting them to imprisonment, which is what the people cannot be subjected to without an act of Parliament'.[16]

The Commons then sought to block Paty's appeal to the House of Lords. A clash between the two houses was only averted when Queen Anne prorogued Parliament, which had the effect of releasing the imprisoned men.

Substantively, *Ashby* and *Paty's Case* have little contemporary relevance. Conceptually, however, they retain significance because of Holt's assertion of parliamentary sovereignty and the rule of law as constitutional principles superior to privilege. That argument has yet to be entirely settled, but, as the following pages suggest, Holt's analysis has gradually gained greater conceptual legitimacy and practical endorsement.

JOHN WILKES

The grievances which antagonised the American colonists were not all engendered by British legislative and executive action undertaken in the colonies. The Americans' disenchantment was added to by the treatment meted out by the Commons and successive British governments to British politicians sympathetic to the Americans' cause. John Wilkes' role as a critic of government policy has already been alluded to;[17] his career now merits further consideration.

Wilkes' early attachment to 'democratic' principles seemed tenuous; in 1757 he bought his way into the Commons by bribing and treating the electors of (ironically) Aylesbury. Wilkes nevertheless moved in radical political circles, and in the 1760s edited a journal, *The North Briton*, which disseminated vehement criticism of the government. Issue No 45 castigated the measures contained in the King's Speech opening the 1763 parliamentary session:

'Every friend of this country must lament that a prince of so many great and admirable qualities . . . can be brought to give the sanction of his sacred name to the most odious measures and the most unjustifiable public declarations . . .'

No 45 was broadly perceived as an attack upon the Monarch as well as his Ministers. Wilkes then published a potentially blasphemous and seditious tract called *An Essay on Women*. The combined effect of the two publications provoked the government to prosecute him for libel and the Commons to expel him. Wilkes meanwhile fled the country, and was declared an outlaw when he did not appear at his trial. On returning to England in June 1768, he was sentenced to two years' imprisonment.

16 (1705) 2 Salk 503, 91 ER 431 at 433. Holt's method provides an obvious precedent for the reasoning subsequently deployed by Lord Camden in *Entick*; see pp 59–61 above.

17 Pp 53–54 above. Information in the following section is drawn largely from Rude G (1962) *Wilkes and liberty* (Oxford: Clarendon Press). See also Maier op cit.

To modern eyes, the events of the next year have a farcical hue, but they were of considerable significance to shaping emergent understandings of the relationship between the Commons, statute, and the electorate. If a member is expelled, the seat becomes vacant and a by-election is held. Wilkes did not contest his Aylesbury seat after his first expulsion. But Wilkes' status as a convicted prisoner was not then a legal impediment to standing for election or taking a seat.[18] Thus in 1769, Wilkes stood as a candidate for Middlesex, where many electors endorsed his views. Wilkes was elected to the house on 16 February – and expelled by the Commons on 17 February. Wilkes was returned again on 16 March – and was expelled the next day. In April, he was again elected. This time, rather than expel Wilkes and trigger another election, the Commons declared Wilkes' defeated opponent the 'winner', and admitted him to the house.

The Commons' defiance of the electorate's wishes prompted many English constituencies (and some American colonists) to petition both the Commons and the King to have the 'result' of the election reversed. One of Wilkes' supporters tabled a motion inviting the Commons to resolve that; 'no person eligible by law can be incapacitated from election by a vote of the House, but by Act of Parliament alone'. The motion was defeated by 226 to 186. The house carried (by 224 to 180) a government motion that Wilkes' expulsion was 'agreeable to the law of the land'.[19]

That conclusion was not put to a legal test. Wilkes did not challenge his exclusion in the courts, and thereby missed the opportunity to set up a potentially momentous dispute between the 'rights' of the electorate and the 'privileges' of the Commons. One can only speculate as to whether the courts would even have accepted jurisdiction to entertain such proceedings, and, had they done so, as to the decision they would have reached. Instead, Wilkes turned his attention towards becoming Lord Mayor of London, an office to which he was elected in 1774. By then, sentiment in the Commons had swung sufficiently to allow him to take the seat for Middlesex which he won (yet again) in December 1774.

One might initially attribute the house's conduct towards Wilkes to the era's political context. The Commons then made no claim to be 'democratic'; 60 years had still to pass before the Great Reform Act would set Britain on the long, slow path towards a universal franchise. In formal terms, Wilkes' repeated expulsion was a defensible expression of the Commons' traditional autonomy. From a functional perspective, the house's action could be construed as a collective expression of Burke's portrayal of the MP as representative rather than delegate: MPs were sparing an ill-advised, intemperate electorate from the consequences of its folly. If so, one might then assume that as the franchise became more extensive and the electorate more 'mature', and the legitimacy of the Commons' legislative role rested increasingly on the assumption that it

18 See the discussion of *Goodwin and Fortescue's Case* (1604) in Plucknett op cit pp 372–374; Keir D (8th ed 1966) *The constitutional history of modern Britain* pp 175–177 (London: Adam and Charles Black).

19 Rude op cit pp 119, 133. See also Wittke op cit pp 115–123. One might ask whether this was decision of 'the Commons' or an early example of effective government control of the lower house.

represented 'the people', the house could no longer defensibly invoke its privileges to exclude an elected member. But as the experience of Charles Bradlaugh suggests, any such assumption would be ill-founded.

CHARLES BRADLAUGH

Bradlaugh, a radical journalist and political campaigner, had achieved considerable notoriety by 1870 both for founding an atheistic organisation known as the National Secular Society, and for being prosecuted for publishing a book on birth control.[20] Such notoriety apparently appealed to the voters of Northampton; in 1880 they returned Bradlaugh as their MP.

Bradlaugh's difficulties began when he tried to take his seat. MPs had been placed under a statutory obligation during Elizabeth I's reign to take an oath of allegiance to the Monarch and the Protestant faith before assuming their seats.[21] The oath (administered by the Speaker on the floor of the house) was intended to exclude Roman Catholics from the Commons, but also caught Protestant non-conformists and Jews. The oath was modified to admit Catholics in 1829; legislation in 1866 introduced an oath acceptable to members of the Jewish faith, and the Promissory Oaths Act 1868 permitted members of dissentient religious sects to 'affirm' their loyalty rather than swear it. The legislation did not actually exclude members from the house if they had not taken the oath or affirmed, but fined them £500 (even in 1880 an enormous sum) for each occasion when they sat and voted without having done so.

On entering the house, Bradlaugh (having previously announced himself an atheist) wished to affirm rather than swear his loyalty. The house, however, resolved that he could not do so. Bradlaugh's subsequent attempt to take the oath instead was also blocked by a resolution. On declining to leave the house, Bradlaugh was forcibly ejected. The majority in the Commons then expelled him in April 1881. He was returned at a by-election a week later, at which point the then Speaker had evidently concluded that: 'the house would do well and wisely, according to the constitution, to admit him without question'.[22] The majority nevertheless expelled him again. Bradlaugh was subsequently physically ejected by Commons' officials. Undeterred, he re-entered the house and adopted the extraordinary course of administering the oath to himself and then assuming his place on the backbenches. He was once again expelled; and yet again returned at the ensuing by-election.

The Commons' continued refusal to admit Bradlaugh seemingly negated the impact of the Great Reform Act and Disraeli's 1867 franchise legislation in respect of the electors of Northampton. For those voters, the extended franchise was worthless,

[20] Arnstein W (1983) *The Bradlaugh Case* ch 1 (University of Missouri Press: Columbia, Miss). Arnstein provides an illuminating insight into the man and his times. For legalistic analysis of Bradlaugh's subsequent difficulties with the Commons see Wittke op cit pp 160–169; Anson W (5th edn 1922) *The law and custom of the constitution* pp 93–98, 195–196 (Oxford: Clarendon Press).

[21] This oversimplifies the issue rather. See Anson op cit pp 93–95.

[22] Arnstein op cit p 104.

since their chosen candidate was unable to represent them. For Bradlaugh the legal and moral position was clear. He, and his electors were the victims of:

'the arbitrary and illegal action of the House of Commons. It is a melancholy exhibition of the tyranny of orthodoxy when we see one branch of the legislature taking upon itself to nullify laws which the whole legislature itself has sanctioned'.[23]

He then sought to challenge this 'arbitrary and illegal action' before the courts. The action in *Bradlaugh v Gossett*[24] was directed against the Commons Serjeant-at-Arms, who, obeying a Commons resolution, had intimated that he would use physical violence to prevent Bradlaugh entering in future. Bradlaugh's suit asked the court to issue an injunction preventing the Serjeant-at-Arms from so doing. As Stephen J indicated, the case raised a straightforward clash between the authority of statute and of privilege:

'Suppose that the House of Commons forbids one of its members to do that which an Act of Parliament requires him to do . . . is such an order one which we can declare to be void and restrain the executive officer of the House from carrying out'.[25]

The judgment held that no statute could impliedly alter the Commons' power to exercise complete control over its internal proceedings. Neither was the house's jurisdiction in such matters overridden by common law. In reaching this conclusion, Stephen J was influenced by a sense of judicial deference to the Commons:

'The House of Commons is not a Court of Justice, but the effect of its privilege to regulate its own internal concerns practically invests it with a judicial character when it has to apply to particular cases the provisions of Acts of Parliament. . . . If its determination is not in accordance with the law, this resembles the case of an error by a judge whose decision is not subject to appeal . . . [I]f we were to attempt to erect ourselves into a Court of Appeal from the House of Commons, we should consult neither the public interest, nor the interests of Parliament and the constitution, nor our own dignity'.[26]

Since swearing or affirming were procedures conducted entirely within the house, the regulation of the process was a matter solely for the house. In contrast, the house would have no authority to interfere with those aspects of the processes affecting its composition which occurred outside its boundaries; such as, for example, a citizen's common law or statutory entitlement to vote in a parliamentary election. This would be consistent with Holt's opinions in *Ashby* and *Paty's Case*, and reiterates the point that the courts claimed the power to identify the extent of privilege, but not to interfere with its exercise within those identified boundaries. But Stephen J seemed decidedly uncertain as to the courts' response if the house chose to exceed its jurisdiction in this way:

'I should in any case feel a reluctance almost invincible to declaring a resolution of the

23 Arnstein op cit p 147. 24 (1884) 12 QBD 271. 25 (1884) 12 QBD 271 at 278.
26 (1884) 12 QBD 271 at 286.

House of Commons to be beyond the powers of the house . . . Such a declaration would in every case be unnecessary and disrespectful'.[27]

In effect, the court was abdicating its role as the guardian of the rule of law and allowing the Commons to determine the meaning of legislation. Given the vituperative clashes between the Commons, Lords and Monarch over the terms of nineteenth century enfranchisement legislation, which had led to considerable modification of the initial bills,[28] it is implausible to assume that Parliament impliedly granted such jurisdiction to the Commons. The judgment thus entirely subverts orthodox understandings of parliamentary sovereignty.

The Bradlaugh saga was eventually ended after the 1885 general election, in which Bradlaugh was for the seventh time returned as Northampton's MP. The solution was, from a legal perspective, unsatisfactory. After the election, the house had chosen a new Speaker, the former Liberal MP Sir Arthur Peel. When the house assembled, Peel maintained that the house's previous resolutions preventing Bradlaugh from taking the oath had lapsed. The Speaker also made it clear that he would not accept any new motion on the same issue:

'I have no right, original or delegated to interfere between an honourable member and his taking of the oath. . . . It is not for me, I respectfully say, it is not for the House, to enter into any inquisition as to what may be the opinions of a Member when he comes to the table to take the oath'.[29]

That Peel ended the controversy in so simple a fashion is a forceful testament to the disciplinary authority a determined Speaker may exercise over the house, even when his/her views are not supported by most members. Yet the solution, as much as the controversy itself, also indicates the extent to which both the Commons and the courts considered themselves competent to deny the electors of Northampton the services of their chosen representative.

The Bradlaugh episode neatly illustrates the so-called 'dualism' which attaches to the constitutional status of the houses' privileges:

'Thus there may be at any given moment two doctrines of privilege, the one held by the courts, the other by either House, the one to be found in the law reports, the other in Hansard, and no way of resolving the real point at issue should conflict arise'.[30]

And as the following sections suggest, the practical problems raised by dualism are not limited solely to the question of the admission of members to their respective house.

FREEDOM FROM IMPRISONMENT, ARREST AND MOLESTATION

The first recorded instance of the Commons asserting its privilege to force the release of one its members from imprisonment seems to be *Ferrer's Case* in 1543.[31] The

27 (1884) 12 QBD 271 at 282. 28 See pp 227–228 above.
29 Quoted in Arnstein op cit p 310. 30 Keir and Lawson op cit p 255.
31 Plucknett op cit pp 249–250. See also Wittke op cit pp 33–35.

privilege has an obvious functional basis in the pre-revolutionary era, namely to ensure that the members summoned by the King were not impeded from travelling to London and thereafter going about their parliamentary business, whether by unlawful interference or by legal proceedings initiated in any of the courts of inferior jurisdiction. A 1604 statute 'recognised' the privilege as encompassing both a power to set free a member duly imprisoned by a court of law, and the power to punish any person arresting a member.[32] Neither house was obliged to protect its members from detention. Rather the privilege was a power the house might waive when it saw fit.

The privilege was not invoked in respect of criminal charges, even if the impugned conduct had occurred within the Commons or Lords itself. There have been relatively few occasions in the modern era on which MPs have faced criminal charges. Several Irish MPs were imprisoned during the 1880s and again in 1918 for criminal activities arising from the Irish struggle for independence. On none of these occasions did the house make any suggestion that it would interfere with the court proceedings.

A more conceptually difficult case concerned Captain A Ramsay MP, a member with alleged fascist sympathies, detained in 1940 under the regulations at issue in *Liversidge*. Ramsay's detention was referred to the Committee of Privileges as a potential breach of the arrest privilege. The Committee (and subsequently the house) was divided on the question, although the majority concluded no breach had occurred. That many MPs doubted the legitimacy of the government's action presumably stemmed from the fact that Ramsay's detention was not the result of a criminal conviction; the only 'crime' he had committed (like Liversidge) was to have aroused the Home Secretary's suspicions as to his loyalty to Britain's war effort. Ramsay remained in detention until 1944.[33]

The Parliamentary Privilege Act 1770

The arrest privilege nevertheless had considerable practical significance in respect of civil suits, especially while it remained possible to be imprisoned for debt. Immediately after the revolution, the houses' growing sense of self-importance led them to claim an ever greater scope for the arrest privilege, encompassing not just the persons of members, but also their land, their moveable property and their servants. The extended privilege was frequently invoked as an expedient way for MPs and their retinues to evade numerous legal obligations – a practice which provoked considerable public criticism.[34]

Public pressure eventually led Parliament to reduce the privilege's scope. In 1700, legislation was enacted entitled 'An Act for preventing any inconveniences that may happen by privilege of Parliament'. Its main provision, as restated in the Parliamentary Privilege Act 1770, s 1, was that:

'Any person may at any time commence and prosecute any action or suit against any Lord of Parliament or any . . . [member] of the House of Commons . . . or any other person intitled

32 Plucknett (1960) op cit pp 333–334.

33 Simpson op cit pp 113–114, 393–395, 404.

34 See Wittke op cit pp 39–43.

to the privilege of Parliament . . . and no such action shall at any time be impeached, stayed or delayed by or under colour or pretence of any privilege of Parliament'.

If interpreted literally (ie *any* privilege), s 1 seems to abolish all aspects of privilege in so far as they restricted access to the courts, including Article 9. The Commons and the judiciary appeared to have reached a shared (and much less expansive) understanding of the Act's impact in 1958, when the Commons (without surrendering its claimed jurisdiction to judge the extent of privilege) invited the Privy Council (in its judicial capacity) to interpret the scope of the 1770 Act.[35]

The court applied the mischief rule rather than the literal rule to s 1. It considered that the 'mischief' in issue was solely MPs' increasing predilection to invoke privilege as a blanket immunity against all civil actions, and not MPs' entitlement to freedom of speech in the house. The Privy Council considered this freedom to have been so central a value in the 1688 settlement that it was inconceivable that Parliament would have curtailed its scope just 12 years later. The court thus concluded that the Act reached only those legal actions whose origins did not lie in a 'proceeding in Parliament'.

But this opinion left a crucial question unanswered: namely who was to decide if the action concerned had been precipitated by a 'proceeding in Parliament' – the Commons or the courts? It is generally assumed that the constitution confers the responsibility of statutory interpretation on the courts. Determining the meaning of 'proceedings' would thus be a judicial function. This presumption could however be rebutted in two ways. Firstly, one might argue that this privilege (or indeed privilege in general) enjoyed a special constitutional status, which (unlike the prerogative or other common law rules) rendered it immune to implied repeal. The court seemed to accept this viewpoint, by observing that the free speech privilege was 'solemnly *reasserted* in the Bill of Rights'.[36] The notion of 'reassertion' suggests that the legal status of privilege was such that it co-existed with Article 9 – that the statutory provision was merely declaratory and not transformative of the substantive entitlements the house had hitherto enjoyed. A second argument, which the court did not entertain, was that the Bill of Rights itself (or indeed any other statute touching upon privilege) impliedly ousted the courts' jurisdiction and bestowed it on the house.

Lord Denning dissented from the court's opinion.[37] He concluded that the clear meaning of the 1770 Act was that the Commons would be acting illegally if it made any attempt to interfere with a legal action initiated against one of its members. The Act was a command from Parliament to one of its component parts not to undertake such action. But this did not mean such a suit could be argued, still less succeed. For Lord Denning also held that the courts remained obliged by Article 9 to refuse to entertain action which 'questioned' a 'proceeding in Parliament'.

Denning nonetheless made the important point that whatever jurisdiction the

35 *Re Parliamentary Privilege Act 1770* [1958] AC 331, [1958] 2 All ER 329, PC.

36 [1958] AC 331 at 350, PC (emphasis added).

37 The Privy Council did not then permit dissents. Denning's opinion was neither recorded nor published in the report itself. See Lord Denning 'Re Parliamentary Privilege Act 1770' (1985) *Public Law* 80–92.

Commons might have possessed to determine the extent and meaning of its free speech privilege before 1689 had been overridden by Parliament when Article 9 was enacted. Article 9 therefore did not 'reassert' the house's privilege. Rather it extinguished the privilege and created a new statutory protection for the Commons and its members. Nor did Article 9 contain any implied grant of interpretive authority to the Commons. Privilege thus enjoyed no higher status vis à vis statute than did the common law:

'This means of course that it is for the courts to say what is a "proceeding in Parliament" within the Bill of Rights – which is just what the House of Commons do not wish to concede'.[38]

Support for Denning's analysis was offered by Scarman J in *Stourton v Stourton*, a 1963 case concerning the applicability of the freedom of arrest privilege to peers:

'I do not think however, that I, sitting in the High Court . . . must necessarily take the law that I have to apply from what would be the practice of the House. I think I have to look to the common law as deduced in judicial decisions in order to determine in the particular case whether the privilege arises, and if so its scope and effect'.[39]

We will revisit this issue below. Before doing so however, we might usefully turn to a second facet of the role played by the Commons' privileges in regulating the relationship between the house and the people.

II. THE PRINCIPLE OF INFORMED CONSENT?

The American revolutionaries attached much importance to the principle that the proceedings of Congress, and especially the speeches and voting behaviour of legislators, should be matters of public record. The presumption that the people should be furnished with the information needed to make informed choices about their preferred representatives was afforded explicit legal protection within the Constitution's text.

At that time, neither the Commons nor the Lords were under any statutory or common law obligation to do likewise. Such publicity as was given to the houses' affairs was a matter for the houses themselves to decide; and their preference then seemed to be for limited disclosure. Both the pre- and post-revolutionary Commons had passed resolutions contending that unauthorised publication of any reports of its proceedings was a breach of privilege.[40] In 1762, the house had declared:

'That it is an high Indignity to, and a notorious breach of the Privilege of this House . . . for any printer or Publisher of any printed Newspaper . . . to give therein any Account of the

[38] (1985) *Public Law* 80–92 at 85.

[39] [1963] 1 All ER 606 at 608. See also Leopold P (1989) 'The freedom of peers from arrest' *Public Law* 398–406.

[40] Wittke op cit p 51.

Debates or other Proceedings of this House . . . and this House will proceed with the utmost severity against such offenders'.[41]

The resolution is quite inconsistent with any notion that the electoral process rested upon voters' informed consent. As the century wore on, so the legitimacy and the legality of the Commons' stance were increasingly questioned by emergent radical factions; by 1770 several newspapers published regular reports of Commons' debates and votes. An acute controversy flared during Wilkes' exclusion from the Commons. Press coverage of the affair made copious and scathing use of MPs' speeches; several editors took what might now be regarded as the eminently 'democratic' view that electors should know which MPs spoke in favour of Wilkes' admission, which members opposed it, and which labelled signatories of petitions supporting Wilkes as 'scum'.

The government's Commons majority resolved that several editors had breached the house's privileges by publishing such reports. When the editors defied the house, the Commons authorised its officers to arrest them. This brought the house into conflict with the Lord Mayor of London, who in his capacity as a magistrate held a judicial jurisdiction over criminal acts undertaken within the city's boundaries. On attempting to seize one of the impugned editors, the Commons' officer found himself arrested for assault and summoned to appear before the Lord Mayor. This in turn led the Commons to resolve that the Lord Mayor had breached the house's privilege by interfering with its officer's execution of its resolution, and thereafter to imprison him in the Tower. When presented with a writ for habeas corpus on the Lord Mayor's behalf, the courts declined to examine the Speaker's warrant maintaining that the Lord Mayor had been committed for a breach of privileges.

While the house had successfully asserted its formal authority, the episode appeared to undermine its practical legitimacy, for unauthorised publication of its proceedings continued apace. One would however be mistaken in assuming that this practical victory for the principle of informed consent was thereafter accorded a legal basis. The house revoked the motion in 1971, but there is still no legal requirement that either house publish records of its business.[42] Such information as is released is a matter entirely for each house itself.

III. THE JUSTICIABILITY OF 'PROCEEDINGS IN PARLIAMENT'

There has as yet been no indication that the courts consider themselves able to force the publication of any aspect of either house's proceedings. However, the question of what use the courts might subsequently make of such records has been (and remains) an issue of appreciable importance and controversy.

41 Cited in Marshall (1979) op cit.

42 Griffith and Ryle op cit p 95.

ACTIONS IN DEFAMATION

Speeches made by MPs in either house which defame other citizens clearly raise a potential conflict with the courts. The fear of losing a defamation action could act as a considerable impediment to MPs' freedom of speech, yet the common law has always provided extensive remedies enabling people to protect their 'right' to a good reputation.[43] In such circumstances, the conceptual problem of 'dualism' is particularly acute. In practice however, the courts and the houses appeared to have reached a shared understanding of the scope of law and privilege on this question.

The plaintiff in *Dillon v Balfour*[44] was a midwife in Ireland. Balfour[45] was then a Minister in Ireland. During the passage of the Criminal Procedure (Ireland) Bill in 1887, Balfour made various remarks about Dillon which she felt undermined her professional reputation, in respect of which she sought substantial damages. Balfour applied for the action to be struck out, contending that speeches made in the house could not be the subject of a defamation suit.

The judgment offers a paradigmatic example of the conceptual obfuscation which attends many analyses of the legal status of such speeches. Palles CB began his judgment by turning to Article 9.[46] However he construed Article 9 not as creating a statutory protection, but as declaratory of pre-revolutionary privilege. To complicate matters further, he then observed that the privilege was an 'ancient right and liberty of the realm',[47] suggesting it had a common law source.

The basis of his judgment, which struck out the plaintiff's action, was equally unclear. Palles CB held that the courts had jurisdiction in a defamation action only to ask if the words in issue were spoken/written as a 'proceeding in Parliament'. Whatever its source, the court's jurisdiction was 'ousted' (though by what he did not explain) if it determined that the words were a 'proceeding in Parliament'. Any such statement enjoyed complete immunity from actions in defamation.[48]

It is unfortunate that the court was not more conceptually precise in identifying the source of this rule. It may also be thought that the substantive protection afforded by the case affords MPs an unnecessarily expansive legal immunity. There is no doubt force in the argument that MPs should be able to use the privilege to raise matters of public concern which subsequent investigation proves to be well-founded. However, MPs may also shelter behind privilege to raise unfounded allegations. The Conservative MP, Geoffrey Dickens, caused considerable controversy in 1986 when he availed himself of privilege to accuse a clergyman of having sexually abused young children. The

43 See Brazier M (9th edn, 1993) *Street on Torts* ch 23 (London: Butterworths).

44 (1887) 20 LR Ir 600. 45 See pp 179–180 above.

46 This in itself was problematic, as it is by no means clear that the Bill of Rights applies to Ireland; see Lock G (1989) 'The 1689 Bill of Rights' *Political Studies* 541–561 at pp 557–558.

47 (1887) 20 LR Ir 600 at 612.

48 In the same era, the courts had concluded that such protection extended to newspapers which produced accurate reports of such 'defamatory' proceedings, if the report was circulated to inform the citizenry of what was happening in Parliament rather than as a malicious attempt to discredit the person criticised: see *Wason v Walter* (1868) LR 4 QB 73.

person concerned had already been subject to a police investigation, and the police had concluded there was no basis for a prosecution.[49] More recently, two Northern Irish Unionist MPs named individuals as terrorist murderers, an accusation which as well as being defamatory presumably exposed the persons named to considerable personal danger. In such circumstances, an MP's behaviour is no doubt more reprehensible if she knows the allegation to be false, or has taken no care to establish its accuracy, than if she is acting in good faith. The damage to the reputation of the individual or company concerned has nevertheless been done irrespective of the MPs' motive.

Dickens made his allegation in a speech on the floor. There is seemingly no doubt this was a 'proceeding in Parliament'. But as suggested in chapter five, much of the Commons' work takes place outside the chamber, and much takes the form of written rather than oral communication. The question then arises of just what is meant by 'proceedings in Parliament'.

WHAT ARE 'PROCEEDINGS IN PARLIAMENT'?

The Privy Council had stressed in *Re the Parliamentary Privilege Act 1770* that it offered no view on the meaning of 'proceedings in Parliament'. Nor did it address the more contentious question of whether the power to determine that meaning lay within the jurisdiction of the courts or the respective houses. The Commons' reference to the Privy Council had been triggered by an episode involving Labour MP George Strauss. Strauss had sent a letter to a Minister criticising the London Electricity Board (LEB). The Minister forwarded the letter to the Chairman of the LEB. The Chairman considered Strauss' comments defamatory, and threatened a libel action. Strauss thereupon referred the matter to the house, claiming the threat was a breach of privilege.

The issue turned on whether the letter was a 'proceeding in Parliament'. There are strong arguments for assuming that it was. Such communications about matters within a Minister's competence would be a frequently occurring and important part of the MP's role, both as a party politician and as a constituency representative. The Committee of Privileges concluded that the letter was a 'proceeding', and that a breach had occurred. However the house rejected the Committee's conclusion. In contrast, the house had accepted in 1938–1939 that communications between members and Ministers which were initiated with a view to placing a question would be 'proceedings'. A fortiori, oral or written questions themselves would also come within the scope of the privilege. Even if we were to accept that the houses are constitutionally competent to give an authoritative definition of the concept, it is clear that they have not done so. Griffith and Ryle's suggestion that there are many 'grey areas' is perhaps a polite understatement.[50]

49 Leopold P (1986) 'Leaks and squeaks in the Palace of Westminster' *Public Law* 368–374.

50 Op cit p 88. For an absurd interpretation see *R v Graham-Campell, ex p Herbert* [1935] 1 KB 594.

The Commons Committee of Privileges recommended in 1977 that the concept be given a clearer, legislative meaning. However the house chose not to act upon the proposal, presumably because the passage of such legislation would imply that Parliament had removed the houses' claimed competence to interpret the term. 'Proceedings in parliament' thus remains a legally obscure area of the constitution. That obscurity has in the past triggered acute controversy.

Stockdale v Hansard (1839)

The constitutional clash between the courts and the Commons which was avoided over Wilkes' admission in the 1760s eventually occurred in the late 1830s. The trigger for the dispute was mundane. A report by the Inspector of Prisons, published on the house's instructions, had made libellous comments about a medical textbook circulating in a gaol. Stockdale, the book's author, commenced defamation proceedings against Mr Hansard, the Commons' printer.[51]

The house instructed Mr Hansard not to contest the case on its merits, but to inform the court that the house had resolved that the report was a proceeding in Parliament, and as such not subject to judicial jurisdiction.[52] The court, for which Lord Denman CJ gave the leading judgment, rejected the Commons' assertion of privilege, categorising it as:

'a claim for an arbitrary power to authorise the commission of any act whatever, on behalf of a body which in the same argument is admitted not to be the supreme power in the state'.[53]

Lord Denman concluded that such a contention was irreconcilable with orthodox understandings of parliamentary sovereignty and the rule of law. The Commons' (or Lords') constitutional competence in matters of privilege stretched only to the application of existing privilege. With that jurisdiction, the ordinary courts would not interfere. But neither house could grant itself new privileges. Furthermore, the power to determine the boundaries of those existing privileges lay not with either house through resolutions, but with the courts through the common law. Parliament might grant either house a jurisdiction which exceeded the existing boundaries, and give the house the power that it claimed in this case, but the Commons could not achieve that result itself:

'The House of Commons is not Parliament, but only a co-ordinate and component part of the Parliament. That sovereign power can make and unmake the laws; but the concurrence of the three legislative estates is necessary; the resolution of any one of them cannot alter the law . . . '.[54]

51 *Stockdale v Hansard* (1839) 9 Ad & El 1. The text that follows presents a simplified account of a judgment which merits close scrutiny.

52 The house was evidently not offering an interpretation of Article 9 of the Bill of Rights qua statute, but construing it as declaratory of a continuing privilege with pre-revolutionary origins.

53 (1839) 9 Ad & El 1 at 107–108.

54 (1839) 9 Ad & El 1 at 108.

Lord Denman's reasoning follows that of Holt CJ in *Ashby v White* and *Paty's Case.* Just as Holt saw the right to vote as a common law entitlement that could only be overridden by Parliament, so Lord Denman viewed the common law right to protect one's reputation against libellous criticism as immune to anything other than statutory regulation. Lord Denman considered that 'proceedings in Parliament' could not form the subject of a defamation action. However he would not accept that reports subsequently circulated outside the house enjoyed such protection. Lord Denman adopted what to modern eyes would be a teleological interpretive strategy by suggesting that the protections the houses possessed under Article 9 extended only to matters 'necessary' for them to perform their duties. He also held, crucially, that assessing the issue of necessity was a matter for the courts, not for the Commons. Since Lord Denman saw no 'necessity' for the publishers of this particular report to be immune from a libel action, Stockdale could proceed with his action.

The Case of the Sheriff of Middlesex

Stockdale won his action. However, the Commons did not accept the court's conclusion. Acting on the house's instructions, Mr Hansard refused to comply with the judgment. The Sheriff of Middlesex, an officer of the court, then sought to enforce the judgment. The Commons ordered that the Sheriff be committed to the Tower for having breached the house's privileges. The Commons' stance on this question is obviously hypocritical, given its long history of opposition in the pre-revolutionary era to the Crown's repeated efforts to invoke a similarly arbitrary power to detain anyone who displeased it. The Sheriff had been detained because he was complying with the court's instructions. In crude terms, he had been punished by the Commons for upholding the rule of law. One might therefore have expected that his subsequent habeas corpus action would lead the courts to order his immediate release.[55]

The Serjeant at Arms' return to the writ stated simply that the Sheriff had been committed for 'a breach of privilege and contempt'. The court, for which Lord Denman gave the leading judgment, declined to question the adequacy of the return. Lord Denman held that so long as the Commons complied with the mere formality of stating that the committal was for 'contempt', no court was competent to order the prisoner's release. It would be, he suggested, 'unseemly' for a court to doubt the Commons' bona fides in such circumstances.

The decision is closely comparable with the opinion offered by the judges in the *Resolutions in Anderson* some 300 years earlier; the only difference being that the court was now permitting the Commons rather than the Crown to make a mockery of habeas corpus. The decision also completely undermined *Stockdale.* Lord Denman began his opinion in *Middlesex* by observing that *Stockdale* was 'in all respects correct'. Yet there is little point in a judgment being 'correct' if the same court subsequently permits it to be evaded.

55 (1840) 11 Ad & El 273. For a fuller discussion see Wittke op cit pp 152–156: Stockdale E (1989) 'The unnecessary crisis: the background to the Parliamentary Papers Act 1840' *Public Law* 30–49.

Neither the Commons nor the judiciary emerge with credit from the *Stockdale* controversy. The specific legal problem that the case raised was subsequently resolved by Parliament in the Parliamentary Papers Act 1840. The Act empowered the Speaker to issue a certificate staying any legal proceedings in respect of documents published by order of either house. But the episode did not provide 'an ultimate political fact' with which to resolve the problem of 'dualism' in the more general sense. It may however be that a recent decision of the House of Lords has opened the way for that particular gap to be filled.

'REDEFINING PARLIAMENT' – *PEPPER V HART*

One rule to which students of British law were traditionally exposed early on in their studies was that judges would not refer to the records of debates in *Hansard* to clarify the meaning of ambiguous or nonsensical legislative terminology. The legal roots of the 'exclusionary rule' are not entirely clear.[56] It might be simply a common law rule concerning the admissibility of evidence. An alternative perspective is that the courts were deferring to a statutory command in Article 9 of the Bill of Rights, wherein the notion of 'questioned' extended to considering the content of debate to aid statutory interpretation. A third argument contends that the courts' refusal to consult *Hansard* was an element of privilege, existing alongside the common law but immune to judicial jurisdiction.

The rule's source is significant when considering whether and how it might be revised. If it was a common law concept, there would be no constitutional barrier to prevent the House of Lords changing it. In contrast, if the rule derived from Article 9, the courts could not simply overrule it. That would be inconsistent with parliamentary sovereignty. However, as a law-maker in the interpretative sense, the House of Lords could alter its previous definition of Article 9. The concept of 'questioned' could, for example, be narrowed, perhaps so that it embraced only a defence to defamation proceedings.[57] If the rule was part of privilege, judicial amendment would be constitutionally problematic rather than impossible. If we accept (per *Stockdale*, Denning's dissent in *Re the Parliamentary Privilege Act 1770*, and *Stourton*) that the common law sets the boundaries to privilege, the courts might legitimately conclude that they had previously misinterpreted those boundaries and that the correct scope of privilege did not preclude reference to *Hansard*. This could however provoke a conflict between the houses and the courts, since it is unlikely that either house would wish to cede its claimed jurisdiction over such questions.

[56] The exclusionary rule was of late Victorian rather than venerable vintage. One can find both pre- and post-revolutionary cases in which the courts made explicit reference to parliamentary debate as an aid to statutory interpretation; see *Ash v Abdy* (1678) 3 Swan 664; *Millar v Taylor* (1769) 4 Burr 2303; *Re Mew and Thorne* (1862) 31 LJ Bcy 87. From a separation of powers perspective, the decision in *Ash v Abdy* is notable, since the judge deciding the case had himself introduced the relevant legislation to Parliament.

[57] This interpretation appealed to Popplewell J in *Rost v Edwards* [1990] 2 QB 460, [1990] 2 All ER 641. However, he considered himself bound to accept the broad meaning. Re-interpretation would have to await a decision by the House of Lords.

The rule's purposes are more readily discernible. Four reasons have been advanced in recent cases. Lord Wilberforce in *Beswick v Beswick*[58] fastened on a question of 'constitutional principle'. The task of interpreting legislation rested solely on the courts; for the judiciary to allow their view of the meaning of a statute to be determined by the speech of a Minister made during the bill's passage would in effect delegate their interpretative role to that Minister. This would turn parliamentary sovereignty into government sovereignty. This reason is perhaps overstated, and loses force if one suggests that *Hansard* should merely be of persuasive not determinative authority.

In the same case, Lord Reid identified 'purely practical reasons' for the rule. Access to *Hansard* would increase the time and expense of litigation, since lawyers would feel compelled to read debates in their entirety in pursuit of statements supporting their clients' cases. This, too, seems a weak justification. The same reasoning might plausibly be applied to law reports; counsel might avidly scrutinise every judgment ever delivered on the point in issue, hoping to uncover some forgotten judicial subtlety buttressing their client's position. Moreover, it seems unlikely that lawyers would not prioritise their use of information cost-effectively. Access to a wider range of materials could lead lawyers to be more discerning in selecting arguments.

Lord Scarman offered a third justification in *Davis v Johnson*.[59] He suggested that *Hansard* was an unreliable guide to a statute's meaning. The content of debate, suffused with the need to score party political points, would be unlikely to convey governmental intent precisely. This objection ostensibly seems convincing, but on reflection is overly simplistic. While many Commons or Lords exchanges may lack the rationality with which one might hope to find laws expressed, *Hansard* also contains calm, deliberate speeches in which ministers precisely describe the objectives they expect a bill to achieve. Lord Scarman's point might be met by selective resort to debate; total abstinence seems unnecessary.

A fourth reason, noted by Lord Diplock in *Fothergill v Monarch Airlines Ltd*,[60] was that 'elementary justice' demanded that all the materials on which the citizen might depend in litigation should be readily accessible. Lord Diplock felt *Hansard* did not meet this criterion. This is also a weak argument. One would doubt that citizens would find Hansard any more esoteric or inaccessible than the *All England Law Reports*. In so far as Lord Diplock's point raises a valid informed consent issue, it amounts to an argument not for excluding *Hansard* from the courts but for ensuring that its contents are more widely known and more easily available.

Sporadic challenges to the traditional position were made in the 1960s and 1970s. Dissenting in *Warner v Metropolitan Police Comr*, Lord Reid reaffirmed the rule but added: 'there is room for an exception where examining the proceedings in Parliament would almost certainly settle the matter immediately one way or the other'.[61] Lord Denning also appeared reluctant to accept the rule. On occasions he simply

58 [1968] AC 58, [1967] 2 All ER 1197, HL.

59 [1979] AC 264, HL.

60 [1981] AC 251, [1980] 2 All ER 696, HL.

61 [1969] 2 AC 256 at 279, HL.

disregarded it altogether or circumvented it by referring not to *Hansard* itself, but to extracts from debates reproduced in legal textbooks or periodicals, or by confessing to taking illicit peeks at *Hansard* when not in court.[62]

Perhaps more significantly (from a practical if not 'legal' perspective), the Commons resolved in 1980 that the courts need no longer petition the house for permission to make 'reference' to *Hansard*. The Commons appeared to root the rule solely in Article 9 of the Bill of Rights, though it was not clear if the house was waiving what it perceived to be a statutory protection or an aspect of its privilege.[63] It subsequently became clear that the Commons' interpretation of 'reference' was restricted: the house would regard use of *Hansard* to clarify the meaning of an ambiguous statute as exceeding the concept of 'reference'.[64] The stage nevertheless seemed set for revision of the rule.

Opening Pandora's box?

Pepper v Hart[65] was triggered by a textual ambiguity in legislation concerning the taxation of a particular benefit. The taxpayers maintained that a Minister had made a clear statement during debate which favoured their interpretation. This argument could not be sustained without recourse to *Hansard*. The taxpayers were therefore asking the court to overturn the exclusionary rule.

Lord Browne-Wilkinson's leading judgment departed substantially if cautiously, from previous orthodoxy. His central conclusion was that:

> 'reference to parliamentary material should be permitted as an aid to the construction of legislation which is ambiguous or obscure or the literal meaning of which leads to an absurdity . . . where such material clearly discloses . . . the legislative intention lying behind the ambiguous or obscure words'.[66]

The rationale underpinning Lord Browne-Wilkinson's judgment lay in what he referred to as an issue of constitutional principle. His principle, however, appeared at odds with the principle advanced by Lord Wilberforce in *Beswick*. He observed that legislators might sometimes be genuinely mistaken as to the legal meaning of the statutory formula they enacted. In such circumstances, the courts would be frustrating rather than fulfilling their constitutional subordination to 'Parliament' by not referring to *Hansard*. This analysis requires one to define parliamentary sovereignty not in the formalistic, Diceyan sense of blind obedience to statutory words, but in a more functionalist vein of giving effect to legislative intent, in which the courts

62 See his judgment in the Court of Appeal in *Davis v Johnson* [1979] AC 264 at 276–277. Such peeking perhaps explains his ostensibly heretical observation in *Magor* some 20 years earlier that the judicial function was to make sense of Ministers' words as well as Parliament's.

63 This again returns us to the question of whether Article 9 is declaratory or transformative of pre-revolutionary privilege. See Leopold P (1981) 'References in court to Hansard' *Public Law* 316–321; Miers D (1983) 'Citing Hansard as an aid to interpretation' *Statute LR* 98–102.

64 See the letter from the Clerk of the House to the Attorney-General quoted from in *Pepper v Hart* [1993] 1 All ER 42 at 55, HL.

65 [1993] AC 593, [1993] 1 All ER 42, HL. 66 [1993] 1 All ER 42 at 64, HL.

assume responsibility for protecting citizens from legislators' readily ascertainable mistakes.

Lord Browne-Wilkinson attempted to meet Lord Scarman's aforementioned concerns about the cut and thrust of debate by limiting the type of speech to which judges may refer to statements by the Minister or member promoting the Bill. He was, however, less accommodating to other previous judicial justifications for the rule. He observed that New Zealand and Canada had both recently allowed their courts to refer to legislative proceedings; neither jurisdiction had found that the cost or duration of litigation had increased unacceptably as a result. Orders for costs against the offending party should be sufficient deterrent to lawyers who invited the courts to examine irrelevant parliamentary material. Nor did Lord Browne-Wilkinson attach any weight to the argument that *Hansard* was insufficiently accessible to litigants, for such a weakness was equally attributable to legislation.

His Lordship was less than precise about the rule's source, suggesting it could derive from all three sources outlined above. He consequently dealt with each in turn. If the rule was judge-made self-regulation, there was no barrier to the House of Lords remaking it in a more contemporarily relevant form. Should the rule have a statutory base, Lord Browne-Wilkinson concluded that Article 9 should be reinterpreted in the narrow sense canvassed in *Rost v Edwards*:

> 'In my judgment, the plain meaning of art 9, viewed against the historical background in which it was enacted, was to ensure that members of Parliament were not subjected to any penalty, civil or criminal for what they said [in either House]'.[67]

Finally his Lordship addressed the question of parliamentary privilege. Referring to the 1980 Commons resolution, he suggested that the House viewed its privileges as co-extensive with the scope of Article 9. Consequently, given his redefinition of Article 9, recourse to *Hansard* could not impinge upon privilege. One might doubt that the house would accept this reasoning, for it 'confirms' the subordinacy of privilege to the common law. Whether this last point has now joined the constitution's array of 'ultimate political facts' is at present an unanswerable question, determinable only when the Commons and the courts again adopt contradictory positions over a question of the magnitude of those posed by Wilkes, Stockdale and Bradlaugh.

Lord Browne-Wilkinson appeared to take some care to frame his judgment in very cautious terms.[68] However the tests that he laid out were quite rapidly relaxed both by the House of Lords itself and by lower courts.[69] Lord Browne-Wilkinson seemed to take the view that this relaxation had gone too far. In *Melluish (Inspector of Taxes) v BMI (No 3) Ltd*,[70] he confirmed that *Pepper v Hart* should not be read as a justification for making reference to *Hansard* a routine element of the process of statutory interpretation.

67 [1993] 1 All ER 42 at 87, HL. 68 Zander op cit pp 153–157.

69 See generally Marshall G (1998) 'Hansard and the interpretation of statutes', in Oliver and Drewry op cit: Mullan K (1999) 'The impact of *Pepper v Hart*', in Carmichael and Dickson op cit.

70 [1996] AC 454, [1995] 4 All ER 453, HL.

This evident unease with the way in which the case was being used was forcefully reiterated by the House of Lords in *R v Secretary of State for the Environment, Transport and the Regions, ex e Spath Holme Ltd*[71] The case centred on the extent of the government's power under the Landlord and Tenant Act 1985 to make regulations controlling rent levels in certain types of private sector housing. The 'Hansard' issue which arose was whether a court could properly take account of ministerial speeches made in either house during the enactment of a bill as an aid not – as in *Pepper v Hart* – to ascertain the meaning of particular statutory text, but to identify the intended scope of a statutory power.

The Court was unanimous in stressing that the principle in *Pepper v Hart* should be used sparingly and cautiously. The point was perhaps put most clearly by Lord Bingham:

'I think it important that the conditions laid down by the House in *Pepper v Hart* should be strictly insisted upon. Otherwise, the cost and inconvenience feared by Lord Mackay, whose objections to relaxation of the exclusionary rule were based on considerations of practice not principle, will be realised. The worst of all worlds would be achieved if parties routinely combed through Hansard, and the courts dredged through conflicting statements of parliamentary intention (see [1993] 1 All ER 42 at 61, [1993] AC 593 at 631), only to conclude that the statutory provision called for no further elucidation or that no clear and unequivocal statement by a responsible minister could be derived from Hansard'[72]

Lords Bingham, Hutton and Hope further considered that there could be very few circumstances where resort to Hansard would be permissible to seek to identify the scope of a statutory power. Lords Hope and Cooke, in contrast, saw no reason to treat the issues of the scope of a power and the meaning of a particular statutory phrase any differently. In both circumstances, Hansard could be an appropriate interpretive aid.

The court's circumspection in *Spath Holme* as to the use of Hansard was enthusiastically endorsed in a forceful analysis of the *Pepper v Hart* principle by Aileen Kavanagh.[73] Kavanagh suggests that the case may be read as elevating ministerial statements to the status of a source of law. This is seen to be problematic in two respects. Firstly it undermines the role of Parliament as a collective assembly in which MPs engage in a careful and informed process of debate and evaluation which eventually leads to the production of a legislative text which accurately expresses the wishes of members who voted for it. Secondly, it undermines the role of the courts as the body with responsibility for determining the meaning of the laws that Parliament has enacted.

This argument has much to commend it in terms of abstract constitutional theory. In a more practical sense, it ought perhaps to be qualified somewhat. Two points might be made.

Firstly, the notion that MPs uniformly and consistently make informed choices as to the measures for which they vote is perhaps poorly based in empirical terms.

[71] [2001] 1 All ER 195. [72] Ibid, at 212.

[73] Kavanagh A (2005) '*Pepper v Hart* and matters of constitutional principle' 121 *LQR* 98–122.

Cowley's previously discussed study of the voting behaviour of backbench Labour MPs since 1997 casts an illuminating and rather unsettling light on the realities of this part of the law-making process.[74] Some of Cowley's findings are almost comic. He cites for example occasions when MPs mistakenly walk through the wrong door when casting their votes. A more frequently occurring scenario is illustrated by a discussion of the extraordinarily esoteric provisions of an obscure provision in the Finance Bill 2005. The provision was so complicated, and an understanding of its impact so thoroughly contingent on an understanding of the existing complicated law, that it is simply absurd to assume that more than a handful of MPs appreciated the effect the measure would have when enacted. The matter is put in rather more prosaic and systemic terms by one of Cowley's MP respondents: 'I go through the lobby a great number of times not knowing a fuck about what I am voting for'.[75] The reality in such cases is that MPs are simply doing whatever the party whips ask them to do.[76]

The second point is that one might as readily argue that *Pepper v Hart* enhances rather than reduces the power of the courts vis a vis than of the 'executive'. If one means by 'the executive' the government which is currently in power, invocation of Hansard as an interpretive aid may well **reduce** executive power. It is entirely possible that the legislative text in issue was promoted by a previous government with quite different political views from the administration currently in power, and with a quite different understanding from the present government as to the meaning of the relevant 'ambiguous or obscure' statutory provision.[77] More broadly, the conditions which *Pepper v Hart* attaches to use of Hansard are all discretion-laden and thus open to judicial manipulation. Is a statutory term ambiguous if literally construed? Would such construction led to an absurd result? Did a minister make a clear statement as to the government's intended meaning of the provision? Such questions will often be answerable quite defensibly as either 'yes' or 'no'. Which means of course that the courts have a choice as to whether or not Hansard is to be used at all, and if it is to be used as to what significance is attached to the information it contains.

Pepper v Hart is undoubtedly a decision with significant constitutional implications. This relates in part to its recognition of the political reality of government dominance of the legislative process and thus of shifts in the nature of the separation of powers within the contemporary constitution. But in respect of the rather narrower issue of parliamentary privilege, the judgment's greater importance lies in the court's implicit claim that it, rather than the two houses, is the only body possessing the constitutional competence to determine the meaning of privilege. This means that the courts are in effect denying that the Commons has any authority to claim immunity from orthodox understandings of parliamentary sovereignty and the rule of law. There may well be many aspects of privilege with which the courts feel unable to

74 (2005) op cit. 75 Ibid, p34. 76 Ibid, pp 28–34.

77 A judgment which attached determinative significance to a ministerial statement in such circumstances would also enhance – at least in theoretical terms – the role of the House of Commons and House of Lords qua legislative assemblies, since in order to change the law in issue the present government would have to promote new legislation.

interfere. But that decision would seemingly now be based on the functionalist criterion of the non-justiciable nature of the privilege in question, rather than the formalist consideration of its source.

But Lord Browne-Wilkinson's judgment has more profound, as yet undeveloped implications. For, paradoxically, by asserting the supremacy of Parliament over its component parts in all aspects of their respective proceedings, *Pepper v Hart* adds considerable force to arguments which attack the doctrine of parliamentary sovereignty itself. We return to this argument in the final chapter. But as the following two sections suggest, it might readily be assumed that many MPs would be reluctant to tolerate further judicial intrusion into the houses' regulation of privilege.

IV. 'CONTEMPT' OF THE HOUSE

The privileges of each house are now supposedly a closed category. Just as the Crown may not create prerogative powers which it did not possess in 1688, neither can the Commons or the Lords create 'new' privileges. But as chapter four suggested in discussing the *Northumbria* case, the prerogative's formally 'residual' nature has little meaning if the courts permit the government to discover 'lost' powers. That point would have equal force in respect of privilege even if it were accepted (which it manifestly, at least by the Commons is not) that the courts possessed sole jurisdiction to define its limits. If the Commons is regarded as the legitimate guardian of those boundaries, claims as to the 'residual' character of privilege would be quite misleading.

Furthermore, the Commons has traditionally claimed the power to punish 'contempts' – a power which the house seems to regard as so expansive that it is in effect claiming an unlimited jurisdiction. *Erskine May* defines contempt as:

> 'any act or omission which obsructs or impedes either House in the performance of its functions, or which obstructs or impedes any Member or officer of such House in the discharge of his duty, or which has a tendency, directly or indirectly, to produce such results'.[78]

Were this a statutory concept, one might assume that Parliament had granted the two houses an arbitrary and illegitimate power. That assumption is reinforced when one realises that the houses also claim that they may punish contempts with fines or imprisonment. Neither sanction has been imposed in the modern era, but the Commons made frequent use of its imprisonment power in the eighteenth and nineteenth centuries.[79]

Contempts may be committed either by MPs themselves or by non-members.

[78] Op cit p 143.

[79] It was invoked in both the Wilkes and Bradlaugh sagas. For further examples see *Erskine May* ch 9.

Allegations of contempt may be raised by an individual MP with the Speaker, who will then decide if the matter should be referred for investigation to the Committee of Privileges. The Speaker effectively enjoys an unconfined discretion on whether to refer, while the Committee itself enjoys similar discretion in determining how it investigates any matter brought to its attention.

Many instances in which a contempt complaint has been upheld have related to matters which could conceivably have amounted to criminal offences. One might point for example to citizens who engaged in a riot outside the house in the hope of intimidating MPs, or assaults upon individual members.[80] Others, while not intrinsically criminal, have related to behaviour which directly hinders the houses' performance of their work. Obvious examples are failure to attend a committee hearing; refusing to answer questions at such a hearing; offering obstructive or misleading responses to questions posed; or disrupting the proceedings of the house.[81]

The Commons has also had a long tradition of upholding contempt complaints against journalists or political commentators who have criticised either the house itself or its individual members. In 1702, the Commons resolved that publishing any material reflecting upon its proceedings or members was 'a high violation of its right and privileges'.[82] The rationale for this power is evidently that criticism (apparently even if well founded) detracts from the house's dignity and undermines the public respect which the house seemingly assumes it deserves. This category of contempt is not however a mere historical anachronism. In the twentieth century it has been applied to MPs who claimed to have seen other MPs drunk in the house, and to journalists who suggested that MPs were getting extra petrol rations in the 1950s.[83]

Perhaps of rather more interest are the numerous efforts made by individual MPs to have the most trivial issues investigated. The petrol rationing episode in the 1950s triggered press comment that the house was invoking privilege to stifle freedom of speech. This in turn led some MPs to have the newspapers concerned charged with contempt. Similarly several Labour MPs sought to initiate contempt proceedings against *The Spectator* magazine when it suggested that they were sympathetic to the North Vietnamese communist regime.[84] The Strauss case is perhaps the most graphic example of the house's apparent capacity to endow its members with an inflated sense of self-importance. Strauss had suggested the mere threat of defamation proceedings against him could constitute a contempt. The suggestion that a citizen should be punished simply for seeking to establish if her common law rights have been infringed is a quite bizarre contention, utterly irreconcilable with any mainstream understanding of the rule of law.

80 *Erskine May* pp 119–120. For a more subtle example of more recent vintage see Leopold P (1984) 'Parliamentary privilege and an MP's threats' *Public Law* 547–550.

81 See Marshall (1979) op cit pp 217–220.

82 Quoted in *Erskine May* p 121 n 9.

83 Marshall (1979) op cit pp 229–231.

84 For further examples see Seymour-Ure C (1964) 'The misuse of the question of privilege in the 1964–5 session of Parliament' *Parliamentary Affairs* 380–388.

THE 1967 REPORT OF THE PRIVILEGES COMMITTEE

Commenting on such cases, Marshall suggested that they had done much 'to bring the House's privilege jurisdiction into disrepute'.[85] The house itself appeared to recognise this in the late 1960s. A Privileges Committee report in 1967 concluded that MPs were 'too sensitive to criticism'.[86] The house appears to have accepted this advice – the contempt jurisdiction has been invoked with decreasing frequency since 1967.[87]

Yet one might wonder if there is any need for the Commons or the Lords to possess such sweeping powers. Contempts which amount to criminal offences (such as assaulting MPs) can be addressed in the courts. Nor is there any strong justification for either house to have the power to punish criticism of its members or of the institution itself (even if the punishment consists only of the ritual of being called to the house to be scolded and offer an apology). It is unfortunate that newspaper editors called in recent times to retract their newspapers' criticisms of the Commons have not simply denied the house's jurisdiction and challenged the legality of its contempt proceedings before the courts.[88] For as we enter the twenty-first century, there would seem to be several good reasons for regarding the Commons as an intrinsically inadequate institution. Its minimal capacity to control the Cabinet is an illustration of this point, as is the way in which its electoral system distorts the wishes of voters. Both those weaknesses are collective in nature, pointing to defects in the house's institutional basis. Of more significance to the question of the legitimacy of maintaining the privileges of the Commons is the house's apparent failure to address the ethical shortcomings of some of its members.

V. THE REGULATION OF MPS' ETHICAL STANDARDS

The summer of 1995 presented the British public with the extraordinary spectacle of a backbench Conservative MP, Sir Jerry Wiggin, tabling amendments during the committee stage of a Bill's passage in the name of another Conservative, Sebastian Coe, without Coe's permission. Wiggin had a financial interest in the issue; he was a consultant for an organisation which would benefit from the amendment. He had used Coe's name for fear that the amendment's prospects of success would be compromised if the house knew its mover had been paid by a commercial organisation to

85 (1979) op cit pp 229.

86 Sills P (1968) 'Report of the Select Committee on Parliamentary Privilege' 31 *MLR* 435–439; Seymour-Ure C (1970) 'Proposed reforms of parliamentary privilege: an assessment in the light of recent cases' *Parliamentary Affairs* 221–231.

87 For a list of examples see Griffith and Ryle op cit pp 98–102.

88 That they have not done so is presumably due primarily to the fact that the house also claims sole jurisdiction to determine which newspapers are granted facilities within the house to report its proceedings. MPs may thus 'punish' a newspaper's supposed contempt by reducing the number of 'lobby passes' offered to the paper's reporters, or temporarily banning some or all of its reporters from the precincts of the house.

promote it. Press coverage of the episode was hugely critical of Wiggin, and he found few supporters even on the Conservative benches. One might have thought that his action was prima facie a gross contempt. However the Speaker declined to refer the matter to the Committee of Privileges; in her opinion Wiggin's misbehaviour merited no greater punishment than that he apologise to the house.[89]

Until 1975, MPs were under no obligation to declare either the sources or amounts of any income they received over and above their MP's salary. Parliament had not enacted legislation on the subject: nor had the house concluded that it should itself require such disclosure. This lacuna had significant implications for the concepts of informed consent, both within the Commons itself and in terms of the relationship between an MP and her electors. One could not be sure, for example, that individual MPs were not supporting or opposing particular pieces of legislation, making speeches in the house, or putting questions to Ministers because they had been paid to do so by commercial interests rather than because they honestly believed in the intrinsic rectitude of the course they were following. It is quite plausible to conclude that many electors might decline to support a particular candidate if they knew that she was receiving financial benefits from sources of which they disapproved.

THE REGISTER OF MEMBERS' INTERESTS

A considerable scandal broke in the early 1970s, when a prominent Labour politician, T Dan Smith,[90] was convicted of various offences of corruption. The scandal was exacerbated by the revelation that Edward Short, then Labour Leader of the House, had accepted a 'gift' of £250 from Mr Smith in 1963 'provided it can be kept a confidential matter between the two of us'.[91]

The episode generated extensive press coverage dwelling on the many opportunities for corrupt and sharp practice which became available to MPs as a result of their membership of the house. There was never any suggestion that such behaviour was endemic or even widespread within the Commons. However given the effective dominance of the legislative process which the Commons by then possessed, even one MP who was prepared to engage in improper financial relationships would be one too many. Without an effective mechanism to regulate such matters, the house could not realistically claim to be above suspicion.

Among the more far-reaching proposals aired in the aftermath of the Smith affair was the suggestion that legislation should be introduced requiring MPs to make their income tax returns available for public inspection. The house apparently regarded this as an intolerable intrusion into MPs' private affairs, and opted for a far more modest system of self-regulation. In May 1974 the Commons resolved that:

89 The Speaker's decision astonished seasoned observers, within and outside the house; see *The Guardian* 23 May 1995.

90 Smith was not an MP, but the leader of Newcastle city council.

91 See *The Economist* 4 May 1974.

'in any debate or proceeding of the house. . .or communications which a Member may have with other Members or Ministers or servants of the Crown, he shall disclose any relevant pecuniary interest or benefit of whatever nature, whether direct or indirect, that he may have or may be expecting to have'.[92]

The house also resolved to create a Register of Members' Interest, on which MPs would record certain sources of income. An ad hoc select committee was established to produce detailed proposals. It is perhaps worth recalling that the Labour government then had only a bare Commons majority; there was thus no prospect of the government simply pushing through its own preferences. That the house endorsed such anodyne reforms is perhaps a powerful indication of its members' (irrespective of party) continuing arrogance and self-righteousness.

The house adopted the select committee's recommendations in 1975. The Register would serve:

'to provide information of any pecuniary interest or other material benefit which a Member of Parliament may receive which might be thought to affect his [sic] conduct as a member of Parliament or influence his [sic] actions, speeches or votes in Parliament'.[93]

The Register covers a wide range of financial interests, including such matters as directorships of companies, income from practice in the professions, paid employment (which includes 'public relations' and 'consultancy' activities), and overseas visits not financed from public funds.[94] The names of any employers or clients should also be disclosed whenever the income the member derives from the relationship pertains 'in any manner' to her/his membership of the house. However, there was no requirement that members disclose how much income they received from each source. The information that the Register disclosed was thus of limited value. The house also created a 'Select Committee on Members' Interests' to consider amendment to the Register and hear complaints about alleged breaches of its terms. But it was not clear what sanctions, if any, would be imposed on MPs whose entries in the Register were found to be inaccurate.

Edward Short, introducing the report to the house, observed that it amounted to no more than 'broad guidelines within which Members should proceed with good sense and responsibility'.[95] Nevertheless, its measures still proved too much for some MPs. Thus the Conservative MP John Stokes, seemingly oblivious to press coverage and public opinion, argued that: 'there is no demand for all this cumbersome machinery to register Members' interests'.[96]

Quite how effective the Register proved is an open question. One MP, Enoch Powell, simply refused to disclose any interests. No action was taken against him. Nor does it appear that the Register became more effective with age. Appreciable controversy arose in 1994, when press stories suggested that Conservative MP Neil Hamilton had failed to disclose that he had enjoyed an expensive six-day stay at the Ritz hotel in

[92] *Erskine May* p 384. [93] *Erskine May* p 386. [94] For a full list see *Erskine May* pp 386–387.
[95] *HCD*, 12 June 1975 c 737. [96] 12 June 1975 c 737 at c 749.

Paris paid for by a foreign businessman, Mohammed Al-Fayed, who was then under investigation by the Department of Trade and Industry. The Privilege Committee's 'investigation' of the Hamilton episode thoroughly undermined any contention that the house eschewed party political considerations in such matters. Conservative MPs acquiesced in the government's wish to have a whip on the committee. His presence could serve no purpose but to ensure that other Conservative members did nothing to jeopardise party interests. Opposition MPs eventually walked out of the Committee, which then reached the extraordinary conclusion that while Hamilton had failed to make a relevant disclosure, this amounted to no more than 'imprudence' and did not merit any punishment.[97] This particular case was however merely symptomatic of an apparently wider malaise.

'CASH FOR QUESTIONS' AND THE REPORT OF THE NOLAN COMMISSION

In 1974, the Labour MP Joe Ashton was found to have committed a serious contempt by alleging that members were prepared to raise issues in the house at the behest of commercial organisations in return for payment.[98] Whether Ashton's claim was then ill-founded is a matter for speculation. It is however clear that some 20 years later the house contained at least two Conservative MPs who, for a sizeable fee, were prepared to do just what Ashton alleged.

Acting on rumours about some MPs' rather lax ethical standards, two *Sunday Times* journalists posed as representatives of a foreign company wishing to raise a question in the house and willing to pay £1,000 to the MP who placed it. The journalists approached ten Labour MPs and ten Conservative MPs. The Labour members refused to take money for such purposes, as did seven Conservatives. The eighth Conservative, Bill Walker, agreed to table a question for a fee given to charity. Two Conservatives, Graham Riddick and David Tredinnick (both parliamentary private secretaries), agreed to table a question and accept the fee.

In the ensuing furore, the Speaker granted an emergency debate to discuss the issue, and referred the case to the Privileges Committee. After a lengthy investigation, the Privileges Committee, dominated by a Conservative majority, imposed a punishment of 10 and 20 days' suspension on the offending MPs. The 'punishment' was laughably lenient. And it is perhaps an indication of the extraordinary values adhered to by many MPs that suggestions were aired that *The Sunday Times* should be charged with contempt of the house for exposing their colleagues' moral frailties.

The 'cash for questions' scandal generated such hostile press coverage that the government established a committee of inquiry, chaired by Nolan LJ, with a wide-ranging remit to inquire into 'Standards in Public Life'.[99] Rumours rapidly began to circulate that the Committee would recommend extensive reforms, whereupon

97 See *The Guardian* 8 June 1995.

98 Marshall (1979) op cit p 228.

99 See Rush M (1998) 'The law relating to members' conduct', in Oliver and Drewry op cit.

Conservative MPs equally rapidly began to cast aspersions on its impartiality and competence. Yet the recommendations contained in the Committee's first report were feeble. Its most significant proposal was that MPs should in future disclose not just the source but also the amount of income they received for the performance of services arising from their membership of the house. Nolan also urged the creation of a body 'independent' of the Commons to investigate MPs' behaviour. The model he favoured was that of a 'Parliamentary Commissioner for Standards', who would report to the Privileges Committee. The obvious weakness of the recommendation was that the Nolan Committee had apparently accepted that MPs' ethical standards should remain a matter for the house. Neither proposal was to have a statutory basis; rather they were to be matters for the Commons itself to introduce.

Although the Conservative government initially welcomed the report, many of its backbenchers (those, one assumes, who received substantial 'consultancy' payments) signalled that they would not support its implementation. Rather than carry the proposals into force by relying on opposition votes, the government decided to refer the Nolan Report to a special select committee for further consideration.

The Committee had a Conservative majority. It divided on party lines on the main question before it. The Conservative members rejected – while all the Opposition members accepted – the Nolan proposal that the house's rules should require MPs to divulge the amount as well as the source of their 'consultancy' payments. The Committee's recommendation was subsequently endorsed by the Cabinet. However when the Committee's report was put before the house, some 23 Conservative MPs voted with the Opposition in support of requiring disclosure of the amount of income MPs received for these activities.[100] The Commons did accept that the post of Parliamentary Commissioner for Standards (PCS) should be created. It also subsumed the former role of the Privileges Committee and the Committee on Members Interests into a new Committee on Standards and Privileges (CSP).

Whether this new regime would prove more effective than its predecessor was open to question. The disclosure requirement is not a 'law' enforceable in the independent arena of the courts; it is merely an internal rule of the house. Its adequacy is entirely dependent on MPs attaching greater importance to financial candour than to party loyalties. The new rule would presumably be most effective if the house were to expel or suspend those members who fail to make accurate disclosures. But one might doubt that MPs in a governing party with a small Commons majority would take such drastic steps should some of their number be found wanting on a question of financial integrity. The outcome of the 'cash for questions' scandal was thus something of a damp squib.

The Blair government took no steps to place the Nolan Commission's recommendations on a statutory basis, nor to strengthen the controls on MPs' disclosure of financial rewards. The Nolan Committee has however metamorphasised into a long-term feature on the political landscape, subsequently chaired by Lord Neill and

100 *The Guardian* 2 November 1995; 8 November 1995.

charged with a general remit to investigate ethical standards in a wide range of governmental bodies. But the need for financial candour has evidently yet to impress itself fully on MPs; the press continues to field a steady stream of stories reporting members' failures to declare relevant sources of income.[101]

Many of these stories related to extremely trivial issues, and indicated that the rather serious questions of MPs' financial ethics had been subsumed beneath the cloak of party political bickering. But in a more serious vein, some Labour ministers proved little less susceptible to the temptation to engage in financial practices of dubious ethicality than their Conservative predecessors. Elizabeth Filkin succeeded Sir Gordon Downey as the PCS. She rapidly made it clear that she would take a vigorous and rigorous approach to her duties. This included conducting investigations into the affairs of Keith Vaz, a Minister of State at the Foreign Office, and John Reid, then Secretary of State for Northern Ireland. Ms Filkin considered that both men had deliberately obstructed her inquiries. In her view, Reid had gone so far as to threaten a witness who Ms Filkin wished to interview. She received little support from the Commons however, or from the government. The CSP rejected her highly critical report on John Reid, and she left her post in 2002 amid press stories of a concerted effort by the government and many backbenchers to sabotage her work.[102]

In 1975, Enoch Powell MP had opposed the creation of the Register of Interests on the grounds that: 'we degrade ourselves by implying that our honour and traditions are not adequate to maintain proper standards in this house'.[103] Similar sentiments were voiced in 1995 by Conservative MPs who opposed the Nolan recommendations.[104] Yet MPs' 'honour and tradition' are clearly entirely inadequate guarantors of 'proper standards'. The circumstances surrounding Ms Filkin's departure from her post would suggest that – most unfortunately – the majority of MPs continue to refuse to accept this.

THE DEFAMATION ACT 1996 S 13 AND THE HAMILTON LIBEL ACTIONS

That we might more sensibly rely on the press than the Commons to bring corrupt MPs to account was powerfully illustrated by events following Neil Hamilton's 'acquittal' by his party colleagues on the Privileges Committee. Hamilton promptly began a libel action against *The Guardian*. That action was then derailed by the Privy Council decision in *Prebble v Television New Zealand Ltd.*[105] *Prebble* held that since Article 9 of the Bill of Rights prevents parliamentary proceedings being used as part of the defence in a libel action, in litigation where such proceedings formed the main

[101] See Rush (1998) op cit pp 115–116.

[102] See generally Doig A (2002) 'Sleaze fatigue in 'The House of ill-repute' *Parliamentary Affairs* 389. Ms Filkin detailed her complaints in a letter to the Speaker and a series of press interviews; see *The Guardian* 26 November 2001: *The Times* 5 December 2001.

[103] *HCD* 12 June 1975 c 743.

[104] See *The Times* 19 May 1995: *The Guardian* 19 May 1995.

[105] [1995] 1 AC 321, [1994] 3 All ER 407, PC.

plank of the defence case, it would be unjust to allow the case to proceed as no effective defence could be offered. In the interests of justice, the action would therefore have to be stayed. While not strictly binding in English law, *Prebble* was invoked by May J to stay Hamilton's action against *The Guardian*, since the paper had hoped to use such forbidden evidence in its defence.[106]

Hamilton subsequently put his action back on course by persuading his party colleagues in the Commons and Lords to vote for an amendment to the Defamation Bill then before the two Houses. The Bill began its life as a technical piece of law reform. Its contents endorsed recommendations made by a committee, chaired by Neill LJ, charged with formulating proposals to streamline the resolution of libel suits.[107] The Bill would have excited discussion among libel lawyers, but was hardly a measure of constitutional significance. May J's decision to stay proceedings in Hamilton's action against *The Guardian* changed its status entirely.

Section 13 of the Defamation Act first surfaced as a proposed amendment at the Lords Committee stage.[108] The nub of the proposal was that an individual MP should be given the power to permit house proceedings to be used as evidence in any libel litigation in which she was involved; ie to 'waive' Article 9. Several peers opposed the amendment, primarily on the grounds that, irrespective of the merits of the proposal, the process through which it had been introduced was precipitate: so significant an amendment to the Bill of Rights of 1688 should be the subject of investigation by a joint committee of both houses. A profound substantive difficulty with the proposal was also identified. The immunity privilege in Article 9 had traditionally been regarded as belonging to each house as a collectivity: the amendment would enable an individual MP to override either house's collective view. Quite what would happen if an individual sought to invoke the power, and the house concerned wished to prevent the evidence being put before the court, was far from clear.

The government had maintained that the amendment, while introduced into a government Bill, would not be whipped. Members could vote on it as they wished. Yet over 200 peers voted on the amendment at third reading – an extraordinarily high number. The vote was 157 in favour and 57 against. The suspicion that a de facto, if not de jure, whip was operating was reinforced by events in the Commons. The amendment was bundled through at second reading. The prevailing mood on the Conservative benches at third reading was best illustrated by Sir Peter Tapsell, who described the amendment as saving MPs from 'persecution . . . from what many people regard as an over-mighty press that is owned, for the most part, by foreigners'.[109] The initial amendment was approved, and the Bill received the Royal Assent in the autumn.

106 The judgment has not been reported. See the news reports in *The Guardian* and *The Times* 22 July 1995.

107 (1991) Supreme Court Procedure Committee Report on Practice and Procedure in Defamation (London: HMSO).

108 See Sharland A and Loveland I (1997) 'The Defamation Act 1996 and political libels' *Public Law* 113–124.

109 *HCD*, 24 June 1996 c 58.

Section 13 is a shocking example of the way in which the Major government was willing to invoke its Commons and Lords majorities for the most partisan of ends, even when so doing involved the reversal of a Privy Council judgment, and the rejection of a supposedly fundamental moral principle outlined in the Bill of Rights. It is perhaps a pleasant irony that Hamilton, the instigator of this unpleasant legislative episode, subsequently had cause to regret it.

Hamilton rapidly invoked s 13 to relaunch his suit against *The Guardian*. He then abandoned the case on the eve of the trial. In Mr Hamilton's account, he took this decision because he could no longer afford to pay his legal fees. *The Guardian's* explanation for this unexpected turn of events was that Mr Hamilton now feared that the paper would convince the jury that its claims were true.

Following the Labour Party's victory at the 1997 general election, the claims against Hamilton had been investigated by Sir Gordon Downey, the Parliamentary Commissioner for Standards (PCS). He concluded that there was compelling evidence that Hamilton had indeed taken cash payments from Al-Fayed.[110] The Committee on Standards and Privileges (which by then – November 1997 – contained an overwhelming Labour majority) subsequently endorsed Sir Gordon's findings and concluded that: 'Mr Hamilton's conduct fell seriously and persistently below the standards which the House is entitled to expect of its members'.[111]

The PCS and CSP were addressing a question which in most democratic countries is left to the criminal law: had a member of the legislature accepted bribes to perform his public duties?

There are three reasons for treating the question in this way. Firstly, the behaviour in issue constitutes a grave breach of public trust, and if proven might be thought to merit substantial punishment. Secondly, given the severity of the punishment, great care must be taken to ensure that punishment is imposed only if it can be established beyond any reasonable doubt that the person accused had actually committed the alleged misconduct. The procedural safeguards granted to the accused in a criminal trial are obviously an effective way to attempt to allay this concern. Thirdly – relatedly – the voting public must be given strong grounds for believing that such serious charges will only be proven on the basis of a dispassionate analysis of relevant evidence untainted by party political bias. The procedures used by the PCS and CSP in the Hamilton investigation fell far short of what a defendant might expect to receive in a criminal trial. In addition to an absence of cross-examination of witnesses and the exclusion of counsel, the inquiry suffered the obvious defect of being conducted largely in private. It also stretches credibility to accept that the deliberations and conclusion of the CSP in disciplinary proceedings would invariably be free of any taint of party political influence.[112] Mr Hamilton subsequently made

110 Committee on Standards and Privileges, First Report, HC 30 (1997–98) Vol 1 pp 110–120.

111 Committee on Standards and Privileges, Eighth Report, HC 261 (1997–98) para 7. The Committee's conclusion was couched in rather ambiguous language.

112 See Leopold P (1998) 'The application of the civil and criminal law to members of Parliament and parliamentary proceedings', in Oliver and Drewry op cit.

much of the point that he had not been given 'a fair trial' by the Labour-dominated Committee.

Hamilton v Al-Fayed

Mr Hamilton then sued Mr Al-Fayed over his repetition on television of allegations that he had indeed handed over substantial sums of money to Hamilton in return for various parliamentary services. Hamilton presumably hoped that the jury in a libel action would conclude that he had not accepted cash from Al-Fayed. The direct result of that would be a vindication of his own reputation. Its indirect result would be to cast doubt on both the substantive and procedural adequacy of the PCS and CSP investigations. In addition to pleading that the claims were true, Al Fayed sought to rely on the PCS and CSP reports to bring the case within the *Prebble* principle and have the action stayed.

That the Commons' disciplinary procedures fall woefully short of the standards of rigour and impartiality demanded of executive and judicial decision-makers by the common law is a matter often critically remarked upon by academic commentators.[113] The judge who heard *Hamilton v Al-Fayed* also expressed reservations: '[B]ecause of the inherent flaws in the inquisitorial system adopted and the inadequacy of the appeal procedure, I do not believe that the plaintiff had a full opportunity of contesting the decision'.[114] The parliamentary inquiry into the episode should thus be seen as: 'a frail basis upon which to oust the jurisdiction of the courts'.[115] The action should therefore proceed.

On further appeal, the Court of Appeal followed Lord Browne-Wilkinson's narrow construction of Article 9 in *Pepper v Hart*,[116] and held that there were no grounds for concluding that allowing Mr Hamilton's action to proceed would breach Article 9:

> 'The most that can be said is that the court might arrive at a different result on some aspects of the factual merits of the "cash for questions" issue from that arrived at by the PCS and (at least) not departed from or objected to by the CSP or the House of Commons'.[117]

This decision was subsequently upheld in the House of Lords.[118] Hamilton then went on, in a barrage of publicity, to lose the action against Mr Al-Fayed, thereby bankrupting himself and destroying what little remained of his political reputation. *The Guardian's* initial claims were thus vindicated. The point that might be stressed here is that in so far as the electorate was eventually provided with the 'truth' about the sleaze scandal, it had gained that insight more as a result of the efforts of the press and the courts than of the House of Commons.

113 See for example Robertson G and Nicol A (3rd edn, 1992 *Media Law* pp 398–400 (Harmondsworth: Penguin); Leopold (1998) op cit; Bradley A and Ewing K (11th edn, 1993) *Constitutional and administrative law* pp 236–237 (London: Longman).

114 The quote is taken from the Court of Appeal's judgment; [1999] 3 All ER 317 at 327, CA.

115 [1999] 3 All ER 317, CA.

116 See the quotation at p 287 above.

117 [1999] 3 All ER 317 at 335, CA.

118 [2001] 1 AC 395.

CONCLUSION

Media coverage of the cash for questions scandal and the Nolan report was perhaps most notable for revealing the casual equation frequently made, both by seasoned media commentators and by MPs themselves – and even by the Court of Appeal in *Hamilton v Al-Fayed* – of the House of Commons with Parliament, and relatedly of the privileges of the house with legislation. This may perhaps be seen as a realistic interpretation of the contemporary balance of power between Parliament's three constituent parts. As noted in chapter six, the Commons is now much the more powerful of the two houses, and we shall see in chapter nine that the Monarch no longer plays a meaningful role in the legislative process.

The equation is however theoretically inept, and in practical terms both dangerous and underdeveloped, because it fails to take the further realistic step of observing that the Commons is generally just a vehicle for the promotion of factional, party interest. The Commons alone (except on those very rare occasions when no party commands a majority) does not in any sense perform the role that the revolution bestowed upon Parliament. As suggested in chapter five, the notion that the Commons plays a significantly independent role either as an actor within the legislative process or as a monitor of executive behaviour is quite fallacious in the contemporary political context.

Shortly after the 1997 general election, the two houses established a Joint Committee, chaired by a Law Lord, Lord Nicholls, to review the whole area of privilege. The Committee produced an extensive report, which contained significant proposals for change.[119] Most importantly, the Committee advocated that many issues relating to privilege – and in particular the various elements of Article 9 (ie 'proceedings in Parliament' 'questioned'; 'place out of Parliament') – now be given a much more tightly defined statutory base. Responsibility for interpreting those provisions would presumably therefore rest with the courts, not with either house. The Report also recommended amendment of s 13 of the Defamation Act 1996, so the waiver of privilege in *Prebble*-type situations would become a matter for the house, not an individual. In an attempt to allay public concern about corruption, the Committee also proposed a new statutory offence of bribery of MPs be created. This would, again, be a matter for the courts to control. The Report also addressed some of the evident weaknesses in the houses' internal disciplinary procedures by proposing that the CSP's hearings should in future adopt a more 'judicial' approach in its investigations.

These are all worthy recommendations. But they are of little value if they are not put on a statutory basis. Whether the Blair government will find time in its legislative programme to promote the necessary Bills is at present unclear.

It is perhaps an exaggeration to suggest that our examination of the Commons'

[119] See generally Leopold P (1999) 'Report of the Joint Committee on parliamentary privilege' *Public Law* 604–615; Lock G (1999) 'Report of the Joint Committee on parliamentary privilege' *Study of Parliament Group Newsletter*, Summer, 13–19.

legislative and supervisory roles, of the electoral system through which its members are chosen, and of the privileges within which MPs wrap themselves, leads to the conclusion that the lower house as presently constituted and regulated can defensibly be described as unrepresentative, incompetent, and corrupt. Such hyperbole perhaps contains more than a grain of truth, but it would as yet be premature to form firm conclusions as to the adequacy of our present parliamentary institutions. The next three chapters take us rather further towards the position from which a firm conclusion might more plausibly be drawn. Chapter nine addresses a further set of non-legal principles of the constitution which regulate governmental and parliamentary behaviour, while chapters ten and eleven assess the uses to which the executive's dominance of the legislature has been put in respect of perhaps the most important of constitutional values in a nominally democratic society – namely the extent to which 'the people' can effectively express the divergent political and moral beliefs which they hold.

9

CONSTITUTIONAL CONVENTIONS

Thus far we have focused primarily on legal regulation of constitutional behaviour. Such controls may be construed as performing a political or moral function – to ensure that the constitution respects the demands of democracy and the rule of law. Chapter six addressed more clearly the constitutional inter-relationship between legal principle and political practice by discussing the changing functions of the House of Lords, especially instances of tension between the Lords' *legal* powers and shifting *conventional* understandings of its legitimate legislative role. This chapter assesses the nature and purpose of constitutional conventions more systematically.

We might begin by considering several hypothetical situations. Assume, for example, that the Queen personally opposes a government's policy to cut old age pensions. She decides that when the Bill promoting the policy is sent for the Royal Assent she will not sign it. She justifies her action on the grounds that 'the people' dislike the policy (observing that the government did not win a majority of votes at the last election) and claims her first loyalty is to her people, not to the Houses of Parliament or the government. Alternatively, assume that the Queen no longer wants Tony Blair as Prime Minister, and concludes that if the Labour Party win the next election she will invite Gordon Brown to assume that office, even though Tony Blair remains Labour Party leader.

Giving the Royal Assent and appointing a Prime Minister are aspects of the residue of prerogative powers still exercised by the Monarch personally. The courts have never indicated that such prerogatives are justiciable. Thus, if the Queen chose to adopt either course, there is no apparent legal obstacle in her way. Nor does it answer this problem to suggest that Parliament could pass legislation preventing such behaviour – for such legislation could only emerge if the Queen assented to the relevant Bill. But it is not just the Queen who wields potentially important yet clearly non-justiciable constitutional powers.

Let us suppose, as a third hypothetical scenario, that the Conservative Party wins the next election with a two seat Commons majority, but with fewer votes than Labour. Tony Blair claims that Labour has 'won' the election, refuses to resign as Prime Minister, and he and his Cabinet resolve (with the Queen's support) to stay in office as a minority government.

We will find neither an Act nor a common law rule indicating that the law of the constitution has been breached in any of those situations. But it seems most unlikely such events could ever occur. Could the Queen veto the wishes of the Commons? Or impose an unwanted Prime Minister on the Commons' majority party? Would a Prime Minister really have to be dragged out of Downing Street after a general election defeat? That such hypotheses belong in the realm of fantasy is a result of their political impracticality – or, in other words, of their 'unconstitutionality'. They indicate that vital pillars of our constitutional structure may be built upon foundations with no obvious legal basis – foundations which we might call constitutional conventions.

THE DICEYAN PERSPECTIVE – LAWS AND CONVENTIONS DISTINGUISHED

Dicey's *Law of the Constitution* identified two distinct types of constitutional rule:

> 'The one set of rules are in the strictest sense "laws", since they are rules (whether derived from statute or . . . the common law) enforced by the courts;. . . . The other set of rules consists of conventions, understandings, habits or practices which, though they may regulate the conduct of . . . officials, are not in reality laws at all since they are not enforced by the courts'.[1]

Dicey does not distinguish laws from conventions because of their importance, or the role they fulfill, but in terms of whether they are enforceable by the courts. A particular rule *is not a convention* if its breach is actionable in the courts. The utility of that proposition is discussed below. But first, it may be useful to approach constitutional conventions from another angle. In Jennings' view, a convention was characterised not just by its legal non-enforceability, but also because there was a reason for the rule.[2] We might therefore ask what constitutional role conventions supposedly play, a question answered in part by exploring the mechanisms through which they come into existence.

THE FUNCTIONS AND SOURCES OF CONVENTIONS

A simple, if incomplete, way to characterise conventions' constitutional function is that they fill in the gaps within the legal structure of government. However this notion operates at different levels of generality. Very narrowly, conventions provide a moral framework within which government Ministers or the Monarch should exercise non-justiciable legal powers. Slightly more broadly, they function as one means of regulating the relationship between Ministers within central government. In a wider vein, conventions also regulate the relationship between the different branches of government – especially between the Monarch and the Cabinet, between central government and the House of Commons and the House of Lords, and between

[1] Op cit pp 23–24. [2] (1959) op cit p 136.

central government and local government. We analyse that final relationship in chapters ten and eleven. This chapter explores the first three. Before turning to conventions' function and substance however, we should give some thought to their source.

The sources of constitutional conventions

As noted in chapter six, George V refused Asquith's requests for a mass creation of Liberal peers to overcome the Lords' Conservative majority during the 1909–1911 controversies. The King had sought advice from senior Conservative politicians. Asquith had described the Lords' intransigence as 'a breach of the constitution'. That breach was of a conventional, rather than legal nature. Asquith took a similar view of George V's recourse to opposition party politicians for advice. In a minute to the King, Asquith explained why:

> 'The part to be played by the Crown, in such a situation as now exists, has happily been settled by the accumulated traditions and unbroken practice of more than 70 years. It is to act upon the advice of the Ministers who for the time being possess the confidence of the House of Commons. . . . It follows that it is not the function of a Constitutional Sovereign to act as arbiter or mediator between rival parties and policies, still less to take advice from the leaders on both sides, with the view to forming a conclusion of his own'.

Asquith assumed that the reason for the convention that the Monarch 'act upon the advice of the Ministers who possess the confidence of the Commons' was to ensure that the preferences of the party with majority Commons support were always given legal effect whenever personal prerogatives were deployed. We can see an obvious 'democratic' (albeit majoritarian) justification for the convention, since the party with a Commons majority usually represents the largest section (if not a majority) of the electorate.

Asquith also suggests three possible sources of conventions: 'tradition', 'unbroken practice', and a lengthy time span, in this case 70 years.[3] We might reasonably assume that if a particular (non-legal) aspect of the government process possesses all three characteristics it can be regarded as a convention. Whether we could so regard a practice having but one or two such features is a more difficult question.

The idea that there are minimum requirements to become a convention is reinforced by the argument that there are also a set of non-legal constitutional rules inferior to conventions. Dicey used such phrases as customs, practices, and usages to describe these lesser rules of behaviour. Jennings agreed with Dicey on this point. He suggested that these informal practices could be divided into those that eventually became conventions and those that did not. As already noted, Jennings additionally insisted that a convention only arose if there was an important 'reason' for its existence, ie that its provisions had substantial political significance.

[3] A period which of course (from 1909) takes us back to the decade in which the Great Reform Act was passed; see pp 226–228 above.

Determining when a practice matures sufficiently to be a convention is a question defying authoritative answer. Chapter six suggested the Salisbury doctrine was a convention. Griffith and Ryle's *Parliament* approves that classification. But another eminent commentator, Colin Turpin, concludes: 'It may be doubted whether these principles have sufficient clarity, or are supported by a sufficient agreement to give them the status of conventions'.[4]

Such disagreement over so important an element of constitutional history implies we may never find analytical tools which tell us when a custom assumes conventional status. We might nonetheless proceed by assuming that a crucial test of whether a custom is a convention is whether the rule is respected by the people it supposedly controls. This suggests that convention spotting is more an empirical than a theoretical task. Consequently, the only way to decide how to classify rules of political behaviour is to examine situations where a supposed convention has either been respected or ignored. The rules on which we initially focus are the concepts of collective and individual ministerial responsibility.[5]

I. COLLECTIVE MINISTERIAL RESPONSIBILITY

The Cabinet, like the office of Prime Minister, has no identifiable legal source. It assumed a recognisably modern form after about 1720, when we can also see the first Prime Minister emerging as the 'first among equals' within it. Both the office of Prime Minister and the institution of the Cabinet are therefore creatures of convention. As suggested in chapter five, except in periods when a ruling party has a small Commons majority, and must be acutely sensitive to its MPs' wishes, the Cabinet is the hub of the legislative and executive arms of government: it is there that government policies are formulated and refined. Consequently, for a government with a reliable Commons majority, parliamentary sovereignty is in effect Cabinet sovereignty. Given the Cabinet's obvious importance, it may seem odd that it operates without any appreciable legal structure. But the absence of legal controls on Cabinet behaviour does not mean that there are no principles regulating its activities.

The convention of ministerial responsibility is perhaps the most important non-legal rule within our constitution. Its concern is with regulating the conduct of government (and especially Cabinet) activities, both in respect of Ministers' relations with each other, and with the two Houses of Parliament. The convention is divided into collective and individual branches. We consider individual responsibility in section four. Firstly, however, we address collective responsibility. This convention has three sub-divisions; the confidence rule, the unanimity rule, and the confidentiality rule.

[4] (1990) op cit p 491.

[5] See generally – and with particular relevance to recent episodes – the excellent study by Diana Woodhouse (1994) *Ministers and Parliament* (Oxford: Clarendon Press).

CONFIDENCE

The confidence rule originally required a government to resign if it could not command majority Commons support – if the House had 'lost confidence' in the government. Initially the rule applied if a government was defeated on a major policy issue.[6] During the mid-nineteenth century such resignations were commonplace: we noted several over electoral reform in chapter seven; Jennings records five between 1852 and 1859.[7]

It is difficult to define 'major' issues. Presumably the Shops Bill on which the Thatcher government was defeated in 1986 did not meet that criterion.[8] But this does no more than tell us that an issue is not sufficiently important to require a government's resignation if the government does not resign when it is defeated. That test would be entirely circular. Furthermore, there have been several instances of modern governments enduring Commons defeats on important issues, but continuing in office regardless. The 1974–1979 Labour administrations suffered frequent defeats. Its expenditure plans were rejected by the Commons in March 1976. It is difficult to disagree with the then Leader of the Opposition, Margaret Thatcher, that this policy was so fundamental a part of the government's raison d'être that defeat demanded resignation. The Cabinet declined to do so however. The government also refused to resign when defeated in an attempt to raise income tax levels in 1977, clearly a matter of major importance.

The experiences of the mid-1970s suggest that the convention's initial form no longer binds Cabinet behaviour. If a necessary feature of conventional status is that politicians consider themselves obliged to follow a given course of action, it is clear that the confidence rule of the 1850s is not a conventional feature of the contemporary constitution. But it would be inaccurate to claim the convention has disappeared entirely; rather, it has evolved into a different form.

The rule's modern version seems to require the government to resign only if defeated on an explicit no-confidence motion. The function of this shift in conventional understandings is readily discernible. Governments are rarely elected because of their policy on a single issue, but because of the overall package of policies and personalities they offer. A government's failure to command a Commons majority on a particular issue need not mean it cannot do so in all other policy areas. Defeat in an explicit no-confidence motion, in contrast, implies the Commons considers the government incompetent in all matters.

As such, the reason behind the new convention is clear. In one, somewhat abstract sense, it stresses that the executive is accountable to the Commons, and so provides a rather different illustration of the principle of legislative supremacy. More prosaically, in the age of nationalised party politics, it provides an indirect means for the people, via their MPs, to signify withdrawal of their consent to a particular government.[9]

6 Norton P (1978) 'Government defeats in the House of Commons: myth and reality' *Public Law* 360–378.

7 (1959) op cit pp 512–519.

8 Pp 145 above.

9 Although, as noted below, a successful no-confidence motion might lead not to a dissolution, but to the formation of a new administration from within the existing Parliament.

However we have only rather barren historical soil in which to root the new convention. There has been just one occasion since 1945 when the convention has been tested. James Callaghan's minority Labour government resigned in 1979 when defeated by one vote on an explicit no-confidence motion. One might doubt that this amounts to a tradition or long term unbroken practice.

Only one other Prime Minister has resigned in comparable circumstances after such a defeat in the twentieth century, that one being Stanley Baldwin in 1924. Baldwin led a minority Conservative administration, which failed to gain Commons approval for the legislative programme outlined in the King's speech. (At the 1923 election the Conservatives won 258 seats, Labour 191, and the Liberals 159). Ramsay MacDonald subsequently formed a minority Labour administration from within the same Parliament, which survived for barely 11 months. That administration was also defeated on a confidence vote, although that vote led to a dissolution rather than simply a change of government.[10] It thus seems that the contemporary confidence rule, if rarely invoked in practice, is straightforward in principle. The second limb of collective responsibility, the unanimity rule, seems quite the opposite.

UNANIMITY

The unanimity rule requires all Cabinet Ministers to offer public support for all cabinet decisions, even if a Minister opposed the policy concerned in Cabinet. Ministers who find a particular policy unacceptable should resign from office. As Lord Salisbury explained in 1878:

> 'For all that passes in Cabinet every member of it who does not resign is absolutely and irretrievably responsible and has no right afterwards to say that he agreed in one case to a compromise, while in another he was persuaded by his colleagues.'[11]

The rule also supposes that ministerial differences of opinion have been aired in Cabinet. The convention demands collective loyalty to collective decisions. It could therefore be undermined either by Ministers who openly signalled their disagreement with government policy, or by Cabinet decision-making procedures which prevent Ministers having any say in policy formation.

The rule originally arose in the seventeenth century to protect Ministers from the King's attempts to undermine their power by exposing or encouraging public arguments. Since the Cabinet is no longer in conflict with the Monarch, the rationale for the rule has changed. The contemporary argument suggests the rule is needed to maintain public and business confidence in the unity and purpose of government. It is alleged that public Cabinet divisions would trigger such dire consequences as reduced investment from overseas, a run on the pound, or various other forms of economic or political instability.

[10] Norton (1978) op cit; Jennings (1959) op cit pp 28–30.

[11] Quoted in Ellis D (1980) 'Collective ministerial responsibility and collective solidarity' *Public Law* 367–396.

There seem to be three ways to test whether the rule has conventional status. The first, and most elusive, would be to identify occasions when a Minister strongly opposed a particular policy, made and lost her argument in Cabinet, and then resolutely kept her dissent a secret from outside observers. Unfortunately, it is in the nature of a secret event that we do not know that it happened. We may, in retrospect, gain some insight by the eventual release of Cabinet papers (currently embargoed for at least 30 years), or (more promptly) by the memoirs of former Ministers, although the latter may present a skewed interpretation of events. The second test would seek instances when irreconcilable disagreement between Cabinet members led to resignations or dismissals of Ministers. Such episodes would reinforce the claim that the convention effectively determined government behaviour. The third test, which would seem to disprove the rule's conventional status, would search political history for public intra-Cabinet disputes in which all protagonists stayed in office. It is an indicator of the unfortunate indeterminacy of conventional rules that one readily finds examples to satisfy all three tests.

Michael Heseltine's resignation from Thatcher's second administration in 1985 over the Westland affair offers a powerful illustration of the convention taking effect. Heseltine, then Defence Secretary, was embroiled within Cabinet in an argument as to whether the financially troubled Westland helicopter company should be rescued by American or European firms. Heseltine favoured the European option, but the Cabinet majority preferred the American bid. It is not clear if Heseltine would have resigned solely because of his disagreement with the substance of Cabinet policy. His own account stresses that he left office because the Cabinet did not accept the second limb of the unanimity convention – namely that a Minister may argue her case fully before her colleagues. Heseltine alleged that a Cabinet meeting scheduled for him to make his argument had been cancelled by the Prime Minister in order to force through the American takeover, a strategy which he interpreted as confirming that the Cabinet no longer operated in a collective manner.[12]

A similar accusation that Margaret Thatcher rejected collective forms of decision-making was made by Nigel Lawson. Lawson resigned as Chancellor of the Exchequer in 1989, claiming his position had been undermined by the Prime Minister's preference for taking advice on economic policy from her personal adviser, Professor Alan Walters, rather than from her Chancellor. Lawson's decision to leave office has several obvious Conservative predecessors. In 1886, Lord Randolph Churchill, Chancellor in Lord Salisbury's administration, was isolated in Cabinet over his plans to cut military spending. Rather than defer to majority sentiment, Churchill quit the government altogether.[13] A similarly principled stand was taken by Chancellor Peter Thorneycroft and two junior Ministers in 1958, who felt the Cabinet was not committed to sufficiently rigorous anti-inflation policies. Neither the Churchill nor Thorneycroft departures dealt a fatal blow to their respective government's stability. Prime Minister

[12] The episode repays close attention; see especially Hennessy (1986) op cit.

[13] For further details see Madgwick P (1966) 'Resignations' *Parliamentary Affairs* 59–76.

Harold Macmillan famously minimised the impact of the 1958 events by referring to them as 'a little local difficulty'. The impact of Lawson's resignation will be considered further below.

Illustrations supportive of the rule are not limited solely to the Conservative Party. In 1951, two members of the Labour Cabinet (Nye Bevan and Harold Wilson) resigned from Attlee's government in protest at plans to introduce prescription charges into the newly founded National Health Service. The action was widely construed as revealing a deep ideological split within the party.[14] It pales in comparison, however, to the events of 1931. The 1929–1931 Labour government was a minority administration. Its tenure coincided with the Great Depression, which wrought severe distress on most western economies. A cabinet committee proposed large cuts in public expenditure to address the crisis. These were opposed by eight Cabinet members. Faced with so profound a split in his government, MacDonald tendered its resignation to the King.

At the Prime Minister's invitation, George V played a pivotal role in brokering a solution to the crisis. The suggestion for a coalition government headed by MacDonald was made by Sir Herbert Samuel, the leader of the Liberal Party, and enthusiastically pressed on Stanley Baldwin, the Conservative leader, by the King. The Liberals and Conservatives agreed to join a coalition administration, on the understanding that Parliament would be dissolved as soon as emergency legislation enacting the cabinet committee's recommendation was passed. Only three of the Labour Cabinet's 18 ministers agreed to serve in a 'National' coalition government, in which MacDonald led what he described as 'a Cabinet of Individuals' – most of whom were Conservatives. At the subsequent general election, the National government, led by MacDonald, was returned with a substantial Commons majority.

Reactions to Disraeli's proposals for the 1867 Reform Act also illustrate the operation of the unanimity rule. Three members of Lord Derby's Cabinet, all opposing further democratisation, resigned rather than support the Bill.[15] Similarly, Richard Crossman's *Diaries* reveal that the 1966–1970 Labour Cabinet was deeply divided over lowering the voting age to 18.[16] Such disagreement was not made public (at least not until the *Diaries* were published some years later!). Ministers opposed to the reform stifled their dissent; the government could thus present the Bill as a measure enjoying unanimous Cabinet support.

But electoral reform also provides quite contradictory examples, seemingly disproving the convention's existence. In 1883, for example, Joseph Chamberlain campaigned vigorously for continued extension of the franchise, to which the rest of Gladstone's Cabinet was clearly opposed.[17] Similarly, Asquith's various cabinets were openly divided on the issue of women's votes, as indeed were previous Liberal and Conservative administrations.[18]

14 Pilot op cit pp 160–165; Hennessy P (1992) *Never again* pp 415–417 (London: Jonathan Cape).

15 Cowling op cit pp 163–165.

16 Op cit pp 493–494, 500–501.

17 Jones op cit p 106.

18 Rover op cit p 102.

Asquith presented the last example as 'an agreement to differ', suggesting that the convention could be 'suspended' for matters crossing party political boundaries. The same argument was invoked by McDonald's coalition National Government to justify patent Cabinet disagreement over the question of import controls, although we might wonder if we could expect collective solidarity in a 'Cabinet of Individuals'. This 'suspension' principle has latterly been deployed by both Labour and Conservative Cabinets over government policies towards the European Community.[19] In 1975, the Labour Prime Minister Harold Wilson allowed Cabinet members to campaign on both sides in the referendum on whether Britain should remain in the EEC. Wilson explained his decision by saying that the split reflected a similar rift within public opinion.[20] James Callaghan, Labour Prime Minister between 1976 and 1979, supported the idea of selectively applied conventions. Callaghan permitted his Cabinet openly to hold differing views in 1979 about the type of electoral system to be used for elections to the EEC Parliament. When accused of acting unconstitutionally, he replied that collective responsibility would always apply 'except in cases where I announce that it does not'.[21] More informally, the second Major government was noticeably divided between 'Euro-sceptics' and 'Euro-enthusiasts', a point explored more fully in chapter twelve.

As an organising principle, 'suspension' has little merit – a practice cannot be a binding rule if it can be disregarded at the whim of those it purportedly controls. Moreover, such arguments do not explain the 1883 Cabinet's tolerance of Chamberlain's independent line. The Cabinet portrayed Chamberlain's 1883 dissent as an example of a principle of 'Ministerial freedom of speech', but such a concept is manifestly incompatible with a unanimity convention. Chamberlain's behaviour was accepted because his dismissal or resignation was impractical from a party political perspective; it would have alienated many Liberal voters, with dire electoral results. He could thus defy the supposed convention and advance both his own prospects within the party and the prospects of more radical electoral reform being enacted.

A similar combination of personal ambition and policy preference seems to underlie James Callaghan's very evident dissent, when Home Secretary, from the industrial relations policies of the second (1966–1970) Wilson administration. The government wished to impose legal sanctions on workers who took industrial action without trade union approval. Callaghan clearly aligned himself with trade union opposition to this proposal. Subsequently, he announced, without having sought Cabinet approval, that the government would take no new measures to regulate wage and price inflation. Many Cabinet members apparently considered that Callaghan was seeking to establish himself as the trade unions' preferred successor to Harold Wilson, and demanded he be disciplined for disregarding the unanimity rule.[22] No action was taken however,

[19] See chs 12 and 13 below.

[20] This episode is discussed more fully in ch 12.

[21] *HCD*, 16 June 1977 at c 552.

[22] According to Crossman's *Diaries*; op cit at pp 497–500. Crossman notes that Callaghan himself protested that there was nothing unconventional about his behaviour.

since the government, facing an imminent general election, could not risk losing the political and financial support the unions provided.

The inference we might draw from these examples is that whatever 'reason' one might adduce for the rule of cabinet unanimity, it is ignored for reasons of party political expediency too frequently for us to conclude that Asquith's threefold test for conventional status is met. One might refine the convention by suggesting it operates differently for Conservative and Labour governments. Writing in 1980, Ellis argued Labour governments contained a wider range of opinion than Conservative administrations, and their members were less inclined than Conservatives to compromise ideological preferences to preserve party unity.[23] So fractious an atmosphere was inimical to effective functioning of the unanimity rule, especially since, as noted in chapter seven, until very recently most Labour governments have had precarious Commons majorities. Ministers representing distinct party factions may see no need to respect the unanimity rule if their faction's continued support is a prerequisite of the government's survival.

CONFIDENTIALITY

Lawson and Heseltine withheld their explanation of the events leading to their departures from Cabinet until after they had resigned. In so doing, they respected the unwritten letter of the unanimity rule. It is also however a convention of the constitution that Ministers who resign are afforded the opportunity to offer reasons and justifications for their action to the Commons (or, if they are peers, to the Lords). As we shall see in chapter thirteen, such speeches can have a devastating political effect. This is another manifestation of the confidence rule, since it enables MPs to evaluate the government's performance after having heard both sides of the argument.

Once out of Cabinet, Lawson and Heseltine explained their actions in detail, both in the Commons and in the media. In so doing, they drew attention to another facet of collective responsibility, namely that all Ministers owe their cabinet colleagues a duty of confidentiality. Ministers should not reveal how colleagues argued or voted in particular disputes: to do so would seriously undermine the unanimity rule and also inhibit Ministers from speaking their minds.

To date this rule seems to have been respected, at least formally. However, reports of Cabinet discussions are leaked to the press with sufficient regularity to suggest that in practice some Ministers ignore it. A more contentious issue is whether confidentiality should continue after a Minister leaves the Cabinet. And if so for how long, and how stringently? The rule's status, and the political and legal consequences which flowed from ignoring it, came before the courts in *A-G v Johnathan Cape Ltd*, popularly known as the *Crossman Diaries* case.[24]

[23] Op cit. [24] [1976] QB 752.

Can conventions become laws? 1: The Crossman Diaries case

Crossman, a member of Wilson's cabinet between 1964 and 1970, wanted to provide a detailed account of Cabinet government in operation. Consequently, he kept a comprehensive diary of Cabinet decisions, intending to publish it following his retirement. Unfortunately for Crossman, he died prematurely; but his widow decided to publish the *Diaries*.

After extracts appeared in *The Sunday Times*, the government sought an injunction preventing further publication. It argued that the courts should preserve the confidentiality of three types of ministerial information: firstly, the views of individual Ministers; secondly, confidential advice to Ministers from civil servants; and thirdly, discussions about the appointment or transfer of senior officials. Crossman's publishers argued that the duty of Cabinet confidentiality had no legal basis; it was merely a moral obligation, respected or ignored according to the Minister's conscience.

Lord Widgery did not find history a helpful guide: 'I find overwhelming evidence that the doctrine of joint responsibility is generally understood and practiced, and equally strong evidence that it is on occasion ignored'.[25] Widgery eventually delivered a puzzling judgment. Firstly, he accepted that Ministers owed each other a legally enforceable duty of confidentiality. However, this duty did not derive from the convention turning into a law. It was created by 'stretching' existing common law principles about confidentiality in respect of other types of relationship, particularly marriage and commercial undertakings.[26] But secondly, Widgery held that unless the disclosures threatened national security, the duty would disappear ten years after the relevant events occurred. The government subsequently established a committee of inquiry, headed by Lord Radcliffe, to make recommendations concerning the publication of Ministers' diaries or autobiographies.[27] The committee proposed a 15-year delay on publication of sensitive material. The proposal has not been given statutory force: given the rapidity with which retired Ministers have subsequently marketed their memoirs, it seems safe to assume that it should not be regarded as a convention.[28]

If analysed formalistically, the judgment does not sweep away Dicey's claim that conventions are not enforceable by the courts. Technically, the case is not an example of a court enforcing a convention, but accepting that a convention was coincidentally underpinned by existing common law rules. That may seem a semantic distinction. In functionalist terms, we might argue that the court enforced a convention by cloaking it with a common law label. There is no legal impediment to the courts doing so. The common law is recognised to be a dynamic, unstable set of legal rules. In cases such as

25 [1976] QB 752 at 770.

26 *Argyll v Argyll* [1967] Ch 302, [1965] 1 All ER 611; and *Saltman Engineering Co Ltd v Campbell Engineering Co Ltd* (1948) [1963] 3 All ER 413n, CA, respectively.

27 Radcliffe (1976) *Report on Ministerial Memoirs*, Cmnd 6386 (London: HMSO).

28 Eg Clark A (1993) *Diaries* (London: Weidenfield and Nicolson) – the most revealing of the genre; Baker K (1993) *The turbulent years* (London: Faber); Lawson N (1992) *The view from No 11* (London: Bantam); Ridley N (1991) *My style of government* (London: Fontana).

Burmah Oil, Lain, and *GCHQ,* 'new' common law principles emerged when judges considered that applying traditional ideas would have produced unsatisfactory results. Parliament may restore the former law by legislation reversing a court decision, but (short of passing legislation forbidding the courts from altering common law principles) it has no power to pre-empt judicial innovation. This inter-relationship between convention and common law within the courts is something to which we shall return. For the present, before concluding our discussion of collective responsibility, we must make a detour in our circuitous journey among the constitution's conventional undergrowth to an ostensibly non-justiciable issue – the relationship between the Monarch and her ministers.

II. THE MONARCH

In formal terms, the Monarch retains substantial legal powers. Unlike the House of Lords, she has the legal capacity to veto any Bill passed by the Commons. No court has thus far indicated that it is competent to compel the grant of the Royal Assent. The Monarch also seems to have the legal authority to appoint whomsoever she wishes to be Prime Minister, and to appoint and dismiss other Ministers at will; she may dismiss an entire government if she wishes. And she may at any time, without fear of legal reversal, dissolve Parliament and thereby force a general election to be held. All such actions are elements of the royal prerogative which are 'peculiar and eccentrical' to the Monarch herself, and which, per *GCHQ,* appear non-justiciable. Nor could such prerogatives be altered or abolished by statute without the Monarch's consent. As a legal creature, therefore, the Monarchy appears to possess (at least) co-equal status with the Commons.

Yet there is no part of the contemporary constitution in which the mismatch between legal principle and political fact is more pronounced than in respect of the personal prerogatives. The notion that a single individual should wield substantial legal powers bestowed solely by accident of birth is entirely antithetic to the particular form of parliamentary democracy on which the legitimacy of the constitution rests. This is not to say, as is suggested below, that one could not invoke alternative conceptions of 'democracy' to justify such powers in some circumstances. But as a matter of political instinct, one might readily infer that there would be very convincing reasons for the presence of constitutional conventions which subjected the exercise of the personal prerogatives to the wishes of the government which enjoyed the confidence of the Commons. A brief survey of the past 150 years suggests that such a convention has indeed emerged.

On the advice of her Ministers'? The conventional 'democratisation' of the personal prerogatives

As noted in chapter seven, William IV did not acknowledge that the Great Reform

Act's tentative push towards constitutional democratisation affected his power to remove a government which displeased him. In 1834, he dismissed Lord Melbourne's Whig administration, which he regarded as unacceptably radical.[29] William invited Sir Robert Peel to lead a minority Conservative administration. Peel was more sensitive to the Act's implications, and requested an immediate dissolution of Parliament, hoping to legitimise both his own position and the King's by winning the subsequent general election. The electorate, however, returned the Whigs and their allies with a workable Commons majority. William subsequently deferred to the Commons majority, and did not obstruct the formation of a new Whig administration.

There have been no subsequent examples of such blatant interference by the Monarch. However, Queen Victoria engaged in secretive manoeuvrings to keep Gladstone out of power in 1886. Victoria, like many Liberal MPs, opposed Gladstone's policy of granting home rule to Ireland. She subsequently approached several prominent anti-Gladstonian Liberals to try and ensure that a Gladstone administration could not enact that policy. Her tone was explicitly partisan:

> 'I appeal to you and to all moderate loyal and patriotic men, who have the safety and well-being of the Empire and the Throne at heart, and who wish to save them from destruction, with which, if the government again fell into the reckless hands of Mr Gladstone, they would be threatened, to rise above party and to be true patriots'.[30]

It is possible to defend the Queen's action by characterising her appeal that politicians should forswear party allegiances in pursuit of greater national interests as echoing a Madisonian fear of faction. As an abstract exercise in democratic theorisation, that viewpoint has some substantive attractions, although one might doubt that the process through which such a national interest was defined, namely the Monarch's individual preferences, would satisfy even the most dilute notions of democratic process. But in the context of historical trends in the late nineteenth century, Victoria's initiative was undoubtedly 'unconstitutional'.

By 1886, the Monarch's conventional capacity to engage in independent exercise of her legal powers had been substantially undermined by both the gradual extension of the Commons' electoral franchise to ever greater numbers of 'the people' – and relatedly – by the increasing ascendancy of the Commons vis à vis the Lords within Parliament. Neither trend formally affected the Monarch's legal powers, but both emphasised that electoral accountability rather than accident of birth should regulate access to governmental power. In so far as the legitimacy of her constitutional role depended on her maintaining a studied neutrality between those political parties which each enjoyed substantial electoral support, Victoria's machinations in 1886 revealed a distinct failure to accept (or perhaps to understand) the constitutional implications of the political and social changes the country was undergoing.

29 Brock op cit pp 315–317; Jennings (1959) op cit pp 403–405.

30 Cited in Jennings (1959) op cit p 34. Gladstone himself suggested of Victoria that there was 'no greater Tory in the land'; quoted in Arnstein op cit p 151.

This gradual process of subordinating legal power to political practice is demonstrated by subsequent Monarchs' increasingly tentative interventions in situations of political instability. As we saw in chapter seven, the behaviour of Edward VII and George V in 1909–1911 was less than fully supportive of Asquith's wishes. At that point, the legal context in which the personal prerogatives were to be exercised was virtually the same as in 1886 – the House of Lords remained a co-equal partner to the Commons, and the franchise had not been substantially extended since 1884. Twenty years later, that context had altered significantly. The far more passive role played by George V in forming the 1931 National government can be explained largely by the virtual completion of the democratisation process; since 1928, Britain had had a universal franchise for elections to the Commons, and since 1911 the Lords' inferior status within Parliament had been established as a matter of law, not merely convention. Elizabeth II was admittedly intimately involved in the choice of a Conservative Prime Minister in the mid-1950s, but that was because the Conservative Party had no formal arrangements to choose its leader; the leader traditionally 'emerged' in some mysterious fashion after consultation among the party's senior figures. In the mid-1960s, the Conservative Party established a system in which its leader was chosen through a ballot of its MPs. The Labour Party already had such a process, and it seems inconceivable that it would now be legitimate for a Monarch to appoint as Prime Minister someone who was not the leader of her party. The principle is a powerful, further illustration not just of the primacy of party interests over national interests within Parliament, but also of the ascendancy of convention over law at the very heart of Britain's constitutional identity.

Refusing the Royal Assent

If we borrow Jennings' 'reason' test for conventional status, and (mis)apply it to the 1688 settlement, we might assume that the Monarch's formal co-equality with the Commons and the Lords served to protect both the Queen herself from an alliance of the two houses, and the 'people' from a lower and upper house temporarily seized by a desire to enact oppressive legislation. To suggest that the Queen might ever invoke her veto power would, however, seem utterly to contradict the trend towards democratisation which we employed to explain why the Monarch generally cannot use her personal prerogatives in an independent manner. This leads us yet again to examine the meaning of democracy in the contemporary constitution. If the concept means simply that a political party commanding a reliable Commons majority can pass any law whatsoever, a refusal of the Royal Assent to any Bill would be 'undemocratic'. Yet it is not difficult to imagine scenarios in which we might intuitively regard such action as essential to defend democratic ideals.

Assume, for example, that a government, fearing it will lose the next general election, promotes a Bill to extend the lifetime of a Parliament without opposition party agreement. At present the Lords may veto such legislation, and so, in its anachronistic way, can operate as a 'democratic' safeguard against a dictatorial Commons majority. But the Lords does not (apparently) possess a veto over a third Parliament Act removing that veto power. What conventional understandings should guide the Queen's decision about granting the Royal Assent in the following situations?

Firstly if the Lords also approved the Bill extending the lifetime of the Parliament? Secondly to a new Parliament Bill, introduced against the Lords' wishes under the 1949 procedures, which removed the Lords' veto power on all legislation? And thirdly, if she assented to the second Bill, to a subsequent Bill extending the lifetime of the present Parliament? Alternatively, what course should the Queen follow in respect of a Bill which requires that the next general election be fought on constituency boundaries designed to secure a vast majority for the governing party?

We might suggest all such Bills would be 'unconstitutional', and that the Queen could therefore legitimately withhold her assent. But the argument is a difficult one to sustain. One could contend, for instance, that refusing the Royal Assent would be legitimate because any such Bill would be seeking to change the basis of consent to government within the constitution – to effect, as the Duke of Wellington put it, 'a revolution by due process of law'. The flaw in this argument is that it entrenches contemporary understandings of 'consent', and so suggests that we have now arrived at the ultimate form of democratic government. Yet these allegedly 'unconstitutional' Bills may be no more radical from our perspective than were Grey's Reform Bill or Asquith's Parliament Bill in the eyes of contemporaneous conservative opinion. In the absence of a supra-parliamentary constitution, we simply lack an authoritative yardstick against which to measure the substantive legitimacy of radical constitutional reform.

It is some answer to these questions to observe that no such Bills are ever likely to be produced. In all reasonably foreseeable circumstances, there appears to be no difficulty in concluding that the Monarch's personal prerogatives are exercised in accordance with the wishes of a Prime Minister whose government enjoys the confidence of the Commons. The reason for that convention is to subject the Queen's legal powers to democratic control – in so far as we consider Prime Ministerial control democratic. But that reason disappears when a Prime Minister's government does not possess the lower house's confidence. In such situations, the conventional constraints on the Monarch's legal powers are decidedly ambiguous.

Two such circumstances have constantly exercised the minds of constitutional analysts. The first relates to the appointment of the Prime Minister following a general election in which no party has won a majority of Commons seats. The second concerns a Prime Minister's request for a dissolution, prior to the expiry of the five-year term fixed by the Parliament Act 1911, when an alternative government might be formed from within the existing lower house.

Choosing a Prime Minister in a hung Parliament

In the February 1974 general election, Edward Heath's outgoing Conservative government failed to win an overall majority. But although Harold Wilson's Labour Party had the largest number of Commons seats, it too had no majority. The balance of power was held by small parties, which in combination had only 37 seats.

There is no legal requirement that a government resign after a general election defeat. It does so, as a matter of convention, in deference to an electoral sentiment which indicates that another party is the people's preferred choice. That choice was however far from clear in 1974. While the electorate may have signalled displeasure with the Conservatives, it had not shown obvious enthusiasm for Labour. In these circumstances, Heath decided not to resign immediately, but to conduct negotiations with the smaller parties to see if they would offer him support in a coalition government. None did so. Heath then concluded that the correct course was for him to resign, and advise the Queen to invite Wilson to form a minority administration.

It is possible to argue that Heath should have automatically resigned, on the grounds firstly that Labour had won more seats than the Conservatives and, secondly, that the prospect of a Conservative/Liberal coalition had not been put to the electorate. However, there is neither a legal nor a conventional basis for the claim that the leader of the largest single party has any immediate entitlement to a favourable exercise of the personal prerogatives. Heath, and the Queen, faced a somewhat unusual situation; it would be difficult to describe their behaviour as constitutionally indefensible.[31]

Granting a dissolution after a transfer of party loyalty

A far more difficult question would arise in circumstances which have not yet occurred in the modern era, but which are not wholly implausible. Let us suppose a party gains a majority of 20 seats at a general election. After one or two years of the Parliament's five-year term, following a bitter dispute over economic policy, 20 of its members cross the floor and join the opposition. (Since MPs hold their seats as individuals, not party representatives, they are under no legal obligation to resign and fight a by-election.) As a result, the Leader of the Opposition, rather than the Prime Minister, possesses the confidence of the lower house, a point confirmed when the opposition successfully moves an explicit no-confidence motion.

The Prime Minister, hoping the electorate would return his party with a new majority, requests a dissolution, even though the Leader of the Opposition could form a viable administration. If the Queen granted a dissolution, she would be defying the Commons majority. This suggests dissolution would be unconstitutional, and that the Queen's correct course would be to invite the Leader of the Opposition to become Prime Minister. But the Queen would have to dismiss the current Prime Minister before she could do so. The Prime Minister, however, will neither resign nor advise the Queen to dismiss him and then appoint the Leader of the Opposition as his successor; he maintains that the realities of electoral politics are that voters are motivated by party loyalties, not the merits of individual candidates, and that the new commons majority has no electoral mandate.

In such circumstances, the Queen would have no alternative but to fashion a new constitutional convention. Since there is no Minister with majority support on whose

31 See generally Brazier R (1982) 'Choosing a Prime Minister' *Public Law* 395–417.

advice she can act, she would have to choose her own advisers and form her own opinion on the relative merits of dissolution and dismissal. Yet, even if we limit our notion of 'democracy' to electoral majoritarianism, the democratic solution to this situation is unclear. The 'legal' 'majority' is surely the largest grouping of MPs within the Commons, each of whom has been sent there as the representative of her particular constituency. This majority would clearly prefer dismissal to dissolution. However the 'political' majority might readily be seen as the party which won the greatest share of the vote at the last general election. This majority would obviously prefer dissolution to dismissal. Yet it would seem that for the Queen to grant a dissolution would entail her exercising her prerogative powers in accordance with a version of democracy which Parliament itself has never accepted.[32]

Variations on this theme are as endless as answers are elusive, and neither will be explored at length here.[33] But readers might consider how the Queen should act when one of the 20 defecting MPs in the above example is the Prime Minister, and the opposition party agrees to select her as its new leader. Alternatively, what should happen if the defectors do not include the Prime Minister, but, for example, the Foreign Secretary, who does not resign his office on switching parties, and who is adopted as Leader by the opposition before the Prime Minister asks the Queen to dismiss him, and then satisfies Asquith's criterion of being the Minister commanding a Commons majority? Whatever the Queen did in such circumstances would inevitably be regarded by the 'losers' as an illegitimate exercise of constitutional power, with, as a recent episode of Australian constitutional history suggests, serious consequences for the Monarch's constitutional role.

THE AUSTRALIAN CRISIS OF 1975

Australia's present constitution, which dates from 1901, established a federal system of government with a bicameral central legislature. The Australian Parliament followed the British model in some respects. The lower house, the House of Representatives, corresponds to the House of Commons. The upper house, the Senate, is elected by a form of proportional representation designed to reflect the country's federal nature. The Governor-General (in 1975 Sir John Kerr) exercises certain prerogative powers as the Queen's appointee. These powers include the granting of the Royal Assent, the granting of a dissolution of either or both houses of Parliament, the dismissal of the government and the appointment of a Prime Minister. The text of the Australian constitution (itself a creation in formal legal terms of the Westminster Parliament)

32 The legalistically minded might then wonder if the courts would accept that a justiciable issue had been raised here. The grant of a dissolution might be seen as elevating the prerogative above statute. There is, admittedly, no specific statute in issue here, but it is clear that our electoral law regards MPs as individuals, rather than party representatives. To grant a dissolution on the grounds of the electorate's presumed party allegiances would subvert that statutory scheme.

33 Readers might wonder how the Queen should have responded to Edward Heath in 1974 had he advised her to dissolve Parliament rather than invite Harold Wilson to form a minority administration: see Brazier (1982) op cit.

did not spell out any legal rules to regulate the exercise of these powers, and it was (even in 1975) unclear to what extent Australia's constitution adhered to the British convention that personal prerogatives should be exercised only in accordance with the wishes of a Prime Minister commanding a lower house majority.

In 1975, Gough Whitlam's Labour government held a majority in the lower house, but was in a minority in the Senate. The government had been racked by successive scandals, and Whitlam had been compelled to dismiss two Cabinet colleagues after it was revealed that they had lied to the lower house about certain financial dealings. The Australian economy was also in parlous health, and the Whitlam administration appeared to attract little public support.

We need not dwell on the precise allocation of constitutional powers between House and Senate. It suffices to note that the Senate appeared to have a legal capacity to prevent the government levying the taxation or raising the loans needed to finance public services. As a matter of convention, that power had never been used, even during periods of quite acute party political conflict. But in 1975, the Liberal opposition (led in the House by Malcolm Fraser) resolved to use its greater strength in the Senate to refuse to grant supply in the hope of forcing Whitlam to request a dissolution.[34]

The Senate's position resembles that adopted by the House of Lords towards Lloyd George's 'People's Budget'. It may be overstating the case to describe the Senate as 'Mr Fraser's poodle', but Fraser was clearly deeply involved in the manoeuvrings. Those manoeuvrings culminated in Sir John Kerr dismissing the Whitlam government, and inviting Fraser to form a minority administration on the understandings that he would firstly instruct his party members in the Senate to grant supply and, secondly request an immediate dissolution.

The Governor-General did not act on the advice of the Prime Minister in following this course. Had Whitlam been aware of the Governor-General's intentions, he would surely have asked the Queen to dismiss Sir John Kerr. And since the Queen should by convention act on the advice of her Prime Minister, one assumes she would have complied with any such request.

Sir John Kerr maintained that he was obliged, rather than simply empowered, to dismiss a government that could not maintain a majority in both houses on the supply question. As David Butler has argued, the text of the constitution provides no obvious support for that proposition.[35] Moreover, Butler suggests, the Governor-General's stance may have been politically defensible, if legally contentious in 1901, but the extent to which both the British and Australian constitutions had been democratised since then made his actions untenable.

The Governor-General, and by implication the Queen, were spared further difficulties by the outcome of the subsequent general election; Malcolm Fraser's Liberal Party

[34] This incident may sound a warning to analysts who suggest that the defects of the House of Lords could be cured by making it an elected assembly.

[35] Butler D (1976) 'The Australian crisis of 1975' *Parliamentary Affairs* 201–210.

won a substantial majority. In the longer term, however, the episode triggered a substantial delegitimisation of the Monarch's role within the Australian constitution. It now seems quite anachronistic that a modern western democracy should permit its most acute political problems to be 'solved' by a power which is neither 'democratic' nor domestic. Kerr's actions appear to provide another illustration of the phenomenon of a legal power being conventionally acceptable only while it remains unused.[36]

We revisit the impact of controversies in Commonwealth countries on our domestic constitution in the penultimate section of this chapter. However, we may at this point conclude that as a matter of constitutional practice, albeit not of constitutional law, the Monarch's personal prerogatives are generally exercised by the Prime Minister. This might lead us wonder if our previous discussion of collective cabinet responsibility was incomplete, and to ask just how much effective political power is wielded by the Prime Minister alone in our contemporary constitution?

III. COLLECTIVE MINISTERIAL RESPONSIBILITY REVISITED: FROM CABINET TO PRIME MINISTERIAL GOVERNMENT . . .?

It is perhaps an apocryphal tale that when the Duke of Wellington became Prime Minister, after a career spent in the army rather than the Commons, he remarked on his first Cabinet meeting: 'An extraordinary affair. I gave them their orders and they wanted to stay and discuss them'.[37] We might doubt if there ever was a 'golden age' of Cabinet government in which all Ministers participated fully in decision-making. But in the modern era, James Callaghan's aforementioned belief that he could suspend constitutional conventions whenever he saw fit provides lucid support for the argument that Britain's government is controlled by the Prime Minister rather than the Cabinet.

That argument was first aired in the nineteenth century in Walter Bagehot's leading work on the constitution.[38] Bagehot suggested that the cabinet was becoming a 'dignified' rather than 'efficient' part of the constitution. Its role was increasingly ceremonial or symbolic, while real power was shifting to the Prime Minister and a few of his colleagues.

Bagehot's ideas were forcefully restated in a new edition of his book by Richard Crossman in the 1960s. Crossman's introduction, written before he became a Cabinet Minister, argued that the Prime Minister effectively dominated the Cabinet rather than being just 'first among equals'. Prime Ministers achieved this through three main powers: firstly, by being able to appoint and dismiss Ministers; secondly, by setting

[36] Cf Shell's critque of the House of Lords' evident reluctance to make routine use of its delaying powers after 1949: see p 193 above.

[37] Quoted in Hennessy P (1986a) *Cabinet* p 121 (Oxford: Basil Blackwell).

[38] (1867) *The English constitution* (1963 edn by Crossman R) (London: Fontana).

the agenda for Cabinet discussions, which permitted the Prime Minister to avoid challenges over particular issues by leaving them off the agenda altogether; and thirdly, by controlling the remit and membership of cabinet committees, where particular policies were discussed in more detail.

Crossman argued that collective responsibility had assumed a new meaning by the 1960s. It no longer meant that all Cabinet Ministers were involved in making the decisions which they were obliged to support, but rather that that all Ministers were expected to lend unquestioning support to decisions reached by Cabinet Committees, or a so-called inner Cabinet of senior Ministers, or the Prime Minister. The unanimity rule would thus have undergone a marked shift. If a Minister disagreed with Cabinet policy she would still be expected to either stifle her dissent or resign; she should not however expect to be a full participant in a collective decision-making process.

As we saw above, Michael Heseltine felt this trend had become an established, and (to him) unacceptable feature of the Thatcher cabinets. His resignation was premised, we might say, on his refusal to accept the legitimacy of a Cabinet in which collective decision-making had become entirely a 'dignified' rather than 'efficient' part of the constitution.

Harold Wilson did not invent the committee based form of cabinet decision-making, but did use it more systematically than his predecessors. Nevertheless, Wilson himself disputed the Prime Ministerial government thesis. Writing in 1972, while in opposition, he suggested that 'The Prime Minister's task is to get a consensus of Cabinet or he cannot reasonably ask for loyalty and collective responsibility'.[39]

There are undoubtedly sound justifications for a drift away from a fully collegiate model of Cabinet decision-making. As the government's workload has grown, it has become increasingly implausible to expect all Cabinet members to have the time or expertise to comment usefully on all fields of government activity. One is nevertheless left with the problem of deciding how best to enhance governmental efficiency without concentrating power in too few ministerial hands. The only satisfactory way to gauge the accuracy of Crossman's thesis would be to study the intimacies of Cabinet decision-making over a protracted period. Such a task is beyond the scope of this work;[40] we can however advert briefly to certain important episodes which indicate one can readily find examples which both underpin and undermine Crossman's argument.

There have been perhaps few more important policy decisions made in the post-war era than the 1945–1951 Attlee governments' conclusion that Britain should develop its own atomic weapons capacity. But to talk of this as a decision of the government, or even of the Cabinet, would be quite misleading. Attlee had permitted only a handful of his Cabinet to know about this policy. He recalled some years later that: 'I thought some of them [the Cabinet] were not fit to be trusted with secrets of this kind'.[41] Similarly, James Callaghan preferred to formulate the major strands

39 Quoted in Ellis op cit at p 372.

40 The most accessible and informative guide is perhaps Hennessy (1986a) op cit.

41 Quoted in Hennessy (1986a) op cit p 123.

of economic policy not in Cabinet, but in a small 'Economic Seminar', containing just a handful of Ministers. The role of Cabinet was merely to agree to whatever conclusions the 'Seminar' had reached.

Such dismissive Prime Ministerial treatment of Cabinet colleagues has not been a trait solely of Labour Prime Ministers. A graphic example of the apparently paradoxical way in which the Prime Minister's use of his great power within Cabinet can actually much weaken his position is provided by the notorious 'night of the long knives' in July 1962. As Prime Minister, the Conservative leader Harold Macmillan had cultivated an air of 'unflappability'. The party's electoral appeal was felt to depend largely on public perception that Macmillan could always be relied upon to act in a calm, rational fashion. That perception was shattered in just one day, when Macmillan peremptorily dismissed one third of his Cabinet. Macmillan's initial concern had simply been to replace his Chancellor of the Exchequer, Selwyn Lloyd, who he considered insufficiently interventionist on economic policy issues. However several Conservative defeats in by-elections, coupled with the government's poor standing in public opinion polls, and press rumours of an impending Cabinet reshuffle, led Macmillan to panic rather, and end up sacking seven Ministers, hoping that a new look government would be more electorally appealing.

That a Prime Minister can dismiss so many Ministers in so cursory a fashion cogently illustrates her short term dominance of the Cabinet. Yet, since that Prime Minister may have appointed those Ministers in the first place, their removal casts doubt on the Prime Minister's own competence, for one of her most important tasks is surely to select able colleagues. Macmillan subsequently described the sacked Ministers as 'worn out', and did indeed replace them with much younger colleagues, but his strategy did not attract substantial backbench support. Whether Macmillan could have survived as party leader in the long term after antagonising so large a section of his party, and whether he could have led the Conservatives to victory in another general election, remained unanswered questions, for he resigned as a result of ill health the following year.[42]

There are no legal rules controlling the identity of individuals appointed to ministerial office. Nor does it seem likely that there could be. It seems clear that the Prime Minister's choices are motivated by two factors: maximising her own standing within her party, while simultaneously maximising her party's standing with the electorate. Neither criterion seems even remotely justiciable. We might wonder if the constitution should require a Prime Minister to appoint the most able of her party's members to Ministerial office, but 'ability' is a concept which cannot be objectively defined. There would seem little alternative but to leave evaluation of the Prime Minister's selection and management of her Cabinet to her parliamentary party, and ultimately to the electorate. Both MPs and voters might plausibly be thought to place some pre-emptive limits on the extent to which Prime Ministers can amend conventional understandings of collective responsibility. The difficulty, as Margaret

[42] See generally Horne A (1987) *Macmillan 1957–1986* (London: Macmillan).

Thatcher's tenure of 10 Downing Street eventually revealed, is predicting where those boundaries lie.

Thatcher was often portrayed as placing little faith in the idea of full Cabinet participation in policymaking. Shortly before the 1979 election, she had announced that her government would 'not waste time having any internal arguments'. Her first Cabinet contained many so-called 'wet' Ministers, who were not entirely supportive of her preferred economic policies. To some extent, these Ministers were simply by-passed. Peter Hennessy observes that the Thatcher Cabinet met far less frequently than its post-war predecessors, and also considered far fewer policy documents.[43] A further tactic which the new Prime Minister deployed to control policymaking more tightly was to have Ministers present their initial ideas to her and her personal advisers, rather than to the Cabinet or even to a Cabinet Committee. Furthermore, on those occasions when committees were used, Thatcher had no compunction about 'packing' them with Ministers supporting her viewpoint. This occasionally proved problematic. The decision to withdraw union recognition from GCHQ workers was made by only five Ministers; wider consultation may have identified the constitutional implications that the decision subsequently proved to have.

After the 1983 election, when the Conservative majority increased to over 140 seats, Thatcher 'purged' her Cabinet in a manner almost as draconian as the 'night of the long knives', but secure in the knowledge that she would be antagonising only a limited section of the parliamentary party. By the late 1980s some commentators were suggesting that she had effectively instituted a form of Presidential government.[44] And this supposedly fundamental shift in constitutional arrangements was achieved without any formal legal changes whatsoever. Peter Hennessy concluded his discussion of Thatcher's style of Cabinet government more cautiously:

> 'At worst she has put Cabinet government temporarily on ice. . . . the old model could, and probably will, be restored in the few minutes it takes a new Prime Minister to travel from Buckingham Palace to Downing Street'.[45]

Events were subsequently to prove that the 'old model' had indeed merely been chilled, rather than deep frozen, in the Thatcher years.

. . . AND BACK AGAIN?

At the 1987 general election, the Conservative Party retained a Commons majority of over 100 seats. In such circumstances, one might have expected Thatcher's control of her third government to have become even more personalised in both style and substance. However, while that may indeed have been the Prime Minister's intention,

43 Hennessy (1986a) op cit ch 3.

44 Doherty M (1988) 'Prime Ministerial power and ministerial responsibility in the Thatcher era' *Parliamentary Affairs* 49–67.

45 (1986a) op cit p 122.

her belief that she could amend still further the conventional notion of collective cabinet government was to prove misplaced.

Nigel Lawson's resignation as Chancellor, on the grounds that the Prime Minister was simply ignoring his advice, can be bracketed with Heseltine's earlier suggestion that the Prime Minister was crossing conventional constitutional boundaries. Both resignations threatened the Prime Minister's authority within the Conservative Party, in that they offered figureheads around which dissident backbench opinion might coalesce. However their true significance was subsequently seen to lie in the individual contribution they made to a growing sense of collective unease within the parliamentary party. That unease was given an acute focus by the resignation of Sir Geoffrey Howe as Deputy Prime Minister in 1990, an event which had serious and immediate implications, both for Thatcher herself and the Prime Ministerial government thesis.

Howe resigned because he could no longer accept the Prime Minister's avowedly hostile attitude towards the EC (a matter explored in chapter twelve). In his resignation speech to the Commons, Howe maintained that the Prime Minister had consistently and deliberately undermined the collective decisions which the Cabinet assumed it had reached on EC matters. Howe's account reinforced Michael Heseltine's earlier claims that Thatcher held conventional understandings as to the conduct of Cabinet business in some contempt, and the speech precipitated Heseltine's challenge to Thatcher for leadership of the Conservative Party. That challenge led rapidly to Thatcher's resignation as party leader (and thence as Prime Minister) and her eventual replacement by John Major. As we shall see in subsequent chapters, factors other than her evident disregard for the conventional understandings of Cabinet decision-making processes contributed to Margaret Thatcher's fall from power. But her fate would suggest that her preference for an increasingly Presidential style of government amounted (eventually) to a serious error of political judgment: even the most powerful of Prime Ministers, it seems, must retain the support of senior Ministers.

In reviewing Thatcher's resignation, it is difficult to be sure where the effective political power that removed her actually lay.[46] Was it in the combined resignations of Heseltine, Lawson and Howe? Or with those remaining Cabinet Ministers who intimated to Thatcher that they would resign if she did not? If so, we might plausibly conclude that the convention of collective Cabinet government had merely been dormant during the 1980s, and simply required a sudden jolt to reawaken it. Or did that power lie with the many Conservative MPs who did not vote for Thatcher in the first round of the leadership election? If so, we see a further manifestation of the pre-eminence of party politics within the constitution. Or did the power lie (indirectly) in the electorate, who had indicated in many opinion polls that a Thatcher government could not hope to win another general election, and thereby frightened Conservative MPs in marginal seats into withdrawing support from their Prime Minister?

What is clear, however, is that Thatcher's successor, John Major, did adopt a more

[46] For various perspectives see Brazier R (1991) 'The downfall of Margaret Thatcher' 54 *MLR* 471–491; Alderman and Carter op cit.

collective style of cabinet government.[47] Michael Heseltine's return to Cabinet was one manifestation of this trend, as was Major's apparent concern to ensure that his ministerial team reflected the various factional groupings within his parliamentary party.

Recent history would suggest that Prime Ministerial styles – and the capacity of other Cabinet ministers to influence those styles – are not determined by party political allegiance. Tony Blair's premiership has been characterised by one leading commentator as a 'command and control' approach to governance.[48] Peter Hennessy cites as a particularly cogent illustration of this style the decision taken by Blair, and his Chancellor of the Exchequer, Gordon Brown, to relinquish governmental control of interest rate policy to the Bank of England. This extremely important economic policy decision was taken without any Cabinet discussion at all. Indeed, Hennessy notes, the decision was taken before the first Blair Cabinet had even met.[49] Cabinet meetings in the Blair government have evidently been of far shorter duration that under previous administrations, and they are frequently conducted without the benefit (or perhaps, in the Prime Minister's view, the constraint) of a formal agenda.

Whether Mr Blair's apparent fondness for the authoritarian style of Cabinet government preferred by Margaret Thatcher will lead him to the political fate that ultimately befell her remains to be seen. Yet it would be rash to accept that Thatcher's fall from power demonstrates that conventions are a self-correcting constitutional mechanism, which can be pushed so far, but no further. To reach that conclusion would require consideration of substantially more evidence; evidence which, as sections four and five suggest, undermines such complacent assumptions.

IV. INDIVIDUAL MINISTERIAL RESPONSIBILITY

The second strand of the ministerial responsibility convention is individual ministerial responsibility, which supposedly identifies the situations in which Ministers should resign from government office. Its modern form has two parts. The first addresses the Minister's political or administrative competence; the second her personal morality.

ISSUES OF COMPETENCE

The competence rule originally held Ministers answerable to the Commons for every action undertaken by their departments' civil servants. Ministers took the credit when their officials got things right. Relatedly they took the blame when their staff got things wrong; if the error was sufficiently grave, a Minister would be expected to resign. A corollary of this proposition was that individual civil servants would not face

47 Marshall G (1991) 'The end of Prime Ministerial government?' *Public Law* 1–6.

48 Henessy P (2001) *The Prime Minister* ch 18 (Harmondsworth: Penguin).

49 Henessy P (2001) op cit at pp 480–481.

parliamentary scrutiny or public criticism for their own failures. This is not to say that incompetent civil servants would find their careers unaffected, but that sanctions attached to failure were a managerial matter resolved within the executive, not, as for a Minister, a political matter resolved within Parliament.

In the early 1800s, the idea that a Minister should be personally responsible for everything done in his department was perhaps feasible. But the scale of government has grown so much since 1850 that it has become completely impracticable for a Minister to know everything that is being done by her department's civil servants. So the initial form of this supposed convention has altered. It now seems necessary that a Minister has been personally involved in a particular decision before she must resign.

This redefinition of conventional boundaries began in a series of late nineteenth century episodes,[50] and had hardened sufficiently to merit being described as a rule by the mid-1950s. The resignation of Sir Thomas Dugdale as Minister of Agriculture in 1954 following the Crichel Down controversy is a good illustration. Crichel Down involved a government department's failure to resell land to the family from whom it had been compulsorily purchased for military use just before World War II, in evident breach of assurances to that effect. Dugdale resigned when it became clear he had specific knowledge of his civil servants' activities, but had failed to appreciate the problematic nature of the action being undertaken.

Crichel Down's ramifications went beyond the issue of a Minister's personal culpability.[51] The episode triggered a crisis of confidence in the green light variant of the rule of law which had increasingly structured the government process in the immediate post-war era. The response of the then Conservative government was to promote a wide-ranging 'judicialisation' of the many aspects of the administrative process, entailing more tightly defined legislative rules for executive bodies to follow, the creation of quasi-judicial appeal tribunals for citizens dissatisfied with certain types of government decision, and somewhat easier access to judicial review. The change in emphasis was encapsulated in the Tribunals and Inquiries Act 1958, whose provisions corresponded closely to the theoretical perceptions of the rule of law advanced by analysts such as Harry Jones. Longer term efforts were also made to enhance green light mechanisms of political control: Crossman's select committee initiative has already been mentioned, and another of his innovations is considered further below.

For present purposes, Crichel Down's significance lies in the clear indication that a Minister need not resign in response to the failings of civil servants of which he was not, and could not reasonably be expected to have been aware, irrespective of the gravity of the consequences. This suggests resignation is more likely to be triggered by a failure of policy, rather than implementation, since the former remains more obviously the province of Ministers themselves.

James Callaghan's 1967 resignation as Chancellor from Harold Wilson's second Labour government was clearly precipitated by policy failure, even though the failure

50 See Finer S (1956) 'The individual responsibility of Ministers' *Public Administration* 377–396.

51 Hamson C (1954) 'The real lesson of Crichel Down' *Public Administration* 383–400.

was determined largely by matters beyond his control. The government had struggled for some years to maintain sterling's dollar exchange rate at $2.80. After repeated rumours of devaluation, followed by repeated government denials of any such intention, sterling was devalued. As Chancellor, Callaghan was the chief architect of a manifestly unsuccessful economic strategy. Nevertheless the devaluation arguably owed far more to previous governments' refusal to acknowledge Britain's declining economic status than to Callaghan's errors per se.

A more pertinent, more recent, example is offered by Lord Carrington's resignation as Foreign Secretary following the Argentinean invasion of the Falkland Islands in 1982. Carrington considered he had underestimated the severity of the Argentinean threat, and thought it necessary that somebody accept responsibility for the governmental failure that the invasion betokened.

This redefinition of the convention to require personal knowledge is strengthened by instances when Ministers have not resigned following gross errors by their civil servants. In 1982, for example, a man named Michael Fagan breached security at Buckingham Palace and wandered around unchallenged for hours before having a conversation with the Queen in her bedroom. William Whitelaw, the Home Secretary, was formally 'responsible' for the Metropolitan Police, who provided security at the Palace. Fagan's escapade revealed that security precautions were quite inadequate. Whitelaw's initial instinct was to go, but he was evidently talked out of this by the Prime Minister. Her argument was firstly that no harm had befallen the Queen and, secondly, the Home Secretary could not be expected personally to supervise the minutiae of the Metropolitan Police's activities.

James Prior, Secretary of State for Northern Ireland, invoked a similar argument when 38 IRA prisoners broke out of the Maze prison in 1983. Prior felt that convention would require his resignation only if the escape had resulted from a policy initiative he had taken – for example if he had given instructions to relax prison security measures. When an inquiry concluded that the escape resulted from management errors made by the prison governor, Prior decided not to resign. He sacked the prison governor instead.

The experience of one of Whitelaw's successors as Home Secretary, Kenneth Baker, suggests a Minister need not resign over such errors even when they happen with disquieting frequency. Mr Baker endured an accident-prone tenure at the Home Office. The most serious incident occurred in 1991, when several IRA prisoners escaped from Brixton prison, using a gun which had been smuggled into the gaol. The Chief Inspector of Prisons had reported some months earlier that security at Brixton was inadequate for high-risk prisoners. However the Home Office had neither stopped using Brixton for such detainees, nor improved its security facilities. One might have assumed this was a high level policy matter within the Home Secretary's personal sphere of responsibility. However, Mr Baker contended that responsibility lay with the prison governor.

Baker subsequently resigned from the government when offered the less important post of Welsh Secretary in 1992. But his failings in office continued to haunt him.

In 1993, he achieved the unenviable distinction of being held by the House of Lords in *M v Home Office*[52] to have committed contempt of court by authorising the expulsion of a political refugee in defiance of a court order. We can only speculate as to whether Baker would have seen this as a resigning matter.[53] It seems possible that he would have argued that he was just following the advice of his departmental lawyers. If so, it becomes difficult to conceive of any decision-making error which would require a Minister's resignation.

The competence limb of the convention now seems to be in a fluid, or perhaps fragile, state of health. It may however be rash to conclude that it has now evolved to the point where only the most calamitous incompetence will necessitate resignation. We should perhaps focus our attention not simply on the scale of the mistake, but also on the strength or weakness of the Minister's position within the governing party. This is a point to which we will return.

ERRORS OF JUDGEMENT

The sanction of resignation seems to attach more firmly to Ministers making severe errors of judgement rather than policy or administrative mistakes. In recent times, the Westland Affair provides a graphic example of this convention. The then Trade Secretary, Leon Brittan, had authorised the leaking of a letter from the Solicitor-General criticising the constitutional propriety of Michael Heseltine's behaviour. This leak breached another convention – that Law Officers' advice to Ministers should remain confidential within the government. Although the Cabinet initially disclaimed knowledge of the leak's source, the Solicitor-General's threat to resign if a leak inquiry was not conducted led to the revelation that Brittan had condoned a decision by his Press Officer to release the letter. Facing such evidence, Brittan had no option but to resign, albeit amid suspicions that his departure was intended to conceal the Prime Minister's reputed approval of the leak.[54]

Westland provided yet another illustration of ministerial responsibility when the Prime Minister, Margaret Thatcher, was subsequently compelled to defend her own role in the affair before the Commons in an emergency debate. The potential importance of debate in the House as a mechanism to control executive behaviour is revealed by Thatcher's own belief that a poor performance might result in her own resignation that evening. But an inept speech by Neil Kinnock, then Leader of the Opposition, enabled the Prime Minister successfully both to distance herself from the Westland intrigues and to downplay their constitutional importance.[55]

52 [1993] 3 All ER 537, HL.

53 He had declined to do so when held in contempt by the Court of Appeal; see Marshall G (1992) 'Ministerial responsibility, the Home Office, and Mr Baker' *Public Law* 7–12.

54 Brittan's case also illustrates that resignation even on the grounds of gross personal culpability need not end a Minister's political career. Shortly after resigning, Brittan was appointed as an EEC Commissioner, a post (as we shall see in chapter eleven) of considerable political importance.

55 See Young H (1991) *One of us* pp 454–457 (London: Pan): Clark op cit pp 132–135.

Westland is an unusually important episode in modern constitutional history. Other recent resignations over errors of judgement have been more mundane. Nicholas Ridley, for example, resigned as Secretary of State for Trade and Industry in 1990 after expressing hostile and xenophobic attitudes towards Germany in a press interview. Such sentiments were considered quite inappropriate for a Minister, given the closeness of Anglo-German relations within both the EEC and NATO. Similarly, in 1988, Edwina Currie, a junior Minister, left the government after alleging that almost all UK egg production was infected by salmonella. The statement's accuracy was questionable. Its devastating, if temporary effect on British egg producers was not. Protracted vilification from the farming industry, and repeated media questioning of her abilities, persuaded Mrs Currie to resign. The episode need not have ended her ministerial career. She was invited to join the second Major administration, but declined to do so.

The Blair government did not escape such difficulties. Peter Mandelson, the Secretary of State for Trade and Industry, and Geoffrey Robinson, the Paymaster-General, both resigned from the government in 1999 when it transpired that Robinson had lent Mandelson some £370,000 to buy a house. While it was questionable if the feeble post-Nolan requirements on MPs' disclosure of financial interests was breached here, concealing the loan was manifestly an error of judgement on both men's part, given that the Department of Trade was conducting investigations into the running of companies with which Robinson was closely involved. Mandelson's 'punishment' was however a light one. He returned to the Cabinet less than a year later. Somewhat bizarrely, Mandelson was subsequently compelled by prime ministerial and backbench pressure to resign from the Cabinet a second time, following accusations that he had sought to assist the Indian billionaire Hinduja brothers to gain British citizenship in return for them making a substantial contribution to the government's ill-fated Millennium Dome project.

It is difficult to extract a 'rule' (qua a predictable, binding behavioural code) from these or any other examples of resignation. Finer's celebrated study of the issue suggested party political expediency rather than moral principle was the critical factor in determining both whether a Minister should resign and her subsequent fate.[56] It certainly appears that subsequent resignations have been intended to have symbolic rather than practical effects. Callaghan's aforementioned resignation as Chancellor in 1967 was in effect a sideways transfer, for he simply swapped offices with the Home Secretary, Roy Jenkins. One thus gains the impression that the reason for the resignation was an attempt to wipe the government's economic slate clean before the next general election. Such an interpretation reinforces Finer's earlier (1956) suggestion that a minister's errors will not invariably precipitate resignation unless his/her conduct has alienated a substantial body of opinion within his own party.

But it is not just professional or political misjudgment that can bring the convention of individual ministerial responsibility into play. Questions as to moral or

[56] (1956) op cit.

personal conduct have also been a regular recent source of ministerial resignations. In these circumstances, questions of party solidarity seem less important.

ISSUES OF MORALITY

Few resignations have generated as much public curiosity as John Profumo's in 1963. Profumo, Minister of War in Macmillan's government, had an extra-marital affair with a call girl, Christine Keeler. The liaison had obvious security implications, since Ms Keeler was simultaneously sleeping with a Russian Naval Attache. The affair itself may have been enough to have forced Profumo's departure from office. To choose a mistress who was also a lover of an enemy agent would presumably also have amounted to a gross error of judgement. But Profumo's greatest sin was to lie to the Commons when Richard Crossman raised the matter in the house. When the truth was subsequently revealed, Profumo had no choice but to resign. Macmillan himself thought the episode sufficiently grave to threaten the government's continued existence. In the event, it did not directly do so, but it seems likely the episode added further weight to incidents such as 'the little local difficulty' and the 'night of the long knives' which had already undermined the Conservatives' electoral appeal – Harold Wilson's Labour Party subsequently won the 1964 general election.

The resignations of Lord Lambton and Earl Jellicoe in 1973 from Edward Heath's government also had salacious and security-related overtones. Both peers had been conducting relationships with prostitutes, and Lambton was also reputed to have been using illegal drugs. Neither Minister returned to the government. But sexual indiscretion need not always end a ministerial career. Cecil Parkinson resigned from the Cabinet in 1983 when it was disclosed that he had an affair with Sara Keays, who eventually bore his child. Parkinson's behaviour was considered the more reprehensible as he had allegedly promised Keays he would leave his wife, a promise on which he reneged. However after some years on the backbenches, Parkinson re-entered the Cabinet in 1987.

It is too soon to conclude that the morality rule now demands only that Ministers interrupt rather than abandon their career, although the Mellor and Yeo resignations suggest immediacy in resigning is a fast disappearing element of the convention. Mellor, then a married man with several young children, served in John Major's Cabinet. He attracted voluminous media publicity in 1992 following his affair with a young actress. There was no suggestion of any threat to national security. The episode did however cast doubt on his fitness for office, in the sense both of his personal integrity (or lack thereof) and allegations that he felt too 'knackered' to devote as much energy as previously to government responsibilities. Tim Yeo, a junior environment Minister, suffered similarly extensive and critical publicity over an affair with a young Conservative Party worker, by whom he fathered an illegitimate child.[57]

[57] See Brazier R (1994) 'It is a constitutional issue: fitness for Ministerial office in the 1990s' *Public Law* 431–451.

Both Ministers, evidently with Prime Ministerial support, clung to office for several months hoping to ride out the media storm which engulfed them. Mellor decided to resign only when his adultery and apparent exhaustion were coupled with the revelation that he had accepted gifts from a prominent associate of the Palestine Liberation Organisation. Yeo did not resign until his local party members made it clear that they wished him to do so.

Most 'moral' resignations are triggered by the sexual 'misbehaviour' of male ministers. The weight of evidence suggests there is a respected convention that such activities should lead to resignation, albeit only temporarily. The reason behind the rule is less clear, given that Britain's contemporary social mores indicate that adultery is an activity in which many citizens engage. One suggestion would be that Ministers should set a shining moral example, and are unfit for office if they cannot meet such exacting standards. Another argument would be that resignation is a 'punishment' not for sexual immorality per se, but for the hypocrisy of participating in activities of which the government supposedly disapproves. This contention is especially persuasive in respect of Parkinson, Mellor, and Yeo; all broke their marriage vows while members of Conservative administrations which laid great stress on 'traditional' family values.

Whether a Minister's personal life compromises his discharge of public duties is a large question. An answer is more easily found when one asks if individual ministerial responsibility could assume a legal basis. Designating behaviour as grossly immoral, or quite immoral, or not really immoral at all, is a highly value laden decision. One might assume that when opposition MPs express outrage at a Minister's misbehaviour they are more concerned with embarrassing the government than protecting the nation's moral fibre. The obvious political delicacy of these questions of ministerial morality provides a strong argument against having this aspect of the government process overseen by legal rules. It would be extremely contentious for a judge to say that a Minister was unfit for office because of the way he conducts his personal life.

That point seems equally applicable to questions of ministerial competence or misjudgement. There are no obvious criteria against which a court could measure a Minister's incompetence to decide if it was sufficiently grave to merit dismissal. Nor could a judge reach that conclusion without being accused of taking sides in what will almost invariably be a party political dispute.

This might indicate we could begin to construct some definition of conventions in terms of those parts of the constitution with which the courts could not interfere without jeopardising their supposedly impartial political status. This pushes us towards a suggestion that 'non-justiciability' may be an essential ingredient of conventional status. If a rule is important to the operation of the government process, and can be framed in a justiciable manner, the diluted Diceyan version of the rule of law to which the constitution adheres would suggest it should be given legal form. The role of the courts in promoting that process has been adverted to above in the *Crossman Diaries* case, and we will shortly pursue this argument in greater depth. Before doing so, however, we focus once again on the relationship between conventions and Acts of Parliament.

REFORMING THE EXECUTIVE: 1 – THE PARLIAMENTARY COMMISSIONER FOR ADMINISTRATION

Crichel Down's institutional fall out continued well into the 1960s. We have already noted Richard Crossman's unsuccessful select committee initiative. His reform plans bore more immediate fruit in the creation of the Parliamentary Commissioner for Administration (PCA), colloquially known as the 'Ombudsman'.

The PCA was established by the Parliamentary Commissioner Act 1967. His role can be seen as plugging various holes in the systems of both Parliamentary and judicial supervision of government activities. Section 5 empowered the PCA to investigate any activity of (most) government departments about which he had received a complaint from a member of the public. To emphasise that the PCA was complementing rather than replacing the Commons' own supervisory role, she was only permitted to investigate matters referred to her by an MP. Similarly, to emphasise that the PCA was complementing rather than replacing the supervisory role of the courts, the Act stressed that the PCA could not generally investigate complaints which could be pursued through legal action. The PCA operates with limited resources, but was granted (per s 8) extensive powers to examine government documents and require testimony from Ministers and civil servants. Unlike the courts, the PCA could not impose a remedy on an erring department, but it was widely assumed that governments would comply voluntarily with his suggestions. The PCA's 'independence' is protected in the same way as that of a High Court judge. While she is appointed by the Prime Minister, she holds office during 'good behaviour'; dismissal can only be effected by addresses from both Houses.

The evil to which the PCA's energies were directed was 'maladministration'. This concept has never been precisely defined, either in statute or litigation. The so-called 'Crossman catalogue', offered by Richard Crossman during the Bill's passage remains the primary reference point. This embraced 'bias, neglect, inattention, delay, incompetence, ineptitude, perversity, turpitude and arbitrariness'. It may be, post-*Pepper v Hart*, that Crossman's catalogue now enjoys rather more authoritative legal status than formerly. But it seems we are still reduced to defining maladministration in negative terms; it reaches those aspects of the administrative process which while unsatisfactory, are not unlawful, and so cannot be the subject of an action for judicial review or a claim in tort or contract against the government body concerned.

A detailed assessment of the Ombudsman's (evidently successful and expanding) role in the past 30 years is more appropriately undertaken within a study of administrative rather than constitutional law, and is not attempted here. Our primary concern is her impact on traditional understandings of individual ministerial responsibility, a point best pursued by considering one of her earliest investigations.

Sachsenhausen

The Sachsenhausen controversy arose from an agreement negotiated between the British and German governments in 1964, under which Germany paid Britain £1m to distribute to war-time victims of Nazi persecution.[58] The agreement was an exercise of the prerogative. Foreign Office civil servants administered the funds through prerogative powers. The compensation rules were eminently justiciable. Claimants qualified if they had been detained in 'a concentration camp'; the amount received was a multiple of the time spent in detention. The scheme was however established prior to *Lain*, and there seemed no contemporaneous expectation that decisions would attract full judicial review.

The claims of several servicemen detained in premises adjacent to the Sachsenhausen concentration camp were rejected by Foreign Office officials who decided they had been ordinary prisoners of war, whose maltreatment was not covered by the scheme. Two successive junior Foreign Office Ministers reviewed the claims, as did the Foreign Secretary, George Brown. All confirmed the civil servants' decision.

The PCA's subsequent investigation identified serious flaws in the civil servants' decision-making procedures, and suggested that the decision was substantively indefensible. It is not entirely clear if Ministers personally scrutinised the evidence de novo, or had simply relied on their official's advice. In either event, their decisions merely reiterated the original maladministration, and the PCA recommended that the servicemen be compensated in accordance with the scheme's criteria.

In a subsequent Commons speech, George Brown accepted the PCA's decision, announcing that compensation would be paid. However, he then criticised both the PCA's findings in the Sachsenhausen case itself, and also what he regarded as a more substantial question of constitutional principle:

> 'We will breach a very serious constitutional position if we start holding officials responsible for things that are done wrong. . . . If things are wrongly done, then they are wrongly done by Ministers. . . . It is Ministers who must be attacked, not officials'.[59]

Brown was correct in concluding that the creation of the PCA had forced a redefinition of the convention of individual ministerial responsibility. The PCA's extensive investigatory and reporting powers did raise the possibility that the individual failings of civil servants would be brought into both the parliamentary and public domain, rather than being dealt with as an internal management matter. One might think, as matter of policy, that this could be undesirable both because 'accused' civil servants could not defend themselves against such attack, and also because it raised the possibility that Ministers would evade personal responsibility by hiding behind an impartial report which laid blame at a civil servant's feet.

The constitutional difficulty raised by Brown's speech was that those issues of

[58] Information in the following paragraphs is drawn from Fry G (1970) 'The Sachsenhausen concentration camp case and the convention of ministerial responsibility' *Public Law* 336–357.

[59] *HCD* 5 February 1968 c 123.

policy had already been settled. His speech may therefore itself be seen as a breach of the unanimity rule. He had been a member of the Cabinet which presented the 1967 Act to Parliament. Had he respected conventional principles, he would presumably have been compelled either to resign from the Cabinet before publicly criticising its policy, or kept his disquiet as a matter only for the ears of his Cabinet colleagues. Brown had prefaced his remarks by saying he spoke in a personal rather than Cabinet capacity, but this contention seems even less satisfactory than other manifestations of the 'suspension' principle to which we have already referred. Unanimity cannot be a conventional rule if Ministers may opt in and out of it whenever they wish.

One cannot trace a direct link between Ministers' apparently increasing insulation against resignation as the price for serious error and the expanding role of the PCA. The fact nevertheless remains that the present political climate seemingly makes it acceptable for Ministers such as Prior and Baker to maintain that the chain of responsibility for even very grave mistakes ends with a civil servant, not a politician. The PCA, however, was but a minor innovation compared to the restructuring of the civil service undertaken since the mid-1980s.

REFORMING THE EXECUTIVE: 2 – 'NEXT STEPS' AND PRIVATISATION

The 'Next Steps' reforms initiated by the third Thatcher government divided some parts of the Civil Service into separate 'policy formulating' and 'policy implementation' organisations. While policy formulation remains the province of Ministers and civil servants within traditional government departments, implementation has been entrusted to so-called 'executive agencies'.

Under the new system, the department drafts a 'framework document' which outlines the policies which the agency should apply. The agency thereafter proposes 'performance targets', subject to ministerial approval, which it will seek to meet each year. Agencies are headed by 'Chief Executives', drawn both from government and private sector organisations. Similar reforms had been proposed by Harold Wilson's government in 1968, but had not been adopted. The third Thatcher government implemented the changes with some speed. Some fifty agencies had been established by 1992, including the Royal Mint, the employment service, and the prisons service.

The agencies' relationship with their supervising department appears to be 'quasi-contractual'.[60] This has considerable implications for traditional concepts of individual ministerial responsibility, for it raises the possibility that Ministers may 'contract out' of responsibility for governmental errors which would previously have been made within their departments. The fear that the Next Steps structure would produce a situation in which Ministers might disclaim their accountability to Parliament for agency errors was intensified in late 1994 by a series of failures in prison security.

60 Oliver (1991) op cit p 65. On the reforms more generally see Oliver (1991) op cit pp 64–70; Woodhouse op cit chs 11–12.

An attempted escape by IRA prisoners was rapidly followed by the discovery of live ammunition in one jail, and explosives in another. At the same time, national newspapers ran stories alleging that the government had authorised a marked relaxation of security measures in respect of some IRA and other prisoners. Calls were made, both in the press and from opposition parties, for the resignation of Michael Howard, the Home Secretary.

These events raised the difficult question of identifying at which managerial point within a Next Steps agency a Minister's influence becomes sufficiently acute to make him responsible for the agency's errors. It seems possible that a Minister's responsibility would extend to the contents of the framework document, to the objectives of the annual performance agreements, and the choice of the agency's Chief Executive: imposing an absurd framework, setting ludicrous targets, or appointing a manifestly incompetent Chief Executive would presumably be a personal ministerial decision.

There seems little doubt that the Next Steps initiative has further weakened the already enfeebled convention that a Minister accepts responsibility for a civil servant's failings. Nor has that decline in political accountability been accompanied by an increase in legal regulation. The Major governments produced various 'Citizen's Charters', which set targets for government agencies to meet, in terms of such matters as the speed, accuracy and courtesy with which they address citizen's enquiries or concerns. The charters might be seen as reinforcing the role of the PCA, in so far as they are directed at various types of maladministration. They are not legislative instruments however, and there has thus far been no indication that either successive government or the courts regard them as creating common law rights.[61] The Blair government appeared enthusiastically to support what has now come to be known as 'the new public management'. The Citizen's Charter was promptly renamed 'Service First' in 1998, and a White Paper published in 1999 indicated that there would be no reversal of the trends of the past ten years.[62] Despite its significant impact on the relationship between the government and the Commons, the Next Steps initiative has less profound implications for ministerial responsibility than the extensive programme of 'privatisation' of government functions that has been carried out by the Thatcher and Major administrations.

Privatisation

The first Thatcher administration subscribed enthusiastically to the model of government advocated by Hayek's *Road to Serfdom*, and just as previous Labour governments had used their de facto control of Parliament's sovereignty to 'nationalise' private industries, so the first Thatcher government used its Commons majority to return them to the private sector. The Thatcher administrations regarded activities such as shipbuilding, and car and aerospace manufacturing as purely economic in nature, and thus no legitimate part of the government's responsibilities. Similarly,

61 Drewry G (1993) 'Mr Major's Charter: empowering the consumer' *Public Law* 248–256.

62 See Drewry G (2000) 'The new public management', in Jowell J and Oliver D eds (4th edn, 2000) *The changing constitution* (Oxford: Clarendon Press).

it was thought that services such as the telephone system, the railways, and gas, electricity, and water provision were better run as profit-making private businesses rather than some form of public sector social services.

In addition, the Thatcher and Major governments also believed that more overtly 'governmental' services should also be managed by private sector companies. Unlike the Next Steps reforms, privatisation does not dilute Commons control over service management, but rather removes it altogether. In privatising former public services, the government effectively abolishes ministerial responsibility for matters which may have a significant impact on citizens' lives and welfare. If we regard the constitution as being concerned essentially with structuring both the substance and the processes of the relationship between a country's government and its citizens, it seems that a major part of the constitution has undergone substantial reform in the past 15 years. This too is an aspect of governmental reform which the Blair governments have shown no inclination to reverse. We will return to a further, more important aspect of institutional constitutional amendment in chapter eleven. For the present, to conclude our analysis of conventions, we return to the question of the relationship between convention, statute and the common law – and find that it may be less straightforward than we might have thought.

V. CAN CONVENTIONS BECOME LAWS? 2: PATRIATING THE CANADIAN CONSTITUTION

One can only speculate whether Kerr's intervention in the Australian controversy would have been regarded as more legitimate if the conventional rules surrounding the Queen's prerogative had been placed on a statutory basis which explicitly authorised their use in circumstances of budgetary deadlock. It is possible that in such a hypothetical situation, domestic disquiet over the 'Queen's' role would have triggered a change in the relevant laws. It is unlikely that merely attaching a legal label to the Governor-General's reasoning could so dilute its politically contentious substance as to make it acceptable to Australian parliamentary and public opinion. The episode suggests Australian 'consent' to the Queen's constitutional role was a fiction – existing only if her powers were not used.

Yet in the longer term, non-use of such powers may have the same delegitimising effect. As chapter seven suggested in discussing the Lords' disinclination to invoke its delaying powers under the Parliament Act 1949, there may be areas of constitutional practice in which conventional reluctance to deploy legal authority eventually leads to the law shedding its political legitimacy. This chapter indicates that conventions might plausibly be seen as a melting pot in which differing concentrations of legal and political ingredients are constantly mixed. If so, we might ask if a diametrically opposite process to delegitimisation could occur? Might it ever be possible for conventions to have been respected for so long, become so precisely defined, and be so important, that they could 'crystallise' into laws?

One obvious way to give conventions legal effect is to enact them as statutes. The Parliament Acts are themselves a clear illustration of that process. A more radical proposition is that the courts can achieve that effect through the common law. *Crossman Diaries* suggests the courts can de facto do so by finding that the common law 'coincidentally' mirrors conventional understandings. This is not the same however, either in symbolic or practical terms, as de jure acknowledgement of crystallisation. Events in the early 1980s seemingly offered an opportunity for that constitutional development to occur.

PATRIATING THE CANADIAN CONSTITUTION

The country of Canada, as a legal entity, was created by the UK Parliament's British North America Act 1867. The Act gave Canada a federal structure, which, reflecting the USA's system, granted some powers to the federal (central) government, and others to the (now) ten provincial governments. However, while the USA's constitution could be amended by its 'people', the British North America Act required Canada to ask Westminster to enact amending legislation. In the 1931 Statute of Westminster, the UK Parliament recognised that several of its former colonies had de facto achieved the status of independent nations. Section 4 – which has already been quoted in chapter two in relation to the events leading up to the litigation in *Harris v Donges*[63] – provided:

> 'No Act of Parliament of the United Kingdom passed after the commencement of this Act shall extend . . . to a Dominion as part of the law of that Dominion unless it is expressly declared in that Act that that Dominion has requested, and consented, to the enactment thereof'.

Section 4's political consequence seemed to be that Parliament had sought to bind its successors never to legislate on Canadian issues unless requested to do so by Canada. That consequence would of course be a legal impossibility if one adhered to orthodox notions of parliamentary sovereignty.[64] The 1931 Act also permitted Canada to amend most aspects of the Canadian constitution through domestic procedures. But Canada was still obliged to place a Bill before the UK Parliament to amend the balance of power between the federal and provincial governments.

However, the Act did not specify what was meant by 'Canada'. Was this just the Federal Parliament, or the Federal government, or some or all of the Provinces as well,

[63] See pp 41–43 above.

[64] As a matter of Canadian constitutional law however, one may safely assume that Canadian courts would not obey a subsequent British statute purporting to restore Parliament's previous authority. Nor, one assumes, would Parliament ever legislate in such a way. This 'transfer of sovereignty' to Canada was the source of Lord Sankey's oft-quoted dictum in *British Coal Corpn v R* [1935] AC 500 at 520, PC: 'It is doubtless true that the power of the [UK] Parliament to pass on its own initiative any legislation that it thought fit extending to Canada remains in theory unimpaired. . . . But that is theory and bears no relation to realities'.

and/or the country's various racial and ethnic sub-groups. Nor did the Act say if there were circumstances in which the British Parliament might refuse to enact a measure passed from 'Canada'. During the next 50 years, two conventions filled these legal gaps in the Canadian and UK constitutions. The first was that the Canadian government would not send a Bill to Britain which altered the federal/provincial division of power unless it enjoyed the support of all Provinces. The second was that the British Parliament would always enact Bills sent by the Canadian Federal government. The conventions arose (to adopt Asquith's typology) through 'tradition', 'unbroken practice' (several amendments had been effected in this way) and a lengthy passage of time (some 50 years). Their force was further strengthened by codification in a federal government white paper published in the 1960s.

The reasons for the conventions are readily apparent. The first ensures that the federal nature of Canadian government was safeguarded against unilateral amendment by the central legislature, or factional alteration by a majority or even minority of provincial governments. The particular form of federalism provided for by the allocation of powers between the national government and the provinces, in other words, sat atop Canada's hierarchy of constitutional principles. The second acknowledges that 'Canada' had achieved sufficient economic and political maturity to wield de facto, if not de jure, control of its own constitutional destiny.

In the late 1970s, Pierre Trudeau's Federal government wished to 'patriate' the Canadian constitution – to make all amendments a matter solely of domestic law. The patriation Bill also contained proposals significantly to amend federal/provincial relations. The Bill provoked considerable controversy in Canada; its contents had been supported by only two provincial governments. The Bill's opponents pursued two strategies to prevent its passage. The first attempted to convince the British Houses of Parliament that the Bill had not been sent by 'Canada', and should therefore not be enacted. The second involved litigation before the Canadian Supreme Court to establish firstly that the Canadian constitution recognised a convention that demanded unanimous provincial consent before the Bill could be sent to Westminster; and secondly that the Canadian courts could give that convention legal effect.

The opinion of the British House of Commons

The Canadian crisis presented Mr St John Stevas' newly invigorated Commons Select Committee system with an opportunity to engage in a non-partisan investigation of constitutional principle and practice. The first Thatcher government had indicated that it had no power to look behind a Bill sent from the Canadian government to examine the basis of consent which the measure had attracted. Any such Bill, would, per the second aforementioned convention, be introduced into Parliament. But as we have already established, there is no legal mechanism through which the three constituent parts of Parliament can be compelled to approve a Bill.[65] The question the Select Committee addressed was whether the Commons was morally or politically

65 Although the Lords' objections could be by-passed by use of the Parliament Act 1949.

obliged simply to approve any Canadian Bill, or whether it should satisfy itself that the first of the aforementioned conventions (that the Bill enjoyed unanimous provincial support) had been satisfied. After taking evidence from many expert academic and political sources, the Committee produced a report rejecting the Trudeau government's presumption that Parliament should unquestioningly enact any Canadian Bill.[66] The committee suggested that the Commons was under no conventional obligation to approve a Bill enjoying so little provincial support. But nor need it withhold approval until unanimous support was obtained. Rather, it concluded:

> 'all Canadians (and thus the governments of the provinces too) have, and always have had, a right to expect the UK Parliament to exercise its amending powers in a manner consistent with the federal nature of the Canadian constitutional system . . .'.[67]

This expectation could be met if Parliament required Canadian Bills to enjoy a 'substantial' degree of provincial consent. The committee proposed a complex formula, relating to geographical location and population patterns to determine if substantial consent had been achieved. Without such consent, Parliament could properly refuse to enact a Canadian Bill.

The select committee report nevertheless left several important questions unanswered. For example, if the two houses approved the Bill, would British courts override traditional understandings as to parliamentary privilege and Article 9 of the Bill of Rights and prevent the Bill being sent for the Royal Assent in a manner reminiscent of the *Trethowan* scenario?[68] Equally fascinating was the question of whether, if the British courts refused to intervene, the Queen would breach the convention of acting on her ministers' advice and withhold her assent. Or, assuming assent was given, would a British court disregard the enrolled Bill rule and refuse to apply the statute? No doubt to the regret of constitutional lawyers, most of these questions never required a concrete answer. The eventual solution to Canada's difficulties was provided by its own Supreme Court.

The judgment of the Canadian Supreme Court

In *A-G of Manitoba v A-G of Canada*[69] the Canadian Supreme Court confirmed that there was a convention, established by years of practice and acknowledged by former federal governments, that the British Parliament should only be sent Bills supported by a substantial number of provinces. Two out of ten was not substantial. Consequently the federal government was breaching this constitutional convention. The reason for the convention was to ensure that 'Canada' retained its distinctively federal system of government.

[66] House of Commons Foreign Affairs Committee (1981) *British North America Acts: the role of Parliament* (London: HMSO).

[67] House of Commons Foreign Affairs Committee (1981) op cit at para 103.

[68] See pp 39–40 above.

[69] [1981] 1 SCR 753, sub nom *Reference re Amendment of Constitution of Canada (Nos 1, 2, 3)* 125 DLR (3d) 1. For other critiques from a British perspective see Turpin (1990) op cit pp 102–115; Allan T (1986) 'Law, convention, prerogative: reflections prompted by the Canadian constitutional case' *Cambridge LJ* 305–320.

For two dissentient judges, Martland and Ritchie JJ, the principle of federalism was an 'ultimate political fact' which demanded judicial obedience. The requirement of provincial consent to reform was so vital an element of Canada's constitutional order that it had assumed justiciable status – it had crystallised into law. But more than that, it had become a law possessing higher status than federal legislation.

If transposed to the British context, the implications of the dissenting judgments are revolutionary. Even the most imaginative interpretation of *Crossman Diaries* would maintain only that a convention could crystallise into a common law rule. That process presents no threat to parliamentary sovereignty, for common law rules can be reversed by statute. Rather, the Martland/Ritchie argument would lead us to conclude that some conventions might assume supra-statutory status; *Dr Bonham's Case* would again become a valid constitutional principle, and the extent of Parliament's supremacy would be unclear. That is of course little more than wild speculation. The argument operates at three steps removed from domestic law, since firstly the British constitution is not (as we shall see in chapter ten) a federal structure; secondly, the judgments of another nation's courts have no binding force in British law; and thirdly, the Canadian Supreme Court majority produced a more orthodox decision.

Having recognised a convention of substantial provincial consent, the majority concluded that while a convention could be admissible as evidence in helping judges decide the correct legal response to a particular problem, it could not become a law, no matter how long it had been respected and no matter how important a principle it embodied. Conventions were not justiciable, and could not become so. 'Crystallisation' was a figment of overactive legal imaginations. The Supreme Court could not stop the Trudeau government sending the Bill to Britain.

But by laying such stress on the importance of the convention of substantial provincial consent, the Supreme Court completely undermined the legitimacy of the federal government's efforts to ignore the Provinces. It was not possible as a matter of morality or political practicality for the government to go ahead. The initial Bill was therefore withdrawn, and the Trudeau government re-opened negotiations with the Provinces in order to produce a conventionally legitimate patriation proposal. A Bill was eventually produced which attracted the support of nine Provinces. This Bill was subsequently sent to the Westminster Parliament, where it was enacted as the Canada Act 1982.

Manuel v A-G

The amendment saga had not however fully run its course. Thus far, the dispute as to the meaning of 'Canada' had centred on the federal/provincial relationship. The plaintiffs in *Manuel v A-G*[70] were native Canadian Indians, who maintained their respective tribes were as much a part of 'Canada' as the provincial governments, and that therefore any Bill affecting their constitutional status (as the revised Trudeau Bill did) had not been sent by 'Canada' unless the federal government had secured tribal

[70] [1983] Ch 77, CA.

consent. They thus launched an action in the British courts seeking a declaration that the Canada Act 1982 was ultra vires Parliament's legal powers.

In the High Court, Megarry VC (with admirable understatement) characterised the plaintiff's case as 'bold in the extreme', since it patently rejected the enrolled Bill rule confirmed in *Wauchope* and *Pickin*. The plaintiff's counsel suggested the rule applied only to domestic legislation, and not to statutes enacted as a consequence of the political independence granted to British colonies by the Statute of Westminster. In effect, he contended that such statutes were secondary legislation, their vires set by the 1931 Act.[71] Megarry VC saw no scope for constructing any such hierarchy of statutes. The Canada Act 1982 was an Act of Parliament like any other: 'sitting as a judge in an English court I owe full and dutiful obedience to that Act'.[72] The enrolled Bill rule completely answered the plaintiff's claim.

Slade LJ's Court of Appeal judgment was more ingenious, albeit reaching the same end. Slade LJ observed that s 4 of the 1931 Act did not require that Canada consented 'in fact' to a Bill being sent to Westminster, but merely that such consent was explicitly referred to (as indeed it was in the 1982 Act) in any subsequent British legislation. What s 4 meant in Canadian law was a matter for the Canadian judiciary, but the identity of 'Canada' was not a matter for a British court to pursue; its concern was only with the statute's text:

> 'This court would run counter to all principles of statutory interpretation if it were to purport to vary or supplement the terms of this stated condition by reference to some supposed convention, which . . . is not incorporated in the body of the statute'.[73]

The Court thereby avoided the key question of whether the 1931 Act could function as a 'higher form of law' than subsequent 'statutes' affecting the law of former Dominions. We can only speculate as to how a British court would have viewed an 'Act' which seemed to alter Canadian law but did not contain any reference to Canadian consent to its terms. The Diceyan view would be that any such reference is unnecessary – for the courts to demand it would amount to recognition of 'manner and form' entrenchment as a valid principle of British constitutional law, and thereby create a new 'ultimate political fact'. The whole basis of the constitution would then be undermined; for if we accept one statute is 'special' because of the political substance of its subject matter, there is no logical barrier to prevent other 'special' statutes emerging, and indeed for different statutes to enjoy different degrees of 'specialness' according to the enacting Parliaments' and interpreting courts' perceptions of their political importance. As a political or moral principle, such a 'revolution' may be no bad thing, and we will further consider its merits in chapter thirteen: yet as a matter of orthodox legal theory, it would seem unachievable. But the question of whether constitutional lawyers should regard legal theory as more important than

[71] As we saw in chapter six, such an argument has also been made in respect of 'legislation' passed under the Parliament Acts. Here however one would have four (Commons, Lords, Monarch and 'Canada') rather than two (Commons and Monarch) part 'Parliament'.

[72] [1983] Ch 77 at 87, CA.

[73] [1983] Ch 77 at 107, CA.

political practice is one which we might consider once more in the final section of this chapter.

VI. FROM MINISTERIAL RESPONSIBILITY TO MINISTERIAL ACCOUNTABILITY? THE MATRIX-CHURCHILL CONTROVERSY

The roots of the Matrix-Churchill controversy date back to 1984, during the war between Iran and Iraq.[74] In response to United Nations restrictions on the supply of arms to both countries, the second Thatcher government announced through a written answer to a Commons question that it would not issue the requisite licence approving the export to either country of any military equipment which might prolong or exacerbate the war. In 1988, at the end of the war, three junior Ministers (Lord Trefgarne in the Ministry of Defence, Alan Clark at the Department of Trade, and William Waldegrave at the Foreign Office), decided to change the policy, adopting a far less restrictive approach to Iraq. It is scarcely credible to believe that this was done without Cabinet approval. The restrictive policy was seen to have several disadvantages: firstly, it might reduce profits and employment in the British arms industry; and secondly it might compromise Britain's capacity to exercise political influence on middle east politics. No member of the government thought it appropriate to inform the Commons of this change in policy. Nor was the change revealed when John Major replaced Thatcher as Prime Minister. It seems unlikely that the government's tame majority in the house would have objected to the change in policy when it was made. But to announce the alteration to the house would also have meant announcing it to the press, and thence to the public and the rest of the world community. The government was, it seems, concerned to avoid the opprobrium it might attract from opposition parties, the press and other member states in the United Nations if it became known that it had assisted the efforts of Iraq to re-arm itself. To acknowledge the change some years afterwards would have been even more problematic, given Iraq's subsequent invasion of Kuwait and Saddam Hussein's resultant 'Gulf War' against the US, the UK and their allies.

The hidden change in policy was revealed when the Customs and Excise service, unaware of the Waldegrave/Clark/Trefgarne initiative, commenced a prosecution against the directors of an engineering firm, Matrix-Churchill, for supplying Iraq with arms under the guise of non-military equipment. The defendants maintained that they had been encouraged to supply the weapons, and to lie about their nature, by the Department of Trade. Their lawyers naturally sought documentation from the

[74] The episode has prompted production of a large literature. The most searching analysis is offered by Tomkins A (1998) *The constitution after Scott* (Oxford: Clarendon Press). See also Leigh I and Lustgarten L (1996) 'Five volumes in search of accountability: the Scott Report' *MLR* 695–725.

government to support this claim. The government denied the allegation. Several senior Ministers then returned 'public interest immunity' certificates to the court, claiming that release of any of the documents would threaten national security.[75] To the government's great discomfort, Alan Clark, subpoenaed to attend the trial, confirmed the defendants' claims under cross-examination. His more senior colleagues had seemingly been prepared to let the defendants be convicted and perhaps sentenced to lengthy terms of imprisonment rather than reveal their own roles in the affair.

The government denied any wrongdoing. It claimed that arms sales policy had not been altered, but only 'reinterpreted', and that therefore the Commons and Lords had not been misled by the government's failure to inform them of the initiative. It further contended that Ministers had been legally obliged to issue the PII certificates. Prime Minister Major was nonetheless sufficiently embarrassed by the episode to 'allow'[76] the Commons to request the government to appoint (under prerogative powers) an independent Commission of Inquiry, chaired by Sir Richard Scott, then a member of the Court of Appeal.

Over three years passed between the establishment of the Commission and the publication of its report. The Report spanned some 1800 pages, and was published in five volumes.[77] The inquiry proceedings were marked by constant government obstructionism. Sir Richard was not granted legal powers to compel the attendance of witnesses, nor to require that they give evidence on oath. The eventual Report criticised government recalcitrance and delay in providing requested documents. More significantly, while Ministers gave evidence to the inquiry, senior figures in the Conservative Party, led by the former Foreign Secretary Sir Geoffrey (then Lord) Howe, made systematic attempts pre-emptively to discredit Scott's findings by accusing the inquiry procedure of being biased in nature and partial in effect.

The core conclusion that the inquiry reached was that Ministers had changed policy and that they (especially Waldegrave) had misled the Commons by not announcing the alteration. Scott stopped short of accusing them of deliberate lying, but characterised their position as 'not remotely tenable' and accused Waldegrave of 'sophistry':

> 'The answers to parliamentary questions . . . failed to inform Parliament [sic] of the current state of government policy on non-lethal arms sales to Iraq. This failure was deliberate. . . . The overriding and determinative reason was fear of strong public opposition to the loosening of restrictions'.[78]

The impact of this conclusion was however much reduced by the Report's excessive length and verbosity. It was further reduced by the Major government's grotesquely

75 On this area of law see Tomkins op cit ch 5.

76 The Conservative majority in the house would not have taken such a step in the face of government opposition.

77 (1996) *Report of the Inquiry into the export of defence equipment and dual use goods to Iraq and related prosecutions* (London: HMSO: HC (1995–96) 115); hereafter referred to as 'Scott'.

78 Scott op cit para D4.42.

cynical handling of the Report's publication. The government insisted on being given copies eight days prior to publication. During that time, Ministers familiarised themselves with its contents, and their departments produced highly distortive 'summaries' to give to the press. Commons debate was scheduled for the day of publication. MPs received copies 10 minutes before the debate was to begin. The government had grudgingly allowed the Labour and Liberal Foreign Affairs spokesman an additional three hours to examine the report. In such circumstances, ensuing debate was a farce, and press coverage necessarily slanted to reflect the government's view. The Major administration's unwillingness to permit serious debate may not have amounted to a 'contempt of the house' in a formal sense, but it undoubtedly displayed contempt for the principle that the legitimacy of the government process should rest on the informed consent of the governed.

At an abstract level, the Matrix-Churchill episode is significant in prompting explicit recognition of a further shift in the conventional basis of the government's relationship with the Commons. From both an individual and collective perspective, ministerial *responsibility* seems to have been partially replaced by a notion of ministerial *accountability*.[79] The presumption seems to be that the process of governance has now become so complex and multi-faceted that no Minister can be expected to keep abreast of all policy matters generated in her department; still less could a Cabinet or a Prime Minister have personal knowledge of the full range of government initiatives. To hold a Minister *responsible* for governmental failings is thus unrealistic. To hold her *accountable*, by which is meant that she is comprehensive and candid in informing the Commons of the details of the relevant failing is seen as a more plausible obligation for Ministers to accept. That such a redefinition of convention would excuse ministerial incompetence is perhaps a good reason (per Jennings) for not accepting it in principle. That the Thatcher and Major governments did not voluntarily even pay lip service to the notion of accountability to the Commons over their enthusiasm for selling military hardware to Iraq would suggest that even if a new convention has emerged, its integrity has already been thoroughly undermined.

In practical terms, the lesson one might draw from the Matrix-Churchill episode is perhaps that conventions are essentially useless creatures, and the Commons is an essentially useless institution, when it comes to providing governments of either party with an incentive to temper their enthusiasm for the vast profits made in the armaments industry with a more than rhetorical concern for the respect of democratic principle both at home and abroad.[80]

79 On the rationale for such a shift see Woodhouse op cit ch 13.

80 Cf Leigh and Lustgarten op cit at 724: 'The process by which Ministers responded to the Report and by which Parliament [sic] considered it could hardly have been a more graphic illustration of the central lesson of the entire Arms for Iraq episode; the futility and ineffectiveness of parliamentary scrutiny'.

CONCLUSION – THE CONVENTIONAL BASIS OF PARLIAMENTARY SOVEREIGNTY?

It was suggested in chapters five to seven that the sovereignty of Parliament was de facto the sovereignty of whichever political faction controlled majority support in the Commons. Much of the argument advanced in this chapter has indicated that the concentration of effective political power is often very intense even within a political party; small groups of senior Ministers or even the Prime Minister alone may occasionally be, to all intents and purposes, 'elected dictators'.[81]

One might think that this type of institutional structure would be a recipe for oppressive, if not tyrannical law-making. But while we may question complacent claims that Britain's form of democracy is incapable of improvement, it is absurd to claim that our constitution has proven profoundly insensitive to its citizens' wishes. Yet this result has seemingly been achieved in spite of, rather than because of, the constitution's legal structure. This might prompt us to adopt the argument made by Geoffrey Marshall that:

> 'the most obvious and undisputed convention of the British constitutional system is that Parliament does not use its unlimited sovereign power of legislation in an oppressive or tyrannical way. That is a vague but clearly accepted conventional rule resting on the principle of constitutionalism and the rule of law'.[82]

In the light of the analysis presented thus far in this book, we might qualify that assertion somewhat. Episodes such as the sleaze controversy of the mid-1990s and the Matrix-Churchill affair might make us wonder whether avoiding tyranny and oppression is a sufficiently ambitious target for a modern constitution to set itself? That a democratic constitution may avoid such gross evils does not mean that there is no scope for further improvement in the structure and powers of its governing process.

The second qualification relates to the nature of 'Parliament'. We have now established that legislative sovereignty is frequently de facto wielded by a small faction within a single political party that enjoys only minoritarian electoral support. In that context, we might plausibly conclude that the most important of all constitutional principles are that governing parties (and within them, Cabinets and Prime Ministers) resist the temptation to use Parliament's unfettered legal powers to enact policies intolerable to the majority of the electorate and, moreover, that the electoral majority is not predisposed to consent to laws which impinge substantially on the liberty of minority factions.

The American revolutionaries, and the constitutional architects of most other western democracies, did not have so optimistic a view of their legislators' or their citizenries' political culture. Indeed, Madison and Jefferson saw sound reasons for taking

[81] The phrase is Lord Hailsham's.

[82] Marshall G (1984) *Constitutional conventions* p 9 (Oxford: Clarendon Press).

a particularly pessimistic view of the political morality of Britain's ruling elites. It was precisely because they considered that conventional constraints on governmental power could not be relied upon that the American Framers erected so elaborate a system of procedural entrenchment of basic values to safeguard them against majoritarian intolerance or irrationality. The great paradox of British constitutional development is that its basic principle, the sovereignty of Parliament, was initially premised on a perceived need to protect fundamental values through an even more rigorous form of procedural entrenchment. In 1688, each faction of 'the people' (as then very narrowly defined) could veto legislation of which it disapproved. Yet now 'the people' comprise virtually the entire adult population and, in so far as the people are ridden by factions, their alliances derive from loyalties to a political party. If we transposed the 1688 revolutionaries' 'Three Estates of the Realm' methodology to contemporary British society, the tripartite Parliament in which each limb exercised veto powers would not be the Commons, Monarch and Lords, but the Conservative, Labour, and Liberal Democrat parties. Yet the constitution currently empowers a government to ignore rather than accommodate the wishes of those among the people who support opposition parties.

It would thus seem that the long-term legitimacy of our modern constitutional arrangements rests on the assumption that we have no need for a system of 'higher' or entrenched laws, protecting fundamental constitutional values against the whims of electoral majorities, because government and opposition parties are in broad agreement as to the basic political and moral principles which the constitution should express. In such circumstances, it would not greatly matter if one's preferred party lost a general election, for one could be sure that while the new government would pursue policies with which one disagreed, that disagreement would be of degree rather than kind. A political party might readily be expected to consent to laws that its supporters found unpalatable, but not intolerable. This may be because it accepts the intrinsic legitimacy of majoritarian law-making in respect of non-fundamental issues, and/or (more cynically) because it hopes to win the next general election and expects that its own consent to defeat would be reciprocated in respect of its own unpalatable laws by supporters of the previous government.

It is not possible in this book to delve in great detail into Britain's post-war political history. But at the risk of over-simplification, most commentators accept that the 1945–1975 period was marked by appreciable agreement between Labour and Conservative administrations about both the substance and the style of government.[83] The era is often referred as one of 'Butskellite' consensus. 'Butskell' is an amalgam of the surnames of R A Butler and Hugh Gaitskell, respectively leading figures in the Conservative and Labour parties. Both men adhered to the Keynesian school of economic policy, which advocated extensive government interference in the economy to smooth out the peaks and troughs of the economic cycle. Butskellism embraced a commitment to maintaining full employment, to government ownership of public

[83] See George and Wilding op cit chs 3–4: Gamble (1981) op cit chs 3–4.

utilities such as rail, telecommunications, gas, water, electricity and coal, to an extensive network of social security benefits for the elderly and unemployed, and to a comprehensive, government controlled national health service.

This is not to suggest that general elections in that era were not keenly fought, nor that the identity of the winning party made no discernible difference to the way the country was governed. Rather it stresses that the constitution did not face the problem of a people bitterly divided over basic issues.

Chapter six used the changing historical role of the House of Lords as a vehicle to explore the notion of democracy as a matter of procedural politics – the co-equal legislative status of the upper house had become politically unacceptable because of the consolidation of a conventional principle that 'consent' to government demanded legislators be electorally accountable. But we should be wary, especially given the characteristics of our electoral system, of assuming that periodic voting for members of the Commons is a sufficient guarantor of a democratic constitution. Chapters ten and eleven return to the idea that democracy may also be a matter of substantive politics, by focusing not on the House of Lords, but on the institution of local government, in exploring the importance of inter-party consensus to the legitimacy of our constitutional arrangements.

10

LOCAL GOVERNMENT – I: CONVENTIONAL PLURALISM?

We have thus far encountered federalism, in the sense of political mechanisms dividing governmental power geographically, in several different forms. Chapter one noted the inter-relationship in the USA between the people, the national government, and the State governments. The geographical separation of powers between national and State government was a fundamental political principle underpinning the constitutional settlement, afforded explicit legal protection in the Constitution's text. Chapter nine discussed how the Canadian constitution developed a similarly profound attachment to a national/provincial division of powers as a matter of constitutional convention.

Both Canadian and American federalism rest on the moral premise that the constitutions of large, democratic nations should permit 'the people's' inevitably varying political sentiments to be given constant expression on matters of substantial political significance. A unitary state where legislators face periodic re-election may provide its people with the opportunity to consent in a **sequential** sense, at a national level, to different governmental philosophies. It may have supra-legislative constitutional provisions which ensure that opposition parties have realistic prospects of winning future general elections if they formulate attractive policies. But such societies cannot provide their people with any legally constituent basis for the **simultaneous** co-existence of alternative governmental programmes.

It is also possible, in theory, for a unitary state with a legislature exercising sovereign powers on a bare majority basis to offer its people substantial sequential and simultaneous pluralism within the government process. This would require that whichever political faction controlled a central legislative majority regarded political pluralism as a fundamental constitutional convention. Such legislators would fashion and maintain a governmental system facilitating effective expression of divergent political opinion. The fewer the powers that the national legislature gave to the national government, and the more it allocated to locally elected bodies, the less unitary and thence more 'federal' or 'pluralist' the constitution's conventional basis would be. A country could be very federalist in functional terms, while formally being entirely unitary.

Post-revolutionary England adopted a constitutional structure recognising a unitary state, whose Parliament possessed total legislative competence. Any geographical division of governmental power within English (and later British) society could not have a constituent legal status; it could have only a conventional basis.

That the American and English revolutionaries adopted (and that their successors subsequently maintained) such divergent approaches to the geographical separation of powers might suggest either or both of two things. Firstly, that British society did not then (and has not since) contained geographically based divisions of political sentiment among its people; and/or, secondly, that it has such divisions, and they have been respected by successive parliamentary majorities. It is to exploring these issues, in the period up until 1979, that the rest of this chapter is directed.

I. LOCALISM, TRADITION AND THE 'MODERNISATION' OF LOCAL GOVERNMENT

'Localism' was an important element of seventeenth century English political culture. By then, some areas could already claim several hundred years of self-government. Kingston-upon-Hull was recognised as a unit of local government by 1299, while the town of Beverley traces its local government history back to 1129.[1] Much local government activity was based on a fusion rather than separation of powers. Its origins frequently lay in the need to enforce and maintain law and order, so government officials frequently occupied posts which now appear as much judicial as executive in nature.[2] Indeed, the English '*common law*' emerged from efforts by successive monarchs to impose uniform legal principles on the many divergent inferior jurisdictions which flourished in England since the Middle Ages.[3]

The twin socio-economic forces of urbanisation and industrialisation[4] placed increasing demands on government from 1750 onwards, particularly in respect of maintaining public health and law and order, and providing transport infrastructure. Initially however, Parliament did not address these pressures in a systematic way. Rather, it created ad hoc units of local government in response to perceived social needs in particular areas. Often these government bodies had only one responsibility: for poor relief, or sewerage works, for example. Some, but not all of these office holders were elected (and electorates were then extremely small and entirely unrepresentative of local populations). Most were appointed by central government, which had often delegated that responsibility to powerful locally based politicians. In terms both of the

1 Elcock H (2nd edn, 1986) *Local government* ch 1 (London: Methuen).

2 See Jennings I (4th edn, 1960) *Principles of local government law* ch 2 (London: University of London Press).

3 Plucknett (1960) op cit ch 3.

4 See Loughlin M (1985) 'Municipal socialism in a unitary state', in McAuslan and McEldowney op cit; (1986) *Local government in the modern state* ch 1 (London: Sweet and Maxwell).

type of powers that its office holders exercised, and the way that they were chosen, local government at this time might more appropriately be described as a form of 'magistracy' rather than a manifestation of representative democracy.

The preponderance of single function authorities produced a very complex governmental structure. As well as presenting difficulties in co-ordinating service provision, the profusion of small single issue bodies prevented local government deriving the advantages of economies of scale, and offered many opportunities for corruption and patronage in allocating offices and the performance of public duties. It was not a system well-suited to the social, economic and political demands of a country in the throes of the world's first industrial revolution.

THE MUNICIPAL CORPORATIONS ACT 1835

Following the passage of the 1832 Great Reform Act, the Whigs (Liberals), then led by Lord Melbourne, promised further reform of the country's governmental structures, this time at the local level. Such radicalism triggered one of the last exercises of explicitly partisan monarchical intervention in the political process. William IV dismissed Melbourne's government and dissolved Parliament in the hope that an election would produce a Tory majority. However the January 1835 election returned the Whigs (with Melbourne as Prime Minister with an adequate Commons majority). Melbourne resumed office only after having extracted a pledge of support from the King,[5] and immediately promoted a Bill to reform the country's system of sub-central government.

While the Bill's Commons passage was uneventful, it met determined opposition in the Lords. This is perhaps surprising, given the obvious 'defeat' that the Lords had suffered over the 1832 Great Reform Act. It seems more readily understandable, however, when one considers the Act's impact on aristocratic control over the country's governance. To some contemporary observers, it amounted to revolution:

> 'There never was such a coup as this Bill. . . . It marshalls all the middle classes in all the towns . . . in the ranks of reform: aye, and gives them monstrous power too. I consider it a much greater blow to Toryism than the Reform Bill itself'.[6]

While the 1832 Act had cut a swathe through the foliage of the landed classes' political influence, the 1835 Bill promised to attack that influence at its roots: it signified that the twin economic forces of urbanisation and industrialisation had been joined by the political catalyst of increased pressure for the democratisation of the country's constitutional arrangements. The functionally haphazard, aristocratically dominated structure of sub-central government which then existed offended the emergent middle classes' attachment to the principles of both efficiency and representativeness in public affairs.

[5] Brock op cit p 317.

[6] See Turbeville (1958) op cit p 351; Brock op cit p 317.

The Tories in the Lords campaigned vigorously against the Bill,[7] passing numerous wrecking amendments. The government offered no resistance, seemingly believing that if given enough legislative rope the Tory peers would hang themselves from the scaffold of reformist, middle class public opinion. One contemporary commentator suggested that the government was:

'content to exhibit its paltry numbers in the House of Lords in order that the world may see how essentially it is a Tory body, that it hardly fulfils the conditions of a great independent legislative assembly, but presents the appearance of a dominant party faction'.[8]

As in 1832, the intransigence of reactionary Tory peers finally foundered on Peel's refusal to condone their obstruction of an elected government's policy. Shorn of lower house support, Tory peers subsequently contented themselves with fashioning amendments which the Whig government would accept. This was not however the end of the legal battle over the Act.

The courts as defenders of local democracy – the emergence of the 'fiduciary duty doctrine'

In anticipation of the enactment of the legislation, the officials of several boroughs attempted to prevent corporation assets falling into the hands of the newly enfranchised middle classes by disposing of corporation property to themselves or their nominees. Once the Act came into force, the newly elected authorities (acting through the Attorney General) sought recovery of the assets.

A-G v Aspinall[9] was the first of these cases. The application succeeded, the nub of the judgment being that the controllers of the corporation, whoever they might be, held its property on trust for their successors and that dispositions of such property; 'made collusively for less than full value' were unlawful.[10] Lord Cottenham CJ analysed the case by drawing an analogy from the law of trusts, in which a trustee holding financial resources on trust for a beneficiary is placed under an implied 'fiduciary duty' to exercise her management powers over the resources to the best advantage of the beneficiary. In Lord Cottenham CJ's view, the officers of the now defunct corporations should be regarded as holding corporation assets on trust for the local population:

'I cannot doubt that a clear trust was created by this Act for public, and therefore in the legal sense of the term, charitable purposes of all the property belonging to the corporation at the time of the passing of this Act; and that the corporation in its former state . . . were in the situation of trustees for these purposes . . . and subject to the general obligations and duties of persons in whom such property is vested.'[11]

A clearer indication of what Lord Cottenham LC had meant by 'collusive' in *Aspinall*

7 See generally Turbeville (1958) op cit pp 351–358.

8 Quoted in Turbeville (1958) op cit at p 354.

9 (1837) 40 ER 773; 2 My & Cr 613.

10 (1837) 40 ER 773 at 777.

11 (1837) 40 ER 773 at 777.

was provided in *A-G v Wilson.*[12] The Mayor and Aldermen of the borough of Leeds had greeted the 1835 bill with a resolution to the effect that:

'[T]his Court views with alarm the sweeping measure of corporation reform introduced into the House of Commons by Lord John Russell, as calculated to throw municipal government into the hands of political parties and religious sectaries, opposed to the best and most sacred institutions of the country.'

The Mayor and Aldermen then transferred a substantial portion of the borough's assets to three of their number. On the basis of the evidence before the court, Lord Cottenham CJ concluded that:

'The deed of the 30th May 1835 was avowedly made for the purpose of stripping the corporation of all its property before the bill then in Parliament could pass. . . . These five defendants, being agents and trustees of the corporation funds, though the legal title was not vested in them, by an illegal exercise of the authority of the corporation, procured the funds to be diverted from their legal custody and purpose, and to be placed in other hands. . . .'[13]

These cases indicate that the fiduciary duty doctrine in relation to local authorities emerged within English law to deal with an extreme political problem; namely an attempt by appointed holders of public office to sabotage an Act of Parliament and to undermine the significance of the newly created local electoral process.

An incremental approach to reform

The 1835 legislation reformed only urban areas – the system of rural local government remained intact. Nor did the Act effect a significant transfer of powers to the new borough councils from existing single function bodies. Its importance lay rather in its recognition that councillors should hold office on the basis of periodic elections, and that their continued occupancy of that office should depend on their winning the consent of a local electorate whose right to vote was defined by a uniform, national franchise based on low levels of property ownership.[14]

Parliament nevertheless continued to create single issue bodies to address new social and economic problems at a local level. The Poor Law Amendment Act 1834 had vested responsibility for the administration of poor relief in local Boards of Guardians, rather than granting it to the soon to be reformed boroughs. Similarly, following acute public anxiety in the 1850s over the spread of cholera, Parliament created local boards of health, rather than bestow such powers on the boroughs. It was not until the 1870s that the legislature was ultimately convinced of the desirability of allocating this task to the boroughs.

By the 1880s, the boroughs' 'multi-functional'[15] nature was firmly established. In

[12] (1840) 41 ER 389. [13] (1840) 41 ER 389 at 398.

[14] The local electoral franchise was more expansive than its parliamentary counterpart. This was not only a class matter; as noted in chapter seven, women were enfranchised at the local level some years before being permitted to vote for members of the Commons.

[15] See Loughlin M (1994) 'The restructuring of central–local government relations', in Jowell and Oliver op cit.

addition to their public health powers, they gained extensive responsibilities in the areas of housing provision and town planning. Relatedly, Parliament had in 1871 created a central government department, originally titled the Local Government Board, to co-ordinate and oversee local authority activities.[16]

The system of rural local government was not rationalised in the sense of becoming multi-functional and elected according to a uniform franchise until the enactment of the Local Government Act 1888. A county council for London was created in 1899. The 1902 Education Act further reinforced councils' multi-functional importance by transferring responsibility for state elementary schooling from the specialist school boards established in 1870 to the county councils and the larger boroughs.

During the next two decades, Parliament made further significant extensions to local government's responsibilities for administering the newly emergent welfare state.[17] There were then some 1500 units of elected, multi-functional local government. They were divided on the basis of powers as well as geography. Many authorities existed within a two tier structure, in which different types of authority had different responsibilities.[18] Thus a county council, which provided education and social services throughout its area, might contain within its boundaries several borough councils, each controlling such issues as housing and town planning. The picture was further complicated by some areas which had only a single tier structure; larger boroughs might be granted 'county borough status', and thereby take over the county's responsibilities within the borough's boundaries.

Given their profusion, there was no scope for local councils to exercise powers on a scale comparable to those possessed by the state governments of the USA, or the Canadian provinces. But this does not mean that their powers were politically insignificant. In a welfare state, citizens will be intimately and acutely affected by governmental decisions in such fields as education, housing, social services and town planning. Moreover, the combined impact of these services would be sufficient to enable electors to express appreciably divergent opinions as to the precise content and conduct of citizen-government relations in their respective areas.

By 1920, the democratisation of British society was firmly established. Parliament had introduced a near universal franchise, and the legal reduction in the Lords' powers effected by the Parliament Act 1911 stressed the elected chamber's dominance in the legislative process. It was also the case, as the results of the 1906–1910 general elections made clear, that the 'people's' political allegiance was almost equally divided between the Conservative and Liberal/Labour parties. A powerful local government sector, enjoying appreciable independence from central control, would thus offer defeated voters the opportunity to see their preferred policies given some effect. If our

16 This role successively passed to the Ministry of Health, the Ministry of Housing and Local Government, and, from the 1970s onwards, the Department of the Environment (DoE).

17 Which became firmly established following the eventual passage of Lloyd George's 'People's Budget'. For details of local government's role in this period see Hampson W (2nd edn, 1991) *Local government and urban politics* ch 2 (London: Longman).

18 This presents a simplified picture. For more detail see Hampson op cit pp 17–20.

concept of democracy rests on reasonably sophisticated notions of popular consent to government, it is of crucial importance to consider, as a matter both of law and of convention, the principles which structured the relationship between central government, local authorities, and the national and local electorates from the 1920s onwards.

II. LOCAL GOVERNMENT'S CONSTITUTIONAL STATUS IN THE EARLY TWENTIETH CENTURY – LAW AND CONVENTION

The sophisticated understanding of consent might provide us with (per Jennings) a 'reason' for parliamentary self-restraint in respect of local political pluralism. From this perspective, it makes little sense to begin a search for conventional understandings of central/local relations prior to 1918. That date does offer, from a contemporary vantage point, the advantage of giving us (to borrow from Asquith) a sufficiently lengthy time span to scrutinise in order to see if any clear 'traditions and settled practices' have emerged.

Several strong presumptions as to the 'correct' allocation of power between central and local government were consolidated among politicians of all parties during World War II, when Britain was governed by a Conservative-Labour-Liberal coalition. The parliamentary roots of the Butskellite consensus are highly significant for consent-based theories of constitutional law, since Churchill's war-time administration is the only modern government which can plausibly be portrayed as commanding the level of popular support which, in democracies such as the USA, would be sufficient to redefine 'fundamental' constitutional values.

The election campaigns of 1945, 1950 and 1951 featured hyperbolic denunciations by both parties of their opponent's policies.[19] But the depth of the consensus between mainstream Conservative and Labour policies is well illustrated by Churchill's first Commons speech following his return as Prime Minister in 1951: 'What the nation needs is several years of quiet, steady administration, if only to allow the socialist [ie Labour government's] legislation to reach its full fruition'.[20]

The 'socialist legislation' to which Churchill referred had entailed significant transfers of formerly local responsibilities to newly created national bodies, especially in the fields of health care and the management of gas, water, and electricity supplies. In terms of the multiplicity of its functions, local government in the Butskellite era was thus less important than it had been immediately before the war. It was also subject to more central oversight, insofar as legislation increasingly contained explicit powers

[19] Cf Churchill's ludicrous claim in a June 1945 election broadcast that Labour's economic policies could not be implemented without the creation of a *Gestapo*; see Butler and Sloman op cit p 227.

[20] *HCD*, 4 November 1951; quoted in Jenkins R (1994) 'Churchill: the government of 1951–1955' at p 497, in Blake R and Louis W (eds) *Churchill* (Oxford: Clarendon Press).

which would enable Ministers to interfere with or override council decisions in certain circumstances.[21] However in terms of the scale of its activities, local government had become more important than ever. Local responsibilities lay primarily in the fields of housing, education, land use planning, social work and consumer protection services. Given the substantive importance of such functions in a modern welfare state, their reservation to elected local government could be seen as a guarantor of political pluralism within the government process. Should the Labour, Liberal or Conservative parties win control of councils endowed by Parliament with such significant responsibilities, they might reasonably assume that their respective political preferences would be implemented in some parts of the country, irrespective of the outcome of general elections. This is not to suggest that that local councils would enjoy complete independence in these spheres of activity, but rather that they would possess sufficient autonomy to exceed or modify centrally determined standards.[22]

There was a readily discernible party split along regional lines in general elections during the post war era. Crudely stated, a greater percentage of electors in London, Wales, Scotland and northern England consistently voted Labour rather than Conservative, and that tendency was reversed in the rest of southern England. Powerful and autonomous local councils would ensure that this geographically based divergence of opinion was constantly accommodated within the country's overall government structure. It is plausible to conclude that 'the people' in these regions would more readily consent to defeat at the national level if they could be sure that their respective political preferences could influence the government process on a significant, if limited scale in their particular areas.

The Butskellite view of government also acknowledged reasons of a less profoundly 'constitutional' nature for preserving a powerful and vibrant local government sector.[23] The first might be called the 'local knowledge' factor. This argument assumes that one will improve the efficiency of service provision if it is entrusted to an organisation that has an intimate knowledge of local social and economic conditions, especially if one is dealing with a package of services where trade-offs need to be made between the amount of resources that each is allocated.

A second justification falls under the heading of political education. Councils can serve as training grounds for politicians before they move on to central government. In another sense, local government's role as a political educator draws more people into the government process, thereby making them aware of their rights and responsibilities as citizens. This can be achieved not only through the route of becoming a councillor. Involvement with local pressure groups, or even individual lobbying over such issues as school closures or housing repairs also gives citizens the opportunity to participate in the government process.

21 Hampson op cit ch 10; Buxton R (1971) *Local government* ch 5 (Harmondsworth: Penguin).

22 See especially Griffith J (1966) *Central departments and local authorities* ch 1 (London: Allen and Unwin).

23 See Sharpe J (1970) 'Theories and value of local government' *Political Studies* 153–174.

A third justification sees local government as a vehicle for experimental social policies. The sheer diversity of political opinion to which local councils offer expression makes it likely that some authorities will formulate novel and innovative policies. Relatedly, the small geographical scope of any such authority's jurisdiction offers a guarantee of damage limitation if experimental policies prove unsuccessful.

Broadly stated, this Butskellite perception of local government suggests that there is more to the concept of 'democracy' in a modern multi-party state than a five-yearly stroll to the ballot box to express a preference concerning the party composition of national government. Rather, it indicates that democracy in post-war Britain was widely perceived as a perpetual and multi-faceted process, within which various sub-groups of 'the people' would push and pull 'government' at all levels in contradictory directions, and to which a geographical separation of powers can make a vital contribution.

The remaining sections of this chapter analyse the nature of the geographical separation of powers within the British constitution in the Butskellite era by focusing on four elements of central/local relations: the question of councils' fiscal autonomy; the provision of public housing; the management of state schools; and, pervading all areas, the regulatory role played by administrative law. Before turning to this task however, we briefly address the question of geographical boundaries.

THE PHYSICAL BOUNDARIES OF LOCAL AUTHORITIES

In terms of their physical boundaries, no less than in respect of their powers, local authorities have not enjoyed a sacrosanct, conventional status in the modern era. The Macmillan government had persuaded Parliament to create a Local Government Boundary Commission in 1958, which exercised powers analogous to those of its parliamentary namesake.[24] Boundary redrawing had previously been undertaken on an ad hoc basis, a process clearly vulnerable to accusations of political bias. Macmillan's initiative lent the issue a consensual rather than factional character.

However, the Commission was abolished during Harold Wilson's first administration. Wilson established a Royal Commission (the Redcliffe-Maud Commission) to review the structure of local government in England. Richard Crossman was then the Minister of Local Government, and was largely responsible for determining the Commission's personnel and terms of reference.[25]

Redcliffe-Maud recommended radical reforms. It proposed as a first principle that England should contain just 58 local councils, each exercising all the powers formerly divided between counties, county boroughs, and boroughs. A two-tier system would be retained only in London and several other large conurbations. The Commission also advocated the creation of eight 'provinces', whose governments (indirectly elected

[24] Local Government Act 1958. See Jennings (1960) op cit pp 88–94.

[25] Crossman's *Diaries* suggest that his zeal for 'modernisation' in this process did not always override his concern with party political electoral advantage: op cit at p 201.

from the other local authorities) would exercise broad, strategic economic planning powers.

Redcliffe-Maud suggested that these reforms would eliminate conflict and confusion between different types of authorities with geographically overlapping responsibilities, heighten people's awareness of which government body was responsible for local service provision, and by enhancing both the geographical size and range of powers each council wielded significantly increase the political importance of local government. Had they been implemented, the proposals would have lent the overall structure of English government a distinctly more 'federal' character.

The Labour and Conservative parties divided on the merits of the Redcliffe-Maud proposals, although both rejected the proposal for provincial government. Labour's initial Bill watered down the proposals significantly, although it did not reject in principle the extension of single tier local government. However the Wilson government lost office in the 1970 general election before its measures could be enacted. The Heath government, in contrast, while accepting that England contained too many small authorities, remained attached to the multi-tier principle. The Local Government Act 1972 (which came into force in 1974) abolished many of the 1500 or so small councils which then existed, and merged them into larger units. The 'larger units' were still however numerous and therefore often quite small. In 1974 there were 47 county councils in England and Wales, 36 metropolitan district councils, and 333 district councils.[26] Only the metropolitan districts were single tier authorities in the sense envisaged by Redcliffe-Maud and apparently preferred by the Labour Party. The Bill had been appreciably amended, at least in matters of detail, during its passage, when the government accepted that its original proposals should be adjusted to accommodate local sensitivities.[27] The Bill was nevertheless opposed at second reading by both the Labour and Liberal parties.

The size and range of powers exercised by local councils has obvious implications for the sector's efficacy as a representative of divergent political opinion. The larger a council, and the more extensive its powers, the greater scope it possesses to act as a meaningful 'alternative' to central government for a local electorate which opposes the party commanding a Commons majority. Neither the Conservative nor Labour parties during the Butskellite era saw any merit in creating a conventionally federal model (in the US or Canadian sense) of central/local relations; councils remained too small, too numerous and too functionally heterogeneous for that argument to have any force. But this is not to say either that local authorities therefore lacked a significant degree of political autonomy, or that the British constitution was insensitive to the pluralist nature of its people's political beliefs. Before introducing its Bill, the Heath government had stated that:

26 For a helpful explanation (and even more helpful maps) of the eventual structure see Hampson op cit ch 2.

27 See Burton I and Drewry G (1972) 'Public legislation a survey of the session 1971–1972' *Parliamentary Affairs* 145–185.

'A vigorous local democracy means that authorities must be given real functions – with powers of decision and the ability to take action without being subjected to excessive regulation by central government through financial or other controls . . . [A]bove all else, a genuine local democracy implies that decisions should be taken – and should be seen to be taken – as locally as possible'.[28]

The following pages address the extent to which such rhetoric reflected the realities of central/local relations.

III. TAXATION AND REPRESENTATION: THE FISCAL AUTONOMY OF LOCAL GOVERNMENT

There is a close connection between fiscal and political autonomy within the 'government' process. The notion of 'government' carries within it the idea that elected representatives have the power to raise sufficient revenue to put the policies preferred by their electorate into practice: such limits as were imposed on this power would be a purely political matter regulated by the electoral process. An elected body whose revenue and expenditure was determined entirely by another government organisation would not in any meaningful sense be a 'government' at all, but would be merely an administering agency doing the bidding of its fiscal master. This point illustrates a proposition of general applicability to the British constitution in the modern era; that the more fiscal autonomy the council sector possessed, the greater its capacity to express pluralist political sentiment, and hence the more 'governmental' and less 'administrative' its constitutional role.

The multi-functional, elected local authorities with which Britain entered the modern democratic age traditionally derived their funding from three sources. The first source was grants from central government. The second was income from various trading operations, especially rents from council houses. The third was a locally levied property tax, colloquially known as 'the rates', paid both by local businesses and householders.

As table 10.1 suggests, the trend during the twentieth century until 1980 was for an increasingly larger part of local government's income to be central government grant. In the mid 1970s almost half of a council's income came from grants; barely a quarter derived from the rates.

One reason for this heavy financial input from central government lay in the need to avoid massive inequality in service provision between various councils. Local authorities obviously cover very different areas. There can be significant discrepancies both in their wealth and their needs for welfare services. In general, poorer areas will need more services but have less capacity to pay for them than more affluent regions.

28 DoE (1971) *Local government in England* p 6 (London: HMSO Cmnd 4584).

Table 10.1 Sources of local authority income 1945–1975

Year	Income (£m)	Rates %	Grants %	Trading operations %
1950	966	34	34	32
1955	1415	33	36	31
1960	2182	33	37	30
1966	3767	33	38	29
1970	5511	31	40	29
1984	9764	28	45	27

Source: Extracted from data in Layfield/DoE (1976) *Local government finance* (Cmnd 6453. London: HMSO).

Central grants were allocated according to various complex formulae which tried to take these factors into account – in effect the process involved a transfer of wealth from richer to poorer areas to enable all councils to meet minimum standards of service provision.

But while greater central funding may enhance equality, it also poses the threat of undermining local authorities' political independence from central government. If a local authority could levy and spend only that amount of money which central government was prepared to provide, the local electoral process would be a mere charade; the constitution might just as well provide for a local office of a central government department to administer whatever services central government wished to offer, and abolish local elections altogether.

Several steps were taken to reduce this risk. From the 1950s onwards,[29] central grants were paid in a 'block', rather than being earmarked for specific services. This afforded councils some scope to prioritise expenditure on different activities according to their particular political preferences. Perhaps of more significance was the apparent existence of a conventional rule that central government would not use statute to limit the revenue that local authorities raised through the rates. The question of local taxation levels was presumed to be a matter for a council and its electors. If rates were too high, the appropriate means to reduce them was for local electors to vote the party controlling the council out of office, and replace it with a party committed to lower levels of expenditure on local services. Central government might request an authority to keep its rates within certain limits; it might negotiate about total spending plans and the amounts allocated to particular services; it might even threaten to reduce the grants it provided; but it did not ask Parliament to place legal limits on councils' tax levying 'independence'.

The significance of Parliament's conventional self-restraint on the question of local taxation was forcefully stressed by Jennings in 1960:

[29] Loughlin (1994) op cit.

'Local authorities are elected by the people of the area not to carry out as agents of the central government the policy of that government, but to carry out the policy of the electors of the area. The furtherance of that policy needs expenditure, and for the expenditure and the means of meeting it the local authority is again responsible, not to the central government . . . but to the electors. . . . The importance of this principle cannot be overestimated. . . . so long as the rating power is independent of [central government] control, local government as a whole must be, to a large extent, independent'.[30]

One must beware of exaggerating this degree of 'independence'. Indeed, independence is perhaps an inappropriate word to use here. 'Autonomy' may be a better term to describe local government's constitutional relationship vis à vis central government, given that so substantial a proportion of its financial resources derived from central grants. But 'autonomy' is a complicated concept. Its extent may depend as much on precisely how a council is permitted to spend its resources as on the amount of revenue itself. To explore this issue, we must examine the legal framework regulating council behaviour in rather more detail.

IV. THE ROLE OF THE JUDICIARY

Councils are statutory creations, susceptible to judicial review to ensure that the powers that Parliament has granted them are not exceeded. However the absence of explicit legal limits on a council's rate levying power typified a general trend in legislation defining local government' powers before 1980. Many local government statutes were drafted in very loose language, reflecting the fact that Parliament accepted both the need for local variation in service provision, and the competence of elected councillors to reach those exact decisions.

Consequently, we can find several important cases which suggest that the courts might be reluctant to apply the ultra vires doctrine to local authorities acting under loosely drafted statutes. In *Kruse v Johnson*,[31] for example, the local authority had passed a bye-law[32] making it an offence to play an instrument on the highway within 50 yards of a dwelling house if asked to stop by an occupant or constable. The bye-law apparently expressed the wish of local electors to maintain rigorous standards of peace and quiet in their neighbourhoods. Kruse was charged with the offence, but raised in his defence the assertion that the bye-law was invalid because it was 'unreasonable'. In addressing this question, the court held that because councils were elected bodies accountable to their voters, bye-laws should be 'benevolently' interpreted. While a bye-law would be ultra vires if unreasonable, unreasonable bore a special meaning in this context. The substance of a decision would only be ultra vires

30 (1960) op cit pp 184–186. 31 [1898] 2 QB 91.

32 In effect a piece of delegated legislation whose geographical reach was confined within the council's boundaries.

if it was 'manifestly unjust; or contained elements of bad faith or fraud; or involved gratuitous and oppressive interference with citizens' rights'.[33]

This expansive concept of substantive reasonableness in relation to local authority discretion was reiterated in the 1948 decision in *Associated Provincial Picture Houses Ltd v Wednesbury Corpn*, a case briefly noted in chapter three.[34] In *Wednesbury*, the Court of Appeal refused to interfere with a council decision to use its statutory power to licence cinemas to prohibit children from attending shows on Sunday mornings. The court considered the policy was well within the range of opinions that reasonable people might hold. The courts should only invalidate the substance of such a decision if it was so grossly unreasonable that no reasonable person could have thought it within the powers conferred by the Act.

These two cases both seemed to accept that the courts should be slow to question the merits of council policy decisions. Their rationale appears to be that Parliament has entrusted these democratically elected bodies to govern their particular areas in certain fields. This process necessarily involves the making of value judgements about political issues, a task which, in accordance with traditional notions of the separation of powers, one might reasonably assume that politicians are better equipped to make than judges. But *Kruse* and *Wednesbury* co-existed with another line of cases in which judges placed more restrictive limits on a council's power to pursue its preferred policies. The best known is *Roberts v Hopwood*, a case which reached the House of Lords in 1925.

The 'fiduciary duty' doctrine revisited (and subverted?)

Poplar Council, a small inner-London authority, was controlled by a radical faction of the Labour Party in the 1920s. The councillors had an uneasy relationship with central government over their social policies. This conflict came to a head when the council decided to pay all its employees a flat rate wage much higher than that offered for similar private sector jobs.[35]

Section 62 of the Metropolis Management Act 1855 empowered the council to pay its employees 'such wages as it thought fit'. The council assumed this meant either that there were no limits on its discretion, or at most, that its policy should be 'benevolently' interpreted per *Kruse*. This was the view taken by the Court of Appeal in *Roberts*.

However the House of Lords decided that the council's apparently unfettered statutory power to pay 'such wages as it thinks fit' was subject to a common law 'fiduciary duty' to local ratepayers, analogous to the duty a limited company owes to its shareholders, or trustees owe to the trust's beneficiaries. As noted above, this principle emerged within British constitutional law in order to protect the interests of the local population against the behaviour of electorally unaccountable municipal office

33 [1898] 2 QB 91 at 99. 34 [1948] 1 KB 223, [1947] 2 All ER 680.

35 [1925] AC 578, HL. For background to the case see Keith-Lucas B (1962) 'Poplarism' *Public Law* 52–80; Jones G (1973) 'Herbert Morrison and Poplarism' *Public Law* 11–31.

holders. The origins of the principle seem to have been either overlooked or disregarded in the House of Lords. Neither *Aspinall* nor *Wilson* was cited in any of the opinions delivered by the court. As construed by the House of Lords in *Roberts*, the fiduciary duty doctrine apparently required that local authorities be construed as businesses, operating on a profit and loss basis, rather than as governments which can redistribute wealth in whatever way attracts electoral support. The House of Lords characterised Poplar's policy as the pursuit of 'eccentric principles of socialist philanthropy'. Councillors should not allow their personal political or philosophical preferences to influence their policy choices.

This reasoning entirely ignores the argument that giving effect to local partisan political preferences is one of the main justifications for having elected sub-central government in a democratic unitary state. The decision attracted a stinging, contemporaneous rebuke from Harold Laski, then a professor at the LSE:

> 'the council's theory of what is "reasonable" in the exercise of discretion is, even though affirmed by its constituents, seemingly inadmissible if it does not square with the economic preconceptions of the House of Lords; it is, it appears, a function of the courts to protect the electorate from the consequences of its own ideas'.[36]

Several Poplar councillors were jailed for contempt of court after refusing to amend their policies.[37] However central government (then Conservative-controlled) considered this an extreme sanction, and introduced legislation enabling councillors who approved unlawful expenditure to be personally surcharged and disqualified from office for five years.[38]

Conclusion

One might safely suggest that judicial supervision of council policy-making in the first half of the twentieth century displayed both very expansive and extraordinarily stunted[39] perceptions of local government's role in a modern, 'democratic' state. The next two sections add more historical flesh to this analytical skeleton by examining how central government and judicial control of local authorities was exercised in the Butskellite era in respect of two important areas of council activity; housing and education.

36 Laski H (1926) 'Judicial review of social policy in England' *Harvard LR* 832–848 at p 844. For a retrospective view see Fennel P (1986) '*Roberts v Hopwood*: the rule against socialism' *JLS* 401–422.

37 See Branson N (1979) *Poplarism* (London: Lawrence and Wishart).

38 Board of Guardians (Default) Act 1926; Audit (Local Authorities) Act 1927. For comment see Keith-Lucas op cit.

39 This is perhaps best illustrated by Lord Sumner's comment in *Roberts* that the limits of a council's discretion was reached in such matters as deciding 'the necessity for a urinal, and the choice of its position'; [1925] AC 578 at 605, HL.

V. COUNCIL HOUSING

By 1974, the council sector contained over six million properties and housed seventeen million people.[40] Council housing performed several governmental functions in the Butskellite era in addition to the obvious concern of providing reasonable quality, low cost accommodation for individual families. The 1945 Labour government regarded an expanding council sector as a useful tool for wealth redistribution. Conservative administrations were less attached to this principle, but shared enthusiasm for public housing's role in shaping the environment. And both parties found the labour intensive nature of house building a useful tool to regulate overall demand in the economy.

The public sector's style and scope varied considerably across the country. Local discretion over such macro-issues as stock size and design was not formally structured by tightly defined legislative rules;[41] decisions on such matters were largely determined by local election results. The absence of a precise legal framework might appear peculiar given council housing's important role in central government economic and land development policy. Legal compulsion was however largely unnecessary; councils formulated policies in close consultation with Ministers and civil servants at the Ministry of Housing and Local Government (MHLG) and (subsequently) the Department of the Environment (DoE), in a process which typified the consensual, negotiatory ethos informing central-local government relations between 1945–1970.

However, the 'national-local government system'[42] which dominated housing policy did not offer tenants any significant legal or political control over the management of their homes. Parliament's allocation of power to local authorities in this area was a paradigmatic example of green light theory, which afforded individual citizens few legal 'rights'. The Housing Act 1936 had simply placed the 'general management, regulation and control' of public housing within the discretion of the local authority with no discernible substantive or procedural constraints. With respect both to macro-issues such as the number and types of dwellings built, and to such micro-questions as allocation mechanisms, rent levels, maintenance standards, tenancy conditions, and management styles, council discretion was not closely regulated by statute.

40 For an overview of public sector development see Bowley M (1985) *Housing and the state 1919–1945* ch 1 (London: Allen & Unwin); Merret S (1979) *State housing in Britain* (London: RKP); Malpass P and Murie A (1987) *Housing policy and practice* (1987) ch 2 (London: Macmillan); Forrest R and Murie A (1988) *Selling the welfare state* ch 2 (London: Routledge).

41 Although in the 1960s central government 'encouraged' councils to build particular types of dwelling, and to meet minimum (and, subsequently, maximum) standards of space and amenity provision, by variations in the financial support it offered; see Cullingworth J (1979) *Essays on housing policy* ch 1 (London: Allen & Unwin); Malpass and Murie op cit pp 78–81.

42 See Loughlin (1985a) 'The restructuring of central–local government legal relations' *Local Government Studies* 59–73; Hampson op cit ch 9: and more exhaustively Rhodes R (1986) *The national world of local government* (London: Allen & Unwin).

Nor were the courts eager to subject local authorities' housing powers to the *Wednesbury* principles of substantive and procedural ultra vires. In *Shelley v LCC*,[43] the plaintiff was a tenant summarily served with an eviction notice. Shelley had no opportunity to argue against eviction, nor was evidence offered of any breach of the tenancy agreement. The council's decision would thus seem both procedurally and substantively ultra vires. The House of Lords however declined to intervene, asserting that housing authorities could 'pick and choose their tenants at will',[44] and evict them in similar fashion. Thirty years later, the judgments in *Bristol District Council v Clark* and *Cannock Chase District Council v Kelly*[45] confirmed the *Shelley* rationale; tenants had no recognisable rights in their housing.

Both Parliament and the courts adopted a similarly non-directive role over the issue of the rents that councils charged. Section 83 of the Housing Act 1936 required that rents be 'reasonable'. This did not make it clear to what extent councils might 'subsidise' rents from local taxation. In *Belcher v Reading Corpn*,[46] the court held that 'reasonableness' required councils to balance tenants' interests, (the presumed beneficiaries of public subsidy), with those of ratepayers (the supposed financiers of the subsidy). Romer J held that rent levels would be unreasonably high only if significantly more costly than similar private sector dwellings.[47] Tenants thus had no legal right to subsidised rents. *Belcher* nevertheless upheld local authorities' politically accepted role to use rent policies to *ameliorate* market forces – council house rents would be unreasonably low, and thus breach the council's fiduciary duty, only if *significantly* less expensive than comparable private dwellings. The decision thus took a more 'benevolent' view of local fiscal autonomy than *Roberts v Hopwood.*

Litigation over council tenancies presented the courts both with a question of administrative law between an authority and its tenants, and a question of constitutional convention concerning local autonomy from central control. The 'hands-off' approach adopted by both Parliament and the courts towards public housing administration reflected the wider norms regulating central-local government relations between 1945–1975. Tightly drafted statutes or interventionist case law would have overridden the traditional expectation that councils should *govern* their local areas, rather than simply *administer* centrally defined services on an agency basis. The inference one might draw from this is that legalisation of council/tenant relations might have to await a redefinition of the constitutional relationship between central and local government. Such a redefinition appeared to occur in 1972.

The Housing Finance Act 1972

Notwithstanding its evident commitment to principles of local fiscal autonomy prior to introducing the Local Government Bill 1972 to the Commons, the Heath

43 [1948] 2 All ER 898, HL. 44 [1948] 2 All ER 898 at 900, HL.

45 [1975] 3 All ER 976, [1975] 1 WLR 1443, CA and [1978] 1 All ER 152, [1978] 1 WLR 1, CA.

46 [1950] Ch 380. See also *Summerfield v Hampstead Borough Council* [1957] 1 All ER 221, [1957] 1 WLR 167; *Luby v Newcastle-under-Lyme Corpn* [1965] 1 QB 214, [1964] 3 All ER 169, CA.

47 [1950] Ch 380 at 392.

government adopted a more directive policy towards rental levels in the Housing Finance Act 1972. This legislation sought to raise council house rents to levels analogous to those in the private rented sector, while providing rent rebates to poorer tenants. For many councils, this required a substantial rent increase. The government had anticipated that many councils might not wish to implement this legislation; consequently, the Act also gave the DoE stringent enforcement powers against obstructive authorities.[48]

Several Labour-controlled councils threatened not to apply the Act. Only one authority eventually refused to do so. Clay Cross council in Derbyshire, whose 11 councillors were all Labour Party members, resolutely refused to raise rents.[49] DoE attempts to persuade the councillors to implement the Act failed, and they were subsequently surcharged and disqualified. At the subsequent election, local voters returned eleven new Labour councillors, all committed to maintaining the unlawful policy. The conflict was eventually resolved indirectly, in that Clay Cross was one of the many authorities merged into larger councils when the Local Government Act 1972 came into force in 1974.

The Clay Cross episode raises interesting questions both about the relationship between law and convention, and about the nature of the central/local government partnership convention itself. There is no doubt that the Clay Cross councillors broke the law. In that legalistic sense, the council's behaviour was obviously unconstitutional. In terms of convention, the picture is less clear. The traditional approach to housing policy had been that local authorities should have considerable freedom to set rent levels. Thus the Clay Cross councillors considered the Housing Finance Act to be conventionally 'unconstitutional'. Relatedly, they regarded their own illegal refusal to implement the Act as entirely legitimate. The practical difficulty which this stance presented for them was of course that they could not draw on the Heath government's alleged breach of convention as a defence in legal actions arising from their own breach of the law.

Nor was it entirely clear that convention was on the council's side. There is no great weight of historical practice which supported the notion that councils might legitimately defy the law so flagrantly. Convention seemed to require that councillors kept their political preferences within the legal limits set by legislation. From this perspective, the 'constitutional' course of action for the council to have followed would have been (reluctantly) to have enforced the Act and hope that the Heath government's breach of convention would lead voters to turn it out of office at the next general election.

The objection to such a strategy is that it suggests the disputed policy is tolerable to the factions which oppose it, and thereby dilutes or diffuses popular antagonism to central government's preferences. One then faces the argument that had the American

[48] With which the courts proved reluctant to interfere; see *Asher v Secretary of State for the Environment* [1974] Ch 208, [1974] 2 All ER 156, CA.

[49] Mitchell A (1974) 'Clay Cross' 45 *Political Quarterly* 165–175; Sklair L (1975) 'The Struggle Against the Housing Finance Act', in Miliband R and Smith J (eds) *Socialist Register* (London: Merlin).

revolutionaries, or the 1832 electoral reformers, or the Suffragettes adopted similarly quiescent tactics, they might not have achieved the results we would now regard as entirely justified. It may of course be argued that the issue of local electoral control of council house rents in 1972 is qualitatively distinct from the enfranchisement struggles of the 1770s, 1830s, and 1900s: we might assume that 'democracy' within the British constitution is a concept that reached its fullest expression in 1930, when all adults became entitled to vote in parliamentary elections. From that perspective, there would be no justification for any defiance of any statute, for one would remain at liberty to argue and campaign for its repeal. This is a question to which we will return. For the present however, our attention moves from council housing to perhaps the most important of local government functions – the management of children's education.

VI. EDUCATION

The Education Act 1944 placed a vaguely defined responsibility on both central and local government to provide schooling for all children up to the age of 15. The Act did not specify precisely how this should be done. However there was near universal agreement among central and local government and education professionals that children should be segregated according to academic ability. Consequently a tripartite system of secondary education developed all over the country. Children would attend a common elementary or primary school between the ages of eight and eleven. They would then sit an examination and be placed in one of three types of schools according to their supposed academic abilities. The 'cleverest' children would attend grammar schools; the remainder were sent to either secondary modern schools, or, if they were thought to have technical aptitude, to technical high schools.[50]

The selective system had no explicit legal basis, although it was given an official seal of governmental approval in successive reports and circulars.[51] This legal lacuna is the most graphic example of the extent to which the governance of post-war British society depended upon conventional understandings between different tiers of government. State education policy and practice was shaped by a 'national–local government system', which embroiled central government Ministers and civil servants, local authority councillors and officials, and the leadership of the teaching profession in a complex, inter-active and consensual relationship.[52]

This does not mean that a bland uniformity of opinion prevailed, but rather that

50 See Pedley R (1966) *The comprehensive school* pp 38–49 (Harmondsworth: Penguin).

51 A circular being an official statement of government 'advice' as to its preferred interpretation of particular statutory powers. Circulars have no binding legal force, but are something to which the decision-makers to whom they are directed should have regard when exercising the statutory powers concerned.

52 See Buxton R (2nd edn, 1973) *Local government* ch 8 (Harmondsworth: Penguin); Ranson S (1988) 'From 1944–1988: education, citizenship and democracy' *Local government Studies* 1–19: see also the references at n 42 at p 364 above.

local departures from orthodox practice were insufficiently frequent, and insufficiently radical, to merit a legalistic central government response. The West Riding of Yorkshire County Council, for example, had firmly rejected the selective principle on which national policy was based:

'[Our councillors] have been unable to accept certain suggestions . . . made in Ministerial circulars. They cannot for instance agree that at the age of eleven children can be classified into three recognised mental types and allocated to grammar, modern and technical schools accordingly'.[53]

The West Riding provided a single mixed ability secondary school system (colloquially referred to as 'comprehensive') for its children. A few other councils followed suit. Such action amounted to an important assertion of local autonomy. What is significant for our purposes is that both Labour and Conservative governments appeared content to allow such diversity to occur.[54]

However, just as the administration of council housing had accorded little legal or direct political influence to tenants, so the politicians' and professionals' dominance of education policy gave little obvious scope for the wishes of parents and students to influence the schooling process, other than through the rather indirect mechanism of local elections.

Section 76 of the 1944 Act provided that:

'in the exercise and performance of all powers and duties conferred and imposed upon them by this Act, the Minister and local education authorities shall have regard to the general principle that, so far as is compatible with the provision of efficient instruction and training and the avoidance of unreasonable public expenditure, pupils are to be educated in accordance with the wishes of their parents'.

Literally construed, s 76 might suggest that parental wishes occupied a lowly legal status. This was confirmed by the Court of Appeal in *Watt v Kesteven County Council*. Lord Denning held that parental wishes were merely one factor to which councils should have regard: 'this leaves it open to the county council to have regard to other things as well, and also to make exceptions to the general principle if it thinks fit to do so'.[55]

Watt again exemplifies a green light approach to the government process. Denning LJ's opinion suggests that Parliament had not intended to empower individual parents, nor small groups of parents within a particular local authority, to frustrate the policy choices made by elected councillors. In contrast to the sentiments displayed in *Roberts*, there is no indication here that parents needed 'protection' from the local electoral process.

Moreover, although the Act made no express effort to oust the courts' jurisdiction to supervise ministerial or council behaviour, its terms implied that disputes should

53 Quoted in Pedley op cit p 43.

54 Pedley op cit pp 47–49; (1958) 'Lord Hailsham's legacy' *Journal of Education* (January) 4–5.

55 [1955] 1 QB 408 at 424, CA.

be resolved without ready recourse to the courts. Section 99, for example, permitted parents to make representations to the Secretary of State if they were dissatisfied with their council's policies or practice. The Secretary of State was also empowered under s 68 to issue 'directions' to local authorities which she considered were acting 'unreasonably' in discharging their functions under the Act. Section 68 was apparently envisaged very much as a power of last resort by the 1944 Parliament, to be invoked only in exceptional circumstances.[56] By the mid-1960s, however, both the depth and breadth of consensus within the education branch of the national–local government system began to change.

THE EMERGENCE OF COMPREHENSIVE EDUCATION

By the late 1950s, some authorities, primarily but not exclusively Labour controlled, had embraced the concept of comprehensive secondary schooling. The comprehensive/selective debate was keenly contested, and cut across party lines. Many Labour-controlled councils (and a few of their Conservative counterparts) were attracted by the more egalitarian ethos of the comprehensive system. Other authorities, particularly those with small and scattered populations, favoured it for financial reasons. In contrast, many Conservative (and some Labour) councils wished to retain the tripartite structure.

Harold Wilson's first Labour government, elected in 1964, also supported the comprehensive approach. However, this significant policy shift was not given an explicit legislative base. Instead the government issued Circular 10/65, a document whose legal status was purely advisory, in which the Department of Education and Science (DES) expressed the hope that local authorities would follow central government's preferences. The circular made no suggestion that the government would promote legislation to force compliance with its preferences. The DES 'requested' councils to submit plans for reorganising their selective systems along comprehensive lines. The circular did not specify a preferred model of reform, but outlined several different options. It also stressed that: 'The proper processes of local government must leave initiative on matters of principle and the ultimate responsibility for decisions with the elected representatives of the community'.[57]

Such sentiments may suggest that the Labour government was prepared to allow appreciable divergence from its preferred aims. By introducing the new policy in a circular rather than an Act, the government was not equipping itself with the legal powers to enforce its preferred policy. This may have been because the Wilson government was committed to the principle of local democracy in education matters. Or it may have been because Labour then had a Commons majority of only four, and could not have pushed so radical a Bill through the house.[58]

56 See Harlow and Rawlings (1984) op cit pp 333–334.

57 Circular 10/65 para 41.

58 Pimlott provides some support for the latter view. He records the then Secretary of State, Tony Crosland, as pronouncing (in a private letter); 'If it's the last thing I do, I'm going to destroy every fucking grammar school in England. And Wales.': op cit p 512.

Paragraph 44 of the circular hinted that the DES would only fund new secondary schools if they were comprehensive rather than selective. This was of course an informal enforcement mechanism that the government did not have to pilot through the Commons. If that was indeed the threat underlying para 44, it was one that many councils did not take seriously. The circular had given local authorities two and a half years to submit their reorganisation plans. Some 20% of councils failed to meet that deadline, seemingly more as a result of their rejection of the legitimacy of the policy than simple inefficiency. The government's plans received a further setback in the local elections of 1967 and 1968, in which the Conservative Party enjoyed considerable success,[59] and which produced a substantial increase in the number of councils hostile to the comprehensive system.

The courts continued to leave outcomes to be determined by the political process. In *Wood v Ealing London Borough Council*, the High Court rejected an attempt by a group of pro-selection parents to overturn their council's re-organisation plans. Goff J confirmed that parents had no right to insist upon the retention of grammar schools:

'it has to be observed that the Act nowhere provides for grammar school education, or secondary modern education as distinct from grammar, and in my judgment . . . all that the local education authority has to provide is schools adequate in number, character and equipment for providing a full range of secondary education suitable for the number and kind of pupils for which it has to cater'.[60]

A group of parents achieved rather greater success in *Bradbury v London Borough of Enfield*,[61] when they succeeded in convincing the courts to quash both a local council's reorganisation plans and the Secretary of State's subsequent efforts to provide the council with a way round this legal obstacle. Their victory was based however only on the grounds of procedural impropriety, since both the council and the Secretary of State had displayed a complete disregard for the procedures specified by the Act. The case was not a judicial pronouncement on the merits of selective education.

The Conservatives' local electoral successes in 1967–1968 were followed by victory at the 1970 general election. The 1970–1974 Heath government immediately withdrew Circular 10/65. Margaret Thatcher, then Secretary of State for Education, explained that she disapproved of the circular, apparently because she adhered to the conventional constitutional principle which left such matters to the local electoral process. She considered that the circular had imposed an unwarranted degree of 'compulsion on democratically elected authorities'.[62] It seems unlikely that any councils were in fact co-erced, and indeed the essentially bi-partisan commitment to the introduction of comprehensive schooling was demonstrated by the 1970–1974 Heath

59 See Butler and Sloman op cit pp 338–340; Gyford J (1984) *The politics of local socialism* pp 24–29 (London: Allen & Unwin).

60 [1967] Ch 364 at 384. See also Donaldson J in *Lee v Secretary of State for Education and Science* (1967) 66 LGR 211 at 215: '[T]he court is not concerned with the merits of what is proposed but solely with its legality'.

61 [1967] 3 All ER 434, [1967] 1 WLR 1311, CA.

62 *HCD*, 8 July 1970 c 688.

government's decision to continue to approve local authority reorganisation plans.[63] It was not until the subsequent election of a Labour government in 1974 that the comprehensive question once again assumed a highly controversial political (and legal) status.

Tameside

The case of *Secretary of State for Education and Science v Tameside Metropolitan Borough Council*[64] arose after the Conservatives won control of Tameside council in the May 1975 elections. The Conservatives had pledged in their manifesto that they would scrap the previous Labour council's plan to switch to comprehensive schools in September 1975, and instead retain the authority's existing selective system. This policy contradicted the preferences of the third Wilson government, which, in DES Circular 4/74, forcefully restated its desire to see all councils adopt a comprehensive system.

The Labour government subsequently tried to block the new council's plans, and de facto achieve its Circular 4/74 policy, by resorting to s 68 of the 1944 Act. The Secretary of State concluded that Tameside was acting 'unreasonably', and directed the now Conservative council to reinstate the plans formulated by its Labour predecessor. As noted above, Parliament had intended that s 68 be invoked only in exceptional circumstances. This indicates that the term 'unreasonable' was deployed in the *Wednesbury* sense – was the decision so peculiar that it seems the decision-maker must have taken leave of her senses?

Given the acute division of opinion within both political and educational circles over the merits of comprehensive education, there would have been little scope for the DES to argue that Tameside's preference for a selective system was per se 'unreasonable'. Rather the government argued this criteria was met because the main teaching unions had refused to co-operate with the new council's plans. The DES contended this would make it impossible to set up an accurate selection procedure in the two months remaining before the new school year.

The House of Lords rejected this argument. While it might be difficult for the new council to put its plans into effect, it would not have been impossible. Consequently it was not unreasonable of the council to pursue this policy. Therefore the criterion set out in s 68 which empowered the Secretary of State to intervene had not arisen. In coming to this decision, the House of Lords attached great importance to the election result. Electoral support for the Conservative policy was considered 'vital' in establishing that the policy itself was not unreasonable. If one's starting point is a concern that local government is accountable to its voters, the House of Lords' invocation of electoral approval as a means to establish the legality of the council's plans has considerable force. However it does not fit very easily with the earlier decision in *Roberts v Hopwood*, in which electoral support for Poplar's high wage policy was considered irrelevant.

[63] Pimlott op cit p 512.

[64] [1977] AC 1014, HL.

The obvious conclusion to be drawn from *Tameside* is that the Labour government was acting unlawfully in trying to impose its preferences on the council. But its action would also appear to have been contrary to the long accepted principle that until such time as Parliament made a definite choice between the selective and comprehensive systems, local authorities should remain free to provide schooling in their respective areas in accordance with the wishes of the local electoral majority.

Whether the House of Lords was drawing upon this conventional consideration in deciding its response to the legal issue before it is difficult to decide. As we saw when we looked at the Canadian controversy in 1980, the courts have thus far held that there are no circumstances in which even the most important convention can assume legal status. Of course that does not mean that judges do not allow conventional values to tip the legal balance in difficult cases. *Tameside* may be a good example of that process. Whether we would regard such judicial innovation as legitimate, and against what criteria we might seek to measure its legitimacy, are much larger questions – to which we return in chapter eleven.

The Wilson government seemed unwilling to accept the pluralist implications of *Tameside's* interpretation of the 1944 Act. The Education Bill introduced to the Commons in 1976 was intended, in Wilson's words, to 'abolish selection in state education'.[65] At second reading, the then Secretary of State (Fred Mulley) suggested that the negotiatory, consensual orthodoxies of the 'national–local government system' had broken down. Seven Conservative controlled councils had bluntly refused to implement Circular 4/74:

> 'I should have preferred to deal with this by agreement rather than by legislation. But we face an impasse. We can progress no further by discussion and agreement towards our declared policy of comprehensive secondary education for all. . . . The Bill . . . will, I hope lead to a determined effort by all local education authorities . . . to bring their reorganisation to a speedy and as efficient a conclusion as possible'.[66]

Section 1 of the proposed Act would provide that councils shall:

> 'in the exercise . . . of their powers and duties relating to secondary education, have regard to the general principle that such education is to be provided only in schools where arrangements for the admission of pupils are not based (wholly or partly) on selection by reference to ability or aptitude'.

It is not clear that s 1 would have abolished selection; the notion of a 'general' rather than 'universal' principle necessarily implies the existence of exceptions to the mainstream trend. That was nevertheless how most MPs interpreted the formula at second reading. The debate split on party lines. Conservative MPs expressed opposition both to the comprehensive principle per se, and to the erosion of local autonomy that the Act would seemingly impose. The latter point was perhaps best put by Paul Channon MP, who subsequently served in several of Margaret Thatcher's cabinets:

[65] Wilson op cit p 189. [66] *HCD*, 4 February 1976 cc 1219–1220.

'I had always understood that education was a matter for local people to decide in the light of local interests. Is [Mr Mulley] saying that the government intend to introduce the Bill to flout the democratically-expressed wishes of the parents involved'.[67]

The government won the second reading debate with a majority of 40, and the Bill became law in November 1976. The DES did not anticipate that the Act would immediately bring about a complete end to selection, nor would it impose a uniform model of non-selective education on the local authorities. Quite how much diversity would have remained is a matter for speculation. By 1977 the Labour government was in some disarray, and enforcing the Act slid far down its list of priorities.

CONCLUSION

It is difficult to draw firm conclusions about the constitutional position of local government in the period up to 1980. It is tempting simply to categorise central–local relations in the post-war era as a 'partnership' model,[68] in which governments of both parties adhered to a principle of constitutional morality which accepted that elected local authorities should enjoy appreciable political freedom, and should be persuaded rather than legally compelled to follow central government preferences on those occasions when central government regarded uniformity as desirable. From this viewpoint, we might plausibly conclude that the constitution did indeed by 1975 contain a convention to the effect that legislative majorities should generally tolerate a significant, geographically defined separation of powers – that parliamentary self-restraint in deference to the preservation of political pluralism had, as a matter of 'tradition and settled practice', become a matter of fundamental moral significance.

We should however recall that there was considerable consensus between the main political parties on major issues in this period. It is not politically intolerable from central government's perspective for Parliament to maintain a legal structure which allows local councils to pursue their own preferred policies over such important issues as housing and education if those policies diverge only mildly from central preferences. But in situations where that divergence was significant, such as Clay Cross or Tameside, it is clear that central government would try to invoke formal legal powers in an attempt to force councils to comply with its wishes. Clay Cross and Tameside were however isolated examples, and we might perhaps regard them as the legalistic exceptions which prove the partnership rule. But this conclusion is largely impressionistic, and speaks to general trends rather than absolute truths. Anthony Crosland, a

[67] *HCD*, 4 February 1976 c 1222. Mr Channon had a rather selective notion of local democracy. As Mr Mulley pointed out in reply, Channon had been a Minister responsible for pushing the Housing Finance Act 1972 through Parliament.

[68] See Loughlin (1985a) op cit.

member of Harold Wilson's cabinets, offered a more cynical explanation of Ministers' attitudes towards local autonomy:

'On the one hand, they genuinely believe the ringing phrases they use about how local government should have more power and freedom. . . . On the other hand a Labour government hates it when Tory councils pursue education or housing policies of which it disapproves, and exactly the same is true of a Tory government with a Labour council. This ambivalence exists in everybody I know who is concerned with relations between central and local government'.[69]

Chapter eleven examines the constitutional role that Parliament has allocated to local government since 1980; from that time it seems that both the legal and conventional rules regulating central/local relations have undergone a profound change, in which 'ambivalence' no longer plays a major role.

[69] Quoted in Bogdanor V (1976) 'Freedom in education' *Political Quarterly* 149–159 at 156.

11

LOCAL GOVERNMENT – 2: LEGAL AUTHORITARIANISM?

The 1979–1983 Thatcher administration was not the first modern government to pursue monetarist economic policies fundamentally concerned with reducing public expenditure. The Heath government had done so between 1970 and 1972, as did Wilson and Callaghan's Labour administrations between 1974 and 1979 in response to an economic crisis. Most areas of public expenditure, including local government spending were cut back. The Labour governments sought to control council expenditure through the negotiatory model of central/local relations. Authorities were requested or cajoled to reduce spending, but were not legally obliged to do so. Relatedly, the amount of tax revenue that a council raised was left to be determined at local elections.

Nevertheless, the 'ambivalence' adverted to by Crosland swung markedly in favour of greater central control by 1975. Wilson's government had established a Committee of Inquiry (the Layfield Committee) to investigate local government finance. Layfield suggested that the issue raised profound questions about the nature of British democracy. Close central control over finance and meaningful political diversity could not co-exist. A choice as to which was the more important moral value was required. Layfield's preference was clear: '[T]he only way to sustain a vital local democracy is to enlarge the share of local taxation in total local revenue'.[1]

The Labour government appeared unwilling to accept the pluralist argument. The 1977 DoE policy paper, *Local government finance*, analysed local government's role in a way which relegated localised forms of democracy almost to an afterthought.[2] The 1979–1983 Conservative government also wished to reduce local authority spending, but for the Thatcher government tight control of local government's expenditure plans was one part of a systematic attempt to restructure the constitution's conventional basis.

[1] Layfield/DoE (1976) *Report of the Committee of Enquiry into local government finance*, p 300 (London: HMSO; Cmnd 6453).

[2] See para 2.3 (London: HMSO).

'AUTHORITARIAN POPULISM' – THE IDEOLOGICAL AGENDA OF THE THATCHER GOVERNMENTS

The first Thatcher administration rejected the Keynesian orthodoxies favoured by previous Labour and Conservative administrations. It adhered instead to a Hayekian philosophy stressing a much reduced social and economic role for state institutions.[3] This philosophy entailed substantial reductions in public expenditure on welfare services, areas where local authorities traditionally exercised significant responsibilities and enjoyed appreciable discretion. The Thatcher administration was also determined to impose its preferred moral principles on all levels of government.

This authoritarian outlook did not fit easily with the pluralist model of central/local relations. Nor did it reflect the wishes of even a small majority of the electorate. In the UK as a whole, the Thatcher government had the support of barely 33% of eligible voters. In Scotland, Wales and northern England its levels of support were under 25%. The geographical fragmentation of support for Thatcherism was reinforced by the fact that many local authorities were controlled by opposition parties: the Conservatives suffered further considerable losses in the local government elections of 1980 and 1981.[4] But the limited nature of the 'consent' which 'Thatcherism' enjoyed did not persuade the government that it should moderate its wishes to impose its policies on the entire country. For local authorities, this absence of governmental self-restraint had profound consequences.

The legitimacy of the Thatcher government's plans lay partly in the argument that local authorities were not really 'democratic' institutions. Turnout for local elections since 1945 was low: it rarely exceeded 50%, and in 1975 fell to below 33% in England. This limited participation compares unfavourably with turnout in general elections, which averaged 70%–80% since 1945.[5] The Thatcher administrations suggested these figures revealed a 'silent majority' of local electors who needed to be 'saved' by national government from the unrepresentative and possibly extremist views of the small minority of political activists controlling local councils.[6] Given that the Thatcher governments had themselves attracted the support of barely one third of the national electorate, such arguments might not appear to withstand close scrutiny. The government nonetheless chose to 'protect' local people from elected councils by substantially reducing the powers that authorities could wield.

3 See particularly Hall S (1983) 'The great moving right show', in Hall and Jacques op cit.

4 See Butler D, Adonis A and Travers T (1994) *Failure in British government: the politics of the poll tax*, p 29 (Oxford: OUP).

5 For detailed figures see the first edition of this book at pp 428–429.

6 See Jenkins J (1987) 'The green sheep in Colonel Gadaffi Drive' *New Society*, 9 January 1987.

I. FINANCIAL 'REFORM' 1: GRANT PENALTIES AND RATECAPPING

The Local Government, Planning and Land Act 1980 introduced 'grant penalties'. The DoE calculated a total spending plan for each authority. Councils were not legally obliged to respect the spending target. However if a council's spending exceeded the DoE's expenditure target, the DoE withdrew a specified amount of grant. This meant that ratepayers had to finance both 100% of extra expenditure and the resultant loss of grant.

Many councils nevertheless continued to spend at higher levels than the DoE wished. Consequently, the Local Government Finance Act 1982 increased the rate of grant withdrawal. From the government's perspective, this measure was little more successful than its predecessor. Some councils simply imposed ever-higher rates on local voters, and so received ever-lower central government grants, yet still attracted electoral approval.

Some penalised authorities also initiated judicial review proceedings to challenge expenditure targets. This strategy met with mixed results. In *R v Secretary of State for the Environment, ex p Hackney London Borough Council*,[7] the council argued that expenditure targets should be attainable; if the reductions could not be achieved without large cuts in services, surely the target must be substantively ultra vires? The court refused to enter what it saw as essentially a political dispute between central and local government; this was evidently another non-justiciable issue. Subsequently, in *Nottinghamshire County Council v Secretary of State for the Environment*,[8] the House of Lords indicated that it had no wish to enter this political controversy. Lord Templeman observed that judicial review was not 'just a move in an interminable game of chess'; rather than commence litigation, councils should 'bite on the bullet' and govern their areas within whatever financial constraints the DoE thought appropriate. Notwithstanding the courts' reluctance to participate in this dispute, the DoE rapidly concluded that the grant penalties system was not very effective either in curbing council expenditure or in 'persuading' local electorates not to vote for high spending parties. Some councils overcame the threat of penalties by raising rates to such high levels that they no longer received any grant at all. That situation presumably enhances a council's accountability to its local electorate, given that voters would pay almost the entire cost of the local services their council provided. It would also seem to insulate a council from central government control; threats to withdraw grant will not work if councils receive no grant anyway. Thus the government introduced more direct methods to curb council expenditure.

7 (1985) Times, 11 May, CA. 8 [1986] AC 240, [1986] 1 All ER 199, CA.

RATECAPPING

The post-revolutionary constitution seemed always to have harboured a conventional rule that Parliament would not impose direct legal limits on a council's power to raise revenue through the rates. The grant penalties legislation undermined that convention. In the Rates Act 1984, the Thatcher government cast it aside.

The 1984 Act introduced the practice of 'ratecapping'. This simply permitted the DoE to impose a ceiling on the amount of rates revenue a council could raise. The new control was placed on income rather than expenditure. Twenty authorities were originally targeted for capping; 18 were Labour controlled.

The 'democratic' implications of ratecapping were profound; local voters wishing to choose a council providing extensive services simply could not do so, even if they were prepared to finance such services through increased local taxation. They might vote for any party they chose, but their chosen councillors could raise only that amount of revenue which central government deemed appropriate.[9]

The government had some difficulty in pushing the 1984 Act through Parliament. A few Conservative MPs, and rather more Conservative peers, felt the Act would take too much power away from local authorities and their voters. They shared the sentiments of opposition parties that local government's conventional status as an independent political organ was being too severely undermined. But with a Commons majority of 140, the government's problems in the lower house were only minor, particularly as ready resort was made to the guillotine to stifle debate.[10] In the Lords, opposition, cross-bench and some Conservative peers were sufficiently alarmed by the 1984 Bill's anti-pluralist implications to mount a determined amendment campaign, which on occasion reduced the government's majority to single figures.[11] The Bill nevertheless emerged virtually unscathed. The focus of political opposition then shifted to its implementation.

Some Labour councils attacked the Rates Act as constitutionally illegitimate, and resolved to refuse to apply it. They hoped that widespread defiance would trigger a constitutional crisis which would force the government to return to the conventional, fiscally pluralist model of central/local relations. As the deadline for compliance approached, however, support for illegal defiance melted away. Only two councils eventually refused to abide by the Act's provisions – the London borough of Lambeth and Liverpool city council.[12] Many Lambeth and Liverpool councillors were eventually surcharged and disqualified from office as a result of their non-compliance.

Given the utter inconsistency of the ratecapping principle with conventional understandings of local government's constitutional role, it is understandable that

[9] On the background to the Bill, and for a detailed description of its mechanics, see Jackman R (1984) 'The Rates Bill: a measure of desperation' *Political Quarterly* 161–170. For a more economic analysis see Wilson T (1988) 'Local freedom and central control – a question of balance', in Bailey S and Paddison R (eds) *The reform of local government finance in Britain* (London: Routledge).

[10] See Loughlin (1994) op cit at n 49.

[11] See Welfare op cit.

[12] Butler, Adonis and Travers op cit p 65.

several authorities declined to take Lord Templeman's earlier advice to 'bite the bullet' of government decisions which denied their electorates the power to vote for local services to be administered as they preferred. Both Birmingham and Greenwich councils initiated successful judicial review proceedings against ratecapping in 1986.[13] But these proved short-lived successes. The government had by now tired of defending its policies in the courts; judicial review was a time-consuming process, in which favourable outcomes could apparently not be guaranteed. Consequently, the government began to respond to defeats in the courts by promoting retrospective legislation.

The highly unconventional constitutional character of retrospective legislation has already been adverted to.[14] The Thatcher government saw no impediment to using retrospective legislation to curb local government's financial independence; what had previously been regarded as a presumptively 'unconstitutional' exercise of Parliament's sovereign power, invoked on a cross-party basis in response to extraordinary situations, had evidently become a routinised and partisan feature of government policy.[15]

Grant penalties and rate-capping comprised the first two phases of the Thatcher governments' efforts to redefine conventional constitutional understandings about central/local financial relations. We address the third phase below. Before doing so however, we devote some further attention to the courts' role in determining the limits of local authorities' political and economic autonomy.

II. COLLECTIVE POLITICS AND INDIVIDUAL RIGHTS: THE JUDICIAL ROLE

A notable consequence of the grant penalty and ratecapping policies was that it became accepted as a normal aspect of central/local relations for councils to challenge the legality of government action. Between 1945 and 1980 it was rare for disagreements between central and local government to be resolved in this way.[16] Disputes were generally settled through negotiations which eventually produced acceptable compromise. After 1980, such compromises proved unattainable. But the so-called 'juridification'[17] of the financial relationship between central and local government was not the only issue relating to local democracy in which the courts were embroiled.

[13] *R v Secretary of State for the Environment, ex p Birmingham City Council* (15 April 1986, unreported); *R v Secretary of State for the Environment, ex p Greenwich London Borough Council* (17 December 1986, unreported). Neither case is reported, but both are noted in Loughlin (1994) op cit.

[14] See pp 87–88 above.

[15] Much like it seems, the use of Henry VIII clauses.

[16] Loughlin (1985) op cit; (1994) op cit.

[17] The term is Martin Loughlin's; see (1985) op cit.

'FARES FAIR': *BROMLEY LONDON BOROUGH COUNCIL V GREATER LONDON COUNCIL*

While most of the country had waited until the Local Government Act 1972 for its Victorian local government structures to be modernised, local government in London was overhauled in the mid-1960s. Many small councils were abolished, and new larger authorities created. The London County Council was also replaced by a strategic council with limited functions for the entire capital. The 'Greater London Council' (GLC) assumed responsibility for, among other things, public transport systems, waste collection, major planning proposals and housing provision. An elected 'Inner London Education Authority' (ILEA) was also created, with wide-ranging education functions. The GLC's creation was the result of a prolonged process of negotiation, initiated by a Royal Commission investigation. The Commission's proposals were subsequently introduced as a Bill and, following substantial amendment in response to the wishes of the opposition and various local authorities, enacted in 1965.[18]

The GLC's most noteworthy policy in the 1980s attempted to shift the burden of transport provision in London away from cars towards greater use of buses, tubes, and trains. The GLC's transport role was set out in the London (Transport) Act 1969, a statute introduced by Wilson's second Labour government. Section 1 required the GLC to provide an 'economic, efficient and integrated' transport system for Greater London. The Act did not give the GLC direct control of London's bus and underground networks; rather it created a body called the London Transport Executive (LTE) to co-ordinate and manage services. Following the green light philosophy then prevailing in parliamentary circles, the 1969 Act did not specify precisely how the LTE should operate; but s 7 indicated that the LTE should as far as practicable avoid making a financial loss in successive years. The Act envisaged that the LTE and the GLC would work closely together, and in particular s 3 empowered the GLC to make grants to the LTE for 'any purpose'.

At this point we might ask what 'purposes' the 1969 Parliament intended London Transport to serve. From a social democratic perspective, the system might be seen as a social service, with operating losses subsidised by ratepayers. By encouraging people to use trains and buses rather than cars one presumably reduces traffic congestion and air pollution, speeds up journey times, reduces overcrowding on trains, and makes public transport a more pleasant and reliable way to travel to work and to leisure activities. An alternative, Hayekian view would see London Transport as a business like any other, providing a system that made an overall profit. If the LTE or GLC wanted to run loss-making routes, they would have to subsidise them through profits on other routes, not by taking subsidies from ratepayers.

Scrutiny of the Act, and of *Hansard*, indicates that Wilson's government was unclear about its preferences. When introducing the Bill, the sponsoring Minister had said that:

[18] See Hampson op cit, pp 23–26.

'. . . the GLC might wish . . . the LTE to run services at a loss for social or planning reasons. It might wish to keep fares down at a time when costs are rising and there is no scope for economies. It is free to do so. But it has to bear the costs'.[19]

But the Minister also stressed that the LTE should attempt to break even. Consequently, one could find neither a legislative nor governmental answer to the crucial question of whether the GLC could use s 3 to cancel out successive deficits the LTE might incur if it ran London Transport as a 'social service' rather than a 'business'.

In its manifesto for the 1981 GLC elections, Labour put forward a programme (called 'Fares Fair') to increase bus and tube services, and simultaneously cut fares by 25%. 'Fares Fair' would cost £120 million per year; a sum comprising a £69 million operating deficit, and a £50 million loss in central government grant because the programme took the GLC over its expenditure target. The Labour group planned to raise this money by levying a special rate on all the London boroughs.

Labour won a majority in the GLC elections. A legal challenge to Fares Fair was immediately launched by the Conservative controlled Bromley Council, a suburban London borough liable to pay the supplementary rate. The issue before the court was straightforward: what had Parliament meant when it ordered the GLC to maintain 'economic, efficient and integrated' transport services? Was London Transport a social service, heavily subsidised by London ratepayers? Or a business, whose primary concern should be to avoid operating losses?

The House of Lords decided unanimously against the GLC.[20] The majority held that s 1's reference to an 'economic' service required the GLC to ensure that the LTE ran on a 'break even' basis. The GLC could use s 3 to provide a subsidy to make up for unforeseen losses, or to compensate for exceptional circumstances, but it was not 'economic' deliberately to adopt a s 3 subsidy policy which underwrote a long-term operating deficit. Lord Diplock adopted a slightly different argument. He considered that the argument over the first component of the policy's cost, the £69 million rating loss, was finely balanced. However he did not feel obliged to resolve this question, for the second element of the cost, the loss of £50 million of government grant, clearly breached the council's fiduciary duty to its ratepayers.

The judgments obviously owe much to the *Roberts v Hopwood* misapplication and subversion of the fiduciary duty doctrine. As in *Roberts*, the House of Lords did not consider that electoral approval had any bearing on the policy's legality. This initially seems difficult to reconcile with the *Tameside* decision. In *Tameside*, Lord Wilberforce had concluded that electoral approval for the council's selective education policy was 'vital' in establishing that the policy was not ultra vires. Yet in *Bromley*, Lord Wilberforce held that voter support 'could not confer validity' on Fares Fair.

It is difficult to see why the same judge seems to have adopted such different positions in cases which apparently present similar problems. The decisions can be distinguished in a rather formalistic way, if the GLC's action was ultra vires because

[19] *HCD*, 17 December 1968, cc 1247–1248. [20] [1983] 1 AC 768.

of its alleged 'illegality' rather than (as in *Tameside*) its alleged 'irrationality'. Since irrationality is a concept concerned with bizarre departures from accepted moral standards, it is difficult (but not impossible) to sustain the argument that a local electoral majority can be irrational: a widely shared opinion is unlikely to be morally outrageous. Illegality, in contrast, is a technical question, which only judges, not lay people, are competent to decide. Electoral majorities may form entirely rational opinions as to desired policy outcomes premised on a misunderstanding of the correct legal position; in such circumstances, the electorate's view is irrelevant.

While superficially attractive, that distinction may not withstand close scrutiny. As Lord Greene MR suggested in *Wednesbury*, the various grounds of review run into each other. This raises the suspicion that a judge might classify the question before her as one of irrationality if she wished the electorate's view to prevail, and as one of illegality if she did not.[21]

There is a temptation to explain the divergent outcomes of *Tameside* and *Bromley* simply in terms of judicial bias; Tameside won because a conservative House of Lords approved of grammar schools; the GLC lost because the still conservative House of Lords did not approve of cheap bus fares. This rather simplistic political reductionism (which in effect alleges that the courts are constantly engaged in an anti-Labour conspiracy which subverts the sovereignty of Parliament, the separation of powers, and conventional models of central-local relations) has attracted some support from authoritative commentators.[22] The argument is difficult to sustain. Its weakness in respect of *Tameside* has already been noted. In respect of *Bromley*, one cannot avoid the conclusion that Wilson's government presented Parliament with an ambiguous Bill, which neither house clarified. The Act's text lent itself to two irreconcilable interpretations; it is unsurprising that the judiciary favoured the more fiscally conservative meaning.

Nevertheless, the re-emergence of the warped version fiduciary duty doctrine intensified the juridification process. The high profile it was afforded by *Bromley* led many councils routinely to seek counsel's opinions on the legality of their expenditure plans.[23] Yet it was not simply questions of fiscal autonomy that led local authorities to the courts in the mid-1980s.

WHEELER V LEICESTER CITY COUNCIL

From 1979, the 'new urban left' grouping of Labour controlled councils[24] undertook many experimental social and economic policy initiatives directed towards reducing

21 For an incisive analysis see Himsworth C (1991) 'Poll tax capping and judicial review' *Public Law* 76–92. See further chapter fourteen below.

22 See Griffith J (1985) 'Judicial decision-making in public law' *Public Law* 564–582; Pannick D (1984) 'The Law Lords and the needs of contemporary society' *Political Quarterly* 318–328; McAuslan P (1983) 'Administrative law, collective consumption and judicial policy' *MLR* 1–21.

23 Bridges L et al (1987) *Legality and local politics* (Aldershot: Avebury).

24 On its origins, composition and policy objectives see Gyford J (1985) *The Politics of Local Socialism* (London: George Allen and Unwin).

racial discrimination. Section 71 of the Race Relations Act 1976[25] required local authorities to promote good race relations when discharging their functions. Labour councils invoked s 71 to justify such diverse strategies as promoting ethnic minority cultural and political associations, and requiring contractors to use workforces reflecting the local population's ethnic balance.[26] Councils of all parties also took related initiatives in discharging their education functions, by developing multi-cultural and anti-racist school curricula.

Notwithstanding the fact that the councils pursuing these policies had been elected by local citizens, such activities were described as 'loony leftism' by sections of the national media. Such stories were frequently entirely inaccurate; but Margaret Thatcher evidently saw them as identifying another evil against which local people required protection.[27] However one particular allegation levied at Leicester City Council did have a factual basis, and attracted the attention of the courts as well as the mass media.

During the 1970s and 1980s, political parties and pressure groups in many Commonwealth countries campaigned to discourage sporting links with South Africa, which then still maintained the apartheid regime introduced in 1948. That movement culminated in the 1977 Gleneagles Agreement, in which the Commonwealth states pledged to take 'every practical step' to discourage national teams from playing South African opposition. In Britain, neither Labour nor Conservative governments considered the Agreement an appropriate instrument to incorporate into British law. In 1984, the English Rugby Football Union (ERFU) accepted (despite government disapproval) an invitation to tour South Africa. ERFU denied that it approved of apartheid, and advanced the widely held argument that the best way to hasten reform in South Africa was to maximise its people's exposure to the representatives of democratic nations.

The question of 'representatives' much concerned Leicester city council. Several members of the touring party played club rugby for Leicester RFC. Some councillors – taking a rather odd view of the matter – feared that these players' participation might indicate that Leicester's citizens approved of apartheid. The council's ruling Labour group consequently requested the club to condemn the tour and urge its players not to participate. The club would not do so. Councillors then decided to terminate the club's lease of a council playing field which it had used for some years.

The council justified its behaviour through s 71:

[25] A measure introduced by a Labour government with the broad support of the then Conservative opposition.

[26] See Ousley H (1984) 'Local authority race initiatives', in Boddy M and Fudge C (eds) *Local socialism* (London: Macmillan); Hall W (1986) 'Contracts compliance at the GLC' *Local Government Studies* 17–31.

[27] Haringey council reportedly refused to buy black dustbin bags because associating the colour black with garbage might offend people of African-Caribbean ethnicity. Similarly, Hackney Council allegedly ordered its nursery schools to sing 'Baa Baa Green Sheep' rather than 'Baa Baa Black Sheep'. Subsequent investigation suggested these stories had no sustainable base: see Jenkins (1987) op cit. For a full account of press coverage see Gordon P (1990) 'A dirty war: the new right and local authority anti-racism', in Ball W and Solomos J (eds) *Race and local politics* (London: Macmillan).

'The council considers it appropriate, to encourage racial harmony, to be seen publicly to distance itself from bodies who occupy an important position in the city, which may be seen to be representing the city and which do not actively discourage or condemn sporting contacts with the South African regime which discriminates and oppresses people of the same ethnic origin as a substantial proportion of Leicester's population'.[28]

The club's action to have the council's decision quashed as irrational failed at first instance. In the Court of Appeal, Ackner LJ (supported by Sir George Waller) considered that as the council's action accorded with the Gleneagles Agreement:

'it would be quite wrong to categorise as perverse the council's decision to give an outward and visible manifestation of the club's failure, indeed refusal, "to take every practical step to discourage" the tour, and in particular the participation of its members'.[29]

The court afforded local authorities considerable power to pursue political preferences whose effective expression was dependent upon winning public office. In refusing to quash the council's decision, it defined the issue as one of *political legitimacy*, to be resolved through the local electoral process. The House of Lords, in contrast, proceeded from a different premise and held unanimously in the club's favour.

Lord Roskill's leading judgment found several reasons for declaring the council's action unlawful. The first was that the council's action was irrational. Lord Roskill accepted that the council would not act *Wednesbury* unreasonably if it sought to 'persuade' the club to accept its views:

'But in a field where other views can equally legitimately be held, persuasion, however powerful, must not be allowed to cross that line where it moves into the field of illegitimate pressure coupled with the threat of sanctions'.[30]

But rather than pursuing this argument, Lord Roskill immediately turned his attention to condemning the council's 'request' to the club as too imprecise to permit an affirmative response. He regarded this imprecision as a 'procedural impropriety' which invalidated the council's substantive decision; it was on this ground that he eventually decided the case.

Lord Templeman based his decision on wider grounds:

'My Lords, the laws of this country are not like the laws of Nazi Germany. A private individual or a private organisation cannot be obliged to display zeal in the pursuit of an object sought by a public authority and cannot be obliged to publish views dictated by a public authority'.[31]

The casual equation of the council's behaviour with that of the Hitler government is an asinine analogy, and does much to undermine the credibility of Templeman's opinion. In a less absurd vein, Lord Templeman accepted that the council was not bound to allow its property to be used by an organisation which contravened the

28 *Wheeler v Leicester City Council* [1985] AC 1054; affidavit evidence of the council's Chief Executive, quoted by Ackner LJ in the Court of Appeal, at 1059.

29 Ibid, at 1061. 30 Ibid, at 1078. 31 Ibid, at 1080.

spirit of the Race Relations Act 1976. He did not explain what the spirit of the 1976 Act might entail, but some further judicial guidance was promptly forthcoming.

R V LEWISHAM LONDON BOROUGH COUNCIL, EX P SHELL UK LTD

The issue before the High Court in *R v Lewisham London Borough Council, ex p Shell UK Ltd*[32] was whether s 71 empowered a council to boycott products manufactured by a company with extensive South African interests. Lewisham had sought assurances from Shell UK that the company would sever these links. When such assurances were not given, the council decided to boycott Shell products.

Lewisham took pains to establish that its actions were legally defensible. Councillors were apprised by their solicitors of the fiduciary duty doctrine. The council decided that the boycott would extend only so far as was financially 'feasible'. It established that alternative suppliers were available, and that the boycott's total cost would not exceed £2000 per year. The council also sought counsel's opinion before implementing the policy. This emphasised the limits imposed by *Wheeler*, and also advised that if the council sought to justify the boycott per s 71, councillors:

> 'must be guided, not by their abhorrence of the Apartheid system in itself, but their judgement as to the effect on race relations in their Borough of taking or not taking action. . . .'.[33]

Given that advice, it is surprising that the letter to Shell UK in which the council announced its boycott not only stressed its wish to promote good race relations but also observed that the authority was 'keen to ensure that we are not inadvertently contributing to Apartheid via our pension fund investments and purchase of goods'.[34]

Like the rugby club in *Wheeler*, Shell responded by reiterating its abhorrence of apartheid, and observed that disinvestment was merely one of several competing views on how to hasten South Africa's progress towards democracy. Shell subsequently sought a declaration that the boycott was ultra vires, alleging it to be *Wednesbury* unreasonable; to have breached the council's fiduciary duty; to have been reached without investigation as to whether it reflected the views of local electors; and to have been motivated by a wish to punish the company and induce a change of policy.

Neill LJ felt that the council's decision was not irrational; the boycott was a plausible way to promote good race relations. Nor need the council adduce evidence confirming electoral support for the decision; this was a conclusion the authority might lawfully reach 'on the basis of its own experience and perception'.[35]

In finding for Shell, Neill LJ followed *Wheeler*. He observed: 'though the scope of s 71 of the 1976 Act is wide and embraces all the activities of the council, a council cannot use it . . . to punish a body or person who had done nothing contrary to English law'.[36] The remaining issue was therefore to determine if the boycott was a bona fide attempt to promote good race relations or a 'punishment'. The court thus

[32] [1988] 1 All ER 938. [33] Ibid, at 945. [34] Ibid, at 945. [35] Ibid, at 952.
[36] Ibid, at 951.

turned to the council's reasons for its decision. Neill LJ accepted that the motives underlying government action could be complex and multi-faceted. Some might be lawful, others unlawful. However the applicable legal principle was clear: '[W]hen . . . two reasons or purposes cannot be disentangled and one of them is bad . . . the court can interfere to quash the decision'.[37] Neill LJ concluded that Lewisham's 'wish to change the Shell policy towards South Africa was inextricably mixed up with any wish to improve race relations . . . and this extraneous and impermissible purpose has the effect of vitiating the decision as a whole'.[38]

SECTION 17 OF THE LOCAL GOVERNMENT ACT 1988

Both *Lewisham* and *Wheeler* exposed the courts to accusations of interfering with an arguably non-justiciable problem. On this occasion, the government appeared to agree. The Local Government Act 1988, s 17 addressed the contract compliance initiatives at issue in *Lewisham*. Local authorities were now obliged to exercise their contractual powers 'without reference to . . . non-commercial matters . . .'. These included, inter alia:

(c) any involvement of . . . contractors with irrelevant fields of government policy;

(e) the country of territory of supplies to, or the location in any country or territory of the business activities or interests of contractors;

(f) any political industrial or sectarian affiliations or interests of contractors . . .

Nicholas Ridley, the Environment Secretary, regarded s 17 as a necessary response to Labour councils' 'loony left' excesses:

'Although as yet only a small minority of councils go in for such posturing, the disease is spreading. Already more than 40 local authorities impose contract conditions relating to links with South Africa. Too many councillors seem to find it more fun to play at national politics at their ratepayers' expense than to deal with the real local challenges and problems'.[39]

Ridley attached little consequence to arguments that a council's electoral accountability ensured that council activities attracted popular approval: 'ratepayers do not elect the councils; in many . . . areas a very small minority of the electorate pays full rates'.[40]

[37] Ibid, at 951. [38] Ibid, at 952. [39] HCD 6 July 1987, cc 83–84.

[40] Ibid, c 84. Ridley's suggestion that effective voting rights should depend on an ability to pay is reminiscent of the political philosophy underpinning the 1832 Great Reform Act, but seems inconsistent with modern notions that make voting rights contingent merely on being an adult, mentally competent citizen. As we shall below, the idea that a citizen should have to 'pay' to vote was then exercising considerable influence on central government.

III. INSTITUTIONAL AND IDEOLOGICAL REFORM

In the context of Britain's existing constitutional order, one cannot question the legality of the s 17 restrictions. Nevertheless, they reinforced the argument that the Thatcher governments had little sympathy with that pluralist, tolerant, view of local government's constitutional role. But s 17 was not the most extreme example of authoritarian legislation passed in that era.

THE ABOLITION OF THE GLC AND THE METROPOLITAN COUNTIES

The Local Government Act 1985 was a straightforward measure to abolish the GLC. The commitment to do this was belatedly slipped into the Conservative Party's 1983 election manifesto by the Prime Minister.[41] The governmental investigations preceding the creation of the GLC had spanned several years and comprised several thousand pages of investigation and proposals. The DoE report recommending abolition, *Streamlining the cities*,[42] took two months to produce, spanned 31 pages, and involved no significant consultation with opposition parties, local authorities, or the people of London. Its recommendation was that the council should be abolished and its functions given to the London boroughs or boards appointed by central government. The GLC was simply presumed to be an unnecessary tier of government, which added to bureaucracy without producing any worthwhile benefits.[43]

The GLC campaigned skilfully against abolition. The campaign questioned the constitutional legitimacy of simply doing away with an elected local authority which represented over five million people, and on the technical efficiency of scrapping an authority which provided co-ordinated strategic services for one of the world's most important cities. The GLC attracted considerable public support. It also seemed that some Conservative MPs and many Conservative peers would vote against the government on this issue, as they had over ratecapping. The government's abolition timetable had two parts. The Local Government (Interim Provisions) Bill 1984 proposed that the GLC elections scheduled for May 1985 would be scrapped. Arrangements for transferring the GLC's powers to new bodies would not be effective until April 1986, and would be introduced in a subsequent Bill early in 1985. Parliament was thus being asked to approve the details of abolition before debating the merits of the central question. This procedural objection was compounded by the Bill's substantive effect. During the 11 month gap between May 1985 and April 1986, the GLC's powers would be wielded by 'interim councils' based on the various London boroughs, which in effect would give the Conservative Party majority control of powers which the GLC's electorate had bestowed on the Labour Party.

41 Butler, Adonis and Travers op cit, pp 37–39.

42 (1983) (London: HMSO: Cmnd 9063).

43 For an analysis of the motives behind abolition see O'Leary B (1987) 'Why was the GLC abolished?' *International Journal of Urban and Regional Research* 192–217; (1987) 'British farce, french drama and tales of two cities' *Public Administration* 369–389.

The Lords inflicted a substantial defeat (191 votes to 143) on the government in Committee. The government then conceded that the existing GLC councillors could remain in office until the abolition in 1986.[44] The government did not however concede on the cancellation of the 1985 elections, presumably because it feared that London's voters might use it to signify massive popular disapproval of the abolition proposal. The Lords' stance did much to enhance its resurgent reputation; *The Times* hailed the government's defeat as 'a triumph for the principles of constitutionalism and specifically for the principle of a bicameral Parliament'.[45] Upper house opposition continued when the abolition Bill itself was debated. An amendment creating an elected 'co-ordinating authority' to supervise all of the GLC's former powers was lost by only 17 votes.

That the Bill was ultimately enacted virtually unscathed illustrates the fragility of conventional constitutional principles when they are opposed by a determined central government with a large Commons majority. The geographical boundaries of local government have been restructured many times before. But in the modern era, the process has not been conducted in so pre-emptory a way, nor on the basis of substantive terms prompting so much party political dispute and public opposition, and not without the creation of a new elected body to assume the powers of the abolished authorities.

IV. PRIVATISING LOCAL GOVERNMENT

The abolition of the capital city's elected council is perhaps the most graphic example of local government's declining constitutional significance since 1980. But it is merely one part of a more complex tapestry. The GLC abolition Bill, seen in conjunction with the previous reforms to local government finance, was described in 1984 as the 'most determined assault on local government autonomy in recent history'.[46] It is overly simplistic to suggest that this assault was 'anti-democratic' in nature. Rather it represented the triumph of a highly centralised, authoritarian perception of minoritarian democracy over a decentralised, consensual perception of pluralist democracy. This trend raises large questions as to the adequacy of Britain's contemporary constitutional arrangements; but before turning to that issue it is appropriate to examine several other legislative innovations enacted from the mid-1980s onwards.

44 See Welfare op cit; Shell (1992) op cit, pp 168–173.

45 30 June 1984; quoted in Shell (1992) op cit, p169.

46 Jackman op cit, p161.

THE WIDDICOMBE REPORT

The Widdicombe Committee of Inquiry into the Conduct of Local Authority Business,[47] was established by the DoE in 1985 following the GLC abolition imbroglio. The Committee's title perhaps hints at the kind of recommendations the government was hoping the report would produce – the concern apparently being more with 'business' than with 'government'. If so, the government was disappointed both by the Committee's investigations and its conclusions. Widdicombe identified an important role for party politics in the local government sector, and produced a package of recommendations which would seemingly have strengthened councils' capacities to pursue distinctive political agendas.[48]

The resultant legislation, the Local Government and Housing Act 1989,[49] was highly selective in the principles it accepted from the Widdicombe report. The DoE policy statement which preceded the Act announced that the reforms were intended 'to ensure that local democracy and local accountability are substantially strengthened'.[50] However, the government chose to define 'democracy' in terms which increased the likelihood that the outcome of locally based decision-making procedures would accord with central government preferences.

Thus the Act responded to the fact that many Labour councillors were the employees of other councils by prohibiting such 'twin-tracking',[51] but refusing to accept that councillors should be paid for the tasks they performed. Relatedly, the Act created so-called 'politically restricted' posts in local authorities. Citizens employed in such jobs were not permitted to engage in such political activities as holding office in a political party, canvassing at elections, or speaking or writing in public in a way that might affect support for a political party. The Act made several other significant intrusions into local authorities' internal management processes, often by simply making provision for the DoE to issue regulations to control particular aspects of council behaviour. The Act exemplifies, as McAuslan suggests, a perception of democracy in a unitary state in which 'in so far as local government has a role in the governance of the United Kingdom . . . it is to carry out and obey central government policies in the manner required by central government'.[52]

Forcing local government, either indirectly through ratecapping, or directly via such legislation as the LGA 1988 s 17, to conduct its activities along business lines is one method by which a government with a legislative majority can ensure that local electorates which prefer social democratic forms of government cannot vote for councils which can implement those principles. It is not however the only method.

47 (1986) (London: HMSO: Cmnd 9797). For comment see McAuslan P (1987) 'The Widdicombe Report: local government business or politics' *Public Law* 154–162.

48 See Leach S (1989) 'Strengthening local democracy? the government's response to Widdicombe', in Stewart J and Stoker G (eds) *The future of local government* (London: Macmillan).

49 See Ganz G (1990) 'The depoliticisation of local authorities: the Local Government and Housing Act 1989, Part I' *Public Law* 224–242.

50 DoE (1988) *The conduct of local authority business* p v (London: HMSO: Cmnd 433).

51 Except in respect of teachers.

52 (1988) op cit, pp 157–158.

Rather than force elected councils to act like businesses, central government might simply decide to remove certain powers from the council sector altogether, and give them to individuals or bodies more likely to share central government's political predispositions. This section examines two major areas of local government activity which have been 'privatised' in this way.

HOUSING – INDIVIDUATED AND COLLECTIVE PRIVATISATION

A corollary of councils' traditional autonomy in the area of housing management was that neither Parliament nor the courts granted tenants legally enforceable rights against their landlords over the way that their homes were managed. Many councils evidently thought that tenants' 'rights' were unnecessary, considering councils' 'democratic accountability . . . a sufficient safeguard against any abuses'.[53] But by 1975, it was widely accepted that council house management could often justifiably be accused of inefficiency and insensitivity to tenants' wishes.[54]

The Callaghan government's 1979 Housing Bill included a 'Tenant's Charter'. The Charter limited councils' eviction powers, forbade certain restrictive tenancy conditions, and would have required authorities to establish a Tenants' Committee which was to be consulted on all aspects of housing management, including allocation policies and rent levels. The Bill fell with the Labour government in 1979.

The Tenants' Charter enacted in the Thatcher government's Housing Act 1980 superficially resembled Labour's Bill. The new legislation added a 'right to buy' for existing tenants, and dropped the Tenants' Committees proposal. The 1980 Act fundamentally recast the legal basis of a council's relationship with its tenants. In granting tenants legally enforceable rights, the Thatcher government necessarily curtailed local authority autonomy, at least at the formal level. From a functionalist perspective, however, the change did not appear to have either an immediate or a substantial effect.

A wide-ranging study of the Charter's implementation was carried out between 1980 and 1983 by the City University Housing Research Group (CUHRG).[55] The Tenant's Charter was introduced with several other major housing initiatives. All authorities had to allocate considerable administrative resources to handling 'right to buy' sales; councils in London had the additional task of inheriting former GLC properties; and the entire local government sector was adjusting to the new financial regime created by the Local Government, Planning and Land Act. These various demands led councils to prioritise their housing management resources: CUHRG reported that many housing managers were concerned more with: 'coping with these other priorities and keeping their basic activities going, than with introducing the tenants' rights'.[56] The survey's 'most striking' result was that many authorities did not

53 Cited in Laffin op cit, n 6, p 194.

54 See for example Cullingworth op cit, pp 38–47; Merret op cit, ch 8.

55 Kay A, Legg C and Foot J (1985) *The 1980 Tenant's Rights in Practice* (London: City University).

56 Ibid, pp 18 and 22.

realise that the Act's provisions were part of the tenancy agreement; only 56% of authorities had incorporated the Act's security of tenure requirements into their leases.[57] But in respect of the 'right to buy', a different picture emerged.

The right to buy

The Housing Act 1980's 'right to buy' entitled council tenants of three years standing to buy their home at a discount of 33% on its market value, with an extra 1% for each year of additional occupancy, to a 70% maximum. Over a million units were sold during the 1980s.

The right to buy was a controversial policy in 1980. Some Labour councils decided they did not want to apply it: several decided to make it difficult for tenants to become owner-occupiers.[58] The 1980 Act had given the DoE sweeping interventionist powers against authorities suspected of obstructing sales. Section 23 provided that where it appears that to the Minister that the tenants are experiencing difficulty in buying their houses, the Minister may send in centrally appointed Housing Commissioners to take over the sales process.[59]

Following complaints from tenants in Norwich, the Minister invoked s 23. The council challenged the use of this power, arguing it had deployed staff on other responsibilities which it was obliged to undertake and so there was nothing 'unreasonable' about the delays that tenants experienced. In *Norwich City Council v Secretary of State for the Environment*, the Court of Appeal characterised s 23 as: 'draconian . . . without precedent in legislation of this nature'.[60] But whether the council's action was reasonable was irrelevant. The person whose conduct was in question was the Minister – was his intervention *Wednesbury* unreasonable? As no sales at all had been completed in Norwich in the first seven months of the Act being in force it would seem difficult to categorise his action in that way. His intervention was clearly a 'legal' exercise of executive power. Whether s 23 was itself a 'legitimate' exercise of legislative power is a different and more difficult question.

The right to buy enabled many less wealthy householders to become owners, and therefore to benefit from long-term increases in property values and to escape from a restrictive landlord-tenant relationship. The policy's full impact on local government's role as a housing provider is however only evident when one also considers central government policies towards the building of new council housing. The Thatcher administrations placed significant restrictions on new construction. Proceeds from the right to buy exceeded nine billion pounds by 1986. But councils were permitted to spend only a fraction of those receipts on new housing. Fewer council houses were

[57] Ibid, table 3.1.

[58] Ascher K (1983) 'The politics of administrative opposition – council house sales and the right to buy' *Local Government Studies* 12–20.

[59] An analysis of the power and subsequent case law is provided in Loughlin (1986) op cit, n 44, pp 104–110.

[60] [1982] 1 All ER 737 at 748, per Kerr LJ. For an analysis of events see Murie and Maplass op cit, pp 233–240.

built in the 1980s than in any decade since 1920. While over one million units were sold, only 330,000 were built.[61]

'Opting out' and Housing Action Trusts

Nevertheless, over 20% of the population still lived in council houses in 1988. Few of these tenants could afford to buy their homes. Consequently the DoE sought other methods further to reduce the local authority's landlord role. The Housing Act 1988 empowered tenants to 'opt out' of local authority control and 'vote' for a new, government approved landlord. Early votes indicated little tenant support for wholesale privatisation. This perhaps suggests that tenants, if not central government, continued to see councils as legitimate and desirable providers of subsidised housing.

Part III of the 1988 Act also introduced the 'Housing Action Trust' (HAT). HATs were government appointed boards which assumed control of public housing and land use planning in government designated inner-city areas. HATs were to act as temporary landlords, responsible for upgrading the housing and thereafter selling it, either to current occupants or new private sector landlords. HATs attracted little support from council tenants initially. Seven estates were originally targeted for HAT schemes. By late 1990, none had voted to leave council control. Several estates subsequently chose HAT status in 1991. This was perhaps not an entirely 'free' choice, insofar as prospective HATs were offered funds for refurbishment and redevelopment not available to local authorities.[62]

'Ring-fencing' housing revenue accounts

Legislative initiatives also reduced local authorities' traditionally loosely confined discretion to set rent levels. Significant reductions in DoE rent subsidies since 1980[63] compelled many councils to raise rents well above prevailing inflation rates. Councils' scope to subsidise rents from their general revenue was obviously curbed by general DoE expenditure constraints during the 1980s. The Housing and Local Government Act 1989 reinforced this indirect pressure by 'ring fencing' councils' housing budgets. Local authorities could no longer use their general revenue for housing purposes; council stock must run on a 'break even' basis. Ring fencing provoked vigorous criticism from Labour and Conservative authorities. Many considered it an unwarranted, further limitation on council autonomy. Twenty authorities increased rents by over 30% in 1990, with Conservative controlled Canterbury DC and South Buckinghamshire DC levying 54% and 53% rises respectively.[64]

[61] See Loveland I (1992) 'Square pegs, round holes: the "right" to council housing in the post-war era' *Journal of Law and Society* 339–364.

[62] Owens R (1991) 'If the HAT Fits' ROOF 17 (November/December); Woodward R (1991) 'Mobilising opposition: the campaign against housing action trusts in Tower Hamlets' *Housing Studies* 44–56.

[63] Loughlin (1985) op cit, p 104: Malpass and Murie op cit, pp 110–113.

[64] See Ward M (1988) 'Priced out' (1988) *Housing 9* (October); Warburton M and Malpass P (1991) 'Riding the rent rocket' ROOF 27 July/August.

THE MANAGEMENT OF STATE SCHOOLS

When 'ring-fencing' is combined with compulsory sales, little new building, and the opting out proposals, it becomes clear that the constitutional legitimacy of council housing has been increasingly undermined by central government since 1980. What has traditionally been an important vehicle for councils to apply the benefits of local knowledge, political education, political pluralism, and policy innovation to the government of their respective areas has been appreciably weakened. But housing is not the only area of local authority responsibility to be reformed in such a way.

The Education Act 1986

In 1947, Quintin Hogg MP (who as Lord Hailsham subsequently sat in several Thatcher cabinets) stressed the need for cross-party consensus on education policy:

> 'Education is a matter which must be handled by statesmen on pragmatical and objective lines . . . not the least valuable feature of the 1944 Education Act is that it has placed the general framework of our educational system beyond the range of party politics'.[65]

Hogg seemed to suggest that education policy was too important to be left to a political process in which outcomes may be shaped by the transient, populist desires of a faction of 'the people'. His concern was largely allayed by the pervasively bipartisan character of British party politics in the Butskellite era. But by the mid-1960s, a forceful critique of the educational consensus coalesced around a group of educators and politicians associated with the Conservative Party's right wing. This ideological standpoint had three primary foci: firstly, it vehemently opposed comprehensive education: secondly it feared that the 'traditional' concern of equipping children with adequate literacy abilities, numeracy skills and knowledge of 'British' history and culture had been sacrificed to the 'trendy' ideas of the teaching profession and DES policymakers; and thirdly it contended that the (allegedly always sensible) wishes of parents were being subverted by the extremist preferences of local politicians.[66]

Under Edward Heath's leadership of the Conservative Party, such sentiments enjoyed little influence, even though his Education Secretary during the 1970–1974 government, Margaret Thatcher, was a right-wing sympathiser.[67] However Thatcher's emergence as party leader in 1975, and the Conservatives' general election victory in 1979, raised the prospect, in respect of local government's role in education, of a significant redefinition of conventional constitutional understandings.

The changes initiated by the Thatcher governments were couched in terms of enhancing 'parental choice' within education. Two strands of these early reforms merit mention here; the first concerned the powers of parents to determine which school their child would attend; the second the powers of school governors.

65 (1947) *The case for Conservatism*, pp 143–144 (Penguin: West Drayton).

66 See especially Dale R (1983) 'Thatcherism and education', in Ahier J and Flude M (eds) *Contemporary education policy* (London: Croom Helm); Centre for Contemporary Cultural Studies (1981) *Unpopular education* pp 201–207 (London: Hutchinson).

67 For an account of Thatcher's tenure at the DES see Young op cit, ch 6.

Parental choice of school. As noted in chapter ten, s 76 of the 1944 Act did not entitle parents to insist that their child attend a particular school; individual parental preferences were clearly subordinated to the council's judgements as to its area's overall requirements. That emphasis was altered by the Education Act 1980, which the DES presented as a device granting parents enhanced 'rights of choice'.[68] Section 6 provided that:

> '(1) every local education authority shall make arrangements for enabling the parent of a child in the area of the authority to express a preference as to the school at which he wishes education to be provided for his child . . .
>
> (2) it shall be the duty of a local education authority . . . to comply with any preference expressed in accordance with the arrangements'.

Section 6(3) then provided that an LEA need not comply with parental preference when to do so would 'prejudice the provision of efficient education or the efficient use of resources'.

Parents could appeal to a special tribunal (composed of LEA nominees) if the LEA did not grant their preference.[69] In the procedural sense, the admissions process was thus reconstituted on a distinctly more juridified basis. The substantive change however was perhaps less significant. The courts generally construed s 6(3) as granting LEAs substantial latitude to determine questions of efficiency.[70] Furthermore, the Act did not remove the LEA's power to decide when a school was 'full'. Thus if an LEA wished to restrict pupil numbers at particular schools to ensure that other schools still attracted sufficiently large student populations, it was free to do so.

An LEA could not however refuse to accommodate a parent's wishes because they rested on an objectionable moral basis. In *R v Cleveland County Council and Secretary of State for Education, ex p Commission for Racial Equality*, the Court of Appeal confirmed that s 6 obliged councils to defer to parental wishes even if the parent's motive was to place her child in an all-white school because she harboured a racist dislike of ethnic minorities.[71] The government had anticipated such segregation might occur, but did not regard it as a problem. During the Act's passage, Baroness Hooper, government spokeswoman in the Lords, commented: 'If we are offering freedom of choice to parents, we must allow that choice to operate. If it ends up with a segregated system, then so be it'.[72]

68 The following paragraphs draw heavily on Harris N (1993) *Law and education*, ch 5 (London: Sweet and Maxwell).

69 See Bull D (1980) 'School admissions: a new appeals procedure' *Journal of Social Welfare Law* 209–233.

70 *R v Greenwich London Borough Council, ex p Governors of John Ball Primary School* (1989) 88 LGR 589, CA; *R v Governors of Bishop Challoner Roman Catholic Comprehensive Girls' School, ex p Choudhury* [1992] 2 AC 182, sub nom *Choudhury v Governors of Bishop Challoner Roman Catholic Comprehensive School* [1992] 3 All ER 277, HL.

71 [1993] 1 FCR 597. For analysis see Loveland I (1993) 'Racial segregation in state schools: the parent's right to choose?' *Journal of Law and Society* 341–355.

72 Quoted in the *Times Educational Supplement*, 4 December 1987.

Governing bodies. The Education Act 1902 had required local authorities to establish boards of 'managers' to assume responsibility for routine management decisions in schools. Councils had virtually unfettered discretion in regard to appointing managers under these provisions, which were retained in 1944. By the early 1970s, in a manner mirroring the growth of tenant discontent with the management of council housing, considerable dissatisfaction had arisen with the often remote and insensitive way in which councillors controlled school administration.[73]

The Education Act 1980 was in part a response to this dissatisfaction. Sections 1–5 renamed managers as 'Governors' and limited the LEA's appointment powers. Each governing body would henceforth be required to have two parent governors (elected by parents with children at the school) and a teacher governor.

Initial research on the new system suggested that councils and teachers rather than parents were continuing to exercise the greatest influence on governing bodies.[74] The Education Act 1986 thus increased the level of parental representation, and also required LEAs to seek co-opted governors from the local business community. The Act dictated the relative weight which each 'interest' should have on the governing body, and ensured that parents and co-opted governors would form a majority. What the Act could not do was ensure that parental or co-opted governors would not hold the same opinions as the local authority-appointed governors with whom they shared the school's management powers. It came as a disappointment to central government to learn that few governing bodies saw any need to reject the prevalent basic understandings about good school practice. The 1986 Act did not come into force until 1988, but by then the government had apparently already decided that its efforts to persuade parents to accept DES orthodoxies would prove unsuccessful. More coercive measures were therefore introduced.

The Education Reform Act 1988

The Education Reform Act 1988 attacked local authority autonomy in three ways; firstly by creating a new central government body, the National Curriculum Council, which exercised virtually unfettered control over the curriculum that children were taught; secondly by forcing councils to delegate the financial management of schools to schools themselves; and thirdly by enabling schools to 'opt out' altogether from local authority control.[75]

The national curriculum. Section 23 of the 1944 Act had formally left the question of the curriculum that schools should teach to the discretion of the LEA. In practical terms, curriculum development and delivery exemplified the pluralist, multi-

73 Taylor/DES (1977) *A new partnership for our schools* (London: HMSO).

74 For an overview see Golby M (1993) 'Parents as school governors', in Munn op cit.

75 See particularly Ransom S and Thomas H (1989) 'Education reform: consumer democracy or social democracy', in Stewart and Stoker op cit; Raab C (1993) 'Parents and schools: what role for education authorities?', in Munn P (ed) *Parents and schools* (London: Routledge).

institutional approach to policymaking which characterised central-local relations in the Butskellite era. The DES exercised appreciable advisory influence on local authority behaviour, as did the universities and teacher training colleges. Relatedly, this particular facet of the 'national-local government system' left considerable leeway for individual councils to experiment with newly emergent pedagogic techniques. The DES might invoke s 68 in extreme circumstances, but, as Harris suggests, this was not regarded as a routine feature of the governmental process:

> . . . 'central government viewed its powers to intervene in respect of deficiencies in curricular provisions by LEAs to be dangerously punitive and a matter of last resort'.[76]

The Education Reform Act 1988 radically altered this position. As originally conceived, the legislation would give the Secretary of State the power to prescribe through delegated legislation the detailed contents of lessons which would fill most of the school timetable.[77] Various 'foundation' subjects were identified, within which English, mathematics and combined sciences were to serve as a core. The National Curriculum Council would draw up extremely detailed 'programmes of study' which all LEA schools would be obliged to follow. The national curriculum reform represented a substantial centralisation of power; the legislation contained no provisions to ensure that centralised decision-making procedures take account of, still less accommodate, divergent opinions.

'Open enrolment' and local management of schools. The 1988 Act also transferred various LEA functions, including such significant matters as the employment and dismissal of teachers, to individual schools. The extent to which the DES had embraced a 'business' ethos is neatly illustrated by the fact that the preliminary investigations on which the so-called 'local management of schools' (LMS) reforms were based were conducted not by a Royal Commission, nor by central or local government bodies, but by Coopers and Lybrand, a firm of management consultants.[78]

The Act subsequently required that decision-making powers over how to spend some 90% of the school's budget (which would necessarily include the appointment and dismissal of teachers) should be delegated to governing bodies. This significantly reduced LEA control of the school management process. The notion that it enhanced parental control is however somewhat illusory, since the governors' obligations to implement the national curriculum placed tight limits on their discretion. In effect therefore, local management of schools amounts, indirectly, to DES management of schools. In other parts of the Act, the DES's wish to oust local authorities from school management was more clearly expressed.

76 Harris op cit, p 200. See also Pedley (1978) op cit, pp 97–103.

77 See generally Simon B (1988) *Bending the rules*, ch 4 (London: Lawrence and Wishart).

78 Coopers and Lybrand (1988) *Local management of schools* (London: Coopers and Lybrand).

'Open enrolment' coupled the parental choice provisions of the 1980 Act with the removal of the LEA's power to determine the size of each school's population. Parents would be entitled to send their child to a given school as long as it was not physically 'full'. A school was defined as 'full' only if its pupil numbers exceeded those it had in 1979 (historically a year of very high enrolment). This provision essentially removed a council's power to plan its overall admissions policies in order to achieve an acceptable balance in its overall provision.

'Opting out'. The Act also made provision for the creation of a small number of 'City Technology Colleges' (CTCs). These would be new schools, funded directly by central government (at levels which significantly higher than provided for LEA schools), entirely free from any local authority control, able to select their pupils on the basis of ability, and not required to follow the national curriculum. Opponents of the measure suggested CTCs would have an indirect delegitimising effect on nearby council schools, in so far as they would 'cream off' the most able pupils.

The Act's provisions on 'opting out', which mirror those available to council tenants under the Housing Act 1988, were more significant. The governors (or 20% of parents) could call for a ballot on the question of whether the school should be removed entirely from local authority control and thereafter operate as a 'Grant Maintained' (GM) school receiving its funding direct from central government. A simple majority of parents participating in the ballot would be sufficient to trigger the change. The DES offered significant financial inducements to schools which opted out, yet by 1992 fewer than 2% had chosen to do so. Despite its small size in absolute terms, the GM sector can cause severe disruption to LEA efforts to plan its overall school provision.

Conclusion

The Major government found itself in early 1995 facing considerable pressure and criticism from both LEAs and many governing bodies over continuing cutbacks in school funding. The focus of that discontent on the question of finance forcefully demonstrates the largely illusory nature of the 'choice' which the successive education Acts passed since 1980 created. For neither parents, nor schools, nor local authorities possess the legal competence to provide education services whose overall costs exceed the sum which central government deems appropriate. The Thatcher and Major reforms to the education system were concerned with curtailing ideological as well as fiscal pluralism in the local authority sector, but it is frequently difficult to disentangle the two issues. The penultimate section of this chapter consequently returns to questions of local government finance, in discussing the rise and fall of the 'poll tax'.

V. FINANCIAL 'REFORM' 2: THE COMMUNITY CHARGE

By 1980, the rates had long been seen by all political parties as having several defects. Since they were levied on householders, many citizens were not legally obliged to pay them. Consequently many people were presumed to be immune from the financial consequences of voting for increased local authority spending. And since business ratepayers had no vote at all, their only way to register disapproval of council policies was to relocate – an often impractical option. A second flaw was that there was no direct link between the size of a rates bill and the services provided. Since rates were based primarily on property values, the amount a householder or business paid could depend more on the value of her house or shop than her council's spending plans. Thirdly, rates were not sensitively related to ability to pay. People could live in an expensive house but have only a limited income: the apocryphal little old lady living in her family home on a widow's pension is the obvious example. On the positive side, rates were easy to administer, and, since they were levied on properties not people, were difficult to evade. Rates reform was thus a popular but impractical political slogan. When Leader of the Opposition, Thatcher had promised her first administration would abolish the rates; that pledge was quietly forgotten.[79] Indeed, the Thatcher government concluded in 1983 that: 'rates should remain for the foreseeable future the main source of local revenue for local government'.[80]

Reform re-appeared on the political agenda in 1986, when a DoE report, *Paying for Local Government*, recommended replacing the rates with a 'community charge' or 'poll tax'. The government's volte face seems to have been triggered by the evident failure of grant penalties and rate-capping to curb the spending of Labour controlled local authorities. The poll tax would be levied on a flat rate basis on everyone resident in a local authority area, and would thus require councils to compile a residence register. Some groups would be exempt, and there would be a limited rebate scheme for people on extremely low incomes. Local councils would set the community charge for their respective voters; central government would set a uniform rate for businesses. Under the rates, councils had set both figures.

The government assumed that a flat rate, universal tax would convey to voters the true cost of electing a council providing expansive (and expensive) services. What is less clear is whether the government intended that such transparency would ensure that local electoral choices would be made on the basis of fully informed consent (in which case they would presumably have to be respected as meaningful exercises in democratic practice), or whether it hoped that opposition parties would be 'priced out' of office.

As originally conceived, the community charge would not be subject to capping.

[79] Butler, Adonis and Travers op cit, p 22.

[80] DoE (1983) *Rates*, p 14 (London: HMSO: Cmnd 9008).

This suggests that the government was willing to give local electorates unimpeded freedom to determine their council's expenditure. However when it became apparent that many councils still proposed to finance high spending through very high community charge levels, the government introduced capping powers into the Bill.[81] Charge capping seems completely inconsistent with the principle of increased political accountability between a council and its electorate. If a council is capped, voters who want lots of services and are prepared to pay for them cannot do so.

Furthermore, the poll tax's very nature suggests the latter objective was predominant. A flat rate tax is necessarily highly regressive – it falls with disproportionate severity on taxpayers with low incomes. This evidently led some Cabinet ministers, foremost among them Nigel Lawson, to regard it as an ill-advised venture. Leon Brittan (then Home Secretary) also voiced doubts, on the basis that compulsory registration for the tax might lead some people to 'disappear' from the electoral register to evade payment: the charge might thus be portrayed as a tax on voting. But in accordance with the unanimity limb of the convention of collective ministerial responsibility, neither Lawson nor Brittan resigned over the issue; their dissent was kept secret until they published their memoirs.

The Bill which eventually became the Local Government Finance Act 1988 met sustained opposition in the Commons and the Lords. In the Commons, the government's greatest difficulties were caused by one of its own backbenchers, Michael Mates, who moved an amendment relating the amount of poll tax levied to the individual's ability to pay. Government whips exerted considerable pressure on Mates to withdraw. When he declined to do so, they turned their attention (with more success) to Conservative MPs expressing support for the amendment. Notwithstanding such efforts at 'persuasion', 38 Conservative MPs voted with Mates, while 13 abstained.[82] In the Lords, a similar amendment was defeated by mobilising the backwoodsmen.[83]

Local authority efforts to challenge the Act's implementation in the courts were unsuccessful.[84] However a more broadly-based political campaign against the poll tax proved considerably more effective.

A STEP TOO FAR? THE DEMISE OF THE POLL TAX

Many local authorities had opposed the poll tax because of its regressive nature and the threat that it posed to their political autonomy. This disquiet straddled party boundaries; Conservative councillors were among the fiercest of critics, some resigning the party whip in protest. Concern among councils increased markedly when they were faced with the prospect of collecting the tax.

81 See Himsworth (1991) op cit.

82 Butler, Adnois and Travers op cit, pp 118–121.

83 Welfare op cit.

84 See *R v Secretary of State for the Environment, ex p Hammersmith and Fulham London Borough Council* [1991] 1 AC 521, sub nom *Hammersmith and Fulham London Borough Council v Secretary of State for the Environment* [1990] 3 All ER 589; and more generally Himsworth op cit.

The legislation subjected householders to fines, initially of £50, and thereafter £10 per day, for not providing details of people living in their properties. If registered individuals refused to pay the tax, a local authority could seek a 'liability order' from the magistrates' court. This allowed councils to use various enforcement measures, including attachment of earnings, deductions from welfare benefits, and distress – an archaic remedy which enables private bailiffs to seize and sell a debtor's property. Refusal to pay the poll tax could (and did) ultimately lead to imprisonment.[85] Moreover, since the legislation made a designated individual liable for his/her spouse/cohabitee's payment, it was also possible to be jailed for someone else's non-payment.

The Labour Party had pledged to repeal the legislation if it won the next general election, but did not advocate non-payment. This reflected a legalistic interpretation of appropriate constitutional behaviour; how could the party present itself as an alternative government if it set a precedent for ignoring legislation, a precedent which might be used against future Labour administrations? Unofficially, however, many Labour Party members (including several MPs and many councillors) supported non-payment.

Opposition to the tax was magnified by a loose-knit group called the *All-Britain Anti-Poll Tax Federation.*[86] Its leaders had links to far-left parties, but the membership appeared to cross party lines and included people who had not previously been politically active. The Federation's techniques included encouragement of non-payment, marches and demonstrations, offering legal assistance to individuals facing court action, and a practice called 'scum-busting', in which members formed a human barrier around the houses of people issued with liability orders, thereby preventing bailiffs from seizing goods.

Due in part to the success of the Federation's activities, non-payment rates reached 50% in some areas.[87] There was initially appreciable variation in the enthusiasm with which local authorities approached the collection process. However, when faced with the income shortfall caused by mass non-payment, even some of the more radical Labour councils began to make full resort to all collection processes.[88]

The *Anti-Poll Tax Federation* also promoted legalistic techniques to frustrate administration of the community charge. The *Federation* assumed that the magistrates' courts could only process large numbers of poll tax cases if people did not turn up to contest them. The *Federation* reasoned that if citizens resisted liability orders, if only by insisting that technical requirements be satisfied, the courts would be overloaded, making enforcement impossible. The strategy had some successes. The Conservative controlled Medina council tried to push 2000 cases through the courts on 2 and 3 June 1990. But after several liability orders had been made, one defendant noticed that the council had not allowed enough time between sending its final

[85] See Luba J (1991) 'Legal eye' ROOF January/February: Dickman J (1989) 'Debt and the poll tax' *Municipal Review* (May).

[86] See Nally S and Dear J (1990) 'No surrender' *Municipal Journal*, 12–18 October.

[87] Institute of Fiscal Studies (1990) *Local government finance: the 1990 reforms* (London: IFS).

[88] See Hill D (1991) 'A job to do' *New Statesman and Society*, 8 March.

demand for payment and commencing legal proceedings. The remaining 1950 summonses were withdrawn. Similarly chaotic scenes occurred elsewhere.

In the abstract, such outcomes are demanded by the Diceyan principle of the rule of law. Executive bodies should not be permitted to impose losses on individuals without lawful authority. In practice, some magistrates' courts were equivocal about their role as the guardian of individual rights. On 5 July 1990, Wandsworth Council sought 200 liability orders. The first case, which was contested, lasted 90 minutes. The other 199, not contested, took 10 minutes – three seconds each. Given the Act's technical complexities, it seems likely that some summonses were issued without legal authority.

The non-payment campaign continued on a grand scale, which in turn obliged local authorities to make frequent resort to the courts. The Audit Commission, a central government watchdog of local authority finance, predicted that as many as four million people might have to be taken to court in 1991 and 1992 to collect poll tax arrears.[89]

CONCLUSION

If the story ended here, it would be difficult not to regard the poll tax policy as revealing major deficiencies in Britain's constitutional structure. One might point to minority electoral approval for the principle; to rebellions within the parliamentary Conservative Party when the tax was enacted; to clear public opposition to the policy in opinion polls; to the display of more overt dissatisfaction through widespread non-payment; to very limited enthusiasm on the part of the local politicians and professional officers responsible for the tax's collection; and to a breakdown of basic legal principles in the enforcement process. Despite all this, the poll tax's legality remained beyond challenge. As previous chapters have already suggested however, the operation of the British constitution is shaped as much, if not more, by issues concerning the legitimacy of government behaviour than questions over its legality. And from the perspective of legitimacy, the poll tax proved to have significant defects.

As chapter thirteen reveals, Thatcher's fall from power in 1990 was caused in part by her attitude towards the European Community. But her association with the poll tax also made her an electoral liability for many Conservative MPs, who feared that they would lose their seats at the next general election if the tax was not removed. Unsurprisingly, therefore, Michael Heseltine's challenge to Thatcher for the party leadership in 1990 was coupled with an announcement that he would, if elected, institute a thorough review of the community charge. John Major made a similar commitment when announcing his candidacy for the leadership. His government subsequently introduced a Bill replacing the poll tax with a so-called 'council tax', based primarily on property values. While less regressive and easier to collect than its predecessor, the council tax did not indicate any resurgence of pre-Thatcherite conventions concerning local authority fiscal autonomy: the DoE retained the power to

[89] The Audit Commission (1990) *The administration of the community charge* (London: HMSO).

'cap' council tax levels. Nor did the Major government make any attempt to restore local autonomy in such as areas as housing and education policy. Notwithstanding the demise of the community charge, the 'partnership', pluralist model of central-local relations was by 1997 becoming evermore clearly a feature of past constitutional history rather than current constitutional practice.

VI. THE BLAIR GOVERNMENT'S REFORMS

The Blair governments have not introduced any substantial reversal of this general trend. Labour's 1997 election manifesto offered several abstract statements which might be thought to herald the restoration of much of local government's former autonomy, for example that: 'Local decision-making should be less constrained by central government, and also more accountable to local people'.[90] But on the crucial issue of councils' fiscal powers, the manifesto promised only minor tinkering with rather than reversal of the existing legal position: 'Although crude and universal council tax capping should go, we will retain reserve powers to control excessive council tax rises'.[91] Nor did the manifesto envisage any substantial restoration of local authorities' influence over education policy, housing provision or transport services.[92] The suggestion that the Labour Party had accepted the Thatcherite position that councils' freedom of political judgement extended only to doing things of which central government approved was powerfully conveyed by the following passage:

'Every council will be required to publish a local performance plan with targets for service improvement, and be expected to achieve them. The Audit Commission will be given additional powers to monitor performance and promote efficiency. On its advice, [central] government will where necessary send in a management team with full powers to remedy failure'.[93]

In a major policy statement, published in 1998 as a pamphlet entitled *Leading the Way*,[94] Prime Minister Blair suggested that local authorities' proper constitutional role is to serve as the agents of central government:

'However much government does at the centre it will often be dependent on others to make things happen on the ground where it matters. And that is where local government comes in. The delivery of the government's key pledges and policies also requires modern local government helping to make change happen'.[95]

The Prime Minister's message was blunt. If local authorities do just what the government wants them to do:

90 At p 34. 91 Ibid, p 34.

92 For a suggestion that there has been a shift in kind, if not quality, see Vincent-Jones P (2000) 'Central-local relations under the Local Government Act 1999' *MLR* 84–103.

93 Ibid. 94 London: IPPR. 95 Ibid, p 6.

'You can look forward to an enhanced role and new powers. Your contribution will be recognised. Your status enhanced. If you are unwilling or unable to work to the modern agenda then the government will have to look to other partners to take on your role'.[96]

The notion that local government has a legitimate constitutional role to play in enabling voters to express opposition or antagonism to central government policy did not enter the Prime Minister's argument. In that very important respect, the present Prime Minister seems to share common constitutional ground with his two immediate predecessors. The policy objectives underlying the Local Government Acts 1999 and 2000 went some way, albeit only a short way, towards refuting that assumption.

THE LOCAL GOVERNMENT ACTS 1999 AND 2000

The central policy objective contained in the 1999 Act is to subject all local authority decision-making to a 'Best Value' regime. The 'Best Value' principle is rather more expansive than a crude statutory reassertion of the *Roberts/Bromley* notion of the fiduciary duty, but is essentially a notion of 'efficiency' in which central government has the sole responsibility to determine what 'efficient' actually means. Councils are to be subject to rigorous inspection by central government bodies – primarily the bizarrely-named Best Value Inspectorate – to establish that these efficiency targets are being met. Those councils which are successful when measured against this yardstick will be rewarded with extra responsibilities and resources. Those which fail may find that their powers are removed and transferred to government-appointed boards.

The Blair governments' understanding of 'efficiency' in the local government context does not encompass the principle that local electorates should be able to instruct their authorities to pursue policies with which central government disagrees. The Best Value regime indicates that central government remains contemptuous of the principle that local councils should govern rather than simply administer their areas.[97]

The most significant innovation provided for by the 2000 Act points in a rather more pluralist direction. The Act permits local authorities to hold a referendum in which voters may decide if they wish their council to be headed by a directly elected Mayor, who would wield a substantial portion of the authority's (admittedly very limited powers). A directly elected Mayor of cities such as Manchester, Birmingham or Leeds would exercise significant political authority, even though she would actually wield few governmental powers. As we shall see in subsequent chapters, the Blair administration's local government reforms have been introduced alongside measures which grant substantial political powers to new governmental bodies in Wales and Scotland and which also significantly extend the courts' powers to control executive behaviour.[98]

96 Ibid, at p 22.

97 See Wilson D (2001) 'Local government: balancing diversity and uniformity' *Parliamentary Affairs* 289–307.

98 In chapters twenty-one and twenty-two respectively.

This might indicate that the current government is sincerely attempting to reverse the authoritarian, centralising ethos of the Thatcher and Major governments.

The new policy did not however seem to attract much enthusiasm from local voters. By February 2002, referenda had been held in only 22 areas. In fifteen of those areas, voters had rejected the directly elected Mayor option.[99]

THE GOVERNANCE OF LONDON

In this general context, the Blair government's plans to introduce a new tier of elected local administration in London seem oddly out of place; for they raised the very real possibility that the Blair government would create a new locus of political power which might afford it substantial discomfort in both the short and longer term.

A Mayor and Assembly for London

A government white paper published in 1998, began by suggesting that:

> 'Since the abolition of the GLC in 1986, London has lacked strategic direction and leadership. Londoners and London organisations have complained about confused responsibilities, duplication of effort, conflicting policies and programmes and a general sense of drift. No one was in charge or able to speak up for London'.[100]

Rather than recreate the GLC, the government proposed to establish a 'Greater London Authority' (GLA), composed of a directly elected Mayor and an elected Assembly of some 25 members. The proposals were subsequently enacted in virtually unamended form in the Greater London Authority Act 1999. The Assembly would be the junior partner in the enterprise; it seemed likely to be a body possessing little political influence and even less political power.[101] The proposals for the Mayor, in contrast, presented a considerable constitutional curiosity, for the government's plans envisaged an office which exercises little practical political authority but which may prove extraordinarily important in terms of political influence.

The GLA has been given some practical responsibility for several areas of governmental activity – including transport, land planning, economic development, environmental protection, and policing.[102] The Mayor is empowered to act both as the formulator and executor of most policy decisions, advised by a 'Cabinet' of her own choosing. The Assembly has a potentially significant checking and amendment role in respect of the GLA's budget, and some entitlement to be consulted by the Mayor over the formulation of policy. The Assembly may also initiate reports and investigations

[99] *The Times*, 18 February 2002.

[100] Department of the Environment, Transport and the Regions (1998) *A Mayor and Assembly for London*, para 1.6 (London: HMSO: Cm 3897).

[101] Greater London Authority Act 1999, ss 59–60.

[102] Policing powers are among the more important of the GLA's functions, if only because the Police Authority for the London area is at present the Home Secretary: see Part VI of the Act.

on matters of concern to the administration of the city, and is empowered to require the Mayor to explain and defend her activities in an annual report to its members.

Financial autonomy

The government's explanation of the motives behind the financial system it intends to impose on the GLA sounded distinctly Thatcherite in tone:

'The new finance system will. . . . meet the government's objectives of efficiency and value for money in public spending, while keeping the overall tax burden as low as possible. The finance system will incorporate incentives to be efficient, be durable and robust, and seek to minimise the scope for conflict with central government'.[103]

The GLA has not been granted any powers to levy income tax, or a property tax, or a sales tax directly on local residents and businesses. It can raise income through the council tax, but it will do this indirectly by charging a precept to local authorities within the GLA area which will be quantified on each borough's own council tax forms.[104] The GLA's precepting power is subject to capping under the same rules as currently apply to other local authorities' council tax levies. The GLA will also derive income from government grants, charges for services, and the sale of capital assets. The white paper made no attempt to quantify the relative importance of these various sources of finance within the GLA's overall budget, which it suggested would initially be some £3.3 billion.

The GLA's fiscal power is limited to decisions about viring sums of money within its overall budget from one function to another. Even here, however, the GLA's discretion is tightly restrained. A substantial proportion of the GLA's grant revenue – particularly in respect of transport and economic development matters – is earmarked by central government for specific capital or recurrent expenditure. The GLA has no viring power at all over such monies. To put the matter bluntly, the GLA has no significant degree of budgetary autonomy.

This lacuna strikes a powerful blow at the heart of the government's claim that the GLA is substantially enhancing the democratic basis of London governance. A meaningful notion of 'government' surely demands that multi-function government institutions enjoy appreciable autonomy to raise and spend tax revenues, while a meaningful notion of democratic accountability surely demands that voters have some appreciable say in how much tax revenue their elected representatives raise and spend on their behalves. The GLA demonstrably fails both tests.

The electoral process

The Mayor is chosen by the supplementary vote (SV) system.[105] Electors may select a first and second choice candidate. Should any candidate not receive 50%+1 of the first

103 Department of the Environment, Transport and the Regions op cit, para 6.7 (hereafter cited as DETR op cit).

104 Greater London Authority Act 1999, ss 82–84.

105 Greater London Authority Act 1999, ss 3–4, 17 and Sch 2.

preference votes, all but the two candidates attracting the most first preference votes are eliminated. Any second preference votes of defeated candidates which were given to the top two candidates will then be reallocated, leaving the person with the greater number of first and second preference votes as the winner. First and second preference votes will apparently be weighted equally at this stage, thus raising the possibility that the election will actually be won by a candidate who received fewer first preference votes than the eventual runner-up. To discourage frivolous or crank candidates, a 'significant deposit' would be required, which would be returned only if the candidate gains 5% or more of the vote. Candidates also have to be nominated by a 'significant number' of registered voters from each borough. These proposals will presumably restrict the field to the representatives of established political parties.

Assembly candidates must pay a 5% threshold deposit and be nominated by a set number of voters in their chosen constituency. The Assembly is elected by the additional member system (AMS). Fourteen seats are allocated to constituencies, which will return members on a first past the post basis. The remaining 11 members are drawn from party lists, in numbers which ensure that party representation closely reflects the overall distribution of the vote. The use of AMS means it is improbable that the Assembly will contain a single party majority, a fact which may have some significant impact in the way in which the Assembly goes about discharging its (limited) governmental duties.

Conclusion

In an interesting break with tradition, the government had promoted legislation allowing a referendum to be staged in London on the desirability of proceeding with the GLA proposals. The vote was held on 7 May 1998. Some 70%+ of those voting supported the government's plans. Turnout however was barely 35%, so the government could hardly claim a ringing democratic mandate for its plans.

The low turnout is not inconsistent with the participation levels recorded in local authority elections in general in recent years. Nor indeed was the present government's response to that low turnout significantly out of line with that of previous Conservative governments. It appeared unimpressed by the argument that voters may not turn out for local elections because they believe (quite justifiably) that local authorities no longer have any substantial political role. A substantial expansion of local power as a cure for low turnout was not on the government's agenda.

CONCLUSION – FROM AMBIVALENCE TO INTOLERANCE?

It was suggested in chapter nine that legislative self-restraint in deference to 'traditionally fundamental' political and moral principles might be the most important of Britain's constitutional conventions. There is room to dispute the precise conventional understanding of central/local relations in the modern era, but the preponderance of evidence suggests that prior to 1980 governments of both parties considered that maintaining some significant simultaneous political pluralism within the overall structure of government was an important constitutional principle.

We might argue whether that principle should be regarded as a 'convention' in the orthodox sense, but there is little scope for disagreement as to its importance in the context of modern British society. The recent history of local government suggests that the pluralist principle was ignored by the Conservative administrations which enjoyed a Commons majority from 1979 onwards. The Thatcher and Major governments' defiance of accepted conventional norms was not limited exclusively to the question of the geographical separation of powers; their ready resort to the guillotine in Commons debates,[106] Ministers' increased disinclination to accept personal responsibility for departmental failings,[107] and the creation of Next Steps Agencies within central government in respect of which Ministers do not accept accountability to the Commons, also indicate a political readiness (married with a legal capacity) to flout long-established moral values.

But it is in the area of local government that (to borrow from the Duke of Wellington) 'the revolution through due process of law' wrought on the constitution since 1979 is most evident. The paradox, of course, is that the 'revolution' to which Wellington referred was intended to introduce a more sophisticated notion of popular consent to government in British society. The Thatcher and Major administrations' incremental local government revolution appeared to seek quite the opposite result.[108]

As noted in chapter ten, some contemporary commentators regarded the Municipal Corporations Act 1835 as having a more radical impact on the allocation of political power than the Great Reform Act 1832. The reasons underpinning this interpretation are not difficult to discern. Elected, multi-functional and fiscally autonomous local authorities would permit differences in political opinion to be given constant expression. Once rooted at some (albeit modest) point in the governmental structure, political ideologies which reject central government orthodoxies may gain a familiarity and hence legitimacy which might lead more and more of 'the people' to evaluate the merits of divergent policies and exercise their power to vote accordingly, whether at the local or national level. If the ideas which had controlled the government process were to hold sway in post-1835 society, they would do so because of their intrinsic merits, not because Parliament had granted their proponents monopolistic control over the allocation of government power. Simply put, such commentators recognised (and feared) that a powerful local government sector would prove a vital vehicle for cultivating and maintaining the informed consent of the people in a large modern democracy.

Those principles are no less valid in the context of early twenty-first century British

[106] See pp 141–142 above. [107] See pp 328–329 above.

[108] The most incisive critique of this period is now offered by Loughlin M (1998) *Legality and Locality* (Oxford: Clarendon Press).

society. Consequently, it is quite misleading to suggest that the restructuring of central-local relations enacted since 1980 has left the constitution's democratic basis unchanged simply because the electorate has remained free to return a Labour or Liberal government at successive general elections. The notion that political powers may become delegitimised through prolonged disuse has already been raised in respect of the House of Lords and the personal prerogatives of the Monarch.[109] The idea has equal force with respect to local government. In the Butskellite era, the local electoral process functioned as a perpetual 'market place of ideas',[110] within which competing political philosophies were formulated by politicians, selected by voters, tried and tested in practice, and thereafter re-affirmed or rejected according to the success they had achieved. The Thatcher and Major government 'reforms' reduced the scope for alternative ideas to be put into practice, thereby denying the voters power to make informed choices about party policy and ultimately undermining the basis of popular consent to the government process.

The Thatcher and Major governments' efforts to delegitimise social democratic policies by preventing their implementation at the local level should, moreover, be seen in conjunction with the increase in the number of 'governmental' functions, formerly exercised by local authorities, which are now controlled by single issue, (often) non-elected bodies, whose members are frequently appointed by government Ministers. It is inherent in the nature of such 'quangos'[111] that their policies are dictated by central government, not determined by local electors. The trend has led one commentator to identify 'a new magistracy' occupying more and more positions of political power.[112] The label, redolent with the aura of Britain's pre-1830 local government structure, starkly conveys the highly antiquated notion of democracy which Parliament has latterly pursued.

Yet it is a profound paradox of constitutional history that just as the Thatcher and Major governments so successfully deployed their Commons' and Lords' majorities to dismantle the country's internal structures of post-war pluralism and eradicate the influence of Butskellite philosophy on the government process, so they faced increasingly formidable opposition to their ideological agenda from a hitherto unexpected quarter. Chapters twelve and thirteen address the impact on traditional constitutional understandings of Britain's membership of the European Community.

109 See pp 193–194 and 316–320 above.

110 The concept is borrowed from Holmes J (of the US Supreme Court) in *Abrams v United States* 250 US 616 (1919).

111 The acronym originally stood for 'quasi-non-governmental organisations'. A new acronym, quacgos, would perhaps be more appropriate – 'quasi-central government organisations'.

112 Stewart J (1993) *Defending public accountability* (London: Demos). See also Davies H and Stewart J (1994) *The growth of government by appointment: implications for democracy* (Local Government Management Board: Birmingham).

12

THE EUROPEAN ECONOMIC COMMUNITY 1957–1986

As chapter two suggested, the UK's accession to the European Economic Community[1] has markedly affected traditional constitutional understandings; especially, but not exclusively, in respect of parliamentary sovereignty. This chapter and the next will not examine developments in the EEC's institutional structure in detail;[2] our primary concern is to chart the way in which this country's membership of the Community has prompted changes in the domestic constitutional order. It is nevertheless essential broadly to understand the EEC's history to appreciate its importance to modern British constitutional theory and practice.

The pervasive historical theme revolves around the meaning of European 'federalism'. Madison's classical account of a federal constitution divides the ordinary structure of government both horizontally and vertically. Each governmental unit has particular powers, into which other units cannot intrude, prescribed by a higher form of law, and alterable only by a cumbersome, super-majoritarian law-making process. Federalism in its pure sense is thus a legal rather than conventional doctrine. But, 'federalism', like democracy or the rule of law, may take many forms: the governmental divisions which federal constitutions adopt vary enormously.

As we saw in discussing Madison's views on federalism as a legal rule, the conventional versions of the concept which influenced British central–local government relations between 1945 and 1975, and Canadian provincial–central relations prior to 1982, federalism is usually adopted for a particular 'democratic' purpose. That purpose is to provide an institutional means within a country's overall governmental structure to enable large sections of 'the people' whose favoured party does not control the national legislature and/or executive to have a significant, if subsidiary influence on how their country is governed.

One of the questions presented by the creation of the EEC in the late 1950s was to what extent one could sensibly describe its objectives and structure as 'federal'.

[1] There were technically three communities, the EEC, the ECSC and Euratom, which 'merged' in 1965. These two chapters deal only with the EEC. Since the coming into force of the Treaty of Maastricht in 1994, the European Economic Community (EEC) has been formally renamed the European Community (EC), and its member states also established a body known as the European Union (EU). This book refers to the 'EEC' in relation to pre-1986 events, and to the 'EC' thereafter.

[2] On which see Craig P and DeBurca G (3rd edn, 2003) *EU law* ch 2.

The Community came into being as the result of a treaty agreed between six sovereign nations. Countries had for many years signed treaties with each other, promising to respect particular undertakings. But treaties were traditionally seen as agreements between countries. They could not therefore create 'federal' legal orders in the strict sense. For constitutional theorists, the crucial questions raised by the EEC are: firstly, is its legal system 'different' from those created by all other treaties; secondly, what impact does the EEC's legal system have on its Member States' constitutions; and thirdly, is that impact sufficient to demand that we now attach a new meaning to the concept of 'federal' government?

I. THE TREATY OF ROME 1: FOUNDING PRINCIPLES

The European Economic Community was created in 1957 by six countries who signed the Treaty of Rome (West Germany, Italy, France, Holland, Belgium and Luxembourg). The EEC's immediate origins can be traced to the foundation by the same six states of the European Coal and Steel Community (ECSC) under the Treaty of Paris in 1951. The most basic concern of the founders of the ECSC was to prevent another war between France, Germany and Italy. The ECSC was intended to integrate its member countries' coal and steel industries so closely that war between the states would become impossible. The ECSC was also motivated by a belief among many politicians that co-ordinated rebuilding of these basic industries would hasten the Member States' economic recovery from the devastation inflicted by World War II. More amorphously, the ECSC offered a means for Italy and Germany to demonstrate that they could function as civilised, democratic societies.[3]

The Treaty of Rome appeared to be intended to push the idea of political co-operation through economic integration several steps further. The preamble to the Treaty began by asserting that the signatory States were; 'DETERMINED to lay the foundations of an ever closer union among the peoples of Europe'. The preamble continued by identifying a series of economic policy objectives which it was felt would promote that purpose. The Treaty's primary purpose (outlined in Arts 2 and 3) was to create a 'common market' between the members of the European Economic Community. The common market would eventually require free movement of goods, workers, services, and capital across national boundaries; a common policy on agriculture; uniform rules governing competition law; and community rules regulating imports of goods from non-Member States. It seems plausible that the Treaty's architects envisaged that increased economic interdependence would slowly lead to some kind of political union, but quite how widely such sentiments were shared within the six original Member States is a matter for speculation.[4]

[3] For an overview see Craig and DeBurca (op cit) ch 1; Pinder J (2nd edn, 1995) *European Community* ch 1.

[4] On which there is now a vast body of literature. For an introduction see Pinder op cit; Urwin D (1995) *The community of Europe: a history of integration.*

The organisation established by the Treaty of Rome was not a single country, and thus not 'federal' in the orthodox, de jure, sense. However, we have seen in previous chapters that constitutional behaviour may owe more to issues of practical politics than to legal theory. It may therefore be defensible to suggest that 'federalism' may be a de facto construct, and that specific allocations of powers between different organs of government can be of sufficient significance for us to conclude that a federal system has indeed emerged.

We will draw a fuller picture of the EC's substantive role in the next two chapters. At this introductory stage, there are five essentially procedural issues to address. These are: firstly, the various types of EEC law; secondly, the various types of law-making process within the EEC; thirdly, the status of EEC laws compared with the domestic laws of the six Member States; fourthly, the ways in which EEC laws are enforced; and, fifthly, the relationship between law and politics (or, to use familiar terminology, between legal and conventional rules) within the EEC's constitution.

THE TYPES OF EEC LAW AND LAW-MAKING PROCESSES

This book has suggested at various points that most modern democracies accept the principle that their constitutions should recognise a hierarchy of laws. The more important the political value at stake, the more difficult it should be to amend it. That principle is clearly expressed within the Treaty of Rome.

The Treaty itself is the original source of EEC law. In the context of the EEC's own legal order, the Treaty is a constituent document. The various governmental organisations which the Treaty created are bodies of limited competence; they can only do those things the Treaty permits. There is no doctrine equivalent to parliamentary sovereignty available to any EEC institution. The 'sovereign law-maker' within the EEC is identified by Art 236 of the Treaty. Article 236 provided for a process through which the Treaty could be amended. Amendment entails cumbersome procedures, involving an Inter-Governmental Conference between the signatory nations, and their unanimous support in accordance with their respective constitutional amendment mechanisms for any changes. So there was no possibility of a tyranny of a majority, or even of an overwhelming majority, concerning the basic scope of EEC law. Even tiny Luxembourg had a power of veto on Treaty amendment. The terms of the Treaty are therefore deeply entrenched in a procedural sense. The Treaty is often referred to as 'primary legislation' within the EEC's legal order. From a British perspective, that label can be misleading. A better characterisation might be to describe the Treaty as the Community's 'fundamental law'.

Many of the Treaty's provisions are drafted in loose terms. The Treaty is a 'traite cadre' rather than a 'traite loi'. Its text contains broadly framed objectives and basic principles about institutional structures and law-making procedures, rather than precise rules detailing what the Community can do and exactly how it must do it. Consequently, most EEC law is made without the need for Treaty Amendment. But within the Treaty, there is a clear hierarchy (or, perhaps more accurately, heterogenity) of laws.

The Council of Ministers

Most EEC laws are in formal terms made by a body called the Council of Ministers. Each Member State has one representative on the Council of Ministers. This is generally the Minister whose domestic responsibilities coincide with the issue the Council is addressing.[5] The Council was empowered (per Art 148) to make laws through three types of voting system. In some areas of EEC activity, the Treaty required unanimous Member State approval. In other fields, the Council may proceed by a qualified majority, in which each Member State's voting power is (crudely) adjusted according to its population size. Thirdly, the Treaty also permits some laws to be made by a simple majority system, which gives all Member States equal weight.

These differential voting systems illustrate a theme pervading the EEC's institutional structure; namely a tension between inter-nationalism and supra-nationalism. A purely inter-national Community, in which every action required the consent of all Member States, would permit short-term national interests (or temporary political pressures within a particular country) to frustrate achievement of Community policy. In contrast, too strong an emphasis on supra-national objectives and law-making processes might have dissuaded some countries from joining the EEC at all, or alternatively have convinced Member States that they could not adequately protect their national interests within the Community, and would therefore have to leave it.

In crude terms, we might conclude that the more important an issue was to the national interests of Member States, the more likely it was that the Treaty would require unanimous voting—the most inter-national law-making process. Qualified majority voting originally weighted the Member States' votes according to the following formula: Germany 4; France 4; Italy 4; Luxembourg 1; Netherlands 2; Belgium 2. Twelve votes were required to pass the law. This is a more supra-national process than unanimity, but nevertheless permitted one big state plus one other to invoke shared national interests to block integrationist legislation. Simple majority voting is clearly the most supra-national of the three processes—perhaps unsurprisingly it was rarely provided for in the EEC's initial development.

But the Treaty did not envisage that the inter/supra-national balance within the Council's voting process would be static. Its framers presumed that as the EEC became more firmly established as an essential part of each Member State's constitutional structures, national suspicion of supra-national sentiment would diminish, in turn permitting a gradual move from the unanimous voting system towards qualified majority and ultimately simple majority voting. Consequently, the Treaty set out several phases in the Community's development (transition periods) by which certain EEC objectives were to be achieved. At the expiry of these periods, unanimous voting

[5] This would obviously mean that the personnel on the Council would constantly be changing; or, in practical terms, that the 'Council' would always exist in a multiple form; see Pinder op cit, pp 30–31. To enable the Member States to maintain a 'permanent' presence on the Council, Art 151 allowed the Council to create a Committee of Representatives to perform whatever tasks the Council thought appropriate. The body established is known by the acronym COREPER. Each state's delegation to COREPER is staffed by domestic civil servants and headed by each country's Ambassador to the Community.

would be replaced with either the qualified or simple majority system in certain areas of Community activity. This provided an incentive for Member States to reach unanimous agreement—a failure to legislate might mean a less desirable law would subsequently be imposed on a recalcitrant member. However, the complex balance of international and supra-national forces within the law-making processes sketched by the Treaty extends far beyond the Council's voting mechanisms. To appreciate this point, we must consider the roles of two of the Community's three other main[6] institutions: the Commission, and the Parliament.

The Commission and the Parliament

Unlike the Council, the Commission was intended to be an avowedly supra-national body. It had nine members, not more than two of whom could be nationals of the same Member State. Per Art 158, Commissioners were appointed for four-year terms by the common accord of the Member States. One Commissioner, selected by the common accord of the Member States, would serve as President of the Commission. A 'convention' emerged that Member States would approve each other's nominees. The Treaty did not specify how the nominations should be made. However, per Art 157, Commissioners were to be 'chosen for their general competence and of indisputable independence.' This independence was presumably to be from national pressures—whether directly, or indirectly from the Council—for Art 157(2) provided that Commissioners 'shall not seek or accept instructions from any Government or other body.' Per Art 163, the Commission would act by a simple majority. It also adopted a principle of collective responsibility—arguments among Commissioners were not made public.[7]

Article 155 charged the Commission with various powers of promoting, implementing and monitoring measures: 'with a view to ensuring the functioning and development of the Common Market.' It was also the Commission's task to introduce much of the legislation on which the Council would vote: the Council had minimal powers of legislative innovation. Thus the supra/inter-national complexities of the Council's various voting systems would be applied to measures which had themselves passed through the supra-national filter of the Commission's collective decision-making process. The Commission was also endowed with a limited amount of autonomous legislative power. Especially in the field of competition policy, the Commission was able to issue decisions without the need to make any reference to the Council of Ministers. Legislation of this sort clearly had a very supra-national character.

The Parliament (originally styled as the 'Assembly') was composed of delegates chosen by each Member State from their own legislatures in (crude) proportion to their population size.[8] It had few powers. Some parts of the Treaty specified that the

[6] Since these chapters deal with the EEC only in broad terms, its minor institutions are not examined here.

[7] The 'reason' presumably being to stop the Council or Member States exploiting divisions among the Commissioners.

[8] Germany 36; France 36; Italy 36; Netherlands 14; Belgium 14; Luxembourg 6.

Council had to consult the Parliament before enacting legislation, but the Treaty did not compel the Council to take any notice of the Assembly's opinions. The Parliament also had to be consulted by the Council over the Community's budgetary process, but again its views did not bind the Council's eventual decisions.[9]

Under Art 144, the Assembly could sack the entire Commission if two thirds of the members present so voted.[10] It could not, however, dismiss individual Commissioners, which further strengthens the presumption that the framers anticipated that the Commission should act as a collective body. The dismissal power was so crude an instrument that it was unlikely ever to be used.

The forms of EEC 'law': Article 189

The Treaty's sensitivity to supra and inter-national tensions is further evidenced in Art 189, which empowers the EEC to produce various types of secondary legislation to fill in the gaps left by the Treaty's nature as a traite cadre. Article 189's text identified five types of 'law.'

'Regulations' were to be 'binding in their entirety.' They were to have 'general application', a concept which presumably meant that they would bind not just national governments, but also citizens and companies in EEC countries. Regulations were also 'directly applicable', a concept initially taken to mean both that they assumed legal force as soon as they emerged from the EEC's law-making process, and that Member States need take no steps to incorporate them into domestic law. These legal characteristics of 'universality' and 'completeness' suggest that regulations would be the most supra-national form of EEC legislation.[11]

The form of secondary legislation – which Art 189 referred to as 'directives' – made more concessions to inter-national sentiment. Article 189 provided that directives would not be generally applicable, but could be addressed only to Member States. Directives would bind Member States, but only as to the result the EEC sought; the means of achieving that result would be left to each Member State's discretion. Article 189 does not expressly say that directives could be directly applicable. This suggests that the Treaty would permit Member States either simply to incorporate a directive verbatim into domestic law, or to 'translate' it through their own law-making processes into the form of a domestic legal instrument.

'Decisions' were to be more supra-national in character than directives. They were to bind their addressee, and were unlikely to give Member States any discretion in implementation. However unlike regulations, decisions would not be generally

[9] Article 200 initially required the following contributions from the Member States to the EC budget: Germany 28%; France 28%; Italy 28%; Belgium 7.9%; Netherlands 7.9%; Luxembourg 0.2%. It was expected that the Community would eventually be self-financing from the tax revenues placed on imported goods; but initially, the Budget was an area of potentially significant inter-state disagreement. Anticipating this problem, Article 203 provided that the Budget could be approved by a qualified majority.

[10] And this comprised an absolute majority.

[11] See Winter J (1972) 'Direct effect and direct applicability: two distinct and different concepts . . .' *CML Rev* 425.

applicable: they would bind only the individual, company, or Member State to whom/which they were addressed.[12] Most of the Commission's autonomous legislative power was to be exercised in this way.

The Treaty's individual articles specified the type of legislation to be used for particular EEC objectives. If one links this heterogeneity with the Council's tripartite voting system and with the Commission's initiatory role and the Parliament's consultative powers, it is clear that the Treaty of Rome created a very elaborate law-making structure, with many checks and balances curbing the powers of the EEC's own institutions and of its Member States.

Since that elaborate structure could be amended only by the cumbersome Art 236 procedure, the EEC established a very complex separation of powers within its constitutional structure. But this separation does not comfortably correspond to orthodox British understandings of that concept. No part of the EEC was directly elected by its citizens, which clearly raises some questions as to the Community's democratic base. Such electoral control as citizens exercised on EEC law-making would pass through the indirect filter of their respective government's representative on the Council of Ministers, and their governments' nominees to the Commission and Assembly. But we should resist the temptation of adopting an oversimplistic definition of democracy. For in another sense, the EEC could be seen as bolstering democratic principles, by creating the possibility that citizens of a Member State who did not vote for their own government would find that other governments on the Council would more accurately reflect their own preferences on matters within the EEC's competence, and thereby block or dilute a national government's majoritarian or minoritarian preferences.

In British terms, the Commission appears to serve as the executive branch of the Community's government, but one should qualify this in several ways. As already noted, it has some legislative powers which it may exercise independently of the Council. More significantly, the Commission was (and remains) a small organisation and, consequently, could not realistically be involved in the detailed implementation of community law. For that task, the EEC was to rely primarily on Member State governments.

The EEC Parliament was obviously not comparable to Parliament in the British sense. That it was not an elected body would seem of little import, given that it had no significant powers. But this perhaps raised the longer-term question of whether the EEC should contain a powerful, directly elected legislative branch. Quite where the Parliament would stand on the supra/inter-national axis was initially unclear. Its members' status as governmental appointees, rather than directly elected representatives, suggested it might simply reproduce inter-national tensions on the Council. But there was also the possibility that its members would form alliances according to political ideology rather than national origin, so that it might evolve into

[12] Article 189 also identified two 'legislative' measures, recommendations and opinions, which, according to the text of the Treaty, were not to have binding effect.

a pan-European forum. Article 138(3) required the Parliament to draw up proposals for an electoral system to choose its members. The proposals had to be approved unanimously by the Council, which seemed in no hurry to do so.[13] This is perhaps unsurprising, since endowing the Parliament with elected status may have enhanced its legitimacy in democratic terms, and thereby strengthened the case for increasing its powers, and so shifting the institutional balance within the Community firmly in a supra-national direction.

The roles of the Court of Justice (ECJ)

As stressed above, the Treaty is a constituent document. It was thus necessary that its framers devise some mechanism to ensure; firstly that the substance of the laws made via Art 189 and the processes by which those laws were made respected the limits imposed by the Treaty; and secondly that all the other activities of the EEC's institutions had a defensible legal base, either in the Treaty's text, or in secondary legislation lawfully passed under its authority.

Under Art 164, the ECJ was to ensure that 'in the interpretation and application of this Treaty the law is observed'. The ECJ initially had seven judges. They were (like Commissioners) to be people whose 'independence is beyond doubt', and who would be eligible for high judicial office in their own countries or were eminent legal scholars. The judges were to be appointed by common accord of the Member States for six-year terms. The Court would be assisted by officials known as Advocates-General, who would offer the judges a non-binding opinion on the merits of the cases brought before them.

The Treaty appeared to give the ECJ two distinct jurisdictions. The first might be styled as 'internal': its concern being to ensure that the Community's institutions and officials acted within the boundaries of the powers given to them by the Treaty. The second jurisdiction is best characterised as having an 'external' character; its focus was on the question of whether Member States were complying with their Treaty obligations.

The internal jurisdiction had two main elements. The most important arose under Art 173. Article 173 empowered the ECJ – as a court of first instance[14] – to review the legality of acts of the Council or Commission at the instigation of the Council, Commission or a Member State. Article 173 also seemed to enable individuals in certain circumstances to initiate such proceedings. The grounds of illegality against which the acts of the EEC's institutions should be measured were also laid out in Art 173. Per Art 174, the ECJ could declare illegal acts void. This is obviously consistent with the notion that the Treaty should be regarded as 'fundamental law', and that the EEC's institutions could exercise only those powers granted to them by the Treaty. The second element of the internal jurisdiction arose under Art 215. This empowered

[13] Lasok D and Bridge J (1991) *Law and institutions of the European Communities* pp 246–253 (London: Butterworths).

[14] And of final instance as well, as the Treaty did not subject ECJ judgments to any appellate jurisdiction.

the ECJ to impose tortious liability on the Community's institutions or officials in respect of losses they caused to individuals or companies.

The Court's 'external' jurisdiction also had two elements. Articles 169–170 empowered the ECJ, if requested by the Commission or a Member State respectively, to determine if a Member State had breached its Treaty obligations. Such a power would in itself appear rather confrontational. The potential for conflict was softened by requiring the Commission to seek a negotiated settlement before passing the matter to the ECJ, and by the absence of any measure forcing an errant state to comply with a judgment against it. Any conclusion that the ECJ reached would have only declaratory status. The judgment's efficacy as a means to ensure that the relevant Member State complied with EEC law would be wholly dependent on the Member State being willing to do so. Neither Arts 169–170 nor any other provision of the Treaty empowered the ECJ to quash domestic legislation or executive action.

The second element of the Court's external jurisdiction was less clearly spelled out. Article 177 of the Treaty indicated that some role would be played by national courts in relation to litigation which raised questions as to the meaning of EC law. Article 177 granted to the ECJ alone the power to interpret the Treaty or to decide upon the meaning or validity of any EEC secondary legislation; (and so by implication denied any such power to national courts). Article 177 also indicated that national courts and tribunals could in certain circumstances ask 'questions' of the ECJ concerning issues of EC law, relating to the meaning of a treaty provision or the validity and meaning of secondary legislation, which arose in the course of domestic proceedings. This 'preliminary reference' procedure did not de jure present the ECJ as exercising an appellate jurisdiction over national courts. The procedure evidently envisaged that a domestic court would suspend or adjourn its proceedings pending the ECJ answering the question that had been raised, whereupon the domestic legal proceedings would resume. Quite what effect and impact Art 177 was intended to have was far from clear. More broadly, neither Art 177 nor any other Treaty provision revealed what should happen if the 'preliminary reference' procedure produced an answer from the ECJ which suggested EEC law was incompatible with domestic law

THE STATUS OF EC LAW WITHIN THE LEGAL SYSTEMS OF THE MEMBER STATES

The Art 169–170 jurisdiction replicated what was then regarded as an orthodox international law dispute settlement mechanism. A treaty creates a set of laws operating in the sphere of international law. The treaty also creates a specialised forum – again operating in the sphere of international law – for the resolution of disputes; and grants to signatory states or specially created enforcement bodies the power to initiate proceedings. To state the matter very simply, international law is taken to create legal relationships between countries but not within them. A treaty's terms are not presumptively enforceable in the domestic courts of a signatory State by or between individuals. Signatory States might wish a particular treaty to have such an internal legal effect. This would entail them making such an intention clear in the terms of the treaty which they create; and/or organising their own constitutions in a fashion which automatically gave international law an enforceable status within their respective territories.

To frame the matter more simply still, the dominant view at the time that the Treaty of Rome was created was that the status of international law within the legal system of a nation state was a matter for each nation state to determine.[15] Within this notion of the domestic 'status' of international law, three essential questions arise.

The first might be classed as one of 'accessibility'; and is itself divisible into several component parts. Which domestic courts would be competent to apply international law norms to control legal relationships within the domestic territory? Who (or what) would be permitted to invoke international law rules before national courts; ie who could be a claimant? And who (or what) could those rules be invoked against; ie who could be a defendant?

The second question is one of 'hierarchy'. Assuming that some or all domestic courts can apply some or parts of a particular body of international law in domestic litigation, which rule of law should a domestic court apply if it finds that international law and domestic rules demand different solutions to the case before it?

The third question – which perhaps logically precedes the first two – might be styled as one of 'interpretive competence.' Which body has the power to give authoritative answers to questions concerning the accessibility and hierarchical position of international law within a country's domestic legal system?

It is readily defensible to conclude that in 1957 most politicians and lawyers in the six founding States of the EEC[16] would have concluded that the answer to the third question was: 'Whichever body is given such power by the respective constitution of each signatory State'. But while one might find widespread transnational agreement on that issue of legal competence, the ways in which individual States used that competence to answer questions relating to the accessibility and hierarchal position of international law within their particular constitutional order was remarkably variegated. Even among the six founding States of the EEC, constitutional orthodoxies as to the domestic status of international law were profoundly different.[17]

In 1957, the constitution of the Netherlands[18] afforded an extremely high status to

[15] For a helpful introduction to a topic which is far more contentious than is suggested above, see inter alia, Brownlie I (4th edn, 1990) *Principles of public international law* ch 2: Jackson J (1992) 'Status of treaties in domestic legal systems . . .' *American Journal of International Law* 310–345.

[16] Indeed in virtually all western nations.

[17] And of course could be altered at any time in accordance with whichever amendment procedure the relevant constitution required. Furthermore, a country's constitution might also provide that different Treaties (or parts thereof) could have different internal legal effects.

[18] Articles 65–66 of the Constitution, as amended in 1953. See Claes M and DeWitte B 'Report on the Netherlands', in Slaughter A, Stone Sweet A and Weiler J (eds) *The European courts and national courts.* For present purposes, it suffices to say that the Dutch constitution was framed on an American model, with the constitution operating as a fundamental law which limited the competence of the national legislature and executive.

international law agreements to which the Netherlands was a party. If an international law rule protected the rights of an individual, the Dutch constitution provided both that the rule had a higher status than any rule of domestic law and that the rule was automatically and immediately enforceable by any claimant against any defendant in any national court.

The then extant Belgian constitution granted international law a much lowlier internal status. A Treaty's provisions became accessible in domestic courts only when they were expressly incorporated by an Act of the Belgian Parliament. Once incorporated, the terms had a domestic status equivalent to a statute. They would override previously enacted statutes and place limits on the powers of the executive. But – since a Treaty was, in domestic terms, a statute – the Treaty's hierarchical position in Belgian law would be overridden by a subsequently enacted statute.[19]

The other four Member States each had different constitutional arrangements.[20] If the Treaty of Rome was simply an orthodox instrument of international law, the legal status of its provisions in the legal systems of Members States would vary substantially from one country to another, as no explicit steps were taken by the six Member States when the Treaty came into force to modify their constitutional arrangements in a way which would give EEC law an identical (and entrenched) status within the respective domestic legal systems.

The answers offered by a constitution to questions concerning the internal legal status of international law have profound implications for the allocation of that country's law-making powers. These implications operate in both a trans-national and an intra-national sense. And those implications may acquire an extremely tangled character if either or both of the international law and domestic law arenas contain complicated law-making structures and internal legal hierarchies. This is an issue perhaps best illustrated by a series of concrete examples than by abstract hypothesis, and so it will be returned to at various points below.

For the present, we might note that the text of the Treaty of Rome was virtually silent on each of the three 'status' questions. This silence is ostensibly surprising. It must have been appreciated by the framers of the Treaty that – even if all Member State legislatures and governments consistently made bona fide attempts to ensure that national law was compatible with EEC law – numerous occasions would arise when the two sources of law were mutually inconsistent. And one would have had to have been remarkably naïve not to have assumed that in some situations, Member State governments or legislatures might wilfully seek to contravene EEC law norms.

Almost 200 years earlier, such concerns about inconsistencies between rules of law emanating from different spheres of government had been very much in the minds of the framers of the United States' Constitution. As noted in chapter one, substantial (and potentially overlapping) powers were given by the Constitution to the various branches of the national government and to the States. To Madison and his

19 Bribosia H (1998) 'Report on Belgium', in Slaughter et al op cit.
20 See generally the collection of essays in Slaughter et al op cit.

contemporaries, it was 'self-evident' that conflict would arise between provisions of the Constitution itself, laws enacted by Congress, and the laws produced by the various States. It was equally evident that the Constitution itself should give clear instructions as to according to what hierarchical criteria and in which fora such conflicts should be addressed. Article VI of the Constitution was framed in the following terms:

'This Constitution, and the Laws of the United States which shall be made in pursuance thereof; and all treaties made or which shall be made, under the Authority of the United States, shall be the supreme Law of the Land; and the Judges in every State shall be bound thereby, any thing in the Constitution or Laws of any State to the contrary notwithstanding.'

Article VI is phrased in what now seems a rather archaic style. But its meaning is clear. Article VI lays out a clear hierarchy of legal norms: the Constitution is superior to laws enacted by Congress, which in turn are superior to any laws produced by a State. Article VI also addresses questions of accessibility; all judges – and thus every court in the country – are bound by the stated hierarchy of laws. That principle necessarily entails that litigants in all State courts can invoke and rely upon the Constitution and Congressional legislation to override any inconsistent State law. Article VI is concerned to ensure both the uniform impact and the ready enforceability of the Constitution and Acts of Congress throughout the United States. No State may 'opt out' of any provision of the Constitution and Acts of Congress. Relatedly, by providing for the enforcement of those legal norms in all courts, Art VI provides individual citizens en masse with a vast number of local and familiar fora in which to protect their entitlements. Use of the United States Constitution as a comparator against which to analyse the Treaty of Rome is necessarily of limited utility. The American framers were seeking to create a country. The politicians who designed the Treaty of Rome ostensibly had no such grand ambitions. But both instruments were much concerned with dividing governmental powers between different spheres of government, and – one would assume – with ensuring that the proposed divisions were effective in practice. Why then did the Treaty of Rome not address the three status issues in clear terms? Three explanations might be advanced.

The first is that the framers of the Treaty did not expect EEC law to operate as anything other than international law, and thus pinned their hopes for its uniform and effective application throughout the six Member States on the political goodwill of the countries' respective legislatures and governments. Some support for that presumption is found in Art 5 of the Treaty:

'Member States shall take all . . . measures which are appropriate for ensuring the carrying out of the obligations arising out of this Treaty or resulting from the acts of the institutions of the Community. They shall facilitate the achievement of the Community's aims. . . . They shall abstain from any measures likely to jeopardise the attainment of the objectives of this Treaty.'

Article 5 makes no express references to domestic legal systems, nor domestic courts, nor to the hierarchical relationship of EEC and domestic law. It appears to be no more than a declaration of political good faith.

The second – and perhaps the least likely – hypothesis is that the presumptions that EEC law should be hierarchically superior to all domestic law and immediately enforceable in domestic courts were so obviously essential to the effective creation of a 'common market' that there was no need to express them explicitly. They were instead 'taken for granted' principles.

A third explanation is that the framers of the Treaty appreciated the importance of those presumptions, but were unwilling to articulate them clearly in the Treaty for fear that political or public opinion in the intended Member States would find such ideas so unacceptable that support for joining the Community would evaporate. Their hope or expectation may have been that such principles could be expressly accepted by a subsequent amendment to the Treaty and the Member States' respective constitutions, or that the principles might be found to be already present, albeit in hidden and fragmentary form, in the original Treaty itself.

At this point, a further reference to the way in which the United States Constitution addresses the issue of the status of the country's various types of law is perhaps apposite. Article VI deals with questions of hierarchy and accessibility. It does not broach the issue of interpretive competence: which governmental body had the authority to determine if an Act of Congress conflicted with the Constitution; or if a State law was inconsistent either with the Constitution or an Act of Congress?

Article III of the Constitution provides, inter alia, that: 'the judicial power of the United States shall rest in one Supreme Court. . . .' As noted in chapter one, Alexander Hamilton in *The Federalist Papers No 78* had argued that the Court should have the power to invalidate national or State laws which were inconsistent with the Constitution. There is however no express statement in the text of the Constitution to the effect that the 'judicial power' entitles the Supreme Court to invalidate Acts of Congress or State laws if it considers them to breach the Constitution. The Court itself concluded in a series of cases decided in the early nineteenth century that the Constitution implicitly granted it such powers,[21] and the 'correctness' of that conclusion was never subject to serious political or legal challenge. Observers of the development of the EEC did not have to wait long to see the European Court of Justice embarking upon a similar jurisprudential journey.

QUESTIONS OF ACCESSIBILITY 1: THE 'DIRECT EFFECT' OF TREATY ARTICLES

The Court's initial response to the question of the accessibility of EEC law within domestic legal systems law was to conclude that parts of the Treaty possessed a status which the ECJ termed 'direct effect'. The ECJ first articulated the principle in 1962.

[21] *Marbury v Madison* (1803) 1 Cranch 137: *Fletcher v Peck* (1810) 109 US 87: *Martin v Hunters Lessee* (1816) 14 US 304: *Cohens v Virginia* (1821) 19 US 264.

Van Gend en Loos

Article 12 of the Treaty forbade Member States from increasing customs duties on goods imported from other EEC countries. Dutch legislation subsequently redesignated certain chemicals into an already existing tax band which imposed a higher duty. Van Gend challenged the legality of this redesignation before a Dutch court, asking that the court refuse to apply the Dutch law because it amounted to a new tax contravening Art 12. The Dutch court invoked Art 177 to refer two questions to the ECJ. The first concerned the substantive issue of the Netherlands' government's claim that the reclassification was not a tax increase. Unsurprisingly, the ECJ decided against the Netherlands on that point.[22]

The second, more significant issue, was the jurisdictional question of whether the Dutch court could entertain the action at all. As a matter of Dutch constitutional law, the Dutch court could do so if Art 12 created 'rights' for individuals. The ECJ concluded on that point that Art 12 did create individual rights. Although Art 12 was framed in terms of a restraint on governmental power, the corollary of that restraint was an individual entitlement. If governmental authorities cannot levy a new tax, the targeted taxpayer has a right not to pay any such tax.

From the viewpoint of the Dutch court, these answers were all that were required for it to resolve the case before it. As a result of the way in which the Dutch constitution treated international law, Art 12 immediately overrode the inconsistent provision of the domestic statute. The ECJ's primary concern was however with a quite different issue. Manifestly, the Dutch constitutional rule that Art 12 was accessible in Dutch courts would be of no significance in Germany or Italy or any other Member State. The ECJ's concern was therefore whether or not Art 12 of the Treaty was accessible in the domestic courts of all of the Member States simply and solely because of rules of EEC law? This question would seem in turn to raise two issues. Did EEC law require Art 12 to have that characteristic of pan-Community accessibility? And if so, did EEC law override any domestic legal rule to the contrary.

The ECJ answered the first question in the affirmative. The crucial element of its reasoning for this conclusion was an assertion that the Treaty of Rome was not 'international law' in the orthodox sense:

'The Community constitutes a new legal order of international law for the benefit of which the states have limited their sovereign rights, albeit within limited fields, and the subjects of which comprise not only Member States but also their nationals. Independently of the legislation of Member States, Community law therefore not only imposes obligations on individuals but is also intended to confer upon them rights which become part of their legal heritage.'[23]

Several Member State governments had intervened in the ECJ proceedings to argue that the Treaty created only one mechanism to assess the compatibility of domestic legislation with EEC law; that mechanism being an action before the ECJ via Art 169

[22] Case 26/62: [1963] ECR 1. [23] Ibid, at 12.

or 170. The ECJ did not however regard this as a sufficient remedy.[24] It reasoned that to restrict legal challenges against Member States to Arts 169–170 'would remove all direct legal protection of the individual rights of [EEC] nationals.'[25] If EEC law was to be effectively enforced, the national courts would have to serve as fora where the conformity of a Member State's laws with the Treaty could be gauged at the instigation of individuals; only domestic courts were sufficiently numerous and proximate and familiar to citizens. As well as acting in defence of their own EEC entitlements, citizens invoking direct effect would police Member States' compliance with EEC law.

The Treaty has no obvious textual basis to support the existence of the direct effect principle. The Court made two rather unconvincing references to particular provisions in the Treaty's text to buttress its conclusion. The first noted the reference in the preamble to the 'peoples' of the Member States as well as to their respective governments.[26] The second referred to Art 177, and suggested that the very presence of that provision in the Treaty indicated that national courts were expected to have the capacity to apply EEC law.[27]

The ECJ found the primary justification for its conclusion in what it termed the 'spirit, scheme, and general wording' of the Treaty. The Court's search for the meaning of EEC law was evidently premised on the assumption that the Treaty should be construed in a 'teleological' or 'purposive' manner. The absence of any explicit statement in the Treaty to the effect that some or all EEC law would be accessible in domestic courts was not an insuperable barrier to the conclusion that the Treaty did actually contain that requirement. Such an interpretive strategy was quite foreign to then accepted principles of statutory interpretation within Britain's constitutional tradition,[28] but it was not uncommon in the contexts of either the constitutional law of continental European countries or dominant tenets of international law.

[24] There would be several disadvantages to accepting Arts 169–170 as the only way to challenge the compatibility of domestic laws with EEC law. The first, logistical, problem is that there was only one ECJ, so it could handle only a very limited workload. Secondly, Arts 169–170 only permit actions to be brought by the Commission or another Member State; they do not allow litigation by individual citizens or private companies. Since the Commission and Member States would constantly be cooperating with each other in the EEC's legislative process, it would be plausible to suggest that some breaches of EEC law would be 'overlooked' in order to maintain harmonious political relations. See the incisive article by Craig (1992) 'Once upon a time in the west: direct effect and the federalisation of EEC law' *Oxford Journal of Legal Studies* 453–479. Since the United Kingdom was not a founding member of the EEC, one should be cautious about using ideas drawn from the Anglo-American legal tradition as tools to analyse the ECJ's initial jurisprudence. It is nonetheless helpful to suggest that exclusive reliance on the Arts 169–170 mechanism to resolve disputes as to the compatibility of EEC and domestic law would not satisfy a red light, Diceyan model of the rule of law, in which citizens may challenge the legality of government action before the 'ordinary courts of the land', nor even Jones' greenishly tinged 'meaningful day in court'; see ch 3 above

[25] [1963] ECR 1 at 13.

[26] The ECJ did not however note that the substantial majority of principles laid out in the preamble made no overt reference to individuals.

[27] A more modest interpretation would be that Art 177 does no more than indicate that the preliminary reference procedure would be available to those Member States who wished to make use of it.

[28] See the discussion of *Magor and St Mellens RDC* at pp 75–76 above.

At the core of the ECJ's judgment lies the assumption that the effectiveness ('l'effet utile') of EEC law was substantially dependent upon there being a multiplicity of mechanisms and fora through which the law might be enforced. Legal rules which were impossible or very difficult to enforce would be of little value to the persons/organisations who/which were presumptively supposed to benefit from or be controlled by them.

The principle of direct effect initially seemed to have limited scope. *Van Gend* itself was concerned with a Treaty article, rather than secondary legislation produced under Art 189. Thus it might sensibly have been assumed that direct effect would only apply to the Treaty itself, and not to Art 189 measures. In addition, the ECJ implied that a Treaty article would only be directly effective if it had certain characteristics:

> 'The wording of Article 12 contains an unconditional prohibition, which is not a positive but a negative obligation. This obligation is not qualified by any reservation on the part of states which make its implementation conditional upon a positive legislative measure enacted under national law. The very nature of this prohibition makes it ideally adapted to produce direct effect in the legal relationship between Member States and their subjects.'[29]

These criteria seem to establish a form of justiciability test—a concept we met in the British context in *GCHQ*. As noted in chapter four, 'justiciablity' is a vague concept; it would have been rash in 1962 to predict how the ECJ would use it. A broad construction of *Van Gend* would suggest that all EEC law – both Treaty article and the various types of secondary legislation produced under Art 189 – had the capacity to be directly effective if it possessed a sufficiently justiciable character.

But perhaps the most significant element of the *Van Gend* judgment is one that can easily be missed on a first reading. The ECJ asserted that Art 12 acquired its status as directly effective law '*independently of the legislation*[30] of Member States' (emphasis added). In other words, the status of EC law within national legal systems was a matter for EEC law to determine. National constitutional rules as to the domestic status of 'international law' would apparently not apply to EEC law. The law of the Community, throughout the Community, was an autonomous legal force.

Shortly after *Van Gend* was decided, the ECJ underlined its view that EEC law was a quite distinct creature from ordinary international law. Its judgment in *Commission v Luxembourg and Belgium (Dairy Products)*[31] – an Art 169 action – concluded that the public international law principle of reciprocity had no place in EEC law. The reciprocity principle provides that a State's breach of an international law rule vis a vis another State is excusable if that other State is also in breach. In *Dairy Products*,

29 [1963] ECR 1 at 13.

30 Ibid, at 12. The term 'law' here perhaps best construed as referring to law in a generic sense (ie any law) rather than to a statute as we would understand that term in the context of the hierarchy of laws within the United Kingdom's constitution.

31 Case 90, 91/63 [1964] ECR 625.

the ECJ indicated that this concept had no general application in the EEC law context.[32]

QUESTIONS OF HIERARCHY 1: THE 'PRECEDENCE' OR 'SUPREMACY' OF TREATY ARTICLES OVER DOMESTIC LEGISLATION

It would seem sensible to suggest that if the Treaty of Rome was to create a 'common market' among the six Member States, then Community law (whether it be in the form of Treaty articles or secondary legislation) on such matters as free movement of goods and persons, on agricultural policy – indeed on all areas of Community activity – would have to override any incompatible domestic laws. As noted above, the constitutions of the Member States adopted varying responses to that question of hierarchy. Thus if the question of 'hierarchy' remained one for Member States' own constitutions to determine, EEC law would not have uniform impact throughout the community. If a Member State could apply its own understanding of the hierarchical relationship between (some or all) EEC law and (some or all) domestic law, it could 'opt out' of EEC law and maintain its own laws in areas where the Treaty gave powers to the EEC. The practical basis of a 'common market' would therefore be substantially undermined. And if one Member State could do this, presumably all the others could as well.

That a Treaty article might be 'directly effective' in the domestic legal systems did not in itself address this problem. Direct effect is concerned with accessibility, not with hierarchy. If a domestic court could apply a provision of EEC law, but that provision was – according to the given Member State's own constitution – of inferior hierarchical status to an inconsistent domestic law, then the EEC law would clearly not determine the outcome of the proceedings.

The question of hierarchy was thus of enormous importance to the functioning of community law. Yet the text of the Treaty did not make any express statement as to the hierarchical relationship within domestic legal systems of the various provisions of EEC and national law. The nearest literal support within the Treaty for that proposition is found in Art 5. As suggested above, it is difficult to extract from this text any strong argument that provisions of EEC law – be they Treaty articles or secondary legislation – were to be regarded as normatively superior to incompatible provisions of domestic law. Nor had the ECJ been prepared squarely to address this matter in *Van Gend*. In that judgment, the Court offered at best an oblique hint that (certain types of) EEC law might be superior to (certain types of) domestic law in its

32 'In fact, the Treaty is not limited to creating reciprocal obligations between the different natural and legal persons to whom it is applicable, but establishes a new legal order which governs the powers, rights and obligations of the said persons, as well as the necessary procedures for taking cognizance of and penalizing any breach of it. Therefore, except where otherwise expressly provided, the basic concept of the Treaty requires that the Member States shall not take the law into their own hands. Therefore the fact that the Council failed to carry out its obligations cannot relieve the defendants from carrying out theirs': ibid, at 629.

observation that; 'the Community constitutes a new legal order of international law for the benefit of which the states have limited their sovereign rights, albeit within limited fields.'[33] Some two years later, the ECJ took a clearer position on this essential question.

Costa v ENEL

Signor Costa was a political activist in Italy who was much opposed to the Italian Parliament's recent legislation which had brought Italy's electricity supply industry under direct government control. The opponents of the legislation had invoked various political and legal challenges to the policy. Signor Costa's part in the episode involved a refusal to pay a trifling sum of his electricity bill, on the basis that: firstly, the relevant legislation was incompatible with various Treaty articles; secondly, the articles concerned were directly effective; and thirdly, that the articles possessed a superior status in domestic law to the legislation. If these three propositions were correct, the outcome would be that the Italian courts would be obliged to refuse to apply the Italian legislation to the extent that it was consistent with EEC law.

That outcome was not required by Italian constitutional law at the time. As a matter of Italian law, the Treaty of Rome had the status of an ordinary statute passed by the national legislature. While it would override pre-existing statutes and lesser forms of domestic law, it was in turn inferior both to provisions of the Italian constitution and to subsequently enacted statutes.

The Italian Constitutional Court had held in Signor Costa's case that the Treaty of Rome had not altered this basic principle of domestic law.[34] Both the accessibility of the Treaty articles concerned and their hierarchical status were matters for Italian law to determine. And as a matter of Italian law, the Treaty articles simply did not exist in the domestic legal system if they were inconsistent with subsequently enacted Italian legislation:

> 'There is no doubt that the State is bound to honour its obligations, just as there is no doubt that an international treaty is fully effective in so far as a Law has given execution to it. But with regard to such Law, there must remain inviolate the prevalence of subsequent laws in accordance with the principles governing the succession of laws in time; it follows that any conflict between the one and the other cannot give rise to any constitutional matter.
>
> From the foregoing we reach the conclusion that for present purposes there is no point in dealing with the character of the EEC.'[35]

Following the position it had laid out in *Van Gend*, the ECJ, in contrast, evidently proceeded on the basis that there was 'no point in dealing with the character of Italian

[33] [1963] ECR 1 at 12. Under Dutch law, of course, Art 12 automatically took precedence over the inconsistent national legislation.

[34] The Constitutional Court's judgment is reproduced along with the judgment of the ECJ in [1964] CMLR 425. For a more detailed treatment of the episode see Ruggeri Laderchi P (1998) 'Report on Italy', in Slaughter et al op cit.

[35] [1964] ECR 585 at 593.

law'; the requirements of Italian constitutional law were irrelevant to the question of the status of EC law in the Member States:

'. . . .By contrast with ordinary international treaties, the EEC Treaty has created its own legal system which, on the entry into force of the Treaty, became an integral part of the legal systems of the Member States and which their courts are bound to apply.'[36]

The ECJ then turned to consider the nature of that 'independent source of law':

'The transfer by the States from their domestic legal systems to the Community legal system of rights and obligations arising under the Treaty carries with it a permanent limitation of their sovereign rights, against which a subsequent unilateral act incompatible with the concept of the community cannot prevail.'[37]

The reason that such 'subsequent unilateral acts' could not prevail over community law had an obvious, teleological, basis. If Member States were able to 'opt out' of community laws which they found unpalatable, there would in effect be no 'common market' in a legal sense. A common market would require that community law had uniform effect throughout the Community: 'The executive force of Community law cannot vary from one State to another in deference to subsequent domestic laws, without jeopardising the attainment of the objectives of the Treaty.'[38]

The ECJ also offered a textual basis for this assertion, which it found in Art 189 of the Treaty:

'The precedence of Community law is confirmed by Art 189, whereby a regulation "shall be binding and directly applicable in all Member States". This provision, which is subject to no reservation, would be quite meaningless if a State could unilaterally nullify its effects by means of a legislative measure which could prevail over Community law.'[39]

The Court concluded with the observation that if its reasoning on this point was rejected, the Community simply could not exist in any meaningful sense:

'It follows from all these observations that the law stemming from the Treaty, an independent source of law, could not, because of its special and original nature, be overridden by domestic legal provisions, however framed, without being deprived of its character as Community law and without the legal basis of the Community itself being called into question.'[40]

The facts of *Costa* produced an apparent conflict between Treaty articles (ie the

[36] Ibid. An alternative way of framing this point – but one which leads to the same substantive result – is that the creation of the Community automatically and invisibly amended the constitutional laws of all of the Member States and, more importantly, thereafter prevented the Member States from amending their respective constitutions in a way that rejected the primacy of community law.

[37] Ibid. The ECJ's reference to 'permanency' is obviously problematic. It perhaps meant that the limitation applies while the country remained in the EEC, not that a member state must stay in the EEC for ever. The Treaty made no explicit arrangements for a country to leave the Community. That result could have been 'legally' achieved through the Art 236 amendment process. But it might be thought that the 'ultimate political fact' was that a member state could leave unilaterally if it wished.

[38] Ibid. [39] Ibid, at 594. [40] Ibid.

highest form of Community law) and domestic Italian legislation (ie a form of domestic law inferior to the provisions of the Italian constitution). If narrowly construed, the ECJ's judgment might be taken to hold only that Treaty articles took precedence over national legislation. From such a perspective, it might be thought that a Treaty article did not take precedence over a national constitutional provision; nor that EEC secondary legislation would take precedence over domestic legislation or constitutional provisions. However, the ECJ's judgment did not – and one assumes by design rather than accident – draw any distinction between different types of community law or national law. Broadly construed, *Costa* asserts the blanket principle that *all* EEC law takes precedence over *all* national law, regardless of the various laws' respective positions in their own internal normative hierarchy. Given the ECJ's evident concern with ensuring the uniform substantive impact of Community law, and given the heterogeneity of normative legal hierarchies within the domestic legal systems of the Member States, adopting a blanket approach to the precedence of community law would make obvious sense.

The judgment did not however seem to require that domestic law incompatible with the community law be quashed or invalidated. The ECJ deployed rather less forceful terminology in identifying the practical way in which the precedence doctrine would be expressed. We are told that the domestic law 'cannot prevail', or that EEC law 'cannot be overridden' by the domestic law. This form of words might have been chosen in part for practical reasons. The ECJ presumably accepted that domestic laws which affected both EC nationals and people or organisations which did not derive any rights from the Treaty could properly be enforced by domestic courts against those non-EC nationals. It also seems likely that the ECJ was searching for a legal formula which – at least in symbolic terms – presented a less blunt challenge to the primacy of national law.

This latter point might be of considerable significance when one notes that the principle of precedence would be intimately linked with the principle of direct effect. If EEC law took precedence over domestic law *and* the EEC law in issue was directly effective then – in the ECJ's view – the responsibility for not allowing domestic law to 'prevail' over EEC law would rest with the domestic courts. This would not cause any domestic constitutional difficulties in the Netherlands, where the constitution already mandated such a result. But in a country such as Italy, the interactive effect of the precedence and direct effect principles on the facts of a case such as *Costa* were utterly irreconcilable with orthodox constitutional understandings.

The trial judge in *Costa* was presented with a decision of her national Constitutional Court which essentially told her that the EC law in issue was of no effect, while the judgment of the ECJ told her that the national law in issue could not be applied if it was inconsistent with directly effective community law. The ECJ is telling the trial judge that domestic constitutional law hierarchies are irrelevant to EC law, while the Italian Constitutional Court is saying that EC law doctrine is irrelevant to national law. One might credibly assume that only a very bold judge in a low level domestic court would conclude that she should follow the rulings of the recently established and 'foreign' ECJ rather than those of her own country's highest court.[41]

That observation highlights in a prosaic sense a point of much broader significance. In practical terms, *Van Gend* and *Costa* were simply declaratory statements of abstract legal principle. The ECJ's judgments were not backed up by any kind of coercive force. If the principles laid out in those cases were to be effective determinants of legal relationships within the Community, those principles would have to be applied by national courts, either with the approval of or in the face of opposition from other governmental actors within the various Member States' respective constitutional systems. In the mid-1960s, informed observers might well have doubted that such approval would be forthcoming.

LAWS, CONVENTIONS AND 'ULTIMATE POLITICAL FACTS': THE 'EMPTY CHAIR CRISIS' AND THE LUXEMBOURG ACCORDS

The doctrines of supremacy and direct effect evidently surprised several Member State governments. *Van Gend* and *Costa* also appeared just as the supra-national acceleration built into the Treaty, in the form of a move towards greater use of majority voting in the Council's legislative process, became an imminent rather than distant reality. For the then French government, headed by General de Gaulle, this supra-national shift represented an unacceptable surrender of national autonomy to its partner states within the community. De Gaulle's government was particularly concerned by the prospect of losing its right of veto in the Council of Ministers over certain aspects of the Community's agricultural policy regime. The possibility obviously arose that other Member State governments' Ministers on the Council acting by qualified majority would enact regulations or directives on agricultural issues which the French government opposed.

The unhappy consequences, from De Gaulle's perspective, of this occurring were exacerbated by the additional possibility – albeit remote – that French courts might accept that *Van Gend* and *Costa* required them to give precedence in the domestic legal system to such EEC secondary legislation even if that legislation conflicted with French law. Formally, the French constitution then in force accorded superior hierarchical status to Treaties to which France was a party than to domestic law. That formal position had no basis in reality however. It appeared to be an accepted political fact within the French constitutional tradition that no court would ever invalidate or refuse to apply domestic legislation on the basis that it contradicted provisions of international law to which France was a party.[42]

[41] It seems credible to assume that the ECJ was aware of this possibility and was anxious to avoid it becoming a reality. A point sometimes overlooked in respect of the *Costa* judgment is that of the four Treaty articles in issue, the ECJ held two not to be directly effective, lent the third a meaning that was essentially irrelevant to the argument Signor Costa raised, and held that the fourth granted the domestic court an extremely wide interpretive discretion. The case could thus be resolved on its facts in a way that accommodated the views of both the ECJ and the Italian Constitutional Court.

[42] See Plotner J (1998) 'Report on France', in Slaughter et al op cit.

In 1965, in what has since become known as 'the empty chair crisis', the French government simply withdrew from the Council, and declined to take part in the Community's legislative process. The French government's wish was that even in respect of issues where the Treaty provided for the replacement of unanimous voting by majority processes, the Council should act only on the basis of unanimity in matters where a Member State's 'vital interests' were at stake.

France's absence from the Council obviously prevented the passage of any EEC legislation requiring unanimous approval. As a matter of EEC law, the other Member States could have continued to pass legislation which required only qualified majority or simple majority support. There would however have been little political point in them doing so if the French government was unwilling for that EEC law to have any effect in France. And even if French courts were to accept, in opposition to the likely view of the French government, that the implication of *Van Gend* and *Costa* was that any such directly effective law should be accorded precedence in domestic law, it would have seemed most unlikely that other Member States would have wished to provoke such internal constitutional conflict in France. It also seems that France's withdrawal from the Council would have breached Art 5, which could in turn have led to an Art 169 or 170 action. Again, however, this would not have been a practical course to pursue: its likely consequence would have been France's departure from the Community.

The French government's position amounted in effect to a denial of the legal basis of the Community and thus of the autonomous force of Community law. The 'empty chair' tactic indicated that the then French government regarded the Community simply as a form of political agreement which could simply be ignored whenever a Member State government found particular Community policies unpalatable.

The crisis was resolved in 1966 in a fashion which suggested that the other Member State governments accepted and approved this anti-legal perception of the nature of the EEC. The solution was laid out in the so-called 'Luxembourg Accords.' These 'reforms' to the Council's voting system were not introduced via a Treaty amendment per Art 236. Rather they were agreed by the Member States entirely outside the Treaty's legal structure, and were quite inconsistent with its terms. The nub of the Accords was an agreement that the Council would not invoke qualified or simple majority procedures on matters affecting a Member State's vital interests, but would delay adoption of any Commission recommendation until such time as unanimity could be achieved. The Accords did not clearly define what a 'vital' interest was; nor specify a timescale in which unanimity had to be achieved.[43]

It is tempting to see the Accords as a 'convention' in the British sense.[44] Whether one can unproblematically apply such terminology is questionable. Yet they clearly amounted to a fundamentally important, but non-legal rule within the EEC's

43 See Nicol W (1984) 'The Luxembourg compromise' *Journal of Common Market Studies* 35–43.

44 The 'reason' for it presumably being that without it France would leave the EEC, and the Community would collapse if it lost such an important member.

constitutional structure. Equally clearly, they refute the argument that the Treaty initially functioned as a de facto federal construct. France's action indicated that, contrary to the ECJ's statement in *Costa*, it had not 'surrendered' its sovereignty in any meaningful sense. It also suggested that 'sovereignty' might more sensibly be regarded as a political, rather than legal concept. Perhaps more accurately, it might be suggested that by the mid-1960s two distinct visions of the Community existed side by side. One vision, propounded by the ECJ, was of a community of law existing above matters of politics. The other, exemplified by the Luxembourg Accords, was of a community of politics for which law was no more than an optional and dispensable tool.

QUESTIONS OF ACCESSIBILITY AND HIERARCHY 2: THE DIRECT EFFECT AND PRECEDENCE OF DECISIONS, REGULATIONS AND DIRECTIVES

The 'empty chair' crisis did not seem to have any immediate impact on the ECJ's evidently supra-national perception of its constitutional role. We may recall that in *GCHQ* the House of Lords concluded that the amenability of a government power to full judicial review should depend on its nature, not on its source.[45] We can see a similar rationale in the ECJ's subsequent expansion of the reach of direct effect. In cases decided in the late 1960s and early 1970s, the ECJ confirmed in express terms the proposition that *Van Gend* identified a principle of broad application: if a provision of EEC law was 'clear and unconditional' in its nature, then its source was irrelevant to the question of its direct effect.

In *Politi*,[46] the ECJ held that if regulations created clearly defined individual rights, a citizen could invoke such rights before her own country's courts. The ECJ did not rely on the 'effet utile' doctrine, or any other aspect of the controversial teleological interpretive strategy. Rather it simply pointed to the text of Art 189. This provided that regulations were to be 'directly applicable' in the Member States. One might wonder if 'direct applicability' means the same as 'direct effect'. This is a complex legal point, but it need not detain us here, since most courts (including the ECJ) and commentators use the concepts interchangeably.[47] Notwithstanding this technical question, one can readily see why the ECJ might invoke a literalist approach to Treaty interpretation: it is less controversial, from an orthodox separation of powers perspective, for the Court to give a meaning to the Treaty's precise words than to conjure a legal principle from its 'spirit, scheme, and general wording'.

The ECJ also intimated – although in less than perfectly clear terms – that a regulation was a hierarchically superior form of law relative to any domestic legal provision: 'The effect of a regulation, as provided for in Art 189, is therefore to

45 See pp 117–120 above. 46 Case 43/71: [1971] ECR 1039.

47 See Winter J (1972) 'Direct applicability and direct effect: two distinct and different concepts in Community law' *Common Market Law Review* 425–438; Pescatore P (1983) 'The doctrine of direct effect: an infant disease of Community law' *European Law Review* 155–177.

prevent the implementation of any legislative measure, even if it is enacted subsequently, which is incompatible with its provisions.'[48] The ECJ's reference to 'any legislative measure' was presumably intended to embrace laws enacted by national or sub-national legislatures. But would it extend also to the fundamental constitutional laws of the Member States?

As in *Costa*, the Court in *Politi* eschewed the language of 'invalidation' or 'quashing' of domestic law when describing the obligation which was imposed by EEC law on domestic courts. The responsibility of the domestic court would be to refuse to implement the domestic legislation to the extent of its inconsistency with directly effective EEC law.

The Treaty text was less helpful in establishing the directly effective potential of decisions. Article 189 did not identify decisions as being directly applicable. Nevertheless, in its 1970 judgment in *Grad*, the ECJ reverted to a teleological form of reasoning to hold a decision could be directly effective:

> 'It would be incompatible with the binding effect attributed to decisions by Article 189 to exclude in principle the possibility that persons affected may invoke the obligation imposed by a decision. Particularly in cases where, for example, the Community authorities by means of a decision have imposed an obligation on a Member State or all the Member States to act in a certain way, the effectiveness ('l'effet utile') of such a measure would be weakened if the nationals of that State could not invoke it in the courts and the national courts could not take it into consideration as part of Community law.'[49]

At the same time, the ECJ turned its attention to the question of whether a directive could have direct effect. The text of Art 189 did not obviously support that conclusion. Article 189 expressly provides that Member States would have discretion in choosing how to achieve the directive's intended result, which implied that *Van Gend's* criteria of negativity, precision, and unconditionality could not apply to this type of law. Yet in *SACE SpA*,[50] the ECJ answered the question before it in distinctly teleological terms. In deciding if a directive could be directly effective: 'it is necessary to consider not only the form of the measure at issue, but also its substance and its function in the system of the Treaty.'[51] The directive at issue in *SACE SpA* identified a date by which certain (clear and unconditional) Treaty obligations had to be fulfilled. The Court held that once that time limit expired, the directive's 'result' element became binding on the Member States to which it was addressed. If that result met the criteria of unconditionality and certainty, it could be directly effective. It did not matter that its source was a directive rather than a regulation or a Treaty article.

Cases like *Grad* and *SACE SpA* further illustrate the ECJ's teleological approach to its task. As well as confirming the 'nature not source' test, *SACE Spa* demonstrated the 'nature' a law must have to be directly effective was not fixed, since the 'result to be achieved' there required positive action by the Member States (ie abolishing all

48 [1971] ECR 1039 at para 9.

49 Case 9/70: [1970] ECR 825.

50 Case 33/70: [1970] ECR 1213.

51 Ibid, at 1233.

customs duties) rather than simply as in *Van Gend*, the negative restraint of not introducing new customs duties.

In contrast to the position adopted in *Politi*, the ECJ in *Grad* offered little guidance on the question of whether a directive was hierarchically superior to any or all inconsistent domestic law, the ECJ had said no more than that domestic courts should be able 'to take into consideration'[52] the provisions of the decision in issue. Such phraseology certainly does not connote that the decision was hierarchically superior to domestic law. The Court was similarly evasive in *Spa SACE*, couching its conclusion on the point in minimalist and obscure terms, observing only that the directive concerned conferred; 'rights which the national courts must protect.

Ending the uncertainty; the precedence of all EEC law over all domestic law?

While there was little scope for ambiguity in the ECJ's conclusion that regulations, directives and decisions were capable of having direct effect, the Court was remarkably inconclusive on the question of whether EEC law also required such EEC measures to possess a superior hierarchical status to some (or all) provisions of domestic law. This abstract jurisprudential question was one of profound political significance. Could it really be the case that EEC law demanded that national courts were required to grant precedence to any directly effective provision of EEC law if that provision was incompatible with a rule of domestic law? To pose the question more starkly: did EEC law require that even a piece of EEC secondary legislation – which a Member State may have opposed in Council, or which (in the case of a decision) might have been created solely by the Commission – overrode even a deeply entrenched provision of a Member State's constitution? The ECJ finally offered an answer to that question in 1970 as it encountered an acute conflict between its own effet utile jurisprudence and the provisions of the German constitution.

The German constitution had been radically remodelled after the Second World War. The country's system of governance was structured on a federal basis, with power divided between a bi-cameral national legislature and executive and a subnational level of government (the Lande). Within the national governmental system, the government would be formed by the political party(ies) which commanded majority support in the lower house (Bundestag) of the legislature. As noted in chapter seven, the electoral system adopted for the Bundestag guaranteed a high level of congruence between a political party's electoral popularity and its representation in the Bundestag. The federal basis of the governmental system was substantively entrenched in the new constitution. The constitution also procedurally entrenched a series of basic human rights norms (the Basic Law) which could not be interfered with by either the national or Lande governments acting by simple majority. Such values could be overridden by a two-thirds majority in the national legislature. Echoing the position in the United States, the German constitution created a Federal

52 [1970] ECR 825 at para 5.

Constitutional Court which was empowered to invalidate any executive or legislative measure which contravened the provisions of the Basic Law.

The *Internationale Handelsgesellschaft* litigation threw up a conflict between an EEC regulation controlling flour exports, and individual rights protected in Germany's 'Basic Law'. A Frankfurt court refused to enforce the regulations – which were accepted to be directly effective – because it considered them 'unconstitutional' under German law. In an Art 177 reference, the Frankfurt Court asked if it was obliged under EEC law to give precedence to the regulations even if they were inconsistent with the Basic Law. The ECJ's response was a forthright 'Yes':

> 'Recourse to the legal rules of concepts of national law in order to judge the validity of measures adopted by the institutions of the Community would have an adverse effect on the uniformity and efficacy of Community law. The validity of such measures can only be judged in the light of Community law. In fact, the law stemming from the Treaty, an independent source of law, cannot because of its very nature be overridden by rules of national law, however framed, without being deprived of its character as Community law and without the legal basis of the Community itself being called in question. Therefore the validity of a Community measure or its effect within a Member State cannot be affected by allegations that it runs counter to either fundamental rights as formulated by the constitution of that State or the principle of a national constitutional structure.'[53]

The ECJ softened its judgment by observing that 'the law' it was charged to uphold by Art 164 included respect for fundamental human rights, implying it would invalidate any EEC secondary legislation which transgressed such principles.[54] This in itself is an innovative conclusion. It has an obvious political basis; Member States would be unlikely to remain in a Community in which other members could require them (through majority voting) to enforce laws violating their basic constitutional values. As such, it might be thought to be an essential part of the effet utile strategy. But its legal roots are obscure. There was no express textual human rights code within the Treaty of Rome against which the legality of regulations, directives or decisions could be measured. Article 119 prohibited gender discrimination in employment, while Art 7 prohibited discrimination based on national origins. However such 'fundamental rights' as freedom of speech, freedom of assembly, or the prohibition of racial discrimination did not feature in the Treaty's text. Given the EEC's initially limited 'common market' focus, the omission is perhaps unsurprising: the community was not (initially) competent in such 'political' matters. For countries such as Germany, whose constitutions safeguarded basic political values from their own legislatures or governments, this was a worrisome lacuna, as some EEC powers might cut across their own 'fundamental rights'.

53 Case 11/70: [1970] ECR 1125 at para 3.

54 This idea had first appeared in a 1969 ECJ judgment, *Stauder v City of Ulm* (Case 29/69) [1969] ECR 419 para 25–27. The initiative has been attributed to a (prescient) concern in the ECJ that unease among the German judiciary about the lack of any human rights constraints on the actions of Community institutions would lead German courts to reject the direct effect and precedence doctrines; see Pescatore P (1972) 'The protection of human rights in the European Communities' *CML Rev* 73–82.

MEMBER STATE JUDICIAL REACTION TO THE DIRECT EFFECT AND PRECEDENCE OF EEC LAW

The ECJ's judgment in *Internationale* essentially told German courts that they were required by EEC law to refuse to give effect to the German Basic Law whenever that law contradicted a directly effective provision of community law. More broadly, the judgment told all national courts – and all national governments and legislatures – that even their most deeply entrenched constitutional values 'could not prevail' over any provision of EEC law. This forceful statement attracted a variety of responses from the courts of the Member States.

The German (judicial) reaction

When the *Internationale* case returned to Germany, the German Federal Constitutional Court[55] accepted that the interpretation given by the ECJ to the regulations in issue meant that the regulations did not contravene Germany's Basic Law. But, more importantly, the Federal Constitutional Court (FCC) refused to accept the ECJ's conclusion of legal principle that any EEC law automatically took precedence over any domestic law. The FCC did not rule out the possibility that this principle could at some future date be consistent with the requirements of the German Constitution. For the time being however, the Community's own constitutional order had two deficiencies which prevented the ECJ's ruling in *Internationale* being accepted by German courts:

'[23] In this, the present state of integration of the Community is of crucial importance. The Community still lacks a democratically legitimated parliament directly elected by general suffrage which possesses legislative powers and to which the Community organs empowered to legislate are fully responsible on a political level; it still lacks in particular a codified catalogue of fundamental rights, the substance of which is reliably and unambiguously fixed for the future in the same way as the substance of the Constitution and therefore allows a comparison and a decision as to whether, at the time in question, the Community law standard with regard to fundamental rights generally binding in the Community is adequate in the long term measured by the standard of the Constitution with regard to fundamental rights . . .'

The FCC claimed it retained the power to evaluate EEC laws against Germany's Basic Law, clearly implying it would not allow inferior German courts to give automatic precedence to EEC laws until the 'fundamental human rights' and 'democratically elected parliament' principles were firmly established within the EEC's own internal constitutional order.[56] (The judgment is widely referred to as '*Solange No 1*': 'so long as' the Community lacks an effective judicial mechanism to ensure that secondary legislation complies with human rights norms and lacks an obviously 'democratic'

55 [1974] 2 CMLR 540.

56 This account is necessarily rather simplistic. For a detailed consideration of a fascinating story see Alter K (2001) *Establishing the supremacy of European law* ch 3 (Oxford: Clarendon Press); Klott J (1998) 'Report on Germany', in Slaughter et al op cit.

legislative process, German law will not afford precedence to EEC secondary legislation which appeared to contradict the Basic Law).

It is important to stress that the FCC was only going so far as to indicate that it might be prepared to allow all EEC law to be directly effective (ie the accessibility issue) in Germany and to take precedence (ie the hierarchy issue) over any inconsistent national law. The FCC was certainly not prepared to accept the ECJ's position on the third element of the domestic law status of EEC law question – namely the location of interpretive competence. If EEC law in Germany was to be directly effective and superior to domestic law it would be so as a matter of German constitutional law, not – as the ECJ maintained – simply because it was EEC law.

The German Court's refusal to accept the autonomous effect of EEC law within Germany may be explained in part by a concern that the precedence principle betokened an unacceptable loss of German national sovereignty to the institutions of the Community. But the implications of the precedence and direct effect doctrines for orthodox understandings of sovereignty within Member States are also profound. A second explanation for the German court's conclusion is that if the ECJ's views were correct, the German government, acting through the mechanism of EC secondary legislation, would be able to achieve legally defensible political objectives that were beyond its power as a matter of domestic constitutional law. To put the matter simply, EEC accession had significant implications not just for the locus of legal sovereignty in a *trans-national* sense (ie flowing from a country to the Community), but also in an *intra-national* sense (ie from one branch of national government to other branches).

The Belgian (judicial) reaction

The differential impact of the ECJ's effet utile jurisprudence on Member States as a result of the variegated constitutional structures within the six countries is neatly illustrated by comparing the reception afforded to the *Internationale* principle by Germany's Federal Constitutional Court with the contemporaneous response made by Belgium's Cour de Cassation. At that point, the orthodox understanding of the relationship between domestic law and international law under Belgium's constitutional arrangements was that international law would be enforceable in domestic courts only if the relevant Treaty had been incorporated by legislation. The Treaty would then – qua statuk – override any previously enacted domestic legislation, but would in turn itself be overridden by any subsequently enacted statute.[57]

The EEC Treaty had been so incorporated by Belgian legislation. The issue before the Cour de Cassation in *Minister for Economic Affairs v SA Fromagerie Franco-Suisse 'Le Ski'*,[58] was whether – as orthodox domestic constitutional theory seemed to demand – Belgian courts should accept that directly effective EEC law was overridden by subsequently enacted and inconsistent Belgian legislation. In *Le-Ski*, the Cour de Cassation turned this traditional understanding on its head:

57 See generally Bribosia H (1998) 'Report on Belgium' in Slaughter et al op cit.

58 [1972] CMLR 330.

'[8] The rule that a statute repeals a previous statute in so far as there is a conflict between the two, does not apply in the case of a conflict between a treaty and a statute.

[9] In the event of a conflict between a norm of domestic law and a norm of international law which produces direct effects in the internal legal system, the rule established by the treaty shall prevail. The primacy of the treaty results from the very nature of international treaty law.

[10] This is a fortiori the case when a conflict exists, as in the present case, between a norm of internal law and a "norm" of Community law. The reason is that the treaties which have created Community law have instituted a new legal system in whose favour the member States have restricted the exercise of their sovereign powers in the areas determined by those treaties. . . .

[12] It follows from all these considerations that it was the duty of the judge to set aside the application of provisions of domestic law that are contrary to this Treaty provision.'

The Cour de Cassation's judgment – which in textual terms clearly drew heavily on *Van Gend* and *Costa* – might initially seem surprising, given that it betokened a substantial transfer of sovereign legal power on a trans-national basis from Belgium's Parliament to the Community. But it also betokened a substantial transfer of power in the intra-national sense, in that the Belgian courts were now claiming to be empowered to refuse to apply certain provisions of domestic legislation; an authority that the Belgian judiciary had previously not possessed. The Cour de Cassation was undoubtedly taking something of a risk in domestic political terms by effectively amending the constitution in this way. It seems however that the Cour could justifiably have concluded that its initiative would not be much opposed by other governmental institutions.[59]

The French (judicial) reaction

The judicial strands of France's constitutional tapestry produced a further complication for any attempts to explain in general terms the impact of the ECJ's effet utile jurisprudence. The French Constitution recognises a functional and institutional split between the legislative, executive and judicial branches of the governmental system. But the French judicial system has long been institutionally fragmented, divided between public law courts (topped by the Conseil d'Etat) and private law courts (topped by the Cour de Cassation). That institutional fragmentation had never been, in ideological terms, a happy one. To put the matter crudely, the Conseil d'Etat was widely regarded – and certainly by its own members – as a far more important and prestigious organisation than the Cour de Cassation.[60] The Conseil d'Etat also claimed the ultimate jurisdiction to decide if a particular matter raised a public law or private law issue. That jurisdiction in effect placed the Conseil d'Etat in a superior constitutional position to the Cour de Cassation.

As noted above, Art 55 of the French Constitution notionally empowered the

59 See Bribosia op cit at pp 18–21.

60 See generally Neville-Brown L and Bell J (5th edn, 1997) *French administrative law* ch 4 (Oxford: Clarendon Press).

Conseil d'Etat to give precedence to international law over domestic legislation. This seemed however to be a power that would never be exercised for political reasons. And the Conseil d'Etat initially showed no inclination to accept that such a result was required in respect of EEC law as a result of France's membership of the Community.

The issue raised before the Conseil d'Etat in *Syndicat Generale des Fabricants de Semoules*[61] was stark and simple. Should the French courts refuse to apply a French statute that was inconsistent with a directly effective EEC regulation? *Semoules* was argued early in 1968, so pre-dated the ECJ's secondary legislation effet utile judgments in *Politi, Grad* and *SACE Spa.* But both *Van Gend* and *Costa* had been decided by this point.

The advisory opinion of the Comissaire du Gouvernement[62] focused briefly on the evident inconsistency between the theory and practice of the constitution in respect of the domestic status of international law:

> 'To be sure, under Article 55 of the Constitution a treaty which has been duly ratified has, as from its publication, an authority superior to that of statutes. The Constitution thus affirms a pre-eminence of international law over internal law and numerous voices (nearly all of the academic writers) have been raised to say that a provision which makes our Constitution one of the most receptive to an international legal order should not remain a dead letter.
>
> But the administrative court cannot make the effort which is asked of it without altering, by its mere will, its institutional position.
>
> It may neither criticise nor misconstrue a statute. That consideration has always led it to refuse to examine grounds based on the constitutional invalidity of a statute. . . .'

The opinion then concluded that the Conseil should not depart from its previous practice. The Conseil itself endorsed this position, holding simply and briefly that the French legislation at issue was a valid law.

Both the Commissaire and the Conseil reached their respective conclusions without making any reference *at all* to either *Van Gend* or *Costa.* The ECJ's effet utile jurisprudence was, it seemed, not just unpersuasive in determining the domestic status of EEC law in France; it was completely irrelevant.

A quite different attitude to EEC law was however taken by the Cour de Cassation in *Administration des Douaines v Societe Cafes Jacques Vebre.*[63] The question raised was whether a domestic court should decline to apply a French statute placing a discriminatory tax on coffee imported from Holland, which tax was apparently inconsistent with the provisions of Art 95 of the Treaty.[64] In complete contrast to the position adopted by the Conseil d'Etat in *Semoules,* the Cour de Cassation upheld the judgment of a lower (private law) court which had given practical effect to Art 55 of the Constitution; namely that international law to which France was a party took

61 [1970] CMLR 395.

62 An officer of the Conseil whose function is analogous to that of the Advocate-General before the ECJ; See Neville-Brown and Bell op cit pp 104–105.

63 [1975] 2 CMLR 336.

64 Which the ECJ had held to be directly effective in *Lutticke* (Case 57/65) [1966] ECR 205.

precedence over contradictory domestic legislation.[65] The Cour de Cassation did not invoke any ECJ authority to sustain this proposition.

This might suggest that the Cour de Cassation was 'simply' adopting a different reading of the requirements of Art 55 of the Constitution from that taken by the Conseil d'Etat. In domestic political terms, that would have been a boldly confrontational course for the Cour de Cassation to adopt, since it strikes at the superior constitutional position of the Conseil d'Etat and at the legislature's practical immunity from the formal requirements of Art 55.

However, the Cour de Cassation also intimated that it was minded to accept the autonomous force principle of EEC law. Article 55 of the French constitution conditioned the (theoretical) domestic precedence of international law on the principle of reciprocity. But the Cour de Cassation rejected the suggestion that the question of whether or not Holland was in compliance with Art 95 had any relevance to the status of Art 95 in France, in essence adopting – but not expressly citing – the reasoning offered by the ECJ over ten years earlier in *Dairy Products*:[66]

'[7] But in the Community legal order the failings of a member-State of the European Economic Community to comply with the obligations falling on it by virtue of the Treaty of 25 March 1957 are subject to the procedure laid down by Article 170 of that Treaty and so the plea of lack of reciprocity cannot be made before the national courts.'

This element of the judgment raises the inference that the Cour de Cassation saw in the effet utile principle a means to call into question or even overcome its previously subordinate position within the French constitutional system.[67]

The Italian (judicial) reaction

By this time, the Italian Constitutional Court was intimating that it had modified its own approach as laid out in *Costa* to the domestic status of EEC law. The issue before the Court in *Frontini v Minister delle Finanze*[68] was whether – as a matter of domestic constitutional law – all EEC secondary legislation was to be regarded as of equivalent status to Italian legislation? The Court's answer to the question was a qualified 'Yes'. In contrast to the concerns raised by the German Federal Constitutional Court, the Italian Court considered that the law-making procedures of the Community and the ECJ's capacity to review the legality of secondary legislation were already sufficient to enable Italian law to extend what we might term a strong but rebuttable presumption of validity to EEC regulations, decisions, or directives.[69] The Court nonetheless

[65] '[5] But the Treaty of 25 March 1957, which by virtue of the abovementioned Article of the Constitution has an authority greater than that of statutes, institutes a separate legal order integrated with that of the member-States. Because of that separateness, the legal order which it has created is directly applicable to the nationals of those States and is binding on their courts. Therefore the Cour d'Appel was correct and did not exceed its powers in deciding that Article 95 of the Treaty was to be applied in the instant case, and not section 265 of the Customs Code, even though the latter was later in date.'

[66] See pp 424–425 above.

[67] See the discussion in Alter op cit ch4; Plotner op cit.

[68] [1974] 2 CMLR 372.

[69] See in particular paras 16–19 of the judgment.

stressed that this result arose as a matter of Italian law, not EEC law; and the judgment carefully noted that in circumstances where it appeared that EEC secondary legislation was incompatible with fundamental values in the Italian constitution: '[T]his Court would control the continuing compatibility of the Treaty with the abovementioned fundamental principles.'[70] The judgment did not obviously resolve the question of the precedence of EEC law vis a vis subsequently enacted domestic legislation. But the tone of the Court's reasoning perhaps suggested that when the *Costa* issue came squarely before it again, its understanding of the domestic legal position would change.

CONCLUSION

These episodes serve as a useful corrective to misleadingly simplistic assertions that conflicts created by community law simply and invariably pit the interests of an homogenous, monolithic EEC against a similarly homogenous, monolithic Member State. Such a bald dichotomy ignores the point that in both ideological and institutional terms the Community itself and its Member States are often likely to be highly fragmented constructs. In an ideological sense, it is entirely likely that major political parties within any given Member State will simultaneously hold quite different views on the desirability of Community intervention in certain fields. A change of government in a Member State may therefore produce a quite different domestic response to particular Community laws or policies. Similarly, in a country organised on a federal basis where the national and sub-national levels of government are controlled by different political parties, EEC initiatives might often attract both enthusiastic support and vociferous opposition from the various tiers of domestic government. And, perhaps most significantly from a constitutional lawyer's perspective, the ECJ's effet utile jurisprudence opened up the possibility of particular branches of a Member State's governmental system stepping beyond the purely domestic constitutional constraints controlling their authority.

It would be equally misleading to assume that the Community can be regarded a single entity, whether in structural or ideological terms. A diversity of political views is likely to exist between the various Member State governments when they sit as lawmakers on the Council of Ministers. It is quite possible that a majority of Member State governments on the Council will disapprove of initiatives proposed by the Commission; that a majority of members of the Assembly/Parliament will take yet another view; and that the ECJ may conclude that any measure that does make its way through the Community's legislative process is unlawful.

It might be thought that these many complications were a readily discernible feature of the Community and Member States' political and legal landscapes in the early 1970s. But in the United Kingdom, where a prolonged and vigorously fought political battle to take the country into the Community was nearing its end, there was no

70 Ibid, at para 21.

obvious evidence that these points had been taken on board by Ministers, by legislators, by the judiciary – and still less by the public at large.

II. UNITED KINGDOM ACCESSION

British governments tried to take the country into the EEC twice during the 1960s. However new states could only be admitted with the consent of all the existing members, and on both occasions the French government vetoed British entry. The then (Conservative) Prime Minister Harold Macmillan regarded membership as a central element of his government's foreign and economic policy, and had assigned Edward Heath the task of negotiating acceptable terms of entry. Macmillan and Heath were however thwarted by De Gaulle's firm belief that British entry would lead to Anglo-American domination of the Community.[71] The Labour Party at that time opposed entry; its then leader, Hugh Gaitskell, suggested membership would mean 'the end of a thousand years of history' of Britain as a sovereign state. Gaitskell's historical sense was obviously somewhat bizarre, but although a significant minority of Labour MPs favoured accession, most (including the next leader, Harold Wilson) then shared his sentiments.[72] Wilson subsequently changed his mind, and his government (supported by many Conservative MPs and opposed by 35 Labour backbenchers) applied for entry in 1967. This too was vetoed by De Gaulle.

British opponents drew on two substantial political arguments against accession. The first related to Britain's world role. Opponents of EEC entry felt that Britain should align itself with the Commonwealth countries and the USA, linking those nations to the EEC, rather than risk merging into a 'European super-state'. The second argument focused on 'sovereignty'. The principles of precedence and direct effect alarmed a small number of British politicians. This faction feared that some of Parliament's powers would be irretrievably lost to Community institutions. Opponents of entry argued that such a transfer of political power was undesirable. But some also argued that it was constitutionally impossible for Britain to honour the obligations EEC membership entailed. We need here to recall two key elements of Diceyan theory: that Parliament cannot bind itself or its successors; and that no British court is competent to say that a statute is unconstitutional.

If we translate *Costa* and *Internationale* into orthodox British constitutional language, we seem to say that Parliament could no longer pass legislation inconsistent with EEC law; that any Parliament which incorporated the Treaty into British law would bind itself and its successors not to breach EEC law in the future. The direct effect principle articulated in *Van Gend, Politi, Grad* and *SACE Spa* is equally problematic from the viewpoint of orthodox, Diceyan theory. The principle demanded

[71] See Horne op cit pp 444–451.

[72] Pimlott op cit pp 245–248; Jenkins R (1991) *A life at the centre* pp 144–146 (London: Pan).

that if Parliament enacted a statute which contradicted a directly effective EEC provision, but which did not also withdraw Britain from the Community, a British court would have to refuse to apply that statute. Thus, the courts, via the medium of EEC law, would have a higher constitutional status than Parliament on EEC matters.[73] Furthermore, the ECJ's teleological approach to Treaty and legislative interpretation was incompatible with British courts' more literalist tradition; EEC membership would thus demand that the constitution abandon its traditional approach to the separation of powers.

EEC MEMBERSHIP AND PARLIAMENTARY SOVEREIGNTY: THE LEGISLATORS' VIEWS – AND THEIR VOTES

With the benefit of hindsight, the earliest efforts of British commentators to analyse the potential impact of EEC membership on the British constitution appear woefully inadequate.[74] By the late 1960s, such analyses were becoming more sophisticated. Professor de Smith produced a prescient article in 1971, identifying the EEC as 'an inchoate functional federation', which while not initially a federal state, was likely to evolve in a direction demanding the 'pooling' of sovereignty.[75] de Smith suggested national sovereignty need not be abandoned if the UK acceded to the Treaty, since it might always withdraw from the Community. Nevertheless, he also presumed (in terms reminiscent of Wade's seminal analysis of parliamentary sovereignty) that 'full recognition of the hierarchical superiority of Community law would entail a revolution in legal thought.'[76] de Smith expected that a 'reformulation' of traditional understandings would suffice to deal with the likely eventuality of unintended conflicts between EEC and domestic law, and that such reformulation might be achieved by the simple expedient of the domestic courts presuming that Parliament never intended to breach EEC law and interpreting domestic legislation accordingly. This 'solution' might of course demand that the notion of 'interpretation' would itself have to be reinterpeted in a manner quite inconsistent with dominant British understandings of the courts' proper constitutional role.

The courts' traditional approach to international law would be inadequate for these purposes. We saw in chapter two that unincorporated treaties have no binding force in domestic law. However, that does not mean they are entirely without legal effect. British courts will assume that Parliament does not intend accidentally to legislate in breach of the country's treaty obligations. Thus in circumstances where a statute's

[73] It seems that few MPs grasped this point. Most viewed Parliament's 'sovereignty' as something which might be lost to the EC, not to the domestic courts; see Nicol D (1999) 'The legal constitution: United Kingdom Parliament and European Court of Justice' *Journal of Legislative Studies* 131–151.

[74] For example Keenan P (1962) 'Some legal consequences of Britain's entry into the European Common Market' *Public Law* 327–343.

[75] de Smith S (1971) 'The constitution and the Common Market: a tentative appraisal' 34 *MLR* 597–614 at pp 597 and 614. Interestingly, the article made no reference at all to *Van Gend.*

[76] Ibid, at p 613.

phraseology could bear more than one meaning, the courts will choose whichever meaning best corresponds to the international obligations. Similarly, if a treaty has been incorporated into domestic law, subsequent statutes will be construed, in so far as their language is ambiguous, in a manner consistent with the obligations enacted in the incorporating statute. This interpretive technique would be of no assistance when a later statute expressly repealed or was impliedly irreconcilable with the incorporating legislation. It would also seem incompatible with the ECJ's characterisation of the Treaty as a 'new legal order', quite unlike other international law.

Professor Wade recommended more radical steps. He suggested either that a standard clause be inserted into every domestic statute enacted after accession, providing that the legislation took effect subject to the precedence of EEC law. Alternatively, Parliament might annually enact (with retrospective effect) a statute reaffirming the precedence principle.[77]

Successive governments remained unconvinced of the need for such measures. Harold Wilson's 1966–1970 Labour government had made the extraordinary suggestion that all EEC measures would take effect in the United Kingdom as delegated legislation,[78] an analysis which betokens the subordinacy rather than precedence of Community law. Edward Heath's 1970–1974 administration, which eventually secured the UK's accession, seemed similarly confused. The government boldly stated that while it would introduce a Bill to incorporate the Treaty into domestic law, 'there is no question of any erosion of essential national sovereignty.'[79] The distinction between 'essential' and (presumably) 'non-essential' sovereignty is a novel one, and was replaced when the aforesaid Bill was before the Commons by a different but equally legally nonsensical proposition. MPs were informed by a government spokesman that nothing in the Bill undermined the 'ultimate' sovereignty of Parliament'. What might happen to Parliament's penultimate or anti-penultimate sovereignty (whatever those strange creatures might be) was unclear! Neither of the main parties seemed willing to accept that it was either desirable or possible to entrench the precedence principle. The 1967 government had seemed to accept the inevitability of the Diceyan perspective, observing that if the UK was to honour its EEC obligations, 'Parliament would have to refrain from passing fresh legislation inconsistent with [Community] law.'[80]

That is however not a legal solution. It may be that politicians of both parties adopted such equivocal positions because they feared that candid recognition of the *Costa, Van Gend* and *Internationale* principles would further harden internal opposition to accession, which, as we see below, already presented a threat to the

[77] (1972) 'Sovereignty and the European Communities' 88 *LQR* 1–5. For a survey of other contemporaneous suggestions see Trinadade F (1972) 'Parliamentary sovereignty and the primacy of community law' 35 *MLR* 375–402.

[78] (1967) *Legal and constitutional implications of United Kingdom membership of the European Communities* para 22 (London: HMSO Cmnd 3301).

[79] (1971) *The United Kingdom and the European Communities* para 29 (London: HMSO Cmnd 4715).

[80] Quoted in Wade 1972 op cit at pp 2–3.

government's European ambitions. Equally plausibly, it may be that they simply did not properly understand the legal significance of the step they were about to take.[81]

THE EUROPEAN COMMUNITIES ACT 1972 – THE PASSAGE

The political question as to the desirability of EC membership exposed some unusual divisions in the, by then, firmly established split between the Labour and Conservative parties. Both the Labour left and Conservative right wings opposed the idea. Both factions disliked the partial 'loss' of sovereignty they assumed accession would entail, since that would reduce their capacity (should they ever form a Commons majority) to promote legislation favouring their respective (very different) political ideologies. The support for membership of some more centrist MPs in both parties depended on the entry terms (especially Britain's budget contribution) that the government negotiated. We will return to these divisions on several occasions, but we might gain an initial appreciation of the EEC's capacity to cut across party lines by examining the Commons' vote on the 1971 Bill.

Accession would have two domestic phases: a Commons vote on whether to accept the entry terms which, if successful, would be followed by the Bill incorporating the Treaty into domestic law. At the 1970 election the Conservatives had won 330 seats, Labour 287, and the small parties 13. A rebellion by fewer than 20 anti-EEC Conservatives would have deprived the Heath government of a majority. Heath himself was passionately pro-accession: the great majority of Conservative MPs supported him, but 40 announced they would not approve the terms.

Labour was more deeply split. As Prime Minister in the late 1960s, Wilson had supported EEC membership, reversing his previous opposition. In 1971, he and most of his Shadow Cabinet again opposed it. The 1971 Labour Party Conference voted overwhelmingly against membership, and Wilson authorised a three line whip instructing Labour MPs to vote against the terms. Sixty-nine Labour MPs, led by the Shadow Chancellor Roy Jenkins, defied the whip and voted with the government; a further 20 abstained. The government majority was 112. Had the whip been respected, the terms would have been rejected. This would probably not have been regarded as a resigning issue, as Heath had allowed Conservative MPs a free vote.

But while many Labour MPs approved the terms, they would not defy the whip on votes during the Bill's passage, in part because Heath had announced that he would treat the second reading as a confidence issue.[82] Only a few (Jenkins foremost among them) elevated what they saw as Britain's national interest in joining the EEC above questions of party loyalty. On the Bill's third reading, the government's majority was just 17. For the moment, at least, the UK had entered the EEC. What now fell to be determined was the constitutional adequacy of the legislation enacted.

81 Cf Nicol D (1999) op cit.

82 Norton (1978) op cit pp 363–364.

THE EUROPEAN COMMUNITIES ACT 1972 – THE TERMS

As we saw in *Mortensen v Peters* and *Cheney v Conn*,[83] a government cannot change British law by using its prerogative powers to sign a treaty. If a treaty's terms are to be effective in British law, they must be incorporated by statute. The Treaty of Rome was incorporated by the European Communities Act 1972 (ECA 1972). Four sections merit attention here, in terms of their consistency both with orthodox British constitutional theory and the ECJ's principles of precedence and direct effect.

Section 1 listed the various treaties to which the Act would apply. It also provided that the government might add new treaties to the list by using Orders in Council. This could be seen as a form of Henry VIII clause, in so far as it effectively allowed the government (via its prerogative powers) to incorporate new treaties into domestic law which, by virtue of the precedence principle, would override existing legislation.

Section 2(1) seems to provide that all directly effective EEC law will be immediately enforceable in domestic courts:

'All such rights, powers, liabilities, obligations and restrictions from time to time arising by or under the Treaties, as in accordance with the Treaties are without further enactment to be given legal effect . . . in the United Kingdom shall be recognised and available in law, and be enforced, allowed and followed accordingly. . . .'

Section 2(2)(a) empowers the government, either through Orders in Council or statutory instruments, to 'translate' any non-directly effective EEC law into domestic law. Section 2(4) then provides that '. . . any enactment passed or to be passed . . . shall be construed and have effect subject to the forgoing provisions of this section.' Section 3(1) then states that:

'For the purpose of all legal proceedings any question as to the meaning or effect of any of the Treaties, or as to the validity meaning or effect of any Community instrument shall be . . . [determined] in accordance with the principles laid down by and any relevant decision of the European Court.'

There are several principles of startling constitutional significance in the ECA's few words. There is no constitutional difficulty in the ECA 1972 telling a court to give effect to EEC obligations even if there is a contradictory domestic law if that domestic law predated the ECA 1972. The ECA, as the later statute, would prevail. But what would happen if the inconsistent British statute was passed after 1972?

The 'passed or to be passed' formula of s 2(4) seemed to instruct the courts that any such Act would not have domestic legal effect. As we saw in chapter two, Parliament had produced such forward-looking legislation before. The Treaty of Union was incorporated by an Act which said some of its provisions would endure forever.[84] But those provisions have been repealed. Similarly, the courts held that s 7(1) of the

[83] See pp 35–36 above.

[84] This is to take a Diceyan view of the Treaty's status, rather than to see it as a 'constituent' document establishing the British state; see pp 47–52 above.

Acquisition of Land Act was repealed by an inconsistent later Act. Why should the ECA 1972 be any different? Indeed, how could it be any different? To recognise it as a 'special' statute would undermine the entire basis of the parliamentary sovereignty doctrine.

How the courts would respond to these novel instructions was a matter for speculation. Writing in an academic journal, prior to the ECA 1972 coming into force, Lord Diplock had argued:

> 'It is a consequence of the doctrine of [parliamentary sovereignty] that if a subsequent Act . . . were passed that was in conflict with any provision of the Treaty which is of direct application . . . the courts of the United Kingdom would be bound to give effect to the Act . . . notwithstanding any conflict.'[85]

For Lord Diplock, it seemed, there could be nothing 'special' about the ECA 1972. Lord Denning was initially rather more equivocal.

PARLIAMENTARY SOVEREIGNTY: A NON-JUSTICIABLE CONCEPT?

Opponents of accession had lost the political argument. In a last effort to prevent entry, they tried a legal approach. In *Blackburn v A-G*,[86] Mr Blackburn asked the Court of Appeal to declare that it would be unconstitutional for the government to sign the Treaty of Rome, because to do so would amount to an irreversible surrender of parliamentary sovereignty.

In terms of domestic constitutional principle, this was an outlandish contention in two senses. Firstly, of course, orthodox constitutional theory wholly rejected the proposition that Parliament could limit its sovereignty, still less that the government could achieve this result. Secondly, for the government to sign the Treaty would require an exercise of the prerogative. In 1971, long before *GCHQ*, hardly any prerogative powers were subject to full judicial review. Even after *GCHQ*, Treaty ratification is a non-justiciable prerogative power, within Lord Roskill's 'excluded categories'. Consequently, the Court of Appeal told Mr Blackburn that it could not intervene.

Mr Blackburn's argument was however quite consistent with the ECJ's judgments in *Van Gend*, *Costa* and *Internationale*. At the risk of being repetitive, it might again be emphasised that those judgments did not simply assert the precedence and direct effect of EEC law; they also asserted that Member States did not have the legal capacity to control the domestic status of EEC law. According to the analysis offered by the ECJ in *Van Gend*, the Heath government's ratification of the Treaty of Accession would curtail the United Kingdom's (by which one means Parliament's) complete autonomy to control its constitution.

While the Court of Appeal did not appear to acknowledge this point in explicit terms, Lord Denning did make some interesting comments about the impact EEC membership would have on parliamentary sovereignty:

85 (1972) 'The Common Market and the common law' *Law Teacher* 3–12 at p 8.

86 [1971] 2 All ER 1380.

'We have all been brought up to believe that, in legal theory, one Parliament cannot bind another and that no Act is irreversible. But legal theory does not always march alongside political reality.'[87]

At this point in his judgment, Lord Denning referred approvingly to Professor Wade's 1955 article on parliamentary sovereignty: the root of the principle lay in ultimate political facts. But what is not clear from *Blackburn* is whether Denning thought that accession might entail the irrevocable surrender of sovereignty or merely the lending of it. The Court of Appeal assumed that Parliament would not legislate contrary to EEC obligations. If it did, what would the courts decide? Lord Denning was non-committal; 'We will consider that event when it happens.'[88] As one might expect, 'it' seemed to happen rather quickly. But in the interim, the ECJ had been continuing its teleological approach to EEC law, and the UK's political argument about membership had reawakened.

THE 1975 REFERENDUM

Labour's two narrow election victories in 1974 brought into power a party deeply split over the desirability of EEC membership. Labour's 1974 manifestos had promised that voters would be given the opportunity to vote on continued membership, by either another general election or a referendum. A third general election was not a plausible option, so a referendum seemed inevitable. The question which then arose was how the referendum should be conducted. Having renegotiated the UK's terms of membership, Prime Minister Wilson set off down a political path along which several constitutional principles fell by the wayside.

The first casualty was the convention of cabinet unanimity. Wilson decided to 'suspend' the convention for the referendum campaign. His justification was that the question transcended party politics, although most commentators suggest his real motivation for both the referendum itself and the suspension was his assumption that there was no other way to keep his party together. The party's National Executive Committee had voted against remaining in the Community.[89] It was then announced that seven (identified) members of Wilson's cabinet opposed continued membership, as did many backbench Labour MPs. A Commons motion approving the new terms was carried by a majority of 226; but only 137 of the 315 Labour MPs voted in favour. The success of government policy was entirely dependent on Conservative support. The second casualty was the Burkean notion of the MP as a representative lawmaker rather than the delegate of her voters. Parliament had in effect chosen to divest itself of its sovereignty on membership, by allowing the people the unusual opportunity of expressing an opinion on a single matter, rather than, as in general elections, on

[87] Ibid, at 1382. [88] Ibid, at 1383.

[89] Irving R (1975) 'The United Kingdom referendum, June 1975' *European Law Review* 3–12; Pimlott op cit pp 654–660 suggests that Wilson feared that, in a repeat of 1931, Roy Jenkins would play the MacDonald role and emerge as the Leader of a predominantly Conservative coalition government.

a package of issues. Neither the government nor Parliament was legally bound to respect the outcome of the referendum, although one imagines it would have been impossible, as a matter of practical politics, to do otherwise.

The EEC thus brought to the forefront of British politics the fundamental question of the desirability of leaving all political issues to be determined by a bare parliamentary majority. Some commentators suggested the EEC referendum might have a 'ripple effect', in convincing Parliament that there were other issues on which the 'the people's' views should be directly ascertained. In the 1890s, Dicey had written approvingly of referendums as devices for 'the people' to express authoritative opinions on matters of great constitutional significance; although given his stunted perception of 'the people', it would be rash to see this approval as espousing an avowedly 'democratic' position.[90]

Such a conclusion is perhaps more justifiable in respect of the 1975 referendum. The campaign was not fought along traditional party lines, but might crudely be described as a contest in which right wing Conservatives and the left of the Labour party united in opposing membership, while the Labour centre-right and Conservative centre-left supported it. Both sides received substantial funds from the government to publicise their arguments. The question was very simple: 'Do you think that the United Kingdom should stay in the European Community (the Common Market)?'. The result was a resounding victory for the pro-EEC lobby; 67.2% to 32.8% on a 65% turnout.

Thereafter, constitutional orthodoxies promptly reasserted themselves. The anti-EEC members of Wilson's cabinet re-embraced the unanimity convention, and traditional inter-party rivalries rapidly reappeared.[91] Nevertheless, the mere fact that a referendum was held, the peculiar political divisions which it exposed, and the overwhelming support it revealed for EEC membership, suggested that the Treaty of Rome was undoubtedly a 'special' ingredient in Britain's constitutional recipe. Yet while British politicians and British voters again raked over the old ground of even belonging to the Community, the ECJ was apparently still pursuing a federalist schemata of Treaty interpretation.

III. THE TREATY OF ROME 2: PRECEDENCE AND DIRECT EFFECT REVISITED

We have seen examples of innovative common law decisions in earlier chapters. But judicial dynamicism is not a trait exclusive to the common law; it was also embraced by the ECJ. And in the mid-1970s the Court took the opportunity to root its effet utile jurisprudence more firmly in the Community's legal soil.

[90] See Irving op cit.

[91] Lent a sharper edge by Thatcher's election as Leader of the Conservative party.

CONFIRMING THE DIRECT EFFECT OF DIRECTIVES

Notwithstanding the ECJ's judgment in *SACE Spa*, governments in several Member States maintained that directives, irrespective of their substance, could never have direct effect. The argument invoked by proponents of this position was that since Art 189 made it clear that directives reserved discretion to the Member States they could not be 'clear and unconditional' per *Van Gend*. However, in 1974, the ECJ confirmed *SACE SpA* in forceful terms.

Van Duyn v Home Office

The secondary legislation at issue in *Van Duyn*[92] was Directive 64/221. The directive contained detailed implementing measures for Art 48, the provision establishing free movement of workers within the EEC. Article 48 was not framed in 'unconditional terms'; Member States may per Art 48(3) derogate from it for reasons of public policy, public health or public security. Article 56 required the EEC to issue directives regulating Member States' use of the Art 48(3) derogations. Directive 64/221 Art 3 demanded that derogation be based solely on the 'personal conduct' of the individuals concerned.

The Home Office wanted to prevent Ms Van Duyn, a Dutch citizen, entering the country to work for the Church of Scientology, a cultish religion of which the government disapproved. She claimed that the government's action infringed Art 48, and challenged the Home Secretary's action before the British courts. In an Art 177 reference,[93] the Court of Appeal asked the ECJ firstly if Art 3 of Directive 64/221 was directly effective, and secondly if membership of the Scientologists could be 'personal conduct' ?

The ECJ held Art 3 directly effective because it confined the discretion accorded to the Member States by Art 48(3) with sufficient precision to make it justiciable: a national court could easily ensure that decisions a Member State made on this question were indeed based on the individual's personal conduct. In language reminiscent of *Van Gend*, the ECJ confirmed that there was no principled reason to exclude the possibility that directives (wholly or in part) could be directly effective:

> 'It is necessary to examine, in every case, whether the nature, scheme and general wording of the provision in question are capable of having direct effects on the relations between Member States and individuals.'[94]

But while the British government's arguments were rejected on this point, the ECJ also decided membership of the Scientologists could be 'personal conduct'. The British court could thus hold that Van Duyn's exclusion did not breach EEC law.

The ECJ's decision might be thought as much an exercise in diplomacy as law-making.[95] Judgment was delivered just before the UK's 1975 referendum. By

[92] Case 41/74 [1974] ECR 1337 [93] Case 41/74: [1974] ECR 1337.

[94] Ibid, at para 12.

[95] For a searching analysis see Weiler J (1986) 'Eurocracy and mistrust . . .' *Washington Law Review* 1103–1142.

permitting the Home Secretary to exclude Ms Van Duyn while simultaneously upholding *SACE SpA*, the Court reaffirmed a principle of long term significance to efforts to enhance EEC law's 'effet utile', while handing British supporters of EEC membership a precedent to refute opponents' claims that remaining in the Community required surrendering control over such basic issues as excluding undesirable foreign citizens. One cannot gauge if *Van Duyn* did influence voting behaviour in the referendum, or ascertain if the ECJ was consciously (if covertly) pursuing an avowedly political agenda, but it would be rash to exclude either possibility.

THE HORIZONTAL DIRECT EFFECT OF TREATY ARTICLES – WALRAVE V KOCH

A common thread in all of the ECJ's effet utile case law discussed so far has been that the 'defendant' was a governmental body of one sort or another. A potentially more complicated question presented itself to the ECJ in *Walrave and Koch v Union Cycliste Internationale*.[96] The defendant was a private sector organisation – the Union Cycliste International. The UCI was the governing body for the sport of cycle racing on roads. In formal terms, it had no governmental basis at all. One of the rules which it applied to cycle racing was that cyclists themselves and their motor-cycle pacemakers had to be of the same nationality. The rule was challenged by two Dutch pacemakers who wished to work for non-Dutch teams. There could be no doubt that if the rule had been imposed by a Member State law then the law would breach various directly effective Treaty provisions: the Art 7 prohibition on nationality-based discrimination; the Art 48 presumption of free movement of (employed) workers; and the Art 59 presumption of free movement of (self-employed) workers. (The ICU's rule would also breach the terms of an important piece of secondary legislation (Regulation 1612/68) which laid down detailed provisions concerning the free movement of workers.) In such circumstances, the Treaty articles and regulation could be said to be *vertically directly effective*; ie the legal action is upwards from a citizen against a government body. The question raised in *Walrave* was whether these provisions were also applicable in legal actions between individuals and/or companies; ie whether the provisions were *horizontally directly effective*. The ECJ considered that the Treaty articles and Regulation 1612/68 were directly effective in both vertical and horizontal planes:

'[17] Prohibition of such discrimination does not only apply to the action of public authorities but extends likewise to rules of any other nature aimed at regulating in a collective manner gainful employment and the provision of services.

[18] The abolition as between Member States of obstacles to freedom of movement for persons and to freedom to provide services, which are fundamental objectives of the Community . . ., would be compromised if the abolition of barriers of national origin could be

96 Case 36/74 [1974] ECR 1405.

neutralised by obstacles resulting from the exercise of their legal autonomy by associations or organisations which do not come under public law.

[19] Since, moreover, working conditions in the various Member States are governed by means of provisions laid down in law or regulations and sometimes by agreements and other acts concluded by private persons, to limit the prohibitions in question to acts of a public authority would risk creating inequality in their application.'

The teleological basis for this conclusion is readily apparent. One such reason related to the fact that very substantial amounts of economic activity within the Community were carried out in the private sector. If all these activities were placed beyond the reach of directly effective EEC law, the substantive scope of the 'common market' would be very tightly constrained. A second reason for according horizontal direct effect to EEC law arose from the differential allocation among the Member States of particular types of economic activity between the public and private sectors. If, for example, railways were run as a governmental concern in Member State A, then relevant EEC laws would affect the operation of the railway system in that country even if the EEC laws were only directly effective in the vertical plane. But if EEC law had only vertical direct effect, it would not affect the operation of railways in Member State B where railways were a private sector responsibility. A third – and obviously related – reason was to remove the possibility that some Member State governments might try to negate the impact of EEC law on some areas of economic activity by formally transferring responsibility for their conduct or supervision from public sector bodies to private sector organisations.

It is notable that the ECJ did not engage at all in *Walrave* with potentially tortuous arguments as to whether the ICU could be regarded as a 'governmental body' for the purposes of EEC law. One could readily offer a plausible rationale to sustain that conclusion; namely that the ICU controlled an important area of economic activity which would presumably have to be regulated by a government body if the ICU did not exist. But the ECJ appeared to assume that the notion that non-governmental bodies were legitimate targets of Community law controls was uncontentious. This seems a logical extension of *Van Gend's* principle that the Treaty bestowed rights on individuals. If effective realisation of those rights depended on other individuals respecting reciprocal obligations, it seemed obvious that those individuals should resolve disputes as to the meaning of EEC law in their national courts. *Walrave* expressly identified horizontal direct effect as a characteristic of Treaty articles and regulations. And it would seem plausible to conclude on the basis of *Walrave* that any Commission decision that was addressed to a private sector organisation would also give rise to horizontal direct effect. If narrowly construed, *Walrave* is perhaps authority only for the proposition that horizontal direct effect reaches only certain private sector regulatory bodies, and not to individuals or companies. However, the ECJ wasted little time in confirming that horizontal direct effect could reach into the smallest nooks and crannies of private sector economic activity.

THE JUSTICIABILITY TEST AND THE HORIZONTAL DIRECT EFFECT PRINCIPLE REAFFIRMED AND EXPANDED – DEFRENNE V SABENA

Just as the form which EEC legislation took could not preclude enforcement by national courts, neither does it assure that end. We saw in *Chandler v DPP*[97] that putting a prerogative power into statutory form did not necessarily make it justiciable. In *Defrenne v SABENA*[98], the ECJ drew a similar conclusion regarding direct effect.

Article 119 required Member States to 'ensure and maintain the principle that men and women should receive equal pay for equal work.' Ms Defrenne worked as an air hostess for SABENA, a Belgian airline which was essentially owned and managed by the Belgian government. SABENA paid its hostesses less than male stewards for identical duties. While admitting discrimination, SABENA claimed Art 119 was not directly effective. SABENA contended that Art 119's principle was too complex an economic concept to be justiciable before national courts; more detailed legislation explaining the meaning of equal pay and equal work would be needed before Art 119's principle became 'unconditional'.

The ECJ was only partly convinced by this argument. It held that gender discrimination could take two forms: 'direct and overt' or 'indirect and disguised'. Direct discrimination arose where (as for Ms Defrenne) differing wages were paid for exactly the same job, or where discrimination was specifically permitted in legislation or collective labour agreements. Such inequality could be detected by: 'purely legal analysis . . . the court is in a position to establish all the facts which enable it to decide whether a woman is receiving lower pay than a male worker.'[99] However indirect discrimination, involving inequality between different jobs or industries could only be established against more detailed legislative criteria. Not until such legislation had been enacted could the prohibition on indirect discrimination become directly effective. Once again, the ECJ stressed that it is the nature, not the source, of the EEC law that determines its enforceability in domestic courts.

An equally important element of *Defrenne* was the ECJ's conclusion that Art 119's justiciable terms were enforceable in national courts in a very expansive horizontal sense. Given that SABENA was in formal terms a public sector body, the case could have been resolved on the basis that Ms Defrenne's action was vertical in nature. However as in *Walrave*, the ECJ rejected any need to find a 'governmental element' to SABENA's activities. Rather, the Court concluded that all economic activity – even to the level of contracts between individuals – were controlled by Art 119:

> '[39] Since Article 119 is mandatory in nature, the prohibition on discrimination between men and women applies not only to the action of public authorities, but also extends to all agreements which are intended to regulate paid labour collectively, as well as to contracts between individuals.'

As we will subsequently see, the horizontal direct effect of directives proved a more

[97] See pp 125–126 above. [98] Case 43/75: [1976] ECR 455. [99] Ibid, paras 22–23.

contentious issue. But before that question was broached, the ECJ once again underscored the unambiguous nature of the precedence principle.

IMMEDIATE PRECEDENCE: SIMMENTHAL

As suggested above, the evident willingness of the Italian Constitutional Court in *Frontini* to reconstrue domestic constitutional principles in a fashion which mirrored the requirements of the effet utile jurisprudence did not immediately lead to a reversal of the Court's judgment in *Costa*. *Simmenthal*[100] concerned the compatibility of certain Italian laws regulating meat imports with EEC law. The Italian court hearing Simmenthal's claim referred two questions to the ECJ. The first related simply to the domestic law's substantive compatibility with the EEC regulations, and need not concern us here. The more important question concerned the consistency with EEC law of the Italian constitution's requirement that Italian legislation which breached international obligations could only be invalidated or disapplied by the Italian Constitutional Court. It could not be disapplied by an inferior court such as the one hearing Simmenthal's claim. Some considerable time would elapse before a case had made its way to the Constitutional Court, during which the Italian law in issue would remain in force.

The ECJ held that it was not enough that a Member State's courts give effect to the precedence of EEC law *eventually*: domestic courts had to do so *immediately*. It was the duty of any national court to 'disregard forthwith' any national law conflicting with EEC law: 'without waiting until those measures have been eliminated by action on the part of the national legislature concerned . . . or of other constitutional authorities.'[101]

Several more years were to pass before the Italian Constitutional Court refashioned Italy's domestic constitutional law principles to mirror this ECJ requirement. In its 1984 judgment in *Spa Granital*, the Court – with some delicacy – held that its previous decisions had to be reconsidered. The gist of its conclusion was that, as a matter of Italian constitutional law, its previous holding in *Costa* was incorrect:

> '. . . .[O]n the basis of Article 11 of the Constitution – as stated above – the full and continuous application of Community law is guaranteed. Directly applicable EEC legal provisions enter and stay in force in Italy on the same basis, without their direct effect being impaired by any municipal statute. It is irrelevant, for this purpose, whether a statute was previously or subsequently enacted. A Community regulation is in any event paramount with regard to the matters it covers. . . .'[102]

In the meantime, a quite different attitude was struck by France's Conseil d'Etat. The

[100] *Administratzione delle Finanze dello Stato v Simmenthal SpA (Simmenthal II):* Case 106/77 [1978] ECR 629.

[101] Ibid, para 7.

[102] *Spa Granital v Ammministrazzione delle Finanze dello Stato* (Decision 170 of 8 June 1984) (1984) CML Rev 756 at 761–762 – unofficial translation.

Conseil's 1980 judgment in *Cohn-Bendit* offered a clear message that not only did it reject the ECJ's claim to have sole jurisdiction to determine the status of EEC law in domestic legal systems, but also that it was not even willing to allow French law to match the ECJ's requirements on the principles of precedence and direct effect. *Cohn-Bendit* bluntly refuted the ECJ's conclusion in *SACE SpA* and *Van Duyn* and held that an EEC directive could not be directly effective at all in certain situations.

EFFET UTILE BEFORE THE CONSEIL D'ETAT: THE COHN-BENDIT CONTROVERSY

In May 1968, student-led protests against the French government threatened the overthrow of the existing constitution. Daniel Cohn-Bendit, a German national studying in Paris, was a leader of the protest. 'Danny the Red', as he was popularly known, was subsequently deported and banned from re-entering France, on the obvious ground that he posed a threat to public order.

Ten years later, Cohn-Bendit's revolutionary fervour had dimmed, and he was offered a job in France. The entry ban was still however in place. He claimed before the French courts that the ban infringed his rights under Art 48, unless it was justified under the Art 48(3) derogations. As we saw in *Van Duyn*, Art 64/221 allowed those derogations to be invoked only if the threat to public order, public safety or public health arose from the individual's personal conduct. Cohn-Bendit was in effect asking the French court to conclude that his personal conduct no longer threatened public order, and thence overturn the banning order.

The French court hearing the case tried to make a reference to the ECJ concerning the direct effect of Directive 64/221, but was forbidden to do so by the Conseil d'Etat. The French government had in the interim revoked the exclusion order, but it invited the Conseil d'Etat to rule whether, as a matter of French constitutional law, Directive 64/221 could be directly effective. The Conseil d'Etat simply concluded that directives could not have direct effect in these circumstances.[103] The Treaty's framers had stated in Art 189 that a regulation would be directly applicable and binding in its entirety; it could therefore be directly effective. That the framers had not said so about directives, but had specifically granted Member States discretion in implementing the law, must mean that they envisaged that directives would not have direct effect.

The Conseil d'Etat restricted its search for the meaning of EEC law solely to the Treaty's text, rejecting the ECJ's teleological approach to interpretation. From a narrowly legalistic perspective, the Conseil's conclusion has some merit, but it is utterly inconsistent with both the *Costa* and *Van Gend* principles. The Conseil d'Etat's judgment rejects the proposition that the interpretation of EEC law is ultimately a matter for the ECJ. If the courts in France could assert an unchallengeable jurisdiction to determine the meaning of EC law in France, no doubt other superior courts in other

[103] *Minister of the Interior v Cohn-Bendit* [1980] 1 CMLR 543.

Member States could assert a similar power in respect of their own countries. In that event, the supremacy and direct effect principles would be completely undermined. One commentator describes *Cohn-Bendit* as: 'a clear and deliberate act of defiance . . . a blow at the foundations of the community.'[104] It is impossible to gauge to what extent the Conseil d'Etat was following a nationalistic political agenda, and how far it was motivated by a genuine belief in the legal integrity of its conclusion. Much the same ambiguity seemingly pervades the UK courts' initial efforts to address the constitutional implications of accession.

IV. EEC LAW, PARLIAMENTARY SOVEREIGNTY AND THE UK COURTS: PHASE ONE

The UK judiciary's earliest encounters with EEC law suggested that the radical principles of *Van Gend, Costa* and *Internationale*, and Parliament's evident attempt to enact those principles in the ECA 1972, would meet a trenchant restatement of orthodox Diceyan theory. Lord Denning's non-committal attitude in *Blackburn* was soon followed with a somewhat firmer view in *Felixstowe Dock and Railway Co v British Docks Board.*[105] The case raised the possibility that the provisions of a Bill shortly to be enacted would contravene Art 86's rules on competition law. However Lord Denning did not think that possibility raised a difficult constitutional issue:

> 'It seems to me that once the Bill is passed by Parliament and becomes a Statute, that will dispose of all this discussion about the Treaty. These courts will have to abide by the Statute without regard to the Treaty at all.'[106]

It is not clear if Lord Denning felt that the ECA 1972 had not limited Parliament's sovereignty, or whether it simply could not do so. Nevertheless, in his view, the ECJ's 'new legal order' had apparently not taken root in British constitutional soil.

Lord Denning seemed to adopt a different approach in respect of the ECJ's adherence to teleological methods of treaty and legislative interpretation. In *H P Bulmer Ltd v J Bollinger SA*, he suggested British judges would have to forgo their traditional, literalist techniques, and:

> 'follow the European pattern. No longer must they examine the words in meticulous detail. No longer must they argue about the precise grammatical sense. They must look to the purpose or intent. . . . They must divine the spirit of the Treaty and gain inspiration from it. If they find a gap, they must fill it as best they can.'[107]

[104] Hartley T (1988) *The foundations of European Community law* p 232 (Oxford: Clarendon Press); ch 8 of Hartley's book offers an interesting discussion of the various Member States' responses to the precedence and direct effect issues.

[105] [1976] 2 CMLR 655, CA.

[106] Ibid, at 659.

[107] [1974] 3 WLR 202 at 216, CA.

Lord Denning's advice[108] extended however only to the Treaty and to EEC legislation, not to British statutes. Domestic legislation, it seemed, even if dealing with EC matters, would still be interpreted according to orthodox principles. It came therefore as a surprise when Lord Denning himself advocated a radical break with constitutional tradition some two years later.

THE END OF THE DOCTRINE OF IMPLIED REPEAL? MACARTHYS V SMITH

Macarthys Ltd v Smith[109] arose from an Art 119 dispute. Mrs Smith was employed at a lower wage by Macarthys than the man who previously did her job. She claimed this breached Art 119. Macarthys contended that the British courts should apply the relevant British legislation (the Equal Pay Act 1970 as amended by the Sex Discrimination Act 1975), which forbade discrimination only between men and women doing the same job for the same employer simultaneously. If Macarthy's interpretation of the domestic legislation was correct, the British courts faced a difficulty. For British purposes, Art 119 came into force in 1973. The Sex Discrimination Act was passed two years later. Should the later Act prevail, as Dicey's theory would suggest? Or should EEC law, per *Costa*, be regarded by the court as the superior form of law?

In the Court of Appeal, Lord Denning thought that a literal reading of the British legislation supported Macarthys' claim. However, following his own advice in *Bulmer*, he rejected a literalist approach. Rather, the Act should be construed subject to the 'overriding force' of the Treaty 'for that takes priority even over our own statute.'[110] Denning's own view of Art 119 was that its prohibition on unequal pay extended beyond 'same time' situations to successive employment.[111] Construing the Treaty and the 1975 legislation: 'as a harmonious whole . . . intended to eliminate discrimination against women',[112] Denning found in Mrs Smith's favour.

Denning suggested he was obliged to adopt this expansive interpretive strategy because of the ECA 1972, s 2. That would in itself give the ECA a somewhat 'special' status, but Denning's argument went beyond technical questions of interpretation. He also concluded that s 2 had abolished the doctrine of implied repeal for British statutes affecting EEC matters. Domestic courts should assume that if ever a British statute was impliedly inconsistent with an EEC obligation the inconsistency arose because Parliament had erred in the language chosen: legislators could not have intended to achieve such a result, so the courts would save them from the consequences of their mistake by according precedence to EEC law.

108 Reiterated, reinforced and also applied to other Treaties in *Jones Buchanan & Co Ltd v Babco Forwarding and Shipping (UK) Ltd* [1977] QB 208, CA.

109 Case 129/79: [1979] 3 All ER 325, CA.

110 Ibid, at 329.

111 Ibid. Denning was in a minority on this point. The majority (Cumming-Bruce and Lawton LJJ) were uncertain as to Art 119's scope, and referred the question to the ECJ. They seemed to agree however with Denning's approach to the constitutional issue.

112 Ibid.

This radical contention endows the ECA with a very 'special' constitutional status.[113] In effect, Denning's judgment in *Macarthys* recognised a weak 'manner and form' entrenchment of the precedence and direct effect of EEC law (the 'manner and form' in issue being a special from of words rather than an enhanced majority). These values were not however substantively entrenched, for:

'If the time should come when Parliament deliberately passes an Act with the intention of repudiating the Treaty or any provision of it . . . and says so in express terms then I should have thought it would be the duty of our Courts to follow the statute of our Parliament. I do not envisage any such situation. . . . Unless there is such an intentional and express repudiation of the Treaty, it is our duty to give priority to the Treaty.'[114]

Denning did not explain how the 1972 Parliament had managed to bind itself and its successors in this (limited) way. There is, as we have repeatedly suggested, no obvious legal principle supporting such a conclusion. One must therefore conclude that Denning was recognising a new 'ultimate political fact' – that accession to the EEC had in some (evidently rather mysterious fashion) 'revolutionised' orthodox constitutional understandings.

This argument rests on the presumption that the political, economic and foreign policy implications of acceding to the Treaty were so profound that the courts had to assume a new, protective role. The presumption operates on two levels. The first, itself controversial, is that Parliament should be protected from the adverse political consequences of unintended breaches of its EEC obligations. The second, more controversial still, is that UK citizens should be protected from unwittingly incompetent or deceptive parliamentary efforts to renege on the UK's EEC commitments.

We might think that, as an exercise in constitution building, such protective devices would be desirable. But they are constituent rather than interpretive values, and as such, beyond conventional understandings of the judicial role. Despite its obscure roots, Denning's judgment staked out new constitutional ground. But the House of Lords showed itself reluctant to disapprove it.

A MATTER OF INTERPRETATION? GARLAND V BRITISH RAIL ENGINEERING LTD

The issue before their Lordships in *Garland*[115] was whether the Sex Discrimination Act 1975 prohibited gender discrimination in relation to concessionary travel facilities extended to BR's retired employees. Such discrimination seemed as though it might contravene Art 119, so the prospect again arose of a conflict between EEC law and a subsequent domestic statute.

Somewhat peculiarly, Lord Diplock (for a unanimous House) made an extensive

[113] An excellent analysis is offered in Allan T (1983) 'Parliamentary sovereignty: Lord Denning's dexterous revolution' *OJLS* 22–33.

[114] [1979] 3 All ER 325 at 329, CA.

[115] [1983] 2 AC 751.

reference to how he would approach the question if the EEC was an ordinary international law treaty:

'it is a principle of construction of United Kingdom statutes . . . that the words of a statute passed after the Treaty has been signed and dealing with the subject matter of the international obligation of the United Kingdom are to be construed, if . . . reasonably capable of bearing such a meaning, as intended to carry out the obligation and not to be inconsistent with it.'[116]

This technique would be incompatible with *Van Gend*'s 'new legal order' principle, and would thus breach the ECA 1972 s 3. It would be not 'irrelevant',[117] as one commentator put it, but legally indefensible.

Lord Diplock perhaps made this point to highlight the innovative nature of EEC law, for he did not decide the case on that basis. Rather he suggested that the ECA 1972 s 2 had introduced a new rule of statutory interpretation to which the courts were now subjected. A UK court should construe all domestic legislation in a manner respecting EEC obligations: 'however wide a departure from the prima facie meaning of the language of the provision might be needed in order to achieve consistency.'[118] In this case, the 1975 Act could be interpreted as compatible with EEC law 'without any undue straining of the ordinary meaning of the language used.'[119] In that respect, Diplock shared Denning's sentiment in *Macarthys*. He also agreed with Denning that UK courts must obey a statute breaching EEC law in 'express positive terms'. He was more circumspect about the doctrine of implied repeal: this was not an appropriate case to decide that question.

Barely ten years after accession, Lords Diplock and Denning had both moved considerably from their previously Diceyan position towards the EEC's constitutional impact. They had not gone far enough to satisfy *Van Gend* and *Costa*, but the dynamicism of their respective approaches to the issue of the impact of EC law on orthodox British constitutional theory is undeniable. Yet while British courts struggled to accommodate long established principles of EEC law, the ECJ was facing jurisprudential difficulties of its own.

V. DIRECT EFFECT – THE SAGA CONTINUES

As noted earlier, the ECJ had concluded that Treaty articles and regulations could be both vertically and horizontally directly effective. This characteristic of 'universal enforcability' of aspects of EEC law is an important part of the effet utile doctrine. But Art 189's text seemingly precluded the horizontal direct effect of directives; it stated

[116] Ibid, at 394–395.

[117] Hood-Phillips O (1982) 'A Garland for the Lords: Parliament and community law again' *LQR* 524–526.

[118] [1983] 2 AC 751 at 771. [119] Ibid.

they are binding only on the addressee Member State. As we have seen, the ECJ had not generally allowed textual considerations to constrain its articulation of 'the law'. We might therefore initially find its judgment in *Marshall* somewhat surprising.

THE HORIZONTAL AND VERTICAL DIRECT EFFECT OF DIRECTIVES? MARSHALL V SOUTHAMPTON AND SOUTH WEST HAMPSHIRE AREA HEALTH AUTHORITY

Marshall[120] returned to the adequacy of the UK's attempts to implement Art 119. Mrs Marshall's employer – which was part of the National Health Service – operated a discriminatory retirement age policy: men could work until 65, women had to retire at 60. This was lawful under the UK's sex discrimination legislation, but seemed incompatible with Directive 76/207.[121] The Court of Appeal asked the ECJ if the Directive precluded discriminatory retirement ages, and, if so, whether Mrs Marshall could enforce the directive against her employer in the national courts.

The ECJ answered both questions affirmatively. However it then made a more general point. Directives could only be directly effective against 'public authorities': they could not be enforced in national courts against private sector organisations or individual citizens. Mrs Marshall's employer was a public or governmental body for these purposes: had she worked for a private hospital, she could not have claimed her EEC entitlements until Parliament had implemented the directive by amending the domestic legislation.

Marshall is a very surprising judgment for several reasons. Firstly, there was no need for the ECJ to address the general question of whether a directive could have horizontal direct effect. Mrs Marshall's case would have been resolved simply on the basis of the conclusion that her employer was a governmental body. Secondly, the judgment is premised on a literalist rather than teleological construction of the Treaty. In *Marshall*, allusions to the 'spirit, scheme and general wording' of the Treaty are notably absent, while a reference to the explicit text of Art 189 (stressing that directives are addressed only to Member States and so cannot have horizontal effect) enjoys an unusually prominent position.

That in itself is somewhat unusual. It becomes more so when one appreciates that in teleological terms the *Marshall* principle appears to run counter to the whole thrust of the ECJ's previous effet utile case law. This takes us to the third reason. *Marshall* manifestly creates the problem of partial application of EEC law that the ECJ took such pains to avoid in *Walrave* and *Defrenne* in respect of Treaty articles. Within any Member State where the same kind of economic activities were carried out in the public and private sectors, the very real possibility arose that its public sector

120 Case 152/84: [1986] ECR 723.

121 A piece of secondary legislation which addressed some aspects of the 'indirect and disguised' discrimination adverted to in *Defrenne*.

employees would have easier access to EEC benefits than private sector workers.[122] Such partiality could also arise in a trans-national sense. In a Member State where, for example, health care services were provided entirely by the government, the substantive contents of directives would automatically be accessible in domestic law in respect of that area of economic activity. In a Member State where health care was largely a private sector activity, the availability of that substantive law would be contingent on the Member State having properly implemented the directive in domestic law. And it need hardly be said that the various Member States had very different traditions concerning allocation of particular economic activities to the public and private sectors.[123] These are hardly subtle points. It must have been apparent to the ECJ that its judgment would create these problems.

The fourth curiosity of *Marshall* is that it fits very unhappily with proposals then being refined by the Commission to invite the Member States to implement some major amendments to the original Treaty. It was evident by the early 1980s that the reality of a truly 'common market' among the Member States had yet to be achieved: a great many national law barriers to the free movement of goods, workers and services remained in place. The amendments being floated by the Commission proposed that the Community embark upon a rigorous 'Single Market' program of legal harmonisation of Member States' laws. [124]The programme was to rely substantially on the use of directives. Its success could hardly be helped, and would more likely be markedly hindered, by the ECJ's conclusion in *Marshall*. This too is an obvious point. All in all, *Marshall*, if viewed in isolation, seems a quite extraordinary judgment.

MAKING SENSE OF MARSHALL? THE EMERGENCE OF 'INDIRECT EFFECT'

We can perhaps begin to find a better explanation for *Marshall* by placing the case in a slightly broader context. Consideration might firstly be given to a judgment delivered shortly before *Marshall* in the combined cases of *Von Colson* and *Harz*.[125] The cases presented the ECJ with blatant examples of gender discrimination; in *Von Colson* by a government employer, and in *Harz* by a private company. The ECJ suggested that the literal meaning of the German law passed to implement the relevant EC Directive (No 76/207) did not give adequate effect to the EC law's intentions. If – as the ECJ was soon to announce in *Marshall* – directives had only vertical direct effect, Ms Von Colson could have relied upon the directive itself, but Ms Harz could not. Rather than approve so patently discriminatory an outcome in the two cases, the ECJ opted for a

122 See Curtin D (1990) 'The province of government: delimiting the direct effect of directives in the common law context' *European Law Review* 195–223; Arnull A (1987) 'The incoming tide: responding to *Marshall*' *Public Law* 383–399.

123 It might also be thought that *Marshall* provided Member States with an incentive to 'privatise' certain public sector activities in order to escape the automatic impact of unwelcome directives.

124 The issue is discussed in more detail in chapter 13.

125 Case 14/83 [1984] ECR 1891; and Case 79/83 [1984] ECR 1921.

strategy which allowed both claimants to enforce their EC rights in the same way. The principle which the ECJ uncovered in *Von Colson* has come to be known as 'indirect effect'. The nub of the ECJ's judgment was that the German courts hearing the *Von Colson* and *Harz* cases were obliged by EC law to interpret domestic law in a manner that facilitated the achievement of EC objectives. The duty of loyalty imposed by Art 5 of the Treaty bound not just national legislatures and governments, but embraced:

'. . . all the authorities of the Member states including . . . the courts. It follows that, in applying the national law and in particular the provisions of a national law introduced in order to implement Directive 76/207, national courts are required to interpret their national law in the light of the wording and purpose of the directive in order to achieve the result referred to in the third paragraph of Art 189. . . . in so far as they are given discretion to do so under national law.'[126]

The above extract typifies the rather ambiguous nature of the ECJ's *Von Colson* judgment. Read superficially, *Von Colson* seems to suggest no more than the uncontroversial proposition that a domestic court interpret ambiguous domestic legislation in a manner that accords with its country's international law obligations. But once the judgment is placed in the context of the EC as a 'new legal order', several rather thorny questions arose.

For example, did 'discretion under national law' include the precedence principle espoused by the ECJ in *Costa, Internationale* and *Simmenthal*, or was it to be restricted to 'purely' domestic legal principles. Similarly, was the national courts' 'interpretive' technique to mirror the ECJ's own teleological, integrationist position, or remain loyal to less adventurous domestic principles? In a country with a literalist interpretive tradition, a narrow construction of the *Von Colson* principle on this point might render the principle quite useless. This point obviously raises a 'uniformity' problem across the Member States.

Relatedly, was 'national law' to be interpreted as a concept entirely at large within the domestic legal system, or one limited solely to legislation introduced specifically to implement a directive? If the former view was taken, national courts could presumably scour all domestic laws for a suitable legal peg on which to hang the EEC law right, or even, in some legal systems, fashion a new law themselves with which to achieve the result sought by the directive. If the latter view prevailed, *Von Colson* would not assist citizens in Member States which had assumed that domestic legislation pre-dating the relevant directive fulfilled the EEC's objectives, or had not introduced any implementing legislation at all.

While providing a route round *Marshall* in some instances, *Von Colson* perhaps raised more questions than it solved. Yet in one sense the judgment might be seen as an extraordinarily clever exercise in supra-national judicial constitution-making, as the ECJ recast the problem of unimplemented directives from being a dispute between the Member State and the ECJ to a dispute between the Member State's

126 Ibid, at paras 26 and 28.

government and/or legislature and its own courts. There are two reasons – each flowing from considerations of domestic constitutional tradition – to assume that domestic courts might be more willing to accept the effet utile principle if it could be pursued through indirect rather than direct effect. Firstly, indirect effect merely enjoins domestic courts to 'interpret'. They are not asked to 'make' or 'impose' law. They are thus engaging in a much more obviously 'judicial' role. Secondly, national courts are required to interpret the Member State's own law, which law one assumes has been promoted by a government and enacted by a legislature[127] in order to give effect to the directive concerned. The national court is thus only giving legal effect to a political value which has already been accepted as legitimate by other governmental actors who have unwittingly failed properly to carry out the State's obligations.

Indirect and direct effect also have quite different implications for the nature of the relationship between the ECJ and national courts. Direct effect creates an ECJ/ national court relationship which is essentially vertically hierarchical. Domestic courts are to all intents and purposes being told that they must simply apply laws whose meanings are determined exclusively by the ECJ. The national court is no more than an agent of the ECJ. Indirect effect accords much more authority and responsibility to national courts. The relationship the principle creates between the ECJ and the national might defensibly be portrayed as one of partnership rather than hierarchy; in which the ECJ is heavily dependent upon the creativity of national courts. *Von Colson* was perhaps intended to signal that the ECJ was radically rethinking the nature of its relationship with domestic courts. The ECJ perhaps further emphasised this point in *Johnston v Chief Constable of the Royal Ulster Constabulary*, when it held that a domestic court should invoke the direct effect of a directive against a government body only if it was unable to achieve the same result through creative interpretation of national law.[128]

This gives rise to the inference that the ECJ's judgment in *Marshall* may have been prompted in part by an ECJ concern – in the light of *Solange (No 1)* and *Cohn-Bendit* – to offer reassurance to national courts which were unwilling even to allow domestic law to mirror the requirements of the effet utile doctrine that the ECJ was sensitive to their concerns. The Conseil d'Etat's judgment in *Cohn-Bendit* presented the ECJ with a profound strategic difficulty. For the ECJ to have expressly criticised the Conseil d'Etat would likely have triggered an escalation in the disagreement between the two courts. Yet the ECJ could hardly be expected to reverse its own conclusion in *Van Duyn*; to do so would compromise the effet utile principle, undermine the ECJ's own jurisprudential integrity in a general sense, and send an invitation to other national courts to challenge the content of ECJ jurisprudence. *Marshall, Von Colson* and *Johnston* can be seen as an ingenious middle way between those two unpalatable and impractical alternatives. *Marshall* signals an end to the seemingly inexorable onward

[127] It is of course possible that in some Member States the power to produce the 'laws' required might rest exclusively with the government.

[128] Case 222/84 [1986] ECR 1651 at paras. 53–54.

march of the direct effect principle, and thus to the de facto subordination of national courts to the ECJ. The judgment, rooted largely in a literalist interpretation of Art 189, makes a methodological nod to the Conseil d'Etat's approach to Treaty construction in *Cohn-Bendit.* The obviously deleterious implications of *Marshall* for the uniform impact of EEC law are then partially ameliorated by *Von Colson,* in a fashion which enhances the role of national courts in determining the meaning of EEC law and offers national courts protection against domestic constitutional criticism. That enhancement is then promptly lent an extended reach in *Johnston.* Quite how this new phase of inter-judicial relationships would develop remained to be seen.

AN ANALYTICAL OVERVIEW: 'NORMATIVE' AND 'DECISIONAL' SUPRA-NATIONALISM

The interplay of law and politics was clearly a pervasive feature of the EEC's early constitutional development. In an influential critique published in 1981, Joseph Weiler suggested that this process was best understood in terms of a distinction between what he termed 'normative' and 'decisional' supranationalism.[129]

Normative supranationalism concerned the formal status of EEC law vis a vis the domestic law of the Member States. In decisions such as *Van Gend, Costa, Internationale* and *Simmenthal,* the ECJ had fashioned principles which indicated that 'the relationship between the legal order of the Community and that of the Member States has come to resemble increasingly a fully fledged (USA type) federal system.'[130] Yet Weiler suggested that just the opposite trend was evident in respect of decisional supranationalism, which concerned the characteristics of the practical reality of institutional relations within the Community's legislative and administrative processes. In this sphere, the EEC had become increasingly inter-governmental in nature. The Luxembourg Accords exemplified this trend; as did the emergence of a body known as the 'European Council', a forum for regular summit meetings of heads of government of the Member States, which (like the Luxembourg Accords) existed entirely outside the Treaty's legal structure, but manifestly had an important influence on the conduct of Community business in the Council of Ministers. Weiler also suggested that a similar, albeit not obviously 'unconstitutional' result was produced by the growing influence of COREPER[131] on the Commission's task of initiating legislation. The combined effect of these developments was that the Council had become a forum for individual countries to engage in 'package deal decision-making' and 'high powered political horse-trading'.[132] Moreover, the Commission and Parliament were ill-equipped to counter this trend, in part at least because of the community's so-called 'democracy deficit.' Without an electoral mandate from 'the people' of the EEC,

[129] (1981) 'The Community system: the dual character of supra-nationalism' *Yearbook of European Law* 267–306.

[130] Ibid, at p 273. [131] See footnote 5 at p 412 above. [132] (1981) op cit at 288.

neither institution could forcefully assert an integrationist agenda against the nationalist wishes of (elected) Member State governments.

Although this normative/decisional divergence presented an apparent paradox, in that the EEC was in one sense increasingly coming to resemble a pure form of federal constitutionalism, while in another it seemed no more than a loose association of entirely autonomous sovereign states, Weiler suggested that, on further consideration, the EEC could not, in the short term, have survived in any other way. By pulling in opposite directions, these forces had created:

> 'an equilibrium which explains a seemingly irreconcilable equation: a large . . . and effective measure of transnational integration, coupled at the same time with the preservation of strong, unthreatened, national Member States.'[133]

Weiler's argument is a contentious one, and since it lies in the realm of constitutional and political theory, cannot be 'correct' in any definitive sense. But for our purposes, it is more important for the questions it raises than any answer it might provide. For if the EEC was by then established as a unique form of governmental authority, if it was indeed unlike anything with which Britain's 300-year-old constitution had previously had to deal, one might plausibly wonder if the stage had not been set for Professor Wade's legal revolution to make its long-awaited appearance? That is a question to which chapter thirteen will turn.

THE REDUCTION OF THE 'DEMOCRATIC DEFICIT' AND THE EMERGENCE OF HUMAN RIGHTS AS GENERAL PRINCIPLES OF EEC LAW

Some tentative steps had been taken to address the Community's 'democratic deficit' in the 1970s, primarily by altering the powers and composition of the Parliament. A Treaty amendment which became effective in 1975 greatly enhanced the Parliament's role in the budgetary process.[134] Perhaps more significantly, from 1979 onwards, the Parliament was to be composed of members directly elected by each nation's electorate, thereby providing it with a 'democratic' basis from which to argue that its powers within the Community's law-making process should be increased.[135]

In the same period, the ECJ also sought to reassure domestic courts as to the substantive legitimacy of EEC law through a more enthusiastic and explicit embrace

133 Ibid, at 292.

134 Ehlermann C (1975) 'Applying the new budgetary procedure for the first time' *Common Market Law Review* 325–343; Lasok and Bridge op cit pp 258–264.

135 British Labour MPs opposed to any such increase 'persuaded' the Callaghan government in 1978 to introduce a bill providing that any Treaty enhancing the EP's powers could not be ratified by the government unless approved by an Act of Parliament. This measure, enacted as s 6 of the European Parliamentary Elections Act 1978, had two effects. The first was to qualify the government's power to incorporate new Treaties into domestic law via Orders in Council. The second, more generally, was to place a clear statutory limit on the government's foreign policy prerogatives. It was not however clear then, some seven years before *GCHQ*, if this statutory limit would prove justiciable.

of an implied doctrine of human rights protection within the Treaty, fleshing out the skeletal jurisprudence adverted to in *Internationale.* In *Nold,*[136] the ECJ suggested it would annul EEC secondary legislation which contravened fundamental constitutional principles common to the Member States, and also indicated it would draw on international human rights treaties for guidance as to what those principles might be. Subsequently, in *Hauer v Land Rheinland-Pfalz,*[137] the ECJ explicitly referred to the European Convention on Human Rights in gauging the 'constitutionality' of EEC secondary legislation. The ECJ did not go so far as announcing the Convention's de facto incorporation into EEC law, yet that seemed an implicit consequence of its judgment. That implication did appear to satisfy Germany's Federal Constitutional Court. That court had never in fact exercised its self-proclaimed power to prevent domestic enforcement of EEC measures which contravened the Basic Law, but in *Wünsche-Handelsgesellschaft,*[138] it indicated that it was – in a manner similar to the position embraced a decade earlier by the Italian Constitutional Court in *Frontini* and reiterated in *Granital* in 1984 – content to assume that the compatibility of EEC secondary legislation with basic human rights norms was now adequately policed by the ECJ.

CONCLUSION

The combined effects of the preliminary 'democratisation' of the Community's institutional structure and the ECJ's continued attachment to the effet utile strategy were not in themselves sufficient, as Weiler had predicted, to maintain the Community's integrationist momentum. The European Parliament had promoted a Draft Treaty on European Union (DTEU) in 1984, which advocated a radical overhaul of Community institutions and (unsurprisingly) a substantial extension of its own powers. The initiative, which seemed to entail significant political as well as economic integration, was not embraced by the Member States. But the mid-1980s, it had become evident that even the pervasive economic integration envisaged by the Treaty's Framers had yet to be achieved. The Commission consequently sought to re-energise the Community, proposing a wide range of measures (both normative and decisional in nature) which eventually led to the first major amendment to the Treaty of Rome, some thirty years after its birth, in the shape of the Single European Act.

[136] Case 4/73: [1974] ECR 491. [137] Case 44/79: [1979] ECR 3727. [138] [1987] 3 CMLR 225.

13

THE EUROPEAN COMMUNITY AFTER THE SINGLE EUROPEAN ACT

This chapter traces the history of the EEC from 1986 to 2006. It begins by analysing the origins and objectives of the Single European Act. It then examines the ways in which the ECJ has continued to develop principles to facilitate the enforcement of EC law, and considers to what extent our domestic courts have applied such ideas. After exploring the controversies engendered by the Maastricht and Amsterdam Treaties, the chapter concludes by assessing in what senses, if any, continued EC membership will entail a loss of the United Kingdom's 'sovereignty' to a federal European constitution and a rebalancing of power within the constitution between Parliament and the courts.

I. THE SINGLE EUROPEAN ACT – THE TERMS

The SEA's roots lay in the Commission's perception that the Community's original objectives were being achieved at a painfully slow rate. The Treaty of Rome had envisaged that the four fundamental freedoms of movement for goods, capital, persons and services upon which the Community was to be based would be achieved by 1970. But even by 1984, this objective remained unfulfilled: national laws still contained many barriers to the creation of a truly 'common market'. That such barriers remained in place is a cogent illustration both of the limits of the ECJ's supra-nationalist competence and the continued vitality of nationalist, protectionist sentiment in the more inter-national arena of the Community's legislative process. The Commission's response to this impasse was to seek new means to realise the Treaty's original ends.

In the 1960s and 1970s, the Commission had sought to create the 'common market' by embarking on a programme of harmonisation through detailed Community legislation. These so-called 'Euronorms' imposed a uniform regulatory structure on each of the member states. By 1984 the 'Euronorm' approach was regarded as inappropriate for several reasons. Firstly, the Commission's small size limited the amount of legislation it could initiate. Secondly, several member states were sceptical about the need to homogenise regulatory structures, suggesting that a 'common market' need not be a uniform market, but could accommodate appreciable geographical divergences in the substance and application of EEC law principles.[1] The third reason, flowing from the second, was that it frequently proved impossible to achieve all the member states' agreement on the intricacies of proposed Euronorm legislation.

The regenerative programme first outlined in the Commission's 1985 White Paper consequently represented a move away from what has been described as the Commission's 'almost theological dogmatism'[2] in pursuit of uniformity. The White Paper attempted to reinvigorate a stalled programme of economic integration by reforming both the methods and substance of the Community's law-making process.

The proposed new Treaty Art 8A announced the intention to create an 'internal market' by 1 January 1993. The shift from an emphasis on the 'common market' to an 'internal market' was not simply a question of relabelling. The internal market proposed that the Community seek enhanced economic integration by rejecting the Euronorm's methodology, and relying instead on a process of 'mutual recognition' of acceptable standards. As Forwood and Clough note, the internal market strategy was based on a 'minimalist approach to economic regulation' in which the notion of 'equivalence' is the key.[3] Goods and services lawfully marketed in one member state should be saleable throughout the community.

However, the White Paper's original integrationist thrust was much diluted when exposed to the nationalistically motivated scrutiny of the successive Inter-Governmental Conferences required by the Article 236 amendment process.[4] That these negotiations were protracted and keenly contested by the member states is sometimes portrayed as a weakness in the Community's decision-making structure. But the tortuous process might equally plausibly be seen as perfectly compatible with that view of democracy which contends that alterations to a constitution's fundamental principles should not be easy to effect.

It is perhaps therefore not surprising that the amendments introduced to the original Treaty by the SEA present an even more complex balancing of inter-national and supra-national forces than provided by the original Treaty.[5] In the supra-national sphere, one can point to an extension of the Community's substantive competence into the fields of environmental protection, regional development, research and technical innovation, and some aspects of social policy.[6]

[1] This is perhaps an obvious conclusion for countries where sub-central units of government have appreciable legislative competence in economic policy; a key ingredient of federal systems of government is that the constitution affords effective legal protection to such diversity.

[2] Edward D (1987) 'The impact of the Single European Act on the institutions' *CML Rev* 19–30 at p 26.

[3] (1987) 'The Single European Act and free movement' *EL Rev* 383–408.

[4] Corbett R (1985) 'The 1985 intergovernmental conference and the Single European Act', in Pryce R (ed) *The dynamics of European Union* (London: Croom Helm).

[5] Constraints of space permit only a very selective analysis of the SEA's provisions here. For further details see Shaw op cit pp 37–42, 78–95 and ch 15; Ehlermann C (1987) 'The internal market following the Single European Act' *CML Rev* 361–409.

[6] See Ehlermann (1987) op cit.

In contrast, the Community's continuing inter-national dynamic was expressed by various Member States during the amendment negotiations with sufficient vigour to recast the Commission's initial internal market strategy in a more circumscribed form. Thus for example the Commission's original intention that art 8A should announce the 'complete removal of all physical, technical and fiscal barriers within the community' eventually emerged with the caveat that the internal market was to be pursued 'without prejudice to the other articles in the Treaty'. This is well illustrated by the progressive dilution of the mutual recognition reforms. The Commission had initially proposed simply to sweep away national powers to obstruct free movement. This step was however too radical a reform for all of the Member States to approve. The subsequent acceptance in Article 100b that the Council of Ministers should retain the power to decide the extent of equivalence required by EC law provides a graphic example of the resolution of questions of economic sovereignty by the evident subordination of supra-national legal principle to inter-national political pragmatism. Furthermore, the bulk of the internal market programme would be implemented through directives, a form of EC law which, as noted in chapter twelve, has a less obviously supra-national flavour than regulations in the light of the ECJ's judgments in *Marshall* and *Von Colson.*

But such concessions to inter-national sensitivity were in turn subject to supranational checks and balances. A specific (albeit apparently not legally binding)[7] date (31 December 1992) was set for achievement of the internal market programme. Relatedly, the 'equivalence' standards underpinning the mutual recognition principle were to be based on 'high standards', and while the new Article 100a para 4 formally permitted member states to derogate somewhat from the free movement principle in defence of major 'needs', their invocation of this power was subjected to close Commission control.

The SEA also enhanced the Community's supra-national profile by extending the use of qualified majority rather than unanimous voting within the law-making process. In particular, Article 100a provided that all internal market measures could be enacted in this way. Such reforms offer an obvious antidote to the frustration of EC objectives by a single member state. However some commentators (no doubt with the Empty Chair crisis in mind) questioned whether imposing such legal compulsion on reluctant states was the best way forward: unanimity may be difficult to achieve, and delay the implementation of integrationist policies, but will produce substantive outcomes from which member states will be less likely to resile.[8]

The SEA acknowledged that many areas of government activity could not sensibly be brought within the EC's legal competence. Perhaps the best example of this is the Declaration attached to the SEA that to the effect that the reforms to the Treaty should not be construed as derogating from the Member States' powers to take such measures

7 See Edward op cit.

8 See for example Ehlermann's analysis (1987 op cit) of the harmonisation of indirect taxation laws within the Community.

as they considered necessary regarding immigration control for regulating the movements of non-EC nationals, combating crime, and preventing terrorism.[9]

It is more difficult to decide whether to locate two other substantial innovations introduced by the SEA on the Community's supra-national or inter-national basis. Title I of the SEA gave a formal legal status to the meetings of the European Council, while Title III formalised the hitherto entirely informal process of 'European Political Co-operation', primarily in the area of foreign policy. But while 'recognised' by the SEA, these two aspects of Community action were not incorporated into the body of EC law; rather they were to exist outside the Treaty in the sphere of traditional international law agreements. From a federalist perspective, their greatest significance perhaps lay in their long term potential to 'normalise' joint member state action in explicitly non-justiciable areas, and thereby pave the way at a future date for the Community's legal competence to extend into avowedly 'political' fields.

REDUCING THE DEMOCRATIC DEFICIT – TREATY AMENDMENT

That the EEC had failed to produce a truly common market by 1986 is unsurprising given the cultural heterogenity, linguistic pluralism, and economic nationalism of the various member states. However, the difficulty might be thought to be exacerbated by the institutional balance of power in the Community legislative process. As suggested in chapter twelve, the original Treaty cast that balance firmly in favour of the internationally constructed Council at the expense of the more supra-national Commission and Parliament.

An increase in the Commission's powers would have offered one route to achieving a more Communitaire balance of legislative power. But any such reform would also have intensified accusations as to the EEC's so-called 'democratic deficit'. The SEA consequently sought a modest rebalancing of the supra/inter-national axis by enhancing the legal status of the European Parliament. Such a reform could plausibly be construed as encouraging pan-European sentiment within the Community while simultaneously defusing criticism that Community decision-making processes are too far removed from electoral influence.

The SEA's amendments fell far short of the Parliament's DTEU proposals,[10] but were nevertheless an advance on the Treaty of Rome's original institutional balance.[11] The most important initiative was the creation of a parliamentary power of 'co-operation' in the legislative process in some areas of Community competence, foremost

[9] The legal status of Declarations is unclear. But as Toth points out, the more expansive scope and pro-nationalist sentiment of the SEA declaration suggests the member states hoped that it would temper the ECJ's integrationist inclinations: (1986) 'The legal status of declarations attached to the SEA' *CML Rev* 803–812.

[10] To the disappointment of some member states. See for example the Luxembourg position in European Council (1986) *Speeches and statements made on the occasion of the signing of the Single European Act* at pp 16–18 (Brussels: EC).

[11] See Boyce B (1993) 'The democratic deficit of the European Community' *Parliamentary Affairs* 458–477.

among them internal market measures per Article 100a, some aspects of free movement of workers, workplace health and safety regulation, environmental protection and the common transport policy. The Council cannot simply ignore the Parliament's views when the co-operation procedure is being employed:[12] the initiative thus gave the Parliament an audible voice in important areas of community activity. Its significance should not however be exaggerated. An early assessment concluded that the Parliament 'is still some way from becoming an equal chamber with the Council in a fully bi-cameral system, but some progress has been made in this direction'.[13] One might plausibly add to that statement that the progress was initially both slight and stilted.[14]

Moreover, the SEA left one of the Parliament's basic weaknesses untouched – namely its lack of a single geographical site. The Parliament has always operated partly in Luxembourg, in Strasbourg and in Brussels. Such fragmentation undermines its efficiency, and deprives it of a coherent physical identity with which to convey its significance within the Community's structure. While the Parliament has repeatedly sought a single site,[15] the power to grant that request lies with the Council, which has thus far failed to respond.

On a more grandiose plane, the SEA's preamble announced that the member states were:

> 'DETERMINED to work together to promote democracy on the basis of the fundamental rights recognised in the constitutions and laws of the Member states, in the Convention for the Protection of Human Rights and Fundamental Freedoms and the European Social Charter, notably freedom, equality and social justice'.

Despite this statement of intent, the SEA did not introduce any substantial scheme of human rights protection into the Treaty's text, nor take the obvious step of incorporating the provisions of the European Convention on Human Rights into Community law. Nevertheless, the preamble may be seen as tacit Member State acceptance of the ECJ's by then evident fondness for concluding that the EC's constitutional order contained implied terms analogous to the ECHR's provisions.

The preamble encapsulates a recurrent feature of Community law-making; namely Member States' acceptance of the abstract legitimacy of political values to which they are not prepared to give explicit legal status. For some commentators, such legal lacunae in the SEA's formal structure were a cause of regret. Ehlerman, for example, seemed to assume the necessity of an almost messianic role for formalistic legal change as a mechanism for effective Community integration in concluding that: 'the

[12] The complexities of the procedure are helpfully explained in Shaw op cit at pp 79–82.

[13] Corbett R (1989) 'Testing the new procedures; the European Parliament's first experiences with its new "Single Act" powers' 7 *Journal of Common Market Studies* 362–372 at p 364.

[14] The increase in the EP's powers did however necessitate explicit statutory approval of the SEA Treaty in the UK in accordance with s 6 of the EPEA 1978, rather than the process of 'incorporation' via Order in Council provided for in the ECA 1972, s 1; see p 377 above.

[15] See *Luxembourg v European Parliament:* Case 230/81 [1983] ECR 255, ECJ.

SEA not only fails to live up to the Commission's expectations, but also leaves much to be desired in its wording'.[16] In contrast, Edward advances a rather more pragmatic view, describing the SEA as a 'political manifesto . . . a moral and political commitment'.[17]

It is perhaps surprising that seasoned EC commentators should place much emphasis on the 'wording' of the SEA. For one could not accurately predict in 1986 what interpretation the ECJ would subsequently give to the amended version of the Treaty. In the first 30 years of the Community's existence, the ECJ had propounded – and (eventually) won Member State acceptance of – a series of integrationist legal principles which do not feature in the Treaty's text. It would seem entirely plausible to assume that the ECJ would subsequently bring such an ethos to bear on the SEA. But for at least one national government, the fear of the EC's 'creeping competence' was triggered not by the ECJ's jurisprudence, but by the integrationist enthusiasm of the President of the Commission.

DOMESTIC DISQUIET: MARGARET THATCHER'S BRUGES SPEECH

The driving force behind the SEA reforms had been the Commission President, Jacques Delors, a Frenchman who had served as a Minister in Francois Mitterand's socialist government. Delors was committed to the incrementalist ideal of furthering political union between the Member States, and suggested in a speech in 1988 that the EC would evolve into a federal government akin to that of the USA.

Such sentiments alarmed Prime Minister Margaret Thatcher, who promptly publicised her own view of the Community's future development in a speech delivered at the College of Europe, Bruges, on 20 September 1988. Thatcher premised her view of Europe's development on what she regarded as the essential issue of preserving British 'sovereignty':

> 'Willing and active co-operation between independent sovereign states is the best way to build a successful European Community . . . It would be folly to try to fit [the member states] into some sort of identikit European personality'.[18]

It would be somewhat misleading to describe this view as defending 'national' sovereignty. Rather it entailed undiluted retention of the UK Parliament's omnicompetent legal authority so that successive Thatcher governments could continue (unhindered by either domestic or EC dissent) to impose their preferred ideological agenda on the people of the United Kingdom:

> 'We have not successfully rolled back the frontiers of the state in Britain only to see them re-imposed at a European level with a European superstate exercising a new dominance from Brussels. . . . The lesson of the economic history of Europe in the 1970s and 1980s is that

16 (1987) op cit p 404. 17 (1987) op cit p 20.

18 The speech is thoroughly reported in *The Times*, 21 September 1988.

central planning and detailed control don't work, and that personal endeavour and initiative do . . .'.[19]

Given the UK's poor economic performance during the 1980s, Thatcher's lauding of Hayekian theory may seem ill-founded, especially since the economically most successful state, Germany, had a highly interventionist government and advocated still closer EC integration. But the speech's main significance was that it suggested that the Thatcher government would adopt a sceptical, obstructionist approach to all integrationist EC initiatives.

The Commission described the Bruges speech as 'unrelentingly naive'. Its contents had not been cleared with the then Foreign Secretary, Sir Geoffrey Howe, who evidently viewed its style and content with 'weary horror'.[20] The speech lent a sharper edge to the fundamental divisions over European policy which had riven the Conservative Party ever since the 1972 Accession rebellion. It was enthusiastically received in the party's Eurosceptic wing,[21] but was met with dismay by several senior Cabinet members and a substantial number of Euro-enthusiast backbenchers.[22] As we shall see below, Thatcher's perception of both the nature and location of what we might term the 'ultimate political fact' of the UK's EC membership was eventually to prove seriously flawed.

In the shorter term, it had a significant effect. In 1989, 11 member states had adopted a *Community Charter of Fundamental Social Rights of Workers*. The so-called '*Social Charter*' advocated a significant extension of the Community competence in social policy matters, to encompass workers' rights to fair remuneration and adequate protection against unfair dismissal, redundancy, and unsafe working conditions. The British government opposed such measures, seeing them as a re-expansion of the 'frontiers of the state'. The Charter was merely a Declaration, not a binding part of EC law. Even in this form, however, it was unacceptable to the Thatcher government, which refused to sign the Declaration.[23]

II. NORMATIVE SUPRA-NATIONALISM – THE ECJ CONTINUES

The passage of the SEA presented the ECJ with continuing as well as new challenges. The following section addresses two issues. The first concerns the domestic legal impact of unincorporated or incorrectly incorporated directives; the second, the nature of 'democracy' within the EC's law-making process.

19 Ibid. 20 Young (1991) op cit p 550. 21 Clark op cit pp 225–227.
22 See Young op cit ch 23. 23 See generally Shaw op cit ch 16.

THE 'INDIRECT EFFECT' OF DIRECTIVES – CONTINUED

Six years after *Von Colson*, in *Marleasing,* the ECJ resolved the temporal ambiguity created by *Von Colson* in concluding that existing domestic legislation, as well as newly introduced measures, would be subject to the *Von Colson* approach to interpretation:

'. . . in applying national law, whether the provisions in question were adopted before or after the directive, the national court called upon to interpret is required to do so, as far as possible, in the light of the wording and purpose of the directive in order to achieve the result pursued by the latter . . .'.[24]

Marleasing also intimated that the ECJ expected domestic courts to take an expansive approach to the question of their interpretive autonomy. The formula used in respect of that issue was re-cast as 'as far as possible', a phrase omitting the reference to 'discretion given by domestic law' that featured in the *Von Colson* judgment. The obvious inference was that domestic courts whose own constitutional orthodoxies limited them to literalist approaches to statutory interpretation should not regard themselves as so constrained in future.

We will shortly consider the impact of both cases in the UK's domestic law. Firstly, however, we turn to ECJ innovations in the regulation of the Community's own law-making process.

REDUCING THE DEMOCRATIC DEFICIT: JUDICIAL INITIATIVES

The Treaty has always required that EC institutions identify the 'legal base' of their legislative actions. This would seem a logical demand in respect of any legislative body which has only limited competence. Prior to 1986, the ECJ was called upon on several occasions via Article 173 proceedings to decide if the acts of a particular institution had any defensible legal base at all within the Treaty.[25]

However the super-imposition of new community competences in the SEA on to the existing Treaty raised the prospect that it would theoretically be possible for the Community to achieve particular objectives through more than one type of law-making process. In such circumstances, the Treaty itself did not specify which process was to be accorded priority. The question was not simply an abstract one; it had substantial implications for both the 'institutional balance' and the supra/international balance within the Community's legislative machinery. It was clear, for example, that the Parliament's relative importance vis à vis the Council would be enhanced if an Act's legal base required the co-operation procedure rather than the consultation process. Similarly, supra-national forces would enjoy greater influence at the expense of inter-national sentiment if legislation could be adopted via qualified

[24] Case C–106/89: [1990] ECR I–4135 at para 8.

[25] *Stölting:* Case 138/78 [1979] ECR 713, ECJ; *France, Italy and United Kingdom v EC Commission*: Case 188–190/80 [1982] ECR 2545, ECJ; *Germany v EC Commission:* Case 281/85, 283–285/85, 287/85 [1987] ECR 3203, ECJ. See generally Biebr R (1984) 'The settlement of institutional conflicts on the basis of Article 4 of the Treaty' *CMLRev* 505–523.

majority or simple majority voting rather than unanimity. In either case, the legal base chosen would be likely to influence the substantive content of the legislation enacted. One might plausibly assume that the enacting institutions should opt for whichever base was most likely to facilitate achievement of Community objectives. However the SEA offered no precise criteria against which to assess that question. This was a legal lacuna which the ECJ rapidly took the opportunity to fill.

The issue before the ECJ in *EC Commission v EC Council (Generalised Tariff Preferences*[26] concerned the legal basis of a Council Regulation fixing the tariff regime for certain imported goods. The Council had adopted the measure via Article 235, which required unanimous voting and consultation of the Parliament. The Commission maintained that the measure should have been adopted via Article 113, which demanded qualified majority voting (but had no role for the Parliament). In upholding the Commission's claim, the ECJ offered a broad statement of principle in respect of legal base questions:

> 'It must be observed that in the context of the organisation of the powers of the Community the choice of the legal basis for a measure may not depend simply on an institution's conviction as to the objective pursued but must be based on objective factors which are amenable to judicial review'.[27]

Quite what was meant by 'objective factors' was unclear. In subsequent litigation,[28] the ECJ conflated this notion of 'objectivity' with the requirement that the Community must always choose the most 'democratic' and integrationist legislative method when a choice is available. Thus a simple majority vote is to be preferred to qualified majority procedures, which are themselves preferable to unanimity. Similarly, processes which demand the co-operation of the Parliament are preferable to those requiring merely consultation.

To label such criteria 'objective' is something of a judicial sleight of hand, for it assumes that supra-nationalism and minimising the democratic deficit are 'natural' or uncontested values.[29] In the context of the ECJ's jurisprudential tradition, those assumptions are readily understandable, but that is to ignore questions as to the legitimacy of the tradition itself. As we have repeatedly seen, that larger question remains distinctly controversial in the eyes of some domestic political and judicial audiences. We return to the issues of institutional balance and democratic deficit in

[26] Case 45/86 [1987] ECR 1493, [1988] 2 CMLR 131, ECJ.

[27] Ibid, at para 11. Readers seeking a domestic analogy might refer to the *De Keyser Royal Hotel* case (pp 104–107 above).

[28] *EC Commission v EC Council*: Case C–300/89 *Titanium dioxide* [1991] ECR I–2867, ECJ; *European Parliament v EC Council*: Case C–295/90 *Student residence rights* [1992] ECR I–4193, ECJ. For an overview see Bradley K (1987) 'Maintaining the balance: the role of the Court of Justice in defining the institutional position of the European Parliament' *CML Rev* 41–64; Crosby S (1991) 'The single market and the rule of law' *EL Rev* 451–465.

[29] The ECJ's predisposition to enhance the Parliament's status within the Community's institutional balance was displayed in decisions which, in apparent contradiction of the terms of the Treaty, afforded the Parliament the capacity to challenge the legality of Acts of the Commission and Council before the Court. See *European Parliament v EC Council*: Case C–70/88 (*Chernobyl*) [1991] ECR I–4529, ECJ.

considering the terms of the Maastricht Treaty. Before doing so however, we address the reception afforded by the UK courts to the principles espoused by the ECJ in *Von Colson* and *Marleasing*.

III. EC LAW, PARLIAMENTARY SOVEREIGNTY AND THE UK COURTS: PHASE TWO

Chapter twelve recorded that the British judiciary took some time to come to terms with the constitutional implications of the precedence and direct effect principles. *Von Colson* and *Marleasing* presented a rather different challenge, since they required national courts to adopt avowedly teleological or purposive interpretive techniques in respect of domestic legislation, and, insofar as 'national law' was a concept broadly construed, to create new common law principles to give practical effect to EC directives. British courts could plausibly point to the ECA, s 2 as a parliamentary command for them to accept the supremacy and direct effect principles. However the literal interpretation of s 2 was that it reached only directly effective EC law; it would thus not apply to any attempt to enforce the provisions of a directive against a non-governmental body. Consequently, if British courts felt that they required a domestic, statutory basis for applying the *Von Colson* and *Marleasing* principles, they would have to turn to the ECA 1972 s 3. Alternatively, British courts might simply amend common law principles of statutory interpretation to achieve the same end. Both techniques would have unorthodox constitutional connotations. But after a hesitant start, the House of Lords responded enthusiastically to the challenge.

DUKE V GEC RELIANCE LTD

Like Miss Marshall, Mrs Duke worked for an employer who required women to retire at 60, but permitted men to work until 65. Such discrimination, Mrs Duke assumed, contravened the Equal Treatment Directive. In *Marshall*, the ECJ held that Directive 76/207 (and indeed all other directives) did not have horizontal direct effect. Miss Marshall could rely on the directive because the area health authority was a government body; but since GEC was a private company, Mrs Duke could not do so. She was forced instead to rely on either the *Von Colson* principle – namely that Article 5 of the Treaty required UK courts to interpret the Sex Discrimination Act 'in so far as it is given discretion to do so under national law' to give effect to the directive's intentions – and/or that the ECA 1972 directed the courts to interpret the SDA 1975 in this way.

The House of Lords rejected both arguments.[30] Section 2(4) could only have the effect Mrs Duke wished in respect of directly effective EC provisions. As noted above,

30 [1988] AC 618, [1988] 1 All ER 626, HL.

that conclusion is unavoidable if s 2 is interpreted in a literalist fashion. However, the court also declined to apply *Von Colson*, not because it considered the ECJ's principle unsound, but because the principle was not relevant to Mrs Duke's factual situation. *Von Colson*, Lord Templeman concluded, did not require national courts to invent new domestic laws empowering them to 'distort' domestic statues in order to give effect to all non-directly effective EC directives. Such 'distortion' would be permissible only in respect of domestic legislation passed to give effect to pre-existing EC law. In respect of UK statutes pre-dating the relevant EC directive, the court could only invoke the traditional interpretive theory applied to international law obligations; namely that an ambiguous statutory term should be given whichever meaning best satisfied the UK's international obligations. Unfortunately for Mrs Duke, Lord Templeman considered that the SDA 1975 s 6(4) unambiguously permitted discriminatory retirement ages; it could not be interpreted in any other way.

The difference between 'interpretation' (which Lord Templeman thought acceptable) and 'distortion' (which he considered illegitimate) may be elusive. Critics of *Duke* suggested that it would have been possible for the House of Lords to have found for the plaintiff.[31] Indeed, its failure to do so created several anomalies, both between the UK and those member states where the directive was fully implemented, and within the UK between women working for public and private sector companies. Nevertheless, *Duke* did indicate that domestic legislation introduced in order to implement a directive would be open to judicial 'distortion' to produce a result consistent with EC law.

PICKSTONE V FREEMANS

The plaintiff in *Pickstone v Freemans plc*[32] contended that she and other women colleagues working as 'warehouse operatives' were paid less than male 'warehouse checker operatives' whose work was of equal value to their own. The SDA 1975 had initially provided that comparative studies of the 'value' of different jobs could be conducted only with the employer's consent: an obstructive employer could therefore prevent women employees establishing that discrimination had occurred. The Commission regarded this 'employer's veto' as in breach of EC law, in so far as it prevented individuals enforcing their EC entitlements. In a subsequent Article 169 action, the ECJ upheld the Commission's claim, holding that EC law required that employers could not be permitted to deny employees access to job evaluation mechanisms.[33]

The UK government (acting per ECA 1972 s 2(2)) subsequently introduced regulations which, according to the speech of the sponsoring Minister in the Commons, were intended to implement the ECJ's judgment. This was done by empowering

31 Fitzpatrick B (1989) 'The significance of EEC Directives in UK sex discrimination law' *Oxford Journal of Legal Studies* 336–355: Szyszczk E (1990) 'Sovereignty: crisis, compliance, confusion, complacency' *EL Rev* 480–488.

32 [1989] AC 66, HL.

33 *EC Commission v United Kingdom*: Case 61/81 [1982] ICR 578, ECJ.

Industrial Tribunals to order job evaluation studies in certain circumstances. However, *Pickstone* revealed a flaw in the regulations' text. On their face, they seemed to preclude an action before a tribunal when a man was employed in exactly the same job at the same pay as the woman complainant. If this was correct, an employer could evade evaluation of different jobs by employing one 'token' male among a predominantly female workforce (as Freemans had allegedly done). The UK would therefore have failed to comply with its EC obligations.

A unanimous House of Lords refused to reach this conclusion. Lord Keith felt that 'Parliament cannot possibly have intended such a failure'.[34] Consequently he thought it appropriate to go beyond the bare words of the regulation, and to construe it 'purposively' by examining *Hansard* to confirm that 'Parliament's' intention was to comply with the Directive. Thus construed, the regulation was consistent with EC law. This technique was in itself a quite radical innovation.[35] But Lord Templeman went a step further. His examination of *Hansard* led him to conclude that: 'In my opinion there must be implied in paragraph (c) . . . the words "as between the woman and the man with whom she claims equality" '.[36]

LITSTER V FORTH DRY DOCK AND ENGINEERING CO LTD

Litster raised a dispute over Directive 77/187, which the EC enacted to 'provide for the protection of employees in the event of a change of employer, in particular to ensure that their rights are safeguarded'. Article 4(1) specifically provided that: 'The transfer of an undertaking, business or part of a business shall not in itself constitute grounds for dismissal by the transferor or the transferee'. The rationale behind the directive was to ensure that employers could not evade unfair dismissal or redundancy payment legislation through the simple expedient of transferring their business to someone else.

The UK tried to incorporate Directive 77/187 through the Transfer of Undertakings (Protection of Employment) Regulations 1981. Regulation 5(1) provided that any transfer did not extinguish the employee's contractual rights, but made them enforceable against the new employer. The problem in *Litster* arose because reg 5(3) then provided that reg 5(1) applied only to employees employed by the transferor 'immediately' before the transfer. The employees in *Litster* were sacked at 3.30pm on the day of the transfer. The transfer happened at 4.30 pm. The new company claimed that this one hour gap meant that the workers were not employed by the transferor 'immediately' before the transfer, and so could not enforce their contractual rights against the new owner.

The ECJ had recently held that workers should be regarded as still employed by the

[34] [1989] AC 66 at 112, HL.

[35] This case of course pre-dated *Pepper v Hart*, and provided part of the justification for the overturning of the traditional rule in the latter case. We will return to the inter-relationship of the two cases below.

[36] [1989] AC 66 at 120, HL.

transferor if the only reason for their dismissal was the projected transfer.[37] It was accepted on the facts that this was indeed the reason for the dismissal in *Litster*, but the employer argued that the British courts were bound to apply the UK legislation in its literal sense; literally construed, a gap of one hour could not amount to immediacy.

The House of Lords accepted that a literal interpretation of 'immediately' supported the transferee's argument.[38] A unanimous House nevertheless found in the employees' favour, albeit through slightly different reasoning. Lord Templeman accepted that *Von Colson* required domestic courts to adopt a purposive approach to domestic law 'issued for the purpose of complying with directives'.[39] However, in contrast to his decision in *Duke*, he saw no need to read words into the domestic legislation. Rather, he preferred to construe reg 5(3):

> '. . . on the footing that it applies to a person employed immediately before the transfer or who would have been so employed if he had not been unfairly dismissed before the transfer for a reason connected with the transfer'.[40]

Lord Oliver referred back to *Pickstone* to justify purposive construction of domestic law introduced to give effect to EEC law 'even though it may involve some departure from the strict and literal application of the words which the legislature has elected to use'.[41] He regarded the employer's strategy as a transparent device to evade the spirit of the regulations. Lord Oliver considered it beholden upon the courts to counter such evasion by implying words into the domestic legislation:

> 'In effect this involves reading reg. 5(3) as if there were inserted after the words "immediately before the transfer" the words "or would have been so employed if he had not been unfairly dismissed in the circumstances described in reg 8(1)".'[42]

PICKSTONE AND LITSTER – USURPING THE LEGISLATIVE FUNCTION?

By adding words to legislation, Lord Templeman in *Pickstone* and Lord Oliver in *Litster* seemed to embrace the position adopted forty years earlier by Lord Denning in *Magor*,[43] a position promptly then dismissed by Lord Simonds as a 'naked usurpation of the legislative function'. There would seem to be two possible ways to explain this development. Both imply there is something 'special' in the constitutional sense about EC membership, but neither presents a direct threat to orthodox theories of parliamentary sovereignty.

Firstly, Lords Templeman and Oliver might argue that ECA 1972 s 3 orders the UK courts to adopt whichever interpretive technique the ECJ currently required of them. The ECA 1972 would thus be unorthodox (indeed perhaps even 'unconstitutional') from a conventional perspective, in so far as it seeks to give the courts pervasive

37 *P Bork International A/S v Foreningen af Arbejdsledere i Danmark*: Case 101/87 [1989] IRLR 41, ECJ.
38 [1990] 1 AC 546, [1989] 1 All ER 1134, HL. 39 Ibid, at 558.
40 Ibid. 41 Ibid, at 559. 42 Ibid, at 577. 43 See pp 68–69 above.

commands about interpretive techniques, a matter traditionally regarded as a question of common law. Such an Act (while obviously not 'illegal') could plausibly be seen as incompatible with traditional understandings of the rule of law and the separation of powers.

The second explanation is less radical, amounting to no more than a judicial recognition that EC membership has triggered such a profound change in social and economic conditions that it is time for the common law to recognise the legitimacy of a new interpretive strategy in order to protect EC law entitlements. That conclusion need have no root in the ECA 1972, nor indeed in any other statute. And until such time as the courts' new presumption is negated or amended by statute, it presents no theoretical threat to Parliament's sovereignty.

Yet while *Litster* and *Pickstone* can be reconciled with Diceyan orthodoxies, they did not meet the ECJ's requirements in *Marleasing*.[44] The reasoning deployed by the House of Lords in *Litster* gives full effect to the narrow interpretation of *Von Colson*. The House appeared to say that it was 'given discretion under national law' (per *Von Colson*) to invent a new common law rule of statutory interpretation in respect of legislation passed specifically to implement pre-existing EC law (or to find such a command in the ECA 1972), but such 'discretion' did not extend (as required by *Marleasing* or the broad interpretation of *Von Colson*) to applying similar rules to domestic legislation pre-dating the relevant EC measure. It is difficult to discern any logical basis in domestic legal theory for such a distinction.[45] Stripped to its bones, the judicial methodology employed in *Duke* and *Litster* is to ask: 'What would Parliament have done if it had realised that the literal meaning of the words it wished to use was incompatible with a new EC law?'. The answer, of course, is that 'Parliament would have used the words which we are now implying into the Act'. The methodology required by *Marleasing* is just the same – namely to ask 'What would Parliament have done if it had realised that it needed to alter the literal meaning of the words in an existing statute in order to avoid incompatibility with a new EC law?'. The answer, of course, is that 'Parliament would have enacted amending legislation containing the words which we are now implying into the original Act'. In both circumstances, the court is putting words into Parliament's mouth. It is no less a radical innovation for a court to do so when Parliament has spoken in error than when it has, again in error, failed to speak at all. The House of Lords appeared to recognise this illogicality shortly afterwards, and in *Webb v EMO Air Cargo*[46] it adopted the temporal aspect of *Marleasing*.

[44] See also *Finnegan v Clowney Youth Training Programme Ltd* [1990] 2 AC 407, [1990] 2 All ER 546, HL.

[45] See the critical comment by Szyszczak (1990) op cit. For an attempt to do so see Steiner J (1990) 'Coming to terms with EC directives' 106 *LQR* 144–159.

[46] [1992] 4 All ER 929, [1993] 1 WLR 49. For comment see Szyszczak E (1993) 'Interpretation of Community law in the courts' *EL Rev* 214–225.

IV. THE END OF PARLIAMENTARY SOVEREIGNTY: OR ITS REAPPEARANCE?

Despite their radical practical implications, *Duke* and *Litster* could be portrayed in theory simply as a new innovation in judicial interpretation of statutes. They did not involve a blunt challenge to legislation which could be reconciled with EC law only by affording the concept of 'interpretation' a meaning that paid no heed at all to linguistic limitations and encompassed the presumably distinct concept of defiance. That challenge, however, was not long in coming.

THE DEMISE OF THE LEGAL DOCTRINE? *FACTORTAME*

The *Factortame* litigation arose from a dispute over fishing rights in British waters. The Merchant Shipping Act 1894 had allowed foreign owned vessels to register as 'British', and thereby gain the right to fish in British waters. By the late 1980s, some 95 boats owned by Spanish companies had done so. The British government, alarmed by the impact this 'foreign' fleet was having on fishing stocks, asked Parliament to enact the Merchant Shipping Act 1988 (MSA 1988). The 1988 Act altered the registration rules to require a far higher level of 'Britishness' in a ship's owners or managers.[47] None of the 95 Spanish ships could meet this test. Factortame, one of the affected companies, subsequently launched an action in the British courts claiming that the 1988 Act was substantively incompatible with EC law.

The High Court referred the substantive question to the ECJ. It was likely that 18–20 months would elapse before the ECJ issued its judgment. The High Court therefore granted Factortame an interim injunction 'disapplying' the Act and ordering the Secretary of State not to enforce it against any ship that met the previous registration criteria.[48] The Court of Appeal set aside the order for an interim injunction, on which point Factortame appealed to the House of Lords.[49]

Lord Bridge gave the sole judgment. He accepted that not issuing an interim injunction would cause irreparable damage, perhaps even bankruptcy to Factortame, since the company had no immediate prospect of using its boats elsewhere. He also accepted that the House of Lords would accord precedence to EC law if the ECJ eventually ruled that the Merchant Shipping Act breached EC law. This apparently clear acceptance of the precedence doctrine goes considerably further than the formulae advanced in *Macarthys* or *Garland*. Lord Bridge suggested that the 1972 Parliament had passed legislation in the form of the ECA 1972 s 2 which in some mysterious

[47] Including, inter alia, requirements that individual owners had to be British citizens or residents, and that corporate owners had to be incorporated in Britain, with 75% of their shares owned by British citizens/residents.

[48] See Gravells N (1989) 'Disapplying an Act of Parliament pending a preliminary ruling: constitutional enormity or common law right' *Public Law* 568–586.

[49] *R v Secretary of State for Transport, ex p Factortame Ltd* [1990] 2 AC 85.

manner was incorporated into every subsequent UK Act which affects a directly effective EC right. The inference thus appeared to be that the courts would no longer obey an Act of Parliament which breached directly effective EC law even if the Act expressly stated it was intended to achieve that result.

But that conclusion was not germane to the present appeal, the nub of which was that a British court should refuse to allow the government to apply an Act of Parliament because of the possibility the Act might subsequently prove incompatible with EC law. Lord Bridge could not find any domestic authority for such a radical proposition. Nor was he ultimately persuaded that there was an overriding principle of Community law requiring the House of Lords to issue the interim injunction. However, Lord Bridge finally concluded that any such duty on the domestic courts arose only in respect of substantive rights already clearly established under EC law. The 'rights' claimed by Factortame had yet to be pronounced upon by the ECJ. Consequently, the House of Lords referred its own question to the ECJ, asking if it should disapply domestic law in order to safeguard as yet unproven EC law rights.

The litigation before the ECJ

Shortly thereafter, the ECJ heard an Article 169 action against the UK which claimed that the Merchant Shipping Act breached the UK's Treaty obligations. In *EC Commission v United Kingdom*,[50] the Commission asked the ECJ to make an interim order per Article 186 ordering the British government not to enforce the 1988 Act. The ECJ saw some merit in the UK's position, since the 1988 Act might prove a defensible means to pursue the EC's own objective of conserving long-term fish stocks. However the Act's overt discrimination against non-British EC nationals seriously undermined the UK's case. Moreover, there was no doubt that enforcement of the Act would inflict extremely heavy losses on the Spanish shipowners. In those circumstances, the ECJ granted an interim order requiring the UK to 'suspend' the 1988 legislation.

The ECJ subsequently gave judgment on the question referred to it by the House of Lords, in *R v Secretary of State for Transport, ex p Factortame (No 2)*.[51] After referring explicitly to the *Simmenthal* principle of immediate supremacy, the Court observed that national courts were obliged by the 'principle of co-operation laid down in Article 5' to ensure that domestic legal systems give practical legal effect to directly effective EC rights. Any provision within the national legal system which impairs this effect contravenes EC law. This principle applied as readily to questions of interim as final relief. Consequently, if the sole obstacle to interim relief is 'a rule of national law', the national court must set aside that rule.

Back in the House of Lords . . .

The House of Lords announced that it had held in Factortame's favour, and would disapply the MSA 1988, in June (1990). Its reasons would be given at a later date. The

[50] *EC Commission v United Kingdom*: Case C–246/89R [1989] ECR 3125, ECJ.

[51] Case C–213/89 [1990] ECR I–2433.

announcement provoked apocalyptic denunciations from Prime Minister Thatcher about losses of national sovereignty to the Commission. The leading judgment in *R v Secretary of State for Transport, ex p Factortame (No 2)*[52] was given by Lord Goff. However Lord Bridge took the opportunity to comment on claims (whose source he diplomatically chose not to name) that the decision 'was a novel and dangerous invasion by a community institution of the sovereignty of the UK Parliament'.[53] Such criticism was misconceived. Parliament had been quite aware of the precedence doctrine in 1972, so any 'limitation' of sovereignty that EC membership entailed was 'voluntary'. The ECA 1972 had ordered domestic courts to respect that 'voluntary limitation', so there was nothing novel in this judgment.[54]

As Lord Goff made clear, the ECJ's decision in *Factortame* did not determine the outcome of the domestic litigation. Rather it required the British courts to reject those principles of domestic law (the non-availability of interim injunctions against the Crown and the courts' incapacity to disapply clearly worded statutes) which presented an absolute bar to Factortame's claims. Lord Goff made only a passing reference to the ECJ's decision, apparently seeing no need to justify or explain it, but accepting it as an uncontentious (if brand new) principle of national law to be integrated into the existing common law rules governing the availability of interim injunctions.

Those rules suggested that interim relief was only available if there was no possibility of the plaintiff eventually gaining damages to cover any loss suffered pending resolution of the main question. No such damages could (at that time)[55] be recovered from the government. The Court had then to ask itself if there was a 'strong prima facie case' indicating that the plaintiff would ultimately be successful. Lord Goff considered that the *EC Commission v United Kingdom* decision suggested that the ECJ would answer the substantive issue in Factortame's favour, which would in itself predispose the court to grant interim relief. However, he also implied that he doubted that the plaintiff needed to show such a high probability of eventual success in this case.

The EC Treaties as 'higher law'

Radical though the 'disapplication' doctrine laid out in *Factortame* undoubtedly was, it might initially have been thought to be a principle of limited application. Was the power to be exercised, for example, only by the House of Lords; or did it extend to all national courts and tribunals? Relatedly, was the power triggered only after a reference to the ECJ via Article 177, or might it be applied whenever a national court considered a statutory provision to be inconsistent with EC law?

52 [1991] 1 AC 603, sub nom *Factortame Ltd v Secretary of State for Transport (No 2)* [1991] 1 All ER 70.

53 [1991] 1 AC 603, at 658.

54 Lord Bridge perhaps oversimplified the issue. As we saw in chapter eleven, British judges and British governments displayed confusion in the late 1960s and early 1970s as to the nature and implications of *Costa* and *Van Gend*. Moreover, many innovative aspects of the ECJ's own constitutional jurisprudence had appeared after the UK's accession.

55 But see now the discussion of *Francovich* and *Brasserie de Pecheur* below.

Simmenthal – to which *Factortame* might be seen as a belated response – would suggest that the power lay with any court, and it arose irrespective of whether any reference to the ECJ was made. The House of Lords subsequently endorsed this position in *R v Secretary of State for Employment, ex p Equal Opportunities Commission*.[56] In the immediate aftermath of this case it became clear that even industrial tribunals, which occupy a lowly position within the United Kingdom's constitutional hierarchy, considered themselves competent to apply the *Factortame* doctrine.[57] In practical terms, the *Factortame* rationale rapidly became – as far as all courts were concerned – an obviously comfortable part of the constitutional furniture.

In a more abstract vein, the unfortunate jurisprudential and political lacuna left unfilled by the *Factortame* litigation is that the House of Lords did not grapple with the fundamental question of just how it was that in 1972 the UK Parliament managed to do something that had always been beyond its predecessors' grasp – namely 'voluntarily' to limit its sovereignty? As H R W Wade has pointed out, Lord Bridge's reasoning makes very little sense, whether as an excursion in legal theory or as a recipe for practical politics.[58] The obvious problem is that if Parliament managed in 1972 to entrench the ECA, on what basis can one sensibly maintain that it could not now or in the future entrench other legislation as well? It might be argued that the EC is 'unique' in this respect, because perhaps of the political significance of its powers and/or its elaborate institutional structure. But that is merely an assertion. It is no less plausible to say that other important moral or political factors could acquire a similar constitutional status, with the result that, as Wade puts it 'the new doctrine makes sovereignty a freely adjustable commodity whenever Parliament chooses to accept some limitation'.[59]

This is perhaps not as alarming a spectre as it may appear. *Factortame* entrenchment is – it seems – of an extremely weak procedural kind. It does not take the form of requiring super-majorities within Parliament, nor that there be resort to any extra-parliamentary device such as a referendum; it merely requires that a bare parliamentary majority expresses itself in unusually blunt language. A new Merchant Shipping Act which said in s 1 that it was intended to repudiate the UK's obligations under the Common Fisheries Policy would presumably have been applied by Lord Bridge and his colleagues. It certainly could not have been disapplied through the judicial techniques ostensibly used in *Factortame* (*No 2*).

Factortame need not therefore be read as suggesting that Parliament can grant itself a power equivalent to that given to colonial legislatures in s 5 of the Colonial Laws Validity Act 1865 to entrench any political values it chooses by altering the legislative 'manner and form' required to change them. An entrenchment mechanism of this

[56] [1994] ICR 317, HL.

[57] See Nicol D (1996) 'Disapplying with relish? The Industrial Tribunals and Acts of Parliament' *Public Law* 579–589.

[58] (1996) 'Sovereignty – revolution or evolution?' *LQR* 568–575.

[59] (1996) op cit p 573.

sort is a dangerous device, as it would enable a bare legislative majority enjoying only minority electoral support to set such high thresholds for the repeal of its preferred laws that they could never be altered. But if Parliament was able to create even a very weak form of entrenchment in 1972, might it not be able to create much stronger entrenchment devices in future?

Wade's conclusion that *Factortame* amounts to a 'judicial revolution' is initially enticing. It maintains in essence that it was not Parliament through the ECA 1972 but the judges themselves who have altered the constitution's rule of recognition. In other words, the old orthodoxy was correct, but it was within the power of the courts to change it at any time. This argument displaces rather than refutes the problems posed by Lord Bridge's analysis. The obvious difficulty is that if the courts have managed in 1990 to entrench the European Communities Act, on what basis can one sensibly maintain that they could not now or in the future entrench other legislation as well? Wade's doctrine 'makes sovereignty a freely adjustable commodity whenever the courts choose to impose some limitation'.

Allan's analysis of *Factortame* is more satisfactory on this issue.[60] Allan has long offered a rather isolated voice in our constitutional discourse to the effect that orthodox understandings of parliamentary sovereignty are, and always have been, ill-conceived.[61] Allan's suggestion that our current constitutional settlement permits the courts to disapply legislation which is irreconcilable with the concepts of democracy and the rule of law offers a fascinating point of departure for discussing the *Factortame* saga.

Allan's thesis rests on the presumption that the orthodox, Diceyan view of parliamentary sovereignty misconceives the political objectives that the English Revolution of 1688 was trying to achieve. The Diceyan position, and its more modern restatements, espouse a purely formalist conception of the relationship between statute and the courts. The courts (and presumably everyone else) 'recognise' statute as the highest form of law simply because the 1688 Revolution was fought (and won) by men who wished to establish the legal superiority of measures enacted by the Commons, Lords and Monarch acting collectively over both the actions of either house, of the Monarch acting under prerogative powers, or of the courts acting under the power of the common law. However, if, following Professor Wade, we regard parliamentary sovereignty as the ultimate political fact of the constitution, it does not seem outlandish to ask (as Dicey and Professor Wade did not) why the revolutionaries wished to achieve this objective? What political or moral purpose was the ultimate political fact intended to serve?

Paul Craig has latterly offered an intriguing answer to this question.[62] Craig's critique begins by noting that 'much of the current literature fails to pay attention to the

60 (1997) 'Parliamentary sovereignty: law, politics and revolution' *LQR* 443–452.

61 See particularly (1983) op cit; (1985) op cit; (1993) op cit.

62 (1991) 'Sovereignty of the United Kingdom Parliament after *Factortame*' *Yearbook of European Law* 221–255.

reasons why Parliament should or should not be regarded as sovereign'.[63] He attempts to fill in this gap by digging deeper into and behind the legal sources underpinning the Diceyan position. Orthodox theories place much reliance, for example, on arguments voiced by Sir William Blackstone, the leading eighteenth century jurist, in his celebrated *Commentaries* on English law. The key passage asserts that Parliament 'can in short do everything that is not naturally impossible . . . True it is, that what the Parliament doth, no authority can undo'. On its face, Blackstone's text provides unequivocal support for the orthodox position.

However, Craig's critique, unlike the analysis offered by Wade in 1955, then asks *why* Blackstone was led to this conclusion. As suggested in chapter two, the notion that sovereignty should lie in a tripartite Parliament, within which each element possessed veto powers, reflected a belief that the Commons, Lords and Monarch acting in unison were the only legitimate arbiters of the national interest. The 1688 Revolution can thus be seen as an attempt to created an anti-majoritarian source of sovereign legal authority. It is this essentially political purpose, Craig suggests, which underlay the acceptance of Parliament as the highest source of law. To put the argument simply, Blackstone and those whose views he represented endorsed the principle of parliamentary sovereignty because they could conceive of no more broadly based mechanism for ensuring that laws enjoyed the consent of the people. Parliament was 'sovereign' for political or moral reasons – namely that it minimised the possibility that the English people[64] would be subjected to factionally motivated legislation.

The sovereign Parliament was not created for a modern society. Its proponents in 1688 had no conception that the powers of the Monarch would diminish to insignificance, nor that the House of Lords would voluntarily acquiesce in the removal of its co-equal powers in the legislative process. Still less would they have envisaged a near universal electorate for the Commons and the emergence of national political parties. Our concept of 'the people' is, of course, now much changed. We regard modern Britain as a mature democracy in which the legitimacy of a sovereign Parliament rests on the periodic consent of the electorate. Yet in our mature democracy Parliament functions as an extremely effective vehicle for the majoritarian or even minoritarian sentiments of a single political party to be given legal effect. While 1688 envisaged Parliament as a consensual forum designed to identify the national interest, it now operates as an arena of conflict intended to promote party interests.

It is at this juncture that Allan's suggestion that notions of 'democracy' and 'the rule of law' can serve as limits on Parliament's legislative competence become significant in relation to the *Factortame* conundrum. The EC Treaties stand in marked contrast to our domestic law-making process. Their terms are not the product of majoritarian or even super-majoritarian law-making. Their every provision has been arrived at through a consensual negotiatory process, demanding the unanimous

63 Ibid, at p 234.

64 Narrowly defined of course as the Monarch, the Lords and the small portion of citizens permitted to participate in electing members of the Commons.

approval of a growing number of nations – nations which themselves represent differing political philosophies and a multiplicity of cultural inheritances. And as the Treaties have been successively amended by the same protracted, negotiatory, consensual law-making process, so the innovate jurisprudence of the European Court and the member states' domestic courts have implicitly been granted a unanimous, cross-national seal of legislative approval. The prospect of an EC Treaty provision being narrowly majoritarian, has been reduced almost to vanishing point. In that functional sense, Treaty provisions are a 'higher' form of law than can be produced by any of the EC's member states within their own legal systems. The Treaties thus represent a modern manifestation of the ideal for which England's seventeenth-century 'revolutionaries' strove.[65]

In comparison with the Treaties, the Merchant Shipping Act fares very poorly when measured against this ideal. It is perhaps unfortunate that legal analysis of the *Factortame* episode has generally been confined to exploring the judgment's impact on the relationship between Parliament and the courts. Even Allan, notwithstanding his concern with substantive values of democracy and the rule of law, approaches the issue in this way. Neither Allan's nor Wade's critique addresses the individual citizen's interest in the case. What has rather been forgotten in respect of *Factortame* is that this particular constitutional episode was triggered by the deliberate decision of a xenophobic minoritarian government to use its Commons and Lords majorities (the one generated by the support of 34% of the electorate; the other derived from the principle of hereditary peerages) to enact a crudely segregationist economic policy which – in addition to clearly breaching the Treaty of Rome – was intended to bankrupt several business enterprises and throw many people into unemployment. It would be a very strange view of 'democracy' which nonetheless accorded legitimacy to such behaviour.

There is little indication that such overtly 'political' reasoning underpinned the *Factortame* decisions. It may well prove to be the case, as Craig has argued, that *Factortame* rests on no more than an adjustment to, or development of, the courts' role as interpreters of legislative intent.[66] That assertion can however only be proven 'correct' as a matter of law if political developments afford the opportunity to put it to a legal test. This could occur in one of two scenarios.

The first would arise if a Euro-sceptic government, commanding a majority in the Commons and Lords, were to promote legislation (perhaps, for example, another Merchant Shipping Act unilaterally withdrawing the UK from the Common Fisheries Policy) which stated in s 1:

'This Act is intended to breach the obligations accepted by the United Kingdom in its capacity as a member state of the European Community. The courts of the United Kingdom are hereby expressly ordered to apply the terms of this Act, irrespective of any rule of law

65 This rationale obviously has less force in respect of EC secondary legislation, especially if that legislation can be enacted by qualified or simple majority vote.

66 (1991) op cit.

deriving from the European Communities Act 1972 or the Treaties establishing the European Community or any judgment of the European Court of Justice'.

We might then suppose that a non-UK EC national who wished to fish in UK waters in accordance with the terms of EC law launched an action in the English courts seeking an injunction to prevent the Act being applied. There would then be no scope for a domestic court to uphold the precedence of EC law through innovative techniques of interpretation. Nor could resort be made to theories distinguishing implied and express statutory commands.

If a domestic court wished to uphold the *Costa* and *Van Gend* principles in this situation, it could do so only by bluntly stating that Parliament had no power to disapply EC law while the UK remained a member of the Community. Building on *Costa* and the 'loyalty duty' contained in Article 5 of the Treaty, the argument would be that EC law cannot be 'supreme' if its supposed supremacy is divisible or suspendable at the whim of a national Parliament. If Parliament wishes unilaterally to terminate the 'effet utile' of EC law in the UK, it may do so only by passing legislation which repeals the European Communities Act 1972 and withdraws this country from the EC. This sounds, of course, like a very speculative hypothesis; but it perhaps takes a far smaller leap of the jurisprudential imagination to go to this point from *Factortame (No 2)*, than it did to reach *Factortame (No 2)* from the views which prevailed in many political and legal circles when the UK joined the EC in 1972.

Yet even this scenario, irreconcilable though it may seem with orthodox constitutional principles, does not betoken a permanent loss of parliamentary sovereignty. The final step in that direction could only be taken if Parliament enacted legislation purporting to withdraw the United Kingdom from the Community and the UK courts then refused to apply the Act. Thus far, little serious thought has been given to the argument that Parliament cannot expect such legislation to be applied by domestic courts.[67] But such an argument is a perfectly logical development of the foundations laid by the European Court over 30 years ago in *Van Gend* and *Costa* and of those set down by the House of Lords in *Factortame (No 2)*.

As noted above, the ECJ told us in *Van Gend* that the EC was 'more than just an agreement between member states'. It was rather:

'. . . a new legal order of international law for the benefit of which the states have limited their sovereign rights, and the subjects of which comprise not only the Member States but also their nationals'.[68]

An alternative way of expressing this principle is to say that we as citizens of the United Kingdom each enjoy certain entitlements (and are subjected to certain obligations) which our domestic organs of government, acting unilaterally, are not legally competent to alter. As the Community's legal competence expanded following the

[67] Wade has hinted at the possibility; (1996) op cit at p 570: 'It may be accepted, at least at this point in time, that Parliament could indeed repeal the Act of 1972 altogether'.

[68] Case 26/62: [1963] ECR 1 at para 12.

Single European Act, new entitlements and obligations have been created, and the original ones bestowed by the Treaty of Rome have become more firmly rooted in our legal and political culture. This would imply that any such alteration in the UK's relationship with the EC could lawfully be accomplished only through the mechanisms of EC law. The question then becomes how can that alteration lawfully be effected.

The Treaty of Rome and the SEA contained no express provisions for Member State withdrawal. The only way that result could lawfully be achieved (as a matter of EC law, and hence, given the supremacy of EC law over contradictory domestic statutes, as a matter of domestic law) is if the EC Treaties were amended to reconstitute the Community with one fewer member. That process, as specified in Article 236, requires the convening of an Inter-Governmental Conference, at which all existing member states must agree to alterations to the Treaty's provisions. From this perspective, as a matter of EC law (and of acute political irony), any one of the other Member States would have a veto power over UK departure from the Community.[69]

To suggest that UK courts might simply refuse to apply the provisions of legislation seeking to withdraw the UK from the Community is, quite clearly, a fanciful argument. The sovereignty of Parliament, as generally understood, would undoubtedly be challenged in the most confrontational of ways by such judicial action. There is nonetheless some force in the contention – for the reasons outlined above – that for the UK courts to deny our modern Parliament the power either expressly to breach EC law, or to leave the Community altogether, would not challenge the sovereignty of Parliament but rather restore its original purpose. Perhaps this would indeed amount to a revolution; but more in the sense of our constitutional order turning a full circle and returning to the anti-majoritarian ethos underpinning the 1688 revolution than of embarking on a wholly new and uncharted political adventure.

THE REAPPEARANCE OF THE POLITICAL DOCTRINE? MONETARY UNION, COLLECTIVE MINISTERIAL RESPONSIBILITY AND THE FALL OF MARGARET THATCHER

Several factors contributed to Conservative MPs' decision to remove Margaret Thatcher as their leader (and thence as Prime Minister) in November 1990. As chapter eleven suggested, the unpopularity of the community charge led many Conservative MPs to fear defeat in the next general election. Thatcher's close personal identification with the poll tax offered an obvious reason for some Conservative MPs to want a new leader. Others remained continuingly unhappy with her evident preference for a presidential style of Cabinet government (a preference which had triggered the resignations of Heseltine in 1985 and Nigel Lawson in 1989). But the catalytic event was Thatcher's attitude towards the UK's EC membership.

[69] Since the EC is (per *Van Gend*) a 'new legal order of international law', the rules in 'ordinary' international law permitting unilateral State withdrawal from treaty arrangements would not apply.

The Treaty of Rome (Title II, Chapter 1) had contained various (seemingly non-justiciable) provisions heralding a co-ordinated approach to macro-economic policy. Member States undertook to maintain the stability of their respective currencies and an approximate equilibrium in their balance of payments. The Commission was empowered to monitor Member States performances in this regard, and to offer financial assistance to member states suffering severe currency or balance of payments crisis.

These modest co-ordinatory policies were seen by some observers as a tentative first step towards full blown 'monetary union', which would ultimately require a single EC currency and a central EC bank controlling the Community's money supply and interest rates. This objective has an obvious economic logic in the context of creating a truly 'common' market, as it removes the transaction costs engendered by currency exchanges and ensures that businesses in particular member states are not advantaged or disadvantaged vis à vis their EC competitors as a result of their own government's monetary policy.

But full monetary union also had profound political implications. A single EC currency and a central EC bank would present a distinct challenge to orthodox notions of national sovereignty. By the late 1960s, it is possible to argue that western economies were sufficiently closely interconnected for it to be practically impossible for any one European country successfully to pursue economic policies entirely independent of those adopted by neighbouring states. Nevertheless, economic and monetary union would remove such practical controls as national governments still possessed, thereby significantly extending the de facto federal nature of the Community and adding further force to arguments for a full political federalisation on the American model.

The EC's first steps towards monetary union had begun in 1969, but rapidly foundered during the recession of the early 1970s. Roy Jenkins, having resigned from the Labour government to become President of the Commission in 1977, put the issue at the top of the Commission's list of priorities, and by 1979 the European Monetary System (EMS) was in place. The EMS existed outside the legal structure of the Treaty, and so was not a Community measure in the strict sense. Its central feature was the Exchange Rate Mechanism (ERM), which placed fairly tight limits on fluctuations in currency exchange rates. Member states were not obliged to join the ERM, and successive Labour and Conservative governments chose not to do so, preferring to retain autonomy in exchange rate and interest rate policies. The SEA itself made scant reference to monetary union, beyond noting the obvious point that giving the EMS and ERM a legal basis within Community law would require further Treaty amendment. However in 1988, the European Council instructed Jacques Delors to produce a phased plan for achieving de facto and de jure economic and monetary union. The 1989 Delors *Report on Economic and Monetary Union* envisaged a three-stage process. Firstly, a gradual 'convergence' of the Member States' economies in respect of such matters as inflation rates, economic growth, and the balance of payments; secondly, the locking of all Member States' currencies into a far tighter ERM, which would tolerate only very small currency fluctuations; and thirdly, the introduction of the single currency.

While many Member State governments welcomed the plan, the UK government expressed reservations. The Conservative manifesto for the 1989 EC elections warned that monetary union would 'involve a fundamental transfer of sovereignty. . . . The report, if taken as whole, implies nothing less than the creation of a federal Europe'.[70] Nevertheless, at the Madrid Summit in 1989, the European Council agreed to begin the first stage in 1990, and to initiate the process of Treaty amendment to establish a timetable for phases two and three. The British government also agreed that it would enter the ERM at some point in the near future.

It seems that the Thatcher government regarded the Madrid summit as a recipe for delay rather than prompt action. However, the other member states took quite the opposite view, with the result that by mid-1990, the Prime Minister and some of her Cabinet colleagues were making distinctly hostile comments about the Delors plan. We noted in chapter nine that Nicholas Ridley, perhaps the Cabinet member most in sympathy with Thatcher's EC views, had resigned in July 1990 after giving an interview critical of Germany. Some parts of that interview merit further attention here. Ridley had suggested that monetary union was simply 'a German racket designed to take over the whole of Europe'; he thought that the scheme posed an intolerable threat to British sovereignty: 'You might just as well give it to Adolf Hitler, frankly'.[71]

Ridley's resignation might have been thought to suggest that Ministers holding such sentiments should at the least not express them in such terms. But the Cabinet was clearly split on the monetary union question. The UK finally joined the ERM in October 1990, yet immediately afterwards the Prime Minister herself engaged in a Ridleyesque tirade against the Delors plan. At the European Council's Rome Summit, the other eleven member states expressed their willingness to accelerate plans for further monetary integration. Thatcher resolutely opposed any such initiative, describing the summit as 'a mess' and her fellow heads of government as living in 'Cloud Cuckoo Land'. On her return to the Commons, Thatcher accused Jaques Delors and the Commission of trying to 'extinguish democracy', and announced she would greet every 'federalist' EC measure with a resounding 'No!'.

Thatcher's outburst prompted Geoffrey Howe (the then Deputy Prime Minster) to resign from the Cabinet. His initial explanation that his resignation was over the question of government policy towards the EC was to be expanded upon in a speech to the Commons on 13 November 1990.[72] Howe was never noted as an inspiring orator. He once earned the memorable soubriquet from Dennis Healey that to be criticised by him in debate was 'like being savaged by a dead sheep'. His resignation speech did not contain any stylistic fireworks; but its content had an explosive political effect.

70 Quoted in Nicoll W and Simon T (1994) *Understanding the new European Community* at p158 (London: Harvester Wheatsheaf).

71 *The Spectator*, 14 July 1990.

72 *HCD*, 13 November 1990, cc 461–465.

Howe attributed many of the country's economic difficulties to the government's refusal to join the ERM in 1985. He then revealed that the government's eventual commitment to join had been extracted from an unwilling Prime Minister only when he (then Foreign Secretary) and Nigel Lawson (the then Chancellor) had threatened to resign from the Cabinet if it did not do so. Yet Howe suggested that the question of ERM membership was merely a symptom of a more pervasive Prime Ministerial distaste for the European Community. Echoing Lord Bridge's oblique criticism in *Factortame (No 2)*, Howe asserted that it was a serious error to regard closer European integration, as the Prime Minister appeared to do, as involving the 'surrender of sovereignty'. Making an overt reference to the Bruges speech, Howe argued that such hyperbolic language served only to create:

'. . . a bogus dilemma, between one alternative, starkly labelled "co-operation between independent sovereign states", and a second, equally crudely labelled alternative, "centralised federal super-state", as if there were no middle way in between'.[73]

Howe observed that the EC's development was more likely to proceed in a direction which coincided with British interests if the government argued its case from the centre of the EC policy-making process, rather than standing on the sidelines and eventually being dragged reluctantly into a reformed Community in which the political agenda had been set to reflect the preferences of its other members. But Howe's criticism of Thatcher did not dwell merely on tactics, it reached also to the question of her basic attitude towards the UK's EC partners. Howe saw no merit in what he termed Thatcher's 'nightmare image' of an EC 'positively teeming with ill-intentioned people, scheming in her words to "extinguish democracy", to "dissolve our national identities" and to lead us "through the back-door into a federal Europe" '.[74] Against such Europhobic 'background noise', it was impossible for the Chancellor of the Exchequer to be taken seriously by other member states in any discussion of EC economic policy.

Howe's speech is a graphic example of the Commons' capacity to serve as a forum for calling the executive to account. The speech revealed not simply a disagreement between a Prime Minister and a senior colleague on a matter of major substantive importance, but also suggested that the country was being governed by a dogmatic leader who held an ill-mannered contempt for any divergent opinion (be it within Cabinet or from other EC member states), and who utterly rejected traditional principles of Cabinet government. Such criticisms of Thatcher had frequently been made by opposition parties; but they were likely to carry more weight with Conservative MPs when delivered by the man who had served as Chancellor and Foreign Secretary for over ten years in Thatcher's Cabinets.

Thereafter, domestic political events moved with great rapidity. Michael Heseltine, five years after leaving the Cabinet, challenged Thatcher for leadership of the Conservative Party. Her failure to win an adequate majority in the subsequent election

[73] Ibid, at c 463. [74] Ibid, at c 464.

held among Conservative MPs led to her resignation as party leader and Prime Minister, and then to John Major's eventual succession.

These events reinforce the presumption that EC membership has wrought significant changes in both orthodox constitutional theory and orthodox constitutional practice. In practical terms, the constitutional history of twentieth century Britain has been dominated (except during the two world wars) by a straightforward party political division, in which single party governments with relatively distinct and coherent ideological beliefs have deployed a Commons majority to use Parliament's legal sovereignty to pursue their preferred policy programmes. But that picture may now be changing. In part, that is attributable to the courts' recognition of supra-legislative constraints on parliamentary sovereignty on EC matters. It may be fanciful to equate *Costa* and *Factortame* with the pre-revolutionary supra-legislative notion of 'common right and reason', but the analogy is not entirely spurious. But perhaps of greater immediate significance to analysts of the British constitution is the argument that the demise of Margaret Thatcher, seen in conjunction with the extraordinary party political alignments produced in the 1972 Accession controversy and the 1975 referendum, indicates that the EC has introduced a profound ideological fault line into the very core of the traditional party political divide. In 1990, it seemed plausible to suggest that neither the Labour nor Conservative Party could any longer rely on its MPs to present a unified front on EC questions. Equally, it appeared that EC questions could never be settled in any definitive sense, for Eurosceptics seemed wedded to the belief that only a bare Commons majority would be needed to unravel whatever EC commitments Parliament had previously undertaken. In combination, these factors held out the prospect of a significant weakening of Prime Ministerial authority vis à vis the Cabinet, and of government authority vis à vis the Commons. We will return to this question in the final section of this chapter. But before doing so, we must make one final journey to the case law of the ECJ.

V. THE *FRANCOVICH* REMEDY

Thatcher's dominance of Britain's political agenda in the 1980s (and thence of much of Britain's constitutional history in that decade), lent her resignation major domestic significance. Yet it was of little moment for the on-going development of the Community's constitutional history. Very rapidly, all eyes turned to the proposals that would eventually feature in the Maastricht Treaty on European Union. But in the interim, the ECJ was continuing its efforts to clarify the relationship between EC law's normative supranationalism and the member states' respective constitutional autonomy.

FRANCOVICH

The EC Directive at issue in *Francovich*[75] (No 80/987) required Member States to institute (by October 1983) a scheme which guaranteed a minimum level of financial protection for workers whose employers became insolvent. The maximum amount of compensation envisaged was modest, being only three months' salary. Nevertheless, Italy chose to ignore the directive. The Commission instituted an Article 169 action against Italy in 1987.[76] The ECJ held Italy to be in breach of its Treaty obligations, but the Italian government still refused to implement the directive. Francovich was owed some six million lira by his employer, who had become insolvent in 1985. An Italian court had given judgment in Francovich's favour against the employer under Italian insolvency laws, but since the employer had no resources, it was not possible for that judgment to be enforced. Mr Francovich consequently sued the Italian state in the domestic courts for the compensation he would have received if Directive 80/987 had been correctly incorporated into national law. In an Article 177 reference, the ECJ was asked; firstly, if the directive was directly effective against the Italian state; and, secondly, if it was not directly effective, could Mr Francovich nevertheless claim damages against Italy to reimburse him for the loss he had suffered as a result of the directive's non-implementation?

It is conceivable that the ECJ might have found Directive 80/987 directly effective, and thereafter simply applied the supremacy principle to 'instruct' the domestic court to award Francovich the minimum compensation the EC law required. However the Court concluded (somewhat unconvincingly)[77] that the measure was not directly effective, since it afforded member states the choice of financing the scheme themselves or requiring it to be underwritten by private sector institutions.

One could suggest two powerful reasons for assuming that the remedy alluded to in the second question would be a very effective means of ensuring that member states complied with their EC law obligations. Firstly, a damages remedy – especially if it embraced punitive as well as compensatory damages – could prove extremely expensive for the government concerned. Secondly, it would be much more difficult in domestic political terms for a government to ignore a judgment of a national court in an action brought by one of its own citizens than a judgment of the 'foreign' ECJ in an action initiated by the Commission. One might equally suggest that the very efficacy of the remedy would explain why it has no explicit existence in the Treaty's text; the original member state governments would surely not have wished to subject themselves to such a regime.

Notwithstanding the absence of any explicit textual base for the claimed remedy, the ECJ found in Francovich's favour on the second question. The Court employed an interpretive methodology very reminiscent of its technique in *Van Gend*, suggesting

75 *Francovich and Bonifaci v Italy*: Cases C–6, 9/90 [1991] ECR-I 5357, [1993] 2 CMLR 66, ECJ.

76 *EC Commission v Italy*: Case 22/87 [1989] ECR 143.

77 Steiner J (1993) 'From direct to *Francovich*: shifting means of enforcement of community law' *EL Rev* 3–22.

that: 'This problem must be examined in terms of the general scheme and basic principles of the Treaty'.[78] This purposive approach led the ECJ to hold that: 'the principle of the liability of the state for damage to individuals caused by a breach of Community law for which it is responsible is *inherent in the scheme of the Treaty*'.[79]

Literalists might suggest that 'inherency' is simply a cloak underneath which the ECJ has invented an entirely novel principle of law, which could legitimately be introduced into the EC's constitution only by an amendment to the Treaty via Article 236. The Court did also suggest that this inherent principle also enjoyed some textual basis in Treaty Article 5, but even that conclusion demands some fairly creative interpretation.

The ECJ continued by identifying three conditions which had to be satisfied before individuals could rely on this newly discovered principle. Firstly, that the relevant EC measure was intended to confer benefits on individuals. Secondly, that the substance of such benefits was clearly defined by the directive. And thirdly, that a causal link existed between the individual's loss and the member state's breach of its Treaty obligations. Since all three conditions were met in Francovich's case, he could recover damages from the Italian state. *Francovich* seemingly opened a new chapter in the history of the domestic impact of EC law. The judgment itself left unanswered many important questions: how tight a causal link would be required between the member state's misfeasance and the loss caused; would liability attach only to egregious and deliberate failure to implement a directive (evidenced by failure to comply with an Article 169 judgment) or extend even to unwitting mistakes; would there be a ceiling on the quantum and heads of damages available; on which particular organ of government would liability ultimately fall; and to what extent would the ECJ be prepared to allow the national courts to devise their own answers to these issues?[80] More broadly, one might wonder if the remedy should be limited simply to failure to implement a directive,[81] or whether it should extend to any breach of EC law?

Yet even if *Francovich* was initially to be narrowly construed, the ECJ's gradual extension of the initially limited concept of direct effect created in *Van Gend* might suggest that *Francovich* would grow into an expansive and highly effective tool for citizens to use to enhance the effet utile of EC law. This supposition was borne out a few years later in *Brasserie du Pêcheur SA v Germany*.[82] The issue before the ECJ in *Brasserie* was whether the damages remedy was to be regarded solely as an alternative to direct effect available only in respect of non-implementation of a directive, or whether it was an additional remedy that might be invoked in respect of any breach of EC law. Unsurprisingly, the ECJ favoured the latter approach:

'[T]he right of individuals to rely on the directly effective provisions of the Treaty is only a minimum guarantee and is not sufficient in itself to ensure the full and complete implemen-

[78] [1993] 2 CMLR 66 at para 30. [79] Ibid, at para 35 (emphasis added).

[80] For initial speculation see Steiner (1993) op cit: Craig P (1993) '*Francovich*, remedies and the scope of damages liability' 109 *LQR* 595–621.

[81] Ie, to plugging the enforceability gap created by Marshall which *Von Colson* and *Marleasing* left unfilled.

[82] Case C–46/93: [1996] ECR I–1029, ECJ.

tation of the Treaty. . . . [I]n the event of a right directly conferred by a Community provision upon which individuals are entitled to rely before the national courts . . . the right to reparation is the necessary corollary of the direct effect of the Community provision whose breach caused the damage sustained'.[83]

When seen in conjunction with *Marleasing, Francovich* and *Brasserie du Pêcheur* also reinforce the supposition that the ECJ is developing its own version of the 'mutual recognition' rather than 'Euronorms' approach to integration which underpinned the Single European Act. Both judgments place responsibility for ensuring the effet utile of Community law firmly in the domestic constitutional arena, the onus being placed on national courts to pull their respective legislatures into line with EC principles. On a grander scale, these might lead us to suggest that the EC is now lending a further, geographical dimension to traditional British understandings of the separation of powers, in the sense that national judiciaries may be beginning to see themselves as sharing more common ground with their counterparts in the ECJ and the other member states than with their own countries' legislative and executive branches. It might be argued, for example, that we can identify a 'ripple effect', in which principles espoused by the ECJ and thereafter applied by the domestic courts in respect of EC matters have also begun to influence judicial decision-making on purely domestic issues. An obvious example of this in the English context is the judgment in *Pepper v Hart*,[84] in which – using *Pickstone* as a springboard – the House of Lords departed from the traditional 'exclusionary rule' and concluded that reference might be made to *Hansard* as a guide to statutory interpretation. That result was not, nor could be, in any sense required by EC law. Rather we might suggest that the constitutional principles of the EC have become sufficiently firmly established in the minds of British judges to begin to merge into the courts' constantly evolving conceptions of the contemporary role of the common law. If the hypothesis about a 'ripple effect' is proved accurate, then a further, significant shift towards a purely federalist constitution has slipped, indirectly, and largely unnoticed via the EC's 'new legal order' into the domestic legal system. Other shifts, in contrast, played out in the political rather than judicial arenas, have attracted rather more attention.

VI. MAASTRICHT AND AMSTERDAM

The substantive reforms to the Community's legal structure introduced by the Maastricht Treaty on European Union (TEU) in 1993 were perhaps less far-reaching than those in the Single European Act.[85] Yet the amendment process proved extremely problematic in several states.

[83] Ibid, at paras 20 and 22. [84] See pp 284–290 above.

[85] For a longer, but accessible guide see Hartley T (1993) 'Constitutional and institutional aspects of the Maastricht Agreement' 42 *International and Comparative Law Quarterly* 213–237.

Before that political process ran its course, however, France's Conseil d'Etat took a significant step towards accepting that French law should fully accept the precedence and direct effect doctrines. The Conseil's judgment in *Rauol Georges Nicolo*[86] did not reverse *Cohn-Bendit* in express terms, but certainly indicated that the status of EC law within France had undergone a profound change. In *Nicolo*, the Conseil accepted the advisory opinion from the Commissaire du Gouvernement that French law should now rest on the basis that Art 55 of the French Constitution did require the domestic courts to attach precedence to EC treaty articles even if they were inconsistent with the requirements of subsequently enacted French legislation. Shortly afterwards, in *Boisdet*[87], the Conseil d'Etat extended this principle to accept the applicability of the precedence and direct effect principles in respect of EC secondary legislation. *Boisdet* effectively did overrule *Cohn-Bendit.* Once again, however, the point must be made that the Conseil d'Etat offered these developments as changes in French constitutional law. Neither judgment accepted the ECJ's insistent contentions as to the autonomous status of Community law.

THE TERMS OF THE MAASTRICHT TREATY

The least controversial of the amendments was one of nomenclature; the Community was formally renamed as the EC rather than the EEC. Questions of labelling retained a symbolic importance throughout the negotiatory process. The British government insisted that any reference to the creation of a 'federal' Europe be deleted from the TEU's text. An ambivalent formula was eventually adopted; that the TEU would be 'a new stage in the process of creating an ever closer union among the peoples of Europe, in which decisions are taken as closely as possible to the citizen',[88] but which would respect the 'national identities' of member states.

The TEU introduced several minor extensions in the EC's competence.[89] The Community gained powers over consumer protection, industrial policy, and some education and cultural matters. More significantly, a specific timetable was set for phases two (1 January 1994) and three (1 January 1997 or 1999) of Delors' plan for monetary union.

Further modest efforts were made to reduce the Community's continuing democratic deficit. A new type of law-making process, requiring 'co-decision' between the Parliament and the Council in some areas, has increased the Parliament's influence. Some effort was also made to strengthen the links between the Community and individual citizens by creating a (largely symbolic) status of EU 'citizenship', and by empowering EC nationals to stand for office and vote in local or European elections anywhere in the Community.[90] The TEU also created a 'Committee of the Regions' within the EC's institutional structure, intended to give a voice (but little

86 [1990] 1 CMLR 173. 87 [1991] CMLR 3. 88 TEU, Article A.

89 See by Lane R (1993) 'New Community competences under the Maastricht Treaty' *CML Rev* 939–980.

90 Raworth P (1994) 'A timid step forwards: Maastricht and the democratisation of the EC' *EL Rev* 16–33.

power) in the Community to sub-central units of government within the member states.[91]

The Maastricht negotiations emphasised the plurality of meanings attached to the concept of federalism, both by different member states, and by different political parties within an individual country.[92] The constitutional device eventually adopted to paper over these ideological cracks was the concept of 'subsidiarity'. This in itself is a term bearing several meanings relating to decentralisation of decision-making power.[93] The TEU defined it in what is now Article 3b of the EC Treaty:

'In areas which do not fall within its exclusive competence, the Community shall take action . . . only if and in so far as the objectives of the proposed action cannot be sufficiently achieved by the Member states and can therefore, by reason of the scale or effects of the proposed action, be better achieved by the Community'.

The TEU also introduced significant reforms in respect of the Social Charter. Eleven of the twelve member states had wished to place the 1989 Declaration on a legal basis within the Treaty of Rome, thus making it directly effective in all member states. The Major government rejected this reform. This resulted in the rather peculiar legal creature of a Protocol on Social Policy, attached to the TEU, in which the other eleven states agreed to incorporate the Charter, and all twelve states agreed that the eleven could use Community institutions (including the ECJ) to administer it.

But for both proponents and opponents of a United States of Europe, other aspects of the TEU may have seemed of greater long-term importance. The TEU provided that the EC itself was now to be seen as merely one 'pillar' of the 'European Union' (EU). The other two pillars would be Common Foreign and Security Policy (CFSP) and Justice and Home Affairs (JHA), which in combination substantially extend the range of the former system of 'European Political Co-operation' introduced by the Single European Act. In formal, legal terms, the CFSP and JHA were not part of the EC, and should perhaps be seen as an exercise in traditional inter-governmental co-operation rather than another 'new legal order' operating in parallel to the Community. However they are serviced by the EC's institutions, and there can be little doubt that many proponents of the Maastricht reform anticipated that all three pillars would eventually merge into a single legal order. CFSP and JHA take the member states into far less justiciable territory than that covered by the EC. Nationalist sentiment is likely to be most intense over questions of foreign and defence policy;

[91] Consistent with its dismissive attitude towards local government, the Major administration (uniquely among the Member States) proposed that the UK's representatives on the Committee be central government appointees rather than local authority councillors from the areas concerned. The government was defeated on this in the Lords. Given the obviously 'anti-democratic' character with which its preference could be painted, the government accepted the defeat, thereby once again enabling the non-elected upper house to don the mantle of guardian of electoral democracy.

[92] See Koopmans T (1992) 'Federalism: the wrong debate' *CML Rev* 1047–1052.

[93] Peterson J (1994) 'Subsidiarity: a definition to suit any vision' *Parliamentary Affairs* 116–132; Emiliou N (1994) 'Subsidiarity: panacea or fig leaf', in O'Keeffe D and Twomey P (eds) *Legal issues of the Maastricht Treaty* (London: Wiley Chancery Law).

national governments would seem unlikely to wish to cede control over so emotive an issue as involvement in foreign wars, which may dilute EU responses to the point that they are utterly ineffective. Certainly the first test of the EU's ability to operate as an effective foreign policy player, the war in former Yugoslavia, suggested that the framers of the TEU had underestimated the difficulties that would attend joint initiatives in this area.

The inference that Maastricht may have gone too far too fast may also be drawn from consideration of the fate of the plans to achieve monetary union within the EC. The ERM collapsed late in 1993, before the TEU came into effect. The member states could not maintain exchange rate stability in the face of massive speculation on the international money markets against the weaker currencies. Consequently several countries, including Britain, left the system. The Community's failure to resist these forces undermined its credibility in the eyes of supporters of further integration, and was construed as a sign of more pervasive weakness by its opponents. It is therefore unsurprising that the ratification and incorporation of the Treaty proved so tortuous in several Member States.

THE RATIFICATION AND INCORPORATION OF THE MAASTRICHT TREATY

Under the terms of Article 236 of the Treaty of Rome, those parts of the TEU which amended the EC Treaty could not come into force until it had been ratified by all the member states in accordance with their own constitutional procedures. The people of Denmark had initially rejected the terms of the Treaty in a referendum. Some rapid renegotiation between the Member States ensued, whereupon the TEU was approved by a tiny majority in a second Danish referendum. Public opinion was also sharply divided in France, in which the requisite referendum produced a very small majority in favour of the Treaty. In Germany, the political argument was clearly won by pro-Maastricht forces, although the German government subsequently faced an (unsuccessful) legal challenge which argued that the TEU was inconsistent with provisions of the Basic Law.[94]

'Ratification' of the TEU presented considerable political difficulties in the UK. The non-EC pillars of the Treaty were unproblematic; since there was no need to incorporate their provisions into domestic law, the government could satisfy its international law obligations simply by ratifying the measures through an exercise of the prerogative.

In contrast, the TEU's reforms to the EC would have to be incorporated. Since the TEU increased the powers of the European Parliament, the government was bound by the European Parliamentary Elections Act 1978 s 6 to gain parliamentary approval of the TEU before ratifying it. Given the then small size of the government's Commons majority,[95] and the presence of a dozen anti-EC backbenchers within Conservative

94 *Brunner v European Union Treaty* [1994] 1 CMLR 57.

95 The Conservative majority at the 1992 election was 21.

ranks, it was not clear that approval would be forthcoming. After a series of complex political manoeuvrings in the Commons,[96] the government was defeated by eight votes on a motion concerning the Social Policy Protocol. The Prime Minister thereupon announced that the government's motion on the Protocol would be the subject of a vote of confidence the next day, and implied that a defeat would lead to a dissolution. For rebel Conservative MPs, the prospect of a general election in which they might lose their seats was sufficiently daunting to bring them back into (the party) line. The government's majority in the confidence vote was 40.

But the controversy had not run its course. In a manner reminiscent of Mr Blackburn's feeble attempt to prevent the UK's accession to the Community in 1971, right-wing Eurosceptics launched a legal action after their cause had been defeated in the Commons.[97] The action was fronted by Lord Rees-Mogg, a crossbench peer and former editor of *The Times*, and financed by Sir James Goldsmith, an expatriate financier. Such arguments as Rees-Mogg could muster against ratification and incorporation were peremptorily dismissed by the High Court, whereupon Goldsmith withdrew his financial support and the plaintiff declined to seek an appeal. The litigation was a trivial event compared to the extraordinary convolutions that had gripped the Commons and divided the Conservative Party in previous months; convolutions that continued in the following months.

At the 1992 Edinburgh Summit, the member states had agreed to a modest increase in the Community Budget from 1995 onwards. When the Major government introduced legislation in November 1994 to incorporate that obligation into domestic law, it encountered a substantial rebellion from backbench Conservative MPs who had opposed the Maastricht reforms. For a government whose majority was then only 14, the prospect of a Commons defeat was very real. The Prime Minister then announced that the second reading vote would be a matter of confidence, evidently on the basis that a government which could not honour its international obligations could not continue in office. Should the government be defeated, the entire Cabinet would resign and the Prime Minister would ask the Queen to grant a dissolution.[98] Rebel Conservatives promptly accused the Prime Minister of constitutional sharp practice in elevating a minor financial matter to the status of a confidence issue, and some discussion ensued as to whether the Queen would be conventionally obliged to grant a dissolution in such circumstances. Such speculation ultimately proved of only academic interest. The threat of a general election at a time when the Labour Party enjoyed a substantial lead in the opinion polls was again sufficient to bring most potential rebels back into the government camp. Nevertheless (in a manner reminiscent of Roy Jenkins' elevation of his perception of national interest over party interest in the 1972 accession votes), eight Conservative MPs abstained at second

[96] These are described at length in the first edition of this book at pp 554–557.

[97] *R v Secretary of State for Foreign and Commonwealth Affairs, ex p Rees-Mogg* [1994] QB 552, [1994] 1 All ER 457. For a detailed analysis see Rawlings R (1994a) 'Legal politics: the United Kingdom and ratification of the Treaty of European Union (part two)' *Public Law* 367–391.

[98] Technically, of course, Mr Major would have to have asked for the dissolution before resigning.

reading. They were subsequently stripped of the party whip, and rumours abounded that their local constituency associations were being pressurised by Conservative Central Office to withdraw their support from the errant MPs at the next general election.

THE TREATY OF AMSTERDAM

The Labour Party's victory at the 1997 general election took much political heat out of the constitutional controversies attending the United Kingdom's membership of the Community. The Labour cabinet was firmly pro-European in outlook, and while a small number of backbench Labour MPs fell into the eurosceptic camp, they were an insignificant grouping within the parliamentary party as a whole. The Conservative Party under its new leader William Hague continued its stridently euro-sceptic tone, but given the size of the government's Commons majority Conservative euro-scepticism had also become wholly insignificant.

The Blair government immediately demonstrated its pro-EC credentials by incorporating the Social Charter into UK law. It stood back however from participating in the launch of the single European currency in 1999. The government's official position on this issue was that it supported the single currency in principle, but would not join it until economic conditions were appropriate. The government also promised that the United Kingdom would not join the agreement unless the electorate voted to do so in a referendum.

The new government also found itself plunged immediately into a new round of Treaty amendment negotiations. The proposals aired in the Amsterdam Treaty were relatively modest in effect.[99] Its most significant innovation was to transfer much of the Justice and Home Affairs pillar of the EU into the EC, thereby bringing its terms within the jurisdiction of the ECJ. While the Amsterdam amendments did not incorporate the European Convention on Human Rights into the EC's legal order, the new Treaty did extend the EC's competence into a range of overtly 'political matters'. Under Article 13, the Community now has powers to address discrimination not just on the basis of nationality, but also gender, sexual orientation, disability, race and ethnicity and religious belief. The Amsterdam Treaty also further refined the Community's institutional balance, enhancing the power of the Parliament by extending the range of legislative matters which had to be taken by the co-decision procedure. The ratification process proved less problematic than was the case with the Maastricht Treaty. It was only in Demark that there seemed any likelihood that the proposals would be rejected. In the event, they were approved by a comfortable majority in a referendum.

It might however be suggested that the proposal of any amendment proposals so soon after Maastricht damaged the EC's credibility. It becomes increasingly difficult to regard the EC treaties as containing 'constituent' principles if those principles are

[99] See Craig P (1998) 'The Treaty of Amsterdam: a brief guide' *Public Law* 351–355.

altered every few years. Such rapid change suggests that the treaties are more appropriately seen as part of the rather sordid world of party politics rather than as a cross-national and cross-party attempt to identify and adhere a series of fundamental political values.

That unfortunate impression was reinforced by events in 1998, when it emerged that several Commissioners had been engaging in unethical and possibly corrupt behaviour, particularly in relation to appointing unqualified friends and political supporters to lucrative jobs within the Commission's bureaucracy. The scandal was sufficiently grave to prompt the Parliament to debate a censure motion directed against the Commission as a whole. Although the motion was narrowly defeated, the Commission eventually resigned *en masse*. While those of its members not implicated in the scandal were re-appointed to office, the others were in effect dismissed, and early in 2000 a criminal investigation was initiated against Edith Cresson, a former Commissioner who had once served as Prime Minister of France.

CONCLUSION

The impression that the EU is now a political and legal order engaged in a process of constant constitutional amendment was reinforced when a further inter-governmental conference met at Nice in 2000. The proposals under consideration at Nice were in part issues left unresolved at Amsterdam. The primary questions to be addressed concerned the admission into the EU of as many as ten new Member States, many of them countries from the former eastern bloc, and the alterations that such enlargement would demand for voting systems within the Council and structure of the Commission and the Court.[100] A proposal was also made that the EU should add its own Charter of Rights to the treaty framework. The United Kingdom was opposed to giving any such Charter justiciable status, and it was eventually agreed that the Charter would have the status of a 'Solemn Proclamation' appended to the new treaty.[101] The amendments were initially rejected by Ireland, and in a manner reminiscent of Denmark's eventual ratification of Maastricht, the proposals were eventually approved by Irish voters late in 2002.

The admission of ten new members, many of them poorly developed in economic terms and lacking any deeply rooted democratic culture, promises to present the EU with substantial challenges in the years ahead. The difficulties of securing consensus among so many and so very different governments and peoples for any further major change to the treaties was graphically illustrated by the ignominious collapse of

[100] A helpful guide is offered in Shaw J (2001) 'The Treaty of Nice: legal and constitutional implications' *European Public Law* 195–207.

[101] See Rogers I (2002) 'From the Human Rights Act to the Charter: not another human rights instrument to consider' *European Human Rights LR* 343–356.

attempts to introduce a 'Constitution' for the Community in 2004 and 2005. The proposed 'Constitution' would have introduced substantial changes to the scope of Community competence, to its institutional structure, and to the status of Community law within the member states. Its terms were decisively rejected in referendums in France and Denmark, and the proposals were withdrawn without being put forward for the approval of the majority of member states. Quite how the Community will develop in the medium and long term is therefore a matter of some considerable uncertainty.

For a British constitutional lawyer, however, these long term political issues have a less compelling effect than the impact that accession to the EC has had on the UK's internal constitutional dynamics. It is undeniable that a substantial and continually increasing proportion of the laws applicable in the United Kingdom are found in the Treaties and secondary legislation. It is similarly clear that the gradual extension of the Community's competence beyond the nominally 'economic' sphere into a range of 'political' issues has lent the EC a far more federal identity than it possessed 20 years ago. In that respect, the effective 'sovereignty' of the UK as a nation has been curtailed. Whether Parliament retains the capacity to reclaim that authority remains to be seen. But even if we accept that the courts do not have power to disapply a statute purportedly withdrawing the UK from the EC, the innovative stream of jurisprudence flowing from *Macarthys* through *Garland* and *Pickstone* and *Litster* to *Factortame* and beyond[102] has substantially restructured the internal balance of constitutional power between the legislature, the executive and the courts. Last, and perhaps not least, the UK's membership of the Community has offered us a political issue which transcends the usual rigidities of ideological loyalty within the Conservative and Labour parties.

In all of those three senses, the EC has proven itself a very 'special' ingredient within the UK's modern constitutional recipe. But perhaps its most special characteristic is simply to alert us to the fact that constitutional orthodoxies are not set in stone. If one set of political changes can trigger significant constitutional change, might not others have the same effect? With that question in mind, this book now moves from the more obviously political dimension of constitutional law to begin to explore its more ostensibly legalistic dimension, by addressing certain facets of administrative law.

102 In 2002, the High Court reaffirmed the proposition that the doctrine of implied repeal was no longer applicable in respect of EC matters; *Thoburn v Sunderland City Council* [2002] 1 CMLR 1461. The judgment suggested that the European Communities Act 1972, along with several other Acts unrelated to Community law, possessed so-called 'constitutional' status, which lent them a different legal character to 'ordinary' Acts. Given that the judgment purports to offer principles which are not confined solely to EC law matters – and thus has broad implications for the continued vitality of the doctrine of parliamentary sovereignty – it is analysed at a later stage of this book.

14

SUBSTANTIVE GROUNDS OF JUDICIAL REVIEW: ILLEGALITY, IRRATIONALITY AND PROPORTIONALITY

The grounds on which the courts have traditionally been prepared to conclude that a government action may be unlawful have been alluded to frequently in earlier chapters. The next two chapters offer a rather more systematic approach to this branch of administrative law, by revisiting some of those previously mentioned decisions in the context of a detailed discussion of other leading cases.

The various grounds of review fall essentially into two spheres. *Substantive* grounds of review are concerned with the content or outcome of the decision made. *Procedural* grounds of review, in contrast address the question of the way in which a decision is made. As we shall see in chapter fifteen, it is entirely possible that the substance of a decision is quite lawful, but the decision itself will be unlawful because of a procedural flaw. In this chapter, we focus on the substantive grounds of review. The courts have traditionally recognised two such grounds – illegality and irrationality.[1] These are addressed in sections one and two below. Section three then considers a third ground, which is an emergent rather than established principle in English law – that of proportionality.[2]

[1] 'Irrationality' is the contemporary usage for the concept once referred to as '*Wednesbury* unreasonableness': see p 72 above. The terms are used interchangeably in the rest of this book.

[2] For the reasons alluded to in the preface to this book, the contents of this chapter address only a limited range of the issues that would be discussed under this heading in a book devoted solely to administrative law. This chapter is intended to be an illustrative rather than exhaustive foray into the realm of illegality. Thus for example (to the certain relief of students and the probable relief of their teachers) I have taken at face value Lord Diplock's suggestion in *GCHQ* that *Anisminic* abolished the distinction between jurisdictional and non-jurisdictional errors of law, and omitted any discussion of that doctrinally rather impenetrable issue.

I. ILLEGALITY

Lord Greene MR's judgment in *Wednesbury*[3] had noted that the various grounds of review were not wholly discrete categories, but might often merge and overlap. The same point might be made about the various sub-categories of each ground of review. For the purposes of this book, illegality has been broken down into the following component parts: excess of power; the relevant/irrelevant considerations doctrine; unlawful delegation of power; unlawful fettering of power; and the estoppel doctrine.

EXCESS OF POWERS

The notion that a government body's decision is unlawful because the body has attempted to exercise a power that it simply does not possess might be thought a very straightforward concept to apply. An obvious example, mentioned in chapter three, would arise if a government body invoked a statute which empowered it to build schools as an authority for it to build houses. Such executive activity could readily be understood as involving what is sometimes termed an 'excess of power'. An alternative, and often used formulation in these circumstances would be to say that the government body has gone 'beyond the four corners of the Act'.[4] The test becomes rather more complicated however when one considers that the content of legislation, in so far as it can be presented as having a geometrical shape, may look less like a neat rectangle and more like a blob of custard dropped from a great height on to a hot plate. And even if the contours of the relevant statute might initially appear to have a readily identifiable shape, the twin processes of their application by the executive and their interpretation by the courts may produce unexpected results.

The much-cited judgment in *A-G v Fulham Corpn*[5] is a helpful way of introducing this topic. The case centred on the powers granted by a series of Baths and Washhouses Acts, passed between 1846 and 1878. Fulham Corporation had operated several such facilities to which people came to have baths and to launder their own clothes. It subsequently decided to offer a home delivery laundry service. The service was projected to make a substantial operating deficit each year, and would be subsidised from local taxation. The vires of this policy were then challenged by the Attorney-General.

[3] *Associated Provincial Picture Houses Ltd v Wednesbury Corpn* [1948] 1 KB 223, [1947] 2 All ER 680, CA; see pp 71–72 above.

[4] That label is obviously inappropriate if it is the limits of a prerogative power that are in question. It should be noted that following the UK's accession to the EEC in 1972, a government action would be 'illegal' in this core sense if it breached a directly effective provision of EC law. It is beyond the scope of this book to offer even a cursory outline of the various substantive provisions of EC law, although some aspects of the ECJ's jurisprudence will be touched upon below. For a smoothly integrated approach to the impact of EC substantive law on UK administrative law see Craig P *Administrative law* (4th edn, 1998) (London: Sweet and Maxwell).

[5] [1921] 1 Ch 440.

The judgment did not rest upon a literal construction of any particular provision of the Act. Sargant J seemed instead to apply the 'golden rule' of statutory interpretation in attempting to establish the overall purpose underlying the legislation. This technique led him to conclude that 'the scheme of the Act appears to be to give washing facilities to persons who are not able to provide for themselves places where they may cleanse themselves or wash their clothes'.[6] He then observed that it was a settled facet of the illegality doctrine that a policy would be intra vires, even if it did not fall squarely within the scheme of the Act if it could be regarded as 'incidental to, or consequent upon, those things which the legislature has authorised'.[7]

The notions of incidentalism or consequentialism would seem substantially to reduce the scope for a policy to be held illegal. On these facts, however, the principle did not assist the Corporation. In Sargant J's view, the provision of a home delivery laundry service was 'a completely different enterprise'[8] from just providing facilities where people could do their own washing.

There is no compelling empirical basis for that conclusion. The case could clearly have been decided the other way just as readily, an observation which highlights the often ambiguous reach of the illegality principle. It seems that Sargant J's decision was probably swayed by a factor which he himself described as irrelevant to the question before him – and which he then considered at some length:

> '[T]he service is being performed at about half . . . of the cost to the Council. That is an instance I think, although it is immaterial for the present purpose, of the light-hearted way in which operations are conducted by persons who have not their own pockets to consider, but who have behind them what they regard as the unlimited or nearly unlimited power of the ratepayers'.[9]

Sargant J's observations on the fiscal feasibility (or lack of it) of the council's scheme might be thought to have set the jurisprudential scene for the House of Lords' judgment in *Roberts v Hopwood* a few years later.[10] In *Roberts*, we may recall, the House of Lords had unanimously concluded that Poplar Council's £4 per week minimum wage policy was void on the ground of illegality. The council had assumed it was acting within the limits of s 62 of the Metropolis Management Act 1855, which empowered it to pay 'such wages as it thinks fit'. The House of Lords had held that s 62 had to be construed subject to a common law 'fiduciary duty' imposed upon governmental bodies. Since the payment made by the council bore no close relation to the market value of the work performed it was not a wage or salary at all, but a 'gift'. As such it was beyond the four corners of s 62.

In the Court of Appeal[11] however, the notion that the council was under a fiduciary duty to its ratepayers – and thus that s 62 had to be construed in that context was rejected. While the court accepted that prevailing market rates had some bearing on

[6] Ibid, at 451.
[7] Ibid, at 450; citing James LJ in *Ashbury Railway Carriage and Iron Co Ltd v Riche* (1875) LR 7 HL 653.
[8] Ibid, at 453. [9] Ibid, at 454. [10] [1925] AC 578, HL.
[11] *R v Roberts, ex p Scurr* [1924] 2 KB 695, CA.

establishing if a payment was indeed a 'wage', it also concluded that the concept of a 'wage' was sufficiently elastic to permit a significant departure from the sums paid in the private sector for similar work.

The origin of the fiduciary duty principle in respect of local government actions was discussed in chapter ten.[12] The doctrine can plausibly be seen as a common law mechanism designed to enhance rather than restrict an elected body's substantive autonomy. The decision of the Court of Appeal in *Roberts* is consistent with that understanding of the principle. The judgment of the House of Lords in *Roberts*, and Sargent J's observations in *Fulham*, appear to reject or ignore it.

Notwithstanding this point, one might question the accuracy of portrayals of the House of Lords' decision in *Roberts* as a simple manifestation of right wing political bias by the judiciary.[13] Quite how well-founded that contention was in respect of the judges involved in *Roberts* is unclear. Insofar as the content of the judgment reflected right wing political views, one might readily suggest that those views accurately reflected the wishes of the 1855 Parliament, whose survey of the then political landscape would not have revealed any 'socialists' controlling government bodies. The ghost of *Roberts* in the guise of the fiduciary duty doctrine re-appeared 30 years later in *Prescott v Birmingham Corpn*,[14] when the court concluded that a council's concessionary fare scheme was illegal; and again, a further 30 years later in *Bromley v GLC*, when the House of Lords invalidated the GLC's 'Fares Fair' policy. As suggested in chapter eleven, the court's reading of the relevant legislation at issue in that case was readily defensible, even if one might just as readily have construed the Act to uphold the GLC's policy.

The point to be drawn here is perhaps that illegality, while ostensibly a straightforward concept, becomes markedly more opaque when it is placed – as it (generally) must be – in the context of the principles of statutory interpretation.[15] *Liversidge v Anderson* offers a compelling illustration of this. In Lord Atkin's view, Liversidge's detention was 'illegal', as Anderson's power to detain Liversidge only arose if Anderson had 'reasonable cause' to believe him to be of hostile origins or association. However, for the majority, that power arose if the Home Secretary had a bona fide belief in Liversidge's hostile associations. As long as that belief existed, the detention would not be illegal.[16]

An equally pertinent illustration of the point can be found if one stays in the rather narrow field of a local authority's fiduciary duty when deciding on its employees' wage rates. The High Court's 1983 judgment in *Pickwell v Camden London Borough*

12 See pp 352–353 above. 13 See Laski op cit; Fennell op cit; pp 315–316 above.

14 [1955] Ch 210, CA.

15 That point would of course not apply when the power in issue was alleged to derive from common law rather than statute.

16 One might make just the same observation regarding the different view expressed by the Court of Appeal and House of Lords in *Rossminster* as to the claimed illegality of the Inland Revenue's search of the applicant's property; see pp 79–81 above.

Council[17] was triggered by the council's decision to end a strike by its employees by offering them a pay deal that was substantially (15%–20%) above the rate subsequently negotiated on a national basis by the relevant union and local authority associations. Forbes J accepted that the council was indeed under an implicit fiduciary duty to spend its money wisely. However, the council's fiduciary duty was now to be read in conjunction with another implicit but equally pervasive obligation 'to provide a wide range of services to its inhabitants'.[18] If high payments were needed to secure that objective, then those payments could defensibly be construed as a wage.[19]

That the nominally simple 'four corners' approach to illegality is more complicated than it might first appear is also well illustrated by the more recent judgment in *R v Secretary of State for Foreign Affairs, ex p World Development Movement Ltd* (popularly known as the *Pergau Dam* case).[20] The Overseas Development and Co-operation Act 1980 s 1 provided that the Foreign Secretary:

'. . . shall have power, for the purpose of promoting the development or maintaining the economy of a country . . . outside the UK, or the welfare of its people, to furnish any person or body with assistance, whether financial, technical or any other nature.'

In the late 1980s, several British firms became involved in a bid to build a dam in Pergau, Malaysia. The initial project was costed at £316m. Officials from the Overseas Development Agency (ODA) subsequently visited Malaysia to examine the proposal. They concluded that the project was 'at the margin of economic viability', and the (Conservative) Foreign Secretary agreed to provide aid of £68m. In April 1989, the anticipated cost of the project was re-estimated at £397m, which led an ODA economist to conclude that the project was now 'clearly uneconomic'. In February 1990, the ODA completed a new appraisal and described the scheme as a 'very bad buy'. The World Bank considered it 'markedly uneconomic' and noted that it could have devastating consequences for the local environment. The Secretary of State nevertheless decided to grant the aid. He took the view that not to do so would 'affect the UK's credibility as a reliable friend and trading partner and have adverse consequences for our political and commercial relations with Malaysia'.[21] The Foreign Secretary maintained that s 1 did not limit the provision of aid to projects that were viable in narrow, economic terms, but also permitted aid which served 'wider political and economic considerations, such as the promotion of regional stability, good government, human rights or British commercial interests'.[22] This argument, perhaps ironically, bears an obvious resemblance to the interpretation of the 'economic, efficient and integrated' formula in s 1 of the Transport (London) Act 1969 urged on the House of Lords by the GLC in the *Bromley* case.[23] Rose LJ followed the Lords' methodology in that case.

[17] [1983] QB 962. [18] [1983] 2 WLR 583 at 603.

[19] A conclusion which seems quite consistent with the original understanding of the fidudiary duty doctrine.

[20] [1995] 1 All ER 611, [1995] 1 WLR 386. [21] Ibid, at 623. [22] Ibid.

[23] See pp 380–382 above.

The issue was a simple one: did s 1 impliedly require that development projects be economically sound?

Parliament could obviously have expressly inserted the word 'sound' into s 1 had it wished to do so. The question for the court was to decide what implications should be drawn from its failure to do so. Does the absence of the word mean, as the government contended, that an aid project that was weak in the narrow economic sense was nonetheless legal if other, broader concerns could be invoked to support it? Or, as the World Development Movement maintained, was the requirement that development projects make good economic sense so obvious that there was no need for Parliament to say so expressly? Rose LJ favoured the latter view:

'As to the absence of the word "sound" from s 1(1), it seems to me that if Parliament had intended to confer a power to disburse money for unsound development purposes, it could have been expected to say so expressly . . . This development, is on the evidence, so economically unsound that there is no economic argument in favour of the case'.[24]

The *Pergau Dam* judgment excited some considerable political controversy,[25] but is a readily defensible exercise in literalist statutory interpretation with obvious antecedents in both *Roberts* and *Bromley*. The judgment essentially construed s 1 as containing an implied fiduciary duty on the government's aid spending. One might question whether or not the common law fiduciary duty doctrine should play any part in regulating government bodies' expenditure plans, but *Pergau Dam* would suggest that the courts do now apply the doctrine on a non-party political basis.

From a jurisprudential perspective, the courts' use of the illegality rule to invalidate government decisions is perhaps more problematic when it is premised not on the literal meaning of particular words or phrases in a statute, but – as in the *Fulham* case – when it purports to ascertain the meaning of a particular provision in the light of the overall scheme or policy of an Act. The House of Lords' judgment in *Padfield v Minister of Agriculture, Fisheries and Food*[26] is an extreme example of this point.

An Act of 1931 had introduced the Milk Marketing Scheme, which required dairy farmers to sell all their milk to regional Milk Marketing Boards. Both consumers and producers had representation on the various Boards. The subsequent Agriculture Marketing Act 1958 made provision for two distinct bodies to hear complaints about the scheme's operation. The Act appeared to envisage that most complaints would be referred to a Consumer's Committee. However s 19(3) provided that:

'A committee of investigation shall . . . (b) be charged with the duty, if the Minister in any case so directs, of considering and reporting to the Minister on . . . any . . . complaint made to the Minister as to the operation of any scheme which, in the opinion of the Minister, could not be considered by a Consumers' Committee.'

In the mid-1960s, producers in the south east region wanted a larger price rise than the

24 [1995] 1 All ER 611 at 626.

25 See the discussion of the 'judicial supremacism' controversy of the 1990s in ch 20 below.

26 [1968] AC 997, [1968] 1 All ER 694, HL.

Regional Board would grant. Their preferred remedy was to rely on a 'Committee of Investigation' to consider the issue, presumably because they thought a Consumers' Committee would not be so sympathetic to their interests. The Minister refused to pass the complaint to a Committee of Investigation, on the basis that in his opinion the matter could satisfactorily be considered by a Consumers' Committee. His understanding of s 19(3) was that referral to a Committee of Investigation would only be appropriate when he felt that the relevant Regional Board was not acting in the public interest.

The text of s 19(3) seems to afford the Minister a very wide discretion. However, the House of Lords proceeded to lend s 19(3) a somewhat unexpected meaning. Rather than adopting the literal rule of construction, Lord Reid's leading judgment followed an interpretative technique with distinctly teleological overtones. He began with the ostensibly uncontroversial proposition that: 'Parliament must have conferred the discretion with the intention that it should be used to promote the policy and objects of the Act'.[27] He then deduced the 'policy and objects of the Act' by examining both its entire text and the historical circumstances surrounding its enactment. This was, he suggested, a statute with an unusual substantive effect:

> 'When these provisions were first enacted in 1931 it was unusual for Parliament to compel people to sell their commodities in a way to which they objected and it was easily forseeable that any such scheme would cause loss to some producers'.[28]

The inference of this would seem to be that all producer complaints should be investigated, to ensure that any losses were fully justified and that producers could know their interests were being fully considered. Lord Reid was therefore led to conclude that: '[I]t is plainly the intention of the Act that even the widest issues should be investigated if the complaint is genuine and substantial, as this complaint certainly is'.[29]

Notwithstanding Lord Reid's constant evocation of parliamentary intent as the source of his decision, cynical observers of judicial behaviour might conclude that his reasoning in *Padfield* seems to pay as little heed to orthodox understandings of the relationship between Parliament and the courts as his contemporaneous judgment in *Anisminic.* In effect, Lord Reid ignored the plain meaning of s 19(3) and converted the power it bestowed upon the Minister into a duty whenever a complaint was 'genuine and substantial'[30] – thereby ensuring that the Minister's failure to refer the complaint to a Committee of Investigation automatically became illegal.[31] The case perhaps

27 Ibid, at 699. 28 Ibid. 29 Ibid, at 700.

30 Lord Morris, the sole dissentient in the case, seemed to rest his judgment on much more orthodox grounds; cf his comment at 705: 'If Parliament had intended to impose a duty on the Minister to refer any and every complaint, or even any and every complaint of a particular nature, it would have been so easy to impose such a duty in plain terms. I cannot read the words in s 19(3) as imposing a positive duty on the Minister to refer every complaint as to the operation of the scheme'.

31 *Padfield* could have been decided on much narrower grounds. It does seem clear that the Minister had misunderstood the scope of the Committee of Investigation's powers of inquiry, and had apparently relied heavily on that misunderstanding in respect of Padfield's complaint. On those facts, the court could simply have quashed the Minister's refusal while also accepting that the Minister, having properly understood the Committee's role, could nonetheless lawfully refuse to refer the complaint.

suggests that the ECJ's contemporaneous embrace of the 'spirit, scheme and general wording' approach to the interpretation of the Treaty of Rome was not quite so alien to the English judicial tradition as one might have initially believed.[32]

The use of what appears de facto to be purposive judicial reasoning to bring government action within the illegality doctrine is also evident in the Court of Appeal's judgment in *Congreve v Home Office*.[33] The Wireless Telegraphy Act 1949, s 1 required that television sets must have a licence. Section 1 also permitted the Home Secretary to issue regulations to charge a fee for such a licence. In 1975, the fee was set at £12 per year. In an attempt to increase the revenue generated by the licence, Harold Wilson's third Labour government announced in February 1975 that the fee would be raised to £18 with effect from 1 April 1975. In the following weeks, several newspapers pointed out that licence holders whose current licences expired shortly after 31 March 1975 might save themselves some £6 by purchasing another licence before 1 April. Many citizens took this advice. The Home Office responded by revoking all such licences, and sending their purchasers letters ordering them to return the £12 licences and buy new £18 licences on the date that their original licence expired. Congreve, a solicitor in a leading city firm, refused to comply, and sought a declaration that the Home Office policy was illegal.

From a purely political perspective, such an action by a government with a Commons majority of two might be thought quite asinine. It was also found to amount to maladministration by the Parliamentary Ombudsman. Neither failing necessarily makes a policy unlawful. But in the view of the Court of Appeal, the Home Office's behaviour was indeed illegal as well.

Lord Denning MR's leading judgment deployed the same melodramatic language that he later invoked in *Rossminster*. He began by expressing some suspicion about the legitimacy of s 1:

> 'The statute has conferred a licensing power on the Minister: but it is a very special kind of power. It invades a man in the privacy of his home, and it does so solely for financial reasons so as to enable the Minister to collect money for the Revenue'.[34]

Denning regarded the purchase of a licence as creating a property right for the buyer. Nothing in the Act clearly forbade an individual from holding two or more licences which overlapped for a short period. Section 1 undoubtedly empowered the Minister to revoke a licence in some circumstances; if the purchase had been premised on fraud, for example. But in the absence of such circumstances, or some other good reason, the Act did not empower the Minister to revoke a licence. For him to attempt to do so simply because it would generate additional revenue for the Treasury was a 'misuse of power'.[35]

Congreve might broadly be construed as supporting the notion that 'misuse of power' is a distinct sub-category of the illegality doctrine. As such, it would demand

[32] See the discussion of *Van Gend en Loos* at pp 422–425 above.

[33] [1976] QB 629, [1976] 1 All ER 697, CA.

[34] Ibid, at 708.

[35] Ibid, at 709.

that courts always be willing to inquire into the motives which underlay the impugned decision. That inquiry was unproblematic in *Congreve* itself, as the Home Secretary candidly stated that his purpose was to raise money. In other cases, where the defendant was less forthcoming, an inquiry into motives could lead the court into rather delicate political territory. The case might therefore better be construed more narrowly, as an illustration of the simple point that the courts have consistently maintained that governmental powers to levy taxation can only be created by explicit statutory language.[36]

The presumption of non-interference with 'basic rights'

This narrow construction of the *Congreve* rule is unproblematic because it speaks to a 'fundamental' constitutional principle which has an explicit basis in a statutory text – namely the Bill of Rights. But one can also find applications of the illegality doctrine which rest on the assumption that certain 'fundamental' or 'basic' rights exist at common law or are implicitly protected by statute, and that the defence of those rights provides a legitimate contextual or background principle against which a statutory text should be construed. We have encountered this point on several occasions already. The House of Lords' construction of the Defence of the Realm legislation in *De Keyser* as being intended to respect the common law rule that the government could only in the most limited circumstances take a citizen's property without paying compensation is a good example of this.[37]

Relatedly, one might offer up *Gilmore* and *Anisminic* as illustrations of a 'basic right' presumption at common law that Parliament cannot deprive citizens of access to the courts other than by the most explicit statutory formulae.[38] *R & W Paul Ltd v Wheat Commission* can also be invoked to support this contention.[39] The Arbitration Act 1889 permitted parties who had agreed to resolve commercial disputes by arbitration rather than litigation to appeal to the High Court on a point of law against the arbitrator's decision. Subsequently, the Wheat Act 1932 created a body called the Wheat Commission to regulate the wheat industry. The Wheat Act s 5 empowered the Commission to make byelaws to give effect to the Act. Byelaw 20 made provision to refer disputes between producers and the Commission to an arbitrator, and appeared to make the arbitrator's decision on all disputes final. The company in this case wished to refer the arbitrator's decision to the courts. Byelaw 20 seemed to preclude this. The question thus raised in this action was whether the Commission had the power to pass byelaw 20. The House of Lords held that the Commission had

[36] Cf Roskill LJ, ibid at 715: 'If the Secretary of State wishes to put his position in this respect beyond all argument, he should seek the necessary Parliamentary powers – if he can obtain them'; and Denning at 710: '[The Home Office letters] were an attempt to levy money for the use of the Crown without the authority of Parliament; and that is quite enough to damn them: see *A-G v Wilts United Dairies*' (1922) 38 TLR 781, HL.

[37] See pp 104–107 above.

[38] See pp 84–87 above.

[39] [1937] AC 139, HL. See the discussion in Browne-Wilkinson, Lord (1992) 'The infiltration of a Bill of Rights' *Public Law* 397–410.

exceeded its powers. Byelaw 20 was illegal because it interfered with the basic right of access to the courts:

> 'The Arbitration Act is a statute of general application, and it confers a valuable and important right of resort to the courts of law. To exclude its operation from an arbitration is to deprive the parties . . . of the rights which the Act confers . . . If that is intended, express words to that effect are in my opinion essential'.[40]

A more recent example of this basic right approach to illegality – and one rooted purely in common law – is provided by *Raymond v Honey*.[41] Under the Prison Act 1952, s 47, the Home Secretary may make rules for the regulation and management of prisons. Rules 33 and 37 seemed to empower prison governors to prevent mail being sent by prisoners in certain circumstances. Raymond, the governor, prevented some of Honey's [a prisoner] mail being sent to Honey's lawyers. Honey subsequently initiated contempt of court proceedings against Raymond. Contempt of court is a broad concept in English law. The accepted definition was offered by Lord Russell in 1900 in *R v Gray*, and encompassed 'Any act done which is calculated to obstruct or interfere with the due course of justice'.[42] The governor's action clearly fell within this definition. His defence to the action was that he had been authorised to obstruct prisoners' mail by the Prison Regulations. This in turn raised the issue of whether s 47 of the Act permitted the Home Secretary to make regulations granting a governor such powers. The House of Lords concluded that s 47 did not have that effect. As Lord Wilberforce put it:

> '. . . under English law, a convicted prisoner, in spite of his imprisonment, retains all civil rights which are not taken away expressly or by necessary implication. . . .
>
> There is nothing in the Prison Act 1952 that confers power to make regulations which would deny, or interfere with, the right of the respondent, as a prisoner, to have unimpeded access to a court. Section 47 . . . is quite insufficient to authorise hindrance or interference with so basic a right'.[43]

At this time, the English courts' use of the 'basic right' principle was patchy and erratic. One could not identify with any precision which 'basic rights' existed, nor the circumstances in which the courts would be ready to invoke them as a means to set a particular interpretative context within which particular statutory powers should be construed. As such, the principle lent the concept of illegality a still more complicated and uncertain character. As we shall see in subsequent chapters, the doctrine has assumed a far more coherent shape in recent years. For the moment however, we continue our analysis of the more clearly established facets of the illegality principle.

Relevant and irrelevant considerations

It has generally been accepted that a decision will be illegal if its contents were arrived at because the decision-maker either took account of irrelevant considerations or

40 [1937] AC 139 at 154, per Lord Macmillan, HL. 41 [1983] 1 AC 1, HL.
42 [1900] 2 QB 36. 43 [1983] 1 AC 1 at 10 and 12, HL.

failed to take account of relevant considerations. *Roberts v Hopwood* can be advanced as the classic illustration of this principle. In *Roberts* in the House of Lords, Lord Atkinson had concluded that the £4 per week wage policy was also unlawful because the council had been influenced by 'some eccentric principles of socialist philanthropy' or by a 'feminist ambition to secure the equality of the sexes in the matter of wages in the world of labour'.[44] One might defend the House of Lords on this point by suggesting that in 1855, when s 62 of the Metropolis Management Act was passed, legislators would not have seen any 'socialists'[45] or 'feminists' in control of local authorities, and so could not have envisaged that s 62 would be used for such ends. Yet, once again, the Court of Appeal had taken a different view on this issue. The stress which both Scrutton LJ and Atkin LJ laid on the representative character of the council implicitly accepts that party political views, be they socialist, social democrat or conservative, are a legitimate influence on the exercise of the elected body's discretionary powers. Both judges also made explicit reference to the council's concern with gender equality. For Scrutton LJ, that was 'a matter of acute controversy, which is hardly for either the auditor or the judges to determine'.[46] In Atkin LJ's view, the fact that the council may have been motivated by this factor had no bearing on the illegality issue.[47]

The great weakness of the relevant/irrelevant consideration principle from a constitutional perspective is that it provides a nominally legitimate vehicle for the courts to steer themselves very close to the political/moral merits of a given decision. Which factors are (ir)relevant to the exercise of a given governmental power is a matter on which Parliament has generally not expressed any (and certainly not an exhaustive) opinion. Unlike the core 'excess of power' limb of the illegality doctrine, this principle is much more difficult to justify in terms of clear judicial obedience to a statutory requirement. The inference thereby arises that the courts are placing tighter constraints on executive autonomy than Parliament had envisaged.[48] The unpredictable nature of the relevancy test also creates difficulties from the perspective of legal certainty; a point graphically illustrated by the differing opinions of the Court of Appeal and House of Lords in *Roberts*.

UNLAWFUL DELEGATION OF POWERS

It would, in contrast, seem quite uncontroversial to assert that the illegality doctrine should place limits on the power of a designated decision-maker to pass on certain of her legal powers to other bodies or individuals. In respect of the exercise of statutory powers, Parliament has one assumes given particular powers to particular people/

[44] [1925] AC 578 at 594, HL.

[45] Except perhaps the remnants of the Chartist movement, which was in any case regarded as illegitimate by most MPs; see pp 229–230 above.

[46] [1924] 2 KB 695 at 721, CA. [47] Ibid, at 729.

[48] A second weakness, which will become apparent in the following section, is that a case might be made for treating this ground of review as a facet of irrationality rather than illegality.

bodies for particular reasons; such as, for example, their expertise in respect of the issue in question or their representative character. Should those powers in effect be exercised by someone/somebody else, Parliament's wishes would clearly be frustrated.

The basic parameters of the rule against delegation are well illustrated in *Ellis v Dubowski.*[49] The Cinematograph Act 1909 had empowered county councils to impose conditions on the grant of licences to operate cinemas in their respective areas. Middlesex County Council's licensing conditions included a provision which banned the showing of any movie which had not been approved by the British Board of Film Censors. The High Court concluded that the provision was unlawful:

> 'The condition sets up an authority whose ipse dixit is to control the exhibition of films. The effect is to transfer a power which belongs to the County Council . . . a condition putting the matter into the hands of a third person or body not possessed of statutory or constitutional authority is ultra vires'.[50]

The statutory scheme did permit the county council to delegate its powers to district councils, or to local magistrates. Nor would it be unlawful for the county council to have taken the BBFC's views about a particular film into account when deciding whether it could be shown in a local cinema. What it could not do, however, was grant the BBFC an effective power of veto on the issue.[51]

The rule was applied with similar clarity in *Allingham v Minister of Agriculture and Fisheries.*[52] The Defence Regulations 1939 under which Mr Liversidge had been imprisoned had a far wider scope than dealing simply with potential enemies and saboteurs. Regulation 62 gave the Minister of Agriculture a sweeping power to control the cultivation of land, be it publicly or privately owned. Regulation 66 then empowered him to delegate his power to a local executive committee. In order to make its decisions more quickly, the committee in Bedfordshire then sub-delegated its power to one of its employees. Allingham was a local farmer, who challenged the instructions he had been given in respect of his land. The basis of his challenge was that the committee had no power to sub-delegate the powers it possessed as a delegate of the Minister.

The court accepted this contention, bringing it within the orthodox maxim of *delegatus non potest delegare.*[53] The committee had no statutory authority to allow others to carry out the tasks with which it had been entrusted. It would have been proper for the committee to allow its officers to make recommendations as to the use of land, and even for it to accord substantial weight to such recommendations in reaching its decisions. But each of those decisions had to be the product of its own collective mind.

H Lavender & Son Ltd v Minister of Housing and Local Government[54] illustrates the

49 [1921] 3 KB 621. 50 Ibid, at 625.

51 For a more recent illustration of precisely the same point see *R v Greater London Council, ex p Blackburn* [1976] 3 All ER 184, [1976] 1 WLR 550, CA.

52 [1948] 1 All ER 780. 53 A delegate has no power to delegate.

54 [1970] 3 All ER 871, [1970] 1 WLR 1231.

point that the rule against delegation works as readily between institutions as within them. Lavender had sought permission from its local council to extract gravel from a farm that it owned. When the council refused permission, Lavender exercised a right of appeal to the Minister of Housing and Local Government (MHLG). The Minister rejected the appeal, noting that as a matter of policy he would not approve such applications unless the Minister of Agriculture raised no objection to the proposal. The High Court concluded that this amounted to a de facto delegation of the MHLG's statutory powers to the Minister of Agriculture. While the MHLG was entitled to seek and consider the views of other Ministers, he was not entitled to bind himself to follow them. As Wills J characterised the situation:

'It was the decision of the Minister of Agriculture not to waive his objection that was decisive in this case, and while that might properly prove to be the decisive factor for the MHLG . . . it seems to me quite wrong for a policy to be applied which in reality eliminates all the material considerations save only the consideration, when that is the case, that the Minister of Agriculture objects'.[55]

The rule that a statutory body can only delegate its powers if it has clear statutory authorisation is complicated a little by the proposition that such authorisation need not have an explicit textual base, but can rather arise as a matter of necessary implication. The leading example is the House of Lords' judgment in *Local Government Board v Arlidge*.[56] In that case it was considered permissible for the LGB to delegate its powers to hold inquiries concerning the closure of unfit properties to a senior official. The court took the view that to hold otherwise would severely compromise the LGB's administrative efficiency. But the principle is not one of general application. In *Barnard v National Dock Labour Board*,[57] for example, the Court of Appeal refused to accept that the NDLB was empowered as a matter of necessary implication to delegate its powers to dismiss or suspend dock workers to a senior manager, notwithstanding the fact that such delegation would have saved the NDLB considerable time and expense.[58] The position is however rather different when one is dealing with the activities of a Minister of the Crown within her own department.

As noted in chapter nine, the convention of individual ministerial responsibility has undergone a significant change in the modern era. It is no longer presumed that a Minister is responsible – in the sense of being under a moral obligation to resign her office – for the failings of her department unless she was personally involved in the

[55] [1970] 3 All ER 871 at 880. [56] [1915] AC 120, [1914–15] All ER Rep 1, HL.

[57] [1953] 2 QB 18, [1953] 1 All ER 1113, CA.

[58] The basis for the distinction is perhaps that while both cases concerned government interference with individual 'liberty' (ie the demolition of Arlidge's house and Barnard's dismissal from his job), the power at issue in *Arlidge* also required the LGB to take into account an obvious and immediate public interest, viz the structural safety and sanitary standards of the neighbourhood; see Viscount Dilhorne in *Arlidge* [1914–15] All ER Rep 1 at 6–7, HL. No such factors were relevant in *Barnard*. The inference would be that where a broad public interest in an issue clearly outweighs an individual interest, the requirement that delegation (if done to promote administrative efficiency) requires clear statutory authorisation will be relaxed. But see further the discussion of the estoppel principle below.

matter concerned. The scope of departmental activity has long been far too wide for such a rule to be practical.[59] This point did not escape the courts' attention when considering to what extent a Minister might lawfully 'delegate' her legal responsibilities.

The leading decision is *Carltona v Works Comrs.*[60] The case arose from the Commissioners use of a power granted by reg 51 of the Defence Regulations 1939 to take possession of any land if it considered it necessary to do so in the interests of public safety or defence. That Parliament should grant any powers to this body was something of an oddity, since the Commissioners had no physical existence. Their powers were actually vested by statute in the Minister of Works and Planning. The notice requisitioning Carltona's property was issued by a senior civil servant in the Ministry of Works and Planning, and it was accepted that the Minister himself had not given any personal attention to the matter. Carltona thus contended that there had been an unlawful delegation of power. In the Court of Appeal, Lord Greene MR concluded that this argument was quite misplaced:

> '[T]he functions which are given to ministers (and constitutionally given to ministers because they are constitutionally responsible) are functions so multifarious that no minister could ever personally attend to them. . . . The duties imposed upon ministers and the powers given to ministers are normally exercised under the authority of the ministers by responsible officials of the department. Public business could not be carried on if that were not the case. Constitutionally, the decision of such an official is, of course, the decision of the Minister'.[61]

In the event that such delegation was inappropriate, Lord Greene considered that the proper remedy was for the Minister to be called to account on the floor of the Commons or Lords rather than in the courts.

Carltona tells us that, in effect, no delegation occurs in these circumstances. The official is not a delegate of the Minister, but is rather her 'alter ego'. The principle has been consistently applied by the courts.[62] It is not however without complications. Six years after *Carltona*, in *Lewisham Metropolitan Borough and Town Clerk v Roberts*, Lord Denning observed that:

> 'Now I take it to be quite plain that when a Minister is entrusted with administrative as distinct from legislative functions he is entitled to act by any authorised official of his department. The Minister is not bound to give his mind to the matter personally. That is implicit in the modern machinery of government . . .. No question of agency or delegation . . . seems to me to arise at all'.[63]

This comment raised the possibility that the alter ego principle applied only to 'authorised' officials, which in turn suggests that in the absence of such authorisation, an unlawful delegation would have occurred. However, it was made clear in *R v*

[59] See pp 326–329 above. [60] [1943] 2 All ER 560, CA. [61] Ibid, at 563.

[62] See generally Lanham D (1984) 'Delegation and the alter ego principle' *LQR* 587–611.

[63] [1949] 2 KB 608 at 621, CA.

Skinner[64] that 'authorisation' could be a very informal affair. The defendant in *Skinner* appealed against his conviction for drink-driving on the basis that the Minister of Transport had unlawfully delegated her statutory power to approve breath test devices of the type used on Skinner to a senior official. The argument did not attack *Carltona* as a general principle, but tried to maintain that in situations where a ministerial decision could impact upon the liberty of the individual, the Minister should act in person rather than through an alter ego. The court saw no legal merit in that contention. The judgment also made it clear that 'authorisation' need not be explicit, but could be found simply in the official's conformity with the relevant department's established administrative routines.[65]

That the legitimate reach of the alter ego principle can be very expansive is illustrated by the House of Lords' decision in *Oladehinde v Secretary of State for the Home Department.*[66] The case involved one of the most explicit of governmental interference's with the liberty of the person; namely the power to deport foreign nationals who had overstayed their right to remain in the UK. Prior to the enactment of the Immigration Act 1988, the decision to deport had been taken in practice by a Senior Executive Officer within the Home Office. Following the passage of the Act, the Home Secretary expressly authorised a number of Immigration Inspectors to take the decision. Oladehinde's counsel suggested that since the Immigration Inspectors were technically employed under statutory powers, and so were not part of the Home Office, they could not be brought within the alter ego principle. The court rejected this proposition, observing that whatever its precise legal status, the Immigration Inspectorate had in practice 'evolved' into the Home Office's organisational structure over the years. Immigration Inspectors were comparable in seniority to the Home Office officials who had previously taken the deportation decision, and as such were appropriate figures to take those decisions after 1988. This supposition was further reinforced by the fact that the Act had explicitly required that the Home Secretary exercise certain powers in person, which raised the inference that there were no legislatively imposed limits on his/her capacity to devolve other parts of the process to his/her officials.

As Lanham has observed, the *Carltona* principle now has an expansive reach:

> '[T]he courts have moved a long way from the rule against delegation so far as powers vested in Ministers are concerned. Not only can persons other than the donee of the power actually exercise the power, there is little control either of the method of authorisation or the suitability of the person by whom the power is exercised'.[67]

This state of affairs undoubtedly oils the wheels of the administrative process within central government departments, increasing the speed and cutting the cost of decision-making. That is – in a narrow sense of the word – 'efficient'. One might however

[64] [1968] 2 QB 700, [1968] 3 All ER 124, CA.

[65] See the extracts from the cross-examination of the official concerned; ibid, at 705–706. For a similar analysis see *Re Golden Chemical Products Ltd* [1976] Ch 300, [1976] 2 All ER 543.

[66] [1990] 3 All ER 393.

[67] Op cit p 611.

wonder if the cost of that efficiency is that some decisions are made by officials who may not be properly fitted to take them. Any suggestion that the courts have been insufficiently rigorous in policing the *Carltona* principle might obviously be rebutted by pointing out that an inapposite use of the alter ego principle can be questioned within Parliament. But, as suggested in chapter five, it is naive to assume that the Commons and Lords exercise much effective control over the minutiae of governmental decision-making.

FETTERING OF DISCRETION

The rule against the fettering of discretion rests on the presumption that – except in situations where a clear statutory or common law rule obliges a government body to reach one and only one particular decision – decision-makers must give a reasoned consideration on an individuated basis as to how a power should be exercised or a duty discharged.

R v LCC, ex p Corrie[68] provides a straightforward application of the rule. The London Council (General Powers) Act 1890 s 14 gave the LCC a broadly framed power to make byelaws regulating the use of its parks. The LCC subsequently passed a byelaw which prohibited the selling of any goods in its parks unless the vendor had previously sought and received the council's permission. In response to a concern that the parks were being used for undesirable commercial activities, the LC then resolved, without changing the byelaw, that no permissions would be granted in future. Corrie wished to sell pamphlets on behalf of a charity for the blind. Her application for permission to sell them was met with the response that, in accordance with the new resolution, no permissions would be granted in future. She then applied to the courts for a writ of mandamus to force the LCC to consider her application on its individual merits, rather than in conformity with its policy.

The court unanimously granted the writ. It concluded that the LCC had been charged with a 'judicial' function, which demanded that attention be given to the individual merits of each application. It also concluded that applicants derived a 'right' from the 1890 Act. This was not a right to receive permission, but to have their applications properly considered. The corollary of this right was that the council was under an obligation to consider each application for a permit on a case-by-case basis.

However, the rule against fettering does not preclude a government body forming strong presumptions as to the way in which discretionary powers should be exercised. In other words, while a government body may adopt a policy to structure the exercise of its powers, it may not adopt a rule which exactly controls the way they are used. This point was clearly expressed by Bankes LJ in *R v Port of London Authority, ex p Kynoch Ltd*:

'There are on the one hand cases where a tribunal in the honest exercise of its discretion has

[68] [1918] 1 KB 68.

adopted a policy, and without refusing to hear an applicant, intimates to him what its policy is, and that after hearing him it will in accordance with its policy decide against him, unless there is something exceptional in his case. . . . [N]o objection could be taken to such a course. On the other hand there are cases where the tribunal has passed a rule . . . not to hear any application of a particular character by whomsoever made. There is a wide distinction to be drawn between these two classes'.[69]

This principle recognises that policy presumptions of this sort greatly ease the administrative process, in much the same way as the delegation of power within an organisation. The decision does of course raise the difficulty of deciding at what point a 'policy' has become so rigid that it mutates into a rule; the 'wide distinction' to which Bankes LJ alluded may on occasion be rather narrow.

The more recent House of Lords judgment in *British Oxygen Co Ltd v Minister of Technology*[70] confirms the broad thrust of the *Kynoch* doctrine, and might in some respects be seen as even more indulgent of administrative expediency. The Minister was empowered by s 1(1) of the Industrial Development Act 1966 to 'make to any person carrying on a business in Great Britain a grant towards approved capital expenditure . . . providing new machinery or plant'. In order to speed its decision-making process – by reducing the number of applications – the Ministry decided to institute a policy of not making grants for items valued at less than £25. British Oxygen, which had sought a grant for a great many gas cylinders costing £20 each, claimed that the 'policy' was de facto a rule, and so an unlawful fetter on the s 1 discretion. The House of Lords rejected this argument. Having approved the 'general principle' outlined in *Kynoch*, Lord Reid (in the leading judgment for a unanimous court) observed that some statutory powers might legitimately be constrained by very tight policy choices:

'I do not think that there is any great difference between a policy and a rule. . . . [A] Ministry or large authority may have had to deal already with a multitude of similar applications and then they will almost certainly have evolved a policy so precise that it could well be called a rule. There can be no objection to that – provided the authority is always willing to listen to anyone with something new to say'.[71]

The point – alluded to in *British Oxygen* – that the legality of any structuring of discretion turned on the precise substance of the statutory power/duty in issue was firmly reinforced in *A G (ex rel Tilley) v Wandsworth London Borough Council*.[72] The council was potentially under a duty to provide housing to families with children through one of two statutory routes. The first duty, under the Housing (Homeless Persons) Act 1977, removed that responsibility if a family was 'intentionally homeless'.[73] The

69 [1919] 1 KB 176 at 184, CA. 70 [1971] AC 610, [1970] 3 All ER 165, HL.

71 Ibid, at 171. Cf Viscount Dilhorne, ibid at 175: 'It seems somewhat pointless and a waste of time that the Board should have to consider applications which are bound as a result of its policy to fail'. For a less indulgent approach see *Eastleigh Borough Council v Betts* [1983] 2 AC 613, [1983] 2 All ER 1111, HL.

72 [1981] 1 All ER 1162.

73 For example because the family had been evicted from its former home because a parent had been in rent or mortgage arrears; see generally Loveland (1995) op cit.

second arose – more obliquely – under s 1 of the Children and Young Persons Act 1963, which obliged local authorities 'to make available such advice, guidance and assistance as may promote the welfare of children by diminishing the need to receive children into or keep them in [local authority] care'. In 1980, Wandsworth had adopted a policy, other than in exceptional cases, to refuse to offer housing to children and their families under the 1963 Act if the child's parents were 'intentionally homeless' and so not entitled to housing under the 1977 Act. There was some dispute at trial as to whether or not the exceptions to the 'policy' were genuine. However the Court of Appeal (upholding the High Court) suggested that even a genuine policy (ie one that admitted of exceptions) would be an unlawful fetter in respect of this particular statutory provision. In Templeman LJ's view:

> 'I am not myself persuaded that even a policy resolution hedged about with exceptions would be entirely free from attack. Dealing with children, the discretion and powers of any authority must depend entirely on the different circumstances of each child before them for consideration'.[74]

The *Tilley* judgment does not undermine the general applicability of the *British Oxygen* rationale. It does however reinforce the point that the rationale is one of general and not universal application. There is no doubt a readily discernible qualitative distinction to be drawn between governmental powers that are premised squarely on an individuated issue (ie the best interests of a child) and those relating to a generic matter (ie applications for industrial grants). One might offer as a guiding principle in this area of the law the suggestion that the permissible rigidity of a policy will vary in accordance with the degree of individuation inherent in the power to which the policy is applied. The formula is essentially tautological however. This is perhaps an area of law where the question of how 'rule-like' a policy may be is best answered by extrapolation from case law dealing with closely analogous powers, rather than by application of more general principle.

ESTOPPEL

The problems posed by the doctrine of estoppel in public law also operate at several levels. The most acute difficulty is that presented by the factual scenario in *Minister of Agriculture and Fisheries v Hulkin*.[75] Let us suppose that a government body, having misunderstood its statutory powers, grants a tenancy to an individual citizen in respect of land when it actually has no power to do so. To permit the tenancy to stand would require that we accept that the government body can act 'illegally', in the core sense of going beyond its legal powers. One might therefore assume that the 'tenancy' should be considered invalid. To hold otherwise would be to undermine the illegality principle, and so jeopardise both the sovereignty of Parliament and the rule of law in

74 [1981] 1 All ER 1162 at 1171.

75 (1948) unreported, CA, but discussed at length in *Minister of Agriculture and Fisheries v Matthews* [1950] 1 KB 148, [1994] 2 All ER 724.

their orthodox senses. Yet this might work a substantial injustice on the 'tenant'. A 'tenant' who has acted in honest reliance on the government body's power to grant a tenancy may very well have taken such steps as giving up a former tenancy, changing her job, moving her children to new schools, or spending substantial sums on decoration or refurbishment of the property. Considerations of substantive fairness might then lead us to assume that the 'tenancy' should be upheld.[76] But the position then becomes further complicated if we suggest that a third party's interests in the land concerned may be substantially compromised if the 'tenancy' is not invalidated.

In *Hulkin*, the Court of Appeal (per Lord Greene MR) had considered the matter easily resolved. Any injustice that might be done to an individual could not be invoked to sustain a substantively unlawful decision:

> '[Accepting] that the Minister had no power under the regulations to grant a tenancy, it is perfectly manifest to my mind that he could not by estoppel give himself such a power. The power given to an authority under a statute is limited to the four corners of the power given. It would entirely destroy the whole doctrine of ultra vires if it was possible for the donee to extend his power by creating an estoppel'.[77]

While obviously defensible in terms of its result, the reasoning informing Lord Greene MR's judgment is conceptually problematic from a constitutional law perspective. Hulkin's objective, to remain as a tenant, cannot be achieved by any 'extension' of the Minister's power. It is a trite point that the executive branch of the UK government has no law-making powers; its legal competence derives either from statute or common law. A Minister is no more able to extend her powers through estoppel than she is by scribbling in an additional section on a statute or announcing that she has found a new common law power. Hulkin therefore cannot succeed by estopping the Minister from 'revoking' the tenancy. The Minister cannot revoke something which she had no power to create. And even if we were to accept this flawed premise, judicial enforcement of an estoppel would not entail the *Minister* extending her powers, but the *court* doing so. An alternative characterisation of the case would be to suggest that in order to retain his 'tenancy', Hulkin would have to establish that the court was estopped from quashing the Minister's decision. This approach is however doubly flawed. The court has no pre-existing relationship with Hulkin in respect of the tenancy, and so could not be the subject of an estoppel. But more importantly, the court has no more power than a Minister to 'extend' the powers granted to the Minister by Parliament.[78] To win his case, in a manner that is compatible with orthodox notions of parliamentary sovereignty, the rule of law and the separation of powers, Hulkin must convince the court that the relevant statute[79] contains a provision to the effect that Parliament has instructed the courts that, in certain limited factual circumstances,

[76] If the grant of the tenancy was 'illegal'. [77] Cited in *Matthews* [1950] 1 KB 148, at 154.

[78] Although it could of course, in the absence of statutory limitations to the contrary, create new powers at common law.

[79] Or the common law, if a prerogative power is in issue.

they should recognise a government action as lawful even if, absent such circumstances, the action exceeds the ostensible limits of the Minister's powers.

One can offer very good reasons for assuming that a court would not embrace this approach. The imputation of such an intention to Parliament would be wholly inconsistent with orthodox principles of statutory interpretation; it would demand that the courts embrace a style of teleological construction which attached overriding importance to the avoidance of substantive injustice in certain situations. In addition to threatening orthodox notions of parliamentary sovereignty, such a strategy would raise acute problems of legal certainty. To which government acts would it apply? What criteria would an applicant have to meet to invoke it? There are thus very good 'constitutional law' explanations for Mr Hulkin not having his tenancy; but they have nothing to do with a Minister extending her powers.

The estoppel problem is much less intractable if it is not certain that binding a government body to uphold a particular course of action would result in an illegal decision. The plaintiff in *Robertson v Minister of Pensions*[80] had suffered what he claimed was a disability caused by a war-related injury. In seeking advice about his pension entitlements in respect of the injury,[81] he approached the Ministry of War. An official in that Ministry informed Mr Robertson unequivocally that the injury was attributable to his war service, and he was entitled to a pension. Acting in reliance on this statement, Mr Robertson did not take any steps to seek further, expert medical confirmation of the cause of his injury. Unbeknown to Mr Robertson, and evidently to the official at the Ministry of War, responsibility for making decisions on this question had been transferred by statute to the Ministry of Pensions some years earlier. The Ministry of Pensions subsequently ordered Mr Robertson to undergo a medical examination, on the basis of which it concluded that he was not eligible for a pension. That conclusion was then upheld by a pensions appeal tribunal, against whose decision Robertson appealed on a point of law to the High Court.

The factual gist of Mr Robertson's case was that had he sought a medical examination when he first approached the War Office, that examination would have supported his claim. His point in law was that the Ministry of Pensions was estopped from resiling from the Ministry of War's letter. Denning J decided in Mr Robertson's favour. His judgment rested on two grounds. The narrower basis of his judgment was that the War Office and the Ministry of Pensions were both part of the 'Crown': a representation or decision made by one department was therefore to be regarded as being made any other department. This is in itself a curious conclusion, insofar as it seems to extend the alter ego principle used in the delegation cases discussed above from being just an intra-departmental device to being an inter-departmental device. The principle is difficult to reconcile with the later judgment in *Lavender*, for example. But *Robertson* is most often cited for Denning J's rather broader statement of principle, evidently as applicable to statutory bodies as to the Crown:

80 [1949] 1 KB 227, [1948] 2 All ER 767.

81 That entitlement hinged on the question of whether the disability was war-related.

'In my opinion, if a government department in its dealings with a subject takes it on itself to assume authority on a matter with which he is concerned, he is entitled to rely on it having the authority which it assumes. He does not know, and cannot be expected to know, the limits of its authority'.[82]

Lord Denning took the opportunity to reiterate that broad statement of principle in the Court of Appeal in *Falmouth Boat Construction Co Ltd v Howell*.[83] Moreover, his judgment intimated that the principle would stretch to cover government officials who had made decisions that they had no legal authority to make. However, in a manner with distinct echoes of his criticism of Denning's judgment in *Magor and St Mellons*,[84] Lord Simmonds flatly rejected the proposition when the case reached the House of Lords.[85] Lord Simmonds began by restating the *Hulkin* principle: 'That which is prohibited cannot be lawfully done . . ., and if it cannot be lawfully done it cannot be the subject of a claim enforceable at law'.[86] He then poured a substantial amount of jurisprudential cold water on Denning's *Robertson* principle:

'My Lords, I know of no such principle in our law nor was any authority for it cited. The illegality of an act is the same whether or not the actor has been misled by an assumption of authority on the part of a government officer however high or low in the hierarchy'.[87]

This is a simple restatement of orthodox constitutional theory, and has compelling force in respect of decisions made in excess of the decision-makers' powers. But it has no obvious bearing on 'estoppel' situations where the citizen is attempting to bind an authority to a decision that would be lawful, but which for policy reasons the relevant authority decides it does not want to respect. For this reason, the High Court's judgment in *Southend-on-Sea Corpn v Hodgson (Wickford) Ltd*[88] is rather unsatisfactory. Hodgson had bought a property with a view to using it as a builder's yard. A senior official in the local authority had told them that the site had long been used for such purposes, and no planning permission was necessary for that use. It subsequently emerged that the official was mistaken. The local authority then decided not to grant planning permission, even though it was arguably entitled to do so as a matter of law. The High Court seemed to conclude that it was not possible in any circumstances for a government body to be bound by such a representation, on the basis that an estoppel would improperly fetter the exercise of its discretion. This seems an unnecessarily inflexible conclusion. A more sensible way to approach the issue might be to suggest that avoiding inflicting a substantial burden on a citizen who has relied in good faith on mistaken advice is a relevant consideration when the authority considers how to proceed. That concern should not determine the eventual outcome, since estopping the authority might work an injustice on third parties. On these facts,

82 [1948] 2 All ER 767 at 770.
83 [1950] 2 KB 16, [1950] 1 All ER 538, CA.
84 See pp 74–76 above.
85 [1951] AC 837, [1951] 2 All ER 278, HL.
86 Ibid, at 844.
87 Ibid, at 845. See also Lord Normand at 849: 'But it is certain that neither a minister nor any subordinate officer of the Crown can by any conduct or representation bar the Crown from enforcing a statutory prohibition or entitle the subject to maintain that there was no breach of it'.
88 [1962] 1 QB 416, [1961] 2 All ER 46.

for example, it is quite likely that had Hodgson applied for planning permission, the application would have been opposed by neighbours, whose opinions may have led the council not to grant permission. If the council is bound by its official's mistake, the third parties are deprived of their entitlement to participate in the decision-making process and suffer the perhaps unwelcome presence of a builder's yard near their homes.

Yet the judicial pendulum seemed to swing too far in the other direction in the Court of Appeal's judgment in *Lever Finance Ltd v Westminster (City) London Borough Council*, a case resting on facts very similar to those at issue in *Hodgson.*[89] Denning suggested that, in practice, many planning authorities de facto delegated their powers to senior officers, even though – until the passage of s 64 of the Planning Act 1968 – they had not de jure been entitled to do so.[90] A citizen acting in good faith was thus entitled to assume that decisions taken by officials within the scope of their 'ostensible authority' would be binding. That this result might prejudice the interests of equally blameless third parties did not seem to enter into Lord Denning's reasoning.[91]

This principle was rejected by a differently constituted Court of Appeal in *Western Fish Products Ltd v Penwith District Council.*[92] The court held that an authority could only be bound to respect a representation mistakenly made by one of its officers – if the representation led to a decision within the scope of its powers – in limited circumstances. The court laid particular stress on the need for the citizen to establish that he/she had strong grounds for believing that the representee actually had the legal power to make the relevant decision. It also intimated that an estoppel should be upheld only if the outcome would not work an injustice on third parties.

The substantive problems raised by the estoppel scenario have continued to exercise the courts in recent years. However, the classification of the problems has undergone a change – even if their substantive content has remained unaltered. As we shall see in chapter fifteen, the *Lever/Western Fish* issue now tends to be seen as a facet of the procedural irregularity doctrine; a reclassification which perhaps offers greater scope for the kind of innovative solution discussed above to the constitutional problem posed by 'illegal' estoppels.[93]

89 [1971] 1 QB 222, [1970] 3 All ER 496.

90 It will be recalled that the *Carltona* alter ego principle applies only to Ministers; it does not embrace non-ministerial government bodies.

91 It is also difficult to characterise Lever Finance as an 'ignorant citizen' on these facts. It was, after all, a property development company, a body one might sensibly expect to be wholly familiar with the legal structure of the planning process.

92 [1981] 2 All ER 204, CA.

93 On the closely related principle of res judicata see: *Re 56 Denton Road, Twickenham* [1953] Ch 51, [1952] 2 All ER 799; *Rootkin v Kent County Council* [1981] 1 WLR 1186, Bradley A (1981) 'Administrative justice and the binding effects of official acts' *Current legal Problems* 1–20: Akehurst M (1982) 'Revocation of administrative decisions' *Public Law* 613–627.

II. IRRATIONALITY

Like the ground of illegality, irrationality is concerned with the substantive content of a government decision. However, it is more readily regarded as being concerned with the political or moral rather than (in the strict sense) legal character of the decision concerned.[94]

The formula used by Lord Diplock in *GCHQ* to define the irrationality doctrine might suggest that very few government decisions could be unlawful on this ground. In Lord Diplock's view, irrationality only arose if a decision was:

'. . . so outrageous in its defiance of logic or of accepted moral standards that no sensible person who had applied his mind to the question to be decided could have arrived at it'.[95]

The test then is not simply that the decision defies logic or accepted moral standards; nor even that it defies these criteria to an outrageous extent; rather it requires the defiance to be *so* outrageous. This form of words is perhaps even more indulgent of executive autonomy on 'moral' grounds than Lord Greene MR's phraseology in *Wednesbury*: 'something so absurd that no sensible person could ever dream that it lay within the powers of the authority'.[96]

It is often suggested that in applying the irrationality test the court has no concern with the substantive merits of the decision being challenged. That is a rather unfortunate and misleading characterisation however. The irrationality test certainly does not permit a court to impose its own preferred solution on the decision-making body. But the court is concerned to establish if the substantive decision has *any merit at all*. If the decision lacks that quality entirely, it will be unlawful. In that limited sense, the irrationality test is concerned with the political merits of government decisions.

A local authority – empowered by statute to employ teachers on such terms as it thinks fit – which refused to employ a teacher because she had red hair would be making an obviously irrational decision. But one which decided to employ only teachers with Master's degrees, or more than five years previous teaching experience, would not be acting irrationally, even if many other authorities set much less exacting standards. If irrationality is construed in this expansive way, it is easy to see why the policies in issue in such cases as *Kruse v Johnson*,[97] or *Wednesbury*[98] itself, did not come within the test. We have already seen however that the irrationality test seems

[94] For a more sophisticated account, which breaks the ground down into several discrete sub-heads, see Walker P (1995) 'What's wrong with irrationality' *Public Law* 556–576.

[95] [1985] AC 374 at 410–411, HL.

[96] [1948] 1 KB 223 at 229, CA. Although one might suggest that subsequent commentators have overlooked Lord Greene MR's use of the word 'dream', rather than for example 'consider' or 'conclude'. Departures from normality are an integral element of dreams; irrationality would presumably then only arise if the content of the decision lay not just in, but at the extreme edge of the realm of fantasy.

[97] A ban on playing loud musical instruments in residential areas; see pp 361–362 above.

[98] Excluding children from the cinema on Sunday mornings; see pp 361–362 above.

sometimes to be deployed in a much more restrictive fashion. The Court of Appeal in *Wheeler v Leicester City Council* saw no merit in the suggestion that the council's use of s 71 of the Race Relations Act 1976 was irrational, yet the House of Lords – in a judgment decided at much the same time as *GCHQ* – held that the council's action did fall within the test.[99] This conclusion is difficult to sustain. The council's action may have been misguided, or ineffective, or counter-productive, or just plain stupid; but those characteristics, singly or in combination, do not amount to the extreme departure from logic or prevailing moral standards that the Diplock/Greene tests seemingly require.

The conclusion is even harder to sustain in respect of the House of Lords' judgment in *Roberts v Hopwood*.[100] That a decision is illegal does not mean that it is also irrational. A decision-maker might after the most careful and sensible consideration of a particular course of action proceed on the basis of a misunderstanding of her legal powers. That may be unlawful, but it is a mistake that could be made by the most prudent of persons. But it is extremely difficult to sustain the argument that a decision is irrational if it enjoys widespread support. Poplar's wage policy undoubtedly enjoyed such support among local voters. To conclude that the substance of the policy was per se irrational thus demands that we conclude that the Labour Party's supporters at the local elections had all taken leave of their senses. Collective hysteria is, admittedly, not an unknown phenomenon. But the courts might be venturing into rather dangerous political territory if they were explicitly to maintain that a widely-held belief amounted to an outrageous defiance of accepted moral standards.[101] The opinions offered in the Court of Appeal in *Roberts* seem more satisfactory on this point. Scrutton LJ approached the question of irrationality in the light of the principle of 'benevolent interpretation' propounded by Lord Russell in *Kruse v Johnson*. Poplar's wages were undoubtedly in excess of market equivalents, in some instances substantially so. Such wages might have been irrational if fixed by a non-elected body. But the fact that the council was a representative assembly lent the concept of irrationality an additionally expansive character; it was therefore a test which a council was unlikely to fail.

Yet one can also point to cases in which the courts have explicitly accepted the 'benevolent interpretation' rationale but still invoked irrationality to invalidate government decisions which would appear to have a plausible basis. One such case is the Court of Appeal's decision in *Hall & Co Ltd v Shoreham-by-Sea UDC*.[102] Hall had sought planning permission to develop a plot of land close to a main road for industrial purposes. Councils were empowered by the Town and Country Planning Act 1947, s 14 to grant permission unconditionally or 'subject to such conditions as they think fit'. When approving Hall's application, the council required that the company

[99] [1985] AC 1054; see pp 382–385 above. [100] See pp 362–364 above.

[101] It must be stressed that the level of popular support for a particular policy has no bearing at all on the policy's legality; that is a technical matter which only judges are competent to determine.

[102] [1964] 1 WLR 240, CA.

also provide an ancillary access road, open to public traffic, which would reduce the prospect of delays being caused on the main road. Hall contended, inter alia, that the condition was irrational, as it imposed on the company the burden of building and maintaining what was in effect a public highway. The High Court rejected this argument, concluding that the condition obviously bore a sensible relation to legitimate planning concerns.[103]

This judgment was reversed in the Court of Appeal.[104] Willmer LJ's judgment accepted that; '[planning] conditions imposed by a local authority, like byelaws, should be benevolently construed, and in this connection I would venture to follow the same approach as Lord Russell of Kilowen CJ in *Kruse v Johnson*'.[105] He also accepted that the 'objective' that the planning condition was intended to achieve was 'a perfectly reasonable one'. However, while the objective was acceptable, the means chosen to achieve it were not. This was evidently because the condition imposed an unduly onerous burden on the plaintiffs. The objective would more appropriately be achieved by the council building a new public highway itself. This reasoning is difficult to support. One might accept that there were several 'better' ways for the council to achieve its planning objectives. That does not per se mean that the method actually chosen was irrational.

A similar rationale was deployed by the High Court in *R v Hillingdon London Borough Council, ex p Royco Homes Ltd.*[106] The council had attached several conditions to the grant of planning permission for Royco's proposed housing application. One condition required that the houses be offered to people on the council's own housing waiting list. The court held that the condition was irrational because it 'requir[ed] the applicants to take on at their own expense a significant part of the duty of the council as a housing authority'.[107]

Widgery LJ's own analysis would suggest that both *Hall* and *Shoreham* might better be classified as illegality cases, consistent in effect with a narrow construction of *Conegate*. In both cases the council was essentially levying a tax on the applicants, through the indirect route of demanding that they provide a substantial public service as the price of being granted planning permission.[108]

Two rather more satisfactory applications of the irrationality doctrine have latterly been offered by the House of Lords in *Brind v Secretary of State for the Home Department*[109] and by the Court of Appeal in *R v Ministry of Defence, ex p Smith*.[110] The *Brind* litigation was provoked by the government's efforts to address the problem of terrorism in Northern Ireland. The government formed the opinion that the terrorists' causes would be hindered if the radio and television media were not permitted to broadcast statements made by members of terrorist organisations or by members of political parties which the government designated as supportive of such groups. The

103 (1963) 61 LGR 508. 104 [1964] 1 WLR 240. 105 Ibid, at 245. 106 [1974] QB 720.
107 Ibid, at 732.
108 Cf Willmer LJ in *Hall* [1964] 1 WLR 240 at 249: '[the condition] amounts in effect to a requirement that the plaintiffs shall dedicate the ancillary road when it is built to the public'.
109 [1991] 1 All ER 720. 110 [1996] QB 517, [1996] 1 All ER 257, CA.

ban extended however only to the speaker's actual voice; her words could be quoted verbatim by reporters, or, as frequently happened, dubbed by actors. Prime Minister Thatcher evidently believed the measure would deprive terrorists of the 'oxygen of publicity'.[111] The Home Secretary assumed he could impose the ban on the IBA[112] under the powers granted to him by the Broadcasting Act 1981, s 29:

'. . . the Secretary of State may at any time by notice in writing require the authority to refrain from broadcasting any matter or classes of matter specified in the notice'.[113]

Brind was a journalist who considered that the ban was ultra vires s 29, and thus unlawfully infringed free expression. He based his arguments on several grounds. The first is considered here. The others are addressed at a later stage. Brind firstly contended that the ban was irrational. The court saw little merit in that argument. Lord Bridge thought it was 'impossible' to reach that conclusion: 'In any civilised country the defeat of the terrorist is a public interest of the highest importance . . .. What is perhaps surprising is that the restriction is of such limited scope'.[114]

Similarly, Lord Ackner considered it entirely understandable that the government had concluded that terrorists enhanced their legitimacy by appearing on television and radio. There is little scope for disagreeing with this dismissal of the irrationality point. The test applies only to ludicrously illogical or morally outrageous decisions. The government's decision in *Brind* seems well within the range of views that reasonable people might hold. The policy may indeed have been ill-advised, and was probably counterproductive, but ineffectiveness and a lack of wisdom do not amount to irrationality.

The government policy at issue in *Smith*[115] was the long-standing practice that people of homosexual/lesbian sexual orientation were not permitted to serve in the United Kingdom's armed forces. The prohibition applied simply on grounds of abstract sexual orientation; there was no requirement that the orientation manifest itself in any tangible way. Nor could the prohibition be overcome by a particular soldier's service record; even the most exemplary of recruits would be discharged from the service if it became known that he/she was not heterosexual. The justification for the policy, which was implemented through the government's prerogative powers, was that the presence of known homosexuals/lesbians in the armed forces would compromise military efficiency, expose young recruits to sexual exploitation,

[111] Extracts from the speech made by Douglas Hurd, then Home Secretary, when explaining the ban to the Commons are reproduced in Lord Ackner's opinion at 729. Interestingly (since the case preceded *Pepper v Hart*), Lord Ackner did not seem to think that this reference to *Hansard* was precluded by parliamentary privilege or Article 9 of the Bill of Rights.

[112] The Independent Broadcasting Authority, the body responsible for regulating commercial television and radio services.

[113] In respect of the BBC, the Home Secretary assumed that he could issue the ban under cl 13(4) of the BBC's licensing agreement with the government, which provided that: 'The Secretary of State may from time to time . . . require the Corporation to refrain . . . from sending any matter or matters of any class . . .'.

[114] Ibid, at 724. [115] [1996] 1 All ER 257, CA.

and cause difficulties in the context of the communal living arrangements which the armed forces used.

Like the applicant in *Brind*, Smith contended that the policy was unlawful on several grounds. At this juncture, we consider only the irrationality argument. Smith's counsel contended that one might marshall several arguments to suggest that the policy was ill-advised and unnecessary. A soldier's sexual orientation was not a bar to military service in several other NATO and Commonwealth countries, which would suggest that military effectiveness was not compromised by employing gay men and lesbians. Similarly, within the United Kingdom, gay men and lesbians were permitted to work in the police and fire services; both of which were professions in which co-operative work was essential. It also seemed beyond dispute that – especially during World War II – a great many openly gay men had served with conspicuous distinction in the army, navy and air force. If their presence did not, under those most acute of circumstances, compromise military efficiency, how could the presence of non-heterosexual servicemen do so in the present day?

These might all be regarded as perfectly valid arguments, and in combination would suggest there was much to be said in favour of altering the policy. It also seems evident that both the High Court and Court of Appeal in *Smith* found them to be convincing.[116] As Lord Bingham put it, this shift in public and professional attitudes had a significant bearing on the defensibility of the government's policy:

'I regard the progressive development and refinement of public and professional opinion at home and abroad . . . as an important feature of this case. A belief which represented unquestioned orthodoxy in Year X, may have become questionable by Year Y, and unsustainable by Year Z'.[117]

But mustering a plausible, even a strong argument in favour of changing a governmental policy has no obvious bearing on whether or not that policy is irrational. The pertinent test is whether there is some plausible argument in favour of the policy. In respect of the ban on gay men and lesbians serving in the armed forces, that proviso seemed to be met. The Minister could point to the fact that in both 1986 and 1991 the ban had been reconsidered by the Commons Defence Select Committee; on both occasions the Committee recommended its retention.[118] He had also conducted a survey of opinion within the armed services, which revealed widespread opposition to any removal of the ban. These reinforcements of the government's view precluded the finding that the policy was irrational: 'The threshold of irrationality is a high one. It

[116] For further discussion see Norris M (1996) '*Ex p Smith*: irrationality and human rights' *Public Law* 590–600.

[117] [1996] 1 All ER 257 at 263, CA.

[118] The Court did not address the question – mooted in chapter five – of whether one could plausibly consider Conservative dominated select committees to have been willing and able to form a view independently of the Thatcher and Major governments' wishes on a matter like this.

was not crossed in this case'.[119] In Lord Bingham MR's chronological scheme, Smith was discharged in 'Year Y', and not 'Year Z'.[120]

Smith raises an important issue of what – for want of a better term – we might call common law policy. The Minister's survey of opinion in the armed forces revealed that much opposition to removing the ban was rooted in violent and bigoted beliefs. Illustrative of this point are comments such as:

> 'If a homosexual was on board he will have an accident waiting for him when no-one is looking . . . [Royal Naval able seaman]
>
> I would never serve in a unit where a known homosexual is serving and I like many others would quite happily smash their faces in if I found any in my unit . . . [Corporal, Royal Signals Service]
>
> I would not give first aid to a homosexual under any circumstances [RAF Senior Aircraftsman]'.[121]

The question of principle which then arises is whether the presumption that a government decision which enjoys appreciable levels of public support cannot be irrational should be rebutted if that support is premised on bigoted opinion? In this context, the 'red hair' scenario is an unhelpful analytical tool. One assumes that a ban on redheads serving in the army would be bigoted in a moral sense and also irrational in the legal sense. Yet that particular policy is hardly one that will attract widespread approval. The court would thus be spared the difficulty of deciding how a widely held belief could amount to an 'outrageous defiance of accepted moral standards'. If the government and members of the armed forces and the great majority of the public were to be seized with anti-red haired sentiment, however, it is difficult to conclude that a ban on redheads would be irrational.

A court would enter problematic constitutional territory if it were to assume that 'rationality' must have an objective meaning, irrespective of how widely approved a particular policy may be. Judicial excursions of that sort do perhaps take the common law too close to the moral/political merits of a decision. This is not to say that the decision must therefore be lawful; it may still fail the tests of illegality or procedural fairness. But these tests of course relate to (and here our terminology necessarily becomes rather obscure) the esoteric, legal merits of the decision; not to its exoteric, moral merits. The argument that the courts might legitimately approach that second category of the merits more closely than the irrationality doctrine permits has however been a lively one since 1985, when Lord Diplock suggested in *GCHQ* that the doctrine of 'proportionality' might soon come to play a role in English administrative law.

119 [1996] 1 All ER 257 at 266, CA; per Lord Bingham.

120 Intriguingly however, Lord Bingham MR did indicate that we might have moved from Year Y to Year Z in the two years between Smith being discharged and the court delivering its opinion; ibid, at 266.

121 The quotes are taken from a report in *The Guardian*, 5 March 1996.

III. PROPORTIONALITY – A NEW GROUND OF REVIEW?

By the mid-1980s, the proportionality principle was an established feature in the administrative law of several of the UK's partner countries within the EC. It was also, more pertinently, an integral part of the so-called general principles of community law established by the ECJ.[122] This meant that whenever the UK courts were addressing the legality of government action within the area of Community competence, the doctrine would provide an additional substantive ground of review.

There is no entirely straightforward way to define the principle. But some indication of its scope can be gleaned from consideration of the cases in which it has been applied by the ECJ. A useful example is offered in *Bela-Mühle Josef Bergmann KG v Grows-Farm GmbH & Co KG.*[123] The case concerned a regulation passed by the Council for the purpose of reducing the vast over-supply of skimmed milk powder in the Community. The regulation attempted to compel farmers to use animal feed derived from skimmed milk powder rather than soya. Soya-based feeds were however only 1/3 of the price of the milk products. The legality of the regulation was successfully challenged, on the basis that it imposed far too onerous a burden on farmers, and was thus a disproportionate measure.

The principle is as readily applicable to the actions of member states as to Community institutions. *Re Watson and Belmann*,[124] concerned an attempt by the Belgian government to establish that Treaty Article 48(3) entitled it to deport workers from other member states if they had failed to comply with administrative requirements to register their presence with the local police. The ECJ accepted that member states had a legitimate interest in keeping accurate records of non-national workers. It also accepted that a registration requirement was a lawful means to pursue this end, and that imposing punishments on workers who failed to register was an appropriate way to enforce the requirement. However it also concluded that deportation was too serious a punishment to apply to worker who failed to register. A fine would be the proportionate response in such circumstances.

As Steiner notes in reviewing this strand of the EC's case law, proportionality: 'puts the burden on an administrative authority to justify its actions and requires some consideration of alternatives. In this respect, it is a more rigorous test than one based on reasonableness'.[125] In other words, the test requires that the court looks much

[122] The leading critique is offered by Jowell J and Lester A (1988) 'Proportionality: neither novel nor dangerous', in Jowell J and Oliver D (eds) *New directions in judicial review* (London: Sweet and Maxwell). See for example Hartley T (4th edn, 1998) *The foundations of European Community law* ch 5 (Oxford: Clarendon Press); Craig P and de Burca G (2nd edn, 1998) *EU Law* pp 349–357 (Oxford: Clarendon Press); de Burca G (1993) 'The principle of proportionality and its application in EC law' *YEL* 105–130.

[123] Case 114/76: [1977] ECR 1211, ECJ; popularly known as the 'Skimmed milk powder case'.

[124] Case 118/75: [1976] ECR 1185, ECJ.

[125] (3rd edn, 1992) *EC law* p 58 (London: Blackstone).

more closely at the political merits of a decision than it does under the irrationality doctrine.

In general terms, the proportionality test asks: firstly whether the government body is acting in pursuit of a legitimate objective; if so, it asks secondly whether attaining that objective necessarily demands that the body interfere with a presumptively lawful entitlement possessed by an individual or company; if so, it asks thirdly if the government body had chosen the means to its legitimate end which interferes as little as possible with the presumptive entitlements.

Many of the government actions we have considered against the irrationality principle would no doubt pass a proportionality test. In *Wednesbury*, for example, the council's legitimate aim would be to encourage children to go to church or play sports on Sunday mornings. This interferes both with the children's entitlement to attend the cinema, and the cinema owners' entitlement to sell its seats. But the interference is a modest one. Had the prohibition extended throughout the weekend, it would most likely have failed a proportionality test, but still passed muster against the yardstick of irrationality. Similarly, in *Kruse v Johnson*, proportionality would demand that a breach of the byelaw merited only a modest fine. A large fine, while not necessarily irrational, would probably be disproportionate. Relatedly, one might sensibly conclude that the policy at issue in *Brind* would not have been disproportionate. The Home Secretary's interference with Brind's capacity to do his job as a television reporter was so trivial in scope that it is hard to imagine a less restrictive way for the government to pursue its legitimate aim of depriving terrorist supporters of publicity.

Smith raises rather different issues. Insofar as the government's policy was pandering to bigotry among service personnel, it would not have been pursuing a legitimate aim. As such, it would have fallen at the first stage of the test. And if the aim was the legitimate one of safeguarding operational efficiency, that might have better been achieved by a policy forbidding inappropriate sexual behaviour than one proscribing particular sexual orientations.

Proportionality could thus be seen as constitutionally problematic in both a substantive and jurisdictional sense. The substantive problem arises because proportionality might be characterised as something close to an appellate jurisdiction, which requires courts to substitute their own views of the best way for a government body to achieve a particular objective for that of the designated decision-maker. The second problem arises because appellate jurisdiction is a statutory rather than common law creation. For the courts to modify the common law to produce a new ground of review which came close, in de facto terms, to giving the judiciary an appellate jurisdiction would in a functional if not formal sense amount to a usurpation of legislative power.

These objections were forcefully stated by several members of the House of Lords in *Brind*, in which the plaintiff had invoked proportionality as a second ground of challenge to the Home Secretary's action. As suggested above, it seems unlikely that the policy would have failed a proportionality test. But for the majority of the court, this was not a question that ought even to be asked. Lord Roskill – having referred to

Lord Diplock's suggestion in *GCHQ* that proportionality might some day emerge as a new ground of review – continued:

'I am clearly of the view that the present is not a case in which the first step can be taken for the reason that to apply that principle in the present case would be for the court to substitute its own judgment of what was needed to achieve a particular objective for the judgment of the Secretary of State upon whom that duty has been laid by Parliament'.[126]

For the same reason, Lord Ackner concluded that: 'there appears to me to be at present no basis upon which the proportionality doctrine . . . can be followed by the courts of this country'.[127] Lord Lowry was equally forceful: '[T]here can be very little room for judges to operate an independent judicial review proportionality doctrine in the space which is left between the conventional judicial review doctrine and the admittedly forbidden appellate approach'.[128]

These objections are not compelling. Notwithstanding their Lordships' sentiments to the contrary, proportionality does not by any means demand that the court adopts an essentially appellate jurisdiction. Properly construed, irrationality is such a lax test that there should be plenty of legitimate jurisprudential scope for the courts to place further limits on the political merits of government decisions without setting themselves up as appellate tribunals. The only reason for assuming that no such scope exists is if the courts are actually misapplying the irrationality doctrine, and using it improperly as a device to sail unacceptably close to the detailed political merits of government decisions: to move any closer to the merits from that position would, of course, be to assume a de facto appellate jurisdiction.

There is some indication that this has indeed happened on occasion. *Hall v Shoreham UDC* is perhaps the most obvious example of this, in so far as the court explicitly labelled the council's policy as irrational because there were 'better' ways (ie methods that impacted much less heavily on the applicant) for the council to achieve its policies. Jowell and Lester's influential analysis of the proportionality issue also suggests that Lord Roskill's judgment in *Wheeler* is another example of this phenomenon.[129] Rather less convincingly, they argue that *Congreve* and *Bromley v GLC* can be explained in a similar way. This suggestion perhaps rather blurs the issue, as both cases could readily be defended as instances of the courts using a quite narrow application of the illegality doctrine.

More helpfully, Jowell and Lester identify cases in which the courts seem quite openly to have advocated use of a proportionality test. The most regularly cited illustration of this point is the Court of Appeal's judgment in *R v Barnsley Metropolitan Borough Council, ex p Hook*.[130] Hook was a stall-holder in Barnsley market, whose licence was terminated by the council after he became involved in an abusive altercation with two council street cleaners who had admonished him for urinating in

126 [1991] 1 All ER 720 at 725, HL. 127 Ibid, at 735. 128 Ibid, at 739.

129 (1988) op cit.

130 [1976] 3 All ER 452, [1976] 1 WLR 1052, CA. Jowell and Lester also cite *R v Brent London Borough Council, ex p Assegai* (1987) Times, 18 June.

the street.[131] In attempting to sanction Mr Hook for this behaviour, the council was presumably pursuing a legitimate end, whether it be safeguarding its employees from threatening abuse or encouraging stallholders to respect rudimentary standards of hygiene. Lord Denning nonetheless intimated[132] that the sanction was excessive:

> 'So in this case, if Mr Hook did misbehave, I should have thought the right thing would have been to take him before the magistrates under the bye-laws, when some small fine should have been inflicted. It is quite wrong that the Barnsley Council should inflict upon him the grave penalty of depriving him of his livelihood. That is a far more serious penalty than anything the magistrates could inflict'.[133]

One might plausibly argue that the sanction was not disproportionately severe, given the undesirability of market traders spraying their urine over the streets and verbally abusing the council employees responsible for cleaning up the mess. Herein lies the practical difficulty of the proportionality doctrine; namely that it requires courts to invalidate decisions that many observers might consider quite sensible.

It is hardly surprising that many judges, unlike Lord Denning, might cavil at admitting so candidly that they are placing tight restrictions on the range of politically meritorious decisions that government bodies may lawfully make. Nonetheless, the requirement that proportionality be applied by UK courts in matters raising questions of EC law creates an obvious inconsistency in domestic administrative law, in both jurisdictional and substantive terms. Proportionality would thus have seemed another good candidate to be caught up in the 'ripple effect' of EC law. However as we shall see in subsequent chapters, the courts have latterly been spared the difficulty of taking the step that Lord Diplock canvassed in *GCHQ* by a legislative initiative undertaken by the Blair government.

CONCLUSION

It is readily apparent that the substantive grounds of review comprise a fluid area of administrative law. This is not just because, in the broader sense, wholly new common law grounds of review may gradually emerge. It is also because the boundaries of long-established grounds are themselves somewhat unpredictable in scope. These characteristics are not however unique to the substantive grounds of review. As suggested in the following chapter, much the same argument might be made in respect of the procedural grounds of review.

131 Curiously, most references to the case tend to omit the abusive altercation, which is perhaps a more serious matter than peeing in the gutter.

132 The case was actually decided on an issue of procedural irregularity.

133 [1976] 1 WLR 1052 at 1057–1058, CA.

15

PROCEDURAL GROUNDS OF JUDICIAL REVIEW

One might intuitively wonder what useful purpose would be served by subjecting governmental action to a ground of judicial review concerned not with the content or substance of a given decision, but with the way the decision was made. If the outcome of the decision-making process was neither illegal nor irrational, it would be entirely possible for the government body whose decision was unlawful because of a procedural flaw to remake the decision, this time correcting its procedural error, and to produce precisely the same substantive result. It may be thought that all that is thereby achieved is to slow down, and increase the cost of, government decision-making, while at the same time embroiling the courts in fruitless litigation. Two forceful arguments can be asserted to rebut this proposition.[1]

The first argument speaks to the instrumental value of a concern with procedural standards. It would maintain that there is a linkage between the substance of a decision and the way in which the decision is made. An insistence on a particular type of procedure may enhance the likelihood that the content of the decision is not just legal/rational in the narrow sense, but that it represents – if not the best choice – then at least a good choice within the range of alternatives open to the government body. There is no cast-iron guarantee that this happy state of affairs would be achieved. But it might easily be conceded that there is a fair probability that this would occur.

The second argument is concerned with the intrinsic importance of fair procedures. In a narrow vein, this argument would maintain that individuals who are intimately affected by a particular decision will be more likely to accept its legitimacy if they consider that they have been treated with a sufficient degree of seriousness and respect by the relevant decision-maker. More broadly, it might be thought that we all as citizens are more likely to accept the legitimacy of the governmental process as a whole if government decision-makers are known to be prevented from acting in arbitrary or capricious ways.

Within the Anglo-American political and legal tradition, the paradigmatic example

[1] See Richardson G (1986) 'The duty to give reasons: potential and practice' *Public Law* 437–469: Craig P (2nd edn, 1989) *Administrative law* ch 7 (London: Sweet and Maxwell): Craig P (1994) 'The common law, reasons and administrative justice' *Cambridge LJ* 282–302. For a sophisticated treatment of the issue in the American administrative law context see Mashaw J (1976) 'The Supreme Court's due process calculus for administrative adjudication in *Matthews v Eldridge . . .*' *University of Chicago LR* 28–59.

of procedural fairness is perhaps provided by the criminal trial in respect of a serious crime. It might be thought that in respect of this particular facet of governmental decision-making the most rigorous of procedural standards should apply. This would include such factors as the accused knowing in great detail the nature of the case against her; that she be given ample time to prepare her own arguments; that she be afforded the assistance of expert legal advisers; that she or her counsel be permitted to cross-examine prosecution witnesses and to call witnesses of her own; that there be stringent rules concerning the admissibility of evidence; and that the jury (which would decide guilt or innocence) and the judge (who would preside over the trial and if necessary impose a sentence) would approach their tasks without any pre-existing personal or political bias inclining them towards a guilty verdict. The trial process is distinctly 'red light' in nature, in so far as it is designed to offer substantial protection to the interests of the accused (ie in her continued liberty) against governmental interference.

Such stringent procedures are intended to maximise the possibility that the decision-making process produces the 'correct' outcome. But it is readily apparent that the criminal trial demands extremely heavy investment in time and money. The process is expensive and slow. It would hardly seem feasible to subject all aspects of governmental decision-making processes to such a rigorous procedural regime. And as the scope of governmental intervention in economic or social affairs increases, so the need to distance the conduct of much governmental decision-making from this idealised procedural regime becomes more acute.

That prosaic concern is reinforced by more abstract considerations deriving from the notion of the separation of powers. The determination of guilt in a criminal trial is manifestly a 'judicial' function, in which the court's responsibility is to make a finding as to the precise merits of the issue before it. Since much governmental decision-making has been entrusted by Parliament to the executive rather than the judiciary, it can readily be presumed that there is no legislative expectation that it conform to judicial models. Nonetheless, executive decisions can impact substantially upon questions of great importance to individual citizens. Liversidge's detention by Sir John Anderson is an obvious example of this, as is the Inland Revenue Commissioners' seizure of Rossminster's files and papers. Much executive action is, in contrast, dealing with ostensibly rather trivial issues. One might intuitively suppose that this notion of there being a 'hierarchy of rights' in terms of the substantive impact of government decisions would also be reflected in common law requirements imposing varying levels of procedural rigour on the particular decision in issue.

English law on the question of procedural fairness (or as the issue was traditionally styled, 'natural justice') is essentially concerned with striking a balance between these competing considerations. This area of administrative law is generally accepted to be divisible into two distinct parts. The first is often referred to under the Latin maxim *audi alterem partem*; the literal translation is that 'the other side must be heard', and is generally taken to mean that a person affected by a governmental decision should be afforded some opportunity to present his/her case to the decision-maker and that she should be given a reasonably clear indication of the case that may be made against her. The second, often referred to under the label *nemo iudex sua causa* (literally – 'no-one shall be judge in her own cause'), addresses the question of to what extent it is permissible for a decision-maker to have – or to be suspected to have – a personal bias in respect of a decision she has made.

This chapter attempts to explain the way in which the courts have used the procedural fairness doctrine by focusing on a number of leading cases to identify the values which appear to be shaping the content of the law. The bulk of the chapter is concerned with case law drawn from the 'modern' (ie post 1960) era. But it is perhaps helpful to preface that part of the chapter by paying brief attention to a number of seminal decisions from earlier periods.

I. AUDI ALTEREM PARTEM – THE RIGHT TO A FAIR HEARING

A recurrent (if not ever present) theme in much of the early case law on the *audi alterem partem* principle is the courts' attempt to draw a distinction between, on the one hand, government decisions which affected the 'rights' of individuals and, on the other, those which impacted only on matters of 'privilege'. Relatedly, much judicial energy was expended on determining if a given executive decision should be classified as '(quasi)-judicial' or 'administrative' in nature. These distinctions may be thought to have an obvious jurisprudential root in Diceyan theory as to the purpose of the rule of law. If that purpose is, inter alia, to protect private rights and liberties against the executive, it is important to establish when such rights are in issue, for the consequence of their being put in jeopardy would be that the government's decision-making process (absent a clear legislative indication to the contrary) would be expected to correspond if only in broad terms to a judicial model. Alternatively, it might be contended that Parliament has on occasion – irrespective of whether or not the statutory power in issue affects individual rights – required executive bodies to act in a quasi-judicial fashion. If this has been done explicitly, there is no difficulty in concluding that the bodies' decision-making procedures must closely resemble the judicial model. If the statute is silent on the point, that conclusion becomes more problematic, insofar as it would have to rest on judicial presumptions as to the extent to which Parliament has impliedly 'contracted in'[2] to existing common law principles. The pervasive difficulty however, which is revealed by examining several leading cases, is in finding generalisable criteria with which to draw a distinction between 'rights' and 'privileges' and/or 'quasi-judicial' and 'administrative' functions.

[2] See p 70 above.

THE INITIAL RISE, DILUTION AND FALL OF THE AUDI ALTEREM PARTEM PRINCIPLE

One of the most forceful assertions of the *audi alterem partem* principle in the Victorian era is offered in *Cooper v Wandsworth Board of Works.*[3] Section 76 of the Metropolis Management Act 1855 introduced a limited form of land use planning control. It provided that new buildings should not be erected unless the relevant local Board of Works[4] had been given seven days notice of the project, and also empowered the Board to demolish any buildings erected in breach of this provision. The text of the Act did not expressly require any hearing to be carried out prior to demolition. Cooper had apparently begun to erect a building without giving the requisite notice. The Board then demolished the building overnight.

Mr Cooper commenced proceedings for trespass. The Board contended that it had lawful authority under s 76 of the Act to enter Cooper's land and raze his house. The demolition was clearly not illegal, and was probably defensible in terms of its rationality. The case turned on whether the Board's decision-making process was procedurally acceptable.

The court concluded that the Board had acted unlawfully in not granting Mr Cooper a hearing before deciding to demolish his house. The absence of an express requirement for a hearing in the Act was seen as no obstacle to this conclusion. As Erle CJ put it: 'powers granted by that statute are subject to a qualification that has been repeatedly recognised, that no man is to be deprived of his property without his having an opportunity of being heard'.[5] Byles J made the point in similar terms: 'although there are no positive words in a statute requiring that the party shall be heard, yet the justice of the common law will supply the omission of the legislature'.[6] The more interesting point is why the 'justice of the common law' demanded that such a condition be attached to the exercise of this power?

The various members of the court were divided on whether or not the Board's power was 'judicial' or 'administrative'. Willes J concluded that this was a 'judicial' power, while both Erle CJ and Byles J suggested that the distinction was largely irrelevant, as past case law contained many instances of the audi alterem partem principle being applied to what they considered to be essentially administrative functions. The court was however unanimous in concluding that because the Board's action interfered substantially with Mr Cooper's property rights, it should have afforded him a hearing before reaching its decision.

It is not clear from the judgment how closely this hearing would have to approximate to court procedures. Some indication as to what that requirement might be was subsequently offered by the House of Lords in *Board of Education v Rice.*[7] The case concerned the exercise of what was essentially an appellate jurisdiction conferred

[3] (1863) 14 CBNS 180.

[4] This being one of the ad hoc, subject specific local government bodies created by Parliament in the nineteenth century; see pp 350–351 above.

[5] (1863) 143 ER 414 at 418. [6] Ibid, at 420. [7] [1911] AC 179, HL.

upon the Board to resolve disputes between local education authorities and their employees. The court accepted that such a function, even if were to be described as 'administrative', had to be discharged in accordance with the audi alterem partem principle:

'But I do not think they [the Board] are bound to treat such a question as though it were a trial. They have no power to administer an oath, and need not examine witnesses. They can obtain any information in any way they think best, always giving a fair opportunity to those who are parties in the controversy for correcting or contradicting any relevant statement prejudicial to their view'.[8]

The supposition that judicial methods were an inappropriate reference point to structure the procedures of government bodies, even if the body concerned was exercising a recognisably 'judicial' function, was promptly reinforced in *Local Government Board v Arlidge*.[9] The Housing & Town Planning Act 1909 authorised a local inspector, after holding an inquiry, to issue closing orders in respect of houses he/she considered unfit for human habitation. The statute provided for an appeal against this to the Local Government Board.[10] The statute did not specify the procedures that were to be followed either at the inquiry or the appeal. Arlidge was permitted to appear in person at the inquiry, to be represented by counsel, and to cross-examine witnesses. The inspector nonetheless imposed a closure order on Arlidge's house. Arlidge was allowed to make written representations at the appeal stage, but he was not granted an oral hearing, nor was he allowed to see the Inspector's report. He subsequently maintained that these failings constituted a breach of natural justice, in that they departed too far from a judicial model of decision-making. This argument failed at first instance, but was accepted in the Court of Appeal.

In the House of Lords, the Court of Appeal's judgment was unanimously overruled. Viscount Haldane LC rejected the Court of Appeal's presumption that in the absence of statutorily defined procedures one must assume that Parliament implicitly intended that a body follow judicial procedures. He reached this conclusion notwithstanding the fact that a 'right' was in issue:

'There is no doubt that the question is one affecting property and the liberty of a man to do what he chooses with his own. Such rights are not be affected unless Parliament has said so. But Parliament, in what it considers higher interests than those of the individual, has so often interfered with such rights on other occasions, that it is dangerous for judges to lay much stress on what a hundred years ago would have been a presumption considerably stronger than it is today'.[11]

Haldane's reasoning amounts to a recognition that the substance of government-citizen relations has undergone a profound change, and that governmental

[8] Ibid, at 182 per Lord Loreburn LC.

[9] [1915] AC 120, [1914–15] All ER Rep 1, HL. A different facet of this case was discussed at p 515 above.

[10] The forerunner of the DoE; ie a central government department.

[11] [1914–15] All ER Rep 1 at 6, HL. The methodology is closely comparable to that used by Lord Wilberforce in *Rossminster* 60 years later: see pp 80–81 above.

procedures must therefore change as well. The judgment offers an early but perfectly clear shift from red light to green light theory; or, if one prefers, from a rigid Hayekian concern with judicial process towards Jones' more dilute notion of a 'meaningful day in court'.[12] Somewhat confusingly, Viscount Haldane then indicated that the LGB must – since it was performing an appellate function – act 'judicially'. He followed the lead given in *Rice* in determining the content of this concept in this case. The Board need not offer an oral hearing; granting the opportunity to make written representations would suffice. Nor need it give Arlidge a copy of the Inspector's report. The requirement was simply that the Board:

'deal with the question . . . without bias and . . . give to each of the parties the opportunity of adequately presenting the case made. The decision must be come to in the spirit and with the sense of responsibility of a tribunal whose duty it is to mete out justice . . . Parliament must be taken, in the absence of any declaration to the contrary, to have intended [the Board] to follow the procedure which is its own and is necessary if it is to be capable of doing its work efficiently'.[13]

These sentiments were echoed by Lord Parmoor – 'there is no obligation to adopt the regular forms of legal procedure. It is sufficient that the case has been heard in a judicial spirit'[14] – and by Lord Shaw, whose judgment evinced an explicit concern that the audi alterem partem principle should not be invoked to impede administrative efficiency to an onerous degree:

'Judicial methods may, in many points of administration, be entirely unsuitable, and produce delays, expense, and public and private injury . . . [C]ertain ways of and methods of judicial procedure may very likely be imitated; and lawyer-like methods may find especial favour from lawyers. But that the judiciary should presume to impose its own methods on administrative or executive officers is a usurpation. And the assumption that the methods of natural justice are ex necessitae those of Courts of Justice is wholly unfounded'.[15]

Cooper, Rice and *Arlidge* have in common a clear indication that the courts' concern with audi alterem partem raised two questions. The first, essentially a threshold question, was simply whether or not the principle was applicable to a given decision. (The cases indicate that while a formal distinction was drawn between rights/privileges and judicial/administrative decisions for this classificatory purpose, there were in practice few governmental processes impacting on individual citizens which did not pass the threshold test.) If so, the second question addressed the content of the procedural protection that the applicant should be afforded. A logical consequence of this approach would be that in situations where the first question was answered in the negative, there were no common law restraints on the decision-maker's choice as to

[12] This is perhaps particularly evident in this case because the 1909 Act transferred appeal rights against the council's decision from the courts to the LGB. On Hayek and Jones see pp 66–69 above.

[13] [1914–15] All ER Rep 1 at 6, HL. [14] Ibid, at 14–15. [15] Ibid, at 9.

procedure. This point is well illustrated by the 1920 judgment in *R v Leman Street Police Station Inspector, ex p Venicoff*.[16]

The Aliens Restriction Act 1914 had been enacted during World War I. The Act inter alia empowered the Home Secretary to detain and deport aliens if he considered such action to be conducive to the public good. Venicoff challenged his detention and scheduled deportation on the grounds that the Home Secretary had not granted him an adequate hearing before making the decision.[17] The Court took the view that there was no requirement that the *audi alterem partem* principle be respected here:

'The legislature in its wisdom took from the Courts during the war the power of inquiry into the facts of particular cases . . . In dealing with a regulation such as that with which we are now concerned the value of the order would be considerably impaired if it could be made only after holding an inquiry, because it might very well be that the person against whom it was intended to make a deportation order would, the moment he had notice of that intention . . . take steps to evade apprehension'.[18]

The court reached this conclusion notwithstanding the fact that the decision impacted severely upon Venicoff's 'liberty' in the most obvious of ways. It might be thought that the conclusion could be limited to powers created in time of war, when (*Liversidge* being a primary example) 'normal' administrative law principles were relaxed in order to facilitate the government process. However much the same rationale is evident in Goddard CJ's first instance judgment in *Russell v Duke of Norfolk*.[19] Russell was a race-horse trainer, whose licence was revoked for 'misconduct' by the Jockey Club following allegations of race fixing. As a result, Russell could no longer work in the horse-racing industry. In effect, he had lost his livelihood. He had been granted a rather perfunctory hearing prior to the decision, at which he had been permitted to make a statement but not to challenge in any meaningful way the details of the case against him. Despite the severity of the consequences inflicted upon Russell by the withdrawal of his licence, Lord Goddard CJ could see 'no possible ground' for assuming the *audi alterem partem* principle applied.

Goddard adopted the same approach three years later in *R v Metropolitan Police Comr, ex p Parker*.[20] The Commissioner possessed a (properly) delegated power under the Metropolitan Public Carriage Act 1869 to revoke taxi licences. He revoked Parker's licence following Parker's conviction for various traffic offences and allegations that Parker had been using his cab as part of a prostitution operation. There is little scope to doubt that the revocation was substantively defensible. Parker had also been given the opportunity to rebut the allegations against him at a hearing before a committee chaired by an Assistant Commissioner. His complaint rested on the basis that he had not been allowed to call witnesses in his own defence. Procedures of this sort would

16 [1920] 3 KB 72, DC.

17 The action was for habeas corpus, against the police officer who was detaining Venicoff in accordance with the Home Secretary's instructions.

18 [1920] 3 KB 72 at 80, per the Earl of Reading CJ.

19 [1948] 1 All ER 488.

20 [1953] 1 WLR 1150.

comfortably have satisfied the *Rice/Arlidge* test. However, Lord Goddard indicated that there was no entitlement to natural justice at all in respect of this decision. He offered three reasons for this conclusion.

The first was that Parker had lost only a 'privilege', not a 'right': 'The licence is nothing but a permission'. As a rule, where a licence is granted, the licencor does not have to state why he withdraws his permission'.[21] The second was that the Commissioner's action was an 'administrative' rather than 'judicial' function; it is 'impossible to say that the commissioner . . . was in a judicial or quasi-judicial position. He was in fact exercising a disciplinary authority'.[22] The third explanation was rooted in more obviously policy based concerns, and betokened an extremely 'green light' approach to this facet of administrative law:

> 'it is most undesirable, in my opinion, that [the Commissioner] should be fettered by threats of orders of *certiorari* and so forth, because that would interfere with the free and proper disciplinary exercise of the powers that it may be expected he would otherwise use'.[23]

This approach to the issue was not merely an idiosyncrasy on Lord Goddard's part. In the same year as *Parker* was decided, the Privy Council issued judgment in *Nakkuda Ali v Jayaratne*.[24] The case concerned the power of a Ceylonese government official, the Controller of Textiles, to revoke a trader's licence if he had reasonable grounds to believe that the trader was 'unfit' to hold a licence. The court held that the audi alterem partem principle did not apply to this activity, on the grounds that the licence was a privilege and that its grant and withdrawal were executive and not judicial actions.

Such cases emphasise that the threshold question of whether or not a particular decision-making process was subject to the audi alterm partem principle had become of central importance in the immediate post-war period. That the answer to the question might be unclear is nicely illustrated by the Court of Appeal's judgment in *Russell v Duke of Norfolk*.[25] In contrast to Lord Goddard CJ's decision at first instance, the three judgments offered in the Court of Appeal (by Tucker, Asquith and Denning LJJ) all concluded that the Jockey Club's withdrawal of a trainer's licence was subject to the audi alterem principle. However, the judges also concluded that the principle had not been breached on these facts; in respect of this particular decision, the content of natural justice was quite limited. The point is best put by Tucker LJ:

> 'Throughout this inquiry, [the plaintiff] was . . . given an opportunity of presenting his case . . . It is true that he was not in terms asked: "Have you got any witnesses? Do you want an adjournment?". A layman at an inquiry of this sort is of course at a grave disadvantage compared with a trained advocate . . . Counsel for the plaintiff . . . said "What would be said of local justices who acted in this way?". With all due respect, the position is totally different. This matter is not to be judged by the standards applicable to local justices'.[26]

Tucker LJ continued by noting that the content of a fair hearing would be highly

[21] Ibid, at 1154. [22] Ibid, at 1155. [23] Ibid. [24] [1951] AC 66, PC.
[25] [1949] 1 All ER 109, CA. [26] Ibid, at 118.

context specific: 'The requirements of natural justice must depend on the circumstances of the case, the nature of the inquiry, the rules under which the tribunal is acting, the subject matter that is being dealt with, and so forth'.[27] In so far as there was to be a lowest common denominator, applicable to all decisions to which the audi alterem partem principle applied, it was the rather vague requirement that: 'the person concerned should have a reasonable opportunity of presenting his case'.[28]

That this judgment pre-dated both *Parker* and *Nakkuda Ali*, and that all three cases concerned what was in effect the loss of the plaintiff's preferred livelihood, indicates that the right/privilege and judicial/administrative dichotomies remained a powerful factor in this area of the law. But *Russell* also rather suggested that a plaintiff who successfully passed the threshold test might find herself entitled to such a low level of 'natural justice' that neither the instrumental, nor intrinsic, rationales for imposing procedural restraints on decision-making behaviour were being well-served. This point is well illustrated by the Privy Council's decision in *University of Ceylon v Fernando*.[29] Fernando had been accused of cheating in an exam. If upheld, the charge would have ruined his reputation and career prospects. The Privy Council accepted that these proceedings were quasi-judicial, and subject to the rules of natural justice. However this did not mean that Fernando was entitled to cross-examine (either in person or through counsel) the witnesses against him.

THE RE-EMERGENCE OF THE PRINCIPLE? *RIDGE V BALDWIN*

The 1963 judgment of the House of Lords in *Ridge v Baldwin*[30] appeared decisively to reject the practical difference between judicial/administrative decisions for audi alterem partem purposes, although it did little to indicate that the content of the requisite hearing ought to be strengthened. Ridge was the former Chief Constable of Sussex. He had been tried for corruption, but acquitted. The Police Authority (at that time quaintly named 'the Watch Committee') nonetheless decided to dismiss him. The Committee was empowered to do so per the Municipal Corporations Act 1882, s 191(4) if it thought him 'negligent in the discharge of his duty, or otherwise unfit for the same'. Since Ridge's integrity and competence had been heavily criticised by the judge presiding over his trial, his dismissal would not seem to have been either illegal or irrational. However, he had been sacked immediately after the trial. He had not even been informed that the Committee was considering this course of action, and was given no opportunity to make a case to its members. Following representations from Ridge's solicitor, the Committee agreed to reconvene to permit Ridge the opportunity to persuade them to revoke their decision. Ridge and his lawyer were allowed to make a statement at the hearing, but he was not permitted to call witnesses or cross-examine Committee members. Ridge subsequently sought a declaration that his dismissal was void on the ground that the hearings did not comply with the

27 Ibid, at 118. 28 Ibid. 29 [1960] 1 All ER 631, [1960] 1 WLR 223, PC.
30 [1964] AC 40, [1963] 2 All ER 66, HL.

requirements of natural justice.[31] Neither the High Court nor the Court of Appeal accepted that natural justice applied in this situation, on the basis that the Committee's function was administrative rather than quasi-judicial in nature.[32]

This conclusion was reversed in the House of Lords. Lord Reid's leading judgment suggested that the line of cases typified by *Venicoff, Parker* and *Nakkuda Ali* rested on insecure jurisprudential and political foundations. This was in part because it was inappropriate to attach much significance to judgments addressing the exercise of war powers:

> 'It seems to me to be . . . almost an inevitable inference from the circumstances in which defence regulations were made and from their subject matter that . . . [Parliament's] intention must have been to exclude the principles of natural justice . . . But it was not to be expected that anyone would state in so many words that a temporary abandonment of the rules of natural justice was one of the sacrifices which war conditions required – that would have been almost calculated to create . . . alarm and despondency'.[33]

A second, more pervasive, problem had arisen from a widespread judicial presumption that a government body's duty to act 'judicially' was not – as in *Cooper, Rice* and *Arlidge* – to be inferred as a matter of course whenever its decisions impacted substantially on an individual's interests, but had rather to be 'super-added' either explicitly or as matter of necessary implication by the relevant statutory scheme.[34] Lord Reid saw no need for such a requirement.

He also suggested that the courts had rather misunderstood the changing nature of the relationship between government and the citizenry. It was undoubtedly true that since 1900 Parliament had granted the government more and more extensive powers. Many such powers addressed matters of policy which affected many people en masse. Decisions of that sort need not be subject to the rules of natural justice. However, Lord Reid implied that the courts had extended that presumption too broadly, and had overlooked the fact that many government decisions still involved a power akin to imposing a 'penalty' upon particular individuals. In respect of powers of that type, a common law presumption as to procedural rigour based on nineteenth and (very) early twentieth century precedent was justified.[35]

The presumption was not absolute however, even in situations where what was in issue was the loss of livelihood. Lord Reid drew a careful (if somewhat formalistic) distinction between three types of 'employment' situation. In respect of contracts of employment, there seemed to be no role for common law based principles of natural justice to apply. Such procedural constraints as attached to the exercise of an employer's

[31] Ridge's practical concern was to have the dismissal quashed. This would have the effect of re-instating him in his job. He would then immediately resign before the Committee met again. If he resigned, he retained his pension rights. If he was sacked for negligence or unfitness, he would not do so.

[32] [1963] 1 QB 539, CA; affg [1963] 2 All ER 523.

[33] [1962] 2 All ER 66 at 76. Lord Reid also vindicated Lord Atkin's dissent in *Liversidge* by describing the majority judgment as a 'very peculiar decision': ibid.

[34] Ibid, at pp 77–78.

[35] Cf his criticism of the Privy Council in *Nakkuda Ali* for not considering any cases from before 1911.

powers would have to be found in the relevant contract or in any statutory provisions imposed on the post in question. In the absence of a contract (in effect when the employment of civil servants was in issue),[36] common law restraints on procedure would apply only to office holders who were dismissible for cause (such as Ridge); those who held office at pleasure could be dismissed without any form of hearing.

Contemporary commentators have regarded *Ridge* as something of a landmark decision, comparable in its jurisprudential significance with contemporaneous judgments such as *Padfield* and *Anisminic.* Paul Craig, for example argued that the judgment had two major implications for the audi alterm partem principles:

> 'on the one hand [the majority] rediscovered the nineteenth century jurisprudence which had applied the principle to a broad spectrum of interests and a wide variety of decision-makers. On the other hand they disapproved of some of the impediments which had been erected in the twentieth century'.[37]

It is however important not to overstate the significance of the case. While *Ridge* undoubtedly restored the *reach* of the *audi alterem partem* doctrine to its Victorian extent, it did little to enhance its *content.* Reid's judgment lacks any positive statement on the question of *how much* procedural protection Ridge was entitled to. In a passage towards the end of his judgment,[38] Reid implies that had the Committee actually revoked Ridge's dismissal prior to its second meeting (thereby indicating that it was addressing the issue with an open mind)[39] and given him fuller details of the case against him, it would have satisfied the requirements of natural justice.[40] Nothing in the judgment suggests that Ridge was entitled to a high level of procedural protection.[41]

THE EMERGENCE OF THE PROCEDURAL FAIRNESS DOCTRINE AND THE APPEARANCE OF THE LEGITIMATE EXPECTATION

The indication given in *Ridge* that the common law was now to be more concerned with maximising the reach of the *audi alterem* principle than identifying and

[36] It may be recalled that the courts did not accept that civil servants had 'contracts' of employment until the mid-1980s; see p 118 above.

[37] (1989) op cit p 204. [38] [1963] 2 All ER 66 at 80–81, HL.

[39] Had it done so, one assumes Ridge would not have attended the second hearing, but would have instantaneously resigned to safeguard his pension rights.

[40] On the more general issue of whether a governmental body can cure procedural defects in its original decision by holding a second, procedurally defensible hearing see the judgment of Lord Wilberforce in *Calvin v Carr* [1980] AC 574, [1979] 2 All ER 440; and the analysis by Elliot M (1980) 'Appeals, principles and pragmatism in natural justice' *MLR* 66–69.

[41] One might contrast this position with a contemporaneous academic critique produced in the USA which was to have a profound influence on the development of constitutional and administrative law in that country. In several articles in the *Yale Law Journal,* Charles Reich argued that not only should the reach of the procedural fairness doctrine be extended to all facets of the governmental process which affected individual interests, but that its content should also be modelled on a judicial process; see Reich C (1963) 'Midnight welfare searches and the Social Security Act' *Yale LJ* 1346–1360; (1964) 'The new property' *Yale LJ* 733–787; (1965) 'Individual rights and social welfare: the emerging legal issues' *Yale LJ* 1244–1257.

enhancing its content was quickly reinforced by the High Court's decision in *Re HK*.[42]

Section 2(2) of the Commonwealth Immigrants Act 1962 granted a right of entry to the UK to a citizen of any Commonwealth country who: 'satisfies an immigration officer that he . . . (b) is the . . . child under sixteen years of age of a Commonwealth citizen who is resident in the United Kingdom'. HK, a citizen of Pakistan, claimed to be the 15-year-old son of a resident Commonwealth citizen. However, on his arrival at Heathrow, an immigration officer formed the initial impression that HK was over 16 years old.[43] There followed what seems to have been a rather rapid and rudimentary 'hearing' at the airport, in which HK was examined by a doctor and both HK and his father were interviewed (separately and without any form of expert representation) by immigration officers. The officers were unconvinced that HK was under 16, and arranged for him to be deported back to Pakistan the next day. This decision was challenged on the basis that the procedures adopted by the immigration officers were insufficiently rigorous.

In his leading judgment, Lord Parker CJ followed *Ridge v Baldwin* in suggesting that *Nakkuda Ali*, if not wrongly decided, was certainly poorly expressed. Lord Parker doubted that s 2 imposed a 'judicial' function on immigration officers. Officers were nonetheless subject to 'a duty to act fairly'. Salmon LJ echoed this reasoning:

> 'decisions [under s 2] are of vital importance to the immigrants since their whole future may be affected. In my judgment it is implicit in the statute that the authorities in exercising these powers and making decisions must act fairly in accordance with the procedures of natural justice'.[44]

However, the court also considered that the content of the 'duty to act fairly' was rather anodyne. As Lord Parker put it, the obligation that fell on the officer was merely to: 'give the immigrant an opportunity of satisfying him of the matters in the subsection, and for that purpose let the immigrant know what his immediate impression is so that the immigrant can disabuse him'.[45] The brief interview which HK had been afforded at Heathrow was evidently sufficient to meet this requirement.

One might wonder if any useful purpose – be it of an intrinsic or instrumental kind – would be served by so perfunctory a standard of procedural due process. Furthermore, if so little protection was afforded to an individual interest which was (as Salmon LJ put it) 'vital' to the applicant concerned, the protection offered to 'non-vital interests' would presumably need be little more than barely discernible.

This supposition seemed to be reinforced by a series of cases in the late 1960s and early 1970s in which the courts accepted that a governmental decision was subject to natural justice/fair procedures, but reduced the substance of the protection almost to

42 [1967] 2 QB 617, sub nom *Re K(H)(infant)* [1967] 1 All ER 226.

43 HK's Pakistan passport recorded his date of birth as 29.2.1951; a non-existent date, as 1951 was not a leap year. This anomaly, coupled with HK's mature physical appearance, underpinned the officer's conclusion.

44 [1967] 1 All ER 226 at 233.

45 Ibid, at 231.

vanishing point. Of particular note were the decisions in *R v Aston University Senate, ex p Roffey*[46] and *Breen v Amalgamated Engineering Union*,[47] in which (respectively) the High Court and Court of Appeal indicated that procedural fairness did not always require that the individual be granted a hearing. Similarly, in *Malloch v Aberdeen Corpn*,[48] the House of Lords offered the curious suggestion that in some situations where a hearing would be required the individual need not be given any prior notice of the details of the case which she had to answer. Quite what value (other than the purely symbolic) a hearing might have in such circumstances is difficult to fathom.

It might readily be conceded that in respect of some types of governmental decision there may be strong public policy grounds both for limiting the content of any hearing and for relieving the decision-maker of any obligation to provide precise information of the case an applicant has to answer. An example is offered by *R v Gaming Board for Great Britain, ex p Benaim and Khaida*.[49] The applicants had been refused a licence to run a casino. They had been granted a hearing by the Gaming Board prior to the decision being made. They were not however permitted to know details of the evidence that the Board had considered which had led it to conclude that they were not fit persons to be granted a licence. The Board refused to provide such information, on the basis that it would jeopardise the confidentiality of its sources. This was a consideration of some importance given the suspected links between the gambling industry and organised crime. In the Court of Appeal, Lord Denning held that this was a pertinent factor for the court to consider. He also observed that the plaintiffs were not being deprived of any existing entitlement, but were rather seeking a permission to begin a new venture. In these circumstances, the Board's duty to act fairly demanded that Benaim and Khaida be given:

> 'an opportunity of satisfying them of the matters specified . . . They must let him know what their impressions are so that he can disabuse them. But I do not think that they need quote chapter and verse against him as if they were dismissing him from an office as in *Ridge*: or depriving him of his property, as in *Cooper*'.[50]

Such a conclusion obviously runs the risk that the Board is acting on the basis of flawed evidence, or indeed of no evidence at all. Lord Denning's judgment implies that this is a lesser evil than running the risk that potentially useful sources of information be deterred from offering evidence to the Board.

Lord Denning's own readiness to trust unhesitatingly in the competence and integrity of government decision-makers is perhaps best revealed by his absurd comments a few years later in *R v Secretary of State for Home Affairs, ex p Hosenball*.[51] Hosenball was an American journalist, whose activities were embarrassing the (then Labour) government. The Home Secretary subsequently sought to deport Hosenball. He claimed that 'national security' was in issue, although he declined to give any

46 [1969] 2 QB 538. 47 [1971] 2 QB 175, [1971] 1 All ER 1148, CA.
48 [1971] 2 All ER 1278, [1971] 1 WLR 1578, HL. 49 [1970] 2 QB 417, [1970] 2 All ER 528, CA.
50 [1970] 2 All ER 528 at 534, CA. 51 [1977] 3 All ER 452, [1977] 1 WLR 766, CA.

explanation as to how Hosenball's activities had this effect. In Lord Denning's view, notwithstanding the severe consequences for Mr Hosenball of the Home Secretary's decision, the government was under no obligation to give Hosenball details of the case against him so that he might convince the Home Secretary that the government's suspicions were ill-founded:

'There is a conflict here between the interests of national security on the one hand and the freedom of the individual on the other. The balance between these two is not for a court of law. It is for the Home Secretary. He is the person entrusted by Parliament with the task. In some parts of the world national security has on occasions been used as an excuse for all sorts of infringements of individual liberty. But not in England . . . Ministers . . . have never interfered with the liberty or freedom of movement of any individual except where it is absolutely necessary for the safety of the state'.[52]

These sentiments are redolent of Denning's similarly silly observations in *Hanratty*[53] and do him little credit. The proposition that no government Minister has ever taken inappropriate advantage of the courts' general unwillingness to accept the justiciability of national security issues is risible.[54] To empty the procedural fairness doctrine of all meaningful content in such circumstances may be justifiable, but it is done at the certain cost that the autonomy thereby afforded to the government *may* be abused and the possible cost that it *will* be.[55]

Benaim and Khaida obviously did not raise a 'national security' issue – nor did it concern a ministerial decision – but nonetheless addressed a public policy issue of sufficient sensitivity to persuade the Court of Appeal that only a dilute level of procedural rigour need be attached to the Gaming Board's licencing decisions. The matters in issue in cases such as *Roffey, Breen* and *Malloch* had no such 'delicate' ramifications however.[56] The dilution of the content of procedural fairness in such cases appeared to rest largely on the grounds that it would ease the administrative process. This line of decisions attracted forceful academic criticism from DH Clark, in an article published in *Public Law*.[57] While welcoming the evident extension in the reach of the natural justice principle since *Ridge*,[58] Clark took a less sanguine view of the way in which some decisions had treated the question of its content. His concern essentially was that there was little point in saying that in principle the safeguard of procedural fairness applies to all governmental decisions (unless removed by statute)

52 Ibid, at 461. 53 See p 115 above.

54 See, for example, the discussion of the Matrix-Churchill controversy at pp 297–299 above.

55 See the discussion of *GCHQ* at pp 103–105 above. See also Geoffrey Robertson's analysis of the way in which Denning's hyperbolic rhetoric in *Hosenball* has been deployed in some Commonwealth countries whose democratic credentials are less firmly established than those of the United Kingdom: (1999) *The justice game* ch 10 (Harmondsworth: Penguin).

56 *Roffey* concerned the expulsion of students from university on the grounds of poor academic performance; *Breen* the (non)-appointment of a trade union official; and *Malloch* the dismissal of a teacher.

57 (1975) 'Natural justice: substance or shadow' *Public Law* 27–63. The paper merits careful attention.

58 '*Ridge v Baldwin* restored light to an area benighted by the narrow conceptualism of the previous decade . . . It would not be immoderate to describe as dramatic the pace of consequent advancement beyond the old frontiers': ibid, at 27.

if the concept is so flexible that the benefit thereby bestowed on the individual may be worthless: 'even as the doctrine finds new fields to conquer it is being emasculated from within, honoured in name, but dangerously devalued in substance'.[59] Clark argued in contrast that audi alterem partem ought to be viewed as: 'a basic procedural minimum standard irreducible without negating its raison d'etre';[60] that raison d'etre being to enhance the likelihood that 'good' substantive decisions were produced, and that the legitimacy of the decision-making process be maximised. To achieve those objectives, the 'basic minimum' had to include an entitlement to a hearing and a clear indication of the case that had to be met.

Other commentators took a more positive view of these developments. Mullan, drawing a comparison between recent English, Canadian and New Zealand decisions saw a good deal of merit in what he termed a 'spectrum theory' approach to natural justice.[61] Innovatively, Mullan suggested that the two extreme ends of his 'spectrum' would be set not by archaic or formalistic distinctions between 'rights and privileges' and/or 'judicial and administrative' decisions, but by the criterion of justiciability. The extent to which governmental decisions would be required by the common law to approximate to an idealised, court-based standard of procedural rigour would depend upon the nature of the decision and the immediacy and intensity of its impact upon a particular individual. As a given decision appeared less and less justiciable, so the process of making it would become subject to less and less legalistic procedural constraints, until eventually a concern with due process would almost disappear.

While 'spectrum theory' may have a certain conceptual neatness, and while it might seem a useful analytical tool with which (given the benefit of hindsight) to critique some of the post-*Ridge* case law, its value as a practical, prescriptive tool with which to assess just 'how much fairness' should be applied to particular governmental decisions would appear limited. This was in part due to the intrinsic limitations of the idea itself. But such force as the idea had was also overshadowed by the appearance and rapid consolidation of a new principle in English administrative law – that of the 'legitimate expectation'.

LEGITIMATE EXPECTATION – AN ENTITLEMENT TO A PROCEDURAL BENEFIT OR SUBSTANTIVE BENEFIT?

The notion of the 'legitimate expectation' emerged in the Court of Appeal's 1969 decision in *Schmidt v Secretary of State for Home Affairs*.[62] As noted in chapter twelve,

59 Ibid, at 28. Cf also his suggestion at p 63 that the doctrine was 'undergoing a metamorphosis that would convert it into a mere slogan or ill-defined aspiration'.

60 Ibid, at 37.

61 Mullan D (1975) 'Fairness: the new natural justice' *University of Toronto LJ* 280–316. For (respectively) a more jurisprudential analysis and a helpful critique of this area of administrative law see Loughlin M (1978) 'Procedural fairness: a study of the crisis in administrative law theory' *University of Toronto LJ* 215–241; and Harlow and Rawlings (1984) op cit pp 78–94.

62 [1969] 2 Ch 149, CA.

the British government had by the mid-1970s taken a dim view of the 'religion' of Scientology, to the extent that EC nationals (specifically Ms Van Duyn) found themselves barred from working for the Church of Scientology in the UK.[63] This governmental disapproval had become clear in 1968, when the then Labour government announced that it would take steps to curb the growth of the sect. Among the measures to be taken were a ban on non-British citizens studying at the Church's British headquarters. No new students would be admitted to the country, and those already in the UK would not have their permission to stay in the UK renewed. This new policy posed an acute problem to Mr Schmidt and 50 other non-British citizens studying with the Church, as their permissions to stay would expire before they completed their studies. Their application for an extension of their permission to stay was refused by the Home Secretary. Among various grounds of challenge to this decision was the contention that Schmidt should have been granted a hearing before the Home Secretary reached his decision.

The Court rejected this contention, on the narrow ground that aliens had no right of entry into the UK in the first place, and so had no concomitant right to have any permission to stay that they may have been granted extended. Lord Denning indicated that he thought *Venicoff* to have been correctly decided in terms of its result, although the reasoning underpinning the judgment was now outmoded in so far as it was based on:

> 'the fact that the Home Secretary was exercising an administrative power and not doing a judicial act. But that distinction is no longer valid. The speeches in *Ridge v Baldwin* show that an administrative body, may in a proper case, be bound to give a person who is affected by their decision an opportunity of making representations. It all depends on whether the person has some right or interest, or, I would add, some legitimate expectation of which it would not be fair to deprive him without hearing what he has to say'.[64]

Lord Denning was prepared to accept that Mr Schmidt had a legitimate expectation that he could remain in the UK until the expiry of his permission to stay. In the event that the Home Secretary revoked that permission prematurely, Mr Schmidt would be entitled to a hearing in order to attempt to persuade the Home Secretary not to frustrate his expectation. Non-renewal of permission did not however create such an entitlement. Widgery LJ's judgment also recognised the existence of a legitimate expectation as a trigger for procedural fairness. While no such expectation arose on these facts, he indicated – rather more broadly – that in cases involving the economic interests of citizens a non-renewal of a licence or permission by a government body might be subject to a requirement of procedural fairness. This would suggest that a case such as *Parker* would now have to be decided differently.

Schmidt suggested that while the courts saw no little merit in the judicial/administrative decision dichotomy, they would prefer to embellish rather than abolish the former distinction drawn in natural justice cases between rights and privileges by

63 See pp 449–450 above.

64 [1969] 2 Ch 149 at 170, CA.

adding the legitimate expectation as a third, intermediate category of individual interest. Which individual interests would fall within this new category was however far from certain, as was the level of procedural protection such interests would attract.

That the first question might attract a very broad answer was indicated three years later by the Court of Appeal's judgment in *R v Liverpool Corpn, ex p Liverpool Taxi Fleet Operators' Association*.[65] The decision in issue concerned the council's power to licence taxi-cab drivers in its area. In the late 1960s, the council issued some 300 licences each year for a one-year period. It subsequently considered whether to increase the number of licences. As part of its decision-making process, it invited the trade association representing existing licence holders to make representations to its relevant committee during which the association was represented by counsel. The council decided to increase the number of licences quite substantially, but promised (in writing on several occasions through senior councillors and officers) that no increase would be given effect until the council had succeeded in persuading Parliament to pass a private Act[66] empowering the council to ban the operation of unlicenced mini-cabs in the area. The council subsequently sought to break that promise. The association then asked the court to hold that the council was bound to respect the substance of its promise.

In a narrow sense, one might doubt if *Liverpool Taxi* can properly be regarded as a 'legitimate expectation case', since that phrase does not anywhere appear in any of the three judgments delivered in the Court of Appeal.[67] In Denning's analysis, this was an estoppel case, to be decided in accordance with his own judgments in *Robertson* and *Lever Finance*.[68] He proceeded on the assumptions that: firstly, this particular licencing function was subject to the requirements of procedural fairness; and secondly, the council's promise to delay an increase in the number of licences granted until the relevant Act had been passed was substantively intra vires – ie that it did not unlawfully fetter the council's discretion.[69] Lord Denning then invoked the amorphous notion of 'the public interest' to support the proposition that the council was not at liberty to resile from the substance of its promise:

> 'except after the most serious consideration and hearing what the other party has to say: and then only if they [sic] are satisfied that the overriding public interest requires it'.[70]

The implications of this reasoning are significant. Firstly the entitlement to a hearing (which entails a reasonably high level of procedural protection) seems to be triggered not by the association's economic interest in the decision, but by the council's own promise. This is an innovative, but not radical proposition, resting on the premise that it is per se procedurally unfair for a government body to break clear, substantively

65 [1972] 2 QB 299, sub nom *Re Liverpool Taxi Owners' Association* [1972] 2 All ER 589.

66 On which see p 148 above.

67 By Lord Denning MR, Roskill LJ and Sir Gordon Willmer.

68 See pp 444–446 above. See also Ganz G (1986) 'Legitimate expectation: a confusion of concepts', in Harlow C (ed) *Public law and politics* (London: Sweet and Maxwell).

69 See pp 518–519 above.

70 [1972] 2 QB 299 at 308.

intra vires promises, and then to continue to make a new decision (whatever its content) without affording a new hearing to those individuals intimately affected by the new decision. This was the basis upon which both Roskill LJ and Sir Gordon Willmer decided the case and so should be taken as the opinion of the court.[71] Much more radical – and much more constitutionally problematic – is the second limb of Denning's formula; (which is strictly merely obiter). In effect, Denning is saying that the council's promise has taken it into a position where the court can subject the range of substantive decisions the council may then make in exercising its powers *in so far as they apply to individuals who legitimately expect the promise to be honoured* to much narrower limits than would be applied if the promise had not been made.[72] This is essentially to subject the council to a proportionality test in these particular circumstances, although Denning did not acknowledge (or perhaps perceive) that his judgment had that effect.[73] Roskill LJ and Sir Gordon Willmer made no such allusion; their judgments indicated that as long as a new hearing was held, the council could lawfully make just the same range of decisions as it could if its initial promise had not been made.[74]

The possibility that the legitimate expectation – as Denning construed it – might provide a backdoor route through which courts might in some circumstances come much closer to the political merits of a decision than was permitted by the *Wednesbury* unreasonableness test did not seem to be immediately appreciated after *Liverpool Taxi.* The presumption seemed rather to be – following Roskill and Willmer – that a legitimate expectation, whether it derived from a government body's action or was inherent in an applicant's interest, could give rise only to a procedural benefit. Thus in *R v Hull Prison Board of Visitors, ex p St Germain* the Court of Appeal invoked the concept to conclude (for the first time) that the disciplinary functions of prison Boards of Visitors could be quashed if they failed to conform to the requisite standard of fairness: a prisoner's interest in not being subject to disciplinary punishment was not a right in the orthodox sense, but was an interest of sufficient importance to be

71 An important point to note here is that a hearing would have been required before the council could resile from its promise to delay any increase in licences until the Bill had been passed even if it had not additionally promised to hold such a hearing; ie it was not the promise of a hearing that triggered the requirement of a hearing.

72 It seems tolerably clear that, like Roskill and Willmer, Denning considered that the substantive benefit which the association could legitimately expect was that no new licences would be issued until the Act regulating mini-cabs had been passed, and not simply that the association be given another hearing before that decision was changed.

73 This is a quite distinct position from raising an estoppel in respect of the council's decision. If the court were to estop the council from breaking its promise, the court would essentially be exercising an appellate function by determining the precise outcome of the decision-making process. The 'overriding public interest' formula, in contrast, gives the council some room for substantive manoeuvre, albeit markedly less than it previously enjoyed. Lord Denning was also shortly to stress in *Cinnamond v British Airports Authority* ([1980] 2 All ER 368, [1980] 1 WLR 582, CA) that any expectation on which an applicant sought to rely had to be 'legitimate', a quality that would not attach to (as on these facts) an expectation generated by repeated criminal behaviour.

74 Nor did Roskill LJ make any reference to estoppel as a source for his conclusion. Rather he regarded it as a new administrative law principle which he styled as 'fairness': ibid, at 310.

interfered with only through fair procedures.[75] Mr St Germain had been punished for his part in a series of riots at Hull prison by the revocation of some two years of expected remission of his sentence, a 'punishment' which was clearly of major significance.

The majority in *St Germain* had arguably limited its extension of the procedural fairness doctrine to the disciplinary functions of Boards of Visitors.[76] These were presumed to be 'judicial'. Disciplinary powers exercised by prison Governors were however classified as 'administrative'; (the old dichotomy clearly had not passed into obsolescence). These powers should not be subjected to the natural justice doctrine because (echoing Lord Goddard in *Parker*) that would place too great a burden on the Governor's decision-making behaviour. In *Leech v Deputy Governor of Parkhurst Prison*,[77] the House of Lords rejected this formalistic distinction. It held that a Governor's functions could be divided into disciplinary and management issues, and that the disciplinary element would be subject to the requirements of natural justice. More broadly, Lord Bridge suggested that this principle would extend to any governmental power which affected 'the rights or legitimate expectations' of individuals. In a clear break with the *Parker* rationale, Lord Bridge also attached unusually explicit significance to the intrinsic value of procedural fairness, observing that any burdens this extension of natural justice might impose upon prison Governors would be outweighed by the benefits resulting from prisoners knowing that their grievances about disciplinary decisions would have a full airing at a fair hearing.

The legitimate expectation idea was also used in *McInnes v Onslow Fane*[78] to offer rather more precise guidance on the issue of the content rather than just applicability of the procedural fairness doctrine. Mr McInnes, after an extremely chequered career in and around the fringes of the boxing industry, had by 1976 made five successive but unsuccessful applications to the British Boxing Board of Control for a licence to operate as a manager. All his applications were rejected without him being granted a hearing, and without him being apprised in any detail of the factors which led to the Board's refusals. Megarry VC's judgment suggested that licencing decisions of this sort could be divided into three categories for procedural fairness purposes. The first category was 'forfeiture' cases, in which the decision under challenge had revoked or abridged a still extant licence. The third category was 'application' cases, in which a licence was being sought for the first time. Between these two extremes lay the second

[75] [1979] QB 425, [1979] 1 All ER 701, CA. This case was argued only on a preliminary, jurisdictional question. On the (once again rather low) level of protection subsequently held to be appropriate, see *R v Hull Prison Board of Visitors, ex p St Germain (No 2)* [1979] 3 All ER 545, [1979] 1 WLR 1401. Four years earlier, in *Fraser v Mudge* [1975] 1 WLR 1132, the High Court had hinted that Boards of Visitors might be subject to the rules of natural justice, but did not decide the issue; see the discussion in *St Germain* at 441. *Fraser v Mudge* is revisited in a slightly different context below.

[76] The point is not wholly clear. See the discussion by Webster J in *R v Secretary of State for the Home Department, ex p Tarrant* [1985] QB 251 at 271–272.

[77] [1988] AC 533, [1988] 1 All ER 485.

[78] [1978] 3 All ER 211, [1978] 1 WLR 1520.

category, in which 'the applicant has some legitimate expectation from what has already happened that his application will be granted'.[79]

The first category would attract a high level of procedural protection: 'the right to an unbiased tribunal, the right to notice of the charges, and the right to be heard in answer to the charges'.[80] The mere application cases, in contrast, would apparently merit no worthwhile protection at all. No hearing would be necessary, and the applicant need not be given even the gist of the case against her. Megarry VC did not offer any details of the protection to be provided in the intermediate category; such 'intermediate' decisions would presumably attract an 'intermediate' level of procedural rigour.[81]

That a legitimate expectation might trigger a particular level of procedural protection may have raised practical difficulties in deciding how much was enough, but it was not a conceptually problematic idea. The possibility that a legitimate expectation might have the effect of narrowing a government body's substantive discretion was more contentious. That idea had been given some currency by the Court of Appeal in *Chief Constable of North Wales Police v Evans*, but was then firmly rejected by the House of Lords.[82] Evans was a probationer constable. Under the relevant statutory scheme, the Chief Constable could dismiss a probationer if she considered that he would not be a 'reliable and competent officer'. Evans was dismissed on the basis of unfounded rumours about his personal life, and was not given any form of hearing or other opportunity to rebut the allegations. In the House of Lords, Lord Hailsham had described Evans' treatment as 'little short of outrageous'. Evans' status was clearly comparable to that of Ridge, and as such he was entitled to procedural protection. As in *Ridge*, the court set the content of fairness at a low level. Evans need not be granted an oral hearing, but had to be given at least an opportunity to refute the charge.

However perhaps the most important aspect of the judgment is noted by Craig:

> 'The House of Lords explicitly disapproved of statements made in the Court of Appeal that a court should exercise a general power to consider whether the decision reached was fair and reasonable. It was firmly stated that where review was based upon breach of natural justice the court should only be concerned with the manner in which the decision was reached and not with the correctness of the decision itself'.[83]

Construed in this way, the judgment implicitly rejects Lord Denning's reasoning in *Liverpool Taxi*. But the judgment may also be seen as indicative of a pervasive judicial

[79] Ibid, at 218. Megarry VC intimated that already possessing a licence triggered a legitimate expectation of renewal, as would presumably – although he was not explicit on the point – representations that a licence would be granted by the Board's officials.

[80] Ibid.

[81] This tripartite analysis of licensing decisions has a superficial conceptual neatness. However, it may be difficult to generalise significantly from *McInnes*. Megarry VC paid no obvious attention, for example, to the scale of or public interest in the licence concerned. Should, for example, the revocation of a market stallholder's licence merit greater procedural protection than an application to renew a licence to run a transatlantic airline?

[82] [1982] 3 All ER 141, 1982] 1 WLR 1155, HL.

[83] (1989) op cit at p 213.

failure or unwillingness to distinguish between a proportionality based level of substantive review and an appellate jurisdiction.[84] To decide if the substantive content of a decision is correct is de facto to exercise appellate powers; to decide whether or not it is defensible within a narrower range of options than permitted by the *Wednesbury* unreasonableness test need not have this effect at all. The judgment, whether ill-conceived or not, is nonetheless clear authority for the proposition that a government body's procedural failings should not be used as a stepping stone for a court to narrow its substantive discretion.

This evident clarity was then rather obscured by several decisions in the mid-1980s.[85] The applicant in *A-G of Hong Kong v Ng Yuen Shiu*[86] was an illegal immigrant to Hong Kong from Macau. As part of a general tightening of its policy towards illegal immigration, the Hong Kong government announced that illegal entrants from Macau would not be deported until they had been granted an individuated hearing so that their claim to stay could be carefully considered. Such a hearing was not specifically required by the relevant statutory scheme, but it is clear that the government was acting substantively intra vires in making the promise. Mr Ng was not afforded such a hearing. The Privy Council subsequently held that Mr Ng had a legitimate (or as Lord Fraser styled it 'reasonable') expectation that this promise be honoured. Lord Fraser, who delivered the sole judgment, also held that a legitimate expectation could arise in several ways:

> 'The expectations may be based on some statement or undertaking by, or on behalf of, the public authority which has the duty of making the decision, if the authority has, through its officers, acted in a way that would make it unfair or inconsistent with good administration for him to be denied such an inquiry'.[87]

In other respects, however, the judgment seemed to restrict the scope of the principle. Lord Fraser stressed that 'this is a very narrow case on its facts'.[88] He also emphasised that whatever the source of the legitimate expectation, it could trigger only procedural entitlements which would no have impact on the range of substantive decisions that might eventually be reached.

This seems perfectly clear. The seeds of potential confusion sown by *Ng Yuen Shiu* derive from two sources. The first was that the substantive benefit Mr Ng was seeking was itself a procedural right. All he was asking for was a hearing, not that he be permitted to stay in Hong Kong. As a result, he left the court having succeeded in binding the Hong Kong government to the precise substance of its promise. The second derives from Lord Fraser's reliance on *Liverpool Taxi*, and his failure to note the significantly different implications of Lord Denning's opinion and the judgments of Roskill LJ and Sir Gordon Willmer in that case. In Lord Fraser's view, those three

84 See the discussion at pp 531–534 above.

85 A very helpful and incisive analysis is provided in Forsyth C (1988) 'The provenance and protection of legitimate expectations' *Cambridge LJ* 238–260.

86 [1983] 2 AC 629, [1983] 2 All ER 346, PC.

87 Ibid, at 350.

88 Ibid, at 352.

judgments all held that the council's substantive autonomy was not changed by its generation of a legitimate expectation on the part of the association. That is however incorrect, and by failing to draw the distinction, and by quoting at length from Lord Denning's opinion, Lord Fraser perhaps lent an unintended credibility to its substantive implications.

Those implications were certainly afforded great credibility in *R v Secretary of State for the Home Department, ex p Khan.*[89] Mr Khan was seeking to adopt his nephew, who then lived in Pakistan. A Home Office policy letter detailed the criteria which a person in his situation would have to meet to bring a child to the UK for adoption. Having complied with these criteria Mr Khan was informed that the letter incorrectly represented Home Office policy, that more restrictive criteria actually applied, and that he could not meet them. Parker LJ's leading judgment in the Court of Appeal invoked *Ng Yuen Shiu* as approving Lord Denning's opinion in *Liverpool Taxi.* Parker LJ held that Mr Khan had a legitimate expectation that the policy outlined in the statement would be followed. This legitimate expectation had no *general* impact on the Home Secretary's power to apply a different policy, located at any point within the boundaries of irrationality. But, the substantive autonomy the Home Secretary retained *in respect of Mr Khan*, and anyone in his position, had apparently shrunk:

> 'The Home Secretary, if he undertakes to allow in persons if certain conditions are satisfied, should not in my view be entitled to resile from that undertaking without affording interested parties a hearing and then only if the overriding public interest demands it'.[90]

In *R v Secretary of State for the Home Department, ex p Ruddock*[91] the intimation that a legitimate expectation placed tight limits on a public body's capacity to depart from published policy promises was made more strongly than in *Khan.* The applicant was a prominent member of CND, who suspected her phone was being tapped by the security services. If her suspicion was correct, the security services were acting in breach of guidelines issued by the Home Secretary which identified the criteria she/he would invoke to authorise such tapping.[92] The Court of Appeal concluded that the policy statement created a legitimate expectation (presumably to all citizens) that phones would not – absent overriding public policy considerations – be tapped unless the guideline criteria were satisfied. This would have to be more than a procedural benefit; given the nature of the power in issue, the idea that a potential surveillance target be invited to a hearing to discuss whether the policy should be changed is absurd.[93] The substantive benefit claimed is however a modest one; the Home Secretary

89 [1985] 1 All ER 40, [1984] 1 WLR 1337, CA.

90 Ibid, at 46. Cf also at 48: 'vis a vis the recipient of such a letter, a new policy can only be implemented after such recipient has been given a full and serious consideration whether there is some overriding public interest which justifies a departure from the procedures stated in the letter'.

91 [1987] 2 All ER 518, [1987] 1 WLR 1482.

92 It might be noted that some 10 years later, the supposedly subversive Ms Ruddock was serving as a Minister in the first Blair government.

93 Cf Forsyth C (1997) '*Wednesbury* protection of substantive legitimate expectations' *Public Law* 375–384. The point being that a hearing would obviously alert a suspect to the benefit of no longer using her phone.

may change his policy, but must announce he is doing so and may not depart, except in limited circumstances, from whatever policy is currently in force.

Despite the modesty of this jurisprudential ambition, it appeared to be dismissed as constitutionally inappropriate by the House of Lords in *Re Findlay; Re Hogben; Re Honeyman; Re Matthews.*[94] The policy in question in this case was when prisoners became eligible for parole. In late 1983, the Home Secretary altered his policy on this matter. The previous policy was that prisoners became eligible for parole after serving one third of their sentence; under the new policy, half of the sentence would have to be served. The applicants argued, inter alia, that the change of policy was unlawful insofar as it frustrated their legitimate expectations to be eligible for parole after one third of their sentence. This was perhaps far too ambitious an argument to make. It goes much beyond *Khan*, in that it leaves no scope for 'overriding public policy considerations' to enable the Home Secretary to amend the initial policy. As such, it essentially invited the court to adopt an appellate jurisdiction. That invitation was unsurprisingly refused. Lord Scarman's sole judgment held that while the prisoners may have had a legitimate expectation, it could only be an expectation to be treated in a procedurally fair fashion in accordance with whatever policy the government had in force at the time: 'Any other view would entail the conclusion that the unfettered discretion conferred by the statute upon the minister can in some cases be restricted so as to hamper, or even to prevent, changes of policy'.[95] It is unfortunate that Lord Scarman should suggest that the Home Secretary's discretion in this matter was 'unfettered', as it was obviously subject to *Wednesbury* constraints. The thrust of his conclusion is however clear; that no procedural failing can initiate a change in the scope of a government body's substantive discretion.[96]

The opposing lead counsel in *Findlay* (Stephen Sedley QC for the applicant and John Laws for the government) were both sitting as High Court judges in the mid-1990s, when they produced very different opinions on the substantive legitimate expectation issue. In *R v Secretary of State for Transport, ex p Richmond-upon-Thames London Borough Council*,[97] Laws J faced an attempt by several London councils to bind the Secretary of State – unless overriding public policy reasons justified a contrary decision – to respect the substance of a promise made to limit the number of flights permitted to land at and depart from Heathrow airport. Richmond's counsel, Richard Gordon QC, invoked Lord Denning in *Liverpool Taxi* and Parker LJ in *Khan*

94 [1985] AC 318, [1984] 3 All ER 801, HL.

95 Ibid, at 338.

96 Astute commentators might have suggested that Lord Scarman's endorsement of orthodox principle was confined to this particular power, as, following the above quotation, he continued: 'Bearing in mind the complexity of the issues which the Secretary of State has to consider and the importance of the public interest in the administration of parole I cannot think that Parliament intended the discretion to be restricted in this way': ibid. This supposition is rather contradicted, however, by Lord Diplock's approval of Lord Scarman's reasoning in *Hughes v Department of Health and Social Security* ([1985] AC 776 at 788, HL), a case concerning the ostensibly far more justiciable issue of civil servants' retirement ages. It was at this time, we might recall, that Lord Diplock floated in *GCHQ* the possibility that proportionality could become a ground of review. He too evidently saw no link between proportionality and the recognition of substantive legitimate expectations.

97 [1994] 1 All ER 577, [1994] 1 WLR 74.

to support the existence of this limited notion of a substantive legitimate expectation. Laws J dismissed Mr Gordon's argument as 'barren'. One might however suggest that Laws J's approach perpetuated the judiciary's familiar unwillingness to accept that there is a clear distinction to be drawn between ordering a minister to reach one particular decision (ie an appellate jurisdiction) and limiting his/her room for substantive manoeuvre to decisions underpinned by overriding public policy considerations. The scope inherent in the latter concept may be substantial; it will just not be so wide as permitted by the irrationality test.[98]

Sedley J's judgment in *R v Ministry of Agriculture, Fisheries and Food, ex p Hamble (Offshore) Fisheries Ltd*[99] seemed to be the product of a rather more fertile legal imagination. Sedley J accepted in this case that the creation of a legitimate expectation by a government body did entitle the court to assess if a decision which would disappoint that expectation was 'fair' in substantive terms. He recognised that this did not equate to the court assuming an appellate jurisdiction (although he did not explicitly characterise his principle as a proportionality test):

> 'To postulate this is not to place the judge in the seat of the minister . . . [I]t is the court's task to recognise the constitutional importance of ministerial freedom to formulate and to reformulate policy; but it is equally the court's duty to protect the interests of those individuals whose expectation of different treatment has a legitimacy which in fairness outtops the policy choice which threatens to frustrate it'.[100]

The principle may better have been framed with a qualifying adverb ('clearly' or 'markedly' perhaps) attached to 'outtops'; unqualified, the verb does rather hint at an (almost) appellate power. Unqualified or no, however, Sedley J's reasoning was promptly refuted as 'heretical' and explicitly overruled by the Court of Appeal in *R v Secretary of State for the Home Department, ex p Hargreaves.*[101] Hargreaves' position was closely analogous to that of Findlay, although the benefit in issue in his case was a prisoner's entitlement to 'home leave' rather than parole. At the time of Hargreaves' commitment to prison, the Home Secretary's policy was that prisoners would be eligible for home leave, subject to good behaviour, after serving a third of their sentence. This policy was outlined in a letter given to prisoners on arrival in gaol. Prisoners also signed something called a 'compact', in which they were informed that certain benefits (including home leave) would be available to them if their behaviour was satisfactory. After Hargreaves was gaoled, the Home Secretary altered his policy on home leave, extending the qualifying period from one third to one half of the sentence.[102]

Rather curiously, the Court of Appeal held that no legitimate expectation arose on the facts of this case, on the basis that no clear indication had ever been given to the prisoners that home leave became available at a particular point in their sentences.[103]

98 See especially the passage at ibid, 596–597. 99 [1995] 2 All ER 714. 100 Ibid, at 731.
101 [1997] 1 All ER 397, [1997] 1 WLR 906.
102 There was no suggestion that this was an irrational decision.
103 See the forceful criticism of the court's conclusion on this point in Forsyth (1997) op cit.

Even if such an expectation had arisen, however, it could do no more than had been identified in *Findlay*; that is entitle Hargreaves to have his case considered in accordance with whatever (rational) policy was in force at the time. The court approved the reasoning as well as the result of Lord Scarman's judgment in *Findlay.*[104]

It seems likely that widespread judicial acceptance of even a partial substantive legitimate expectation will have to await judicial recognition of proportionality as a legitimate ground of substantive review. It is manifestly no coincidence that the notion of a substantive legitimate expectation has long been an element of the ECJ's general principles of law existing alongside, and indeed often closely overlapping with, the principle of proportionality. Indeed, it might sensibly be argued that several of the cases often invoked as examples of the ECJ applying the substantive legitimate expectation principle could better be classified as examples of the ECJ applying the proportionality test, insofar as the legitimate expectation was held to trigger a substantial narrowing of the government body's substantive discretion rather than to empower the court to specify exactly the content of the decision made.[105] There have been some instances when the ECJ has invoked the concept to bind a Community body to the precise detail of a particular representation,[106] but in the main the principle has been used to reduce rather than eliminate the decision-maker's discretion.

The judgment of the Court of Appeal in *R v North and East Devon Health Authority, ex p Coughlan*[107] appeared to circumvent this potentially thorny question by labelling the ground of substantive review that the courts should apply in such circumstances as 'unfairness' or 'abuse of power'. Ms Coughlan was a severely disabled person, who had been placed by the health authority in a particular residential facility and promised that the facility would be 'a home for life'. For financial reasons, the authority subsequently wished to close the facility and relocate Ms Coughlan. The Court of Appeal expressly approved the reasoning deployed in *Khan* and *Hamble Fisheries*; the health authority should be permitted to resile from the substance of its promise to Ms Coughlan only to satisfy 'an overiding public interest'. More significantly, the Court confirmed that the evaluation of whether there was such an interest was a matter for the court itself. On the basis of the information before it, the Court of Appeal concluded that no such overriding public interest existed.

The 'fairness' label has a pedigree in legitimate expectation case law. As noted above, it formed the basis of Roskill LJ's decision in *Liverpool Taxi Fleet.* In that case however, its reach was limited to procedural rather than substantive matters. Its invocation in *Coughlan* as a ground of substantive review lends an unnecessary opacity to

[104] A differently constituted Court of Appeal has cast doubt on *Hargreaves*, in *R v North and East Devon Health Authority, ex p Coughlan* [2001] QB 213, [2000] 3 All ER 850, CA; see below.

[105] See especially the discussion of *Mulder v EC Council and EC Commission*: C-104/89, C-37/90 [1992] ECR I-3061, ECJ in Forsyth (1997) op cit and Craig P (1996) 'Substantive legitimate expectations in domestic and Community law' *Cambridge LJ* 289–312. See also *Sofrimport SARL v EC Commission*: C-152/88 [1990] ECR I-2477, ECJ, and *CNTA SA v EC Commission*: 74/74 [1975] ECR 533, ECJ.

[106] Most notably the 'staff salaries' case *EC Commission v EC Council*: 81/72 [1973] ECR 575, ECJ.

[107] [2001] QB 213, [2000] 3 All ER 850, CA.

this point of law. At one point in the Court's judgment, Lord Woolf MR observed that; 'labels are not important'.[108] This might be thought rather disingenuous. While no doubt of little significance to Ms Coughlan and the health authority, the label applied by the Court to the ground of review on which it premised its judgment is important in constitutional terms. De facto, the Court of Appeal's judgment was subjecting the health authority to proportionality review. It is perhaps unfortunate that the Court did not say so explicitly, as it thereby exposes itself to the accusation that it was seeking to expand the reach of judicial review by covert rather than transparent means.[109]

The Court of Appeal confirmed its preference for the notion of 'abuse of power' as a covering label for the analysis of legitimate expectation cases in *R v London Borough of Newham, ex p Bibi*.[110] The Court also suggested that no distinction need be drawn between substantive and procedural expectations; the same approach should be adopted in either situation. The Court's reasoning, which drew heavily on Professor Craig's analysis[111] of the problem, suggested that:

> 'In all legitimate expectation cases, whether substantive or procedural, three practical questions arise. The first question is to what has the public authority, whether by practice or promise, committed itself; the second is whether the authority has acted or proposes to act unlawfully in relation to its commitment; the third is what the court should do.'

In *Bibi*, the local authority has mistakenly believed itself to be under an obligation to grant a secure tenancy[112] in one of its own properties to the applicant. Having promised to do so, the authority then realised that it was not under any such obligation, and resiled from its representation. The Court was not prepared to apply the *Coughlan* test on these facts; ie to insist that a secure tenancy be granted unless the local authority could demonstrate overriding public policy reasons to justify why that should not be done. The judgment that the local authority had acted unlawfully was ultimately premised on the local authority's failure to consider what weight it should attach to the fact that it had actually made the promise before deciding not to provide the substantive benefit in issue.

In addition to subsuming the legitimate expectation concept within a wider notion of 'abuse of power', *Bibi* also weakened the relevance of the principle of estoppel in the administrative law context. The Court considered that it was not necessary to

108 Ibid, at 878.

109 The Court indicated that the principle of a substantive legitimate expectation should be limited to; 'cases where the expectation is confined to one person or a few people, giving the representation the character of a contract'; (ibid, at 872). One might also note that the judgment does not necessarily mean that Ms Coughlan will indeed have a 'home for life' in that particular facility. The authority might well succeed at some future date in convincing a court that changing circumstances have lent an 'overriding' character to its wish to close the facility down.

110 [2001] EWCA Civ 607; [2002] 1 WLR 237.

111 Craig P (5th edn, 2003) *Administrative law* pp 418–431.

112 This being the type of tenancy introduced by the Housing Act 1980: see p 390 above.

found a legitimate expectation – as it would be to found a claim in estoppel – that the claimant had relied to her detriment on the representation made.[113]

The severance between the legitimate expectation and estoppel principles was subsequently underlined by the House of Lords in *R v East Sussex County Council, ex p Reprotech Ltd*.[114] The case rested on facts similar to those in the *Lever Finance* and *Western Fish* litigation, but the House of Lords indicated that such facts should in future be approached in a quite different way:

'It is true that in early cases such as . . . *Lever (Finance) Ltd v Westminster Corp* . . ., Lord Denning MR used the language of estoppel in relation to planning law. At that time the public law concepts of abuse of power and legitimate expectation were very undeveloped and no doubt the analogy of estoppel seemed useful. In the *Western Fish* case the Court of Appeal tried its best to reconcile these invocations of estoppel with the general principle that a public authority cannot be estopped from exercising a statutory discretion or performing a public duty. . . . It seems to me that in this area, public law has already absorbed whatever is useful from the moral values which underlie the private law concept of estoppel and the time has come for it to stand upon its own two feet'.[115]

It has been suggested that the *Reprotech* decision marks the 'end of estoppel' as a ground of judicial review.[116] That contention seems soundly based in respect of land use planning law, and indeed in respect of other areas of government activity which raise broad questions of public interest. Whether it will have a pervasive effect remains to be seen.

But, notwithstanding the innovations which appear to have been introduced by *Coughlan*, *Bibi* and *Reprotech*, it must be emphasised that all of the cases discussed in this section have involved attempts to bind government bodies to substantively intra vires decisions. The argument that the common law could recognise the concept of a substantive legitimate expectation as a device to overcome the classic *Hulkin* estoppel dilemma (ie whether one should, to avoid substantive injustice to an innocent citizen bind a government body to a decision it had no power to reach) has yet to be successfully made.[117] It would at present seem no more feasible to reach that destination through the legitimate expectation route than through the mechanism of estoppel.[118] That it is possible to sustain that result in EC law – or, the example deployed in Forsyth's influential critique, German law[119] – is of little relevance to domestic law. In both EC and German law, the powers ostensibly bestowed by a 'legislature' on an executive body are themselves subject to higher legal rules; the Treaty and the ECJ's own general principles of law within the Community's legal system, and the terms of

[113] [2002] 1 WLR 237 at paras 27–31. See pp [442–447 3rd ed] above.

[114] [2002] UKHL 8; [2002] 4 All ER 58.

[115] Idem, at para 35.

[116] Purdue M (2002) 'The end of estoppel in public law' *Journal of Planning and Environmental Law* 509.

[117] See pp 520–521 above.

[118] It does now seem that such an outcome could arise through the provisions of the Human Rights Act 1998; see *Stretch v United Kingdom* [2003] EHRR 320.

[119] (1988) op cit.

the constitution in Germany. In these legal systems, the ultra vires problem is much less acute than in the UK.[120]

THE CONTENT OF PROCEDURAL FAIRNESS – LEGAL REPRESENTATION AND AN OBLIGATION TO GIVE REASONS FOR DECISIONS

An entitlement to representation by counsel is regarded as an essential element of the procedural protection afforded to litigants in a criminal trial. The entitlement is however far less widely available in respect of hearings held by governmental bodies other than courts.

The applicant in *Pett v Greyhound Racing Association Ltd*[121] had been accused of doping his greyhounds. The Association, which policed the ethics of greyhound racing, announced that he would be subject to disciplinary proceedings and refused to allow him to be represented by counsel. Pett subsequently sought an interlocutory injunction to prevent the hearing being held until he had established whether he had a right to counsel at the hearing. Lord Denning indicated that he thought Pett's claim was well-founded:

> 'It is not every man who has the ability to defend himself on his own. He cannot bring out the points in his own favour, or the weaknesses in the other side. He may be tongue-tied or nervous, confused or wanting in intelligence . . . If justice is to be done he ought to have the help of someone to speak for him. And who better than a lawyer . . .'.[122]

Lord Denning (supported by Davies and Russell LJJ) appeared to limit the reach of this principle to cases where a person's reputation and livelihood was at stake. The above passage was however strictly obiter. At the full trial, *Pett v Greyhound Racing Association Ltd (No 2)*,[123] Lyell J reached the conclusion that even applicants in Mr Pett's position had no automatic right to representation. That their reputations and livelihoods might be at stake was not sufficient to trigger this level of protection.

Nor was the Court of Appeal prepared to accept that this entitlement should be extended to prisoners facing disciplinary proceedings by a Governor or Board of Visitors. In *Fraser v Mudge*, Roskill LJ offered what – from a policy perspective – might be regarded as the other side of the coin to the reasoning advanced by Lord Denning in *Pett*:

> 'One looks to see what are the broad principles underlying these rules. They are to maintain discipline in person by proper, swift and speedy decisions, whether by the governor of the visitors; and it seems to me that the requirements of natural justice do not make it necessary that a person against whom disciplinary proceedings are pending should as of right be entitled to be represented by a solicitor or counsel or both'.[124]

[120] It would of course arise if the executive decision in question was ultra vires the EC Treaties or the German constitution respectively.

[121] [1969] 1 QB 125, CA. [122] Ibid, at 132. [123] [1970] 1 QB 46, [1969] 2 All ER 221.

[124] [1975] 1 WLR 1132 at 1134, CA.

A parallel line of case law addressed the separate question of whether, even if an applicant had no automatic right of representation, the decision-maker might nonetheless be obliged to consider if in the circumstances of the particular case, such representation should be permitted. The Court of Appeal had lent this principle a potentially expansive reach in *Enderby Town Football Club Ltd v Football Association Ltd*,[125] emphasising that no body should adopt a rigid rule never to permit representation.

In *R v Secretary of State for the Home Department, ex p Tarrant*,[126] the High Court held that it would be irrational for a Board of Visitors to refuse to allow representation where there was scope for doubt as to whether a prisoner's behaviour fell within the legal definition of a particular offence (in this case 'mutiny'). Representation need not however be permitted if all that was in issue was a question of fact, even if the offence charged (in this case assault) could attract substantial penalties. Some indication that *Tarrant* applied this principle too generously was subsequently given by the House of Lords in *R v Board of Visitors of HM Prison, The Maze, ex p Hone*, in which the court stressed that allowing legal representation on a routine basis would have the unwelcome results of causing: 'wholly unnecessary delays in many cases, to the detriment of all concerned including the prisoner charged, and to wholly unnecessary waste of time and money, contrary to the public interest'.[127]

The common law had until very recently been as reluctant to recognise a general duty that government bodies give reasons for their decisions as it has been to grant applicants an entitlement to legal representation. In the aftermath of the Crichel Down controversy,[128] Parliament imposed such a duty on a wide range of statutory bodies in the Tribunals and Inquiries Act 1958. That bodies were not brought within the remit of this Act might imply that Parliament did not intend that the common law should subject them to a similar obligation. The argument against the recognition of this doctrine as a general facet of procedural fairness is largely one of the time and expense that it would impose upon decision-makers. A lesser argument is that giving reasons may compromise the anonymity of informants, as for example in *Benaim and Khaida*. It is however clear that both the instrumental and intrinsic justifications for a concern with procedural fairness have especial resonance in respect of this particular content issue.[129] In addition, the giving of reasons would make subsequent review of or appeal against the decision in question more straightforward. These factors may explain the courts' evidently greater willingness to apply the doctrine in a more extensive, if piecemeal fashion in recent years.

The Court of Appeal's judgment in *R v Civil Service Appeal Board, ex p Cunningham*[130] is a good illustration of this trend. The Civil Service Appeal Board performed the role of an industrial tribunal in relation to civil servants. Under the terms of the Civil Service Code, the CSAB was to treat civil servants no less favourably than

125 [1971] Ch 591, [1971] 1 All ER 215, CA.
126 [1985] QB 251, [1984] 1 All ER 799.
127 [1988] 2 WLR 177 at 186, HL.
128 See p 327 above.
129 Richardson G (1986) op cit; Craig (1993) op cit pp 310–316.
130 [1991] 4 All ER 310, CA.

they would be treated by an industrial tribunal applying the terms of the Employment Protection (Consolidation) Act 1978. Cunningham, a prison officer, maintained that the compensation awarded to him by the CSAB was far lower than he would have been given by an industrial tribunal. The CSAB had not offered any reasons for its decisions. The Court of Appeal rejected the proposition that the common law imposed a general duty to give reasons on government bodies. It nonetheless concluded that reasons should be given in this situation. This was in part because the CSAB's function 'mirrored' that of industrial tribunals, which were required to give reasons; in part because the Code had generated a legitimate expectation that reasons should be given; and in part because the imposition of that requirement would not have any obviously adverse implications for the administrative process. The obligation was however to be limited to 'outline reasons'; the CSAB did not have to provide full details of its reasoning. In Lord Donaldson MR's opinion 'fairness requires a tribunal such as the board to give sufficient reasons for its decision to enable the parties to know the issues to which it addressed its mind and that it acted lawfully'.[131]

Subsequently in *R v Parole Board, ex p Wilson*,[132] the Court of Appeal imposed a similar duty on the Parole Board's decision as to whether a prisoner serving a life sentence should be refused parole on the basis that his release would pose a danger to the public. The principle was extended in *R v Secretary of State for the Home Department, ex p Doody*[133] to encompass the Home Secretary's powers to fix the minimum period that prisoners sentenced to life had to serve before they became eligible for parole.[134] This conclusion was presented by Lord Mustill as part of; 'a perceptible trend towards an insistence on greater openness, or if one prefers the contemporary jargon, "transparency", in the making of administrative decisions'.[135]

This approach appeared to spill over into other areas of the government process. In *R v London Borough of Lambeth, ex p Walters*, the High Court held that such a duty to give reasons attached to all aspects of the homelessness provisions of the Housing Act 1985, notwithstanding the fact that a local authority was placed under specific statutory duty to give reasons in respect of particular decisions under the Act.[136] *Walters* was however promptly disapproved by the Court of Appeal in *R v Kensington and Chelsea Royal London Borough Council, ex p Grillo*.[137] The court ruled that this was not an area where the common law 'should supply the omission of the legislature'. While the giving of reasons might be desirable as an element of 'good and courteous administration', the terms of the Act negated the inference of any general duty to do so.

131 Ibid, at 320. 132 [1992] QB 740, [1992] 2 All ER 576, CA.

133 [1994] 1 AC 531, sub nom *Doody v Secretary of State for the Home Department* [1993] 3 All ER 92, HL.

134 See Craig P (1994) 'The common law, reasons and administrative justice' *Cambridge LJ* 282–302.

135 [1993] 3 All ER 92 at 108.

136 [1994] 2 FCR 336. For comment see Loveland (1995) op cit pp 344–346. The rationale of the authority's argument was that the explicit requirement that an authority give reasons in respect of particular parts of the Act implied that it need not do so in respect of the remaining parts of the Act.

137 [1996] 2 FCR 56, 28 HLR 94.

Sedley J's judgment in *R v Higher Education Funding Council, ex p Institute of Dental Surgery* reinforced the view that there would be limits to the scope of the duty to give reasons. The decision in issue was an evaluation of the research activity of an academic institution. Sedley J regarded this as an essentially non-justiciable question, and thus one which the common law would not require to be supported with reasons.[138] The judgment was also however notable for Sedley J's suggestion that certain classes of decisions should be subject to a duty to give reasons; these being those which affected personal liberty or which appeared aberrant in substantive terms.

These categories were extended by the Court of Appeal in *R v Secretary of State for the Home Department, ex p Fayed.*[139] Fayed had made an unsuccessful application for British nationality under the terms of the British Nationality Act 1981, which had been rejected by the Home Office in the most cursory of terms; ('after careful consideration your application has been refused'). Section 44(2) of the Act expressly provided that the Home Secretary need not give any reasons for any decision granting or refusing citizenship. The Court concluded that but for that provision, the common law would have imposed a duty to provide clear reasons for a refusal of citizenship, given the importance of the decision to the applicant concerned.

CONCLUSION

The *Fayed* decision exemplifies the argument that in recent years the courts have been applying a more stringent set of procedural criteria to the making of governmental decisions. In addition to extending the reach of the procedural fairness principle, the courts have been taking (modest) steps also to enhance its content. This area of law still retains however a considerable degree of imprecision, especially on the question of exactly what procedural fairness entails. The point is perhaps best put by Lord Bridge's now oft-quoted comment in *Lloyd v McMahon*:

> 'My Lords, the so-called rules of natural justice are not engraved on tablets of stone ... [W]hat the requirements of fairness demand when any body ... has to make a decision which will affect the rights of individuals depends on the character of the decision-making body, the kind of decision it has to make and the statutory or other framework in which it operates ... [T]he courts will not only require the procedure in the statute to be followed, but will readily imply so much and no more to be introduced by way of additional procedural safeguards as will ensure the attainment of fairness'.[140]

138 'It may be a misfortune for the applicant that the court, which in *Cunningham's* case could readily evaluate the contrast between what the board awarded and what an industrial tribunal would have awarded, cannot begin to evaluate the comparative worth of research in clinical dentistry; but it is a fact of life': [1994] 1 All ER 651 at 670.

139 [1997] 1 All ER 228, [1998] 1 WLR 763.

140 [1987] 1 All ER 1118 at 1161.

II. THE RULE AGAINST BIAS

The second limb of the natural justice doctrine has proven rather less complicated than the *audi alterem partem* principle.[141] The rule against bias (*nemo iudex sua causa* – 'no-one may be a judge in his own cause') is concerned to ensure that government decision-makers do not have a personal interest in decisions that they take. This has long been held to be a fundamental tenet of English public law. The strength and longevity of the rule is neatly illustrated by recalling *Dr Bonham's Case.*[142] The legislation which Coke CJ had suggested was 'against common right or reason' in that case had in effect allowed a governmental body to settle disputes in which it was a party. In the post-revolutionary era, Parliament may if it wishes (subject now to the constraints of EC law) permit such bias, but the undesirability of such situations is now so deeply embedded in the common law that only the most explicit of statutory authorisations could achieve that effect.

The types of bias considered problematic at common law might crudely be labelled as either 'financial' or 'ideological' interests. Such interests may give rise (depending on the intensity of the interest) to the automatic disqualification of a particular decision-maker, or to disqualification if it is established that a suspicion of bias could be thought to be well-founded. The courts' concern has generally been focused not on *actual* bias, but on the possibility that bias may arise. Much of the case law in this area has been concerned with 'judicial' decision-making, a term broadly defined to include judges per se, magistrates, jurors and executive bodies performing judicial or quasi-judicial functions: its relevance to purely 'administrative' decisions is less pronounced.

DIRECT FINANCIAL INTERESTS

The objections to a decision-maker having a direct financial interest in a given decision are obvious. She may favour her own financial concerns above the public interest and so produce a substantively undesirable decision; and even if she does not do so anyone else affected by the decision might reasonably suspect that she has. The rule against bias had been forcefully applied in this situation.

The leading case is *Dimes v Grand Junction Canal.*[143] The case involved a claim that Lord Cottenham LC had sat in proceedings involving a company in which he had shares. There was no suggestion that he had acted in a biased way; the applicant's objection was to the obvious risk that Lord Cottenhams' financial involvement would undermine public confidence in the court's impartiality. The judgment thus had to be set aside. Lord Campbell put the point very clearly:

141 A thorough and incisive view of the complexities of this issue is offered in Beatson and Matthews op cit ch 7.

142 See p 22 above.

143 (1852) 3 HL Cas 759, 10 ER 301, HL.

'it is of the last importance that the maxim that no man is to be a judge in his own cause should be held sacred . . . This will be a lesson to all inferior tribunals to take care not only that in their decrees they are not influenced by their personal interest, but to avoid the appearance of labouring under such an influence'.[144]

The incompatibility of a judge's financial interest with the unbiased administration of justice was reiterated in 1866 by Blackburn J in *R v Rand*: 'There is no doubt that any direct pecuniary interest, however small, in the subject of inquiry, does disqualify a person from acting as a judge in the matter'.[145] A judge who has such an interest is subject to what was later termed 'automatic disqualification' from the case concerned. The strength of the suspicion that has to arise before bias is established is largely unproblematic when direct[146] financial interests are at stake, but it becomes a much more difficult question when the financial interest is rather more oblique.

INDIRECT FINANCIAL INTERESTS – A MERE SUSPICION OR A REAL LIKELIHOOD

The difficulties that may be caused by claims of indirect financial bias are well illustrated by the judgments in *R v Sussex Justices, ex p McCarthy*[147] and *R v Barnsley Licensing Justices, ex p Barnsley and District Licensed Victuallers' Association.*[148] *McCarthy* arose because a solicitor who acted on a part-time basis as clerk to the Justices had sat in a criminal case concerning a car accident which involved a defendant who a client of his firm was suing in a civil action arising from the same accident. There was no suggestion that the clerk/solicitor had actually acted in a biased fashion during the criminal case. But this was not a relevant issue. Lord Hewart CJ again stressed that it was appearances that mattered:

'A long line of cases shows that it is . . . of fundamental importance that justice should not only be done, but should manifestly and undoubtedly be seen to be done . . .

Nothing is to be done which creates even a suspicion that there has been an improper interference with the course of justice'.[149]

The notion of a mere 'suspicion' is however a very wide test; it seems to suggest there need only be a possibility of bias, not a strong probability. This was narrowed somewhat by the presumption that the 'suspicion' is supposed to arise in the mind of a dispassionate observer, not a party to the proceedings (who would of course be likely, because of her own bias, to magnify any suspicions as to the impartiality of the decision-maker).

144 10 ER 301 at 315, HL.

145 (1866) LR 1 QB 230 at 232. The court nonetheless concluded that the financial interest in issue in this case – local justices' status as trustees of a hospital and friendly society which had a financial stake in the outcome of the decision – did not amount to a direct interest.

146 This is in itself a potentially troublesome issue.

147 [1924] 1 KB 256.

148 [1960] 2 All ER 703, CA.

149 [1924] 1 KB 256 at 259.

In *R v Barnsley Licensing Justices, ex p Barnsley and District Licensed Victuallers' Association*, the decision at issue was the justices' grant of a licence to sell alcohol to the local co-operative society – an organisation of which all the justices were members. As such, they were entitled to a share of any profits that the society might make. The Court of Appeal concluded that this interest was sufficient to raise a real likelihood of bias. The case is however most notable for Devlin LJ's judgment, in which he intimated that Lord Hewart CJ's 'even a suspicion' test in *McCarthy* was too broadly stated:

'[I]n my judgment, it is not the test. We have not to inquire what impression might be left on the minds of the present applicants or on the minds of the public generally. We have to satisfy ourselves that there was a real likelihood of bias, and not merely satisfy ourselves that that was the sort of suspicion which might reasonably get abroad'.[150]

Both Ormerod LJ and Lord Evershed MR also used the 'real likelihood' formulation in their judgments, which led to the suggestion that the bias test would now be less easily satisfied than hitherto.

The law was then thrown into a state of some confusion by the subsequent Court of Appeal judgment in *R v London Rent Assessment Panel Committee, ex p Metropolitan Properties Co (IFGC) Ltd*.[151] Lannon was a solicitor who also chaired a rent assessment committee. His father was in dispute with his (the father's) landlord. Lannon was advising his father. Lannon subsequently sat on a rent assessment committee which set the rents (at an extremely low level) at another property owned by the landlord. Lord Denning MR accepted that Mr Lannon's financial interest in the rent level set was 'remote . . . indirect and uncertain'. He nevertheless quashed the committee's decision. He did so by invoking the 'real likelihood' formula, but lent that formula a meaning that seemed to come close to the 'even a suspicion' test by observing that in *Barnsley* Devlin LJ 'appears to have limited [the *McCarthy*] principle considerably, but I would stand by it'.[152] He then offered a test which seemed to include elements of both Lord Hewart CJ's and Devlin LJ's ostensibly disparate approaches to this issue:

'[I]n considering whether there was a real likelihood of bias . . . the court looks at the impression which would be given to other people . . . [I]f right-minded persons would think that, in the circumstances, there was a real likelihood of bias on his part, then he should not sit . . . Nevertheless, there must appear to be a real likelihood of bias. Surmise or conjecture is not enough . . . The reason is plain enough. Justice must be rooted in confidence: and confidence is destroyed when right-minded people go away thinking; "The judge was biased".'[153]

The result of this rather opaque reasoning was that administrative law now seemed to harbour two formulae in respect of indirect pecuniary interests; 'suspicion of bias' (on the part of dispassionate observers) or 'real likelihood of bias' (in the view of the court). Presumably these two formulae did not mean the same thing; the latter test

[150] [1960] 2 All ER 703 at 715. [151] [1969] 1 QB 577. [152] Ibid, at 599.
[153] Ibid.

seems to be harder to satisfy. As Beatson and Matthews suggest,[154] this uncertainty generated a good deal of contradictory case law, including judgments which advanced the unlikely proposition that the two formulae did indeed produce just the same test.[155] The point was not subject to exhaustive analysis by the House of Lords until 1993, in *R v Gough*.[156]

CLARIFYING THE LAW? THE *GOUGH* FORMULAE

Gough had been convicted of robbery. After the trial, he recognised one of the jurors as his brother's next door neighbour, and made the rather speculative assertion that this created a suspicion of bias sufficient for the verdict to be quashed. The claim received short shrift from the court. The primary concern in the judgment was to clarify what Lord Goff referred to as the 'bewildering' state of the law on this point.

Lord Goff (with whom the rest of the court concurred) rooted this uncertainty primarily in the co-existence of the 'suspicion' and 'real likelihood' formulae. He attempted to clarify matters by confirming that a direct pecuniary interest should lead to automatic disqualification. In respect of indirect financial interests – and it seems non-financial interests – the court offered the following test:

> 'I think it unnecessary . . . that the court should look at the matter through the eyes of the reasonable man, because the court in cases such as these personifies the reasonable man . . . [H]aving ascertained the relevant circumstances, the court should ask itself whether, having regard to those circumstances, there was a real danger of bias on the part of the relevant member of the tribunal in question, in the sense that he might unfairly regard . . . with favour or disfavour, the case of a party to the issue'.[157]

Lord Goff stressed that he was thinking in terms of a possibility rather than probability of bias, but also managed to convey the impression that his 'real danger' formula was not a simple assertion of the 'mere suspicion' test. The test formulated by Lord Woolf in his concurring judgment seemed, in contrast, to owe rather more to Devlin LJ's views, being framed in terms of: 'a real danger of injustice having occurred as a result of the alleged bias'.[158] One might doubt that *Gough* has allayed the doctrinal confusion that has attended this issue in recent years, but its significance has latterly come to be overshadowed by an evident extension of the automatic disqualification principle to ideological as well as financial interests.

IDEOLOGICAL BIAS IN 'JUDICIAL' DECISIONS

The question before the House of Lords in *R v Bow Street Metropolitan Stipendiary Magistrate, ex p Pinochet Ugarte (No 2)*[159] was triggered by the attempts of the Spanish

[154] Op cit at pp 287–290.
[155] *R v Liverpool City Justices, ex p Topping* [1983] 1 All ER 490, [1983] 1 WLR 119.
[156] [1993] 2 All ER 724, HL. [157] Ibid, at 738. [158] Ibid, at 738.
[159] [2000] 1 AC 119, [1999] 1 All ER 577, HL.

government to have Pinochet, the Chilean dictator, extradited from Britain to face trial in Spain for various human rights abuses committed against Spanish citizens in Chile. In *Pinochet*,[160] the House of Lords had approved the extradition by a majority of 3–2. Somewhat unusually, the court had allowed various interested parties, including Amnesty International, to participate in the proceedings by offering their respective views of the relevant law.

It then emerged that one of the majority, Lord Hoffmann, in addition to being a member of Amnesty, served as a director of an associated charity. Pinochet then argued that this interest amounted to bias which should automatically have excluded Lord Hoffmann from sitting.

The House of Lords subsequently reconvened and concluded that Lord Hoffmann was disqualified from sitting, and that the judgment had to be 'set aside'. The principle outlined in Lord Browne-Wilkinson's leading judgment was clearly expressed:

> 'if the absolute impartiality of the judiciary is to be maintained, there must be a rule which automatically disqualifies a judge who is involved, whether personally or as a Director of a company, in promoting the same causes in the same organisation as is a party to the suit'.[161]

It might readily be thought that Lord Hoffmann's interest was sufficiently remote on these facts to preclude any finding of automatic disqualification. The *Gough* test would then have come into play, and it would have been for Pinochet to establish that there was 'a real danger of injustice having occurred'. That would seem a stiff test to surmount on the facts, even if one accepts the questionable contention that a judge's support for an organisation whose raison d'etre is to promote respect for international law could amount to 'bias' in the first place.

The judgment does imply that no automatic disqualification would have arisen if Amnesty had not actually intervened in the case, or if Hoffmann had – in previous judgments or academic writings – expressed support for Amnesty's view of the law but was not a member of the group. Whether the *Gough* test would be met in such circumstances is a matter for speculation.[162]

The supposition that *Pinochet* might prompt a flood of spurious bias claims from disgruntled litigants appeared to be borne out by the various cases joined in *Locobail (UK) Ltd v Bayfield Properties Ltd.*[163] The alleged bias in *Locobail* itself was that the judge (who was a QC sitting in a part-time capacity) was a partner in a firm of city solicitors which was acting for a client which was suing the husband of the (de facto) defendant in the action. The contention was that this 'conflict of interest' might be thought to dispose the judge to find in the plaintiff's favour. The Court of Appeal

160 [2000] 1 AC 61, [1998] 4 All ER 897, HL. 161 [1999] 1 All ER 577 at 588, HL.

162 See Malleson K (2000) 'Judicial bias and disqualification after *Pinochet (No 2)*' *MLR* 119–127: Jones J (1999) 'Judicial bias and disqualification in the *Pinochet* case' *Public Law* 391–398.

163 [2000] QB 451, [2000] 1 All ER 65, CA. The case was joined with *Timmins v Gormley; Wiliams v Inspector of Taxes; R v Bristol Betting and Gaming Licensing Committee, ex p O'Callaghan.*

concluded that any financial interest the judge might have was far too tenuous to fall within the *Dimes* principle of 'automatic disqualification'.[164]

Nor did it think the *Gough* test was met. The judge had no knowledge that his firm (which was very large) was acting against the defendant's husband; thus, as the court put it: 'How can there be any real danger of bias, or any real apprehension or likelihood of bias, if the judge does not know of the facts that, in argument, are relied upon as giving rise to the conflict of interest'.[165]

The same rationale was invoked to dismiss the bias claim raised in *O'Callaghan*. Here the judge's family firm owned property which was leased to a company against which the applicant was conducting extensive litigation. The judge had no knowledge of the leases, and played no active part in the firm's business decision. His interest was 'nominal and indirect', and thus could not substantiate a bias claim.

The allegation in *Williams* was wholly absurd. The applicant was engaged in litigation for sexual harassment and racial discrimination against the Inland Revenue. Having lost her claim before an industrial tribunal, Williams then claimed that the *Gough* test was met because the tribunal chair, some 40 years earlier, had spent three years working for the Inland Revenue. The Court saw no merit in this claim: '[N]o right-thinking person knowing of the connection of [the chair] with the Inland Revenue would feel that there was any danger of bias in this case. The suggestion that there might be was fanciful'.[166]

However, in *Timmins*, the Court did accept that the *Gough* test was met. The litigation was a personal injury action, in which the plaintiff had been awarded an ostensibly surprisingly large sum. The defendant's insurance company claimed that the judge fell within *Gough* because he had in recent years written several scathing critiques in professional journals about the way in which insurance companies attempted to refute or minimise their liability in personal injury cases. The Court of Appeal saw no basis for assuming that a judge's extra-judicial writings could per se amount to apparent bias. But a judge who engaged in such activities had to be 'circumspect in the language he uses and the tone in which he expresses himself. It is always inappropriate for a judge to use intemperate language about subjects on which he has adjudicated or will have to adjudicate'.[167] Because the judge in question had used particularly trenchant language in his articles, a real danger of bias could be thought to arise.

[164] The Court of Appeal did seem somewhat to limit the extensive meaning that could be lent to *Dimes* and *Rand*, noting that: 'In the context of automatic disqualification the question is not whether the judge has some link with a party involved in a cause before the judge but whether the outcome of that cause could, realistically, affect the judge's interest' (at 70–71). It also intimated that it approved recent Australian decisions on this issue which accepted that a de minimis exception should apply to the automatic disqualification principle.

[165] [2000] 1 All ER 65 at 84, CA. This does not imply that *McCarthy* was wrongly decided. The Court stressed in this case that the solicitors' firm in question was very large, employing some 500 lawyers; there could be no sensible expectation that any partner could be familiar with its entire caseload.

[166] Ibid, at 93–94. [167] Ibid, at 91.

Locobail will no doubt deter bias allegations based on a judge's indirect and tenuous financial interest or institutional affiliations.[168] *Timmins* may however prompt dissatisfied litigants to trawl academic and professional journals for any hint that a judge holds them or their ilk in disfavour. The Court noted it reached its conclusion with 'misgiving'; which may indicate that the judgment was an unfortunate one which ought soon to be reversed. As in *Pinochet* itself, the conclusion raises the unwelcome inference that we must assume that judges are incapable of recognising and discounting their 'political' views when presiding over litigation.

FURTHER CLARIFYING THE LAW? THE *PORTER V MAGILL* FORMULA

The flurry of litigation on the bias point following *Pinochet* and *Gough* promptly led the Court of Appeal, and thereafter the House of Lords, to offer a further refinement of the correct test to apply in respect of this aspect of the procedural fairness doctrine. The Court of Appeal in *Re Medicaments and Related Classes of Goods (No 2)*[169] concluded that:

> 'The court must first ascertain all the circumstances which have a bearing on the suggestion that the judge was biased. It must then ask whether those circumstances would lead a fair-minded observer to conclude that there was a real possibility, or a real danger, the two being the same, that the tribunal was biased.'[170]

The House of Lords subsequently endorsed this test in *Porter v Magill*[171], save for the further minor modification that the reference to 'real danger' be removed from the formula.

It might be suggested that this drift in the case law evinces a concern to attach greater significance to the second of the two 'intrinsic reasons' identified at the start of this chapter for applying procedural fairness rules to the activities of governmental bodies. But it might also be argued that this strand of administrative law doctrine was becoming bedevilled with an evermore elaborate linguistic superstructure which positively invites disgruntled litigants to engage in ingenious semantic arguments in attempting to overturn unfavourable decisions.

The Court of Appeal's robust conclusion in *Taylor v Lawrence*[172] might therefore be welcomed as sending such litigants a clear signal that claims of tenuous bias would not succeed. The claimed bias in *Taylor* arose from the fact that the judge in the case had previously instructed the firm of solicitors representing the successful party to draw up his will. The Court of Appeal held that this was not a matter that could be thought to have any bearing on the judge's conduct. The Court also indicated that it could see little scope for assuming that any credible suspicion of bias could arise simply because a judge and a party's lawyers had a pre-existing professional relationship.

[168] See now also *Taylor v Lawrence* [2003] QB 528; discussed below. [169] [2001] 1 WLR 700.
[170] Ibid, at para 85. [171] [2002] 2 AC 357. [172] [2003] QB 528.

BIAS IN NON-JUDICIAL PROCEEDINGS

A further way of holding that Poplar council's wage policy that was in issue in *Roberts v Hopwood* was unlawful would be to suggest that the council had succumbed to bias in making its decision. This bias would be found in the councillor's evident embrace of 'eccentric principles of socialist philanthropy' and 'feminist ambition', motives which the House of Lords considered wholly improper. The obvious problem with such a rationale is that it wholly excludes any legitimate role for political ideology in the making of governmental decisions, a proposition which is obviously nonsensical in the modern era.

It was subsequently made clear in *Franklin v Minister of Town and Country Planning*[173] that a decision-maker was not 'biased' simply because she formulated policy in accordance with her pre-existing political beliefs. Lord Thankerton indicated that the nemo iudex rule has no application to this type of 'political decision':

> 'My Lords, I could wish that the use of the word "bias" should be confined to its proper sphere. It proper significance, in my opinion, is to denote a departure from the standard of even handed justice which the law requires from those who occupy judicial . . . or quasi-judicial office . . . .'[174]

Personal financial interests will however be just as unacceptable in this context as in respect of judicial decisions. This is clearly illustrated by *R v Hendon RDC, ex p Chorley*,[175] in which it was held that a suspicion of bias arose if a member of a council planning committee was an estate agent with a financial interest in a piece of land being considered for a grant of planning permission.

CONCLUSION

The concept of procedural fairness has generated a vast body of case law in the modern era, and will no doubt continue to do so in future. But the law on this point, even when seen in conjunction with the law relating to the traditional substantive grounds on which government action can be held unlawful, offers only a partial picture of the way in which administrative law fits into the broader constitutional principles of the rule of law and the sovereignty of Parliament. Chapters sixteen and seventeen add to that picture by exploring two vital, related issues: which legal procedures must an applicant follow when challenging a government decision; and who is entitled to initiate legal proceedings?

173 [1948] AC 87, HL. 174 Ibid, at 92, HL. 175 [1933] 2 KB 696.

16

THE APPLICATION FOR JUDICIAL REVIEW

Questions of procedure have assumed a heightened importance within English administrative law in the past 25 years. This trend was triggered by a modification to the Rules of the Supreme Court, introduced in 1977, which was then given statutory form in the Supreme Court Act 1981. The reform introduced a procedural device called the 'application for judicial review' (hereafter referred to as AJR). The terminology is itself apt to cause confusion, as a very substantial part of litigation conducted in the field of constitutional and administrative law – which in its entirety is often referred to loosely as 'judicial review' – was not initiated through the AJR process or its immediate predecessors.

The starting point for analysing this subject is the historical duality within English administrative law of the mechanisms through which citizens might challenge the lawfulness of government action.[1] This duality might be categorised as one between 'private law' and 'public law' remedies. In many instances, legal actions against government bodies might take exactly the same procedural form as actions against private individuals. *Entick v Carrington*, for example, was technically an action for trespass – that is a private law tort – even though its real concern was to establish the lawfulness or otherwise of the government's claimed power to suppress sedition through the use of general warrants. Similarly, *Liversidge v Anderson*, an action for unlawful imprisonment, was nominally a private law action (as was habeas corpus), even though its true purpose in that case was to ascertain the meaning of the government's powers of detention under reg 18B. Equally, the question of whether a government body's actions were illegal, irrational, or procedurally unfair might arise in an action for breach of contract or restitution. In addition, the private law stream contained the remedies of declaration or injunction; (the former designed to 'declare' the law on a particular point, the latter being a coercive order requiring a defendant to cease a particular course of behaviour). These remedies might be sought through procedural devices known as a 'writ' or 'originating summons'.

The 'public law' stream contained the three so-called 'prerogative remedies' of certiorari, prohibition and mandamus. Certiorari was a device to quash (or

[1] The most helpful, detailed introduction to this issue is provided in Craig P (3rd edn, 1994) *Administrative law* ch 14 (London: Sweet and Maxwell).

invalidate) unlawful decisions; prohibition had the same effect as the injunction; and mandamus was intended to force a government body to exercise its legal powers when it was refusing to do so.

The private and public law streams had developed for different reasons, and had quite different characteristics. The declaration and injunction were initially designed solely to regulate disputes between private individuals. (This is evidenced quite clearly in the way such cases are styled; eg *Anisminic v Foreign Compensation Commission.*) The actions took for granted firstly that litigants would have a direct interest in the dispute, and secondly that trivial or vexatious litigation would rarely occur. The development of the private law remedies was informed by two central assumptions. Firstly, that the court's role would often be as finder of both fact and law; ie it would make decisions on the precise merits of a particular issue. Secondly, because the action was designed to resolve disputes between 'individuals', the efficient administration of government would rarely be compromised by such litigation.[2]

The prerogative remedies, in contrast, developed as a means of ensuring that all government bodies remained within the limits of their lawful powers; individual litigants here were theoretically acting on behalf of the monarch in seeking to establish if the law had been breached.[3] Had *Anisminic* been an action for certiorari, it would have been styled *R v Foreign Compensation Commission, ex p Anisminic.*[4] One obvious consequence of this is that the prerogative remedies were traditionally assumed not to be available against the Crown, on the basis that the Crown could not bring legal proceedings against itself.[5] The development of the remedies also rested on the presumptions firstly that the court's role would generally be simply to establish if an obviously unlawful decision had occurred (ie it would not be looking closely at questions of fact nor reaching any conclusion as to the detailed merits of the governmental decision in issue); and secondly that all prerogative remedy applications would necessarily have implications for the efficient administration of government.

To put the matter crudely, remedies in the private law stream – whether the remedy sought be an action in breach of contract or in tort or an attempt to seek a declaration or injunction through the writ or originating summons route – offered applicants several substantial procedural advantages compared to the prerogative remedies.

Firstly, the private law stream had much longer time limits than the prerogative remedies. Time limits for the declaration or injunction could be as long as six years, while for the prerogative remedies they were generally limited to six months. This difference could obviously be vital if evidence of unlawful government action did not

[2] The one – major – caveat to this point being that the Crown was regarded as an 'individual' for the purposes of a declaration. It was not possible until the enactment of the Crown Proceedings Act 1947 to sue the Crown de jure in contract or tort. Instead, litigants had to proceed through the arcane device of a 'petition of right', in which a nominated official would stand in the place of the Crown as a defendant, and the Crown would underwrite the official's liability; see the first edition of this book at pp 98–99.

[3] See the reference to *Baggs' Case* at p 71 above.

[4] Similarly *R v Sussex Watch Committee [Baldwin], ex p Ridge.*

[5] They would however be available against Ministers if the Minister was exercising a statutory power which had been given to the Minister in her personal capacity, rather than to the Crown per se.

come to light until a year or more after the decision in issue was made. If a six-month limit was enforced, the lawfulness of such decisions could not be assessed, a consequence which would obviously compromise purist understandings of the rule of law. On the other hand, the short time limits for the prerogative remedies served an obvious purpose. Once the limit had expired, a government body could be sure that its decisions could not be quashed by the courts, a factor which might be of great significance to activities such as land or property development.

Secondly, the prerogative remedies required that the applicant be granted 'leave' to proceed by the court before a full hearing was initiated. Leave was a filter mechanism intended to protect government bodies (and indeed the courts themselves) from having to spend large amounts of time dealing with hopeless or mischievous cases. If the court took the view – on a brief perusal of the applicant's case – that the claim was wholly unmeritorious, leave would be refused, and no time need be spent on assessing the details of the claim. The application for leave, which placed the burden of proof on the plaintiff, was not required for a private law action. Unmeritorious claims could only be struck out at the instigation of the defendant.

Thirdly, the private law remedies came with a strong presumption that extensive discovery of documents and cross-examination of witnesses would be permitted. This was an obvious consequence of the assumption that private law remedies dealt with matters of fact as well as of law, and would often be concerned with imposing a detailed solution on the merits. Discovery and cross-examination were, in contrast, not widely available within the public law stream, as the prerogative remedies had not been designed as fact-finding mechanisms. Clearly, if a government body's allegedly unlawful activity was 'hidden' in its papers or the minds of its officers, the private law stream would have been far more useful to an applicant. Additionally, it was possible to combine declaratory or injunctive relief with damages, which were not available with the prerogative remedies.

Simply put, if the allegedly unlawful nature of the government body's decision was not immediately apparent, a plaintiff was much more likely to win if she could proceed by the declaration or injunction rather than one of the prerogative remedies. In more theoretical terms, this public/private dichotomy can readily be presented as raising a rule of law issue. The more widely that private law procedures were available to applicants, the more rigorously the decisions of government bodies would be examined by courts. It is important to stress the significance of the inter-linkage between what might on their face seem to be 'mere' matters of procedure within administrative law and the grounds of review themselves. There would be little point in having, for example, rules against unlawful delegation of power, or the fettering of discretion, or rules requiring fair procedures, if strict time limits prevented many decisions from being challenged, or if restrictive provisions as to discovery and cross examination meant that vital information could not be obtained.

There were nonetheless some disadvantages to the declaration and injunction. They were accepted to be remedies available only at the court's discretion, not as a matter of right. A court might conclude that an application was made too late, or that discovery and cross-examination were not appropriate. Or it might even hold that a claim was well-founded but then refuse to grant relief. Furthermore, it was traditionally held (a tradition which lasted until *Factortame (No 2)*) that injunctions were not available against the Crown. This placed a substantial portion of central government beyond the reach of the injunction, although it was never wholly clear exactly which parts of central government should be regarded as 'the Crown' for these purposes.[6] Both the declaration and injunction were also subject to restrictive tests of 'locus standi' or 'standing'. We consider this issue in detail in chapter seventeen. At this point we might simply note that it was appreciably more difficult for many applicants to convince the courts that they had locus standi for a declaration or injunction than for the public law remedies. And if an applicant did not have standing (ie was not permitted to 'stand' before the court and argue her case), she could not pursue her action at all.[7]

The detailed history of the inter-relationship between the public and private law streams of administrative law is too complex a matter to be addressed here.[8] For our limited purposes, it suffices to say that in the first half of the twentieth century the courts appeared to be reluctant to permit the declaration and injunction to be widely used as a means to challenge the exercise of governmental powers. Insofar as challenges were permitted, they were steered primarily through the public law route.[9] In effect, this amounted to the courts favouring a diluted version of the rule of law.

THE TURNING POINT? *BARNARD V NATIONAL DOCK LABOUR BOARD*

The applicant in *Barnard v National Dock Labour Board*[10] was a dock worker who had been suspended from his job. The power to suspend workers had been given by Parliament to the NDLB. The applicant suspected that, as a matter of routine, this power had been unlawfully delegated to the port manager.[11] There was however no way of establishing this from the notice of suspension. Proof of the point could only be gathered through having discovery of the NDLB's documents and/or by cross-examining its members. Barnard therefore sought a declaration; certiorari would have been a useless remedy. Rather oddly, the defendant made such documents available on receipt of the writ, instead of arguing immediately that the declaration was an

6 In *Nireaha Tamaki v Baker* [1901] AC 561, the Privy Council had held that an injunction could lie against a Minister acting in a personal capacity, but not against a Minister acting in an official capacity, when she was in theory the Crown itself. As noted above, this was also an issue in respect of the scope of the prerogative remedies, since the Crown could not act against itself. The Crown could however in theory act against central government bodies which were not part of the Crown. This is too complex an issue to be addressed in this book. For an indication of the difficulties it may pose see the discussion of *Oladehinde* at p 517 above.

7 Standing is discussed in depth in ch 17.

8 Successive editions of Craig's *Administrative law* again provide the most incisive detailed analysis of this issue.

9 As noted in ch 15, this was also the period in which the courts frequently took the view that the rules of natural justice did not apply to 'administrative' decisions, or those affecting 'privileges' rather than 'rights'.

10 [1953] 2 QB 18, [1953] 1 All ER 1113, CA.

11 See p 515 above.

inappropriate remedy in this case. The unlawful delegation was thereby revealed. It was not until the case came to court that the NDLB sought to have the action struck out on procedural grounds.

Given that the court knew for sure that the NDLB's action had been substantively unlawful in this case, the striking out motion was unlikely to succeed. The rationale informing the judgment was well put by Denning LJ:

'If the tribunal does not observe the law, what is to be done? The remedy by certiorari is hedged round by limitations and may not be available. Why, then, should not the court intervene by declaration and injunction? If it cannot so intervene, it would mean that the tribunal could disregard the law . . . In certiorari there is no discovery, whereas in an action for a declaration there is. The plaintiffs only discovered the true position shortly before the trial, about two and a half years after the suspension. That shows that, but for these proceedings, the truth would never have been known'.[12]

Whether the court would have been so ready to lift any procedural barriers to Mr Barnard gaining a substantively just result if he had come to court only with a strong suspicion that unlawful delegation had occurred is open to question. The case is nonetheless of crucial significance in illustrating the intimacy of the linkage between matters of 'mere' procedure and the substantive reach of administrative law. Had the court taken the view that certiorari was the appropriate remedy, the result would have been that both the rule of law and the sovereignty of Parliament (in their orthodox senses) would have been compromised. In broad terms, *Barnard* can be seen as heralding a shift in the courts' attitudes both towards government bodies (ie being more willing to subject executive action to scrutiny) and towards the citizen (ie being more willing to protect individual interests against government encroachment). In broader terms, it represented a step towards a more purist understanding of the rule of law.

The *Barnard* rationale was reinforced by the 1959 decision in *Pyx Granite Co Ltd v Ministry of Housing and Local Government.*[13] The applicant was attempting to challenge the lawfulness of conditions attached to planning permission. It was out of time to proceed by certiorari, and so sought to use a declaration. The MHLG argued that certiorari should be seen as an exclusive remedy in these circumstances. The court rejected the contention that the public law route should be the only means through which a plaintiff might challenge the lawfulness of decisions of this sort:

'I know of no authority for saying that if an order or decision can be attacked by certiorari the court is debarred from granting a declaration in the appropriate case. The remedies are not mutually exclusive, though no doubt there are some orders, notably convictions before justices, where the only appropriate remedy is certiorari'.[14]

This judicial initiative was reinforced in a political sense by the report of the Franks Committee in the mid-1950s in response to the Crichel Down episode.[15] Franks had

12 [1953] 2 QB 18 at 41, CA.

13 [1960] AC 260, [1959] 3 All ER 1, HL.

14 Ibid, at 8; per Lord Goddard CJ.

15 See pp 327–328 above.

urged that a far more judicialised approach ought to be taken to the administrative decision-making processes. This created a climate of opinion which regarded government with suspicion, thereby legitimating more extensive court intervention through the relaxation of procedural barriers to effective redress. A good many of the seminal administrative law decisions of the 1960s and 1970s would not have happened without the procedural innovation accepted in *Barnard*. *Anisminic* is perhaps the best example, but we might also recall that both *Ridge v Baldwin* and *Padfield* were initiated through private law rather than public law procedures. In the early 1960s, there was, Craig suggests, a presumption that: 'The declaration was meant . . . to be the shining white charger cutting through outmoded limitations encrusted upon the pick and shovel prerogative orders'.[16] That this did not in fact happen seems to be due in large part to the restrictive standing tests applied to the declaration.[17] The result was that by the early 1970s English administrative law, notwithstanding the large strides that were being made in respect of the grounds of judicial review that might be invoked to challenge government action, was riven with a profound procedural ambiguity. An ambiguity which, in some cases, might mean that entirely meritorious cases were never properly argued in court.

THE ORDER 53 REFORMS

The Law Commission turned its attention to this conceptual confusion in 1971. Its first proposal was that English administrative law should recognise an entirely separate procedural system for public law matters, akin in some senses to the rigid divide between public and private law in France. This proposal attracted substantial criticism, on the grounds that the Law Commission had not satisfactorily defined what was meant by 'public law', that the proposal was not compatible with the English legal tradition, and that an exclusive public law system – if modelled on the existing prerogative remedies – might substantially weaken the courts' capacity to subject government decision-making to effective scrutiny.

The reforms the Commission proposed in 1976 were nominally much simpler.[18] They envisaged a dual procedure in which the declaration and injunction would be available either through private law procedures (technically the 'writ' or 'originating summons') or, along with the prerogative remedies, through a new mechanism known as the 'application for judicial review' (AJR). Actions in contract or tort against governmental bodies would not be affected by the new procedure.

The Commission's proposals represented a balanced approach towards the supposedly competing concerns of protecting citizens against unlawful executive decision-making, and protecting lawful government decision-making from vexatious or frivolous applicants. It is certainly clear that (following the sentiments expressed in *Pyx Granite*) the Law Commission did not intend the AJR to be an exclusive remedy;

16 (1994) op cit p 549.

17 Ibid; the issue is discussed in detail in ch 17 below.

18 Law Commission (1976) *Report on remedies in administrative law* (Cmnd 6407; London: HMSO).

that is to say there would be some situations (although precisely which was unclear) where an applicant would seem to have a choice of using either the AJR or the declaration or injunction through a writ or originating summons.

The reforms were initially implemented by an amendment to the Rules of the Supreme Court, which introduced a modified Order 53. The changes were subsequently given a statutory basis in s 31 of the Supreme Court Act 1981.[19] The new Order 53 encompassed all the prerogative remedies and the declaration and injunction in a single procedural form.[20] The declaration and injunction could be granted in situations where any of the prerogative remedies are available, if having considered all the circumstances of the case in issue, the court considered it just and convenient to do so. The AJR retained the requirement of leave, and also introduced a strict time limit of three months. However, even within that period, an application could be ruled out of time if there had been undue delay. These two factors obviously indicated that the reform was intended to protect public bodies against tardy and vexatious claims. In contrast, r 8 seemed to relax the previously tight limits on the availability of discovery and cross-examination; these could now be granted at the discretion of the court in respect of all five remedies. There was nothing explicit in the text of the new Order 53 to confirm that the declaration or injunction would no longer be available through the writ or originating summons procedure, although it was by no means clear what the relationship between the public and private law streams would be. Some hint was given by r 9(5), which empowered the court to transfer applications begun through the AJR to private law procedures, but did not permit movement in the other direction. This raised the possibility that some applicants could find that the substantive merits of their cases would not be heard simply because they have chosen the wrong procedure. Initially, however, it seemed that the courts might interpret Order 53 in a way that did not permit procedural technicalities to have such an important substantive effect.[21]

[19] For the rest of this chapter, the term 'Order 53' is used to include the relevant provisions of s 31.

[20] Order 53 r 1 is framed in the following terms:

(1) An application for (*a*) an order of mandamus, prohibition or certiorari, or (*b*) an injunction under section 9 of the Administration of Justice (Miscellaneous Provisions) Act 1938 restraining a person from acting in any office in which he is not entitled to act, shall be made by way of an application for judicial review in accordance with the provisions of this Order.

(2) An application for a declaration or an injunction (not being an injunction mentioned in paragraph (1)(*b*)) may be made by way of an application for judicial review, and on such an application the Court may grant the declaration or injunction claimed if it considers that, having regard to (*a*) the nature of the matters in respect of which relief may be granted by way of an order of mandamus, prohibition or certiorari, (*b*) the nature of the persons and bodies against whom relief may be granted by way of such order, and (*c*) all the circumstances of the case, it would be just and convenient for the declaration or injunction to be granted on an application for judicial review.

[21] It should also be noted that some more prosaic reforms were introduced in an attempt to speed up the judicial process in administrative law cases. From 1981 onwards, a single judge (rather than the previous three) would be able to hear both leave applications and inter partes hearings, and a more concerted attempt was made to ensure that the High Court contained a de facto 'administrative division'; see Blom-Cooper L (1982) 'The new face of judicial review: administrative changes in Order 53' *Public Law* 250–261.

THE INITIAL ORDER 53 CASE LAW

The crucial issue to be resolved was whether the applicant had a choice between the private law and public law procedures. The policy implications of this issue are obvious. If the applicant is given the choice, it would suggest that the courts are more concerned with protecting citizens' interests, and ensuring that the executive acts within legal limits, than with protecting government from scrutiny and thereby expediting administrative processes.

In *De Falco v Crawley Borough Council*,[22] Lord Denning's Court of Appeal evidently favoured that approach. The case concerned a challenge to a council's decision under the homeless persons legislation (then the Housing (Homeless Persons) Act 1977). The challenge had been initiated as a breach of statutory duty action, in effect a private law action in tort. Lord Denning (while finding for the council on the merits) rejected the council's suggestion that Order 53 was now the sole route for applicants to challenge decisions under the 1977 Act:

'[T]he Housing (Homeless Persons) Act 1977, contained nothing about remedies . . . It has been held by this court that, if the council fails to provide accommodation as required by s 3(4), the applicant can claim damages in the county court: see *Thornton v Kirklees Metropolitan Borough Council* [1979] 2 All ER 349, [1979] QB 626. I am very ready to follow that decision and indeed to carry it further, because this is a statute which is passed for the protection of private persons, in their capacity as private persons. It is not passed for the benefit of the public at large . . . No doubt such a person could, at his option, bring proceedings for judicial review under the new RSC Ord 53 . . . So the applicant has an option'.[23]

Lord Denning's advocacy of a procedural choice for applicants challenging homelessness decisions might be contrasted with Goulding J's judgment in *Heywood v Board of Visitors of Hull Prison*.[24] Heywood, like Mr St Germain,[25] had been involved in the Hull prison riots, and had subsequently been punished by the prison board of visitors by loss of remission. He had sought a declaration through the private law route of a writ. The board argued that he must use Order 53. If so, he would be time barred, and the litigation would never reach the merits of his claim. Goulding J supported this argument:

'[I]t is obviously undesirable that the plaintiff should seek relief by action rather than by application for judicial review . . .

There are very good reasons (among them an economy of public time and the avoidance of injustice to persons whom it is desired to make respondents) for that requirement of preliminary leave. If an action commenced by writ or originating summons is used instead of the machinery of Ord 53, that requirement of leave is circumvented'.[26]

22 [1980] QB 460, [1980] 1 All ER 913, CA.
23 Ibid, at 468.
24 [1980] 3 All ER 594, [1980] 1 WLR 1386.
25 See pp 552–553 above.
26 [1980] 1 WLR 1386 at 1390.

Goulding J was particularly concerned that what he considered (evidently notwithstanding Order 53, r 8) the much more generous rules relating to discovery and cross-examination available through the private law route would have an undesirable impact on the board's decision-making:

> '[T]he machinery of an action as to discovery and giving of evidence may result in placing members of the tribunal concerned in a position not really compatible with the free and proper discharge of their public functions, or at least result in attempts to put them in that position . . .'.[27]

Goulding J distinguished *De Falco*, on the basis that the homelessness legislation was designed to create individual rights (ie it raised a *private law issue*), while the prison system is run for the public interest (ie it raised a *public law issue*). There is no express indication in the text of Order 53 that such a distinction should be drawn. Nor, one might add, that it should not. *De Falco* and *Heywood* thus seemed to present quite divergent, policy-driven interpretations of the reforms.

The twin issues of homelessness and prison discipline continued to lend an aura of uncertainty to the impact of the Order 53 reforms. In *Parr v Wyre Borough Council*,[28] another homelessness case, Lord Denning's Court of Appeal again implied that applicants should have a choice of procedure, although here the suggestion was that an Order 53 action could sometimes prove more effective, and considerably quicker, than a county court action. However, Lord Denning then (without proper explanation) appeared to conclude that his approach in *De Falco* and *Parr* had been misconceived. In *Lambert v Ealing London Borough Council*,[29] he indicated that the AJR should be an exclusive remedy in homelessness cases. This ambiguity then appeared equally starkly in respect of prison disciplinary proceedings.

I. O'*REILLY V MACKMAN*

O'Reilly v Mackman[30] was another case emerging from the aftermath of the Hull Prison riots. The action was not begun until some three years after the impugned decision (here the imposition of a loss of remission by the board of visitors) was made. The applicants were time-barred from proceeding via Order 53. Additionally, they claimed that their action would require extensive discovery and cross-examination, which rendered it more suitable to proceed in the private law rather than public law stream.

In the High Court, the Board invoked *Heywood* as authority for a rule that only the AJR could be used in such circumstance. To accept that argument would necessarily mean that Mr O'Reilly would have no effective remedy. Peter Pain J rejected the

[27] Ibid, at 1390–1391. [28] (1982) 2 HLR 71, CA. [29] [1982] 2 All ER 394, CA.

[30] [1982] 3 All ER 680, QBD and CA; [1983] 2 AC 237, HL. For an extremely cogent analysis of the litigation see McBride J (1983) 'The doctrine of exclusivity and judicial review' *Civil Justice Quarterly* 268–281.

argument and its consequences, and indicated that *Heywood* had been wrongly decided:

'The law offers the plaintiff a choice . . . It seems to me to be an abuse of language to say that the plaintiff is abusing the process of the court because he exercises the choice in the way he thinks best in his own interest'.[31]

The 'rule of law' argument underpinning Peter Pain J's conclusion is well brought out by his observation that only express words in a statute could convince him that Order 53 was intended to operate as an 'exclusive' remedial route. This is redolent of Lord Denning's approach to the ouster clause in issue in *Gilmore*,[32] and serves to emphasise the point that a judicial decision to consign a case to a worthless procedure amounts de facto to the court ousting its own jurisdiction.

It is perhaps therefore ironic that Lord Denning was a member of the Court of Appeal in *O'Reilly* that overturned Pain J's judgment. Building upon his rejection of *De Falco* in *Lambert*, Lord Denning (supported by Ackner and O'Connor LJJ) concluded that that the availability of the AJR should preclude applicants resorting to the declaration through the private law stream, not only for challenges to homelessness decisions and those of prison Boards of Visitors, but for all governmental decisions. To allow such actions to proceed in the private law stream:

'would open the door to great abuse. Nearly all these [applicants] are legally aided. If they were allowed to proceed by ordinary action, without leave, I can well see that the public authorities of this country would be harassed by all sorts of claims, long out of time, on the most flimsy grounds'.[33]

Lord Denning MR observed that the Law Commission's insistence that its proposed reforms should not be an exclusive remedy 'does not appeal to me, at any rate so far as the remedy by action for a declaration is concerned'.[34] To allow such an action would be 'an abuse of process of the court'. Lord Denning seemed to assume that the purpose of the Order 53 reforms was to provide additional protection to government bodies by the requirement of leave, the limited availability of discovery, and the equally limited availability of cross-examination – which should be 'rarely allowed'.[35]

The Court of Appeal's judgment was upheld, albeit in a somewhat diluted form, in the House of Lords, where Lord Diplock issued the sole judgment.[36] The crucial point on which the House rested its decision (a point not made in the Court of Appeal) was that, for procedural purposes, a sharp distinction had to be drawn between matters of 'private law' and 'public law'. While Mr O'Reilly stood to spend substantially more

[31] [1982] 3 All ER 680 at 688. He took the view that a loss of remission was no less a 'private right' from the individual applicant's perspective than an entitlement to be rehoused.

[32] See pp 84–85 above. [33] [1982] 3 All ER 680 at 694.

[34] Ibid, at 692. It is not clear if Lord Denning intended to limit his argument solely to declarations. This passage supports that assumption, but he also expressly disapproved *Thornton*, which was a breach of statutory duty action.

[35] Ibid, at 694. [36] [1983] 2 AC 237, [1982] 3 All ER 1124.

time than he had expected in prison if the Board's conclusion was not overturned, this did not amount to a private right. As Lord Diplock put it:

'It is not, and it could not be, contended that the decision of the board awarding him forfeiture of remission had infringed or threatened to infringe any right of the appellant derived from private law, whether a common law right or one created by a statute. Under the Prison Rules remission of sentence is not a matter of right but of indulgence . . .'.[37]

Lord Diplock acknowledged that before 1977, the prerogative remedies did not adequately protect applicants' interests, and it was therefore quite acceptable, and often indeed necessary, for the courts to allow an applicant to proceed by way of declaration or injunction. But, he continued:

'The position of applicants for judicial review has been drastically ameliorated by the new Ord 53. It has removed all those disadvantages, particularly in relation to discovery, that were manifestly unfair to them and had, in many cases, made applications for prerogative orders an inadequate remedy if justice was to be done . . .'.[38]

Since Order 53 had now removed these obstacles. Lord Diplock concluded that:

'Therefore it would in my view as a general rule be contrary to public policy, and as such an abuse of the process of the court, to permit a person seeking to establish that a decision of a public authority infringed rights to which he was entitled to protection under public law to proceed by way of an ordinary action and by this means to evade the provisions of Order 53 for the protection of such authorities'.[39]

Lord Diplock's presumption that discovery and cross-examination would be much more readily available under the Order 53 procedure than they had been previously in respect of the prerogative writs could be little more than speculation at that stage, given the limited body of Order 53 litigation by then undertaken.[40] The integrity of *O'Reilly* would thus depend in large part on the way in which the High Court would respond to applicants' requests for discovery and cross-examination.

If Lord Diplock's presumption on this point was to prove correct, then the 'protection' that was being extended to public authorities via Order 53 was limited essentially to the matters of leave and of short time limits. As a policy choice, this conclusion is readily understandable. The rationale in respect of short time limits necessarily accepts that the arguably (or even obviously) unlawful actions of government bodies

[37] Ibid, at 1127. As noted above, Peter Pain J at first instance had concluded that O'Reilly was raising an issue of private rights.

[38] Ibid, at 1134. [39] Ibid.

[40] The case law then decided offered little support for Lord Diplock's view; see *George v Secretary of State for the Environment* (1979) 38 P & CR 609, CA, and *Air Canada v Secretary of State for Trade (No 2)* [1983] 2 AC 394, HL. Both cases indicate that discovery should only be granted sparingly under Order 53, and *Air Canada* intimates that it should only be granted in exceptional cases. See also *Khawaja v Secretary of State for the Home Department* [1984] AC 74 per Lord Bridge at 117: 'it may be that the express discretion conferred on the court to permit cross-examination by the new procedure for judicial review has been too sparingly exercised'. One might note that in *Rossminster* (1980) the House of Lords had explicitly indicated that the discretion should be used sparingly.

will go unremedied; but this (it can be argued) is a price worth paying if it means that government decisions acquire a veneer of legal certainty within a short time, and thereby enable policies to be pursued and decisions to be acted upon.

Whether that price was worth paying in Mr O'Reilly's case might give us pause for thought. The outcome of the case is that we simply do not know if the Board acted lawfully in revoking his remission; his argument on the merits was never made because he failed to surmount a procedural obstacle. He had undoubtedly come very late to court – some three years after the Board of Visitors' decision. The delay was however readily explicable. The legal rule that Boards of Visitors were subject to the rules of natural justice had only been established in 1979 – by Mr St Germain, one of Mr O'Reilly's fellow rioters.[41] O'Reilly himself (and Mr Heywood) could not have known that he had any legal remedy available until the *St Germain* case had run its course. To deprive a plaintiff in this situation of a remedy seems, in terms of substantive justice, a harsh decision for the court to reach; a point which perhaps goes some way to explaining Peter Pain J's judgment at first instance. Order 53 did leave the courts a residual discretion to extend the three-month time limit if they wished to do so; but it would seem that a generous approach to that issue would undermine the 'protection' that Lord Diplock assumed the legal reforms were intended to introduce.[42]

It should also be noted that Lord Diplock took some considerable care to root his 'exclusivity principle' in parliamentary intent, rather than – as Lord Denning had done – to present it as a judicial choice.[43] This is perhaps because the House of Lords did not wish to take full responsibility for a procedural initiative which might well increase the likelihood that unlawful government action would go unchecked.

EXCEPTIONS TO THE GENERAL PRINCIPLE?

Lord Diplock's 'exclusivity principle' was not however to be a principle of universal application. It would, it seemed, apply only to 'public law' issues. There was an unfortunate lacuna in the judgment, in so far as Lord Diplock did not explain how – over the broad range of government activities – we might distinguish 'public law' and 'private law' matters for these purposes. Craig has argued that it is doubtful if we could find a convincing theoretical rationale for distinguishing between the two types of interest:

'statements that a public body must have a sufficiently "public" element or must be exercis-

[41] See pp 552–553 above.

[42] Order 53 initially required applications to be made promptly and at most within three months. Section 31 then appeared to change the test to one of 'undue delay', but was drafted in a way that did not repeal the Order 53 provisions. There has been no clarifying statute, but case law suggests that three months is a maximum; cases brought within that limit may be refused on grounds of delay; see for example *R v Stratford-on-Avon, ex p Jackson* [1985] 1 WLR 1319, CA; *Caswell v Dairy Produce Quota Tribunal for England and Wales* [1990] 2 AC 738, HL. It might be thought that three months or less is too short a time.

[43] Order 53 had by this point been given a statutory root in s 31 of the Supreme Court Act 1981.

ing a public duty cannot function as anything other than conclusory labels for whatever we choose to pour into them: they cannot guide our reasoning in advance'.[44]

Craig has suggested that there are three possible ways to construct a predictable distinction, but notes that all of them have flaws. The first would be to focus on the *source* of the decision. If the defendant organisation was a government body we might safely assume that a public law issue arose. However, there are obvious problems in defining 'government'. This is a familiar problem in the context of the vertical direct effect of EC directives,[45] and would be no less difficult to resolve in the purely domestic sphere. Equally, it is perfectly clear that government bodies often engage in purely 'private' activities, such as making contracts or acting negligently. Is it to be assumed that the identity of the defendant would override the basis of its relationship with the applicant for procedural purposes?

A second approach might be to focus on the *nature* of the power. A decision would be a public law matter, irrespective of the identity of the defendant, if its content impacted significantly on the public interest. But it would not seem any easier to define the 'public interest' than to define 'government'.

A third, rather formalistic approach might be to equate 'public law' with the traditional scope of the prerogative remedies. But as Craig notes, the scope of these remedies has always been dynamic, and would therefore offer a rather unstable test.

The elusive nature of 'public law' can be seen as a major definitional fault line running through Lord Diplock's opinion in *O'Reilly*. Assuming we could identify the concept however, Lord Diplock also anticipated that even when a public law issue was raised, there would be two – and perhaps more – exceptions to the requirement that the AJR be invoked:

'My Lords, I have described this as a general rule; for, though it may normally be appropriate to apply it by the summary process of striking out the action, there may be exceptions, particularly where the invalidity of the decision arises as a collateral issue in a claim for infringement of a right of the plaintiff arising under private law, or where none of the parties objects to the adoption of the procedure by writ or originating summons. Whether there should be other exceptions should, in my view, at this stage in the development of procedural public law, be left to be decided on a case to case basis . . .'.[46]

II. THE POST-*O'REILLY* CASE LAW

O'Reilly appeared to have created the clear split between public law and private law which the Law Commission had toyed with in the early 1970s, but then rejected in its 1976 report. The policy implications of *O'Reilly* were potentially profound, in that the case moved away from the Law Commission's advocacy of procedural choice towards a procedural regime apparently balanced in favour of protecting public bodies.

44 (1989) op cit p 420.

45 See pp 459–462 above.

46 [1982] 3 All ER 1124 at 1134.

That *O'Reilly* should not be read in quite so draconian a fashion was hinted at by a subsequent House of Lords' judgment issued on the very same day. In *Cocks v Thanet District Council*,[47] the court arrived at the convoluted and essentially nonsensical proposition[48] that the homelessness legislation could be divided into 'private law' and 'public law' issues for procedural purposes. It also emphasised that most such decisions would fall within the AJR procedure.

The suggestion that *O'Reilly* and *Cocks* may have been underpinned by a judicial concern that government bodies were being subjected to too many challenges – especially in the fields of housing and immigration – was underpinned by the House of Lords' extraordinary 1985 decision in *Puhlhofer v Hillingdon London Borough Council*.[49] In *Puhlhofer*, the court (per Lord Brightman) explicitly disapproved of the use of judicial review to challenge local authority decision-making towards homeless persons. Since *Cocks* had already restricted the availability of private law procedures in this area, *Puhlhofer* effectively placed homeless persons in a position of having virtually no effective protection against ultra vires decision-making. In effect, it seemed, the courts had read an ouster clause into the legislation.

Contemporary empirical evidence suggested that such judicial concerns were misplaced. Sunkin's innovative 1987 study found no evidence that government bodies were being, or ever had been, deluged by legal challenges.[50] In respect of the homelessness legislation, for example, Sunkin noted that local authorities had received some 219,000 applications in 1986. Some 32 of these decisions had led to an Order 53 application.

It was also evident, following the *GCHQ* decision, that there was an arguable inconsistency between the House of Lords' evident readiness to pull more types of governmental decision-making within the field of judicial supervision, and its unwillingness to allow challenges to be raised through the most effective procedural route. This possible tension perhaps underlay the House of Lords' clear statement in *Davy v Spelthorne Borough Council*[51] that an action for damages in negligence against a government body was not precluded by the availability of the Order 53 procedure. Describing the case as 'a sequel' to *O'Reilly*, Lord Fraser saw no grounds for thinking that the litigation was a 'public law' matter at all: 'The present proceedings, so far as they consist of a claim for damages, appear to me to be simply an ordinary action for tort. They do not raise any issue of public law as a live issue'.[52] More broadly,

47 [1983] 2 AC 286, HL.

48 See Loveland I (1993) 'An unappealing analysis of the public-private law divide: the case of the homelessness legislation' *Liverpool LR* 39–59.

49 [1986] AC 484, [1986] 1 All ER 467, HL. For a discussion of the case see Loveland (1995) op cit pp 98–101.

50 Sunkin M (1987) 'What is happening to applications for judicial review?' *MLR* 432–467. See also Sunkin M (1987) 'Myths of judicial review' *LAG Bulletin* (September) 8; (1991) 'The judicial review caseload' *Public Law* 490–499.

51 [1984] AC 262, HL.

52 Ibid, at 273. Cf Lord Fraser's approval of Fox LJ's comment in the Court of Appeal (1983) 81 LGR 580 at 596: 'The claim, in my opinion, is concerned with the alleged infringement of the plaintiff's rights at common

Lord Wilberforce appeared to caution counsel and judges against regarding the 'public-private divide' as an organising principle for procedural purposes:

'the expressions "private law" and "public law" have recently been imported into the law of England from countries which, unlike our own, have separate systems concerning public and private law. In this country they must be used with caution, for, typically, English law fastens, not upon principles, but upon remedies'.[53]

In *Wandsworth London Borough Council v Winder*[54] the House of Lords offered a further exception to the *O'Reilly* principle. Wandsworth used the evidently broad discretion left to it by the Housing Act 1980 over the matter of council house rents[55] to raise rents by some 50%. Mr Winder, a tenant refused to pay the entire increase, but paid his old rent plus an amount to cover inflation. Over a year later, the council began possession proceedings against Mr Winder in the county court – in effect an action for breach of contract. Mr Winder then sought to raise the defence that the rent rise was irrational and thus void, with the result that he had not breached the terms of his lease. The council claimed that this was a public law issue, which could only be addressed via Order 53. The administrative consequences if Mr Winder was permitted to raise the defence and then win on the merits would have been profound; every rent that Wandsworth had collected for the past year might have been unlawful, money might have had to be returned to thousands of tenants, a new rent (with retrospective effect) would have to be set and then collected. This would seem to be just the type of scenario against which Lord Diplock might have wished public bodies to be protected. Mr Winder could obviously have initiated Order 53 proceedings as soon as the rent increase was passed. However, the House of Lords held that *O'Reilly* did not prevent a public law matter being raised in private law proceedings in these circumstances. There appeared to be two reasons for this conclusion. The first was that Mr Winder was addressing a public law matter that impacted on his existing private legal right, ie his tenancy. Secondly, perhaps more importantly, Mr Winder himself had not chosen the form of action. He was merely responding to the council's challenge to his legal right. In Lord Fraser's view:

'It would in my opinion be a very strange use of language to describe the respondent's behaviour in relation to this litigation as an abuse or misuse by him of the process of the court. He did not select the procedure to be adopted. He is merely seeking to defend proceedings brought against him by the appellants. In so doing he is seeking only to exercise the ordinary right of any individual to defend an action against him on the ground that he is not liable for the whole sum claimed by the plaintiff'.[56]

law. Those rights are not even peripheral to a public law claim. They are the essence of the entire claim, so far as negligence is concerned'.

53 [1984] AC 262 at 276, HL. 54 [1985] AC 461, [1984] 3 All ER 976.

55 See pp 364–366 and pp 390–391 above.

56 [1984] 3 All ER 976 at 981. For a review of these cases, and a powerfully persuasive analysis of the flaws in *O'Reilly*, see Forsyth C (1985) 'Beyond *O'Reilly v Mackman*: the foundations and nature of procedural exclusivity' *Cambridge LJ* 415–434. See also Beatson J (1987) '"Public" and "private" in English

THE FLIP SIDE OF THE *O'REILLY* COIN

As indicated in the *Pett* decisions discussed in chapter fifteen,[57] prior to the Order 53 reforms it appeared to be broadly accepted that the activities of bodies regulating sports industries could be challenged by private law proceedings. However in *Law v National Greyhound Racing Club Ltd*,[58] the NGRC argued that a trainer who alleged that there were procedural flaws in his suspension following a dog-doping accusation should have to proceed through the AJR. The NGRC argued in effect that it performed a 'governmental function' in regulating the greyhound racing industry; ie that the activity was so important that 'but for' the existence of the NGRC itself, the government would have to step in to perform this role. As such, the NGRC should benefit from the protections alluded to by Lord Diplock in *O'Reilly*.

While the Court of Appeal could readily see why the NGRC was making this argument,[59] it considered that the contention had little merit. Even if one could identify a 'public law' element in the NGRC's activities, the nature of the relationship between the Club and Mr Law was the quintessentially private law matter of a contract. In consequence, a private law procedure was the only suitable route for the applicant to take.[60]

In *Law* and the other cases discussed so far, the applicant has been seeking to gain access to the private rather than public law stream, on the basis that that stream is the most likely to lead her to her desired outcome. However, there are some situations in which an applicant might actually prefer to proceed through a public law mechanism while the government defendant wished to have her steered into a private law remedy.

Employment disputes are a primary example of this. The United Kingdom now has a substantial body of law (much of it EC generated) protecting employees against their employers. But it is only in very rare circumstances that these statutory provisions offer employees the remedy of 'specific performance' – namely that they are re-instated in their jobs. Certiorari would however have this effect; if the employee's dismissal was quashed and thus held to be void, she would never have been dismissed at all.

administrative law' *LQR* 34–65. For an extremely critical 'judicial' analysis of *Winder* see Woolf H (1986) 'Public law – private law: why the divide' *Public Law* 220–230.

57 See pp 562–565 above. 58 [1983] 3 All ER 300, [1983] 1 WLR 1302, CA.

59 Ibid, at 307; per Slade LJ: '[I]t is easy to understand why the NGRC would prefer that any person who seeks to challenge the exercise of its disciplinary functions should be compelled to do so, if at all, by way of an application for judicial review. In this manner the NGRC would enjoy the benefit of what Lord Diplock in *O'Reilly v Mackman* described as "the safeguards imposed in the public interest . . . on the validity of decisions made by public authorities in the field of public law". Notwithstanding recent procedural changes, these safeguards are still real and substantial. Leave is required to bring proceedings . . . here is a time-bar of three months . . . The court retains firm control over discovery and cross-examination . . .'.

60 Cf Lawton LJ, ibid at 303: 'In my judgment, such powers as the stewards had to suspend the plaintiff's licence were derived from a contract between him and the defendants . . . A stewards' inquiry under the defendants' rules of racing concerned only those who voluntarily submitted themselves to the stewards' jurisdiction. There was no public element in the jurisdiction itself . . . [T]he courts have always refused to use the orders of certiorari to review the decisions of domestic tribunals'.

This concern underpinned the applicant's procedural choice in *R v BBC, ex p Lavelle.*[61] Ms Lavell had been sacked from the BBC following allegations of theft. She sought to argue that because the BBC was a publicly financed body, created by royal charter, its activities should all be regarded as raising a public law issue. Woolf J rejected this contention. Following *Law,* he concluded that Ms Lavell's dispute with the BBC was a pure master/servant question, which should be resolved through private law remedies.

A rather different approach was taken by Hodgson J at first instance in *R v East Berkshire Health Authority, ex p Walsh,* in which he had concluded that the political significance of the National Health Service in modern Britain was sufficiently pronounced to make the dismissal of NHS employees a 'public law' matter as well as a case of breach of contract.[62] This conclusion was promptly overturned in the Court of Appeal, on the basis that the existence of a contractual relationship precluded an action via Order 53.

Notwithstanding the fact that he had been overruled in *Walsh,* Hodgson J felt able to conclude in *R v Home Secretary, ex p Benwell*[63] that employment as a prison officer fell within the scope of Order 53. This conclusion seems readily defensible, since at that time (pre-*GCHQ*) it was assumed that prison officers did not have contracts. Unless the AJR was available to such applicants, there would be no means at all of assessing whether their employer had acted lawfully.[64]

A 'NATURE' NOT 'SOURCE' OF POWER TEST – THE *DATAFIN, AGA KHAN* AND *WACHMANN* DECISIONS

The 'but for' argument that had failed to sway the Court of Appeal in Law was made with greater success in *R v Panel on Take-overs and Mergers, ex p Datafin.*[65] The Take-over Panel, which was created in 1968, was the body responsible for policing the ethics of merger and take-over activities in the United Kingdom. It was neither a statutory nor common law body, nor were any of its members (some 12 in number) government appointees. The Panel's members were representatives of major financial institutions, and applied a non-binding code of ethical practice to firms engaged in take-over or merger activities. Breach of the code did not entail legal sanctions, but

61 [1983] ICR 99.

62 The judgment appears to have been reported, only at (1983) Times, 15 November, and is discussed in the Court of Appeal's decision: [1984] ICR 743.

63 [1985] QB 554, [1984] 3 All ER 854. The judgment contains a splendidly petulant criticism of the Court of Appeal's decision in *Walsh.*

64 An excellent analysis of this area is offered in Walsh B (1989) 'Judicial review of dismissal from employment: coherence or confusion?' *Public Law* 131–155. Subsequently, in *McClaren v Home Office* [1990] ICR 824, the Court of Appeal took the view that prison officers should be regarded as having an employment relationship with the government which, if not contractual in the narrow sense of the term, was nonetheless sufficiently contractual to permit challenges to the Home Office's decisions to be made through private law proceedings.

65 [1987] 1 All ER 564, CA.

would in effect lead to the blackballing of the firms concerned. The Panel effectively exercised monopolistic control over this area of economic activity. Datafin had complained to the Panel that it had been the victim of unethical practices by another firm. Its complaint was investigated but rejected. Datafin then sought judicial review of the Panel's decision.

The Panel argued that since it was de jure a non-governmental body, its decisions could not be challenged via Order 53. Since it did not have a contractual relationship with any of the firms whose activities it policed, there was no possibility of a breach of contract action being initiated. Nor did there seem to be any realistic prospect of Datafin being able to found an action in negligence against the Panel. If the Panel was not subject to challenge via Order 53, its activities would seemingly be wholly beyond judicial control.

Hodgson J had accepted this consequence at first instance. His judgment was then reversed in the Court of Appeal. Sir John Donaldson MR's leading judgment offered several reasons which, in combination, led him to the conclusion that the Panel was subject to judicial review.[66]

The first was that the quantitative significance of the Panel's activities – in contrast to that of the NGRC for example – was immense. The Panel dealt with issues involving tens of millions of pounds, and in so doing affected the financial interests of hundreds of thousands of shareholders. Secondly, it was clear that 'but for' the Panel, the government would have to take a central role in this field. Indeed, it was already apparent that the Department of Trade played a significant background role underpinning the Panel's activities. Thirdly, since the Panel exercised monopolistic powers in this area, it would be inappropriate to suggest that Datafin had 'consented' to its supervision. Fourthly, as applicants would not have any plausible remedy in either contract or negligence, or through the somewhat esoteric action in unlawful restraint of trade, against the Panel, Order 53 provided the only means of legal control. Citing the celebrated judgment of Scrutton LJ in *Czarnikow v Roth Schmidt & Co*,[67] Sir John Donaldson reasoned that: '. . . to exclude this safeguard for the administration of the law is contrary to public policy. There must be no Alsatia in England where the King's writ does not run'.[68] He then concluded that: '[I]t is really unthinkable that, in the absence of legislation such as affects trade unions, the panel should go on its way cocooned from the attention of the courts'.[69]

This conclusion seems wholly defensible. To have upheld Hodgson J's first instance judgment would, in effect, have been to issue the government with an invitation to manoeuvre governmental behaviour beyond the reach of judicial supervision by

[66] Datafin failed on the merits, on the basis that it was essentially asking the court to exercise an appellate rather than supervisory jurisdiction over the substance of the Panel's decisions.

[67] [1922] All ER Rep 45 at 50, CA.

[68] [1987] 1 All ER 564 at 568, CA 'Alsatias' being a colloquial name for the medieval areas known as 'sanctuaries', where criminals could shelter from the attentions of the criminal law.

[69] Ibid, at 577.

transferring public functions to private sector bodies.[70] That outcome would have been difficult to reconcile with any meaningful notion of the rule of law.

In terms of its financial significance, the Jockey Club lies somewhere between the NGRC and the Takeover Panel. Since 1970, when it was granted a Royal Charter, the Jockey Club's legal origins have lain in the prerogative. As such it has – in contrast to the NGRC and the Take-over Panel, a de jure 'governmental' source. Despite these distinctions, in *R v Jockey Club, ex p Massingberd-Mundy*,[71] the High Court considered that it was bound by the Court of Appeal's judgment in *Law* to the effect that anyone who had a contractual relationship with the Jockey Club (as in fact did everyone involved in the horse racing industry) should challenge its decisions through private law rather than public law procedures.

This analysis was upheld in *R v Disciplinary Committee of the Jockey Club, ex p Aga Khan*.[72] One of the Aga Khan's horses had 'won' the Oaks at Epsom in 1992. The horse was subsequently disqualified after traces of a prohibited substance were detected in its urine. A challenge to this decision through contract, even if successful, could not have given the Aga Khan the outcome that he desired – namely to have his horse reinstated as the winner of the race. Consequently, he attempted to proceed via Order 53 in order to have the disqualification quashed. His counsel marshalled several arguments to convince the court that the AJR procedure was appropriate. Firstly, the Jockey Club's source in the prerogative lent it a governmental character. Secondly, it performed functions of such public importance that 'but for' its existence, an explicitly governmental body would have to take over its role. Thirdly, its role gave it monopolistic control over a major industry; anyone wishing to participate in the horse racing industry had to submit to its terms and conditions.

The Court of Appeal found these arguments unconvincing. At least in respect of applicants who had a contractual relationship with the Club, private law procedures were the appropriate mechanism to bring challenges. The court did imply that the AJR procedure might be available to applicants who did not have a contractual relationship with the Club, but declined to decide the point.[73]

The High Court was presented with a problem of a rather different nature in *R v Chief Rabbi of the United Hebrew Congregations of Great Britain and the Commonwealth, ex p Wachmann*.[74] Wachmann was a rabbi who had been suspended by the Chief Rabbi following an investigation into complaints about Wachmann's alleged professional misconduct. The Chief Rabbi's conclusion in effect made Wachmann unemployable as a rabbi. Wachmann did not have a contractual relationship with the Chief Rabbi, which indicated that the only possible means of legal challenge

[70] See Forsyth C (1987) 'The scope of judicial review: "public duty" not source of power' *Public Law* 356–367.

[71] [1993] 2 All ER 207. [72] [1993] 2 All ER 853, [1993] 1 WLR 909, CA.

[73] For comment see Bamforth N (1993) 'The scope of judicial review: still uncertain' *Public Law* 239–248. See for example the factual situation raised in *R v Jockey Club, ex p RAM Racecoures Ltd* [1993] 2 All ER 225. See also *R v Football Association, ex p Football League* [1993] 2 All ER 833.

[74] [1993] 2 All ER 249.

(Wachmann claimed bias and procedural irregularities in the Chief Rabbi's decision) would be the AJR. The court held that Mr Wachmann was not raising a public law issue, although the tone of Simon Brown J's judgment rather suggests that he felt Mr Wachmann was not even raising a justiciable issue:

'[T]he court is hardly in a position to regulate what is essentially a religious function – the determination whether someone is morally and religiously fit to carry out the spiritual and pastoral duties of his office. The court must inevitably be wary of entering so self-evidently sensitive an area . . .

[T]o entertain this challenge would involve a clear departure from and extension of the principles established by the *Datafin* case'.[75]

III. RETREATING FROM *O'REILLY*? THE *ROY* CASE

The applicant in *Roy v Kensington and Chelsea and Westminster Family Practitioner Committee*[76] was a general medical practitioner working in the National Health Service. General practitioners in the NHS have a statutory entitlement to a scale of fees based on a statutory formula. However, Family Practitioner Committees are empowered to withhold a portion of those fees if they consider a practitioner to have failed to carry out his/her duties adequately. The dispute in Roy's case arose when the FPC withheld part of his fee. Roy challenged the decision by seeking a declaration via a writ that he was entitled to the full sum. The FPC's initial response was that since its relationship with Dr Roy was not contractual, he was raising a purely public law issue and could thus proceed only via Order 53.

Lord Lowry's leading judgment for a unanimous House created the strong impression that *O'Reilly*, if not misconceived per se, had certainly been lent an inappropriate interpretation in subsequent years. Lord Lowry accepted counsel's suggestion that *O'Reilly* could be construed in two ways.[77]

The 'broad view' of the case – which would reduce the scope of the exclusivity principle – was that the AJR would be the sole remedy to be used only where there was no private law element at all to the decision in issue. The 'narrow view' – which would extend the reach of the exclusivity principle – was that the AJR would be the sole remedy whenever a public law issue is raised, unless the case comes within the specified exceptions.[78]

[75] Ibid, at 255–256.

[76] [1992] 1 AC 624, [1992] 1 All ER 705, HL. For contemporaneous comment see Cane P (1992) 'Private rights and public procedure' *Public Law* 193–200.

[77] Neither of which – unfortunately – was very clearly formulated.

[78] 'The "broad approach" was that "the rule in *O'Reilly v Mackman*" did not apply generally against bringing actions to vindicate private rights in all circumstances in which those actions involved a challenge to a public law act or decision, but that it merely required the aggrieved person to proceed by judicial review only when private law rights were not at stake. The "narrow approach" assumed that the rule applied

Lord Lowry observed that he instinctively preferred the 'broad view', an observation which one assumes the House of Lords intended lower courts to follow in future. However, he managed to decide the case in Dr Roy's favour by adopting the 'narrow view'. He suggested that that there were three reasons for regarding Dr Roy's claim as an exception to the exclusivity principle. The first of these was that while Dr Roy's relationship with the FPC was not contractual in the orthodox sense, it nonetheless had 'contractual echoes', in that Dr Roy was laying claim to what Lord Lowry characterised as a 'private statutory' right. The second was that the private right 'dominated' the public law issue in the case. The third reason was that the claim required examination of a disputed issue of fact.

The second point is little more than a re-affirmation of the *Winder* principle. The first point illustrates quite neatly the instability of the public right or private right dichotomy offered in *O'Reilly*. The scope of that case could be fundamentally altered without modifying the exclusivity principle at all by the alternative mechanism of lending a 'private' character to previously 'public' rights. That technique would of course simply displace rather than solve the dilemma that *O'Reilly* throws up, and has the added disadvantage of exposing the courts to accusations that they are engaging in a jurisprudential sleight of hand in order to evade, rather than overrule, an inconvenient principle.[79] The third point – the reference to disputes as to fact – is significant, for it implies that the House of Lords did not envisage that discovery and cross-examination (which would be vital if factual disputes were in issue) would be routine elements of AJR proceedings.

That supposition was echoed by Rose LJ in *R v Secretary of State for Foreign Affairs, ex p World Development Movement Ltd*, in rejecting the WDM's request for access to detailed minutes of the Foreign Secretary's deliberations on the Pergau dam aid grant:

> '[It is] common ground that in judicial review proceedings general discovery is not available as it is in a writ action under Ord 24, rr 1 and 2, that an application can be made under Ord 24, r 3, which by virtue of Ord 24, r 8 will be refused if discovery is not necessary for disposing of the case fairly'.[80]

Despite Lord Diplock's predictions to the contrary in *O'Reilly*, it appears that this issue remains of considerable importance over twenty years later.

It may however be that the most significant element of the *Roy* judgment is Lord Lowry's clear intimation that the House of Lords was no longer as exercised by the prospect of applicants 'abusing the process of the court' as Lord Diplock and his colleagues had been:

> 'unless the procedure adopted is ill-suited to dispose of the question . . ., there is much to be said in favour of the proposition that a court having jurisdiction ought to let a case be heard rather than entertain a debate concerning the form of proceedings'.[81]

generally to *all* proceedings in which public law acts or decisions were challenged, subject to some exceptions when private law rights were involved': ibid, at 728.

79 See also the discussion by Cane P (1992) 'Private rights and public procedure' *Public Law* 193–200.

80 [1995] 1 All ER 611, [1995] 1 WLR 386.

81 [1992] 1 All ER 705 at 730, HL.

This apparent reassertion of the courts' primary responsibility as being to establish if an applicant's claim is well-founded, rather than to be bogged down in arguments as to procedure, has obvious (if much less melodramatic) echoes of Lord Denning's judgment in *Barnard*.[82] But any hopes that *Roy* would lead the courts to clarify rather than complicate this area of the law were at least initially disappointed by the judgment in *Bugg v DPP*.[83]

IV. PUBLIC LAW PRINCIPLE AS A DEFENCE IN CRIMINAL PROCEEDINGS

From the mid-1980s onwards, Mr Bugg had been making a considerable nuisance of himself to the Ministry of Defence. He was one of a number of anti-nuclear protesters who (updating Mr Chandler's preferred form of activism in the 1960s)[84] had engaged in persistent incursion into MoD airbases. Such incursions nominally amounted to a breach of certain criminal bye-laws, produced by the MoD under statutory powers. Mr Bugg had taken great delight in frequently demonstrating that he and his colleagues had not breached the bye-laws or – the issue at stake in this case – that the bye-laws concerned were themselves ultra vires.

In *Bugg v DPP*,[85] Mr Bugg convinced the High Court that several MoD bye-laws under which he and his colleagues had been prosecuted were indeed invalid. However the case is most notable for its procedural implications. The prosecutions had taken place in a magistrates' court. When Mr Bugg had attempted to raise the alleged invalidity of the bye-laws as a defence, the prosecuting authorities – building on *O'Reilly* – had contended that this issue could only be addressed via an AJR. Mr Bugg would obviously have been long out of time to pursue this course. Unless he could raise the defence, the risk arose that he would be prosecuted, convicted and sentenced in respect of a 'crime' which might lack any lawful basis.

In a most peculiar judgment, the High Court[86] concluded that a defendant in such circumstances could plead the unlawful nature of the bye-law as a defence if that claim was rooted in either illegality or irrationality. However she could not do so if the claim lay in procedural impropriety. The court did not contend that such a defence would amount to 'an abuse of process', so the case should not strictly be seen as an extension of *O'Reilly*. Rather Woolf LJ concluded that the criminal courts had no jurisdiction to enter such an enquiry and were not 'properly equipped to do so'.[87] The distinction was evidently drawn because illegality and irrationality would be obvious

82 See also the judgment of the Court of Appeal in *Clark v University of Lincoln and Humberside* [2000] 3 All ER 752, [2000] 1 WLR 1988, CA.

83 [1993] QB 473, [1993] 2 All ER 815.

84 See p 125 above.

85 [1993] QB 473, [1993] 2 All ER 815.

86 [1993] QB 473, [1993] 2 All ER 815; Woolf LJ and Pill J.

87 The form of words was perhaps inspired by Lord Lowry's closing comments in *Roy*.

flaws, which would not require any examination of 'evidence', whereas procedural impropriety might well be identifiable only after extensive perusal of such evidence.

Quite what rationale underpinned this analysis is something of a mystery, as the distinction is entirely nonsensical in several senses. A criminal court, concerned as it must be with detailed evaluation of evidence, is perfectly competent in the technical sense to consider factual allegations about procedural impropriety. If Woolf LJ's point was really intended to suggest that criminal courts lacked the expertise to apply principles of administrative law, two further problems arise. The first is that High Court judges who deal with administrative law litigation often sit as trial judges in criminal cases; their administrative law expertise presumably does not disappear when they do so. Secondly, while it is plausible to argue that a lay magistrate may lack the legal skills properly to apply the legal esoterica of the procedural impropriety jurisprudence, she would presumably be equally at sea when faced with a problem rooted for example in the rule against unlawful delegation, or the fettering of discretion, or whether irrelevant considerations had been taken into account. More obviously, it is readily apparent that procedural impropriety (in the form for example of bias or a complete failure to hold a hearing or consult statutorily specified parties) could be discerned without any detailed evidential questions being addressed, and that conversely (*Barnard* and *Anisminic* being prime examples) substantive illegality may be well hidden within the decision-making body.[88]

The judgment also represented a departure from recent[89] and more long-established authority. In the latter category, *DPP v Head*[90] is perhaps the most helpful of cases. Head was prosecuted under the Mental Deficiency Act 1915, s 56(1) for having sex with a person classified as 'mentally defective' under s 9 of that Act. At trial, it emerged that the victim of the crime may not have been lawfully classified under s 9. If this was correct, she was not 'a mental defective', and Head would not have committed the s 56 offence. Head obviously had not challenged the victim's classification (nor had anyone else) at the time it was made. Even under the more generous pre-1977 time limits, a certiorari action would have been time barred. In the view of the majority of the House of Lords, there was no room to doubt that Head should be able to rely on this defence:

> 'It is conceded that the court had material before it which would have led to the [classification] being quashed on certiorari or other appropriate proceedings. The next question, as it appears to me, can be stated in this way. Is a man to be sent to prison on the basis that an order is a good order when the court knows it would be set aside if proper proceedings were taken? I doubt it'.[91]

The House of Lords had rejected the suggestion that any distinction could be drawn

[88] See Feldman D (1993) 'Collateral challenge and judicial review: the boundary dispute continues' *Public Law* 37–48.

[89] *DPP v Hutchinson* [1990] 2 AC 783, [1990] 2 All ER 836, HL: *Plymouth City Council v Quietlynn* [1987] 2 All ER 1040.

[90] [1959] AC 83, HL.

[91] Ibid, at 687; per Lord Somervell.

between different types of unlawful order for these purposes. As such the judgment is a forceful assertion of an expansive notion of the rule in respect of criminal liability. *Bugg* clearly compromised that principle.

The correctness of Woolf LJ's reasoning in *Bugg* was questioned by the House of Lords in *R v Wicks*,[92] although the decision was not overruled. Mr Wicks had rebuilt his house in a manner which required planning permission without having troubled himself to seek it. He then refused to stop the rebuilding, and was eventually served by his council with an enforcement notice under s 172 of the Town and Country Planning Act 1990. He nonetheless continued with his building, even though non-compliance with an enforcement notice is a criminal offence. At the subsequent criminal trial – having unsuccessfully exercised a statutory right of appeal under the 1990 Act to the Secretary of State for the Environment – he attempted to argue that the enforcement notice was unlawful. The House of Lords accepted that the common law recognised a 'guiding principle' that a defendant should always be able to raise the alleged invalidity of a government measure which formed the root of a criminal prosecution. The substantial judgments delivered by Lords Hoffmann and Nicholls overtly cast doubt on the *Bugg* distinction. The court was nonetheless prepared to conclude that Mr Wicks should not be able to raise this administrative law point in the criminal proceedings. The 'guiding principle' could be rebutted by considerations specific to the decision in issue. In this case, the provision of a statutory appeal against the enforcement notice in addition to a potential AJR proceeding afforded the defendant an adequate remedy, and the intensity of the public interest in having planning laws promptly enforced militated against permitting a challenge other than by way of Order 53.

The unworkable distinction introduced by *Bugg* was subsequently removed entirely by the House of Lords in *Boddington v British Transport Police*.[93] Boddington was an inveterate smoker, who took exception to the fact that the operator of his daily train into London had exercised powers under a bye-law wholly to forbid smoking on trains. Boddington decided to ignore the ban and, when subsequently prosecuted for so doing, sought to raise the alleged irrationality of the bye-law as his defence. Predictably, the BTP contended that a challenge of this sort could only be initiated under Order 53. The magistrate accepted this argument. Boddington was convicted and fined £10. He then appealed against his conviction to the High Court, claiming that he should have been permitted to raise the public law defence.

This view was rejected at first instance by Auld J. Auld J appeared to extend the reach of *Bugg*, by holding that a magistrate's court would not be competent to entertain any challenge to the validity of a bye-law or of delegated legislation in the course

[92] [1998] AC 92, [1997] 2 All ER 801, HL. See Bradley A (1997) 'Collateral challenge to enforcement decisions – a duty to apply for judicial review?' *Public Law* 365.

[93] [1999] 2 AC 143, [1998] 2 All ER 203, HL. See Forsyth C (1999) 'Collateral challenge and the foundations of judicial review: orthodoxy vindicated and procedural exclusivity rejected' *Public Law* 364–370: Craig P (1998) 'Collateral attack, procedural exclusivity and judicial review' *LQR* 535–538.

of criminal proceedings. To allow this to happen would, he suggested, cause chaos in the criminal courts.

The House of Lords reversed Auld J's judgment, and unanimously concluded that Boddington was entitled to raise the defence. Lord Steyn offered a carefully argued judgment which convincingly married detailed points of administrative law with broader questions of constitutional principle and condemned *Bugg* as 'contrary to authority and principle'.[94]

In the first field, Lord Steyn (apparently adopting the broad view of *O'Reilly* alluded to by Lord Lowry in *Roy*) observed that *O'Reilly's* exclusivity principle should be limited to 'situations in which an individual's sole aim was to challenge a public law act or decision'.[95] The principle did not apply when private rights were at stake, or when an individual was defending an action initiated by a government body. Lord Steyn also rejected the idea that Woolf LJ's distinction between procedurally and substantively unlawful decisions had a defensible base, either in pragmatic[96] or conceptual terms.[97]

In a more overtly constitutional vein, Lord Steyn observed that: 'the rule of law requires a clear distinction to be made between what is lawful and what is unlawful. The distinction put forward in *Bugg's* case undermines that axiom of constitutional principle'.[98] The constitutional consequences of *Bugg*, namely that a person might be convicted of a 'crime' which might be found not to exist if subject to legal challenge were 'too austere and indeed too authoritarian to be compatible with the traditions of the common law'.[99] This was not however to be an absolute rule. Rather it should be construed as an extremely strong presumption which could only be rebutted if the statutory scheme surrounding the decision in issue made it wholly clear that a departure from orthodoxy was warranted.

Lord Irvine's judgment is perhaps more effective in identifying the constitutional implications of the Order 53 litigation. In forceful terms, he concluded that Boddington had to be allowed to raise his defence: 'It would be a fundamental departure from the rule of law if an individual were liable to conviction for contravention of some rule which is itself liable to be set aside by a court as unlawful . . .'.[100]

94 Ibid, at 226. 95 Ibid, at 226.

96 'An issue of substantive illegality may involve daunting issues of fact . . . In such a case, the issues of law may also be complex. In contrast, an issue of procedural invalidity of a bye-law may involve minimal evidence . . . And the question of law may be straight-forward': ibid at 224.

97 'There is also a formidable difficulty of categorisation created by *Bugg's* case. A distinction between substantive and procedural invalidity will often be difficult to draw . . . In *Wednesbury*, Lord Greene MR pointed out that different grounds of review "run into one another" ': ibid.

98 Ibid, at 225. 99 Ibid, at 227.

100 Ibid, at 209. It would nonetheless seem that *Wicks* is still good law. Lord Irvine's judgment in *Boddington* drew a clear distinction in respect of governmental actions which precipitated criminal liability between bye-laws issued to the world at large (as in *Boddington*) and administrative decisions targeted at a specific individual (as in *Wicks*). In the latter scenario, the individual would have ample opportunity to impugn the lawfulness of the decision, whether by – as in Mr Wick's case – a statutory appeal and then an AJR application, or through an AJR alone. We might note, for the sake of completeness, that the House of Lords saw no merit in Boddington's irrationality defence, and upheld the conviction.

CONCLUSION

To accept *Boddington* as (for the moment) the last word on Order 53 issues would be rather ill-advised. Notwithstanding the grand constitutional terms in which Lords Steyn and Irvine dressed their judgments in that case, *Boddington* deals only with a narrow area of the public law-private law divide. The case tells us little about the way in which procedural questions should be resolved when the action in issue is being instigated rather than defended by the individual citizen. It may be that we might apply the same constitutional logic found in *Boddington* to the broader *O'Reilly* issue, and find that it points us very strongly in the direction of (at least) adopting the 'broad view' of *O'Reilly* propounded by Lord Lowry in *Roy*.[101] But it would seem unlikely that this technique could plausibly take us as far as re-embracing the unhindered procedural duality that seemed to be offered in *Barnard* and *Pyx Granite* and which was apparently supported by the Law Commission in 1976.

In October 2000, various technical and linguistic changes were introduced to the application for judicial review procedure. Order 53 was replaced by what is now Part 54 of the Civil Procedure Rules. A 'claimant' (rather than a 'plaintiff') now makes a 'claim' (rather than an 'application') for judicial review. The names of the prerogative remedies were also altered: certiorari became a 'quashing order'; mandamus became a 'mandatory order'; and prohibition became a 'prohibitory order'. De jure recognition was also given to a state of affairs long existing de facto, namely that the High Court contained a specialist Administrative division. The style of citation of judicial review cases was also amended; from *R v Government Body, ex p Claimant* to *R (Claimant) v Government Body*.

The object underlying the alterations was to simplify and expedite the conduct of litigation raising administrative law issues.[102] Whether the changes have that effect remains to be seen. What they are unlikely to do is finally resolve the conceptual difficulties generated by *O'Reilly v Mackman* and its progeny.[103]

Notwithstanding its intrinsic complexity, the Order 53/part 54 case law is of great importance in constitutional terms, since it lays out so clearly the extent to which our legal system's understanding of the rule of law and the sovereignty of Parliament

[101] See for example *Mercury Communications Ltd v Director General of Telecommunications* [1996] 1 All ER 575, [1996] 1 WLR 48, HL. A caveat against this point is raised by a short line of cases addressing the interrelationship between the AJR and habeas corpus. See in particular *R v Secretary of State for the Home Department, ex p Muboyayi* [1992] QB 244, CA, and the critique by Sir William Wade (1996) 'Habeas corpus and judicial review' *LQR* 55–70.

[102] See Fordham M (2001) 'Judicial review: the new rules' *Public Law* 4–10: Cornford T and Sunkin M (2001) 'The Bowman Report: access and the recent reforms of the judicial review procedure' *Public Law* 11–20.

[103] See Ingman T (2002) *The English legal process* pp 607–610 (Oxford: OUP).

are conditioned not so much by the content of judicially generated constraints on governmental behaviour, as by the issue of access to them. But the Order 53 debate forms only one element of this 'access to justice' question within our modern constitutional law. Of equal significance is the topic to which we turn in chapter seventeen – the matter of locus standi.

17

LOCUS STANDI

One obvious question that would arise from any discussion of the public/private divide that informed the procedural element of administrative law prior to 1977 is: 'Why would any applicant ever have chosen to challenge government action through one of the prerogative remedies rather than seek a declaration or injunction via a writ or originating summons?' Pursuing one of the public law remedies would not seem a rational choice for an applicant to make, since she would be handicapped by short time limits, by quite restrictive rules as to discovery of documents and cross-examination of witnesses, and by the non-availability of damages.

The answer is in part offered by the historical intricacies of the ways in which the various remedies developed. Among the more significant of these esoterica was the rule – which survived until *Factortame* – that injunctions could not (generally) be issued against the Crown.[1] Declarations were available against the Crown, but as indicated by *Dyson v A-G* in 1911[2] – there remained some uncertainty as to their exact scope. As noted in chapter sixteen, the reach of the various administrative law remedies has never been fixed,[3] and the possibility always existed that an applicant might persuade a court to step in hitherto untrodden directions. But notwithstanding such intricacies concerning the reach of the remedies, an important influence on the form of remedy an applicant sought was provided by the law of locus standi (standing).

As chapter sixteen suggested, the division between public law and private remedies raises rule of law questions at a fairly sophisticated level. We saw in chapter three that one of the most obvious challenges to orthodox understandings of the rule of law is posed by Parliament's use of ouster clauses, which – unless imaginatively construed by the courts as in *Gilmore* and *Anisminic* – preclude any applicant from arguing her case in the courts at all. The rule of law issue raised in cases such as *O'Reilly* is a more subtle one. Mr O'Reilly was not de jure being denied access to the courts to challenge the government body's decision. Rather he was directed down a procedural route which made it much less likely that he could win his case.[4] In rule of law terms, locus

[1] See Beatson and Matthews op cit ch 9. For a helpful examination of the exceptions to this general rule see Wade (1988) op cit pp 588–590.

[2] [1911] 1 KB 410, CA. [3] See p 586 above.

[4] It might be suggested he was de facto so excluded, both because under the public law route he was out of time and – even if he had been within time – he could not have won his case without being able to have discovery of the Board's documents and cross-examination of its members.

standi raises, like ouster clauses, the question of whether the applicant can gain access to the courts at all. We might characterise the law on locus standi as asking: 'Who is allowed to stand before the court to challenge a government action?' If an applicant was not granted standing, she simply could not reach the question of whether the government action she was challenging was unlawful. This might mean that 'unlawful' government actions were not quashed, a consequence with obvious (and presumably adverse) implications for orthodox perceptions both of the rule of law and the sovereignty of Parliament.

This topic is intimately connected to the application for judicial review, both because of the present law's roots in Order 53 and the Supreme Court Act 1981, and because of the competing policy issues that it throws up. Those policy concerns are essentially threefold. How does administrative law balance the protection of individual citizens' rights and interests with the desire to ensure that government decision-making remains within legal limits and with the concern to protect government bodies (including the courts) from vexatious litigants? The concept of locus standi is perhaps the most important way in which administrative law deals with this complex question.

For our present purposes, the subject is best studied by a three-part chronological division. The first period addresses the law which existed prior to the introduction of the Order 53 reforms in 1977. The second covers the short period between the introduction of those reforms and the House of Lords' decision in *IRC v National Federation of Self-Employed and Small Businesses* ('*IRC*').[5] The third runs from the mid-1980s to the present day.

I. THE 'OLD' CASE LAW

The law on locus standi developed in quite distinct ways in respect of the public law (certiorari, mandamus and prohibition) and the private law remedies (declaration or injunction).[6] At the risk of some oversimplification, one might at this initial stage suggest that the courts applied more stringent standing tests for the declaration and injunction than for the public law remedies. This is the primary explanation for what might on occasion seem the surprising fact that an applicant chose to proceed (assuming the choice were available) by prerogative writ rather than a declaration or injunction. While an action for certiorari or prohibition might offer lesser prospects of succeeding at trial than an action for a declaration, it offered much better prospects of surmounting the standing test and so being able to begin the action at all.

The force of this point is reinforced when one considers that standing was widely perceived as a 'threshold issue' – ie it was an obstacle an applicant had to surmount

[5] [1982] AC 617, [1981] 2 All ER 93, HL.

[6] Standing is not an issue in private law actions such as tort or breach of contract.

before she was permitted to argue the merits of her case. If this view was correct, then the ostensible strength of an applicant's legal argument and the political significance of the decision she was contesting would be irrelevant to the standing question, which would presumably have to focus solely on the identity of the applicant and the intimacy of her connection to the decision being challenged. Although this notion of locus standi being a preliminary issue enjoyed widespread judicial and academic approval,[7] it was something of a legal fiction. As is suggested below, many of the leading standing judgments were clearly influenced by the respective court's views of the merits of the applicant's claim, and in many cases where one might have thought there was considerable doubt as to the applicant's standing, the question was never broached at all.

A close examination of the many subtleties and complexities thrown up by the 'old' law of standing is best reserved for a specialised administrative law text.[8] The following pages sketch out the main currents in the orthodox view of standing prior to 1977, and also identify some decisions which might suggest we should regard the orthodoxy with some scepticism.

DECLARATION AND INJUNCTION – A RESTRICTIVE TEST?

A cursory glance at several leading judgments might lead the reader to assume that the courts have consistently – over a long period – set very high tests for the grant of standing to pursue these two remedies. In the 1858 case of *Ware v Regent's Canal Co*,[9] the applicant landowner sought a declaration that the defendant had carried out works on his land which were not authorised by the relevant private Act of Parliament permitting construction of a canal. In the course of his judgment, Lord Chelmsford LC offered what Professor Wade describes as a 'classic statement' of this restrictive perception of standing:

> 'Where there has been an excess of the powers given by an Act of Parliament, but no injury has been occasioned to any individual, or is imminent and of irreparable consequences, I apprehend that no-one but the Attorney-General on behalf of the public has a right to apply to this court to check the exorbitance of the party in the exercise of the powers confided to him'.[10]

Much attention has also been given to Buckley J's judgment in *Boyce v Paddington Borough Council*.[11] Boyce owned a block of flats adjacent to a churchyard owned by the council. Statutory provisions limited the types of development that could be carried out in the churchyard. In order to prevent Boyce claiming the arcane right of

[7] Cf Cane P (1980) 'The function of standing rules in administrative law' *Public Law* 303–328 at 303–304: Harlow and Rawlings (1984) op cit pp 284–285.

[8] On which see successive editions of Craig's *Administrative Law*.

[9] (1858) 3 De G & J 212.

[10] Ibid, at 228; quoted in Wade (1988) op cit p 690, fn 7. On the role of the Attorney General in this respect see the discussion of *Gouriet* at pp 115–116 above.

[11] [1903] 1 Ch 109.

'ancient lights', the council erected a billboard in the churchyard pending more permanent development. Boyce subsequently sought a declaration that the billboard was a 'building' of a type prohibited by the statute.

The council argued that individuals could never have standing to seek a declaration against it. Buckley J rejected this argument, and suggested that standing for a declaration could be satisfied on two grounds. The first, more restrictive ground, was that the applicant had a '*private legal right*' which was affected by the decision being challenged. The second, less restrictive ground (often referred to as 'special damage') was that the applicant was *atypically and intensely affected* by the decision's adverse impact on a *public right.*

One can discern obvious reasons for a restrictive standing test for these two remedies. In formal terms, their origin in the private law field would point to their availability being dependent upon infringement of private law rights. From a functionalist perspective, a difficult standing test offered important protections to the defendant against the lengthy time limits and presumptive entitlement to discovery of documents and cross-examination of witnesses that an action for a declaration/injunction brought with it.

The rule in *Ware v Regent's Canal* clearly compromises both the sovereignty of Parliament and the rule of law in their purist, orthodox senses, in so far as it hindered a citizen's attempt to prove that a government body has acted unlawfully. But it did not ignore either concept entirely. In particular, as Lord Chelmsford stressed, the court's view was shaped by the fact that the applicant had known about the works in issue for some eighteen months before he began his action. Had he come promptly, the court's conclusion may have been different. Furthermore, Lord Chelmsford accepted that the applicant had other legal paths open to him, provided for by the Act itself. And it should also be noted that while the court denied the applicant standing, it nonetheless examined the merits of his claim – and found it unproven.

A skilled lawyer would have little difficulty in constructing a plausible argument to the effect that *Ware* offered a rule of narrow rather than general application. And even if *Ware* was construed broadly, the judgment in *Boyce* would suggest that its scope had been somewhat attenuated by the 'public right' limb of Buckley J's two-part formula.

It must also be remembered that Parliament could at any time have introduced a more relaxed standing test through statute had it wished to do so. That Parliament did not take such an initiative is an indication that legislators were content with the common law position, even if this might mean that some unlawful government actions would never be corrected.

Case law of more recent vintage was markedly ambiguous in its approach to this issue. Some of the seminal cases discussed in earlier chapters which were initiated as actions for a declaration clearly fell within even the *Ware* test of locus standi. The applicant's interest in *Anisminic*[12] was money; in *Barnard* and *Ridge v Baldwin*[13] it was continuance in employment. Standing was not an issue in those cases. Yet the

[12] See pp 84–87 above.

[13] See pp 515 and 543–546 respectively.

applicant in *Prescott v Birmingham Corpn*[14] also sought – and was granted – a declaration. Prescott successfully challenged the legality of the council's policy to offer concessionary bus fares to old age pensioners. His interest (as a ratepayer) did not fall within either *Ware* or *Boyce*, but the standing issue was not even argued in that case, still less addressed by the court at first instance or on appeal.

The suspicion that the grant or refusal of standing for a declaration or injunction was determined in large part by the courts' views of the merits of applicants' claims rather than the nature of the applicants' interests is reinforced by examination of several leading cases from the 1960s and 1970s. The issue raised in *Gregory v Camden London Borough Council*[15] was the grant of planning permission to open a school on the site of a former convent. There was allegedly a procedural flaw in the grant of permission. But before reaching that question, the court had to decide if Gregory, who lived next door to the site in question and was concerned by the additional noise and traffic that the school would generate, had standing? The court concluded that he did not:

> 'One has to consider the legal rights of someone. . . . I may be very much affected by the noise of the children coming out to play, by the shouts, by the laughter and everything else. But unless I can establish it is a nuisance then I have lost no legal right. . . .
>
> The next point is this. In this case no question of public rights is involved, as where there is interference with the highway. . . .'[16]

The court was obviously influenced in reaching this decision however by its view that to grant a declaration would be a useless remedy in the circumstances. Paull J indicated that had the applicant sought an injunction, which might have had some practical effect, the court might have taken a different view on the standing point.

The paradigmatic 'hopeless case' is perhaps *Thorne v BBC*.[17] Thorne was seeking an injunction to prevent the BBC broadcasting what he regarded as anti-German propaganda. He claimed that the programmes breached s 6 of the Race Relations Act 1965, which created a criminal offence of incitement to racial hatred. The applicant's bizarre statement of claim[18] would suggest he was mentally disturbed, but the Court of Appeal saw no need to address this issue. In this case, standing was treated as a threshold issue. As Lord Denning put it:

> 'It is a fundamental rule that the court will only grant an injunction at the suit of a private individual to support a legal right. . . . [The applicant] does not allege, and indeed he does not have, any legal right in himself personally in this matter'.[19]

The court[20] observed that the very high standing test set for a declaration served an important political purpose in situations such as this; namely to prevent individual

14 [1955] Ch 210, CA; p 506 above. 15 [1966] 2 All ER 196, [1966] 1 WLR 899.

16 Per Paull J, [1966] 2 All ER 196 at 201–202. On this second test see for example *Brownsea Haven Properties Ltd v Poole Corpn* [1958] Ch 574. The plaintiff owned a hotel in a road which he claimed had been unlawfully designated as a one way street. The standing issue was not even broached in this case.

17 [1967] 1 WLR 1104, CA. 18 Reproduced in full at ibid, 1106–1107.

19 Ibid, at 1109. 20 Danckwerts and Winn LJJ concurred with Lord Denning.

citizens invoking civil law remedies as a means to pre-empt or second guess governmental decisions as to whether or not to initiate criminal law proceedings.

Gregory and *Thorne* appear difficult to reconcile with the Court of Appeal's decision in *Blackburn v A-G.*[21] The merits of Blackburn's challenge to the UK's ratification of the Treaty of Rome were discussed in chapter twelve.[22] What is pertinent here is that the application was for a declaration and that the applicant's substantive claim was quite outlandish. Blackburn manifestly had no 'private legal right' in issue here; nor could he plausibly maintain that he would be atypically affected by the public law consequences of the UK's accession to the Community. Yet Lord Denning MR's leading judgment certainly did not treat the locus standi question as a preliminary issue. He did not reach it until the end of his judgment, and dealt with it in the following way:

'[Standing] is not a matter which we need rule on today. [Mr Blackburn] says that he feels very strongly and that it is a matter in which many persons in this country are concerned. I myself would not rule him out on the ground that he has no standing'.[23]

Whether the court would have 'ruled Mr Blackburn out' on that ground if the merits of his case indicated that he might have won his action is a matter for speculation.

There is some further indication that Lord Denning's Court of Appeal was willing to allow the declaration and injunction to be invoked by citizens with no particular link to the government decision being challenged if they had (in the court's view) a strong case on the merits. *A-G (ex rel McWhirter) v Independent Broadcasting Authority*[24] is a good example. McWhirter sought an injunction against the Independent Broadcasting Authority. His specific concern was to prevent the television broadcast of a documentary about Andy Warhol, which he considered to be obscene.[25] The point of law on which he relied arose under s 3(1) of the Television Act 1964, which required members of the IBA Board to 'satisfy themselves' that broadcast programmes did not offend against good taste. On the facts, it appeared that the Board's members had unlawfully delegated that responsibility to their officials. While McWhirter seemed to have a strong case on the merits, the suggestion that he fell within either of the categories identified in *Boyce* is risible. But the court did not rule out the possibility that an applicant in such circumstances could have standing. Lord Denning expressed this point in grandiloquent language:

'I regard it as a matter of high constitutional principle that if there is good ground for supposing that a government department or a public authority is transgressing the law . . . in

[21] [1971] 2 All ER 1380, [1971] 1 WLR 1037.

[22] At p 446 above.

[23] [1971] 2 All ER 1380 at 1383, CA.

[24] [1973] QB 629, CA.

[25] The case is a mark of how far notions of obscenity have relaxed since 1973. Much press indignation (papers had been given a pre-broadcast screening of the film) was engendered by scenes which might appear only comical today. Thus, per the *Sunday Mirror*, the film was: 'the most permissive shocker to be shown on British screens. . . . It includes: A FAT GIRL, stripping to the waist, daubing her breasts with paint and then painting a canvas with them. She also throws paint down a lavatory pan to form weird patterns. This one she calls Flush Art': ibid, at 633.

a way which offends or injures thousands of Her Majesty's subjects, then in the last resort any one of those injured or offended can draw it to the attention of the courts and seek to have the law enforced'.[26]

This conclusion is readily defensible if we assume that the primary purpose of an injunction is to prevent what seems prima facie to be unlawful government[27] activity. If its purpose is however to protect private rights, the majority's conclusion is absurd. Lord Denning was aware of the shaky doctrinal foundations of his conclusion, observing that: 'in these days we have to mould procedural requirements so as to see that the duty which the statute ordains is fulfilled'.[28] 'Moulding' is perhaps a polite way of describing what the court did to traditional doctrine. A more satisfactory approach would have been for the court explicitly to break with past practice and to suggest that in cases of what appeared to be manifestly unlawful government behaviour, any citizen would be competent to bring an action for an injunction or a declaration.[29]

We have seen in earlier chapters that Lord Denning's time in the Court of Appeal was marked by occasional disagreement on matters of constitutional principle with the House of Lords; *Magor and St Mellons RDC* and *Rossminster* being primary examples.[30] A similar tension was evident in *Gouriet v Union of Post Office Workers*.[31] The background to this case was outlined in chapter four, which addressed the question of whether the Attorney-General's power to initiate relator proceedings was susceptible to full review. Gouriet had also sought to proceed in his own right, seeking a declaration that the proposed mail boycott was illegal and an injunction to prevent it taking place. The Court of Appeal had unanimously concluded that Gouriet had standing to seek a declaration. Since he had unsuccessfully sought a relator, the declaration was presumably (per *McWhirter*) his remedy of 'last resort'.

The House of Lords rejected this conclusion. Lord Wilberforce forcefully restated the rule in *Boyce*: 'where there is no interference with a private right and no personal damage, declaratory relief cannot be sought without joining the Attorney-General as a party (sc as relator)'.[32] (As noted in chapter four, the House of Lords also concluded that the High Court had no jurisdiction to examine the merits of the Attorney-General's refusal to begin relator proceedings.) One might argue that Mr Gouriet would have fared better on the standing question had he been able to present himself to the court as the owner of a business that communicated frequently with South African customers, or if he had friends in South Africa with whom he regularly

[26] Ibid, at 649.

[27] 'Government' in the context of an injunction at this time did not, of course, include the Crown.

[28] [1973] QB 629 at 635, CA.

[29] In the event, McWhirter was not given standing. His own action was not 'the last resort', as he could have attempted to persuade the Attorney General to initiate relator proceedings.

[30] See pp 75–76 and 79–81 respectively.

[31] [1978] AC 435, [1977] 3 All ER 70, HL.

[32] Ibid, at 85. Cf also Viscount Dilhorne at 94: 'In my opinion the cases establish that the courts have no jurisdiction to entertain such claims by a private individual who has not suffered and will not suffer damage'. These comments presumably mean that *Prescott, Blackburn* and *McWhirter* should not be regarded as 'authorities' on the locus standi issue.

corresponded.[33] It is conceivable that he might then, particularly on the first ground, have fallen within Lord Wilberforce's rule. This would however demand that we ignored the political context in which the judgment was issued, which would perhaps be unwise. Lord Wilberforce had indicated that a grant of standing would be futile, since Gouriet was challenging a decision that was so intensely political in nature that it was effectively non-justiciable.

In discussing the House of Lords' judgment, Paul Craig suggested that: 'The decision illustrates a conception of standing which in itself reflects a view of administrative law: the vindication of private rights'.[34] Craig's comment is readily defensible. But their Lordships' decision in *Gouriet* offered just *one* conception of locus standi. As this relatively cursory discussion of the early case law has suggested, other conceptions could readily be found, some of which intimated that in certain circumstances the declaration and injunction could be available to litigants with only the most remote of personal connections to the substantive question in issue. As Craig noted a few pages after the comment quoted above: 'To describe the common law as unnecessarily confused would be to pay it a compliment'.[35] That view applied as readily to the prerogative orders as to the declaration and injunction.

CERTIORARI AND PROHIBITION – AN EXPANSIVE TEST?

Since the prerogative remedies initially developed as mechanisms to control the activities of government bodies, one might expect that they would incorporate a broader test of standing than the declaration and injunction. Their original purpose was, after all, not to protect private rights but to ensure that government bodies did not exceed their jurisdiction.[36] The dominant view appeared to be that standing for certiorari could be satisfied on either of two grounds. These are perhaps best illustrated by the Court of Appeal's judgment in *R v Thames Magistrates' Court, ex p Greenbaum*.[37]

The case concerned the allocation of licences for market pitches. Greenbaum, a licencee, complained that the magistrates court had exceeded its statutory jurisdiction in ordering that a rival trader be given a specific pitch which had previously been allocated to him. Greenbaum clearly had a pecuniary interest in this decision, and it seems plausible that he would have had standing for a declaration had he sought one. He undoubtedly met the first of the two standing tests for certiorari; namely was he 'a person aggrieved'? This test bears some resemblance to the second limb of the *Boyce* test for a declaration. As Lord Ellenborough put it in *R v Taunton St Mary Inhabitants*:

'Certainly a person does not answer to the character of a person aggrieved who is only in

[33] Cf Cane P (3rd edn, 1996) *An Introduction to Administrative Law* pp 43–44 (Oxford: Clarendon Press).

[34] (1989) op cit p 354. Cf Beatson and Matthews: 'A survey for locus standi prior to *Gouriet* would have revealed that consistency was also lacking in respect of that remedy'; op cit p 482.

[35] Craig (1989) op cit p 358.

[36] Cf Wade (1988) op cit p 625: 'Nominally [prohibition and certiorari] are granted to the Crown and the Crown always has sufficient interest to call upon public bodies to act lawfully'.

[37] (1957) 55 LGR 129.

common with the rest of the subjects inconvenienced by the nuisance; but here it appears that persons have by reason of their local situation, a grievance of their own'.[38]

Greenbaum confirmed the proposition that a person aggrieved would be given standing *ex debito justiciae*, that is as a matter of right. Lord Denning also confirmed that standing for certiorari could be granted to a 'stranger' to the challenged decision. In these circumstances, standing would be granted if the court considered it in the public interest for the action to proceed. Lord Denning was not explicit as to which factors would be weighed in the balance to determine this issue. He referred to the 1870 decision of *R v Surrey Justices*[39] to illustrate this point, but all that this case tells us is that standing is unlikely to be granted to a stranger if 'no good would be done to the public' by the applicant succeeding in the action.[40] One would assume that 'the public good/interest' embraced matters relating to the merits of the case, and in particular the apparent strength of the applicant's legal argument and the political significance of the decision being challenged. If those factors were indeed to be taken into account, one cannot plausibly maintain that locus standi was a threshold question.

That 'strangers' could seek certiorari is a strong indication that the court was willing to accept what is sometimes referred to as a 'citizen's action' or 'acto popularis' basis for standing for this remedy. Private rights are an irrelevance under this conception of standing, which regards the purpose of the remedy as a means to control unlawful government decision-making.

The Court of Appeal seemed to step further in this direction in *R v Paddington Valuation Officer, ex p Peachey Property Corpn Ltd*,[41] in which Lord Denning suggested that one could be a 'person aggrieved' (and so entitled to standing as of right) even if one had no financial interest affected by the challenged decision. Peachey Property was a landlord whose purpose built flats had been given a higher rateable value than similar converted flats. It sought to have the rating list quashed on the grounds that the valuation was unlawful. The company clearly had a financial interest in the rateable value of its property, but Lord Denning indicated that this was not necessary for it to be a 'person aggrieved':

'I do not think grievances are to be measured in £.s.d.. If a ratepayer or other person finds his name included in a valuation list which is invalid, he is entitled to come to the court and apply to have it quashed. He is not to be put off by the plea that he has suffered no damage'.[42]

The judgment thus seemed to widen the category of individuals who could expect to be granted standing *ex debito justiciae* to seek certiorari. Lord Denning also held that the courts should construe the notion of a 'stranger' broadly, suggesting that the

[38] (1815) 3 M & S 465 at 472. [39] (1870) LR 5 QB 466.

[40] Ibid, at 473, per Blackburn J. The case is in fact not about standing at all, but rather about the analytically distinct issue of whether the court should withhold a remedy from an applicant who has standing and succeeds on the merits.

[41] [1966] 1 QB 380, CA. [42] [1966] 1 QB 380 at 401, CA.

only type of litigant who would not satisfy this test was 'a mere busybody who was interfering in things which did not concern him'.[43]

The 'busybody' seemed to be a rather narrow residual category. Mr Blackburn appeared again as the applicant in *R v Greater London Council, ex p Blackburn*.[44] His complaint was that the Greater London Council had unlawfully delegated its film censorship functions to the British Board of Film Censors by automatically accepting the Board's classification of particular pornographic films rather than evaluating the films itself. He sought an order of prohibition forbidding the GLC from acting in this way. Lord Denning's judgment is of interest because (rather like his treatment of locus standi for an injunction in *McWhirter*) it manifestly views standing for prohibition as being concerned almost exclusively with ensuring that public bodies do not act unlawfully, regardless of whether the impugned decision affects individual rights:

> 'I regard it a matter of high constitutional principle [that] if the government transgresses the law . . . in a way which offends thousands . . . anyone offended can draw it to the attention of the courts'.[45]

The standing test to be adopted was therefore a (very) loose one:

> 'Mr Blackburn is a citizen of London. His wife is a ratepayer. He has children who may be harmed by the exhibition of pornographic films. If he has no sufficient interest, no other citizen has'.[46]

Lord Denning's test is apparently even more expansive than the one deployed in *McWhirter*, since he has here dropped any reference to an individual's action being admissible only as a matter of last resort.

But, unlike in *McWhirter*, there is an obvious flaw in Lord Denning's reasoning on the matter of 'high constitutional principle' here. One could not know if a government body had 'transgressed the law' until the court issued judgment. Mr Blackburn could at most 'draw the attention of the courts' to a strong prima facie argument that an unlawful act had occurred.[47] Denning's text rather suggests that he did not turn his attention to the standing question until after he had reached a conclusion on the merits; which in turn raises the inference that he allowed his answer on locus standi to be determined by his view on the substantive law. One might be forgiven for concluding that all that was required to gain standing for certiorari and prohibition was that an applicant present a prima facie convincing legal argument in respect of a decision which the court regarded as touching upon a matter of some political or moral importance.

MANDAMUS – BROAD OR NARROW TEST?

Case law on the standing requirements for mandamus offers support for the conflicting views that the remedy demanded an applicant to have something approximating

[43] Ibid. [44] [1976] 3 All ER 184, [1976] 1 WLR 550, CA. [45] Ibid, at 192.
[46] Ibid, at 191. [47] This is the point Lord Denning made in *McWhirter*.

the *Boyce* 'special damage' interest and that he/she need only be a concerned citizen.[48] The first line of case law is best illustrated by *R v Hereford Corpn, ex p Harrower*;[49] the second by *R v Metropolitan Police Comr, ex p Blackburn*.[50]

Harrower was a building and electrical contractor who had tendered unsuccessfully for a contract with the council. The applicants alleged that the council had failed to comply with its own standing orders in allocating the contract, and that its decision was therefore ultra vires on the grounds of procedural irregularity. Harrower applied for an order of mandamus to make the council go through the tendering process again.

The court considered the issue of the merits – finding in the applicant's favour – before broaching the standing issue. Lord Parker CJ felt that the test set was a high one:

> 'It has always been recognised that there is a quite different criterion of interest which would justify an application for certiorari and one which would justify an application for mandamus. It is said that a far more stringent test applies in the case of mandamus, and that the applicant must have, as it is put, a specific legal right'.[51]

This 'right' was not satisfied by the mere fact that the applicants had an economic interest qua potential contractor in the outcome of the tendering process; nor by the fact that the company was a ratepayer in the council's area. However Lord Parker CJ held that the combined effect of these two rather dilute economic interests was sufficient to give the applicant standing on these facts. The judgment implies that the applicant would have to show a specific pecuniary interest in the decision made by the council. The case is certainly not authority for the proposition that being a ratepayer is per se sufficient to give standing for mandamus.

However, the Court of Appeal took a rather different view in *R v Metropolitan Police Comr, ex p Blackburn*.[52] Blackburn alleged that the Metropolitan Police Commissioner had taken a policy decision not to enforce the anti-gambling laws since he considered such enforcement an inefficient use of manpower. Blackburn sought mandamus to compel the Commissioner to reverse this policy. As in *R v GLC, ex p Blackburn*, Lord Denning approached the case from an explicitly constitutional perspective. He seemed to doubt that Mr Blackburn had standing:

> 'it is I think an open question whether Mr Blackburn has a sufficient interest to be protected. No doubt any person who was adversely affected by the action of the commissioner in making a mistaken policy would have such an interest. The difficulty is to see how Mr Blackburn himself has been affected'.[53]

Lord Denning saw no need to decide this issue however. Instead he moved straight away to considering whether the policy was unlawful. Observing that 'The rule of law must prevail', Lord Denning characterised the non-enforcement of the gambling

[48] Compare for example *R v Lewisham Union Guardians* [1897] 1 QB 498, requiring a 'specific legal right', with *R v Cotham* [1898] 1 QB 802, demanding only a 'substantial interest'.

[49] [1970] 3 All ER 460, [1970] 1 WLR 1424.

[50] [1968] 2 QB 118, [1968] 1 All ER 763, CA.

[51] [1970] 3 All ER 460 at 463.

[52] [1968] 2 QB 118, CA.

[53] Ibid, at 137.

laws as 'a deplorable state of affairs'.[54] The Commissioner's policy was undoubtedly unlawful.

The judgment suggests that the court's concern was primarily with the legality of police policy, irrespective of the policy's impact on Blackburn himself. The case certainly indicates that the merits of the case and the applicant's standing were intertwined issues. In the event, the commissioner had reversed his policy before judgment was issued, so no remedy was granted.

II. SECTION 31(3) OF THE SUPREME COURT ACT 1981 AND THE *INLAND REVENUE COMMISSIONERS* CASE

It is apparent that prior to 1977 the law on standing varied markedly not just between remedies but also within them.[55] This is not necessarily an undesirable state of affairs. If one sees the purposes of standing 'rules' as ensuring that the courts have a wide discretion to ration access to judicial review, the diversity in the case law would be quite satisfactory. From an applicant's perspective however, the uncertainty could be problematic. There would for example be little reason for an applicant to seek prohibition or certiorari rather than a declaration or injunction if the court adopted the very relaxed test of standing for the declaration favoured in *Blackburn v A-G*, or ignored the standing question altogether as in *Prescott v Birmingham*. But it would have been foolhardy for counsel to affirm with any certainty whether a court would take that line in an individual case. From that perspective, the law was ripe for reform.

The same policy issues that underlay the amended application for judicial review informed the changes that Order 53, and subsequently the Supreme Court Act 1981, s 31(3), promised to bring with respect to standing. Section 31(3) provided that – at the leave stage – standing would be granted to an applicant who had a 'sufficient interest in the matter to which the application relates'. The text of s 31 did not differentiate between the five remedies in this respect. But while the standing test was now nominally a statutory rather than common law issue, s 31(3) was cast in very loose terms. The notion of 'sufficient interest' is itself a flexible concept.[56] When one adds to this the 'in the matter to which the application relates' limb of the formula, the legitimate scope for judicial discretion in deciding whether a given applicant

54 Ibid, at 138.

55 But see Cane P (1981) 'Standing, legality and the limits of public law' *Public Law* 322–339 at p 335: 'The "old" law of standing was, it is true, couched in terms of greater or lesser vagueness – legal rights, special damage, genuine grievance. But the content of these vague concepts was in principle and in practice capable of being rendered relatively concrete and certain. . . . Rules of standing could be stated in terms of classes of plaintiffs – ratepayers, commercial competitors, neighbours, taxpayers'.

56 Cf Cane 1980 op cit pp 325–326.

meets the test seems virtually boundless.[57] It was also unclear if s 31(3)'s explicit reference to the leave stage meant that locus standi was not to be considered at the full hearing stage; or, if it was to be considered, whether the 'sufficient interest . . .' formula was the test to be applied. Two further issues in particular remained to be resolved by subsequent case law. The first was whether s 31(3) introduced a uniform locus standi test for all five remedies? The second was whether, irrespective of the answer to the first question, s 31(3) should be taken as indicating a parliamentary preference for the relaxation or the restriction of standing requirements?

The House of Lords offered answers to these questions shortly afterwards, in *IRC v National Federation of Self Employed and Small Businesses*.[58] The IRC had given a tax 'amnesty' to casual workers in the newspaper industry who had previously evaded taxes in return for accurate returns in future. The National Federation subsequently sought a declaration to have the amnesty declared illegal and mandamus to force the IRC to assess and collect the tax.

All five judges hearing the case issued judgments. Although there were many points of agreement between the opinions, there were also some significant differences, which makes it very difficult to identify the clear ratio of the case. It would perhaps be more accurate to suggest that the various judgments laid out a series of principles which might be expected to exert a strong influence on the development of the law on locus standi in future.

The judges differed on the question of whether s 31 had created a uniform standing test. Lord Diplock clearly felt that a uniform test was now in place. Lords Scarman and Roskill appeared to support this view. Lord Wilberforce, in contrast, firmly rejected the idea of a uniform test. Lord Fraser was more equivocal, suggesting that not all of the old law had been swept away.

With the exception of Lord Fraser,[59] the court took the view that standing should no longer be seen as a preliminary or threshold issue. There might on occasion be situations where an applicant's interest in the matter was so tenuous that she could be denied standing at the leave stage. In most cases however, the questions of standing and the merits of a claim would be explicitly fused. This fusion implied that if an applicant approached the court with an ostensibly convincing legal argument in respect of a gross illegality committed by a government body she could expect to be granted leave even if she herself had only a remote, personal interest in the matter.[60]

[57] On the background to the new test see Harlow and Rawlings (1984) op cit pp 299–301; Craig (1989) op cit pp 358–359.

[58] [1982] AC 617, [1981] 2 All ER 93, HL. Despite the styling of the case (ie *NFSESB v IRC*), it was argued before the House of Lords as an AJR, not as a private law stream case. The significance of this point is returned to below.

[59] '[W]hether the respondents have a sufficient interest to make the application at all is a separate, and logically prior, question which has to be answered affirmatively before any question on the merits arises': ibid, at 107.

[60] Cf Lord Diplock: 'If on a quick perusal of the material then available, the court thinks that it discloses what might on further consideration turn out to be an arguable case in favour of granting to the applicant the relief claimed, it ought, in the exercise of a judicial discretion, to give him leave to apply for that relief': ibid, at 106.

This reasoning indicated that the court was rejecting a pre-occupation with formal rules of standing, and embracing instead a functionalist approach; that function being not so much the protection of private rights, but ensuring that potentially unlawful government action did not escape judicial scrutiny. In Lord Diplock's opinion:

'It would in my view be a grave lacuna in our system of public law if a pressure group, like the federation, or even a single public spirited taxpayer, were prevented by outdated technical rules of locus standi from bringing the matter to the attention of the court to vindicate the rule of law and get the unlawful action stopped'.[61]

On the facts of the case, all five Law Lords concluded that the Federation did not have standing. This was in (small) part because the relationship between the IRC and taxpayers was regarded as confidential, and should not be open to breach by third parties. The primary reason for denying standing however lay in the fusion of locus with the merits. Simply put, the court considered that the IRCs' actions had been well within the limits of their statutory discretion:

'the Inland Revenue were acting in this matter genuinely in the care and management of the taxes, under the powers entrusted to them. This has no resemblance to any kind of case where the court, at the instance of a taxpayer, ought to intervene'.[62]

The judges nonetheless did not rule out the possibility that there might be some types of allegedly unlawful IRC behaviour in respect of which any taxpayer would be granted standing; a conclusion which certainly countenances the possibility of an acto popularis basis to the locus standi issue.[63]

Lord Wilberforce rooted the explicit fusion of standing and merits in the wording of s 31(3); ie that the applicant show 'sufficient interest *in the matter to which the application relates*'.[64] Lord Diplock, in contrast, indicated that this step was a natural progression in the evolution of common law understandings of the courts' role in regulating the relationship between citizens and government bodies. Whether we see the source of the *IRC* principle in statute or common law, its policy implications are clear. Craig characterised the judgment as confirming that: 'archaic limitations on standing should be discarded in order that public law can meet the new challenges of a developing society'.[65]

Yet it would be a mistake to assume that the *IRC* case is the *starting point* for the current law of standing. It is perhaps more instructive to view it as a *turning point*. Its constitutional significance can only properly be understood if the judgments are set in the contexts of both of the previous case law and the competing policy objectives that case law was attempting to address. Professor Wade suggested in the sixth edition of his influential *Administrative law* textbook that in the *IRC* case:

[61] Ibid, at 107. [62] Ibid, at 100; per Lord Wilberforce.

[63] There is obviously another side to the 'fusion' coin. An applicant who had a close connection to the matter in dispute, but who came to court with an apparently weak legal argument in relation to a trivial matter, could be denied standing.

[64] [1981] 2 All ER 93 at 96 (original emphasis). [65] (1983) op cit p 362.

'The House of Lords gave a new and liberal but somewhat uncertain character to the law of standing. . . . In general [the decision] may be said to crystallise the elements of a generous and public-oriented doctrine of standing which had previously been sporadic and uncoordinated'.[66]

STANDING IN THE PRIVATE LAW STREAM

The extent to which the 'new' law of standing has lent that liberality a more coherent form is the subject we address in the remainder of this chapter.[67] Before doing so, however, it is important to note that whatever liberalisation of locus standi the *IRC* decision produced, it was a liberalisation that operated only in the public law stream of remedies. The judgment was concerned only with locus standi for the AJR: it had no obvious bearing on the standing test for a declaration or injunction sought via a writ or originating summons. *O'Reilly v Mackman* was to be decided shortly after *IRC*. After that judgment was issued, it was apparent that a relaxation of the standing test for a declaration or injunction through Order 53 might not in fact make it any easier at all for an applicant to gain access to the long time limits and entitlement to cross-examination and discovery associated with the private law stream. A grant of standing might therefore prove of limited utility to some (or perhaps many) applicants.

In *Steeples v Derbyshire County Council*,[68] decided in 1981, Webster J had concluded that the standing test for both the public law and private law routes to a declaration should be the same. To hold otherwise 'would seem to me to make an ass of the law'.[69] However, this view was not widely shared.

Thus in *Barrs v Bethell*,[70] decided shortly after *IRC*, the High Court refused to grant standing for a private law route declaration to a ratepayer who alleged that Camden council had unlawfully mismanaged its finances. Warner J indicated that he felt standing should not have been granted in *Prescott*, and doubted that some of Lord Denning's more extravagant locus standi claims were supported by authority. In Warner J's view, the fact that that an applicant might satisfy the s 31(3) test did not mean she had standing for a declaration in the private law stream. The *Boyce* test would still apply in these circumstances. And it would apply in order to ensure that the protections (by way of leave and short time limits) offered to public bodies by Order 53 could not be circumvented by applicants who lacked an intimate interest in the matter in issue.[71]

Similarly, in *Ashby v Ebdon*,[72] Warner J held that s 31(3) and *IRC* had made no difference to the *Gouriet* rationale.[73] An applicant could not seek a declaration through a writ if the effect of so doing would be to sidestep the need to gain the

66 (1988) op cit p 701.

67 Cf Cane's suggestion that *IRC* would create 'a large degree of uncertainty and unpredictability' (1981) op cit p 339.

68 [1984] 3 All ER 468.

69 Ibid, at 500.

70 [1982] Ch 294, [1982] 1 All ER 106.

71 Warner J placed considerable reliance on *Heywood* (see pp 581–582 above) in support of this point.

72 [1985] Ch 394, [1984] 3 All ER 869.

73 See pp 607–608 above.

Attorney-General's consent to a relator action in circumstances where the civil law was to be used as an indirect means of pursuing criminal proceedings, unless the applicant could demonstrate that she fell within the *Boyce* test. This view was upheld by the House of Lords in *Stoke-on-Trent City Council v B & Q (Retail) Ltd.*[74] The court held that the council had no standing to seek an injunction through a writ against B&Q in an attempt to stop the store breaching the provisions of the Sunday Trading Act 1950, that breach being a criminal offence.

III. POST-*IRC* DEVELOPMENTS

Notwithstanding the court's evident unwillingness to allow the supposedly more relaxed locus standi regime identified in *IRC* to cross over into the private law stream, several cases decided shortly after *IRC* indicated that Lord Diplock's preference for more liberal standing rules within the AJR was well supported in the lower courts. The applicant in *R v HM Treasury, ex p Smedley*[75] approached the court 'in his capacity of British taxpayer and elector'. Mr Smedley's complaint was that the government was about to make a payment of some £120 million to the EC in an unlawful manner. The Court of Appeal concluded that his claim was ill-founded on the merits. Lord Donaldson MR did not expressly decide the standing issue, but indicated he would be 'extremely surprised'[76] if he found himself upholding the government's submission that Mr Smedley did not have sufficient interest in this matter. Slade LJ was more explicit: 'I do not feel much doubt that Mr Smedley, if only in his capacity as a taxpayer, has sufficient locus standi to raise this question . . .'.[77]

The case is perhaps a good indication that the 'matter' identified in s 31(3) could include the scale of the practical consequences of the decision under challenge as well as the prima facie flagrancy of its breach of legal norms. Mr Smedley's argument appeared to be weak on its merits, but since £120 million was in issue the 'matter' he raised was a serious one. Slade LJ's grant of locus to Mr Smedley qua taxpayer does not contradict *IRC*, since the applicant was not seeking confidential information about another individual.

The *Smedley* decision is not without pre-*IRC* precedent. It may be recalled that the Court of Appeal in *Blackburn v A-G* had permitted a 'concerned citizen' to seek a declaration, on quite hopeless grounds, concerning the legality of the government's ratification of the Treaty of Accession. *Smedley* may help us to explain that decision as prompted by the court's concern about the consequences (enormous) of accession. Given that the UK's accession to the EC has prompted radical alteration to the doctrine of parliamentary sovereignty, it would be unsurprising if it has also prompted the courts effectively to abandon any concern with the status of the applicant in cases

[74] [1984] AC 754, [1984] 2 All ER 332, HL. [75] [1985] QB 657, CA.
[76] Ibid, at 667. [77] Ibid, at 670.

raising important, EC-related constitutional questions. Lord Rees-Mogg's challenge to the government's ratification of the Maastricht Treaty reinforces that hypothesis.[78] He was granted standing – in respect of an argument as legally feeble as that deployed by Mr Blackburn 35 years earlier – because of his 'sincere concern for constitutional issues'.

There is however reason for believing that a locus test of this breadth is not confined to EC matters, but may extend to other 'constitutional issues'. The applicant in *R v Felixstowe Justices, ex p Leigh*[79] was a journalist who sought – inter alia – a declaration that an apparent policy adopted by the Felixstowe magistrates courts of concealing the identity of magistrates in certain types of case was unlawful. Having concluded that Mr Leigh's argument succeeded on the merits, the court then accepted that he met the s 31(3) test, on the basis that he had initiated the action as 'the guardian of the public interest in the maintenance and preservation of open justice in the magistrates' courts, a matter of vital concern in the administration of justice'.[80]

Watkins LJ then went rather further, and held that any 'public spirited citizen' would have standing in this matter. This raises the inference that, as in *Smedley*, it was the political significance of the impugned government action, rather than the ostensible strength of the applicant's legal argument, that drove the decision on locus.

The argument that *IRC* was de facto if not de jure pushing the courts towards accepting a citizen's action test is buttressed by *R v Independent Broadcasting Authority, ex p Whitehouse*.[81] The case concerned the IBA's decision to broadcast a controversial movie, *Scum*, about life in a gaol for young offenders. Whitehouse sought a declaration that the IBA's members had acted unlawfully by delegating the decision about whether to screen the film to its Director General. The court held that she had sufficient interest in the matter. Watkins LJ indicated that every television licence holder would have standing in litigation relating to the broadcast of television programmes likely to give offence to children or adults. That the applicant identified herself as a licence-holder, rather than simply a citizen or viewer, or – as Whitehouse was – the leader of a long-established pressure group concerned with broadcasting standards – suggests that the courts were still looking for a pecuniary interest as a justification for granting standing. But that interest is so remote in this case that the licence holder point seems little more than a fig leaf to conceal a locus decision driven wholly by the merits of the case.

The Court of Appeal's judgment in *R v Monopolies and Mergers Commission, ex p Argyll Group plc*[82] lent a somewhat more complicated gloss to the position by suggesting (building on the intimations given in *IRC*) that standing was to be regarded both as a threshold issue at the leave stage and as an issue fused with the merits of the claim at the full hearing. As Lord Donaldson MR put it:

[78] *R v Secretary of State for Foreign and Commonwealth Affairs, ex p Rees-Mogg* [1994] QB 552, [1994] 1 All ER 457; see p 499 above.

[79] [1987] QB 582. [80] Ibid, at 598. [81] (1984) Times, 14 April.

[82] [1986] 2 All ER 257, CA.

'The first stage test, which is applied on the application for leave, will lead to a refusal if the applicant has no interest whatsoever and is, in truth, no more than a meddlesome busybody. If, however, the application appears to be otherwise arguable and there is no other discretionary bar, such as dilatoriness on the part of the applicant, the applicant may expect to get leave to apply, leaving the test of interest or standing to be re-applied as a matter of discretion on the hearing of the substantive application. At this second stage, the strength of the applicant's interest is one of the factors to be weighed in the balance'.[83]

It would of course make little sense for the court to make precisely the same inquiry at both the leave and full hearing stage. In practical terms, a distinction between a 'quick glance' and a 'close scrutiny' test for locus standi at the leave and full hearing stages has much to commend it. Lord Donaldson's test is however rather difficult to square with the wording of s 31(3): it requires something of a feat of the interpretive imagination to construe 'sufficient interest in the matter to which the application relates' as 'so long as she is not a busybody'. The case perhaps confirms the point that in this particular field, statutory provisions have little substantive impact on the way in which the courts are developing the law.

'REPRESENTATIVE STANDING'

The cases discussed in the previous section would suggest that *IRC* had triggered a pervasive shift towards a more expansive notion of standing. All of them had however involved actions brought by an individual citizen. In a sense, each applicant was 'representing' a broader constituency. This is most evident in respect of Mrs Whitehouse, who provided a legal mouthpiece for her pressure group. Smedley and Rees-Mogg were in effect acting as representatives of that swathe of political opinion which is hostile to the UK's membership of the EC. Leigh, more broadly, represented the public at large, albeit not in any formal, organisational capacity.

The courts are presented with a rather different standing issues when the prospective applicant is a formal, organised group, created for the purpose of pursuing a particular political agenda.[84] The applicant itself may very well not have an interest in any sense comparable with the private right/special damage test of standing.[85] It would however seem evident that granting standing to representative bodies increases the prospect that an unlawful government action will be challenged. An interest group is likely to have greater financial resources than an individual and is less likely to be intimidated by the potentially adverse personal consequences of beginning an action. It is also probable that an expert pressure group will have the knowledge and experience to present a case to the court in the most pertinent and effective way. These considerations would of course also offer government defendants an incentive to

83 Ibid, at 265.

84 'Political' is used in a broad sense here, to encompass cross-party or non-party political concerns such as health or environmental issues, social policy matters and so on.

85 Although of course it could have such an interest, for example in respect of planning permission decisions affecting its own land and premises.

argue that standing should not be granted; that is if we adopt the essentially cynical position of assuming that government bodies are invariably predisposed to exceed the limits of their powers and to resist being called to legal account for doing so. Furthermore, the ready grant of standing to such applicants raises the potential problem that the courts would find themselves being used as a surrogate or alternative political process, by interest groups which had failed to convince the government of the merits of adopting its particular view on a given political issue.[86]

The High Court had shown a willingness to permit such representative actions shortly after *IRC* in *Covent Garden Community Association Ltd v Greater London Council.*[87] The applicant company had been formed by residents and traders living in the Covent Garden neighbourhood of central London, with the specific purpose of promoting their particular view of how the area should be developed. The litigation concerned a GLC decision to grant planning permission for an office development on a site previously allocated for residential use. The Association alleged that there had been a breach of natural justice in the decision-making process. It was unable to convince the court on this point. Woolf J was nonetheless prepared to accept that the Association had standing. His reasoning seemed to rest primarily on the fact that the Association was an aggregation of the interests of many individuals who, because they had been consulted about and participated in the planning process, each had an individual entitlement to locus standi.

It is perhaps neither conceptually nor empirically problematic to grant standing to a representative group when many or all of the members of the group would have been entitled to standing qua individuals. Indeed, it may not even be appropriate to regard such bodies as 'representative' at all, but rather to see them as 'associational' bodies.[88] A slightly different issue is thrown up when the court is dealing with an interest group whose members would not obviously be granted standing in an individual capacity. This question arose in *R v Secretary of State for Social Services, ex p Child Poverty Action Group.*[89] The case concerned a challenge by the CPAG to a government decision which had occasioned substantial delays in the payment of welfare benefits. The Court of Appeal did not explicitly decide the locus standi issue, but indicated that it would have been prepared to grant standing to the CPAG on the grounds that:

'the issues raised are agreed to be important in the field of social welfare and not ones which individual claimants for supplementary benefit could be expected to raise. Furthermore, the CPAG . . . play a prominent role in giving guidance, advice and assistance to such claimants'.[90]

86 For an illuminating discussion of the issue in both the English and American contexts see Cane P (1995) 'Standing, representation and the environment', in Loveland (1995a) op cit. The 'surrogate political process' label is taken from Stewart R (1975) 'The reformation of American administrative law' *Harvard LR* 1667–1812 at 1670; see the discussion in Harlow and Rawlings (1984) op cit pp 307–309.

87 [1981] JPL 183.

88 Cane (1995) op cit.

89 [1989] 1 All ER 1047, CA.

90 Ibid, at 1048.

The presumption that the courts would invariably welcome representative actions from responsible and expert bodies was however rebutted by Schieman J's judgment in *R v Secretary of State for the Environment, ex p Rose Theatre Trust*.[91] The case concerned the site of the sixteenth century Rose Theatre in London, which was newly rediscovered in the 1980s. Property developers wished to build on the site. The Rose Theatre Trust was formed specifically to lobby to save the site from development. The Trust comprised archaeologists, actors and writers, and other members interested in preserving the country's cultural heritage. The Trust wished to have the Theatre site 'listed' under the Ancient Monuments and Archaeological Areas Act 1979. The Secretary of State refused to list the building, reasoning that the developers had agreed to delay their works to facilitate archaeological digs at the site and that economic development was more important than preserving the site.

Schieman J denied standing to the Trust.[92] His judgment was driven by explicit policy considerations. He did not accept that standing rules should invariably be interpreted to facilitate challenges to government decisions, even if those challenges were brought by informed, well-intentioned and non-partisan applicants. But neither did he assume that standing would invariably be granted even to an applicant who possessed a legal right in the matter in dispute. As Schieman J put it, the fact that a government body may have acted unlawfully did not in itself mean *anyone at all* had the right to challenge the decision:

'the law does not see it as a function of the courts to be there for every individual who is interested in having the legality of an administrative action litigated . . . We are not all given by Parliament the right to apply for judicial review'.[93]

According to Schieman J, the reason for standing rules was 'to avoid chaos'. By this he seemed to mean in part that locus standi was a mechanism to protect the courts from being overloaded with litigation, and, more important, to lend a degree of certainty to government decisions by safeguarding them from legal challenge.[94] As Cane has suggested, this perspective has little to commend it.[95] If the avoidance of 'chaos' in respect of a particular area of government activity is of paramount importance, Parliament could make that clear by using an ouster clause. Similarly, the imposition of a three-month maximum time limit for initiating litigation under Order 53 /Part 54 protects government bodies against the possibility of having to undo major works should they turn out to be premised on unlawful actions. Furthermore, it is always open to the court to find in an applicant's favour and yet avoid 'chaos' by either denying a remedy or tailoring that remedy in a fashion sensitive to the facts of a particular case.[96]

91 [1990] 1 QB 504, [1990] 1 All ER 754.

92 Schieman J devoted most of his judgment to the merits, and concluded the SOSE's action was lawful. He only turned to the issue of standing at the end of his opinion.

93 [1990] 1 QB 504, [1990] 1 All ER 754.

94 For a fuller exposition of the judge's views see Schiemann K (1990) 'Locus standi' *Public Law* 342–353.

95 (1990) 'Statutes, standing and representation' *Public Law* 307–312.

96 Schieman J's judgment on this point might be contrasted with Lord Denning's 1968 decision in *Bradbury v Enfield London Borough Council* ([1967] 1 WLR 1311 at 1319): 'If a local authority does not fulfil

There would seem to be good reasons for thinking that the Trust should have been granted standing for its challenge. The site was arguably of great importance to the country's cultural heritage. The Trust represented a collectivity rather than just an individual, and thus increased the likelihood that the application was motivated by 'serious' and 'non-partisan' consideration. Schieman J was unconvinced by any of these points. Even though the Trust was not a 'busybody', it had no locus standi. He laid considerable stress on the point that mere 'weight of numbers' could not produce standing: if the members of the Trust qua individuals lacked standing, they could not gain it by banding together into an association.[97] *Rose Theatre* was not taken to appeal. Had that happened, it seems probable that Schieman J's decision would have been reversed. That the judgment was something of a restrictive aberration within a generally facilitative trend is suggested by several subsequent cases.

In 1993, British Nuclear Fuels wished to begin to test a new method of treating radioactive waste, involving the discharge of waste into the sea at the Sellafield nuclear reactor. In order to do so, BNF needed a licence from the Inspectorate of Pollution under the Radioactive Substances Act 1960. The inspectorate issued the licence. In *R v HM Inspectorate of Pollution, ex p Greenpeace Ltd (No 2)*,[98] Greenpeace contended that the method was not safe, and sought certiorari to quash the Inspectorate's decision plus an injunction to prevent BNFL discharging any more waste.

As in *Rose Theatre*, the court examined the merits first. Again as in *Rose Theatre*, the court concluded that the impugned action was lawful. But it took a different view on standing. In holding that Greenpeace did satisfy s 31(3), the court emphasised the following factors. Greenpeace had 5,000,000 members worldwide, 400,000 in the UK and (of especial importance) 2,500 living close to Sellafield. This might be seen as rejecting the *Rose Theatre* presumption that individuals who all lacked standing qua individuals could gain it by acting as a group. It should however be noted that each of the 2,500 local members might have been granted standing in an individual capacity. It may be that what most strongly influenced the court were the considerations that: firstly, Greenpeace was a long established and widely respected body (the court noted that the United Nations has given Greenpeace consultant status on pollution issues); and secondly, Greenpeace had far more expertise on this question than an individual living near Sellafield would have and could thus assist the court in evaluating the issues. Otton J indicated that this conclusion was not compatible with *Rose Theatre*.

the requirements of the law, this court will see that it does fulfil them. It will not listen readily to suggestions of "chaos". The . . . authority are [sic] subject to the rule and must comply with it, just like everybody else. Even if chaos should result, still the law must be obeyed'. Consider also *Peachey Property*, in which the court granted standing, found for the applicant on the merits, but avoided the 'chaos' that might result from invalidating the entire rating list by granting a remedy that required the compiling of a new list but did not quash the old list until the new one was produced.

[97] Cf Lord Wilberforce in *IRC* [1981] 2 All ER 93 at 99: 'an aggregate of individuals each of whom has no interest cannot of itself have an interest'. It would however seem plausible that Lord Wilberforce was here alluding to the specific issue of the relationship between taxpayers and the Inland Revenue, rather than advancing a rule of general application.

[98] [1994] 4 All ER 329.

but stressed that his judgment should not be seen as de facto abolishing standing tests in representative actions; 'it must not be assumed that Greenpeace (or any other interest group) will automatically be afforded standing for judicial review in whatever field it and its members may have an interest'.[99]

That there is now a strong, if not 'automatic' presumption that 'respectable' pressure groups will be granted standing in representative actions was underlined in *R v Secretary of State for Foreign Affairs, ex p World Development Movement Ltd.*[100] The merits of the applicant's case were considered in chapter fourteen.[101] At this point, we might ask on what basis did the WDM have standing? It had no personal financial interest in the outcome? Nor did its members have a direct financial interest. It might perhaps have been argued that all citizens had a remote financial interest in the project, in so far as the tax we pay goes in part towards this activity? However the court did not follow this line: rather, it dwelt on two different issues.

The first concerned the 'expertise' and 'respectability' of the WDM. Rose LJ stressed the WDM attracted members from all political parties and none; ie it was not a partisan troublemaker. It had 13,000 members in the UK, with 200 local branches, so could not be dismissed as part of a lunatic fringe. It also enjoyed official consultative status with UNESCO and the OECD; ie it is recognised by powerful bodies as a source of useful advice and so would not be wasting the court's time with spurious argument. All these factors pointed toward the grant of standing. The second issue was a more familiar one. Rose LJ observed that if the WDM did not have standing, no-one else would have it either. This would mean that the legality of the decision would be left unquestioned, a state of affairs compatible neither with (at a theoretical level) a rigorous understanding of the rule of law nor with (in more prosaic terms) the satisfactory stewardship of large amounts of taxpayers' money. In combination, these considerations brought the WDM comfortably within what Rose LJ referred to as 'an increasingly liberal approach to standing'.[102]

CONCLUSION

It would be a rash commentator who suggested that trends in this area of the law had now been set with cast iron certainty. The *Greenpeace* and *Pergau dam* cases did suggest that there is now a strong body of case law indicating that the courts' key concern when interpreting s 31(3) is with establishing the legality of government action. That the issue remains riven by ambiguity was however forcefully illustrated by two contrasting 1997 High Court decisions, in respect of similar facts, in *R v North*

[99] Ibid, at 351. [100] [1995] 1 All ER 611, [1995] 1 WLR 386. [101] See pp 507–508 above.

[102] Ibid, at 620. As noted in ch 16, success on the standing point did not mean that the WDM received discovery of the government documentation that it considered necessary to support its case; see p 594 above.

Somerset District Council and Pioneer Aggregates (UK) Ltd, ex p Garnett[103] and *R v Somerset County Council and ARC Southern Ltd, ex p Dixon.*[104] In each case, the objectors were local residents who contended that the challenged decisions, which granted quarrying rights on publicly owned land, would have substantial adverse effects on their use and enjoyment of the land. Neither applicant could plausibly be regarded as a 'busybody'. In each case, the court (Popplewell J in *Garnett* and Sedley J in *Dixon*) concluded that the applications failed on the merits. In *Garnett*, the applicant was denied standing. Popplewell J did not explain his reasoning on this point, although his suggestion that the applicant had not acted promptly might suggest he was endorsing Schieman's locus standi version of 'chaos theory'. In *Dixon*, in contrast, Sedley J did grant standing, and did so on the basis of a carefully reasoned and explicitly constitutional law rationale:

'Public law is not at base about rights, even though abuses of power may and often do invade private rights; it is about wrongs – that is to say misuses of public power; and the courts have always been alive to the fact that a person or organisation with no particular stake in the issue or the outcome may, without in any sense being a meddler, wish and be well placed to call the attention of the court to an apparent misuse of public power'.[105]

In this particular case, the applicant was:

'neither a busybody nor a mere troublemaker. . . . He is, on the evidence before me perfectly entitled as a citizen to draw the attention of the court to, what he contends is an illegality in the grant of a planning consent which is bound to have an impact on our natural environment'.[106]

The decision thus appears to recognise a citizen's action basis to standing when major planning applications are in issue. Indeed, by alluding only to the applicant's 'contention' of illegality, Sedley J seems almost to be 'de-fusing' the question of standing and the merits, and recasting locus as a preliminary question to be answered on the basis not of the identity of the plaintiff and her relationship to the issue in question, but of the substantive content of the issue itself. That Sedley J's judgment is flatly irreconcilable with *Garnett* is perhaps of little significance, given the patent inadequacy of Popplewell J's reasoning in that case. That *Dixon* goes rather further towards the acto popularis may be attributable to its particular facts, or it may herald a further extension of the principles articulated by the House of Lords in *IRC*.

The relaxation of locus standi rules, together with the House of Lords' subsequent retreat from the strict public/private dichotomy propounded in *O'Reilly v Mackman*, gives a clear indication that the procedural obstacles to the enforcement of a rigorous notion of the rule of law in respect of government action have become less substantial in recent years. More citizens are now able to question the legality of government action in court, and more are able to do so under a procedural regime which enhances

103 [1997] JPL 1015. 104 [1997] JPL 1030. 105 Ibid, at 1037. 106 Ibid.

their prospects of ultimate success.[107] It is appropriate at this juncture to recall the *GCHQ* case. In chapter four, the House of Lords' judgment in *GCHQ* was presented as a radical break with past orthodoxies on an important matter of the courts' jurisdiction.[108] But it occurred at much the same time – the mid-1980s – as the courts were also reforming the key procedural elements of administrative law. As such, it should be seen as part of a wider, judicially-led rebalancing of the separation of powers between Parliament, the executive, the courts and the citizenry.

In the next two chapters of this book we continue to explore this rebalancing by focusing not on matters of procedure, nor on questions of jurisdiction, but on the grounds for review of administrative action. Chapters fourteen and fifteen dealt in the main with traditional grounds of review. Some cases discussed there had what we might now regard as 'human rights' or 'civil liberties' implications, in so far as the government actions in issue touched upon the political values which the Americans had so long ago identified in their Bill of Rights. The lack of entrenched values in the UK's constitution presented an obvious obstacle to the construction of a systematic body of 'human rights' jurisprudence within our constitutional and administrative law.[109] But the concern has, in a somewhat erratic and eclectic form, frequently been visible either on or just below the surface of judicial decisions: as noted in chapter fourteen, the courts have long recognised the (admittedly patchy and elusive) principle that certain 'basic rights' are recognised at common law and may be invoked as yardsticks to measure the lawfulness of government action.[110] Chapters eighteen to twenty-one trace the way in which that episodic presence has latterly – as a result of judicial, governmental and finally parliamentary intervention – been lent a far more expansive and coherent form.

[107] Cf Harlow and Rawlings (1984) op cit at p 299 presciently offered the following comment from an even more prescient (but unpublished) paper by David Feldman, written in 1981: 'Arguments which concentrate on the position of the individual applicant, to the extent of excluding the social interest in maintaining the rule of law, are not properly admissible in a public law context. Others may benefit more than the applicant. In particular, society may benefit as a whole when the courts impress on government agencies the need to act strictly within their legal powers'.

[108] Pp 117–122 above.

[109] Any such 'rights' would of course be enforceable only against government bodies, and not (as in the USA) against the legislature.

[110] See pp 511–512 above.

18

HUMAN RIGHTS AND CIVIL LIBERTIES 1: TRADITIONAL PERSPECTIVES

As chapter one suggested, the Framers of the US constitution reached a broad consensus concerning the moral values which should not be left at the mercy of the federal legislature or executive. Madison's assumption that 'the people' could not always rely on the integrity and competence of government institutions was expressed in part by imposing a rigid separation of powers on the national government, and by constituting America as a federal country where States retained extensive law-making authority.

America's third anti-majoritarian/minoritarian safeguard was that the constitution should provide deeply entrenched legal protection for the various civil liberties identified in the Bill of Rights. The Bill of Rights amendments outlined broad principles, based on ideas which several States had already accepted as fundamental tenets of their own constitutional orders. The Bill of Rights was in no sense a detailed code, but its constitutional purpose was, and remains, clear. One hundred and fifty years after it was framed, the moral values underpinning Madison's creation were powerfully restated by the US Supreme Court:

'The very purpose of a Bill of Rights was to withdraw certain subjects from the vicissitudes of political controversy, to place them beyond the reach of majorities and officials and to establish them as legal principles to be applied by the courts. One's right to life, liberty, and property, to free speech, a free press, freedom of worship and assembly, and other fundamental rights may not be submitted to vote; they depend on the outcome of no elections'.[1]

Within the British constitution, it has traditionally been presumed that every social value is constantly prey to 'the vicissitudes of political controversy'; that no moral principles were 'beyond the reach of majorities'; that no constituent concepts enjoyed protection from the 'outcome of parliamentary elections'. The UK's EC membership has perhaps imbued EC law with constituent, 'fundamental' status. That question has

[1] *West Virginia State Board of Education v Barnette* 319 US 624 (1943) per Jackson J.

yet however to be put to a determinative test. (Nor, at least on its face, does the EC Treaty reach the 'political' or 'moral' principles safeguarded in the US Bill of Rights.[2]) Leaving this question aside for the moment, the organising principle in respect of civil liberties in Britain is that citizens (a concept which includes government officials) may engage in any activity not prohibited by statute or common law. Relatedly, neither other individuals nor government officials may interfere with an individual's legal entitlements unless they can identify a statutory or common law justification for so doing.

The principle is very clear. Civil liberties or human rights in United Kingdom law are 'residual' concepts. Citizens may do anything which is not legally forbidden. The principle is also, as a practical long-term guide to the substance of citizen-state relations, quite meaningless. This relates in part to the discretion exercised by the courts when interpreting statutes or developing the common law. As we saw in cases such as *Liversidge v Anderson* and *Aninismic*, judges sometimes produce unexpected decisions. More significantly, the principle accommodates the blunt political reality that Parliament can at any time forbid activities hitherto permitted, or conversely, permit activities previously forbidden. Civil liberties in Britain are extremely precarious **legal** concepts.[3] They may enjoy a more assured **conventional** status, in so far as the courts, the executive and the legislature may fear the political or moral consequences of undermining them; but, as we saw in chapters nine, ten and eleven, conventional understandings about constitutional morality may themselves be nebulous creatures.

This chapter does not offer a substantial survey of either the history or current status of civil liberties in Britain; so large a task is quite beyond its scope.[4] Instead, more modestly, it focuses on several discrete issues raising principles of general applicability. Sections I–III address the traditional approach taken by Parliament and the courts to the regulation of public protest, the protection of personal privacy, and to certain aspects of freedom of expression.

[2] It now seems to be doing so indirectly however, albeit only in respect of a limited range of issues. See Phelan D (1992) 'Right to life of the unborn v promotion of trade in services' *MLR* 670–689; Coppell J and O'Neill A (1994) 'The European Court of Justice: taking rights seriously' *Legal Studies* 227–245.

[3] One might respond to this by saying that any values contained in the US constitution are also 'precarious' – the constitution's text may be changed via the Article 5 amendment process. Similarly, the EC Treaties may be altered via the Article 236 process. Both mechanisms are however highly cumbersome, time-consuming and also extremely visible. Amendment is difficult to achieve. In contrast, any aspect of the UK constitution could be changed in a day by a government enjoying majority support in the Commons and Lords.

[4] It has however been admirably undertaken recently by several authors. See particularly Feldman (1993) op cit; and successive editions of Bailey S, Harris D and Jones B (1st edn, 1977; 2nd edn, 1992; 3rd edn, 1998) *Civil Liberties* (London: Butterworths).

I. PUBLIC PROTEST AND PUBLIC ORDER

Earlier chapters have discussed several instances in which citizens engaged in formally unlawful behaviour to protest against, and seek to change, legal principles to which they felt unable to consent. The American revolutionaries, the Chartists and the Suffragettes all broke laws which formally denied them legal rights to which they considered themselves morally entitled. It is not difficult to defend such actions in terms of 'democratic' principle, since all the groups concerned were excluded from the electoral process.

We have also encountered more recent episodes of unlawful protest, when, clearly, the justification of disenfranchisement could not be invoked.[5] It may however be too simplistic to assume that such protests are necessarily 'unconstitutional' simply because they are unlawful. That conclusion would demand that we draw no distinction between the legality and legitimacy of the laws promulgated by Parliament and the courts, and relatedly, that we ascribe to the formalist notion that whatever laws a governing party persuades Parliament to enact are invariably 'democratic' simply because that party won a majority of seats in the House of Commons at the previous general election. It may therefore also be similarly simplistic to assume that a universal franchise is in itself an adequate guarantor of what many people might regard as fundamental civil liberties.

THE CLASSIC DILEMMA – *BEATTY V GILLBANKS*

Public meetings or processions may be an extremely effective way for citizens to draw the attention both of law-makers and the wider public to particular causes, and thereby, in the longer term, promote legal reform. The size of a march or meeting can itself be a forceful indicator of an idea's popularity; a crowd of thousands rather than a few dozen may suggest to observers that the protestors' sentiments merit further consideration. Timing and location may also substantially affect a protest's impact on public and political opinion; a protest against a planned school closure is likely to prove more effective in stimulating discussion if held outside the town hall while councillors are discussing their policy than if conducted in a distant park weeks after the closure decision has been taken.

It seems plausible to conclude that citizens must enjoy extensive rights to engage in public, collective displays of their feelings over political or moral questions if the consent of the people to the laws under which they live is to be informed in any expansive sense. It is equally clear that extensive protection of that value will impose certain burdens on other individuals or groups within the community. At a trivial level, marches, processions and rallies entail a degree of noise and obstruction to local

[5] Mr Cheney's refusal to pay his income taxes, the Clay Cross episode and the some of the activities of the Anti-Poll Tax Federation being obvious examples; see pp 36, 365–366 and 400–401 above.

highways and other public places. But in a 'democratic' society, such factors will presumably weigh only lightly in the scales when counterbalanced against the principle of free expression. However, there perhaps comes a point when they assume sufficient weight to pose law-makers, be they legislators or judges, a rather more evenly balanced question.

Beatty v Gillbanks[6] was triggered by the Salvation Army's plans to hold a march in Weston-super-Mare in 1882.[7] An earlier march had been abandoned when the Salvation Army was attacked by a violent mob, calling itself the 'Skeleton Army'. Local magistrates, fearing further violence and disorder, which had obviously alarmed and disturbed local residents, issued a notice forbidding any public assemblies in the town. The Salvation Army ignored the notice, and planned another march, led by Mr Beatty. When the march began, members of the Skeleton Army also appeared. On being asked to stop the march by a constable, Mr Beatty refused to do so and was arrested and subsequently convicted of causing a breach of the peace.

The High Court subsequently concluded that the Magistrates' notice was unlawful. Field J observed that there was nothing intrinsically illegal about Beatty's behaviour. Nor would it be correct to suggest that he had 'caused' any breach of the peace. That responsibility lay squarely on the Skeleton Army. The magistrates' reasoning was therefore fundamentally flawed, for it meant in effect that 'a man may be convicted for doing a lawful act if he knows that his doing it may cause another to do an unlawful act. There is no authority for such a proposition . . .'.[8]

The magistrates' decision amounted to approval for what has subsequently been termed the 'heckler's veto': that citizens opposing a particular viewpoint could hinder its dissemination by suggesting that they would be provoked to violence if it was advocated at a public meeting or procession. Field J's judgment implies that the correct response for the government to make in such circumstances was not to ban the Salvation Army's intrinsically lawful march, but to arrest and prosecute any member of the Skeleton Army who violently tried to disrupt it. That might prove an expensive and difficult task; but Field J is presumably suggesting that it is a price society must pay.

Even at that time however, the extent of residual liberty citizens possessed at common law was unclear. The appellant in the 1864 Irish case of *Humphries v Connor*[9] was a Protestant extremist living in Ireland. Humphries had entered a predominantly Catholic area wearing an orange lily, a symbol then grossly offensive to Catholics. Connor, a constable who feared that some Catholic citizens might be provoked to violence by the display, asked Humphries to remove the lily. When Humphries refused to do so, Connor, using only minimal force, removed it himself. Humphries subsequently sued Connor for assault. Connor contended that his action could not be construed as an assault, since qua constable he was subject to an overriding duty to

[6] (1882) 9 QBD 308.

[7] For discussion of and the background to the case see Bailey, Harris and Jones (1992) op cit pp 217–221.

[8] (1882) 9 QBD 308 at 314.

[9] (1864) 17 ICLR 1.

take whatever steps were 'necessary' to preserve the Queen's peace. The court accepted this conclusion as a matter of law. Whether a constable's action in particular circumstances was indeed necessary was a question of fact to be left to the jury. There would seem little doubt that in circumstances such as these, so minimal an intrusion would be considered necessary. One is then left with the difficult question of whether Humphries has been denied freedom of expression by a potentially violent mob, or whether she has merely been prevented from engaging in a course of conduct designed to provoke a riot?

Similarly, in *O'Kelly v Harvey*, decided the year after *Beatty*, the court appeared to proceed on altogether different principles: 'I have always understood the law to be that any needless assemblage of persons in such numbers and manner and under such circumstances as are likely to provoke a breach of the peace, was itself unlawful'.[10] This rather begs the question of what is meant by 'needless'. Narrowly construed, the concept might encompass only actions required to save life or limb. A wide construction, in contrast, might maintain that a democratic society always 'needs to protect citizens' who wish to express their opinion on matters of political controversy against violent opponents.

Beatty and *O'Kelly* seemingly occupy very different points on that interpretative spectrum. One might reasonably assume that the common law was sufficiently ambiguous to require legislative clarification. Yet while a statute might clarify the legal position, it may leave rather broader political questions unresolved. At present, there are many Acts which conceivably regulate public protests.[11] A systematic survey cannot be undertaken here; the following pages focus on just two such measures – the Public Order Acts of 1936 and 1986.

THE PUBLIC ORDER ACT 1936

The 1936 legislation was enacted as a direct response to the public disorder created by Oswald Moseley's fascist party in the 1930s.[12] Its contents were however phrased in general terms, rather than being targeted solely at fascists. Nor was the Act repealed after World War II, by which time Moseley's influence had waned to vanishing point.

Section 3(1) empowered the chief officer of police in a particular area to 'impose such conditions as appear to him necessary to maintain public order' on any public procession which he had reasonable grounds to believe might cause serious public disorder. If the chief officer concluded that a breach of the peace would inevitably

[10] (1883) 15 Cox CC 435.

[11] See for example *Duncan v Jones* [1936] 1 KB 218; *Arrowsmith v Jenkins* [1963] 2 QB 561, [1963] 2 All ER 210; *Papworth v Coventry* [1967] 2 All ER 41, [1967] 1 WLR 663. For a radical critique see Ewing K and Gearty C (1990) *Civil liberties under Thatcher* ch 5 (Oxford: OUP).

[12] On the background see Cross C (1961) *The fascists in Britain* ch 8 (London: Barrie Books); Skidelsky R (1968) 'Great Britain', in Woolf S (ed) *European fascism* (London: Weidenfield and Nicolson).

occur, s 3(3) empowered her, with the Home Secretary's consent, to ban all marches in her area for up to three months.[13]

Section 5 provided that:

> 'Any person who in any public place or at any public meeting – (a) uses threatening, abusive or insulting words or behaviour . . . with intent to provoke a breach of the peace or whereby a breach of the peace is likely to be occasioned, shall be guilty of an offence'.[14]

On its face, s 5 appeared to subject abusive or insulting language to a heckler's veto. This could be construed as a significant intrusion into freedom of expression, since there may be occasions on which an idea's force would be much reduced if it had to be delivered in a polite, respectful manner. An audience which would be provoked to violence by abuse or insults, irrespective of the reasonableness of the views expressed or the intolerance of the audience itself, could seemingly prevent a hitherto lawful protest being made. Similarly, s 3 raised the prospect that the force that an idea might gain by being visibly advocated by large numbers of marchers could be undermined if its opponents threatened violent disruption of the procession. There would of course be no legal obstacle to Parliament choosing to achieve either result, but the political legitimacy of such a departure from 'traditional' (if ambiguous) common law principles would be open to question.

Many difficulties which surround legislative provisions such as s 3 or s 5 arise from the fact that the right to free expression is often claimed by speakers in whose ideas it is difficult to see any substantive merit. This is not to say simply that one views the ideas as odd or ill-advised, as no doubt would many observers of the Salvation Army's evangelism. Nor is it because the speaker is advocating a mainstream political ideology with which one happens to disagree. Rather it assumes that the ideas are so vile and extreme in content, and/or delivered in such a reprehensible fashion, that society could not possibly derive any benefit from their expression.

The obvious problem with this argument is that vileness and extremism are not concepts with an ahistorical, objective meaning. Ideas once broadly perceived as entirely subversive of orthodox constitutional morality may after the passage of (even a relatively short) time be seen as no more than imprudent or as quite acceptable. A further difficulty arises if the legal principles which regulate such speech or behaviour are cast in loose, potentially expansive terms. This is what has been referred to as 'the slippery slope' argument.[15] The argument suggests (in a manner recalling Dicey's cynical view of governmental predispositions) that the executive is always likely to be tempted to use its power to constrain speech or expression which it finds unpalatable, but which is by no means comparable to the initially egregious problem which

[13] For a helpful collection of instances when the power has been invoked see Bailey, Harris and Jones (1992) op cit pp 182–184.

[14] For a survey of and comment on prosecutions under s 5 see Bailey, Harris and Jones (1992) op cit pp 202–214.

[15] For an account, and rebuttal of the argument see Barendt E (1987) *Freedom of speech* ch 3 (Oxford: Clarendon Press).

prompted Parliament to legislate. In such circumstances, respect for parliamentary sovereignty and a Diceyan perception of the rule of law would require either that a subsequent government did not seek to invoke the statute for purposes that the enacting Parliament had not envisaged, or, if the government sought to do so, that the courts would find its actions unlawful as being beyond the powers the Act conferred. The following cases offer some insight into the way such conventional understandings might influence the application and interpretation of legal powers.

Jordan v Burgoyne

Jordan was a senior figure in a fascist political party which had organised a rally in Trafalgar Square. Many communists, and members of CND and Jewish organisations were attending the meeting to barrack the fascist speakers. When Jordan heaped fulsome praise on Nazi Germany,[16] his opponents stormed the speakers' platform and a violent melee ensued.

Jordan was subsequently prosecuted under s 5.[17] His first defence, that s 5 per se was 'unconstitutional' because it curtailed the ancient liberty of free expression, was in effect an attack on the doctrine of parliamentary sovereignty. Unsurprisingly, it failed. A second defence seemed to have rather more legal merit. Jordan argued that s 5 applied only to language or behaviour which would provoke 'a reasonable man' to breach the peace; the communists and CND supporters who stormed his platform had attended the rally intending to engage in violent opposition to his speech; hence they were not 'reasonable men' and so he had not breached s 5.

As a matter of abstract principle, one might discern some force in this argument, in so far as it draws on the heckler's veto concept. However, the court saw no reason to assume that Parliament had impliedly accommodated this reasoning in the 1936 Act. Lord Parker CJ concluded that the legislation was intended to preserve public order, an issue not affected by the 'reasonableness' or otherwise of the audience:

> 'if words are used which threaten, abuse or insult . . . then that person must take his audience as he finds them, and if those words to that audience . . . are likely to provoke a breach of the peace, then the speaker is guilty of an offence'.[18]

Lord Parker CJ continued by suggesting that s 5 did not restrict free speech in any sense. This is a curious contention, for the Act, as interpreted by the court, clearly did punish certain types of speech. Whether Parliament's intrusion into the realm of free expression was *legitimate* is a difficult (and essentially political) question, with which Lord Parker CJ evidently saw no need to grapple.

Brutus v Cozens

The subsequent decision in *Brutus* nevertheless suggested that the courts could

[16] For an account of the application of public order legislation to explicitly fascist and racist speech and behaviour see Wolffe W (1987) 'Values in conflict: incitement to racial hatred and the Public Order Act 1986' *Public Law* 85–95; Loveland I (1995a) 'The criminalisation of racist violence', in Loveland (1995) op cit.

[17] [1963] 2 QB 744. [18] Ibid, at 749.

interpret s 5 quite narrowly by taking such 'political' questions into account. Brutus, an anti-apartheid campaigner, disrupted a tennis match at Wimbledon in which a South African was playing. Brutus' action enraged many spectators – some assaulted him as he was escorted away. A breach of the peace had certainly occurred. However the House of Lords concluded that Brutus had not 'insulted, abused or threatened' the spectators. Lord Reid's leading judgment approached the task of interpreting s 5 within a paradigm which afforded considerable importance to the principle of preserving free expression:

'Parliament had to solve the difficult question how far freedom of speech or behaviour must be limited in the general public interest. It would have been going much too far to prohibit all speech or conduct likely to occasion a breach of the peace because determined opponents may not shrink from organising or at least threatening a breach of the peace in order to silence a speaker whose view they detest'.[19]

Lord Reid's opinion suggested that an 'insult' had to be targeted directly at the spectators. Brutus, in contrast, had merely displayed contempt of or indifference to the spectators' right to watch tennis without interference. That might amount to an annoyance or an irritation, but it was not an insult. If Parliament wished to make annoying behaviour a criminal offence, it would have to enact more sweeping legislation.[20]

Kent v Metropolitan Police Commissioner

The Campaign for Nuclear Disarmament (CND) attracted considerable public support in the late 1970s and early 1980s. In 1980, some 70,000 people attended a CND rally in central London. CND subsequently proposed to hold a major march through London in 1981, to protest against the government's decision to allow the American air force to keep cruise missiles on its British bases. These plans were disrupted when the Metropolitan Police Commissioner (per s 3) sought and received the Home Secretary's approval to ban all processions in London for a four-week period. There had been several outbreaks of rioting in Britain in 1980 and 1981 in inner-city areas, notably the Brixton district of London and St Pauls in Bristol. The Commissioner had apparently formed the view that any political protest march in London at that time might lead to further outbreaks of violence.

Bruce Kent, a senior figure in CND, challenged the legality of the ban.[21] Lord Denning's judgment contained some stirring rhetoric about the importance of public protest:

19 [1972] 2 All ER 1297 at 1299–1300.

20 Reid's judgment poses an interesting question as to the interpretive technique he was using. His phraseology suggests that he was indulging in strict literalism – what did 'insulting' mean? Yet one might plausibly suggest his reasoning indicated he was applying either the mischief rule, or even the (then still heretical) teleological approach advocated by Denning in *Magor*. Whichever technique he was using, he appeared to be proceeding on the premise that legislative interference with freedom of expression should be narrowly construed.

21 (1981) Times, 15 May, CA.

'it was in the public interest that individuals should possess and exercise a right to protest and demonstrate on issues of public concern ... it was often the only way by which grievances could be brought to the knowledge of those in authority'.[22]

Lord Denning also accepted that there was no suggestion that CND itself sought to instigate violence. But his conclusion rather belied his earlier sentiments. Adopting an interpretative technique which is difficult to reconcile with the one he had used in *Rossminster*,[23] Lord Denning assumed that Parliament had granted the Commissioner a very wide discretion under s 3 in deciding what measures were necessary to preserve public order. Given the prevalence of serious disorder on the streets in recent months, a temporary moratorium on public marches could not be thought to exceed that discretion. Ackner LJ, concurring, seemed to suggest that the ban was for the benefit of CND members, as it protected them from likely violence, observing that 'it was hooligans the police were trying to control, not members of peaceful marches'.[24]

This might lead one to ask why the court did not require the police to direct their energies towards curbing the obviously illegal actions of the alleged 'hooligans' rather than the apparently lawful activities planned by CND and other marchers. The court may be regarded as having been unduly deferential to the Commissioner's evaluation. It certainly appeared to reject the assumption that s 3 should be interpreted in accordance with the principle articulated in *Beatty v Gillbanks*.

THE PUBLIC ORDER ACT 1986

Writing in the 1880s, Dicey concluded his survey of the common law's regulation of public meetings and processions by noting that:

'the government has little or no power of preventing meetings which to all appearances are lawful, even though they may turn out when actually convened to be unlawful because of the mode in which they are conducted. This is certainly a singular instance of the way in which adherence to the principle that the proper function of the state is the punishment, not the prevention, of crimes, deprives the executive of discretionary authority'.[25]

What Dicey neglected to add at that juncture however was the equally authoritative constitutional principle that a government that wished to enjoy such discretionary authority need only convince Parliament to pass legislation to that effect. As we have seen, modern governments experience little difficulty in persuading Parliament to enact their preferred policies. The Public Order Act 1936 revealed the impermanence of the common law presumptions to which Dicey referred. The Public Order Act passed some 50 years later impinged more severely on traditional understandings of constitutional morality.[26]

22 Ibid. 23 See pp 79–80 above. 24 (1981) Times, 15 May, CA.

25 Dicey op cit p 282.

26 For a caustic critique of the 1986 Act see Scraton P (1985) ' "If you want a riot, change the law": the implications of the 1985 White Paper on public order' *Journal of Law and Society* 385–393; Bonner D and Stone R (1987) 'The Public Order Act 1986: steps in the wrong direction?' *Public Law* 202–230.

Section 11 of the 1986 Act requires organisers of most public processions to give advance notice of their plans to the police at least six days prior to the march. The notice must specify the time and route of the procession, and identify the organisers. Section 11 operates in conjunction with s 12, which empowers the police to impose on the procession whatever conditions they think necessary to preserve public order, or prevent serious damage to property, or avoid 'serious disruption to the life of the community'. Section 12 seems to extend the powers the police exercised under s 3 of the 1936 Act; 'serious disruption' presumably encompasses obstruction of the highway or other public places, and loud noise – inconveniences which do not in themselves amount to a breach of the peace. Section 14 also enhances the police's powers to control public assemblies which are confined to one location; conditions may be attached to such meetings on the same basis as under s 12. In contrast, the police's power to ban marches altogether continues to be triggered only if the chief police officer in a given area fears that 'serious public disorder' would inevitably result if a march took place.

The 1986 Act also created a new offence of 'criminal trespass' under s 39. The new provision was seemingly introduced to deal with the problem posed by 'new age travellers', who periodically gathered en masse on privately owned land (especially Stonehenge in mid-summer).[27] Section 5 introduced another new offence, by extending the reach of s 5 of the 1936 Act to include insulting, abusive or threatening behaviour which is likely to cause 'harassment, alarm or distress' to anyone nearby. The government suggested that it expected s 5 to be used only to control rowdy, antisocial behaviour, which served no worthwhile political purpose. Yet it seems s 5 has been invoked against clearly political activities, such as wearing a tee-shirt satirising Margaret Thatcher and producing a poster criticising government policy towards Northern Ireland.[28] It thus seems to offer a potent example of the slippery slope problem.

Notwithstanding such use of s 5, it would be an exaggeration to claim that the implementation of the 1986 Act per se has thus far amounted to gross interference with the citizenry's entitlement to engage in political protest and argument. It is however equally clear that the Act does facilitate greater governmental control of free expression. As such it exacerbates rather than counterbalances recent anti-pluralist trends in other areas of the constitutional structure – primarily the increasing limitations of the House of Commons as a forum for meaningful political debate, and the significant constraints imposed on local government's capacity to express and indulge political sentiments with which central government disagrees. The Act's true significance perhaps lies therefore in its addition of several further threads to an increasingly complex tapestry of political orthodoxy with which the Thatcher and Major governments cloaked the conventionally more pluralist features of the constitution.

27 See Vincent-Jones P (1986) 'The hippie convoy and criminal trespass' *Journal of Law and Society* 343–370; Ewing and Gearty op cit pp 125–128.

28 Ewing and Gearty op cit pp 122–124.

II. PRIVACY

The actions of the government officials in *Entick v Carrington* clearly amounted to a tortious intrusion against both Mr Entick's home and his possessions. His home was physically invaded, and his belongings were physically removed from his control. The tort in issue was however trespass. At that time, English common law did not recognise that individuals enjoyed a right to 'privacy' in any broader sense. Had Carrington gathered evidence of Mr Entick's allegedly subversive activities by, for example, hiding in a tree on a public street outside Entick's house and eavesdropping on Entick's conversations with John Wilkes, he would not have acted unlawfully. Such intrusive behaviour would – perhaps ironically – be part of the 'residue' of individual liberty that neither statute nor common law yet had removed.

As we saw in our discussion of *Rossminster*,[29] Parliament has in recent times explicitly authorised government bodies to engage in activities for law enforcement purposes which would otherwise amount to trespass in the most obvious of senses: the 'invasion' of Rossminster's premises at issue in that case had a 'clear' statutory base.[30] But it would be a mistake to assume that such authorisation is needed to lend a lawful character to governmental attempts to investigate even the most intimate elements of citizen's life. The 'invasion' suffered by Mr Malone in the late 1970s took a much less tangible form.

SPEECH AND COMMUNICATION

The Metropolitan Police Commissioner, suspecting Malone was involved in criminal activities, arranged with the Post Office for a tap to be made on Malone's phone calls. This was done by Post Office engineers in Post Office premises recording Mr Malone's phone calls and passing tapes to the police. The tap therefore did not involve physical interference with Malone's home or property, and so was not a trespass in any traditional sense. The tap was thus not obviously unlawful. However, the Commissioner could not point to any statutory or common law power expressly permitting taps to be made.

Mr Malone subsequently challenged the legality of the Commissioner's action by seeking a declaration (through a writ rather than the AJR) that the tapping was unlawful. His argument rested in part on provisions of the European Convention on Human Rights, which we consider in chapter nineteen. But he also made contentions based purely on domestic law. In effect, Mr Malone was asking the court to recognise that the common law had (by 1979) developed sufficiently to treat telephone tapping by government bodies with the same opprobrium that Lord Camden had regarded a physical trespass in *Entick* 200 years earlier: to restrict the concept of trespass to

29 See pp 79–80 above.

30 To the House of Lords, if not in the view of the Court of Appeal; see p 80 above.

tangible interference with a person's body or possessions would be to adopt an unduly formalist interpretation of the law. In the modern era, he argued, listening-in to a person's phone conversations should be seen as just as much of a trespass as confiscating her books or letters. To frame the matter somewhat differently, Malone was contending that the common law should now recognise an individual right to privacy which could be protected through legal action in the courts against interferences which were not authorised by common law or statute.[31]

In considering, and rejecting, Malone's argument, Megarry VC offered a cogent analysis of the common law's innovatory power:

> 'I am not unduly troubled by the absence of English authority: there has to be a first time for everything, and if the principles of English law . . . together with the requirements of justice and common sense, pointed firmly to such a right existing, then I think the court should not be deterred from recognising the right'.[32]

However, Megarry VC's perception of 'justice and common sense' did not lead him to accept that the common law now recognised a right to 'privacy' which could be compromised by phone taps only if the listener had explicit legal authority for her intrusion. Since neither Parliament nor the common law had prohibited phone tapping, the practice was not unlawful, irrespective of who conducted it. And since it was not unlawful, it could not infringe Mr Malone's legal rights.

Megarry VC's opinion was it seems heavily influenced by questions of justiciability. He suggested that the whole question of privacy in telecommunications was so complex that it could only be settled by legislation. No such package of rights could properly 'spring from the head of a judge'.

Megarry's judgment is open to several criticisms.[33] His reasoning on the privacy argument is wholly circular. The Commissioner's action was not unlawful because it did not affect Mr Malone's legal entitlements:[34] and Mr Malone's legal entitlements were not affected because the Commissioner's action was not unlawful. Admittedly, a decision in Mr Malone's favour would have been similarly tautological in conceptual terms. The question which then arises however is, in the event of uncertainty, should the courts construe the common law in a manner that facilitates or impedes governmental interference with a citizen's privacy? That Megarry VC chose the former course is perfectly defensible as a matter of narrow legalism; whether his choice shares that characteristic in respect of its political legitimacy is a rather different question.

The justiciability point is also quite specious. Mr Malone was not asking the court

[31] Mr Malone placed great reliance on an academic article, published in the *Harvard Law Review* in the 1890s, which suggested that such a right was already discernible in English law at that time. The article had subsequently exercised much influence on the development of American law – and virtually none on English law; Warren S and Brandeis L (1890) 'The right to privacy' *Harvard LR* 193–220.

[32] [1979] Ch 344 at 372.

[33] See Bevan V (1981) 'Is anybody there?' *Public Law* 431–453; Ewing and Gearty op cit pp 56–61.

[34] The court nonetheless seemed to accept without argument that Mr Malone had locus standi to seek a declaration through private law procedures; ie Malone had either suffered interference with a private legal right or had suffered 'special damage'; see pp 603–608 above.

to create an elaborate scheme to regulate all interceptions of telecommunications.[35] He sought merely to establish that the tap made in his case was unlawful. It seems entirely plausible that had he succeeded on this point, the government would have found space in its legislative timetable to introduce the comprehensive statutory scheme which Megarry VC evidently thought desirable. If we (cynically) accept that governments are happiest when their actions escape legal control, it makes little sense merely to invite them to promote legislation subjecting unregulated powers to judicial supervision. If the court's purpose was to seek legislative clarification of ambiguous common law principles, it would be more likely to achieve that purpose if it resolved ambiguities in a manner which inconvenienced central government. It is not surprising that the first Thatcher government declined Megarry VC's invitation.

The existence of statutory authority does not settle the question of the legitimacy of intrusive governmental action, even if it does – following judicial interpretation – settle the question of its legality. Whether or not the substance of the MPC's activities at issue in *Malone* was defensible in political or moral terms is an obviously debatable issue. A case of rather more recent vintage, however, throws up a 'privacy' issue in which even the question of the legality of government behaviour – when measured against traditional, domestic yardsticks – seems to prompt quite different answers.

SADO-MASOCHISTIC SEXUAL BEHAVIOUR

The United Kingdom's domestic law had maintained several sharp distinctions prior to the late 1960s in the way it treated private, consensual sexual activity between adults, depending upon whether the participants were engaging in heterosexual or homosexual behaviour. Until the passage of s 1 of the Sexual Offences Act 1967, consensual sexual relations between adult men were a crime. Section 1(1) decriminalised the activity when it involved only two participants, although retained a much higher age of consent (21 years old) for homosexual activities than for heterosexual ones (16 years old). The discrimination between heterosexual and homosexual private consensual acts was not wholly eliminated, however, as homosexual activities involving more than two persons remained a crime, whereas group sex among heterosexuals was not illegal.

The law did not evidently draw any further distinction between homosexual and heterosexual behaviour when the acts concerned involved physical violence. English law on assault had been (somewhat imprecisely) codified in the 1861 Offences against the Person Act. The Act recognised, inter alia, an offence of assault occasioning actual bodily harm (s 47) and the more serious offence of assault resulting in wounding or grievous bodily harm (s 20). The common law offence of assault did not require that

[35] One might recall here the ECJ's reasoning in *Defrenne*, namely that a court should not tolerate a 'direct and overt' interference with a loosely defined individual entitlement simply because it can also conceive of many other 'indirect and disguised' infringements which could only become justiciable when defined by a legislature; see pp 452–453 above.

any bodily harm be inflicted. It had long been accepted that a common law assault did not arise if the 'victim' had consented to the physical contact concerned. It also appeared to be accepted – conversely – that it was not possible for a victim of 'wounding or grievous bodily harm' per s 20 to consent to such injury, in the sense that his/her consent was irrelevant to the question of the assailant's guilt. It was rather less clear if consent was a relevant issue in respect of the infliction of actual bodily harm.[36] The courts had accepted that the infliction of actual or grievous bodily harm, or wounding, would not be an offence if the injury was the incidental result of the victim's consensual participation in certain types of lawful activity – surgery, cosmetic procedures such as tattooing or body piercing, and contact sports such as boxing or rugby, being obvious examples. The previously unresolved question presented to the Court of Appeal in *R v Donovan*[37] was whether the victim's consent was a relevant issue in respect of a s 20 injury inflicted upon her by a man for the purpose of sexual gratification.[38] The court concluded that:

> 'As a general rule, although it is a rule to which there are well-established exceptions, it is an unlawful act to beat another person with such a degree of violence that the infliction of bodily harm is a probable consequence, and where such an act is proved, consent is immaterial'.[39]

The court also held that it would be 'absurd' and 'repellent to the ordinary intelligence' to classify this kind of nominally deviant sexual activity as one of the exceptions to the rule.

Some 60 years later, the defendants in *R v Brown*[40] found themselves facing prosecution under s 20 and s 47. The defendants were all homosexual men, who had over a period of some years engaged in a range of consensual sado-masochistic activities, involving burning, beating and wounding of each other's bodies, and sometimes carried out under the influence of drugs and alcohol. They were convicted at trial. On appeal before the House of Lords, the gist of their defence was to argue that *Donovan* should no longer be regarded as good law, and that infliction of injury in the course of private, consensual sexual activities should not be regarded as an offence unless the injury was sufficiently severe to impose costs upon the public at large, either because the 'victim' required hospital treatment or became eligible as a result of the injury for some kind of social security benefit. The House of Lords rejected this argument. The texts of the majority judgments[41] indicate that their authors' conclusions were driven in part by policy considerations, and in part by the way in which the judges organised their analyses.

The majority judges appeared to take as their analytical starting point the presumption that, prima facie, a crime of violence had been committed by the accused. The

36 See the variously phrased judgments in *R v Coney* (1882) 8 QBD 534.

37 [1934] 2 KB 498, [1934] All ER Rep 207, CCA.

38 The conduct in question being the whipping of the victim's backside with a cane.

39 [1934] All ER Rep 207 at 210, per Swift J.

40 [1994] 1 AC 212, [1993] 2 All ER 75, HL.

41 Lords Jauncey, Lowry and Templeman.

secondary question was then whether the circumstances of the particular activities in question fell within an exception to the presumption. The secondary question raised matters of public policy. While the majority could see a policy argument in favour of permitting an exception for such activities as boxing, they could see little to invoke in favour of granting an exemption for sado-masochistic sex. They could in contrast see many good policy reasons for not exempting such activities from the general rule: for example that being in a state of sexual arousal would compromise the 'sadist's' capacity to notice a 'masochist's' withdrawal of consent; that the use of alcohol and drugs undermined the certainty that consent was properly informed; that wounding might lead to infections; and that the drawing of blood raised the possibility of the transmission of disease, particularly HIV and Aids. If consent was to be a relevant factor in such circumstances, the legal initiative should come from Parliament through new legislation rather than from the courts through a re-interpretation of the 1861 Act. Lord Jauncey appeared neatly to sum up the majority's rationale in the following passage:

> 'If it is to be decided that such activities as the nailing by A of B's foreskin or scrotum to a board or the insertion of hot wax into C's urethra followed by the burning of his penis with a candle or the incising of D's scrotum with a scalpel to the effusion of blood are injurious neither to B, C and D nor to the public interest then it is for Parliament with its accumulated wisdom and sources of information to declare them to be lawful'.[42]

The convictions were upheld by a 3–2 majority. The two dissenting judgments (by Lords Slyn and Mustill) approached the analytical task before the court in a quite different way, and – presumably as a result of this divergence in approach – viewed the policy considerations informing their reasoning in a very different light. The point is best put by the opening words of Lord Mustill's judgment: 'My Lords, this is a case about the criminal law of violence. In my opinion it should be a case about the criminal law of private sexual relations, *if about anything at all*'.[43] Lord Mustill's analytical starting point appeared to be a presumption that an interference with the accused's entitlement to engage in consensual sexual activities had been committed by the government. The secondary question was then whether the circumstances of the particular interference in question fell within the limits on individual autonomy contained in ss 20 and 47:

> 'The point from which I ask your Lordships to depart is simply this, that the state should interfere with the right of the individual to live his or her life as he or she may choose no more than is necessary to ensure a proper balance between the interests of the individual and the general interests of the individuals who together comprise the populace at large'.[44]

Lord Mustill could discern no overriding force in the public policy arguments advanced by the majority to justify conviction. In consequence, he could not accept that any crime had been committed.

42 [1993] 2 All ER 75 at 92, HL.

43 Ibid, at 101 (emphasis added).

44 Ibid, at 116.

III. FREEDOM OF SPEECH

One could point to a great many celebrated judicial pronouncements by American judges concerning the centrality of the First Amendment's protection of freedom of speech and freedom of the press to the American constitutional tradition. In the landmark case of *Palko v Connecticut*, Cardozo J characterised freedom of speech as 'the matrix, the indispensable condition of nearly every other form of freedom'.[45] Brandeis J's judgment in *Whitney v California* enjoys a similarly oft-quoted status. In his view the First Amendment existed to protect the principle that:

'freedom to think as you will and to speak as you think are indispensable to the discovery and spread of political truth; that without free speech and assembly discussion would be futile; . . . that public discussion is a political duty; and that this should be a fundamental principle of the American government'.[46]

Judge Learned Hand advanced a similarly expansive view in *United States v Associated Press* in 1943:

'The First Amendment presupposes that right conclusions are more likely to be gathered out of a multitude of tongues, than through any kind of authoritative selection. To many, this is, and always will be, folly; but we have staked upon it our all'.[47]

William Brennan's celebrated judgment in *New York Times v Sullivan*[48] formulated a legal rule which rested on the broadest of political foundations: '[W]e consider this case against the background of a profound national commitment that debate on public issues should be uninhibited, robust, and wide-open'.[49]

The functional core at the heart of this presumption is that whenever freedom of speech questions arise before a court, the starting point for analysis of the issues involved is the principle that the citizenry has an entitlement to disseminate and receive all kinds of information, and that any attempt by a governmental agency – be it legislative, executive or judicial – to erode that entitlement should be regarded with the most intense suspicion. Brennan characterised this ethos as 'a fundamental departure from the English and other forms of government . . . [it] was this country's great contribution to the science of government'.[50] Quite how wide a departure the Americans made from the English tradition is the question addressed – albeit in a limited fashion – in the following pages.[51]

OFFICIAL SECRECY

The Official Secrets Act 1911 was enacted at the instigation of Asquith's Liberal government. The legislation was prompted by a public panic about the supposed

45 302 US 319 at 327 (1937). 46 274 US 357 (1927). 47 52 F Supp 362 at 372 (1943).
48 376 US 254 (1964). 49 376 US 254 at 270 (1964). 50 Op cit at 11.
51 For a more detailed treatment see the essays in Loveland I (ed) (1998) *Importing the First Amendment?* (Oxford: Hart Publishing).

presence of German spies and saboteurs, at a time when war with Germany no longer seemed a distant prospect.[52] The Act passed all of its Commons stages in one hour. This might suggest that it was not subject to searching scrutiny and consideration, an omission which is perhaps all the more surprising when one notes the very wide terms in which it was framed.

As we saw in our earlier discussion of *Chandler v DPP*,[53] s 1 forbade entry to any 'prohibited place' for 'any purpose prejudicial to the safety or interests of the State'. Section 1 also criminalised the making of any 'note, sketch or plan' for such purposes, or the communication to any other person of any information 'which is calculated to be or might be or is intended to be directly or indirectly useful to an enemy'. Section 2 was drafted in even broader terms; it penalised the passing of *any* official information (irrespective of whether the information compromised national security) to anybody 'other than a person to whom he is authorised to communicate it, or a person to whom it is in the interest of the State his duty to communicate it'. The potential reach of s 2 was subject to frequent criticism; the most oft-quoted being that of Sir Lionel Heald that the act 'makes it a crime . . . to report the number of cups of tea consumed per week in a government department'.[54]

Legal rules which punish or otherwise restrict the publication of information which arguably compromises the security of the state invariably raise difficult questions.[55] The evident flaw of s 2 however was that it was not restricted to national security questions. Nor did it appear to offer the discloser any opportunity to defend his/her actions on the basis that disclosure was in the public interest.[56] It is not difficult to envisage circumstances in which such disclosure might be desirable; when for example it exposed corruption in the award of arms contracts, or revealed that government officials were misleading Ministers, or that Ministers were misleading the Commons. On its face, s 2 could, as the following cases suggest, be invoked simply to punish the disclosure of information which the government for reasons of either administrative expediency or party political convenience preferred to keep secret.

The *Tisdall* and *Ponting* cases

In the early 1980s considerable controversy arose over the Thatcher government's decision to allow the United States to keep cruise missiles at its air force bases in Britain. The government had apparently decided to announce the missiles' arrival at the very end of Commons questions to the Defence Secretary, Michael Heseltine. Heseltine would then leave the chamber without giving MPs the chance to question him immediately. A civil servant, Sarah Tisdall, subsequently leaked a memo disclosing this plan to *The Guardian* newspaper. Tisdall evidently believed that Heseltine's

52 French D (1978) 'Spy fever in Britain 1900–1915' *Historical Journal* 355–370.

53 See pp 125–126 above.

54 See Bailey, Harris and Jones (1992) op cit pp 421–422.

55 For a helpful discussion see Marshall G (1986) 'Ministers, civil servants and open government', in Harlow C (ed) *Public law and politics* (London: Sweet and Maxwell).

56 See *R v Fell* [1963] Crim LR 207, CCA; *R v Berry* [1979] Crim LR 284.

planned behaviour was 'immoral', in so far as it denied the Commons the opportunity to question the government on a policy question of major significance.[57]

The government demanded the return of the memo, seemingly because markings on the text would enable the leak's source to be identified. *The Guardian* claimed it was not obliged to return the documents. The Contempt of Court Act 1981, s 10 empowered the courts to order disclosure of the media's sources only if 'necessary in the interests of justice or national security'.[58] The government contended that national security questions did make such disclosure necessary in this case. The information itself posed no such threat, but the government contended that the mere presence of a leaker within the Defence Ministry would so undermine our allies' confidence in the government's defence capabilities that it was vital that she/he be identified.

The High Court and the Court of Appeal accepted the government's argument, and ordered *The Guardian* to return the documents.[59] Tisdall was subsequently identified as the leaker, convicted under s 2 and imprisoned for six months. The House of Lords (by a 3–2 majority) later upheld the Court of Appeal's interpretation of s 10 and its application of s 10 to these facts.[60] On the next occasion that the government resorted to a prosecution under s 2 of the Official Secrets Act 1911, however, the outcome was perhaps not what it had expected.

Clive Ponting was, in the early 1980s, an apparently high-flying civil servant in the Ministry of Defence, who had been singled out for praise by the Prime Minister. However, after the Falklands War, Ponting formed the conclusion that his Secretary of State, Michael Heseltine, was systematically misleading the Commons over the circumstances surrounding the sinking of the Argentine battleship, the *Belgrano*. Ponting subsequently leaked information which he regarded as accurate to Tam Dalyell, a backbench Labour MP who had been harrying the government on this question. Dalyell passed the information to the Chair of the Commons Foreign Affairs Select Committee, who (in an act exemplifying the Committee's deference to the executive) returned it to Heseltine.[61]

Ponting was subsequently prosecuted under s 2.[62] The government accepted that the information released did not compromise national security. The issue was simply one of enforcing the civil servant's supposed duty of confidentiality to the Crown.

57 See Ewing and Gearty op cit pp 137–142; Barker R (1986) 'Obedience, legitimacy and the state', in Harlow (ed) op cit.

58 On the origins of this legislation see ch 20 below.

59 *Secretary of State for Defence v Guardian Newspapers Ltd* [1984] Ch 156, [1984] 1 All ER 453, CA.

60 [1985] AC 339, [1984] 3 All ER 601, HL. Lord Scarman and Lord Fraser dissented. Neither felt a threat to national security had been established. Lord Scarman, describing the leaked memorandum as 'innocuous' in national security terms, seemingly thought that the government's main motive was to spare itself party political embarrassment; ibid, at 618.

61 See Drewry G (1985b) 'Leaking in the public interest' *Public Law* 203–212; Thomas R (1987) 'The British Official Secrets Act 1911–1939 and the Ponting case', in Chapman R and Hunt M (eds) *Open government* (London: Routledge).

62 *R v Ponting* [1985] Crim LR 318.

Ponting did not deny leaking the information. He claimed however that Mr Dalyell was a person 'to whom it was in the interest of the State' that the information be passed. The nub of Ponting's argument was that Heseltine was deliberately misleading the House of Commons, and thereby subverting the doctrine of ministerial responsibility.[63] It could not be in 'the interests of the state' that the Commons (and thence the public) formed conclusions about government behaviour based on information which the government knew was false. Since Mr Dalyell would raise the matter in the house, giving him the information would in fact advance the public interest.

However at Ponting's trial, McCowan J instructed the jury that this argument had no legal basis. Section 2, he maintained, adopted a highly factionalised interpretation of 'the interests of the state'. This was not a matter that concerned 'the people', nor even the House of Commons. Rather:

> 'The policies of the State mean the policies laid down by the those recognised organs of government and authority . . . The government and its policies are for the time being the policies of the State'.[64]

In formal terms, therefore, Ponting was guilty. The jury nevertheless declined to convict him. British juries are not permitted to disclose their reasoning, but it seems plausible to assume that the jurors hearing Ponting's case concluded that the government was invoking narrowly legal means to justify broadly immoral ends, and decided it should not be permitted to do so. Parliament had thus far not introduced legislation permitting such legally perverse acquittals to be reversed, presumably because the concept that a citizen should only be tried for serious crimes before a randomly selected jury was too deeply embedded a principle of constitutional morality.[65] The jury nevertheless remains a somewhat unreliable defender of 'just' solutions when faced with clear legal arguments: Tisdall's jurors seemingly took a less robust view of constitutional morality than their counterparts in *Ponting*.

Spycatcher

The Thatcher government was obviously not unique in invoking legal proceedings to restrain publication of information which would enable the Commons and the electorate to make more informed choices about the adequacy of government behaviour. The *Crossman Diaries* case,[66] instigated by a Labour government, served in effect the same purpose as the Tisdall and Ponting trials – namely to deter people with access to sensitive information about government behaviour from making their knowledge available to the general public. But the Thatcher government was perhaps atypical in respect of the patently absurd lengths to which it was prepared to go in order to deter civil servants and the media from revealing 'secret' information.

63 For a less benevolent view of Ponting's motives and behaviour see Marshall (1986) op cit.

64 [1985] Crim LR 318.

65 As evidenced by its inclusion in both the US *Declaration of Independence* and England's earlier *Declaration of Right*.

66 See pp 313–314 above.

Peter Wright had been employed in the 1960s and 1970s by MI5, one of the security services.[67] Just exactly what Wright did in that capacity remains unclear. He was however disgruntled with the financial benefits the work provided, and some years after retiring published a book, *Spycatcher*, alleging that MI5 agents had plotted to destabilise Harold Wilson's Labour governments.[68] Rather than ensure that such extraordinary accusations (which amounted, if proven, to treason) were thoroughly and publicly investigated, the Thatcher government devoted its energies to trying to prevent Wright's story being made available to the British public.

The facts of the case raise several rather different issues. One might readily suggest that Mr Wright should not have been permitted to profit financially from any disclosures he made, irrespective of their content. However that presumption is quite separate from the question of whether or not his allegations should have been discussed in the press. If the allegations posed a present threat to national security, one could see strong arguments for prohibiting disclosure. Yet if they exposed illegal or treasonable behaviour, one would presumably favour disclosure in the expectation that public discussion and criticism might lead both to the prosecution and conviction of those engaged in such treasonable plots and prevent a recurrence of such activities in future. The practical difficulty attending either viewpoint is of course that citizens could not form a view on whether the allegations threatened national security or revealed subversive behaviour until they had been made public. Essentially therefore, the issue is reduced to a question of whether one can (or should) trust government to identify and remedy any wrongdoing among agents of the security services. Diceyan or Madisonian orthodoxies might suggest that would be a dangerous assumption to make; especially when the allegations apparently have a party political dimension, and the government is composed solely of members of one political party.

As noted in earlier chapters, the British courts have tended to adopt a very deferential stance towards government claims that litigation raised 'national security' questions. One can trace an unbroken thread of judicial acquiescence from *Shipmoney*, through to *The Zamora*, to *Liversidge v Anderson*, to *Chandler v DPP* and on to *GCHQ*.[69] The *Spycatcher* litigation suggested that this tradition still enjoyed appreciable judicial support in the late 1980s.[70]

Mr Wright had taken the precaution of going to live in Tasmania before publishing his book. He could thus not be prosecuted under s 2. The government therefore resorted to the civil law to stop publication and discussion of the book. As we saw in the *Crossman Diaries* case, the common law principle of confidentiality was an elastic

67 The exact nature of the security services, their effective powers, and the extent to which they are meaningfully controlled by elected politicians is, as one might expect, a mystery. For an overview see Lustgarten L and Leigh I (1994) *In from the cold: national security and parliamentary democracy* (Oxford: Clarendon Press).

68 Wilson had long held the view that such plots had been hatched against him; Pimlott op cit pp 697–715.

69 At pp 103, 76–79, 125–126 and 117–121 respectively.

70 For an overview see Barendt E (1989) 'Spycatcher and freedom of speech' *Public Law* 204–212; Ewing and Gearty op cit pp 152–174.

concept. In the *Spycatcher* litigation, the government suggested that Wright owed his employer (the Crown) a lifelong duty of confidentiality in respect of any official information he acquired during his employment. The government argued that this duty prevented Wright from publishing any such material, and that if he did so, any profits made would belong to the Crown. But the government further contended that its interest in maintaining confidentiality also prevented *the media* from reporting or commenting on Wright's allegations.

In 1986, both *The Observer* and *The Guardian* ran stories commenting on Wright's claims. The government immediately sought a temporary injunction prohibiting such stories, pending a full trial to determine if such publication could be prevented permanently. This was granted by Millet J. It remained in place for a year, until the newspapers persuaded the High Court to lift it. The judge, Sir Nicolas Browne-Wilkinson, saw no point in retaining the injunction, given that the book had by then been published in the USA and its contents were widely known to British citizens who had access to foreign newspapers or had imported copies from foreign sellers.[71] However both the Court of Appeal and the House of Lords reinstated the constraint on publication.[72]

The Lords' decision in *Spycatcher (No 1)* upheld the injunctions, albeit only by a 3–2 majority. The majority were strongly influenced by the government's claim that publication would damage the public interest in maintaining efficient security services, because it would undermine officers' morale. Lord Bridge's dissent took a different view of the 'public interest', employing grandiloquent language reminiscent of Lord Atkin's speech in *Liversidge*:

'Freedom of speech is always the first casualty under a totalitarian regime. . . . The present attempt to insulate the public from information which is freely available elsewhere is a significant step down that very dangerous road. . . . [The government's] wafer thin victory in this litigation has been gained at a price which no government committed to upholding the values of a free society can afford to pay'.[73]

The Thatcher administration seemed however quite ready to pay this price. In *Spycatcher (No 2)*, the government sought permanent injunctions against *The Guardian* and *The Observer*, and against *The Sunday Times* which intended to publish Wright's book in serial form. At first instance, Scott J discharged the temporary injunction and refused to grant permanent restraints.[74] His decision was upheld by a 2–1 majority in the Court of Appeal, and by a 4–1 majority in the House of Lords.[75] However Lord Keith's leading judgment in the Lords seemingly did not wish to be drawn into consideration of the large constitutional issues which the government's conduct appeared to raise:

'I do not base this upon any balancing of public interests nor upon any considerations of freedom of the press, nor upon any possible defences of . . . just cause or excuse, but simply

71 *A-G v Guardian Newspapers Ltd* [1987] 3 All ER 316.
72 Ibid.
73 Ibid, at 346–347.
74 *A-G v Guardian Newspapers (No 2)* [1990] 1 AC 109.
75 Ibid.

upon the view that all possible damage to the interest of the Crown has already been done by the publication of *Spycatcher* abroad and the ready availability of copies in this country'.[76]

It would thus be misleading to characterise the decision as a forceful judicial assertion of the constitutional right of the British people to be informed of their government's alleged inadequacies. The protection afforded by *Spycatcher (No 2)* to free expression seems at best oblique, premised on the fact that the laws of other countries had permitted both the publication and export of Wright's allegations.

In the interim, the government had also trailed around the courts of the world in an effort to prevent publication of *Spycatcher* in foreign jurisdictions. The government suffered defeats in Australia and New Zealand, before obtaining the dubious benefit of a victory in Hong Kong – a British colony which then had no elected legislative assembly. There was no point in pursuing such an action in the USA, where publication would clearly have been protected by the First Amendment. It is instructive to compare the House of Lords' judgments in *Spycatcher (No 1)* and *(No 2)* with the decision of the US Supreme Court in *New York Times v United States*, the famous 'Pentagon Papers' case.[77] The Pentagon Papers were a comprehensive (and secret) analysis of the US involvement in Vietnam. The papers were leaked to *The New York Times*, which planned to publish them. The court rejected the government's efforts to prevent publication. Its rationale for so doing was best expressed by Black J:

'In the First Amendment the Founding Fathers gave the free press the protection it must have to fulfil its essential role in our democracy. The press was to serve the governed, not the governors. The government's power to censor the press was abolished so that the press would remain forever free to censure the government. The press was protected so that it could bare the secrets of government and inform the people. Only a free and unrestrained press can effectively expose deception in government'.[78]

THE OFFICIAL SECRETS ACT 1989

These were not sentiments for which the Thatcher government showed any greater enthusiasm than had the majority of the House of Lords in the *Spycatcher* litigation. The combined impact of the Ponting and *Spycatcher* embarrassments prompted the third Thatcher government to reform the 1911 Official Secrets Act.[79] The 1989 Act did remove the catch all provisions of s 2 of its 1911 predecessor, but it is difficult to portray the new legislation as an exercise in enhancing the transparency and accountability of the government to its citizens. One commentator has suggested that the Act's:

'stated purpose . . . is to reduce the amount of information protected by criminal sanctions to areas where disclosure would be harmful to the public interest. Yet it is tempting to

[76] Ibid, at 260. [77] 403 US 713 (1971). [78] Ibid, at 739.

[79] For a helpful summary and critique see Palmer S (1988) 'In the interests of the state' *Public Law* 523–535; (1990) 'Tightening secrecy law: the Official Secrets Act 1989' *Public Law* 243–256.

conclude that the primary rationale behind this reform is to tighten the criminal law of secrecy, with the aim of making convictions more likely'.[80]

Section 1 imposes an absolute and permanent duty of confidentiality on all members and ex-members of the security services. Any disclosure of any official information by any such person under any circumstances is now a crime. Thus, to take an extreme example, it would apparently be illegal for an MI5 or MI6 agent to reveal that her superior officers were planning to assassinate the Prime Minister. At the other extreme, even the most trivial of information may not be disclosed by security service officers. There is no requirement that the prosecution prove the disclosure to have damaged the national interest. Nor may officers argue that their action was designed to defend the public interest. Furthermore, under s 1(1)(b) the government may extend this absolute obligation to any person it wishes.

Other civil servants and government contractors are caught by widely framed provisions which criminalise the disclosure of 'damaging' information in the specific areas of defence (s 2), international relations (s 3) or the investigation of crime (s 4). This is clearly a less expansive prohibition than the one contained in the former s 2. Additionally, accused persons have a defence if they can establish that disclosure would not be 'damaging'. However, the Act does not permit a 'public interest defence' – it is a crime to reveal 'damaging' information even if one believes one thereby exposes government behaviour that would be even more 'damaging'.

Palmer rather overstates the case in suggesting that Lord Keith's judgment in *Spycatcher (No 2)* approved the principle that:

> 'It is unacceptable in our democratic society that there should be a restraint on the publication of information relating to government when the only vice of that information is that it enables the public to discuss, review and criticise government action'.[81]

It would be more accurate to suggest that Lord Keith's judgment piggybacked on the judgment of the US Supreme Court in the *Pentagon Papers* case – a judgment expressing moral values subsequently adopted by the constitutions of other western democracies – which ensured that Peter Wright's book was published and subjected to extensive press analysis in many other parts of the world. Palmer is however surely correct in observing that the Thatcher government seemed wholly unpersuaded by this principle. The thrust of the 1989 Act appears to be a rejection of the idea that government employees' duty of loyalty lies anywhere other than to the government of the day. That a government should make such an assumption is an entirely logical consequence of the supposed 'ultimate political fact' of the contemporary constitution – namely that having a Commons majority generally enables a government to do whatever it wishes. This is, as suggested in earlier chapters, a theme which pervades every aspect (except perhaps issues involving EC law) of our current constitutional

80 Palmer (1990) op cit p 243. For similarly critical comment see Ewing and Gearty op cit pp 189–208.

81 (1990) op cit p 247, citing Lord Keith's approval of the quote by Mason J of the Australian High Court in *Commonwealth of Australia v John Fairfax & Sons Ltd* (1980) 147 CLR 39 at 51–52.

arrangements. We turn to the broad question of whether and how this ultimate political fact might be reformed in the final chapter of this book. Yet while litigation involving freedom of expression often arises as a result of governmental attempts to curb public access to information that allegedly has a 'national security' dimension, official secrecy is by no means its only trigger.

BLASPHEMY

In addition to providing safeguards for freedom of speech and the press, the First Amendment provides in specific terms that 'Congress shall make no law respecting an establishment of religion, nor prohibiting the free exercise thereof'. The Supreme Court concluded in *Watson v Jones* in 1872 that 'the law knows no heresy, and is committed to the support of no dogma, the establishment of no sect'.[82] It was thus impossible for blasphemy to be made an offence either by Congressional statute or federal common law. Despite its trenchant rhetoric, *Watson* provided little practical protection for speech attacking religious beliefs, since at that time it was assumed that the First Amendment did not control the activities of state governments.[83] By the early 1950s however, the Court had concluded that a criminal offence of blasphemous libel – whether fashioned by an organ of federal or state government – was wholly incompatible with First Amendment principles. This conclusion was powerfully laid out in *Joseph Burstyn Inc v Wilson*:

> '[F]rom the standpoint of freedom of speech and the press, it is enough to point out that the state has no legitimate interest in protecting any or all religions from views distasteful to them.... It is not the business of government in our nation to suppress real or imagined attacks upon a particular religious doctrine, whether they appear in publications, speeches or motion pictures'.[84]

The *Wilson* decision stands in stark contrast to the British constitutional tradition, within which the common law offence of blasphemous libel continues to impose an acute restraint on freedom of speech.

Prior to the litigation in *R v Lemon*[85] in the mid–1970s, a prosecution for blasphemy had not been brought in England for over 50 years. The offence emerged within the common law in the seventeenth century. It was closely linked to the crime of sedition. Sedition dealt with attacks on the integrity and adequacy of the government; blasphemy addressed attacks on the integrity and adequacy of the established church and the Christian religion. In its initial form, the offence did not concern itself with the style of the attack.[86] A calm and measured assault upon Christian doctrine

82 20 L Ed 66 at 676 (1872) – quoted in Feldman op cit, p 690.

83 The court began to apply aspects of the First Amendment to the States in *Gitlow v New York* 45 S Ct 625 (1925).

84 343 US 495 at 505 (1952).

85 [1979] QB 10, CA; affd [1979] AC 617, HL.

86 See generally Kenny C (1922) 'The evolution of the law of blasphemy' *Cambridge LJ* 127–142; Feldman (1993) op cit pp 684–695.

was as much blasphemy as the most abusive or offensively presented criticism. This principle was relaxed in the mid-nineteenth century, so that religious criticism expressed in temperate terms unlikely to insult or ridicule believers in Christianity would not be blasphemous.[87]

Lemon was the publisher of *Gay News*, a magazine intended primarily for a non-heterosexual readership. The June 1976 edition contained an illustrated poem, entitled 'The love that dares to speak its name'. The poem drew on the imagery of Jesus Christ being executed, and alluded to a homosexual relationship between him and John the Baptist. This poem apparently outraged the delicate religious sensibilities of Mrs Mary Whitehouse, who having failed to persuade the Attorney General to initiate a prosecution, did so herself.

It is perhaps indicative of the very primitive understanding of freedom of expression principles that then informed English law that the *Lemon* case was not argued on the grounds of the basic, substantive point that the common law in a modern, multi-faith and largely secular democratic society should find no place for an offence such as blasphemy to restrict debate about religious matters. Judgment turned instead on a narrow question of law, relating to the mens rea element of the offence. The first possibility was that the prosecution need only prove that the defendant intended to publish a blasphemous article. The second possibility was that the prosecution also has to prove that the defendant intended to offend, shock and arouse resentment among adherents to the Christian faith. It is evident that had the House of Lords accepted that the more expansive version of mens rea was the correct one, the reach of the offence would have been reduced, if not necessarily substantially.

However, by a 3–2 majority, the House of Lords held that the prosecution need only prove an intention to publish. It appeared to be common ground among the court that, as Lord Russell put it: 'The authorities embrace an abundance of apparently contradictory or ambivalent comments. There is no authority of your Lordships' House on the point. The question is open for decision'.[88] The question was answered without any systematic consideration being given to the way in which blasphemy laws, however construed in terms of mens rea, interfered with the freedom of expression of publishers and readers on religious matters. Neither Lord Diplock (dissenting) nor Lord Russell and Viscount Dilhorne made any mention at all of freedom of expression in their judgments. Lord Scarman, the third member of the majority, briefly addressed the free expression issue only to note that the common law did not permit people to publish offensive criticisms of Christianity. Indeed, in Lord Scarman's view, the real vice of the blasphemy law was that it covered only Christianity, and did not also restrict freedom of expression in respect of other religions as well. The only judge to accept that promoting freedom of expression on religious matters was a factor that should push the court towards accepting the more expansive mens rea test was Lord

[87] *R v Hetherington* (1841) 4 State Tr NS 563.

[88] [1979] AC 617 at 657, HL.

Edmund-Davies,[89] the second dissentient. It might also be noted that the arguments offered by Lemon's counsel were equally silent on the significance of free expression principles to the decision before the court.

That the principle of freedom of expression was either (for three judges) wholly irrelevant or (for two) of marginal significance to the content of the law of blasphemy is indicative of a broader ambivalence within the judiciary in this era. *Lemon* is a startling illustration of the potential illiberality of the common law. Even if we accept – and this is a dubious premise – that a majority of the population adhered sincerely to the Christian faith, the existence of blasphemy as a discrete offence is a blatant example of the common law pandering to majoritarian intolerance. Neither Mrs Whitehouse, nor any other Christian of delicate sensibilities was in any sense compelled to read the poem. Nor were they likely to encounter it by chance. In essence the crime permits self-righteous proponents of the Christian faith to rest secure in the knowledge that anyone who has the temerity to cause them offence on a matter of religious doctrine or practice faces the prospect of a substantial fine or a prison sentence. Lord Scarman's professed wish to extend the reach of the offence is even more unpalatable, in so far as it would grant the same repressive entitlement to a still larger proportion of the population.

But as the following case suggests, it would be quite misleading to conclude that the public's interest in being able to read and evaluate certain types of information – as opposed to the publisher's interest in being able to disseminate it – was never accorded importance by the courts. Yet the principle was undoubtedly invoked inconsistently, and certainly did not enjoy the status of being deployed as the starting point for judicial analysis.

CONTEMPT OF COURT

A-G v Times Newspapers Ltd[90] was triggered by two newspaper articles scheduled for publication in *The Sunday Times*. Both articles dealt with the on-going controversy caused by the drug thalidomide. The drug had been marketed in the 1960s as a remedy for morning sickness suffered by pregnant woman. The drug caused severe birth defects in thousands of children throughout the world. Litigation against Distillers was initiated in the UK by several hundred parents of the affected children. The key issue to be decided was whether Distillers had been negligent in testing the drug before its release. The litigation had not been concluded by the early 1970s, as Distillers and some of the plaintiffs were conducting protracted negotiations about the terms of a possible settlement.

In September 1972, *The Sunday Times* published a long article which urged

[89] Ibid, at 652–653; quoting a sentiment expressed in a textbook as to 'the splendid advantages which result to religion and truth from the exertion of free and unfettered minds'.

[90] [1974] AC 273, [1973] 3 All ER 54, HL. For a more detailed treatment of the litigation than is possible here see Miller C (1976) *Contempt of court* pp 126–134 (London: Paul Elek); Duffy P (1980) 'The Sunday Times case: freedom of expression, contempt of court and the ECHR' *Human Rights Review* 17–53.

Distillers not to stand on whatever legal defences it might muster, but rather to make a generous settlement to ensure that justice – in a broad, moral sense – was done. Distillers claimed that the article amounted to a contempt of court, but the Attorney-General did not accept that view and declined to begin proceedings. *The Sunday Times* then prepared a second article, which examined the evidence that might be put before a trial court on the negligence issue. The paper sent the article to the Attorney-General prior to publication. The Attorney-General concluded that this article would amount to contempt. His assumption was that the article would prejudice the fairness of any subsequent trial, by creating a climate of opinion in which Distillers would already stand condemned. This would compromise the overwhelming public interest in ensuring that litigation was conducted free from inappropriate external pressure. The Attorney-General thus sought an injunction preventing publication of the article. The injunction was granted in the High Court.

The injunction was promptly discharged by the Court of Appeal. All three members of the court were clearly influenced by what they regarded as a legitimate public interest in citizens knowing what progress was being made in settling the thalidomide controversy. This was never, it seems, to be regarded as a dominant interest, but in some circumstances could be a powerful one. Lord Denning MR expressed the point in the following way:

> 'It must always be remembered that besides the interests of the parties in a fair trial or a fair settlement of the case there is another important interest to be considered. It is the interest of the public in matters of national concern, and the freedom of press to make fair comment on such matters. The one interest must be balanced against the other'.[91]

When set in the context of his opinion as a whole, however, Lord Denning's above-quoted characterisation of the problem before the court is somewhat misleading. The key factor in his decision seems to have been that the litigation against Distillers was dormant, and that there was no likelihood of any hearings actually beginning in the foreseeable future. Since there was no trial in prospect, there was no possibility that its fair conduct could be jeopardised.

Readers of Lord Denning's judgment could be forgiven for concluding that the purpose of contempt of court in such circumstances was to protect one or other of the parties to the litigation. As was made abundantly clear in the House of Lords, its actual purpose is to protect the public's interest in the proper administration of justice.[92] Nonetheless, the House of Lords framed the question raised in much the same way as the Court of Appeal. In Lord Reid's view, the court was faced with responsibility of balancing 'the public interest in freedom of speech and the public

[91] [1973] QB 710 at 739.

[92] This point is conveyed with great clarity in the opening paragraph's of Lord Diplock's opinion. See also Lord Reid, ibid at 294: 'The law on this subject is and must be founded entirely on public policy. It is not there to protect the private rights of the parties. It is there to prevent interference with the administration of justice'.

interest in protecting the administration of justice from interference'.[93] Lord Reid and his colleagues reached however a different conclusion from that adopted in the Court of Appeal.

The court saw no scope for accepting that the first *Sunday Times* article could amount to contempt. For a newspaper or broadcaster to urge a powerful litigant such as Distillers to accept a moral obligation not to stand on its legal rights was quite legitimate as long as the persuasion was delivered in 'a fair and temperate way and without any oblique motive'.[94] The second article, however, was seen as much more problematic. Lord Reid considered that *The Sunday Times'* analysis of the negligence issue raised a real risk of pre-judging the issue that would be of vital importance at any trial. He observed that: 'There has long been and there still is in this country a strong and generally held belief that trial by newspaper is wrong and should be prevented'.[95] In Lord Reid's view, *The Sunday Times'* second article would have that effect; it was thus quite proper for the court to suppress its publication.[96]

Judicial law-making by the invocation of slogans – in this case 'trial by newspaper' – might immediately raise suspicions that the decision produced may lack a rigorous logical basis. Lord Reid's judgment explicitly acknowledged this point by suggesting it was much driven by intuitive feelings which defied written elucidation.[97]

Those feelings led Lord Reid to offer the following principle as a guide to the way in which such issues should be resolved:

> 'Responsible "mass media" will do their best to be fair, but there will also be ill-informed, slapdash or prejudiced attempts to influence the public. If people are led to think that it is easy to find the truth disrespect for the processes of the law could follow and, if mass media are allowed to judge, unpopular people and unpopular causes will fare very badly. . . . I do not think that the freedom of the press would suffer, and I think that the law would be clearer and easier to apply in practice if it is made a general rule that it is not permissible to prejudge issues in pending cases . . . .'[98]

This principle was to apply only to litigation at first instance. In Lord Reid's opinion, it was evidently 'scarcely imaginable' that Law Lords or Lord Justices of Appeal could ever be swayed in discharging their judicial functions by any stories in the press. This comment makes explicit an assumption on Lord Reid's part that seems to permeate the court's reasoning. The result produced takes a very condescending view of the

[93] Ibid, at 301. [94] Ibid, at 299. [95] Ibid, at 300.

[96] The House of Lords also took the view that the litigation was not dormant, but was simply in something of a negotiatory lull.

[97] For example the following passage at [1974] AC 273 at 300, HL: 'If we were to ask the ordinary man or even a lawyer in his leisure moments why he has that feeling, I suspect that the first reply would be – well look at what happens in some other countries where that is permitted. As in so many other matters, strong feelings are based on one's general experience rather than on specific reasons, and it often requires an effort to marshall one's reasons. But public policy is generally the result of strong feelings, commonly held, rather than of cold argument. If the law is to be developed in accord with public policy we must not be too legalistic in our general approach. No doubt public policy is an unruly horse to ride but in a chapter of the law so intimately associated with public policy as contempt of court we must not be too pedestrian . . . .'.

[98] Ibid.

citizenry's capacity to draw a meaningful distinction between a newspaper's view of a legal issue and the way that issue should be dealt with in a court. The crux of the conclusion is that citizens cannot be trusted with such material.

As one might expect, the informed consent philosophy underpinning the First Amendment had led the US Supreme Court to adopt a far more robust approach to the analytical capacity of American citizens than that favoured in respect of their British counterparts even by the Court of Appeal in the *Sunday Times* case. In *Nebraska Press Association v Stuart*,[99] decided in 1976, the Supreme Court affirmed a line of case law that indicated there were virtually no conceivable circumstances in which an injunction could be granted to restrain publication of press stories analysing either the moral or legal merits even of ongoing, still less pending litigation.[100] A similarly profound distinction between 'traditional' American and English law is also evident in respect of the final topic we consider in this chapter – the issue of political libels.

POLITICAL LIBELS

The tort of libel is something of a curiosity within the field of tort law as a whole. In general, a plaintiff in a tort action has to prove that the defendant's actions have caused her a quantifiable loss. She usually also has to demonstrate that the loss was caused by some level of fault (usually negligence) on the defendant's part. The damage at issue in a libel action is to the plaintiff's reputation, which has allegedly been undermined by a book or article published by the defendant. In a libel action, damage is presumed to flow automatically from the publication of libellous material; ie material that damages the reputation of the victim in the eyes of fair-minded observers. That the material is true is a defence, but it is for the defendant to prove truth. In general, under English law, the publisher has no defence if she did not know the material was false even if she had taken reasonable care to establish its accuracy.

America – a constitutional law perspective

In the United States, the English law of libel has come to be seen as imposing an unacceptable restriction on freedom of speech in relation to political issues. This is because it is feared that politicians and government bodies would be able to suppress media criticism of their activities by threatening a libel action. If the publisher was not wholly confident she/he could prove truth – which might be difficult in respect of many political stories – she might be deterred by the prospect of a large damages award against her from running stories which might well prove to be true. Consequently, by the early twentieth century, many American states had accepted the principle that a *government body* should not be able to initiate any form of legal action

[99] 427 US 539 (1976).

[100] For a concise analysis of the leading cases see Lockhart W, Kamisat Y, Choper J and Shiffrin S (6th edn, 1986) *Constitutional law* pp 830–836 (West Publishing: St Paul, Minnesota).

at all to suppress criticism of its activities – unless the speech concerned threatened an imminent breach of the peace. The leading case is *City of Chicago v Tribune Co.*[101]

The press stories which provoked the litigation had accused the Mayor and the city council of Chicago of being so corrupt and incompetent that the city itself was bankrupt. Such stories could obviously undermine the city's reputation, both as an institution of government and as a commercial actor. Yet the Illinois Supreme Court, its unanimous opinion delivered by Thompson CJ, held that the city could do nothing at all to suppress the dissemination of such stories.

The judgment was formally rooted in Art 2, s 4 of the Illinois Constitution: 'Every person may freely speak, write and publish on all subjects, being responsible for the abuse of that liberty', but the reasoning the court deployed had an overtly functionalist base. Thompson CJ observed that State and federal government in the USA were 'founded upon the fundamental principle that the citizen is the fountain of all authority'.[102] Such powers as government bodies possessed were granted on trust by the relevant electorate. Informed electoral choices demanded that citizens be afforded *absolute* protection against prosecution for criticising government bodies, except in the narrow instance of criticism likely to promote violent disorder.

Having thus limited the legitimate scope of criminal libel, Thompson CJ drew an analogy between criminal and civil actions. He suggested that civil actions could be substantially more effective prohibitors of speech than criminal prosecutions: civil libel actions, unlike criminal prosecutions, did not grant the defendant the presumption of innocence; they imposed a lesser standard of proof on the plaintiff; and there was no ceiling to the damages that might be awarded.

Thompson CJ stressed that the protection against civil liability for criticising a government body was *absolute*; no action of any sort would be permissible. There was no question of the Court trying to strike a 'balance' between freedom of political speech and the government's reputation; the government body had no corporate or public interest in its reputation to weigh in the scales.

Thompson CJ accepted that the rule the court had propounded would sometimes lead to unfounded and malevolent criticism being aired. This however was a price worth paying:

'[I]t is better that an occasional individual or newspaper that is so perverted in its judgment and so misguided in his or its civic duty should go free than that all of the citizens should be put in jeopardy of imprisonment or economic subjugation if they venture to criticise an inefficient or corrupt government'.[103]

[101] 139 NE 86 (1923). For a detailed discussion and analysis of the case see Loveland I (1998) '*City of Chicago v Tribune Co* – in contexts', in Loveland I (ed) *Importing the First Amendment* (Oxford: Hart Publishing).

[102] 139 NE 86 at 90 (1923).

[103] Ibid, at 91. The passage echoes Madison's celebrated observation, which Thompson CJ. had earlier quoted (at 89), that: 'Some degree of abuse is inseparable from the proper use of everything, and in no instance is this more true than in that of the press. It has accordingly been decided by the practice of the states that it is better to leave a few of the noxious branches to their luxuriant growth than by pruning them away to injure the vigour of those yielding the proper fruits'.

American states which adopted this principle recognised that there would be little point in preventing government bodies launching libel actions if such bodies could indirectly achieve the same deterrent effect on freedom of political speech through actions initiated by individual politicians under the ordinary libel laws. Thus, importantly, these states also accepted that individual politicians or government officials could only succeed in a libel action in relation to their political beliefs and behaviour if they could prove that the defendant had knowingly or recklessly published false information.[104] The device used to achieve this objective was the long recognised English law defence of 'qualified privilege', which in English law had only ever been applied to a narrow range of types of information, such as commercial or familial matters, in which it was assumed that both the disseminee and the recipient of the libellous information were under a duty to exchange it.[105] The American rationale, not embraced in England, was that in a representative democracy all citizens (and all media organisations) were under a reciprocal duty to disseminate, analyse and discuss political information in so far as it related to the fitness for office of elected politicians, candidates for such office, and senior appointed government officials. By the 1960s, these principles had been embraced by the US Supreme Court in the landmark case of *New York Times v Sullivan*,[106] and applied through the First Amendment to all of the American States.

Britain – a tort law perspective

English law had, in contrast, adopted a very limited understanding of the extent to which individuals and the press should be protected from the ordinary law of libel when publishing political information. In the 1868 case of *Wason v Walter*,[107] the court accepted that newspapers which offered verbatim accounts of parliamentary proceedings should enjoy a common law protection analogous to that bestowed upon proceedings in Parliament by Article 9 of the Bill of Rights. The court's reasoning in *Wason* – unusually in the English context – framed the issue as one essentially of constitutional law and political morality. Common law libel rules should not be allowed to prevent voters reaching informed conclusions about what was happening in the Houses of Parliament. The task of the common law was to give expression to the public interest; and, as Cockburn CJ saw the matter: 'There is perhaps no subject matter in which the public have a deeper interest than in all that relates to the conduct of public servants of the state'.[108]

Perhaps ironically, it was the reasoning in this case which provided the inspiration which led American courts in the next 50 years to extend protection for political libels

[104] See especially *Coleman v McClennan* 98 PAC 201 (1908) (Kansas); *Ambrosious v O'Farrell* 199 Ill App 265 (1905) (Illinois); *Briggs v Garrett* 11 Pa 406 (1886) (Pennsylvania); *Salinger v Cowles* 191 NW 167 (1922). For a detailed discussion of these cases see Loveland (1998) op cit.

[105] See Loveland I (2000) *Political libels* ch 1 (Oxford: Hart Publishing).

[106] 376 US 254 (1964). The case is discussed in some detail in Loveland (2000) op cit ch 5; and in great detail in Lewis A (1991) *Make no law* (New York: Vintage Books).

[107] (1868) LR 4 QB 73.

[108] Ibid, at 89.

to a much wider range of political information, on the grounds that coverage of legislative proceedings was by no means sufficient to enable citizens to acquire the knowledge they would need in order to offer their informed consent to the government process.[109] Such developments were as often rooted in common law as in interpretation of the texts of state constitutions. These courts took Cockburn's CJ's reference in *Wason* to 'all' political information quite literally.

Notwithstanding English law's evident fondness for literalism as a jurisprudential technique, this American development was not systematically mirrored either by Parliament or the courts in the United Kingdom,[110] with the result that even by the 1980s English law drew no obvious distinction between libels dealing with political issues and those affecting purely private matters. Two cases illustrate this point with great clarity.

The defendant in *Bognor Regis UDC v Campion*[111] had waged a campaign against what he claimed was corruption in his local authority. The suit was triggered by a pamphlet authored by Campion which contained an hysterical polemic accusing the ruling group on the council of ineptitude and dishonesty. Rather than ignore the pamphlet, the council's ruling group resolved that the council itself should sue Mr Campion in libel.

The issue before Browne J in the High Court was whether the authority could maintain such an action. He saw no difficulty in concluding that it could. A council was simply an individual for these purposes:

> 'Just as a trading company has a trading reputation which it is entitled to protect by bringing an action for defamation, so in my view the plaintiffs as a local government corporation have a "governing reputation" which they are equally entitled to protect in the same way. . . .'[112]

Judgment was eventually delivered against Mr Campion. The award of damages was only £2,000, but this was accompanied by an order to pay the council's costs, which amounted to some £30,000.[113] A bill of £32,000 (at 1972 prices) might be thought to have a decidedly deterrent effect on citizens or newspapers wishing to criticise a local authority's behaviour. But there is nothing in Browne J's judgment to indicate that he perceived the case to have any 'political' or constitutional dimension at all. The action was characterised simply as a matter of tort law.

Some ten years later, in *Blackshaw v Lord*,[114] the Court of Appeal did acknowledge the argument that political libels might raise a 'constitutional law' issue; but having acknowledged the argument, the judges accorded it no weight.

The litigation concerned a *Daily Telegraph* story written by Lord which alleged that the Department had apparently breached Treasury guidelines and overpaid some

109 Loveland (2000) op cit ch 3.

110 For an account of some exceptions to this general trend see ibid, chs 4 and 6.

111 [1972] 2 QB 169. 112 Ibid, at 175.

113 Weir A (1972) 'Local authority v critical ratepayer – a suit in defamation' *Cambridge LJ* 238–249.

114 [1984] QB 1, CA.

£52m in grants to various oil companies. Several civil servants were reprimanded following internal disciplinary proceedings. The Commons Public Accounts Committee investigated the affair, and issued a report. The article linked the report to the resignation of a senior civil servant, Blackshaw, who held the rank of Under-Secretary. The Permanent Secretary at the Department of Energy had told the PAC that an Under-Secretary had been reprimanded. Just after Lord's story ran, the Permanent Secretary informed the PAC that this was false; no Under-Secretary had been reprimanded. Blackshaw claimed that the story libelled him, in that it implied that his professional incompetence had cost the taxpayer £52m.

At trial, Lord claimed that a story dealing with so obviously political a matter should attract qualified privilege. This argument was accepted by the trial judge. His conclusion was however overturned in the Court of Appeal, which held that the press had no duty to publish stories of this type to the public at large. Fox LJ doubted that the general public had any 'audience interest' in this sort of story. He concluded simply that 'an allegation of improper or negligent conduct against a public servant may be privileged if made to persons having a proper interest to receive it – such as the police or senior officials'.[115] The electorate had no legitimate interest in such information.

CONCLUSION

Fox LJ's suggestion that the electorate had 'no proper interest' in being provided with press analysis (which was neither deliberately dishonest nor reckless as to truth) of important political issues offers a most compelling illustration of the antediluvian state of the common law's human rights jurisprudence in the mid–1980s. It is no answer to this criticism to explain it away as a necessary consequence of the doctrine of parliamentary sovereignty; that, in the absence of a codified statement of entrenched, fundamental civil liberties such as those in the USA's Bill of Rights, the courts simply had no legitimate scope to fashion a systematic approach to the issue of human rights protection. Even within the constitutional constraints imposed on the judiciary by the existence of a sovereign legislature, there was scope for such principles to have emerged and hardened as moral yardsticks against which to measure responses to purely common law problems or to structure the task of statutory interpretation. As we have seen in this, and previous chapters, there were undoubtedly exceptions to this general proposition. But English law could not lay any plausible claim at this time even to have addressed, still less embraced, any systematic methodology for the identification and protection of human rights issues. The lacuna is perhaps all the more surprising because by the mid–1980s the United Kingdom had been for almost 40 years a signatory to what had by then become an extensive body of international law dealing with civil liberties questions – the European Convention on Human Rights.

115 Ibid, per Fox LJ at 41.

19

HUMAN RIGHTS AND CIVIL LIBERTIES II: EMERGENT PRINCIPLES

This chapter offers a limited and partial introduction to the European Convention on Human Rights. It now seems increasingly likely that the Convention will begin to be treated as a topic in its own right in many British law schools. It is certainly the case that the breadth and complexities of its provisions cannot be addressed in a properly detailed fashion within a year or semester-long course on constitutional and administrative law. An initial familiarity with the Convention is however of some appreciable importance in the areas both of constitutional and administrative law. The following pages consequently have two objectives. Section I discusses the main procedural and substantive features of the Convention itself. Section II assesses the status and use of the Convention in English law up until (approximately) the early 1990s. And sections III and IV examine the leading judgments of the European Court on Human Rights in the areas of privacy and freedom of expression which were addressed in chapter eighteen.

I. THE EUROPEAN CONVENTION ON HUMAN RIGHTS – INTRODUCTORY PRINCIPLES

The European Convention on Human Rights is an international treaty, whose origins lie, like those of the EC, in the reconstruction of Europe's political order following World War II. In 1949, 25 European states formed a body known as the Council of Europe.[1] The Council's broad concern was to foster the growth and entrenchment of democratic government within western Europe. One means of doing so was to persuade its members to become signatories to the Convention.

[1] Which, despite the similarity of its name, should not be confused either with the EC's Council of Ministers or the EU's European Council. On the background to the Council of Europe's formation, and the subsequent production of the Convention, see Robertson A and Merrill J (3rd edn, 1994) *Human rights in Europe* ch 1 (Manchester: Manchester UP).

The Convention's terms cover a wide sweep of political issues, broadly comparable to those outlined in the USA's Bill of Rights. Article 2 safeguards the right to life. Article 3 prohibits the use of torture, and the infliction of degrading or inhuman treatment and/or punishment. Articles 5 and 6 are aimed primarily at the conduct of criminal proceedings. Article 7 places strict limits on retrospective criminal laws. Article 8 addresses the right to privacy and family life, while Art 12 concerns the right of adults to marry and found a family. Articles 9 and 10 focus on freedom of thought, conscience, religious belief and expression,[2] and Article 11 addresses the right to freedom of assembly and association, including the right to join a trade union.

INSTITUTIONAL AND JURISDICTIONAL ISSUES

The Council of Europe also established several institutions to enforce and monitor the Convention's provisions. The European Commission of Human Rights (EComHR) was established to perform both an investigatory and conciliatory role. Its members were distinguished lawyers, their number being equal to the number of states which have ratified the Convention; no state could have more than one of its nationals sitting on the Commission.[3] The Commission was the body to which complaints of a breach of the Convention were initially notified. The Commission was also empowered to determine if the complaint was admissible. The Commission would not admit complaints which it considered 'manifestly ill-founded'. Furthermore, per Art 26, the applicant must have exhausted all effective domestic remedies before the Commission would intervene. Nor could the Commission act if the applicant was raising a question which was 'substantially the same' as one with which the Commission or Court had already dealt. Admissibility proved a formidable hurdle for applicants to surmount. By 1990, the Commission had entertained over 17,000 applications; fewer than 700 were admitted.[4] It would thus be quite inaccurate to portray the Commission as a body which was constantly interfering with internal affairs of the Convention's signatory states.

Should the Commission have concluded that the complaint was justified, it attempted to negotiate a 'friendly settlement' between the parties. If no settlement could be reached, the Commission drafted an 'opinion' detailing its view of the breach, which was sent to the Committee of Ministers (comprising the foreign ministers of each signatory state). The Committee could either (by a two-thirds majority) produce its own 'judgment', or could refer the case to the European Court of Human Rights (ECtHR). The term 'judgment' is used guardedly. The Convention does not require the Committee to adopt court-style procedures. Its decision-making process is conducted in secret, and the impugned member state can vote on the outcome. This

2 The scope of the initial Convention has subsequently been expanded by various protocols, although not all of the original signatory states have acceded to all of these.

3 See Robertson and Merrill op cit ch 7.

4 Bailey, Harris and Jones (1992) op cit p 757.

process is obviously unsatisfactory from a narrowly legalistic perspective, but it does alert observers to the important fact that the Convention retains a substantial 'inter-national' element.

Approximately 25% of the Commission's opinions have been dealt with in this way. The great majority have in contrast been referred to the European Court on Human Rights (ECtHR). The Court's members were selected by the Committee of Ministers, generally for a nine-year term; the Court's total membership could not exceed the number of signatory states, and no state could have more than one of its nationals sitting on the bench. The applicant was not formally a party to the ECtHR proceedings, although she could appear and be legally represented. Her case was presented on her behalf by the Commission, although the Commission's role in such proceedings was technically to act as the 'defender of the public interest', rather than as the applicant's advocate.

The Convention provides that the ECtHR's judgments 'bind' the signatory states. Responsibility for ensuring compliance is entrusted to the Committee of Ministers. Compliance generally requires the offending state to alter its domestic law in a manner which satisfies the ECtHR's judgment. Thus far, such amendments have almost always been forthcoming. The Convention has therefore to some extent 'federalised' the constitutional orders of some of its signatory nations. Its provisions are the supreme source of legal authority in some states. For those countries whose constitutions provide that Treaty obligations automatically become part of domestic law, or have made specific arrangements to accord the Convention that status, it is also (to borrow familiar terminology) 'directly effective'; their own courts must apply the ECtHR's case law, a situation which greatly speeds their citizen's access to their Convention entitlements. Yet there is no requirement in the Convention itself that signatory states make its provisions directly effective in domestic law; it does not demand that its terms can be enforced by national courts. In many states, citizens were instead required to exhaust all their domestic remedies before invoking a right of direct complaint to the Commission itself. However, the Convention does not even insist that signatory states grant individuals this right of petition to the EComHR. In those countries, the Convention operates more as a source of diplomatic rather than legal obligation; it exists in the realm of international law rather than constitutional law. The conformity of such states' laws with the Convention can be challenged only at the instigation of another signatory state.[5]

The absence of a direct effect requirement within the Convention has meant that citizens of states which granted the right of petition might find that pursuing a complaint all the way to the Court proved a very time-consuming process. Suits are rarely concluded in under two years, and time spans of five years between the first action in a domestic court and the eventual ECtHR judgment were not uncommon.

In 1999, in a significant procedural reform, the Commission and the Court merged

[5] Ie the equivalent of an Article 170 action under the Treaty of Rome: see p 417 above. There have been very few such actions under the Convention: see Bailey, Harris and Jones (1992) op cit pp 756–757.

into a single body, styled as the ECtHR.[6] It was hoped that the reform would make the ECtHR more accessible to citizens, speed up the process of litigation and also reduce its costs. The merged Court is substantially larger than its predecessor, and will do much of its work in 'Chambers' of a few members, rather than in a plenary session in which all judges will sit.[7]

THE JURISPRUDENTIAL METHODOLOGY OF THE CONVENTION

In one important sense, albeit not necessarily a supra-legislative legal sense, the Convention articulates a series of 'higher law' moral principles ostensibly embedded within the political cultures of its signatory states. It might readily be thought that in some of those states, where democratic traditions enjoy only a precarious foothold in political culture, accession to the Convention was intended more as a sop to international opinion rather than a sincere attempt to restrain the potential abuse of governmental power.[8] Yet one should not equate the Convention's embrace of supposedly fundamental moral principles with the imposition of a rigid constitutional orthodoxy on those signatory states which have committed themselves bona fide to respect its terms.

The Convention does not impose a uniform coda of detailed legal rules. Its text is itself liberally sprinkled with provisions allowing states to derogate from its formal provisions. Article 15, for example, is a derogation clause of wide application in respect of many Convention entitlements, through which a state can seek permission de jure to 'opt out' of Convention obligations for limited periods. Similarly, the 'rights' protected in specific articles of the Convention are often immediately qualified by provisions permitting state interference. For example, the 'right to life' protected in Art 2 contains an exception for 'the execution of a sentence of a court following . . . conviction for a crime for which this penalty is provided by law'. Similarly, while Art 10(1) announces the 'right to freedom of expression' – and expressly provides that this includes the entitlement to receive as well as disseminate information[9] – Art 10(2) provides that the right:

'may be subject to such formalities, conditions, restrictions or penalties as are prescribed by

[6] For the background to the reform, and an indication of its details, see Schermers H (1993) 'The European Court of Human Rights after the merger' *European Law Review* 493–505.

[7] On the final shape of the reforms see Mowbray A (1999) 'The composition and operation of the new European Court of Human Rights' *Public Law* 219–231.

[8] In 2000, for example, the countries adhering to the Convention included Romania, Bulgaria and the Ukraine, in which it was quite far-fetched to suggest that the governmental system was in any meaningful sense democratic. It might of course be argued that such countries should ratify the ECHR, in the hope that so doing might make a contribution to the consolidation of democratic governance within their constitutional orders.

[9] Article 10.1. Everyone has the right to freedom of expression. This right shall include freedom to hold opinions and to receive and impart information and ideas without interference by public authority and regardless of frontiers. This Article shall not prevent States from requiring the licensing of broadcasting, television or cinema enterprises.

law and are necessary in a democratic society, in the interests of national security, territorial integrity or public safety, for the prevention of disorder or crime, for the protection of health or morals, for the protection of the reputations or rights of others, for preventing the disclosure of information received in confidence, or for maintaining the authority and impartiality of the judiciary'.

This constitutional methodology pervades the Convention. In the main, the Convention's articles define and afford protection to a broadly defined civil right (what we might call 'the presumptive entitlement'); the text then permits signatory states to interfere with the presumptive entitlement in defence of certain specified objectives (what we might call 'legitimate interference'); but it then in turn requires that intrusion to comply with certain safeguards; ie that it be 'prescribed by law' and 'necessary in a democratic society'.

The same scheme of reasoning can be seen in the text of Art 8, which protects 'privacy and family life':

'1. Everyone has the right to respect for his private and family life, his home and his correspondence.

2. There shall be no interference by a public authority with the exercise of this right except such as is in accordance with the law and is necessary in a democratic society in the interests of national security, public safety or the economic well-being of the country, for the prevention of disorder or crime, for the protection of health or morals, or for the protection of the rights and freedoms of others.'

The way in which this textual methodology has been applied by the ECtHR is perhaps best illustrated by examining the Court's decision-making process in Art 10 cases. Its technique can be broken down into four stages. Firstly, the Court will ask if a governmental body has in some way interfered with the applicant's presumptive entitlement to free expression?

Secondly, if the first answer is 'Yes', the ECtHR will ask if the government body has interfered with the entitlement in pursuit of a legitimate objective arising from one or more of the factors identified in Art 10(2); ie national security, territorial integrity etc. This test is generally unproblematic from a state's perspective.

If the answer is again 'Yes', the Court moves to stage three, in which it considers if the restriction is 'prescribed by law'; ie is its content accurately identified in the domestic legal system?[10] The primary point of reference for the meaning of this concept is now provided by the ECtHR in its 1979 judgment in *Sunday Times v United Kingdom*:

'a norm cannot be regarded as a "law" unless it is formulated with sufficient precision to enable the citizen to regulate his conduct; he must be able, if need be with appropriate advice – to foresee to a degree that is reasonable in all the circumstances, the consequences which a given action may entail'.[11]

[10] The text sometimes uses the formula 'according to law'. There do not appear to be any differences between the two formulae.

[11] (1979) 2 EHRR 245 at para 49. The case, which dealt with the *A-G v Times Newspapers* litigation (see pp 650–651 above) is discussed in detail below.

The ECtHR has not accepted that a measure can only be 'prescribed by/according to law' if it has a legislative base. The Court has recognised that a body of judge-made rules such as the common law may pass that test, even if – as is the case with common law – the state's indigenous legal principles permit the substance of that law to change in response to altered social and economic circumstances or moral perceptions. Thus, in *The Sunday Times* case, the ECtHR continued after the above quotation in the following way:

'Those consequences need not be attainable with absolute certainty: experience shows this to be unattainable. Again, whilst certainty is highly desirable, it may bring in its train excessive rigidity and the law must be able to keep pace with changing circumstances. Accordingly many laws are inevitably couched in terms which, to a greater or lesser extent, are vague and whose interpretation and application are questions of practice'.[12]

Should the government's interference fail that test, a breach of Art 10 is established. The 'prescribed by law' test speaks to what was earlier described as the 'How?' element of the rule of law.[13] Its concern is – to put the matter somewhat simplistically – with the procedural rather than the substantive dimension of the relationship between government and citizens.[14]

If the interference in issue is considered to be 'prescribed by law', the ECtHR then moves to the fourth and final stage of its analysis: is the measure taken 'necessary in a democratic society'. This is the most complex and controversial area of the ECtHR's jurisprudence. Its concern is explicitly with the 'What?' element of the rule of law; namely what substantive restraints may a signatory state legitimately impose upon its citizens?

In interpreting this aspect of the Convention, the ECtHR has developed a principle known as 'the margin of appreciation'. In formulating its approach to the 'necessary

[12] Ibid. The ECtHR has shown itself to be quite accommodating to this common law tradition. The best illustration of the point is perhaps provided by the Court's eventual decision in the *R v R (marital rape exemption)* case: [1992] 1 AC 599, [1991] 4 All ER 481, HL: see pp 88–90 above. The ECtHR's judgment is given in *SW v United Kingdom; CR v United Kingdom* (1995) 21 EHRR 363. R challenged his conviction on the basis that the House of Lords' judgment had breached the Art 7 prohibition on retrospective criminal laws. The ECtHR saw no merit in this argument. The Court held that the orderly evolution of the common law did not per se amount to retrospectivity. On this particular issue, the Court considered that it was perfectly clear by the time R 'raped' his wife that the scope of the marital consent defence was diminishing and that it was plausible to assume that it might at any point be narrowed further or be removed altogether. This might suggest that retrospective legislation would have breached Art 7 or (possibly) that a sudden and complete judicial reversal of a long-established common law rule would have done so. However it should also be noted that the ECtHR laid some stress in its judgment on the grossly reprehensible moral nature of R's activities: 'What is more, the abandonment of the unacceptable idea of a husband being immune against prosecution for rape of his wife was in conformity not only with a civilised concept of marriage but also, and above all, with the fundamental objectives of the Convention, the very essence of which is respect for human dignity and human freedom': ibid, at para 44/42. This may indicate that 'orderly evolution' at common law may breach Art 7 in respect of morally anodyne offences.

[13] See p 56 above.

[14] The term 'citizen' is used here in a loose sense, simply to denote any individual who happens to fall within the state's jurisdiction at any given time.

in a democratic society' provision, the ECtHR has repeatedly stressed that it does not see the Convention's role as imposing a series of common, detailed legal rules on all of the signatory states. The Court's jurisdiction is not de jure appellate, nor – in most situations – could its jurisdiction be so classified in a de facto sense. In much of its activity, the Court's task could be seen – if one were searching for an indigenous British comparator – as supervisory in a rather loose, almost *Wednesbury* irrationality sense. Neither does the Court quash or invalidate national laws. Its remedial role is essentially declaratory in nature, although it also has the power under Art 41 to order a state to pay 'damages' (the term used in the text is 'just satisfaction') to successful applicants. Subsequent compliance with the Court's judgments is a matter for the signatory state concerned.

This point is well conveyed by the ECtHR's judgment in *Handyside v United Kingdom.*[15] Handyside had been convicted under English obscenity laws for producing a publication called *The Little Red Schoolbook.*[16] Before the ECtHR, the UK government argued that this interference with freedom of expression was justified 'for the protection of morals'. Having accepted this argument, and agreed that the UK's obscenity laws met the 'prescribed by law' test, the Court then turned to consider whether the laws were 'necessary in a democratic society'. The Court stressed that when questions of 'the protection of morals' were in issue, it would be reluctant to conclude that state measures were not necessary:

> 'By reason of their direct and continuous contact with the vital forces of their countries, state authorities are in principle in a better position than the international judge to give an opinion . . . on the necessity of a "restriction" or "penalty".[17]

This did not mean that the ECtHR had no role to play in such circumstances; but rather that its jurisdiction would be secondary, almost residual, in nature:

> 'Nevertheless, Article 10(2) does not give the contracting states an unlimited power of appreciation. The Court is empowered to give the final ruling on whether a "restriction" or "penalty" is reconcilable with freedom of expression as protected by Article 10'.[18]

This principle speaks to a limited notion of justiciability in both a substantive and trans-national sense. The Court accepts that the classification and regulation of 'obscene' material is an intensely 'moral' question. This does not per se render the matter non-justiciable, since prosecutions for obscenity are necessarily judged on their detailed merits by national courts. However, moral questions evidently acquire a much less justiciable status when they are exported beyond their indigenous national boundaries. In describing itself as an 'international' rather than 'constitutional' court, the ECtHR seems to suggest that it lacks the cultural competence to conduct a close examination of the merits of a state's laws. Thus, while the Court would insist that a measure was only 'necessary' if it met what the Court termed 'a pressing social need'

[15] (1976) 1 EHRR 737.

[16] See Fiengold C (1978) 'The Little Red Schoolbook and the ECHR' *Human Rights Review* 21–47.

[17] (1976) 1 EHRR 737 at para 48.

[18] Ibid, at para 49.

and was 'proportionate' in the sense of not interfering unduly with the presumptive entitlement, it would not subject the state's own conclusions on these points to rigorous scrutiny.

The consequences of this relaxed standard of review could be spun in either a positive or negative light. It could be seen as having the desirable outcome of respecting the autonomy of signatory states on moral matters. Alternatively, it might be viewed as abandoning the liberties of individuals or small minorities to the intolerance of national majorities.[19]

It is however clear that as a matter of general principle – we explore the point in a more detailed context below – the breadth of the margin of appreciation afforded to signatory states (and thence the practical nature of the EComHR's and the Court's jurisdiction) is not uniform in respect of all the Convention's provisions; rather it varies according to the particular presumptive entitlements and/or legitimate interferences in issue. In many situations, the ECtHR will seem to function more as a 'constitutional' than 'international' court; it will look closely at the merits of the legitimate interference, and will accept that it is 'necessary' only if the Court itself is convinced that, given the detailed circumstances of the case, the measure has indeed been undertaken to satisfy a 'pressing social need' and if the means chosen to achieve the desired end are 'proportionate' in the sense of interfering as little as possible with the presumptive entitlement. An examination of the intricacies of the way in which the Court has pursued this approach across the whole spectrum of Convention entitlements is beyond the scope of this book.[20] We return to the issue below, but at this point we might just note that the Court subjects state laws to quite varying standards of scrutiny depending on the issue at stake.

II. THE INITIAL STATUS OF THE ECHR IN DOMESTIC LAW

It is perhaps worth repeating the point that, in contrast to the status of EC law, the Convention does not require that its terms be given 'direct effect' in the legal systems of its signatory states. Nor did the Convention even require that states grant their citizens direct access to the Commission and the ECtHR. In countries where the Convention is neither directly effective, nor actionable by individuals before the ECtHR itself, compliance with its terms would be a matter to be resolved through the political rather than the legal process.

[19] For a powerful critique from this perspective see Jones T (1996) 'The devaluation of human rights under the European Convention' *Public Law* 430–449. See also Warbrick C (1998) 'Federalism and free speech', in Loveland I (ed) *Importing the First Amendment?* (Oxford: Hart Publishing).

[20] Both Janis, Bradley and Kay op cit and Harris, O'Boyle and Warbrick op cit undertake the task admirably.

Although Attlee's 1945–1950 Labour government was closely involved in drafting and promoting the Convention, his Cabinet was bitterly divided on the question of whether this country should even be a signatory.[21] Atlee's government did eventually accede to the Convention. However, it was not until the mid–1960s that a UK government (Harold Wilson's first Labour administration) allowed UK citizens the right of direct access to the EComHR. And, prior to 1997, no post-war government ever introduced a bill to incorporate the Convention into domestic law. UK citizens were thus apparently unable to enforce its terms before their courts.

POLITICAL RESPONSES – WHY DID PARLIAMENT NOT INCORPORATE THE ECHR?

Parliament's failure to incorporate cannot be explained on simple party political grounds. Both Labour and Conservative governments consistently refused to promote the necessary legislation. It is also misleading to suggest that this reluctance stemmed from an objectively defensible concern to ensure that the wishes of a democratically elected legislature are not frustrated by the unelected judiciary. That argument fails on several counts. The shortcomings in 'Parliament's' democratic credentials have already been alluded to; the Commons' electoral system was (and remains) crudely minoritarian, and the Lords' composition was until 1999 entirely indefensible.[22] Moreover, if the ECtHR were to be incorporated (on terms analogous to those used in the ECA 1972), the government and Parliament's subordination would not be to the domestic courts, but to the ECtHR, on whose behalf the British courts would act as an agent. Rather, the Convention's formal constitutional status as merely international law seems to derive from the traditional unwillingness of either the Labour or Conservative parties to accept the moral premise that they are not each entitled to make whatever use they wish of Parliament's sovereignty whenever their electoral fortunes afford them a Commons majority.

The legal education of many law students in Britain in the past 20 years has included exposure to successive editions of Professor John Griffith's celebrated work on *The Politics of the Judiciary*. Griffith promoted considerable controversy in suggesting that the judiciary's social and educational background predisposed most judges to adopt a highly conservative attitude when faced with contentious political questions. Griffith was not accusing judges of acting in a crudely party political sense:

'But it is demonstrable that on every major social issue which has come before the courts during the last 30 years – concerning industrial relations, political protest, race relations, governmental secrecy, police powers, moral behaviour – the judges have supported the conventional, established and settled interests. And they have reacted strongly against challenges to those interests'.[23]

[21] On the Atlee government's views see Lester A (1984) 'Fundamental rights: the United Kingdom isolated' *Public Law* 46–72.

[22] Quite how defensible it is now is obviously a matter of some controversy: see pp 207–209 above.

[23] Op cit pp 239–240. The 30 years in question being from the mid-1940s to the mid-1970s.

Griffith suggested that such judicial bias may explain the Labour Party's historic reluctance to embrace the idea of a supra-legislative constitution. The point was echoed by other commentators. Wallington and McBride observed for example that any enthusiasm the third Wilson government might have had for such reform was snuffed out by the ostensibly pro-Conservative decision in *Tameside*.[24] Yet from any sophisticated view of democratic government, the Tameside saga reflects poorly on the Labour government rather than on the courts. *Tameside* was defensibly decided both as a matter of law and of broader constitutional morality. The Labour government's efforts to ignore the clear meaning of the 1944 Education Act (an Act promoted by an all-party coalition government) so that it could impose a particular educational ideology on all parts of the country, irrespective of local preferences, forcefully disproves assertions that only the Thatcher and Major governments succumbed to the minoritarian vice of assuming that having a Commons majority entitles them to do whatever they like to whoever they wish whenever they choose.

The Griffith thesis draws much of its force from its attachment to such a crude notion of 'democracy'. The unelected judiciary's 'conservatism' was undesirable because it obstructed the policies preferred by the 'democratically elected' government of the day. Such assumptions are themselves vulnerable to criticism on the ground that they leave a rather more important question unasked – namely whether it is 'democratic' for a constitution to permit barely majoritiarian or even minoritarian ideologies to exercise ultimate control of the law-making process? In a democracy which had placed its basic moral principles beyond the reach of bare majorities, one would of course expect the judiciary to adopt a conservative stance in defence of constituent moral values. By doing so, they evince loyalty to a rather broader conception of 'the people' than one is likely to find in a transient electoral majority. This might suggest that in so far as judicial conservatism reveals a 'problem' within the constitution, it is a problem that stems from the doctrine of parliamentary sovereignty rather than from the courts.

Nonetheless, the notion that it was 'undemocratic' to place supra-legislative authority in the hands of the judges – both domestic and European – exercised a sufficiently strong grip on both the Labour and Conservative Party leaderships to make legislative incorporation of the Convention a non-issue in British political circles until the late 1990s. The notion that the Convention should restrain the power of Parliament itself was regarded as absurd, and even the more modest proposition that the Convention should operate as a de jure check on government power in the field of administrative law attracted minimal political support.

The suggestion that this opposition to incorporation rested on an implacable hostility to the possibility of the imposition of 'foreign' legal solutions to domestic political problems is not easy to sustain. The UK's record in complying with adverse ECtHR judgments through the eventual enactment of legislation is almost flawless. As

[24] Wallington P and McBride J (1976) *Civil liberties and a Bill of Rights* pp 28–29 (London: Cobden Trust), cited in Bailey, Harris and Jones (1992) op cit p 15. On *Tameside*, see pp 371–372 above.

noted in section 1 of this chapter, it is also generally misleading to suggest that the Convention imposes rules on signatory states. Defeat before the Court usually means no more than that the signatory state must accept that its discretion in respect of certain matters is not quite as broad as it would like. And, as is indicated by the cases discussed in the final sections of this chapter, it has often been the case that the EComHR and the Court have found governmental decisions which generated acute political controversy in the UK to be perfectly compatible with the demands of the Convention. Before reaching that question however, it is helpful to spend some time exploring the way in which the Convention has been deployed in domestic law by the courts.

LEGAL RESPONSES – THE ECHR AS A SOURCE OF PRINCIPLE AT COMMON LAW

Murray's Hunt's influential analysis of the Convention's role in domestic law records that for the first twenty years of its existence – between 1953 and 1973 – the Convention was cited only once in domestic law reports, and that in a case involving the institutional status of the EComHR.[25] The first allusions made to it (Hunt describes the allusions as 'fleeting' and 'passing' references)[26] as a potential influence on individual rights under English law appeared in *Cassell & Co Ltd v Broome*,[27] a House of Lords' judgment on damages in libel cases, and *Waddington v Miah*,[28] an immigration case which addressed whether a particular statutory provision imposed retrospective criminal liability.[29]

The virtual invisibility of the Convention in domestic law in this period is something of a puzzle. As was made clear in the discussion in chapters two and twelve of the relationship between statute and international law,[30] English courts had long accepted that while the terms of an unincorporated treaty could not override the clear meaning of an Act of Parliament, they could be invoked as an aid to the interpretation of ambiguous statutory provisions. Thus the fact that the Convention had not been incorporated into domestic law by Parliament did not mean that it was invariably irrelevant in domestic proceedings. This principle as to the general status of international law had been clearly recognised in *Mortensen v Peters*.[31] As Lord Kyllachy put it – in somewhat equivocal terms:

'[I]t may probably be conceded that there is always a certain presumption against the legislature of any country asserting or assuming the existence of a territorial jurisdiction

[25] (1997) *Using human rights law in English courts* p 131 (Oxford: Hart Publishing). I am much indebted to this book in the following pages.

[26] Ibid.

[27] [1972] AC 1027, [1972] 1 All ER 801. See Loveland I (2000) *Political libels* pp 90–91 (Oxford: Hart Publishing).

[28] [1974] 2 All ER 377, [1974] 1 WLR 683.

[29] Which is forbidden by Art 7 ECHR.

[30] See pp 35–37 and 442–443.

[31] (1906) 14 SLT 227; see pp 35–36 above.

going beyond limits established by the common consent on nations – that is to say by International law'.[32]

The principle was reiterated in a much more forceful and expansive form some 60 years later by Diplock LJ in *Salomon v Customs and Excise Comrs:*

'If the terms of the legislation are clear and unambiguous they must be given effect to whether or not they carry out Her Majesty's treaty obligations. . . . If the terms of the legislation are not clear, however, but are reasonably capable of more than one meaning, the treaty itself becomes relevant, for there is a prima facie presumption that Parliament does not intend to act in breach of international law . . .; and if one of the meanings that can reasonably be ascribed to the legislation is consonant with the treaty obligations and another or others are not, the meaning which is consonant is to be preferred'.[33]

That neither counsel nor the judges made any resort to the Convention as an interpretive aid when faced with ambiguous legislation or common law rules impacting upon civil liberties may perhaps be explained by a complacent assumption that UK law – being the product of a 'democratic' legislature and an independent judiciary – was invariably as protective of human rights as the Convention itself. *Jordan v Burgoyne*,[34] for example, in 1963 and *Brutus v Cozens*[35] ten years later, were both cases affecting freedom of expression and assembly (protected by Arts 10 and 11 ECtHR) which turned on issues of statutory interpretation. Neither case made any reference to the Convention.

Yet in 1975 – if only initially for a brief period – the Convention seemed suddenly to have acquired prominent (even perhaps dominant status) in domestic law. As Hunt notes, this may be attributable to the fact that the first few cases against the UK had by then made their way to the ECtHR.[36] It may also stem from the fact that as a result of applying (directly effective) EC law, domestic judges had become much more aware of other 'European' treaty provisions.

Whatever the explanation, Lord Denning was among the first to recognise that – at the very least – the normal status of international law attached to the ECtHR. In *Birdi v Secretary of State for Home Affairs*, he indicated that the imaginative rules of statutory interpretation he was later to apply in respect of EC law in *Macarthys v Smith* should also apply to the Convention:

'[judges] – could and should take the Convention into account in interpreting a statute. An Act of Parliament should be construed so as to conform with the Convention'.[37]

It should be noted that Lord Denning does not require ambiguity in statutory provisions as a trigger for considering the ECtHR: his assumption seems rather to be that the Convention would always be a relevant factor. In the same case, Lord Denning also made the claim (which Hunt, with admirable understatement describes as

[32] (1906) 14 SLT 227 at 232. [33] [1966] 3 All ER 871 at 875, per Diplock LJ, CA.
[34] [1963] 2 QB 744; see p 631 above.
[35] [1973] AC 854, [1972] 2 All ER 1297, HL; see pp 632–633 above. [36] Op cit pp 135–136.
[37] (1975) 119 Sol Jo 322, CA.

'surprising')[38] that the ECtHR might be viewed as a higher form of law than statute: '[I]f an Act of Parliament did not conform to the Convention, I might be inclined to hold it invalid'.[39]

If acted upon, this would have been a quite 'revolutionary' proposition. It would entail the denial of parliamentary sovereignty, not by virtue as subsequently seems to have been the case in respect of EC law of an entrenching statute passed by Parliament itself,[40] but as result of a judicial assertion (triggered by successive government's continuing affirmation of the Convention treaties) of the supreme legal status of the moral values laid out in the ECtHR's text.

It thus came as no surprise that Lord Denning promptly stepped back from his position in *Birdi*. In *R v Secretary of State for the Home Department, ex p Bhajan Singh*,[41] Lord Denning dropped any suggestion that the Convention could be used to 'invalidate' legislation. He retained, however, his presumption that it could be used as an aid to statutory interpretation even if there was no apparent ambiguity in the relevant statutory text.[42]

For no obviously discernible reason however, the courts (led by Lord Denning) then discarded this more radical interpretive principle and reasserted the orthodox understanding of the use that might be made of international law. Thus, in *R v Chief Immigration Officer, Heathrow Airport, ex p Salamat Bibi*,[43] a case turning on the meaning of provisions of the Immigration Act 1971, Lord Denning made the following statement:

'The position, as I understand it, is that if there is any ambiguity in our statutes or uncertainty in our law, then these courts can look to the convention as an aid to clear up the ambiguity and uncertainty. But I would dispute altogether that the convention is part of our law. Treaties and declarations do not become part of our law until they are made law by Parliament'.[44]

The courts were still holding firmly to this proposition in the early 1990s. There was nothing 'special' about the ECtHR which required that its status in domestic law could be any different from any other unincorporated treaty. Thus, for example, in *R v Secretary of State for the Home Department, ex p Brind*, Lord Ackner observed that: 'It is well settled that the convention may be deployed for the purpose of the resolution of an ambiguity in English primary or subordinate legislation'.[45] In the

[38] Op cit at p134. [39] (1975) 119 Sol Jo 322, CA.

[40] See the discussion of *Factortame* at pp 480–483 above. [41] [1976] QB 198, CA.

[42] A similar presumption seemed to have been embraced at this time in respect of purely common law rules; see Hunt op cit pp 139–140.

[43] [1976] 3 All ER 843, CA.

[44] [1976] 3 All ER 843 at 847, CA. Cf also Geoffrey Lane LJ at 850: 'It is perfectly true that the convention was ratified by this country. Nevertheless the convention, not having been enacted by Parliament as an Act, does not have the effect of law in this country. Whatever persuasive force it may have in resolving ambiguities it certainly cannot have the effect of overriding the plain provisions of the 1971 Act and the rules made thereunder'.

[45] [1991] 1 AC 696, sub nom *Brind v Secretary of State for the Home Department* [1991] 1 All ER 720, HL. On the background to the case, see the initial discussion at pp 527–528 above.

absence of such an ambiguity however – and Lord Ackner felt that s 29 of the Broadcasting Act 1981 was unambiguous in bestowing an extremely wide discretion on the Home Secretary – the Convention was not a relevant factor for the court to consider.[46] Nor did Lord Ackner discern any merit in Mr Brind's suggestion that, as matter of domestic law, the court should at least insist that the Home Secretary considered whether or not the ban was consistent with Art 10. Lord Ackner suggested that accepting this argument: 'inevitably would result in incorporating the convention into English law by the back door'.[47] That contention is poorly founded. Requiring Ministers to pay attention to the Convention as part of the government's decision-making process does not in itself bind them to follow the ECtHR's judgments.

We will revisit the question of the Convention's changing status at common law at the beginning of chapter twenty. Before doing so however, we consider the judgments that the ECtHR eventually reached in respect of the controversial English 'human rights' cases discussed in the previous chapter in an attempt to form a preliminary conclusion on the question of how much difference the ECtHR actually makes to the substance of civil liberties and human rights protection in the UK's constitutional order.

III. THE IMPACT OF THE ECHR ON DOMESTIC LAW 1: PRIVACY

The United Kingdom's record before the Court has not been an entirely happy one, although it is overly simplistic to suggest that British law has been found wanting significantly more often than that of the Convention's other signatories.[48] Successive governments have generally responded to defeats before the ECtHR by introducing bills to amend domestic law,[49] although if one adds the time needed to pass legislation to the lengthy time period required to bring a claim before the ECtHR, it is clear that British citizens did not enjoy speedy access to the Convention's protection. Mr Malone, for example, found himself having to wait some five years before his challenge to Megarry VC's High Court judgment in his case was heard.

46 'Ambiguity' is of course itself an ambiguous concept. What might seem tolerably clear or even perfectly straightforward to one court might seem to be pervaded by doubt and uncertainty to another. This is a point returned to below.

47 [1991] 1 All ER 720, HL.

48 For a helpful analysis of the statistics see Bradley A (1991) 'The UK before the Strasbourg court', in Finnie W, Himsworth C and Walker N (eds) *Edinburgh essays in public law* (Edinburgh: Edinburgh University Press). For a listing of the cases involving the UK up until 1993 see *HCD*, 17 December 1993 c 964. See also Farran S (1996) *The UK before the European Court of Human Rights* (London: Blackstone Press).

49 See Bradley (1991) op cit.

SPEECH AND COMMUNICATION

In the course of his judgment in *Malone v Metropolitan Police Comr*, Megarry VC had paid a considerable amount of attention to the requirements of the ECtHR. He had in particular examined the ECtHR's decision in *Klass v Germany*[50] in some detail. *Klass* addressed the compatibility with Art 8 ECtHR of Germany's legislation authorising the interception of mail and the tapping of phone conversations. German law constrained such powers very tightly, and established an elaborate series of legal and political controls which had to be complied with before the powers could be used. In the light of these extensive controls, the ECtHR concluded that the German rules were both 'in accordance with the law' and 'necessary in a democratic society'.

Malone had been argued shortly after *Salamat Bibi* had been decided, and Megarry VC intimated that he was not certain to what extent this judgment had modified the principle expressed in *Birdi*. He thus concluded that: 'I take note of the Convention, as construed in the *Klass* case, and I shall give it due consideration in discussing English law on the point'.[51] That consideration led Megarry VC to suggest that the wholly unregulated nature of domestic law on telephone tapping was certainly in breach of Art 8:

> '[I]t is impossible to read the judgment in the *Klass* case without its becoming abundantly clear that a system which has no legal safeguards whatever has small chance of satisfying the requirements of [the ECtHR]'.[52]

This proved of no help to Mr Malone in the High Court however. Megarry VC observed that had he been faced with an ambiguity in domestic law, he would have resolved that ambiguity in accordance with the *Klass* formula. But here there was no ambiguity in the law; there simply was no law at all. The court was faced with a legal void. In such circumstances, Megarry VC suggested, the court would be compromising traditional understandings of the separation of powers if it granted Mr Malone a remedy:

> 'It seems to me that where Parliament has abstained from legislating on a point that is plainly suitable for legislation, it is indeed difficult for the court to lay down new rules of common law . . . that will carry out the Crown's treaty obligations, or to discover for the first time that such rules have always existed'.[53]

When Mr Malone's case finally reached the ECtHR,[54] the Court saw no difficulty in concluding that telephone conversations were within Art 8's concepts of 'private life' and 'correspondence'. Accepting also that the MPC's interference had been in pursuit of a legitimate Art 8(2) objective – namely the prevention of crime – the question which then arose was whether the Commissioner's interference with this right had been exercised 'according to law'. The meaning afforded to it in *Malone* was broadly in line with the test laid out in *The Sunday Times* case:

[50] (1978) 2 EHRR 214. [51] [1979] Ch 344 at 366. [52] Ibid, at 379.
[53] Ibid. [54] *Malone v United Kingdom* (1984) 7 EHRR 14.

'law must be sufficiently clear in this terms to give citizens an adequate indication as to the circumstances in which and the conditions on which public authorities are empowered to resort to this secret and potentially dangerous interference with the right to respect for private life . . .'.[55]

No such clarity could be found in British law. The Post Office Act 1969 s 80 required the Post Office to pass information to the police when requested to do so. However the Act itself did not specify the circumstances under which such a requirement arose. Furthermore, William Whitelaw (when Home Secretary) had explained to the Commons in 1980 that he considered such guidance as existed regarding use of s 80 unsuited to enactment.[56] These factors led the Court to conclude that the tapping power had not been exercised 'according to law'. The Court answered the question before it in terms evocative of Diceyan principle: 'it would be contrary to the rule of law for the legal discretion granted to the executive to be expressed in terms of an unfettered power'.[57]

On this occasion, the government appeared willing to amend domestic law accordingly. The Interception of Communications Act 1985 (ICA 1985) introduced a statutory framework to regulate phone tapping. Unauthorised tapping has been made a criminal offence, although the Act grants government bodies extensive discretion to authorise taps in a wide range of circumstances.[58]

SADO-MASOCHISTIC SEXUAL BEHAVIOUR

The 3–2 basis of the House of Lords' decision in *R v Brown* indicated that the criminal nature of sado-masochistic sexual behaviour was a precarious concept in domestic law. Brown subsequently came before the ECtHR as *Laskey, Jaggard and Brown v United Kingdom*.[59] Unlike the House of Lords, the Court was unanimous in its judgment: Brown's prosecution and conviction did not breach Art 8. The ECtHR observed (obiter) that it rather doubted that there had been any interference with private life at all in this case, on the rather curious basis that the group nature of Brown's activities implied that they could not be regarded as private.[60] Nonetheless, accepting that there had been such interference, it was also accepted by all parties that the interference was undertaken in pursuit of a legitimate objective (the protection of health or morals) and was imposed according to law. The court confined its observations to the

55 Ibid, at para 67.

56 The ECtHR it seems did not feel compelled to respect restrictive interpretations of parliamentary privilege or Article 9 of the Bill of Rights concerning the justiciability of proceedings in either house. This case was of course decided before *Pepper v Hart*: see pp 284–287 above.

57 (1984) 7 EHRR 14 at para 68.

58 See Ewing and Gearty op cit pp 66–81: Leigh I (1986) 'A tapper's charter' *Public Law* 8–18.

59 (1997) 24 EHRR 39.

60 Ibid, at para 36. Cf the concurring judgment of Judge Pettiti: 'in my view . . . [Article 8] was not even applicable in the instant case. The concept of private life cannot be stretched indefinitely. . . . The protection of private life means the protection of a person's intimacy and dignity, not the protection of his baseness or the promotion of criminal immoralism': ibid at 61.

protection of health, and offered no clear indication of the breadth of the margin of appreciation that the UK would have been granted if its objective had been limited solely to protecting morals.[61] The breadth accorded on health grounds, however, was sufficient for the Court to conclude that Brown's conviction had been 'necessary in a democratic society'. Rejecting any assertion that the prosecution or conviction had been prompted by the fact that the defendants had been engaging in homosexual rather than heterosexual practices, the Court noted both that the 'extreme' activities undertaken had caused serious injuries in practice and had the potential to cause even more serious damage. It thus endorsed the Commission's view that: 'The state authorities therefore acted within their margin of appreciation in order to protect its citizens from real risk of serious physical harm or injury'.[62]

IV. THE IMPACT OF THE ECHR ON DOMESTIC LAW 2: FREEDOM OF EXPRESSION

The contrasting outcomes (from the government's perspective) of *Malone* and *Brown/Laskey* indicate the varying impact that the Convention would be likely to have on domestic treatment of civil liberties issues. The following section continues to explore that question by focusing on a series of Commission and Court judgments in the area of freedom of expression.

OFFICIAL SECRECY

That the ICA 1985 affords the government wide discretion is itself a powerful reminder that compliance with the Convention does not impose detailed or uniform standards on its signatory states. That point is reinforced when one considers the reasoning and conclusions of the ECtHR when the *Spycatcher* litigation eventually came before it.

The litigation concerned both the temporary and continuing injunctions granted against *The Guardian* and *The Observer* in *Spycatcher (No 1)* by Millet J and the House of Lords respectively. The ECtHR's judgment in *Observer and Guardian v United Kingdom*[63] began by articulating two general principles which might initially seem redolent of the ethos which has informed the US Supreme Court's interpretation of the First Amendment:

'(a) Freedom of expression constitutes one of the essential foundations of a democratic society; subject to para (2) of Art 10, it is applicable not only to "information" or "ideas" that are favourably received or regarded as inoffensive or as a matter of indifference, but also

[61] Cf para 42: 'The scope of this margin of appreciation is not identical in each case but will vary according to the context. Relevant factors include the nature of the Convention right in issue, its importance for the individual and the nature of the activities concerned'.

[62] Ibid, at para 41.

[63] (1991) 14 EHRR 153.

to those that offend, shock or disturb. Freedom of expression, as enshrined in Art 10, is subject to a number of exceptions which must be narrowly interpreted and the necessity for any restrictions must be convincingly established.

(b) These principles are of particular importance as far as the press is concerned. While it must not overstep the bounds set, inter alia, "in the interests of national security".... it is nevertheless incumbent upon it to impart information and ideas on matters of public interest. Not only does the press have the task of imparting such information: the public also has a right to receive them. Were it otherwise, the press would be unable to play its vital role of public watchdog'.[64]

On a closer reading, this statement seems to attach very great significance to the Art 10(2) exceptions, a significance only partly reduced by the subsequent assertion that the scope for legitimate interference with freedom of expression should be narrowly constrained. It is clear that the Court's application of these principles in *Spycatcher* did not amount to an expansive protection of freedom of expression. Despite the intensely political content of the information contained in Wright's book, the Court concluded that the initial injunction did not contravene Art 10: it was entirely reasonable for Millet J to have assumed that the book may have contained information that jeopardised national security; in such circumstances, pending a full trial, a temporary restraint could be regarded as 'necessary in a democratic society'. However, the Court also held that the House of Lords' continuation of the injunction did breach Art 10. Since the book had by then been published in the USA, its contents were common knowledge; the ban on media discussion therefore served no useful purpose.

For advocates of an expansive notion of 'informed consent', the ECtHR's judgment is rather unsatisfactory, in that it seemed to hinge (as did the House of Lords' decision in *Spycatcher (No 2)*, on the fact that the book had been published in the USA. As Ian Leigh has suggested,[65] one might therefore wonder if the Convention per se would have permitted the newspapers to discuss *Spycatcher* if not for the more extensive protection of free expression afforded to the book in America under the First Amendment.

POLITICAL LIBELS

There would however appear to be a divergence between domestic law and the requirements of the Convention in respect of libel actions initiated by politicians. By the early 1990s, the ECtHR had yet to be faced with a civil law libel action initiated either by a politician or a government body. It had however delivered several judgments declaring convictions for criminal libel against journalists disseminating political information to be in breach of Art 10.

The Court's decision in *Lingens v Austria*[66] seemed to rest on an organising principle concerned with the *effect* rather than the *form* of restraints on freedom of

[64] Ibid, at para 59.
[65] Leigh I (1992) 'Spycatcher in Strasbourg' *Public Law* 200–208.
[66] (1986) 8 EHHR 407.

expression. The *Lingens* litigation arose following Lingens' publication of two articles in a political magazine which suggested that Austria's then Chancellor, Kreisky, had shielded the leader of a minor political party from investigations into that person's alleged role in Nazi atrocities in order to secure the smaller party's participation in a coalition government. Kreisky issued private criminal proceedings against Lingens under Article 111 of the Austrian Criminal Code. This provided that the publisher of material which accuses any person of 'possessing a contemptible character or attitude or of behaviour contrary to honour or morality and of such a nature . . . to lower him in public esteem' could be fined or imprisoned for up to a year. The disseminator had a defence if he proved truth, or that he had a reasonable belief that the material was true. Lingens was convicted by the Austrian courts.

The ECtHR began its judgment with a broad evaluation of the functions to be performed by Art 10. In the Court's view, the Convention recognised freedom of speech as 'one of the essential foundations of a democratic society and one of the basic conditions for its progress and for each individual's self-fulfilment'.[67] Freedom of speech on political questions enjoyed an elevated status: 'freedom of political debate is at the very core of the concept of a democratic society which prevails throughout the Convention'.[68]

That the Austrian law in issue did not impose a restraint on political debate by preventing publication of the article at all was regarded as irrelevant by the ECtHR. Fines or gaol sentences imposed after publication could still deter journalists from voicing useful political information and opinions in future, thereby depriving the public of access to political discussion and undermining the press' role as a watchdog on governmental behaviour.

The ECtHR held that the 'core' status of political speech had significant implications for the extent to which states could restrict its dissemination in order to protect the reputation of individuals. Politicians did not forfeit all entitlement to have their reputations protected by defamation laws, but nor could they expect to be treated as 'private citizens'. In respect of attacks on a politician's political beliefs and behaviour: 'the requirements of such protection have to be weighed in relation to the interests of the open discussion of political issues'.[69] In the Court's view, that weighing demanded that: 'The limits of acceptable criticism are accordingly wider as regards a politician as such than as regards a private individual'.[70] The unavoidable inference to be drawn from this conclusion is that the obstacles presented by domestic libel law to a politician plaintiff in respect of stories concerning her political beliefs or behaviour must be appreciably more onerous than those facing a private plaintiff suing over a non-political story.

This point seemed however to elude the Court of Appeal, which invoked *Lingens* as a persuasive authority in *Derbyshire County Council v Times Newspapers Ltd*, a case triggered by a *Sunday Times*' story alleging that Derbyshire had been improperly using its pension funds. When sued for libel by the council, the *Sunday Times* argued

[67] Ibid, at para 41. [68] Ibid, at para 42. [69] Ibid, at para 42. [70] Ibid.

that local authorities lacked the legal capacity to bring a libel action over criticism of their 'governing reputations'. This contention was initially rejected by Morland J, who followed the lead given some 20 years earlier by Browne J in *Bognor Regis UDC v Campion.*[71] A unanimous Court of Appeal reversed Morland J's decision.[72] All three judges (Balcombe, Ralph Gibson, and Butler Sloss LJJ) thought that the common law position on this question was ambiguous. Consequently, the Court felt that it was appropriate to examine the provisions of the Convention to assist it in finding the 'correct' solution to the problem before it. Indeed, both Balcombe LJ and Butler Sloss LJ, while observing that the Convention was not formally part of domestic law, went so far as to say they considered it appropriate to 'apply' the case law of the ECtHR in this instance. On examining the ECtHR's case law, the Court of Appeal concluded that allowing a local council to launch a libel action was an 'unnecessary' restriction on free expression.

This conclusion was reached in large part because the court considered that the council could deploy other legal remedies to defend its reputation. It would be possible, for example, for the council to initiate a criminal prosecution for libel. It might also begin an action in malicious falsehood. This tort is less helpful to plaintiffs than libel, as they must prove the falsity of the material published and that the publisher was motivated by 'malice' in disseminating it. Thirdly, the council's reputation could be indirectly protected through a libel action begun by a councillor or officer libelled in the relevant story, who could evidently proceed on the same basis as a private individual.

The Court of Appeal had apparently misunderstood the implications of Art 10 by failing to draw a distinction between elected politicians and private individuals for libel law purposes. Its failure to do so was technically obiter rather than part of the ratio of the judgment, but the substance of the point was perfectly clear. The presumption that the court had misconstrued Art 10 was strengthened by the ECtHR's decision in *Castells v Spain*, delivered shortly after the Court of Appeal's judgment in *Derbyshire.*

The applicant in *Castells v Spain*[73] was a member of the Spanish Senate. He had published articles in a Basque newspaper which accused 'the government' of complicity in violence against the Basque people. He was convicted under Art 162 of Spain's criminal code, which made it a crime to 'insult, falsely accuse or threaten the government'. Art 162 did not permit a defence of truth.

The Court accepted that the government had brought this action not to protect any person's reputation, but to preserve public order – the Basque area was in considerable turmoil when the articles were published in 1979. The restraints 'necessary' to achieve this objective were more severe than those justified by the protection of reputation: criminal law sanctions could be imposed against untruths or accusations 'formulated in bad faith'. However, if such sanctions were to comply with Art 10, the defendant had to have the chance (denied to Castells) to prove the truth of his claims and his good faith.

71 See pp 655–656 above.

72 [1992] QB 770, [1992] 3 All ER 65, CA.

73 (1992) 14 EHRR 445.

Like *Lingens, Castells* has no direct bearing on civil defamation law. But the conceptual framework surrounding the Court's narrow holding was broadly framed. Thus the Court observed that:

'[T]he pre-eminent role of the press in a State governed by the rule of law must not be forgotten . . . [F]reedom of the press affords the public one of the best means of discovering and forming an opinion on the ideas and attitudes of their political leaders'.[74]

Building from this political presumption, the Court suggested that domestic legal systems had to recognise a tri-partite division within their defamation laws. The Court observed that 'the limits of political criticism are wider with regard to government than in relation to a private citizen, or even a politician'.[75] This clearly implies that the 'government' qua corporate body must endure more criticism than a 'politician', who in turn must endure more than a private citizen. The Court of Appeal in *Derbyshire* correctly predicted the first part of the *Castells* formula, but seemed to neglect the second.

As will be suggested in chapter twenty, the common law has subsequently been amended in a manner which would seem to satisfy Art 10. For the present, however, we return to litigation in which the ECtHR held that English law on freedom of expression fell far short of the Convention's requirements.

CONTEMPT OF COURT

The ECtHR's judgment in *Sunday Times v United Kingdom*[76] case was eventually delivered in April 1979, almost six years after the House of Lords had upheld the injunction forbidding publication of the paper's article on the thalidomide controversy.[77] The EComHR had concluded – albeit not unanimously – that the injunction had breached Art 10. The Court subsequently reached the same conclusion. There could be no doubt that the injunction had amounted to an interference with freedom of expression. The ECtHR also accepted without difficulty that the purposes served by the contempt jurisdiction were intended to promote one of the legitimate objectives identified in Art 10(2) to justify such interference – namely to protect 'the authority and impartiality of the judiciary'.[78] The Court further accepted that the interference with free expression imposed by contempt of court met the 'prescribed by law' criterion of Article 10(2). As noted above, the Court's formulation of that principle in this case now serves as the standard point of reference for its meaning. The outcome of the case turned on whether the grant of the injunction had been 'necessary in a democratic society'.

74 At para 43. 75 Ibid, para 46. 76 (1979) 2 EHRR 245.

77 See pp 650–652 above. The House of Lords had issued judgment on 25 July 1973.

78 On this point, the ECtHR concluded that it was not relevant to ask if the litigation was dormant: 'preventing interference with negotiations towards the settlement of a pending suit is no less legitimate an aim under Article 10(2) than preventing interference with a procedural situation in the strictly forensic sense' (1979) 2 EHRR 245 at para 64.

In addressing this issue, the Court stressed that the nature of its jurisdiction in respect of Art 10 would vary according to which of the legitimate objectives identified in Art 10(2) was in issue. The approach to the margin of appreciation doctrine laid out in *Handyside* (ie that 'State authorities are in principle in a better position than the international judge to give an opinion on the exact content of these requirements') – was not appropriate in this case. The governmental interference with free expression under consideration in *Handyside* – a case involving obscenity – was pursued 'for the protection of morals'. 'Moral' principles might legitimately vary very substantially among the signatory states. The ECtHR's jurisdiction in such matters would be of a loosely supervisory kind. However, the Court reasoned that:

'[T]he same cannot be said of the far more objective notion of the "authority" of the judiciary. The domestic law and practice of the Contracting States reveal a fairly substantial measure of common ground in this area. . . . Accordingly, here a more extensive European supervision corresponds to a less discretionary power of appreciation'.[79]

To frame the matter rather differently, one might suggest that evaluating interferences with judicial authority was a far more 'justiciable' task than gauging moral standards.[80] In consequence, the Court could legitimately exercise a jurisdiction which came very close to being appellate rather than just supervisory in character. The ECtHR thus went on to make its own evaluation of the facts at issue in the litigation. The Court laid particular stress on what it regarded as the even-handed substance of the censored article, and doubted that so balanced a piece could in any meaningful sense prejudge the result of any trial.[81] Perhaps more broadly, the Court observed that stories addressing important matters of public controversy 'did not cease to be a matter of public interest merely because they formed the background to pending litigation'.[82] Indeed, it was suggested that publication of *The Sunday Times* article could actually enhance rather than prejudice the conduct of any subsequent trial: 'By bringing to light certain facts, the article might have served as a brake on speculative and unenlightened discussion'.[83]

It is tempting to assume that the ECtHR reached a different conclusion from the House of Lords largely because the two courts adopted different analytical starting points. In the House of Lords, preserving the impartial administration of justice was the initial consideration. In the ECtHR, that value was assigned only secondary status, as a potential justification for an interference with the dominant value of freedom of

[79] Ibid, at para 59.

[80] It might be suggested that this raises a 'political' question – not in the *GCHQ* sense of being non-justiciable – but in the sense which the ECtHR later emphasised in *Lingens* and *Castells* that freedom of expression on political/governmental issues (which would include judicial law-making) lies at the 'core' of Art 10, and thus any interference with it must be subject to exacting standards of review.

[81] 'The proposed *Sunday Times* article was couched in moderate terms and did not present just one side of the evidence or claim that there was only one result at which a court could arrive': (1979) 2 EHR 245 at para 63.

[82] Ibid, at para 66. [83] Ibid.

expression.[84] It should however be noted that the Court's judgment was an 11–9 majority verdict. This rather precludes the conclusion that the English law of contempt was 'clearly' incompatible with Article 10, and also emphasises the point that there is a certain contingency about the substance of the ECtHR's jurisprudence. It would seem quite plausible to expect that the same issue could be decided quite differently within a few years simply as result of a change of personnel on the Strasbourg bench.

The judgment was accorded a mixed reception from British commentators. In a splendidly melodramatic critique, Mann condemned the majority's reasoning as 'diffuse and imprecise',[85] and castigated the decision as: '[T]he gravest blow to the fabric of English law that has ever occurred'.[86] In Mann's view, the judgment evidently posed an immediate threat to the integrity of the British legal system. One might note that Mann's critique afforded no explicit significance to the public's interest in reaching informed conclusions about the thalidomide saga, and offered the extraordinary suggestion that the House of Lords decision was perfectly consistent with the First Amendment.[87] Other commentators offered a more measured response.[88]

The Contempt of Court Act 1981

Notwithstanding the potential ephemerality of the ECtHR's judgment – and the criticism it had attracted – the first Thatcher government moved promptly to bring domestic law into line with the ruling by promoting a Contempt of Court Bill in the Commons, which was enacted in 1981. The Bill was not wholly a response to the ECtHR's judgment; it was also intended to implement some of the recommendations of a *Report on contempt of court*, chaired by Phillimore LJ, which had conducted a general review of the contempt jurisdiction.[89]

Section 2(2) of the Act addressed *The Sunday Times* judgment. It provided that contempt in respect of pressurising litigants or prejudging issues would only arise if a particular story created 'a substantial risk that the course of justice in the proceedings in question will be seriously impeded or prejudiced'. The Act also made it clear (in

84 For a very detailed critique of the judgment see Duffy P (1980) 'The Sunday Times case: freedom of expression, contempt of court and the European Convention on Human rights' *Human Rights Review* 17–53.

85 Mann F (1979) 'Contempt of Court in the House of Lords and the European Court of Human Rights' *LQR* 348–354.

86 Ibid, at p 349.

87 For a rather more sensible (and expert) view on that point see Nathanson N (1979/1980) 'The Sunday Times case: freedom of the press and contempt of court under English law and the European Convention on Human Rights' *Kentucky Law Journal* 972–1025; noting at p 972: 'the gulf between constitutional law of freedom of the press and the British common law on the same subject'.

88 Cf Gray C (1979) 'European Convention on Human Rights – freedom of expression and the thalidomide case' *Cambridge LJ* 242–245 at p 245: 'Perhaps this case will remind English courts of the potentially embarrassing consequences of ignoring the existence of the ECHR and encourage in them a more constructive approach to its application'.

89 (1974, Cmnd 5794) (London: HMSO). Phillimore LJ had sat in the Court of Appeal in *A-G v Times Newspapers*. For contemporaneous critiques of the Act see Lowe N (1981) 'Contempt of Court Act' *Public Law* 20–28: Boyle A (1981) 'The Contempt of Court Act 1981' *Human Rights Review* 148–150: Bailey S (1982) 'The Contempt of Court Act 1981' *MLR* 301–316.

schedule 1) that in a civil action 'proceedings' were only occurring if a date had been set down for trial; if no date was set, proceedings would be 'dormant' and so no possibility of contempt could arise. A contemporary commentator suggested that s 2 did enhance press freedom in respect of issues such as the thalidomide controversy: '[T]he fact that the matter under discussion is one of legitimate public interest and concern and that the issues are addressed in a fair and balanced way will now weigh more strongly in favour of allowing publication, where previously these factors would have been discounted'.[90] Others were more sceptical. Lowe commented that, notwithstanding s 2(2): 'The Act nevertheless maintains the basic stance of the ultimate supremacy of the administration of justice over free speech, although it does attempt to shift the balance a little further in favour of the latter'.[91] Lowe doubted that s 2(2) actually met the ECtHR's requirements. Given that the margin of appreciation doctrine – even when narrowly construed – grants states some appreciable discretion, that claim was perhaps overstated. But as we shall see below, the Act – or at least its interpretation by the House of Lords – was subsequently to prove an inadequate response to the ECtHR's interpretation of the Convention.

BLASPHEMY

Observers who assumed that Article 10 might protect freedom of expression to an extent closely comparable to that provided by the First Amendment in the USA would also have been dismayed by the outcome of the *Lemon v United Kingdom* litigation. Lemon's challenge to the House of Lords' judgment did not even reach the ECtHR: the Commission dismissed it as manifestly 'ill-founded'.[92]

Lemon v United Kingdom

The Commission recognised that Lemon's conviction interfered with the entitlement to freedom of expression, but it found little merit in the rest of his contentions. The EComHR considered that blasphemy laws did pursue a legitimate Art 10(2) objective, namely the 'protection of the rights of others':

> 'The Commission considers that the offence of blasphemous libel as it is construed under the applicable common law in fact has the main purpose to protect the right of citizens not to be offended in their religious feelings by publications'.[93]

This is an extremely expansive proposition, which simply endorses without question the common law presumption that Christians in the UK – unlike adherents to other religious faiths or atheists – need not endure scathing criticism of their beliefs, even if that criticism is published in a forum which it is unlikely that any of them will ever encounter in their day to day lives. This constitutes a markedly illiberal approach to the question of freedom of expression.

[90] Boyle (1981) op cit p 148.
[91] Lowe op cit p 28.
[92] (1982) 5 EHRR 123.
[93] Ibid, at para 11.

Lemon's argument under Article 10 rested in part on the contention that the crime of blasphemy was too imprecisely defined to be 'prescribed by law'. The Commission rejected this argument. While the fact that the House of Lords' judgment had been divided 3–2 indicated that the law was somewhat uncertain, the Commission concluded that the majority judgment: 'did not go beyond the limits of a reasonable interpretation of the existing law' – the decision was: 'reasonably foreseeable with the assistance of appropriate legal advice'.[94] That would seem a largely uncontentious conclusion. Much more problematic, in contrast, was the Commission's conclusion on the final stage of its inquiry – was the law of blasphemy 'necessary in a democratic society'?

The EComHR's views on this point were evidently determined by its earlier conclusion that the law pursued a legitimate objective:

'If it is accepted that the religious feelings of the citizen may deserve protection against indecent attacks on the matters held sacred by him, then it can also be considered as necessary in a democratic society to stipulate that such attacks, if they attain a certain level of severity, shall constitute a criminal offence at the request of the offended person'.[95]

There is little independent logical force to the Commission's argument on this point. It seemed to rest wholly on the twin propositions that because Mary Whitehouse was so offended by the poem, and because the judges considered the poem blasphemous, the law was necessary. That Whitehouse may have been unduly sensitive, or ideologically intolerant, or a religious zealot, were not matters that the Commission addressed. Nor did it entertain the point that the absence of blasphemy prosecutions in the 50 years prior to *Lemon* indicated that the law was obsolescent. In effect, the Commission was extending an extremely wide margin of appreciation to the UK on this point, with the result that its own jurisdiction was clearly perceived as supervisory in the most relaxed (perhaps comatose) of forms, and could in no sense be seen as involving quasi-appellate functions.

It might readily be thought that the legitimate objective which the Commission upheld in *Lemon* – namely that Christian sensibilities should not be offended – is very difficult to reconcile with the principle subsequently outlined by the ECtHR in *Spycatcher*; namely that freedom of expression extends 'not only to "information" or "ideas" that are favourably received or regarded as inoffensive or as a matter of indifference, but also to those that offend, shock or disturb'.[96] The reasoning deployed in *Lemon* would suggest that the Art 10(1) entitlement to publish and receive information and ideas which 'offend' others is trumped by those others' Art 10(2) entitlement not to be offended. One cannot of course – unless one adheres to a ludicrously formalistic notion of law – publish 'offensive' material if nobody is offended by it.

A further point that was not specifically addressed by the Commission in *Lemon*

[94] Ibid, at para 10. [95] Ibid, at para 12.

[96] *Observer and Guardian v United Kingdom* (1991) 14 EHRR 153 at para 59.

was whether blasphemy should be seen as 'political/public interest' speech in the sense to which the ECtHR subsequently alluded in *Lingens*. The irresistible inference to be drawn from this omission is that the Commission did not consider that blasphemy raised political questions at all, but simply moral ones. Quite how one draws the line between 'political' and 'moral' is unclear, but one might have thought the divide was particularly obscure in the British context, given the privileged legal status enjoyed by the Church of England.[97]

Otto-Preminger Institute v Austria and Wingrove v United Kingdom

Some 12 years later, in *Otto-Preminger Institute v Austria*,[98] the ECtHR confirmed both that religious speech was not 'political' speech in the *Lingens* sense, and that the entitlements of citizens who wished to publish or consume religiously offensive material could indeed be subordinated to the interest of adherents to the particular religion not being offended.

The applicant was an arts organisation located in Innsbruck, Austria. The Institute had arranged to exhibit a movie, *Das Liebeskonzil*, which presented a forceful attack on the Catholic church. A very substantial majority of citizens in the Institute's area were practising Catholics, and the state authorities took the view that showing the movie would both cause grave offence to such people and raise the possibility of public order offences. The film was therefore banned under Austria's blasphemy laws, and the Institute's copy of it was seized and destroyed.

The ECtHR found no breach of Art 10 on these facts. At the core of its judgment lay the proposition that Art 10's protection would not extend to expression that did 'not contribute to any form of public debate capable of furthering progress in human affairs'.[99] *Das Liebeskonzil* evidently fell into this pariah category of expression, and could thus be banned entirely. The Court drew a distinction between offensive attacks on political issues (presumptively of some value) and those addressing religious questions (presumptively worthless):

> 'Whereas there is little scope for restrictions on political speech or on debate of questions of public interest . . . a wider margin of appreciation is generally available to the Contracting States when regulating freedom of expression in relation to matters liable to offend intimate personal convictions within the field of morals or, especially, religion'.[100]

The Court's insistence on 'depoliticising' religious belief seems rather myopic in this situation, given that such beliefs are likely to exercise a considerable influence on political issues. It is a formalistic rather than functionally-based differentiation. The judgment has been subjected to a compelling critique by Warbrick, who suggest that it

[97] For a happily unsuccessful attempt to extend the intolerance of the blasphemy laws to non-Christian religions in the wake of the publication of Salman Rushdie's satirical novel, *The Satanic Verses*, see Modood T (1990) 'British Asian muslims and the Rushdie affair' *Political Quarterly* 143–160: *R v Chief Metropolitan Stipendiary Magistrate, ex p Choudhury* [1991] 1 QB 429, [1991] 1 All ER 306; *Choudhury v United Kingdom* (1991) 12 *Human Rights LJ* 74.

[98] (1994) 19 EHRR 34. [99] Ibid, para 49. [100] Ibid, at para 58.

'makes an unfortunate collapse of the nature of the expression in issue and the justification for interfering with it'.[101] In particular, Warbrick observes that the court has been less than astute in appreciating the 'political' or 'public interest' dimension of ideological attacks on the supposed sanctity of (some) religious sentiment.

The Court's decision was by a 6–3 majority. The three dissentients took particular issue with the majority's suggestion that some ideas were per se incapable 'of furthering progress in human affairs'. To allow a state to impose that opinion: 'could be detrimental to that tolerance on which pluralist democracy depends'.[102] The ratio of the dissent was however rather timid, resting primarily on the fact that the Institute had taken steps to ensure that the film was not seen by young people or those with strongly held Catholic beliefs.

The Court endorsed its decision in *Otto-Preminger* in its 1996 judgment in *Wingrove v United Kingdom*.[103] Wingrove was a movie director, who had made a short video entitled *Visions of Ecstacy*. The film was either – depending upon your moral sensibilities – a bravely satirical attempt to challenge the misogyny of the Catholic church or a piece of soft pornography. Its main image was of a young woman having sex with Jesus Christ during his crucifixion, interspersed with scenes in which the same woman was undressed and caressed by another female character. Mr Wingrove was not subjected to a prosecution for blasphemy, but the government body responsible for licensing videos for sale (the Video Appeals Committee) refused to grant a certificate for *Visions of Ecstacy*, on the grounds that it was blasphemous. The Committee relied on *R v Lemon* as its guide to the law on this issue.

By a 10–2 majority, the EComHR held that Mr Wingrove's challenge to the VAC's refusal was admissible. The Commission concluded that the complete ban on sale of the movie was not 'necessary in a democratic society'. Its primary reason for reaching this decision was that the video could have been licensed for sale solely in specialised outlets, selling only 'adult' films. In such circumstances, the film was unlikely to be seen by children or members of the public generally. This would evidently distinguish the case from *Lemon*, since *Gay News* was on sale in all kinds of non-specialist outlets.

Only two members of the Court supported the Commission's conclusion. The majority, having stressed that states retained a substantial margin of appreciation in such cases, felt there was nothing 'arbitrary or excessive' about the VAC's refusal to licence the film. It was unimpressed by the EComHR's suggested that the video could have been restricted for sale in specialist shops, noting that the film could subsequently have been resold into general circulation.

Lemon, Otto-Preminger and *Wingrove* offer a line of authority which graphically illustrates the limits of the Convention as a guarantor of effective human rights protection.[104] The cases make a nonsense of the evidently robust principle articulated by the Court in *Spycatcher*. The jurisprudential sentiment they embody is best

[101] (1998) op cit p 189. [102] (1994) 19 EHRR 34 at 61. [103] (1996) 24 EHRR 1.

[104] See Warbrick (1998) op cit: Ghandi S and James J (1998) 'The English law of blasphemy and the European Convention on Human Rights' *European Human Rights LR* 430–451.

expressed by the following passage from *Wingrove*, in which the Court outlined the principle that would inform its reasoning on whether the UK's blasphemy laws were 'necessary in a democratic society':

'The Court recalls that freedom of expression constitutes one of the essential foundations of a democratic society. As para 2 of Art 10 expressly recognises, however, the exercise of that freedom carries with it duties and responsibilities. Amongst them, in the context of religious beliefs, may legitimately be included a duty to avoid as far as possible an expression that is, in regard to objects of veneration, gratuitously offensive to others and profanatory'.[105]

The poverty of the ECtHR's ambition in this respect, and the consequent feebleness of its jurisprudence, provide perhaps the most compelling of rebuttals to any of those opponents of incorporating the Convention into UK law whose case rested on the argument that the ECtHR would impose alien cultural values on our domestic law.

CONCLUSION

Despite the UK's evidently mixed record before the ECtHR on freedom of expression issues, it was not uncommon in the early 1990s to encounter judicial pronouncements that the common law and the Convention bestowed identical levels of civil liberties protection on British citizens. A typical example is Lord Goff's comment in *A-G v Guardian Newspapers Ltd (Spycatcher) (No 2)*:

'I can see no inconsistency between English law on this subject and art 10. . . . This is scarcely surprising, since we pride ourselves on the fact that freedom of speech has existed in this country perhaps as long as, if not longer than, it has existed in any other country in the world'.[106]

Such protestations would seem poorly based. *Spycatcher* was decided in the same way both in the House of Lords and the ECtHR, as was *Wingrove*, but there is little doubt that the Court of Appeal's judgment in *Derbyshire* was irreconcilable with *Lingens*. This spasmodic rather than pervasive consistency between domestic law and Art 10 is reinforced if one contrasts *Brind* with the *Morgan Grampian/Goodwin* litigation.

Mr Brind's efforts to raise his case before the ECtHR did not even win the approval of the Commission. In July 1994, the Commission concluded that Brind's application was ill-founded. Even if – and the Commission seemed to have doubts on this point – the government's policy amounted to an interference with freedom of expression, that interference was undoubtedly in pursuit of a legitimate objective, it was prescribed by law, and it was necessary in a democratic society. That the policy was just plain silly did not seem to found an Art 10 claim.[107] This conclusion was perhaps surprising, but

105 Ibid, at para 52.

106 [1990] 1 AC 109 at 283, HL.

107 For a critical comment see Pannick D 'No logic behind gagging terrorists' empty rhetoric' *The Times*, 2 August 1994.

it did perform the useful function of suggesting that advocates of incorporating the Convention overestimated its capacity to forbid government behaviour which impinged upon freedom of expression, while opponents of incorporation had a similarly exaggerated view of the extent to which it would impinge upon the sovereignty of Parliament and the autonomy of the government.

The *Goodwin* case, in contrast, revealed a substantial (if not obviously predictable) divergence between UK law and Art 10.[108] Mr Goodwin was a journalist, working for *The Engineer*, a specialist trade magazine. Goodwin was provided with some sensitive financial information about a firm Tetra (the 'X' in the case name) by a source who must have been either a disloyal Tetra employee or a thief who had stolen the information. Goodwin then wrote an article about the firm, drawing on the leaked information. Before *The Engineer* published any story, Tetra successfully applied to the High Court for an injunction preventing publication. Tetra also sought a court order requiring the publishers and Mr Goodwin to identify their source.

Prior to 1981, the question of whether a court could order a journalist to reveal her sources had been a matter of common law. The courts accepted that competing interests might be at stake in such circumstances. An order to disclose could have a 'chilling effect' – much like the threat of a libel action – on press freedom, insofar as sources might not come forward in future and so potentially valuable stories might not be written. That interest would of course be particularly strong in respect of leaked information revealing criminal behaviour, or unethical or incompetent activities by government bodies. On the other hand, allowing the press to keep their sources secret could mean that a firm like X would have to continue to operate knowing that it may be employing a disloyal employee, and that none of its operations (which may be wholly legal and ethical) could be kept secret from commercial rivals.

In *British Steel Corpn v Granada Television Ltd*, decided in 1980,[109] the House of Lords ordered Granada to identify the source who had provided it with 250 confidential BSC documents. BSC, then a state-owned industry, was in the throes of major industrial action by its workers. It had for many years been making vast operating losses. The leaked documents charted major incompetence within the firm, and revealed that the Thatcher government – contrary to its public protestations – was taking covert steps to assist BSC to break the strike. Granada argued that the documents concerned a matter of acute public interest, and that an order to disclose its source would have the effect of deterring comparable leaks in future, with the result that the public would be denied access to important political information.

The High Court, Court of Appeal and four members of the House of Lords rejected this argument.[110] In a manner that foreshadowed the Court of Appeal's decision in *Blackshaw v Lord* a few years later,[111] the majority in the House of Lords failed to

[108] *X Ltd v Morgan-Grampian (Publishers) Ltd* [1991] 1 AC 1, [1990] 2 All ER 1, HL.

[109] [1981] 1 All ER 417.

[110] The cases are reported together at [1981] 1 All ER 417.

[111] See p 656 above.

see any 'political' or 'constitutional' issue at stake in the case. As Lord Wilberforce put it: 'this case does not touch on freedom of the press even at its periphery'.[112] His sentiment was echoed by Lord Russell: 'this case has not even marginal connection with any concept of "the freedom of the press" '.[113]

The principle on which the majority decided the case was framed in the following way; newspapers, television stations and journalists 'have no immunity based on public interest which protects them from the obligation to disclose in a court of law their sources of information, when such disclosure is necessary in the interest of justice'.[114] While such a public interest might arise in respect of information exposing criminality or wrongdoing, no such activities were in issue here. All that was at stake was the continued confidentiality of commercially sensitive information. The 'interest of justice' – namely that BSC not be subjected to breaches of confidentiality or thefts – therefore demanded that the source be revealed.

Lord Salmon issued a powerful and wholly convincing dissent. He started from the premise that this case was primarily about the freedom of the press, and especially about the public's interest in knowing about huge mismanagement of public funds by a state-owned industry. BSC was as much a governmental body as a commercial enterprise. He thus had no difficulty in concluding that Granada need not disclose its source:

> 'The freedom of the press depends on this immunity. Were it to disappear, so would the sources from which [press] information is obtained; and the public would be deprived of much of the information to which the public of a free nation is entitled'.[115]

Section 10 of the Contempt of Court Act 1981 ostensibly attempted to strengthen press protection in such circumstances by replacing the common law rule with a new statutory formula. The presumption would be against disclosure unless disclosure was 'necessary in the interests of justice or national security or for the prevention of disorder or crime'. Whether s 10 actually modified the *BSC* decision is debatable;[116] much would obviously depend on the way the new provision was interpreted. As noted in the previous discussion of the *Tisdall* case, s 10 was not being lent an expansive definition in the mid-1980s.[117]

The *X v Morgan Grampian* case seemed to lack the 'political' or 'constitutional' overtones of either *BSC* or the *Tisdall* episode. In contrast to its decision in *BSC*, the House of Lords clearly recognised that the case did raise freedom of expression questions, even if no 'political' information was in issue. It also indicated – the point is put most clearly by Lord Bridge – that it accepted that s 10 had tipped the balance in favour of maintaining the confidentiality of press sources:

112 Ibid, at 455.

113 Ibid, at 481. 114 Ibid, at 456; per Lord Wilberforce. 115 Ibid, at 475.

116 Cf Boyle (1981) op cit p 149: 'the section appears to do no more than adopt the very test employed by the majority judgments in [*BSC*]'.

117 See pp 641–642 above.

'In this balancing exercise it is only if the judge is satisfied that disclosure in the interests of justice is of such preponderating importance as to override the statutory privilege against disclosure that the necessity will be reached'.[118]

On these facts, there was no obvious public interest in disclosure of the relevant information, while the continued presence of a potential leaker within Tetra posed an acute and serious problem for the company. It thus seems unobjectionable from a human rights perspective that Morgan Grampian and Mr Goodwin were ordered to disclose their source. Mr Goodwin – who had not revealed the source to his employers – chose not to comply with the court order. He was thus fined £5000 for contempt. While this was an unfortunate consequence for Mr Goodwin – and while one might admire his (in the court's view misguided) determination to respect his source's confidentiality[119] – the judgment need not have any 'chilling effect' on sources providing political or public interest information; it can be seen as limited solely to cases involving purely 'private' information.

Lord Bridge's methodology in *X* has obvious similarities to the ECtHR's approach to Art 10 claims. It was perhaps therefore something of a surprise that Mr Goodwin's subsequent Art 10 action before the ECtHR was successful.[120] The Court adopted an essentially appellate role in remaking the balancing equation that the House of Lords had conducted. On the Court's view of the facts, Tetra's interest in uncovering the identity of the leaker/thief did not outweigh 'the vital public interest in the protection of the applicant's journalist's source'.[121] The House of Lords' order – and Mr Goodwin's subsequent committal for contempt – therefore breached Art 10.

Goodwin is a manifestly unsatisfactory decision, marred by the ECtHR's peculiar failure – given the position it had staked out in *Lingens* and *Castells* – to draw any distinction between different types of information. Had it respected the 'core status' of political speech identified in those two cases, its judgment would presumably have approved the House of Lords' decision since there was no 'political' element to Tetra's internal financial secrets. One could hardly cast any blame on the English courts for failing to conform with Art 10 on this point, since the ECtHR seemed to go markedly further than its previous case law would suggest was possible.

Even if one were to accept that proposition that domestic law on freedom of expression issues was generally in conformity with the Convention in the early 1990s, it was certainly arguable that the protection thereby obtained often fell far short of that provided in the USA by the First Amendment. On this issue at least, the Convention does not in the main set particularly exacting civil liberties standards. It was nonetheless the case that by this time the Convention had become a quite 'normal'

118 [1990] 2 All ER 1 at 9, HL.

119 Cf Lord Bridge, ibid, at 13: 'To contend that the individual litigant, be he a journalist or anyone else, has a right of "conscientious objection" which entitles him to set himself above the law if he does not agree with the court's decision, is a doctrine which undermines the rule of law and is wholly unacceptable in a democratic society'.

120 (1996) 22 EHRR 123.

121 Ibid, at para 45.

ingredient of domestic administrative law – albeit in a context in which 'normalcy' meant it enjoyed only a limited effect. In chapter twenty, our attention turns to the way in which the constitution's approach to the issue of civil liberties and human rights has altered in the past 15 to 20 years; an alteration which while falling some way short of a 'revolution', has nonetheless involved evolution at an unusually rapid pace and lent that 'normalcy' a rather different – and initially constitutionally problematic – character.

20

HUMAN RIGHTS AND CIVIL LIBERTIES III: NEW SUBSTANTIVE GROUNDS OF REVIEW

That United Kingdom law was so frequently found to have breached the Convention by the ECtHR is explained in large part by the fact that the Convention had not been incorporated into domestic law. If the provisions of the Convention had been incorporated into national law by a statute on terms which gave them a superior status to common law rules, to delegated legislation, or to previously enacted statutes, many cases which eventually reached the Court would have been resolved within the UK. It is entirely likely that some national law would have been held to have breached the Convention; but those outcomes would have been produced by judgments of domestic courts, not the ECtHR. Moreover, such judgments would not have been enforcing the Convention directly, but would rather have been applying the statute through which the Convention had been given domestic legal effect.

Members of the House of Lords frequently tried to incorporate the Convention through private members' Bills from 1970 onwards. Some Bills proposed unambiguously supra-legislative, entrenched status for the Convention. An alternative scenario was that an incorporating statute should seek to protect Convention rights from implied, but not express repeal. The most modest proposals envisaged only that the Convention should be used as additional grounds of review in administrative law, with no binding effect on Parliament. These initiatives invariably triggered brief media interest in the question of fundamental rights, and as such exemplify the Lords' useful role as a forum for debate on issues of public concern. No such Bill, however, even came close to being enacted.[1] In the early 1990s, several senior judges also advocated incorporation of the Convention in their academic writings.[2] The Liberal Party had long been committed to incorporation, and by the mid-1990s the Labour Party (under the leadership of John Smith and then Tony Blair) also accepted this position.

[1] See Bailey, Harris and Jones (1992) op cit pp 19–20.

[2] Scarman L (1987) 'Human rights in an unwritten constitution' *Denning LJ* 129–139: Bingham T (1993) 'The European Convention on Human Rights: time to incorporate' *LQR* 390–400.

I. JUDICIAL INCORPORATION OF THE CONVENTION?

Advocates of incorporation had consistently assumed that it could only be achieved through legislation, whether as an isolated instance of constitutional reform or as part of a broader process of political restructuring. As a matter of strict legal theory however, there was never any impediment to the House of Lords (qua final court of appeal) concluding (as Lord Denning had hinted at in *Birdi*)[3] that the Convention should be construed, de jure, as an authoritative source of law, binding on all executive bodies and directly effective in British courts.

THE CONVENTION IN DOMESTIC LAW

As suggested in chapters two and four, the formal rule that treaties have no binding force in domestic law until incorporated by legislation had an obvious functional basis in 1688. In the absence of such a rule, the Crown could have overridden legislation by using its prerogative powers to undertake international obligations. Affording treaties binding legal status would have subverted a revolutionary settlement which supposedly established the supremacy of Parliament vis à vis the Crown. That functional basis does not exist in the modern era. The fusion of the executive and legislative branches, coupled with the consolidation of the party system, has meant that in general the government effectively controls the legislature. 'Parliament' thus has no need of judicial protection against executive law-making in the international law arena.

There is a subsidiary justification for the rule. This derives from the courts' historical deference to the personal prerogatives of the Monarch. The point was clearly expressed in the 1876 case of *Rustomjee v R*, by Lord Coleridge CJ, who observed that 'as in making the treaty, so in performing the treaty, [the Queen] is beyond the control of municipal law, and her acts are not to be examined in her own courts'.[4] *Rustomjee* was quoted approvingly by Lord Denning in *Blackburn v A-G*,[5] and identified as the source of the traditional rule.

However, there were obvious flaws, both intrinsic and contextual, in adhering to this reasoning in the 1990s. In 1876, given Queen Victoria's manifest reluctance to acknowledge the process of democratisation which the constitution was undergoing,[6] it was conceivable to assume that the Monarch played a significant role in influencing the Treaty terms to which her government adhered. To suggest that the present Monarch does so is a nonsense; as Lord Roskill observed in *GCHQ* in response to the argument that the Monarch personally had abrogated her civil servants' rights of trade union membership: 'To talk of that act as the act of the sovereign savours of the

[3] See p 669 above. [4] (1876) 2 QBD 69 at 74, CA.
[5] See p 446–447 above. [6] See p 315 above.

archaism of past centuries.'[7] Archaism has no greater validity in respect of foreign policy than of employment conditions.

The intrinsic flaw lies in the fact that the *Rustomjee* rationale conflates the two quite distinct issues of the government's power to conclude a treaty and that treaty's subsequent impact in domestic law. The first issue *is* essentially non-justiciable in nature. Whether it is advantageous for this country to accept a particular set of obligations vis à vis other countries is a political question in the broadest sense; it is not an issue for judicial determination. However, where those obligations are expressed in terms of legal rules, and are purportedly intended to bestow legal rights on individual citizens, they are manifestly justiciable in character.

This elision of discrete phenomena was nevertheless restated by Lord Oliver in 1989 in *Maclaine Watson & Co Ltd v Department of Trade and Industry*:

> 'A treaty is not part of English law until it has been incorporated into the law by legislation . . . [I]t is outside the purview of the court [ie unenforceable] not only because it is made in the conduct of foreign relations, which are a prerogative of the crown, but also because as a source of rights and obligations, it is irrelevant'.[8]

The reasoning in the final clauses of Lord Oliver's quotation is completely tautological; the court cannot enforce a treaty because it is irrelevant to the domestic legal issue before it, and it is irrelevant because the court will not enforce it. Irrelevance and unenforceabilty are just different names for the same concept. The pertinent question is to ask **why** treaties are irrelevant/unenforceable? Lord Oliver's evident answer – namely that a treaty is an exercise of the 'foreign relations' prerogative – is not convincing in the post-*GCHQ* era. As suggested in *Everrett*,[9] 'foreign relations' is a blanket term which covers a wide range of both justiciable and non-justiciable issues. The question of whether a government body has contravened the Convention in its dealings with a citizen is no less justiciable than the question of whether a passport has been withheld on unlawful grounds.

The traditional rule is thus reduced to one based on pure formalism. The Convention (or any other treaty) is not enforceable in domestic courts because its *source* lies in an exercise of the prerogative rather than statute. There is no doubt that the *nature* of the Convention (in contrast perhaps to the contents of many other treaties) is eminently justiciable: its meaning is found in the judgments of the ECtHR. If the traditional rule was no more than a common law presumption, the House of Lords would have been competent to reverse it, and to have concluded that courts should now presume that a treaty whose terms are justiciable and intended to bestow rights and obligations upon individual citizens would be part of domestic law once ratified by the government until such time as Parliament says it is not.

In conceptual terms, that conclusion would be no more radical than the ones taken in *GCHQ* or *Pepper v Hart*. In all three cases the court is simply giving legal expression

[7] [1984] 3 All ER 935 at 956, HL.

[8] Popularly known as *The International Tin Council* case [1990] 2 AC 418 at 500, HL.

[9] See pp 123 above.

to the obvious political fact that the government is generally the dominant actor on the constitutional stage, and as such should expect all its justiciable actions to be subject to the High Court's supervisory jurisdiction unless Parliament ousts that jurisdiction in the most explicit of terms. Nor would judicial incorporation infringe upon Parliament's legal sovereignty. That challenge would only arise if a government subsequently convinced Parliament to enact legislation which explicitly forbade the domestic courts from applying the Convention and the courts refused to obey it: in that event, we would indeed be in a 'revolutionary' situation. Judicial incorporation de jure of the Convention would have been unexpected, unorthodox, and even perhaps so unconventional that many observers would have considered it unconstitutional. But it is difficult to sustain the argument that it would have been illegal.

It would however seem that a domestic court determined to allow its judgments to be shaped by the law of the Convention could often achieve that result, if only episodically, in rather less speculative ways. As noted in chapter twelve, the ECJ has embraced the idea that the provisions of the Convention are analogous to the 'fundamental human rights' contained in the EC's 'general principles of law'.[10] The member states declined to incorporate the Convention into community law de jure at either Maastricht or Amsterdam. Nevertheless, the TEU's preamble offers explicit support for the ECJ's more circuitous approach to the same end:

> 'The Union shall respect fundamental rights, as guaranteed by the European Convention for the Protection of Human Rights . . . and as they result from the constitutional traditions common to the Member States, as general principles of Community law'.[11]

This has significant implications for British courts, in so far as it would seem to oblige them (post-*Factortame*) to disapply any domestic statutory or common law provision (in an area within the EC's competence) which could not be construed to comply with the Convention.[12] This development does not of course answer the methodological question of how *any* EC law obligation has assumed such 'special' constitutional status within the UK, but its substantive impact seems uncontentious.[13] A question of greater interest arises when one wonders whether the alleged 'ripple effect' of EC law would carry with it into matters purely of domestic law some or all of the Convention's legal principles, or indeed, if the ECtHR's jurisprudence possesses its own 'ripple effect'. If this were to have happened, it would have entailed at the least a radical alteration of accepted common law principles and thence of techniques of statutory interpretation, and could, if enthusiastically embraced by the courts, have provided a moral launch pad for more far-reaching redefinition of orthodox constitutional understandings.

[10] Pp 464–465 above. [11] TEU, Art F(2) TEU.

[12] See the development of this argument by Grief N (1991) 'The domestic impact of the ECHR as mediated through Community law' *Public Law* 555–567: and in Lord Browne-Wilkinson (1992) 'The infiltration of a Bill of Rights' *Public Law* 397–410.

[13] See Grief op cit: Browne-Wilkinson op cit.

II. THE (RE-)EMERGENCE AND CONSOLIDATION OF FUNDAMENTAL HUMAN RIGHTS AS AN INDIGENOUS PRINCIPLE OF COMMON LAW

Constraints of space preclude any systematic analysis of judicial use of human rights principles in the area of administrative law since 1990.[14] The following section focuses instead on several leading decisions in which the courts appeared to recognise that the common law contained a significant and as yet under-explored capacity to mirror the moral principles contained in the Convention.

DERBYSHIRE COUNTY COUNCIL V TIMES NEWSPAPERS LTD IN THE HOUSE OF LORDS

Lord Keith delivered the leading judgment in the Lords. Unlike the judges in the Court of Appeal,[15] he did not either 'apply' the Convention, nor resort to judgments of the ECtHR to resolve a common law 'ambiguity'. Lord Keith considered the common law quite clear. There was no ambiguity: *Bognor Regis UDC v Campion* had simply been wrongly decided:

> '[N]ot only is there no public interest favouring the right of organs of government, whether central or local, to sue for libel, but it is contrary to the public interest that they should have it . . . because to admit such actions would place an undesirable fetter on freedom of speech'.[16]

In reaching this conclusion, Lord Keith had focused on the function served by criticism of government in a modern democratic society. He thought this purpose was best described by Lord Bridge in *Hector v A-G of Antigua and Barbuda*:

> '[T]hose . . . responsible for public administration must always be open to criticism. Any attempt to stifle or fetter such criticism amounts to political censorship of the most insidious and objectionable kind . . . [T]he very purpose of criticism . . . is to undermine public confidence in their stewardship and to persuade the electorate that the opponents would make a better job of it than those presently holding office'.[17]

Lord Keith found further support for his perception of the requisite 'public policy' concerns in several United States' decisions, primarily *City of Chicago v Tribune Co*[18] and *New York Times v Sullivan.*[19]

Lord Keith's concern was obviously to remove an undesirable fetter on free speech. As such, his judgment can readily be seen as enhancing the protection afforded to

[14] See on that issue Hunt M. (1997) *Using human rights law in English courts* (Oxford: Hart Publishing).

[15] See pp 676–677 above.

[16] [1993] 1 All ER 1011 at 1019.

[17] [1990] 2 All ER 103 at 106, PC.

[18] 139 NE 86 (1923); p 654 above.

[19] 376 US 254 (1964); p 655 above.

freedom of expression.[20] However, on closer reading, both the substance of the judgment and the methodology that underpinned it are flawed. The substantive problems are twofold. Firstly, like the Court of Appeal, Lord Keith placed no additional barriers in the path of libel actions brought by elected politicians. This omission provided an obvious route to sidestep the ratio of the judgment. Secondly, the ratio itself is problematic, as indeed is that of the *Chicago* judgment on which Lord Keith relied. A complete ban on libel actions initiated by government bodies provides the press and political parties with a perverse incentive to tell deliberate lies on political matters; that is knowingly and wilfully to mislead voters. If one's primary concern when addressing freedom of expression issues concerning political matters is to promote informed consent, such an incentive may well prove counter-productive.

The methodological flaw lies in the House of Lords' evident failure to appreciate the subtle question of balance between encouraging the circulation of information and restricting the circulation of misinformation that the US Supreme Court struck in *Sullivan*. The judgment seems to have been read rather simplistically, and used to underpin propositions which it did not really support. This raises a danger of general application when civil liberties questions are in issue in domestic law; namely that courts may invoke authorities from other jurisdictions to buttress innovative common law developments without properly appreciating the reasons for and implications of the judgments concerned.[21]

R V SECRETARY OF STATE FOR THE HOME DEPARTMENT, EX P LEECH (NO 2)

The expansion of the notion of fundamental rights at common law in respect of freedom of expression issues continued – this time rooted in wholly indigenous principles – in *R v Secretary of State for the Home Department, ex p Leech (No 2)*.[22] As noted in the previous discussion of *Raymond v Honey*,[23] the common law has long accepted that 'access to the courts' should be regarded as a 'basic right', in the sense that it could only be abridged by legislation either explicitly or by necessary implication. *Raymond* concerned a prison Governor's attempts to prevent a prisoner initiating legal action, a power which the court held had not been given to him by the loosely framed powers created under s 47 of the Prison Act 1952. The applicant in *Leech* was seeking to extend that principle.

Mr Leech, a prisoner, was an inveterate litigator on matters of prison discipline. His action was aimed at preventing the prison authorities from intercepting or stopping his letters to his solicitor. The relevant prison rules which the prison governor invoked to justify this activity were said to be authorised by s 47. The case was concerned simply with deciding whether those rules were ultra vires s 47.

20 For so long, of course, as Parliament chose not to overrule the judgment through legislation.

21 See generally on this point Loveland I (1995) 'Introduction: should we take lessons from America?' in Loveland I (ed) *A special relationship?* (Oxford: Clarendon Press).

22 [1994] QB 198, CA.

23 [1983] 1 AC 1, HL: p 512 above.

Two rules were in issue. Rule 33(3) provided that:

'Except as provided by these Rules, every letter or communication to or from a prisoner may be read or examined by the governor . . . and the governor may at his discretion, stop any letter or communication on the grounds that its contents are objectionable or that it is of inordinate length.'

Rule 37A removed this limit in respect of correspondence between an inmate and his/her solicitor in respect of ongoing litigation.[24] It did not however apply to letters preparatory to actual or potential litigation. It was correspondence of this sort with which Mr Leech was concerned. His action failed in the High Court, but that judgment was then reversed by a unanimous Court of Appeal, for which Steyn LJ delivered the sole judgment.

The opinion was framed in terms which bore an obvious resemblance to the jurisprudence of the ECtHR. Steyn LJ accepted that a 'presumptive entitlement' was in issue; 'It is a principle of our law that every citizen has a right of unimpeded access to a court . . . Even in our unwritten constitution it must rank as a constitutional right'.[25] The significance of the 'constitutional right' designation was that the entitlement could be removed or abridged only by explicit legislation or as a matter of necessary implication from the relevant statutory text. Steyn LJ made it clear that courts should be reluctant to accept implied statutory interferences with such rights:

'. . . in relation to rule-making powers alleged to arise by necessary implication, it can fairly be said that the more fundamental the right interfered with, and the more drastic the interference, the more difficult becomes the implication'.[26]

While one might welcome this conclusion, the methodology is open to criticism on two obvious grounds. The first is the absence of any supra-judicial catalogue of 'constitutional rights'. They are purely common law creations, susceptible to change at any time. The second is Lord Steyn's suggestion that the common law recognises a hierarchy of constitutional rights, some 'more fundamental' than others. If the rights themselves are elusive, their respective positions on the constitutional ladder are even more so. What Steyn LJ did de facto here was to incorporate Arts 6 and 10 ECHR into the Prison Act 1952, but, presumably for the reasons discussed above, he was unable to acknowledge this explicitly.

Having established its methodology. the Court defined the notion of 'access to a court' quite broadly. Steyn LJ argued that the common law clearly recognised that:

'a prisoner's unimpeded right of access to a solicitor for the purpose of receiving advice and assistance in connection with the possible institution of civil proceedings in the courts forms an inseparable part of the right of access to the courts themselves'.[27]

Lord Steyn's reasoning on the latter point is somewhat disingenuous. That the reach

24 This amendment had been introduced in response to an ECtHR judgment which had found r 33(3) standing alone to breach Art 6 of the Convention: see *Golder v United Kingdom* (1975) 1 EHRR 524.

25 Ibid, at 548. 26 Ibid, at 547. 27 Ibid, at 548.

of that proposition extended to a prisoner in Leech's situation was made entirely clear only by Steyn LJ's own judgment. His purpose perhaps was to suggest that the Court of Appeal was merely declaring existing law rather than creating new law. That is an unconvincing distinction. The conclusion is obviously teleological in its source, resting on the premise that a prisoner is likely to be deterred from initiating legal actions at all if he/she knows that she cannot discuss the pros and cons of such action with her/his legal advisers on a confidential basis.

While the court accepted that s 47 – as a matter of necessary implication – authorised *some* interference with prisoner's mail, the question to be answered was whether r 33(3) was drawn too widely. In addressing this issue, Steyn LJ effectively adopted a proportionality test:

'The question is whether there is a self-evident and pressing need for an unrestricted power to read letters between a prisoner and a solicitor and a power to stop such letters on the ground of prolixity and objectionality'.[28]

In applying the test, the Court looked unusually closely – given that this was an AJR action – at the merits of the policy issues involved. It considered the Home Office's arguments on this point to be unconvincing. Drawing on a recent Canadian authority,[29] Steyn LJ offered a series of 'illustrative' safeguards which might be attached to such a governmental power in order to make it compatible with the prisoner's right of access to the courts. Since the Prison Rules contained no such safeguards, rule 33(3) was ultra vires s 47 of the 1952 Act.[30]

R V SECRETARY OF STATE FOR SOCIAL SECURITY, EX P JOINT COUNCIL FOR THE WELFARE OF IMMIGRANTS

In February 1996, Peter Lilley (then Secretary of State for Social Security) introduced delegated legislation[31] denying welfare benefits to any asylum seekers who did not declare themselves as such immediately upon entering the UK and to those who chose to appeal (as they were entitled by statute to do) against an initial refusal of their application. Such people would have to rely on charitable support. The measure attracted much criticism, on the basis that many asylum seekers were likely to be too afraid or disorientated to approach the Home Office straight away and that, de facto, the change would abrogate rights of appeal. In June 1996, the Court of Appeal held the policy unlawful.[32] The Court reached this conclusion by in effect applying the

28 Ibid, at 550. He framed the test in somewhat different terms, even more redolent of the proportionality principle, at 555; 'The authorised intrusion must, however, be the minimum necessary to ensure that the correspondence is in truth bona fide legal correspondence'.

29 *Solosky v R* (1979) 105 DLR (3d) 745.

30 This technique invites comparison with Lord Donaldson MR's much less assertive strategy in *Malone*: see pp 635–637 above.

31 The Social Security (Persons From Abroad) Miscellaneous Amendments Regulations 1996, SI 1996/30.

32 *R v Secretary of State for Social Security, ex p Joint Council for the Welfare of Immigrants* [1996] 4 All ER 385, CA.

'fundamental human rights' rationale: indeed, the argument deployed had undertones of a 'natural law' philosophy. Simon Brown LJ expressed his conclusion in very forceful terms:

'[T]he 1996 regulations necessarily contemplate for some a life so destitute that, to my mind, no civilised nation can tolerate it. So basic are the human rights here at issue, that it cannot be necessary to resort to the [ECHR] . . . Nearly 200 years ago Lord Ellenborough CJ in *R v Eastbourne (inhabitants)* ((1803) 102 ER 769 at 779) said: "As to there being no obligation for maintaining poor foreigners . . . the law of humanity, which is anterior to all positive laws, obliges us to afford them relief, to save them from starving" '.[33]

The Court considered that when Parliament had passed the relevant 'parent Act', it had not given the government any power to negate this common law principle. Simon Brown LJ concluded by observing that:

'Parliament cannot have intended a significant number of genuine asylum seekers to be impaled upon the horns of so intolerable a dilemma – the need either to abandon their claims to refugee status or alternatively to maintain themselves as best they can but in an utter state of destitution. Primary legislation alone could in my judgement achieve that sorry state of affairs'.[34]

III. THE 'JUDICIAL SUPREMACISM' CONTROVERSY

The increasing assertiveness of the domestic courts, coupled with a series of forceful judgments by the ECJ and the ECtHR in the mid-1990s, triggered something of a political controversy in the early to mid-1990s. The controversy was kindled and stoked by a mix of government ministers (the second Major government then being in power), backbench MPs, and right-wing newspapers. It was cast in terms of a need to defend 'sovereignty' and 'democracy', which were apparently both being undermined by a judicial conspiracy embracing domestic judges and the 'foreigners' sitting on the two European courts, all of whom were supposedly intent on giving themselves a more powerful, essentially illegitimate constitutional role within the United Kingdom.

JUDGMENTS OF THE ECJ AND THE ECtHR

In November 1995, the ECJ delivered its judgment in *R v Secretary of State for the Home Department, ex p Gallagher*.[35] Gallagher was an Irish citizen, who had been convicted in Ireland some years previously of firearms offences. The then Home Secretary, Michael Howard, invoked powers under the Prevention of Terrorism

[33] Ibid, at 400. [34] Ibid, at 402.

[35] Case C–175/94: [1995] ECR I–4253, [1996] 1 CMLR 557. See the comment by O'Leary S (1996) *'R v Secretary of State for the Home Department, ex p Gallagher' Common Market LR* 777–793.

(Temporary Provisions) Act 1989 to exclude Gallagher from the UK. Gallagher challenged his exclusion before the English courts on the basis that it breached his EC-derived right of free movement as a worker. Like Ms Van Duyn,[36] Gallagher relied specifically on Directive 64/221, Art 9 of which required that an individual be able to challenge any exclusion decision before a 'competent authority'. Following a reference from the Court of Appeal, the ECJ indicated that the UK's procedures on this point were incompatible with EC law. The judgment was hardly surprising, being well-rooted in existing ECJ judgments.[37] Nor was it as far reaching as it might have been. The ECJ did not require, for example, that prospective deportees be provided with reasons for the government's actions. Its effect and legitimacy were nonetheless derided by Conservative ministers and backbench MPs,[38] who were it seems distinctly disturbed to see how the nominally 'economic' basis of Community law could cut across into 'human rights issues'.[39]

Their indignation was rather more forceful in response to the ECJ's judgment in *Factortame (No 3)/Brasserie du Pêcheur*,[40] handed down on 5 March 1996. The judgment extended the *Francovich* damages remedy to breach of any provision of EC law, not simply failure to implement directives, and so raised the possibility that an English court might soon award Factortame substantial damages for losses caused by the Merchant Shipping Act 1988. The notion that – in effect – Parliament could be liable in damages was not welcomed by the Major government and Conservative MPs. The then Fisheries Minister, Tony Baldry, described the judgment as; 'a crazy law'.[41] A backbench MP, Iain Duncan Smith, proposed drastic action to prevent any damages being awarded:

'The government should therefore act now to stop these cases going ahead until it had resolved the matter. It should pass a simple act of Parliament amending the European Communities Act 1972 to stop the ruling applying in English courts'.[42]

Duncan-Smith's presumption that the government could pass an Act is itself a telling indictment of the extent to which Conservative MPs had discarded orthodox understandings of the separation of powers. It is perhaps unfortunate that Parliament did not enact such a Bill. Factortame would no doubt have sought to have the resultant statute disapplied. The ensuing litigation would have provided a marvellous opportunity for the courts to confirm just how significantly the UK's accession to the Community had compromised traditional understandings of the sovereignty of Parliament.

[36] See pp 449–450 above. [37] See the discussion in O'Leary op cit.

[38] See *The Times* and *The Guardian*, 1 December 1995.

[39] Cf O'Leary op cit at 787: 'indeed it is surprising that the PTA was adopted and successively renewed in the form it was, given the clear rulings of the Court of Justice . . . Perhaps it was thought that national anti-terrorist legislation did not come within the scope of Community law'.

[40] Cases C–46/93 and C–48/93: [1996] 1 CMLR 889: see pp 417–419 above.

[41] *The Guardian*, 6 March 1996.

[42] 'This writ should not run over us' *The Times*, 12 March 1996. Duncan Smith was elected as leader of the Conservative Party in 2001. He proved remarkably inept in that role.

Factortame (No 3) was immediately followed by the judgment in the '*Working Time Directive*' case.[43] The litigation – which turned on a 'legal base' question[44] – threatened the government with a possible erosion of the UK's 'opt-out' from the EC Social Charter.[45] The Council had enacted Directive 93/104 to place maximum limits on the hours that employees could be required to work. The Council claimed it had the power to do so under Art 118a of the Treaty of Rome; which provided, inter alia, that: 'Member States shall pay particular attention to encouraging improvements, especially in the working environment, as regards the health and safety of workers . . .'. Limiting working hours (to a maximum of 48 per week) would seem obviously to be a 'health and safety' matter. The Major government, which opposed the substance of the measure, was unable to veto it in Council, because Art 118(a) allowed secondary legislation to be adopted by a qualified majority. It thus argued that the measures of this sort were properly regarded as parts of the 'internal market' strategy,[46] and should thus be enacted under Art 100a. Since Art 100a required unanimity in the Council, success on this point would enable the government to veto the measure altogether. The Advocate-General's preliminary opinion found against the UK, and was met with the comment from the Prime Minister that: 'It is precisely because of legislation like this and stupidities like this that the EU is becoming uncompetitive and losing jobs to other parts of the world'.[47] When the ECJ subsequently upheld the Advocate-General's opinion, the most splenetic reaction came from John Redwood, one of the Prime Minister's Cabinet colleagues: 'The court is off the leash and on the loose, overturning Acts of Parliament, destroying our fishing industry, and changing our employment laws. Parliament should immediately assert its rights'.[48]

Shortly afterwards, in *P v S and Cornwall County Council*,[49] the ECJ held that the notion of 'gender' within the Equal Treatment Directive[50] included trans-sexualism. Thus a person who was dismissed from his job because he had undergone surgical and hormonal treatments to change his sex from male to female had been unlawfully discriminated against under EC law. No such protection (of course) existed under domestic law. The gist of the political reaction within the Conservative Party on this issue was nicely characterised by a leading article in the right-wing newspaper *The Daily Mail*, on 2 May 1996:

> 'Until and unless we have a government prepared to mount a fundamental and unyielding challenge to the supremacy of this alien jurisdiction, then Britain will continue to face nothing less than the death of its nationhood by a thousand cuts of the Euro-scalpel'.

The government received a number of similarly unwelcome setbacks before the ECtHR in this period. In June 1996, the Court's judgment in *Benham v United Kingdom*[51]

43 *United Kingdom v EU Council:* C–84/94 [1996] ECR I–5755. 44 See pp 473–474 above.
45 See p 497 above. 46 See pp 467–468 above. 47 *The Guardian*, 13 March 1996.
48 *The Times*, 13 March 1996.
49 Case C–13/94: [1996] ECR I–2143. Judgment was given on 1 May 1996.
50 Directive 76/207: see p 459 above. 51 (1996) 22 EHRR 293.

found the UK in breach of Art 6 ECHR.[52] Benham had refused to pay his poll tax, and was eventually gaoled for 30 days for continuing to withhold payment. He had not been able to afford to employ counsel at his trial, and no legal aid was available to pay for legal representation at such hearings. In the light of the severity of the punishment he faced (ie a gaol sentence), and the complexity of the legal issues that the trial raised, the ECtHR considered that the government's failure to provide legal representation had denied Mr Benham a fair hearing.[53]

Benham followed the judgment in *Hussain v United Kingdom.*[54] Hussain had been convicted of murder while a juvenile, and had been sentenced to be detained 'at her Majesty's pleasure'. Under domestic law, the question of his release was a matter for the Home Secretary. The applicant argued that this amounted to a breach of Art 5(4) ECHR.[55] The Court accepted this submission, thereby in effect requiring a transfer of particular sentencing powers from the government to the courts.

To Conservative MPs, however, the ECtHR's most controversial judgment was *McCann v United Kingdom.*[56] McCann was an Art 2 case.[57] The applicants were relatives of several IRA terrorists, who, while plotting to explode a bomb in Gibraltar, had been shot dead by British soldiers. In a judgment which involved an extremely detailed examination of the facts of the episode,[58] the Court concluded by a 10–9 majority that the killings could not be justified under Art 2(2).

In response to these decisions, the Major government evidently gave serious consideration to withdrawing UK citizens' right of individual petition to the Commission. It decided instead to try to pressurise the Council of Europe to curb the ECtHR's jurisdiction and to set much wider limits to the 'margin of appreciation' doctrine. A Foreign Office memorandum to the Council (leaked to the British press) contained the extraordinary proposal that the Court be required to respect 'long-standing laws and practices' within member states even if they were 'manifestly contrary to the Convention'.[59]

52 Art 6 (1): 'In the determination of his civil rights and obligations or of any criminal charge against him, everyone is entitled to a fair and public hearing within a reasonable time by an independent and impartial tribunal established by law . . .'

53 The judgment goes substantially further than domestic administrative law rules concerning the 'right' to legal representation: see pp 562–563 above.

54 (1996) 22 EHRR 1. Judgment given on 21 February 1996.

55 Article 5 (4): 'Everyone who is deprived of his liberty by arrest or detention shall be entitled to take proceedings by which the lawfulness of his detention shall be decided speedily by a court . . .'

56 (1995) 21 EHRR 97.

57 '1 Everybody's right to life shall be protected by law. No-one shall be deprived of his life intentionally save in the execution of a sentence of a court following his conviction of a crime for which this penalty is provided by law.

2 Deprivation of life shall not be regarded as inflicted in contravention of this Article when it results from use of force which is no more than is absolutely necessary:

(a) in defence of any person from unlawful violence;
(b) in order to effect a lawful arrest or to prevent the escape of a person lawfully detained;
(a) in action lawfully taken for the purpose of quelling a riot or insurrection.'

58 Ie the ECtHR was in effect exercising an appellate jurisdiction.

59 See *The Guardian*, 2 April 1996.

The Council of Europe was apparently unimpressed by these suggestions. This is hardly surprising, for by then it was wholly clear that the Major government's penchant for making unlawful decisions arose as often in respect of matters of domestic law as it did in respect of the law of the EC and the ECHR.

JUDGMENTS IN DOMESTIC COURTS ON IMMIGRATION POLICIES

Two of the more important judgments which figured in the judicial supremacism controversy have already been discussed in previous chapters. The *Pergau Dam* case proved a substantial embarrassment to the Major government, as did the House of Lords' decision in the *Fire Brigades Union* litigation. Neither judgment could be regarded as particularly radical in nature. *Pergau Dam* turned on a long-rooted principle of statutory interpretation,[60] while *Fire Brigades Union* was concerned with safeguarding the sovereignty of Parliament from governmental misuse of the royal prerogative.[61] The government's most acute and consistent cause for concern however lay in a series of judgments dealing with its immigration policies, especially in relation to the treatment of people who had come to the UK to escape from what they claimed was political persecution in their home countries.

Michael Howard's legal difficulties as Home Secretary prompted much of the Conservative MPs' anti-judicial ire in this period. However his predecessor, Kenneth Baker, had set the scene for this supposed conflict between the Home Office and the courts through a course of action which ultimately led to the House of Lords' judgment in *Re M*.[62]

Re M

M was a teacher from Zaire who sought political asylum in Britain, claiming that he would be subject to political persecution if he returned to his homeland. The Home Secretary[63] decided he did not qualify for asylum under the relevant legislation, and ordered his deportation. M's counsel then presented new evidence to the court. By this time, M was on his way to Heathrow airport. The judge, Garland J, considered that the Home Office's counsel had given the court an undertaking that M would not be deported until the new evidence was heard, and made an order (which was in effect an interim injunction) in those terms. However, M was then flown to Paris and placed on a flight to Zaire. M's solicitor then woke up Garland J in the middle of the night, and the judge immediately (by phone) ordered the Home Secretary to return M to Britain. The Home Secretary was then informed by his legal advisers that Garland J had no power to make such an order, and the Home Secretary decided to ignore it. The case raised several important issues. Much of the argument centred on complex

[60] See pp 507–508 above. [61] See pp 110–111 above.

[62] [1994] 1 AC 377, sub nom *M v Home Office* [1993] 3 All ER 537.

[63] It appears that the decision was actually made by a junior minister, and that the Home Secretary himself, Kenneth Baker, was not familiar with the case.

questions of administrative law, which need not concern us here.[64] There are however, two points of constitutional significance which we need to address. Firstly, did the High Court have the power to issue an injunction against the Crown, represented here by the Home Office? And if so, was Kenneth Baker, the Home Secretary, in either his personal or ministerial capacity, in contempt of court for ignoring it?

If we recall *Entick* and *Liversidge*, we see that the citizen's legal actions were not against the 'government' (or the Crown), but against individual government officials. In both instances, the government official was being sued for allegedly committing a tortious action; trespass in *Entick* and false imprisonment in *Liversidge*. In neither 1765 nor 1942 was it possible for those actions to be commenced against the Crown per se. As previously noted, while the 1688 revolution had established the supremacy of statute over common law, it did not in itself alter common law principles in any systematic way. One such principle, encapsulated in the aphorism that 'the King could do no wrong', was that the courts had no jurisdiction to entertain suits in tort or contract against the Crown. Citizens could pursue such actions only via 'the petition of right' device. Relatedly, it had always been thought that an injunction could not lie against the Crown per se.[65] Similarly, while an individual government official who deliberately defied an injunction against her would be in contempt of court, the non-availability of such a remedy against the Crown would logically imply that there could be nothing in respect of which the Crown per se could be in contempt.

It was not until the Crown Proceedings Act 1947 that Parliament exercised its sovereign legal power to abolish the petition of right device. The Act made it clear that the Crown itself could now be sued in contract or tort. However the Act did not explicitly confirm that injunctions and the contempt jurisdiction could also issue against the Crown per se, rather than just against individual officials. Prior to the *M* case, the weight of judicial authority in matters purely of domestic law suggested such remedies were not available. In effect, this case law seemingly suggested that remedies which citizens might enforce against other citizens were only available against the Crown when Parliament had explicitly legislated to that effect.

This left something of a gap in the legal regulation of government activity. On the facts of *M*, for example, an interim injunction against Mr Baker in person would not have prevented other Home Office Ministers or employees from placing M on the plane to Zaire. Had Mr Baker wilfully defied the courts and breached such an order, he personally would have been in contempt, but that consequence would neither be of assistance to M nor underline the principle that the government as a corporate body must respect court orders. Thus, if the 'rule of law' was not to be undermined in practice, we would have to rely on the integrity of government in never doing anything that might be the subject of an injunction or a contempt order, a reliance that fits uneasily with the Diceyan principle that the rule of law demands that we should always be suspicious of government's bona fides. In the context of EC law, that

64 See Gould M (1993) '*M v Home Office*: government and the judges' *Public Law* 568–578.

65 See further pp 576–577 above.

position had been changed by the *Factortame* judgments,[66] but it did not necessarily follow that this principle would spill over into domestic law.

The leading judgment in *M* was given by Lord Woolf. The court concluded that the High Court had the power to issue an interim injunction against the Crown, that the Crown was in theory amenable to the contempt jurisdiction, and that, on the facts of this case, such a contempt had been committed. Lord Woolf's judgment is much concerned with technical questions of administrative law. For our purposes, perhaps the key passage in the decision comes from Lord Templeman's speech:

'[T]he argument that there is no power to enforce the law by injunction . . . against a Minister in his official capacity would, if upheld, establish the proposition that the executive obey the law as a matter of grace and not as a matter of necessity, a proposition which would reverse the result of the civil war'.[67]

The logic of his contention seems unassailable; namely that the revolution had created a situation in which the Crown's legal status was equivalent to that of an ordinary legal person; thus all legal remedies which are available against individuals should be available against the Crown, unless Parliament has clearly provided to the contrary.

Lord Woolf drew on similarly expansive principles in confirming the availability of the contempt jurisdiction. The Home Secretary, in either his personal or official capacity, could be in contempt for disregarding the terms of such an injunction. The only bodies capable of overturning the order of a High Court judge would be the Court of Appeal and House of Lords; if ministers could ignore the courts on the basis of the advice of their lawyers, the rule of law would clearly be being subverted. As Lord Woolf explained:

'[T]he ability of the court to make a finding of contempt is of great importance. It would demonstrate that a government department has interfered with the administration of justice. It will then be for Parliament to determine what should be the consequences of that finding'.[68]

M should thus be seen as a long overdue embrace of traditional principle. The judgment plugged an unfortunate gap in the coverage of the rule of law principle in modern society, while making it perfectly clear that if Parliament took the view that it was appropriate for government Ministers to enjoy this immunity (in non-EC matters) it could create it for them in statute.

R v Secretary of State for the Home Department, ex p Moon

Kenneth Baker's successor as Home Secretary, Michael Howard, threw further fuel onto the political fire by making a series of patently unlawful decisions which were subsequently invalidated in the courts. In *R v Secretary of State for the Home Department, ex p Moon*,[69] Sedley J quashed Howard's attempt to exclude the Revd Sun Il

66 See pp 480–483 above.

67 [1994] 1 AC 377 at 395.

68 [1994] 1 AC 377 at 425.

69 (1995) 8 Admin LR 477.

Moon – the leader of the 'Moonie' religious cult – from the UK under powers granted by the Immigration Acts. The decision promoted an outcry among Conservative MPs and the tabloid and broadsheet press, who felt Moon was so unpleasant a character that he should never be allowed into the country. This response was wholly ill-informed about both the nature of the decision and the basic features of the judicial review jurisdiction. Sedley J had not held that Howard could not exclude Moon. His decision was based on a procedural irregularity in the Home Secretary's decision-making process. The judgment held simply that Howard could exclude Moon only after giving him an opportunity to argue that he should be admitted: ie it was a straightforward application of the procedural fairness doctrine. Having heard such arguments, the Home Secretary could admit or exclude Moon as he thought fit, subject only to *Wednesbury* irrationality constraints.

One might expect tabloid papers to misrepresent or misunderstand such principles. But it was more surprising to find *The Times* displaying similar ignorance. In a leader engagingly entitled 'Judicial Moonshine', *The Times* castigated Sedley's judgment on the grounds that Moon was a thoroughly undesirable alien who should never be allowed into Britain. That substantive conclusion may have much to commend it; but it has nothing to do with Sedley J's judgment, which concerned only the procedures through which the Home Secretary acted. *The Times* was either misinformed or mendacious in suggesting the judgment overturned established legal understandings.

The al-Mas'ari case

Professor al-Mas'ari's legal action against the Home Secretary had rather graver implications. Saudi Arabia, while an important economic and political ally for the UK, could hardly be described as having a constitutional system which operated as a model of enlightened and humane government. The regime is intolerant of internal political opposition, and dissidents who escape imprisonment tend to conduct their political campaigns from abroad. Professor al-Mas'ari was one such dissident who had sought political asylum in the UK. The Home Secretary, again exercising statutory powers, declined to grant asylum. His reasons for so doing were fear that Saudi Arabia's government would be less inclined to buy British arms and other goods if the UK sheltered one of its critics.

Al-Mas'ari's legal challenge to this refusal was unsurprisingly successful. The case turned on a simple and long-established administrative law point; were calculations as to arms' sales a 'relevant consideration' in the exercise of statutory powers concerning asylum decisions? In this case, Judge Pearl had little difficulty in concluding that considerations of commercial advantage were not relevant factors. On relevant grounds – such as the asylum seeker's personal characteristics, the regime from which she or he fled, the likelihood that she or he would suffer harm if returned there – al-Mas'ari presented a strong case. For the Home Secretary to allow such factors to be trumped by the prospect of losing arms' sales was an abuse of the powers Parliament had granted him. The government did not appeal against this judgment, which indicates it realised that its legal position was untenable.

However, the government did not let the matter rest. Rather than challenge the judgment in court, the government attacked it in the media. On Radio 4's *Today* programme on 14 March 1996, John Major elided the *al-Mas'ari* judgment with recent terrorist outrages in Israel and suggested that Parliament might reconsider whether Britain should shelter critics of 'friendly' regimes. His government could have asked Parliament to enact legislation achieving such an outcome; or providing specifically for al-Mas'ari's deportation; or expressly permitting the Home Secretary to take into account the beneficial impact on arms' sales that deporting political dissidents might have. Should Parliament have enacted such laws, a future Home Secretary could follow Howard's lead without fear of court intervention. That the Major government did not choose to pursue any of these options might suggest it knew the ends it sought might be regarded as immoral by both the Commons and the Lords.

The court's decision can therefore be seen as protecting not just Professor al-Mas'ari, but also the principle of parliamentary sovereignty, against government whims. Both the *Moon* and the *al-Mas'ari* cases, as well as the *Fire Brigades Union* and *Pergau Dam* judgments, underline this basic constitutional truth. Ministers may do only what Parliament permits. The limits of parliamentary intent are, and always have been, policed by the High Court. If ministers find these limits uncongenial, they must ask Parliament to change them.

R v Secretary of State for Social Security, ex p Joint Council for the Welfare of Immigrants

Perhaps the most graphic example of Conservative MPs either denying or not understanding this principle was provided in the aftermath of the *R v Secretary of State for Social Security, ex p Joint Council for the Welfare of Immigrants* judgment.[70] As noted above, the Court of Appeal had concluded in that case that only primary legislation could achieve 'the sorry state of affairs' of removing all benefit entitlements from certain categories of asylum seekers. Spectators in the Commons' public gallery the week after judgment was issued saw Lilley announce new legislation to achieve that objective.[71] The minister did not enter debates about judicial supremacism. His back-bench colleagues showed no such restraint, and coupled their copious indignation with magnificent ignorance.

Tony Marlow MP simply failed to grasp the essential distinction between primary and delegated legislation. His contribution to the debate was to ask: 'Have I missed something? Do the judiciary now have a democratic mandate to decide which laws are acceptable?'[72] His colleague Toby Jessell apparently found the distinction between politics and law too confusing to grasp: 'My constituents [do not] expect the Court of Appeal to do other than uphold public policy. [They] do not expect the Court of Appeal to make up the law as it goes along'.[73]

[70] [1996] 4 All ER 385, CA. [71] *HCD*, 24 June 1996, cc 37–38.
[72] Ibid, at c 42. [73] Ibid, at c 44.

The answer to both of Marlow's questions is manifestly: 'Yes'. Mr Marlow had apparently 'missed' the Glorious Revolution, the structure of constitutional law built upon its foundations, and the long-established principle that the courts do indeed have a 'democratic mandate': namely, to ensure that the executive in making delegated legislation does not exceed the limits of powers delegated by the parent Act. What Marlow and his ilk on the Tory backbenches did not understand was that what the court invalidated in the *JCWI* case was not 'a law' at all, but government abuse of the law.

There is a certain comedy in listening to MPs' politically closed minds rattling around in their legally empty heads, but the comedy is underpinned by a serious constitutional point. The MPs' substantively illiterate criticism of the court was echoed in much of the press, which accused Simon Brown LJ in particular of overstepping the limits of his powers. It might be argued that the style of Simon Brown LJ's judgment was atypically trenchant. It might even be suggested that his recognition of what was in essence a 'fundamental human right' to subsistence, abrogable only by explicit statutory language, somewhat extended the reach of the courts' resurgent fundamental rights jurisprudence.[74] But the judgment can hardly be seen as an example of judicial supremacism. It would be much more accurate to categorise it as removing an element of 'executive supremacism'.

'Executive supremacism' is of course not a concept which sits happily in a constitution where, in theory, sovereign authority lies with Parliament rather than the government. However, as has been suggested repeatedly in earlier chapters of this book, 'executive supremacism' would seem an accurate description of the way the constitution works in practice, insofar as a government is generally able to 'persuade' both Houses of Parliament to enact whatever legislation it wishes. The defining feature of the judicial supremacism episode was that ministers, Conservative MPs and much of the press seemed either to ignore or forget that point. Their argument was, in effect, that as long as a Commons majority approves of what a Minister does, nothing more need be said about the legality of her or his behaviour. A governing party which had for over fifteen years possessed a substantial and generally loyal majority in both houses may well have forgotten that the constitution requires the house's majority views to be placed on a statutory basis before the courts accord them legal significance. It is no more the task of backbench MPs, individually or en masse, to determine if a minister's action is legal than it is for a minister to do so.

A JUDICIAL RESPONSE

Michael Howard's criminal justice policies also brought him into public confrontation within the political arena with several senior judges and ex-judges. In December 1995, Lord Donaldson, the former Master of the Rolls, suggested in a *Guardian* article that the government and its media supporters were mounting 'a campaign of abuse

[74] Cf his own acknowledgment of the relevance of *Leech* to his judgment: [1996] 4 All ER 385 at 400–401.

and criticism of the judiciary as a whole'.[75] In so doing, the government was attacking orthodox understandings of the rule of law and thereby opening a path towards despotic government. As Lord Donaldson acknowledged, Parliament could enact any policy which the government wanted to pursue. But he argued that it was wholly unacceptable that ministers should, by constantly vilifying judicial decisions, seek to intimidate the courts into toeing the government line.

The former Lord Chief Justice, Lord Taylor, also joined the fray, arguing in a speech at King's College London in March 1996 that Howard's plans to impose mandatory sentences for particular kinds of criminal offence were dictated by 'the vagaries of fashion'. The Home Secretary responded to the Lord Chief Justice's speech on the *Today* programme the following morning, suggesting that Lord Taylor was 'soft on crime'. One particular line of Howard's diatribe was reprinted as the front-page headline of the same day's London *Evening Standard* in the form of a question to Lord Taylor: 'DO YOU WANT RAPISTS TO GO FREE?' The question is absurd – a gratuitous insult, which could not be taken seriously by any rational observer. But that does not mean it was ineffective. Rather, it suggested that if judges offered reasoned criticism of any aspect of the Major government's policy agenda, they would face a ministerial reply designed only to foster prejudice and intolerance among the public.

Any thought that Lord Donaldson's claim that the judiciary was being subjected to an orchestrated government campaign was the result of paranoia was dispelled in December 1995 by the curious episode of Lord Mackay's non-existent speech. *The Daily Telegraph* ran a story on 7 December headed 'Judges Warned to Keep in Line', explaining that the Lord Chancellor, the formal head of the judiciary, would deliver a speech that evening warning the judges not to exceed their powers. That day's *Times* predicted that Lord Mackay would tell judges to 'refrain from using their judicial powers to challenge ministerial decisions'. Lord Mackay evidently intended no such thing. He had circulated a paper on recent judicial decisions for internal Cabinet discussion; in it he defended traditional understandings of the courts' powers. He had no wish to make his views public. However, the then Conservative Party Chairman, Brian Mawhinney, evidently thinking that such comment from the head of the judiciary would undermine the position of 'liberal' judges, arranged (without Lord Mackay's approval) to leak the paper to the *Telegraph.* Mawhinney's initiative reinforced what *The Times* had already identified on 3 November 1995 as an acute judicial concern: that the government was fanning, in one judge's words, 'a hate campaign coming through sections of the media, to pour poison on the views of the judiciary'. A judge quoted in *The Times* felt the campaign was a pre-emptive strike, designed to discredit the conclusions of the Scott and Nolan reports prior to their publication.[76] If that view is correct, the government would seem to have been deliberately undermining accepted constitutional principles to garner a brief party political

[75] *The Guardian*, 11 December 1995. Lord Donaldson was not regarded as a particularly liberal judge: see the discussion of *Malone* at pp 635–637 above.

[76] See pp 344–345 and pp 295–297 above.

advantage. Another judge who was quoted felt, more charitably, that the government's behaviour resulted not from mendacity, but from ignorance: ministers and backbench MPs simply did not understand the basic constitutional principles underpinning the role of judicial review, had no grasp of the legitimacy of the common law as a dynamic source of legal authority, and did not appreciate the distinction between parliamentary majorities and Parliament itself.[77]

These points are axiomatic as to the way the constitution has been structured since 1688. That structure also makes it clear that the *only* way ministers can ultimately be rendered answerable to *Parliament* is through judges in the courts ensuring that ministers do not deploy powers that Parliament has not given them. Of course, members of the judiciary may misconstrue Parliament's intentions in their interpretation of statutes. If Parliament considers a court has misconstrued its intention, it may pass legislation amending the court's decision. A Commons majority plays a vital part in that process – but only a part.

LORD MUSTILL'S ANALYSIS

Perhaps the most coherent and revealing exposition of the relationship between the courts and the Thatcher and Major governments is offered by a lengthy passage in Lord Mustill's (dissenting) judgment in the *Fire Brigades Union* case.[78] The passage merits substantial reproduction here, as it raises important and controversial questions as to the inter-relationship of the sovereignty of Parliament, the rule of law and the separation of powers in late twentieth century British society:

'The courts interpret the laws, and see that they are obeyed. This requires the courts on occasion to step into the territory which belongs to the executive, to verify . . . that the powers asserted accord with the substantive law created by Parliament . . .

Concurrently with this judicial function Parliament has its own special means of ensuring that the executive, in the exercise of delegated functions, performs in a way which Parliament finds appropriate. Ideally, it is these latter methods which should be used to check executive errors and excesses; for it is the task of Parliament and the executive in tandem, not of the courts, to govern the country. In recent years, however, the employment in practice of these specifically Parliamentary remedies has on occasion been perceived as falling short, and sometimes well short, of what was needed to bring the performance of the executive into line with the law . . . To avoid a vacuum in which the citizen would be left without protection against a misuse of executive powers the courts have had no option but to occupy the dead ground in a manner, and in areas of public life, which could not have been foreseen 30 years ago. For myself, I am quite satisfied that this unprecedented judicial role has been greatly to the public benefit. Nevertheless, it has its risks, of which the courts are well aware. As the judges themselves constantly remark, it is not they who are appointed to administer the country. Absent a written constitution much sensitivity is required of the

[77] For a more detailed treatment of this issue see Loveland I (1997) 'The war against the judges' *Political Quarterly* 162–171.

[78] *R v Secretary of State for the Home Department, ex p Fire Brigades Union* [1995] 2 AC 513, HL.

parliamentarian, administrator and judge if the delicate balance of the unwritten rules evolved (I believe successfully) in recent years is not to be disturbed . . .'.[79]

In a fascinating critique of judicial politics during the Thatcher and Major eras, Simon Lee argued that the courts effectively donned the mantle of 'the opposition' to the minoritarian preferences of the elected central government.[80] But this was not 'opposition' in a party political sense; the judiciary was not simply plugging the constitutional holes left by the feebleness of the Labour Party during the 1980s, or more systemically, by the Commons' pervasive inadequacy as a monitor of and restraint on governmental extremism. Lee is not suggesting that the courts' allegedly more interventionist ideas are intended to compete on equal terms with those of politicians, but rather that they exist above party political dispute, in a kind of constitutional moral stratosphere.

Lee's thesis receives some support from essays and articles written by members of the judiciary in addition to Lord Mustill's critique in *Fire Brigades Union*. In a series of academic articles, Sir John Laws characterised the judiciary's more interventionist stance in administrative law as an attempt to give legal expression to a series of moral principles; 'about whose desirability there can be no serious argument'.[81] Sir John Laws suggests that much of the impetus for this development has come from the judiciary's increasing exposure to the constitutional orders of the EC, the European Convention, and the domestic legal systems of the EC's and the Convention's member states.

A perhaps more significant analysis, given its author's then status as a Law Lord, was offered by Lord Browne-Wilkinson.[82] Lord Browne-Wilkinson also acknowledged that the ECHR and the ECJ had had a significant influence on the judicial consciousness. However he also suggested that British courts have increasingly been returning to a more rigorous (and often overlooked) schemata of statutory interpretation, in which judges should assume that; 'a presumption in favour of individual freedom almost certainly reflects the true intention of Parliament'.[83]

79 Ibid, at 567.

80 Lee S (1994) 'Law and the constitution', in Kavanagh D and Seldon A (eds) *The Major effect* (London: Macmillan).

81 Sir John Laws (1993) 'Is the High Court the guardian of fundamental constitutional rights?' *Public Law* 59–79. See also (1995) 'Law and democracy' *Public Law* 72–93; (1998) 'The limitations of human rights' *Public Law* 254–265.

82 Browne-Wilkinson op cit.

83 Ibid, at p 408. Lord Browne-Wilkinson suggests *R & W Paul Ltd v Wheat Commission* [1937] AC 139, HL; *National Assistance Board v Wilkinson* [1952] 2 QB 648; and *Raymond v Honey* [1983] 1 AC 1, HL, as examples.

CONCLUSION

It would however be rash to assume that such sentiments pointed towards an inviolable truth in recent judicial decisions. The common law has always been, and remains, a pluralistic source of legal authority. Its balance may shift, but it is implausible to expect either that the new balance will be set in stone, or that even firmly established trends could not be reversed. More significantly, notwithstanding the force of Lord Mustill's speech in *Fire Brigades Union*, there will always be doubts raised as to the legitimacy of judges determining the meaning of 'human rights' or 'individual liberties' without the benefit of guidance from a supra-parliamentary constitution. With such an instrument to hand, courts may plausibly claim not to be imposing their own values on governmental bodies, but to be demonstrating instead a loyalty to 'the people' who decided upon the values to be placed beyond governmental reach. In the 1990s, the domestic courts were – with the limited exception of EC law – denied such luxuries. Every innovative principle – even any traditional principle – invoked to defend individual rights could be expected to serve as a trigger for political controversy should it inconvenience a government not prepared to accept orthodox constitutional principles.

The Labour Party evidently harboured few such fears in the mid-1990s. Its attraction to the idea of incorporating the Convention was evidently growing stronger, for it committed itself to do so while in opposition. That commitment was reiterated in the party's 1997 election manifesto. In little more than a year after coming to power in May 1997, the Blair government had successfully piloted the Human Rights Act 1998 through Parliament. In chapter twenty-one, we consider both the terms of the Act and its initial impact on the status of human rights principles in the United Kingdom's constitutional law.

21

HUMAN RIGHTS AND CIVIL LIBERTIES IV: THE HUMAN RIGHTS ACT 1998

The Labour Party's 1997 election manifesto commitment to redefine the status of the ECHR in domestic law was placed within the departmental remit of Lord Irvine, the Lord Chancellor, following the formation of the first Blair administration. In a speech made shortly after the election, Lord Irvine outlined the government's intentions;

'The government's position is that we should be leading in the development of human rights in Europe, not grudgingly driven to swallow the medicine prescribed for us by the Court in Strasbourg when we are found in breach of the Convention. Our citizens should be able to secure their human rights not only from a court in Strasbourg but from our own judges.'[1]

The detailed contents of the proposed Act were signalled in a Labour government white paper – *Rights Brought Home: the Human Rights Bill*[2] – which proposed that the Convention be given substantially enhanced status in domestic law. The white paper identified several cogent reasons for dissatisfaction with the current position of the ECHR in the UK's constitutional structure:

'1.14 . . . It takes on average five years to get an action into the ECtHR . . .; and it costs an average of £30,000. Bringing these rights home will mean that the British people will be able to argue for their rights in the British courts – without this inordinate delay and cost. It will also mean that the rights will be brought much more fully into the jurisprudence of the courts throughout the United Kingdom and their interpretation will thus be far more subtly and powerfully woven into our law . . .

1.15. Moreover, in the government's view, the approach which the United Kingdom has so far adopted towards the Convention does not sufficiently reflect its importance . . .'[3]

The white paper's main proposals were reflected in a Bill published in October 1997, the contents of which were in broad terms subsequently enacted in the 1998 legislation.

[1] Lord Irvine (1997) 'Constitutional reform and a Bill of Rights' *European Human Rights LR* 483–489 at 485.

[2] (1997) (Cm 3782: London: HMSO).

[3] Ibid. Publication of the white paper coincided with the ECtHR concluding that – for the fiftieth time, United Kingdom law was in breach of the Convention; see *Johnson v United Kingdom* [1997] 27 EHRR 296. Mr Johnson's case had taken some four years to reach the ECtHR.

In a limited sense, the Act makes (to borrow terminology familar in the EC law context) certain provisions of the Convention either 'directly effective' or 'indirectly effective' in United Kingdom courts.[4] As such, it has been widely portrayed in the popular press as tantamount to a 'Bill of Rights' – an analogy which is presumably intended to suggest that Parliament has succeeded by embracing European jurisprudence in Americanising the United Kingdom's constitutional order. Campaigners for constitutional reform had afforded the Bill a warm welcome. The then chairperson of the pressure group Charter 88 hailed the Bill as a measure which would; 'tip the balance of power from politicians to the people'.[5] The director of the human rights group Liberty announced that; 'We're absolutely delighted'.[6] As we shall see below, the Act has already had an important effect on domestic administrative law, but any suggestion that it has lent fundamental status (in the American sense of the term) to human rights norms would seem to be a substantial exaggeration.

I. THE TERMS OF THE ACT

Few legislative measures passed in the last 25 years have attracted so much political, academic and professional scrutiny as the Human Rights Act 1988.[7] The analysis of the Act offered in this chapter makes no attempt to be comprehensive. Such a task is more appropriately undertaken in a text dealing specifically with human rights issues. In a generalist public law text of this sort, more modest objectives need to be set. The first part of this chapter discusses the main provisions of the Act itself, and identifies some of the Act's obvious – and less obvious – implications for the understandings we attach to the core constitutional principles of parliamentary sovereignty, the rule of law and the separation of powers.[8] Part II then turns to a brief analysis of the way in which the courts have interpreted and applied the main provisions of the Act in the first few years of its existence.

[4] See pp 423–425 and 460–461 above. The distinction will be explained further below. In crude terms some parts of the Convention seem to have acquired directly effective and superior status to rules of common law and some delegated legislation, while they have only indirect effect vis à vis statutes and other types of delegated legislation. The EC law analogy should not be assumed to be perfectly applicable to the Human Rights Act, but it does provide a helpful frame of reference.

[5] *The Guardian*, 25 October 1997. [6] Ibid.

[7] For a variety of perspectives see Lord Irvine (1997) 'Constitutional reform and a Bill of Rights' *European Human Rights LR* 483–493; Boateng P and Straw J (1996) *Bringing Rights Home* (London: Labour Party); (1997) 'Bringing rights home: Labour plans to incorporate the ECHR into UK Law' *European Human Rights LR* 71–80; Tierney S (1998) 'The Human Rights Bill' *European Public Law* 299–311; Ewing K (1999) 'The Human Rights Act and parliamentary democracy' *MLR* 79–99; Bamforth N (1998) 'Parliamentary sovereignty and the Human Rights Act 1998' *Public Law* 572–582; Loveland I (1999) 'Constitutional law or administrative law? The Human Rights Act 1998' *Contemporary Issues in Law* 124–140.

[8] The analysis offered here is necessarily somewhat cursory. For a detailed treatment see Wadham J and Mountfield H (1999) *The Human Rights Act 1998* (London: Blackstone Press).

AN INCORPORATION OF FUNDAMENTAL RIGHTS?

The device of 'entrenching' basic human rights by requiring super-majoritarian legislative procedures to alter their content is now a firmly and widely established feature within the constitutions of western democratic nations. As we have seen in previous chapters, there is substantial variation on the types of entrenching techniques deployed in different countries, as well as in the depth of the entrenchment thereby achieved. The various methods are however all underpinned by a common rationale – namely that those moral and political principles considered fundamental to societal ordering must not be left at the mercy of transient political majorities which might temporarily control a national legislature.

The European Convention articulates just such a set of fundamental moral and political principles. And in many of the Convention's signatory states, its terms have been afforded supra-legislative constitutional status. That status enables those countries' courts to invoke the Convention terms as a moral yardstick against which to measure national legislation, and thereafter to strike down or disapply such legislation if it falls short of the necessary standards.

The Human Rights Act makes no attempt to achieve similar results in the United Kingdom; it does not seek to endow the Convention with an 'entrenched', supra-legislative legal status which would override any *future* legislation that breached its terms. It should also be noted that the Human Rights Act does not even 'incorporate' the Convention in the much more limited sense of permitting the courts to invoke the Convention to invalidate *pre-existing* legislation. The Blair government did not intend to achieve that objective.[9] The preamble to the statute identifies a rather more modest purpose; 'An Act *to give further effect to* rights and freedoms guaranteed under the European Convention on Human Rights'.[10]

The white paper reiterated the orthodox proposition that Parliament lacks the legal capacity to entrench an Act against repeal by a future Parliament through the simple majority plus royal assent formula; even if the (then) present Parliament and the government – wished to do so. Almost a decade after *Factortame (No 2)* has been decided, that does seem a very odd view to adopt.[11] By quite what constitutional mechanism directly effective EC law has achieved a minimal degree of entrenchment in United Kingdom law remains conceptually unclear,[12] but the principle does seem to have become embedded ('entrenched' being perhaps too loaded a word) in contemporary understandings of constitutional propriety. Unless we accept the contention

[9] Cf Lord Irvine at the report stage of the Bill in the House of Lords; 'I have to make this point absolutely plain. The ECHR under [the HRA] is not made part of our law . . . it does not make the Convention directly justiciable'; *HLD* January 29 1998, c 421.

[10] Emphasis added.

[11] In so far as the *Factortame* principle is limited to matters within the EC's competence, it is admittedly not a 'general' power in the sense that the White Paper may be using that term. But given the very wide competence that the EC now enjoys (post-Amsterdam), it is hardly credible to suggest that the *Factortame* rationale is not applicable to broad swathes of legislative activity.

[12] See pp 480–486 above.

that EC law is a unique jurisprudential creature, the political fact that it has achieved embedded status in United Kingdom law would indicate that other moral values might also – in similarly mysterious fashion – acquire that characteristic.

That the Blair government has not even tried to entrench the Human Rights Act indicates that for New Labour the old constitutional orthodoxies retain a potent force. The government's unwillingness to try to tackle the entrenchment issue would suggest that the Human Rights Act is, in formal legal terms, a statute just like any other. Its provisions may be amended or repealed by legislation at any point in the future. Advocates of incorporation who accept that the Convention cannot be entrenched in the legal sense, have suggested that a measure such as the Human Rights Act might gain a degree of 'moral entrenchment', in that its hold on the political consciousness of politicians of all mainstream parties might quickly become so firmly established that no government would promote a Bill seeking to dilute its effect. But one might readily doubt if a future right-wing Conservative government which has re-embraced the rigours of Thatcherite authoritarianism would feel morally constrained not to introduce a Bill substantially amending or wholly repealing the Human Rights Act.

The Blair government's evident reluctance to seek to achieve such unconventional constitutional objectives as entrenching a panoply of fundamental moral principles can perhaps be explained by its members' intrinsic attachment to Diceyan orthodoxies. More cynically, one might suggest, the government had no wish to place limits on the lawmaking autonomy it enjoyed as a result of its de facto control of Parliament's unlimited legislative powers. What is rather more difficult to understand is why the Blair government set its face against the principle that the Human Rights Act should empower courts to invalidate *previously enacted* statutory provisions which were incompatible with the ECHR. The white paper portrayed this scenario as politically undesirable:

'To make provision in the Bill for the courts to set aside Acts of Parliament would confer on the judiciary a general power over the decisions of Parliament which under our present constitutional arrangements they [sic] do not possess, and would be likely on occasions to draw the judiciary into serious conflict with Parliament.'[13]

The Blair government was vigorously opposed to the proposal floated at the Nice Summit that the EC treaties should be amended to include a fundamental human rights element. Such an amendment to EC law would – post-*Factortame* – have empowered domestic courts and tribunals to disapply both existing and future legislation which was inconsistent the requirements of EC human rights jurisprudence.[14] Having set its face so firmly against such innovations as an element of EC law, there was little likelihood that the Blair administration would attempt to produce a similar effect through engineering a 'revolutionary' change to domestic law. It is this lack of

[13] Ibid, at para 2.13. One should also note that the Act contains a broad definition of 'legislation', to include not just statutes but also certain elements of the prerogative: s 21.

[14] Craig P and DeBurca B (2002, 3rd edn) *EU law* pp 358–369 (Oxford: OUP). See also Rogers I (2002) 'From the Human Rights Act to the Charter . . .' *European Human Rights LR* 343–356.

will or ambition in the Act's reach which perhaps most clearly points to its status as an innovation in administrative rather than constitutional law. As we shall see below, its innovation in this regard is substantial, and – for so long as it remains in force – the Act promises to work important changes in orthodox understandings of the relationship between the various branches of government. But its impact is likely to fall far short of triggering a constitutional revolution in the sense of placing judicially enforceable, 'higher law' constraints on Parliament's legislative power. The point was put with perfect clarity by the then Home Secretary, Jack Straw, at the Bill's second reading in the Commons:

> 'What the [HRA] makes clear is that Parliament is supreme, and that if Parliament wishes to maintain the position enshrined in an Act that it has passed, but which is incompatible with the Convention in the eyes of a British court, it is that Act which will remain in force.'[15]

SECTION 3 – NEW RULES OF STATUTORY INTERPRETATION?

Section 1 of the Act identifies various parts of the ECHR as 'Convention Rights' within domestic law. It is these parts of the Convention to which the Human Rights Act 1998 has lent a new and enhanced legal status. Those parts of the Convention which are not identified as 'Convention Rights' continue to have effect in domestic law only to the extent that orthodox common law principles permit.

Section 2 then imposes a clear duty on any court or tribunal which is hearing litigation in which a Convention Right is in issue. The duty is that the court or tribunal must 'take into account' any judgment of the ECtHR, opinion of the EComHR or decision of the Committee of Ministers when considering the case before it. Section 2(1) makes it clear that it is for the domestic court or tribunal to decide if any such judgment, opinion or decision is indeed relevant. Section 2 does not therefore expressly attribute binding status to ECHR jurisprudence.

At an abstract, theoretical level, s 3 of the Act seems to mark a clear departure from orthodox understandings of the separation of powers.[16] As suggested in chapter three, Parliament has traditionally regarded the question of the principles which courts should apply when interpreting legislation as a matter of common law; that is, as an issue to be determined by the courts. Legislation rarely seeks to instruct the courts as to the principles of statutory interpretation which they should deploy. An exception is provided by ss 2–3 of the European Communities Act 1972;[17] but as we have seen, the issue of EC membership occupies an apparently distinct position within the United Kingdom's constitutional law. Section 3 of the Human Rights Act contains an instruction to courts and tribunals couched in the following terms:

> '(1) So far as it is possible to do so, primary legislation and subordinate legislation must be read and given effect to in a way which is compatible with Convention rights.
> (2) This section –

[15] *HCD*, 16 February 1998, c 773. [16] See pp 74–77 above. [17] See pp 445–446 above.

(a) applies to primary legislation and subordinate legislation whenever enacted;

(b) does not affect the validity, continuing operation or enforcement of any incompatible primary legislation.'

Section 3 would manifestly affect both criminal and civil law matters. The Human Rights Act cannot be invoked as a defence by defendants accused of statutory crimes defined in a manner that does not permit of Convention-compliant interpretation, as it does not empower the courts to invalidate legislation. That scenario seems unlikely to arise with any frequency. But many statutory offences are not cast in rule bound terms. Public order legislation – involving for example picketing, demonstrations, or public marches and speeches – provides an obvious example of this. Such statutes would have to be interpreted in a fashion that conforms to the Convention's protection of freedom of expression and association in Arts 10 and 11 ECHR. The same consideration would also apply to the construction of statutes in the civil law area; concerning for example the government's regulation of the media or the refusal of permission for public marches and demonstrations. It may also be noted that s 21(1) of the Act extends the notion of 'primary legislation' to Orders in Council made under the prerogative.

The constitutional significance of s 3 depends in large part on the meaning which courts attach to the notion of 'possible'. This is a term which might plausibly be thought to bear several meanings. Narrowly construed, s 3 requires courts to reject literalist approaches to statutory interpretation if such approaches would produce results incompatible with Convention Rights, and to adopt instead other indigenous, established techniques (viz the golden rule or the mischief rule) if those techniques would produce a Convention compatible outcome. More broadly construed, s 3 might be taken as requiring courts to embrace a teleological or purposive approach to interpretation in the sense advocated by Lord Denning in *Magor and St Mellens RDC*[18] if use of any established techniques would not render a statutory term consistent with the requirements of Convention rights; (the purpose being of course to respect Convention Rights). If lent a broad meaning, s 3 could be seen as authorising domestic courts to adopt the type of interpretive techniques proposed by the ECJ in *Marleasing*.[19] It is perhaps worthy of note that the phrase 'so far as it is possible to do so' in HRA, s 3 is an almost verbatim repetition of the ECJ formula concerning the scope of domestic courts' interpretive autonomy in *Marleasing*. As noted in chapter thirteen, *Marleasing* has been viewed by the House of Lords as justifying the de facto insertion of additional clauses into legislation by the courts; a technique which is very hard to reconcile with traditional understandings of the courts' interpretive role.

As one might expect, varying views were expressed in political, judicial and academic fora as to how s 3 itself should be interpreted. The government's white paper suggested that the instruction given to the courts by s 3 goes; 'far beyond the present rule which enables the courts to take the Convention into account in resolving any

[18] See pp 74–75 above. [19] See pp 473–474 above.

ambiguity in legislative provisions'.[20] At the Bill's committee stage in the Commons, the Home Secretary appeared to favour giving s 3 a narrow meaning; '[I]t is not our intention that the courts, in applying [s 3] should contort the meaning of words to produce implausible or incredible results'.[21] He then went on to offer a magnificently tautological construction of the term 'possible' in s 3; 'It means, "What is the possible interpretation?" Let us [ie the courts] look at this set of words and the possible interpretations'.[22] Lord Irvine, in a public lecture, indicated that he anticipated that s 3 would empower the courts to adopt a *Marleasing*-type approach to the construction of legislation: it would be acceptable for the courts to; 'strain the meaning of words or read in words which are not there'.[23]

Quite what the government intended s 3 to do – and quite what the courts would make of it – prompted considerable debate among academic commentators. Geoffrey Marshall suggested that 3 was; 'a deeply mysterious provision'.[24] Bennion's view that; 'There was much vagueness and confusion in the minds of the Act's promoters about the intended meaning of the rule'[25] seems eminently defensible.[26] Some hint as to the judiciary's view of the effect of s 3 was offered by Lord Cooke (a former President of the New Zealand Court of Appeal, and then sitting as a law lord), during the Bill's Committee Stage in the Lords. Lord Cooke suggested that s 3; 'enjoins a search for possible meanings as distinct from the true meaning which has been the traditional approach'; it would require courts and tribunals to adopt not; 'a strained interpretation, but one that is fairly possible'.[27]

Notwithstanding such divergences of opinion, it would seem safe to conclude that the real question raised by s 3 would not be *whether* it required the courts to make a radical break with orthodox interpretive principles – but rather *to what extent* it required them to do so. One can readily identify individual judgments decided before 1998 in which British courts pursued unorthodox interpretive strategies in order to safeguard human rights values.[28] But s 3 could sensibly be construed as requiring all domestic courts in all cases to match the most imaginative and expansive use of the Convention occasionally made by some courts prior to 1998.

Section 3 of the HRA 1998 was modelled on the approach taken by the New

[20] At para 2.7. [21] *HCD*, 3 June 1998, c 421. [22] Ibid, at c 423.

[23] Cited in Klug F (1999) 'The Human Rights Act 1998, *Pepper v Hart* and all that' *Public Law* 246–273 at p 254.

[24] Marshall G (1998) 'Interpreting interpretation in the Human Rights Bill' *Public Law* 167–171 at 167.

[25] Bennion F (2000) 'What interpretation is "possible" under s 3(1) of the Human Rights Act?' *Public Law* 77–91 at 88.

[26] See also Pannick D (1998) 'Principles of interpretation of Convention Rights . . .' *Public Law* 545–551: Klug F (1998) op cit: Lester A (1998) 'The Act of the possible. . . .' *European Human Rights LR* 665–680.

[27] Lord Cooke's views might be thought particularly persuasive here, given his status as a senior Law Lord and his previous role as President of the Court of Appeal of New Zealand, where he heard many cases involving the New Zealand Bill of Rights, a measure which strongly influenced the design of the HRA 1998 itself.

[28] The Court of Appeal's judgment in *Ex p Leech* [1994] QB 198 being a clear example of this: see pp 695–696 above. See also the Court of Appeal's judgment in *Rantzen v Mirror Group Newspapers (1986) Ltd* [1994] QB 670; discussed in Loveland (2000) op cit pp 129–132.

Zealand Parliament when it enacted a Bill of Rights.[29] The thinking behind both countries' adoption of this technique is rooted in a concern to preclude the courts from straying into the legislative arena; by explicitly identifying the judiciary's competence as one of 'interpretation', it might be thought possible to present the Act as an initiative which does not impinge upon traditional understandings of the separation of powers and therefore does not compromise the sovereignty of Parliament.

This is perhaps a naive assumption, and one which rests on a rather limited understanding of the relationship between Parliament and the courts. If we are to accept that orthodox perceptions of parliamentary sovereignty hinge upon the presumption that courts will generally adopt a literalist approach to statutory interpretation, s 3 does impact upon – at least in de facto terms – the sovereignty of Parliament. The UK's experience with EC law indicates that judges may on occasion be tempted to apply 'interpretive' techniques so outlandish in the meaning they attach to statutory texts that they do not in any but the most formalistic of senses appear to be 'interpretation' at all.[30] It was after all judgments, both of domestic courts and the ECJ and ECtHR, couched in the language of interpretation which so enraged many backbench Conservative MPs during the judicial supremacism controversy.[31] Labour Ministers in the Blair governments might be thought less likely than their Conservative predecessors to indulge media and backbench hysteria concerning alleged 'judicial usurpations of legislative functions' in respect of innovative 'interpretations' of legislative provisions that might in future emerge from the courts, but whether they would be able wholly to resist the temptation to engage in a little cheap political populism at the judiciary's expense remained to be seen.

SECTION 4 – THE 'DECLARATION OF INCOMPATIBILITY

While the Act does not empower any court to question the *legality* of primary legislation, it does seem to offer the superior courts[32] the opportunity to challenge a statute's *legitimacy*. Section 4 introduces a device called the 'Declaration of Incompatibility'. Section 4 is directed at those statutory provisions which a court cannot interpret in a fashion that is compatible with a Convention Right, even if those provisions are subjected to the unorthodox canons of constructions evidently introduced by s 3. Again, we might note that the notion of 'primary legislation' includes Orders in Council made under the prerogative.

The declaration of incompatibility empowers – but does not oblige – a court to

29 Lord Cooke (1997) 'Mechanisms for entrenchment and protection of a Bill of Rights: the New Zealand experience' *European Human Rights LR* 490–495.

30 Cf *Pickstone v Freemans plc* [1989] AC 66, HL, and *Litster v Forth Dry Dock and Engineering Co Ltd* [1990] 1 AC 546, HL: see pp 476–479 above. It is perhaps odd, given the white paper's invocation of New Zealand as a model for Britain to follow, that no mention was made, either in the white paper or by ministers during the parliamentary debate on the bill, of the interpretive strategies that courts in that country have deployed when applying its Bill of Rights: see Lord Cooke op cit.

31 See pp 698–709 above.

32 In England and Wales these are the High Court, the Court of Appeal and the House of Lords: s 4(5).

identify the way in which the statutory provision breaches the Convention. Section 4(6) makes it quite clear that the declaration itself does not invalidate the provision concerned: the court is obliged to apply the incompatible parts of the statute. Nor does the Act contain any requirement the government or Parliament take remedial action to repeal or modify the statute in issue. Section 4 cannot therefore be seen as an entrenching device in the traditional sense of the term.

The purpose of the Declaration of Incompatibility mechanism seems to be twofold. Firstly, assuming the government's pro-Convention *bona fides*, a Declaration will alert the government to unintended breaches of the Convention which it might then seek to remedy. Or secondly, in the event that the government wishes to condone a breach of the Convention, the Declaration will expose ministers to the pressure of public and/or opposition opinion to take remedial action.

In either case, the Declaration mechanism relieves the courts of the responsibility of having to deploy controversial interpretative strategies which might lead to them being accused of 'usurping the legislative function'. Section 4 empowers judges openly to express their loyalty to the values laid out in the Convention while simultaneously avoiding any covert undermining of Parliament's intentions.

The mechanism has strong echoes of the tactic adopted by the Canadian Supreme Court in the early 1980s when it found itself faced with a federal government attempt to amend the Constitution in a way which was constitutional in the narrow legal sense, but which was clearly in breach of firmly established constitutional conventions. The Supreme Court's judgment in *A-G of Manitoba v A-G of Canada*[33] confirmed that there were no legal obstacles in the government's path, but did so in language so condemnatory of the political mores of the government's plans that it became impossible for the government to proceed.[34]

The Canadian episode was an isolated instance of a court undermining the moral foundation of governmental and parliamentary intentions, and one fashioned by the Supreme Court rather than the national legislature. That the United Kingdom Parliament has created a similar device, without knowing with any certainty how often a declaration of incompatibility might be made, may be thought a rather radical innovation. Section 4 does not bind the legislature in a legal sense, but it could be read as inferring that the judiciary need no longer adhere to the traditional administrative law notion that courts should adopt a deferential attitude towards Parliament's clearly expressed intentions.[35] A judge may not be empowered by the Act to overturn legislation, but she has it seems been invited, even perhaps instructed, to make clear her reasons for assuming it lacks a defensible moral base.

The frequency with which the Declaration device would be used would be likely to turn in large part on the way in which the courts construed their powers under s 3. The more expansive the courts' interpretive jurisdiction, the less likely it would be that a particular statutory provision could not be reconciled with the pertinent

33 [1981] 1 SCR 753. 34 See pp 337–342 above.

35 As will be suggested below, this inference has apparently not commended itself to the judiciary.

Convention Right. One might sensibly suggest that if the courts were to construe s 3 (per the approach taken to *Marleasing* in *Litster*)[36] as authorising the insertion of qualificatory clauses into the text of legislation, then the Declaration of Incompatibility would become a relevant factor only in respect of statutory provisions which were stated in express terms as being intended to breach a Convention Right. The interplay between s 3 and s 4 of the Act thus promised to pose the courts a complicated question to answer. The Blair government – implicitly endorsing an expansive interpretation of s 3 – evidently expected that Declarations would rarely be necessary. As the Home Secretary put it during the Bill's committee stage; 'We want the courts to strive to find an interpretation . . . that is consistent . . . and only in the last resort to conclude that legislation is simply inconsistent'.[37]

SECTION 6 – THE REACH OF THE ACT: VERTICAL (AND HORIZONTAL?) DIRECT EFFECT

Similar difficulties could be thought to attend the question of the reach that the Act might have. Perhaps the most complex and opaque provision of the legislation is s 6. Section 6(1) expressly provides that it is unlawful for a 'public authority' to act in a fashion that it is incompatible with a Convention right. In essence, this provision makes all those parts of the Convention which have been given Convention Right status sub-categories of the illegality ground of judicial review of government action.[38] Many of the Convention's provisions require that the legality of government action be measured against a rigorous standard: the requirements that interferences with Art 8 or Art 10 rights be 'necessary in a democratic society' are obvious examples.[39] This level of judicial scrutiny of the lawfulness of government action would in many circumstances be akin to what English administrative lawyers would regard as proportionality review. As noted in chapter fourteen,[40] English courts have traditionally rejected suggestions that the common law should recognise proportionality as new ground of review. Section 6 might be thought to render such judicial innovation unnecessary when Convention Rights are in issue.

A major difficulty thrown up by s 6(1) is identifying which decision-makers are caught by this expanded notion of review; ie what is the meaning of 'public authority'. The issue of how to draw a line between 'public' and 'private' organisations/individuals has been a vexed question both in domestic administrative law and EC law over the past 30 years.[41] Lord Irvine ran into difficulties on this issue when the Bill was published when he clearly stated that the Press Complaints Commission would not be a public authority. On being presented with an opinion written by David Pannick QC

[36] See pp 473–474 and pp 477–478 above. [37] *HCD*, 3 June 1998, cc 421–422.

[38] See pp 504–524 above. [39] See pp 661–662 above. [40] See pp 531–534 above.

[41] The line of case law flowing from *O'Reilly v Mackman* [1983] 2 AC 237, HL, is now both voluminous in scale and tortuous in complexity: see ch 16 above. On the EC position, see especially Curtin D (1990) 'The province of government' *EL Rev* 195–217.

which drew the opposite conclusion, Lord Irvine changed his mind and accepted that the PCC would be subject to the restraints imposed by the Convention.

The white paper had offered a reasonably lengthy list of 'public authorities'. This included:

> '. . . central government (including executive agencies); local government; the police; immigration officers; prisons; courts; and, to the extent that they are exercising public functions, companies responsible for areas of activity which were previously within the public sector, such as privatised utilities'.[42]

The Human Rights Act, in contrast, makes no attempt to identify in detail all the various bodies which Parliament envisages should be regarded as 'public authorities'. The definition offered in s 6 of the Act includes 'courts and tribunals'[43] and – in a disquieting display of imprecision in s 6(3)(b) – 'any person certain of whose functions are of a public nature'.[44] Section 6(3)(b) offers a limited, negative definition of the public authority concept. The sub-section states that neither house of Parliament is a public authority for these purpose, nor is a person 'exercising functions in connection with proceedings in parliament'. Parliamentary privilege has not been brought within the limits on governmental autonomy laid out by the Convention.

Much interpretative work would thus have to be done by the courts to decide whether a particular person or body was a 'public authority', or whether she or it was performing functions having 'a public nature'. This prospect evidently alarmed several Conservative MPs who criticised the vagueness of the 'public authority' formula during the Bill's passage. It remained to be seen whether the courts' definition of public authorities would borrow wholesale from common law doctrine on this question, or follow the ECJ's reasoning, or blend common law and EC law, or create a whole new line of ECHR specific 'public authorities'. It would be most unfortunate if we were to end up with three quite distinct streams of law on this question for domestic, EC and ECHR purposes. But as the Act stands, we will be dependent on the courts to tie up this particular legislative loose end. Given the many threads which are still dangling from our jurisprudence on what is a public law issue for the purposes of an application for judicial review,[45] we could no doubt expect that the loose ends would be tied with many knots.

[42] At para 2.2.

[43] An obvious problem arises from the inter-relationship between s 2 and s 6. Section 2 does not give binding effect in domestic law to ECtHR jurisprudence: the section merely requires domestic courts to consider such jurisprudence when it is relevant. However, a domestic court which – having considered ECtHR case law – then produced a judgment which was manifestly incompatible with the Convention's requirement presumably breaches s 6(1) and an appellate or reviewing court would be bound so to hold. Unless s 6(2) – discussed immediately below – could be invoked, that result essentially means that the domestic court is controlled by ECHR precedent. This may prove to be a technical quibble with little practical effect.

[44] Section 6(5) then tells us that: 'In relation to a particular act, a person is not a public authority by virtue of subsection (3)(b) above if the nature of the act is private'.

[45] See ch 16 above. See also Forsyth (1987) op cit; Pannick D (1988) 'What is a public authority?', in Jowell J and Oliver D (eds) *New directions in judicial review* (London: Sweet and Maxwell) Bamforth (1993) op cit.

Lawful breaches of Convention Rights by public authorities

The Act does not designate a specific procedure through which Convention Rights issues may be raised. Section 7 makes it clear that such issues can be addressed; 'in any legal proceedings'. Section 8 then provides that if a public authority is found to have acted unlawfully per s 6(1), the court may; 'grant such relief or remedy, or make such order, within its powers as it considers just and appropriate'.[46]

However, s 6(2) provides that a public authority which breaches a Convention Right does not act unlawfully if it is required to adopt the course it has taken by 'primary legislation'. The bite of s 6(2) – which effectively provides public authorities with a justification for breaching Convention Rights – would be contingent on the way in which the courts construed s 3 of the Act.

Should a court conclude that the statutory provision under which the public authority was proceeding could be construed in a manner compatible with Convention Rights, s 6(2) would not come into play. In these circumstances, a court exercising a judicial review jurisdiction (which does not permit it to substitute its own judgment for that of the initial decision-maker)[47] would invalidate the initial decision and remit it to be determined afresh in accordance with a Convention compliant construction of the relevant statutory provision.[48] If the Convention Right issue was raised in private law litigation, such as an action in tort or contract, the court's jurisdiction could of course extend to substitution of judgment.[49] If, in contrast – in either a judicial review or private law action context – the court concluded that the public authority's breach of a Convention Right was unavoidable, s 6(2) precludes a finding of unlawfulness. A court empowered to issue a Declaration of Incompatibility would then consider whether its s 4 power should be invoked.

Section 6(2) clearly has no bearing on government action taken through a direct exercise of prerogative powers, although per s 21 it would impact upon prerogative powers exercised through Orders in Council. Nor would s 6(2) apply to criminal offences or civil law relationships existing purely at common law. Section 6(1) would seem to require that courts qua 'public authorities' should 'unrecognise' common law crimes that breached Convention Rights: if a court convicted a defendant in such circumstances the court would presumably be acting unlawfully per s 6(1). Similarly, a court should not allow other public authorities to benefit from existing common law rules in such areas as contract or tort law if those rules were incompatible with the court's understanding of Convention requirements.

Section 6(2) is obviously another manifestation of the principle that the Human

[46] Subsequent provisions of s 8 indicate that courts should be slow to award damages against public authorities for breaches of Convention Rights; and if they do so, awards should be set at a low level.

[47] See pp 70–73 above.

[48] If the courts accept that the Human Rights Act requires application of proportionality review to some or all interferences with Convention Rights, a judicial review jurisdiction will more closely approach a substitution of judgment power; see the discussion at pp 531–534 above.

[49] As noted above, the Act does not designate an 'exclusive' procedure through which Convention Right questions may be raised.

Rights Act does not affect the sovereignty of Parliament. The provision's impact was characterised above as providing public authorities with a justification for breaching Convention Rights. An alternative characterisation would be to regard s 6(2) as affirming Parliament's capacity to order executive bodies to act in defiance of accepted human rights norms. That conclusion might be regarded as undesirable in moral or political terms. Its legal impact is nonetheless quite clear. On another important question, however, s 6 seems to be woefully lacking in clarity.

Do convention rights have 'horizontal effect'?

It is an important characteristic of the 'fundamental' nature of many provisions of EC law that the rights and obligations they create are both 'vertically' and 'horizontally' directly effective; that is enforceable against both government bodies (vertically) and private companies or individuals (horizontally).[50] Similarly, many common law rules are as readily enforceable against companies or individuals as they are against government bodies. Whether the Human Rights Act bestows this universalistic character on the Convention rights was not however made clear by the text of the Act itself. Might an individual, for example, invoke Art 8's right to privacy against a newspaper which publishes stories about her sex life?[51] Could a court apply Art 9 to prevent a plc from refusing to hire Buddhist or Muslim employees? Would a newspaper, qua defendant in a libel action brought by a politician, be able to rely on *Lingens* and *Castells*?

There is no explicit, textual provision in the Human Rights Act to the effect that individual or private sector organisations are legally required to respect Convention Rights. Had Parliament wished the Act to have horizontal effect, such a term could certainly have been placed in the legislation.[52] The absence of any such provision can be taken as strong evidence that Parliament intended that Convention Rights operate only in the vertical plane.

That inference can be reinforced in a contextual sense by considering the reach of the Convention itself as an international law instrument. In proceedings before the ECtHR, the 'defendant' is invariably one of the Convention's signatory states. As already noted, the Convention contains provisions which enable (but do not require) a state to empower its citizens to initiate actions against it before the ECtHR. The ECHR does not make any provision however for individual citizens to litigate against other individuals or private sector organisations before the Strasbourg court. Actions before the ECtHR instigated by individuals are always 'vertical' in nature;[53] at least in formal terms.[54]

It is not fanciful however to suggest that s 6 can be read as implicitly lending

50 See pp 450–453 above.

51 See for example Markesinis B (1986) 'The right to be let alone versus freedom of speech' *Public Law* 67–81; (1990) 'Our patchy law of privacy' *MLR* 802–809.

52 Ie s 6(1) might read; 'It is unlawful for a public authority or any natural or legal person . . .'.

53 Although one might suggest – semantically – that actions initiated by one state against another are 'horizontal' in one sense.

54 The reason for this caveat is outlined below.

Convention Rights horizontal effect. The starting point for this argument is the fact that s 6(3) designates courts as 'public authorities'. Per s 6(1), therefore, it is 'unlawful' for a court to act in a way that is incompatible with a Convention Right; (unless of course it is required so to act by legislation which cannot be interpreted in a Convention compliant manner). So far, so simple. But the jurisprudential map drawn by s 6 becomes much more difficult to read from this point on.

A problem arises because it is possible to take rather different points of view as to who – or what – is really the defendant in human rights litigation. The view taken on this question in turn has profound consequences for the effective horizontality or otherwise of the Act's effect. The uncertainties can be illustrated by considering a series of quite mundane hypothetical scenarios.

Scenario 1. A judicial review action brought by citizen A against the Home Secretary's use of a prerogative power. Since no statutory power is in issue, neither s 3 nor s 6(2) are relevant. In this scenario, we would assume that the action is vertical. The Home Secretary is obviously a 'public authority'. If the High Court concludes that the Home Secretary's action does not breach a Convention Right, we might assume that in any subsequent appeal the Home Secretary would still be the defendant. However, it could also be suggested that the breach of the Convention is triggered here by the High Court's first instance judgment; that the High Court qua public authority is breaching s 6(1); and that the 'real' defendant on appeal is the High Court. The identity of the defendant is of no obvious significance in this scenario – all of the candidates are 'vertical' entities.

Scenario 2. We might reach a similar conclusion in scenario 2. Here, a judicial review action is brought by citizen A against the Home Secretary's use of a statutory power. The Home Secretary is a public authority. The High Court is also a public authority, and is additionally obliged by s 3 to interpret the relevant statutory provision in a manner consistent with the Convention Right. Again, it could be suggested that if the first instance judgment is in the Home Secretary's favour, either she or the High Court could be seen as the 'real' defendant on appeal. Again, the identity of the defendant is of no obvious significance in this scenario as all of the candidates are 'vertical' entities.

Scenario 3. An action brought by citizen A against company B, the solution to which turns on the conclusion reached by the court as to the meaning of a particular statutory provision. An action of this sort is nominally horizontal. Company B is not a public authority; (and we may assume that s 6(3)(b) is not relevant here). Three questions then arise. Firstly; notwithstanding the lack of a public authority defendant at first instance, is the court nonetheless obliged by s 3 to give the relevant statutory term a Convention compliant interpretation? Secondly; alternatively or additionally, does s 6 require the court to construe the term in a manner compatible with the Convention; the rationale being that if the court adopted an orthodox, Convention non-compliant meaning of the provision the court itself would be acting unlawfully? Thirdly, assuming that neither of the first two questions are answered affirmatively, would the first instance court nonetheless become de facto the defendant in a subsequent appeal?

Scenario 4. An action brought by citizen A against company B, the solution to which turns on the conclusion reached by the court as to the content of the common law. S 3 would not bite here, as no statutory term is in issue. But the second and third questions outlined in scenario 3 above would still be pertinent.

The argument made in scenarios 3 and 4 would afford the Human Rights Act at least de facto horizontal effect through the indirect mechanism of placing the courts through either s 3 or s 6 under a duty to ensure that domestic law conforms to Convention requirements. This is an imaginative but by no means implausible reading of the text of the Act.

What might be termed the implicit textual justification for according Convention Rights de facto horizontal impact can also be buttressed by contextual considerations. It is clear that the ECtHR has interpreted some elements of the Convention as founding what would seem to be a 'horizontal' remedy. This situation can arise in one of two ways.

Firstly, it arises when the action before the Strasbourg court has emerged from what was ostensibly horizontal litigation in the domestic sphere. *Goodwin v United Kingdom*, discussed in chapter nineteen,[55] is a good example of this. The litigation began as a suit between private parties, but turned on the interpretation of the Contempt of Court Act 1981, s 10. Before the ECtHR, the 'real' defendant was s 10 itself as interpreted by the House of Lords in *X Ltd v Morgan-Grampian (Publishers)*.[56] The ECtHR's judgment is illustrative of the proposition that a signatory state may breach the Convention if its laws allow individuals to invoke legal protections which unacceptably hamper other individuals' access to rights identified by the Convention.

The second situation is illustrated by cases such as *X and Y v The Netherlands*.[57] X was the father of a mentally handicapped teenager (Y) allegedly raped in the residential facility where she lived. The crux of the Court's judgment was that both the father and child's Art 8 rights to private and family life were breached because Dutch criminal law made no effective provision for the prosecution of such alleged crimes. The ECtHR concluded that Art 8 imposed a positive obligation on the Netherlands to introduce such a law because; 'This is a case where fundamental values and essential aspects of private life are at stake. *Effective deterrence* is indispensible in this area . . .'.[58] Similarly, in *Marckx v Belgium*,[59] the ECtHR held that Belgium was in breach of Art 8 because Belgian law did not allow parents and their illegitimate children to enjoy any legally recognised family relationship at all. The Court's decision in *Malone v United Kingdom* can be analysed in a similar way. The United Kingdom was in breach of Art 10 because domestic law contained no provisions at all to safeguard Mr Malone's Art 8 rights against intrusion by government tapping of his phone. In all three cases, the state's first step in remedying the breach would be to introduce *some* law dealing with the relevant issues.[60] There is an unhappy lack of clarity in the ECtHR's jurisprudence as to which articles of the Convention – and in what circumstances – can create such a 'positive obligation'. But the principle per se lends weight to the argument that the

55 At pp 686–688 above. 56 See ibid above. 57 (1985) 8 EHRR 235.

58 Ibid, at para 27 (original emphasis). 59 (1979) 2 EHRR 330.

60 That law would in turn be subject to evaluation against the yardsticks (cf the 'necessary in a democratic society' test) applied by the Convention.

Human Rights Act may impose a comparable responsibility on domestic courts in some instances of ostensibly horizontal litigation.

Prior to the Human Rights Act coming into force, academic and judicial opinion on the horizontal effect issue was sharply divided. The argument against horizontal effect was most strongly put by Buxton LJ in an article in the *Law Quarterly Review*.[61] Buxton LJ's argument rested primarily on the fact that, under the Convention itself, actions are brought only against signatory states; ie that they are only vertically effective. The argument is supposedly buttressed, as a matter of implication, by the very mention of 'public authorities' in s 6; the inference being that had Parliament intended the Act to be horizontally and vertically effective, it would have inserted the clause 'or any natural or legal person' into s 6.

The counter argument has been raised by Professor Wade and Murray Hunt.[62] Their central contention is that since a major element of the courts' role as 'public authorities' is to settle disputes between individuals, the Act's horizontal impact arises as a matter of necessary implication. Wade further makes the point that accepting the horizontality of the Act would much reduce the problem of deciding whether or not a body is a 'public authority' for this purpose.[63] Hunt also suggests that the Fourteenth Amendment jurisprudence of the US Supreme Court on the construction of common law ruled as 'State action' may prove particularly instructive to United Kingdom judges on this issue. The Fourteenth Amendment is notionally directed only at 'State action' which infringes certain human rights principles, notably a freedom from racial discrimination. However the US Supreme Court's 1948 judgment in *Shelley v Kramer*[64] clearly gave the Fourteenth Amendment an effective horizontal impact. In *Shelley*, the Court held that a racist restrictive covenant negotiated between individuals could not be enforced as any judgment to that effect issued by a court would amount to 'state action' within the Fourteenth Amendment.

One might also note that if Buxton LJ's view is correct, an applicant whose 'Convention rights' have been infringed by a 'private body' will still be able to make an application direct to the ECtHR to begin an action against the UK government for failure to protect the right concerned.[65] If the point of the Act is indeed to 'bring rights home' that consequence would seem rather silly.

Anthony Lester and David Pannick urged the courts to adopt a more subtle

[61] (2000) 'The Human Rights Act and private law' *LQR* 48–67.

[62] Wade HRW (2000) 'Horizons of horizontality' *LQR* 217–224; Hunt M (1998) 'The "horizontal effect" of the *Human* Rights Act' *Public Law* 423–443. See also Bamforth N (1999) 'The application of the Human Rights Act to public authorities and private bodies' *Cambridge LJ* 159–170; Phillipson G (1999) 'The Human Rights Act, "horizontal effect" and the common law: a bang or a whimper' *MLR* 824–849.

[63] (2000) op cit at p 223. The obvious point against this assertion is that the Act expressly recognises in s 6(5) that persons who are 'public authorities' when discharging functions of a 'public nature' are not public authorities when discharging functions of a private nature. This seems implicitly to accept a public/private or vertical/horizontal divide within the Act.

[64] 334 US 1 (1948).

[65] Wade cites *Young, James and Webster v United Kingdom* (1981) 4 EHRR 38 and *A v United Kingdom* (1998) 27 EHRR 611 to support this point; (2000) op cit at p 219.

technique to give Convention Rights horizontal effect. Their proposition essentially suggested that the court should regard the Human Rights Act as a parliamentary invitation to accelerate innovation at common law in order to prevent individuals interfering unjustifiably with other people's Convention Rights:

'The correct way involves approaching the Convention rights through domestic law rather than round domestic law. . . . The central legislative purpose [of the 1998 Act] is that of bringing the Convention rights home, that is of domesticating them so that they are not regarded as alien rights protected exclusively by a "foreign" European Court. . . . [I]t is especially important to weave the Convention rights into the principles of the common law and of equity . . .'[66]

Which of these various views would prove the more compelling to the courts remained to be seen. It is however a shocking indictment of Parliament's approach to this legislation that so important a matter has not been clearly settled by the text of the Act itself. Reference to Hansard along the lines permitted by *Pepper v Hart*[67] will apparently not provide the courts with obvious assistance on this point. Lord Irvine made the following comment at the Bill's second reading in the Lords:

'[I]t is right as a matter of principle for the courts to have the duty of acting compatibly with the Convention not only in cases involving other public authorities but also in developing the common law in deciding cases between individuals. Why should they not? In preparing this Bill, we have taken the view that it is the other course, that of excluding Convention considerations altogether from cases between individuals, which would have to be justified.'[68]

While that passage seems to point firmly towards the conclusion that the Act was intended to have horizontal effect, at a later point in his speech Lord Irvine made the observation that; '[The Act] should apply only to public authorities, however defined, and not to individuals'.[69] Lord Irvine's evidently inconsistent views have unsurprisingly been invoked as persuasive authority by both Buxton LJ and Professor Wade to support their respective arguments. One can also find passages in Lord Irvine's speeches on the Bill in the Lords which seem strongly to approve the Lester/Pannick strategy.[70] The only conclusion we might safely draw from this is that resort to Hansard is by no means a panacea to cure all the interpretative ills caused by textual ambiguities in legislation.

At the point when the Bill was enacted, commentators could do little more than surmise that it seemed possible that once the Act comes fully into force, a significant portion of domestic administrative law would have to concern itself with regulating relationships between individuals, rather than between individuals and various state bodies. In effect, the Act could introduce a public law dimension to what have previously been regarded as issues purely of private law.

[66] (2000) 'The impact of the Human Rights Act on private law: the knight's move' *LQR* 380–392 at 383.

[67] See pp 284–290 above.

[68] *HLD*, 24 November 1997, c 783.

[69] Ibid, at cc 1231–1232.

[70] See for example *HLD*, 24 November 1997, at cc 784–785.

A SPECIAL STATUS FOR CHURCHES AND THE PRESS?

Few substantial amendments were made to the Bill during its passage. The Church of England expressed grave concern – voiced by the bishops in the House of Lords – that its religious freedom would be unacceptably curbed if it were to be subject to the Act. The government was evidently moved by these plaintive representations, although whether from a belief in their intrinsic desirability or a concern to avoid possible obstruction of the Bill in the Lords is not entirely clear. Section 13 of the Act now requires that courts pay 'particular regard' to the Convention's protection of religious freedom. The inference would seem to be that should, for example, the Church of England or any other religious body wish to discriminate against its employees on grounds of race, gender or sexual orientation, it might be able to invoke the principle of freedom of religious belief to trump these competing entitlements. The amendment is a substantive obscenity, as are the sentiments of the Church of England which lies behind it – namely that there is no obvious linkage between Christian values and respect for human rights. It is unfortunate that the concession was made, and one might hope that it proves of little substantive value to its progenitors when it comes to be interpreted by the courts.

The press was evidently also much concerned that the Act would curb media freedom, primarily by stimulating the growth of an indigenous privacy law. The concern seemed hugely overstated, as the European Court on Human Rights has shown little willingness to allow privacy considerations to trump press freedom in respect of news coverage with a political or public interest dimension.[71] Lobbying of ministers, particularly by Lord Wakeham, the Chairman of the Press Complaints Commission, nonetheless led to the insertion of what would seem a wholly superfluous amendment. Mirroring the favoured status afforded to religious groups in s 13, s 12 requires courts to have 'particular regard' to freedom of expression principles when, inter alia, the litigation before it concerns information which it would in the 'public interest' to be published.

QUESTIONS OF PROCEDURE

While the Act undoubtedly expands the substantive scope of administrative law, its position on procedural questions seems markedly more ambiguous. The Act's *locus standi* requirements raise a potentially awkward problem for the courts to resolve.[72] As noted above, s 7 permits Convention Rights issues to be raised in; 'any legal proceedings'. However, s 7 also provides that only a 'victim' of an alleged infringement of the Convention may bring an action under the Act. The concept of 'victim' is borrowed

[71] See the survey of ECHR cases in Tierney S (1998) 'Press freedom and public interest' *European Human Rights LR* 419–431.

[72] See Marriot J and Nicol D (1999) 'The Human Rights Act, representative standing and the victim culture' *European Human Rights LR* 730–741.

from Art 25 of the Convention itself.[73] The concept is a narrow one, which requires claimants to be personally affected by the action being impugned. The ECHR test is undoubtedly more expansive than the restrictive notion of a 'private legal right' which used to govern the grant of standing for the declaration and injunction in English law prior to the introduction of the Order 53 reforms in 1977.[74] Thus, for example, in *Dudgeon v United Kingdom*[75] and *Norris v Ireland*,[76] the gay male applicants would have been regarded as 'victims' of their countries' criminalisation of homosexual practices even though they themselves had not been subject to a prosecution. Conversely, in *Leigh, Guardian Newspapers Ltd and Observer Ltd v United Kingdom*,[77] the Commission was not prepared to accept that all journalists were 'victims' of a House of Lords' decision upholding a lower court's refusal to disclose documents to journalists even though the documents concerned had been read out in court.

There is an obvious tension in the ECtHR's case law on this point. On the one hand, as the Court made clear in *Klass v Germany*, it was not willing to allow procedural questions to frustrate achievement of the Convention's substantive objectives.[78] This concern points towards a liberal interpretation of Art 25. On the other hand, a more restrictive test would be helpful in ensuring that cranks and busybodies are excluded from the Court, in reducing the likelihood that litigation is used by pressure groups as in effect a surrogate political process, and in preventing the Court being overwhelmed with work.

Domestic courts will now also be faced with this tension. But the Act's importation of Art 25 into domestic law creates a further problem for United Kingdom judges. The Act does not abolish – but rather expressly preserves in s 11 – an individual citizen's right to maintain an action for an infringement of an existing common law right as an addition or alternative to an action alleging breach of a Convention entitlement.[79]

This raises a difficulty from a *locus standi* perspective, since, as noted in chapter seventeen, the UK courts have in recent times made it appreciably easier for individuals and pressure groups to challenge the legality of government decisions against a common law yardstick. Recent judgments on standing have taken significant steps towards the point where a reputable claimant with a plausible legal argument can use a judicial review action and the publicity such hearings provide as an alternative or supplement to the political process. But none of the claimants which feature in these cases are obviously 'victims' in the sense envisaged by the Human Rights Act. They are

[73] For a helpful summary of the European Court's case law on Art 25 see Harris, O'Boyle and Warbrick op cit pp 630–638.

[74] See pp 603–607 above. [75] (1981) 4 EHRR 149. [76] (1988) 13 EHRR 186.

[77] (No 10039/82) (1984) 38 DR 74. [78] (1978) 2 EHRR 214.

[79] Section 11. Safeguard for existing human rights.

A person's reliance on a Convention right does not restrict–

(a) any other right or freedom conferred on him by or under any law having effect in any part of the United Kingdom; or

(b) his right to make any claim or bring any proceedings which he could make or bring apart from sections 7 to 9.

more accurately seen as 'representatives' of victims.[80] They are arguably performing a useful public service in bringing potentially unlawful government action into a forum where that action's lawfulness can be assessed.

That they should not be permitted to do so in respect of alleged breaches of human rights seems most curious. Many individuals who are personally affected by an alleged breach of the Convention may lack the financial resources and the expertise to marshall an effective legal argument, particularly as the Act has been introduced at a time when the legal aid budget is being reduced. It also seems improbable that many lawyers will accept contingency fee arrangements to pursue Convention cases, given that the European Court has traditionally set 'damages' for breaches of the Convention at a very low level. Section 8 of the Act explicitly links any awards of damages for a breach of Convention rights to the ECtHR's 'just satisfaction' principles. While it is conceivable that a court might under s 8 depart from these principles or that the courts will recognise breach of human rights as a head of damage at common law – it seems at present most unlikely that the quantum available will be substantial. Some lawyers may expand their provision of *pro bono* work to pick up Convention litigation, particularly in high profile cases, but this offers no guarantee of effective representation on any systemic scale.

The Act's attempts to use standing rules to close the Convention door to well-resourced, expert pressure groups might thus be thought appreciably to reduce the efficacy of its substantive provisions. During the Bill's passage, the government acknowledged in the House of Commons that it was quite likely that groups such as Amnesty and Greenpeace could achieve *locus standi* de facto by sponsoring and funding any action launched by a 'real' victim. If that is indeed to be the case, the Act's restrictive position de jure seems unnecessary. Even at its most benevolent, the English law of standing has never opened the doors of the courts to cranks, busybodies and vexatious litigants.

We are thus faced with the unwelcome prospect that our public law procedures could contain two streams of administrative law controls on government running side-by-side. The one a common law stream which offers claimants easy access to the courts but limited grounds against which to measure the acceptability of the impugned government action. The other a Convention stream which, while offering significantly more extensive grounds of review, will be more difficult for a claimant to enter.

The government made some attempt to address this problem in what is now s 7(3) of the Act. This provides that a claimant who raises a Convention claim via proceedings for judicial review will only have 'sufficient interest in the matter to which the application relates'[81] if she is a 'victim' of the action impugned. This seems on its face an unnecessarily illiberal provision. But it would also seem to be ineffective. This becomes apparent when one considers that our courts have been suggesting with increasing frequency that many Convention principles already have precise

80 See the discussion of this issue by Cane (1995) op cit.

81 The formula is taken from s 31(3) of the Supreme Court Act 1981.

counterparts in the common law. The non-victim applicant could therefore seek *locus standi* for an application for judicial review on the basis that a common law right, not a Convention Right, has been infringed. Having been granted standing in accordance with our increasingly liberal domestic law, she might then argue that the common law right she is invoking should now be construed in a way that mirrors the protections offered by the Convention. By adopting this strategy, the claimant will by-pass the Human Rights Act's less accommodating *locus standi* rules without depriving herself de facto of the substantive protection the Act is intended to provide.

The courts would seem to have two choices in attempting to resolve this contradiction. The first would be to adopt a more expansive interpretation of 'victim' than is favoured by the ECtHR. That would seem undesirable, both because it runs counter to Parliament's evident intentions and because it would involve disobedience to the ECtHR itself. The second would be for our domestic law of standing to become rather more restrictive. There is no legal impediment to the courts reversing the recent trend towards more liberal standing laws, but it would seem unlikely that they would be willing to do so given that the consequences of such a reversal would be to reduce the extent to which government action is subject to judicial scrutiny. Neither option seems particularly attractive, which would suggest that in respect of this part of the Act the unhappy result the courts will have to pursue is to decide which choice amounts to the lesser evil.

This concern is reinforced when one considers the issue of time limits. The rather brief presumptive three-month limit for initiating actions via judicial review has been one of the main reasons for claimants seeking to challenge government action through private law proceedings, in which time limits are considerably more generous. Section 7(5)(a) of the Act imposes a maximum time limit of one year on the commencement of action relying on Convention rights, while s 7(5)(b) provides that this 'is subject to any rule imposing a stricter time limit in relation to the procedure in question'. This presumably means that any Convention based challenge brought by way of judicial review will have to be begun at most within three months.[82]

It would seem that if a claimant wishes to raise a Convention argument in an action in tort, contract or restitution, she must begin that action within a year, or run the risk of the Convention points being struck out.[83] Section 7(5)(b) grants the court a power to disregard the time limit if it considers that would be equitable in the circumstances, but this is a provision which – to put it kindly – is rather vague.

[82] See Nicol D (1999) 'Limitation periods under the Human Rights Act 1998 and judicial review' *LQR* 216–220.

[83] The stricter limit clearly does not apply in relation to Convention points which are raised as a defence in proceedings initiated by another person or institution, but does apply to counter-claims initiated in response to another action.

ON THE SEPARATION OF POWERS

There appear to be firm grounds for accepting the argument that the Act gives too much power to the government at the expense of 'Parliament'. In its original form, cl 10 of the Human Rights Bill proposed to empower the government to respond to a declaration of incompatibility by issuing an Order in Council amending or repealing the relevant statutory provision concerned. Except in 'urgent' cases, the Order would not have legal effect unless issued in draft form and subsequently approved by a resolution of both houses within 60 days. In urgent cases however, a draft Order would have immediate effect, and while it would lapse if it were not approved by a resolution of both houses within 40 days, the government could have re-issued it (seemingly ad infinitum).

From a separation of powers/parliamentary sovereignty perspective, the objections to these proposals were obvious. In an 'urgent' case, cl 10 would empower the government to repeal legislation even if it could not command majority support for its views in both houses. Assessing 'urgency', it seemed, was to be a matter for the subjective discretion of the relevant Secretary of State. In non-urgent cases, cl 10 would have required the government to command majority support for its proposed remedy in each house. What it did not require was that the measure receive the same degree of scrutiny – and hence the same level of publicity – as would attach to a proposed reform effected by new primary legislation.

The clause clearly proposed a substantial extension of de facto legislative power to the government, a step which is manifestly incompatible with the constitutional presumption that Parliament is the only legislative body within the United Kingdom. The government's response to such criticisms of cl 10 was rather modest. As enacted, s 10(2) provides that;

'If a Minister of the Crown considers that there are compelling reasons for proceeding under this section, he may by order make such amendments to the legislation as he considers necessary to remove the incompatibility'.

Professor Ewing has suggested that s 10(2) represents a substantial concession by the government: 'The result is to restore the principle that primary legislation should be amended or repealed only by primary legislation'.[84] The 'compelling reasons' caveat is seen as a residual power, and one that will in any event be subject to judicial review. This seems a curious conclusion. The initial responsibility for deciding if an issue is 'compelling' will rest with the minister. While framed in subjective terms, her power under s 10(2) is obviously subject to the limitations imposed by administrative law. But it is arguable that these will be extremely loose constraints. If one takes human rights seriously, it might be thought any breach of the Convention provides 'compelling' grounds for immediate remedial action. What is being infringed is, after all, a fundamental human right. At most, judicial control of this particular power is likely

[84] (1999) op cit at p 93.

to be premised on grounds of *Wednesbury* unreasonableness. It seems rather improbable that a court would be pre-disposed to obstruct a ministerial action which is intended to remedy a legal wrong which a superior court had itself identified a short time previously.

It could of course be suggested that this entire debate on the way the 1998 Act affects the balance of power between 'Parliament' and the executive is a silly indulgence in abstract theorisation, and one which has minimal relevance to the realities of political power. Governments with reliable Commons majorities have for most practical (ie legislative) purposes been Parliament in the post-war era. This might suggest that the only sensible way to give some worthwhile empirical effect to an idealised understanding of the separation of powers is to break the link between bare Commons majorities and legislative authority when fundamental human rights are in issue. But this is one thing the Human Rights Act makes no attempt to do.

POLITICAL ENTRENCHMENT? A NEW 'RIGHTS' CULTURE WITHIN GOVERNMENT AND PARLIAMENT

Whether the Act produces a degree of 'moral entrenchment' for Convention rights will be dependent as much on ministers' and Parliament's ability to avoid taking decisions or enacting statutes which breach the Convention as on their readiness to respond to judicial condemnation of measures which already exist. The Human Rights Act contains several provisions designed to prevent, rather than just cure, contravention of Convention principles.

Section 19 requires a minister piloting a Bill through either house to certify prior to the second reading either that she is satisfied that the measure is compatible with the Convention, or that she believes it to be incompatible but nevertheless wishes it to proceed. The white paper argued that this obligation; 'will ensure that all ministers, their departments and officials are fully seized of the gravity of the Convention's obligations in respect of human rights'.[85] The white paper also anticipated that the requirement would lead to the creation of inter-departmental working groups of lawyers and administrators within central government; 'meeting on a regular basis to ensure that a consistent approach is taken and to ensure that developments in case law are well understood'.[86] This would seem to be laudable objective. How far it is achieved in practice remains to be seen.

What actually happens within Parliament in respect of s 19 may also raise contentious legal questions. MPs who fancy themselves – with or without good cause – as legal experts will surely not resist the temptation to challenge the accuracy of the minister's certification. This would obviously make the Bill's conformity with the Convention a subject of sustained debate during second reading, at the committee and report stages, and again at third reading. The white paper does not seem to anticipate this. The Commons in particular is much pressed for time in discharging its

[85] At para 3.4. [86] At para 3.5.

legislative business. Section 19 is likely to encourage every opponent of a government Bill[87] to eat up significant amounts of time by questioning the measure's vires vis à vis the Convention. The probable result of this is that less legislation will be passed, or that the substantive merits (above and beyond their conformity with the Convention) of many Bills will receive an even more cursory examination in the Commons than is offered at present.

Nor is it clear what the legal position would be if a minister fails to make a s 19 certification, or is alleged to have done so in bad faith, or to have come to a wholly unsustainable conclusion as to the Bill's compatibility with the Convention. There will presumably not be any scope for a court subsequently to hold that an Act which has not been certified in accordance with s 17 is invalid, since that would entail a rejection of parliamentary sovereignty.

A more interesting question is whether a claimant might, (in a manner echoing the *Trethowan* situation),[88] seek injunctive relief against the government to prevent the Bill going to third reading, or to the other house, or for the Royal Assent. Since that claim would not rest on a breach of the Convention per se, the Act's exclusion of a person acting during a proceeding in Parliament from being construed as a 'public authority' would be inapplicable.[89] We would thus be thrown back to considering whether the Minister's duty under s 19 is a 'proceeding in Parliament' within the meaning of Art 9 of the Bill of Rights, and so something that cannot be 'impeached or called into question' in a court? The likely answer to that question would seem to be 'Yes'. But this does not settle the issue. For the next question which arises is whether s 19 should be construed as having impliedly repealed Art 9 in so far as challenges to ministerial certification are concerned? That is perhaps a matter best reserved for (speculative) discussion elsewhere.

CONCLUSION

The government's rapid and determined efforts to convince Parliament to pass the Human Rights Act offers clear confirmation that members of the first Blair administration did not share the simplistic view of 'democracy' embraced by the Conservative Party during the judicial supremacism episode. The 1998 Act may obviously be criticised on the basis that it transfers a dangerous amount of political power from the government to the judges. But the sentiments evinced by many Conservative MPs on this issue had little to commend them from a constitutional perspective. Properly construed, Convention rights have no role at all to play within the field occupied by mainstream party politics. Rather, their whole purpose is to try to lift certain basic moral values **above** the sphere of party politics. The Convention offers an understanding of democracy which has a substantive rather than just a procedural dimension. It is concerned not just with how governmental power is won, but also with how it is

[87] Section 19 seems not to reach to private members bills or private bills.

[88] See pp 39–40 above.

[89] See p 722 above.

subsequently used. It rejects the simple homily that everything a democratically elected government does must be democratic just because the government was elected.

The Convention represents an attempt to fashion a wide-ranging substantive notion of democracy based on broad consensus. It rests on moral principles which are assumed to cut across not just party political boundaries, but also historical and geographical frontiers. It is unarguable that a judgment of a UK court which concludes that the action of a public authority has breached the Convention, or a declaration that a statute is incompatible with its provisions, does indeed disclose 'undemocratic' behaviour. However it is not necessarily the court's behaviour which has that characteristic; rather it may be the behaviour of the government or Parliament. What the Blair government has clearly understood – and the point that eludes critics of so-called 'judicial supremacism' – is that the Human Rights Act does not subordinate government to the courts, but to the moral principles articulated in the Convention. The courts figure in this new constitutional equation only because Parliament has taken the view that judges are better equipped than politicians to draw the **preliminary** conclusion as to whether those moral principles have been compromised.

This is however an innovation – albeit a radical one – which operates only in the sphere of administrative law. For it leaves the power to draw the **final** conclusion in the same hands – namely those of a bare majority of members of the Commons[90] who between them may have garnered the electoral support of barely one third of the voting population. The Human Rights Act thus readily lends itself to characterisation as a repository of legally contingent political values. It provides further mechanisms for preventing the exercise of political power in extremist directions, be they to the left or the right, only for so long as centrist political sentiment commands the support of a majority of members of the House of Commons. What it does not do is provide any long term legal underpinnings for centrist values if majoritarian sentiment should at some future date lurch violently to the left or right. For this reason, it is regrettable the Blair government seemed to write off any attempt to engineer a new legal settlement premised on legally entrenched fundamental rights. It is not until a government grasps that particular nettle that talk of a constitutional revolution will be well-founded.

While the Act received the Royal Assent in 1998, most of its provisions did not come immediately into effect. Section 22(3) granted the Home Secretary the power to decide at what date(s) the other parts of the legislation would be effective. The government had made it clear that full implementation of the Act could not occur until the many tribunal members, magistrates and judges who would be required to apply its terms had received extensive training with respect both to the Act itself and the relevant provisions of the Convention. This process evidently took longer than the

[90] I assume that the Commons majority could if necessary invoke the Parliament Act 1949 to override a Lords veto.

government had initially expected, with the result that the target date for bringing the Act fully into force was set for October 2000.[91] Further delay was apparently caused by the government's dawning realisation that the impact of the Act would touch upon many more areas of domestic law than had hitherto been anticipated.[92] In the interim period, however, the status of fundamental rights at common law had not been standing still.

Rather than construe the Act as a legislative 'takeover' of the common law's emergent fundamental human rights jurisprudence, some judges seem to have seen it a spur to continuing innovation. In *R v Secretary of State for the Home Department, ex p Simms*,[93] the House of Lords substantially extended the principle set out by the Court of Appeal in *Leech*.[94] In *Simms*, the Court broadened still further the concept of 'access to the courts' to include a prisoner's entitlement to conduct face to face interviews with journalists who the prisoner was trying to persuade to investigate his claims that he was the victim of a miscarriage of justice. In a similar, if more significant, extension of the common law's protection of freedom of expression, the House of Lords accepted in *Reynolds v Times Newspapers Ltd*[95] that the qualified privilege defence would frequently be available to defendants who had published libellous stories about elected politicians. In *Fitzpatrick v Sterling Housing Association Ltd*,[96] the House of Lords offered an illustration of the way in which developments of common law principles – here the approach taken to statutory interpretation – could render the vertical/horizontal debate in respect of the Human Rights Act quite redundant. The judgment contained an innovative reading of legislation passed in the 1920s which recognised that non-heterosexual couples could be regarded as members of each other's families for the purposes of inheriting a tenancy in a flat owned by a private sector organisation. Such developments indicated that the courts would approach the implementation of the Human Rights with a considerable degree of enthusiasm for the project of 'giving better effect to' Convention jurisprudence.

II. THE INITIAL IMPACT OF THE HUMAN RIGHTS ACT

Some five to six years (spring 2006) after the Human Right Act had come into force, a substantial body of case dealing with its effect had already accumulated.[97] No attempt is made here to survey the overall impact that the Act has initially had on all the

[91] On the status of the Act itself prior to this date see the apparently contrasting conclusions drawn by the High Court and the House of Lords in *R v DPP, ex p Kebilene* [1999] 4 All ER 801.

[92] *The Times*, 5 May 1999.

[93] [1999] 3 All ER 400, HL.

[94] See pp 695–697 above.

[95] [1999] 4 All ER 609.

[96] [2001] 1 AC 27.

[97] All of the cases involving Convention Rights are listed in Selgado E and O'Brien C (2001) 'Table of cases under the Human Rights Act' *European Human Rights Law Review* 376; Arkinstall J and O'Brien C (2002) 'Table of cases under the Human Rights Act' *European Human Rights LR* 364–388.

various sub-branches of domestic law.[98] It seems entirely likely that the effect or reach of the Act will quickly prove to be so broad that treatises dealing with most legal subjects will soon have to be amended in a fashion which approaches ECHR jurisprudence as an integral element of domestic law. The second part of this chapter seeks merely to focus on a small number of leading cases in which the courts have addressed different aspects of the Act, and to draw out the constitutional implications of the courts' preliminary conclusions. The issues addressed are: firstly, the approach to statutory interpretation mandated by s 3; secondly, the use of Declarations of Incompatibility; thirdly, the appearance of the doctrine of judicial 'deference' to legislative judgment; fourthly, the 'horizontality' of the Act; and fifthly, the status of proportionality as a ground of review of executive action.

THE APPROACH TO STATUTORY INTERPRETATION MANDATED BY S 3 AND THE USE OF DECLARATIONS OF INCOMPATIBILITY

The interactive effect of ss 3–4 is perhaps the most important issue raised by the Act. To what extent have the courts accepted that s 3 requires them to abandon traditional attachments to literalist approaches to statutory interpretation and adopted instead a teleological technique in which the telos (purpose) is to uphold Convention Rights in a manner consistent with ECHR jurisprudence? It is undoubtedly possible to identify judgments in which the courts have embraced very expansive understandings of s 3. It would however be an exaggeration to suggest that such an approach had become a new dominant paradigm within domestic law.

As suggested above, one of the most radical departures from orthodox approaches to statutory interpretation is the *Marleasing/Litster* methodology mandated by EC law. This technique requires courts to add 'missing' clauses to domestic legislation in order to secure compatibility with EC law. In *R v A (No 2)*,[99] the House of Lords made it clear that it accepted that HRA, s 3 could have a similar effect in relation to Convention Rights.

The legislation at issue in *R v A (No 2)* concerned the admissibility of evidence in a rape trial relating to a complainant's previous sexual behaviour. Section 41 of the Youth Justice and Criminal Evidence Act 1999 seemed to bar any evidence being adduced during a rape trial which might support the assertion that the defendant had had a consensual sexual relationship with the alleged victim unless the evidence related to consensual sexual relations which occurred (per s 41(3)(b); 'at or about the same time' as the alleged rape. Section 41 had been enacted to prevent defence counsel seeking to discredit alleged rape victims by subjecting them to intrusive and irrelevant questioning about past sexual behaviour. The difficulty the provision raised from a

[98] See Klug F and Starmer K (2001) 'Incorporation through the "front door": the first year of the Human Rights Act' *Public Law* 654–665.

[99] [2001] UKHL 25, [2001] 3 All ER 1.

Convention perspective was that it could rule out the admission of evidence relevant to the trial, and thereby breach the 'fair trial' requirements of Art 6 ECHR.

Lord Steyn's leading judgment suggested that domestic courts should not make immediate resort to s 3 in construing other legislation. If it appeared prima facie that a literal construction of a statutory provision would breach a Convention Right, courts should first consider whether; 'ordinary methods of purposive and contextual interpretation'[100] could yield Convention compliant results. Only if 'ordinary methods' were inadequate should s 3 be invoked.

In the instant case, Lord Steyn doubted that 'ordinary methods' would suffice. He thus turned to s 3, the impact of which he characterised in the following way:

'The interpretive principle under s 3 of the 1998 Act is a strong one. . . . [It] goes far beyond the rule which enabled the courts to take the Convention into account in resolving any ambiguity in a legislative provision. . . . In accordance with the will of Parliament as reflected in s 3 it will sometimes be necessary to adopt an interpretation which linguistically may appear strained. The techniques to be used will not only involve the reading down of express language in a statute, but also the implication of provisions . . .'[101]

Adopting this approach, Lord Steyn construed the relevant statutory provision in a way compatible with the Convention by reading into s 41 an addendum that permitted use of such evidence where it was obviously relevant to the particular case.

In contrast, Lord Hope issued a dissenting judgment which indicated that he felt Lord Steyn's approach to s 3 overstepped appropriate constitutional boundaries:

'The rule of construction which s 3 lays down is quite unlike any previous rule of statutory interpretation. There is no need to identify an ambiguity or an absurdity. Compatibility with convention rights is the sole guiding principle. That is the paramount objective which the rule seeks to achieve. But the rule is only a rule of interpretation. It does not entitle the judges to act as legislators'.[102]

As previous parts of this book have suggested, it is not problematic to support the abstract assertion that our constitutional traditions allocate the task of making legislation to Parliament and of interpreting such legislation to the courts. It is lending practical meaning to such abstractions that causes difficulty.

In the context of Human Rights Act adjudication, that task is further complicated by the presence of the higher courts' s 4 power to issue declarations of incompatibility in respect of statutory provisions which cannot be construed in a way that lends them a Convention compliant character. Lord Steyn's judgment in *R v A (No 2)* had echoed the Home Secretary's assumption during the passage of the HRA that the courts' s 4 power would not often be invoked: 'A declaration of incompatibility is a measure of last resort . . . It must be avoided unless it is plainly impossible to do so.'[9] As suggested in part I of this chapter, the frequency with which s 4 is used will depend largely on the way in the courts construe their interpretive powers under s 3. Lord Steyn's 'last resort' approach to s 4 obviously has greater credibility when viewed in conjunction

[100] Ibid, at 15. [101] Ibid, at 17. [102] *R v A (No 2)* [2001] UKHL 25, [2001] 3 All ER 1 at 35.

with his readiness to 'strain' or 'add to' the text of ostensibly Convention non-compliant statutory terms. In contrast, the more conservative interpretive technique advocated by Lord Hope in *R v A* might be thought to lead to more frequent use of declarations of incompatibility

That Lord Steyn and Lord Hope's respective analyses in *A* were indicative of a diversity of views within the judiciary as to the nature of s 3 (and thence the role of s 4) is illustrated by the Court of Appeal's almost contemporaneous treatment of an ostensibly Convention non-compliant statutory provision in *Wilson v First County Trust (No 2)*.[103] The case concerned s 127 of the Consumer Credit Act 1974 – a statute which might not initially be thought to raise Convention issues at all. Section 127 of the Act placed an absolute bar on recovery of assets by a creditor from a debtor if certain formalities had not been complied with when the credit agreement between the parties had been concluded. In *Wilson*, counsel for the creditor succeeded in convincing the trial court and the Court of Appeal that this provision, if literally construed, would breach Art 1 of the First Protocol to the ECHR (which is concerned with the protection of people's property) and also the fair trial provisions of ECHR Art 6. The Court of Appeal construed s 3 in rather opaque terms:

'The court is required to go as far as, but not beyond, what is legally possible. The court is not required, or entitled, to give words a meaning which they cannot bear . . .'[104]

In following this approach, the Court reached the conclusion that it could not use s 3 to read words into s 127 which would limit the provision's effect to situations where recovery would work an injustice on the debtor, and thereby render s 127 compatible with the Convention. The immediate consequence of this conclusion was that the Court of Appeal issued a declaration of incompatibility with respect to s 127.

A similar rationale was employed in *R (on application of H) v London North and East Mental Health Review Tribunal*.[104a] S 73 of the Mental Health Act 1983 seems to provide – literally construed – that persons detained in a mental hospital because they have committed serious crimes cannot be released unless they prove that they are not a danger to society. The Court of Appeal regarded this as a deprivation of personal liberty and reversal of the burden of proof in a criminal matter, and so incompatible with Art 5 and Art 6 ECHR. As in *Wilson*, the Court did not consider that s 3 would permit the reading in of a qualification to the 1983 Act. This breach of the Convention could be cured only by new legislation.

Quite what qualitative difference can be drawn in methodological terms between reading in a clause to s 41 of the Youth Justice and Criminal Evidence Act 1999 which made evidence of consensual sexual relationships admissible when it was obviously relevant to the charge before the court, and reading in a saving proviso to s 127 of the Consumer Credit Act which lifted the bar to recovery of assets in situations where

103 [2001] EWCA Civ 633, [2001] 3 All ER 229.

104 Ibid, at para 42.

104a [2002] QB 1.

non-compliance with legal formalities had not worked any substantive injustice on the debtor, is less than obvious.[105]

In subsequent cases, the Court of Appeal seemed to identify a more principled means to determine when innovative judicial construction of a statutory term stops being 'interpretation' and becomes 'legislation' instead. In *Poplar Housing and Regeneration Community Association Ltd v Donoghue*, Lord Woolf offered the following suggestion:

'If it is necessary in order to obtain compliance [with the Convention] to radically alter the effect of the legislation this will be an indication that more than interpretation is involved.'[106]

We might instinctively agree that the notion that 'radical' change to a statute's meaning is beyond s 3 is attractive in formal or rhetorical terms. We would presumably also ask what does 'radical' really mean in this context? A helpful indication on this point was offered in *R (International Transport GmbH) v Secretary of State for the Home Department*.[107] The case was triggered by the government's use of provisions in the Immigration and Asylum Act 1999 which empowered the Home Secretary to impose automatic fines on transport companies on whose lorries or trains asylum seekers had hidden as a means to enter the United Kingdom illegally. Nearly 1000 fines had been imposed by 2001. This seemed incompatible with the fair trial provisions of Art 6 ECHR. The Court of Appeal (per Simon Brown LJ) considered s 3 did not assist here:

'It appears to me quite impossible to recreate this scheme by any interpretive process as one compatible with Convention rights . . . To achieve fairness would require a radically different approach . . . As the authorities clearly dictate, the Court's task is to distinguish between legislation and interpretation and confine itself to the latter. We cannot create a wholly different scheme . . . so as to provide an acceptable alternative means of immigration control. That must be for Parliament itself'.[108]

As in *Wilson*, the Court of Appeal's reasoning on the scope of s 3 led it to issue a declaration of incompatibility in respect of the relevant statutory provisions.

This tentative distinction between what we might term 'schematic' and 'isolated' legislative incompatibility with Convention Rights may provide a helpful way of demarcating the boundary lines between s 3 and s 4 of the Act. Where a non-literal reading of a specific statutory provision would have the effect of unravelling a wide-ranging regulatory system, it may be that courts will and should be unwilling to construe their s 3 powers in broad terms. In those circumstances, of course, the Human Rights Act does offer the courts a mechanism through the s 4 declaration of

[105] One might of course suggest that the impact on the individual of the alleged breach of Convention Rights would be far more severe in *R v A (No 2)* than in *Wilson*, and that a court's readiness to 'stretch' the notion of interpretation should be greater in cases involving serious criminal charges than issues of civil law. Section 3 itself does not expressly support any such distinction.

[106] [2001] EWCA Civ 595, [2001] 4 All ER 604 at para 76.

[107] [2001] 02 LS Gaz R 27.

[108] Ibid, at 30.

incompatibility to pass responsibility for securing compliance with the Convention to the government and to Parliament.

There is obvious scope for the argument to be made that greater judicial resort to s 4 – which would be the result of adopting a less expansive understanding of the power arising under s 3 – would better fit with traditional understandings of the separation of powers. Lord Steyn's judgment in *A* was for example criticised as being 'outlandish' and 'far-fetched' by Professor Nicol, on the basis that Lord Steyn's method could not convincingly be categorised as 'interpretation' in any meaningful sense.[109] Professor Nicol also suggests that in several subsequent judgments, the House of Lords has taken a less expansive view of the interpretive obligation imposed by s 3.

In *Re S (Care Order: Implementation of Care Plan*),[110] the Court of Appeal had invoked s 3 to create an entirely new procedure within the Children Act 1989 in order to make the provisions of that Act in relation to care proceedings compatible with Arts 6 and 8. The 1989 Act had largely removed the High Courts' previous jurisdiction to supervise in any detailed fashion the way in which a local authority implemented orders made by the court which placed children in the care of the local authority. The Court of Appeal in *S* considered that this scheme was inconsistent with Arts 6 and 8, and so read into the 1989 Act a judicial power for the court to specify particular targets in the care order which, if breached by the local authority, would entitle the court to intervene.

Lord Nicholls, delivering the only substantial judgment in the House of Lords,[111] offered a principle of general application to the scope of s 3:

> '[39] . . . Interpretation of statutes is a matter for the courts; the enactment of statutes, and the amendment of statutes, are matters for Parliament.
>
> [40] Up to this point there is no difficulty. The area of real difficulty lies in identifying the limits of interpretation in a particular case. This is not a novel problem. . . . For present purposes it is sufficient to say that a meaning which departs substantially from a fundamental feature of an Act of Parliament is likely to have crossed the boundary between interpretation and amendment. This is especially so where the departure has important practical repercussions which the court is not equipped to evaluate. In such a case the overall contextual setting may leave no scope for rendering the statutory provision Convention compliant by legitimate use of the process of interpretation . . .'.

In this 'particular case', Lord Nicholls considered that the Court of Appeal had undermined a 'fundamental feature' of the Children Act 1989; namely that Parliament had sought to prevent the courts exercising the kind of supervisory role within the child care system which would be created by the Court of Appeal's conclusion.[112] This reasoning underlines the presumption that s 3 cannot be used to alter the schematic nature of particular statutory regimes, but is instead limited in scope to statutory provisions which have an essentially isolated or free-standing character.

109 Nicol D (2004a) 'Statutory interpretation and human rights after *Anderson*' *Public Law* 273–283.

110 [2001] EWCA Civ 757; [2001] 2 FCR 450.

111 [2002] UKHL 10; [2002] 2 All ER 192.

112 See especially paras [42]–[44] of the judgment.

Lord Nicholls also advanced a further principle which would likely restrict the range of substantive results which s 3 could be invoked to achieve:

'[41] .... When a court, called upon to construe legislation, ascribes a meaning and effect to the legislation pursuant to its obligation under s 3, it is important the court should identify clearly the particular statutory provision or provisions whose interpretation leads to that result. Apart from all else, this should assist in ensuring the court does not inadvertently stray outside its interpretation jurisdiction.'

This observation seems to re-inject a dose of literalism into the s 3 interpretive process, and might be thought to make it more difficult to justify a *Litster/Marleasing* approach to s 3 which empowers a court to read particular words or even entire phrases into a statutory text. That is of course what was done in *R v A*, albeit in respect of an 'isolated' rather than 'schematic' legislative provision. Lord Nicholls did not in terms disapprove the method used in *R v A*, but it is difficult to conclude otherwise than that his judgment in *S* could sensibly be read by judges in lower courts as intended to limit the circumstances in which such an approach could be applied.[113]

This conclusion is perhaps reinforced by the subsequent House of Lords decision in *Bellinger v Bellinger*,[114] in which Lord Nicholls again gave the leading judgment. The claimant in *Bellinger* had been classified (correctly as a matter of then extant law) as a male at birth. The claimant subsequently underwent gender reassignment treatment, and had conducted herself as if she were a woman since 1975. In 1981, the claimant underwent a marriage ceremony with a male partner. Under the terms of the Matrimonial Causes Act 1973, s 11(c), any 'marriage' would be void if the partners were not respectively a 'man' and a 'woman'. Domestic law equated gender for this purposes with the gender assigned to a person at birth. Thus the claimant and her husband were both 'men', and consequently no marriage had occurred. The Bellingers subsequently contended that domestic law was incompatible with Arts 8 and 12 ECHR.[115]

In a series of decisions in the 1980 and 1990s,[116] the ECtHR had held that the United Kingdom's refusal to allow post-operative trans-sexual persons to alter their legal gender classification was not incompatible with the Convention. However, by the time the Bellingers' case reached the House of Lords, the ECtHR had changed its view on this issue, and had concluded in *Goodwin v the United Kingdom*[117] that domestic law was inconsistent with Art 12 in so far as it prevented a transsexual person marrying another person of a different gender.[118]

[113] Nicol also invokes the House of Lords' judgment in *R (on the application of Anderson) v Secretary off State for the Home Department* [2002] UKHL 46, [2003] 1 AC 837 in support of this argument. For an alternative perspective see Kavannagh A (2004) 'Statutory interpretation and human rights after *Anderson*: a more contextual approach' *Public Law* 537–545.)

[114] [2003] UKHL 21, [2003] 2 AC 467.

[115] Which concern the right to marry.

[116] *Rees v United Kingdom* (1986) 9 EHRR 56; *Cossey v United Kingdom* [1993] 13 EHRR 622.

[117] [2002] 2 FCR 577.

[118] Under domestic law, the claimant in *Bellinger* would have been able to marry a person classified at birth as a 'woman'. This would be so even if that person had subsequently undergone gender reassignment treatment in order to appear and live as a 'man'.

The primary question before the House of Lords was whether s 3 of the Human Rights Act empowered the Court to read s 11 of the Matrimonial Causes Act 1973 – and specifically the terms 'man' and 'woman' in a fashion which rendered domestic law consistent with the ECtHR's judgment in *Goodwin*. All members of the Court held that the answer to this question was 'No', but the unanimous conclusion rested on rather different reasons.

Lord Hope appeared to conclude that since it is presently beyond the capacity of medical science to provide a person with what he termed 'the equipment'[119] needed to make that person fertile in his/her chosen gender identity, it is simply not 'possible' as a matter of objective fact for 'man' and 'woman' within s 11(c) to mean anything other than the gender assigned at birth.

The other substantive judgments (by Lords Hobhouse and Nicholls respectively) approached the issue in a fashion which was perhaps better attuned to the sensitivities of the claimant and people in her position. Both opinions seemed to accept that 'whether a person was a 'man' or a 'woman' – either in a general sense of for specific purposes – was a question of law, not of biological fact. The question to be answered was not whether the claimant was a 'man' or a 'woman', but which law-makers could legitimately decide that point. Lords Hobhouse and Nicholls evidently took the view that Mrs Bellinger's claim raised a profoundly systemic question. Whether or not she was a 'woman' was a question which had implications going far beyond the matter of the validity of her marriage. Lord Nicholls identified; 'education, child care, occupational qualifications, criminal law (gender specific offences), prison regulations, sport, the needs of decency and birth certificates'[120] as areas of social policy on which gender reassignment would have a significant and obvious impact. Equally problematic, in Lord Nicholls' view, was what degree of trans-gender medical treatment would a person have to undergo before he/she should be regarded as having altered his/her initial gender for a particular purpose?[121]

The initial cogency of this 'systemic implications' justification for concluding it was not 'possible' to use s 3 in this case should perhaps be questioned. It was manifestly open to the House of Lords to limit the ratio of *Bellinger* to the question of the validity of a marriage. Mrs Bellinger could be a 'woman' for that purpose. Whether she, or persons in like circumstances, would be a 'woman' for other legal purposes would then be left to be litigated on a case-by-case basis as and when particular questions arose. That conclusion would have no disabling effect upon Parliament's legal capacity to revisit the 'marriage' question in any subsequent legislative initiative dealing with the legal gender classification of persons who had undergone gender reassignment treatment. A judgment to that effect would perhaps have injected an

119 At para 57. 120 Ibid, para 45.

121 Ibid, paras 39–44. For more extensive comment see Kavannagh (2004) op cit; Nicol D (2004) 'Gender reassignment and the transformation of the Human Rights Act' *LQR* 194–198.

additional sense of urgency and importance into the respective minds of government ministers and MPs as they considered how best to respond to this issue.[122]

The point to be made here is a simple, if somewhat cynical, one. Whether a particular statutory provision has a systemic or isolated character is itself a matter for judicial determination. The use of such dichotomous classification criteria as tools with which to structure the use of s 3 displaces rather than resolves the difficult question which s 3 creates.

Bellinger also offered further guidance on the use of s 4. There is no requirement in the HRA that a court which cannot 'save' a Convention non-compliant term through s 3 must then go on to issue a declaration of incompatibility. Section 4 creates a power: it does not impose a duty. The government intervened in the proceedings to argue that, inter alia, no declaration should be issued in this case as it accepted that domestic law breached the Convention and was formulating proposals for new legislation on the issue. The House of Lords evidently saw little weight in this contention. It is perhaps not an exaggeration to suggest that *Bellinger* is authority for the proposition that s 4 should properly be read as creating a very strong, if not quite irrebuttable, presumption that a declaration of incompatibility should be made whenever a statutory term's breach of a Convention right cannot be avoided by use of s 3.

That this aspect of HRA jurisprudence remains mired in uncertainty is confirmed by the House of Lords' judgment in *Ghaidan v Godin-Mendoza*.[123] Mr Godin-Mendoza was the same-sex partner of a man who had occupied a house leased from Mr Ghaidan with the status of a 'protected tenant' under the Rent Act 1977. Under the terms of the 1977 Act (as amended in 1988) the husband or wife or spouse (a term taken to include non-married cohabitees of different genders) of a deceased protect tenant was able to succeed to a statutory continuation of the tenancy. A 'family member' (if he/she had resided in the property for the year prior to the tenant's death) was entitled to succeed to a less beneficial 'assured' tenancy.[124] A resident who was neither a spouse nor family member had no extra-contractual occupancy rights at all on the death of the tenant. Shortly before the HRA came into effect, the House of Lords had held in *Fitzpatrick v Sterling Housing Association*[125] that a person in Mr Ghaidan-Mendoza's position could properly be regarded as a 'family member' of the deceased tenant, but could not be regarded as his/her spouse. The outcome clearly discriminated against same sex couples on the basis of their sexual orientation.

Shortly after *Fitzpatrick* was decided, the ECtHR held for the first time that sexual

[122] The position adopted by the House of Lords – and the criticism that can be levied at it – are of course precisely the same as those arising from Megarry VC's conclusion in *Malone* that he should not recognise even a very narrowly drawn limited right to privacy at common law; see pp 635–637 above.

[123] [2004] UKHL 30, [2004] 2 AC 557. For comment of the House of Lords' judgment see Young A (2005) *Ghaidan v Godin-Mendoza*: avoiding the deference trap' *Public Law* 23–34. On the judgment of the Court of Appeal and the background to the issue see Loveland I (2003) 'Making it up as they go along: the Court of Appeal on succession rights in tenancies to same sex partners' *Public Law* 222–235.

[124] The main difference between the two types of tenancy being that a protected statutory tenancy is subject to rent control, while an assured tenancy is not.

[125] [2001] AC 127; see p 737 above.

orientation discrimination was presumptively prohibited by Art 14 ECHR.[126] Mr Ghaidan-Mendoza was therefore able to argue that the Rent Act 1977 breached his Convention Right not to be subjected to unjustifiable sexual orientation discrimination.

The precise wording of the phrase in issue within the relevant statutory provision[127] was: 'a person who was living with the original tenant as his husband or wife shall be treated as the spouse of the original tenant. . . .' The gist of Mr Mendoza's argument was that para 2(2) should be read to include some additional words which would expand the literal formulation 'as his husband and wife' beyond mere categories of physical gender – which if *Bellinger* is to be taken as correct are concepts beyond judicial redefinition – to include the particular types of emotional and physical relationship which characterised a marriage or heterosexual cohabitation partnership and which could just as readily be met in a same-sex partnership.

In accepting this argument, Lord Nicholls took the opportunity to review and attempt to clarify the body of principle which had built up around the use of s 3. He began his analysis with a question:

'[27]. . . . What is the standard, or the criterion, by which "possibility" [in s 3] is to be judged? A comprehensive answer to this question is proving elusive. The courts, including your Lordships' House, are still cautiously feeling their way forward as experience in the application of s 3 gradually accumulates.'

The point at which Lord Nicholls seemed to have arrived was that courts should eschew use of s 3 to lend Convention compliant meanings to statutory terms if to do so would produce a meaning 'inconsistent with a fundamental feature of [the] legislation.'[128] What this notion of 'fundamental' appears to mean is that the court should satisfy itself that the meaning it might give to a statutory provision is consistent with the policy objectives that Parliament was seeking to achieve when the term was enacted. In addition to introducing this 'fundamental feature' barrier to an expansive use of s 3, Lord Nicholls also reiterated the views expressed in *Re S* and *Anderson* that it was not constitutionally appropriate for courts to deploy s 3 to produce results that would have far-reaching systemic implications.

If neither a fundamental nor systemic matter was in issue however, Lord Nicholls indicated that it was appropriate for s 3 to be used to achieve what would from a traditional understanding of the sovereignty of Parliament and the separation of powers be regarded as very unorthodox results:

'[32]. . . . Section 3 enables language to be interpreted restrictively or expansively. But s 3 goes further than this. It is also apt to require a court to read in words which change the meaning of the enacted legislation, so as to make it convention-compliant. In other words, the intention of Parliament in enacting s 3 was that, to an extent bounded only by what is

126 *Salgueiro v Portugal* (2001) 31 EHRR 47.

127 Rent Act 1977, Sch 1, para 2(2).

128 Ibid, para 33.

"possible", a court can modify the meaning, and hence the effect, of primary and secondary legislation.'

Lord Nicholls saw no systemic implications for a modification of the previously accepted meaning and effect of the Rent Act provision in issue.[129] Nor did he consider that construing that provision to include same-sex partners ran counter to the social policy purpose underlying the legislation, which policy he took to be extending the benefit of succession to; 'couples living together in a close and stable and relationship'.[130]

It would therefore be appropriate for the court to change the original meaning of para 2.2 by reading in additional words. Perhaps surprisingly, Lord Nicholls did not think any particular linguistic precision was needed in this regard: 'The precise form of words read in for this purpose is of no significance. It is their substantive effect which matters.'[131]

While Lord Steyn agreed with both the result reached by Lord Nicholls and the reasons underlying it, his judgment might readily be taken as advocating a rather more forceful approach to s 3 and – consequentially – less frequent use of s 4. Lord Steyn had not sat in *Bellinger*. In *Mendoza*, he expressed concerns that courts when faced with a non-Convention compliant statutory term were making insufficient use of s 3. Lord Steyn identified 25 such cases. In ten, the incompatibility had been removed by use of s 3. In 15, a s 4 declaration had been issued. These statistics, Lord Steyn suggested, 'reinforce the need to pose the question whether the law has taken a wrong turning'.[132]

That 'wrong turning' arose from the relative priority afforded to s 3 and s 4 as remedial devices in the event of a Convention right being breached. Lord Steyn asserted that s 3 was intended by Parliament to be the dominant remedy in such circumstances. As such, the notion of 'possible' within s 3 should be accorded a very expansive meaning. In notable contrast to Lord Nicholls, Lord Steyn held that *Marleasing* and the consequential judgments of the House of Lords in *Pickstone* and *Litster*[133] provided the proper guide to the potential of s 3 as an interpretive device. Lord Steyn appeared to accept that s 3 should not be used to undermine the scheme of a particular statute, but in terms of principle his approach towards s 3 is rather difficult to reconcile with the arguments offered by Lord Nicholls in the same case.

Notwithstanding the statistics noted by Lord Steyn in *Mendoza*, there is as yet little indication of any deluge of declarations of incompatibility flooding across the United Kingdom's legal landscape. This consequence can be seen as – in part – an indication of the judiciary's willingness to read ss 3–4 of the Human Rights Act as an invitation to redefine the courts' interpretive role in a radical fashion. We might also attribute it

[129] That he reached this conclusion without offering any considered discussion of the point is perhaps a nice illustration of the way in which displacement tools can be invoked to gloss over difficult analytical questions.

[130] Ibid, at para 35. [131] Ibid, para 35. [132] Ibid, para 39.

[133] See pp 473, 476, and 477 above.

however to the emergence of a new common law principle informing the courts' approach to human rights issue.

THE NOTION OF 'DEFERENCE' TO LEGISLATIVE JUDGMENT

In an early review of the court's use of the Human Rights Act,[134] Paul Craig argued that the Court of Appeal and House of Lords have developed a doctrine of 'deference' in respect of questions arising under the Act; that deference being owed by the courts to the decisions made by elected executive and legislative bodies. The doctrine is an indigenous version (and variation) of the 'margin of appreciation' principle within the jurisprudence of the EComHR and the ECtHR.[135]

The margin of appreciation principle is generally taken as recognising that the Convention requires that signatory states be afforded a measure of autonomy in determining if a prima facie derogation from a Convention entitlement can be permitted; ie it is a doctrine existing in international law, the purpose of which is to 'save' or 'justify' a nation's intrusion into the sphere of a given Convention Right. However, in Craig's view, the emergent concept of deference in domestic law goes rather further than this:

'*[I]t is equally clear that deference may be of relevance in determining the initial scope and applicability of Convention rights, as well as the application of limitations placed on those rights*. . . . The early jurisprudence has however applied deference at an earlier stage. It has done so as part of the initial determination as to the scope of the right in question . . .'[136]

To use the terminology deployed in chapter twenty Craig's argument is that domestic courts appear to be accepting that the scope of the 'presumptive entitlement' element[137] of certain Convention Rights is a matter for political as well as judicial definition. Professor Craig draws on several authorities raising Art 6 issues to support this proposition.

The issue before the Court of Appeal in *R v Lambert, Ali and Jordan*[138] was the compatibility of various provisions of the Homicide Act 1957 and the Misuse of Drugs Act 1971 with Art 6 ECHR. In the course of finding that neither provision was incompatible with the Convention, Lord Woolf CJ (giving the sole judgment) offered a general statement of principle as to the appropriate method for the courts to follow in Human Rights Act cases:

'It is also important to have in mind that legislation is passed by a democratically elected [sic] Parliament and therefore the Courts under the Convention should, as a matter of constitutional principle, pay a degree of deference to the view of Parliament as to what is in the interest of the public generally when upholding rights of the individual under the Convention'.[139]

134 Craig P (2001) 'The courts, the Human Rights Act and judicial review' *LQR* 592–612.

135 See pp 633–634 above.

136 Craig (2001) op cit p 592; original emphasis.

137 See p 662 above.

138 [2001] 2 WLR 211.

139 Ibid, at para 17.

This principle was reiterated by Lord Hoffman in the House of Lords in *Alconbury*, a case concerning the compatibility of aspects of the land use planning system with Art 6 ECHR:

'In a democratic country, decisions as to what the general interest requires are made by democratically elected bodies or persons accountable to them....

There is no conflict between human rights and the democratic principle. Respect for human rights requires that certain basic rights of individuals should not be capable in any circumstances of being overridden by the majority, even if they think that the public interest so requires. Other rights should be capable of being overridden only in very limited circumstances. These are rights which belong to individuals simply by virtue of their humanity.... But outside these basic rights there are many decisions which have to be made every day (for example about the allocation of resources) in which the only fair method of decision is by some person or body accountable to the electorate.'[140]

Lord Hoffman's dichotomy between 'basic rights' (in respect of which courts should be unwilling to defer to legislative conclusions) and 'allocation of resources' questions (in respect of which deference to legislative opinion is more appropriate) echoes the analysis offered by Lord Hope of Craighead in *R v DPP, ex p Kebilene*:

'The Convention should be seen as an expression of fundamental principles rather than as a set of mere rules . . .

In some circumstances, it will be appropriate for the courts to recognise that there is an area of judgment within which the judiciary will defer, on democratic grounds, to the considered opinion of the elected body or person whose act or decision is said to be incompatible with the Convention.... It will be easier for it [ie deference] to be recognised where the questions involve issues of social or economic policy, much less so where the rights are of high constitutional importance or are of a kind where the courts are especially well placed to assess the need for protection'.[141]

This judicial recognition of a 'hierarchy' of Convention Rights jurisprudence lends a further layer of elaboration to the way in which the Human Rights Act can be applied by the courts. The need for s 3 to be applied in an expansive fashion – or for s 4 to be invoked – is reduced if one accepts that the presumptive scope of certain Convention Rights has an elastic meaning.

This is illustrated by the outcome of *Wilson v First County Trust* in the House of Lords[142] The view taken by the Court was that s 127 of the Consumer Credit Act 1974 was not incompatible with Art 1 of the First Protocol ECHR. While it was accepted that s 127(3) worked 'drastic' or 'harsh' consequences even on a lender who had acted throughout in good faith[143], the court approached its assessment of s 127 vis a vis Art 1 with a clear preconception as to the correct allocation of decision-making responsibility on such a question:

140 *R (Alconbury v Secretary of State) for the Environment, Transport and the Regions* [2001] 2 All ER 929 at paras 69–70.

141 [1999] 3 WLR 972 at 994.

142 [2003] UKHL 40, [2003] 4 All ER 97; p 740 above.

143 Per Lord Nicholls at para 72.

'[70] In approaching this issue . . . courts should have in mind that theirs is a reviewing role. Parliament is charged with the primary responsibility for deciding whether the means chosen to deal with a social problem are both necessary and appropriate. Assessment of the advantages and disadvantages of the various legislative alternatives is primarily a matter for Parliament. The possible existence of alternative solutions does not in itself render the contested legislation unjustified. . . . The court will reach a different conclusion from the legislature only when it is apparent that the legislature has attached insufficient importance to a person's convention right. The readiness of a court to depart from the views of the legislature depends upon the circumstances, one of which is the subject matter of the legislation. The more the legislation concerns matters of broad social policy, the less ready will be a court to intervene.'[144]

If lent a broad meaning, as in *Wilson* in the House of Lords, the 'deference' principle might often spare courts the difficulty of grappling with the meaning of s 3 and thence the inter-relationship between s 3 and s 4. This might seem an attractive proposition. It becomes much less so when one considers that deference' has the potential to be a mechanism for the abdication of judicial responsibility, in that it transfers interpretive authority from the courts to the legislature. If lent too broad a meaning, the deference principle could substantially compromise the 'fundamental' (in the sense of supra-party political) nature of Convention Rights. A second concern is more prosaic in nature. The notion of a hierarchy of rights may seem to be a coherent concept in principle, but will surely prove to be very complex and prone to inconsistency when put into practice. At present, however, its complexity rather pales in comparison to the challenges posed by the question of the extent to which the HRA should be taken to have 'horizontal' effect.

THE HORIZONTALITY OF THE ACT

The courts have also initially been charting a rather erratic course through the murky waters of s 6 of the Act. As commentators on the Act predicted, two major questions have arisen. The first relates to the breadth of the concept of a 'public authority' for s 6(1) purposes. The second concerns the impact that the Act has had on legal relationships between private parties.

As suggested above, the definition of 'public authority' within s 6 of the Act was a question likely to generate considerable litigation. The answer given by the courts on this point might have a substantial bearing on the impact of the Act, insofar as that answer would determine which legal actors were bound to respect Convention Rights. The point also bears closely on the distinction between de facto and de jure understandings of the 'horizontal effect' argument.

In a superficial sense, the identification of a particular individual or body as a 'public authority' means that any action against her or it based on the HRA 1998 would be (nominally) 'vertical' in nature. But one must beware of allowing labels to

144 Per Lord Nicholls.

obscure realities. By interpreting the notion of a public authority in very broad terms, the courts could pull a great many ostensibly 'private' individuals or corporations within s 6 without formally recognising horizontal effect all. Conversely, a narrow construction of the public authority principle would be largely irrelevant if the courts were to assume that s 3 of the Act and their own status as public authorities per s 6 compelled them to issue Convention-compliant judgments irrespective of the identities of the parties to the litigation before them.

The meaning of 'public authorities'

An ostensibly straightforward question as to the reach of the public authority principle was raised in *Aston Cantlow and Wilmcote with Billesley Parochial Church Council v Wallbank*.[145] The Chancel Repairs Act 1932 empowers parochial church councils (PCCs) to impose costs of maintaining church buildings on owners of land which was once owned by the church. The defendants in the action had been issued with a substantial bill by their local PCC, and claimed that this infringed Art 1 of the First Protocol to the Convention. The Court of Appeal accepted that the PCC was a public authority within s 6. In part this was because the PCC derived its powers from statute. This should not per se be regarded as a conclusive point however. It may be that an equally or more important factor underpinning the court's conclusion was the nature of the PCC's power. The power in issue was regarded by the Court of Appeal essentially one of taxation, which is generally seen as a government function.[146]

A different factual situation arose in *Poplar Housing and Regeneration Community Association v Donoghue*.[147] The appellant was a notionally private sector housing association. However, in de facto terms the housing association was essentially a management takeover of the housing operation previously controlled by the London Borough of Tower Hamlets.[148] The litigation was triggered by the association's attempt to evict one of its tenants; a tenant whose tenancy had been granted when the housing was owned by the local authority.

For present purposes, the central issue before the Court of Appeal was whether the association fell within the scope of s 6(3)(b); ie was it – a 'person certain of whose functions are of a public nature'. Lord Woolf CJ's leading judgment accepted that the notion of public authority in s 6: 'should be given a broad definition'.[149] Lord Woolf suggested that guidance as to the meaning of public authority could be found in administrative law cases concerned with whether particular bodies should be subject to judicial review.[150] But, in terms of broad principle, the Court of Appeal rejected the

145 [2001] EWCA Civ 713, [2001] 3 All ER 393.

146 The court went on to conclude that the tax imposed on the defendants breached Art 1 of the First Protocol, in that it was arbitrary and disproportionate as it bore no relation to the value of the land itself. For further discussion, see Dawson I and Dunn A (2002) 'Seeking the principle: chancel, choices and human rights' *Legal Studies* 238–258: Oliver D (2001) 'Chancel repairs and the Human Rights Act' *Public Law* 651–653.

147 [2001] EWCA Civ 595, [2001] 4 All ER 604.

148 See the discussion of the privatisation of council housing at pp 390–393 above.

149 [2001] EWCA Civ 595, [2001] 4 All ER 604 at 619.

150 See the discussion in ch 16 above.

suggestion that private individuals or organisations which contracted with public authorities to provide the means for those authorities to discharge legal obligations themselves became public authorities for s 6 purposes:

> 'The fact that a body performs an activity which otherwise a public body would be under a duty to perform cannot mean that such a performance is necessarily a public function. A public body in order to perform its public duties can use the services of a private body. S 6 should not be applied so that if a private body provides such services, the nature of the functions are inevitably public'.[151]

On the facts of the case, the Court of Appeal considered that the Association should be regarded as performing a public function because it was 'so closely assimilated' with the local authority.

Application of what might be termed the 'close assimilation' test led to a different conclusion on the s 6 point in *R (Heather) v Leonard Cheshire Foundation.*[152] The National Assistance Act 1948, s 21(1) places a duty on local authorities to provide accommodation for certain vulnerable people. Section 26 then allows local authorities to discharge the s 21 duty by placing people in facilities owned and run by charities. Several local authorities placed residents in a home run by a charity, the Leonard Cheshire Foundation, for people in need of intensive care. The Foundation subsequently decided that it wished to close the particular home where Mrs Heather lived. The Court of Appeal concluded that the Foundation was not a public authority. The Court accepted that *Poplar* required that s 6 be given a broad interpretation. However it distinguished the factual position of the Foundation and the Housing Association in *Poplar*. The Court saw no reason for assuming that there was a 'close assimilation' between the local authorities and the Foundation. This conclusion was clearly driven by policy concerns as to the reach of the Act. As in *Poplar*, the Court evidently saw no merit in the argument that every privately-owned hotel or nursing home should be regarded as a public authority just because a government body bought its services to house people to whom the government body owed a duty.[153]

The House of Lords took a distinctly different approach to the issue when it heard the appeal in *Aston Cantlow.*[154] The House of Lords indicated that s 6 required a distinction to be drawn between what may be termed 'core' and 'hybrid' public authorities. This dichotomy was substantially shaped by a consideration which had not been pursued before the Court of Appeal. Article 34 of the Convention empowers the ECtHR to receive petitions from 'persons, groups of individuals and non-governmental organisations'. Section 7 of the HRA identifies such petitioners as

151 [2001] EWCA Civ 595, [2001] 4 All ER 604 at 619.

152 [2002] EWCA Civ 366, [2002] 2 All ER 936.

153 *Leonard Cheshire* could plausibly have been decided differently. It is not an extravagant proposition to assert that a private company whose commercial relationship with an individual citizen exists only because a government body is under a legal obligation to the individual should be regarded as stepping into the government body's shoes for human rights purposes.

154 [2003] UKKL 37, [2003] 3 WLR 283.

potential 'victims' of infringements of Convention rights for the purposes of domestic law. The House of Lords in *Aston Cantlow* was much concerned to avoid the potential difficulty of defining 'public authorities' under s 6 in a fashion which effectively negated the capacity of a 'non-governmental organisation' ever to present itself as a 'victim' in respect of Convention rights. That incapacity should apply only to a 'core' public authority.

There is obviously a certain circularity in this form of reasoning.[155] But members of the Court did offer some freestanding criteria to be used in assessing whether a body was a 'core' body for this purpose. Lord Nicholls' formulation was perhaps the most expansive:

'[T]he phrase "a public authority" in s 6(1) is essentially a reference to a body whose nature is governmental in a broad sense of that expression. It is in respect of organisations of this nature that the government is answerable under the convention. Hence, under the Human Rights Act a body of this nature is required to act compatibly with convention rights in everything it does. The most obvious examples are government departments, local authorities, the police and the armed forces. Behind the instinctive classification of these organisations as bodies whose nature is governmental lie factors such as the possession of special powers, democratic accountability, public funding in whole or in part, an obligation to act only in the public interest, and a statutory constitution. . . .'[156]

No member of the Court felt that the PCC could be classified in this way:

'Its functions. . . . clearly include matters which are concerned only with the pastoral and organisational concerns of the diocese and the congregation of believers in the parish. It acts in the sectional not the public interest. . . . [I]t is essentially a domestic religious body. The fact that the Church of England is the established Church of England may mean that various bodies within that Church may as a result perform public functions. But it does not follow that PCCs themselves perform any such functions.'[157]

The Court's conclusion on this point was reinforced by the ECtHR's own decision in *Holy Monasteries v Greece*[158] in which the ECtHR held that the 'established' Greek Church was able to bring an action against the Greek state in respect of the confiscation of its property. Somewhat unusually, the House of Lords also drew upon German constitutional law principle to support its conclusions.[159]

Nor did the House of Lords accept that the Parochial Parish Council was performing a 'function of a public nature' within s 6(3)(b)in this case. The Court indicated

[155] And we can now expect complications to arise on the domestic impact of the ECtHR's jurisprudence on this point: cf Davis H (2005) 'Public authorities as victims under the HRA' *Cambridge LJ* 315–328: Quane H (2006) 'The Strasbourg jurisprudence and the meaning of a "public authority" under the HRA' *Public Law* 106–123.

[156] Ibid, at para 7. [157] Ibid, per Lord Hobhouse at para 86.

[158] (1994) 20 EHRR 1. In emphasising the importance of the ECtHR's case law on this point, the House of Lords also indicated that no great reliance should be placed for s.6 purposes on the ostensibly similar issue of whether a body was amenable to judicial review under domestic law or whether – in the context of EC law it was an 'emanation of the state' for *Marshall* purposes: see pp 590 and 459 above.

[159] See the judgment of Lord Hope at para. 62.

that it would not be possible to offer any definitive answer to what might amount to a public function for these purposes. Any such answer would have to be substantially dependent upon the factual character of the particular body and the particular function in issue. On the facts of *Aston Cantlow* itself, the Court concluded that the 'function' under consideration lacked a 'public' character. Rather than characterise what the PCC was doing as analogous to levying a tax, the House of Lords regarded the PCC as simply enforcing a private law obligation comparable to a restrictive covenant or a civil debt.[160]

The impact of *Aston Cantlow* was promptly considered in the Court of Appeal in *R (on the application of Beer) v Hampshire Farmers Market Ltd*[161] Hampshire Farmers Market Ltd was de jure a private company. However it had initially been created and operated by Hampshire County Council as a device to stimulate the agricultural sector of the local economy by promoting weekend markets at which local farmers sold their produce direct to the public. The Council subsequently decided to hand control of the operation to the local farmers involved. It assisted them in establishing a limited company, provided office space and logistical support to the company, and a former council employee took on senior position in the new company. The company was given control, inter alia, of granting licences to farmers who wished to participate in the market sales. Mr Beer was refused a licence, in a fashion which – by the time the case reached the Court of Appeal – was accepted to have been procedurally unfair. The issues before the Court were whether the company was subject to judicial review at common law, and whether it was a public authority within s 6.

Dyson LJ's judgment observes that the answer to these two questions would often – but not always – be the same on any given set of facts. Two factors in this case led him to conclude that the company was both a 'hybrid' public authority and amenable to judicial review. The first was the very close assimilation between the company and the county council; the council had created the company; the company 'stepped into the council's shoes' in terms of its functions; and the council continued to provide substantial support to the company. This element of the judgment is essentially an endorsement of the Court of Appeal's reasoning in *Poplar*. The second, and perhaps more idiosyncratic, factor was that the venues where the markets were held had traditionally been regarded as places to which the general public had a right of access. As such, the company was in a sense acting as a steward of a public rather than private interest.

These cases could be taken to suggest that the courts have given little credence to arguments that the Act should be afforded an expansive horizontal effect in practical

[160] See generally Meisel F (2004) 'The *Aston Cantlow* case: blots on English jurisprudence and the public/private law divide' *Public Law* 2–10: Donnelly C (2005) '*Leonard Cheshire* again and beyond: private contractors, contract and s 6(3)(b) of the Human Rights Act' *Public Law* 785–805: Sunkin M (2004) 'Pushing forward the frontiers of human rights protection; the meaning of public authority under the Human Rights Act' *Public Law* 643–658.

[161] [2004] 1 WLR 233. For an interesting discussion of the legal context of the case see Hough B (2005) 'Public regulation of markets and fairs' *Public Law* 586–607.

terms through the route of extending an extremely broad reach to s 6. But the judgments by no means settle the question as to the reach of the Human Rights Act. Of equal or perhaps greater significance on that point is the way in which the courts have dealt with cases raising what were referred to above as 'scenario 3' and 'scenario 4' situations.

Imposing Convention Rights on private individuals and organisations

As suggested above, the Court of Appeal's judgment in *Wilson v First County Trust (No 2)*[162] took a rather conservative approach to the impact of s 3. The House of Lords saw no need to tackle that issue as it concluded that the relevant statutory provision was compatible with the Convention. But the decision also has implications for the Act's reach into the ostensibly 'private' sphere.

It will be recalled that *Wilson* concerned the construction of the Consumer Credit Act 1974, s 127. Insofar as s 127 regulates the relationship between private lenders and borrowers it creates a 'horizontal' relationship. The Court of Appeal however (without evidently giving any thought to the horizontality question) 'verticalised' the dispute by in effect treating the first instance judgment as the defendant on appeal.[163] The Court (whether by design or happy accident is not clear) cut through much of the conceptual difficulty attending the horizontal/vertical effect debate by essentially making Parliament – in the sense of s 127 as construed by the trial court – the 'defendant'. The action in the case was 'horizontal' only inasmuch as Ms Wilson provided the procedural peg on which the substantive argument as to the compatibility of the Consumer Credit Act 1974 s 127 with the Convention could be hung. The question of horizontality was not pursued before the House of Lords. To put the point differently; one issue of principle which could be extracted from *Wilson* is that Human Rights Act litigation in which the substance of the relationship between the parties turns on the interpretation of statutory provisions is always 'vertical' in nature irrespective of the identity of the parties.[164]

Precisely the same conclusion can be drawn from the *Mendoza* decision. No issue appears to have been raised by either counsel or the various courts which heard *Mendoza* as to the 'horizontality' of the action. Mr Mendoza's landlord was manifestly not a public authority in either a core or functional sense. The 'real' defendant, as in *Wilson*, was the statutory term which mandated a particular outcome in any dispute between private parties in the respective positions of the litigants in these cases.

Aston-Cantlow might initially be thought to complicate this picture somewhat, in so far as that case was concerned primarily with whether a PCC was a public authority and the PCC's capacity to recover the costs of chancel repairs had a statutory basis. However, the statutory provisions at issue in *Aston-Cantlow* had only a procedural (or

162 [2001] EWCA Civ 633, [2001] 3 All ER 229.

163 Ibid, at paras 18–19; per Sir Andrew Morrit VC.

164 This would not require the conclusion that *Leonard Cheshire* was wrongly decided. On the facts of that case, there was no direct statutory relationship between the Foundation and the applicant. The parties were rather indirectly linked together through their respective statutory relationships with a local authority.

jurisdictional) rather than substantive character. The primary effect of the Chancel Repairs Act 1932 was to remove disputes over repairs from the ecclesiastical courts and transfer them to the county courts. The 1932 Act did not require any particular outcome to such disputes, and could sensibly be characterised as placing PCCs on the same footing as any other private litigant seeking to enforce a contractual term.

On this reading of the Act, the designation of courts as 'public authorities' within HRA, s 6 simply reiterates their s 3 obligation when questions of statutory interpretation arise. The consequences of the courts' designation as 'public authorities' within s 6 for the purposes of 'horizontalising' Convention Rights in actions between private parties then becomes pertinent only in respect of litigation which raises the question of whether existing common law rules should be modified or – if the court faces a legal void – whether new common law rules should be recognised/created to limit the autonomy of private parties in their dealings with each other. The initial case law on this point suggested that the courts might be inclined de facto – but certainly not de jure – to give certain Convention Rights horizontal effect.

The applicants in *Douglas and Zeta-Jones v Hello! Ltd*[165] were unlikely candidates for the roles of flag-bearers of a right to privacy in English law. As noted above, prior to 2000 neither the courts nor Parliament had thought it desirable to introduce such a law.[166] Douglas and Zeta-Jones, both film stars, had signed a lucrative deal with a popular magazine – *OK* – for exclusive coverage of their wedding. Elaborate security precautions were put in place to prevent any unauthorised photos or sound recordings being made. Another magazine nonetheless managed to acquire some photos of the event and planned to feature them in its next edition. Douglas and Zeta-Jones then sought an injunction to prevent publication. This was granted at first instance.

The Court of Appeal subsequently lifted the injunction, but did so in a judgment which initially appeared to have significant implications for both the emergence of a right to privacy at common law and the likely horizontal impact of the Human Rights Act. All three judges[167] in the Court of Appeal appeared to approve the approach to horizontality advocated by Pannick and Lester;[168] namely that the courts should see the Human Rights Act as providing a legislative spur for more rapid development of indigenous common law principles.[169] For Sedley LJ, the spur was sufficient for him to accept that; 'We have reached a point at which it can be said with confidence that the law recognises and will appropriately protect a right of personal privacy'.[170] Keene LJ appeared to endorse this view. Brooke LJ adopted a more conservative approach,

[165] [2001] QB 967, CA. [166] See the discussion of *Malone* at p 636 above.

[167] Sedley, Brooke and Keene LJJ. [168] See pp 727–728 above.

[169] Cf Sedley LJ [2001] 2 All ER 289 at 321; '[I]f the step from confidentiality to privacy is not simply a modern restatement of the scope of a known protection but a legal innovation – then I would accept . . . that this is precisely the kind of incremental change for which the Human Rights Act is designed . . .': Keene LJ at 330: '[T]he courts as a public authority cannot act in a way which is incompatible with a convention right: s 6(1). That arguably includes their activity in interpreting and developing the common law, even where no public authority is a party to the litigation'.

[170] [2001] 2 All ER 289 at 316.

preferring to conclude that the claimants would find a remedy in an extended version of the tort of breach of confidence.

The subtleties of the various judgments unsurprisingly prompted some divergence of opinion as to the degree of horizontalisation which the Act might subsequently attain.[171] Even cautiously construed however, *Douglas and Zeta-Jones* provides clear support for the proposition that the passage of the Human Rights Act has provided a sharp stimulus to the courts to stretch the reach of existing common law principles to cover interferences with Convention rights by bodies other than 'public authorities'. The court considered that the existing law of breach of confidence could be extended in these circumstances to protect the claimant's Art 2 and Art 8 rights.[172] That assumption was subsequently reinforced by the House of Lords in *Campbell v MGN*[173] in which the Court held (unanimously in principle but by a 3–2 majority on application of the facts) that the famous model Naomi Campbell had a remedy in breach of confidence in respect of the publication by a newspaper of photographs of her attending a drug rehabilitation programme.[174]

Further powerful support for that viewpoint was provided by a High Court judgment – *Venables v Newsgroup Newspapers Ltd*[175] – issued shortly after *Douglas.* Venables had been convicted of murder when he was a child. He was shortly to be released from imprisonment, and feared he would be the subject of vigilante vengeance attacks if his identity and whereabouts became matters of public knowledge. He therefore sought an injunction against all media sources to prevent publication of any information that could reveal his new identity and home, on the basis that such publicity would unacceptably jeopardise his right to privacy under Art 8 ECHR and his right to life under Art 2 ECHR.

Dame Butler Sloss P followed the reasoning in *Douglas* in drawing the following conclusion:

'That obligation [ie of s 6(1)] on the court does not seem to me to encompass the creation of a free standing cause of action based directly on the articles of the convention. . . . The duty on the court, in my view, is to act compatibly with convention rights in adjudicating on existing common law causes of action, and that includes a positive as well as a negative obligation.'[176]

The House of Lords subsequently addressed this issue in *Wainright v Home Office*[177] *Wainright* was not a case in which horizontality was strictly in issue, as the defendant was a public authority. However the judgment offered important guidance as to the intensely important question in respect of both 'horizontal' and 'vertical' actions of

171 On subsequent developments see Beyleveld D and Pattinson S (2002) 'Horizontal applicability' *LQR* 623–647: Morgan J (2002) 'Questioning the "true effect" of the Human Rights Act' *Legal Studies* 259–275.

172 [2004] UKHL 22, [2004] 2 AC 457.

173 For (a very) critical comment see Morgan J (2004) 'Privacy in the House of Lords, again' *LQR* 563–566.

174 See Moreham N (2001) '*Douglas v Hello! Ltd* – the protection of privacy in English private law' *Modern LR* 767–775: Young A (2002) 'Remedial and substantive horizontality: the common law and *Douglas v Hello! Ltd*' *Public Law* 232–241.

175 [2001] 1 All ER 908.

176 Ibid, at 918.

177 [2003] UKHL 53; [2003] 4 All ER 969.

whether or not the HRA directly or indirectly created a right to privacy at common law. The claimants had been strip searched – in a fashion which was accepted to breach Home Office guidelines – while visiting a family member in prison. One had been subject to a battery which subsequently caused him psychiatric damage. The other claimant had not been the victim of a battery, but was left feeling humiliated and offended by the search. That one claimant had an existing remedy in damages in respect of the battery was uncontentious. The difficult point before the House of Lords was whether the claimants also had an action for breach of privacy.

The House of Lords rejected the assertion that English law should recognise a general remedy for breach of privacy in English law. The Court approvingly referred to Megarry VC's analysis in *Malone*[178] to explain why it was inappropriate for such an initiative to be taken at common law. Nor did the Court consider that such a wide-ranging right was required by the Convention. Its reading of the ECtHR's jurisprudence led it to conclude that what was required was that remedies be available to deal with specific instances of breaches of Art 8. Nor, on the facts of the case, did the Court accept that a breach of Art 8 had even occurred. That the claimants were distressed or humiliated by the search was did not in itself amount to an invasion of the claimants' privacy entitlement under the ECHR.

The extent to which the HRA has a horizontal impact has presented the courts with a very difficult question to which we have thus far been given a complicated answer and not fully reasoned answer. Several propositions might however be advanced.

Firstly, where the substantive outcome of litigation is dependent upon the meaning attached to a statutory provision, the identity of the parties is irrelevant. All such situations are lent a vertical character by s 3.

Secondly, the courts have adopted a sufficiently expansive approach to the meaning of 'public authority' per s 6 to ensure that some notionally horizontal actions acquire a vertical character because of the identity of the claimant/defendant.

Thirdly, if no statutory provision is in issue and neither party is a public authority, the court qua public authority per HRA s 6:

(a) is obliged where the substantive outcome of the case is dependent on an existing rule of common law to alter that rule of common law to ensure that the common law is Convention-compliant;

(b) is obliged where the existing common law does not produce a Convention-compliant outcome but could do so if it were extended in a modest and orderly fashion to make that extension;

(c) is not obliged, where no extendable rule of common law exists, to create an entirely new rule to render the relationship between the parties Convention-compliant.

Indeed, it might (tentatively) be suggested that the notion of 'horizontal' effect is

[178] Pp 635–637 above.

something of a jurisprudential red herring. A different and perhaps better way of framing the issue is in terms of differing types of 'verticality'. Four types of verticality might be identified, only one of which is concerned at all with the identity of the parties. Type 1 arises when the party allegedly contravening a Convention right is a public authority. Type 2 occurs when the outcome of litigation depends upon the meaning given by the court to a legislative provision. Type 3 is in issue when the outcome of litigation depends upon the meaning given by the court to an existing rule of common law. And type 4 comes into play when the outcome of litigation depends on the courts' capacity to extend an existing rule of common law.

The only certain conclusion which might yet be drawn on this question is that a good deal of judicial and academic attention will be focused on the search for a comprehensive answer during the next few years.

PROPORTIONALITY AS A GROUND OF REVIEW OF EXECUTIVE ACTION

As noted in chapter fourteen,[179] domestic courts have traditionally been unwillingly (at least overtly) to apply proportionality as a ground of review of executive action. It is quite clear however that the 'necessary in a democratic society' test used in many provisions of the Convention demands that courts subject the merits of government action to far more rigorous scrutiny than would be required by orthodox principles of English administrative law. This proposition has been endorsed albeit rather cautiously by domestic courts, with the result that government actions interfering with Convention Rights will in some circumstances be subjected to proportionality review.

This development is well-illustrated by the House of Lords' judgment in *R (Daly) v Secretary of State for the Home Department.*[180] The case concerned the legality of a policy adopted by the Home Secretary to exclude prisoners from their cells while the cells were being searched. Daly contended that the policy breached Art 8 ECHR, inasmuch as such searches could be conducted even if the prisoner had legally privileged correspondence in his cell at the time. The policy had been adopted to minimise the possibility that searches for contraband material could be compromised by prisoners being able to intimidate, obstruct or otherwise influence prison officers during the search. These are obviously rational objectives, and there would be little scope for assuming such a policy to be irrational per se in the *Wednesbury/GCHQ* sense. Daly's challenge to the policy's lawfulness was tightly focused: he argued that it was not 'necessary' per Art 8(2) to achieve those objectives to leave privileged correspondence in the cell during the search.

Lord Steyn framed the issue in the following way:

'There is an overlap between the traditional grounds of review [irrationality] and the approach of proportionality. Most cases would be decided in the same way whichever

[179] See pp 531–533 above. [180] [2001] UKHL 26, [2001] 3 All ER 433.

approach is adopted. But the intensity of review is somewhat greater under the proportionality approach . . .'[181]

The primary distinction between the two approaches was, in Lord Steyn's view, that: 'the doctrine of proportionality may require the reviewing court to assess the balance which the decision-maker has struck, not merely whether it is within the range of rational or reasonable decisions'.[182] On the facts of the case, the House of Lords suggested that the policy was disproportionate. To be compliant with Art 8, the policy should be modified to permit legally privileged correspondence to be safely sealed prior to any search.

Both Lord Steyn and Lord Bingham indicated that proportionality review would arise in respect of Convention Rights as a result of the requirements imposed on the courts by the Human Rights Act. They did not advocate that it should be accepted as a principle of domestic common law. Lord Cooke's concurring judgment seemed to take that larger step. He concluded that the very loose test of irrationality put forward by Lord Greene MR in *Wednesbury*: 'was an unfortunately retrogressive decision in English administrative law, in so far as it suggested that there are degrees of unreasonableness and that only a very extreme degree can bring an administrative decision within the legitimate scope of judicial invalidation'.[183]

Lord Slynn had appeared to adopt a similar viewpoint – which was not expressly shared by his colleagues – in *R (Alconbury Developments) v Secretary of State for the Environment*.[184] The case concerned the compatibility of the land use planning system with Art 6 ECHR, and in particular the degree of judicial scrutiny which should be applied to planning decisions taken by the Secretary of State for the Environment in which central government had a financial interest. The House of Lords concluded in *Alconbury* that if a Convention Right was engaged by a government decision that could be characterised as being a 'policy' matter, a loose regime of judicial supervision akin to *Wednesbury* irrationality might suffice to make the overall process Convention compliant.

It would be premature to seek to identify principles on which one could firmly predict the rigour which domestic courts should scrutinise particular governmental interferences with Convention Rights.[185] It might be suggested that this issue will lead the courts to develop a more elaborate notion of justiciability than the (in retrospect) rather crude test outlined in *GCHQ*.[186] It also seems tolerably clear that the question of intensity of review will be closely related to the 'hierarchy of rights' concept discussed above in the context of the deference principle. Nonetheless, it is obviously safe

181 Ibid, at 446. 182 Ibid.

183 Ibid, at 447. This may be seen as advocating the same kind of 'ripple effect' from Convention Rights into the whole field of administrative law as has been seen in respect of some EC law principles; see pp 476–478 above.

184 [2001] UKHL 23, [2001] 2 All ER 929.

185 For a helpful discussion of the early cases on the point see Leigh I (2002) 'Taking rights proportionately' *Public Law* 265–280.

186 See pp 117–120 above.

to conclude that as a result of the Human Rights Act a substantial amount of governmental activity will receive more exacting judicial examination than has hitherto been the case.

CONCLUSION

There is no doubt that the Human Rights Act has already had significant and far-reaching effects on domestic administrative law and has triggered – at least for the moment – extensive changes in the balance of power between executive bodies and the courts. This assertion is perhaps best illustrated by considering the judgment of the House of Lords in *A v Secretary of State for the Home Department*[187] and the subsequent response of the Blair government and the two houses of Parliament to the court's decision.

The statutory provision in issue in *A* was s 23 of the Anti-Terrorism, Crime and Security Act 2001. Section 23 was one element of a 129-section Bill which was pushed through both houses after just a few days of debate, following the terrorist attacks in New York on 11 September 2001. Section 23 empowered the Home Secretary to detain without criminal charge for an indefinite period any foreign national whom the Home Secretary certified to be a terrorist if the person did not consent to being deported to his home country. The policy – which rested in part on a presumption that the government would not be able to prove that suspects had committed any criminal offence – was prima facie incompatible with Art 5(1) ECHR. The government therefore sought to avoid the possibility of a declaration of incompatibility in respect of s 23 by claiming that the threat posed by terrorists was such as to justify a derogation under Art 15 ECHR from Art 5 ECHR, on the basis that the United Kingdom was faced by a 'public emergency threatening the life of the nation'.[188]

The House of Lords – sitting as a nine-judge court to emphasise the importance of the case – accepted (over a notable dissent by Lord Hoffman) that the requisite 'public emergency' existed. However, also it held that s 23 did not meet the additional requirement in Art 15 that any derogation be limited to 'the extent strictly required by the exigencies of the situation.' The Court considered that s 23 clearly failed to satisfy a key element of the proportionality test. The supposed purpose of s 23 was to protect the public against terrorist attacks. But since a putative detainee could in effect free herself from detention by agreeing to be deported, the Court understandably reasoned that s 23 was not a rational means to achieve that purpose. The notion that a 'terrorist' would be unable to plot terrorist attacks against targets in Britain from

[187] [2004] UKHL 56; [2005] 2 AC 68.

[188] The mechanism by which the HRA gives domestic effect to a derogation is per s 14 by empowering the government to issue a 'derogation order' – which is strictly speaking a statutory instrument. A prima facie breach of a Convention Right loses its unlawful domestic nature if the derogation is in force.

her/his homeland and then to re-enter the country and carry out the attacks and/or use other individuals to do so was clearly risible. The Court also concluded that s 23 breached Art 14's prohibition on nationality based discrimination. Assuming there was indeed a real emergency in existence, there was no convincing basis for assuming that terrorist attacks would not be planned or carried out by British nationals.[189] Given that s 23 lent itself to only one Convention non-compliant meaning, no issue arose as to the use of s 3 of the HRA. The Court therefore issued a declaration of incompatibility.[190]

The judgment was (predictably) denounced in some media and political quarters as an affront to democracy. As has been suggested repeatedly in this book, the presumption that any political value favoured by elected law-makers is 'democratic' simply because its makers are elected is at best grossly over-simplistic and at worst dangerously misleading. Any sophisticated notion of democratic governance would identify two major objections to s 23. The first would relate to the rushed and truncated nature of the deliberative process within the Commons and Lords as to the merits of the proposed Act. The second would focus on the ludicrously ineffective and grossly discriminatory substantive provisions. If one's understanding of democratic governance embraces the proposition that politicians should be prevented from giving legal effect to policies which impose grotesque restrictions on basic liberties, or even the more modest proposition that it should very difficult for politicians to achieve such results, s 23 was an obscenity and in saying so the House of Lords was upholding rather than undermining notions of democratic governance.

While the judgment of the House of Lords is per se significant as an indicator of the way in which the HRA has led the courts to feel they may now appropriately venture into areas of political controversy which might previously have been regarded as having a demonstrably 'non-justiciable character', it may be that we should attach even more importance to the way in which the government responded to the judgment. The government did not choose, as it was legally entitled to do, to proceed on the basis that s 23 should remain in effect notwithstanding its incompatibility with the Convention. Instead, the government promoted – and Parliament enacted – a new provision which would replace s 23 with a less draconian 'control order' applicable to nationals and non-national which restricted the movements of suspected terrorists.

To frame this episode in somewhat grandiose theoretical terms, it might be suggested that the declaration of incompatibility delegitimised s 23 to such an extent that the government felt it was under a political obligation to promote amending legislation.[191] As such, the *A* judgment and its aftermath certainly mark a significant point in the development of our constitution. But it would be a gross overstatement to regard

[189] Indeed, the only Al-Qaeda related terrorist attack in Britain – the bombings of July 2005 – were carried out by four British citizens.

[190] See further Dwyer D (2005) 'Rights brought home' *LQR* 359–364: Feldman D (2005) 'Proportionality and discrimination in anti-terrorism legislation' *Cambridge LJ* 270–272.

[191] Cf the discussion of the impact of the Canadian Supreme Court's judgment in the patriation dispute; see pp 338–342 above.

the Human Rights Act as having had in any systemic sense a revolutionary effect in the sphere of constitutional law. The crucial point to be laboured (perhaps painfully) here is that the HRA does not – and makes no attempt to – endow the Convention with the status of a constituent framework of political values, existing beyond the reach of reform or repeal by a simple legislative majority. The protection offered to civil liberties by the Human Rights Act is in legal terms ephemeral and (at this point in time) in political terms precarious. Its substance may be promptly modified by whichever political faction can command even a bare Commons and Lords majority. Rights recognised as 'fundamental' at common law prior to the HRA coming into force are obviously no less ephemeral. The Human Rights Act does not even attempt to embrace the basic moral principles that, over two hundred years ago, Jefferson, Madison and their colleagues articulated in the US Constitution: namely that, as Madison put it, in the United States: 'the censorial power is in the people over the government, and not in the government over the people'.[192]

Once made, this observation raises a larger question. It takes little reflection to lead one to ask whether the greatest threat to the pervasive, long-term respect for human rights in modern British society stems from the doctrine of parliamentary sovereignty. The final chapter of this book thus returns to the question of whether it is possible in legal terms to entrench fundamental values within the UK's constitution, and, if so, which values should be chosen and how should they be protected. The penultimate chapter, however, examines the issues of sovereignty and entrenchment in a political rather than legal sense. Its focus is on what may prove to be the most significant of the constitutional reforms promoted by the first Blair administration – the devolution of governmental power to Scotland and Wales.

[192] Perhaps the best guide to Madison's views on the point are offered by his speech in the House of Representatives on June 1789, when he spoke to move adoption of the First Amendment to the Constitution; see Fisher L (1996, 3rd edn) *Constitutional law* vol 2, pp 551–555 (Minneapolis: McGraw-Hill).

22

SCOTS AND WELSH DEVOLUTION

The *McCormick v Lord Advocate*[1] litigation in the 1950s indicated that at least some of the Scots people rejected the orthodox view of the Treaty of Union that Scots MPs were simply absorbed into the English Parliament.[2] Since Scotland's population was far smaller than England's, the principle of approximate parity of constituency sizes adopted in respect of parliamentary elections since 1948 necessarily meant that Scotland sent only a small minority of MPs to the Commons.[3] Scotland's 'separateness' was to some extent recognised by the creation of a Secretary of State for Scotland in 1926, and by the existence of a Scots 'Grand Committee' in the Commons,[4] yet neither initiative afforded Scotland any constituent political autonomy. Its Secretary was merely one member of the Cabinet; the Grand Committee merely a small fraction of MPs.

But Scots discontent was not limited solely to questions of parliamentary representation. Rather it expressed in an acute form a more general perception that Scotland's historical status as a 'nation', and its contemporary status as a discrete area of the United Kingdom whose people had a distinctive political and cultural identity, had been unacceptably submerged beneath a legislative and governmental structure pervasively and perpetually dominated by 'English' concerns. Such sentiments appeared to be gaining wider support from the early 1960s onwards, when Scots (and Welsh) nationalist parties began to attract substantially increased electoral support. In response to this pressure, both the Conservative and Labour parties had indicated in the late 1960s that they would be prepared to introduce legislation creating distinctively Scots and Welsh 'national' governments. The second Wilson government established a Royal Commission (the Kilbrandon Commission) to address the question of the relationship between the various countries of the United Kingdom. Its report,

[1] See pp 50–51 above.

[2] Dicey was perhaps the prime example of this theory. As Vernon Bogdanor notes, Dicey's analysis of Anglo-Scots relations spoke always of the Act (rather than the Acts) of Union, a linguistic sleight of hand which implicitly rejects the merger theory of union: see Bogdanor V (1979) 'The English constitution and devolution' *Political Quarterly* 36–49.

[3] Some 11% of MPs represented Scots constituencies.

[4] See Turpin (1990) op cit pp 183–188.

published in 1973, recommended that Parliament enact potentially far-reaching schemes of 'devolution'.[5]

Neither Conservative nor Labour governments in the 1970s ever suggested that Wales or Scotland should become independent sovereign states, nor even that the United Kingdom should become a federal country like the USA. Any such proposal would of course run into the legal difficulty of the sovereignty of Parliament. In terms of strict legal theory, any grant of 'independence' that Parliament might make to Wales or Scotland (or indeed England), or any legislation that sought to reconstruct the UK's unitary state on a federal basis, would lack constituent legal status; a subsequent Parliament could at any time restore the previous arrangements. As we saw in respect of Canada, such legal niceties may be swept aside by the brute force of new political facts. But the political realities which shaped the Kilbrandon report offered no obvious, immediate threat to the legal structure of the constitution. They did, however, point to a significant redefinition of conventional understandings.

Kilbrandon's concept of 'devolution' was an idea quite distinct from either federalism or independence in the formal, legal sense of those terms. The idea suggests that Parliament is delegating or lending legal competence in certain areas of government activity. But it is not giving its sovereignty away, for it reserves the power to revoke or redefine the nature of the delegation at any future date. Scotland was to have an elected Assembly (often colloquially referred to as the Scottish Parliament), whose members were to be chosen through a process analogous to that used for the Commons. In technical terms, however, it would be quite inaccurate to describe a body implementing devolved powers as a legislature, or to label its 'laws' as legislation. The Scots Assembly would be an executive body, just like a local council, empowered to produce byelaws in certain specified fields. It might indeed prove, as a matter of practical politics, to be a tier of local government unlike any other the British constitution had ever contained; but it would nevertheless depend (at least until political realities dictated otherwise) for its continued legal existence on the whim of Parliament.

THE SCOTLAND ACT 1978 AND THE WALES ACT 1978

The schemes of devolution ultimately enacted[6] in the Scotland Act 1978 and Wales Act 1978 were presented to the Commons by the then Prime Minister James Callaghan as:

'... a great constitutional change ... There will be a new settlement among the nations that

[5] For a useful summary of the Commission's investigations, the varying views of its members, and its conclusions see Mackintosh J (1974) 'The report of the Royal Commission on the Constitution 1969–1973' *Parliamentary Affairs* 115–123.

[6] The Bill was resolutely opposed by the Conservative Party. Its Commons passage was secured because the Labour government, by then in a Commons minority, had the support of the Liberals and the Scots and Welsh nationalist parties.

constitute the United Kingdom. We shall be moving away from the highly centralised State that has characterised our system for over two and a half centuries'.[7]

Whether the Acts would mark a first step in a longer march towards significant constitutional change is an open question. But there was little in the Scotland Act itself to merit such hyperbolic language.[8] Although the government firmly rejected any suggestion that enacting its Bills would 'federalise' the constitution, it would nevertheless be the case that the more powers that the Scots and Welsh Assemblies possessed, the more defensibly one might describe the UK's new system of government (if only in the conventional sense) as federal in nature.

It is difficult to determine from the Act's text how substantial a devolution of power it would effect.[9] The powers which were clearly not devolved included all of the major issues reserved to the federal government in the United States (foreign policy, the control of military forces, the issuance of currency), but also many others which in America would be regarded as primarily state rather than national government responsibilities (such as the electoral system, industrial strategy and aspects of labour relations and land development). Perhaps most importantly, the Assembly was not granted any tax raising powers at all, nor was it permitted to raise loans. All of its income would derive from a block grant provided by the Westminster Parliament; (although the Assembly could divide that grant as it wished among the services it was responsible for providing). In one very significant sense therefore, the Assembly would (in functional as well as formalist terms) be an 'administrative' rather than a 'governmental' body.

The scope of the Assembly's 'administrative' powers initially seemed quite extensive, but close examination of the Act reveals a very tortuous legal position. One commentator was moved to suggest that; 'The allocation of powers to the Assembly . . . is the most complex part of the Act, and one unlikely to be understood by most Assembly members and the public'.[10]

The Act's method was to outline in Part I of Sch 10 a series of 'groups' of powers over which the Assembly would enjoy complete autonomy. These seemed very far-reaching. For example, group 2 embraced 'social welfare'; group 3 covered 'education'; group 6 encompassed 'land use and development'; and group 7 dealt with 'pollution'. However Part II of Sch 10 then listed a great many specific functions within each group which were not devolved. Thus all matters relating to universities were excluded from the education group. Similarly, all social security benefits were excluded from the social welfare group. Furthermore, Part III of Sch 10 contained a lengthy list of powers within particular statutes which were not to be devolved. In combination, these specific exceptions could effectively negate the delegation apparently made in Part I. Thus Part III reserved so many detailed land use and

[7] *HCD*, 13 December 1976 c 993.

[8] The Wales Act was even less radical. The discussion that follows focuses solely on the Scots legislation.

[9] What follows is a much simplified and selective description of the Act.

[10] *Current Law Statutes Annotated 1978*, ch 51 – General Comments para d (London: Sweet and Maxwell).

development powers (group 6) to central government that it was a nonsense to suggest that the Assembly exercised such responsibilities in any meaningful form. In contrast, however, the Assembly would have virtually unfettered control of the structure and revenue raising capacity of Scots local government.

The Scotland Act came closest to an American form of federalism in the provision it made for the resolution of disputes between the Assembly and Parliament on the question of whether a Scots Bill intruded into the sphere of competence retained by the UK Parliament. Per s 19, such questions were to be referred to the Privy Council (in its judicial capacity). If the Law Lords considered the Bill ultra vires the 1978 Act, the Bill would not be enacted into law. It need hardly be added that should central government ever have found itself in disagreement with a judicial decision on such a question, it could have invited Parliament to amend the Scotland Act to overrule the Privy Council's opinion. The retention of so many powers by Parliament (including the 'ultimate political fact' of its legal sovereignty) suggests that the Scots Assembly would initially have been little more than a glorified local authority, albeit one with 'national' geographical boundaries. The extent of its 'autonomy', would, as with local government more generally, be contingent entirely on parliamentary self-restraint. Quite how willing national government would be to tolerate (and more importantly to fund) the preferred policies of a Scots Assembly controlled by a different political party was a matter of conjecture.

No answer was ever given to that question however, since the provisions of the Act never came into force. The Labour government had broken to some extent with the tradition of 'parliamentary government' by including in both the Scotland and Wales Act a provision that required the proposed changes to be approved by a referendum conducted among the Scots and Welsh electorates respectively before they could be implemented.[11] The Acts required not simply that a majority of those voting supported devolution, but also that any such majority comprised at least 40% of the eligible electorate. The government was empowered to repeal the Act if its terms were not approved by the electorates. In Wales, on a mere 59% turn-out, 80% of voters rejected the devolution proposals. In Scotland, 55% of voters approved the change. However, since the turnout was only 64%, the 40% threshold was not reached.[12]

The outcome of the referendums suggests that there was no great enthusiasm among the Scots or Welsh for the Labour government's proposals. Scots Nationalist MPs nevertheless saw the election result as sufficient reason to vote against the Labour government in a subsequent vote of confidence, with the result that the government resigned, Parliament was dissolved, and the first Thatcher administration was returned at the ensuing general election. The Thatcher and Major governments deployed their majorities in the Commons and Lords to repeal the Scotland and Wales

[11] This being perhaps another example of the 'ripple effect' of EC membership on the domestic constitution. The Wilson government had deployed a referendum on the question of EEC membership in 1975; see pp 447–448 above.

[12] See Balsom D and McAllister I (1979) 'The Scottish and Welsh devolution referenda of 1979: constitutional change and popular choice' *Parliamentary Affairs* 394–409.

Acts, and saw no need to introduce devolution Bills of any sort, notwithstanding the fact that their share of the Scots vote in successive general elections was so small that barely a dozen of Scotland's 72 MPs were Conservatives. Throughout the 1980s, therefore, Scotland was governed by a party pursuing policies that enjoyed the support of only a small minority of the Scots people. In the 1995 local government elections, the Conservatives were unable to win a majority of seats on any Scots local authority. By this time, the Scots Nationalists were stridently committed to the creation of an independent Scots state, while the Labour and Liberal parties advocated a more extensive form of devolution (including the crucial power to levy taxation) than that proposed in the Scotland Act. The status quo was preferred only by a party which had attracted little more than 40% of the popular vote in general elections since 1979; but as we have already seen on many occasions, such minoritarian support is quite sufficient to control every level of the law-making process under the British constitution's particular form of democratic government.

I. THE SCOTLAND ACT 1998

At the 1987 general election, the Conservatives won only ten of Scotland's 70 Commons seats. They nevertheless had a large majority in the Commons overall. The evident unpopularity of the Conservatives in Scotland – and a growing sense of injustice that the country should be governed by an 'English' Conservative administration – led the Labour and Liberal parties in Scotland, along with various other small parties and some trade union and church groups, to convene a 'Scottish Constitutional Convention' to debate the case for radical reform to Scotland's governmental system.[13]

The Convention's discussions continued throughout the 1990s,[14] and culminated in 1995 in the publication of a policy document entitled '*Scotland's Parliament, Scotland's Right*', which urged the creation of a Scots legislature and executive which would exercise substantial political powers and enjoy a large degree of autonomy from the Westminster Parliament. Much of the letter and some of the spirit (albeit in diluted form) of the Convention's proposals found their way into the Labour Party's manifesto proposals for the 1997 general election. The manifesto highlighted Scots devolution as one of the most urgent priorities for a Labour government. The extent to which the Conservative government had lost any plausible claim to legitimacy within Scotland was forcefully underlined by the result of the 1997 general election. The Conservatives did not win a single seat in Scotland in 1997. This dire performance

[13] The Scottish Nationalist Party boycotted the Convention, on the basis that it regarded complete independence for Scotland as the only acceptable reform. See McClean R (1999) 'A brief history of Scottish home rule', in Hassan G (ed) *A guide to the Scottish Parliament* (Edinburgh: Centre for Scottish Public Policy).

[14] The Conservatives had in the meantime managed to win 12 Scots seats at the 1992 general election. The Major government remained implacably opposed to any reform of Scotland's governmental system.

was in part the result of the first past the post system; in all the Conservatives attracted some 17.5% of the Scots popular vote.

The new government lost little time in acting on its manifesto commitment. A white paper, *Scotland's Parliament*,[15] was published in July 1997. In a preface to the white paper, the Prime Minister characterised Scotland as 'a proud historic nation' and stated that his government's reform programme was designed to enhance the Scots people's control over domestic Scottish politics. The government's plans did not extend as far as the Constitutional Convention had urged, but nevertheless outlined a reform programme which appeared to offer the Scots electorate a substantial measure of political autonomy.

The white paper proposed that the new structure of government within Scotland would be modelled on the existing United Kingdom system. There would be a fusion rather than separation of powers between the 'legislature' and the 'executive'. The Scots government would be headed by a First Minister, whose administration would be drawn from, and hence have to command the support of, a majority of members of the Parliament.[16]

It was proposed that the Parliament would contain 129 members. Its electoral system would be markedly different from the straightforward first past the post method used for the House of Commons, and would be loosely based on the process used to elect members of the German Bundestag.[17] Each elector would have two votes. Some 73 of MSPs[18] would represent the same constituencies[19] as the Scots members of the UK Parliament, and would be chosen by the orthodox first past the post system. The electors' second vote would be for a party rather than an individual candidate. The other 56 MSPs would be selected from eight regional party lists, with allocation of additional members being designed to ameliorate – if not eliminate – any seats won/votes cast discrepancies arising in the constituency seat section. This system makes it very likely that, unless one party managed to gain an extremely high percentage of the popular vote,[20] that the Scots Parliament will always be hung. This in turn would suggest that the Scots government would be either a minority or coalition administration.

The Constitutional Convention had begun its activities with the announcement that: 'We, gathered as the Scottish Constitutional Convention, do hereby acknowledge the sovereign right of the Scottish people to determine the form of government suited to their needs'.

[15] London: HMSO; Cm 3658.

[16] The white paper did not use the formal label of 'the Cabinet' to describe the senior members of the Scots government, but it seems likely that this will be the commonplace terminology.

[17] See p 260 above.

[18] MSP being the accepted abbreviation for 'Member of the Scottish Parliament'.

[19] There were in fact only 72 Scots constituencies at Westminster. The Orkney and Shetland constituency is split into two for the Scottish Parliament.

[20] Although, given that Scotland has four major political parties, it would be technically possible for a single party to win all 73 constituency seats with less than 30% of the constituency vote and without receiving any party list votes at all.

The echoes that this statement had of the US Declaration of Independence were studiedly ignored in the white paper. Its text laid repeated emphasis on the legal fact that the creation of a Scots Parliament did not and could not in any way detract from the continuing sovereignty of the Westminster legislature.[21] This position implicitly repudiates any notion that the Scots people possess in the legal sense 'sovereign rights', whether over their form of government or any other matter. The government also stressed, in a less legalistic fashion, that the United Kingdom would remain as a unitary state. There was no suggestion that the reform would in legal terms attempt to restructure the constitution on a federal basis, still less that Scotland would become an independent, sovereign nation. The envisaged legislation was not to be a latter day equivalent of the 1931 Statute of Westminster.[22]

In addition to believing that substantial devolution was an intrinsically correct policy to pursue, the Labour government appeared to have concluded that granting Scotland a substantial degree of self-governance would reduce rather than intensify growing pressure among some sections of the Scots electorate – particularly the Scottish Nationalist Party – for full independence. The notion that Scotland might survive and flourish as an independent nation was much less outlandish in 1997 than it would have been 20 years earlier. The substantial expansion of the EC's competence since 1980 made the Westminster Parliament less significant in economic terms to Scotland than it had hitherto been, and advocates of independence could also point to the rapid emergence of small sovereign states in eastern Europe following the collapse of the Soviet Union to buttress the feasibility of their position. Whether the Blair government judged this issue correctly remained to be seen.[23]

The white paper advocated that the division of political power between the UK and Scottish Parliaments be conceived in a manner quite distinct from the arrangements contained in the 1978 legislation. In that Act, the Scots Assembly had been treated in the same manner as any other local government body; ie it would only be permitted to exercise those specific powers explicitly granted to it by statute. The white paper advocated a different approach. Certain matters would be 'reserved' to the UK Parliament. But any matter not so reserved in the Act would be presumed to have been devolved to the Scottish legislature.

It was readily apparent that the new Scots Parliament would have more extensive powers than its aborted predecessor. By a process of deduction (ie by seeing which powers were to be reserved), one could see that the Scots Parliament would enjoy substantial control over inter alia; all levels of education, over local government, over land development and environmental regulation, over many aspects of transport

21 One might note that the white paper maintained a diplomatic silence on the issue raised in *McCormick v Lord Advocate* to the effect that that the Treaties of Union may impose some limits on the Westminster Parliament's powers; see pp 47–52 above.

22 See however Bogdnaor's suggestion that the relationship between the Scots and UK legislatures will in effect be quasi-federal: (1999a) 'Devolution: decentralisation or disintegration' *Political Quarterly* 185–194.

23 See the discussion in Bogdanor (1999a) op cit: and Brazier R (1999) 'The Constitution of the United Kingdom' *Cambridge LJ* 96–128.

policy, over the national health service, over the legal system (both civil and criminal law), over agriculture and fisheries, and over sports, arts and cultural heritage policy. Those matters to be reserved to the UK Parliament and government included constitutional reform, foreign policy, defence, macro-economic policy and social security law.

As was suggested in the previous discussion of local authorities, granting a government body a nominally long list of political powers has only limited meaning if the body concerned does not have the fiscal competence to exercise those powers in the way that its voters consider appropriate. The raising and spending of revenue would be of crucial significance to the degree of autonomy that the Scots Parliament would enjoy.

The white paper envisaged some substantial and some rather modest changes to the previous financial system. From the late 1970s onwards, under what has come to be known as the 'Barnett formula', Scotland's share of the public revenues has been based increasingly on its pro rata share of the UK's overall population.[24] A 'block grant' has been allocated to Scotland, which the Secretary of State was at liberty to allocate to different services as he/she thought appropriate. Under the devolved system of government, the block grant system remains unchanged, save for the fact that it will be for the Scots government and executive to determine just how that revenue should be spent. This would of course enable the Scots government substantially to increase expenditure on a given service, for example schooling, but only if it reduced expenditure by the same amount in other areas.

The devolution proposals also envisaged that the Scots Parliament should enjoy what was described as a 'limited' tax-raising/reducing capacity of its own. This would comprise a power to increase or cut the rate of income tax by up to three pence in the pound. The Blair government's insistence that macro-economic policy be a 'reserved' matter precluded the grant of any substantial fiscal autonomy to the Scots Parliament. The 'three pence in the pound formula' is however little more than tokenism, and makes something of a mockery of the notion that a government must possess significant tax raising powers if it is to govern in accordance with the wishes of its own electors rather than simply administer in conformity with the preferences of a hierarchically superior authority.

That the devolution proposals have as much a symbolic as practical dimension was indicated by the white paper's insistence that a devolution Bill would only be tabled if Scots voters approved the principle of devolution in a referendum. Legislation providing for a referendum was rapidly enacted, and the vote was scheduled for 11 September 1997. The referendum posed two questions. The first was whether voters approved in principle the creation of a Scots Parliament with a substantial array of devolved, 'legislative' powers. The second was whether those powers should include a capacity

24 Scotland has historically enjoyed a higher per capita share of public expenditure than England. That advantage has been reduced, but not eliminated by the Barnett formula; see Mait C and McCloud B (1999) 'Financial arrangements', in Hassan op cit.

to vary the rate of income tax levied by the UK Parliament by up to three pence in the pound.

The Scottish Nationalist Party – having boycotted the Constitutional Convention whose deliberations underpinned the white paper – decided to support the proposals in the referendum, albeit with the evident intention of wishing to seek full independence for Scotland at a later date. The Conservative Party maintained the stance it had adopted at the general election; that devolution was an irreversible step towards independence, and that to support it would signal the disintegration of the United Kingdom as a single country.[25] Such sentiments evidently did not deter Scots voters. In marked contrast to the result of the 1979 referendum, the 1998 poll produced large majorities for a 'Yes' answer (on a high turnout) for both questions. The Blair government subsequently proceeded to lay a devolution Bill before the Commons and Lords.

THE TERMS OF THE ACT

It was a sign of the strength of the first Blair government's Commons majority that the terms of the white paper were approved without serious quibble in the House of Commons. (The House of Lords, mindful no doubt of the fact that any obstruction of the Bill would be both a breach of the Salisbury Convention and a clear defiance of the referendum result, offered no resistance to the Bill.) It would nonetheless be rash to laud the promptness of the Bill's passage as a tribute to representative democracy. Given the substantial complexities of the Act's eventual provisions,[26] one cannot help but be left with the feeling that rather few Labour and Liberal Democrat backbenchers had any detailed understanding of just exactly what they were voting for.[27] It is perhaps unrealistic to expect backbenchers to have a lawyerly grasp of all the subtleties and complications of the Bill, but its rapid enactment can be seen as a further illustration of the Commons' persistent failure to act as an effective evaluator of the government's policy proposals.

The government's drafting of the Bill was evidently not designed to facilitate backbench scrutiny. As Brazier notes: 'Even passages of fundamental constitutional importance are not given the prominence which it may be said that they deserve, but are tucked away in the 132-section statute, leaving it to the assiduous reader to find them'.[28] That assiduity is a trait in which the Commons en bloc has been singularly lacking in recent years perhaps need not be further remarked upon.

The Act is too lengthy a document to be examined in detail here, but some of its key sections might be noted. Section 1 begins with the bald announcement that; 'There

25 See for example 'MP with no enemies goes into battle to preserve the UK' *The Guardian* 9 March 1998.

26 The Act has over 130 sections, as well as 6 schedules. In its annotated form in Current Law Statutes it covers some 217 pages of text.

27 See Craig P and Walters M (1999) 'The courts, devolution and judicial review' *Public Law* 274–306 for a helpful outline of the intricacies of the Act.

28 (1999) op cit p103.

shall be a Scottish Parliament'. Sections 1–10 then sketch out the electoral system through which MSPs are to be chosen. Under the terms of ss 2–3, Parliament may sit for a maximum of four years between elections, although provision is made for more frequent elections in exceptional circumstances. Sections 22–27 and s 36 delineate the rules surrounding the legislature's internal proceedings. Section 19 creates the position of Presiding Officer (the Scots Parliament's equivalent of the Speaker of the Commons), and provides for her/his election by a majority of MSPs. The structure and powers of the Scots government are laid out in ss 44–58. Rules relating to the allocation of the block grant and the Parliament's tax raising powers are contained in ss 64–80.

The autonomy of the Scots Parliament

Sections 28 and 29 are among the most significant of the Act's provisions. Section 28 confirms that the Parliament will have the power to pass legislation on Scots matters. Section 29 then places various substantive limits on the Parliament's legislative competence.[29] Section 33 introduces a form of pre-enactment judicial scrutiny of Bills at the request of the UK or Scots government's law officers. Should a Bill be thought to exceed the Parliament's powers – in the Act's parlance 'to raise a devolution issue' – it may be referred to the Judicial Committee of the Privy Council (ie to the Law Lords) for consideration. A Bill may not be enacted unamended if the Law Lords conclude it would breach s 29. The UK government is also empowered under s 35 to block enactment of any Scots Bill which it has reasonable grounds to believe to affect national security, international relations, or any reserved matter.[30]

The Act envisages that the Parliament may enact Bills which are not understood at the time to contravene s 29. Provision is therefore made for so-called 'devolution issues' to be raised by litigants in subsequent court proceedings. Schedule 6 of the Act sets out a referral procedure, (loosely modelled on the EC's Article [177] 234 device), through which lower courts may interrupt the proceedings before them to seek the opinion of the the High Court or Court of Appeal (the Inner Court of Session if the proceedings are taking place in Scotland) on whether a particular legislative provision breaches s 29. A further appeal on that question lies to the Privy Council.

It seems quite likely that 'devolution issues' will trigger a great deal of litigation in

[29] The Parliament may not legislate on any reserved matter. These are laid out in great detail in Schedule 5 to the Act. In addition, it may not legislate with extra-territorial effect, nor in breach of any provision of European Community law. The impact of the Human Rights Act 1998 in Scotland and Wales will also be rather more dramatic than in the UK as a whole. The Scots Parliament and the Welsh Assembly (discussed below) are both subjected to the Convention's provisions in a way that the UK Parliament is not. All of the 'laws' that they produce, irrespective of the form that the laws take, will be liable to invalidation by the courts on the grounds of their incompatibility with the Convention. See Lord Hope (1998) 'Devolution and Human Rights' *European Human Rights LR* 367–375.

[30] There is no ouster clause explicitly precluding judicial review of the exercise of this power, but it seems likely that its use would be regarded as a non-justiciable issue. Conversely, the Act also contains what amounts to a Henry VIII clause in respect of s 29 in s 63. This enables the UK government to transfer additional powers on matters relating to Scotland to the Scots government by Order in Council.

the first few years of the Scots Parliament's existence. The text of the Act will itself provide much scope for lawyers to argue about the meaning the UK Parliament intended to convey. In the aftermath of *Pepper v Hart*,[31] counsel in such litigation will no doubt also resort to Commons and Lords debates on the Bill to support divergent interpretations of the Act.

The legislation itself contains a rather unusual provision in s 101. This is essentially an instruction to the courts to interpret ambiguous Scots legislation as being within, rather than beyond, the Parliament's competence if either meaning is possible. Section 101 offers a statutory echo of a much broader common law principle that has been largely obsolete in United Kingdom law for some years. Like the Scots executive, the Scots Parliament is technically a statutory executive body. When exercising justiciable powers, most statutory bodies are presumptively[32] subject to judicial review on the grounds of illegality, irrationality, and procedural impropriety. That presumption will undoubtedly apply to actions taken by the Scots government. There is however an historical exception to this general rule, rooted in Britain's former status as a colonial power,[33] which supports the argument that Scots '**legislation**' could only be subject to review on the grounds of illegality.

The Parliament's subjection to the provisions of the European Convention and EC law makes this less of a legal lacuna than would previously have been the case. Many governmental decisions previously quashed on the basis of irrationality or procedural unfairness would also fall foul of one or other provision of the Convention or of EC law, to which s 29 of the Act requires the Parliament to conform.[34] (The Scots Parliament's subjection to the Convention stands in marked contrast to the position which the Convention has in respect of the United Kingdom Parliament, and serves as a reminder of the non-sovereign status of the Scots legislature). The lacuna would however be significant in respect of Scots legislation which impinged neither on Convention rights nor EC law.[35] It is in respect to these powers that some rather aged case law may acquire a new significance.

Colonial case law on legislative autonomy

The issue before the Privy Council in *R v Burah*[36] concerned the validity of a statute

31 See pp 284–290 above.

32 Ie in the absence of an ouster or limitation clause in the relevant statute.

33 See in particular the analysis offered by Craig and Walters *op cit* at pp 288–293.

34 One might suggest that s 29 renders the common law ground of illegality redundant. Section 29 of the Scotland Act is in essence a statutory restatement (and expansion) of the illegality principle in administrative law.

35 The extent to which the courts will be prepared to regulate the Parliament's non-legislative activities remains unclear. The Act affords the Parliament substantial discretion in respect of many facets of its internal proceedings. Section 29 obviously requires that those proceedings – unlike those of the Westminster legislature – respect the requirements of the European Convention; (as noted in ch 20, the Human Rights Act 1998 expressly exempts 'proceedings in Parliament' from the need to conform to the Convention). Whether the courts will also impose administrative law standards of rationality and procedural fairness on Scots parliamentary proceedings is an intriguing and thus far rather neglected question.

36 (1878) 3 App Cas 889.

passed by the Indian legislature which sought to alter the jurisdiction of the court system established by the British statute which created the Indian constitution. In the course of its judgment, the Privy Council made it quite clear that Indian legislation could be overturned on the basis of illegality; ie that the Parliament was interfering with issues that the British legislature had not granted it authority to address. However the courts would not entertain challenges based on irrationality or procedural impropriety:

'If what has been done is legislation, within the general scope of the affirmative words which give the power, and if it violates no express condition or restriction by which that power is limited . . . it is not for any Court of Justice to inquire further, or to enlarge constructively those conditions and restrictions'.[37]

The essentially non-democratic nature of the Indian legislature at that time (1878) perhaps makes *Burah* a precedent of limited utility in respect of the Scots Parliament.[38] More assistance might be derived from Privy Council decisions on Canadian constitutional law. *Riel v R*[39] turned on the meaning to be attributed to the proviso in the British North America Act 1867 to the effect that the Canadian Parliament could pass legislation; 'for the administration, peace, order and good government' of the country. Riel contended that this provision required the courts to consider whether the policy enacted in legislation did indeed amount to 'good government'. The Privy Council saw no merit in this argument: '[T]here is not the least colour for such a contention. The words of the statute are apt to authorise the utmost discretion of enactment'.[40]

The decision in *Edwards v A-G for Canada*[41] is perhaps the most interesting judgment however; in part because of its relative historical proximity to the present day, and in part because of its subject matter, which spoke very clearly to matters both of individual human rights and the representativeness of the governmental system. As noted in chapter two, British courts had held in the nineteenth and early twentieth century that women were incapable at common law of being regarded as 'men' or

37 Ibid, at 905; per Lord Selborne.

38 See also *Middelburg Municipality v Gertzen* (1914 AD 544) in which the Appellate Division of the South African Supreme Court held that South Africa's four provincial councils (whose boundaries were the same as the four self-governing colonies which had merged to form South Africa in 1909; see ch 2 above) enjoyed a similarly expansive legal competence. If one is seeking a 'democratic' justification for a relaxation of judicial controls on the Parliament's decision-making, this case (like *Burah*) offers little assistance. The South African constitution under which *Middelburg* was decided was a blatantly racist and anti-democratic arrangement; see generally Loveland (1999) op cit ch 4. It could of course be argued that the argument of relaxed judicial supervision applies with even more force to a democratically elected legislature, as the activities of such a Parliament (particularly if elected by a form of proportional representation) are subject to reasonably effective censure or approval by voters.

39 (1885) 10 App Cas 675.

40 Ibid, at 678; per Lord Halsbury. A similar rationale had been applied two years earlier to the activities of Canada's various provincial legislatures vis à vis the national Parliament in *Hodge v R* (1883) 9 App Cas 117, PC.

41 [1930] AC 124.

male 'persons' for the purposes of voting in elections to the Commons.[42] By the late 1920s, the UK Parliament had reversed that assumption through legislation, as had most of the provincial legislatures in Canada. Women were also by then eligible under statute to sit in the British and Canadian Houses of Commons. The question which arose in *Edwards* was whether women could sit in the Canadian Senate. Section 24 of the British North America Act 1867 provided that 'persons' could sit in the Senate. In the late 1920s, several Canadian women sought a declaration from the Canadian courts that s 24 included women. The Canadian Supreme Court held, placing much reliance on *Chorlton v Lings* and *Nairn v University of St Andrews*, that women were not 'persons' within s 24.[43]

On further appeal, the Privy Council reversed this judgment. At the core of its decision lay the proposition that the British North America Act 1867 was a 'constitution' rather than an ordinary statute, and so should not be subjected to orthodox techniques of statutory interpretation. As Lord Sankey put it, in a passage replete with splendidly mixed metaphors:

> 'The British North America Act planted in Canada a living tree capable of growth and expansion within its natural limits. Their Lordships do not conceive it to be [their] duty . . . to cut down the provisions of the Act by a narrow and technical construction, but rather to give it a large and liberal interpretation so that [Canada] to great extent . . . may be mistress in her own house.'[44]

In essence, the Privy Council appeared to be holding that the intention of the British Parliament in enacting the British North America Act in 1867 was to permit the courts in future years to attach new meanings to the Act's text in response to changing political, economic and social circumstances within Canadian society. That the Act itself made no explicit textual allusion to this principle was irrelevant; the principle was evidently to be regarded as inherent in any Westminster statute which creates a 'constitution'. On the particular facts of the case, the Privy Council concluded that gratuitous gender discrimination in relation to occupancy of legislative office had become an obsolete moral principle in Canada by 1930, an (ultimate?) political fact that was firmly evidenced by national and provincial statutes entitling women to vote in legislative elections and to occupy elected political office.

It would require something of a leap of the imagination to accept that the Scotland Act has fashioned a 'constitution' in this sense. Nonetheless, *Edwards* and the other cases mentioned above have led Craig and Walters to suggest that 'there is considerable scope for an interpretative approach [to the Scotland Act] that is sensitive to the fact that the courts will be reviewing the actions of democratically elected bodies'.[45] This could be considered a rather limited objective for the common law to pursue – and rather underplays the significance of the colonial case law – since just the same

[42] See the discussion of *Chorlton v Lings* and *Nairn v University of St Andrews* at pp 52–53 above.
[43] [1928] SCR 276.
[44] [1930] AC 124 at 136.
[45] Op cit, at p 292.

observation might be made in respect of the actions of local authorities.[46] Indeed, Craig and Walters' suggestion is strongly reminiscent of Lord Russell's judgment in *Kruse v Johnson*[47] that a council's power to make byelaws be construed 'benevolently'. Adequate judicial recognition of the very different political (and thence constitutional) status of the Scots Parliament and local authorities would suggest that the courts should go considerably further than simply being 'benevolent' when assessing if the Parliament has exceeded its powers.

There is an obvious temptation to assume that the courts' approach to matters concerning the Scots Parliament will be driven by the purposive jurisprudence which is now so firmly established as a tenet of EC law. That the Scotland Act does not instruct the courts to adopt this interpretative technique is no bar to them doing so: with the exception of the provision contained in s 101,[48] the choice of interpretative principles remains a matter of common law. Any allusion to purposive interpretation obviously begs the question of just what 'purpose' the Scotland Act is intended to serve. The Act itself does not contain any preamble answering this question. A plausible line of speculation would be to suggest that the judiciary will allow its task of interpreting the Scotland Act (and subsequent related legislation, whether Scots or United Kingdom in origin) to be influenced (but obviously not determined) by the 'sovereign right of the Scots people' thesis which underpinned the final recommendations of the Scottish Constitutional Convention.[49] Re-casting this sentiment in more constitutionally orthodox terms, the courts might readily be expected to assume that the purpose underpinning the Scotland Act is to maximise the extent to which the Scots electorate, acting through its representatives in the Scots Parliament, determines the outcome of Scots political questions. To address this point, we need also to consider what impact – if any – the Act will have on the sovereignty of the UK Parliament.

The continuing sovereignty of the UK Parliament?

The question of how much autonomy the courts afford to the Scots Parliament will also be affected by the meaning that the courts attach to s 28(7) of the Scotland Act. Section 28(7) seems, from a traditionalist constitutional standpoint, to be a wholly unnecessary provision. It states simply that the power given to the Scots Parliament to enact legislation for Scotland; 'does not affect the power of the United Kingdom Parliament to make law for Scotland'. In essence, the clause is saying that Parliament cannot entrench the initial autonomy it grants to the Scots legislature. This statutory

[46] The vast difference between the court's perception of the *vires* of a colonial parliament and a domestic local authority is forcefully conveyed if one recalls that *Edwards* was decided at much the same time as *Roberts v Hopwood*.

[47] See pp 361–362 above.

[48] Which could perhaps be seen as a (very) mild endorsement of teleological jurisprudence.

[49] Craig and Walters *op cit* note that an analogous principle has been adopted by the Canadian Supreme Court in interpreting the Canadian constitution, even though that constitution initially derives from an Act of the Westminster parliament; see *Reference Re Secession of Quebec* [1998] 2 SCR 217. Canada is of course a sovereign state, which Scotland manifestly is not.

restatement of orthodox Diceyan principle has perhaps been included in the Act in response to the new constitutional climate engendered by *Factortame (No 2)*, which does indicate that Parliament can now (in a limited sense) safeguard some political values against future repeal. Section 28(7) is perhaps intended to deter the courts from allowing the *Factortame* principle to seep into non-EC related constitutional contexts. It is also likely to be invoked by the UK government to rebut Scots accusations of undemocratic behaviour should the Westminster Parliament choose to pass legislation on a devolved matter. But its inclusion in the Act may have unexpected legal consequences.[50]

The Labour government's evident unwillingness deliberately even to attempt to entrench any part of the Scotland Act stands in marked contrast to the recommendations of the Constitutional Convention. The Convention had advocated that any devolution legislation should include an entrenching device – (reminiscent of s 4 of the Statute of Westminster)[51] – namely that the Westminster Parliament should not be able to enact future legislation reducing the powers of the Scots legislature unless the Scots legislature consented to the Act in question. The white paper made no reference to this proposal, nor to the issue of entrenchment generally.[52] The presence of s 28(7) in the Act would suggest that this omission arose because the Blair government regarded entrenchment as politically undesirable, rather than legally unachievable.[53]

Notwithstanding *Pepper v Hart*, a government's wishes cannot determine a court's interpretation of a statutory provision. A court which accepted the presumption that the Scotland Act was indeed intended to maximise the autonomy of the Scots electorate would not be sailing (and here the potential influence of the EC becomes apparent) into wholly uncharted constitutional waters if it held that s 28(7) requires the courts to apply UK legislation affecting matters devolved to the Scots Parliament by the 1998 Act only if the subsequent UK statute expressly states that the Scotland Act is being amended. To take the argument further, it might be suggested that s 28(7) could even be construed as confirming only that the Westminster Parliament can repeal the Scotland Act in its entirety. And unless and until it does so, any UK Act purportedly interfering with a devolved power will have no legal effect.

Professor Brazier has offered a hypothetical but quite plausible scenario that would put a thesis of this sort to an exacting test. The Scots Nationalist Party has committed itself, should it ever form a government in Scotland, to conduct a referendum to ascertain if the Scots people wish Scotland to become an independent nation. In Professor Brazier's view, an attempt by the Scots Parliament even to hold a referendum

50 It is also very difficult to reconcile with the Blair government's forceful statement vis à vis the ECHR in *Rights brought home* to the effect that it is not possible to entrench legislation in the United Kingdom; see pp 714–715 above.

51 See p 41 above.

52 See Myles A (1999) 'Scotland's Parliament White Paper', in *Hassan* op cit.

53 One might note that the government's unwillingness to countenance entrenchment in respect of the Human Rights Act was couched at least as much in terms of the legal impossibility of entrenchment as its political undesirability; see pp 714–715 above.

on this issue would be ultra vires s 29, as it is a 'constitutional' matter and so reserved to the UK Parliament.[54] This is a debatable point. For the Scots Parliament to seek to discover if the electorate would welcome further constitutional reform does not necessarily amount to constitutional reform per se. Whether it does or does not do so will be dependent on the background principles that the courts invoke when interpreting ss 28–29. A court which adopted a variant of the *Edwards* rationale in determining the legal consequences of the Scotland Act would presumably conclude that it does not.

These are presently fanciful conjectures. They will become less so if the UK Parliament makes no early attempt to reduce the powers of the Scots legislature, and markedly less so if those powers are actually increased by subsequent Westminster legislation. In either event, the conventional status of the Scots Parliament's legislative autonomy will be strengthened by the mere passage of time, by the observance of the principle by Westminster legislators, and by the continued vitality of the reason for its existence – namely the Scots people's legitimate democratic desire to exercise control over matters of Scottish domestic politics.

THE FIRST SCOTTISH PARLIAMENT AND GOVERNMENT

The results of the first Scottish general election, held in May 1999, were perhaps not altogether what the Labour government had hoped for. The Party failed to win an overall majority of seats in the new legislature, and also fell substantially short of gathering a clear majority of votes cast. As had been widely predicted, the election produced a hung Parliament. One cannot be sure that electors would have voted in the same way if the Parliament was to be chosen solely on the basis of the first-past-the-post system. But if one assumes they would have done so, it is evident that the opposition parties (the SNP and the Conservatives) have benefitted hugely from the Blair government's readiness to promote legislation which provided for a proportional system.

Table 22.1 Scottish general election May 1999

Party	constituency vote		party list vote		total
	%	seats	%	seats	seats
Labour	38.8	53	33.8	3	56
Liberal	14.2	12	12.5	5	17
Conservative	15.6	0	15.4	18	18
SNP	28.7	7	22.0	28	35
Others	2.7	1	11.4	2	3

54 (1999) op cit.

A coalition administration was eventually formed between the Labour and Liberal Democrat parties, within which Liberal MSPs would occupy several positions of appreciable political significance. Donald Dewar, the then Secretary of State for Scotland, became First Minister.[55] Dewar had already indicated that he saw his political future as lying in Scotland rather than Westminster, and that he would not seek re-election to the House of Commons. The Act itself is somewhat ambiguous on the issue of individuals fulfilling a dual political role in Scotland and at Westminster. A minister in the Scots Executive is not permitted to serve as a minister in the UK government, although Scots ministers and MSPs are not required to resign from the House of Commons.[56] After the 1999 election, some MSPs also had seats at Westminster. It is difficult to believe that they could adequately perform both roles, and many of the members with seats in both legislatures indicated that they would not contest seats in the Commons at the next general election.

Given that Donald Dewar was a senior member of the Blair cabinet, it was unlikely that his administration would take any policy initiatives which were incompatible with the Blair government's preferences. This point had indeed been made prior to the Scottish election: the Labour Party had announced in its Scots election manifesto that a Scots Labour government would not ask the Parliament to exercise its tax-raising powers in the foreseeable future. In the run-up to the 1999 election, the Liberal Democrats had stressed that the abolition of university tuition fees would be an essential component of their governmental programme. That commitment was quietly diluted in the subsequent coalition negotiations. There thus seemed no likelihood of any significant ideological friction between the Blair and Dewar governments in the first few years of the Scots Parliament's existence.

CONCLUSION

There is a clear danger of both exaggerating and understating the constitutional significance of the Scotland Act 1998. As with any Act (except perhaps the European Communities Act 1972)[57] orthodox theory would have it that the Scotland Act could be amended or wholly repealed by the United Kingdom Parliament at any point in the

[55] Per s 44, the First Minister is formally appointed by the Queen following nomination by the Parliament.

[56] This raises the rather puzzling prospect of the First Minister (and other senior Scots ministers), qua backbench MPs at Westminster, speaking from the backbenches on matters affecting Scotland which have been reserved to the Westminster Parliament. This would seem odd even when both governments are controlled by the same party. It will seem even stranger if and when they are controlled by different parties.

On a related point, Speaker Boothroyd indicated that she would not allow questions in the house to the Secretary of State for Scotland on matters devolved to the Scots Parliament. This is an interesting, if curious stance for the Speaker to adopt. In legal terms, the Scots parliament is a statutory body much like any local authority. There has never been any suggestion that the Secretary of State for the Environment is not required to answer questions in the house on matters assigned by statute to local government. The Speaker's attitude would suggest that she at least saw the Scots Parliament as enjoying 'special' constitutional status. Whether subsequent Speakers will adopt that view remains to be seen.

[57] See pp 480–488 above.

future. In a narrow legalistic respect, therefore, the Act is of limited significance. As suggested above, it is not wholly implausible to argue that the domestic courts might eventually attribute the same 'special' constitutional status to the Scotland Act as they have afforded to the European Communities Act 1972. But in the short term, this seems unlikely. The texts of the two statutes treat the issue of entrenchment in different ways, and, unlike the 1972 legislation, the Scotland Act is not emerging into a pre-existing legal context which demands that the sovereignty of the UK Parliament be modified to accommodate the principles of the direct effect and supremacy of a supra-national source of law. From a purely domestic perspective, the courts may regard the Scotland Act as 'special' in so far as they may deploy interpretative principles as to the vires of the new Parliament's activities derived from case law concerning colonial legislatures rather than indigenous statutory bodies. While this would be an interesting innovation, it is hardly a revolutionary one.

The Act does however provide a graphic example of the way in which the constitution can be seen as harbouring a profound dichotomy between the legal and political conceptions of sovereignty.[58] In legal terms, the comment of a Scots Nationalist MSP on the opening day of sitting of the new Parliament to the effect that the pre-Act of Union Scots legislature had come back into being was quite asinine. Yet as a statement of political realities, it contains some force.

In the aftermath of the referendum, senior members of the Conservative Party made it quite clear that they – in common with the Blair government – regarded devolution as having instantly acquired a degree of moral entrenchment, in the sense that a future Conservative government would not promote a Bill to repeal the devolution legislation. It might be rash to assume that this commitment will be adhered to in the long term. But – unless there is a dramatic shift of opinion in favour of repeal in Scotland itself – the political illegitimacy of any initiative markedly to reduce the Scots Parliament's powers would seem to make it an impractical course for any UK government to follow. There seems every likelihood that a convention will emerge to the effect that the Scots Parliament's powers should not be reduced without the consent of MSPs or the Scots electorate.[59]

In the short term, the tensions between the 'political' and 'legal' understandings of sovereignty in Scotland will probably manifest themselves in much more prosaic ways. A Scots government may well find for example that notwithstanding its [illegible] powers to raise its own income tax – reductions in public expenditure in the UK as a whole preclude the financing of Scots public services at the level that it and its supporters in Parliament and the electorate desire.

It is also probable that some judgments which the courts produce on devolution issues will displease either the Scots or the United Kingdom government. The Act lends the higher courts the status of a 'Constitutional Court' in a sense that they have

58 See particularly the lucid discussion of this issue in Brazier (1999) op cit.

59 The convention regulating the relationship between the provincial and national legislatures in Canada offers an obvious point for comparison; see pp 338–342 above.

not hitherto possessed, and they may in consequence be drawn much more often into making ostensibly party political judgments, especially in periods when the Scots and United Kingdom governments are controlled by different political parties. This is an important issue, and one that may have implications for the role of the courts that go above and beyond matters limited just to Scotland.[60]

That the Scots Parliament had succeeded rapidly in establishing its political autonomy within the United Kingdom is evidenced by the successions to the office of First Minister which followed the untimely death of Donald Dewar. The second incumbent as First Secretary was a man named Henry MacLeish, who was little known in Westminster circles. His tenure of office proved brief, as he was forced to resign following a scandal over his apparent misuse of the office expenses previously paid to him while he was an MP at Westminster. His successor, Jack McConnell, had no political reputation to speak of in United Kingdom circles. The choice of Scotland's First Minister, it seems, has become a matter wholly of Scots domestic politics.

II. THE GOVERNMENT OF WALES ACT 1998

The Blair government's proposals for devolution to Wales were an altogether more modest affair than those anticipated for Scotland. Their successful implementation also proved to be more problematic than those applied in Scotland. The level of popular support for Welsh devolution was pathetically low. Some 50.3% of the voters who took part in the referendum voted in favour of devolution, while 49.7% opposed. Moreover, the turnout was a dismal 51%. This meant that the devolution proposal was positively supported by barely 25% of eligible voters. Any subsequent legislation could thus lay no convincing claim to be legitimised by popular consent, a case which could clearly be made in respect of Scots devolution. The initially ponderous momentum the proposals enjoyed was further slowed shortly after the referendum when Ron Davies, Secretary of State for Wales and the designated leader of the Labour Party in the projected Assembly, resigned from the government and his post as leader of the party in Wales, in the aftermath of a sex scandal.

The modesty of the government's ambitions,[61] enacted virtually unamended in the Government of Wales Act 1998, was reflected in the names attached to the new system of Welsh government. Wales would not, like Scotland, have a Parliament, but an 'Assembly'. The Welsh government would not be headed by a First Minister, but by a 'First Secretary'. And her 'cabinet' colleagues would not be Ministers, but Assembly

60 See Craig and Walters op cit: Tierney S (2000) 'Constitutionalising the role of the judge: Scotland and the new order' *European LR* 49–72; (2000a) Devolution issues and s 2(1) of the Human Rights Act' *European Human Rights LR* 380–392.

61 See Welsh Office (1997) *A voice for Wales* (London: HMSO; Cm 3718).

Secretaries. The Assembly itself does not have 'legislative powers', but rather 'enacts' policy through transfers of authority from the Secretary of State for Wales.[62]

The scope and nature of Welsh devolution were also markedly different from the model used in Scotland. Rather than grant the Assembly a general competence and then reserve specific powers to the UK Parliament, the Government of Wales Act treats the Assembly as if it were a local authority; that is it is given specific powers. The powers themselves are a mere shadow of those enjoyed by the devolved government in Scotland. The Assembly and the Welsh executive undoubtedly amount to a powerful instrument of *local* governance, but they could in no sense be seen as a structure of *national* governance.

The Assembly and executive nonetheless rapidly proved to be of some considerable political significance. This was primarily the result of the electoral process chosen by the government to select the Labour Party's candidate as First Secretary and by the electoral process created by Parliament to select the Assembly's members. It rapidly became apparent that Labour Party members in Wales wished Rhodri Morgan, an independently-minded backbench MP, to be their candidate as First Secretary. The Blair government thought Morgan too 'independent' for its taste, and so devised a rigged electoral college that ensured the candidacy was won by Alun Michael, a cabinet minister. The Assembly itself, like the Scots Parliament, was to be elected by a mix of first-past-the-post and a list system. The result of the election left Alun Michael as First Secretary of a minority Labour administration. He subsequently lost a vote of confidence in the Assembly, and resigned, to be replaced by Morgan. The devolved government thus rapidly established itself as a mechanism for delivering a salutary – if largely symbolic – rebuke to the centralising tendencies of central government.

CONCLUSION

That the Scotland Act 1998 and Government of Wales Act 1998 fall far short of 'federalising' the United Kingdom's constitution in any legal sense is undeniable. Yet their constitutional significance should not be underestimated. Their most significant feature is the substantial step they take towards the assertion of *simultaneous political pluralism*[63] as a fundamental (if conventional) tenet of British constitutional morality. For the first time in twenty years, a British government has knowingly and enthusiastically invited Parliament to enact legislation which creates new governmental bodies within the United Kingdom constitution which – in addition to possessing significant political power – were by no means guaranteed to be controlled by the

[62] See generally Brazier (1999) op cit; Craig and Walters op cit: Rawlings R (1998) 'The new model Wales' *Journal of Law and Society* 461–512.

[63] See pp 349–350 above.

Labour Party. That a government was willing to entertain the probability that its policy initiatives would reduce its own power marks a complete break with the authoritarian ethos of the Thatcher and Major eras. In addition, the adoption of a system of proportional representation for electing the Scots Parliament and Welsh Assembly makes it very unlikely that legislative policy in Scotland and Wales will ever be determined by political parties enjoying only minoritarian electoral support. The adequacy of the Commons' electoral system and the minoritarian governments it almost invariably produces will thus be exposed to a constant, indigenous source of comparison. Perhaps even more importantly, the notion that a 'Parliament' can and should be a body possessing limited law-making competence will begin to become normalised within British political culture. At present, predictions as to the future development of the Scots and United Kingdom Parliaments seem to be dominated by the supposition that the former will become more like the latter.[64] We may find in the longer term that the reverse argument acquires increasing force.

64 One minor consequence of the initial 'success' of the devolution experiment is that the number of Scots seats in the Westminster Parliament has been reduced (by 12) so that the 'electoral quota' for Scots and English constituencies is the same; see p 238 above.

23

CONCLUSION – ENTRENCHMENT OF FUNDAMENTAL LAW REVISITED

The question of constitutional reform is in itself worthy of book length examination. This final chapter does not offer a detailed prescription of the ways in which the United Kingdom's constitution should be structured. Its concern rather is to address two questions that logically precede any discussion of the substance of radical constitutional reform. Firstly, whether it is legally possible to entrench legislation in a manner which safeguards it from repeal by the traditional 'simple majority in Commons and Lords plus royal assent' formula? And secondly, if such a legal device can be found, under what political circumstances might it legitimately be employed?

I. ISSUES OF LEGALITY AND LEGITIMACY

As suggested in chapter two, it now seems rather less difficult to construct a legal argument supporting the idea of entrenched legislation than it was in the 1950s, when the *Harris* and *McCormick* cases triggered a rash of interest in the possibility of finding domestic limitations to Parliament's evidently sovereign legal status. The orthodox Diceyan view, so persuasively restated by Professor Wade in 1955, need not be repeated here. The argument that such orthodoxy need no longer be construed as binding rests on several premises, both formalist and functionalist in nature. Some of these were evident but underdeveloped when Wade and indeed Dicey himself outlined the traditionalist viewpoint; others have emerged far more recently, as a result both of modern political history and contemporary judicial practice.

The first issue we might address is a problem raised by linguistic imprecision, an imprecision that has in turn produced considerable conceptual confusion. The conceptual confusion may arise if one fails to distinguish between two quite different routes to achieve the same moral/political ends. If one should somehow succeed in legally 'binding' future Parliaments to respect particular values, then one has necessarily succeeded in entrenching those values. But one need not necessarily have to achieve the former result to bring about the latter consequences; it may be that one can now entrench legislation without having to destroy 'Parliament's' legal sovereignty. This argument assumes that entrenchment need not need place any limits at all on 'Parliament's' legislative capacities; rather it need only convince the High Court that it has – if invited to do so by Parliament in a particular political context – an appropriate role to play in controlling the internal proceedings of the Commons and the Lords and the prerogative powers of the Monarch.

To illustrate this argument, we might begin with a hypothetical entrenching provision, contained in a 'Constitution Act' passed in the ordinary manner. The Constitution Act specifies that a statutory provision (whether enacted prior or subsequent to the Constitution Act) affecting an entrenched value detailed in the Constitution Act (which would include the entrenching provision itself) would have legal force only if the court was satisfied that the following criteria had been met:

1. the Act concerned had begun its parliamentary passage in the Commons;
2. the Commons had voted for it by a two thirds majority at third reading before sending it to the Lords;
3. the Lords had voted for it by a two thirds majority at third reading before sending it for the Royal Assent;
4. the Monarch had granted the Royal Assent only after establishing that the requisite majorities had been achieved in both houses.

We may then assume that a subsequent 'Parliament' purports to pass an 'Act' by the traditional simple majority plus royal assent formula that contains terms breaching the provisions of the Constitution Act.

It is tempting to conclude simply that a citizen who asked the court to obey the Constitution Act and disapply or invalidate a later statute would be asking the judiciary to override the wishes of Parliament, which had seemingly enacted the subsequent provision. However, steps 1–3 of the entrenchment process can be analysed in a rather different way. They could be seen as merely asking the courts to 'question' the proceedings adopted in each house in respect of a Bill. Step 4, in contrast, could be seen as simply requiring the courts to undertake the now uncontentious task of reviewing an exercise of the prerogative.[1]

The argument assumes that 'Parliament' has the legal capacity to regulate the powers of its component parts – that the Commons, the Lords, and the Monarch as parts of Parliament are legally inferior to Parliament itself. If this view is accepted, it seemingly follows that Parliament may enact legislation placing specific limits on the legal competence of either house or of the Monarch. The hypothetical Constitution

[1] It is perhaps feasible to argue that the granting of the Royal Assent is itself a 'proceeding in Parliament'. This would however seem implausible, given that privilege and Art 9 emerged as devices to protect the two houses against the Monarch. But for the purposes of this argument, the legal source of the royal assent is irrelevant.

Act essentially provides that the Commons would be acting ultra vires its powers in sending a Bill which infringed the Constitution Act to the Lords if the Bill had not attracted a two thirds majority; similarly, the House of Lords would be acting ultra vires in sending that Bill for the royal assent if it was not supported by that enhanced majority of peers; while the Monarch would be acting ultra vires if she assented to such a measure without having established that the requisite majorities in each house had been achieved.

There is similarly a need here for precision in describing what the High Court would be doing if it declined to disapply a subsequent statute which infringed the Constitution Act, on the basis of the orthodox theory that no Parliament can bind its successors. In refusing to disapply such a statute, the courts would in effect be concluding that the privileges of each house (steps 1–3)[2] and/or privilege plus the royal prerogative (steps 1–4) and/or the royal prerogative alone (step 4) outrank legislation in the constitution's legal hierarchy.

This rationale would draw us into a rather bizarre series of conclusions. It was suggested in chapter two that the orthodox view does indeed recognise one limit on Parliament's sovereign authority – namely that it cannot bind itself and its successors. But the orthodox view seemingly also requires us to accept three further constraints to Parliament's omnipotent legal power – namely that it cannot remove the Commons and Lords' powers to approve a Bill by simple majority vote, nor attach conditions to the Monarch's legal capacity to give the Royal Assent. To accept one limit to a nominally unlimited power might perhaps be accommodated as an inconvenient necessity: to accept four suggests that the integrity of the central argument is seriously flawed.

It is most unfortunate that the common elision in constitutional parlance of Parliament itself and the two houses of Parliament (but particularly the Commons) has so thoroughly pervaded analysis of the question of sovereignty as well as the question of privilege.[3] A perfect example of this is provided by Lord Simon's previously quoted observation in *Pickin*,[4] that the exclusive right of each house to control its own proceedings is a 'concomitant' of the sovereignty of Parliament. That view is however fundamentally misconceived, as a matter both of simple logic and of constitutional history. To allow each house an unfettered and apparently unfetterable power to control its own proceedings is not a concomitant of parliamentary sovereignty, but a blatant denial of it. By suggesting that each house has such an 'exclusive power', Lord Simon is setting privilege above both common law and statute. One thus finds oneself facing the oxymoronic proposition that Parliament possesses its legal sovereignty not because it cannot bind itself and its successors, but because it cannot bind its component (and hence inferior) parts.

The suggestion that one might entrench legislation in Britain by placing limits on the powers of the respective houses of Parliament rather than on those of Parliament

[2] *Wauchope* and *Pickin* might thus be reclassified as cases which did not concern the sovereignty of Parliament at all, but the non-justiciability of the privileges of the two houses.

[3] See pp 300–301 above. [4] At p 33 above.

itself is not, it should be stressed, a novel idea. Heuston had advanced a very similar thesis in 1964.[5] Heuston chose to support his argument with reference to the litigation in Commonwealth countries which we discussed in chapter two. This might be thought to weaken both the legal and political force of his thesis. As Wade observed in 1955, there is little point in invoking this case law in the British context.[6] The entrenchment formulae in issue in *Trethowan* and *Harris* each enjoyed a certain, unambiguous legal and political status because they were 'created' by a British statute which the 'peoples' of New South Wales and South Africa had accepted as expressing their preferred constituent moral values.[7] Since the British Parliament has no 'creator' in this sense, we might assume (as traditionalists always have) that the 'manner and form' principle cannot be applied here.

But this involves perhaps too ready a dismissal of the *Trethowan* rationale. Heuston's argument has also been offered more recent support by Paul Craig, in a thesis premised on a discussion of basic, indigenous constitutional principles rather than a speculative importation of inapposite foreign case law.[8] This was discussed at some length in chapter twelve in the context of the *Factortame* judgments.[9] Both authors operated under something of a disadvantage when advancing their ideas. Heuston, writing in 1964, laboured under the handicap of courts' adherence to the principle that exercise of the prerogative was not reviewable under any circumstances, a common law rule which would presumably incline the judiciary to consider the royal assent beyond legal scrutiny. In post-*GCHQ* era, that principle no longer presents an obstacle to entrenchment. Similarly, both Heuston and Craig's critiques were formulated when the courts were seemingly not prepared to examine events that occurred in either house during the passage of a Bill in order to ascertain the meaning of a statute. In the aftermath of *Pepper v Hart*, it seems clear that Article 9 of the Bill of Rights (whatever its legal status)[10] is no longer regarded by the courts as an insuperable barrier to questioning either house's proceedings.

There is a clear danger here that one simply ends up suggesting that entrenchment is now possible because the courts have embraced an increasingly expansive notion of justiciability, in which the legitimacy of judicial intervention is determined not by the legal identity of the institution whose actions are being impugned, but by the nature of the question the courts assume they are being asked. (In the hypothetical Constitution Act, the terms of the entrenchment procedure itself simply require the courts to perform a simple arithmetic calculation, and are thus obviously justiciable. Care would also have to be taken that the Act's substantive terms were similarly amenable to judicial analysis: we might accept here for the sake of argument that those terms simply embraced the provisions of the Convention, which are also clearly matters

[5] Heuston R (2nd edn, 1964) *Essays in constitutional law* ch 1 (London: Stevens and Sons).

[6] See pp 43–45 above.

[7] In the case of South Africa, 'the people' was obviously an extremely narrow concept, which would not be regarded as legitimate in the modern context.

[8] (1991) op cit. [9] See pp 480–488 above. [10] See pp 267–269 above.

courts can address).[11] To do so would in effect return us to Jennings' view that the 'rule of recognition' is a common law concept.[12] This would however be no solution at all to the entrenchment conundrum, rather it makes the legal problem even more vexed.

As Jennings suggested, accepting that the rule of recognition was a common law concept implies that it could be redefined by Parliament. But equally, (and this is a point on which we did not dwell in chapter two) it could be redefined by the courts without any parliamentary initiative having been undertaken at all. In formal terms, if the rule of recognition is a purely common law phenomenon, there is no legal barrier to the House of Lords suddenly deciding that it would not 'recognise' any statute that impinged upon particular moral or political values, or that it would 'recognise' such statutes only if they had been enacted with an enhanced Commons and/or Lords majority. Jennings' thesis, taken to its logical conclusion, suggests that the common law is legally superior to Acts of Parliament, that the courts and not the legislature are the ultimate source of legal authority, and that we might, as a matter of law, find that at any moment the courts had exercised a power explicitly to refuse to apply statutes of which they disapproved. The extravagant interpretation of the principle espoused in *Dr Bonham's Case* would thereby be reasserted, and the 1688 revolution would have been waged in vain.

Some commentators – one thinks primarily of Professor Griffith – might find that alarming prospect made rather too real by Laws LJ's judgment in *Thoburn v Sunderland City Council*.[13] *Thoburn* was an EC-related case, focused on the ostensibly prosaic issue of whether fruit and vegetables had to be sold in metric rather than imperial measurements. In the course of his judgment, Laws LJ endorsed the presumption that the European Communities Act 1972 possessed 'special' constitutional status, and was as such immune to the doctrine of implied repeal. Laws LJ also made two assertions of perhaps broader interest. The first was that the doctrine of implied repeal was itself a creature of the common law – rather than, as Wade's analysis of orthodox theory would suggest – an element of the constitution's 'ultimate political fact'. As a creature of the common law, of course, the doctrine of implied repeal would always be subject to extension, contraction or abolition at the behest of the higher courts. The second was that other statutes – which Laws LJ termed 'constitutional' statutes – enjoyed the same status as the European Communities Act:

'We should recognise a hierarchy of Acts of Parliament: as it were "ordinary" statutes and "constitutional" statutes. The two categories must be distinguished on a principled basis. In my opinion a constitutional statute is one which (a) conditions the legal relationship between citizen and State in some general, overarching manner, or (b) enlarges or diminishes the scope of what we would now regard as fundamental constitutional rights. . . .

[11] Although one lesson that we should learn from the *Harris* saga in South Africa is that the requirement of super-majorities to protect entrenched rights can be sidestepped by cynical governments unless both the mechanism for selecting members of the legislature and the process of appointing judges are themselves entrenched values; see further pp 63–64 above and Loveland (1999) op cit ch 11.

[12] See pp 38–39 above. [13] [2002] 1 CMLR 1461.

...e Magna Carta, the Bill of Rights 1688, the Act of Union, the Reform Acts ...uted and enlarged the franchise, the HRA, the Scotland Act 1998 and the ...nt of Wales Act 1998. The ECA clearly belongs in this family'.[14]

...rn was not appealed to the Court of Appeal. It presently stands therefore as ...e more than a point of departure for further speculation about the nature of ...arliament's legislative authority. As a mechanism within the sphere of administrative law to force Parliament in the text of legislation – and by extension the government in the text of the Bills it promotes – to be utterly candid about the objectives an Act it is intended to achieve, Laws LJ's conclusion perhaps has much to commend it. Characterised in this way, the judgment may be seen as little more than an extension of developing principles of statutory interpretation. Even generously construed, however, the judgment cannot be seen as advocating a 'revolutionary' limitation of Parliament's law-making powers.

Further judicial fuel was however added to this particular jurisprudential fire by the obiter comments of several members of the House of Lords in *R (on the application of Jackson and others) v Attorney-General.*[15] Lord Steyn put the point in this way:

'81. . . . But, apart from the traditional method of law making, Parliament acting as ordinarily constituted may functionally redistribute legislative power in different ways. For example, Parliament could for specific purposes provide for a two-thirds majority in the House of Commons and the House of Lords. This would involve a redefinition of Parliament for a specific purpose. Such redefinition could not be disregarded.'

Lord Hope made similar observations:

'104. . . . . Our constitution is dominated by the sovereignty of Parliament. But Parliamentary sovereignty is no longer, if it ever was, absolute. It is not uncontrolled in the sense referred to by Lord Birkenhead LC in *McCawley v The King* [1920] AC 691, 720. It is no longer right to say that its freedom to legislate admits of no qualification whatever. Step by step, gradually but surely, the English principle of the absolute legislative sovereignty of Parliament which Dicey derived from Coke and Blackstone is being qualified.

105. For the most part these qualifications are themselves the product of measures enacted by Parliament. Part I of the European Communities Act 1972 is perhaps the prime example.'

Baroness Hale took the argument one step further:

'163. If the sovereign Parliament can redefine itself downwards, to remove or modify the requirement for the consent of the Upper House, it may very well be that it can also redefine itself upwards, to require a particular Parliamentary majority or a popular referendum for particular types of measure. In each case, the courts would be respecting the will of the sovereign Parliament as constituted when that will had been expressed. But that is for another day.'

It is readily apparent that any search for a purely legal solution to the entrenchment

[14] [2002] 1 CMLR 1461 at para 62.

[15] [2005] UKHL 56. See pp 213–219 above.

question in that more expansive sense – namely that Parliament cannot through even the most express of statutory formulae achieve certain objectives – is likely to be severely hampered by the conceptually tangled constitutional undergrowth which has now grown so luxuriantly from the soil of the 1688 settlement. But Craig's critique is also helpful to advocates of entrenchment in that it asks us to consider not what the traditional rule is, but what the traditional rule is **for?** This approach then forces us to consider that entrenchment should not be analysed as a legal issue, but as a moral one. The central question that is raised is 'Are there sound reasons for regarding particular political values as so important that they should not be subject to amendment or repeal by simple parliamentary majorities?'

QUESTIONS OF LEGITIMACY

The parliamentary sovereignty doctrine appears to have emerged as a crude device to prevent enactment of factional legislation in a pre-democratic society. Yet it is quite clear that by the early twentieth century, shifts in the political context in which the doctrine operated meant that it had evolved into a constitutional device which would in most circumstances facilitate achievement of entirely the opposite result. The combined impact of the Commons' dominance within Parliament, and of minoritarian governments within the Commons, generally places uninhibited legislative power within the grasp of political factions which represent the preferred political views of only a minority of the population. It is perhaps in this political reality, rather than in tortuous arguments about legal practicality, that the real difficulties posed by entrenchment actually lie. For in such a context, we might plausibly wonder whether even if the entrenchment of particular political values was possible as a matter of law, would it be defensible as a matter of morality if it was triggered simply by a legislative initiative enacted by Parliament?

The entrenching device upheld by the Privy Council in *Trethowan* offers a very poor model for the creation of fundamental, supra-parliamentary values in the British context. The effect of such a provision would be to place the power to entrench laws in the hands of a barely majoritarian or even minoritarian faction. There would seemingly have been no legal impediment to a legislature introducing 'manner and form' legislation which rooted the preferences of the then governing party so deeply that they could not in practice be changed – by insisting for example on 75% or 80% majorities in both houses, or requiring similar levels of support in a referendum.

Transposed to the modern British context, this would have permitted the Thatcher or Major governments to impose their own preferred brand of minoritarian ideology on the substantial majority of the electorate which consistently chose not to support them. Similarly, a future Labour government which took the view that it should attempt to entrench certain social democratic moral values against an extremist right wing administration would be doing so with (on the most optimistic of electoral predictions) 50% of the vote on an 85% turnout.

One would have to embrace a rather peculiar view of democracy to discern any moral legitimacy in a process which allowed minority factions within modern British society to impose entrenched 'fundamental' political values on the entire population. Such 'reform' would be the very antithesis of the supra-majoritarianism required to shape the outlines of the US Constitution and the unanimity needed to fashion and subsequently amend the provisions of the EC Treaties. Its terms would be not consensual but coercive: its rationale would be not pluralist but authoritarian: its effect would be not to empower 'the people' but to oppress them.

Thus even if we assume entrenchment is legally possible, we do not thereby prove that it is constitutionally desirable. As has been stressed throughout this book, constitutional law forms but one ingredient (albeit an important one) of a complex constitutional recipe. Issues of politics and morality as well as mere legality pervade the much larger and more complex issue of constitutionality.

There would seem to be only two ways that entrenchment could plausibly claim to have a legitimate constitutional basis. The legitimacy of constituent moral values appears to depend primarily on the breadth of consensus that they attract. The rationale underpinning this principle was perhaps best articulated, as we saw in chapter one, in Madison's celebrated critique of factionalism: the higher the level of support required to enact a law, the less likely it is that the law concerned will be arbitrary, oppressive or intolerant, because its terms will express a compromise between groups of citizens holding different moral and political views. The Americans chose the 'two thirds of Congress plus three quarters of the States' rule to protect the terms of this initial compromise. We have seen that other constitutions have adopted devices which differ in their detailed form – the 'substantial provincial support' formula discovered by the Canadian Supreme Court in 1982, or the two-thirds of both chambers sitting in joint session criterion originally upheld by the South African Supreme Court in *Harris (No 1)* and *Harris (No 2)*, or the legislative majority plus referendum approach favoured in New South Wales – but which serve a broadly similar function.[16]

Two-thirds or three-quarters legislative majorities clearly do not eliminate the possibility that a country will produce oppressive laws. Such countries are however less likely to do so than those whose constitutions permit unfettered minoritarian or bare majoritarian law-making. But in the British context, this 'enhanced legislative majority' route to entrenchment could be followed only by a government which enjoyed hitherto unachieved levels of electoral support, in terms both of Commons seats and share of the popular vote. There would seem no prospect of a single political party coming remotely close to achieving such levels of popular approval. The position could presumably only be reached if the Labour Party won a comfortable Commons majority, attracting perhaps 45% of the vote, but rather than govern as a single party chose to initiate major constitutional reform with the support of a Liberal Party which had maintained its recent average electoral support of around 20%. Ideally, such a coalition would also detach at least a handful of MPs from the left-wing of the

[16] See respectively pp 339–340, 41 and 39–40 above.

Conservative Party, and attract the support of Scots, Welsh and Irish nationalist members of the Commons. The legitimacy of such reform would be further enhanced if the various governing parties had announced their intentions prior to the general election; the government could then more convincingly argue that the consent of their supporters to a constitutional revolution was informed.

In the absence of such a broad coalition, a minoritarian or barely majoritarian government seeking to entrench certain basic values could only stake a plausible claim to legitimacy by promoting substantive reforms which would both reduce its own share of political power and enhance the political influence wielded by opposition parties. The claim would however be a weak one, since many observers might genuinely doubt that any political party could ever be motivated by such selfless objectives. In these circumstances, a reformist government would necessarily be embarking on an elitist and ostensibly unrepresentative course of action.

It would nevertheless be rash to assume a reform of this nature could not be 'democratic'. The moral quandary such a government would face forces us rather to focus again on the intimate linkage between matters of substance and process in the context of constitution building which were adverted to in chapter one. One should perhaps add that this observation applies, albeit perhaps with less force, to a context in which reform attracted overwhelming popular support. Even a super-majoritiarian coalition government could not defensibly claim much legitimacy for its plans unless it sought to entrench principles which both restricted its own authority and increased the political power exercised by citizens who did not support its 'revolution'.

Legitimacy in process? A Liberal Democrat proposal

The Liberal Democrat Party offered a relatively detailed vision of a reformed British constitution in a 1990 policy paper, entitled *'We the people...'*. As might be surmised from its title, the paper drew heavily on the American constitutional model, in matters both of abstract theory and practical detail. *We the people* devoted considerable attention to planning a reform process which would enhance the legitimacy of the 'fundamental' values it hoped to introduce.

As suggested above, any attempt by a single party government returned under the existing electoral system to entrench constitutional values with any significant degree of fixity would be most unlikely to have a legitimate moral base; the breadth of popular consent such a government attracted would simply be too narrow to justify the imposition of constituent principles. *We the people* clearly recognised this difficulty, and offered an ingenious mechanism to overcome it.

Had the Liberals won a Commons majority at the 1992 general election, its government would have promoted Bills to reform the Commons' electoral system on the basis of the single transferable vote (STV) mechanism, and to establish a body to be called the 'Constituent Assembly'. Parliament would then be dissolved, and a general election fought on the basis of the new STV electoral system. The Constituent Assembly would be composed of the members of the Commons returned under the basis of the new STV electoral system. The Assembly would have been empowered by the previous Parliament to adopt (by a two-thirds majority) a new constitutional settlement, within which certain political values (inter alia the ECHR, the STV electoral system, and (extensive) devolved powers to the Scots, Welsh and Northern Irish and regional governments) would all assume supra-parliamentary status. These values would be entrenched in the procedural sense; they could be amended only with the approval of two thirds of both houses sitting separately.

In legal terms, using the Constituent Assembly to implement a constitutional revolution might be thought something of a nonsense: Parliament presumably cannot create something more powerful than itself. It would however seem that *We the people* proceeded on the assumption that its proposals were at root designed to achieve a political rather than legal objective. By requiring a two-thirds majority of a body chosen by the STV system to create the new constitution, the Liberal programme ensured that its terms could not be given legal effect unless they enjoyed a very high level of popular support. The proviso that the Commons should in effect wear a different political hat when assessing the merits of fundamental reform would also have served a useful legitimising purpose, insofar as it would focus both MPs and the public's attention on the gravity of the task being undertaken.

For adherents to a pluralist perception of democracy, the Liberal Party's inability to mobilise greater electoral support is something of a disappointment. There is no doubt that *We the people* offered a radical and far-reaching programme to modernise Britain's constitutional arrangements. One might of course suggest that the Liberals' limited electoral support is in itself indicative of 'the people's' disinclination to have the constitution reformed in any meaningful way. The only immediate prospect of the Liberal programme being implemented would be for the party to hold the balance of power in a hung Commons, and to convince one of the main parties that pursuing its reforms was an acceptable price to pay for the benefit of forming a coalition government for one parliamentary term. It would however seem unlikely that either the Labour or Conservative parties would accept such reasoning. Nor would the reforms enjoy much legitimacy if their opponents could plausibly argue that the major partner in the coalition had been 'blackmailed' into accepting them.

CONCLUSION

Prime Minister Blair stressed in the preface to the *Scotland's Parliament* white paper that Scots devolution was best seen as just one part of a much broader programme of constitutional reform. There is no doubt that – in terms of its commitment to establishing a pluralist political culture – the Blair governments stand head and shoulders above any of their twentieth century predecessors. This is obviously evidenced in its devolution legislation. But it is also apparent in the government's embrace of the ECHR and the provisions of the Amsterdam Treaty: the protection of individual rights is an essential element of a diverse democratic polity. The same observation may be made about the Blair government's promotion of the Constitutional Reform Act 2005. The Act's objective is more modest than its grandiose title might suggest. The Act will (eventually) transfer the judicial functions of the House of Lords to a new Supreme Court, remove the judicial elements of the office of Lord Chancellor, and perhaps most importantly – create a new Judicial Appointments Commission which will assume effective responsibility for the selection of members of the judiciary.

Yet these initiatives, desirable though they may be, can hardly be seen as engineering a constituent reformation of our political system. Their longevity is by no means assured. It is perhaps something of a misnomer to speak at all of the **law** of the British constitution, whether we are considering legislation of great or recent vintage, or rules of common law. This misdescription does not simply arise from the obvious fact that so much of the organisation and behaviour of contemporary government rests on the non-justiciable basis of convention. More seriously, it derives from the constant vulnerability of those principles which are expressed in justiciable form to whichever political faction has temporary control of the House of Commons. To search for constitutional law in a society which has thus far rejected the concept of subjecting its system of governance to constituent legal principles is to embark upon a generally fascinating, often frustrating but ultimately always fallacious journey.

Having begun the journey into this book with a quotation from Thomas Jefferson's *Declaration of Independence*, we might, in the interests both of substantive and stylistic symmetry, end it with the words of Jefferson's great friend and colleague, James Madison:

> 'No doctrine can be sound that releases a legislature from the control of a constitution. The latter is as much a law to the former, as the acts of the former are to individuals; and although alterable by the people who formed it, it is not alterable by any other authority; certainly not by those chosen by the people to carry it in to effect. This is so vital a principle . . . that a denial of it cannot possibly last long or spread far'.[17]

Britain has of course denied the principle for over 300 years. To many observers that may suggest the principle is an unnecessary ingredient of a democratic society. To others, it may in contrast indicate that an attempt to grapple with this elemental ingredient of constitutional morality is long overdue.

[17] Padover S (ed) (1953) *The complete Madison* p 344 (Norwalk, Conn; Easton Press).

BIBLIOGRAPHY

Adonis A (1988) 'The House of Lords in the 1980s' *Parliamentary Affairs* 380–401.

—— (1990) *Parliament today* (Manchester: Manchester University Press).

—— (2nd edn, 1993) *Parliament today* (Manchester: Manchester University Press).

Ahier J and Flude M (eds) (1983) *Contemporary education policy* (London: Croom Helm).

Akehurst M (1982) 'Revocation of administrative decisions' *Public Law* 613–627.

Alder J (1994) *Constitutional and administrative law* (London: Macmillan).

Alderman R and Smith M (1990) 'Can British Prime Ministers be given the push by their parties?' *Parliamentary Affairs* 260–276.

Alderman R and Carter N (1991) 'A very Tory coup: the ousting of Mrs Thatcher' *Parliamentary Affairs* 125–139.

Allan T (1983) 'Parliamentary sovereignty: Lord Denning's dexterous revolution' *Oxford Journal of Legal Studies* 22–33.

—— (1985) 'Legislative supremacy and the rule of law' *Cambridge LJ* 111–143.

—— (1986) 'Law convention and prerogative' *Cambridge LJ* 305–320.

—— (1993) *Law, liberty and justice* (Oxford: Clarendon Press).

—— (1995) 'Equality and moral independence: public law and private morality', in Loveland I

—— (1995a) *infra.*

—— (1997) 'Parliamentary sovereignty: law, politics and revolution' *LQR* 443–452.

Alter K (2001) *Establishing the supremacy of European law* (Oxford: OUP).

Anderson O (1967) 'The Wensleydale peerage and the position of the House of Lords in the mid-nineteenth century' *English Historical Review* 486–502.

Anson W (5th edn, 1922) *The law and custom of the constitution* (Oxford: Clarendon Press).

Arkinstall J and O'Brien C (2002) 'Table of cases under the Human Rights Act' *European Human Rights LR* 364–388.

Arnstein W (1983) *The Bradlaugh case* (Columbia, Missouri: University of Missouri Press).

Arnull A (1987) 'The incoming tide: responding to *Marshall*' *Public Law* 383–399.

Ascher K (1983) 'The politics of administrative opposition – council house sales and the right to buy' *Local Government Studies* 12–20.

Atrill S (2005) 'Nulla poena sine lege in comparative perspective ...' *Public Law* 107.

Audit Commission (1990) *The administration of the community charge* (London: HMSO).

Bagehot W (1963 ed by Crossman R) *The English constitution* (London: Fontana).

Bailey S (1982) 'The Contempt of Court Act 1981' *MLR* 301–316.

Bailey S and Paddison R (eds) *The reform of local government finance in Britain* (London: Routledge).

Bailey S, Harris D and Jones B (1977; 2nd edn, 1992; 3rd edn, 1998) *Civil liberties* (London: Butterworths).

Bailyn B (1967) *The ideological origins of*

the American revolution (Cambridge, Mass: Harvard University Press).

BAINES P (1985) 'The history and rationale of the 1979 reforms', in DREWRY G (ed) *The new Select Committees* (Oxford: Clarendon Press).

BAKER D, GAMBLE A, and LUDLUM (1993) 'Whips or scorpions? The Maastricht vote and Conservative MPs' *Parliamentary Affairs* 147–166.

BAKER K (1993) *The turbulent years* (London: Faber).

BALDWIN N (1999) 'The membership and work of the House of Lords', in DICKSON and CARMICHAEL (eds) *The House of Lords: its parliamentary and judicial roles* (Oxford: Hart Publishing).

BALL W, GULAM W and TROYNA B (1990) 'Pragmatism or retreat? funding policy, local government, and the marginalisation of anti-racist education', in Ball and Solomos *infra.*

BALL W and SOLOMOS J (eds) *Race and local politics* (London: Macmillan).

BALSOM D and MCALLISTER I (1979) 'The Scottish and Welsh devolution referenda of 1979' *Parliamentary Affairs* 394–409.

BAMFORTH N (1993) 'The scope of judicial review – still uncertain' *Public Law* 239–248.

—— (1998) 'Parliamentary sovereignty and the Human Rights Act 1998' *Public Law* 572–582.

—— (1999) 'The application of the Human Rights Act to public authorities and private bodies' *Cambridge LJ* 159–170.

BANNER C and BOUTLE T (2004) 'Challenging the Commons' *New law Journal* 1466.

BARENDT E (1987) *Freedom of speech* (Oxford: Clarendon Press).

—— (1989) 'Spycatcher and freedom of speech' *Public Law* 204–212.

—— (1993) 'Libel and freedom of speech in English law' *Public Law* 449–464.

—— (1995) 'Constitutional law and the Criminal Injuries Compensation Scheme' *Public Law* 357–366.

—— (1998) *An Introduction to Constitutional Law* pp 86–93 (Oxford: Clarendon Press).

BARKER R (1986) 'Obedience, legitimacy and the state', in HARLOW C (ed) *Public law and politics* (London: Sweet and Maxwell).

BASH L and COULBY D (eds) *The Education Reform Act: competition and control* (London: Cassell).

BATES St J (1988) 'Scrutiny of administration', in RYLE M and RICHARDS P (eds) *The Commons under scrutiny* (London: Routledge).

BEALEY F (1988) *Democracy in the contemporary state* (Oxford: Clarendon Press).

BEARD C (1990) 'An economic interpretation of the Constitution', in BIRMBAUM J and OLLMAN *infra.*

BEATSON J (1987) ' "Public" and "private" in English administrative law' *LQR* 34–65.

BEATSON J and MATTHEWS M (2nd edn, 1987) *Administrative law* (London: OUP).

BEIBR R (1984) 'The settlement of institutional conflicts on the basis of Article 4 of the Treaty' *CMLRev* 505–523.

BENNET P and PULLINGER S (1991) *Making the Commons work* (London: Institute for Public Policy Research).

BENNION F (2000) 'What interpretation is "possible" under s.3(1) of the Human Rights Act?' *Public Law* 77–91

BEVAN V (1981) 'Is anybody there?' *Public Law* 431–453.

BEYLEVELD D and PATTINSON S (2002) 'Horizontal applicability' *LQR* 623–647.

Bingham T (1993) 'The European Convention on Human Rights: time to incorporate' *LQR* 390–400.

Birmbaum J and Olmann B (eds) *The United States Constitution* (New York: New York University Press).

Blake R and Louis W (eds) *Churchill* (Oxford: Clarendon Press).

Blom-Cooper L (1982) 'The new face of judicial review: administrative changes in Order 53' *Public Law* 250–261.

Boateng P and Straw J (1996) *Bringing rights home* (London: Labour Party).

—— (1997) 'Bringing rights home: Labour plans to incorporate the ECHR into UK law' *European Human Rights LR* 71–80.

Bogdanor V (1976) 'Freedom in education' *Political Quarterly* 149–159.

—— (1979) 'The English constitution and devolution' *Political Quarterly* 36–49.

—— (1983) *What is proportional representation?* (Oxford: Martin Robertson).

—— (1988) 'Introduction', Bogadnor V (ed) *Constitutions in democratic politics* (Dartmouth Publishing: Aldershot).

—— (1999) 'Reform of the House of Lords: a sceptical view' *Political Quarterly* 375–381.

—— (1999a) 'Devolution: decentralisation or disintegration' *Political Quarterly* 185–194.

Bonner D and Stone R (1987) 'The Public Order Act 1986: steps in the wrong direction?' *Public Law* 202–230.

Borthwick R (1973) 'Public Bill Committees in the House of Lords' *Parliamentary Affairs* 440–453.

—— (1979) 'Questions and debates', in Walkland S (ed) *The House of Commons in the twentieth century* (Oxford: Clarendon Press).

—— (1988) 'The floor of the house', in Ryle M and Richards P (eds) *The Commons under scrutiny* (London: Routledge).

Boulton C (ed) (21st edn, 1989) *Erskine May's treatise on the law, privileges, proceedings and usage of Parliament* (London: Butterworths).

Bowley M (1985) *Housing and the state 1919–1945* (London: Allen & Unwin).

Boyce B (1993) 'The democratic deficit of the European Community' *Parliamentary Affairs* 458–477.

Boyle A (1982) 'The Contempt of Court Act 1981' *Human Rights Review* 148–150.

—— (1986) 'Political broadcasting, fairness and administrative law' *Public Law* 562–596.

Bradley A (1981) 'Administrative justice and the binding effects of official acts' *Current Legal Problems* 1–20.

—— (1988) 'Police powers and the prerogative' *Public Law* 298–303.

—— (1991) 'The UK before the Strasbourg Court', in Finnie W, Himsworth C and Walker N (eds) *Edinburgh essays in public law* (Edinburgh: Edinburgh University Press).

—— (1997) 'Collateral challenge to enforcement decisions – a duty to apply for judicial review' *Public Law* 365–370.

Bradley K (1987) 'Maintaining the balance' *Common Market LR* 41–64.

Branson N (1979) *Popularism* (London: Lawrence and Wishart).

Brazier M (9th edn, 1993) *Street on torts* (London: Butterworths).

Brazier R (1992) *Constitutional reform* (Oxford: OUP).

—— (1990) *Constitutional texts* (Oxford: OUP).

—— (1994) 'It is a constitutional issue: fitness for Ministerial office in the 1990's' *Public Law* 431–451.

—— (1999) 'The constitution of the United Kingdom' *Cambridge LJ* 96–128.

Bridges L *et al.* (1987) *Legality and local politics* (Aldershot: Avebury).

Briggs A (ed) *Chartist studies* (London: Macmillan).

Brock M (1973) *The Great Reform Act* (London: Hutchinson).

Brogan H (1986) *History of the USA* (Harmondsworth: Pelican).

Brown K (ed) *The first labour party* (London: Croom Helm).

Brown L and Kennedy T (1994) *The Court of Justice of the European Communities* (London: Sweet and Maxwell).

Brown R (1987) 'The Beard thesis attacked: a political approach', in Birmbaum and Olson *supra.*

Brown W (1899) 'The Hare system in Tasmania' *LQR* 51–70.

Browne-Wilkinson, Lord (1992) 'The infiltration of a Bill of Rights' *Public Law* 397–410.

Bull D (1980) 'School admissions: a new appeals procedure' *Journal of Social Welfare Law* 209–233.

Burton I and Drewry G (1972) 'Public legislation a survey of the session of 1971–1972' *Parliamentary Affairs* 145–185.

—— (1978) 'Public legislation: a survey of the sessions of 1975/77' *Parliamentary Affairs* 140–162.

Bush M (1983) 'The Act of Proclamations: a reinterpretation' *American Journal of Legal History* 33–53.

Butler D (1953) *The electoral system in Britain 1918–1951* (Oxford: Clarendon Press).

—— (1976) 'The Australian crisis of 1975' *Parliamentary Affairs* 201–210.

Butler D, Adonis A and Travers T (1994) *Failure in British Government: the politics of the poll tax* (Oxford: OUP).

Butler D and Bogdanor V (eds) *Democracy and elections* (Cambridge: CUP).

Butler D and Kavanagh D (1984; 1988; 1993; 1998) *The British general election of 1982; 1987; 1992; 1997* respectively (London: Macmillan).

—— (2002) *The British general election of 2002* (London: Macmillan).

—— (2005) *The British general election of 2005* (Basingstoke: Palgrave Macmillan).

Butler D, Penniman H and Ranney A (1981) *Democracy at the polls* (Washington DC: American Enterprise Institute).

Butler D and Sloman A (1975) *British political facts* (London: Macmillan).

Buxton, Lord Justice (2000) 'The Human Rights Act and private law' *LQR* 48–67.

Buxton R (2nd ed, 1973) *Local Government* (Harmondsworth: Penguin).

Cane P (1980) 'The function of standing rules in administrative law' *Public Law* 303–328.

—— (1981) 'Standing, legality and the limits of public law' *Public Law* 322–339.

—— (1992) 'Private rights and public procedure' *Public Law* 193–200.

—— (1995) 'Standing, representation and the environment', in Loveland I (ed) *A special relationship?* (Oxford: Clarendon Press).

—— (3rd edn, 1996) *An introduction to administrative law* (Oxford: Clarendon Press).

Cannon J (1973) *Parliamentary reform 1640–1832* (Cambridge: CUP).

Centre for Contemporary Cultural Studies (1981) *Unpopular education* (London: Hutchinson).

Chapman R and Hunt M (eds) (1987) *Open government* (London: Routledge).

CHESTER N (1977) 'Questions in the House', in WALKLAND S and RYLE M (eds) *The Commons in the seventies* (London: Martin Robertson).

CHESTER N and BOWRING M (1962) *Questions in parliament* (London: OUP).

CLARK A (1993) *Diaries* (London: Weidenfeld and Nicolson).

CLARK D (1975) 'Natural justice: substance or shadow' *Public Law* 27–63.

COLEMAN D and SALT J (1992) *The British population* (Oxford: OUP).

COLLEY L (1996) *Britons* (London: Vintage).

CONSTITUTION UNIT (2001 – December) *Monitor* p 2.

COOKE, LORD (1997) 'Mechanisms for entrenchment and protection of a Bill of Rights: the New Zealand experience' *European Human Rights LR* 490–495.

COOPERS and LYBRAND (1988) *Local management of schools* (London: Coopers and Lybrand).

COPPEL J and O'NEILL A (1994) 'The European Court of Justice: taking rights seriously' *Legal Studies* 227–245.

CORBETT R (1985) 'The 1985 intergovernmental conference and the Single European Act', in PRYCE R (ed) *The dynamics of European integration* (London: Croom Helm).

—— (1989) 'Testing the new procedures; the European Parliament's first experiences with its new "Single Act" powers' *Journal of Common Market Studies* 362–372.

CORNFORD T and SUNKIN M (2001) 'The Bowman Report: access and the recent reforms of the judicial review procedure' *Public Law* 11–20.

CORWIN E (1928) 'The higher law background of American constitutional law (parts I and II)' *Harvard LR* 149–175 and 365–409.

COULBY D (1989) 'From educational partnership to central control', in BASH L and COULBY D (eds) *The Education Reform Act* (London: Cassell).

COWEN D (1952) 'Legislature and judiciary: part I' *Modern Law Review* 282–296.

—— (1953) 'Legislature and judiciary: part II' *Modern Law Review* 273–298.

COWLEY P and STUART M (2001) 'Parliament: a few headaches and a dose of modernisation' *Parliamentary Affairs* 238 at 253–255.

—— (2002) 'Parliament: mostly continuity, but more change than you'd think' *Parliamentary Affairs* 270.

COWLING M (1967) *1867: Disraeli, Gladstone and revolution* (Cambridge: CUP).

CRAIG J (1959) 'Parliament and Boundary Commissions' *Public Law* 23–45.

CRAIG P (1991) 'Sovereignty of the UK Parliament after *Factortame*' *Yearbook of European Law* 221–255.

—— (1992) 'Once upon a time in the west: direct effect and the federalisation of EEC law' *Oxford Journal of Legal Studies*.

—— (1993) '*Francovich*, remedies and the scope of damages liability' 109 *LQR* 595–621.

—— (1994) 'The common law, reasons and administrative justice' *Cambridge LJ* 282–302.

—— (3rd edn 1994) *Administrative Law* (London: Sweet & Maxwell).

—— (1996) 'Substantive legitimate expectations in domestic and Community law' *Cambridge LJ* 289–312.

—— (1997) 'Formal and substantive conceptions of the rule of law' *Public Law* 467–487.

—— (1998) 'The Treaty of Amsterdam: a brief guide' *Public Law* 351–355.

—— (1998a) 'Collateral attack, procedural

exclusivity and judicial review' *LQR* 535–538.

—— (4th edn, 1998b) *Administrative law* (London: Sweet and Maxwell).

—— (2001) 'The courts, the Human Rights Act and judicial review' *LQR* 592–612.

Craig P and de Burca G (2nd edn, 1998) *EU law* (Oxford: Clarendon Press).

Craig P and DeBurca B (3rd edn, 2002) *EU law* (Oxford: OUP) pp 358–369.

Craig P and Walters M (1999) 'The courts, devolution and judicial review' *Public Law* 274–308.

Crosby S (1991) 'The Single market and the rule of law' *ELRev* 451–465.

Crosland C (1952) 'The transition from capitalism', in Crossman R (ed) *New Fabian Essays* (London: Turnstile).

Cross C (1961) *The fascists in Britain* (London: Barrie Books).

Cross J (1967) 'Withdrawal of the Conservative party whip' *Parliamentary Affairs* 169–175.

Cullingworth J (1979) *Essays in housing policy* (London: Allen & Unwin).

Curtice J (2005) 'Turnout: electors stay home again' *Parliamentary Affairs* 776–785.

Curtin D (1990) 'The provice of government delimiting the direct effect of directives in the common law context' *ELRev* 195–223.

Dale R (1983) 'Thatcherism and education', in Ahier J and Flude M (eds) *Contemporary education policy* (London: Croom Helm).

Dauses M (1985) 'The protection of fundamental rights in the Community legal order' *ELRev* 398–417.

Davies H and Stewart J (1994) *The growth of government by appointment: implications for democracy* (Birmingham: Local Government Management Board).

—— (1994) 'A new agenda for local governance' *Public Money and Management* (October) 29–36.

Davis H (2005) 'Public authorities as victims under the HRA' *Cambridge LJ* 315–328.

Dawson I and Dunn A (2002) 'Seeking the principle: chancel, choices and human rights' *Legal Studies* 238–258.

de Burca G (1993) 'The principle of proportionality and its application in EC law' *YEL* 105–130.

Denning, Lord (1985) 'Re Parliamentary Privilege Act 1770' *Public Law* 80–92.

de Smith S (1951) 'The prerogative writs' *Cambridge LJ* 40.

—— (1955) 'Boundaries between Parliament and the courts' *Modern Law Review* 281–286.

—— (1971) 'The constitution and the Common Market: a tentative appraisal' 34 *MLR* 597–614.

—— (5th edn, 1985) *Constitutional and administrative law* (by Brazier R and Street H) (Harmondsworth: Penguin).

Dickman J (1989) 'Debt and the poll tax' *Municipal Review*, (May) 13–15.

Dickson B and Carmichael P (eds) *The House of Lords* (Oxford: Hart Publishing.

Dike C (1976) 'The case against parliamentary sovereignty' *Public Law* 283–297.

Diplock, Lord (1972) 'The common market and the common law' *The Law Teacher* 3–12.

DoE (1971) *Local government in England* p 6 (London: HMSO; Cmnd. 4584).

—— (1976) *Report of the Committee of Inquiry into local government finance* (London: HMSO; Cmnd 6453).

—— (1977) *Housing policy: a consultative document* (London: HMSO).

—— (1983) *Rates* (London: HMSO; Cmnd 9008).

—— (1983) *Streamlining the cities* (London: HMSO; Cmnd 9063).

—— (1986) *Paying for local government* (London: HMSO; Cmnd 9414).

—— (1988) *The conduct of local authority business* (London: HMSO; Cmnd 433).

Department of the Environment, Transport and the Regions (1998) *A Mayor and Assembly for London* (London: HMSO; Cm 3897).

Doherty M (1988) 'Prime Ministerial power and ministerial responsibility in the Thatcher era' *Parliamentary Affairs* 49–67.

Doig A (2002) 'Sleaze fatigue in "The House of ill-repute" ' *Parliamentary Affairs* 389–401.

Donnelly C (2005) '*Leonard Cheshire* again and beyond: private contractors, contract and s 6(3)(b) of the Human Rights Act' *Public Law* 785–805.

Donoughmore, Lord (1932) *Report of the Committee on Minister's powers* (London: HMSO; Cmnd 4060).

Drewry G (1983) 'The National Audit Act – half a loaf' *Public Law* 531–537.

—— (ed) (1985) *The new select committees* (Oxford: Clarendon Press).

—— (1985a) 'Select committees and backbench power' in Jowell J and Oliver, D (eds 2nd edn) *The changing constitution* (London: OUP).

—— (1985b) 'Leaking in the public interest' *Public Law* 203–212.

—— (1988) 'Legislation', in Ryle M and Richards P (eds) *The Commons under scrutiny* (London: Routledge).

—— (1993) 'Mr Major's Charter' *Public Law* 248–256.

Drewry G and Butcher T (1988) *The civil service today* (Oxford: Basil Blackwell).

Du Bois W (1990) 'Slavery and the Founding Fathers', in Birmbaum and Olson *supra*.

Duffy P (1980) 'The Sunday Times case: freedom of expression, contempt of court and the ECHR' *Human Rights Review* 17–53.

Dunleavy P, Jones G and O'Leary B (1990) 'Prime Ministers and the Commons: patterns of behaviour 1868–1987' *Public Administration* 123–140.

Dwyer D (2005) 'Rights brought home' *LQR* 359–364.

Edelman M (1964) *The symbolic uses of politics* (Urbana: University of Illinois Press).

Edward D (1987) 'The impact of the Single European Act on the institutions' *CMLRev* 19–30.

Ehlermann C (1975) 'Applying the new budgetary procedure for the first time' *CMLRev* 325–343.

—— (1987) 'The internal market following the Single European Act' *CMLRev* 361–409.

Elcock H (2nd ed, 1986) *Local government* (London: Methuen).

Electoral Commission (2002) *Modernising elections* (London: Electoral Commission).

—— (2004) *The funding of political parties* (London: Electoral Commission).

—— (2005) 'Spending by political parties and campaign groups at the 5 May UK parliamentary election' www.electoralcommission.org.uk.

Elliot M (1980) 'Appeals, principle and pragmatism in natural justice' *MLR* 66–69.

Ellis D (1980) 'Collective ministerial reponsibility and collective solidarity' *Public Law* 367–396.

Elton G (1953) *The Tudor Revolution in government* (Cambridge: CUP).

—— (1960) 'Henry VIII's Act of Proclamations' *English Historical Review* 208–222.

Emiliou N (1994) 'Subsidiarity: panacea or fig leaf', in O'Keefe D and Twomey P (eds) *Legal issues of the Maastricht Treaty* (London: Wiley).

Ewing K (1987) *The funding of political parties in Britain* (Oxford: Clarendon Press).

—— (1999) 'The Human Rights Act and parliamentary democracy' *MLR* 79–99.

Ewing K (2001) 'Transparency, accountability and equality: the Political Parties, Elections and Referendums Act 2000' *Public Law* 542–565.

Ewing K and Gearty C (1990) *Civil liberties under Thatcher* (Oxford: OUP).

Farran S (1996) *The UK before the European Court of Human Rights* (London: Blackstone Press).

Feldman D (1993) *Civil liberties and human rights in England and Wales* (Oxford: Clarendon Press).

—— (1993a) 'Collateral challenge and judicial review: the boundary dispute continues' *Public Law* 37–48.

—— (2005) 'Proportionality and discrimination in anti-terrorism legislation' *Cambridge LJ* 270–272.

Fennel P (1986) '*Roberts v Hopwood*: the rule against socialism' *Journal of Law and Society* 401–422.

Fiengold C (1978) 'The little red schoolbook and the ECHR' *Human Rights Review* 21–47.

Finer S (1956) 'The individual responsibility of Ministers' *Public Administration* 377–396.

Finnie W, Himsworth C and Walker N (eds) *Edinburgh essays in public law* (Edinburgh: Edinburgh University Press).

Fitzpatrick B (1989) 'The significance of EEC Directives in UK sex discrimination law' *Oxford Journal of Legal Studies* 336–355.

Fordham M (2001) 'Judicial review: the new rules' *Public Law* 4–10.

Forrest R and Murie A (1988) *Selling the welfare state* (London: Routledge).

Forsyth C (1985) 'Beyond *O'Reilly v Mackman*: the foundations and nature of procedural exclusivity' *Cambridge LJ* 415–434.

—— (1987) 'The scope of judicial review: "public duty" not "source of power"' *Public Law* 356–367.

—— (1988) 'The provenance and protection of legitimate expectations' *Cambridge LJ* 238–260.

—— (1997) '*Wednesbury* protection of substantive legitimate expectations' *Public Law* 375–384.

—— (1999) 'Collateral challenge and the foundations of judicial review: orthodoxy vindicated and procedural exclusivity rejected' *Public Law* 364–370.

Forwood N and Clough M (1986) 'The Single European Act and free movement' *ELRev* 383–408.

Fowler N (1988) *Ministers decide* (London: Chapman).

Freedland M (1995) 'Privatising *Carltona:* Part II of the Deregulation and Contracting Out Act 1994' *Public Law* 21–27.

French D (1978) 'Spy fever in Britain 1900–1915' *Historical Journal* 355–370.

Friedmann W (1950) 'Trethowan's case, parliamentary sovereignty and the limits of legal change' 24 *Australian Law Journal* 103–108.

Fry G (1970) 'The Sachsenhausen concentration camp case and the convention of ministerial responsibility' *Public Law* 336–357.

Gamble A (1981) *Britain in decline* (London: Papermac).

Ganz G (1986) 'Legitimate expectations: a confusion of concepts', in Harlow C (ed)

Law and politics (London: Sweet and Maxwell).

—— (1990) 'The depoliticisation of local authorities: the Local authorities: the Local Government and Housing Act 1989' *Public Law* 224–242.

Gash N (1953) *Politics in the age of Peel* (London: Longmans).

Genn H and Richardson G (eds) (1994) *Administrative law and government action* (Oxford: Clarendon Press).

George V and Wilding P (1976) *Ideology and state welfare* (London: RKP).

Ghandi S and James J (1998) 'The English law of blasphemy and the European Convention on Human Rights' *European Human Rights LR* 430–451.

Golby M (1993) 'Parents as school governors', in Munn P (ed) *Parents and schools* (London: Routledge).

Gordon P (1990) 'A dirty war', in Ball and Solomos *supra*.

Gough I (1983) 'Thatcherism and the welfare state': in Hall and Jacques *infra*.

Gould M (1993) '*M v Home Office*: government and the judges' *Public Law* 568–578.

Gravells N (1989) 'Displaying an Act of Parliament pending a preliminary ruling: constitutional enormity or common law right' *Public Law* 568–586.

Gray C (1979) 'European Convention on Human Rights – freedom of expression and the thalidomide case' *Cambridge LJ* 242–245.

Grief N (1991) 'The domestic impact of the ECHR as mediated through Community law' *Public Law* 555–567.

Griffith J (1966) *Central departments and local authorities* (London: Allen and Unwin).

—— (1974) *Parliamentary scrutiny of government bills* (London: Allen & Unwin).

—— (1985) 'Judicial decision making in public law' *Public Law* 564–582.

—— (1993) *Judicial politics since 1920* (Oxford: Basil Blackwell).

Griffith J and Ryle M (1989) *Parliament* (London: Sweet and Maxwell).

Griswold E (1952) 'The coloured vote case in South Africa' *Harvard LR* 1361–1374.

Gyford J (1985) *The politics of local socialism* (London: Allen and Unwin).

Hall S (1983) 'The great moving right show' in Hall and Jacques *infra*.

Hall S and Jaques M (eds) *The politics of Thatcherism* (London: Lawrence and Wishart).

Hall W (1986) 'Contracts compliance at the GLC' *Local Government Studies* 17–24.

Hampson W (2nd ed, 1991) *Local government and urban politics* (London: Longman).

Hamson C (1954) 'The real lesson of Crichel Down' *Public Administration* 383–400.

Hansard Society (2000) *The challenge for Parliament: making government accountable* (London: Vacher Dod).

Harlow C (1986) (ed) *Public law and politics* (London: Sweet and Maxwell).

—— (1995) 'A special relationship? American influences on judicial review in England', in Loveland (1995a) *infra*

Harlow C and Rawlings R (1984) *Law and administration* (London: Weidenfeld and Nicolson).

Harris N (1993) *Law and education: regulation, consumerism and the education system* (London: Sweet and Maxwell).

Hart H (2nd edn, 1994) *The concept of law* (Oxford: Clarendon Press).

Hart J (1992) *Proportional representation: critics of the British electoral system 1820–1945* (Oxford: Clarendon Press).

HARTLEY T (2nd ed, 1988) *The foundations of European Community law* (Oxford: Clarendon Press).

—— (1993) 'Constitutional and institutional aspects of the Maastricht Agreement' *International and Comparative Law Quarterly* 213–237.

—— (3rd edn, 1994) *The foundations of European Community law* (Oxford: Clarendon Press).

—— (4th edn, 1998) *The foundations of European Community law* (Oxford: Clarendon Press).

HASSAN G (ed) (1999) *A guide to the Scottish Parliament* (Edinburgh: Centre for Scottish Public Policy).

HATTERSLEY R (1992) 'The beggaring of PM's question time' *The Guardian* January 28.

HAWES D (1992) 'Parliamentary select committees: some case studies in contingent influence' *Policy and Politics* 227–235.

HAY J (1975) *The origins of the Liberal welfare reforms 1906–1914* (London: Macmillan).

HAYEK F (1944) *The road to serfdom* (London: RKP).

HENNESSY P (1986) 'Helicopter crashes into Cabinet: Prime Minister and constitution hurt' *Journal of Law and Society* 423–432.

—— (1986a) *Cabinet* (Oxford: Basil Blackwell).

HEUSTON R (1964) *Essays in constitutional law* (London: Stevens).

—— (1970) 'Liversidge v Anderson in retrospect' *LQR* 33–68.

HIMSWORTH C (1991) 'Poll tax capping and judicial review' *Public Law* 76–92.

—— (1995) 'The delegated powers scrutiny committee' *Public Law* 34–44.

HOBSBAWM E (1969) *Industry and empire* (Harmondsworth: Penguin).

HOGG Q (1947) *The case for Conservatism* (West Drayton: Penguin).

HOLDEN B (1988) *Understanding liberal democracy* (Oxford: Phillip Allan).

HOLDSWORTH W (1919) 'The power of the Crown to requisition British ships in a national emergency' *LQR* 12–42.

HOME OFFICE (1993) *Compensation for victims of violent crime* (London: HMSO; Cm 2434).

—— (1997) *Rights brought home* (London: HMSO; Cm 3782).

HOOD-PHILLIPS O (1982) 'A Garland for the Lords: Parliament and Community law again' *LQR* 524–526.

HOPE, LORD (1998) 'Devolution and Human Rights' *European Human Rights LR* 367–375.

HORNE A (1987) *Macmillan 1957–1986* (London: Macmillan).

HORWITZ H (1974) 'Parliament and the glorious revolution' *Bulletin of the Institute of Historical Research* 36–52.

HOUGH B (2005) 'Public regulation of markets and fairs' *Public Law* 586–607.

HOUGHTON, LORD (1976) *Report of the committee on financial aid to political parties* (London: HMSO; Cmnd 6601).

HOUSE OF COMMONS FOREIGN AFFAIRS COMMITTEE (1981) *British North America Acts* (London: HMSO).

HOUSE OF COMMONS PUBLIC ADMINISTRATION SELECT COMMITTEE (2002) *Continuing the reform* (HC 4941 2001–2002)(London: HMSO).

HUGHES D and POLLARD D (1990) *Cases and materials on constitutional and administrative law* (London: Butterworths).

HUME D (1978) 'Of the original contract', in LOCKE J (ed) *Social contract: essays by Locke, Hume and Rousseau* (London: OUP).

Hunt M (1997) *Using human rights law in English courts* (Oxford: Hart Publishing).

—— (1998) 'The "horizontal effect" of the Human Rights Act' *Public Law* 422–423.

Hutton R (1985) *The Restoration* (Oxford: Clarendon Press).

Ingman T (9th edn, 2002) *The English legal process* (London: OUP).

Institute of Fiscal Studies (1990) *Local government finance* (London: IFS).

Irvine, Lord (1997) 'Constitutional reform and a Bill of Rights' *European Human Rights LR* 483–493.

Irving R (1975) 'The United Kingdom referendum, June 1975' *ELRev* 3–12.

Irwin H (1988) 'Opportunities for backbenchers', in Ryle and Richards *infra.*

Jackmann R (1984) 'The Rates Bill: a measure of desperation' *Political Quarterly* 161–170.

Jackson P (1964) 'The royal prerogative' *MLR* 709–717.

—— (1965) 'War Damage Act 1965' *MLR* 574–576.

Jaffe L and Henderson G (1956) 'Judicial review and the rule of law: historical origins' *LQR* 345.

Jenkins J (1987) 'The green sheep in Colonel Gadaffi Drive' *New Society*, 9 January 1987.

Jenkins R (1952) 'Equality' in Crossman R (ed) *New Fabian Essays* (London: Turnstile).

—— (1968) *Mr Balfour's Poodle* (London: Heinemann).

—— (1991) *A life at the centre* pp 144–146 (London: Pan).

—— (1994) 'Churchill: the government of 1951–1955', in Blake and Louis *supra.*

—— (1999) *Report of the independent commission on the voting system* (London: HMSO).

Jennings I (5th edn, 1959) *The law and the constitution* (London: Hodder and Stoughton).

—— (3rd edn, 1959) *Cabinet government* (Cambridge: CUP).

—— (4th edn, 1960) *Principles of local government law* (London: University of London Press).

Jennings I and Tambiah H (1952) *The dominion of Ceylon* (London: Stevens and Sons).

Jensen M (1990) 'The Articles of Confederation', in Birmbaum and Ollman *supra.*

Johnson N (1988) 'Departmental select committees', in Ryle and Richards *infra.*

Joint Committee on House of Lords Reform (2002) *First Report* (HL 171/HC 17)(London: HMSO).

Jones A (1972) *The politics of reform 1884* (Cambridge: CUP).

Jones G (1973) 'Herbert Morrison and Popularism' *Public Law* 11–31.

—— (1973) 'The Prime Minister and parliamentary questions' *Parliamentary Affairs* 260–272.

Jones H (1958) 'The rule of law and the welfare state' *Columbia LR* 143–156.

Jones T (1996) 'The devaluation of human rights under the European Convention' *Public Law* 430–449.

—— (1999) 'Judicial bias and disqualification in the *Pinochet* case' *Public Law* 391–398.

Jowell J and Lester A (1988) 'Proportionality: neither novel nor dangerous', in Jowell J and Oliver D (eds) *New directions in judicial review* (London: Stevens and Sons).

Jowell J and Oliver D (eds) (1985; 2nd edn, 1989; 3rd edn, 1994) *The changing constitution* (London: OUP).

Judson M (1936) 'Henry Parker and the theory of parliamentary sovereignty', in

WITTKE C (ed) *Essays in honour of McIlwain* (Cambridge, Mass: Harvard University Press).

KAVANAGH D and SELDON A (eds) *The Major effect* (London: Macmillan).

KAVANNAGH A (2004) 'Statutory interpretation and human rights after *Anderson:* a more contextual approach' Public Law 537–545.

—— (2005) '*Pepper v Hart* and matters of constitutional principle' 121 *LQR* 98–122.

KAY A, LEGG C and FOOT J (1985) *The 1980 Tenant's Rights in Practice* (London: City University).

KEENAN P (1962) 'Some legal consequences of Britain's entry into the European Common Market' *Public Law* 327–343.

KEIR D (1936) 'The case of ship-money' *LQR* 546–574.

KEIR D (8th edn, 1966) *The constitutional history of modern Britain* (London: Adam and Charles Black).

—— (6th edn, 1978) *Cases in constitutional law* (Oxford: Clarendon Press):

KEITH-LUCAS B (1962) 'Popularism' *Public Law* 52–80.

KELLY A, HARBISON W and BEIZ H (1983) *The American Constitution* (New York: W.W. Norton).

KENNY C (1922) 'The evolution of the law of blasphemy' *Cambridge LJ* 127–142.

KENT S (1989) *Sex and suffrage in Britain 1860–1914* (New Jersey: Princeton University Press).

KLOTT J (1998) 'Report on Germany' in SLAUGHTER A, STONE SWEET A and WEILER J (eds) *The European courts and national courts* (Oxford: Hart Publishing).

KLUG F (1999) 'The Human Rights Act 1998, *Pepper v Hart* and all that' *Public Law* 246–273

KLUG F and STARMER K (2001) 'Incorporation through the "from door": the first year of the Human Rights Act' *Public Law* 654–665.

KOOPMANS T (1992) 'Federalism: the wrong debate' *CMLRev* 1047–1052.

LAFFIN M (1986) *Professionalism and policy* (Aldershot: Gower).

LANE R (1993) 'New Community competencies under the Maastricht Treaty' *CMLRev* 929–980.

LANHAM D (1984) 'Delegation and the alter ego principle' *LQR* 587–611.

LARDY H (2001) 'Democracy by default: the Representation of the People Act 2000' *Modern LR* 263–281.

LARGE D (1963) 'The decline of the party of the Crown' *English Historical Review* 669–695.

LASKI H (1926) 'Judicial review of social policy in England' *Harvard LR* 832–848.

LASLETT P (1998) 'The social and political theory of Two Treatises of Government', in Laslett *infra.*

—— (1988) 'Two Treatises of Government and the revolution of 1688', in Laslett *infra.*

LASLETT P (ed) (1988) *Locke – Two Treatises of Government* (Cambridge: CUP).

LASOK D and BRIDGE J (1991) *Law and institutions of the European Community* (London: Butterworths).

LAUNDY P (1979) 'The Speaker and his office in the twentieth century' in WALKLAND S (ed) *The House of Commons in the twentieth century* (Oxford: Clarendon Press).

LAW COMMISSION (1976) *Report on remedies in administrative law* (London: HMSO; Cmnd 6407).

LAWS, SIR JOHN (1993) 'Is the High Court the guardian of fundamental constitutional rights?' *Public Law* 59–79.

—— (1995) 'Law and democracy' *Public Law* 72–93.

—— (1998) 'The limitations of human rights' *Public Law* 254–265.

LAWSON N (1992) *The view from No. 11* (London: Lawrence and Wishart).

LEACH S (1989) 'Strengthening local democracy? the government's response to Widdicombe', in STEWART J and STOKER G (eds) *The future of local government* (London: Macmillan).

LEE S (1985) 'Prerogative and public principles' *Public Law* 186–193.

—— (1994) 'Law and the constitution' in KAVANAGH D and SELDON A (eds) *The Major effect* (London: Macmillan).

LEIGH I (1986) 'A tapper's charter' *Public Law* 8–18.

—— (1992) 'Spycatcher in Strasbourg' *Public Law* 200–208.

—— (2002) 'Taking rights proportionately' *Public Law* 265–280.

LEIGH I and LUSTGARTEN L (1996) 'Five volumes in search of accountability: the Scott Report' *MLR* 695–725.

LE MAY G (1957) 'Parliament, the constitution and the doctrine of the mandate' *South African Law Journal* 33–42.

LENEMAN L (1991) 'When women were not "persons": the Scottish women graduates case, 1906–1908' *Juridical Review* 109–118.

LEOPOLD P (1981) 'References in court to Hansard' *Public Law* 316–321.

—— (1984) 'Parliamentary privilege and an MP's threats' *Public Law* 547–550.

—— (1986) 'Leaks and squeaks in the Palace of Westminster' *Public Law* 368–374.

—— (1989) 'The freedom of peers from arrest' *Public Law* 398–406.

—— (1998) 'The application of the civil and criminal law to members of Parliament and parliamentary proceedings', in Oliver and Drewry *infra.*

—— (1999) 'The report of the Joint Committee on parliamentary privilege' *Public Law* 604–615.

LESTER A (1984) 'Fundamental rights: the United Kingdom isolated' *Public Law* 46–72.

LESTER A (1998) 'The Act of the possible. . . .' *European Human Rights LR* 665–680.

LESTER A and PANNICK D (2000) 'The impact of the Human Rights Act on private law: the knight's move' *LQR* 380–392.

LEVY L (1987) 'Introduction', in LEVY L (ed) *The Making of the Constitution* (New York: OUP).

LEWIN J (1956) 'The struggle for law in South Africa' *Political Quarterly* 176–181.

LEWIS A (1991) *Make no law* (New York: Vintage Books).

LIDDINGTON J and NORRIS J (1979) *One hand tied behind us* (London: Virago).

LOACH J (1990) *Parliament under the Tudors* (Oxford: Clarendon Press).

LOCK G (1988) 'Information for Parliament', in Ryle and Richards *infra.*

—— (1989) 'The 1689 Bill of Rights' *Political Studies* 541–556.

—— (1999) 'The report of the Joint Committee on parliamentary privilege' *Study of Parliament Group Newsletter* (summer) 13–19.

LOCKHART W, KAMISAT Y, CHOPER J and SHIFFRIN S (6th edn, 1986) *Constitutional law* (West Publishing: St Paul, Minnesota).

LOCKE J (1988) *Two treatises of government* (Cambridge: CUP).

LOUGHLIN M (1978) 'Procedural fairness: a study of the crisis in administrative law theory' *University of Toronto LJ* 280–316.

—— (1985) 'Municipal socialism in a unitary state', in MACAUSLAN P and

McEldowney J (eds) *Law, legitimacy and the constitution* (London: Sweet and Maxwell).

—— (1985a) 'The restructuring of central-local government legal relations' *Local Government Studies* 59–73.

—— (1986) *Local government in the modern state* (London: Sweet and Maxwell).

—— (1992) *Public law and political theory* (Oxford: Clarendon Press).

—— (1994) 'The restructuring of central-local government relations', in Jowell and Oliver *supra.*

—— (1988) *Legality and locality* (Oxford: Clarendon Press).

Loveland I (1992) 'Labour and the Constitution: the "right" approach to reform' *Parliamentary Affairs* 173–187.

—— (1993) 'Racial segregation in state schools: the parent's right to choose? *Journal of Law and Society* 341–355.

—— (1993a) 'An unappealing analysis of the public-private divide: the case of the homelessness legislation' *Liverpool LR* 39–59.

—— (1994) 'Defamation of government: taking lessons from America?' *Legal Studies* 61–80.

—— (1995) *Housing homeless persons* (Oxford: Clarendon Press).

—— (1995a) (ed) *Frontiers of criminality* (London: Sweet and Maxwell).

—— (1995b) (ed) *A special relationship?* (Oxford: Clarendon Press).

—— (1995c) 'The criminalisation of racist violence', in Loveland (1995b) *supra.*

—— (1995d) 'Introduction: should we take lessons from America?', in Loveland (ed) *A special relationship?* (Oxford: Clarendon Press).

—— (1996) *Constitutional law* (London: Butterworths).

—— (1997) 'The war against the judges' *Political Quarterly* 162–171.

—— (1998) *Importing the First Amendment* (Oxford: Hart Publishing).

—— (1998a) '*City of Chicago v Tribune Co* – in contexts', in Loveland I (ed) *Importing the First Amendment* (Oxford: Hart Publishing).

—— (1999) *By due process of law: racial discrimination and the right to vote in South Africa 1850–1960* (Oxford: Hart Publishing).

—— (1999a) 'Constitutional law or administrative law? The Human Rights Act 1998' *Contemporary Issues in Law* 124–140.

—— (2000) *Political libels* (Oxford: Hart Publishing).

—— (2003) 'Making it up as they go along: the Court of Appeal on succession rights in tenancies to same sex partners' *Public Law* 222–235.

Lowe N (1979) 'Contempt of Court Act' *Public Law* 20–28.

Lustgarten L (1989) *The governance of police* (London: Sweet and Maxwell).

Lustgarten L and Leigh I (1994) *In from the cold: national security and parliamentary democracy* (Oxford: Clarendon Press).

MacCormick N (1978) 'Does the United Kingdom have a constitution?' *NILQ* 1–20.

Mackintosh J (1962) *The British Cabinet* (London: Stevens and Sons).

—— (1974) 'The report of the Royal Commission on the Constitution 1969–1973' *Parliamentary Affairs* 115–123.

Madgwick P (1966) 'Resignations' *Parliamentary Affairs* 59–76.

Magnus P (1963) *Gladstone* (London: John Murray).

MAIDMENT R (1992) *The Supreme Court and the New Deal* (Buckingham: Open University Press).

MAIER P (1963) 'John Wilkes and American disillusionment with Britain' *William and Mary Quarterly* 373–395.

MAIT C and MCCLOUD B (1999) 'Financial arrangements', in Hassan *infra.*

MAITLAND F (1908) *The Constitutional history of England* (Cambridge: CUP).

MALLESON K (2000) 'Judicial bias and disqualification after *Pinochet (No.2)*' *MLR* 119–127.

MALPASS P and MURIE A (1987) *Housing policy and practice* (1987) (London: Macmillan).

MANDLER P (1990) *Aristocratic government in the age of reform* (Oxford: Clarendon Press).

MANN F (1979) 'Contempt of court in the House of Lords and the European Court of Human Rights' *LQR* 348–354.

MARKESENIS B (1973) 'The royal prerogative revisited' *Cambridge LJ* 287–309.

—— (1986) 'The right to be let alone versus freedom of speech' *Public Law* 67–81.

—— (1990) 'Our patchy law of privacy' *MLR* 802–809.

MARRIOT J (2005) 'Alarmist or relaxed? Election expenditure limits and free speech' *Public Law* 764–784.

MARRIOT J and NICOL D (1999) 'The Human Rights Act, representative standing and the victim culture' *European Human Rights LR* 730–741.

MARSHALL G (1954) 'What is Parliament? The changing concept of Parliamentary Sovereignty' *Political Studies* 193–209.

—— (1979) 'The House of Commons and its privileges', in Walkland *infra.*

—— (1984) *Constitutional conventions* (Oxford: Clarendon Press).

—— (1986) 'Ministers, civil servants and open government' in Harlow *supra.*

—— (1992) 'Ministerial responsibility, the Home Office and Mr Baker' *Public Law* 7–12.

—— (1998) 'Hansard and the interpretation of statutes', in Oliver and Drewry *infra.*

MARSHALL G and LOVEDAY B (1994) 'The police: independence and accountability', in Jowell and Oliver *supra.*

MASHAW J (1976) 'The Supreme Court's due process calculus for administrative adjudication in *Matthews v Eldridge* . . .' *University of Chicago LR* 28–59.

MASON D (1985) *Revising the rating system* (London: Adam Smith Institute).

MATHER F (1962) 'The government and the Chartists', in BRIGGS A (ed) *Chartist studies* (London: Macmillan).

MATTHEW C (1986) *Gladstone 1809–1874* (Oxford: Clarendon Press).

MAUDE A and SZEMEREY J (1981) *Why electoral reform? The case for electoral reform examined* (London: Conservative Political Centre).

MCAUSLAN P (1983) 'Administrative law, collective consumption and judicial policy' *MLR* 1–21.

—— (1987) 'The Widdicombe Report: local government business or politics' *Public Law* 154–162.

MCAUSLAN P and MCELDOWNEY J (eds) *Law, Legitimacy and the constitution* (London: Sweet and Maxwell).

MCBRIDE J (1983) 'The doctrine of exclusivity and judicial review: *O'Reilly v Mackman*' *Civil Justice Quarterly* 268–281.

MCCLEAN I (1999) 'The Jenkins Commission and the implications of electoral reform for the UK' *Government and Opposition* 145–160.

McClean R (1999) 'A brief history of Scottish home rule', in Hassan *supra.*

McEldowney J (1985) 'Dicey in historical perspective', in McAuslan and McEldowney *supra.*

—— (1988) 'The contingencies fund and the Parliamentary scrutiny of public finance' *Public Law* 232–245.

McKay D (1989) *American politics and society* (Oxford: Basil Blackwell).

Meisel F (2004) 'The *Aston Cantlow* case: blots on English jurisprudence and the public/private law divide' *Public Law* 2–10.

Merret S (1979) *State housing in Britain* (London: RKP).

Miers D (1983) 'Citing Hansard as an aid to interpretation' *Statute LR* 98–102.

Miliband R and Smith J (eds) *Socialist Register* (London: Merlin).

Miller C (1976) *Contempt of court* (London: Paul Elek).

Miller J (1982) 'The Glorious Revolution: "contract" and "abdication" reconsidered' 25 *The Historical Journal* 541–555.

Mitchell A (1974) 'Clay Cross' *Political Quarterly* 165–175.

Moddod T (1990) 'British asian muslims and the Rushdie affair' *Political Quarterly* 143–160.

Montesquieu C (1989) *The spirit of the laws* (Cambridge: CUP).

Moreham N (2001) '*Douglas and others v Hello Ltd* – the protection of privacy in English private law' *Modern LR* 767–775.

Morgan J (2002) 'Questioning the "true effect" of the Human Rights Act' *Legal Studies* 259–275.

—— (2004) 'Privacy in the House of Lords, again' *LQR* 563–566.

Morris G and Fredman S (1991) 'Judicial review and civil servants' *Public Law* 485–490.

Mount F (1992) *The British constitution now* (London: Heinemann).

Mowbray A (1999) 'The composition and operation of the new European Court of Human Rights' *Public Law* 219–231.

Mullan D (1975) 'Fairness: the new natural justice' *University of Toronto LJ* 280–316.

Mullan K (1999) 'The impact of *Pepper v Hart*' in Carmichael and Dickson (eds) *The House of Lords: its parliamentary and judicial roles* (Oxford: Hart Publishing).

Munn P (ed) *Parents and schools* (London: Routledge).

Munro C (1976) 'Elections and expenditure' *Public Law* 300–304.

—— (1987) *Studies in constitutional law* (London: Butterworths).

—— (2nd edn, 1989) *Studies in constitutional law* (London: Butterworths).

Murdie A (1990) 'Bailiffs, Henry III, the community charge and all that' *Municipal Journal* August 17–23.

Myles A (1999) 'Scotland's Parliament White Paper', in Hassan *supra.*

Nally S and Dear J (1990) 'No surrender' *Municipal Journal*, October 12–18.

Nathanson N (1979/1980) 'The Sunday Times case: freedom of the press and contempt of court under English law and the European Convention on Human Rights' *Kentucky LJ* 971–1025.

Neville-Brown L and Kennedy T (1994) *The Court of Justice of the European Communities* (London: Sweet and Maxwell).

Nicol D (1996) 'Disapplying with relish? The Industrial Tribunals and Acts of Parliament' *Public Law* 579–589.

—— (1999) 'The legal constitution: United Kingdom Parliament and European Court of Justice' *Journal of Legislative Studies* 131–151.

—— (1999a) 'Limitation periods under the Human Rights Act 1998 and judicial review' *LQR* 216–220.

—— (2004) 'Gender re-assignment and the transformation of the Human Rights Act' *LQR* 194–198.

—— (2004a) 'Statutory interpretation and human rights after Anderson' *Public Law* 273.

Nicol W (1984) 'The Luxembourg compromise' *Journal of Common Market Studies* 35–43.

Nicol W and Simon T (1994) *Understanding the new European Community* at p 158 (London: Harvester Wheatsheaf).

Nixon J and Nixon N (1983) 'The social services committee' *Journal of Social Policy* 331–355.

Norris M (1996) '*Ex p Smith*: irrationality and human rights' *Public Law* 590–600.

Norton P (1979) 'The organisation of parliamentary parties', in Walkland *infra.*

Norton P (1978) 'Government defeats in the House of Commons' *Public Law* 360–378.

—— (1979) 'The organisation of parliamentary parties', in Walkland *infra.*

—— (1980) *Dissension in the House of Commons 1974–1979* (London: Macmillan).

—— (1982) ' "Dear Minister" . . . The importance of MP to minister correspondence' *Parliamentary Affairs* 59–72.

—— (1985) *The Commons in perspective* (London: Martin Robertson).

—— (1988) 'Opposition to government', in Ryle and Richards *infra.*

—— (2nd ed, 1991) *The British polity* (London: Longman).

O'Keefe D and Twomey P (eds) *Legal issues of the Maastricht Treaty* (London: Wiley).

O'Leary B (1987) 'Why was the GLC abolished' *International Journal of Urban and Regional Research* 192–217

—— (1987) 'British farce, French drama amid tales of two cities' *Public Administration* 369–389.

O'Leary C (1962) *The elimination of corrupt practices in British general elections 1868–1911* (Oxford: Clarendon Press).

O'Leary S (1996) '*R v Secretary of State for the Home Department, ex parte Gallagher*' *Common Market LR* 777–793.

Oliver D (1982) 'Why electoral reform? The case for electoral reform examined' *Public Law* 236–239.

—— (1990) *Government in the United Kingdom* (Buckingham: Open University Press).

—— (1992) 'Written constitutions: principles and problems' *Parliamentary Affairs* 135–152.

—— (1999) 'An Electoral Commission: an ingenious idea' *Public Law* 585–588.

—— (2001) 'Chancel repairs and the Human Rights Act' *Public Law* 651–653.

Oliver D and Drewry G (eds) (1998) *The law and parliament* (London: Weidenfeld and Nicolson).

Ousley H (1984) 'Local authority race initiatives', in Body and Fudge C (eds) *Local socialism* (London: Macmillan)

Padover S (ed) (1953) *The complete Madison* (Norwalk, Conn: Eastern Press).

Palmer S (1988) 'In the interests of the state' *Public Law* 523–535.

—— (1990) 'Tightening secrecy law: the Official Secrets Act 1989' *Public Law* 243–256.

Pannick D (1984) 'The Law Lords and the needs of contemporary society' *Political Quarterly* 318–328.

—— (1994) 'No logic behind gagging terrorists' empty rhetoric' *The Times* August 2.

—— (1988) 'What is a public authority?', in Jowell J and Oliver D (eds) *New directions in judicial review* (London: Sweet and Maxwell).

Pedley R (1958) 'Lord Hailsham's legacy' *Journal of Education* 4–5.

—— (1966) *The comprehensive school* (Harmondsworth: Penguin).

Pescatore P (1972) 'The protection of human rights in the European Communities' *CMLRev* 73–79.

—— (1983) 'The doctrine of direct effect: an infant disease of Community Law' *ELRev* 155–177.

Peterson J (1994) 'Subsidiarity: a definition to suit any vision' *Parliamentary Affairs* 116–132.

Phelan D (1992) 'Right to life of the unborn v promotion of trade in services' *MLR* 670–689.

Phillimore, Lord Justice (1974) *Report on contempt of court* (London: HMSO; Cmnd 5794).

Phillipson G (1999) 'The Human Rights Act, "horizontal effect" and the common law: a bang or a whimper?' *MLR* 824–849.

Pimlott B (1992) *Harold Wilson* (London: Harper Collins).

Plotner J (1998) 'Report on France' in Slaughter A, Stone Sweet A and Weiler J (eds) *The European courts and national courts* (Oxford: Hart Publishing).

Plucknett T (1928) '*Dr Bonham's Case and judicial review*' *Harvard LR* 30–70.

—— (11th ed, 1960) Taswell-Langmead's *English constitutional history* (London: Sweet and Maxwell).

Plumb J (1937) 'Elections to the Convention Parliament of 1689' *Cambridge Historical Journal* 235–254.

Pryce R (ed) (1985) *The dynamics of European Union* (London: Croom Helm).

Pugh M (1980) *Women's suffrage in Britain 1867–1928* (London: The Historical Association).

—— (1985) 'Labour and women's suffrage', in Brown K (ed) *The first Labour Party* (London: Croom Helm).

Pulzer P (1983) 'Germany', in Butler and Bogdanor *supra.*

Punnet R (1968) *British government and politics* (London: Heinemann).

Purdue M (2002) 'The end of estoppel in public law' *Journal of Planning and Environmental Law* 509–510.

Quane H (2006) 'The Strasbourg jurisprudence and the meaning of a "public authority" under the HRA' *Public Law* 106–123.

Raab C (1993) 'Parents and schools: what role for education authorities?', in Munn *supra.*

Radcliffe, Viscount (1976) *Report on Ministerial Memoirs, Cmnd* 6386 (London: HMSO).

Ranson S (1988) 'From 1944–1988: education, citizenship and democracy' *Local Government Studies* 1–19.

Ranson S and Thomas H 'Educational reform: consumer democracy or social democracy', in Stewart J and Stoker G (eds) *The future of local government* (London: Macmillan).

Rawlings H (1988) *Law and the electoral process* (London: Sweet and Maxwell).

Rawlings R (1994) 'Legal politics: the UK and ratification of the Treaty on European Union (parts one and two) *Public Law* 254–278 and 367–391.

—— (1998) 'The new model Wales' *Journal of Law and Society* 461–512.

Raworth P (1994) 'A timid step forwards:

Maastricht and the democratisation of the EC' *ELRev* 16–33.

Raz J (1977) 'The rule of law and its virtue' *LQR* 195–211.

Reich C (1963) 'Midnight welfare searches and the Social Security Act' *Yale LJ* 1346–1360.

—— (1964) 'The new property' *Yale LJ* 733–787.

—— (1965) 'Individual rights and social welfare: the emerging legal issues' *Yale LJ* 1244–1257.

Reid (Lord) (1972–1973) 'The judge as lawmaker' *Journal of the Society of Public Teachers of Law* 22–28.

Rhodes R (1986) *The national world of local government* (London: Allen and Unwin).

Richards P (1970) *Parliament and conscience* (London: Allen and Unwin).

Richardson G (1986) 'The duty to give reasons: potential and practice' *Public Law* 437–469.

Richardson T (1995) 'The War Crimes Act 1991', in Loveland (1995a) *supra.*

Ridley N (1991) *My style of government* (London: Fontana).

Robertson A and Merrill J (3rd edn) *Human rights in Europe* (Manchester: Manchester UP).

Robertson G (1999) *The justice game* (Harmondsworth: Penguin).

Robertson G and Nicol A (3rd edn 1992) *Media law* (Harmondsworth: Penguin).

Robinson R (1988) 'The House of Commons and public money', in Ryle and Richards *infra.*

Rodger (Lord) (2005) 'A time for everything under the law: some reflections on retrospectivity' *LQR* 57–71.

Rogers I (2002) 'From the Human Rights Act to the Charter: not another human rights instrument to consider' *European Human Rights LR* 343–356.

Rose H (1973) 'The Immigration Act 1971: a case study in the work of Parliament' *Parliamentary Affairs* 69–91.

Rousseau J (1987) *The social contract* (edited and translated by C Betts) (Oxford: OUP).

Rover C (1967) *Women's suffrage and party politics in Britain* (London: RKP).

Rowbottom J (2005) 'The electoral Commission's proposals on the funding of political parties' *Public Law* 468–476.

Rude G (1962) *Wilkes and liberty* (Oxford: Clarendon Press).

Rush M (1998) 'The law relating to members' conduct', in Oliver and Drewry *supra.*

Russell C (1971) *The Crisis of Parliaments* (Oxford: Clarendon Press).

Russell M (2000) *Reforming the House of Lords. Lessons from overseas* (London: OUP).

Ryle M and Richards (1988) *The Commons under scrutiny* (London: Routledge).

Scarman, Lord (1987) 'Human Rights in an unwritten constitution' *Denning LJ* 129–139.

Schermers H (1993) 'The European Court of Human Rights after the merger' *European LR* 493–505.

Schiemann K (1990) 'Locus standi' *Public Law* 342–353.

Scraton P (1985) '"If you want a riot, change the law": the implications of the White Paper on Public order' *Journal of Law and Society* 385–393.

Sedley S (1994) 'Governments, constitutions and judges', in Genn and Richardson *supra.*

Selgado E and O'Brien C (2001) 'Table of cases under the Human Rights Act' *European Human Rights Law Review* 376.

Seymour C (1970) *Electoral reform in*

England and Wales (Newton Abbot: David and Charles).

Seymore-Ure C (1964) 'The misuse of the question of privilege in the 1964–65 session of Parliament' *Parliamentary Affairs* 380–388.

—— (1970) 'Proposed reforms of parliamentary privilege' *Parliamentary Affairs* 221–231.

Shannon R (1982) *Gladstone Vol. 1* (London: Hamish Hamilton).

Sharland A and Loveland I (1997) 'The Defamation Act 1996 and political libels' *Public Law* 113–124.

Sharp A (1983) *Political ideas of the English civil war* (London: Longman).

Sharpe J (1970) 'Theories and value of local government *Political Studies* 153–174.

Shaw J (1993) *EC law* (London: Macmillan).

—— (2001) 'The Treaty of Nice: legal and constitutional implications' *European Public Law* 195–207.

Shell D (1985) 'The House of Lords and the Thatcher government' *Parliamentary Affairs* 16–32:

—— (1992) *The House of Lords* (London: Harvester Wheatsheaf).

—— (1999) 'The future of the second chamber' *Political Quarterly* 390–395.

—— (2000) 'Reforming the House of Lords' *Public Law* 193.

Silk P (1992) *How Parliament works* (London: Longman).

Sills P (1968) 'Report of the Select Committee on parliamentary privilege' *MLR* 435–439.

Simon B (1988) *Bending the rules* (London: Lawrence and Wishart).

Simpson A (1991) *In the highest degree odious* (Oxford: Clarendon Press).

Skidelsky R (1968) 'Great Britain', in Woolf S (ed) *European facism* (London: Weidenfeld and Nicolson).

Sklair L (1975) 'The Struggle Against the Housing Finance Act', in Miliband R and Smith J (eds) *The Socialist Register* (London: Macmillan).

Slaughter A, Stone Sweet A and Weiler J (eds) *The European courts and national courts* (Oxford: Hart Publishing).

Slaughter T (1981) ' "Abdicate" and "contract" in the Glorious Revolution' *The Historical Journal* 323–337.

Smith E (1992) *The House of Lords in British politics and society 1815–1911* (London: Longman).

Smith T (1957) 'The Union of 1707 as fundamental law' *Public Law* 99–121.

Speck W (1986) *Reluctant revolutionaries* (Oxford: Clarendon Press).

Steiner J (1990) 'Coming to terms with EC directives' *LQR* 144–159.

—— (3rd edn, 1992) *EC law* (London: Blackstone).

—— (1993) 'From direct to *Francovich*: shifting means of enforcement of community law' *ELRev* 3–22.

Stellman H (1985) 'Israel: the 1984 election and after' *Parliamentary Affairs* 73–85.

Stewart J (1983) *Defending public accountability* (London: Demos).

Stewart J and Stoker G (eds) *The future of local government* (London: Macmillan).

Stewart R (1975) 'The reformation of American administrative law' *Harvard LR* 1667–1812.

Sunkin M (1987) 'What is happening to applications for judicial review' *MLR* 432–467.

—— (1987a) 'Myths of judicial review' *LAG Bulletin* (September) 8.

—— (1991) 'The judicial review caseload, 1987–1989' *Public Law* 490–499.

—— (2004) 'Pushing forward the frontiers of human rights protection; the meaning of public authority under the Human Rights Act' *Public Law* 643–658.

Szyszczak E (1990) 'Sovereignty: crisis, compliance, confusion, complacency' *ELRev* 480–488.

—— (1993) 'Interpretation of Community Law in the courts' *ELRev* 214–225.

Taylor/DES (1977) *A new partnership for schools* (London: HMSO).

Taylor P and Gudgin G (1976) 'The myth of non-partisan cartography' *Urban Studies* 13–25.

Thomas R (1987) 'The British Official Secrets Act 1911–1939 and the Ponting case', in Chapman R and Hunt M (eds) *Open government* (London: Routledge).

Thompson E (1975) *Whigs and hunters* (London: Penguin).

Thompson R and Game C (1985) 'Section 137: propoganda on the rates?' *Local Government Studies* 11–18.

Thorne S (1938) *'Dr Bonham's case'* *LQR* 543–552.

Tierney S (1998) 'The Human Rights Bill: incorporating the European Convention on Human Rights into UK law' *European Public Law* 299–311.

—— (1998a) 'Press freedom and public interest' *European Human Rights LR* 419–431.

Tierney S (2000) 'Constitutionalising the role of the judge: Scotland and the new order' *European LR* 49–72.

—— (2000a) 'Devolution issues and s 21(1) of the Human Rights Act' *European Human Rights LR* 380–392.

Titmuss R (1971) 'Welfare rights, law and discretion' *Political Quarterly* 133–151.

Tomkins A (1998) *The constitution after Scott* (Oxford: Clarendon Press).

—— (2005) *Our republican constitution* (Hart: Oxford).

Toth A (1986) 'The legal status of declarations attached to the SEA' *CMLRev* 903–812.

—— (1994) 'Is subsidiarity justiciable?' *ELRev* 268–285.

Trinadade F (1972) 'Parliamentary sovereignty and the primacy of community law' *MLR* 375–402.

Turbeville A (1927) *The House of Lords in the eighteenth century* (Oxford: Clarendon Press).

—— (1958) *The House Lords in the Age of Reform* (London: Faber and Faber).

Turpin C (1985; 2nd edn, 1990) *British government and the constitution* (London: Weidenfeld and Nicolson); (3rd edn, 1995) (London: Butterworths).

Underdown D (1985) *Revel, riot, and rebellion* (Oxford: Clarendon Press).

Upton M (1989) 'Marriage vows of the elephant: the constitution of 1707' *LQR* 79.

Vile M (1967) *Constitutionalism and the separation of powers* (Oxford: Clarendon Press).

Vincent-Jones P (1986) 'The hippy convoy and criminal trespass' *Journal of Law and Society* 343–370.

Wade HRW (1955) 'The basis of legal sovereignty' *Cambridge LJ* 172–197.

—— (1969) 'Constitutional and administrative aspects of the Anisminic case' *LQR* 198–212.

—— (1972) 'Sovereignty and the European Communities' *LQR* 1–5.

—— (1977) 'Judicial control of the prerogative' *LQR* 325–327.

—— (1980) *Constitutional fundamentals* (London: Steven & Sons).

—— (1985) 'The civil service and the prerogative' *LQR* 190–199.

—— (1996) 'Sovereignty – revolution or evolution' *LQR* 568–575.

—— (1996a) 'Habeas corpus and judicial review' *LQR* 55–70.

—— (2000) 'Horizons of horizontality' *LQR* 217–224.

WADE HRW and FORSYTH C (1994) *Administrative law* (Oxford: Clarendon Press).

WAKEHAM COMMISSION (2000) *A House for the future* (London: HMSO; Cm 4534).

WALKER C (1987) 'Review of the prerogative: the remaining issues' *Public Law* 63–84.

WALKER P (1995) 'What's wrong with irrationality?' *Public Law* 556–576.

WALKLAND S (ed) *The House of Commons in the twentieth century* (Oxford: Clarendon Press).

WALKLAND S and RYLE M (eds) (1977) *The Commons in the seventies* (London: Martin Robertson).

WALLINGTON P and MCBRIDE J (1976) *Civil Liberties and a Bill of Rights* pp 28–29 (London: Cobden Trust).

WALSH B (1989) 'Judicial review of dismissal from employment: coherence or confusion' *Public Law* 131–155.

WARBRICK C (1998) 'Federalism and free speech', in LOVELAND I (ed) *Importing the First Amendment?* (Oxford: Hart Publishing).

WARBURTON M and MALPASS P (1991) 'Riding the rent rocket' *ROOF* 27 July/August.

WARD J (1973) *Chartism* (New York: Harper Row).

WARD M (1988) 'Priced out' (1988) *Housing* 9 (October).

WARREN S and BRANDIES L (1890) 'The right to privacy' *Harvard LR* 193–220.

WEARE V (1964) 'The House of Lords – prophecy and fulfilment' *Parliamentary Affairs* 422–433.

WEILER J (1981) 'The Community system: the dual character of supra-nationalism' *Yearbook of European Law* 267–306.

—— (1986) 'Eurocracy and distrust . . .' *Washington Law Review* 1103–1152.

WEILER J and LOCKHART N (1995) 'Taking rights seriously: the European Court and its fundamental rights jurisprudence (parts one and two)' *CMLRev* 51–94 and 579–627.

WEIR A (1972) 'Local authority v critical ratepayer – a suit in defamation' *Cambridge LJ* 238–249.

WELFARE D (1992) 'The Lords in defence of local government' *Parliamentary Affairs* 205–219.

WESTON C (1965) *English constitutional theory and the House of Lords* (London: RKP).

WICKS E (2001) 'A new constitution for a new state? The 1707 union of England and Scotland' *LQR* 109.

WILLIAMS G (1978) *Textbook of criminal law* (London: Stevens).

WILSON D (2001) 'Local government: balancing diversity and uniformity' *Parliamentary Affairs* 289–307.

WILSON H (1979) *Final term* (London: Weidenfeld and Nicolson).

WILSON T (1988) 'Local freedom and central control – a question of balance', in BAILEY and PADDISON (eds) *The reform of local government finance in Britain* (London: Routledge).

WINTER J (1972) 'Direct applicability and direct effect: two distinct and different concepts in Community law' *CMLREv* 425–438.

WINTERTON G (1976) 'The British grundnorm: parliamentary sovereignty re-examined' *LQR* 591–617.

—— (1981) 'Parliamentary supremacy and the judiciary' *LQR* 265–275.

Wittke C (ed) (1936) *Essays in history and political theory in honour of Charles Howard McIlwain* (Cambridge, Mass: HUP).

—— (1970) *The history of English parliamentary privilege* (New York: Da Capo Press).

Wolffe W (1987) 'Values in conflict: incitement to racial hatred and the Public Order Act 1986' *Public Law* 85–95.

Woodhouse D (1994) *Ministers and Parliament* (Oxford: Clarendon Press).

Woodward R (1991) 'Mobilising opposition: the campaign against housing action trusts in Tower Hamlets' *Housing Studies* 44–56.

Woolf H (1986) 'Public law – private law: why the divide?' *Public Law* 220–238.

Woolf S (ed) *European fascism* (London: Weidenfeld and Nicolson).

Young A (2002) 'remedial and substantive horizontality: the common law and *Douglas v Hello! Ltd*' *Public Law* 232–241.

—— (2005) *Ghaidan v Godin-Mendoza*: avoiding the deference trap' *Public Law* 23–34.

Young H (1991) *One of us* (London: Pan).

Zander M (1994) *The law-making process* (London: Butterworths).

INDEX